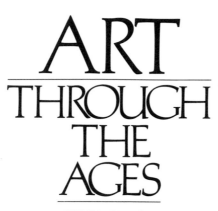

ART
THROUGH
THE
AGES

EIGHTH EDITION

II
RENAISSANCE
AND
MODERN ART

GARDNER'S
ART
THROUGH
THE
AGES

EIGHTH EDITION

II
RENAISSANCE
AND
MODERN ART

Horst de la Croix

Richard G. Tansey

HARCOURT BRACE JOVANOVICH, PUBLISHERS
San Diego   New York   Chicago   Atlanta   Washington, D.C.
London   Sydney   Toronto

ISBN: 0-15-503763-3 (hardbound)
0-15-503764-1 (paperbound, Vol. I)
0-15-503765-X (paperbound, Vol. II)
Library of Congress Catalog Card Number: 85-60874 (hardbound)
85-80092 (paperbound)

Printed in the United States of America

New illustrations by Felipe Fernandez.

PREFACE

Since publication of the first edition in 1926, Helen Gardner's *Art through the Ages* has been a favorite with generations of students and general readers, who have found it an exciting and informative survey. Miss Gardner's enthusiasm, knowledge, and humanity have made it possible for the beginner to learn how to see and thereby to penetrate the seeming mysteries of even the most complex artistic achievements. Every effort has been made in this volume to preserve her freshness and simplicity of style and, above all, her sympathetic approach to individual works of art and to the styles of which they are a part.

Miss Gardner completed the third edition shortly before her death in 1946. The fourth edition was prepared in 1959 by Professor Sumner Crosby and his colleagues at Yale University. Our fifth edition was published in 1970, the sixth in 1975, and the seventh in 1980. We were led to prepare this edition by the popularity of those earlier editions and by suggestions we received for further improvement. The eighth edition of Gardner's *Art through the Ages,* we hope, will continue a tradition of 60 years as a standard and reliable survey of the history of world art.

In this edition, in addition to emendations made throughout the book, the text and the number of pictures have been expanded to include works of art recently discovered, restudied, or considered by the editors to be particularly characteristic of their periods and illustrative of developmental trends. Fuller treatment has been given to periods and monuments when warranted. Many new pictures are in color, and a large number of black-and-white pictures in previous editions have been converted to color in this edition. Every effort has been made to accommodate the results of recent research in as comprehensive and detailed a survey of the material as the physical limits of a textbook of this scope permit.

In making a balanced historical introduction to the art of the whole world, which *Art through the Ages* uniquely achieves, the hardest task is selection—in effect, limitation—of the monuments to be discussed and illustrated. Though a corpus of monuments essential to the art-history survey course has long been forming, and though there seems to be considerable agreement as to what constitutes it, there will naturally be differences of choice deriving from differences of emphasis. A radical departure from the corpus might well obliterate the outlines of the study. To avoid the random, systemless distribution of material that might result, we have generally adhered to the corpus and occasionally introduced monuments not well known, newly discovered, or not customarily treated in a survey. Our aim throughout has been to present and interpret works as reflections of an intelligible development rather than merely as items of a catalogue or miscellany. We have tried particularly to give coherence to the best assortment of materials by stressing—in the descriptions of sculpture and painting—the theme of representation as it passes through the many historical variations behind which operate the crucial transformations of humankind's view of itself and of the world.

Various teaching aids accompany the eighth edition of *Gardner's Art through the Ages*. A Study Guide by Kathleen Cohen and Horst de la Croix contains chapter-by-chapter drills on identification of geographical locations, time periods, styles, terms, iconography, major art movements, and specific philosophical, religious, and historical movements as they relate to particular works of art examined in the text. Self-quizzes and discussion questions enable students to evaluate their grasp of the material. A geographical index of locations of works of art illustrated in the eighth edition is also included.

A computer-generated, coded key is available to adopters for use in obtaining commercial slides of the works and monuments illustrated in the eighth edition. In addition, a computer disk will generate printed slide labels for all illustrations in the eighth edition, as well as printouts of lists of illustrations categorized by artist, title, date or period, medium, genre, and geographical location.

A note on style. Given a contemporary sensitivity, reported by some of our readers, to traditional English usage that would seem to disparage women, the editors disclaim at the outset any prejudice in the use of words like "man" or "mankind." These, through centuries of English speech and writing, have been generic terms for humanity and the human race and are inclusive of both sexes. Our disclaimer extends to such locutions as "the artist . . . he," which could not, we feel, be altered without clumsy misuse, neologism, or circumlocution destructive of English sense and style; nevertheless, we have made changes wherever they were appropriate and neither obtrusive on good form nor offensive to our readers' feelings. We would deeply appreciate the forbearance of concerned readers in this matter, especially since we do not believe ourselves to have the authority or the competence to introduce extraordinary changes in the language as it now stands.

A work as extensive as a history of world art could not be undertaken or completed without the counsel and active participation of experts in fields other than our own. In some cases, this took the form of preparation of chapters or portions of chapters; in others, of reviews of work in progress or already prepared. For such contributions to this edition and to previous ones, we offer our sincere thanks to Professor James Ackerman, Harvard University; Professor Marjorie P. Balge, University of Virginia; Professor Jacques Bordaz, University of Pennsylvania; Professor Louise Alpers Bordaz, Columbia University; Professor James Cahill, University of California, Berkeley; Professor Herbert M. Cole, University of California, Santa Barbara; Professor George Corbin, Lehman College, City University of New York; Professor Mary S. Ellett, Randolph-Macon Woman's College; Professor Roger K. Elliott, Central Virginia Community College; Professor Ian Fraser, Herron School of Art; Professor Oleg Grabar, Harvard University; Professor M.F. Hearn, University of Pittsburgh; Professor Howard Hibbard, late of Columbia University; Professor Joel Isaacson, University of Michigan; Professor M. Barry Katz, Virginia Commonwealth University; Professor Robert A. Koch, Princeton University; Professor William L. MacDonald, formerly of Smith College; Professor A. Dean McKenzie, University of Oregon; Professor Diane Degasis Moran, Sweet Briar College; Dr. Harry Murutes, University of Akron; Professor Edith Porada, Columbia University; Professor Bruce Radde, San José State University; Professor Raphael X. Reichert, California State University at Fresno; Professor Grace Seiberling, University of Rochester; Dr. Peter Selz, University of California, Berkeley; Professor David Simon, Colby College; Professor Pamela H. Simpson, Washington and Lee University; Professor Richard Vinograd, University of Southern California; Professor Joanna Williams, University of California, Berkeley; and the Art History Department, Herron School of Art, Indiana University–Purdue University at Indianapolis. We owe a special debt of gratitude to Luraine Collins Tansey, art librarian and slide consultant, who compiled the bibliography and made valuable suggestions on its content. In addition, she designed the geographical index for the Study Guide, prepared the computer-generated coded key, and completed and made available the personal computer diskette. Rod Scher, HBJ Electronic Publishing, and also Charles Edgin and Jo Ellen Hardester Herrick, CCOC Computer Center, San Jose, managed the technical problems in the diskette's production. Edith Crowe did indispensable bibliographical research.

Among those who have contributed their efforts, often in demanding and painstaking capacity, to the efficient management of an enormously detailed manuscript are our editors, Albert Richards, Mary George, and Andrea McCarrick; our art editor, Susan Holtz, and her assistants on this project, Avery Hallowell, Alice Harmon, and Rebecca Lytle; our designer, Jamie Fidler; and our production manager, Sharon Weldy.

We should like, as we thank all those who have helped immeasurably in the production of this book, to affirm that we alone are responsible for whatever may be its deficiencies.

Horst de la Croix
Richard G. Tansey

A Note on the Paperbound Version

This volume is one of two that constitute the paperbound version of *Gardner's Art through the Ages*, Eighth Edition. The two volumes exactly reproduce the text of the one-volume version, including its pagination. The first of these volumes contains Part I, The Ancient World; Part II, The Middle Ages; and Part III, The Non-European World. The second volume contains Part IV, The Renaissance and the Baroque and Rococo; and Part V, The Modern World. The Introduction, glossary, bibliography, and index appear in both volumes. The two-volume printing is intended for those who have occasion to use only half of *Art through the Ages*. The differences between the one-volume and the two-volume versions of the book are differences in form only.

CONTENTS

ART
THROUGH THE AGES

EIGHTH EDITION

II
RENAISSANCE
AND
MODERN ART

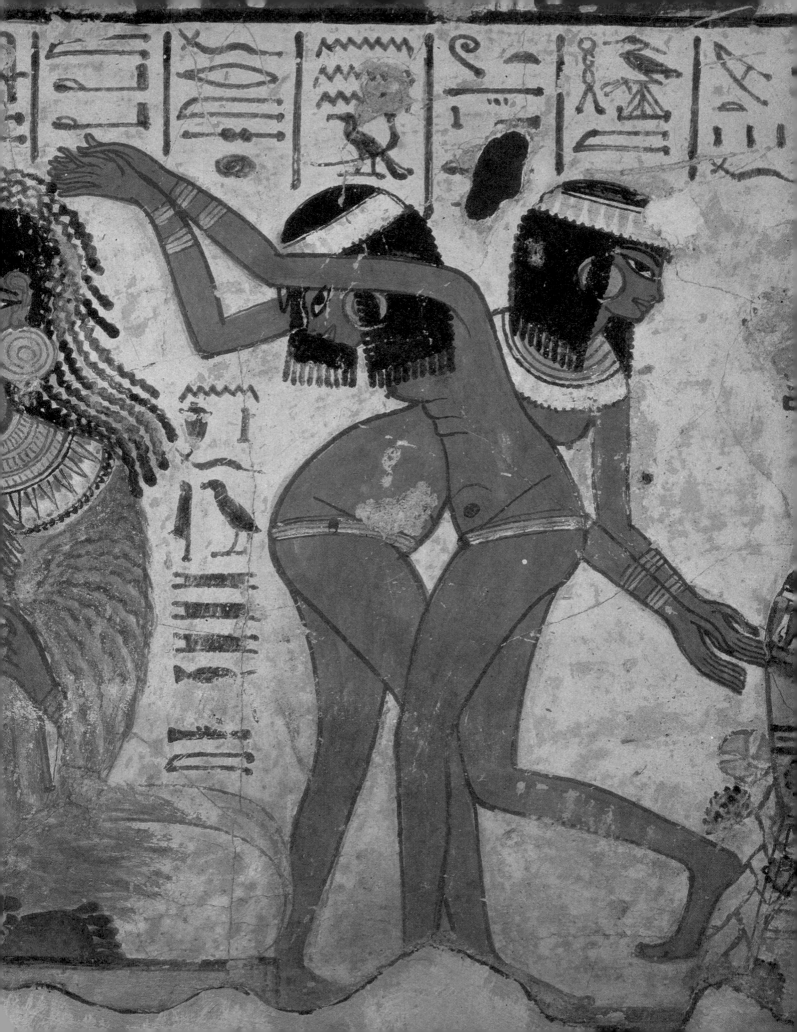

INTRODUCTION

The goal of art history—the subject of this book—is the discerning appreciation and enjoyment of art, from whatever time and place it may have come, by whatever hands it may have been made. Outside the academic world, the terms *art* and *history* are not often juxtaposed. People tend to think of history as the record and interpretation of past (particularly political) human actions, and of art—quite correctly—as something *present* to the eye and touch, which, of course, the vanished human events that make up history are not. The fact is that a visible and tangible work of art is a kind of *persisting event.* It was made at a particular time and place by particular persons, even if we do not always know just when, where, and by whom. Although it is the creation of the past, art continues to exist in the present, long surviving its times; Charlemagne has been dead for a thousand years, but his chapel still stands at Aachen.

THE BASES OF ART HISTORY

Style

The time in which a work of art was made has everything to do with the way it looks—with, in one key term, its *style.* In other words, the style of a work of art is a function of its historical *period.* The historiography of art proceeds by sorting works of architecture, sculpture, and painting into stylistic classes on the bases of their likenesses and the times or periods in which they were

Dancers (detail of FIG. 3-35), wall painting from
the tomb of Nebamun (?), Thebes, *c.* 1450 B.C.

produced. It is a fundamental hypothesis of art history that works of art produced at the same time (and, of course, in the same place) will generally have common stylistic traits. Of course, all historiography assumes that events derive their character from the time in which they happen (and perhaps from their "great men," also products of their time); thus, we can speak of the Periclean Age, the Age of Reason, even—as with the title of a recent historical work—of the Age of Roosevelt. We also must know the time of a work if we are to know its meaning—to know it for what it is. Yet if the work of art still stands before us, persisting from the past, isn't this sufficient? By virtue of its survival, isn't the work in a sense *independent* of time? May not a work of art speak to people of all times as long as it survives? The key to this last question is the word "speak." Indeed, it may speak, but what is its language? What does it say to us? Art may be more than a form of communication, but it is certainly that; and it is the business of art history to learn the "languages" of the art of many different periods as they are embodied in the monuments from their respective times. We can assume that artists in every age express in their works some sort of meaning that is intelligible to themselves and others. We can get at that meaning only by setting a particular work in relation to other works like it that were made about the same time. By grouping works in this way, we can infer a community of meaning as well as of *form*; a style will then be outlined. In a chronological series of works having common stylistic features, we may find that the later and the earlier works show stylistic *differences* as well. The art historian tends to think of this phenomenon as reflecting an evolution, a *development*.

It is obvious that before stylistic development can be inferred it is necessary to be sure that the chronological sequence is correct (that each monument is correctly dated); without this certainty, art-historical order and intelligibility are impossible. Thus, an indispensable tool of the historian is *chronology*, the measuring scale of historical time; without it there could be no history of style—only a confusion of unclassifiable monuments, impossible to describe in any sequence of change.

The table of contents of this book reflects what is essentially a series of periods and subperiods arranged in chronological order—the historical sequence that embraces the sequence of art styles. Until the later eighteenth century, the history of art was really a disconnected account of the lives and the works of individual artists. We now regard art history as a record of the dynamic change of styles in time, and the art of individual masters as substyles of the overall period styles. Although one speaks of "change" in the history of art, the objects themselves obviously do not change; as we have said, they persist, although each naturally suffers some material wear and tear with time. But the fact that works of art from one period look different from those of other periods leads us to infer that *something* changes. This something can only be the points of view of the human makers of works of art with respect to the meaning of life and of art. Modern historiography is much influenced by modern philosophies of change and evolution, and, from the terms and data of biological science, our modern history of art was bound to borrow a sense of continuous process to help explain art-historical change.

In art history, as in the sciences and in other historical disciplines, we have gone far in knowing a thing once we have classified it. Art historians, having done this, resemble experienced travelers who learn to discriminate the different "styles" peculiar to different places. Such travelers know that one must not expect the same style of life in the Maine woods as on the Riviera, and when they have seen a great many places and peoples—like art historians who are familiar with a great many monuments—they are not only at ease with them, but can be said to know and appreciate them for what they are. As their experience broadens, so does their discrimination, or perception of distinctive differences. As world travelers come to see that the location contributes to the unique quality and charm of a town, so students of art, viewing it in the historical dimension, become convinced that a work's peculiar significance, quality, and charm are a function of the time of its making.

But isn't the historical "placing" of a work of art, so visibly and tangibly present, irrelevant to the *appreciation* of it? After all, isn't art-historical knowledge *about* a work of art different from the direct experience of it? The answers lie in the fact that uninstructed appreciators, no matter how sincere, still approach a work of art with the esthetic presuppositions of their own time, rather than of the time of the work itself. Their presuppositions can be tantamount to prejudices, so that their appreciation, even if genuine, may well be for the wrong reasons; it will, in fact, be undiscerning and indiscriminate, so that dozens of works of art may be viewed in the same way, without any savor of the individual significance and quality of each. Thus, as a work of art is intended for a particular audience at a particular time and place, so may its *purpose* be quite particular, and its purpose necessarily enters into its meaning. For example, the famous *Vladimir Madonna* (FIG. 7-62, p. 291) is a Byzantine–Russian icon, a species of art produced not as a work of "fine art" so much as a sacred object endowed with religio-magical power. It was considered, moreover, the especially holy picture of Russia that miraculously saved the city of Vladimir from the hosts of Tamerlane, the city of Kazan from the later Tartar invasions, and all of Russia from the Poles in the seventeenth century. We may admire it for its innate beauty of line, shape, and color, its expressiveness, and its craftsmanship, but unless we are aware of its special historical function as a wonder-working image, we miss the point. We can admire many works of art for their form, content, and quality, but we need a further characterizing experience; otherwise, we are admiring very different works without discriminating their decisive differences. We will be confused, and our judgment will be faulty.

Although our most fundamental way of classifying works of art is by the time of their making, classification by *place of origin* is also crucial. In many periods, a general style (Gothic, for example) will have a great many regional variations: French Gothic architecture is strikingly different from both English and Italian Gothic. Differences of climate helped to make French Gothic an architecture with no bearing walls (and with great spaces for stained-glass windows) and Italian Gothic an architecture with large expanses of wall wonderfully suited to mural painting. Art history, then, is also concerned with the spread of a style from its place of origin. Supplementing time of origin with place of origin therefore adds another dimension to the picture of art monuments in the process of stylistic development.

The *artist*, of course, provides a third dimension in the history of art. Early "histories" of art, written before the advent of modern concepts of style and stylistic development, were simply biographies of artists. Biography as one dimension is still important, for, through it, we can trace stylistic development within the career of the artist. We can learn much from contemporaneous historical accounts, from documents such as commission contracts, and from the artist's own theoretical writings and literary remains. All of this is useful in "explaining" an artist's works, although no complete "explanation" exhausts the meaning of them. Relationships to their predecessors, contemporaries, and followers can be described in terms of the concepts *influence* and *school*. It is likely that artists are influenced by their masters and then influence or are influenced by fellow artists working somewhat in the same style at the same time and place. We designate a group of such artists as a *school*; by this, we do not mean an academy, but a classification of time, place, and style. Thus, we may speak of the Dutch School of the seventeenth century and, within it, of subschools like those of Haarlem, Utrecht, and Leyden.

Iconography

The categories of time and place, the record of the artist, influences, and schools are all used in the composition of the picture of stylistic development. Another kind of classification, another key to works of art, is *iconography*—the study of the subject matter of and symbolism in works of art. By this approach, paintings and sculptures are grouped in terms of their themes rather than their styles, and the development of subject matter becomes a major focus of critical study. Iconographic studies have an ancillary function in stylistic analysis; they are often valuable in tracing influences and in assigning dates and places of origin.

Historical Context

Another very broad source of knowledge of a work of art lies outside the artistic region itself, yet encloses it and is in transaction with it. This is the *general historical context*—the political, social, economic, scientific, technological, and intellectual background that accompanies and influences specifically art-historical events. The fall of Rome, the coming of Christianity, and the barbarian invasions all had much to do with stylistic changes in architecture, sculpture, and painting in the early centuries of our era. The triumph of science and technology had everything to do with the great transformation of the Renaissance tradition that took place in what we call "modern art"—the art of our own time. The work of art, the persisting event, is, after all, a historical document.

THE WORK OF ART

The work of art is an object as well as a historical event. To describe and analyze it, we use categories and vocabularies that have become more-or-less standard and that are indispensable to an understanding of this book.

General Concepts

Form, for the purposes of art history, refers to the shape of the "object" of art; in the made object, it is the shape that the expression of content takes. To create forms, to make a work of art, artists must shape materials with tools. Each of the many materials, tools, and processes available has its own potentialities and limitations; it is part of the artists' creative activity to select the tools most suitable to their purpose. The technical processes that the artists employ, as well as the distinctive, personal way in which they handle them, we call their *technique.* If the material that artists use is the substance of their art, then their technique is their individual manner of giving that substance form. Form, technique, and material are interrelated, as we can readily see in a comparison of the marble statue of *Apollo* from Olympia (FIG. 5-40, p. 149) with the bronze *Charioteer of Delphi* (FIG. 5-37, p. 148). The Apollo is firmly modeled in broad, generalized planes, reflecting the ways of shaping stone that are more-or-less dictated by the character of that material and by the tool used—the chisel. On the other hand, the Charioteer's fineness of detail—the crisp, sharp folds of the drapery—reflects the qualities inherent in cast metal. However, a given medium (the material used) can lend itself to more than one kind of manipulation. The technique of Lehmbruck's bronze *Seated Youth* (FIG. 1), for example, contrasts strikingly with Rodin's *The Thinker* (FIG. 2), also in bronze. The surfaces of Lehmbruck's figure are smooth, flowing, quiet; those of Rodin's figure are rough, broken, and tortuous. Here, it is not so much the bronze that determines the form as it is the sculptor's difference of purpose and of personal technique.

Space, in our common-sense experience, is the bounded or boundless "container" of masses of objects. For the analysis of works of art, we regard space as bounded and susceptible of esthetic and expressive organization. Architecture provides us with our most common experience of the actual manipulation of space; the art of painting frequently projects an image (or illusion) of our three-dimensional spatial world onto a two-dimensional surface.

Area and *plane* describe a limited, two-dimensional space and generally refer to surface. A plane is flat and two-dimensional—like this page and like elements dealt with in plane geometry (a circle, square, or triangle). An area, which also can be described in terms of plane geometry, is often a plane or a flat surface that is enclosed or bounded. Bernini created an area when he defined the essentially plane surface in front of St. Peter's by means of his curving colonnades (FIG. 19-3, p. 714).

Mass and *volume*, in contradistinction to plane and area, describe three-dimensional space. In both architecture and sculpture, mass is the bulk, density, and weight of matter in space. Yet the mass need not be solid; it can be the exterior form of enclosed space. For example, "mass" can apply to a pyramid (FIG. 3-7, p. 78), which is essentially solid, or to the exterior of Hagia Sophia (FIG. 7-41, p. 278), which is essentially a shell enclosing vast spaces. Volume is the space that is organized, divided, or enclosed by mass. It may be the spaces of the interior of a building, the intervals between the masses of a building, or the amount of space occupied by three-dimensional objects like sculpture, ceramics, or furniture. Volume and mass describe the exterior as well as the interior forms of a work of art—the forms of the matter of which it

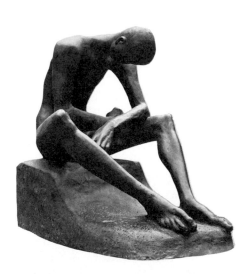 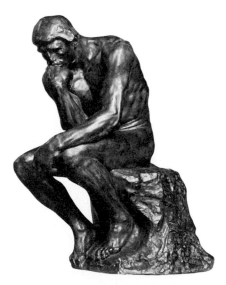

1 WILHELM LEHMBRUCK, *Seated Youth*, 1918. Bronze. Wilhelm-Lehmbruck-Museum, Duisburg.

2 AUGUSTE RODIN, *The Thinker*, 1880. Bronze. Metropolitan Museum of Art, New York (gift of Thomas F. Ryan, 1910).

is composed *and* the forms of the spaces that exist immediately around that matter and interact with it. For example, in the Lehmbruck statue (FIG. 1), the expressive volumes enclosed by the attenuated masses of the torso and legs play an important part in the open design of the piece. The absence of enclosed volumes in the Rodin figure (FIG. 2) is equally expressive, closing the design, making it compact, heavy, and locked in. (Yet both works convey the same mood—one of brooding introversion.) These closed and open forms, manifest throughout the history of art, demonstrate the intimate connection between mass and the space that surrounds and penetrates it.

In the definition of mass and volume, *line* is one of the most important, but most difficult, terms to comprehend fully. In both science and art, line can be understood as the path of a point moving in space, the track of a motion. Because the directions of motions can be almost infinite, the quality of line can be incredibly various and subtle. It is well known that psychological responses are attached to the direction of a line: a vertical line being positive; a horizontal line, passive; a diagonal line, suggestive of movement, energy, or unbalance; and so on. Hogarth regarded the serpentine or S-curve line as the "line of beauty." Our psychological response to line is also bound up with our esthetic sense of its quality. A line may be very thin, wire-like, and delicate, conveying a sense of fragility, as in Klee's *Twittering Machine* (FIG. 22-30, p. 914). Or it may alternate quickly from thick to thin, the strokes jagged, the outline broken, as in a 600-year-old Chinese painting (FIG. 12-20, p. 455); here, the effect is of vigorous action and angry agitation. A gentle, undulating, but firm line, like that in Picasso's *Bathers* (FIG. 3), defines a *contour* that is restful and quietly sensuous. A contour continuously and subtly contains and suggests mass and volume. In the Picasso drawing, the line is distinct, dark against the white of the paper. But line can be felt as a controlling presence in a hard edge, profile, or boundary created by a contrasting area, even when its tone differs only slightly from the tone of the area it bounds. A good example of this can be seen in the central figure of the goddess in Botticelli's *The Birth of Venus* (FIG. 16-60, p. 690).

When a line serves as an element along which forms are organized, it is known as an *axis*. The axis line itself may not be evident; there may be several axis lines (usually with one dominant), as in the layout of a city. Although we are most familiar with directional axes in urban complexes, they occur in all the arts. A fine example of the use of axis in large-scale architecture is the plan

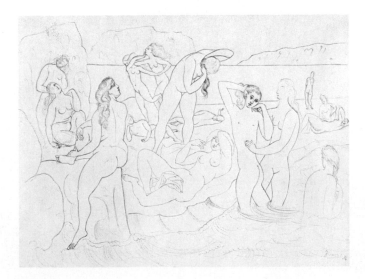

3   PABLO PICASSO, detail of *Bathers*, 1918. Pencil drawing. Fogg Art Museum, Harvard University, Cambridge, Massachusetts (bequest of Paul J. Sachs).

of the Palace of Versailles and its magnificent gardens (FIG. 19-67, p. 761). Axis, whether vertical, horizontal, or diagonal, is also an important compositional element in painting.

Perspective, no less than axis, is a method of organizing forms in space, but perspective is used primarily to create an illusion of depth or space on a two-dimensional surface. Because we are conditioned by exposure to Western, single-point perspective, an invention of the Italian Renaissance (see pp. 600–630), we tend to see perspective as a systematic ordering of pictorial space in terms of a single point—a point at which lines converge to mark the diminishing size of forms as they recede into the distance (FIG. 17-17, p. 612). Renaissance and Baroque artists created masterpieces of perspective illusionism. In Leonardo's *The Last Supper* (FIG. 4), for example, the lines of perspective (dashed lines) converge on Christ and, in the foreground, project the picture space into the room on the wall of which the painting appears, creating the illusion that the space of the picture and the space of the room are continuous. Yet we must remember that Renaissance perspective is only one of several systems for depicting depth. Others were used in ancient Greece and Rome; still others, in the East. Some of these other systems, as well as the Italian Renaissance perspective, continue to be used. There is no final or absolutely correct projection of what we "in fact" see.

Proportion deals with the relationships (in terms of size) of the parts of a work. The experience of proportion is common to all of us. We seem to recognize at once when the features, say, of the human face or body are "out of proportion"—if the nose or ears are too large for the face or the legs are too short for the body. An instinctive or conventional sense of proportion leads us at once to regard the disproportionate as ludicrous or ugly. Formalized proportion is the mathematical relationship in size of one part of a work of art to the other parts within the work, as well as to the totality of the parts; it implies the use of a denominator that is common to the various parts. Recently, it has been shown that the major elements of Leonardo's *Last Supper* exhibit proportions found in harmonic ratios in music—12:6:4:3 (FIG. 4).

4 LEONARDO DA VINCI, *The Last Supper, c.* 1495–1498. Fresco. Santa Maria delle Grazie, Milan. (Perspective lines are dashed; lines indicating proportions are solid white or black.)

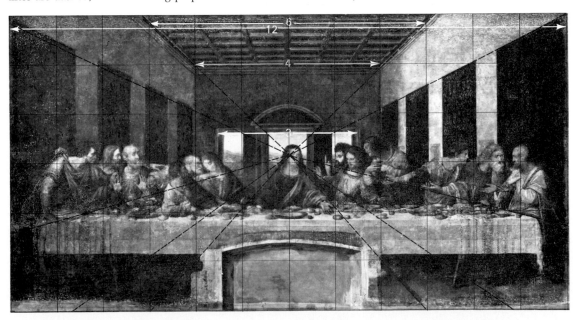

These figures (with the greatest width of a ceiling panel taken as one unit) are the horizontal widths, respectively, of the painting, the ceiling (at the front), the rear wall, and the three windows (taken together and including interstices); they apply to the vertical organization of the painting as well. Leonardo found proportion everywhere: "not only in numbers and measures, but also in sounds, weights, intervals of time, and in every active force in existence."* The ancient Greeks, who considered beauty to be "correct" proportion, sought a canon (rule) of proportion, not only in music, but also for the human figure. The famous Canon of Polykleitos (p. 161), expressed in his statue of the *Doryphoros* (FIG. 5-61, p. 160), long served as an exemplar of correct proportion. But it should be noted that canons of proportion differ from time to time and culture to culture and that, occasionally, artists have deliberately used disproportion. Part of the task of the students of art history is to perceive and adjust to these differences in an effort to understand the wide universe of art forms. Proportional relationships are often based on a *module,* a dimension of which the various parts of a building or other work are fractions or multiples. A module might be the diameter of a column, the height of the human body, or an abstract unit of measurement. For example, the famous "ideal" plan of the ninth-century monastery of St. Gall (FIG. 8-19, p. 331) has a modular base of $2\frac{1}{2}$ feet, so that all parts of the structure are multiples or fractions of this dimension.

Scale (like proportion) refers to the dimensional relationships of the parts of a work to its totality (or of a work to its setting), usually in terms of appropriateness to use or function. We do not think that a private home should be as high as an office building or that an elephant's house at the zoo should be the size of a hencoop—or vice versa. This sense of scale is necessary to the construction of form in all the arts. Most often, but not necessarily, it is the human figure that gives the scale to form.

Form, with which we began this list of fundamental concepts, is mediated primarily by *light.* The function of light in the world of nature is so pervasive that we often take it for granted. Few of us realize the extraordinary variations wrought by light alone, whether natural or artificial, on our most familiar surroundings—as daylight, for example, changes with the hour or season. Few of us realize the full extent to which light affects and reveals form. One who did—the French artist Monet (pp. 855–57)—painted the reflections in a waterlily pond according to their seasonal variations and, in a series of more than 40 canvases of the façade of Rouen Cathedral, revealed its changing aspect from dawn until twilight in different seasons (FIG. 5 and FIG. 21-55, p. 856). Light is as important for the perception of form as is the matter of which form is made.

One function of light is *value.* In painting, and in the graphic arts generally, value refers to lightness, or the amount of light that is (or appears to be) reflected from a surface. Value is a subjective experience, as FIG. 6 shows. In absolute terms (if measured, say, by a photoelectric device), the center bar in this diagram is uniform in value. Yet where the bar is adjacent to a dark area, it *looks* lighter, and where the bar is adjacent to a lighter area, it looks darker. Value is the basis of the quality called, in Italian, *chiaroscuro* (*chiaro,* or light; *scuro,* or dark), which refers to the gradations between light and dark that produce the effect of *modeling,* or of light reflected from three-dimensional surfaces, as exemplified in Leonardo's superb rendering of *The Virgin and Child with St. Anne and the Infant St. John* (FIG. 17-2, p. 602).

In the analysis of light, an important distinction must be made for the realm

*Thomas Brachert, "A Musical Canon of Proportion in Leonardo da Vinci's *Last Supper*," *Art Bulletin*, Vol. 53, No. 4 (December 1971), pp. 461–66.

of art. Natural light, or sunlight, is whole or additive light, whereas the painter's light in art—the light reflected from pigments and objects—is subtractive light. Natural light is the sum of all the wavelengths composing the visible spectrum, which may be disassembled or fragmented into the individual colors of the spectral band. (Recent experiments with lasers—*l*ight *a*mplification by *s*timulated *e*mission of *r*adiation—have produced color of incredible brilliance and intensity, opening possibilities of color composition that, until now, were unsuspected. The range and strength of color produced in this way approach, although at considerable distance, those of the sun.) Although the esthetics of color is largely the province of the artist and can usually be genuinely experienced and understood only through intense

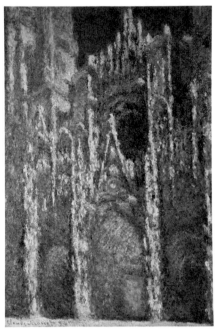

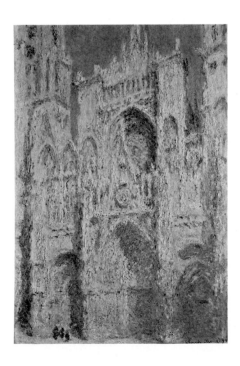

5 CLAUDE MONET, façade of Rouen Cathedral, early 1890s. *Left:* Museum of Fine Arts, Boston (bequest of Hanna Marcy Edwards); *below:* National Gallery of Art, Washington, D.C. (Chester Dale Collection).

6 Effect of adjacent value on apparent value. Actual value of center bar is constant.

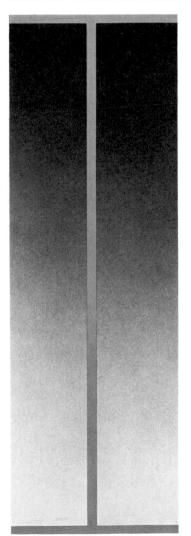

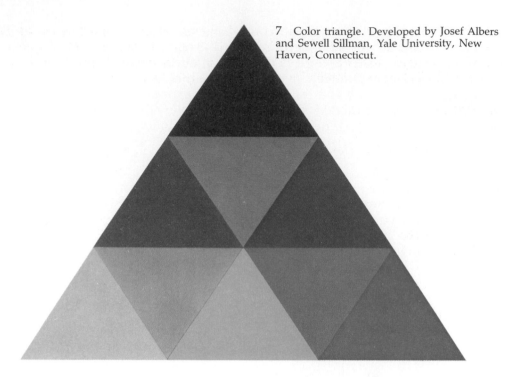

7 Color triangle. Developed by Josef Albers and Sewell Sillman, Yale University, New Haven, Connecticut.

practice and experimentation, some aspects can be analyzed and systematized. Paint pigments (as well as those of the human body) produce their individual colors by reflecting a segment of the spectrum while absorbing all the rest. "Green" pigment, for example, subtracts or absorbs all the light in the spectrum except that seen by us as green, which it reflects to the eye. (In the case of transmitted, rather than reflected, light, the coloring matter—as in stained glass—blocks or screens out all wavelengths of the spectrum except those of the color we see.) Thus, theoretically, a mixture of pigments that embraced all the colors of the spectrum would subtract all light—that is, it would be black; actually, such a mixture of pigments never produces more than a dark gray.

The name of a color is its *hue*—red, blue, yellow. Although the colors of the spectrum merge into each other, artists usually conceive of their hues as distinct from each other, giving rise to many different devices for representing color relationships. There are basically two variables in color—the apparent amount of light reflected and the apparent purity; a change in one must produce a change in the other. Some terms for these variables are (for lightness) *value* and *tonality* and (for purity) *chroma, saturation,* and *intensity*.

One of the more noteworthy diagrams of the relationships of colors is the triangle (FIG. 7), once attributed to Goethe, in which red, yellow, and blue (the *primary colors*) are the vertexes of the triangle and orange, green, and purple (the *secondary colors,* which result from mixing pairs of primaries) lie between them. Colors that lie opposite each other (such as red and green) are called *complementary* colors, because they complement, or complete, one another, each absorbing those colors that the other reflects and resulting in a neutral tone or gray (theoretically, black) when mixed in the right proportions. The inner triangles in FIG. 7 are the products of such mixing.

Color also has a psychological dimension—red and yellow, quite naturally, connoting warmth; blue and green, coolness. Generally, *warm* colors seem to *advance* and *cool* colors seem to *recede*.

The quality of a surface (rough, smooth, hard, soft, shiny, dull) as revealed by light is *texture*. The many painting media and techniques permit the creation of a variety of textures. The artist may simulate the texture of the materials represented, as in Kalf's *Still Life* (FIG. 19-56, p. 752), or create arbitrary surface differences, even using materials other than canvas, as in Picasso's *Still Life with Chair-Caning* (FIG. 22-14, p. 902).

Specialized Concepts

The terms we have been discussing have connotations for all the visual arts. Certain observations, however, are relevant to only one category of artistic endeavor—to architecture, or to sculpture, or to painting.

IN ARCHITECTURE

Works of architecture are so much a part of our environment that we accept them as given, and scarcely notice them until our attention is summoned. People have long known how to enclose space for the many purposes of life. Of all the arts, it is in architecture that the spatial aspect is most obvious. The architect makes groupings of enclosed spaces and enclosing masses, always keeping in mind the function of the structure, its construction and materials, and, of course, its design—the correlative of the other two. We experience architecture both visually and by moving through and around it, so that we perceive architectural space and mass together. The articulation of space and mass in building is expressed graphically in several ways; the principal ones follow.

A *plan* is essentially a map of a floor, showing the placement of the masses of a structure and, therefore, the spaces they bound and enclose (FIG. 7-44, p. 280). A *section*, like a vertical plan, shows placement of the masses as if the building were cut through along a plane—often one that is a major axis of the building (FIG. 3-8, p. 78). An *elevation* is a head-on view of an external or internal wall, showing its features and often other elements that would be visible beyond or before the wall (FIG. 5-56, p. 158).

Our response to a building can range from simple comfort to astonishment and awe. Such reactions are products of our experience of a building's function, construction, and design; we react differently to a church, a gymnasium, and an office building. For one thing, the very movements we must make to experience one building will differ widely and profoundly from the movements required to experience another. These movements will be controlled by the continuity (or discontinuity) of the plan or by the placement of its axes. For example, in a central plan—one that radiates from a central point, as in the Pantheon in Rome (FIG. 6-53, p. 223)—we perceive the whole spatial entity at once; but in the long axial plan of a Christian basilica (FIG. 7-27, p. 268) or a Gothic cathedral (FIG. 10-17, p. 383), our attention tends to focus on a given point—the altar at the eastern end of the nave. Mass and space can be interrelated to produce effects of great complexity, as, for example, in the Byzantine Church of the Katholikon (FIG. 7-48, p. 283) or in Le Corbusier's church at Ronchamp (FIG. 22-106, p. 964). Thus, our experience of architecture will be the consequence of a great number of material and formal factors, including training, knowledge, and our perceptual and psychological makeup, which function in our experience of any work of art.

The architect must have the sensibilities of a sculptor and of a painter and, in establishing the plan of a building, must be able to use the instruments of a mathematician. As architects resolve structural problems, they act as (or with) engineers who are cognizant of the structural principles underlying all architecture (FIG. 8). Their major responsibilities, however, lie in the manner in which they interpret the *program* of the building. We are not talking in architectural terms when we describe a structure simply as a church, a hospital, an airport concourse, a house. Any proposed building presents an architect with problems peculiar to it alone—problems related to the site and its surroundings, the requirements of the client, and the materials available, as well as the function of the building. A program, then, deals with more than function; it addresses itself to all the problems embodied in a specific building.

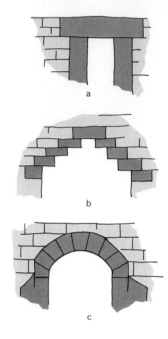

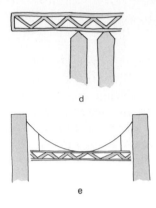

8   Basic structural devices: (a) post and lintel; (b) corbeled arch; (c) arch; (d) cantilever; (e) suspension.

IN SCULPTURE

Like architecture, sculpture exists in the three-dimensional space of our physical world. But sculpture as image is closer to painting than is architecture. Until recently, sculpture has been concerned primarily with the representation of human and natural forms in tangible materials, which exist in the same space as the forms they represent. However, sculpture also may embody visions and ideals and has consistently presented images of deities and people in their most heroic as well as their most human aspects (FIGS. 17-20, p. 616, and 5-77, p. 170). Today, sculpture often dispenses with the figure as image, and even with the image itself, producing new forms in new materials and with new techniques (FIGS. 22-79 through 22-86, 22-89, and 22-91, pp. 946–53).

Sculpture may be intimately associated with architecture, often to such a degree that it is impossible to disassociate the two (FIG. 10-14, p. 381). Sculpture is called *relief* sculpture when it is attached to a back slab or back plate (FIG. 3-42, p. 100); *high relief*, if the figures or design project boldly (FIG. 5-79, p. 171); and *low relief*, or *bas-relief*, if the figures or design project slightly (FIG. 3-42, p. 100).

Sculpture that exists in its own right, independent of any particular architectural frame or setting (FIG. 17-47, p. 636), is usually referred to as *freestanding* sculpture, or "sculpture in the round," although, in the art of Greece and of the Renaissance, freestanding sculpture has been closely allied to architecture on many occasions. Indeed, sculpture is such a powerful agent in creating a spatial as well as an intellectual environment that its presence in city squares or in parks and gardens is usually the controlling factor in creating their "atmosphere" or general effect (FIG. 19-74, p. 765).

Some statues are meant to be seen as a whole—to be walked around (FIG. 17-47, p. 636). Others have been created to be viewed only from a restricted angle. How a sculpture is meant to be seen must be taken into account by the sculptor, and by those who exhibit the work. The effect of ignoring this is illustrated in FIG. 9. The left photograph is taken directly from the front, as the piece is now seen in the museum; the right photograph is taken from below, at approximately the same angle from which the statue was originally meant to be seen in its niche on the facade of the cathedral of Florence.

In sculpture, perhaps more than in any other medium, textures, or tactile values, are important. One's first impulse is almost always to handle a piece of sculpture, to run one's finger over its surfaces. The sculptor plans for this, using a great variety of surfaces from rugged coarseness to polished smoothness (FIGS. 10-56, p. 407, and 16-50, p. 581). Textures, of course, are often intrinsic to a material, and this influences the type of stone, wood, plastic, clay, or metal that the sculptor selects. There are two basic categories of sculptural technique: *subtractive* and *additive.* Carving, for instance, is a subtractive technique; the final form is a reduction of the original mass (FIG. 10). Additive sculpture is built up, usually in clay around a framework, or armature; the piece is fired and used to make a mold in which the final work is cast in a material such as bronze (FIG. 16-52, p. 583). Casting is a popular technique today, as is the direct construction of forms by welding shaped metals (FIG. 22-80, p. 947), also an additive technique.

Within the sculptural family, we must include ceramics and metalwork, and numerous smaller, related arts, all of which employ highly specialized techniques described in distinct vocabularies. These will be considered as they arise in the text.

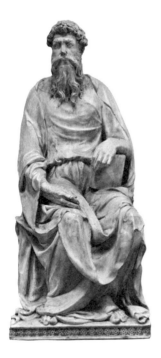

9 DONATELLO, *St. John the Evangelist,* 1412–1415. Marble. Museo del Duomo, Florence. *Left:* as seen in museum; *right:* as intended to be seen on façade of Florence Cathedral.

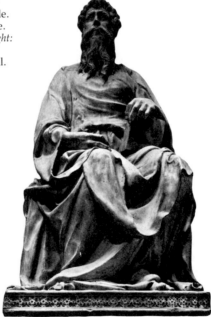

IN THE PICTORIAL ARTS

The forms of architecture and sculpture exist in actual, three-dimensional space. The forms of painting (and of its relatives, drawing, engraving, and the like) exist almost wholly on a two-dimensional surface, on which the artist creates an illusion—something that replicates what we see around us or something that is unique to the artist's imagination and corresponds only vaguely or slightly to anything we can see in the optical world. Human discovery of the power to project illusions of the three-dimensional world onto two-dimensional surfaces goes back thousands of years and marks an enormous step in the control and manipulation of the things we perceive. To

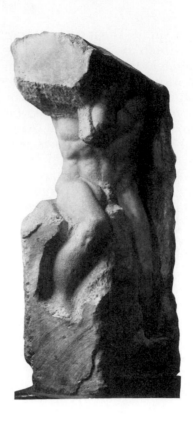

10 MICHELANGELO, *Unfinished Bound Slave,*
1519. Marble. Accademia, Florence.

achieve this illusion, the artist configures images or representations drawn
from the world of common visual experience. Throughout the history of art,
this has been interpreted in an almost infinite variety of ways. Undoubtedly,
there is much that all people *see* in common and can agree on: the moon at
night, a flying bird, an obstacle in one's path. They may differ, though, in
their interpretation of the *seen,* for seeing and then representing what is seen
are very different matters. The difference between *seeing* and *representing*
determines the variability of artistic styles, both cultural and personal. For
what we *actually* see (the optical "fact") is not necessarily reported in what we
represent. In other words, in art, there is and need be little agreement
between the *likeness* of a thing and the *representation* of it. This makes for a
persisting problem in the history of art. How are we to interpret or "read"
images or replicas of the seen? Is there a "correct" vision of the "real" world?

THE PROBLEM OF REPRESENTATION

The conundrum of seeing something and making a representation of it is
artfully illustrated in FIG. 11, a cartoon of a life-drawing class in ancient Egypt
that Gombrich uses to introduce his invaluable work *Art and Illusion.* The
cartoon and the actual representation of an Egyptian queen (FIG. 12) raise
many questions: Did Egyptian artists copy models exactly as they saw them?
(Did Egyptians actually *see* each other in this way?) Or did they translate what
they saw according to some formula dictated by conventions of representation
peculiar to their culture? Would we have to say—if what was seen and what
was recorded were optically the same—that this is the way Egyptians must
have looked? Or wished to look? Beginning students usually have questions
somewhat like these in mind when they perceive deviations in historical
styles from the recent Western realism to which they are conditioned. They

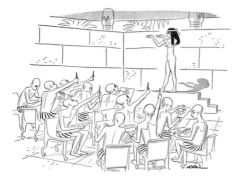

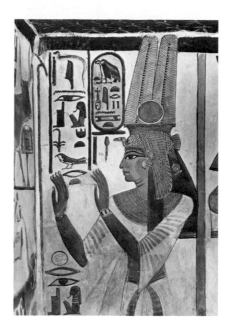

12 *Queen Nofretari,* from her tomb at Thebes, *c.* 1250 B.C. Detail of a painted bas-relief.

will ask whether the Egyptians, or other artists, were simply unskilled at matching eye and hand, so to speak, and could not draw from what they saw. But such a question presupposes that the objective of the artist has always been to match appearances with camera-like exactitude. This is not the case, nor is it the case that artists of one period "see" more "correctly" and render more "skillfully" than those of another. Rather, it seems that artists represent what they *conceive* to be real, not what they *perceive.* They bring to the making of images conceptions that have been instilled in them by their cultures. They understand the visible world in certain unconscious, culturally agreed-on ways, and thus bring to the artistic process ideas and meanings out of a common stock. They record not so much what they *see* as what they *know* or *mean.* Even in the period of dominant realism in recent western European art, great deviations from camera realism have set in. Moreover, in our everyday life there are images familiar to all of us that distort optical "reality" quite radically; consider, for example, the images of the ubiquitous comic strip.

Solutions to the problem of representation compose the history of artistic style. It is useful to examine some specimens of sharp divergence in representational approach. Compare, for example, the lion drawn by the medieval artist Villard de Honnecourt (FIG. 13) and lions drawn by the Renaissance artist Albrecht Dürer (FIG. 14). In the de Honnecourt lion— which, it is important to notice, the artist asserts was drawn from life—the figure is entirely adequate for identification but preconceived and constructed according to the formulas of its time. Dürer's lions, drawn some three centuries later, obviously are a much different report of what the artist saw. So are the Assyrian lions of the hunting reliefs (FIG. 2-30, p. 61), the *Lion from the Processional Way* of the Ishtar Gate (FIG. 2-32, p. 62), the lion in Henri Rousseau's *The Sleeping Gypsy* (FIG. 21-77, p. 876), or (in slight shift of species) Barye's sculpture of a jaguar in his *Jaguar Devouring a Hare* (FIG. 21-8, p. 814). In each case, *personal vision* joins with the *artistic conventions* of time and place to decide the manner and effect of the representation. Yet, even at the same

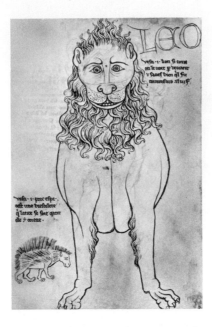

13 Villard de Honnecourt, *Lion Portrayed from Life*, c. 1230–1235. Drawing. Cabinet des Manuscripts, Bibliothèque Nationale, Paris.

14 Albrecht Dürer, *Two Lions*, c. 1521. Drawing. Staatliche Museen Preussischer Kulturbesitz, Kupferstichkabinet, Berlin.

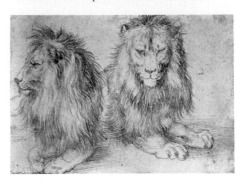

time and place (for example, nineteenth-century Paris), we can find sharp differences in representation when the opposing personal styles of Ingres and Delacroix record the same subject (FIGS. 21-24 and 21-25, pp. 826–27).

A final example will underscore the relativity of vision and representation that differences in human cultures produce. We recognize, moreover, that close matching of appearances has mattered only in a few times and places. Although both portraits of a Maori chieftain from New Zealand (FIG. 15)—one by a European, the other by the chieftain himself—reproduce his facial tatooing, the first portrait is a simple, commonplace likeness that underplays the tatooing. The self-portrait is a statement by the chieftain of the supreme importance of the design that symbolizes his rank among his people. It is the splendidly composed insignia that is his image of himself, the European likeness being superficial and irrelevant to him.

Students of the history of art, then, learn to distinguish the works before them by scrutinizing them closely within the context of their time and place of origin. But this is only the beginning. The causes of stylistic change in time are mysterious and innumerable; and it is only through the continuing process of art-historical research that we can hope to make the picture even fragmentarily recognizable, never complete. Incomplete though the picture is, the panorama of art, changing in time, lies before the students; and, as their art-historical perspective gains depth and focus, they will come to perceive the continuity of the art of the past with that of the present. It will become clear that one cannot be understood without the other and that our understanding of the one will constantly change with changes in our understanding of the other. The great American poet and critic T.S. Eliot has cogently expressed this truth for all of art in a passage that suggests the philosophy and method of this book:

> . . . what happens when a new work of art is created is something that happens simultaneously to all the works of art which preceded it. The existing monuments form an ideal order among themselves, which is modified by the introduction of the new (the really new) work of art among them. . . . Whoever has approved this idea of order . . . will not find it preposterous that the past should be altered by the present as much as the present is directed by the past.*

*T.S. Eliot, "Tradition and the Individual Talent," in *Selected Essays 1917–1932* (New York: Harcourt Brace Jovanovich, 1932), p. 5.

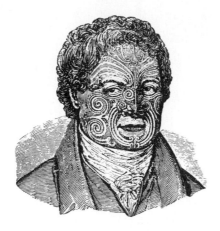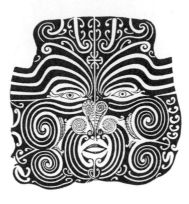

15   *The Maori Chief Tupai Kupa, c.* 1800. *Left:* after a drawing by John Sylvester; *right:* a self-portrait. From *The Childhood of Man* by Leo Frobenius, 1909. Reproduced by permission of J.B. Lippincott Company.

As new works of art continue to be created, old ones, buried by time, are recovered and others, known to have existed, disappear. Many come to light by chance, and many are destroyed by catastrophe or neglect. Restoration and reconstruction either damage or rescue them. The whole domain of art constantly shifts in outline and population, as does our knowledge of it. Identification of a work of art may be accepted at one time, rejected at another. Attribution of certain works to certain artists may be challenged. The chronology of stylistic change may be readjusted; the dating of particular works, debated and revised. Critics may disagree as to the number of works to be ascribed to a single artist. (Some allow Rembrandt as many as 600 paintings; some, as few as 350.) Reinterpretation of the meanings and functions of works of art is an ongoing process, as is the reassessment of their artistic value and stylistic importance. Our knowledge of art history is as much in flux as artistic creation itself; what seems to be certain at one time proves to be inconclusive or erroneous at another. Evidence for our conclusions is never all in; more of it is always turning up, and much of it cannot be found.

Students are therefore cautioned not to expect this book to contain an outlay of facts that are incontestable beyond all alteration. The facts are the works of art themselves, as made palpable to our senses; our descriptions of these works—our dating, attributions, classifications, interpretations—are forever provisional and open to doubt. What is not open to doubt is the presence in our world of a small universe of objects of art that expresses, in myriad, arresting forms, the highest values and ideals of the human race. It is essential to the quality of our own experience to encounter, comprehend, appreciate, and preserve these precious works of human hands.

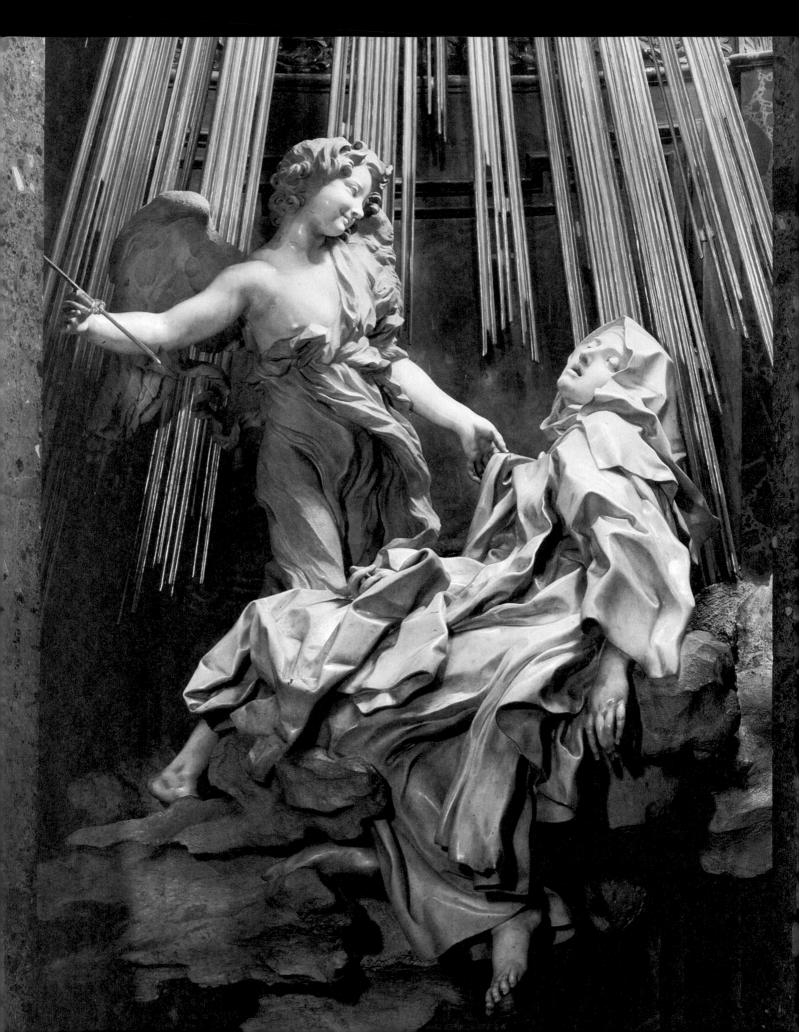

IV
THE RENAISSANCE AND THE BAROQUE AND ROCOCO

The Medieval period was once regarded as a thousand dark and empty years separating the "good" eras—Classical antiquity and modern times, the Renaissance being thought of as "early modern." But beginning in the nineteenth century, a more cosmopolitan and tolerant taste and a more discerning and accurate historical method readjusted the view, and to us the Middle Ages are no longer so "dark" as once depicted. In the same way, the

GIANLORENZO BERNINI, *The Ecstasy of St. Theresa*, 1645–1652. Marble, life-size. Cornaro Chapel, Santa Maria della Vittoria, Rome.

Renaissance ("rebirth"), spanning roughly the fourteenth through the sixteenth century, no longer seems, as it was once thought to be, the abrupt onset of the modern world suddenly shining forth in the fifteenth century to illuminate Medieval darkness with the rekindled light of Classical antiquity. Much of the Renaissance has its roots in epochs that long "preceded" the Middle Ages, and much that is Medieval continues in the Renaissance and even much later. Since the mid-nineteenth century, when Jacob Burckhardt wrote his influential and still highly valuable work *The Civilization of the Renaissance in Italy*, the precise dividing line between the Middle Ages and the Renaissance and even the question of whether there ever was a Renaissance have been disputed. Without reopening these issues, it may be useful to examine the Renaissance characteristics that, although originating in the earlier period, seem to have matured and to have become influential during the period from the fourteenth through the sixteenth century.

Medieval feudalism, with its patchwork of baronial jurisdictions and sprawling, inefficient local governments, yielded slowly to the competition of strong cities and city-states, which were increasingly in league with powerful kings, both being the natural political enemies of the countryside barons. The outlines of the modern state, with its centralized administrations, organized armies, aggressive expansionism, and "realistic" politics, began to become firm about this time. The discovery of the world outside Europe—especially the Western Hemisphere and Africa, itself so dramatically expressive of Renaissance expansiveness—brought vast treasures of gold and silver into Europe, beginning its transformation into a money economy, a process already begun in the thirteenth century in the commercial cities of Italy. Increasingly, religion came under the direction of the clergy of the cities, particularly of such orders as the Dominicans and the Franciscans; the claims of the popes to temporal as well as spiritual supremacy were surrendered, and they became merely splendid Italian princes. Eventually, with the upheaval of the Protestant Reformation, which fractured the old Medieval religious unity, religion became almost a branch of the state, with kings and princes well in control of its secular manifestations. Dramatic events in science, like Nicolaus Copernicus' enunciation of the heliocentric theory of the solar system, set the scene for the development of the first successful empirical science—mathematical physics. The opening of the heavens to Western man's scrutiny was attended by the renewed physical exploration of the globe and, until recently, by the increasing subjugation of it to the will of Europe. Technological advances in navigation, metallurgy, mechanics, and warfare helped greatly to that end.

The religious fanaticism that had launched the Crusades—Europe's first extended contact with non-European civilizations—was replaced during the Renaissance by motives of calculated economic interest mingled with the genuine and fruitful curiosity of the explorer. Indeed, the Renaissance was precisely what it has often been called, an "age of discovery," when Europe saw before it an almost fantastic realm of possibility open to all men of merit who could perceive it.

Accompanying the great events that quite clearly set the Middle Ages and the Renaissance apart were subtler changes of human attitude. There was a slow turning away from the ideas and values of a supernatural orientation and toward those concerned with the natural world and the life of man. The meaning of the world and of human life came to be couched in terms that were not exclusively religious. The spirit and dogma of Medieval religion— even its emotional color—were modified as the worldly philosophy of the Greco–Roman tradition revived and took on new strength. But the process of humanization had begun well before the full influence of the pagan tradition was felt; the twelfth century had seen its beginning. In the thirteenth century, the teachings of St. Francis had humanized religion itself and had called man's attention to the beauty of the world and of all things in it, even though he understood the physical beauty he celebrated as a manifestation of the spiritual; nevertheless, his emphasis was clear, and the Franciscan message calls attention to the God-made beauties of the natural order. This message had special significance for the naturalism of proto-Renaissance art. The duty of Medieval man—the focus of his life—was to procure, through the sacred offices of the Church, the salvation of his immortal soul. In the Renaissance, though the obligation and concern remained and the institutions of the Church retained power, nature and the relations among human beings simply became *more interesting* than theological questions. Theology, like institutional Christianity, persisted; so also, for centuries, did fervent Christian devotion. But there can be no doubt that they were affected by a new spirit—the spirit of pagan humanism—which curiously joined with and reinforced the Christian humanism of St. Francis. The intellectual and artistic history of the modern world is as much the history of Christianity's reaction to this new spirit as it is a history of the challenge of that spirit to Christianity. Actually, the challenge and the reaction interacted, modifying each other. The dialogue between the late Greco–Roman world and nascent Christianity commenced again in the Renaissance; since that time, it has been supplemented and amplified by other, even stronger voices, especially those of modern science.

Whereas the veritable face and body of the human being emerged in the transition from Romanesque to Gothic sculpture, Renaissance art brings Western humanity rapidly into full view—a phenomenon that resembles the manifestation of the human figure in Greek art in the sixth and fifth centuries B.C. The Renaissance stresses the importance of the individual, especially men of merit. In life and in art, the focus is sharpened; at last, individuals are real, are solid, and cast a shadow. Medieval man saw himself as corrupt and feeble of will—in fact, capable of acting only by the agency of God's grace. Although many thinkers, both Protestant and Catholic, insisted on this view for centuries, the Renaissance view is different: man may make himself. He is assumed to have a power of agency—God-given, to be sure—that, in the greatest of men, becomes the divine gift of "genius." Thus, in the Renaissance, those who think may overcome the curse of original sin and, in so doing, rise above its devastating load of guilt to make themselves, if they will, what they will. In his *Oration on the Dignity of Man* (the very title of which constitutes a bold new claim), Giovanni Pico della Mirandola, an ingenious and daring Renaissance philosopher, represents God giving the following permission to all in a way that reflects a sharp departure from the Medieval sense of man's natural helplessness:

> The nature of all other beings is limited and constrained within the bounds of laws prescribed by Us. Thou, constrained by no limits, in accordance with thine own free will . . . shalt ordain for thyself the limits of thy nature. We have set thee at the world's center . . . and have made thee neither of heaven nor of earth, neither mortal nor immortal, so that with freedom of choice and with honor . . . thou mayest fashion thyself in whatever shape thou shalt prefer.*

This option would have been almost unthinkable in the Middle Ages: could one really aspire beyond the angels or debase oneself below the beasts and inanimate nature, given one's place in the carefully articulated "chain of being" that God had made permanent?

---

*Giovanni Pico della Mirandola, *Oratio de hominis dignitate* (1485), trans. by E.L. Forbes, in Ernst Cassirer et al., eds., *The Renaissance Philosophy of Man* (Chicago: University of Chicago Press, 1956), pp. 224–25.

Whether or not one could indeed so rise or fall, the leaders of the Renaissance were acutely aware of the new possibilities open to their talents and did not fail to recognize, and often advertise, the powers they were confident they possessed. The wide versatility of many Renaissance artists—like Alberti, Brunelleschi, Leonardo da Vinci, and Michelangelo—led them to experimentation and to achievement in many of the arts and sciences and gave substance to that concept of the archetypal Renaissance genius—*l'uomo universale*, "the universal man." Class distinctions and social hierarchies had loosened, and the ambitious and talented could now take their places even as the friends, companions, and advisers of princes. Such persons could win the award of everlasting fame, and what has been called the "cult of fame" went naturally with the new glorification of individual genius. Indeed, the immortality won through fame may have been more coveted by many great men of the time than the spiritual immortality promised by religion. When the painter Fra Filippo Lippi died in 1469, the town of Spoleto requested that it be allowed to keep his remains on the grounds that Florence, his native city, already had many celebrated men buried within the bounds of its walls.

Petrarch, the great Italian poet and scholar of the fourteenth century, who may fairly be said to have first propounded those peculiarly Renaissance values of versatile individualism and humanism nourished by the study of Classical antiquity, has been called the high priest of the "cult of fame" and, by many, the founder of the Renaissance. Petrarch himself was crowned with the ancient symbol of triumph and fame, the laurel wreath, on the Capitoline Hill in Rome; the occasion was a celebration of his superb sonnets (written in native Italian), which open the age of Renaissance literature. Petrarch, in his development of the "cult of fame," postulated that public recognition is never given to an unworthy work or talent and that, therefore, public glory is proof of excellence. After Petrarch, it would be possible to call both great works and great men "divine," as if they belonged to a kind of religious congregation of a new elect; thus it was with the *Divina Commedia* of Dante and with Michelangelo after his death.

Petrarch's embracement of a new concept of Humanism encouraged the resurrection of the spirit of Classical antiquity from a trove of ancient manuscripts, which were eagerly hunted, edited, and soon to be reproduced in books made by the new process of mechanical printing. With the help of a new interest in and knowledge of Greek (stimulated by the immigration of Byzantine refugee-scholars after the fall of Constantinople to the Turks), the Humanists of the later fourteenth and fifteenth centuries recovered a large part of the Greek as well as the Roman literature and philosophy that had been lost, unnoticed, or cast aside in the Middle Ages. Their greatest literary contribution was, perhaps, the translation of these works, but they also wrote commentaries on them, which they used as models for their own historical, rhetorical, poetic, and philosophical writings. What the Humanists perceived with great excitement in classical writing was a philosophy for living in this world, a philosophy of human focus primarily, that derived not from an authoritative and traditional religious dogma but from reason, which was supposed to be awarded directly to anyone of intelligence and taste. The model, thus, for the Renaissance is no longer the world-despising holy man but rather the great-souled, intelligent man of the world.

Though the Humanism inspired by Petrarch matured and flourished between the late fourteenth and early sixteenth centuries in Renaissance Italy, it was a phenomenon of great complexity, with varying tendencies and emphases, diverging as well as converging doctrines, and personalities often in wordy conflict with one another. Thus, Humanism is not easy to define with comprehensive sureness; the modern philosophy called "humanism," for example, is quite different in many ways from that of the Renaissance. Yet we can say that the early Humanism embraced the ideal of a new kind of practical knowledge, extracted from the literature of Classical antiquity and applied to the problems of secular and civil life prevailing in the city culture of the Renaissance. The Humanists thought of themselves as a new kind of professionals, distinct from the clergy, who could improve the human condition by propagating the new knowledge through education and public service. They were educators, publicists, administrators, secretaries, and advisers to princes just as much as they were philosophers, scholars, historians, and poets—and, as we shall see, important for Renaissance art. Though they prized literature and scholarship for their own sake, they sought not so much to recover Classical antiquity in all its completeness and correctness, but rather to use it as a basis for pointing a new way to the understanding, conduct, and enjoyment of life.

Medieval scholars were in possession of vast learning embodied in the inherited culture of antiquity, but they had viewed this heritage in a different light from that prevalent in the Renaissance. The Medieval scholar, usually a theologian, had valued classical learning mostly for its usefulness in arguing Christian dogma; thus, Aquinas could use Aristotle as the authority for arguments based on scriptural revelation, while others could point to secular classical literature as a tool for tempting souls to damnation through atheism and sensuality. The Renaissance Humanists found inspiration in the heroes of antiquity, especially in the accounts of their careers in Plutarch's *Parallel Lives:* by the fifteenth and sixteenth centuries, even the lives of prominent contemporaries were viewed as appropriate exemplars of life's rule of reason intelligently and nobly followed. The biographies of famous men no longer dealt exclusively with the heroes of antiquity, and artists painted portraits of illustrious contemporaries. The confident, new, "modern" tone rings in Alberti's treatise *On Painting,* in which he congratulates his generation on its achievements:

> And I reveal to you, that if it was less difficult for the ancients, having as they had so very many to learn from and imitate, to rise to a knowledge of those supreme arts that are so toilsome for us today, then so much the more our fame should be greater if we, without teachers or any model, find arts and sciences unheard of and never seen.*

Almost prophetically, Alberti asserts that the moderns will go beyond the ancients; but the ancient example had first to be given—both as a model and a point of departure.

Although the Humanists of the Renaissance received the new message from pagan antiquity with enthusiasm, they did not look on themselves as pagans. It was possible, for example, for the fifteenth-century scholar Lorenzo Valla to prove the forgery of the *Donation of Constantine* (an early Medieval document purporting to record Constantine's bequest of the Roman empire to the Church) without feeling that he had compromised his Christian faith. The two great religious orders founded in the thirteenth century, the Dominicans and the Franciscans, were as dominant in setting the tone of fourteenth- and fifteenth-century Christian thought as they had been earlier, and they continued to be patrons of the arts. Within these established religious orders, Humanist clerics strengthened rather than weakened the reputation of the Church. Humanists, sometimes while members of religious orders, were appointed to important posts in city governments; the Florentine office of chancellor, for example, was held by distinguished men of letters. On the other hand, secular lords like Federigo da Montefeltro, Lord of Urbino—a

*In E.G. Holt, ed., *Literary Sources of Art History* (Princeton, N.J.: Princeton University Press, 1947), p. 109.

skilled general, generous governor of his people, Humanist patron of the arts and letters, and renowned lover of books—chose to die in the arms of the Church after a long and pious spiritual preparation. Here and there, the antagonism between the pagan and the Christian traditions may have manifested itself—and certainly it was bound to continue to exist—but, in general, the Renaissance achieved a natural, sometimes effortless, reconciliation of the two.

Not least among the leaders of the new age were the artists who, it appears to a number of modern historians, were among its most significant producers. Indeed, the products of the plastic arts may have been the most characteristic and illustrious of the Renaissance. Although we now perceive much more of the value of Renaissance literature, philosophy, and science, these branches of human creativity seem, in comparison with the plastic arts, to have been less certain, complete, and developed. But it is noteworthy that the separation of the great disciplines was not as clear-cut as it now is; mathematics and art, especially, went hand in hand, many Renaissance artists being convinced that geometry was fundamental to the artist's education and practice. In *The School of Athens* (FIG. 17-17), Raphael places his portrait and the portraits of his

RAPHAEL, detail of *The School of Athens* (FIG. 17-17). Raphael appears second from the extreme right in the foreground grouping.

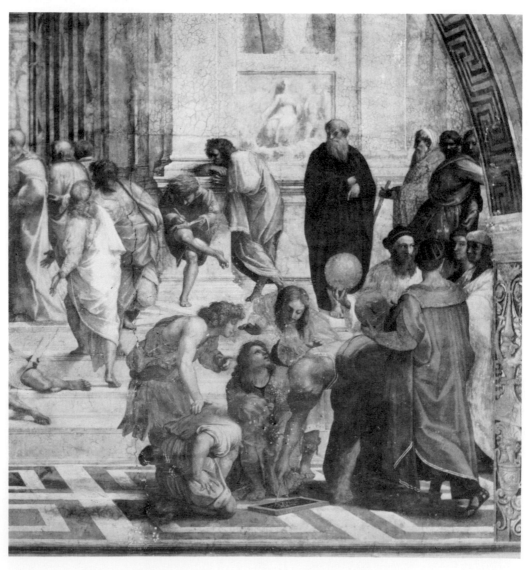

colleagues among the mathematicians and philosophers, not among the poets. The Medieval distinction of *ars* and *scientia* is replaced by a concept (becoming current again) that views them as interrelated. Albrecht Dürer will insist that art without science—that is, technique without a theory relating the artist's skills and observations—is fruitless. The careful observations of the optical world made by Renaissance artists and the integration of these observations by such a mathematical system as perspective (derived from Medieval optics) foreshadow the formulations of the natural sciences. The twentieth-century thinker and mathematician, Alfred North Whitehead, believes that the habit and temper of modern science are anticipated in the patient and careful observation of nature practiced by the artists of the Renaissance. The methodical pursuit of a system that could bring order to visual experience may necessarily precede the scientific analysis of what lies behind what we see. Thus, the art of the Renaissance may be said to be the first monument to Western man's later search for order in nature.

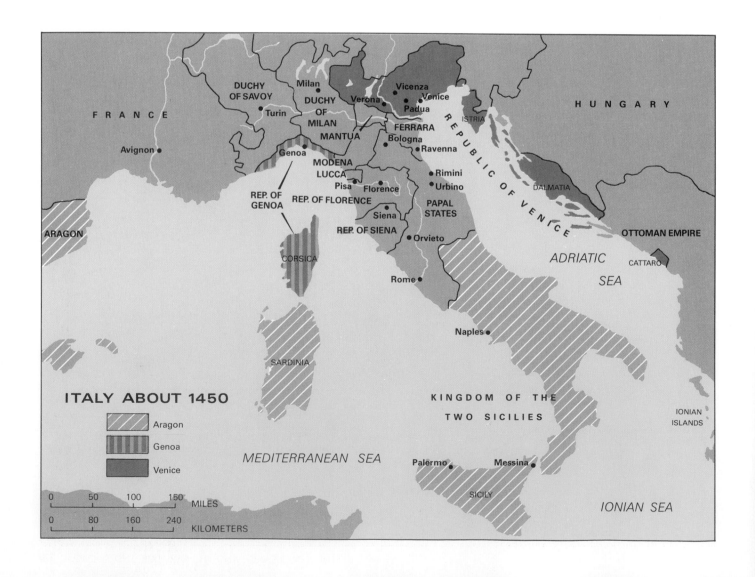

ITALY ABOUT 1450

Aragon
Genoa
Venice

0   50   100   150   MILES
0   80   160   240   KILOMETERS

FRANCE

DUCHY OF SAVOY
Turin
Avignon

Milan
DUCHY OF MILAN
MANTUA
Genoa
REP. OF GENOA
MODENA
LUCCA
Pisa
REP. OF FLORENCE
Florence
Siena
REP. OF SIENA
Orvieto
Rome

CORSICA

SARDINIA

Verona
Vicenza
Venice
Padua
FERRARA
Bologna
Ravenna
Rimini
Urbino
PAPAL STATES

REPUBLIC OF VENICE
ISTRIA
DALMATIA

HUNGARY

OTTOMAN EMPIRE
CATTARO
ADRIATIC SEA

Naples

KINGDOM OF THE TWO SICILIES

MEDITERRANEAN SEA

Palermo   Messina

SICILY

IONIAN ISLANDS

IONIAN SEA

ARAGON

15

THE "PROTO-RENAISSANCE" IN ITALY

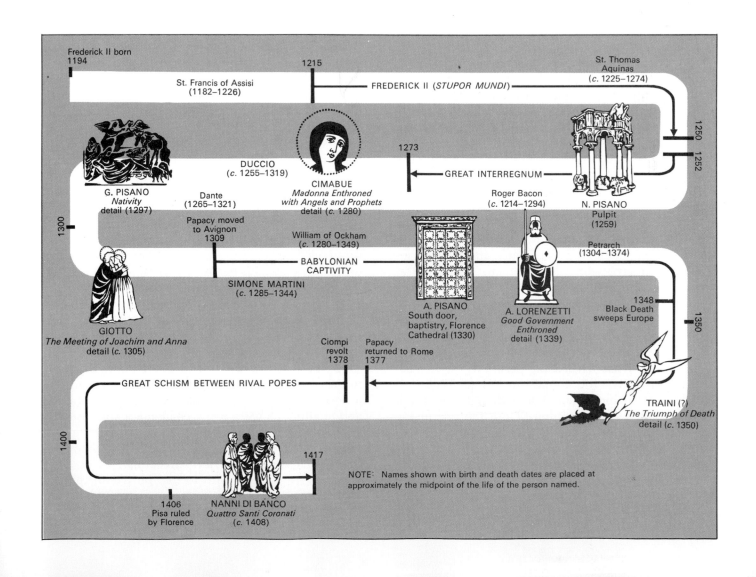

Frederick II born
1194

St. Francis of Assisi
(1182–1226)

1215

FREDERICK II (*STUPOR MUNDI*)

St. Thomas
Aquinas
(*c.* 1225–1274)

1250

1252

DUCCIO
(*c.* 1255–1319)

CIMABUE
*Madonna Enthroned
with Angels and Prophets*
detail (*c.* 1280)

1273

GREAT INTERREGNUM

Roger Bacon
(*c.* 1214–1294)

G. PISANO
Nativity
detail (1297)

Dante
(1265–1321)

N. PISANO
Pulpit
(1259)

1300

Papacy moved
to Avignon
1309

William of Ockham
(*c.* 1280–1349)

BABYLONIAN
CAPTIVITY

SIMONE MARTINI
(*c.* 1285–1344)

Petrarch
(1304–1374)

GIOTTO
The Meeting of Joachim and Anna
detail (*c.* 1305)

A. PISANO
South door,
baptistry, Florence
Cathedral (1330)

A. LORENZETTI
*Good Government
Enthroned*
detail (1339)

1348
Black Death
sweeps Europe

1350

Ciompi
revolt
1378

Papacy
returned to Rome
1377

GREAT SCHISM BETWEEN RIVAL POPES

TRAINI (?)
The Triumph of Death
detail (*c.* 1350)

1400

1417

NOTE: Names shown with birth and death dates are placed at
approximately the midpoint of the life of the person named.

1406
Pisa ruled
by Florence

NANNI DI BANCO
Quattro Santi Coronati
(*c.* 1408)

SCHOLARS HAVE LONG been uncertain about how to classify the art of the late thirteenth and the fourteenth centuries. Most of it still looks quite Byzantine or Gothic; in the countries outside Italy, Gothic traits last into the sixteenth century; but in Italy, a new spirit begins to be felt in art in the late thirteenth. As this new spirit is in fact that of the emerging Renaissance, it is misleading to define its monuments exclusively as "Gothic," even though Gothic traits are obvious in them. (To be sure, Gothic art itself represents a quickening of naturalism, although not the naturalism of the Renaissance; Gothic naturalism is a principal ingredient in the stylistic complex of the Late Medieval world.) What appears in Italy in the thirteenth century is destined to commence a new epoch, one that will have a quite recognizable continuity for centuries—indeed, almost until our own times. To stress the initiative that Italian art takes at this time and to prevent the new epoch from being cut off from its beginnings, we have classified Italian art of the later thirteenth and the fourteenth centuries as "proto-Renaissance." Although it is not until the fifteenth century that Renaissance art makes its not always clear break with the Gothic, one can discern in the "proto-Renaissance" the advance of novel tendencies that will lead to the new era.

Of course, Italy does not come into historical view only with the Renaissance. After the long disorganization of Europe, attendant on the passing of Rome and the age of the migrations, the Italian peninsula held a commanding position in the Mediterranean world, commercially and politically, from the eleventh until the fifteenth century. The power of its city-states on the one hand and of the papacy on the other kept Italy largely independent of the rest of Europe while broadly influencing it; during this time, the country remained politically divided. Economic life as we know it had its beginnings in Italy. Via their fleets, the merchants of Pisa, Genoa, and Venice controlled commerce with Islamic Spain, North Africa, Byzantium, Russia, the Near East, and, overland, with China. The banking houses of Florence and Milan managed the finances of Europe. Southern Italy and Sicily were the site of cosmopolitan civilizations. Indeed, Italy was powerful and influential centuries before what we call the period of the Renaissance. Ironically, the Renaissance had begun to flower at the time when Italian dominance in the Mediterranean was declining before the rise of the Ottoman Turks in the east and of Spain in the west.

French Gothic art had risen and flourished in the regions around Paris under the patronage of the kings of France. In Italy, the art of the Renaissance was supported by the prosperous merchant classes that ruled the cities after ousting the aristocracies. The reconstitution and expansion of city culture, which began as early as the eleventh century, had increasingly broken down old feudal barriers to the advancement of ambitious people of merit from all classes. Communal government (the Italian city-republics were called *communes*) came into the hands of guilds of merchants and bankers. This rule of magnates and their families was not by hereditary right but by the authority of power—a power that, often as not, favored republican institutions; thus, the Medici came to rule in Florence, not as raw tyrants but as a kind of "first among equals." Behind their power was commercial success (their own as well as the city's) and their skill in business government. During the "proto-Renaissance," the growth in wealth and power of many Italian cities corresponded with a rise in their wool trade. Florence, in particular, was noted for finished cloth that was sold all over Europe. As their wealth increased, the guilds, including the powerful wool guild, commanded ever-greater political influence; eventually the city—and, with it, much of the patronage of art—was in their hands. Commercial setbacks or jealousies within the guild coalitions created a highly unstable government, in which authority frequently changed hands overnight.

The Ciompi revolt of 1378 in Florence, when the workmen attempted to wrest the government from the merchant guilds, was only one of many social upheavals that followed the disaster of the great plague (the "Black Death") in 1348, which almost depopulated Europe. All over Europe, there were revolts of peasants in the countryside and of laboring men in the cities. A great and desolating war, destined to last a hundred years, broke out between France and England. The papacy suffered a humiliation that would ultimately destroy its prestige; the popes became puppets of the French monarchy and their residence moved from Rome to Avignon in southern France. Their sojourn there for some 70 years was climaxed by the Great Schism, when the throne of St. Peter was claimed simultaneously by three popes, who excommunicated one another. Christendom was permanently changed by this scandal, which contributed mightily to the advent of the Protestant Reformation in the sixteenth century.

Yet, despite turbulence and devastation, a powerful vitality was stirring, and confusion was but one aspect of significant and beneficial change. Old ideas and institutions were being challenged and, to a degree, discredited, and people of merit—in this age of Petrarch and Giotto—could feel that the times encouraged setting off in new directions.

Events from the twelfth to the fourteenth century constitute a kind of long overture, announcing the advent of full, naturalistic representation in European art. Whether we regard the "proto-Renaissance" as the end of the overture or the raising of the curtain on the first act, the event, especially in painting, is singularly dramatic. The Medieval artist had for centuries depended chiefly on prototypes (pictures and carvings) for representations of the human figure, with an occasional searching glance at objects and persons in the optical world. Now it is the optical world that offers prototype and authority to the artist—though not all at once, of course. Not until the fifteenth century will the "imitation of nature" as an objective give the artist direction, and not until the sixteenth will it become theory and doctrine. In the "proto-Renaissance," the artist's procedure is tentative, as if he were suspicious of an approach involving fleeting appearances and devoid of traditionally authoritative formulations. Nevertheless, as the artist carefully treads the threshold of discovery, his experimental groping and the somewhat unsystematic, yet hopeful and often confident, spirit of the period are unmistakable.

Artists are not philosophers, although in the Renaissance they come very close to sharing in the philosophical enterprise. Certainly, in the fourteenth century, the way was opening to new and tremendous possibilities that would have to be thought through as well as worked through. In many ways, the situation was similar to that of art today: so many possibilities and such diverse directions that, though rich conclusions may be anticipated, the way to them seems confused.

As the Christian Middle Ages evolved out of the disintegration of the Roman empire, so a new way of looking at the world emerged from the disintegration of what might be called the Medieval style of thought. Distinct from and in opposition to the balanced Scholasticism of Aquinas, the new views were only in part products of the Christian humanism of St. Francis and the secular Humanism of Petrarch and the classicizing scholars. The attack on the rationalism of Aquinas made by the *later* Scholastics and theologians led to the discrediting of philosophy as a valid form of knowledge and to the unseating of reason, with its logical method, as the ruling faculty that produces it. The unity of theology and philosophy, which Aquinas had achieved by bringing together Christian dogma and Aristotelian thought, was broken—theology going off in the direction of mysticism and pure faith, and philosophy yielding to skepticism and the first faint manifestation of that inquisitive bent of mind that would later mature into experimental science. If knowledge of God was impossible to achieve through philosophy and pure reason, so also was knowledge of nature and the world, God's crea-

tion. Thus, pure reason came to be despised for its failure to make the mysteries of faith or of the world intelligible. In the fifteenth century, Nicholas of Cusa would disparage philosophy as mere "learned ignorance"; in the sixteenth, Martin Luther would call reason a "whore."

A new approach was needed to understand and explain nature and God, and it is necessary to examine the great changes in the Western view of nature that lie behind and accompany fundamental changes in art. William of Ockham, one of the most subtle and ingenious Scholastics who attacked the rationalism of Aquinas, seemed to be providing such an approach when, on the verge of a great insight, he stressed the importance of the role of intuitive knowledge and individual experience in the process of knowing: "Everything outside the soul is individual . . . [and] knowledge which is simple and peculiarly individual . . . is intuitive knowledge . . . . Abstractive individual knowledge presupposes intuitive knowledge . . . our understanding knows sensible things intuitively."

The placement of intuition before abstraction was common to *both* the mystical and skeptical critics of Aquinas in the fourteenth century and, in effect, put human intuition squarely in front of individual knowledge, whether of God (for the mystic) or of the world (for the skeptic). This elevation of direct human experience constitutes a kind of exaltation of the knowing, human agent. Of course, since Early Christian times and especially since St. Augustine in the fifth century, the tradition of Christian mysticism had been that the experience of God must be personal; knowledge otherwise must be the result of divine illumination. Thus, the fourteenth-century advocacy of intuitive experience is a kind of renewal of the idea that prevailed before the conviction held by Abelard and Aquinas in the twelfth and thirteenth centuries—that truth could be achieved by the intellect only by following rules of rational demonstration. Even in the thirteenth century, the importance of experience in acquiring knowledge had been stressed by the remarkable Roger Bacon, the English philosopher, who bore out his convictions on this point with many astonishingly precocious discoveries and inventions in what now would be called the physical sciences and technology. Calling attention to the existence and necessity of experimental science, he insisted that the experimenter "should first examine visible things . . . without experience nothing can be known sufficiently . . . argumentation [that is, logical rational demonstration in Aquinas' manner] does not suffice, but experience does." In the universities (especially Oxford) of the fourteenth century, the followers of men like Bacon and Ockham discussed questions in physics (the acceleration of freely falling bodies, inertia, the center of gravity, and the like)—anticipating by centuries the age of Galileo.

Particularly noteworthy about the later thirteenth- and fourteenth-century mystical and skeptical thinkers, who emphasized personal intuition and experience in seeking divine and natural knowledge, is the fact that a large majority were Franciscans. In view of St. Francis' humanizing of Medieval religion—making it a matter of intense personal experience and drawing attention to the beauty of natural things, the handiwork of God—it is natural that his successors should inspect nature more closely, with a curiosity that would lead to scientific inquiry. St. Francis' independence and his critical posture toward the religious establishment were passed down to many Franciscans, the more radical of whom were often accused by the Church of association with outright "heretics." The Franciscans—conspicuously, William of Ockham—challenged the papacy itself, especially its claim of secular lordship over all Christendom. In these challenges, there already rings the rebelliousness that will take mature shape in the Protestant Reformation.

What might be called Franciscan "radicalism," then, stresses the primacy of personal experience, the individual's right to know by experiment, the futility of formal philosophy, and the beauty and value of things in the external world. It was in the stimulating intellectual and social environment created in part by the Franciscans that the painters and sculptors of the "proto-Renaissance" began a new epoch—an epoch in which the carved and painted image took its shape from the authority of the optical world and what could be found of that authority in the Classical antique. The individual artist, breaking with the formal traditions of a thousand years, now came to depend on his own inspection of the world before his eyes. Applying the Baconian principle of personal discovery through experience—in the artist's case, the experience of *seeing*—he began to project in painting and sculpture the infinitely complex and shifting optical reticulum that we experience as the world.

SCULPTURE

Many imitations of the art of Classical antiquity may be encountered during the Carolingian, Ottonian, Romanesque, and French Gothic periods. The statues of the *Visitation* group on the west façade of Reims Cathedral (FIG. 10-33) show an unmistakable interest in Late Roman sculpture, even though the modeling of the faces reveals their Gothic origin. However, the thirteenth-century sculpture of NICOLA PISANO (active *c.* 1258–1278), contemporary with the Reims statues, exhibits an interest in the forms of the Classical

antique unlike that of his predecessors—perhaps due in part to the humanistic culture of Sicily under its brilliant king, Holy Roman Emperor Frederick II, who, for his many intellectual gifts and many other talents, was known in his own time as "the wonder of the world." Frederick's nostalgia for the grandeur that was Rome fostered a revival of Roman sculpture and decoration in Sicily and southern Italy before the mid-thirteenth century. It may have been in this environment that Nicola received his early training, although recently it has been suggested that his style continues that of Romanesque Pisa. After Frederick's death in 1250, Nicola traveled northward and eventually settled in Pisa, which was then at the height of its political and economic power and a place where a proficient artist could hope to find rich commissions.

In typically Italian fashion, Nicola's sculpture was not applied in the decoration of great portals; thus, it is quite unlike the French sculpture of the period. Nicola carved marble reliefs and ornament for large pulpits, the first of which he completed in 1260 for the baptistry of Pisa Cathedral (FIG. 15-1). Some elements of the pulpit's design carry on Medieval traditions (for example, the lions supporting some of the columns and the tri-lobed arches), but Nicola is evidently trying to retranslate into Classical terms a Medieval type of structure. The large, bushy capitals

15-1 NICOLA PISANO, pulpit of the baptistry of Pisa Cathedral, 1259–1260. Marble, approx. 15' high.

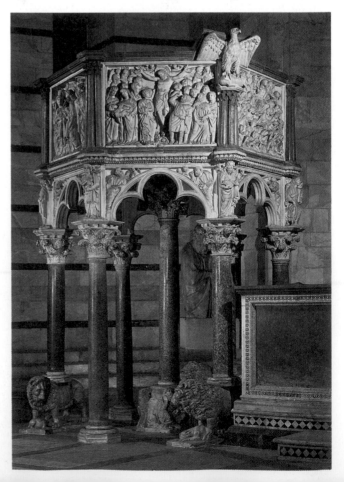

are a Gothic variation of the Corinthian; the arches are round rather than ogival; and the large, rectangular relief panels, if their proportions were slightly altered, could have come from the sides of Roman sarcophagi. The densely packed, large-scale figures of the individual panels seem also to derive from the compositions found on Late Roman sarcophagi. In one of these panels, representing *The Annunciation and the Nativity* (FIG. 15-2), the Virgin of the Nativity reclines in the ancient fashion seen in Byzantine ivories, mosaics, and paintings. But the face-types, beards, coiffures, and draperies and the bulk and weight of the figures are inspired by Classical models and impart a Classical flavor to the relief that is stronger than anything seen in several centuries.

Nicola's classicizing manner was strongly reversed by his son GIOVANNI PISANO (c. 1250–1320). Giovanni's version of *The Annunciation and the Nativity* (FIG. 15-3) from his pulpit in Sant' Andrea of Pistoia, finished some 40 years after the one by his father in the Pisa baptistry, offers a striking contrast to Nicola's thick carving and placid, almost stolid presentation of the theme. Giovanni's figures are loosely and dynamically arranged; an excited animation twists and bends them, and their activeness is emphasized by spaces that open deeply between them, through which they hurry and gesticulate. In the Annunciation episode, which is combined with the Nativity (as in the older version), the Virgin shrinks from the sudden apparition of the angel in an alarm touched with humility. The same spasm of diffidence contracts her supple body as she reclines in the Nativity scene. The principals of the drama share in a peculiar, nervous agitation, as if they are all suddenly moved by spirit-

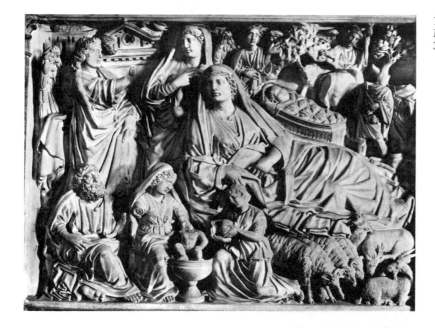

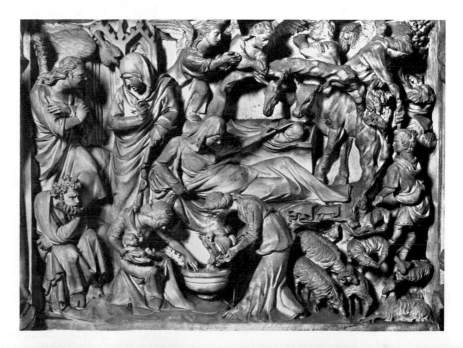

15-2   NICOLA PISANO, *The Annunciation and the Nativity* (detail of FIG. 15-1). Marble, approx. 34″ × 45″.

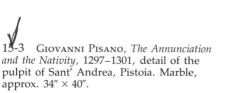

15-3   GIOVANNI PISANO, *The Annunciation and the Nativity*, 1297–1301, detail of the pulpit of Sant' Andrea, Pistoia. Marble, approx. 34″ × 40″.

ual passion; only the shepherds and the sheep, appropriately, do not yet share in the miraculous event. The swiftly turning, sinuous draperies, the slender figures they enfold, and the general emotionalism of the scene are features to be found not in Nicola's interpretation but in the Gothic art of the north in the fourteenth century. (These deep currents of Gothic naturalism and linear rhythms are evident in most sculpture in Italy throughout the fourteenth century.) Thus, the art of Nicola and of Giovanni show, successively, two novel trends of great significance for Renaissance art—a new contact with the Classical antique and a burgeoning, native Gothic naturalism.

Sculpture seems to have been more actively pursued in centers other than Florence until ANDREA PISANO (c. 1270–1348), unrelated to Nicola and Giovanni, was commissioned by the city to make bronze doors for the cathedral baptistry (FIG. 15-4). Each door has 14 panels, each enframing a *quatrefoil*, a motif found in Gothic sculpture and illuminations. Within these, as in *The Visitation* panel (FIG. 15-5), Andrea placed low reliefs with smoothly flowing lines admirably adapted to the complex space of the Gothic frame. The gentle sway of the figures and the blade-like folds of their drapery are quite in the general Late Gothic manner, but Andrea's skill at composition and

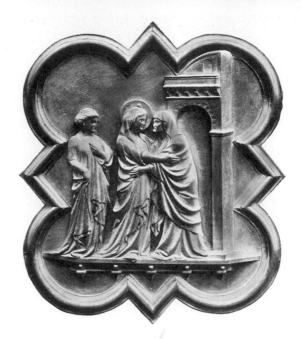

15-5 ANDREA PISANO, *The Visitation* (detail of FIG. 15-4). Gilt bronze, approx. 20″ high.

the quiet eloquence of his narrative make him an outstanding master among the fourteenth-century sculptors who followed the earlier Pisani. The simplicity of Andrea's statements, the amplitude of his forms, and their clear placement in shallow space also point to the influence of his great contemporary, the painter Giotto di Bondone.

PAINTING

Maniera Greca

Throughout the Middle Ages, Italian painting was dominated by the Byzantine style. This Italo–Byzantine style, or *maniera greca*, is shown in a panel of the *St. Francis Altarpiece* (FIG. 15-6) and is a descendant of those tall, aloof, austere figures that people the world of Byzantine art. Painted in tempera (a water-base paint using a binder such as glue or egg yolk) on wood panel, the saint, wearing the cinctured canonicals of the Franciscan order, holds a large book and displays on his hands and feet the stigmata—the wounds of Christ imprinted on him as a sign of Heavenly favor. The saint is flanked by two very Byzantine angels and by scenes from his life, the latter very much suggesting that their source is in Byzantine illuminated manuscripts. A detail of the altarpiece represents *St. Francis Preaching to the Birds* (FIG. 15-7). The figures of St. Francis and his two attendants are carefully aligned against a shallow, stage-property tower and wall, a stylized symbol of a town or city from Early Christian times. In front of the saint is another stage-scenery image of nested, wooded hills populated by alert and sprightly birds and twinkling

15-4 ANDREA PISANO, south door of the baptistry of Florence Cathedral, 1330–1335. Gilt bronze, approx. 17′ high.

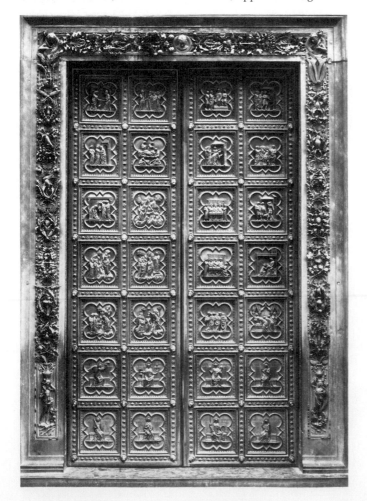

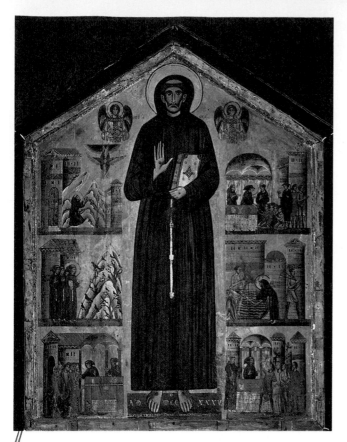

15-6 BONAVENTURA BERLINGHIERI, panel from the *St. Francis Altarpiece*, 1235. Tempera on wood, approx. 60″ × 42″. San Francesco, Pescia.

15-7 BONAVENTURA BERLINGHIERI, *St. Francis Preaching to the Birds* (detail of FIG. 15-6).

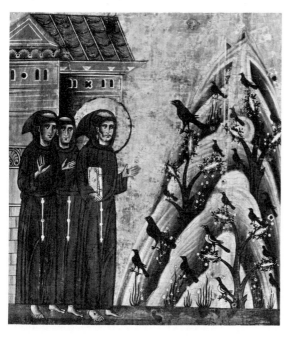

plants. The strict formality of the composition (relieved somewhat by the sharply observed birds and the lively stippling of the plants), the shallow space, and the linear flatness in the rendering of the forms

are all familiar traits of a long and august tradition, now suddenly and dramatically to be replaced.

BONAVENTURA BERLINGHIERI, artist of the *St. Francis Altarpiece* was one of a family of painters in the Tuscan city of Lucca. It was largely in the busy cities of Tuscany (Lucca, Pisa, Siena, Florence) that the stirrings of the new artistic movement began. Florence was destined to lead the great development toward the new pictorial manner of the Renaissance, just as politically it gradually absorbed the other cities in Tuscany to make the Florentine republic. But during the fourteenth century, its defiant rival, Siena, which had long and stubbornly resisted the encroachment of Florence, was the seat of a splendid school of painting of its own.

Duccio

DUCCIO (Duccio di Buoninsegna, active *c.* 1278–1319) represents the Sienese tradition at its best. Among his large altarpieces, the *Maestà,* so called because it shows the Madonna enthroned in majesty as Queen of Heaven amidst choruses of angels and saints, illustrates the major aspects of his mature style. The front of the seven-foot-high panel (which is painted on both sides) represents the formal, monumental side of Duccio's art, which remains essentially Byzantine. On the reverse side, a series of small panels illustrated scenes from the life of Christ. These little pictures, which show Duccio's power of narration, were dismantled in the sixteenth century and are now scattered throughout the museums of the world. Given their narrative purpose—they were meant to be read, as were the windows of Chartres—Duccio could relax the formalism appropriate to the iconic, symbolic representation of the *Maestà* and could reveal his ability not only as a narrator but as an experimenter with new pictorial ideas. In a synoptic sequence on one of the panels, *The Betrayal of Jesus* (FIG. 15-8), the artist represents several episodes of the event: the betrayal of Jesus by Judas' false kiss, the disciples fleeing in terror, St. Peter cutting off the ear of the high priest's servant. Although the background, with its golden sky and its cheese-like rock formations, remains traditional, the figures before it have changed quite radically. They are no longer the flat, frontal shapes of Byzantine art, but have taken on body; they are modeled through a range from light to dark, and their draperies articulate around them convincingly. Only their relation to the ground on which they stand remains somewhat in doubt, as they tend to sway, glide, and incline with a kind of disembodied instability. Even more novel and striking is the manner in which the figures seem to react to the central event. Through posture, gesture, and even facial expression, they display a variety of emotions,

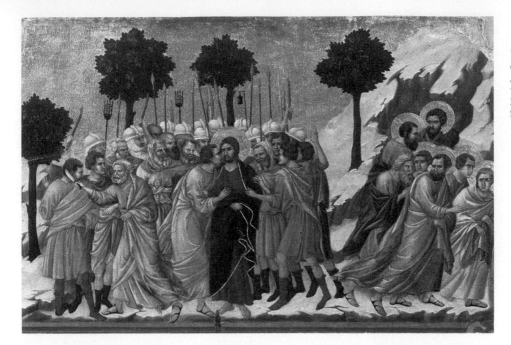

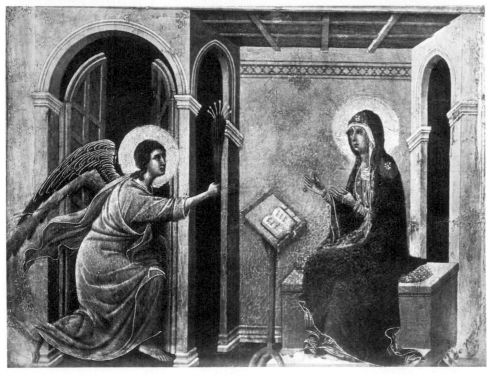

as Duccio extends himself to differentiate between the anger of Peter, the malice of Judas (echoed in the faces of the throng about Jesus), and the apprehension and timidity of the fleeing disciples. No longer the abstract symbols of Byzantine art, these little figures have become actors in a religious drama, which, in a lively performance, is interpreted in terms of thoroughly human actions and reactions. In this and similar narrative panels, Duccio takes a decisive step toward the humanization of religious subject matter— an approach that will become an ever stronger undercurrent in the development of painting in the following centuries.

In *The Annunciation of the Death of Mary* (FIG. 15-9) from the same altarpiece, Duccio shows that, in the study of interior space, he is second to none of his contemporaries. Although his perspective is approximate, he creates the illusion of an architectural space that *encloses* a human figure. If we could be sure that the sophisticated ancient Roman painters had not achieved this effect also, we might say that it had never been done before. Certainly, nothing like it is to be found in painting during the 900 years preceding Duccio, and it must be regarded as epoch-making even though it may have been anticipated by the St. Francis master at Assisi and was accomplished in a similar manner by Giotto in the Arena Chapel in Padua (FIG. 15-17) a few years before Duccio painted his *Maestà*. While the angel's position remains ambiguous, the Virgin has been clearly placed in a cubical space that recedes from the picture plane. The illusion is made quite emphatic by the convergence of the three beams in the ceiling, a phenomenon that Duccio observed and recorded. As yet the perspective is not entirely unified, each of Duccio's planes tending to have its own point of convergence. Nevertheless, the illusion is convincing enough and represents the first step in the progressive construction of a true, geometrically ordered, perspective space that will be completed in the next century.

Giotto

Duccio resolved his problems within the general framework of the Byzantine style, which he never really rejected. His great Florentine contemporary, GIOTTO (Giotto di Bondone, *c.* 1266–1337), made a much more radical break with the past. The sources of Giotto's style are still debated, although one must have been the style of the Roman school of painting represented by PIETRO CAVALLINI (active *c.* 1273–1308). As shown in a detail from Cavallini's badly damaged fresco of *The Last Judgment* (FIG. 15-10) in the church of Santa Cecilia in Trastevere, the style is characterized by a great interest in the sculptural rendering of form. Cavallini, perhaps under the influence of Roman paintings now lost, abandons Byzantine linearism for a soft, deep modeling from light to dark and achieves an imposing combination of Byzantine hieratic dignity with a long-lost impression of solidity and strength. Another, perhaps less significant,

formative influence on Giotto may very well have been the work of the man presumed to be his teacher, GIOVANNI CIMABUE (*c.* 1240–1302). A Florentine, Cimabue must have been an older rival of Giotto, as Dante suggests in *Il Purgatorio* (XI, 94–96): ''Cimabue thought to hold the field in painting, and now Giotto has the cry, so that the fame of the other is obscured.''

Like Cavallini, Cimabue—inspired by the same impulse toward naturalism as Giovanni Pisano and also influenced, no doubt, by Gothic sculpture— pushed well beyond the limits of the Italo–Byzantine style. In an almost ruined fresco of the Crucifixion in San Francesco in Assisi, Cimabue's style can be seen to be—like Giovanni Pisano's—highly dramatic, the figures blown by a storm of emotion. On the other hand, Cimabue is much more formal in his *Madonna Enthroned with Angels and Prophets* (FIG. 15-11), as the theme naturally calls for unmoving dignity and not for dramatic presentation. Despite such progressive touches as the three-dimensional appearance of the throne, this vast altarpiece is a final summing-up of centuries of Byzantine art before its utter transformation. What that transformation looked like in its first phase can be seen in Giotto's version of the same theme (FIG. 15-12).

The art of Cimabue, the art of Cavallini and of the Roman painters like him (whom Giotto must have seen at work in San Francesco), the art of the Gothic sculptors of France (perhaps seen by Giotto himself, but certainly received by him from the sculpture of Giovanni Pisano), and the ancient art of Rome, both sculpture and painting—all must have provided the elements of Giotto's artistic education. Yet no synthesis of these varied influences could have sufficed to

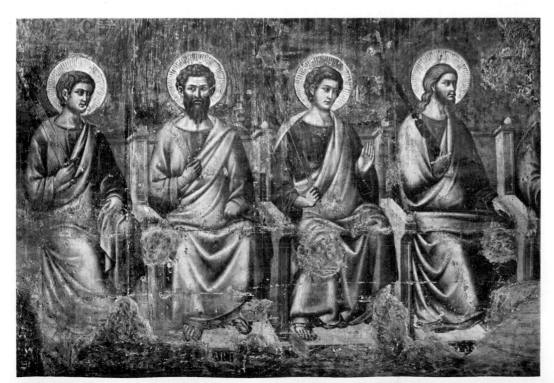

15-10 PIETRO CAVALLINI, *Seated Apostles*, detail of *The Last Judgment*, *c.* 1291. Fresco.* Santa Cecilia in Trastevere, Rome.

*Dimensions for wall paintings will not be given from this point on.

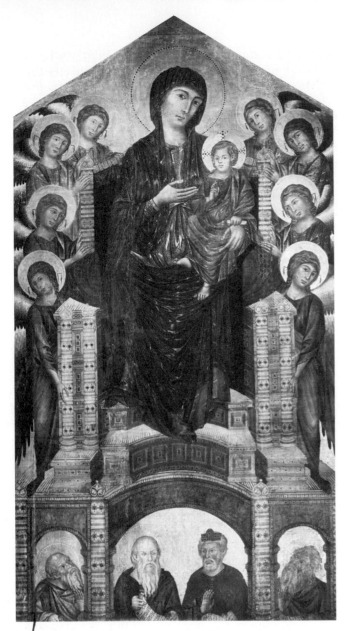

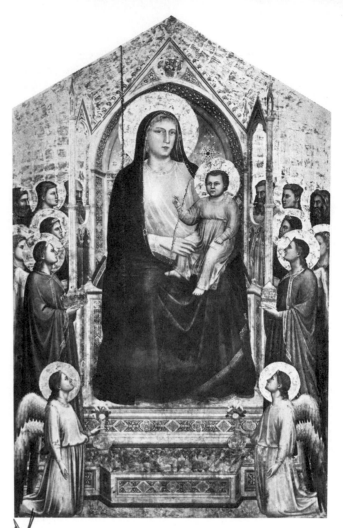

15-12 GIOTTO, *Madonna Enthroned*, c. 1310. Tempera on wood, 10′ 8″ × 6′ 8″. Galleria degli Uffizi, Florence.

15-11 GIOVANNI CIMABUE, *Madonna Enthroned with Angels and Prophets*, c. 1280–1290. Tempera on wood, 12′ 7″ × 7′ 4″. Galleria degli Uffizi, Florence.

produce the great new style that makes Giotto the father of Western pictorial art. Renowned in his own day, his reputation has never faltered. No matter the variety of his materials of instruction, his true teacher was nature, the world of visible things.

Giotto's revolution in painting did not consist only of the final displacement of the Byzantine style, of the establishment of painting as a major art for the next six centuries, and of the restoration of the naturalistic approach invented by the ancients and lost in the Middle Ages. He inaugurated a firm method of pictorial experiment through observation, and, in the spirit of the experimenting Franciscans, opened an age that might be called "early scientific." Giotto and his successors, by stressing the preeminence of the faculty of sight in gaining knowledge of the world—

the visual world must be observed before it can be analyzed and understood—laid the trails that empirical science would follow. Praised in his own and later times for his fidelity to nature, Giotto is more than an imitator of it; he *reveals* nature in the process of observing it and divining its visible order. In fact, he showed his generation a new way of seeing. With Giotto, Western man turns resolutely toward the visible world as the source of knowledge of nature. This new *outward* vision replaced the Medieval *inward* vision that searched not for the secrets of nature but for union with God.

In nearly the same great scale as the Madonna painted by Cimabue, Giotto presents her enthroned with angels (FIG. 15-12) in a work that offers an opportunity to appreciate his perhaps most telling contribution to representational art—sculptural solidity and weight. The Madonna rests within her Gothic throne with the unshakable stability of a marble goddess out of antiquity. The slender Virgins of Duccio and Cimabue, fragile beneath the thin ripplings of their draperies, are replaced by a sturdy, queenly mother, corporeally of this world, even to the swelling of the bosom. The body is not lost; it is asserted. The new art aims, before all else, to construct a figure that will have substance, dimensionality, and bulk—that, like a figure in sculpture, will project into the light and throw a shadow or give the illusion that it does. Thus, in this work the throne is deep enough to contain the monumental figure and breaks away from the flat ground to project and enclose it.

In examining Giotto's work it should be kept in mind that scholars have questioned the attribution of the Assisi frescoes (FIG. 15-13) to Giotto's hand, noting not only a certain inferiority in the execution of the figures and other details but also a crowding or complexity in the composition that is inconsistent with the lucidity and monumentality of his other paintings. All agree that Giotto authored the works at the Arena Chapel (FIGS. 15-14 and 15-17), which must date from about 1304 to 1313, his frescoes in the chapels of Santa Croce in Florence (FIG. 15-15, c. 1320), and the *Madonna Enthroned* (FIG. 15-12, c. 1310). However, a serious controversy revolves around the great cycle of frescoes depicting the life of St. Francis in the Upper Church of Assisi, traditionally attributed to Giotto and dated about 1300. As written evidence is lacking and opinions are based on stylistic analysis, it is probable that opinions will continue to vary. Current scholarship suggests that the St. Francis cycle was painted in the 1290s, and although the influence

15-13 MASTER OF THE ST. FRANCIS CYCLE, *St. Francis Preaching to the Birds*, c. 1296 (?). Fresco. Upper Church, San Francesco, Assisi.

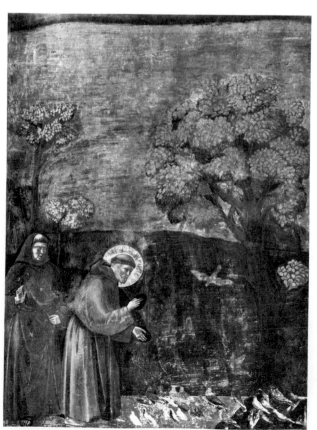

of Giotto's style is not denied, it is felt that it is better exemplified in other works. Scholars now believe that the Assisi frescoes were most likely done by Florentine artists who were influenced by Giotto or who had a similar background. One of these frescoes, *St. Francis Preaching to the Birds* (FIG. 15-13), is certainly Giottesque in its simplicity of statement, in the reduction of the number of figures to the minimum required for the story, and in the sharp psychological touches—the eloquent gesture of the saint as he bends forward to the birds, almost commanding them to attend his words, and the astonishment of his disciple. The modeling of the figures is strong; their sculptural relief, emphatic. If the picture is compared with Berlinghieri's version of the same theme (FIG. 15-7), the nature of the great stylistic change, happening within little more than half a century, can be appreciated. Its attribution to the MASTER OF THE ST. FRANCIS CYCLE reflects the provisional nature of much of our art-historical knowledge. As the history of art moves into an age of known personalities, the vexatious question of attribution arises with increasing frequency. How can the authorship of a work be verified when documentary evidence is scarce and when the internal evidence (evidence from the study of individual styles) is controversial?

The projection on a flat surface of an illusion of solid bodies moving through space presents a duplex problem. The construction of the illusion of a body requires, at the same time, the construction of the illusion of a space sufficiently ample to contain that body. In Giotto's fresco cycles—and he was primarily a muralist—he is constantly striving to reconcile these two aspects of illusionistic painting. His *Lamentation* from the fresco cycle in the Arena Chapel (Cappella Scrovegni) at Padua (FIG. 15-14) is undisputed and shows us his art at its finest. The theme is the mourning of Christ's mother, his disciples, and the holy women over the dead body of the Savior just before its entombment, in the presence of angels darting about in hysterical grief. Giotto has arranged a shallow stage for the figures, bounded by a thick, diagonal scarp of rock that defines a horizontal ledge in the foreground. The rocky landscape links this scene with the adjoining one of the *Resurrection* and *Noli me tangere* (not shown). Giotto links the framed scenes throughout the fresco cycle, much as Dante joins the cantos in his epic poem, the *Divina Commedia*. Though rather narrow, the ledge provides the figures with firm visual support, while the scarp functions as an indicator of the picture's dramatic focal point at the lower left. The centralizing and frontalizing habits of Byzantine art are here dismissed. The figures are sculpturesque, simple, weighty volumes but are not restrained by their mass from appropriate action. Here, postures and gestures

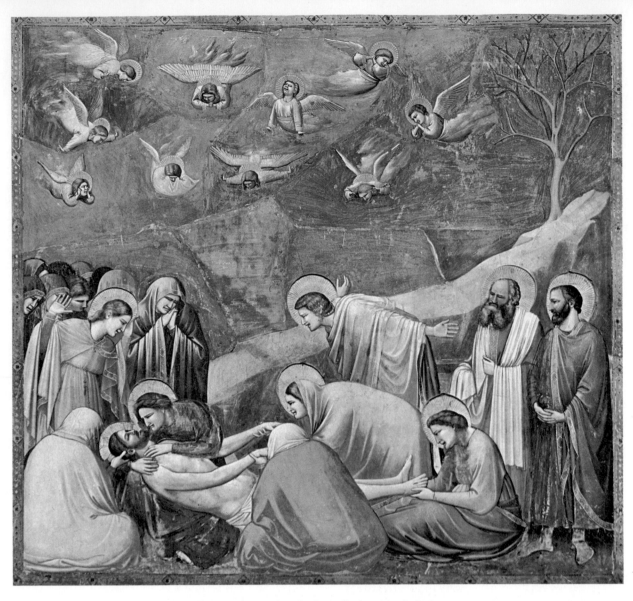

15-14 GIOTTO, *Lamentation, c.* 1305. Fresco. Arena Chapel (Cappella Scrovegni), Padua.

that might have been only rhetorical and mechanical convincingly express a broad spectrum of grief—from the mother's almost fierce despair through the passionate outbursts of Mary Magdalene and John, the philosophical resignation of the two disciples at the right, and the mute sorrow of the two hooded mourners in the foreground. Although Duccio makes an effort to distinguish shades of emotion in *The Betrayal of Jesus* (FIG. 15-8), he does not match Giotto in his stage management of a great tragedy. Giotto has indeed constructed a kind of stage, which will serve as a model for those on which many human dramas will be depicted in subsequent paintings. He is now far removed from the old isolation of episodes and actors seen in art until the late thirteenth century. In the *Lamentation,* a single event provokes a single, intense response within which there are, so to speak, degrees of psychic vibration. This integration of the formal with the emotional composition was scarcely attempted, let alone achieved, in art before Giotto.

The formal design of the *Lamentation* fresco, the way the figures are grouped within the contrived space, is worth close study. Each group has its own definition, and each contributes to the rhythmic order of the composition. The strong diagonal of the rocky ledge, with its single dead tree (the tree of knowledge of good and evil, which withered at the fall of Adam), concentrates our attention on the group around the head of Christ, dynamically off-center in the composition. All movement beyond this group is contained, or arrested, by the massive bulk of the seated mourner in the corner of the painting. The seated mourner to the right establishes a relation with the center group, the members of which, by their gazes and gestures, draw the viewer's attention back to the head of Christ. Figures seen from the back—frequent in Giotto's compositions—emphasize the foreground, helping visually to place the intermediate figures further back in space. This device, the very contradiction of the old frontality, in effect puts the viewer behind the "observer" figures, which, facing the action as spectators, reinforce the sense of stage-craft as a model for paintings with a human "plot." In this age of dawning Humanism, the old Medieval, hieratic presentation of holy mysteries evolved into full-fledged dramas employing a plot. By the thirteenth century, the drama of the Mass was extended first into one- and two-act tableaux and scenes and then into simple shows often presented at the portals of churches. (The portal statuary of the Gothic period suggests a discourse among the represented saints, and the architectural settings serve to enframe and enclose them, as does a stage the movement of its actors.) Thus, the arts of illusionistic painting and of drama were developing simultaneously, and the most accomplished artists of the Renaissance and later periods became masters of a kind of stage rhetoric of their own. Giotto, the first master of the tradi-

tion, was one of the most expert in the matching of form and action; it is difficult to exaggerate his trailblazing achievement.

For the Franciscan church of Santa Croce in Florence, Giotto painted a St. John cycle and frescoes of the life and death of St. Francis. Shown is the *Death of St. Francis*, as restored in the nineteenth century (FIG. 15-15) and with the restorations removed (FIG. 15-16).* Fortunately, despite the removal of the restora-

*This painting exemplifies another aspect of the problem of attribution and authenticity already mentioned. Until the historically sensitive twentieth century, it had long been the custom to "renew" old pictures by painting over damaged or faded areas. Modern scholars, in their zeal to know the "real" painter, have advocated stripping even where this leaves only fragments that are perhaps esthetically unsatisfactory. The practice remains controversial, and the historian of art, the expert, the connoisseur, and, ultimately, the layman always have before them the question of the authenticity of the given work.

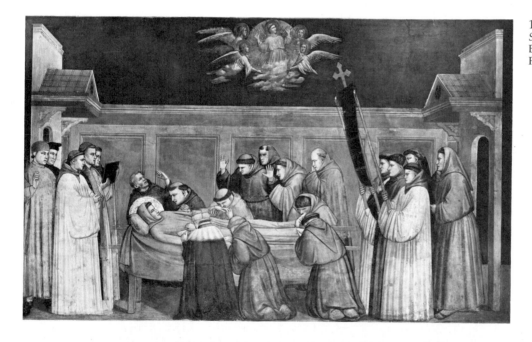

15-15 GIOTTO, *Death of St. Francis, c.* 1320. Fresco. Bardi Chapel, Santa Croce, Florence.

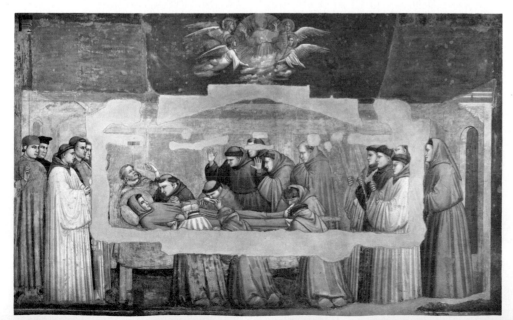

15-16 GIOTTO, *Death of St. Francis,* FIG. 15-15 after removal of nineteenth-century restorations.

tions and the resultant gaps in the composition, there is enough of the original *Death of St. Francis* to give a view of the later style of Giotto. Compared with the *Lamentation,* with which it has considerable spiritual affinity, the St. Francis painting shows significant changes. The Gothic agitation has quieted, and the scene has little of the jagged emotion of the *Lamentation.* It seems, indeed, as if the artist, from off-stage, had watched the solemn obsequies: the saint, at center on his bier, flanked by kneeling and standing monks, the kneeling seen from behind in Giotto's fashion. From left and right come stately processions of friars in profile, as they would be seen in actuality— not frontally, as in a Byzantine procession like that of *Justinian and Attendants* at San Vitale (FIG. 7-36). The figures are carefully accommodated on an architecture-enclosed, stage-like space that has been widened and no longer leaves any doubt that the figures have sufficient room in which to move about. They are taller and have lost some of their former sack-like bulk; Giotto now makes a distinction between the purely form-defining function of the robes and the fact that they are draped around articulated bodies. The impressive solemnity of the procession is enhanced by the omission of the casual and incidental beauties of the world so dear to Sienese and Gothic painters. Giotto sees and records nature in terms of its most basic facts: solid volumes resting firmly on the flat and horizontal surface of this earth. These he arranges in meaningful groups and infuses with restrained emotions, revealed in slow and measured gestures. With the greatest economy of means, Giotto achieves unsurpassed effects of monumentality, and his paintings, because of the simplicity and directness of their statements, belong to the most memorable in world art.

Giotto's murals in the Bardi and Peruzzi chapels of Santa Croce served as textbooks for generations of Renaissance painters from Masaccio to Michelangelo and others later. These later artists were able to understand the greatness of Giotto's art better than his immediate followers, who were never capable of absorbing more than a fraction of his revolutionary innovations. Their efforts usually remained confined to the emulation of his plastic figure description. A good example of a diligent follower is TADDEO GADDI (*c.* 1300–1366), Giotto's foster son and his assistant for many years. The difference between the work of a great artist and that of a competent one is readily apparent if we compare Giotto's *The Meeting of Joachim and Anna* in the Arena Chapel (FIG. 15-17) with Taddeo's version of the same subject in the Baroncelli Chapel in Santa Croce (FIG. 15-18). Giotto's composition is simple and compact. The figures are carefully related to the single passage of architecture (the Golden Gate), where the parents of the Virgin meet in triumph in the presence of splendidly dressed ladies. The latter mock the cloaked servant who refused to believe that the elderly Anna (St. Anne) would ever bear a child. The story, related in the Apocrypha, is managed with Giotto's usual restraint, clarity, and dramatic compactness. Taddeo allows his composition (FIG. 15-18) to become somewhat loose and unstructured. The figures have no clear relation to

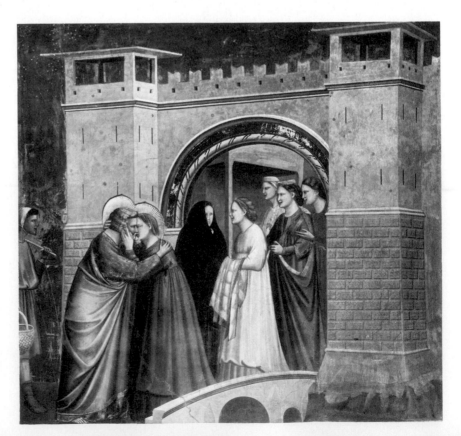

15-17 GIOTTO, *The Meeting of Joachim and Anna,* c. 1305. Fresco. Arena Chapel (Cappella Scrovegni), Padua.

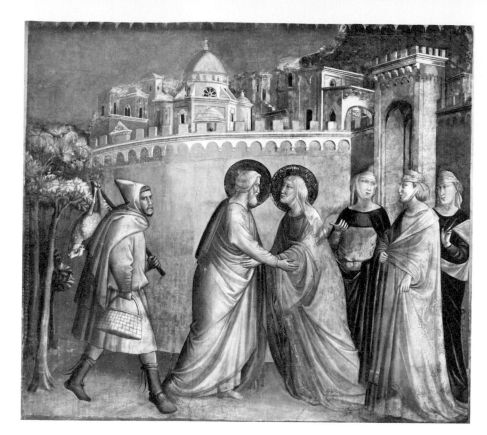

15-18 TADDEO GADDI, *The Meeting of Joachim and Anna*, 1338. Fresco. Baroncelli Chapel, Santa Croce, Florence.

the background; the elaborate cityscape, though pleasant in itself, demands too much attention and detracts from the action in the foreground. Gestures have become weak and theatrical, and the hunter (discreetly cut-off and unobtrusive in Giotto's painting) here strides boldly toward the center of the picture—a picturesque genre subject that weakens the central theme. Although his figures retain much of Giotto's solidity, Taddeo weakens the dramatic impact of the story by elaborating its incidental details. Giotto stresses the essentials and, by presenting them with his usual simplicity and forceful directness, gives the theme a much more meaningful interpretation. Yet we must not seem to disparage Giotto's contemporaries and followers. Taddeo presses forward the investigation of perspective, as his cityscape reveals, and the genre figure attests to the development of a keen interest in realism.

Simone Martini

Duccio's successors in the Siena School display even greater originality and assurance. SIMONE MARTINI (*c.* 1285–1344)—a pupil of Duccio and close friend of Petrarch, who praised him highly for his portrait of "Laura"—worked for the French kings in Naples and Sicily and, in his last years, at the papal court at Avignon, where he came in contact with northern painters. By adapting the insubstantial but luxuriant patterns of the French Gothic manner to Sienese art and, in turn, by acquainting northern painters with the Sienese style, Simone became instrumental in the formation of the so-called International style, which

swept Europe during the late fourteenth and early fifteenth centuries. It was a courtly style that appealed to the aristocratic taste for brilliant color, lavish costume, intricate ornament, and themes involving splendid processions in which knights and their ladies, complete with entourages, horses, and greyhounds, could glitter to advantage. Simone's own style does not quite reach the full exuberance of the developed International style. But his famous *Annunciation* (FIG. 15-19), with its elegant shapes and radiant color, its play of flowing, fluttering line, its weightless figures and spaceless setting, is the perfect antithesis of the style of Giotto—of whom Simone certainly must have been aware, but whose art just as certainly left him untouched. The complex etiquette of the chivalric courts of Europe dictates Simone's presentation. The angel Gabriel has just alighted, the breeze of his passage lifting his mantle, his iridescent wings still beating, the white and gold of his sumptuous gown heraldically representing the celestial realm whence he bears his message. The Virgin, dropping her book of devotions, shrinks demurely from Gabriel's reverent genuflection, appropriate in the presence of royalty. She draws about her the deep blue, golden-hemmed mantle, the heraldic colors she wears as the Queen of Heaven. Despite the Virgin's modesty and diffidence and the tremendous import of the angel's message, the scene subordinates drama to court ritual and structural experiments to surface splendor.

For the Palazzo Pubblico in Siena, Simone painted a very different kind of composition, a large mural

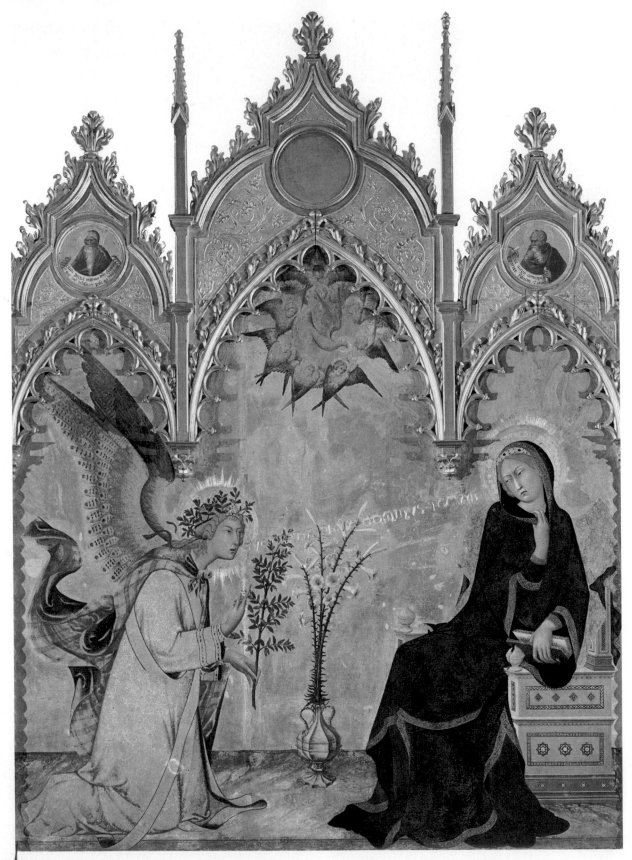

15-19 SIMONE MARTINI, *The Annunciation*, 1333. Tempera on wood, approx. 10' 1" × 8' 8¾". Galleria degli Uffizi, Florence.

representing a soldier of fortune, Guidoriccio da Fogliano, in the service of Siena (FIG. 15-20). This is the first in a long line of equestrian paintings and statues honoring and commemorating those freebooting and ambitious professional soldiers (*condottieri*) who led the armies of the Italian states in their endless petty wars and who often took power themselves. Guidoriccio, who recaptured two small

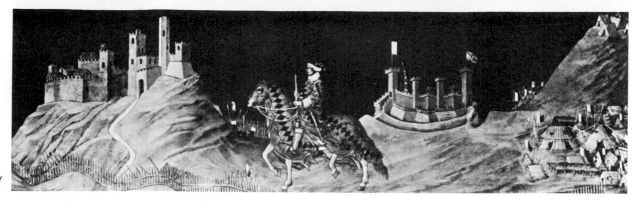

15-20 SIMONE MARTINI, *Guidoriccio da Fogliano*, 1328. Fresco. Palazzo Pubblico, Siena.

Sienese towns from the Pisans, is honored for this solid service to the state by Simone's representation of him cantering in monumental isolation across the barren terrain, his camps to the far right, his banners flying over one city he has just retaken, his resolute and silent course directed toward the hill town at the left still to be conquered. Simone does not concentrate his design around a single episode, as Giotto does, but makes the portrait a kind of sequential description, giving the progress of the general through time. Nor does Simone attempt a single viewpoint; the camp, the towns, and the rider are all seen from different angles. Although this diffuseness is somewhat retrograde, it does not detract from the effectiveness of the great figure on its splendidly caparisoned horse. A quite beautiful touch appears in the diamond pattern shared by horse and rider, which, with the rhythmically fluttering draperies, gives an astonishing illusion of forward motion. The Gothic feeling for line as primarily ornamental is here adroitly employed to produce an illusion of real movement. The subject—a real man in a historically real situation—is itself an innovation and bespeaks the new and irresistible advance of worldly interests into life and art.

Recent scholarly controversy about this great work seems to be leading to a revision of the standard interpretation of it. In the process of its cleaning and restoration, new questions have arisen. Was the figure of Guidoriccio painted later than the landscape? Which cities are represented, and is the one just to the right of the rider not a city but a temporary siege tower? What adjustments of dating must be made? These questions are complicated by the recent discovery of another fresco, just below the larger one of Guidoriccio riding, which represents two figures—the principal one surely Guidoriccio—standing before a captured city. Which city is it? What is its date and significance relative to the equestrian picture? Who was the painter—Duccio, Simone, or some other? Conflicting answers to these questions have been given, and the debate continues. The reader is reminded of how provisional and problematical our art-historical knowledge often is—and of how it is ever-open to revision.

The Lorenzetti

The brothers Lorenzetti, also students of Duccio, share in the general experiments in pictorial realism that so characterize the fourteenth century, especially in their seeking of convincing spatial illusions. PIETRO LORENZETTI (active 1320–1348), going well beyond his master, achieved remarkable success in a large panel representing *The Birth of the Virgin* (FIG. 15-21). The wooden architectural members that divide the panel into three compartments are represented as extending back into the painted space, as if we were looking through the wooden frame (apparently added later) into a box-like stage, where the event takes place. The illusion is strengthened by the fact that one of the vertical members cuts across one of the figures, blocking part of it from view. Whether this architecture-assisted perspective illusion was intentional is problematical; in any case, the full significance of the device of pictorial illusion enhanced by applied

15-21 PIETRO LORENZETTI, *The Birth of the Virgin*, 1342. Tempera on wood, approx. 6' 1" × 5' 11". Museo dell' Opera Metropolitane, Siena.

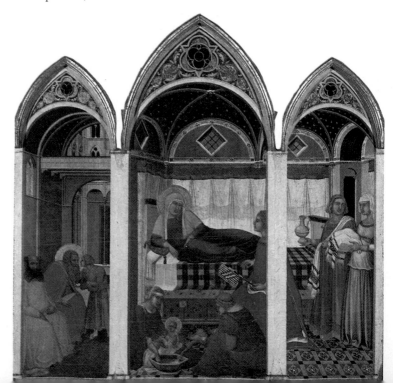

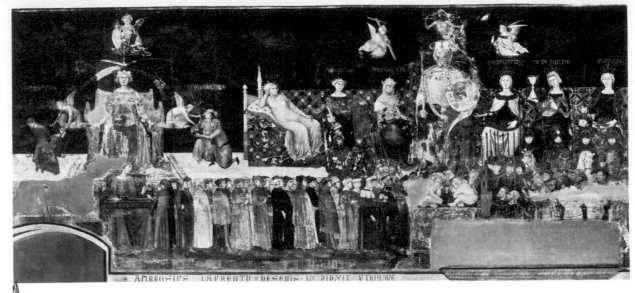

15-22 AMBROGIO LORENZETTI, *Good Government Enthroned*, from the *Good Government* fresco, 1339. Palazzo Pubblico, Siena.

architectural parts was not realized until the next century. There was no precedent for it in the history of Western art, but there was to be a long, successful history during the Renaissance and Baroque periods of such visual illusions produced by a union of real and simulated architecture with painted figures. Pietro made not just a structural advance here; his very subject represents a marked step in the advance of wordly realism. St. Anne, reclining wearily as the midwives wash the child and the women bring gifts, is the center of an episode that takes place in an upper-class Italian house of the period. A number of carefully observed domestic details and the scene at the left, where Joachim eagerly awaits the news of the delivery, place the scene in an actual household, as if we had slid the panels of the walls back and peered within. Thus, the structural innovation in illusionistic space becomes one with the new curiosity that leads to careful inspection and recording of what lies directly before our eyes in the everyday world.

Pietro's brother, AMBROGIO LORENZETTI (active 1319–1348), elaborated in spectacular fashion the Sienese advances in illusionistic representation, as is shown in his vast mural, the *Good Government* fresco, in the Palazzo Pubblico, in which the effects of good and bad government are allegorically juxtaposed. Good Government (FIG. 15-22) is represented as a majestic figure, enthroned and flanked by the virtues of Justice, Prudence, Temperance, and Fortitude, as well as by Peace and Magnanimity; above hover the theological virtues of Faith, Hope, and Charity. In the foreground, the citizens of Siena advance to do homage to Good Government and all the virtues that accompany it. The turbulent politics of the Italian cities, the violent party struggles, the overthrow and reinstatement of governments would certainly have called for solemn reminders of the value of justice in high places, and the city hall would be just the place for a painting like Ambrogio's. Beyond the allegories

and dedication scene stretches the depiction of the fruits of Good Government, both in the city and the countryside. The *Peaceful City* (FIG. 15-23) is a panoramic view of Siena itself, with its clustering palaces, markets, towers, churches, streets, and walls. Commerce moves peacefully through the city, the guildsmen ply their trades and crafts, and a cluster of radiant maidens, hand in hand, perform a graceful, circling dance. The artist fondly observes the life of his city, and its architecture gives him an opportunity to apply Siena's rapidly growing knowledge of perspective. Passing through the city gate to the countryside beyond its walls, Ambrogio's *Peaceful Country* presents a bird's-eye view of the undulating Tuscan countryside—its villas, castles, plowed farmlands, and peasants going about their seasonal occupations (FIG. 15-24). An allegorical figure of Security hovers above the peaceful landscape, unfurling a scroll that promises safety to all who live under the rule of the law. In this sweeping view of an actual countryside, we have the first appearance of landscape since the ancient world. The difference is that now the landscape—as well as the view of the city—is particularized by careful observation, being given almost the character of a portrait of a specific place and environment in a desire for authenticity. By combining some of Giotto's analytical powers with the narrative talent of Duccio, Ambrogio is able to achieve results beyond those of either of his two great predecessors.

The Black Death may have ended the careers of both Lorenzettis; nothing is heard of them after 1348, the year that brought so much horror to defenseless Europe. In an unusual and fascinating painting relating this common late Medieval theme—*The Triumph of Death* (FIG. 15-25) in the Campo Santo at Pisa, attributed to FRANCESCO TRAINI (active *c.* 1321–1363) and, more recently, to BUONAMICO BUFFALMACCO (active early fourteenth century)—three young aristocrats and their ladies in a stylish cavalcade encounter three

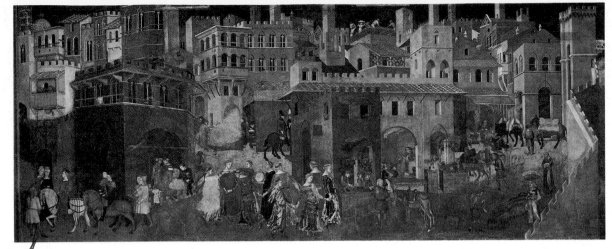

15-23. AMBROGIO LORENZETTI. *Peaceful City*, from the *Good Government* fresco.

15-24. AMBROGIO LORENZETTI, *Peaceful Country*, from the *Good Government* fresco.

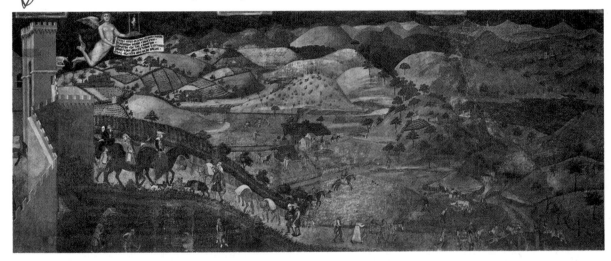

corpses in differing stages of decomposition. As the horror of the confrontation with death strikes them, as the ladies turn away with delicate and ladylike disgust and a gentleman holds his nose (the animals, horses and dogs, sniff excitedly), a holy hermit unrolls a scroll that demonstrates the folly of pleasure and the inevitability of death. In another section, the ladies and gentlemen, wishing to forget dreadful realities, occupy themselves in an orange grove with music, gallantries, and lapdogs, while all around them death and judgment occur and angels and demons struggle for souls. The Medieval message is as strong as ever; but gilded youth refuses to acknowledge it. The painting applies all the stock of Florentine–Sienese representational craft to present the most worldly—and mortal!—picture of the fourteenth century. It is an irony of history that, as Western humanity draws both itself and the world into ever-clearer visual focus, it perceives ever more clearly that corporeal things are perishable.

15-25. BUONAMICO BUFFALMACCO OR FRANCESCO TRAINI (?), *The Triumph of Death*, c. 1340. Fresco. Campo Santo, Pisa.

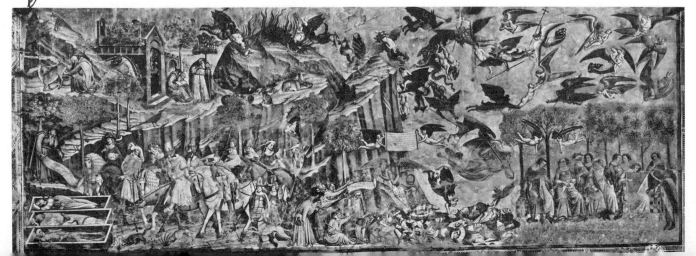

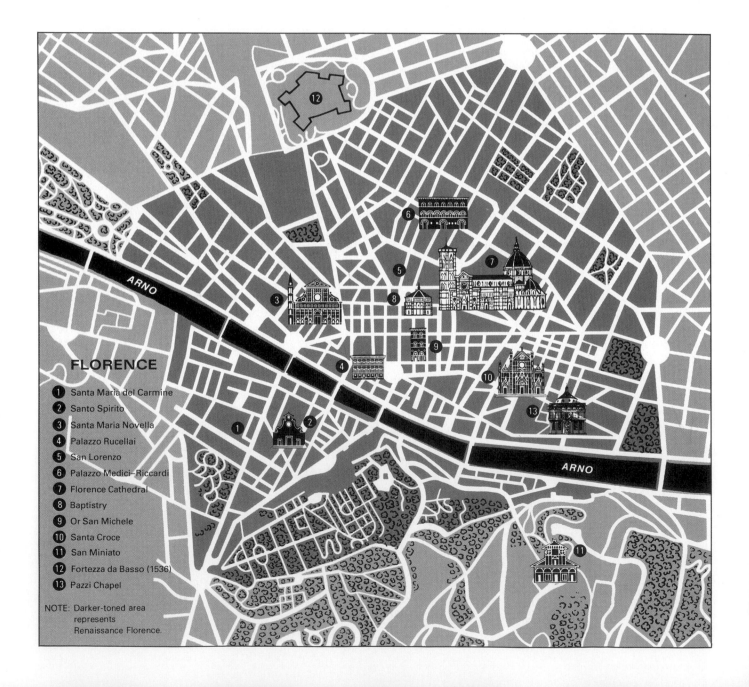

FLORENCE

1. Santa Maria del Carmine
2. Santo Spirito
3. Santa Maria Novella
4. Palazzo Rucellai
5. San Lorenzo
6. Palazzo Medici–Riccardi
7. Florence Cathedral
8. Baptistry
9. Or San Michele
10. Santa Croce
11. San Miniato
12. Fortezza da Basso (1536)
13. Pazzi Chapel

NOTE: Darker-toned area
represents
Renaissance Florence.

FIFTEENTH-CENTURY ITALIAN ART

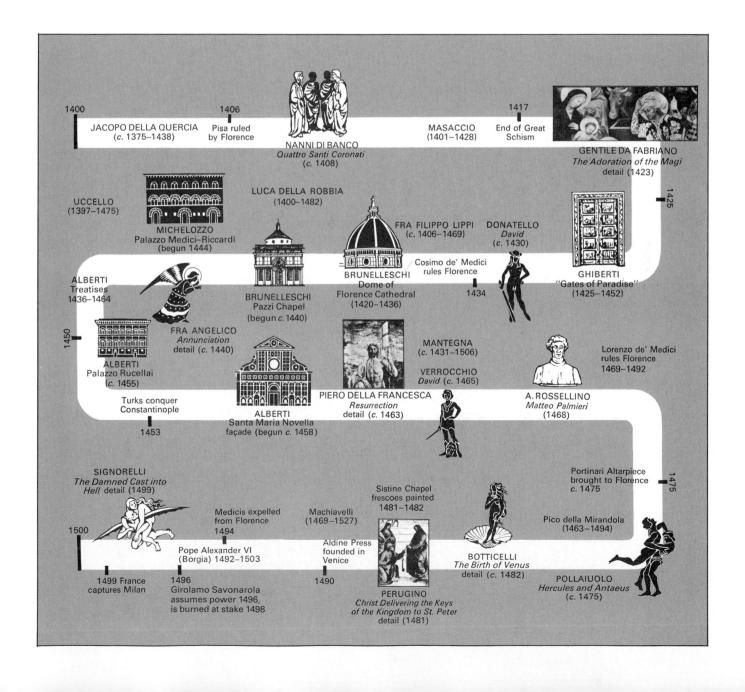

1400

JACOPO DELLA QUERCIA
(c. 1375–1438)

1406 Pisa ruled
by Florence

NANNI DI BANCO
Quattro Santi Coronati
(c. 1408)

MASACCIO
(1401–1428)

1417 End of Great
Schism

GENTILE DA FABRIANO
The Adoration of the Magi
detail (1423)

1425

UCCELLO
(1397–1475)

MICHELOZZO
Palazzo Medici–Riccardi
(begun 1444)

LUCA DELLA ROBBIA
(1400–1482)

FRA FILIPPO LIPPI
(c. 1406–1469)

DONATELLO
David
(c. 1430)

Cosimo de' Medici
rules Florence

GHIBERTI
"Gates of Paradise"
(1425–1452)

ALBERTI
Treatises
1436–1464

BRUNELLESCHI
Pazzi Chapel
(begun c. 1440)

BRUNELLESCHI
Dome of
Florence Cathedral
(1420–1436)

1434

1450

ALBERTI
Palazzo Rucellai
(c. 1455)

FRA ANGELICO
Annunciation
detail (c. 1440)

MANTEGNA
(c. 1431–1506)

VERROCCHIO
David (c. 1465)

Lorenzo de' Medici
rules Florence
1469–1492

Turks conquer
Constantinople

1453

ALBERTI
Santa Maria Novella
façade (begun c. 1458)

PIERO DELLA FRANCESCA
Resurrection
detail (c. 1463)

A. ROSSELLINO
Matteo Palmieri
(1468)

SIGNORELLI
*The Damned Cast into
Hell* detail (1499)

Portinari Altarpiece
brought to Florence
c. 1475

1475

1500

Medicis expelled
from Florence
1494

Machiavelli
(1469–1527)

Sistine Chapel
frescoes painted
1481–1482

Pico della Mirandola
(1463–1494)

Pope Alexander VI
(Borgia) 1492–1503

Aldine Press
founded in
Venice

BOTTICELLI
The Birth of Venus
detail (c. 1482)

POLLAIUOLO
Hercules and Antaeus
(c. 1475)

1499 France
captures Milan

1496
Girolamo Savonarola
assumes power 1496,
is burned at stake 1498

1490

PERUGINO
*Christ Delivering the Keys
of the Kingdom to St. Peter*
detail (1481)

FLORENCE took cultural command of Italy in the early fifteenth century, inaugurating the Renaissance and establishing itself as the intellectual and artistic capital of southern Europe—a position of dominance it was to retain until the end of the century. According to John Addington Symonds, a nineteenth-century historian of the Renaissance:

> . . . nowhere else except at Athens has the whole population of a city been so permeated with ideas, so highly intellectual by nature, so keen in perception, so witty and so subtle, as at Florence. . . . The primacy of the Florentines in literature, the fine arts, law, scholarship, philosophy and science was acknowledged throughout Italy.*

The power and splendor of Florence had long been building; the fifteenth century marked its perfection. Like the Athenians after the repulse of the Persians, the citizens of Florence (who felt a historical affinity with the Athenians) responded with conscious pride to their repulse of the dukes of Milan, who had attempted the conquest of Tuscany. Like the Athenians also, the Florentines developed a culture that was stimulated and supported by a vast accumulation of wealth; but unlike the Athenians, only a few illustrious families controlled that wealth. The Medici, bankers to all Europe, became such lavish patrons of art and learning that, to this day, the name "Medici" means a generous patron of the fine arts. For centuries, the history of Florence is the history of the House of Medici. Early in the fifteenth century, Giovanni de' Medici had established the family fortune. His son Cosimo, called "father of his country" by the Florentines, secured the admiration and loyalty of the people of Florence against the noble and privileged; with this security, the Medici gradually became the discreet dictators of the Florentine republic, disguising their absolute power behind a mask of affable benevolence. Scarcely a great architect, painter, sculptor, philosopher, or Humanist scholar was unknown to the Medici. Cosimo began the first public library since the ancient world, and it is estimated that in some 30 years he and his descendants expended almost $20,000,000 for manuscripts and books; such was the financial power behind the establishment of Humanism in the Renaissance. The Medici, careful businessmen that they were, were not sentimental about their endowment of art and scholarship; Cosimo declared that his good works were "not only for the honor of God but . . . likewise for my own remembrance." Yet the astute businessman and politician had a sincere love of learning, reading Plato in his old age and writing to his tutor, the Neo-

Platonic philosopher Marsilio Ficino, "I desire nothing so much as to know the best road to happiness." This is the very model of the cultivated, Humanist grandee. The grandson of Cosimo, Lorenzo the Magnificent, went, as his name suggests, even beyond his grandfather in munificence. Himself a talented poet, he gathered about him a galaxy of artists and gifted men in all fields, extending the library Cosimo had begun, revitalizing his academy for the instruction of artists, establishing the Platonic Academy of Philosophy, and lavishing funds (often the city's own) on splendid buildings, festivals, and pageants. If his prime motive was to retain the affection of the people and, thus, the power of the House of Medici, he nevertheless made Florence a city of great beauty, the capital of all the newly flourishing arts. His death, in 1492, brought to an end the "golden age" of Florence, and the years immediately following saw the invasion of Italy by—as the Italians called them—the "barbarian" nations of France, Spain, and the Holy Roman Empire. The Medici were expelled from Florence; the reforming, fanatical Girolamo Savonarola preached repentance in the cathedral of Florence; and the Renaissance moved its light and its artists from Florence to Rome. But one of the most prominent patrons of the Roman Renaissance, Pope Leo X, patron of Raphael and Michelangelo, was himself a Medici, the son of Lorenzo the Magnificent. Never in history was there a family so intimately associated with a great cultural revolution. It might safely be said of the Medici that they subsidized and endowed the Renaissance.

THE FIRST HALF OF THE FIFTEENTH CENTURY

Sculpture

The spirit of the Medici and of the Renaissance was nothing if not competitive and desirous of fame. But even before Medici rule, civic competitiveness and pride had motivated the adornment of Florence. The history of the Early Renaissance in art begins with an account of a competition for a design for the east doors of the baptistry of Florence (later moved to the north), the south doors of which Andrea Pisano had designed almost three generations before (FIG. 15-4). LORENZO GHIBERTI (1378–1455), the sculptor who won the competition, describes his victory in terms that reflect the egoism and the "cult of fame" characteristic of the period and of the Renaissance artist himself:

> To me was conceded the palm of the victory by all the experts and by all . . . who had competed with me. To me the honor was conceded universally and with no

*John Addington Symonds, *Renaissance in Italy* (New York: Modern Library, 1935), Vol. 1, p. 125.

exception. To all it seemed that I had at that time surpassed the others without exception, as was recognized by a great council and an investigation of learned men . . . highly skilled from the painters and sculptors of gold, silver, and marble. There were thirty-four judges from the city and the other surrounding countries. The testimonial of the victory was given in my favor by all. . . . It was granted to me and determined that I should make the bronze door for this church. . . .*

This passage also indicates the esteem and importance now attached to art, with leading men of a city bestowing eagerly sought-for commissions and great new programs of private and public works being widely undertaken.

The contestants represented the assigned subject, the Sacrifice of Isaac, within panels shaped like the Gothic quatrefoil used by Andrea Pisano for the south doors of the baptistry. Only those by FILIPPO BRUNELLESCHI and Ghiberti have survived. Brunelleschi's panel (FIG. 16-1) shows a sturdy and vigorous interpretation of the theme, with something of the emotional agitation of the tradition of Giovanni Pisano (FIG. 15-3). Abraham seems all at once to have summoned the dreadful courage needed to kill his son at God's command; he lunges forward, draperies flying, exposing, with desperate violence, Isaac's throat to the knife. Matching Abraham's energy, the saving angel darts in from the left, arresting the stroke just in time. Brunelleschi's figures are carefully observed, and there are elements of a new realism in them. Yet his composition is perhaps overly busy,

and the figures of the two servants and the donkey are not sufficiently subordinated to the main action.

We can make this criticism more firmly when we compare Brunelleschi's panel to Ghiberti's (FIG. 16-2). In the latter, vigor and strength of statement are subordinated to grace and smoothness; little of the awfulness of the subject appears. Abraham sways elegantly in the familiar Gothic S-curve, and seems to feign rather than to aim a deadly thrust. The figure of Isaac, beautifully posed and rendered, recalls ancient Classicism and could be regarded as the first really classicizing nude since antiquity. Ghiberti was trained as both a goldsmith and a painter, and his skilled treatment of the fluent surfaces, with their sharply and accurately incised detail, evidences his goldsmith's craft. As a painter, he shares the painter's interest in spatial illusion. The rocky landscape seems to emerge from the blank panel toward us, as does the strongly foreshortened angel. These pictorial effects, sometimes thought alien to sculpture, are more developed in Ghiberti's later work, a second pair of doors for the baptistry (FIG. 16-10), the execution of which testifies to his extraordinary skill in harmonizing the effects peculiar to sculpture and painting. Here, within the limits of the awkward shape of the panel, Ghiberti achieves a composition that is perhaps less daring than Brunelleschi's but more cohesive and unified, and the jury's choice probably was fortunate for the course of art, despite accusations of collusion by Brunelleschi's biographer, Manetti. One result of the decision was, apparently, to resolve Brunelleschi's indecision about his proper calling. Subordinating sculpture, he became the first great architect of the Renaissance. As for Ghiberti, his conservative style would be greatly modified by the

*In E.G. Holt, ed., *Literary Sources of Art History* (Princeton, N.J.: Princeton University Press, 1947), pp. 87–88.

16-1   FILIPPO BRUNELLESCHI, *The Sacrifice of Isaac*, 1401–1402. Gilt bronze, 21″ × 17″. Museo Nazionale, Florence.

16-2   LORENZO GHIBERTI, *The Sacrifice of Isaac*, 1401–1402. Gilt bronze, 21″ × 17″. Museo Nazionale, Florence.

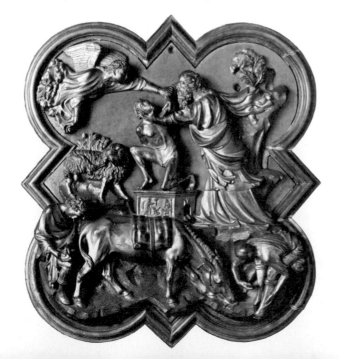

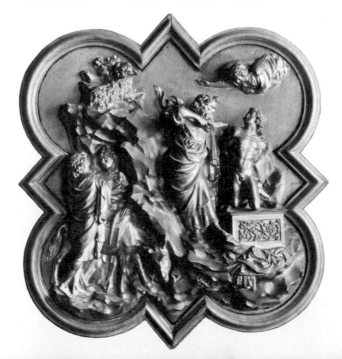

discoveries of his contemporaries, and their influence on him would be visible in the later east doors of the baptistry.

The artists of Florence in the early Renaissance are sometimes classified as "conservative" or "progressive," depending on whether they cling to the International Gothic style or they take up the new pictorial experimentalism. The classification cannot be applied consistently, however, for some artists who keep to the old conventions still occasionally adopt what they can use from their more experimental contemporaries wherever it may be made consistent with their own styles. Whether conservative or progressive, artists may produce work of the highest quality, and we should not think that their excellence is merely a function of their being up-to-date or avant-garde. In some cases, too fertile and inventive an imagination may outrace the artist's powers to systematize his effort and become detrimental to his development.

JACOPO DELLA QUERCIA (c. 1375–1438), a Sienese sculptor competing for the baptistry commission, was perhaps the only non-Florentine sculptor of first rank in the fifteenth century. In comparison with the early work of Ghiberti, Jacopo's is progressive. His panel, *The Expulsion from the Garden of Eden* (FIG. 16-3), from a series of reliefs enframing the portal of San Petronio in Bologna, is carved in shallow relief and set into the frame in a closely knit pattern of curves and diagonals. The figures are constructed so that they seem capable of breaking out of the confines of the relief. A robust energy animates the powerful, heavily muscled forms and recalls the ideal Classical athletes. The conventional Gothic slenderness and delicacy are

16-3 JACOPO DELLA QUERCIA, *The Expulsion from the Garden of Eden*, c. 1430. Istrian stone, 34" × 27". Main portal, San Petronio, Bologna, Italy.

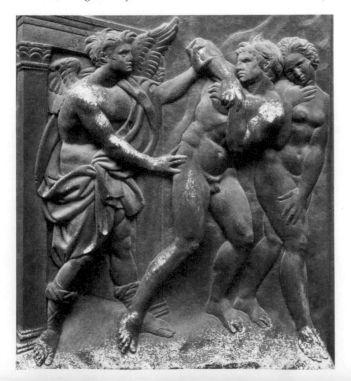

gone, and Jacopo's massive, monumental forms herald the grand style of the Renaissance. Indeed, although his style is without influence in Florence, he was to be rediscovered by Michelangelo at the end of the fifteenth century; the latter's debt to Jacopo is clearly visible in the great Florentine's painting of the same subject in the Sistine Chapel ceiling.

As the Sienese artist turned to the observation of the mechanics of the human body, a Florentine artist, NANNI DI BANCO (c. 1380–1421), began to explore that other popular avenue of Humanistic research, the antique. His life-size figures of four martyred saints, *Quattro Santi Coronati* (FIG. 16-4), represent the patron saints of the Florentine guild of sculptors, architects, and masons. The group, set into the outside wall of the Medieval church of Or San Michele in Florence, is an early near-solution to the Renaissance problem of integrating figures and space on a monumental scale. Here, we are on the way to the great solutions of Masaccio and of the masters of the High Renaissance. The emergence of sculpture from the architectural matrix—seen beginning in such works as the thirteenth-century statues of the west front of Reims Cathedral (FIG. 10-32)—is almost complete in Nanni's figures, which stand in a niche that is *in* but that confers some separation *from* the architecture. This spatial recess permits a new and dramatic possibility for the interrelationship of the figures. By placing them in a semicircle within their deep niche and relating them to one another by their postures and gestures, as well as by the arrangement of draperies, Nanni has achieved a wonderfully unified spatial composition. The persisting dependence on the architecture may be seen in the abutment of the two forward figures and the enframement of the niche and in the position of the two recessed figures, each in front of an engaged half-column. Nevertheless, these unyielding figures, whose bearing expresses—as in Roman art and stoicism—the discipline through which men of passionate conviction attain order and reason, are joined in a remarkable psychological unity. While the figure on the right speaks, pointing to his right, the two men opposite listen and the one next to him looks out into space, meditating the meaning of the words. Such reinforcement of the formal unity of a group with psychological cross-references will be exploited by later Renaissance artists, particularly Leonardo da Vinci.

Nanni has before him the example of the sculpture of antiquity. If we compare his statues with those of the *Visitation* group at Reims (FIG. 10-33) or of Nicola Pisano (FIG. 15-2), we find the Classicism of the older works lacking in authority and, as yet, unsure—hesitant steps in a direction only dimly suspected. The *Quattro Santi Coronati* figures have arrived at a position that, if not identical with the Roman norm, is adjacent to it. The Renaissance artist has begun to

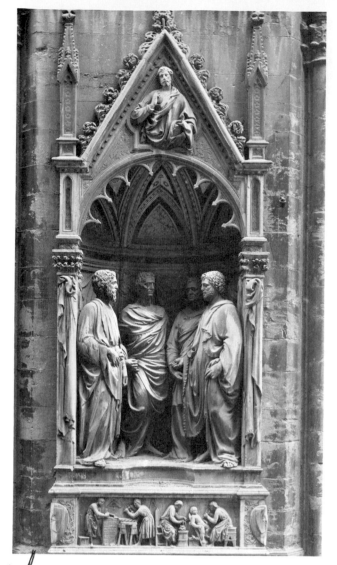

16-4 NANNI DI BANCO, *Quattro Santi Coronati, c.* 1408–1414. Marble, figures approx. life-size. Or San Michele, Florence.

comprehend the Roman meaning, even if he does not duplicate the Roman form. But duplication is not his purpose; rather, it is interpretation or commentary in the manner of the Humanist scholars dealing with Classical texts.

The Humanist, Roman Classicism expressed in the sculpture of Nanni was not exclusively of his devising. The whole city of Florence, in its last, fierce war with the Visconti of Milan at the turn of the century, modeled itself on the ancient Roman republic. The Humanist chancellor of Florence, Coluccio Salutati, whose Latin style of writing was widely influential, exhorted his fellow citizens to take as their own the republican ideal of civil and political liberty they believed to be that of Rome, and to identify themselves with its spirit. To be Florentine was to be Roman; freedom was the distinguishing virtue of both.

A new realism based on the study of man and nature, an idealism found in the study of Classical forms, and a power of individual expression characteristic of genius are the elements that constitute the art and the personality of the sculptor DONATELLO (1386–1466), who, in the early years of the century, carried forward most dramatically the search for new forms capable of expressing the new ideas of the Humanistic Early Renaissance. Working side by side, Donatello and Nanni collaborated on sculpture for the cathedral of Florence and the church of Or San Michele. They shared the Humanistic enthusiasm for Roman virtue and form; their innovations in style, expressive of a new age, are parallel. Donatello's greatness lies in an extraordinary versatility and depth that led him through a spectrum of themes fundamental to human experience and through stylistic variations that express these themes with unprecedented profundity and force.

A principal characteristic of greatness is authority. The great artist produces work that his contemporaries and posterity accept as authoritative; his work becomes a criterion and a touchstone for criticism. Judgments of what is authoritative and "best" will of course vary with time and place, but the greatest artists seem to survive this relativity of judgment, apparently because they reveal something deeply and permanently true about man and broadly applicable to his experience. Shakespeare, for example, seems miraculously familiar with almost the whole world of human nature. Similarly, Donatello is at ease not only with the real, the ideal, and the spiritual, but with such diverse human forms and conditions as childhood, the idealized human nude, practical men of the world, military despots, holy men, derelict prelates, and ascetic old age. Others who follow Donatello in the school of Florence may specialize in one or two of these human types or moods, but none commands them so completely and convincingly. In the early fifteenth century, Donatello defined and claimed as his province the whole terrain of naturalistic and Humanistic art.

Early in his career, Donatello took the first fundamental and necessary step toward depiction of motion in the human figure—recognition of the principle of weight shift (*ponderation*). His *St. Mark* (FIG. 16-5), commissioned for Or San Michele, was completed in 1413; with it, Donatello closed a millennium of Medieval art and turned a historical corner into a new era. We have seen the importance of weight shift in the ancient world, when Greek sculptors, in works like the *Kritios Boy* (FIG. 5-19) and the *Doryphoros* (FIG. 5-61), grasped the essential principle that the human body is not rigid, but a flexible structure that moves by continuous shifting of weight from one supporting leg to the other, the main masses of the body moving in consonance. An illuminating comparison may be made between Donatello's *St. Mark* and Medieval portal statuary, or, for that matter, the sculpture of Nicola and Giovanni Pisano or even of the early Ghiberti; in none of these statues except Donatello's

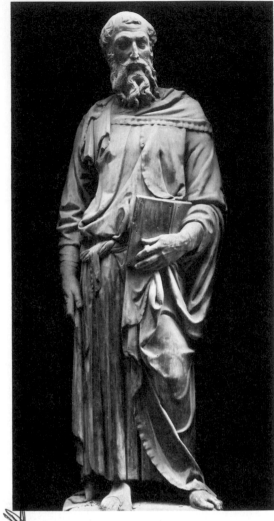

16-5 DONATELLO, *St. Mark*, 1411–1413. Marble, approx. 7′ 9″ high. Or San Michele, Florence.

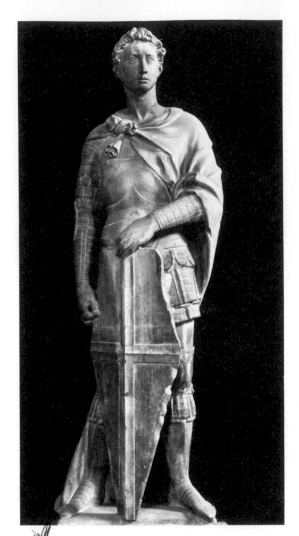

16-6 DONATELLO, *St. George*, 1415–1417, from Or San Michele. Marble, approx. 6′ 10″ high. Museo Nazionale, Florence.

has the principle of weight shift been grasped. Now all at once, with the same abruptness with which it appeared in ancient Greece in Early Classical art (FIG. 5-19), it is rediscovered by Donatello. In sculpture and painting, his successors gradually mastered the representation of bodily motion of the most complex kind.

As the body now "moves," so its drapery "moves" with it, hanging and folding naturally from and around bodily points of support, so that we sense the figure as a draped nude, not simply as an integrated column with drapery arbitrarily incised. This further contributes to the independence of the figure from its architectural setting. We feel that *St. Mark* can and is about to move out of the deep niche, as the stirring limbs, the shifting weight, and the mobile drapery suggest. It is easy to imagine the figure as freestanding, unenframed by architecture, without loss of any of its basic qualities.

In his *St. George* (FIG. 16-6), also designed for Or San Michele (between 1415 and 1417), Donatello provides an image of the proud idealism of youth. The armored soldier-saint, patron of the guild of ar-morers, which commissioned the statue, stands with bold firmness—legs set apart, feet strongly planted, the torso slightly twisting so that the left shoulder and arm advance with a subtle gesture of haughty and challenging readiness—as the dragon ap-proaches. His head is erect, turned slightly to the left; the noble features beneath the furrowed brows are intent, concentrated, yet composed in the realization of his power, intelligence, and resolution. In its regal poise and tense anticipation, the figure contrasts strikingly with its earlier Gothic counterpart, *St. Theodore* (FIG. 16-7), from Chartres Cathedral. *St. Theodore* the soldier, essentially weightless, seems in some mystic reverie, removed from the world and unaware of his surroundings. The elements of his body are not coordinated in the unity of action we find in *St. George*. The Medieval figure conveys the *idea* of the chivalric knight but nothing of the *fact* of the soldier confronting his enemy.

Between 1416 and 1435, Donatello carved five stat-ues for the niches on the campanile of Florence Ca-thedral—a project that, like the figures for Or San Michele, had originated in the preceding century.

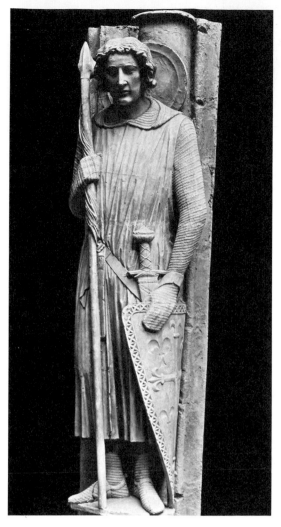

16-7 *St. Theodore*, jamb statue, *c.* 1215–1220. South portal, Chartres Cathedral. Stone, over life-size.

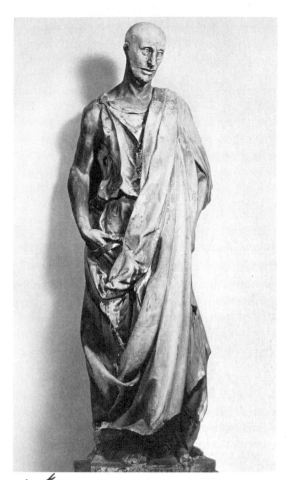

16-8 DONATELLO, prophet figure (*Zuccone*), 1423–1425, from the campanile of Florence Cathedral. Marble, approx. 6' 5" high. Museo dell' Opera del Duomo, Florence.

The most striking of the five figures—a prophet, generally known by its nickname *Zuccone*, or "Pumpkin-Head" (FIG. 16-8)—shows Donatello's peculiar power of characterization at its most original. All of his prophets are represented with a harsh, direct realism reminiscent of ancient Roman portrait sculpture. Their faces are bony, lined, and taut; each is strongly individualized. The *Zuccone* is also bald, a departure from the conventional representation of the prophets. He is dressed in an awkwardly draped and crumpled toga-like garment with deeply undercut folds. At first view, one might suspect Donatello of simply having draped a gaunt, uncouth assistant, placing him in casual stance, and rendering the subject just as he saw it. The head discloses an appalling personality—instinct with crude power, even violence. The deep-set eyes glare under furrowed brows, nostrils flaring, the broad mouth agape, as if the prophet were in the very presence of the disasters that would call forth his declamation.

In a bronze relief, *The Feast of Herod* (FIG. 16-9), on the baptismal font in the baptistry at Siena, Donatello carries his talent for characterization of single figures

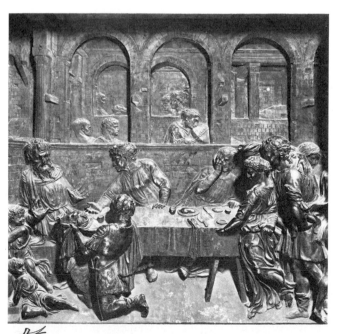

16-9 DONATELLO, *The Feast of Herod*, *c.* 1425. Gilt bronze, approx. 23" × 23". Baptistry, San Giovanni, Siena, Italy.

onto the broader field of dramatic groups. Salome (toward the right), still seems to be dancing, even though she has already delivered the severed head of John the Baptist, with which the executioner kneels before King Herod. The actors recoil in horror into two groups: at the right, one figure covers his face with his hand; at the left, Herod and two terrified children shrink back in dismay. The psychic explosion that has taken place drives the human elements apart, leaving a gap across which the emotional electricity crackles. This masterful stagecraft obscures the fact that on the stage itself another drama is being played out—the advent of rationalized perspective space, long prepared for in the "proto-Renaissance" and recognized by Donatello and his generation as a means of intensifying the reality of the action and the characterization of the actors.

"Proto-Renaissance" artists, like Duccio and the Lorenzetti brothers, had used several devices to give the effect of distance, but with the invention of "true" linear perspective (generally attributed to Brunelleschi), early Renaissance artists were given a way to make the illusion of distance mathematical and certain. In effect, they understood the picture plane as a transparent window through which, from a fixed standpoint, the observer looks *into* the constructed, pictorial world, where all orthogonals (lines perpendicular to the picture plane) meet in a single point on the horizon (a horizontal line that corresponds to the viewer's eye level) and where all objects are unified within a single space system—the perspective. This discovery was of enormous importance, for it made possible what has been called the "rationalization of sight"—the bringing of our random and infinitely various visual sensations under a simple rule that can be expressed mathematically. Indeed, the discovery of perspective by the artists of the Renaissance reflects the emergence of science itself, which is, put simply, the mathematical ordering of our observations of the physical world. It is interesting that the artists of the Renaissance were often mathematicians, and a modern mathematician asserts that the most creative work in mathematics in the fifteenth century was done by the artists. The experimental spirit that had animated many Franciscans, like Roger Bacon, now came firmly to earth; indeed, Bacon's essays on optics had large influence on Renaissance theorists like Alberti. The position of the observer of a picture, who looks "through" it into the painted "world," is precisely that of any scientific observer fixing his gaze on the carefully placed or located datum of his research. Of course, the early Renaissance artist was not primarily a scientist; he simply found perspective a wonderful way to order his composition and to clarify it. But there is little doubt that perspective, with its new mathematical authority and certitude, conferred a kind of esthetic legitimacy on painting by making the picture *measurable* and exact. According to Plato, "the excellence of beauty of every work of art is due to the observance of measure." This is certainly expressed in the art of Greece, and now, in the Renaissance—when Plato was newly discovered and eagerly read—the artists once again exalted the principle of measure as the foundation of the beautiful in the fine arts. The projection of measured shapes on flat surfaces now influenced the character of painting and made possible scale drawings, maps, charts, graphs, and diagrams—those means of exact representation without which modern science and technology would be impossible. At this beginning of the modern world, mathematical truth and formal beauty became conjoined in the minds of the artists of the Renaissance. In his relief panel *The Feast of Herod* (FIG. 16-9), Donatello, using the device of pictorial perspective, opens the space of the action well into the distance, showing two arched courtyards and groups of attendants in the background. This penetration of the panel surface by spatial illusion replaces the flat grounds and backdrop areas of the Medieval past. The ancient Roman illusionism returns, but it is now based on a secure principle never possessed by the ancients.

It is worth comparing Donatello's Siena panel with one from Ghiberti's famous east doors of the baptis-

16-10 LORENZO GHIBERTI, east doors ("Gates of Paradise"), 1425–1452. Gilt bronze, approx. 17' high. Baptistry of Florence Cathedral.

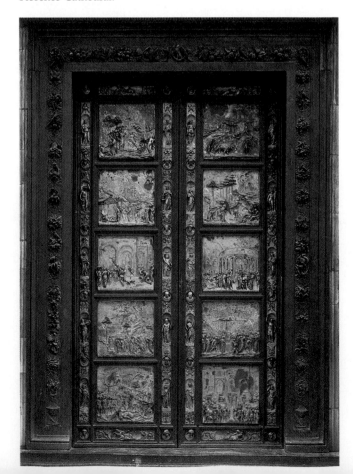

try of Florence Cathedral (FIG. 16-10), later declared by Michelangelo to be "so fine that they might fittingly stand as the Gates of Paradise." The east doors (1425–1452) were composed differently from Ghiberti's earlier north doors. There are three sets of doors on the baptistry. The first was made by Andrea Pisano for the east doorway (1330–1335), which faces the cathedral and is the most important entrance. This set of doors was moved to the south doorway to make way for Ghiberti's first pair of doors (1403–1424), which, in turn, was moved to the north doorway so that Ghiberti's second pair of doors, the "Gates of Paradise," could be placed in the east doorway. After 1425, Ghiberti abandoned the pattern of the earlier doors and divided the space into ten square panels, each containing a relief set in plain moldings. When gilded, the glittering movement of the reliefs created an effect of great splendor and elegance.

The individual panels of Ghiberti's doors, such as *Isaac and His Sons* (FIG. 16-11), clearly recall painting in their depiction of space as well as in their treatment of the narrative; some exemplify more fully than painting many of the principles Alberti formulates in his treatise, *On Painting*. In his relief, Ghiberti creates the illusion of space partly by pictorial perspective and partly by sculptural means. Buildings are represented according to the painter's one-point perspective construction, but the figures (in the lower section of the relief, which actually projects slightly toward the viewer) appear almost in the full round, some of the heads standing completely free. As the eye progresses upward, the relief becomes flatter and flatter until the architecture in the background is represented by barely raised lines, creating a sort of "sculptor's aerial perspective" in which forms are less distinct the deeper they are in space. Ghiberti describes the work as follows:

16-11 LORENZO GHIBERTI, *Isaac and His Sons* (detail of FIG. 16-10). Approx. 31½" × 31½".

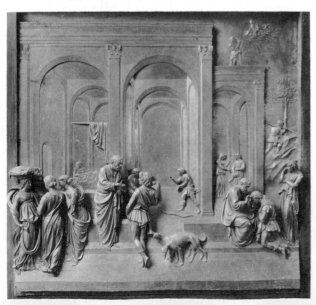

I strove to imitate nature as closely as I could, and with all the perspective I could produce [to have] excellent compositions rich with many figures. In some scenes I placed about a hundred figures, in some less, and in some more. I executed that work with the greatest diligence and the greatest love. There were ten stories, all [sunk] in frames because the eye from a distance measures and interprets the scenes in such a way that they appear round. The scenes are in the lowest relief and the figures are seen in the planes; those that are near appear large, those in the distance small, as they do in reality. . . . Executed with the greatest study and perseverance, of all my work it is the most remarkable I have done and it was finished with skill, correct proportions, and understanding.*

Thus, an echo of the ancient and Medieval past is harmonized by the new science: "proportion" and "skill" are perfected by "understanding." Ghiberti achieves a greater sense of depth than has ever before been possible in a relief. However, his principal figures do not occupy the architectural space he has created for them; rather, they are arranged along a parallel plane in front of the grandiose architecture. (According to Alberti, in his *De re aedificatoria*, the grandeur of the architecture reflects the dignity of events shown in the foreground.) Ghiberti's figure style shows a mingling of Gothic patterning of rhythmic line, Classical poses and motifs, and a new realism in characterization, movement, and surface detail. The Medieval narrative method of arranging several episodes within a frame persists. In *Isaac and His Sons* (FIG. 16-11), the group of ladies in the left foreground attends the birth of Esau and Jacob in the left background; Isaac sends Esau and his hunting dogs on his mission in the central foreground; and, in the right foreground, Isaac blesses the kneeling Jacob as Rebecca looks on (Genesis 25–27). Yet the groups are so subtly placed that there is no crowding or confusion. The figures, in varying degrees of projection, gracefully twist and turn, appearing to occupy and move through a convincing stage space, which is deepened by showing some figures from behind. The Classicism, particularly of the group of visiting ladies, derives from Ghiberti's close study of ancient art. From his biography, we know that he admired and collected Classical sculpture, bronzes, and coins— and their influence is seen throughout the panel. The beginning of the practice of collecting Classical art in the fifteenth century had much to do with the appearance of Classicism in the Humanistic art of the Renaissance.

For a time, Donatello forgot his earlier realism under the spell of Classical Rome, the ruins and an-

*In E.G. Holt, ed., *Literary Sources of Art History* (Princeton, N.J.: Princeton University Press, 1947), pp. 90–91.

tiquities of which he studied at some length. His bronze statue of *David* (*c.* 1430–1432) is the first free-standing nude statue since ancient times, and here Donatello shows himself once more to be an innovator (FIG. 16-12). The nude, as such, proscribed in the Christian Middle Ages as both indecent and idolatrous, had been shown only rarely—and then only in biblical or moralizing contexts, like the story of Adam and Eve or descriptions of sinners in Hell. Donatello reinvented the Classical nude, even though, in this case, we have neither god nor athlete but the young David—slayer of Goliath, biblical ancestor and antitype of Christ, and symbol of the Florentine love of liberty. The classically proportioned nude—a balance of opposing axes, of tension and relaxation—recalls, and is perhaps derived from, Roman copies of Hellenic statues. Although the body has an almost Praxitelean radiance and a sensuous quality unknown to Medieval figures, David is involved in a complex psychological drama unknown to Antique sculpture. The glance of this youthful, still adolescent hero is not directed primarily toward the severed head of Goliath, which lies between his feet, but toward his own graceful, sinuous body, as though, in consequence of his heroic deed, he is becoming conscious for the first time of its beauty, its vitality, and its strength. This self-awareness, this discovery of the self, is a dominant theme in Renaissance art.

In 1443, Donatello left Florence for northern Italy to accept the rewarding commission of an equestrian

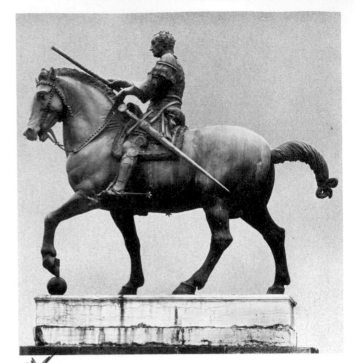

16-13   DONATELLO, equestrian statue of Erasmo da Narni (*Gattamelata*), *c.* 1445–1450. Bronze, approx. 11' high. Piazza del Santo, Padua, Italy.

statue of the Venetian *condottiere* Erasmo da Narni, called *Gattamelata* ("slick cat"), for the square of San Antonio, Padua (FIG. 16-13). With it, Donatello recovered the Roman grandeur of the mounted leader as it existed in the great equestrian statue of Marcus Aurelius (FIG. 6-72), which he must have seen in Rome. The figure stands high on a lofty, elliptical base to set it apart from its surroundings and becomes almost a celebration of the liberation of sculpture from architecture. Massive and majestic, the great horse bears the amored general easily; together, they make an overwhelming image of irresistible strength and unlimited power. Next to the *Gattamelata*, a Medieval equestrian statue like *The Bamberg Rider* (FIG. 10–55), still attached to the wall, looks positively fragile, even ghost-like. The Italian rider, his face set in a mask of dauntless resolution and unshakable will, is the very portrait of the Renaissance individualist: a man of intelligence, courage, and ambition, frequently of humble origin, who, by his own resourcefulness and on his own merits, rises to a commanding position in the world.

Donatello's ten-year activity in Padua (he received additional commissions for statues and reliefs for the high altar of the church of San Antonio) made a deep and lasting impression on the artists of the region and contributed materially to the formation of a Renaissance style in northern Italy. After his return to Florence in 1453, Donatello's style changes once more. His last period is marked by an intensely personal kind of expression, in which his earlier realism returns, but with purposeful exaggeration and distortion. He turns away from Classical beauty and gran-

16-12   DONATELLO, *David,* *c.* 1430–1432. Bronze, approx. 62" high. Museo Nazionale, Florence.

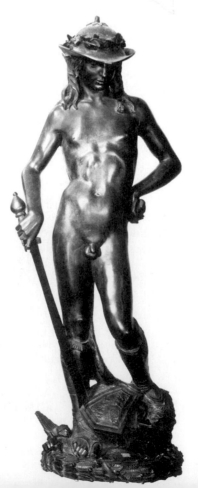

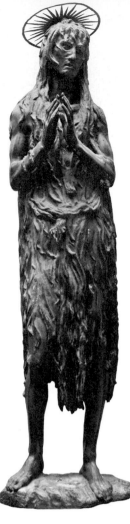

16-14 DONATELLO, *Mary Magdalene*, c. 1454–1455. Wood, approx. 6' 2" high. Museo dell' Opera del Duomo, Florence.

trained as a goldsmith, but his ability as a sculptor must have been well known at that time. Although his biographer, Manetti, tells us that Brunelleschi turned to architecture out of disappointment over the loss of the baptistry commission, he continued to work as a sculptor for several years and received commissions for sculpture as late as 1416. In the meantime, however, his interest turned more and more toward architecture, spurred by several trips to Rome (the first in 1402, probably with his friend Donatello), where he too was captivated by the Roman ruins. It may well be in connection with his close study of Roman monuments and his effort to make an accurate record of what he saw that Brunelleschi developed the revolutionary system of geometric, linear perspective that was so eagerly adopted by fifteenth-century artists.

Brunelleschi's knowledge of the principles of Roman construction, combined with an analytical and inventive mind, permitted him to solve an engineering problem that no other fifteenth-century man could have solved—the design and construction of a dome for the huge crossing of the unfinished cathedral of Florence (FIGS. 16-15 and 10-58). The problem was staggering; the space to be spanned (140 feet)

16-15 FILIPPO BRUNELLESCHI, dome of Florence Cathedral, 1420–1436 (view from the southeast).

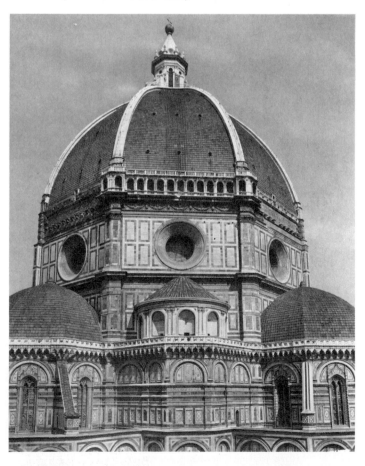

deur toward a kind of expressionism that seems deliberately calculated to jar the sensibilities; he gives us the ugly, the painful, and the violent. He may, in his last years, have felt religious remorse for such works as *David* and may have set about to achieve a kind of anti-esthetic manner, well exemplified in his *Mary Magdalene* (FIG. 16-14). The repentant saint in old age, after years of wasting mortification, stands emaciated, hands clasped in prayer. Donatello, in what appears to be a rekindling of Medieval piety, here rejects the body as merely the mortal shell of the immortal soul. The beautiful woman has withered, but her soul has been saved by her denial of physical beauty. Donatello's originality, independence, and insight into the meaning of religious experience are asserted here as he reinterprets Medieval material in his own terms. But Medieval as *Mary Magdalene* might first appear, we realize that it was carved by the man who made *David*, and Donatello appears as we first described him—a man with the vast versatility that distinguishes the great artist from the good artist.

Architecture

FILIPPO BRUNELLESCHI (1377–1446)—one of the unsuccessful competitors for the commission to do the doors of the baptistry of Florence in 1401—was

was much too wide to permit construction with the aid of traditional wooden centering. Nor was it possible, because of the plan of the crossing, to support the dome with buttressed walls. Brunelleschi seems to have begun work on the problem about 1417; in 1420, he and Ghiberti were jointly awarded the commission. The latter, however, soon retired from the project and left the field to his competitor. With exceptional ingenuity, Brunelleschi not only discarded traditional building methods and devised new ones but also invented much of the machinery that was necessary for the job. Although he might have preferred the hemispheric shape of Roman domes, Brunelleschi raised the center of his dome and designed it around an ogival section, which is inherently more stable, as it reduces the outward thrust around the dome's base. To reduce the weight of the structure to a minimum, he designed a relatively thin double shell (the first in history) around a skeleton of 24 ribs, the eight major ones being visible on the exterior. Finally, in almost paradoxical fashion, Brunelleschi anchored the structure at the top with a heavy lantern (built according to his design, but after his death). This lantern, although adding to the weight of the dome, has the curious effect of stabilizing the entire structure; without the pressure of its weight, the ribs had a tendency to tilt outward from the center, spreading at the top.

Although the dome of Florence Cathedral is Brunelleschi's most outstanding engineering achievement and although he knew of and admired Roman building techniques, the solution to this most critical structural problem was arrived at by the first acknowledged Renaissance architect through what were essentially Gothic building principles. Thus, the dome does not really express Brunelleschi's own ar-

chitectural style, which is shown for the first time in a building that he began shortly before he accepted the commission for the dome—the Ospedale degli Innocenti (Foundling Hospital) in Florence (FIG. 16-16). The basic element of its design—a series of round arches supported by slender columns and framed by pilasters that carry a flat, horizontal entablature—appears to have been inspired either by the church of San Miniato al Monte (FIG. 9-21) or by the baptistry of Florence Cathedral, both Romanesque buildings. The latter was mistakenly believed to be a Roman temple in Brunelleschi's time, but even if he had known better, Brunelleschi may well have mistaken it for an Early Christian building of the fourth or fifth century—a style that he associated closely with Classical Roman architecture and that had just as much authority for him. But the hospital expresses quite a different style from that of its possible Medieval prototypes. The stress on horizontals, the clarity of the articulation, and the symmetry of its design—combined with the use of such Classical elements as Corinthian capitals and pilasters, as well as windows topped by pediments—create an impression of rationality and logic that, in spirit at least, relates the Ospedale degli Innocenti more to Classical than to Medieval architecture.

The same clarity of statement is to be found in the two basilican churches that Brunelleschi built in Florence—San Lorenzo and Santo Spirito. Of the two, the later Santo Spirito shows the architect's mature style (FIGS. 16-17 and 16-18). Begun in 1436 and completed, with some changes, after Brunelleschi's death, the cruciform building is laid out on the basis of either multiples or segments of the dome-covered crossing square in a manner reminiscent of Romanesque planning. But this segmentation is not reflected

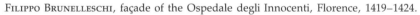

16-16 Filippo Brunelleschi, façade of the Ospedale degli Innocenti, Florence, 1419–1424.

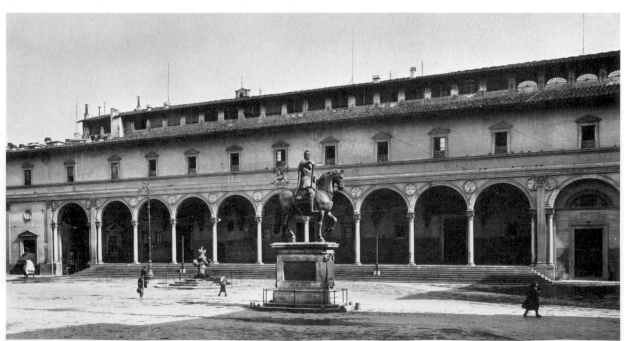

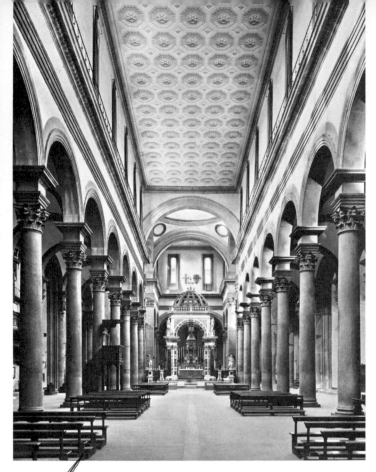

16-17 FILIPPO BRUNELLESCHI, interior of Santo Spirito, Florence, begun 1436 (view facing east).

in the nave, which is a continuous, unbroken space in the tradition of Early Christian basilicas. The aisles—subdivided into small squares covered by shallow, saucer-shaped vaults—run all the way around the flat-roofed central space and have the visual effect of compressing the longitudinal design into a centralized one, because the various aspects of the interior resemble each other, no matter where the observer

16-18 FILIPPO BRUNELLESCHI, early plan of Santo Spirito, Florence (left), and plan as constructed (right).

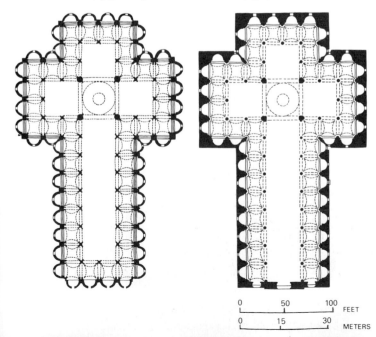

stands. Originally, this effect of centralization would have been even stronger; Brunelleschi had planned to extend the aisles across the front of the nave as well, as shown on the plan (FIG. 16-18). Because of the modular basis of the design, this would have demanded four (instead of the traditional three) entrances in the façade of the building—a feature that was hotly debated during Brunelleschi's lifetime and changed after his death. The appearance of the exterior walls was also changed later, when the recesses between the projecting, semicircular chapels were filled in to convert an originally highly plastic wall surface into a flat one. The major features of the interior, however, are much as Brunelleschi designed them. Compared with those of the Ospedale degli Innocenti, the forms have gained in volume. The moldings project more boldly, and the proportions of the columns more closely approach the Classical ideal. Throughout the building, proportions in a ratio of 1:2 have been used with great consistency. The nave is twice as high as it is wide; arcade and clerestory are of equal height, which means that the height of the arcade equals the width of the nave; and so on. These basic facts about the building have been delineated for the observer by crisp articulations, so that they can be read like mathematical equations. The cool logic of the design may lack some of the warmth of Medieval buildings, but it fully expresses the new Renaissance spirit that places its faith in reason rather than in the emotions.

Brunelleschi's evident effort to impart a centralized effect to the interior of Santo Spirito suggests that he was intrigued by the compact and self-contained qualities of earlier central-plan buildings, such as the Pantheon and Medieval baptistries. His Old Sacristy, built onto the left transept of San Lorenzo, expresses his admiration of the central plan. He nearly realized his ideal with the Pazzi Chapel (FIGS. 16-19, 16-20, 16-21), begun around 1440 and completed in the 1460s, long after his death. The exterior probably does not reflect Brunelleschi's original design, as the narthex, admirable as it is, seems to have been added as an afterthought, perhaps by sculptor–architect GIULIANO DA MAIANO. Behind this narthex stands one of the first independent buildings of the Renaissance to be conceived basically as a central-plan structure. Although the plan is rectangular, rather than square or round, all emphasis has been placed on the central, dome-covered space; the short, barrel-vault sections that brace the dome on two sides appear to be no more than incidental appendages. The articulation of the interior, with dark pilasters on light walls, reflects a subtle and sophisticated system of modular relationships in both plan and elevation and creates a tight network of geometric patterns that ties all parts of the building together and enhances the effect of compact self-sufficiency.

THE FIRST HALF OF THE FIFTEENTH CENTURY 561

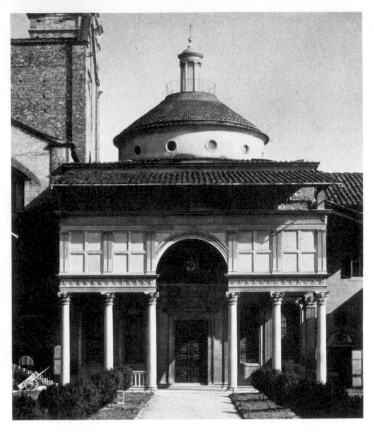

16-19 FILIPPO BRUNELLESCHI, west façade of Pazzi Chapel, begun c. 1440. Santa Croce, Florence.

16-20 FILIPPO BRUNELLESCHI, plan of Pazzi Chapel, Santa Croce, Florence.

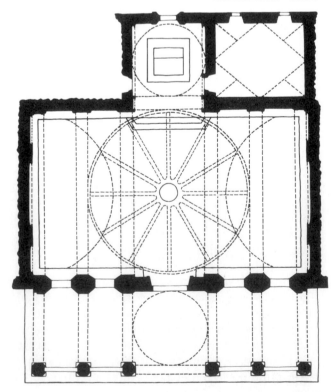

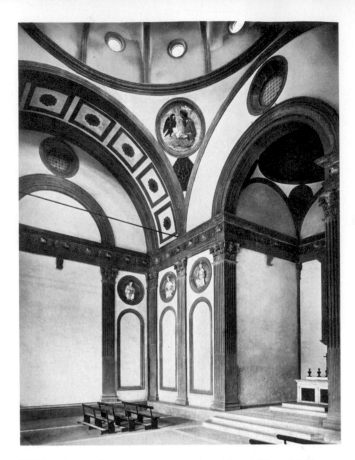

16-21 FILIPPO BRUNELLESCHI, interior of Pazzi Chapel (view facing northeast).

Brunelleschi only approximated the central plan in the Pazzi Chapel; he had planned to give it full realization in Santa Maria degli Angeli (FIG. 16-22). Begun in 1434, the project was abandoned, unfinished, in 1437. The plan shows a central octagon, the corner piers of which were undoubtedly intended to carry a dome. Around this core are arranged eight identical chapels (one was to have served as entrance) that are seemingly carved out of the massive masonry that surrounds them. The plastic handling of both exterior and interior wall surfaces recaptures the ancient Roman ''sculptured'' wall principle and is so far ahead of its time that it does not appear again until

16-22 Plan of Santa Maria degli Angeli, Florence, 1434–1437. (After a sixteenth-century drawing of a design by Filippo Brunelleschi.)

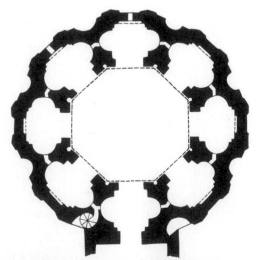

the very end of the fifteenth century. Alberti must have seen the unfinished building and may well have had it in mind when he praised the central plan in his treatise and implanted a taste for it in generations of later architects.

It seems curious that Brunelleschi, the most renowned architect of his time, did not participate in the upsurge of palace-building that Florence experienced in the late 1430s and 1440s and that testified to the soundness of the Florentine economy and the affluence and confidence of its leading citizens. His efforts in this field were confined to work on the Palazzo di Parte Guelfa and to a rejected model for a new palace that Cosimo de' Medici intended to build. Cosimo evidently felt that Brunelleschi's project was too imposing and ostentatious to be politically wise. Instead, he awarded the commission to MICHELOZZO DI BARTOLOMMEO (1396–1472), a young architect who had been Donatello's collaborator in several sculptural enterprises. Michelozzo's architectural style was deeply influenced by Brunelleschi, and, to a limited extent, the Palazzo Medici–Riccardi may reflect Brunelleschian principles (FIG. 16-23). Built for the Medici and later bought by the Riccardi family, who almost doubled the length of the façade in the eighteenth century, the palace is a simple, massive structure; heavy rustication on the ground floor accentuates its strength. The building block is divided into stories of decreasing height by long, unbroken horizontal bands (stringcourses), which give it articulation and coherence. In the upper stories, the severity of the ground floor is modified by dressed stone, which presents a smoother surface with each successive story, so that the building appears progressively lighter as the eye moves upward. This effect is dra-

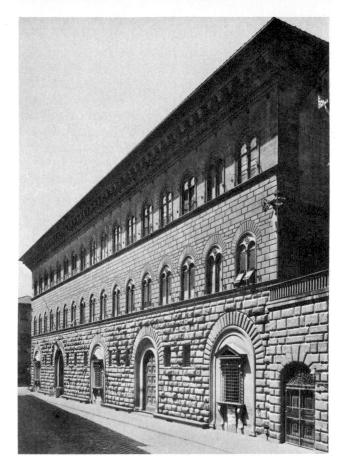

16-23 MICHELOZZO DI BARTOLOMMEO, Palazzo Medici–Riccardi, Florence, begun 1444.

matically reversed by the extremely heavy, classicizing cornice, which Michelozzo related not to the top story but to the building as a whole. It is a very effective lid for the structure, clearly and emphatically defining its proportions. The palace is built around an open, colonnaded court that most clearly shows

16-24 MICHELOZZO DI BARTOLOMMEO, court of the Palazzo Medici–Riccardi.

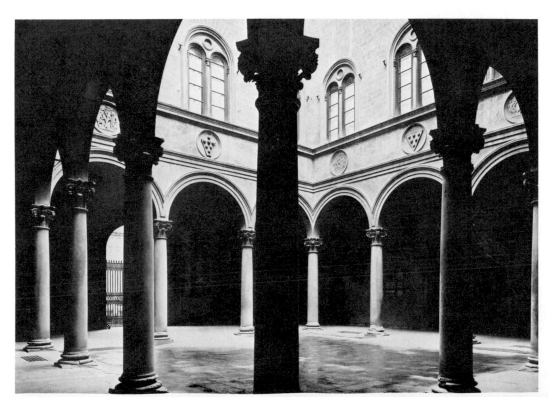

Michelozzo's debt to Brunelleschi (FIG. 16-24). The round-arched colonnade, although more massive in its proportions, closely resembles that of the Ospedale degli Innocenti; however, Michelozzo's failure to frame each row of arches with piers and pilasters, as Brunelleschi might have, causes the structure to look rather weak at the angles. Nevertheless, this *cortile* was the first of its kind and was to have a long line of descendants in Renaissance domestic architecture.

Painting

The youngest of the three leading innovators of the early fifteenth century, with Donatello and Brunelleschi, was the painter MASACCIO (Tommaso Guidi, 1401–1428). To understand the almost startling na-

ture of his innovations, we should look again at the International style in painting, which was the dominant style around 1400 and persisted well into the fifteenth century, side by side with the grand new style of Masaccio and his followers. GENTILE DA FABRIANO (*c.* 1370–1427), who was working in Florence at the same time as Masaccio, produced what may be the masterpiece of the International style, *The Adoration of the Magi* (FIG. 16-25). Gentile's purpose is to create a gorgeous surface, spreading across it scores of sumptuously costumed kings, courtiers, captains, and retainers accompanied by a menagerie of exotic and ornamental animals—all in a rainbow of color with much display of gold. Here is all the pomp and ceremony of chivalric etiquette, a picture that proclaims the sanctification of aristocracy in the presence of the Madonna and Child. There is little basic

16-25 GENTILE DA FABRIANO, *The Adoration of the Magi*, 1423. Tempera on wood, approx. 9' 11" × 9' 3". Galleria degli Uffizi, Florence.

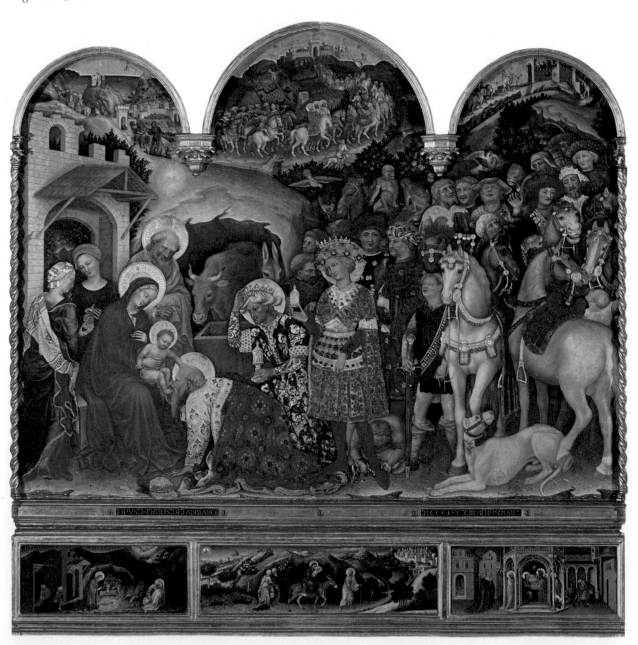

difference between the stylistic apparatus of Gentile and that used in the century following the junction of Gothic and Sienese painting. Into this traditional framework, however, Gentile inserts striking bits of radical naturalism. Animals are seen from a variety of angles and are convincingly foreshortened, as are tilted human heads and bodies. (Note the man removing the spurs from the standing magus in the center foreground.) On the right side of the *predella*, the Presentation scene is shown in a "modern" architectural setting. (The arcade in the right background looks much like Brunelleschi's Ospedale degli Innocenti, FIG. 16-16.) And on the left side of the predella, Gentile paints what may be the very first nighttime Nativity in which the light source is introduced into the picture itself.

Thus Gentile da Fabriano, although dominantly conservative, shows that he is not oblivious to contemporary experimental trends and that, with great skill and subtlety, he is able to blend naturalistic and inventive elements with a traditional composition without sacrificing Late Gothic coloristic splendor.

Masaccio was much less compromising. Although his presumed teacher, MASOLINO DA PANICALE, had worked in the International style, Masaccio moved suddenly, within the short span of only six years, into wide-open, unexplored territory. No other painter in history is known to have contributed so much to the development of a new style in so short a time as Masaccio, whose creative career was so short and whose death at 27 was so untimely. Masaccio is the artistic descendant of Giotto, whose calm, monumental style he revolutionized through a whole new repertory of representational devices that generations of Renaissance painters would study and develop. Masaccio also knew and fully understood the innovations of his great contemporaries Donatello and Brunelleschi and introduced into painting new possibilities for both form and content.

We can see his breakthrough best in his frescoes in the Brancacci Chapel of Santa Maria del Carmine in Florence. In *The Tribute Money* (FIG. 16-26), painted shortly before his death, Masaccio groups three episodes. In the center, Christ, surrounded by his disciples, tells St. Peter that in the mouth of a fish he will find a coin to pay the imperial tax demanded by the collector who stands in the foreground, his back to the spectator. At the left, in the middle distance, St. Peter struggles to extract the coin from the fish's mouth, while at the right, with a disdainful gesture of great finality, he thrusts the coin into the tax collector's hand. Masaccio's figures recall Giotto's in their simple grandeur, but they stand before us with a psychological and moral self-realization that is entirely new. Masaccio realizes the bulk of the figures not through generalized modeling with a flat, neutral light without identifiable source, as Giotto does, but by means of a light that comes from a specific source outside the picture, striking the figures at an angle, illuminating the parts of the solids that obstruct its path and leaving the rest in deep shadow. This placement of light against strong dark gives the illusion of deep sculptural relief. Between the extremes of light and dark, the light is a constantly active but fluctuating force, independent of the figures and almost a tangible substance. As Masaccio and Donatello's generation learn the separation of body and drapery and the functional interrelation of them as independent fabrics, so light, which in Giotto is merely the modeling of a mass, in Masaccio comes to have its own nature, and the masses we see are visible only because of the direction and intensity of the light. We

16-26 MASACCIO, *The Tribute Money*, c. 1427. Fresco. Brancacci Chapel, Santa Maria del Carmine, Florence.

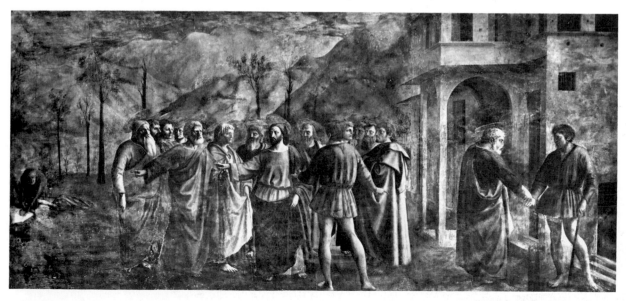

imagine the light as playing over forms—revealing some and concealing others, as the artist directs it. In the creation of a space filled with atmosphere, Masaccio anticipates the achievements of the High Renaissance; few painters between Masaccio and Leonardo da Vinci have so realistically created the illusion of space as a substance of light and air existing between our eyes and what we see.

The individual figures in *The Tribute Money* are solemn and weighty, but they also express bodily structure and function, as do Donatello's statues. We feel bones, muscles, and the pressures and tensions of joints; each figure conveys a maximum of contained energy. Both the stately stillness of Nanni di Banco's *Quattro Santi Coronati* (FIG. 16-4) and the weight-shifting figures of Donatello (FIG. 16-5) are here. The figure of Christ and the two appearances of the tax collector make us understand what the biographer Vasari* meant when he said: "Masaccio made his figures stand upon their feet."

Another important invention, for so we might call it, is the arrangement of the figures. No longer do they appear as a stiff screen in the front planes. Here, they are grouped in circular depth around Christ, and the whole group is shown in a spacious landscape, rather than in the confined stage space of Giotto's frescoes. The foreground space is generated by the group itself, as well as by the architecture on the right, shown in a one-point perspective construction in which the location of the vanishing point coincides with the head of Christ. The foreground is united with the distance by aerial perspective, which employs the diminution in light and the blurring of outlines that come with distance. This device, used by Roman painters, was forgotten during the Middle Ages and rediscovered by Masaccio, apparently independently. Masaccio realized that light and air interposed between ourselves and what we see are part of the visual experience we call "distance." With this knowledge, the world as given to ordinary sight can become for the painter the vast pictorial stage of human action.

In an awkwardly narrow space in the Brancacci Chapel (FIG. 16-27), Masaccio has painted the theme already seen in Jacopo della Quercia's slightly later relief, *The Expulsion from the Garden of Eden* (FIG. 16-3). The representational innovations are all present in Masaccio's work: the sharply slanted light from an outside source, creating deep relief by the placement of lights and darks side by side and acting as a strong unifying agent; the structurally correct motion of the

*GIORGIO VASARI (1511–1574), a versatile painter and architect, is best known for his *Lives of the Most Eminent Italian Architects, Painters, and Sculptors* (1550)—a series of biographies, which, although not always reliable, remains one of the most important art-historical sources for the Italian Renaissance.

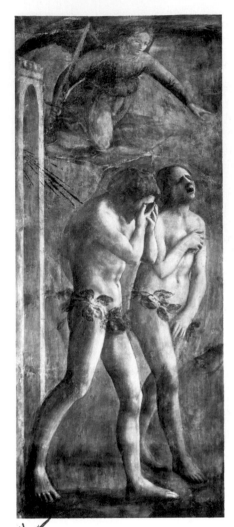

16-27 MASACCIO, *The Expulsion from Eden, c.* 1425. Fresco. Brancacci Chapel, Santa Maria del Carmine, Florence.

figures; their bodily weight and substantial contact with the ground; the hazed, atmospheric background that gives no locale but suggests a space around and beyond the figures. Masaccio's *Expulsion* is one of the supreme masterpieces of Renaissance art and an interpretation of the tragic scene of man's fall that is perhaps unsurpassed even by Michelangelo's Sistine Chapel ceiling. Adam's feet, clearly in contact with the ground, mark man's presence on earth, and the cry issuing from Eve's mouth voices the anguish of humanity deprived of God. Adam and Eve do not resist; there is no physical contact with the angel, nor are the figures crowded against the frame. Rather, they stumble on blindly, driven by the will of the angel and their own despair. The composition is starkly simple, its message incomparably eloquent.

In *The Holy Trinity* fresco in Santa Maria Novella (FIG. 16-28), the dating of which is still in dispute, Masaccio gives a brilliant demonstration of the organizing value of Brunelleschi's perspective; indeed, so much is it in the Brunelleschian manner that some have thought the great inventor of perspective may have directed Masaccio. The composition is on two

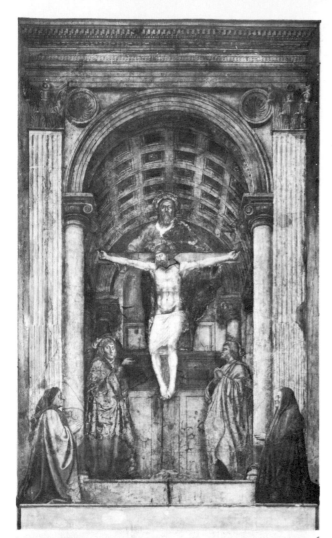

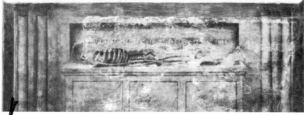

16-28 MASACCIO, *The Holy Trinity*, 1428 (?). Fresco. Santa Maria Novella, Florence.

levels of unequal height. Above, in a coffered, barrel-vaulted chapel, the Virgin Mary and St. John are represented on either side of the crucified Christ, whose arms are supported by God the Father, while the Dove of the Holy Spirit rests on Christ's halo. The donors, husband and wife, kneel just in front of the pilasters that enframe the chapel. Below the altar—a masonry insert in the painted composition—is a tomb containing a skeleton, said to represent Adam. An inscription in Italian reminds the spectator that "I was once what you are, and what I am you will become." Masaccio places the vanishing point, to which all the orthogonals of the perspective converge, at the center of the masonry altar. This is at the eye level of the spectator, who looks up at the Trinity and down

at the tomb. About 5 feet above the floor level, the vanishing point pulls the two views together, creating the illusion of an actual structure, the interior volume of which is an extension of the space in which the spectator is standing. This adjustment of the spectator to the pictured space is a first step in the development of illusionistic painting, which so fascinated many artists of the Renaissance and the later Baroque period. Masaccio has been so exact in his metrical proportions that we can actually calculate the numerical dimensions of the chapel (for example, the span of the painted vault is 7 feet; the depth of the chapel, 9 feet). Thus, he achieves not only successful illusion, but a rational, metrical coherence that, by maintaining the mathematical proportions of the surface design, is responsible for the unity and harmony of this monumental composition. *The Holy Trinity*, standing at the very beginning of the history of Renaissance painting, sums up two principal interests: realism based on observation and the application of mathematics to pictorial organization.

Masaccio's discoveries, like Donatello's, led to further experiments by his contemporaries and successors, who tended to specialize in one of the branches of pictorial science that Masaccio founded. PAOLO UCCELLO (1397–1475), a Florentine painter trained in the International style, discovered perspective well along in his career and became obsessed with it, though he was not always successful in harmonizing the old and the new. In *The Battle of San Romano* (FIG. 16-29), one of three wood panels painted for the Palazzo Medici to commemorate the Florentine victory over the Sienese in 1432, Uccello creates a composition that recalls the processional splendor of Gentile da Fabriano's *Adoration of the Magi* (FIG. 16-25). But the world of Uccello, in contrast with the surface decoration of the International style, is constructed of immobilized, solid forms; broken spears and lances and a fallen soldier are foreshortened and carefully placed along the converging orthogonals of the perspective to create a base plane like a checkerboard, on which the volumes are then placed in measured intervals. All this works very well as far back as the middle ground, where the horizontal plane is met abruptly by the up-tilted plane of an International style background. Beyond that, Uccello's sense of design is impeccable. The rendering of three-dimensional form, used by other painters for representational or expressive purposes, became for Uccello a preoccupation; for him, it had a magic of its own, which he exploited to satisfy his amazingly inventive and original imagination. His fascination with perspective had little in common with the rationality in Masaccio's concern for defining the dimensionality of space. Uccello had an irrational passion for arranging the forms of solid geometry in

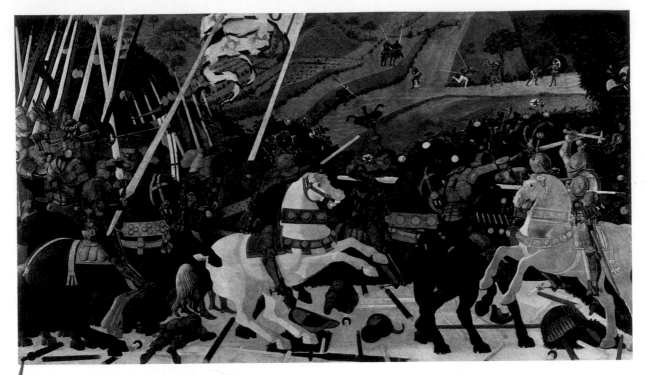

16-29 PAOLO UCCELLO, *The Battle of San Romano, c.* 1455. Tempera on wood, approx. 6′ × 10′ 5″. Reproduced by courtesy of the Trustees of the National Gallery, London.

space, and it is perhaps not surprising that he became one of the favorite masters of the Cubists of the early twentieth century.

ANDREA DEL CASTAGNO (*c.* 1423–1457) interested himself both in perspective and in the representation of imposing, strong, structurally convincing human figures. In his *Last Supper* (FIG. 16-30), painted in the late 1440s and covering a wall of the refectory of the convent of Sant' Apollonia in Florence, we see a severity and clarity of form characteristic of this phase of Florentine painting. Christ and the disciples, with Judas isolated at the front of the table in the traditional manner, are painted as static, sculptural solids.

Here, Andrea faced the problem of setting his figures within a space arranged to give (as in Masaccio's *Holy Trinity*) the illusion that the space of the observer is continuous with that of the marble-paneled alcove where the principals are sitting. But the perspective construction is so strict that it serves to limit action; its rigid frame stiffens the figures it controls, and it will not be until Leonardo's famous version of this theme, painted at the end of the century, that the architectural setting will serve the action rather than constrict it.

Andrea is seen at his best in his group of figures of famous people painted in the Villa Pandolfini near

16-30 ANDREA DEL CASTAGNO, *The Last Supper, c.* 1445–1450. Fresco. Museo di Sant' Apollonia, Florence.

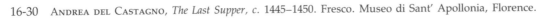

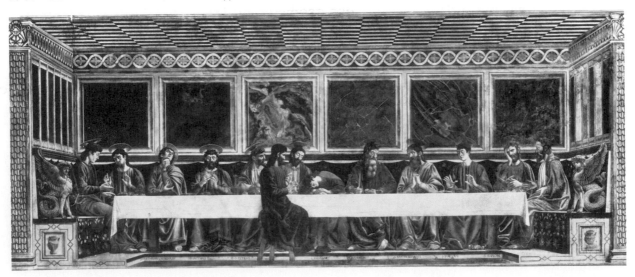

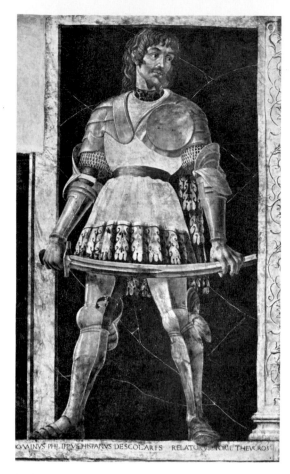

16-31 ANDREA DEL CASTAGNO, *Pippo Spano, c.* 1448. Fresco. Galleria degli Uffizi, Florence.

Florence around 1450, and transferred first to the Castagno Museum in Sant' Apollonia and, more recently, to the Uffizi Gallery. One, a portrait of the general called *Pippo Spano* (FIG. 16-31), is the very image of the swaggering commander—his feet firmly planted, "powerful among peers," and bristling with insolent challenge. The figure is meant to be seen as standing in a *loggia,* the space of which is continuous with that of the spectator. The illusion is reinforced by the heavy, armored, foreshortened foot that seems to protrude over a sill of the opening. If Masaccio first "made his figures stand upon their feet," then Andrea followed him faithfully and made the point more emphatically in this splendid figure so alive with truculent energy. And by having parts of his figure appear to project into the space of the viewer, Andrea takes a step beyond Masaccio's *Holy Trinity* in the direction of Baroque illusionism.

Andrea's sometime collaborator DOMENICO VENEZIANO (*c.* 1420–1461) was born and trained in Venice, but settled in Florence in the late 1430s. The sixteenth-century architect, painter, and biographer Giorgio Vasari tells us that Andrea, in a fit of jealous rage, killed Domenico by hitting him with an iron bar; in fact, Andrea fell victim to the plague some four years before Domenico died. Vasari also claims that Domenico introduced the mixed-oil technique to

Florence, but the artist himself seems to have painted in the traditional tempera. Although he fully assimilates Florentine forms, Domenico retains some International-style traits that he may have acquired from northern painters active in Venice. He may also have brought from Venice his sensitivity to color and outdoor light, which goes well beyond that of his Florentine contemporaries; it is in this field that Domenico makes his major contribution to Florentine art of the mid-century. His *St. Lucy Altarpiece* (FIG. 16-32) is one of the earliest examples of a type of painting that will enjoy great popularity from this time on—a *sacra conversazione* (holy conversation), in which saints from different epochs are joined in a unified space to form a company and seem to be conversing either with each other or with the audience. The clarity and precision of the architectural setting and the individualization, weight, and solemn dignity of the figures show Domenico to be a worthy heir to Masaccio and Donatello. The composition recalls Nanni di Banco's *Quattro Santi Coronati* (FIG. 16-4); here, however, the vaulted niche has been converted to an airy loggia open to the sky and flooded with bright, outdoor light. The brilliant local colors and ornate surfaces of the International style are muted by this directed light, which falls into the loggia from the upper right and bathes the scene with atmospheric luminosity. Reflected from the architecture, it lightens the shadows, and the modeling of the figures becomes less harsh than that in Masaccio, to whom effects of relief were more important than those of color. The resultant overall blonde tonality is characteristic of the paintings of Domenico and his followers.

Domenico's most important disciple and his assistant in Florence during the early 1440s was PIERO DELLA FRANCESCA (*c.* 1420–1492). Piero's art is the projection of a mind cultivated by mathematics and convinced that the highest beauty is found in forms that have the clarity and purity of geometric figures. A skilled geometrician, Piero wrote the first theoretical treatise on systematic perspective toward the end of his long career, after having practiced the art with supreme mastery for almost a lifetime. It is likely that his association with the architect Alberti at Ferrara and at Rimini around 1450–1451 turned his attention fully to perspective (in which science Alberti was an influential pioneer) and helped to determine his later, characteristically architectonic compositions. One can fairly say that Piero's compositions are determined almost entirely by his sense for the exact and lucid structures that mathematics defines. Within this context, he developed Domenico's sophistication in the handling of light and color, so that color became the matrix of his three-dimensional forms, lending them a new density as well as fusing them with the surrounding space.

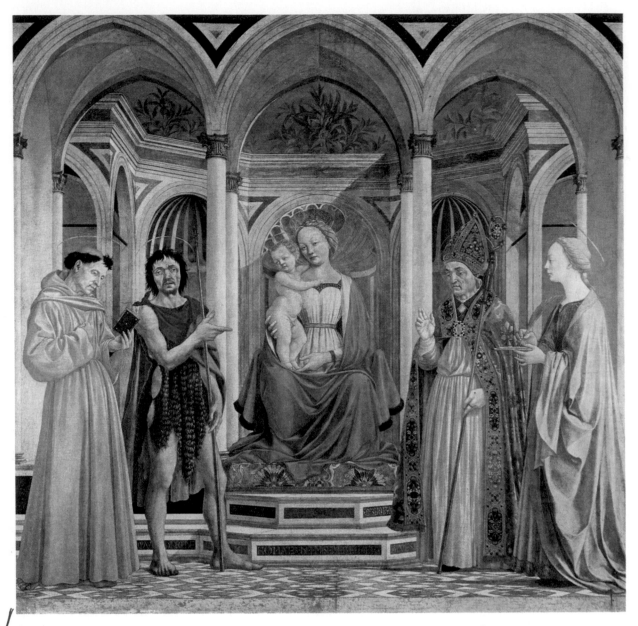

16-32 Domenico Veneziano, *The St. Lucy Altarpiece*, center panel, *c.* 1445. Tempera on wood, approx. 6′ 7½″ × 7′. Galleria degli Uffizi, Florence.

A damaged but still beautiful panel, Piero's *The Flagellation of Christ* (FIG. 16-33), is almost a painted exposition of the rules of linear perspective and its inherent pictorial possibilities. The painting has been designed with such precision that modern architects, using the division of the brick floor paneling along the painting's baseline as a module, have been able to reconstruct accurately the floor plans of the depicted court and building and the positions of the figures within them.

The dating of the panel is uncertain; wide-ranging dates from 1445 to 1472 have been advanced. Since the depicted loggia has a distinctly "modern" (that is, Albertian) look, the painting seems to presuppose Piero's contact with the architect Alberti in the early

1450s, so that its date might fall into the middle of that decade. As exact as the architectural rendering of the portico appears to be, its structure has been modified for pictorial reasons. Stalactite-shaped forms at the beam crossings denote the positions from which two interior columns have been removed in order to create a continuous space that encloses the martyrdom scene and permits a full view of Pontius Pilate, who watches impassively as the executioners raise their whips to chastise Christ. The column to which Christ is tied is topped by a golden statue of a nude man holding a rod in one hand and a ball in the other, attributes that appear on coins of Roman emperors. The meaning of this figure within the context of the flagellation scene is uncertain; apparently a pagan

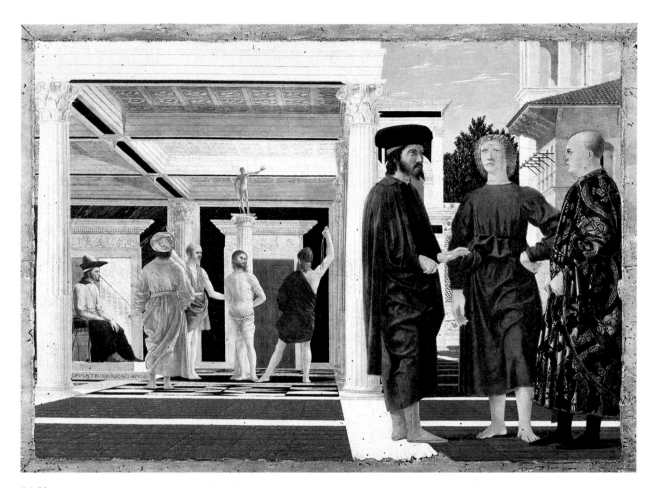

16-33   Piero della Francesca, *The Flagellation of Christ, c.* 1455 (?). Tempera on wood, 32¾″ × 23⅓″. Palazzo Ducale, Galleria Nazionale delle Marche, Urbino.

symbol, it may represent the pagan power that Christianity had to confront and overcome.

The lighting is not as clearly legible as the perspective rendering. All outdoor forms are illuminated from the left, but the interior of the loggia receives its light from the right, either reflected from the buildings across the court or from a stipulated secondary light source behind the second column of the right colonnade. Even more ambiguous are the identities of the three figures in the right foreground and their relation to the central event, which have given rise to unending speculation. None of many tentative identifications, nor their meanings in relation to the central event, have found universal acceptance, and perhaps we should be content with viewing and experiencing the formal aspects of a masterful painting. In a composition that is at once clear, complex, and marvelously subtle, the perspective design is reinforced by visual cross-references that create a compact, pictorial unity. In the foreground figure group, which, at first glance, seems to have little relation to the depicted event, the pose of the central figure is almost identical to that of Christ. And the relation of the turbaned man with his back to us (Herod?) to the

flagellation scene is the same as that of the viewer of the painting to the foreground figure group. Thus, in a unique and ingenious manner, the artist draws the spectator past the foreground triad toward the main subject in the middle ground. With forms that are essentially static, Piero—by manipulating perspective and the disposition of volumes and voids— creates pictorial tension in a composition that is firmly contained within its frame and, at the same time, highly dynamic. By placing the massed volumes of his three foreground figures off-center into a relatively restricted space, Piero poses the question, How much mass balances how large an empty space? The proportional relationships Piero shows us in this painting provide one possible—and certainly most satisfying—answer.

Piero's most important work is the fresco cycle in the apse of the church of San Francesco in Arezzo, which represents ten episodes from the legend of the True Cross (the cross on which Christ died). Painted between 1452 and 1456, the cycle is based on a thirteenth-century popularization of the Scriptures, the *Golden Legend* by Jacobus de Varagine. The *Annunciation* from this cycle (FIG. 16-34) perhaps best illustrates

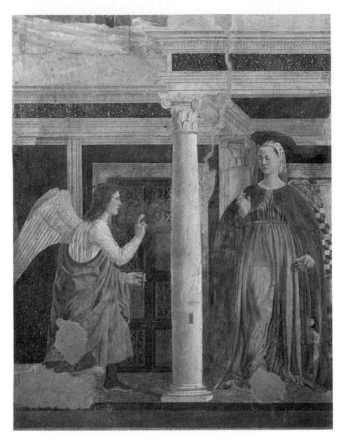

16-34 PIERO DELLA FRANCESCA, *Annunciation, c.* 1455. Detail of fresco. San Francesco, Arezzo, Italy.

16-35 PIERO DELLA FRANCESCA, *The Proving of the True Cross, c.* 1455. Fresco. San Francesco, Arezzo, Italy.

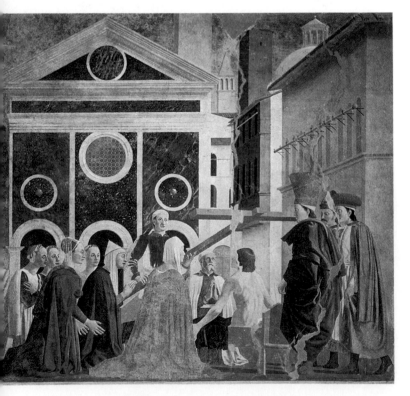

Piero's manner. One of the problems that occupied him all his life was how to establish a convincing architectonic relation between animate and inanimate objects. The key to Piero's solution in this painting is the conspicuously placed column that divides the depicted space into two vertical, cubic sections. The cylindrical shape of the column is echoed in the simplified, solemn, and immobile form of the Virgin. To make his figures conform to the static quality of the architecture that surrounds them, Piero reduces all actions and gestures to the slowest, simplest signals; all emotion is banished. The composition is essentially a cylinder inscribed in a cubic void, and this geometricality of the forms gives the depiction of the event a trance-like and abstract quality.

In the climactic scene of Piero's fresco cycle, *The Proving of the True Cross* (FIG. 16-35), St. Helena, mother of Constantine, accompanied by her retinue, witnesses how the True Cross miraculously restores a dead man (the nude figure) to life. The grouping of the figures is controlled by the architectural background; its medallions, arches, and rectangular panels are the two-dimensional counterparts of the ovoid, cylindrical, and cubic forms placed in front of it. One feels the careful planning behind the placement of each shape and volume; it is almost the procedure of an architect, certainly that of a man entirely familiar with compass and straightedge. As the architectonics of the abstract shapes controls the grouping, so, as in the *Annunciation*, does it impart a mood of solemn stillness to the figures—a quiet rapture shown by unindividualized and emotionless faces, the slow gestures like those of a priest's at an altar. The concourse of all these solid forms yet yields an impression of an otherworldly, mystical and eternally celebrated rite that knows nothing of the passing facts and accidents of this world. We see a union of the unchanging mathematical form with the calm silences of the contemplative spirit.

In addition, of course, Piero's work shows an unflagging interest in the properties of light and color. He suspects that one is the function of the other; he observes that colors turn cool (bluish) in shadow and that they lose intensity with increasing distance from the observer. In his effort to make the clearest possible distinction between forms, he floods his pictures with light, imparting a silver–blue tonality. To avoid heavy shadows, he illumines the dark sides of his forms with reflected light. By moving the darkest tones of his modeling toward the centers of his volumes, he separates them from their backgrounds. As a result, Piero's paintings lack some of Masaccio's relief-like qualities but gain in spatial clarity as each shape becomes an independent unit, surrounded by an atmospheric envelope and movable to any desired position, like a figure on a chessboard.

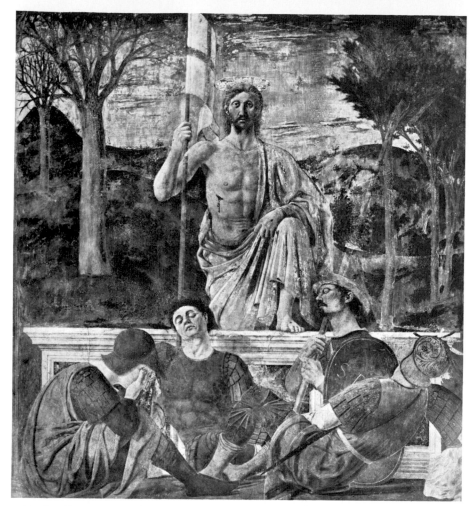

In the *Resurrection* fresco in the town hall of Borgo San Sepolcro (FIG. 16-36), Piero introduces a compositional device that would enjoy great favor with later Renaissance artists—the figure triangle. To stabilize his composition, Piero arranges his figures in a group that can be circumscribed by a triangle centrally placed in the painting. The figure of the risen Christ, standing with columnar strength and in the attitude of eternal triumph at the edge of the sepulcher, occupies the upper portion of a triangular arrangement that rests on the broad base of the sleeping soldiers in the foreground. This triangular massing of volumes around a picture's central axis gives a painting great compositional stability and is one of the keys to the symmetry and self-sufficiency that Renaissance artists strove for in their work.

Piero was at home with realism and could paint exact and unflattering likenesses of human subjects, quite unlike the generalized heads and features of his customary type. His work summarizes most of the stylistic and scientific developments in painting during the first half of the fifteenth century: realism, descriptive landscape, the structural human figure, monumental composition, perspective, proportionality, and light and color.

But other good artists were active during this period whose style remains rooted in an earlier age and whose interest in the new tendencies remained marginal. One, the Dominican painter–monk FRA ANGELICO (*c.* 1387–1455), was conservative by both training and inclination. Although he was fully aware of what was being done by his more experimentally inclined contemporaries, Fra Angelico adopted only those innovations he could incorporate without friction into his essentially conservative style. While accepting realistic details in anatomy, drapery, perspective, and architecture, he rejected Masaccio's heavy modeling, which would have dulled his bright Gothic coloring. In the *Annunciation* (FIG. 16-37)—one of numerous frescoes with which Fra Angelico decorated the Dominican convent of San Marco in Florence between 1435 and 1445—the Brunelleschian loggia is neatly designed according to the rules of linear perspective, but the fact that the vault is too low to allow the figures to stand would have been unacceptable to a Piero della Francesca. However, such considerations were secondary to Fra Angelico; what he wanted above all was to stress the religious content of his paintings, and he did so by using the means, past and present, that he felt were most appropriate. In our example, the simplicity of the statement recalls Giotto, as does the form of the kneeling, rainbow-winged angel; the elegant silhouette of the sweetly shy Madonna descends from Sienese art, and the

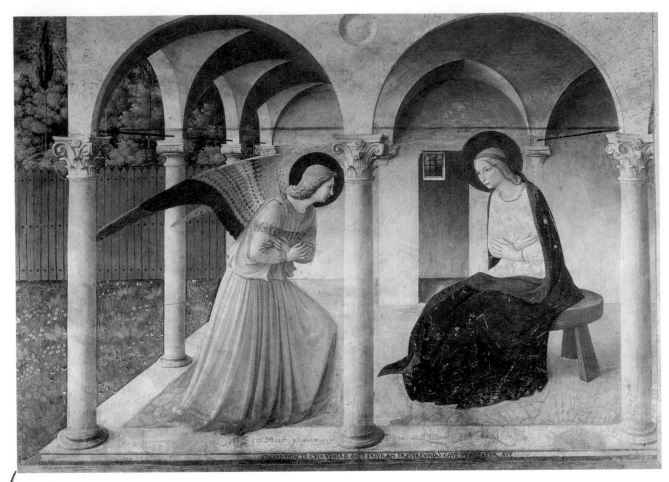

16-37　Fra Angelico, *Annunciation, c. 1440–1445*. Fresco. San Marco, Florence.

flower-carpeted, enclosed garden (symbolic of the virginity of Mary) is a bit of International Gothic. But all these elements have been combined with lyrical feeling and a great sense for decorative effect, so that nothing seems incongruous. Like most of Fra Angelico's paintings, the naïve and tender charm of the *Annunciation* still has an almost universal appeal and fully reflects the character of the artist, who, as Giorgio Vasari tells us, "was a simple and most holy man . . . most gentle and temperate, living chastely, removed from the cares of the world . . . humble and modest in all his works."

A strong—though perhaps somewhat unlikely—contributor to the pictorial humanization of religious subject matter was Fra Filippo Lippi (c. 1406–1469). Like Fra Angelico, Fra Filippo was a monk, but there all resemblance ends. From reports, he seems to have been a kind of amiable scapegrace quite unfitted for monastic life, who indulged in misdemeanors ranging from forgery and embezzlement to the abduction of a pretty nun, Lucretia, who became his mistress and the mother of his son, the painter Filippino Lippi. Only the Medici's intervention on his behalf at the papal court preserved Fra Filippo from severe

punishment and total disgrace, and he was, despite all, able to produce important and influential work. An orphan, Fra Filippo was raised in a monastery adjacent to the church of Santa Maria del Carmine, and, when about 18, he must have met Masaccio there and witnessed the decoration of the Brancacci Chapel. Fra Filippo's early work survives only in fragments, but these show that he tried to work with Masaccio's massive forms. Later, probably under the influence of Ghiberti's and Donatello's relief sculptures, he developed a linear style that emphasizes the contours of his figures and permits him to suggest movement through flying and swirling draperies. A fresh and inventive painting from Fra Filippo's later years, a *Madonna and Child with Angels* (FIG. 16-38) shows his skill in manipulating line at its very best. Beyond noting its fine contours and modeling, we soon become aware of the wonderful flow of line throughout the picture, making precise yet smooth delineations of the forms, whether of the whole figures or of the details within them. Even without the reinforcing modeling, the forms would look three-dimensional and plastic, as the line is handled in a sculptural rather than in a two-dimensional sense.

THE SECOND HALF OF THE FIFTEENTH CENTURY

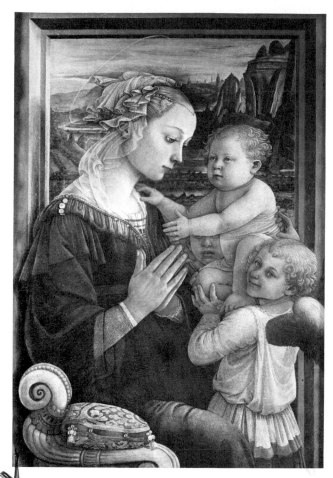

6-38 FRA FILIPPO LIPPI, *Madonna and Child with Angels,*
c. 1455. Tempera on wood, approx. 36" × 25". Galleria degli
Uffizi, Florence.

Fra Filippo's skill in the use of line is rarely surpassed;
in the immediate future, only his most famous pupil,
Botticelli, will use it with greater subtlety.

Fra Filippo has interpreted his subject in a surpris-
ingly worldly manner. The Madonna, a beautiful
young mother, is not at all spiritual or fragile, and
neither is her plump bambino, the child Christ, who
is held up to her by two angels, one of whom turns
toward us with the mischievous, puckish grimace of a
boy refusing to be subdued by the pious occasion.
Significantly, all figures reflect the use of models (that
for the Madonna may even have been Lucretia). Fra
Filippo plainly relishes the charm of youth and
beauty as he finds it in this world; he prefers the real
in landscape also, and the background, seen through
the window, has, despite some exaggerations, recognizable features of the Arno river valley. Compared
with the earlier Madonnas by Duccio (FIG. 15-9) and
Giotto (FIG. 15-12), this work shows how far the humanization of the theme has been carried. Whatever
the ideals of spiritual perfection may have meant to
artists in past centuries, those ideals are now realized
in terms of the sensuous beauty of this world.

In the early fifteenth century, Florence led Italy in the
development of the new Humanism; later, the city
shared its leadership. Under the sponsorship of local
rulers, important cultural centers developed in other
parts of Italy and began to attract artists and scholars:
Urbino under the Montefeltri, Mantua under the
Gonzaga, Milan under the Sforza, Naples under the
kings of Aragon, and so forth.

This later period of Humanism is marked by a new
interest in the Italian language and literature, the
beginnings of literary criticism (parallel to the development of theory in art and architecture), the foundation of academies (especially the Platonic Academy of
Philosophy in Florence), and the introduction of the
printing press—and all that these elements could
mean for the dissemination of culture.

The conquest of Constantinople by the Turks in
1453 caused an exodus of Greek scholars, many of
whom fled to Italy, bringing with them knowledge of
ancient Greece to feed the avid interest in Classical
art, literature, and philosophy. That same conquest
closed the Mediterranean to Western shipping, making it necessary to find new routes to the markets of
the East. Thus began the age of navigation, discovery, and exploration.

In art and architecture, a theoretical foundation
could now be placed under the more-or-less "intuitive" innovations of the earlier generation of artists.
We must emphasize again the high value the Renaissance artist placed on *theory.* In his view, if any occu-
pation or profession were to have dignity and be worthy of honor, it must have an intellectual basis. This is
a requirement we still recognize; a "scientific" pursuit
wins utmost respect in our age, and, for somewhat
similar reasons, the "fine" artist today is likely to consider his pursuit superior to that of the "commercial"
artist. The Renaissance artist strove to make himself a
scholar and a gentleman, to associate with princes
and the learned, and to rise above the long-standing
ancient and Medieval prejudice that saw him as
merely a kind of handicraftsman.

Beginning with Alberti's treatises on painting and
architecture, theoretical studies multiplied. The rediscovered text of the ancient Roman architect and
theoretician, Vitruvius, became the subject of exhaus-
tive examination and interpretation (partly because
the text found was only a copy, which, unlike the
original, was not illustrated, rendering passages that
referred to illustrations obscure and subject to varying interpretations). Brunelleschi's invention of perspective and Alberti's and Piero's treatises on the
subject provided the Renaissance artist with the op-

portunity to demonstrate the scientific basis of the visual arts.

The genius and creative energy required to achieve the new social and intellectual status claimed by the artist were available in abundance. The Renaissance ideal of *l'uomo universale* ("the universal man") here finds its realization; indeed, in Leon Battista Alberti (1407–1472), it finds one of its first personifications. Writing of himself in the third person, Alberti gives us a most revealing insight into the mind of the brilliant Renaissance man—his universal interests, broad capabilities, love of beauty, and hope of fame:

> In everything suitable to one born free and educated liberally, he was so trained from boyhood that among the leading young men of his age he was considered by no means the last. For, assiduous in the science and skill of dealing with arms and horses and musical instruments, as well as in the pursuit of letters and the fine arts, he was devoted to the knowledge of the most strange and difficult things. And finally he embraced with zeal and forethought everything which pertained to fame. To omit the rest, he strove so hard to attain a name in modeling and painting that he wished to neglect nothing by which he might gain the approbation of good men. His genius was so versatile that you might almost judge all the fine arts to be his. . . . He took extraordinary and peculiar pleasure in looking at things in which there was any mark of beauty. . . . Whatever was done by man with genius and with a certain grace, he held to be almost divine. . . .*

It is probably no accident that this autobiography sounds like a funeral oration on a great man.

Architecture

Alberti scarcely mentioned architecture as a prime interest. He entered the profession rather late in life, but today we know him chiefly as an architect. He was the first to study seriously the treatise of Vitruvius *(De architectura),* and his knowledge of it, combined with his own archeological investigations, made him the first Renaissance architect to understand Roman architecture in depth. Alberti's most important and influential theoretical work, *De re aedificatoria,* although inspired by Vitruvius, contains much new and original material. For later architects, some of Alberti's most significant observations were the advocations of a system of ideal proportions, a central-type plan as the ideal Christian church, and the avoidance of the column–arch combination (which had persisted from Spalatum in the fourth century to Brunelleschi in the fifteenth) as incongruous. By arguing that the arch is a wall-opening that should be

supported only by a section of wall (a pier), not by an independent sculptural element (a column), Alberti, with a few exceptions, disposed of the Medieval arcade for centuries.

Alberti's own architectural style represents a scholarly application of Classical elements to contemporary buildings. His Palazzo Rucellai in Florence (FIG. 16-39) probably dates from the mid-1450s. The façade, built over a group of three Medieval houses, is much more severely organized than that of the Palazzo Medici–Riccardi (FIG. 16-23). Each story of the Palazzo Rucellai is articulated by flat pilasters, which support full entablatures. The rustication of the wall surfaces between the smooth pilasters is subdued and uniform, and the suggestion that the structure becomes lighter toward its top is made in an adaptation of the ancient Roman manner by using different articulating orders for each story: Tuscan (resembling the Doric order) for the ground floor, Composite (combining Ionic volutes with acanthus leaves of the Corinthian) for the second, and Corinthian for the third. Here, Alberti has adapted the articulation of the Colosseum (FIG. 6-46) to a flat façade, which does not allow the deep penetration of the building's mass so effective in the Roman structure. By converting the plastic, engaged columns of the ancient model into shallow pilasters that barely project from the wall,

16-39 Leon Battista Alberti, Palazzo Rucellai, Florence, *c.* 1452–1470.

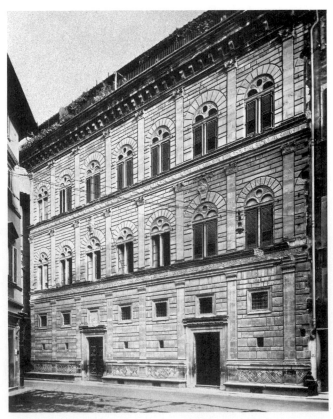

*In J.B. Ross and M.M. McLaughlin, eds., *The Portable Renaissance Reader* (New York: Viking, 1953), pp. 480ff.

Alberti has created a large-meshed, linear net that, stretched tightly across the front of his building, not only unifies its three levels but also emphasizes the flat, two-dimensional qualities of the wall.

The design for the façade of the Gothic church of Santa Maria Novella in Florence (FIG. 16-40) was also commissioned by the Rucellai family. Just as Brunelleschi has done occasionally, Alberti takes his cue from a pre-Gothic Medieval design—that of San Miniato al Monte (FIG. 9-21). Following his Romanesque model, he designs a small, pseudo-Classical portico for the upper part of the façade and supports it with a broad base of pilaster-enframed arcades, incorporating the six tombs and three doorways of the extant Gothic building in the process. But in the organization of these elements, Alberti takes a long step beyond the Romanesque planners. The height of Santa Maria Novella (to the tip of the pediment) equals its width, so that the entire façade can be inscribed in a square. The upper structure, in turn, can be encased in a square one-fourth the size of the main square; the cornice of the entablature that separates the two levels halves the major square, so that the lower portion of the building becomes a rectangle that is twice as wide as it is high; and the areas outlined by the columns on the lower level are squares with sides that are about one-third the width of the main unit. And so, throughout the façade, Alberti defines areas and relates them to each other in terms of proportions that can be expressed in simple numerical relations (1:1, 1:2, 1:3, 2:3, and so on). In his treatise, Alberti uses considerable space to propound the necessity of such harmonic relationships for the design of beautiful buildings. He shares this conviction with Brunelleschi, and it is this dependence on mathematics—the belief in the eternal and universal validity of numerical ratios as beauty-producing agents—that most fundamentally distinguishes both architects from their predecessors.

At San Francesco in Rimini (FIG. 16-41), Alberti once more modernizes a Gothic church—in this case, at the behest of one of the more sensational tyrants of the Early Renaissance, Sigismondo Pandolfo Malatesta, Lord of Rimini. Malatesta wanted a temple in which to enshrine the bones of great Humanist scholars like Gemistus Pletho, who dreamed of a neopagan religion that would supersede Christianity and whose remains Malatesta had brought from Greece. He intended his "temple" also to memorialize his mistress, Isotta. Alberti's thoroughly Roman design is a monument both to the tyrant's love of Classical learning and to his arrant paganism. Alberti redesigned the exterior shell of San Francesco, making a cubic structure, complete within itself, and fronting it with a façade like a Roman triumphal arch. Four massive engaged columns frame three recessed

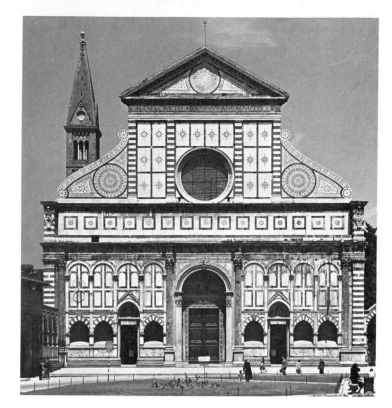

16-40 LEON BATTISTA ALBERTI, west façade of Santa Maria Novella, Florence, c. 1458–1470.

arches and carry a flat entablature that projects sharply, making a *ressaut*, or "jump," above each capital. Alberti intended the second story, which remains incomplete, to have an arched window framed by pilasters. The heavy relief of this façade contrasts with the flat, band-like elements in most of Alberti's other buildings. The deep, arched niches, rhythmically deployed along the flanks of the building and containing sarcophagi for the remains of famous

16-41 LEON BATTISTA ALBERTI, San Francesco, Rimini, Italy, begun 1451 (view from the northwest).

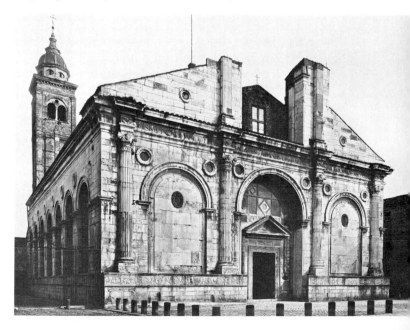

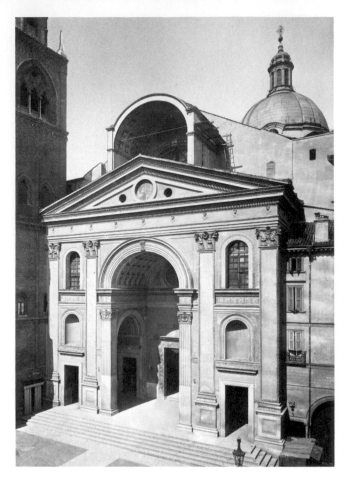

16-42 LEON BATTISTA ALBERTI, west façade of Sant' Andrea, Mantua, Italy, designed *c.* 1470.

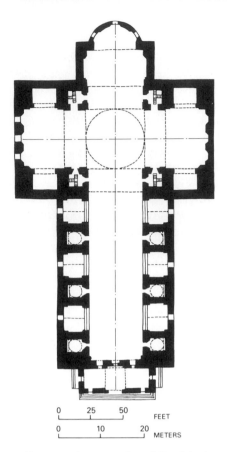

16-43 LEON BATTISTA ALBERTI, plan of Sant' Andrea, Mantua.

men, are in keeping with Alberti's conviction that arches should be carried on piers, not columns. These, along with the elements of the façade, provide an effect of monumental scale and grandeur that approaches ancient Roman architecture.

Adjusting the Classical orders to façade surfaces occupied Alberti throughout his career. In 1470, in his last years, he designed the church of Sant' Andrea in Mantua (FIGS. 16-42, 16-43, 16-44) to replace an older eleventh-century church. In the ingeniously planned façade, which illustrates the culmination of Alberti's experiments, he locks together two complete Roman architectural motifs—the temple front and the triumphal arch. His concern for proportion made him equalize the vertical and horizontal dimensions of the façade, which leaves it considerably lower than the church behind it. This concession to the demands of a purely visual proportionality in the façade and to the relation of the façade to the small square in front of it—even at the expense of continuity with the body of the building—is frequently manifest in Renaissance architecture, where considerations of visual appeal are of first importance. On the other hand, there *are* structural correspondences in Sant' Andrea. The façade pilasters are the same height as those on the interior walls of the nave, and the central barrel

vault, from which smaller barrel vaults branch off at right angles, introduces (in proportional arrangement but on a smaller scale) the system used on the interior. The façade pilasters, becoming part of the wall once more, run uninterrupted through three stories—an early application of the "colossal" or "giant" order that will become a favorite motif of Michelangelo.

16-44 LEON BATTISTA ALBERTI, interior of Sant' Andrea.

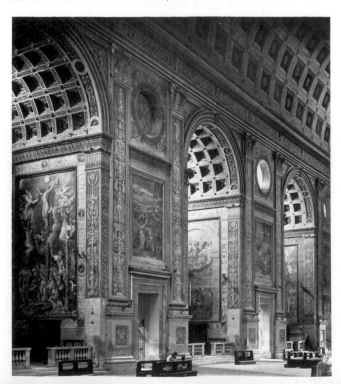

The interior of Sant' Andrea (FIG. 16-44) suggests that Alberti may have been inspired by the tremendous vaults of the ruined Basilica of Constantine (FIG. 6-85). The Medieval columned arcade, still used by Brunelleschi in Santo Spirito, is now forgotten, and the huge barrel vault—supported by thick walls alternating with vaulted chapels and interrupted by a massive dome over the crossing*—returns us to the vast interior spaces and dense enclosing masses of Roman architecture. In his treatise, Alberti calls the traditional basilican plan, in which continuous aisles flank the central nave, impractical, because the colonnades concealed the ceremonies from the faithful in the aisles; hence, his design of a single, huge hall, from which independent chapels branch off at right angles. This break with a thousand-year Christian building tradition was extremely influential in later Renaissance and Baroque planning.

Although Alberti extolls the virtues of the central plan in his treatise, his one attempt to build a church

*It is not known what kind of dome Alberti planned for the crossing; the present dome was added by FILIPPO JUVARA in the eighteenth century.

of this type remains abortive; San Sebastiano in Mantua, begun in 1460, was never completed. To many Renaissance architects and theoreticians, the circle was the ideal geometric figure; without beginning or end and with all points equidistant from a common center, it seemed to reflect the nature of the universe. This is one reason why the central plan was felt to be so appropriate for religious architecture. (Figures that approached the circle, such as polygons, were considered adequate.) But as firm as this conviction of the architects may have been, the clergy was almost as firm in its demands for traditional longitudinal churches, which, of course, are much more practical for Christian religious services. Additional to the main question of how to accommodate the congregation in central-plan churches was the question of where to put the main altar, and architects were permitted to realize their ideal relatively rarely.

A compromise solution, suggested first in Alberti's San Sebastiano in Mantua, was realized by GIULIANO DA SANGALLO (1443–1516) in Santa Maria delle Carceri in Prato (FIGS. 16-45, 16-46, 16-47). Built according to the plan of a Greek cross—with the cross arms so short that the emphasis is on the central, dome-covered square—the building, in fact, very closely approaches the central-plan ideal. Block-like, it is as high as it is wide, the cross arms are twice as wide as they are deep, and the Ionic second story is two-thirds the height of the Doric first floor—in fact, the whole building can be read in terms of the simple numerical relations that Alberti advocates. Interior articulation, however, is much closer to Brunelleschi and resembles that of the Pazzi Chapel (FIG. 16-21).

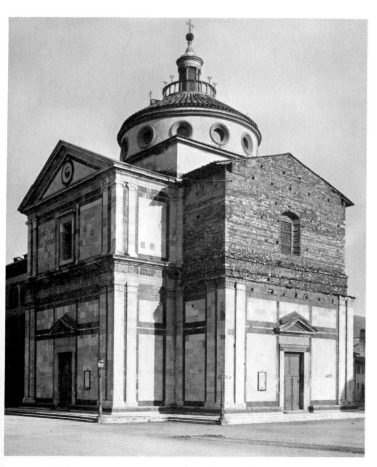

16-45 GIULIANO DA SANGALLO, Santa Maria delle Carceri, Prato, Italy, 1485 (view from the northwest).

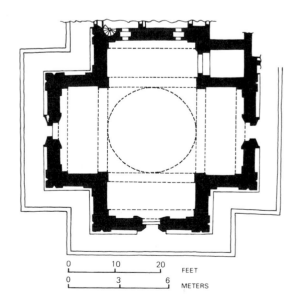

16-46 GIULIANO DA SANGALLO, plan of Santa Maria delle Carceri, Prato.

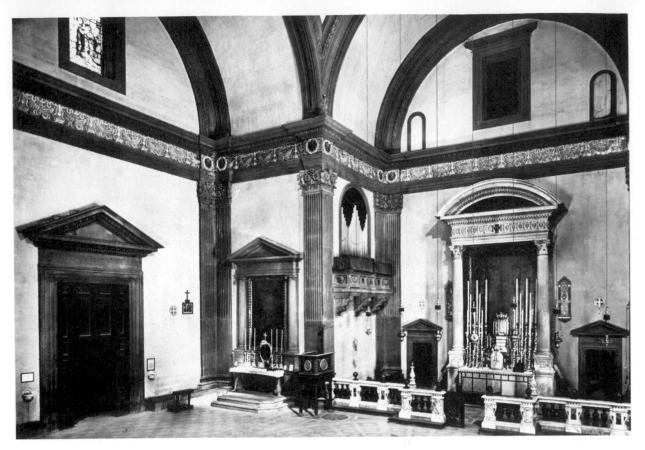

16-47   GIULIANO DA SANGALLO, interior of Santa Maria delle Carceri (view facing northeast).

The building seems to be a hybrid of the styles of Giuliano's two great predecessors, but it is also a neat and compact near-realization of an ideal central-plan Renaissance church.

Sculpture

Like the work of Alberti in the latter half of the fifteenth century, the sculpture of the Florentine School realizes new triumphs of Humanist Classicism. The successors of Donatello refined his innovating art and specialized in its many forms and subjects. No monument made by the following generation expresses more beautifully and clearly this dedication to the values of pagan antiquity than the tomb of Leonardo Bruni in Santa Croce in Florence (FIG. 16-48). Its sculptor, BERNARDO ROSSELLINO (1409–1464)—at one time a resident of Arezzo, like the man whose tomb he built—strove mightily to immortalize the fame of his fellow citizen. The wall tomb has a history that reaches back into the Middle Ages, but Rossellino's version is new and definitive and the expression of an age deliberately turning away from the Medieval past.

Leonardo Bruni was one of the most distinguished men of Italy, and his passing was widely mourned. An erudite scholar in Greek and Latin, a diplomat and apostolic secretary to four popes, and finally a member of the chancery of the city of Florence, Bruni's career sums up the Humanistic ideal. The Florentines particularly praised him for his *History of Florence*. In his honor, the practice of the funeral oration was revived, as was the ancient custom of crowning the deceased with laurel. It is quite possible that the historic event of the crowning of the dead Humanist gave Rossellino his theme and that the tomb is a kind of memorialization of the laureate scene. The forms of antiquity and the event of their restoration are brought together by the call of fame.

The deceased lies on the catafalque in a long gown, the *History of Florence* on his breast, the drapery of his couch caught up at the ends by Imperial Roman eagles. Winged genii at the summit of the arch hold a great escutcheon; on the side of the sarcophagus, others support a Latin inscription that describes the Muses' grief at the scholar's passing. At the base of the niche are Roman funeral garlands. The only Christian reference is a Madonna and Child with angels in the tympanum. As in Alberti's churches, a Humanist and pagan Classicism controls the mood of the design in an evocation of the ancient Greco–Roman world.

Few could hope for a funeral and tomb like Leonardo Bruni's; but in a Humanistic age, many wanted to see their memory, if not their fame, perpetuated. Also, Renaissance man probably enjoyed seeing likenesses of himself. At the time, Roman portrait busts were being found and preserved in ever-greater numbers; given this model, it was almost inevitable that the Renaissance would develop a similar portrait

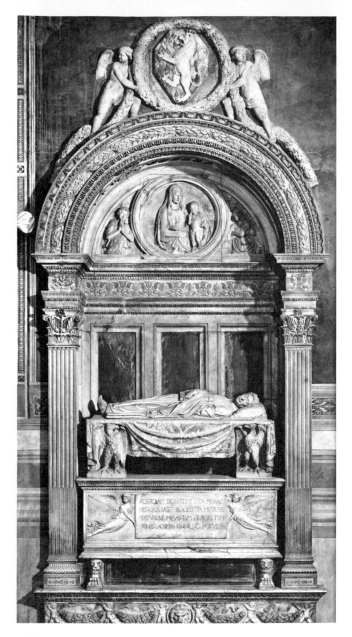

16-48 Bernardo Rossellino, tomb of Leonardo Bruni, c. 1445–1450. Marble, approx. 20' high to top of arch. Santa Croce, Florence.

type. The form may have originated in the shop of Antonio Rossellino (c. 1427–1479), Bernardo's younger brother. An example of Antonio's work is the portrait bust of *Matteo Palmieri* (FIG. 16-49), apostolic delegate for Pope Sixtus IV. Palmieri, who held high rank in Florence, was a learned man and author of a theological poem, *City of Life,* based formally on Dante's work. After his death, parts of the poem were declared heretical because the souls of men were originally represented as fallen angels. However, at the time of his death, Palmieri received a state funeral like Bruni's; his book was placed on his breast and a funeral oration was delivered. Antonio's portrait of Palmieri is extremely realistic but avoids the hardness of Roman Republican visages, which suggest the lifeless exactitude of the death mask—from which, indeed, they must have been made. Palmieri's almost clown-like face, with its enormous nose and endless mouth, is filled with a bright, intelligent animation, and the fine eyes seem those of a man engaged in a quick and subtle dialogue. The unsparing realism in the depiction of the ugly yet beguiling face is not surprising for a subject who probably had little difficulty in detecting flattery and rejecting it.

Donatello has shown the sternly real and the gently idealized in his forms; indeed, realism and idealism are parallel tendencies in the later fifteenth century. Desiderio da Settignano (1428–1464) specialized in the sensitive reading of the faces of women and children, which he idealized without diminishing character, as we may see in his *Bust of a Little Boy* (FIG. 16-50). The proportions and soft contours of the head are wonderfully understood, as is the psychological set—a wondering innocence—captured by Desiderio in the ambiguous pout and in the uplifted brows and large eyes directed wide at an adult world. The marble has been carved to give a remarkable smoothness to the planes, so that the light will be modulated softly and the impression of living, tender flesh con-

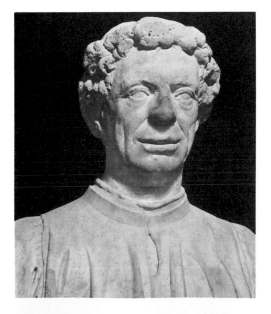

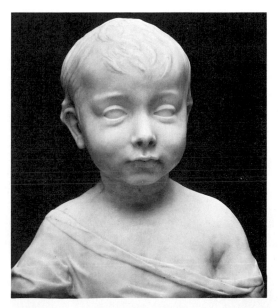

16-49 Antonio Rossellino, *Matteo Palmieri,* 1468. Marble, life-size. Museo Nazionale, Florence.

16-50 Desiderio da Settignano, *Bust of a Little Boy,* c. 1455. Marble, life-size. National Gallery of Art, Washington, D.C. (Andrew W. Mellon Collection).

veyed. The subtlety of Desiderio's surfaces and the consequent effect of life they give have long been admired by the Italians, as is evident in their phrase, *il vago Desiderio, si dolce bello* ("the charming Desiderio, so sweetly beautiful"). A whole school of sculptors worked in this manner, and attributions, often quite uncertain, range from Desiderio to the young Leonardo da Vinci. The soft, misty, shadow effects certainly point ahead to the *sfumato* ("smoky" light and shade) in Leonardo's paintings.

Since the thirteenth and fourteenth centuries, the Madonna and Child theme has become increasingly humanized, until, in the fifteenth century, we might almost speak of a school of sweetness and light in which many sculptors attempt to outdo each other, especially in relief, in rendering the theme ever gentler and prettier. In the latter half of the fifteenth century, increasing demand for devotional images for private chapels and shrines (rather than for large public churches) contributed to an increasing secularization of traditional religious subject matter. LUCA DELLA ROBBIA (1400–1482), a sculptor in the generation of Donatello and a leader of the trend toward sweetness and light, discovered a way to multiply the images of the Madonna so that they would be within the reach of persons of modest means. His discovery (around 1430), involving the application of vitrified potters' glazes to sculpture, led to his production, in quantity, of the glazed terra-cotta reliefs for which he is best known. Because they were cheap, durable, and decorative, these works became extremely popular and the basis for a flourishing family business. The tradition was carried on by his nephew ANDREA, whose colors tend to become a little garish, and by the latter's sons (GIOVANNI and GIROLAMO), whose activity extends well into the sixteenth century, when

16-51   LUCA DELLA ROBBIA, *Madonna and Child, c.* 1455–1460. Terra cotta with polychrome glaze, approx. 6′ in diameter. Or San Michele, Florence.

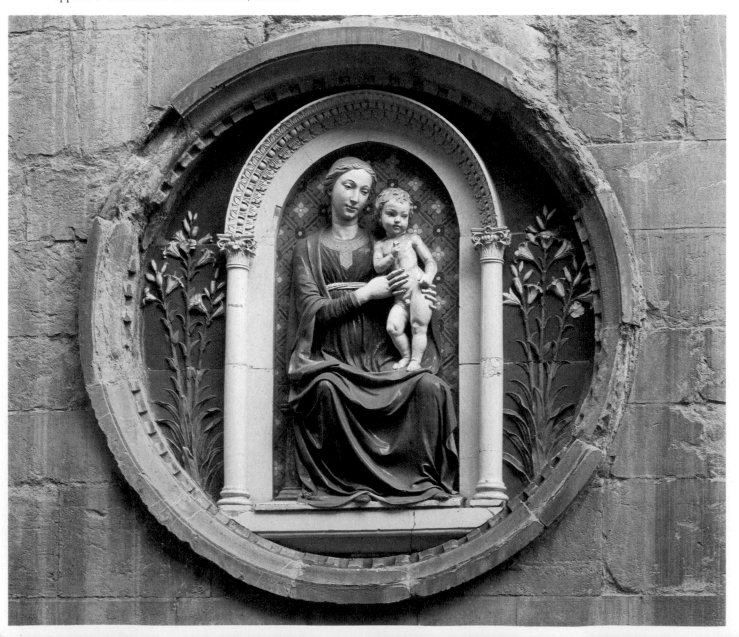

the product tends to become purely commercial; we still speak today of "della Robbia ware." An example of Luca's specialty is the *Madonna and Child* set into a wall of Or San Michele (FIG. 16-51). The figures are composed within a *tondo,* a circular frame that will become popular with both sculptors and painters, particularly the della Robbia family, in the later part of the century. The introduction of high-key color into sculpture adds a certain worldly gaiety to the theme, and the customary light blue grounds (and here the green and white of lilies and the white architecture) suggest the festive season of Easter and the freshness of May, the month of the Virgin. Of course, the somber majesty of the old Byzantine style has long since disappeared. The young mothers who prayed before images like this could easily identify with the Madonna, and doubtless did. The distance between the observed and the observer has vanished.

The most important sculptor of the second half of the century was ANDREA DEL VERROCCHIO (1435–1488). A painter as well as a sculptor, with something of the versatility and depth of Donatello, Verrocchio had a flourishing *bottega* in Florence that attracted many students, among them Leonardo da Vinci. Ver-

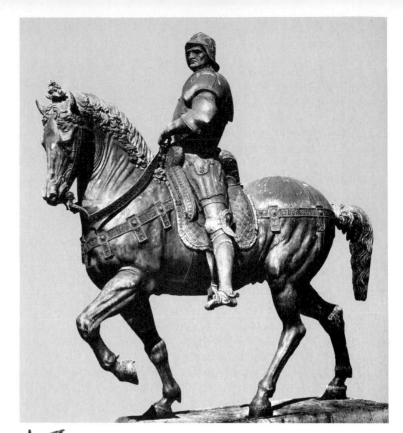

16-53 ANDREA DEL VERROCCHIO, *Bartolommeo Colleoni,* c. 1483–1488. Bronze, approx. 13' high. Campo dei Santi Giovanni e Paolo, Venice.

16-52 ANDREA DEL VERROCCHIO, *David, c.* 1465. Bronze, approx. 49" high. Museo Nazionale, Florence.

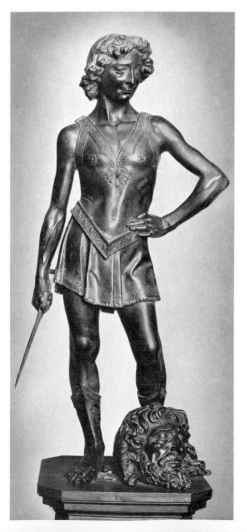

rocchio, also like the great Donatello, had a broad repertory. He too made a figure of *David* (FIG. 16-52), one that strongly contrasts in its narrative realism with the quiet, esthetic Classicism of Donatello's *David* (FIG. 16-12). Verrocchio's *David*—a sturdy, wiry young apprentice clad in a leathern doubtlet—stands with a jaunty pride, the head of Goliath at his feet. He poses like any sportsman who has just won a game, or a hunter with his kill. The easy balance of the weight, the lithe, still thinly adolescent musculature, in which the veins are prominent, show how closely Verrocchio read the text and how clearly he knew the psychology of brash and confident young men. Although the contrast with Donatello's interpretation need hardly be labored, we might note the "open" form of the Verrocchio *David,* the sword and pointed elbow sharply breaking through the figure's silhouette and stressing the live tension of the still alert victor; Donatello's *David,* on the other hand, has a "closed" silhouette, which emphasizes its Classical calm and relaxation. The description of the anatomy of the two figures—specific in the former, generalized in the latter—puts further accent on the difference between them. Both statues are masterpieces and show how two skillful and thoughtful men approach the same theme from very different angles.

Verrocchio competes with Donatello again in an equestrian statue of another *condottiere* of Venice, *Bartolommeo Colleoni* (FIG. 16-53), who, eager to emulate the fame and the monument of Donatello's

Gattamelata (FIG. 16-13), provided for the statue in his will. Both Donatello's and Verrocchio's statues were made after the deaths of their subjects, so that neither artist knew his subject. The result is a fascinating difference of interpretation—like that between the two *Davids*—of what a professional captain of armies would look like. On a pedestal even higher than that of Donatello's *Gattamelata*, Verrocchio's statue of the bold equestrian general is placed so that the dominating, aggressive figure can be seen above the rooftops, silhouetted against the sky, its fierce authority unmistakably present from all major approaches to the piazza (the Campo dei Santi Giovanni e Paolo). In contrast with the near repose of the *Gattamelata*, the Colleoni horse moves in a prancing stride, arching and curving its powerful neck, while the commander seems suddenly to shift his whole weight to the stirrups and, in a fit of impassioned anger, to rise from the saddle with a violent twist of his body. The group is charged with an exaggerated tautness; the bulging muscles of the animal, the fiercely erect and rigid body of the man unify brute strength and rage. The commander, represented as delivering the battle harangue to his troops before they close with the enemy, has worked himself into a frenzy that he hopes to communicate to his men. In the *Gattamelata*, Donatello gives us a portrait of grim sagacity; Verrocchio's *Bartolommeo Colleoni* is a portrait of savage and merciless might. Machiavelli writes that the successful ruler must combine the traits of the lion and the fox; one feels that Donatello's *Gattamelata* is a little of the latter and that Verrocchio's *Bartolommeo Colleoni* is much of the former.

Closely related in stylistic intention to Verrocchio is the work of ANTONIO POLLAIUOLO (c. 1431–1498). Also important as a painter and engraver, Pollaiuolo infuses the nervous movement and emotional expressiveness of Donatello's late style with a new linear mobility, spatial complexity, and dramatic immediacy. He has a realistic concern for movement in all its variety and for the stress and strain of the human figure in violent action. A good example is Pollaiuolo's small-scale group of *Hercules and Antaeus* (FIG. 16-54); not quite 18 inches high, it embodies the ferocity and vitality of elemental, physical conflict. The group illustrates the legend of a wrestling match between Antaeus (Antaios), a giant and son of earth, and Hercules (Herakles). We have already seen this story represented by EUPHRONIOS on an ancient Greek vase (FIG. 5-9). Each time Hercules threw him, Antaeus sprang up again, his strength renewed by contact with earth. Finally, Hercules held him aloft, so that he could not touch earth, and strangled him around the waist. The artist strives to convey the excruciating moment—the straining and cracking of sinews, the clenched teeth of Hercules, the kicking

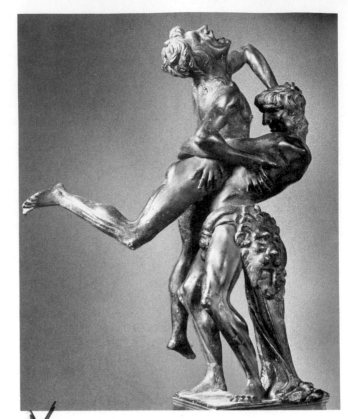

16-54 ANTONIO POLLAIUOLO, *Hercules and Antaeus*, c. 1475. Bronze, approx. 18″ high with base. Museo Nazionale, Florence.

and screaming of Antaeus. The figures are interlocked in a tightly wound coil, and the flickering reflections of light on the dark, gouged surface of the bronze contribute to the effect of agitated movement and fluid play of planes.

Painting and Engraving

The twisting of figures through space shows the growing interest in realistic action among this generation of artists. Now an enthusiasm, this interest is further revealed in Pollaiuolo's *Battle of the Ten Nudes* (FIG. 16-55). Pollaiuolo belongs to the second generation of experimentalists, who, in their pursuit of realism, were absorbed in the study of anatomy, and he may have been one of the first artists to perform human dissection. The problem of rendering human anatomy had been rather well solved by earlier artists like Donatello and Andrea del Castagno, but their figures are usually shown at rest or in restrained motion. Pollaiuolo, as in his *Hercules and Antaeus*, takes delight in showing violent action and finds his opportunity in subjects dealing with combat. He conceives the body as a powerful machine and likes to display its mechanisms; knotted muscles and taut sinews activate the skeleton as ropes pull levers. To show this to best effect, Pollaiuolo developed a figure so thin and muscular that it appears *écorché* (as if without skin or outer tissue), with strongly accentuated articulations at the wrists, elbows, shoulders,

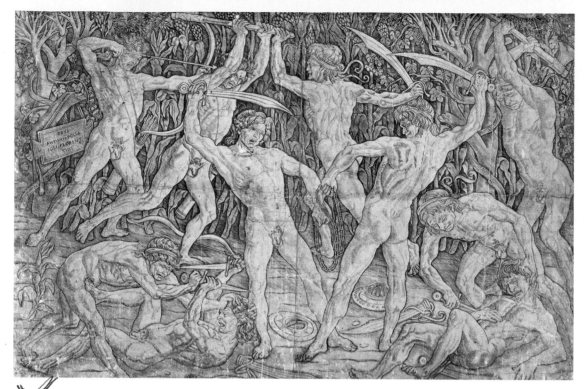

16-55 Antonio Pollaiuolo, *Battle of the Ten Nudes*, *c.* 1465. Engraving approx. 15″ × 23″. Metropolitan Museum of Art, New York (bequest of Joseph Pulitzer, 1917).

and knees. His *Battle of the Ten Nudes* shows this figure type in a variety of poses from numerous points of view. If the figures, even though they hack and slash at one another without mercy, seem somewhat stiff and frozen, it is because Pollaiuolo shows *all* the muscle groups at maximum tension. The fact that only part of the body's muscle groups are involved in any action, while the others are relaxed, was to be observed only some decades later by an even greater anatomist, Leonardo da Vinci.

Pollaiuolo's *Battle of the Ten Nudes* is an *engraving*, a print made by pressing an inked metal plate, into which a drawing has been incised, against a sheet of paper. Developed around the middle of the fifteenth century, probably in northern Europe, engraving proved to be more flexible and durable than the older woodcut, which it gradually replaced during the later part of the century. As numerous prints could be made from the same plate, they were cheap and could be widely circulated, bringing art to the common man and spreading new and stimulating pictorial ideas among artists. Because they were easy to transport, prints were a quick and easy means of inter-artist communication. Italian prints had important influence on such northern painters as Albrecht Dürer, and the prints of that great master of engraving were widely admired among Italian artists.

The versatile Pollaiuolo experimented in painting, especially with the problem of representing figures in a landscape setting. The problem of relating figures to architecture had already been solved by Piero della Francesca, but the landscape setting presented some-

what different requirements, some of which had been met by Masaccio. The panel representing *Hercules and Deianira* (FIG. 16-56), contemporaneous with the sculptured group of *Hercules and Antaeus*, indicates that Pollaiuolo is a master not only of anatomy but also of landscape and light. In this, one of three paintings commissioned by Piero de' Medici for the Medici palace (the subjects of which were the labors of Hercules, the legendary Greek hero), the centaur Nessus has abducted Deianira, the bride of Hercules, and Hercules is in the act of slaying him with a poisoned arrow. The dramatic action and play of muscle and sinew is what we would expect of Pollaiuolo, but here he sets the bounding Nessus, the gesticulating Deianira, and the bow-taut Hercules in a broad landscape, the valley of the river Arno. The winding river takes the viewer's gaze all the way to the horizon, past the city of Florence, dim in the distance. (The cathedral can be seen just beyond Deianira's left hand). Pollaiuolo's observation of deep landscape space and atmospheric effects, like the luminous glaze on the river and the fade-out of the contours of the far distant hills, complements his knowledge of the human figure; the broad, quiet, natural perspective serves to set off the tense movements of the actors. From mid-century on, there is sharply increased interest in the pagan mythologies as subjects for painting and sculpture, an interest that will persist well into the nineteenth century. Here, a mythological subject has been imagined so vividly that it has been made part of the actual Florentine scene. Instead of relating figures and space in a rationally clear

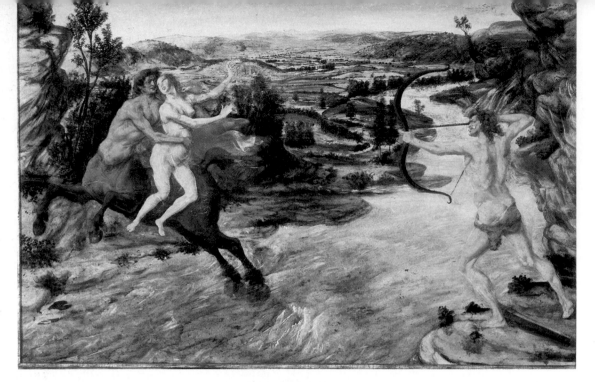

16-56 ANTONIO POLLAIUOLO, *Hercules and Deianira, c.* 1470. Egg tempera and oil (?) on canvas, $21\frac{1}{2}'' \times 31\frac{3}{16}''$. Yale University Art Gallery, New Haven, Connecticut. (University purchase from James Jackson Jarves.)

perspective, abstracted from nature, Pollaiuolo represents human figures in their natural environment. This image of the world is not fixed, like Piero della Francesca's, but fluid and changing.

DOMENICO GHIRLANDAIO (1449–1494) differs in character from Pollaiuolo. Neither an innovator nor an experimenter, Ghirlandaio is rather a synthesizer who, profiting from everything done before, summarizes the state of Florentine art by the end of the century. His works express his times to perfection, and, for this, he enjoyed great popularity among his contemporaries. Ghirlandaio's paintings also show a deep love for his city of Florence, its spectacles and

pageantry, its material wealth and luxury. His most representative pictures—a cycle of frescoes representing scenes from the lives of the Virgin and St. John the Baptist, from which is shown *The Birth of the Virgin* (FIG. 16-57)—are found in the choir of Santa Maria Novella. In the rich interior of a palace room, embellished with fine *intarsia* (wooden mosaic) and sculpture, the mother of the Virgin, St. Anne, reclines, while midwives prepare the infant's bath. From the left comes a grave procession of ladies, led by a member of the Tornabuoni family (the donors of the paintings). This splendidly dressed young woman holds as prominent a place in the composi-

16-57 DOMENICO GHIRLANDAIO, *The Birth of the Virgin*, 1485–1490. Fresco. Santa Maria Novella, Florence.

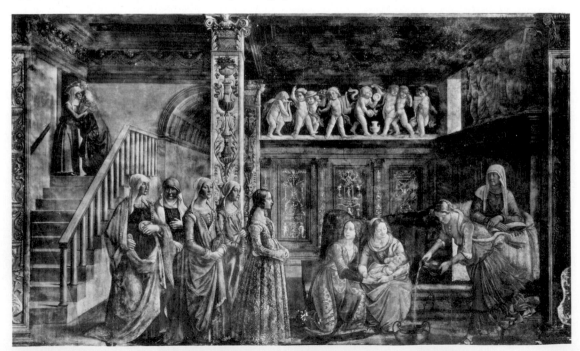

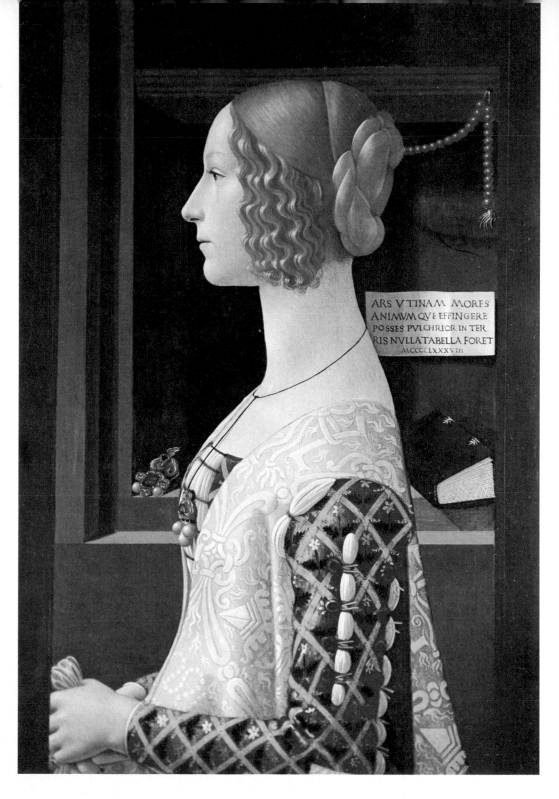

16-58 DOMENICO GHIRLANDAIO, *Giovanna Tornabuoni* (?), 1488. Oil and tempera on wood, approx. 30″ × 20″. Sammlung Thyssen-Bornemisza, Lugano.

ARS VTINAM MORES
ANIMVM QVE EFFINGERE
POSSES PVLCHRIOR IN TER
RIS NVLLA TABELLA FORET
MCCCCLXXXVIII

tion (close to the central axis) as she must have held in Florentine society; her appearance in the painting (a different female member of the house appears in each of the frescoes) is conspicuous evidence of the secularization of sacred themes commonplace in art by this time. Living persons of high rank are now represented not only as present at biblical dramas but, as here, often stealing the show from the saints. The display of patrician elegance absorbs and subordinates the devotional tableau.

The composition epitomizes the achievements of Early Renaissance painting: clear spatial representation; statuesque, firmly constructed figures; and rational order and logical relation among these figures and objects. If anything of earlier traits remains, it is in the arrangement of the figures, which still somewhat rigidly cling to layers parallel to the picture plane.

Giovanna Tornabuoni may be the subject of a portrait by Ghirlandaio (FIG. 16-58), the cool formality of which repeats the lady of the fresco and sets off the proud, sensitive beauty of the aristocratic features. Although the profile pose is not primarily intended to a convey a reading of character, this portrait tells us much about the high state of human culture achieved in Florence, the careful cultivation and prizing of beauty in life and art, the breeding of courtly manners, and the great wealth behind it all.

The profile pose was customary in Florence until about 1470, when three-quarter and full-face portraits began to replace it. From the last quarter of the fifteenth century, we have a three-quarter view, *Portrait of a Young Man* (FIG. 16-59) by SANDRO BOTTICELLI (Alessandro di Mariano dei Filipepi, 1444–1510), the brightest star of the Florentine galaxy in the later part of the century. Earlier in the century, this three-quar-

16-59 SANDRO BOTTICELLI, *Portrait of a Young Man*, late fifteenth century. Oil and tempera on wood, 23″ × 15½″. Formerly in the collection of Sir Thomas Merton, Berkshire, England.

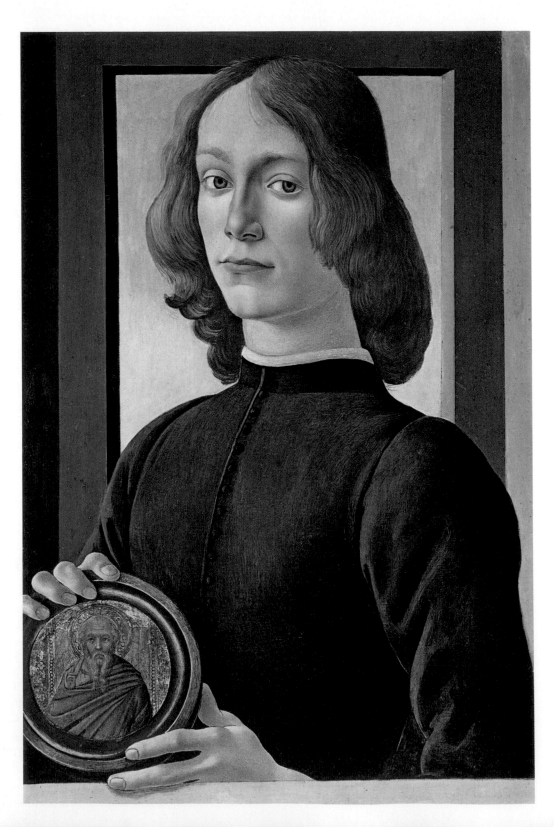

ter view—the head almost full-face, the eyes meeting those of the observer—was made common by the painters of northern Europe. The Italian painters now take it up, perceiving that it greatly increases the viewer's information about the subject's appearance. This almost full view also allows the artist to search and reveal the subject's character, although, for a long while, Italian artists will prefer (and no doubt their sitters would demand) an impersonal formality that presents a calm, undisturbed public face and conceals the private, pyschological man. Thus, Botticelli's young man measures observers with impassive nonchalance, as if expecting them to maintain the proper formal distance.

Botticelli was the pupil of Fra Filippo Lippi, from whom he must have learned the method of "drawing" firm, pure outline with light shading within the contours. The effect is clearly apparent in the explicit and sharply elegant form of the portrait. In the hands of Botticelli, this method will be refined infinitely, and he is known in world art as one of the great masters of line. One of the most important monographs on Botticelli is by a Japanese;* in Botticelli, the Orient recognizes a master from the West.

No discussion of Botticelli can be fully meaningful without some reference to the environment that peculiarly encouraged him—the circle of Lorenzo de' Medici and the Platonic Academy of Philosophy. Here, he studied the philosophy of Plato, or rather of Neo-Platonism, for scholars had not yet developed the critical sense that would distinguish between Plato and the Neo-Platonic mystics of Alexandria, who came centuries after and quite transformed Plato's thought in the direction of a religious system. It was this spiritualized and mystical Platonism that Botticelli absorbed, believing that it was close to Christianity in essence and that the two could be reconciled. He must have heard the Humanists around Lorenzo discourse on these new mysteries in one of the Medici villas, in surroundings highly conducive to reflection. A modern historian writes:

> In a villa overhanging the towers of Florence, on the steep slope of that lofty hill crowned by the mother city, the ancient Fiesole, in gardens which Cicero might have envied, with Ficino, Landino, and Politian at his side, he [Lorenzo] delighted his hours with the beautiful visions of Platonic philosophy, for which the summer stillness of an Italian sky appears the most genial accompaniment.†

Botticelli had the power to materialize the "beautiful visions," and this he did in a number of works for the Medici villas, among them the famous *Birth of Venus* (FIG. 16-60), inspired, it is believed, by a poem

by Politian on that theme. Botticelli is of his generation in his enthusiasm for themes from Classical mythology as well as in his suiting of the ancient pagan materials to a form prepared by the Early Renaissance, a form realistic yet still modified by something of the Medieval past. Competent in all the new representational methods, he seems deliberately to sacrifice them in the interest of his own original manner, rarefying the realism of the Early Renaissance into an inimitable decorative and linear system that generates its own kind of figure and space. Venus, born of the sea foam, is wafted on a cockle shell, blown by the Zephyrs, to her sacred island, Cyprus, where the nymph Pomona, descended from the ancient goddess of fruit trees, runs to meet her with a brocaded mantle. The presentation of the figure of Venus nude was, in itself, an innovation; as we have seen, the nude—especially the female nude—had been proscribed in the Middle Ages. Its appearance on such a scale and its use of an ancient Venus statue of the *Venus pudica* (modest Venus) type as a model could have drawn the charge of paganism and infidelity. But under the protection of the powerful Medici, a new world of imagination could open freely with the new Platonism.

The high priest of the Neo-Platonic cult (for which *The Birth of Venus* could almost have been an altarpiece) was the Humanist Marsilio Ficino, certainly known to Botticelli through Lorenzo de' Medici's circle. Ficino believed that the soul could ascend toward a union with God through the contemplation of beauty, which reveals and manifests the two supreme principles of the Divine: love and light. This kind of mystical approach—so different from the earnest search of the early fifteenth century to comprehend humanity and the natural world through a rational and empirical order—finds expression in Botticelli's strange and beautiful style, which seems to ignore all of the scientific ground gained by experimental art. His style parallels the allegorical pageants in Florence, which were staged as chivalric tournaments but revolved completely around allusions to Classical mythology; the same trend is evident in the poetry of the 1470s and 1480s. Artists and poets at this time did not directly imitate Classical antiquity, but used the myths, with delicate perception of their charm, in a way still tinged with Medieval romance.

In Botticelli's hands, the Classical myth takes on a fresh and fascinating quality. The lovely figure of Venus, strangely weightless and ethereal, is the intellectual or spiritual apparition of beauty, not at all the queen of sensual love whom the Venetian Renaissance will create. The lightness and bodilessness of the Zephyrs move all the figures without effort. Draperies undulate easily in the gentle gusts, perfumed by rose petals that fall on the whitecaps stirred by the Zephyrs' toes. For the Medieval world and for

*Y. Yashiro, *Sandro Botticelli* (London, Boston: 1925, 1929).

†Henry Hallam, in J.A. Symonds, *Renaissance in Italy* (New York: Modern Library, 1935), Vol. 1, p. 477.

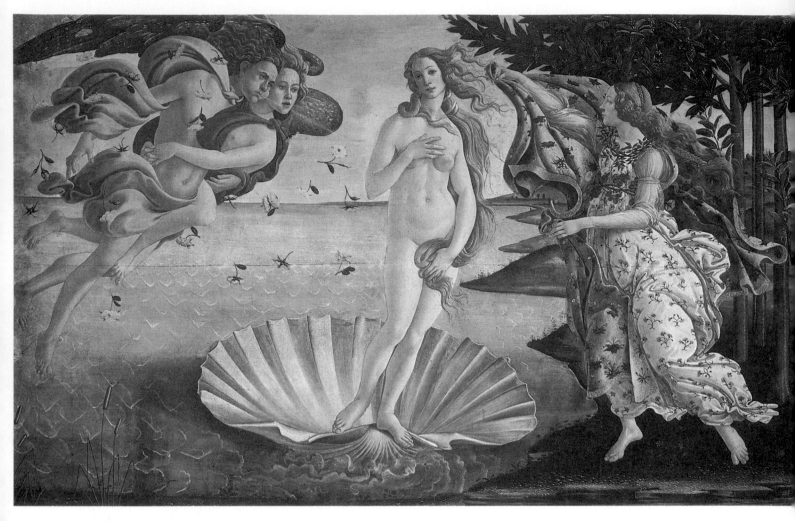

16-60   SANDRO BOTTICELLI, *The Birth of Venus, c.* 1482. Tempera on canvas, approx. 5' 8" × 9' 1". Galleria degli Uffizi, Florence.

that of Neo-Platonism, as distinct from the modern scientific view, everything is linked by infinitely complex lines of affinity. Everything is related to everything else; meanings can be read from objects and events, as the ancients read the future from the stars, the entrails of animals, and prodigies. It does not surprise us, then, that any number of interpretations can be made of a picture like *The Birth of Venus;* doubtless, it was intended to mean many things at the same time and to have, so to speak, many layers of significance. For example, a modern scholar sees, beyond the simple depiction of the myth of the birth of Venus, an allegory of the innocence and truth of the human soul, naked to the winds of passion and about to be clothed in the robe of reason. We can be sure that such abstruse interpretations and hyperinterpretations were made of paintings and texts at the time; it has been a long-enduring habit of the Western mind.

Botticelli's style, the sensitive vehicle of an in-

tensely sensitive mind, changed with the fortunes of Florence; as he responded to the Humanist and Neo-Platonic ideas of the circle of Lorenzo de' Medici, so he responded to the overthrow of the Medici, the incursion of the French armies, and especially to the preaching of the Dominican monk Girolamo Savonarola, the reforming priest–dictator who denounced the paganism of the Medici and their artists, philosophers, and poets. Savonarola called on the citizens of Florence to repent their iniquities, and, when the Medici fled, he prophesied the doom of the city and of Italy and took absolute power over the state. Together with a large number of citizens, Savonarola believed that the Medici had been a political, social, and religious influence for the worse—corrupting Florence and inviting the scourge of foreign invasion. Modern scholarship still debates the significance of Savonarola's brief span of power. Apologists for the undoubtedly sincere monk deny that his actions played a role in the decline of Florentine culture at the end of the century. But he did rail at the Neo-Platonist Humanists as heretical gabblers, and his banishing of the Medici, Tornabuoni, and other noble families from Florence deprived local artists of some of their major patrons. Florence lost its position of cultural leadership at the end of the century and never regained it. Certainly, the puritanical spirit that moved Savonarola—and that was soon to appear throughout Europe in the reforming preachments of the Protestant Reformation—must have dampened considerably the neopagan enthusiasm of the Florentine Early Renaissance.

The sensitive, highly personal, and exotic style of

Botticelli closed the great age of Florentine art on an exquisitely refined note. Artists of his generation outside Florence, but within the circuit of its influence, expanded the experiments of the century. An Umbrian painter, LUCA SIGNORELLI (*c.* 1445–1523), further developed the interest of Antonio Pollaiuolo in the depiction of muscular bodies in violent action in a wide variety of poses and foreshortenings. In the San Brizio Chapel in Orvieto Cathedral, Signorelli's painted scenes depicting the end of the world include *The Damned Cast into Hell* (FIG. 16-61). Few figure compositions of the fifteenth century have the same awesome psychic impact. St. Michael and the hosts of

16-61 LUCA SIGNORELLI, *The Damned Cast into Hell*, 1499–1504. Fresco. San Brizio Chapel, Orvieto Cathedral, Italy.

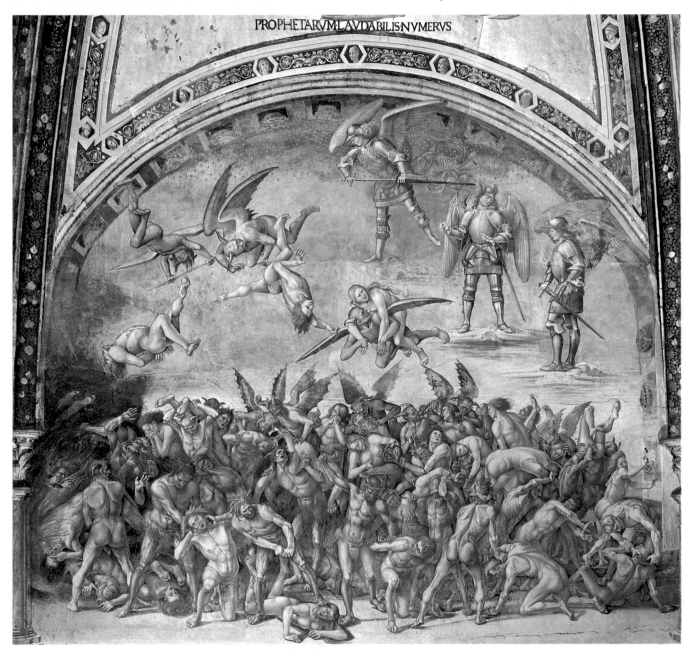

Heaven hurl the damned into Hell, where, in a dense, writhing mass, they are tortured by vigorous demons. The figures—nude, lean, and muscular—assume every conceivable posture of anguish. Signorelli's skill at foreshortening the figure is one with his mastery of its action; and although each figure is clearly a study from a model, he fits his theme to the figures in an entirely convincing manner. Terror and rage pass like storms through the wrenched and twisted bodies. The fiends, their hair flaming and their bodies the color of putrefying flesh, lunge at their victims in ferocious frenzy; we can imagine the appalling pandemonium. Not even Pollaiuolo achieves such virtuosity in the manipulation of anatomy for dramatic purpose. Doubtless, Signorelli influenced Michelangelo, who makes the human nude his sole and sufficient expressive motif. In *The Last Judgment* in the Sistine Chapel, Michelangelo shows that he was much aware of Signorelli's version of the theme.

Signorelli's fellow Umbrian, PERUGINO (Pietro Vannucci, c. 1450–1523), was concerned not with the human figure in violent action, as Signorelli was, but with the calm, geometric ordering of pictorial space. Between 1481 and 1483, Perugino and several other famous artists, including Botticelli, Ghirlandaio, and Signorelli, were summoned to Rome to decorate the walls of the newly completed Sistine Chapel with frescoes. Perugino painted *Christ Delivering the Keys of the Kingdom to St. Peter* (FIG. 16-62)—the event on which the papacy had, from the beginning, based its claim to infallible and total authority over the Church. Christ gives the keys to St. Peter at the center of solemn choruses of saints and citizens, who occupy the apron of a great stage space that marches into the distance (stepped off by the parallel lines of the pavement) to a point of convergence in the doorway of a central-plan temple. Figures in the middle distance complement the near group, emphasizing its density and order by their scattered arrangement. At the corners of the great piazza, triumphal arches resembling the Arch of Constantine (FIG. 6-89) mark the base angles of a compositional triangle having its apex in the central building. The group of Christ and Peter are placed on the central axis, which runs through the temple's doorway, within which is the vanishing

16-62   PERUGINO, *Christ Delivering the Keys of the Kingdom to St. Peter*, 1481–1483. Fresco. Sistine Chapel, Vatican, Rome.

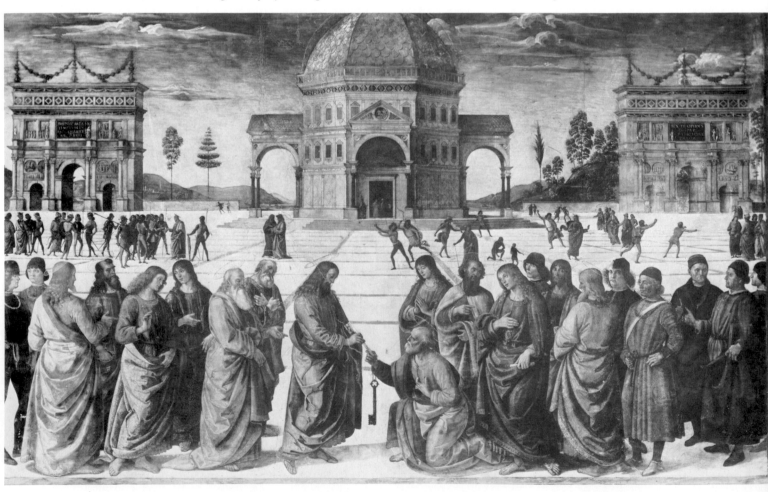

point of the perspective. Thus, the composition interlocks both two-dimensional and three-dimensional space, and the central actors are carefully integrated with the axial center. This spatial science provides a means for organizing the action systematically. Perugino, in this single picture, incorporates the learning of generations. His coolly rational, orderly style and the uncluttered clarity of his compositions left a lasting impression on his best-known student, Raphael.

Many Florentine artists worked in northern Italy: Donatello in Padua; Paolo Uccello, Andrea del Castagno, and Fra Filippo Lippi in Venice. Gradually, the International style, which lingered long in the north, yielded to the new Florentine art. Around mid-century, one of the most brilliant talents of the entire Renaissance, ANDREA MANTEGNA (c. 1431–1506) of Padua, appeared in northern Italy; there he must have met Donatello, who greatly stimulated and influenced his art. With Mantegna's frescoes in the Ovetari Chapel in the Church of the Eremitani in Padua (largely destroyed in the Second World War), northern Italian painting falls into line with the Humanistic art of Florence. *St. James Led to Martyrdom* (FIG. 16-63) reveals the breadth of Mantegna's literary, archeological, and pictorial learning. The motifs that appear on the barrel-vaulted triumphal arch are taken from the Classical ornamental vocabulary. The soldiers' costumes are studied from antique models; the painter strives for historical authenticity, much as did the antiquarian scholars of the University of Padua. Mantegna sets himself difficult problems in perspective for the joy of solving them. Here, the observer's viewpoint is set very low, as if looking up out of a basement window at the vast arch looming above. The lines of the building to the right plunge down dramatically. There are, however, significant deviations from true perspective. Mantegna, using artistic license, ignores the third vanishing point

16-63 ANDREA MANTEGNA, *St. James Led to Martyrdom, c.* 1455. Fresco. Ovetari Chapel, Church of the Eremitani, Padua, Italy (largely destroyed, 1944).

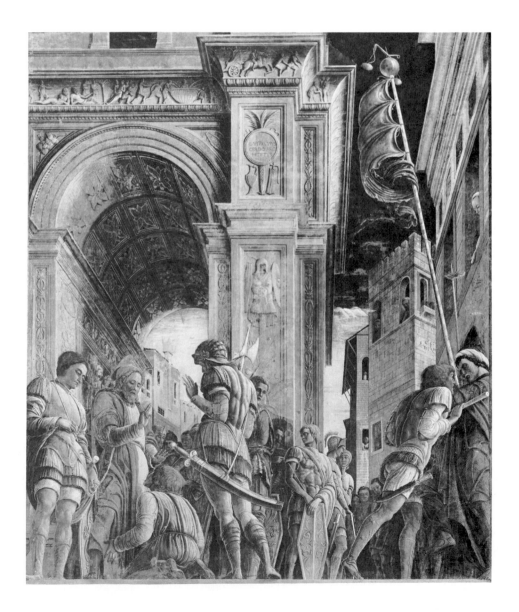

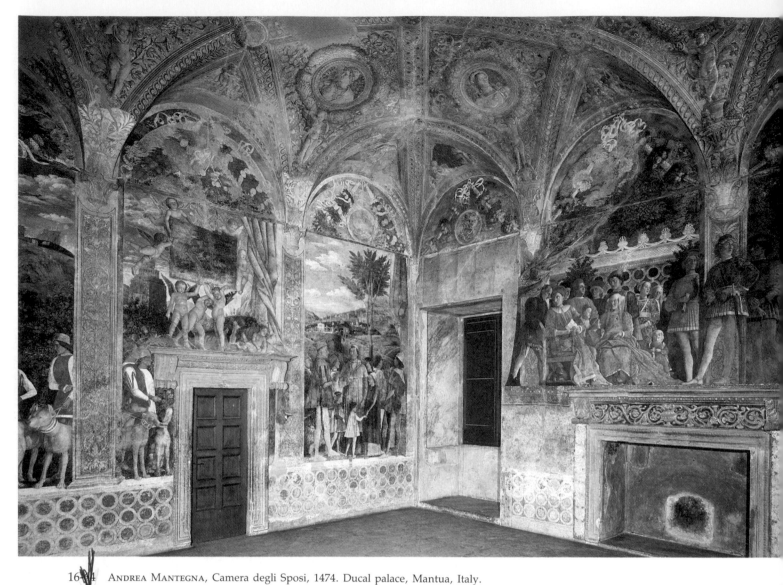

16-64 ANDREA MANTEGNA, Camera degli Sposi, 1474. Ducal palace, Mantua, Italy.

(seen from below; the buildings should converge toward the top). Disregarding the perspective facts, he prefers to work toward a unified, cohesive composition in which pictorial elements are related to the picture frame. The lack of perspective logic is partly compensated for by the insertion of strong diagonals in the right foreground (for example, the staff of the banner).

From about 1460 onward, Mantegna worked predominantly for the Gonzaga family of Mantua, who were great art patrons like the Medici but—unlike the Medici (who were the most powerful members of a merchant oligarchy)—hereditary dukes. In the ducal palace at Mantua, Mantegna performed a triumphant feat of pictorial illusionism, producing the first completely consistent illusionistic decoration of an entire room, the so-called Camera degli Sposi ("Room of the Newlyweds," FIG. 16-64). Utilizing actual architectural elements, Mantegna paints away the walls of the room in a manner that forecasts later Baroque

decoration. He represents members of the House of Gonzaga welcoming home a son, a prince of the Church, from Rome. The family members, magnificently costumed, are shown in both domestic and landscape settings and are rendered carefully in portrait realism. The poses are remarkably unstudied and casual, conveying the easy familiarity of a family reunion. The painting is a celebration of fifteenth-century court life and a glorification of the Gonzaga, as well as the century's only major depiction of a current event. The lunettes are filled with garlands and medallions *all' antica* (in the antique manner), motifs that are standard features in northern Italian painting.

Mantegna's daring experimentalism leads him to complete the room's decoration with the first *di sotto in sù* perspective of a ceiling (FIG. 16-65)—a technique later broadly developed by the northern Italian painter, Correggio, and the Baroque ceiling decorators. We look directly up at figures looking down at

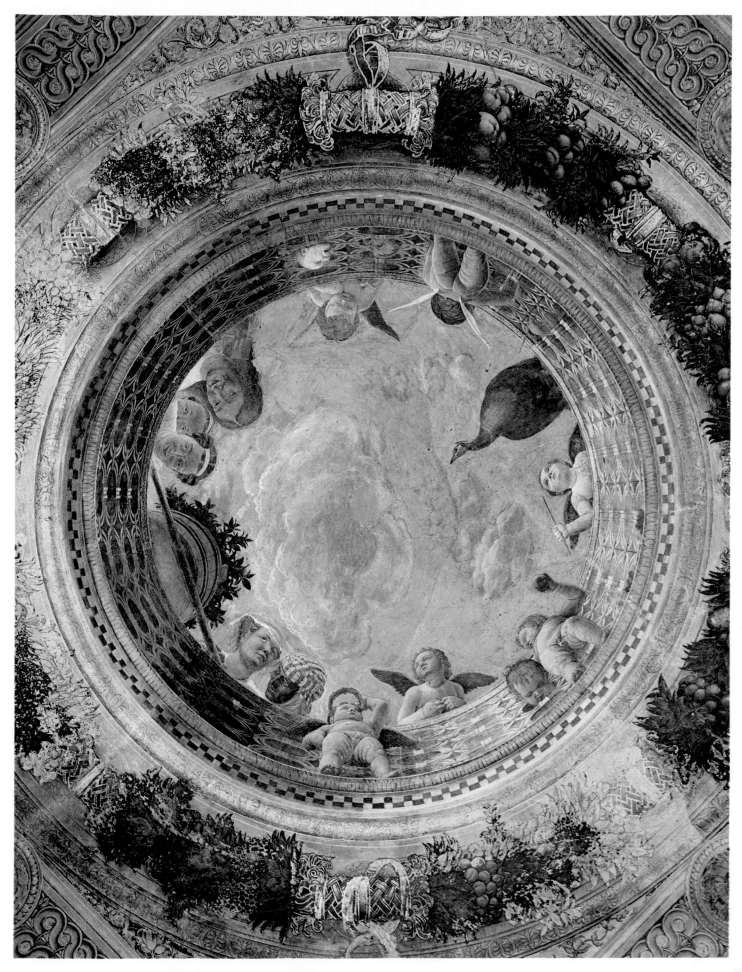

16-65 ANDREA MANTEGNA, ceiling of the Camera degli Sposi, 1474. Fresco. Ducal palace, Mantua.

us. Cupids, strongly foreshortened, set the amorous mood, as the painted spectators smile down on the scene. This *tour de force* of illusionism climaxes almost a century of experiment in perspective.

One of Mantegna's later paintings, *The Dead Christ* (FIG. 16-66), is a work of overwhelming power, despite the somewhat awkward insertion of the two mourning figures on the left. What seems to be a strikingly realistic study in foreshortening, however, is modified by a reduction in size of the figure's feet, which—as every photographer knows and as Mantegna must have known—would cover the body if properly represented. Thus, tempering naturalism with artistic license, Mantegna presents both a harrowing study of a cadaver strongly foreshortened and an intensely poignant presentation of a cosmic tragedy. The harsh, sharp line seems to cut the surface as if it were metal and conveys, by its grinding edge, the corrosive emotion of the theme; one thinks of Ernest Hemingway's "the bitter nail holes in Mantegna's Christ." For Mantegna's presentation is unrelievedly bitter, an unforgiving reproach to guilty mankind. What is remarkable is that all the science of the fifteenth century here serves the purpose of devotion. A Gothic religious sensitivity of great depth and intensity, still lingering in the northern Italian sunset of the Middle Ages, is embodied in an image created by a new science.

Mantegna's influence was great in northern Italy, especially in the school of Ferrara—but also in Venice, where his style had a strong, formative influence on Giovanni Bellini, who may be regarded as the

progenitor of Venetian painting (see FIGS. 17-56, 17-57, 17-58, 17-59). Mantegna's influence went even further, however, for he was a great engraver (the line in *The Dead Christ* certainly suggests engraving), and his prints found their way across the Alps to influence Albrecht Dürer, father of the Northern Renaissance.

By itself, the influence of Mantegna might have stunted Giovanni Bellini's development, and the arrival in Venice of an artist with a style very different from Mantegna's probably was most opportune for Bellini's artistic growth. ANTONELLO DA MESSINA (*c.* 1430–1479) is an enigmatic figure about whose background little is known. He was born in Sicily (the only major artist of the fifteenth century to be born south of Rome) and received his early training in Naples, where he must have come in close contact with Flemish painting. The Flemish influence in some of his works is so strong that it has long been assumed that Antonello actually spent some time in Flanders, a possibility that now seems unlikely. It has also been speculated that Antonello may have had direct contact with the Flemish artist Petrus Christus in Milan during the mid-1450s—a most intriguing possibility, as the styles of the two artists have many similarities. But the presence of either man in Milan at that time cannot be definitely proved. In any case, Antonello arrived in Venice in 1475, with a full mastery of the mixed-oil technique, and made a strong impression there during his two-year stay.

How greatly Antonello's style differs from Mantegna's can be seen in one of his later works, *The Martyrdom of St. Sebastian* (FIG. 16-67), which has none of Mantegna's brittle, sometimes harsh linearity. The forms are modeled in broad, simplified planes, reminiscent of the style of Piero della Francesca, whose work Antonello must have studied very closely indeed. Also Pierfrancescan are the crisp clarity of the spatial composition, the subdued emotion, and the solemn calm with which the saint suffers his martyrdom. But Antonello goes even beyond Piero in bathing his painting in atmospheric luminosity, and his colors tend to be warm rather than cool, with golden brown tones dominating. Compared to earlier works, the painting has a "juicy" colorism that is due, in good part, to Antonello's use of mixed oil—a medium more flexible and wider in coloristic range than tempera or fresco. Thus, by combining elements of Piero's style with Flemish painting techniques, Antonello fuses monumental qualities with coloristic effects of unrivaled richness. Giovanni Bellini was one of the first to appreciate the value of Antonello's gift to Venice and to abandon Mantegna's "hard" style, which, within a decade of Antonello's visit to Venice, became hopelessly outdated.

16-66 ANDREA MANTEGNA, *The Dead Christ*, c. 1501. Tempera on canvas, approx. 26″ × 31″. Pinacoteca di Brera, Milan.

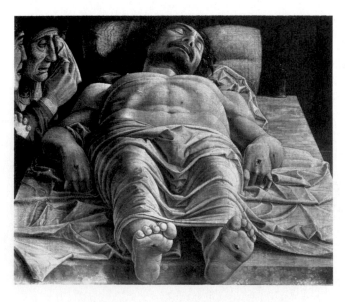

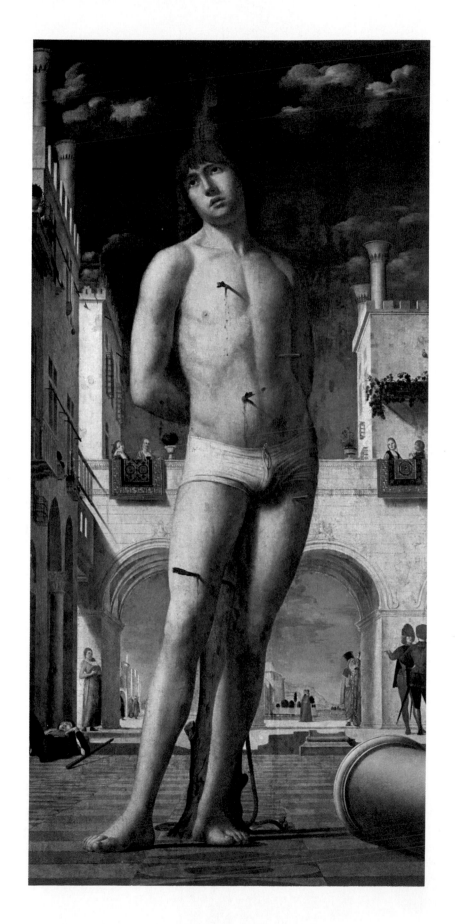

16-67 ANTONELLO DA MESSINA,
The Martyrdom of St. Sebastian,
c. 1475–1477. Oil on wood,
approx. 68″ × 34″. Gemäldegalerie,
Abt. Alte Meister, Staatliche
Kunstsammlungen, Dresden.

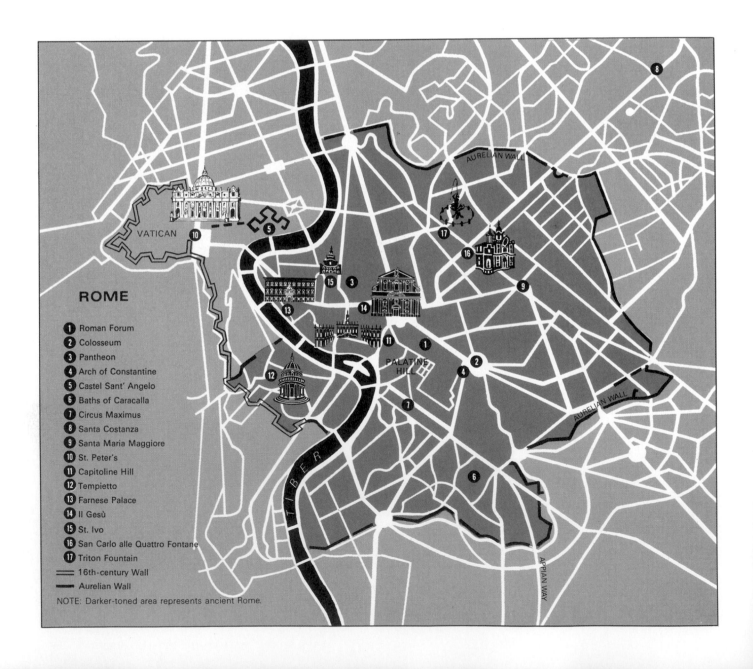

ROME

1. Roman Forum
2. Colosseum
3. Pantheon
4. Arch of Constantine
5. Castel Sant' Angelo
6. Baths of Caracalla
7. Circus Maximus
8. Santa Costanza
9. Santa Maria Maggiore
10. St. Peter's
11. Capitoline Hill
12. Tempietto
13. Farnese Palace
14. Il Gesù
15. St. Ivo
16. San Carlo alle Quattro Fontane
17. Triton Fountain

══ 16th-century Wall
━━ Aurelian Wall

NOTE: Darker-toned area represents ancient Rome.

SIXTEENTH-CENTURY ITALIAN ART

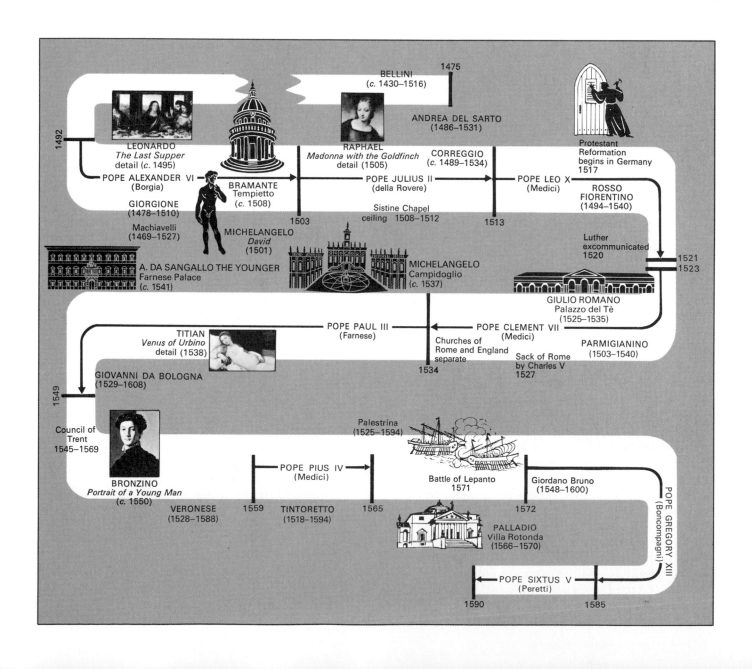

BELLINI (c. 1430–1516)   1475

ANDREA DEL SARTO (1486–1531)

Protestant Reformation begins in Germany 1517

1492

LEONARDO
The Last Supper detail (c. 1495)

RAPHAEL
Madonna with the Goldfinch detail (1505)

CORREGGIO (c. 1489–1534)

POPE ALEXANDER VI (Borgia)

BRAMANTE
Tempietto (c. 1508)

POPE JULIUS II (della Rovere)

POPE LEO X (Medici)

ROSSO FIORENTINO (1494–1540)

GIORGIONE (1478–1510)

Machiavelli (1469–1527)

MICHELANGELO
David (1501)

Sistine Chapel ceiling 1508–1512   1513

1503

Luther excommunicated 1520

1521
1523

A. DA SANGALLO THE YOUNGER
Farnese Palace (c. 1541)

MICHELANGELO
Campidoglio (c. 1537)

GIULIO ROMANO
Palazzo del Tè (1525–1535)

POPE PAUL III (Farnese)

POPE CLEMENT VII (Medici)

PARMIGIANINO (1503–1540)

TITIAN
Venus of Urbino detail (1538)

Churches of Rome and England separate
1534

Sack of Rome by Charles V 1527

GIOVANNI DA BOLOGNA (1529–1608)

1549

Council of Trent 1545–1569

Palestrina (1525–1594)

POPE PIUS IV (Medici)

BRONZINO
Portrait of a Young Man (c. 1550)

Battle of Lepanto 1571

Giordano Bruno (1548–1600)

POPE GREGORY XIII (Boncompagni)

VERONESE (1528–1588)   1559

TINTORETTO (1518–1594)   1565

1572

PALLADIO
Villa Rotonda (1566–1570)

POPE SIXTUS V (Peretti)

1590   1585

BEFORE THE END of the fifteenth century, Florence had lost her unique position of leadership in the arts, and the innovations of her artists had become the property of Italian artists, regardless of local political boundaries. This is not to suggest that Florence no longer produced the artistic giants of an earlier age. Leonardo and Michelangelo called themselves Florentines, even though they spent a great part of their lives outside the city, and the turning point in Raphael's artistic education occurred as a result of his experience of Florentine art. In addition, Florence, with the early work of Leonardo, had already become the source of sixteenth-century style and later shared with Rome the beginnings and growth of Mannerism, a style that was to dominate western Europe during much of the sixteenth century. But Florence was faced with a time of crisis that began with the expulsion of the Medici and the brief and stormy dictatorship of Girolamo Savonarola and ended with the subversion of the Florentine republic by the Spanish and the return of the Medici (a collateral line of the original family) as tyrants under Spanish protection. Finally, in the 1530s, Florentine independence became a thing of the past when the state was made into a grand duchy under the crown of the Hapsburgs.

THE HIGH RENAISSANCE

Between about 1495 and the date of its own invasion and sack in 1527, Rome took the place of Florence and laid claim to its artistic preeminence. A series of powerful and ambitious popes—Alexander VI (Borgia), Julius II (della Rovere), Leo X (Medici), and Clement VII (Medici)—created a new power in Italy: a papal state, with Rome as its capital; and Rome became, at the same time, the artistic capital of Europe. The popes, living in the opulent splendor of secular princes, embellished the city with great works of art, inviting artists from all over Italy and providing them with challenging tasks. In its short duration, this High Renaissance saw works of such authority produced that generations of later artists were instructed by them; the art of Leonardo, Raphael, Michelangelo, and Titian is seen to belong to no school but is, in the case of each, something unique. The masters had of course inherited the pictorial science of the fifteenth century, and they learned from one another. Yet they made a distinct break from the past, occupying new and lofty ground—so lofty as to discourage emulation by their successors.

The High Renaissance not only produced a cluster of extraordinary geniuses, but found in divine inspiration the rationale for the exaltation of the artist–genius. The Neo-Platonists found in Plato's *Ion* his famous praise of the poet: "All good poets compose their beautiful poems not by art, but because they are inspired and possessed. . . . for not by art does the poet sing, but by power divine." And what the poet could claim, the Renaissance artist claimed also, raising visual art to the status formerly held only by poetry. Thus, at the threshold of the modern world, the painter, sculptor, or architect comes into his own, successfully claiming for his work a high place among the fine arts. In the High Renaissance, the masters in a sense created a new profession, having its own rights of expression, its own venerable character, and its own claims to recognition by the great. The "fine" artist today lives—often without realizing it—on the accumulated prestige won by preceding artists, beginning with those who made the first great gains of the High Renaissance.

Leonardo da Vinci

A man who is the epitome of the artist–genius as well as of the "universal man," LEONARDO DA VINCI (1452–1519) has become a kind of wonder of the modern world, standing at the beginning of a new epoch like a prophet and a sage, mapping the routes that art and science would take. The scope and depth of his interests were without precedent, so great as to frustrate any hopes he might have had of realizing all that his feverishly inventive imagination could conceive. We still look with awe on his achievements and, even more, on his unfulfilled promise. His mind and personality seem to us superhuman; the man himself, mysterious and remote. Jacob Burckhardt writes: "The colossal outlines of Leonardo's nature can never be more than dimly and distantly conceived." Although we are here concerned primarily with Leonardo as an artist, we can scarcely hope to do his art credit in isolation from his science; his scientific drawings are themselves works of art, as well as models for that exact delineation of nature that is one of the aims of science. Leonardo's unquenchable curiosity is best revealed in his voluminous notes, liberally interspersed with sketches dealing with matters of botany, geology, zoology, hydraulics, military engineering, animal lore, anatomy, and aspects of physical science, including mechanics, perspective, light, optics, and color. Leonardo's great ambition in his painting, as well as in his scientific endeavors, was to discover the laws underlying the flux and processes of nature. With this end in mind, he also studied the human body and contributed immeasurably to our knowledge of physiology and psychology. Leonardo believed that reality in an absolute sense is inaccessible and that we can know it only through its changing images. Thus, he considered the eyes to be the most vital organs and sight the most essential function, as, through these, the images of reality could be grasped most directly and profoundly. Hence, one may understand Leonardo's insistence, stated many times in his notes, that all his scientific investigations were merely aimed at making himself a better painter.

Leonardo was born near Florence and was trained in the studio of Andrea del Verrocchio. But he left Florence around 1481, offering his services to Ludovico Sforza, Duke of Milan. The political situation in Florence was uncertain, and the Neo-Platonism of Lorenzo de' Medici and his brilliant circle may have proved uncongenial to the empirical and pragmatic Leonardo. It may also be that Leonardo felt that the artistic scene in Milan would be less competitive. He devoted most of a letter to the Duke of Milan to advertising his competence and his qualifications as a military engineer, mentioning only at the end his supremacy as a painter and sculptor:

> And in short, according to the variety of cases, I can contrive various and endless means of offence and defence . . . . In time of peace I believe I can give perfect satisfaction and to the equal of any other in architecture and the composition of buildings, public and private; and in guiding water from one place to another . . . . I can carry out sculpture in marble, bronze, or clay, and also I can do in painting whatever may be done, as well as any other, be he whom he may.*

The letter illustrates the new relation of the artist to his patron, as well as Leonardo's breadth of competence. That he should select military engineering and design to interest a patron is an index, in addition, of the dangerousness of the times. Weaponry had now been developed to the point, especially in northern Europe, that the siege cannon was a threat to the feudal castles of those attempting to resist the wealthy and aggressive new monarchs. When, in 1494, Charles VIII of France invaded Italy, his cannon easily smashed the fortifications of the Italian princes. By the turn of the century, when Italy's liberties and unity were being trampled by the aspiring kingdoms of Europe, not only soldiers and architects, but artists and Humanists, were deeply concerned with the problem of designing a system of fortifications that might withstand the terrible new weapon.

During his first sojourn in Milan, Leonardo painted *The Virgin of the Rocks* (FIG. 17-1)—a group that, although it may derive ultimately from Fra Filippo Lippi, is well on its way out of the older tradition. The old triangular composition now broadens out into three dimensions, making a weighty pyramid. The linear approach, with its musical play of undulating contours and crisp edges, is abandoned, as Leonardo

*In E.G. Holt, ed., *Literary Sources of Art History* (Princeton, N.J.: Princeton University Press, 1947), p. 170.

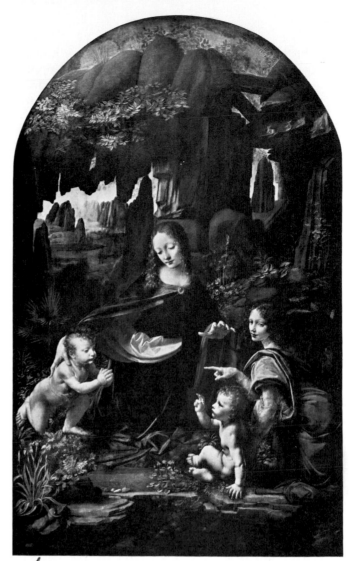

17√ LEONARDO DA VINCI, *The Virgin of the Rocks*, c. 1485. Oil on wood, approx. 6' 3" × 3' 7". Louvre, Paris.

returns through the generations of the fifteenth century to Masaccio's great discovery of *chiaroscuro*, the subtle play of light and dark. What we see is the result of the moving together and interpenetration of lights and darks. "Drawn" representations, consisting of contours and edges, can be beautiful, but they are really not true to the optical facts. Moreover, a painting must embody not only physical chiaroscuro but the lights and darks of human psychology as well. Modeling with light and shadow and the expression of emotional states were, for Leonardo, the heart of painting:

> A good painter has two chief objects to paint—man and the intention of his soul. The former is easy, the latter hard, for it must be expressed by gestures and the movement of the limbs. . . . A painting will only be wonderful for the beholder by making that which is not so appear raised and detached from the wall.*

*In Anthony Blunt, *Artistic Theory in Italy, 1450–1600* (London: Oxford University Press, 1964), p. 34.

The figures in *The Virgin of the Rocks* are knit together not only as a pyramidal group but as figures sharing the same atmosphere—a method of unification first seen in Masaccio's *The Tribute Money* (FIG. 16-26). The Madonna, Christ Child, infant John the Baptist, and angel emerge through subtle gradations and nuances of light and shade from the half-light of the cavernous, visionary landscape. Light simultaneously veils and reveals the forms of things, immersing them in a layer of atmosphere between them and our eyes. The ambiguity of light and shade (familiar in the optical uncertainties of dusk) is in the service of the psychological ambiguity of perception. The group depicted, so strangely wrapped in subtle light and shade, eludes our precise definition and interpretation. The figures pray, point, and bless, and these acts and gestures, although their meanings are not certain, visually unite the figures. The angel points to the infant John, who is blessed by the Christ Child and sheltered by the Virgin's loving hand. The melting mood of tenderness, enhanced by the caressing light, is compounded of yet other moods. What the eye sees is fugitive, as are the states of the soul, or, in Leonardo's term, its "intentions."

The style of the High Renaissance fully emerges in a *cartoon* (a full-size drawing) for a painting of *The*

17-2 LEONARDO DA VINCI, cartoon for *The Virgin and Child with St. Anne and the Infant St. John,* 1498 (?). Charcoal heightened with white on brown paper, approx. 54″ × 39″. Reproduced by courtesy of the Trustees of the National Gallery, London.

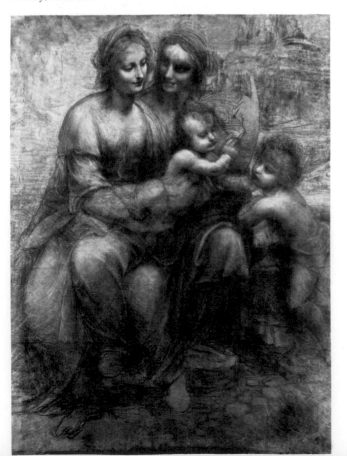

Virgin and Child with St. Anne and the Infant St. John (FIG. 17-2). The glowing light falls gently on the majestic forms and on a tranquil grandeur, order, and balance. The figures are robust and monumental, moving with a stately grace reminiscent of the Phidian sculptures of the Parthenon. Every part is ordered by an intellectual, pictorial logic into a sure unity. The specialized depiction of perspective, anatomy, light, and space is a thing of the past; Leonardo has assimilated the learning of two centuries and applies it wholly, in a manner that is Classical and complete. This High Renaissance style, as Leonardo here authoritatively shows it, is stable without being static, varied without being confused, and dignified without being dull. As in the similar case in Greece, this brief, Classical moment inaugurated by Leonardo unifies and balances the conflicting experiences of an entire culture. This style will prove difficult to maintain. In a rapidly changing world, the artist may either repeat the compositions and forms of the day in a sterile, academic manner or revolt against the time by denying or exaggerating its principles. For these reasons, the High Renaissance was of short duration— even shorter than the brief span of the Golden Age of Athens in the fifth century B.C.

For the refectory of the church of Santa Maria delle Grazie in Milan, Leonardo painted *The Last Supper* (FIG. 17-3). Despite its ruined state (in part the result of the painter's own unfortunate experiments with his materials) and although it has often been ineptly restored, the painting is both formally and emotionally his most impressive work.* It is the first great figure composition of the High Renaissance, and the definitive interpretation of its theme. Christ and the Twelve Disciples are seated in a simple, spacious room, at a long table set parallel to the picture plane. The highly dramatic action of the painting is made still more emphatic by the placement of the group in the austerely quiet setting. Christ, with outstretched hands, has just said, "One of you will betray me." A wave of intense excitement passes through the group, as each disciple asks himself and, in some cases, his neighbor, "Is it I?" Leonardo has made a

*Since 1977, the painting has been undergoing painstaking, scientifically controlled restoration (a square inch at a time!). Although much of it is permanently lost, enough has already been recovered and repaired to reveal Leonardo's actual intentions and performance. The restored portions (at this writing, the group of three disciples at the far right)—freed from 500 years dark accumulation of dirt, mold, glue, and overpainting—reveal bright and strong colors and firm and elegant contours. Restoration also shows that Leonardo's style is firmly rooted in the practice of fifteenth-century Italian painting. Beneath the many mistaken overpaintings, the true characters of the disciples emerge from the blurred, murky, out-of-focus forms of the damaged picture. They are vividly realized individuals, of the kind we find in Leonardo's preserved preparatory drawings, who—through attitudes, gestures, personal traits, and facial expressions—compellingly play the roles Leonardo designed for them, consistent with his own highly personal conception of this drama and its protagonists.

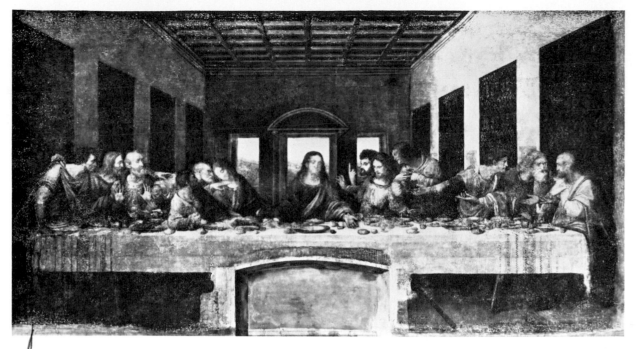

17-3 LEONARDO DA VINCI, *The Last Supper*, c. 1495–1498. Fresco. Santa Maria delle Grazie, Milan.

brilliant conjunction of the dramatic "One of you will betray me" with the initiation of the ancient liturgical ceremony of the Eucharist, when Christ, blessing bread and wine, said "This is my body and this is my blood: do this in remembrance of me." The force and lucidity with which this dramatic moment is expressed are due to the abstract organization of the composition. In the center, Christ is in perfect repose, the still eye of the swirling emotion around him. Isolated from the disciples, his figure is framed by the central window at the back, the curved pediment of which (the only curve in the architectural framework, here serving as a halo) arches above his head, which is the focal point of all perspective lines in the composition. Thus, the still, psychological focus and cause of the action is, at the same time, the perspective focus as well as the dead center of the two-dimensional surface. (One could say that the two-dimensional, the three-dimensional, and the psychodimensional focuses are one and the same.) The agitated disciples, registering a whole range of rationally ordered, idealized, and proportionate responses, embracing fear, doubt, protestation, rage, and love, are represented in four groups of three, united among and within themselves by the gestures and postures of the figures. Leonardo sacrifices traditional iconography to pictorial and dramatic consistency by placing Judas on the same side of the table as Jesus and the other disciples. His face in shadow, Judas clutches a money bag in his right hand and reaches his left forward to fulfill the Master's declaration: "Behold, the hand of him that betrayeth me is with me on the table." The two disciples at either end of the table are more quiet than the others, as if to enclose the overall movement, which is more intense

closer to the figure of Christ, whose calm at the same time halts and intensifies it. We know from numerous preparatory studies that Leonardo thought of each figure as carrying a particular charge and type of emotion. Like a skilled stage director (perhaps the first, in the modern sense), he has carefully read the gospel story and scrupulously cast his actors as their roles are described. With him begins that rhetoric of Classical art that will direct the compositions of generations of painters until the nineteenth century. The silence of Christ is one such powerful rhetorical device. Indeed, Heinrich Wölfflin saw that the Classical element is precisely here, for in the silence following Christ's words, "the original impulse and the emotional excitement continue to echo and the action is at once momentary, eternal and complete."* The two major trends of fifteenth-century painting—monumentality and mathematically ordered space at the expense of movement, and freedom of movement at the expense of monumentality and controlled space—are here harmonized and balanced. *The Last Supper* and Leonardo's career leading up to it are at once a synthesis of the artistic developments of the fifteenth century and a first statement of the High Renaissance style of the early sixteenth in Italy.

If Leonardo's *Last Supper* is the world's most famous religious picture, the *Mona Lisa* (FIG. 17-4) is probably the world's most famous portrait. Since the nineteenth century and perhaps earlier, the enigmatic face has been a part of Western folklore. Painted after Leonardo returned from Milan to Florence, the lady, thought by many to be La Gioconda,

*Heinrich Wölfflin, *Classic Art,* 2nd ed. (London: Phaidon, 1953), p. 27.

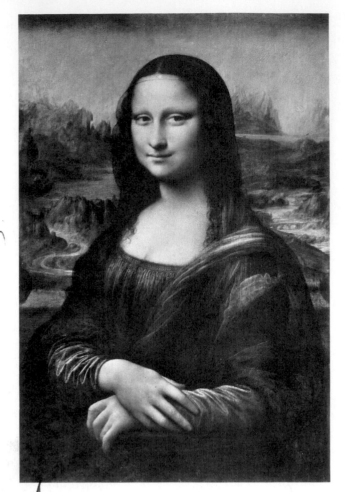

17-4 LEONARDO DA VINCI, *Mona Lisa*, *c*. 1503–1505. Oil on wood, approx. 30″ × 21″. Louvre, Paris.

latter exceptionally beautiful. It may well have been the artist's intention to confuse observers or enchant them by allowing them to interpret the secret personality as they pleased.

Leonardo completed very few paintings; his perfectionism, restless experimentalism, and far-ranging curiosity scattered his efforts. Yet an extensive record of his ideas is preserved in the drawings in his notebooks, one of which was discovered in Madrid, Spain, in the 1960s. Science interested him increasingly in his later years, and he took knowledge of all nature (given first to the eye) as his proper province. His investigations in anatomy yielded drawings of great precision and beauty of execution; an example is the *Embryo in the Womb* (FIG. 17-5), which, despite some inaccuracies, is so true to fact that it could be used in medical instruction today. Although Leonardo may not have been the first scientist of the modern world (at least not in the modern sense of "scientist"), he certainly originated the method of scientific illustration, especially cutaway and exploded views. The importance of this has been stressed by Erwin Panofsky: ". . . anatomy as a science (and this applies to all the other observational or descriptive disciplines) was simply not possible without a method of preserving observations in graphic records, complete and accurate in three dimensions."*

Leonardo was well known in his own time as both sculptor and architect, though no sculpture that is certainly by him has survived and no actual buildings can be attributed to him. From his many drawings of central-plan buildings, it appears that he shared the interest of other Renaissance architects in this building type. In Milan, Leonardo must have been in close contact with the architect Bramante, who may well have remembered a drawing by Leonardo when he prepared his original designs for the great church of St. Peter's in Rome (FIG. 17-7).

As for sculpture, Leonardo left numerous drawings of monumental equestrian statues, one of which ripened into a full-scale model for a monument to the Sforza; used as a target, it was shot to pieces by the French when they occupied Milan in 1499. Leonardo left Milan outraged at this treatment of his work and worked for a while as military engineer for Cesare Borgia, who, with the support of his father, Pope Alexander VI, tried to conquer the cities of the Romagna and create a Borgia duchy. At a later date, Leonardo returned to Milan in the service of the French. At the invitation of the king, Francis I, he then went to France, where he died at the château of Cloux in 1519, without leaving any impression on French contemporary art.

*Erwin Panofsky, "Artist, Scientist, Genius," in *The Renaissance,* ed., Wallace K. Ferguson (New York: Harper & Row, 1962), p. 147.

wife of the banker Zanobi del Giocondo, was originally represented in a loggia with columns that have been cut from the painting. She is shown in half-length view, her hands quietly folded and her gaze directed at the observer. The ambiguity of the famous "smile" is really the consequence of Leonardo's fascination and skill with atmospheric chiaroscuro, which we have seen in his *Virgin of the Rocks* and *Virgin and St. Anne* groups and which here serve to disguise rather than reveal a human psyche. The light is adjusted subtly enough, but the precise planes are blurred (a useful comparison can be made between the *Mona Lisa* and the portraits by Domenico Ghirlandaio and Sandro Botticelli we saw in Chapter 16) and the facial expression is hard to determine. The romantic nineteenth century made perhaps too much of the enigma of the "smile," without appreciating Leonardo's quite scientific concern with the nature of light and shadow. On the other hand, Leonardo himself must have enjoyed the curious effect he achieved here; it was one of his favorite pictures, one with which he could not bear to part. The superb drawing present beneath the fleeting shadow is a triumph in its rendering of both the head and the hands, the

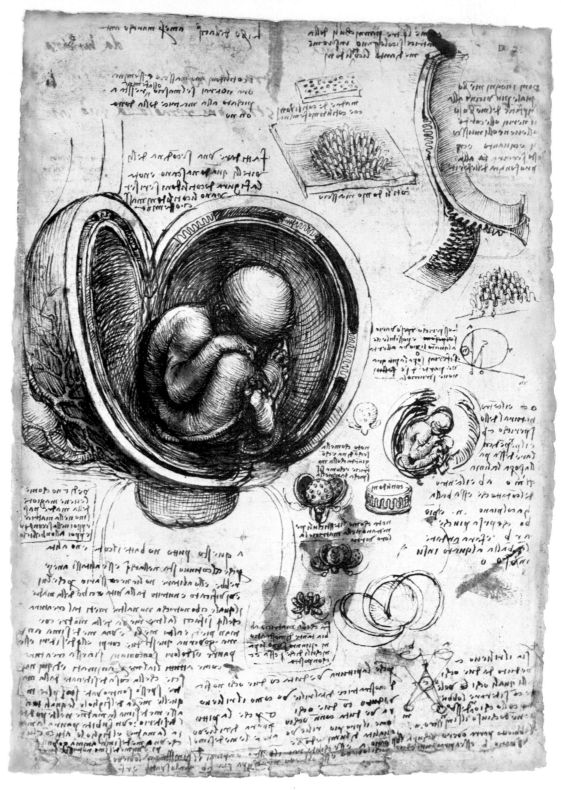

17-5 LEONARDO DA VINCI, *Embryo in the Womb, c.* 1510. Pen and ink. Royal Collection, Windsor Castle. Copyright reserved. Reproduced by Gracious Permission of Her Majesty the Queen.

Bramante and His Circle

The most important artist with whom Leonardo came into contact in Milan was BRAMANTE (Donato d' Angelo, 1444–1514). Born in Urbino and trained as a painter (perhaps by Piero della Francesca), Bramante went to Milan in 1481 and, like Leonardo, stayed there until the arrival of the French in 1499. In Milan, he abandoned painting to become the greatest archi-

tect of his generation. Under the influence of Filippo Brunelleschi, Leon Battista Alberti, and perhaps Leonardo, all of whom had been strongly influenced by the Classical antique, Bramante developed the High Renaissance form of the central-plan church. But it was not until after his arrival in Rome in 1499 that Bramante built what was to be the perfect prototype of Classical, domed architecture for the Renaissance and subsequent periods—the Tempietto (FIG. 17-6),

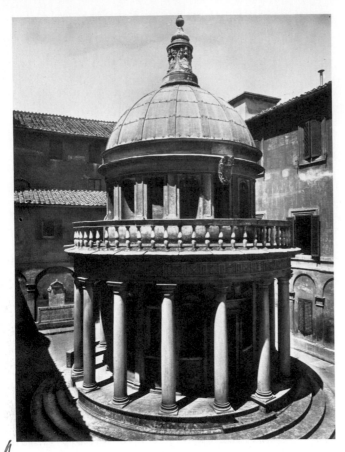

17-6 BRAMANTE, the Tempietto, 1508 (view from the northwest). San Pietro in Montorio, Rome.

so called because it has the aspect of a small pagan temple from antiquity. This building, recently redated to 1508, was to mark the supposed spot of St. Peter's crucifixion and indeed gives the appearance of a solid sculptural reliquary. In fact, it was originally

17-7 BRAMANTE, plan for the new St. Peter's, Rome, 1505.

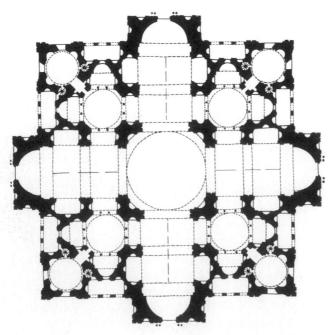

planned to stand, somewhat like a reliquary, in the center of a colonnaded, circular court. All but devoid of ornament, the building relies for its effect on the sculptural treatment of the exterior, which creates a sense of volume in movement (as does High Renaissance sculpture and painting). At first glance, the Tempietto seems unnecessarily formalistic and rational, with its distinct, cool Tuscan order and abstract plan repeated in the colonnade and in the steps of the stylobate. However, Bramante achieves a wonderful harmony among the parts—the dome, drum, and base—and the whole. The balustrade accents, in shorter beats, the rhythms of the colonnade and averts a too-rapid ascent to the drum; the pilasters on the drum itself repeat the ascending motif and lead the eye past the cornice to the ribs of the dome. The strictly regulated play of light and shade around the columns and balustrade and in the alternation of deep-set rectangular windows with shallow, shell-capped niches enhances the experience of the building as an articulated, sculptural mass—a domed cylinder within the wider cylinder of the colonnade.

The significance of the Tempietto was well understood in the sixteenth century. The architect Andrea Palladio, an artistic descendant of Bramante, put it among his survey of ancient temples because "Bramante was the first who brought good and beautiful architecture to light, which from the time of the ancients to his day had been forgotten . . . ." Round in plan, elevated on a base that isolates it from its surroundings, the Tempietto conforms with Alberti's and Palladio's strictest demands for an ideal church, demonstrating "the unity, the infinite essence, the uniformity, and the justice of God."

The same architectural concept guided Bramante's plans for the new St. Peter's, commissioned by Pope Julius II in 1505 to replace the Constantinian basilica, Old St. Peter's (FIG. 7-6). This structure had fallen into considerable disrepair and, in any event, did not suit the taste for the colossal of that ambitious and warlike pope, who wanted to gain sway over the whole of Italy and to make the Rome of the popes more splendid than the Rome of the caesars. As originally designed by Bramante, the new St. Peter's (FIG. 17-7) was to have consisted of a cross with arms of equal length, each terminated by an apse. It was intended as a martyrium to mark St. Peter's grave; Julius also hoped to have his own tomb in it. The crossing would have been covered by a large dome, and smaller domes over subsidiary chapels would have covered the diagonal axes of the roughly square plan. Bramante's ambitious plan called for a boldly sculptural treatment of the walls and piers under the dome. The interior space is complex in the extreme, with the intricate symmetries of a crystal; it is possible to detect in the plan some nine interlocking crosses, five

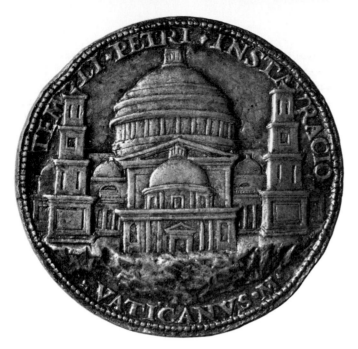

17-8 CHRISTOFORO FOPPA CARADOSSO, medal showing Bramante's design for the new St. Peter's, 1506. British Museum, London.

domed. The scale was titanic; Bramante is said to have boasted that he would place the dome of the Pantheon over the Basilica of Constantine. A commemorative medal (FIG. 17-8) by CHRISTOFORO FOPPA CARADOSSO (1452–1527) shows how Bramante's scheme would have attempted to do just that. The dome is hemispherical, like the Pantheon's, but otherwise the exterior, with two towers and a medley of domes and porticoes, breaks the massive unity, resulting in a still essentially anthropometric design scaled down to human proportions in the Early Renaissance manner. During Bramante's lifetime, the actual construction did not advance beyond the building of the piers of the crossing and the lower walls of the choir. With his death, the work passed from one architect to another and finally to Michelangelo, who was appointed by Pope Paul III in 1546 to complete the building.

After Bramante's Tempietto, the closest realization of the High Renaissance Classical ideals—order, clarity, lucidity, simplicity, harmony, and proportion—is found in the pilgrimage church of Santa Maria della Consolazione at Todi, begun in 1508 (FIGS. 17-9 and 17-10). Its elevated hillside site outside the town makes it visible from far away, and its sturdy, carefully proportioned silhouette offers an attractive goal for the faithful approaching through the valley below. Although the identity of its designer is uncertain, it is quite clearly in the manner of Bramante, and we can call it "Bramantesque." In its plan, the church takes the form of a domed cross, with its lobe-like arms ending in polygonal apses. The interior space, showing a Classical purity of arrangement in which the layout is immediately open to the eye and vol-

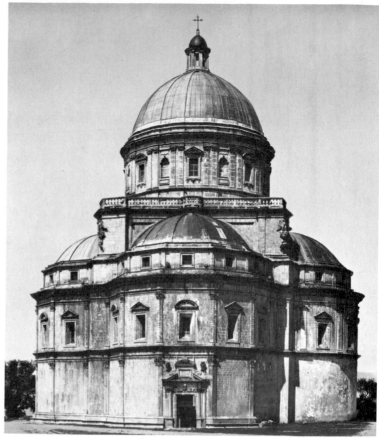

17-9 Santa Maria della Consolazione, Todi, Italy, begun 1508 (view from the south).

umes and spaces are in exquisite adjustment, finds its exact expression on the exterior. Here, each level is carefully marked off by projecting cornices, and there is a steady increase in rhythm from bottom to top. The unfenestrated first story, marked off into blank

17-10 Interior view into the main dome and one of the half-domes, Santa Maria della Consolazione.

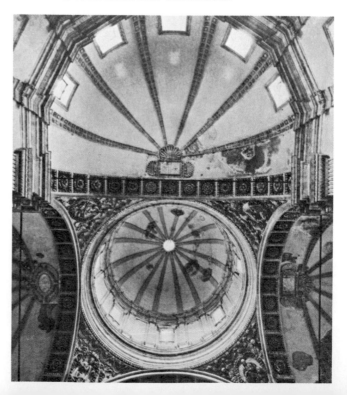

panels by pilasters, provides a firm base for the upper structure; the second story is fenestrated, the windows topped by alternating triangular and segmental pediments. The attic story makes a transition to the half-domes, and the half-domes to the balustraded platform that sets off drum and dome as it makes a transition to them. The rhythm of fenestration of the second floor reappears in the drum, where it is quickened by the interpolation of round-headed niches between the windows, like the appearance of a second voice in a fugue. No matter from which side it is seen, the building presents a completely balanced and symmetrical aspect. Like a three-dimensional essay in rational order, all of its parts are in harmonious relation to each other and to the whole, yet each is complete and independent. To appreciate the wide difference between the Medieval and the High Renaissance views of the nature of architecture, one need only recall the design of a typically Gothic building. In both scale and complexity, Santa Maria della Consolazione stands between the Tempietto and the design for the new St. Peter's. More amply than the former, with greater purity than the latter, it expresses the architectural ideals of the High Renaissance. Its spirit is that of Classical antiquity and, though it is modern, it speaks only the Classical language.

17-11 BRAMANTE, Palazzo Caprini (House of Raphael), Rome. (Drawing attributed to ANDREA PALLADIO.)

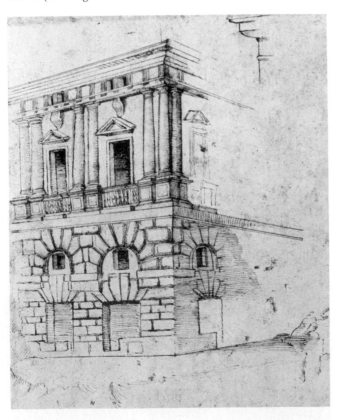

The palaces designed by Bramante have been preserved only in drawings or engravings. His Palazzo Caprini (FIG. 17-11), bought by Raphael in 1517, was torn down during the rebuilding of the area around St. Peter's. Still, it was one of the most important and influential palace designs of the sixteenth century. In it, Bramante reduced the typical three-story façade of the fifteenth century to two stories, with the strongly rusticated first story serving as a robust support for the elegantly articulated *piano nobile*. This arrangement not only differentiates the two stories, but emphatically puts the residential level of the building above the commercial. (The ground floor was occupied by shops and offices.) The pedimented windows of the second story are flanked by pairs of engaged Tuscan columns supporting an entablature in which the frieze is pierced by the windows of an attic story. The total aspect of the building is of rugged plasticity, and its effect on contemporary and later architects, including Palladio and Inigo Jones, was lasting. With Baroque modifications, Bramante's scheme can be recognized in Claude Perrault's Louvre façade (FIG. 19-65), erected almost two centuries later.

Less plastic, perhaps, than Bramante's design, but equally imposing, is the Farnese Palace in Rome (FIGS. 17-12, 17-13, 17-14), designed by ANTONIO DA SANGALLO THE YOUNGER (1483–1546), which fully expresses the Classical order, regularity, simplicity, and dignity of the High Renaissance. Antonio, the youngest of a family of architects, received his early training from his uncles Giuliano, the designer of Santa Maria delle Carceri in Prato (FIGS. 16-45, 16-46, 16-47), and Antonio the Elder. Antonio the Younger went to Rome around 1503 and became Bramante's draftsman and assistant. As Paul III's favorite architect, he received many commissions that might have gone to Michelangelo. He is the perfect example of the professional architect, and his family constituted an architectural firm, often working up the plans and doing the drafting for other architects. Essentially a developer, Antonio has frequently been criticized as unimaginative; but if this is so, it is only by comparison with Michelangelo. He built fortifications for almost the entire papal state and received more commissions for military than for civilian architecture. Although he may not have invented it, Antonio certainly developed the modern method of bastioned fortifications to a high degree and, in this, demonstrated his ingenuity and originality.

The Farnese Palace, built for Cardinal Farnese, (later Pope Paul III), sets a standard for the High Renaissance palazzo. The sixteenth century saw the beginning of the age of the great dynasties that would dominate Europe until the French Revolution. It was an age of royal and princely pomp, of absolute monarchy rendered splendid by art. The broad, majestic

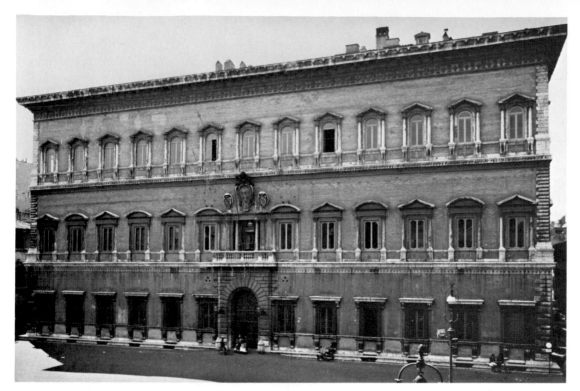

17-12 ANTONIO DA SANGALLO THE YOUNGER, Farnese Palace, Rome, c. 1530–1546 (view from the northeast).

front of the Farnese Palace asserts to the public the exalted station of a great family. This proud frontispiece symbolizes the aristocratic epoch that followed the stifling of the nascent, middle-class democracy of the European—especially the Italian—cities by powerful kings heading centralized states. It is thus significant that the original, rather modest palace was greatly enlarged to its present form after Paul's accession to the papacy in 1534, reflecting the ambitions of the pope both for his family and the papacy. Unfinished at the time of Antonio's death in 1546, the building was completed by Michelangelo.

The façade (FIG. 17-12) is the very essence of princely dignity in architecture. Facing a spacious paved square, the rectangle of the smooth front is framed and firmly anchored by the *quoins* (rusticated building corners) and cornice, while lines of windows (with alternating triangular and segmental pediments, in Bramante's fashion) mark a majestic beat across it. The window casements are no longer flush with the wall, as in the Palazzo Medici–Riccardi (FIG.

17-14 ANTONIO DA SANGALLO THE YOUNGER, courtyard of the Farnese Palace. Third story and attic by MICHELANGELO in 1548.

17-13 ANTONIO DA SANGALLO THE YOUNGER, plan of the Farnese Palace, Rome.

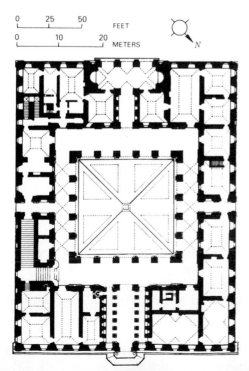

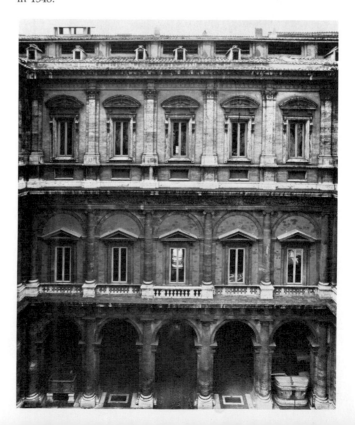

16-23), but project from its surface, so that instead of being a flat, thin plane, the façade becomes a spatially active, three-dimensional mass. Each casement is a complete architectural unit, consisting of a *socle* (a projecting under-member), engaged columns, entablature, and pediment. The variations in the treatment of these units prevent the symmetrical scheme from becoming rigid or monotonous. The rusticated doorway and second-story balcony, surmounted by the Farnese coat of arms, emphasize the central axis and bring the horizontal and vertical forces of the design into harmony. This centralizing feature, not present in the palaces of Alberti or Michelozzo di Bartolomeo, is the external opening of a central-corridor axis that runs through the whole building and continues in the garden beyond; around this axis, the rooms are disposed with strict regularity. The interior courtyard displays stately Colosseum arch-orders on Antonio's first two levels and, on the third, Michelangelo's sophisticated variation on that theme, with overlapping pilasters replacing the weighty columns of Antonio's design.

Raphael

The artist most typical of the High Renaissance is RAPHAEL (Raffaello Santi, 1483–1520). The pattern of his growth recapitulates the sequence of tendencies of the fifteenth century, and although strongly influenced by Leonardo and Michelangelo, Raphael developed an individual style that, in itself, clearly states the ideals of High Renaissance art. His powerful originality prevailed while he learned from everyone; he assimilated what he could best use, and rendered into form the Classical instinct of his age. He worked so effortlessly in the Classical mood that his art is almost the resurrection of Greek art at its height. Goethe, the renowned German poet and critic, said of Raphael that he did not have to imitate the Greeks, for he thought and felt like them. Born in a small town in Umbria near Urbino, Raphael probably learned the rudiments of his art from his father, GIOVANNI SANTI, a provincial painter connected with the court of Federigo da Montefeltro. While still a child, Raphael was apprenticed to Perugino, who had been trained in Verrocchio's shop with Leonardo. We have seen in Perugino's *Christ Delivering the Keys of the Kingdom to St. Peter* (FIG. 16-62) that the most significant formal quality of his work is the harmony of its spatial composition. While Raphael was still in the studio of Perugino, the latter painted a panel of *The Marriage of the Virgin* (not shown), which, in its composition, very closely resembles the central portion of his Sistine Chapel fresco (FIG. 16-62). Perugino's panel, now in the Museum of Caen, probably served as the model for Raphael's *Marriage of the Virgin* (FIG.

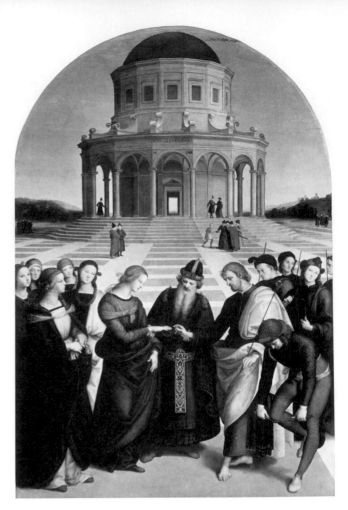

17-15 RAPHAEL, *The Marriage of the Virgin*, 1504. Oil on wood, 67″ × 46½″. Pinacoteca di Brera, Milan.

17-15). Although scarcely 21, Raphael was able to recognize and to remedy some of the weaknesses of his master's composition. By relaxing the formality of Perugino's foreground figure screen and disposing his actors in greater depth, he not only provides them with greater freedom of action but also bridges the gap between them and the background building more successfully. The result is a painting that, although it resembles its model very closely, is nevertheless more fluid and better unified.

Four years in Florence, from 1504 to 1508, were greatly stimulating for Raphael. Here, in the home of the Renaissance, he discovered that the style of painting he had so painstakingly learned from Perugino was already outmoded. The two archrivals Leonardo and Michelangelo were engaged in an artistic battle. Crowds flocked to Santissima Annunziata to see the recently unveiled cartoon for Leonardo's *Virgin and Child with St. Anne and the Infant St. John* (FIG. 17-2), the original version of which was done about 1498. Michelangelo responded with the *Doni Madonna*. Both artists were commissioned to decorate the council hall in the Palazzo Vecchio with pictures memorializing Florentine victories of the past. Although only Leonardo completed his task and although only some small preparatory sketches and some small copies survive, the effect on artists in Florence—especially on one as gifted as Raphael—must have been considerable.

Under the influence of Leonardo, Raphael began to modify the Madonna compositions he had learned in Umbria. In the *Madonna with the Goldfinch (Madonna del Cardellino)* of 1506 (FIG. 17-16), Raphael uses the pyramidal composition of Leonardo's *Virgin of the Rocks* (FIG. 17-1). The faces and figures are modeled in subtle chiaroscuro, and Raphael's general application of this technique is based on Leonardo's cartoon for *The Virgin and Child with St. Anne and the Infant St. John* (FIG. 17-2). At the same time, the large, substantial figures are placed in a Peruginesque landscape, with the older artist's typical feathery trees in the middle ground. Although Raphael experimented with Leonardo's dusky modeling, he tended to return to Perugino's lighter tonalities. Raphael preferred clarity to obscurity, not being, as Leonardo was, fascinated with mystery. His great series of Madonnas, of which this is an early member, unify Christian devotion and pagan beauty; no artist has ever rivaled Raphael in his definitive rendering of this sublime theme of grace and dignity, sweetness and lofty idealism.

Had Raphael painted nothing but his Madonnas, his fame would still be secure. But he was also a great

17-16 RAPHAEL, *Madonna with the Goldfinch (Madonna del Cardellino)*, 1505–1506. Oil on wood, 42″ × 29½″. Galleria degli Uffizi, Florence.

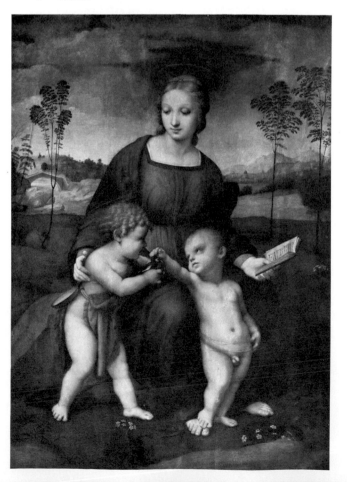

muralist, a master in the grand style begun by Giotto and carried on by Masaccio and the artists of the fifteenth century. In 1508, Raphael was called to Rome to the court of Pope Julius II, perhaps on the recommendation of his fellow townsman, Bramante. There, in competition with older artists like Perugino and Luca Signorelli, Raphael received one of the largest commissions of the time: the decoration of the papal apartments in the Vatican. Of the several rooms (*stanze*) of the suite, Raphael painted the first, the Stanza della Segnatura; the others were done mostly by his pupils, after his sketches. On the four walls of the Stanza della Segnatura, under the headings of Theology, Law, Poetry, and Philosophy, Raphael deploys a host of magnificent figures that symbolize and sum up the learning of the West as understood in the Renaissance. His intention was to indicate the four branches of human knowledge and wisdom, while pointing out the virtues and the learning appropriate to a pope. The iconographic scheme is most complex, and it is likely that Raphael received advice from the brilliant company of Classical scholars surrounding Julius. On one wall, Raphael presents a composition that, of itself, constitutes a complete statement of the High Renaissance in its artistic form and spiritual meaning—the so-called *School of Athens* (FIG. 17-17). The setting is not a "school" but rather a concourse of the great philosophers and scientists of the ancient world, who—rediscovered by the Renaissance—hold a convention, where they teach one another once more and inspire a new age. In a vast hall covered by massive vaults that recall Roman architecture and predict the look of the new St. Peter's, the figures are ingeniously arranged around the central pair, Plato and Aristotle. On Plato's side are the ancient philosophers, concerned with the ultimate mysteries that transcend this world; on Aristotle's side are the philosophers and scientists, concerned with nature and the affairs of men. The groups move easily and clearly, with eloquent poses and gestures that symbolize their doctrines and are of the greatest variety. Their self-assurance and natural dignity bespeak the very nature of calm reason, that balance and measure so much admired by Renaissance men as the heart of philosophy. At the lower left, Pythagoras writes as a servant holds up the harmonic scale. In the foreground, Heraclitus (probably a portrait of Michelangelo) broods alone. Diogenes sprawls on the steps. At the right, students surround Euclid, who demonstrates a theorem. This group is especially interesting; Euclid may be a portrait of the aged Bramante. At the extreme right, Raphael includes his own portrait.

Significantly, this great Renaissance artist places himself among the mathematicians and scientists, and certainly the evolution of pictorial science comes

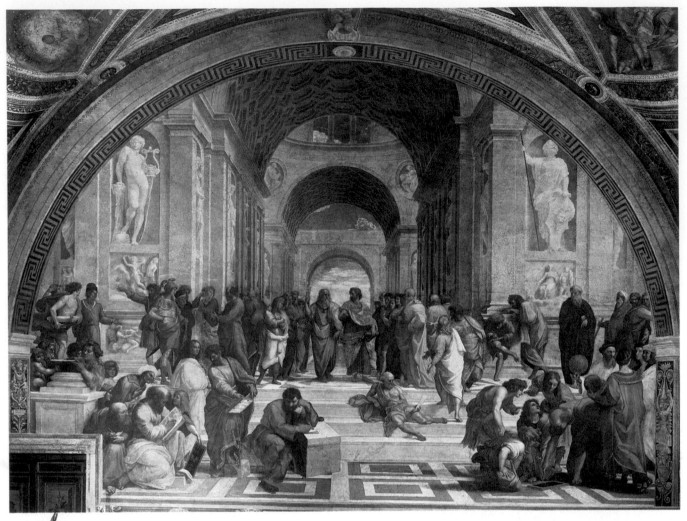

17-17 RAPHAEL, *The School of Athens*, 1509–1511. Fresco. Stanza della Segnatura, Vatican Palace, Rome.

to its perfection in *The School of Athens*. A vast perspective space has been created, in which human figures move naturally, without effort—each according to his own intention, as Leonardo might say. The stage setting, so long in preparation, is complete; the Western artist knows now how to produce the drama of man. That this stage-like space is projected onto a two-dimensional surface is the consequence of the union of mathematics with pictorial science, which yields the art of perspective, here mastered completely. The artist's psychological insight has matured along with his mastery of the problems of physical representation. Each character in Raphael's *School of Athens*, like those in Leonardo's *Last Supper* (FIG. 17-3), is intended to communicate a mood that reflects his beliefs, and each group is unified by the sharing of its members in the mood. The design devices by which individuals and groups are related to each other and to the whole are wonderfully involved and demand close study. From the center, where Plato and Aristotle stand, silhouetted against the

clear blue of the sky within the framing arch in the distance, the groups of figures are rhythmically arranged in an elliptical movement that swings forward, looping around the two forward groups to either side, and then back again to the center. Moving through the wide opening in the foreground along the perspective pattern of the floor, we penetrate the assembly of philosophers and are led, by way of the reclining Diogenes, up to the here-reconciled leaders of the two great opposing camps of Renaissance philosophy. In the Stanza della Segnatura, Raphael reconciles and harmonizes not only the Platonists and Aristotelians, but paganism and Christianity, in the same kind of synthesis manifest in his Madonnas.

Pope Leo X, the son of Lorenzo de' Medici, succeeded Julius II as Raphael's patron, and it was in his pontificate that Rome achieved a splendor it had not known since ancient times. Leo, a worldly, pleasure-loving prince, spent huge sums on the arts, of which, as a true Medici, he was a sympathetic connoisseur. Raphael moved in the highest circles of the papal court, himself the star of a brilliant society—young, handsome, wealthy, and adulated, not only by his followers but by the city of Rome and all Italy. His personality contrasts strikingly with that of the aloof, mysterious Leonardo or the tormented and intractable Michelangelo. Genial, even-tempered, generous, and high-minded, Raphael was genuinely loved. The pope was not his only patron. His friend, the immensely wealthy banker Agostino Chigi, who managed the financial affairs of the papal state, commissioned Raphael to decorate his small but splendid palace on the Tiber, the Villa Farnesina, with scenes from Classical mythology. Outstanding among the frescoes painted there by Raphael is the *Galatea* (FIG. 17-18), which takes its theme from the popular Italian poem by Politian, "La giostra"; Botticelli borrowed the theme for his *Birth of Venus* (FIG. 16-60) from the same work. In Raphael's fresco, Galatea flees from her uncouth lover, the giant Polyphemus, on a shell drawn by leaping dolphins, surrounded by sea creatures and playful cupids. The painting erupts in unrestrained pagan joy and exuberance, an exultant song in praise of human beauty and zestful love. The composition artfully wheels the sturdy figures

17-18 RAPHAEL, *Galatea*, 1513. Fresco. Villa Farnesina, Rome.

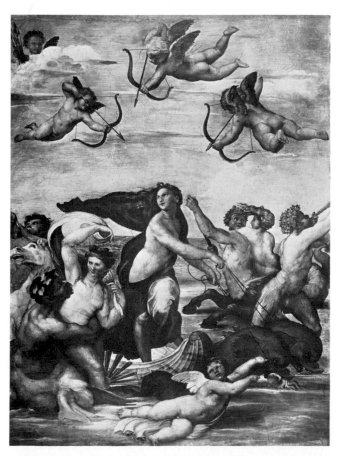

around Galatea in bounding and dashing movements that always return to her as the energetic center. The figures of the cupids, skillfully foreshortened, repeat the circling motion. Raphael's figures are sculpturally conceived, and the body of Galatea—supple, strong, and vigorously in motion—should be compared with Botticelli's delicate, hovering, almost dematerialized Venus. Pagan myth presented in monumental form, in vivacious movement, and in a spirit of passionate delight brings back the kernel substance of which the naturalistic art and poetry of the Classical world was made. Raphael revives the gods and heroes and the bright world they populated, not to venerate them but to make of them the material of art. From Raphael almost to the present, Classical matter will hold as prominent a place in art as religious matter. So completely does the new spirit embodied in the *Galatea* take control that it is as if the Middle Ages had never been.

Raphael was also an excellent portraitist. His subjects were the illustrious scholars and courtiers who surrounded Pope Leo X, among them Count Baldassare Castiglione, a close friend of Raphael and memorable for his handbook on High Renaissance criteria of aristocratic behavior. In the *Book of the Courtier*, Castiglione portrays an ideal type of the High Renaissance, a courageous, sagacious, truth-loving, skillful, and cultivated man—in a word, the completely civilized man, a culmination of the line that runs from the rude barbarian warriors who succeeded to the Roman empire through the half-literate knights and barons of the Middle Ages. Castiglione goes on to describe a way of life based on cultivated rationality in imitation of the ancients. In Raphael's portrait of him (FIG. 17-19), Castiglione, splendidly yet soberly garbed, looks directly at us with a philosopher's grave and benign expression, clear-eyed and thoughtful. The figure is in half-length and three-quarter view, in the pose made popular by the *Mona Lisa* (FIG. 17-4), and we note in both portraits the increasing attention paid by the High Renaissance artist to the personality and psychic state of his subject. The tones are muted and low-keyed, as would befit the temper and mood of the reflective, elderly man; the background is entirely neutral, without the usual landscape or architecture. The composition emphasizes the head and the hands, both wonderfully eloquent in what they report of the man, who himself had written so eloquently in *The Courtier* of the way to enlightenment by the love of beauty. Both Raphael and Castiglione, as well as other artists of their age, were animated by such love, and we know from his poetry that Michelangelo shared in this widely held Neo-Platonic belief that the soul rises to its enlightenment by the progressively rarefied experience of the beautiful.

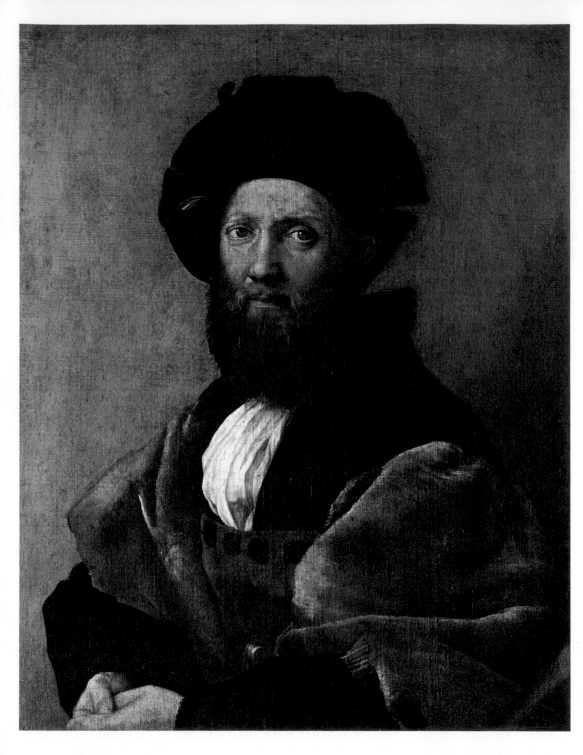

17-19 RAPHAEL, *Baldassare Castiglione, c.* 1514. Oil on wood transferred to canvas, approx. 30¼″ × 26½″. Louvre, Paris.

Michelangelo

MICHELANGELO (Michelangelo Buonarroti, 1475–1564) is a far more complex personality than Raphael, and his art is not nearly so typical of the High Renaissance as Raphael's. Frequently irascible, Michelangelo was as impatient with the shortcomings of others as he was with his own. His jealousy of Raphael, his dislike of Leonardo, and his almost continuous difficulties with his patrons are all well known. Perhaps these personal problems arose out of his strong and stern devotion to his art, for he was always totally absorbed in the work at hand. He identified himself with the task of artistic creation completely, and his reactions to his rivals were often impulsive and antagonistic. In this respect, Michelangelo's character has often been compared with Beethoven's, but the personal letters of both reveal a deep sympathy and concern for those close to them, and a profound understanding of humanity informs their works.

Whatever his traits of character, Michelangelo's career realizes all those Renaissance ideals that we conceptualize as "inspired genius" and "universal man." His work has the authority of greatness we have already attributed to Donatello. His confidence in his genius was unbounded; its demands determined his choices absolutely, often in opposition to the demands of his patrons. His belief that nothing worth preserving could be done without genius was attended by the conviction that nothing could be done without persevering study. Although he was architect, sculptor, painter, poet, and engineer, he thought of himself first as a sculptor, regarding that calling as superior to that of a painter because the sculptor shares in something like the divine power to "make man." In true Platonic fashion, Michelangelo believed that the image produced by the artist's hand must come from the Idea in his mind; the Idea is the reality that has to be brought forth by the genius of the artist. But the artist is not the *creator* of the Ideas he conceives; rather he finds them in the natural world, reflecting the absolute Idea, which, for the artist, is Beauty. In this way, the strongly Platonic strain makes the Renaissance theory of the imitation of nature a *revelation* of the high truths hidden within nature. The theory that guided Michelangelo's hand, though never complete or entirely consistent, appears in his poetry:

> Every beauty which is seen here below by persons of perception resembles more than anything else that celestial source from which we all are come . . .

> My eyes longing for beautiful things
> together with my soul longing for salvation
> have no other power
> to ascend to heaven than the contemplation of beautiful things.*

One of the best-known observations by Michelangelo is that the artist must proceed by finding the Idea—the image, locked in the stone, as it were—so that, by removing the excess stone, he extricates the Idea, like Pygmalion bringing forth the living form:

> The best artist has no concept which some single marble does not enclose within its mass, but only the hand which obeys the intelligence can accomplish that . . . . Taking away . . . brings out a living figure in alpine and hard stone, which . . . grows the more as the stone is chipped away . . . .†

The artist, Michelangelo felt, works through many years at this unceasing process of revelation and "arrives late at lofty and unusual things and . . . remains little time thereafter."

Michelangelo did indeed arrive "at lofty and unusual things," for he broke sharply from the lessons

of his predecessors and contemporaries in one important respect: he mistrusted the application of mathematical methods as guarantees of beauty in proportion. Measure and proportion, he believed, should be "kept in the eyes." Giorgio Vasari quotes Michelangelo as declaring that "it was necessary to keep one's compass in one's eyes and not in the hand, for the hands execute, but the eye judges." Thus, he would set aside Vitruvius, Alberti, Leonardo, Albrecht Dürer, and others who tirelessly sought the perfect measure, being convinced that the inspired judgment could find other pleasing proportions and that the artist must not be bound, except by the demands made by the realization of the Idea. This insistence on the artist's own authority is typical of Michelangelo and anticipates the modern concept of the right of talent to a self-expression limited only by its own judgment. The license thus given to genius to aspire far beyond the "rules" led Michelangelo to create works in architecture, sculpture, and painting that depart from High Renaissance regularity and put in its stead a style of vast, expressive strength with complex, eccentric, often titanic forms that loom before us in tragic grandeur. His self-imposed isolation (Raphael spoke of him as "lonely as the hangman"), his creative furies, his proud independence, and his daring innovations led Italians to speak of the dominating quality of the man and his works in one word, *terribilità*—the sublime shadowed by the awesome and the fearful.

As a youth, Michelangelo was apprenticed to the painter Domenico Ghirlandaio, whom he left before completing his training. He soon came under the protection of Lorenzo the Magnificent and must have been a young and thoughtful member of the famous Neo-Platonic circle. He studied sculpture under one of Lorenzo's favorite artists, BERTOLDO DI GIOVANNI, a former collaborator of Donatello who specialized in small-scale bronzes. When the Medici fell in 1494, Michelangelo fled from Florence to Bologna, where he was impressed by the sculpture of Jacopo della Quercia (FIG. 16-3). Besides his study of Jacopo—although he claimed that in his art he owed nothing to anyone—Michelangelo made studious drawings after the great Florentines, Giotto and Masaccio, and it is very likely that his consuming interest in representing the male nude both in sculpture and painting was much stimulated by Signorelli (FIG. 16-61).

Michelangelo's wanderings took him to Rome, from which he returned to Florence in 1501, partly because the city might permit him to work a great block of marble, called the Giant, left over from an earlier, abortive commission. With his sure insight into the nature of stone and a proud, youthful confidence that he could perceive its Idea, Michelangelo added to his already great reputation by carving his

---

*In Robert J. Clements, *Michelangelo's Theory of Art* (New York: New York University Press, 1961), p. 9. © 1961 by Robert J. Clements. Reprinted by permission of the publisher.

†Ibid., p. 16.

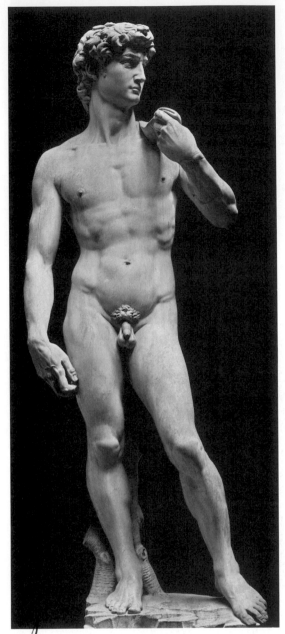

Michelangelo, *David*, 1501–1504. Marble, approx. 13′ 5″ high. Galleria dell' Accademia, Florence.

young David and the large hands and feet, giving promise of the giant strength to come, are not composed simply of inert muscle groups, nor are they idealized by simplification into broad masses. They serve, by their active play, to make vivid the whole mood and posture of tense expectation. Each swelling vein and tightening sinew amplifies the psychological vibration of the monumental hero's pose. Michelangelo doubtless had the Classical nude in mind—Antique statues, which were being found everywhere, were greatly admired by Michelangelo and his contemporaries for their skillful and precise rendering of heroic physique—but if we compare the *David* with the *Doryphoros* (FIG. 5-61), we realize how widely his intent diverges from the measured, almost bland quality of the Antique statue. As early as the *David*, then, Michelangelo's genius, unlike Raphael's, is dedicated to the presentation of towering, pent-up passion rather than calm, ideal beauty. His own doubts, frustrations, and torments of mind passed easily into the great figures he created or planned.

The tomb of Julius II, a colossal structure that would have given Michelangelo the room he needed for his superhuman, tragic beings, became one of the great disappointments of Michelangelo's life when the Pope, for unexplained reasons, interrupted the commission, possibly because its funds had to be diverted for Bramante's rebuilding of St. Peter's. The original project called for a freestanding, two-story

17-21 Michelangelo, *Moses*, c. 1513–1515. Marble, approx. 8′ 4″ high. San Pietro in Vincoli, Rome.

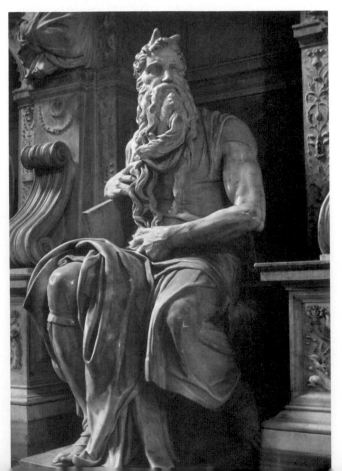

David (FIG. 17-20), still the marvel it was then. The colossal figure again takes up the theme that Donatello and Verrocchio had used successfully, but it reflects Michelangelo's own highly original interpretation of the subject. David is represented not after the victory, with the head of Goliath at his feet, but rather turning his head to his left, sternly watchful of the approaching foe. His whole muscular body, as well as his face, is tense with gathering power. The ponderated pose, suggesting the body at ease, is misleading until we read in the tightening sinews and deep frown what impends. Here is the characteristic representation of energy in reserve that gives the tension of the coiled spring to Michelangelo's figures. The anatomy plays an important part in this prelude to action. The rugged torso and sturdy limbs of the structure with some 28 statues. After the Pope's death in 1513, the scale of the project was reduced step by step until, in 1542, a final contract specified a simple wall tomb with less than one-third of the originally planned figures. The spirit of the tomb may be summed up in the figure of *Moses* (FIG. 17-21), which was completed during one of the sporadic resumptions of the work in 1513. Meant to be seen from below, and balanced with seven other massive forms related in spirit to it, the *Moses* now, in its comparatively paltry setting, can hardly have its full impact. The leader of Israel is shown seated—the tables of the Law under one arm, his other hand gripping the coils of his beard. He may be imagined as resting after the ecstasy of the receiving of the Law on Mount Sinai, while, in the valley below, the people of Israel give themselves up once more to idolatry. Here again,

Michelangelo presents the turned head (as in the *David*), which concentrates the expression of awful wrath that now begins to stir in the mighty frame and eyes. One must study the work in detail to appreciate Michelangelo's sense of the relevance of each detail of body and drapery in forcing up the psychic temperature. The muscles bulge, the veins swell, the great legs begin slowly to move. If this titan ever rose to his feet, says one writer, the world would fly apart. The holy rage of *Moses* mounts to the bursting point, yet must be contained, for the free release of energies in action is forbidden forever to Michelangelo's passion-stricken beings.

Two other figures believed to be intended for the Julius tomb (although this is now doubted by some)— *The Dying Slave* (FIG. 17-22) and *The Bound Slave* (FIG. 17-23), may represent the enslavement of the human

17-22   MICHELANGELO, *The Dying Slave*, 1513–1516. Marble, approx. 7′ 5″ high. Louvre, Paris.

17-23   MICHELANGELO, *The Bound Slave*, 1513–1516. Marble, approx. 6′ 10½″ high. Louvre, Paris.

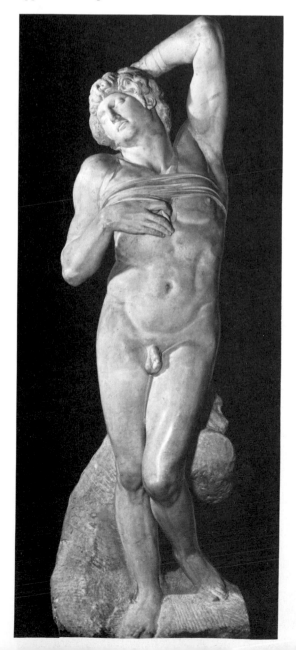

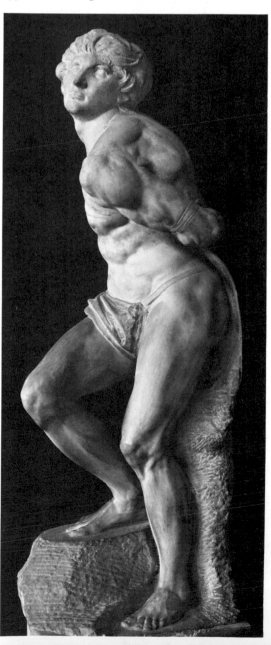

617

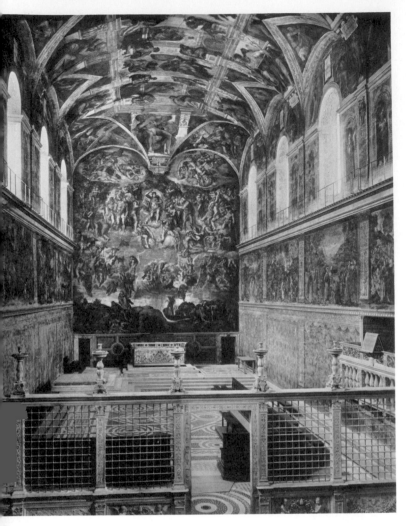

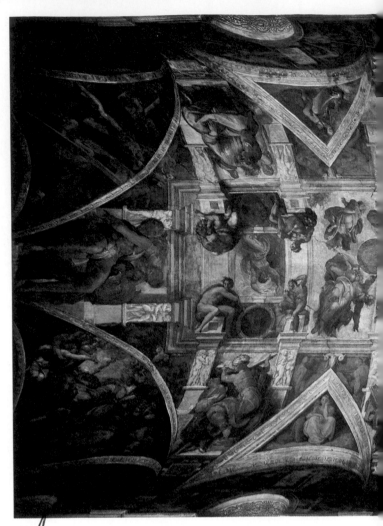

17-24   Interior of the Sistine Chapel (view facing east). The Vatican, Rome.

17-25   MICHELANGELO, ceiling of the Sistine Chapel, 1508–1512. Fresco. The Vatican, Rome.

soul by matter when the soul falls from Heaven into the prison house of the body. With the imprisoned soul slumbering, our actions, as Marsilio Ficino says, are "the dreams of sleepers and the ravings of madmen." Certainly, the dreams and the ravings are present in these two figures. Originally, there were to be some 20 slaves for the tomb, in various attitudes of revolt and exhaustion. In the two slaves, as in the *David* and the *Moses*, Michelangelo makes each body a total expression of the Idea, so that the human figure serves not so much as a representation of a concept, as in Medieval allegory, but as the concrete realization of an intense feeling. Michelangelo's own powerful imagination indeed communicates itself in every plane and hollow of the stone. The beautiful, Praxitelean lines of the swooning captive present—in their slow, downward pull—the weight of exhaustion; the violent contrapposto of the defiant captive is the image of frantic, impotent struggle. Michelangelo's whole art depends on his conviction that whatever can be said greatly through sculpture and painting must be said through the human figure.

A group of four unfinished slaves, one of which is illustrated in the Introduction (FIG. 10), was probably meant for one of the later versions of the tomb. These figures serve not only as object lessons in the subtractive method of sculpture, but also as revelations of the creative process in which abstract ideas—in effect, encased in blocks of stone—are converted into dynamically expressive, concrete forms. If Michelangelo's slaves indeed symbolize the struggle of the human soul to find release from the bonds of its material body, then this idea can find no fuller expression than in these partly finished figures that, with superhuman effort, struggle to cast off the inert masses of stone that imprison them.

With the failure of the tomb project, Julius II gave the bitter and reluctant Michelangelo the commission to paint the ceiling of the Sistine Chapel (FIG. 17-24). The artist, insisting that painting was not his profession, assented only in the hope that the tomb project could be revived. The difficulties facing Michelangelo were enormous: the inadequacy of his training in the art of fresco; the dimensions of the ceiling (some 5,800 square feet) and its height above the pavement (almost 70 feet); and the complicated perspective problems presented by the height and curve of the vault. Yet, in less than four years, Michelangelo pro-

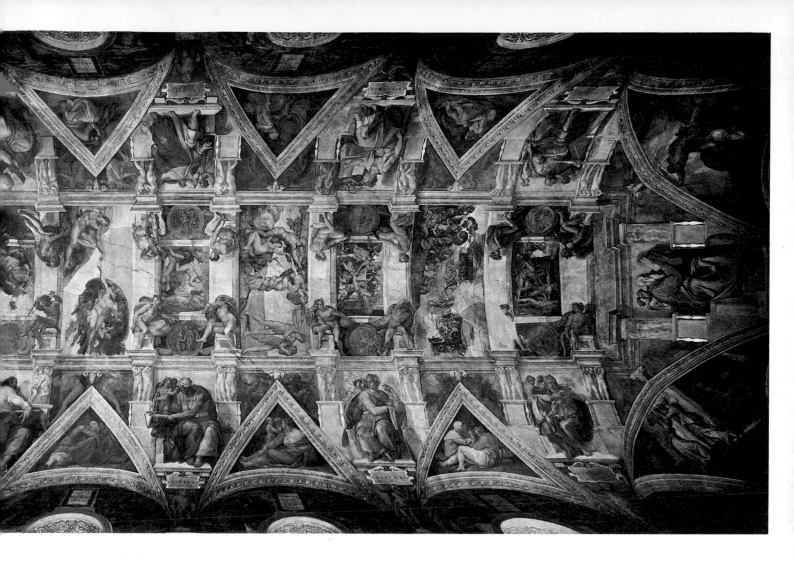

duced an unprecedented work—a one-man master-piece without parallel in the history of world art (FIG. 17-25).* Taking the most august and solemn theme of all—the creation, fall, and redemption of man—he spread a colossal decorative scheme across the vast surface, weaving together more than 300 figures in an ultimate grand drama of the human race. A long corridor of narrative panels describing the creation re-

*Like Leonardo's *Last Supper,* Michelangelo's Sistine Chapel paintings are in the process of restoration. Centuries of accumulated grime, overpainting, and protective glue are being removed, and restorers have already revealed much of the artist's original craft in form, color, style, and procedure. The restoration work, part of a 12-year program, began on the lunettes above the windows of the chapel, where the vault curves down on either side. In these semi-circular spaces, Michelangelo painted figures representing the ancestors of Christ. These figures, once thought to be purposefully dark, now show brilliant colors of high intensity, brushed on with an astonishing freedom and rapidity. Holes in the walls below the windows are believed to have held trusses that supported a bridge-like scaffold covering half the ceiling at a time; this would seem to verify old accounts that the artist worked from a structure that required no floor supports. The success of the restorers in recovering the freshness and vivacity of Michelangelo's paintings in the lunettes is expected to continue as they begin on the prophets and the narrative scenes along the crown of the vault. By 1988, we should be able to view the great artist's work in all its first splendor. Without doubt, our present knowledge of Michelangelo's art, intentions, and influence will need thorough revision at that time.

corded in Genesis runs along the crown of the vault, from God's *Separation of Light and Darkness* to the *Drunkenness of Noah.* On either side, where the vault curves down, are seated the Hebrew prophets and pagan sibyls who foretold the coming of Christ. At the four corner pendentives are four Old Testament scenes with David, Judith, Haman, and the Brazen Serpent. Scores of lesser figures appear: the ancestors of Christ in the triangular compartments above the windows, the nude youths who punctuate the corners of the central panels, and the small pairs of putti in *grisaille* (grey monochrome to imitate sculpture), who support the painted cornice surrounding the whole central corridor. The conception of the whole design is astounding enough in itself; the articulation of it in its thousand details is an achievement little less than superhuman. But Michelangelo *was* human; in the first few months of work, he made mistakes in the technical application of the fresco that spoiled all he had done up to that time. Also, in the first three panels, beginning at the entrance with the *Drunkenness of Noah,* he had not yet estimated the scale properly, and the compositions are crowded, without the simplicity of the panels beginning with the *Temptation and Fall.*

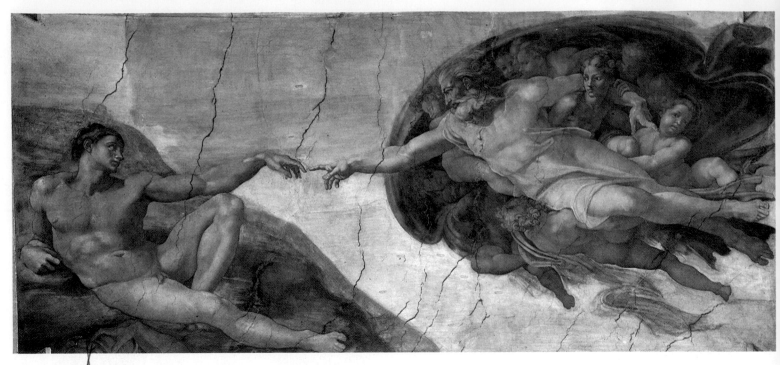

17-26   MICHELANGELO, *The Creation of Adam* (detail of FIG. 17-25).

Unlike the case in Andrea Mantegna's Camera degli Sposi in Mantua (FIG. 16-64), the strongly marked, unifying architectural framework is not used to construct "picture windows" through which we may look up into some illusion just above. Rather, our eyes seize on figure after figure, each sharply outlined against the neutral tone of the architectural setting or the plain background of the panels. Here, as in his sculpture, Michelangelo relentlessly concentrates his expressive purpose on the human figure. To him, the body is beautiful not only in its natural form but also in its spiritual and philosophical significance; the body is simply the manifestation of the soul or of a state of mind and character. Michelangelo represents the body in its most simple, elemental aspect: in the nude or simply draped, with no background and no ornamental embellishment, and always with a sculptor's sense that the figures could be tinted reliefs or full-rounded statues.

One of the central panels of the ceiling will evidence Michelangelo's mastery of the drama of the human figure. *The Creation of Adam* (FIG. 17-26) is not the traditional representation but a bold, entirely Humanistic interpretation of the primal event. God and Adam, members of the same race of superbeings, confront each other in a primordial, unformed landscape of which Adam is still a material part, heavy as earth, while the Lord transcends it, wrapped in his billowing cloud of drapery and borne up by his genius powers. Apprehensively curious but as yet uncreated, the female figure beneath his sheltering arm, long held to represent Eve, has recently been interpreted as the Virgin Mary (with the Christ child at her knee). Life leaps to Adam like an electric spark from the extended and mighty hand of God. The communication between gods and heroes, so familiar in Classical myth, is here concrete: both are made of the same substance; both are gigantic. This blunt depiction of the Lord as ruler of Heaven in the Olympian, pagan sense, is an indication of how easily the High Renaissance joined pagan and Christian traditions; we could imagine Adam and the Lord as Prometheus and Zeus. The composition is dynamically off-center, its focus being the two hands that join the great bodies by the energy that springs between the fingers. The bodies themselves are complementary—the concave body of Adam fitting the convex body of the Lord. The straight, architectural axes we find in the compositions of Leonardo and Raphael are replaced by curves and diagonals; thus, motion directs not only the figures but the whole composition. The reclining poses, the heavy musculature, and the twisting contrapposto are all a part of Michelangelo's stock, which he will show again in the sculptured figures of the Medici tombs.

Following the death of Julius II, patron of the Sistine ceiling paintings, Michelangelo went once again into the service of the Medici popes, Leo X and Clement VII. These pontiffs were little interested in perpetuating the fame of their predecessor by letting Michelangelo complete the tomb of Julius; instead, they commissioned him to build a funerary chapel, the New Sacristy, in San Lorenzo in Florence. Brunelleschi's Old Sacristy was off the left transept of San Lorenzo, and Michelangelo built the new addition off the right. He attempted a unification of architecture and of sculpture, designing the whole chapel as well as the tombs. This relationship between the two arts (and, in this case, painting as well) was a common Medieval feature; we think of the sculptured portals and stained glass of the Gothic cathedral. But the relationship had been broken in the fifteenth century, when sculpture fought free of its architectural matrix and asserted its independence—so much so that Brunelleschi could complain that Donatello's architectural and sculptural additions to his Old Sacristy spoiled the purity of his design. This new integration by Michelangelo, though here unfinished, pointed the way to Baroque art, in which the architectural–sculptural–pictorial ensemble will again become standard.

At opposite sides of the chapel stand the tombs of Giuliano, Duke of Nemours, and Lorenzo, Duke of Urbino, son and grandson of Lorenzo the Magnificent. The tomb of Giuliano (FIG. 17-27) is compositionally the twin of Lorenzo's. Both are unfinished; it is believed that pairs of recumbent river-gods were to be placed at the bottom of the sarcophagi, balancing the pairs that rest on the sloping sides. The composition of the tombs has been a long-standing puzzle. How were they ultimately to look? What is their relationship to one another? What do they signify? The present arrangement seems quite unstable; were the sloping figures meant to recline on a flat surface, or were they to be partly supported by the river-gods below them? We can do little more than state some of

17-27 MICHELANGELO, tomb of Giuliano de' Medici, 1519–1534. Marble, central figure approx. 71" high. New Sacristy, San Lorenzo, Florence.

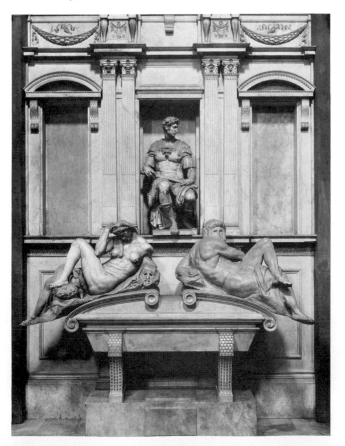

the questions, without attempting to answer them in full. It has been suggested that the arrangement (planned by Michelangelo, but never completed) can be interpreted as the ascent of the soul through the levels of the Neo-Platonic universe. The lowest level, represented by the river-gods, would have signified the underworld of brute matter, the source of evil. The two statues on the sarcophagi would then symbolize the realm of time: the specifically human world of the cycles of dawn, day, evening, and night. Man's state in this world of time is one of pain and anxiety, frustration and exhaustion. At left, the female figure of Night and, at right, the male figure of Day appear to be chained into never-relaxing tensions. Both exhibit that anguished twisting of the masses of the body in contrary directions seen in *The Bound Slave* (FIG. 17-23) and in the Sistine Chapel paintings. This contrapposto is the signature of Michelangelo. Day, with a body the thickness of a great tree and the anatomy of Hercules, strains his huge limbs against each other, his unfinished visage rising menacingly above his shoulder. Night, the symbol of rest, twists as if in troubled sleep, her posture wrenched and feverish. The artist has surrounded her with an owl, poppies, and a hideous mask symbolic of nightmares.

On their respective tombs, the figures of Lorenzo and Giuliano, rising above the troubles of the realm of time, represent the two ideal human types: the contemplative man (Lorenzo) and the active man (Giuliano). They thus become symbols for the two means by which man might achieve union with God: meditation or the active life fashioned after that of Christ. Michelangelo disdained to make portraits of the actual persons; who, he asked, would care what they looked like in a thousand years? What counted was the contemplation of what was beyond the corrosion of time. Giuliano, the active man (FIG. 17-27), his features quite generalized, sits clad in the armor of a Roman emperor, holding the baton of a commander, his head turned alertly, as if in council (he looks toward the statue of the Virgin at one end of the chapel). Across the room, Lorenzo, the contemplative man, sits wrapped in thought, his face in deep shadow. In these works, as in many others, Michelangelo suggests powerful psychic forces that cannot be translated into action but are ever on the verge of it. His prevailing mood is tension and constraint, even in the figures that seem to aspire to the ideal, to the timeless, perfect and unmoving. Michelangelo's style was born to disturb. It brings the serene, brief High Renaissance to an end.

The tensions and ambiguities of Michelangelo's style, which will pass over into the general style called Mannerism, are strongly felt in his architecture. His building activity for the Medici in Florence centered in and around San Lorenzo, and his Laurentian Library, built to house the great collections of the Medici, adjoins it. The building's peculiar layout was dictated by its special function and by its rather constricted site. Michelangelo had two contrasting spaces to work with: the long horizontal of the library proper, and the vertical of the vestibule. In the latter, everything is massive and plastic, but the planes and solids of the reading room are shallow and played down (perhaps so as not to distract the readers). The need to place the vestibule windows high determined the narrow verticality of its elevation (FIG. 17-28).

The vestibule, much taller than it is wide or long, gives the impression of a vertically compressed, shaft-like space. A vast, flowing stairway that almost fills the interior greatly adds to a sense of oppressiveness. Anyone schooled exclusively in the Classical architecture of Bramante and the High Renaissance would have been appalled by Michelangelo's indifference to Classical norms in the use of the orders or in proportion. He uses columns in pairs and sinks them into the walls. He breaks columns around corners. He places consoles beneath columns that are not meant to support them. He arbitrarily breaks through pediments, as well as through cornices and stringcourses. In short, Michelangelo disposes willfully and abruptly of Classical architecture as the High Renaissance knows it. But some features, often called Manneristic, were dictated by structural necessity. The recessed columns, for example, which seem neither to support nor to be supported, have recently been shown to perform a supporting function, in contrast with the standard, applied Classical orders, which are purely decorative. These paired stone columns, due to their greater compressive strength, actually add rigidity to the relatively thin brick walls and support the upper part of the structure. The "ambiguity" of the resulting wall surface is illusory, as the columns clearly have been recessed *into* the wall. In any event, Michelangelo, with his usual trailbreaking independence of mind, has sculptured an interior space that conveys all the strains and tensions we find in his statuary and in his painted figures. But, unlike Mannerist architects—especially his contemporary Giulio Romano in the Palazzo del Tè (FIGS. 17-48 and 17-49)—he never tried to baffle or to confuse. His style in all three arts is wonderfully consistent. The key to that consistency may be found in his own words: "The members of an architectural structure follow the laws exemplified in the human body. He who . . . is not a good master of the nude . . . cannot understand the principles of architecture." His whole inspiration came from the beauty and majesty of the human body: the visible aspect of the human soul.

17-28 MICHELANGELO, vestibule of the Laurentian Library, Florence, begun 1524. Stairway designed 1558–1559.

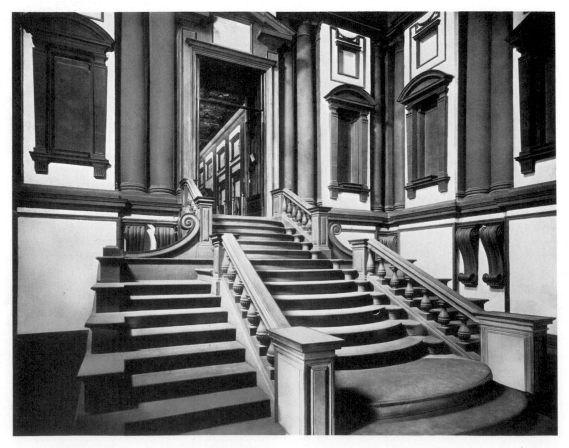

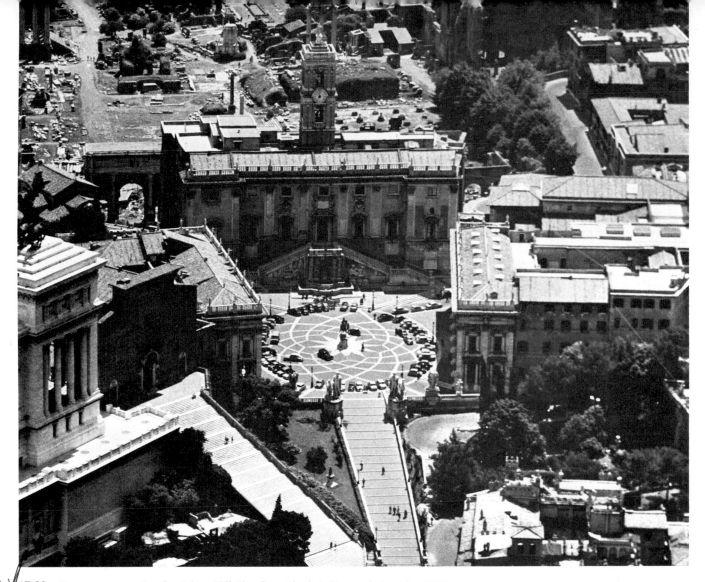

17-29   MICHELANGELO, the Capitoline Hill (the Campidoglio), Rome, designed *c.* 1537.

In his later years, Michelangelo turned increasingly to architecture. In 1537, he undertook to reorganize the Capitoline Hill (the Campidoglio) in Rome (FIGS. 17-29 and 17-30), receiving from Pope Paul III a flattering and challenging commission. The pope wished to transform the ancient hill, which had once been the spiritual as well as political capitol of Rome, into a symbol of power of the new Rome of the popes. The great challenge of the project was that Michelangelo was required to incorporate into his design two existing buildings—the Medieval Palazzo dei Senatori (Palace of the Senators) on the east, and the fifteenth-century Palazzo dei Conservatori (Palace of the Conservators) on the south—and that these buildings formed an 80° angle. These preconditions might well have defeated a lesser architect, but Michelangelo converted what seemed to be a handicap into the most impressive design of a civic unit of the entire Renaissance.

Michelangelo reasoned that architecture should follow the form of the human body to the extent of disposing units symmetrically around a central and unique axis, as the arms are related to the body or the eyes to the nose. It must have been with arguments like this that he convinced his sponsors of the necessity of balancing the Palazzo dei Conservatori, for which he was going to redesign the façade, with a similar unit on the north side of the square. To achieve balance and symmetry in his design, Michelangelo placed the new building (the Museo Capitolino, originally planned only as a portico with single rows of offices above and behind it) so that it stood at the same angle to the Palazzo dei Senatori as the Palazzo dei Conservatori stood, thus arriving at a trapezoidal rather than a rectangular plan for his piazza (FIG. 17-30). All other elements of the design were subsequently adjusted to this unorthodox but basic feature.

The statue of Marcus Aurelius (FIG. 6-72)—the only one of many equestrian statues of Roman emperors to survive the Middle Ages—became the focal point for the whole design. It was brought to the Capitoline Hill on the pope's orders and against the advice of Michelangelo, who might have preferred to carve his

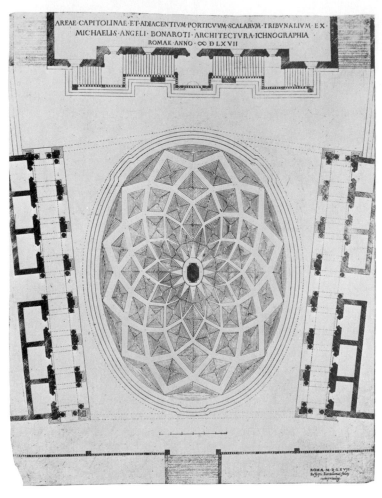

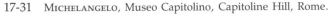

17-30 MICHELANGELO, plan for the Capitoline Hill, Rome. (Engraving by ÉTIENNE DUPÉRAC, c. 1569).

own centerpiece. The symbolic significance of the statue, which seemed to link the Rome of the caesars with the Rome of the popes, must have appealed to Paul III. To connect this central monument with the surrounding buildings, Michelangelo provided it with an oval base and placed it centrally in an oval pavement design (FIG. 17-30), the twelve points of which may have had ancient or Medieval cosmological connotations. Michelangelo's choice of the oval is significant, as it was considered to be an unstable geometric figure and was shunned by older Renaissance architects. But given the trapezoidal shape of the piazza, the oval, which combines centralizing with axial qualities, was the figure best suited to relate the various elements of the design to one another. It was to become the favorite geometric figure of the Baroque period.

Facing the piazza, the two lateral palazzi have identical, two-story façades (FIG. 17-31). They introduce us again to the giant order, first seen in somewhat timid fashion in Alberti's Sant' Andrea in Mantua (FIG. 16-42). Michelangelo uses it with much greater gusto and authority. The giant pilasters not only tie the two stories of the building together but provide a sturdy skeleton that fully expresses its actual function of being the main support of the structure. Walls have been all but eliminated. At ground level, the transition from the massive bulk of the pilaster-faced piers to the deep voids between them has been softened by the interposed columns. These columns carry straight lintels, in the manner advocated by Alberti, but Michelangelo uses them with even greater logic and consistency than Alberti. The façade

17-31 MICHELANGELO, Museo Capitolino, Capitoline Hill, Rome.

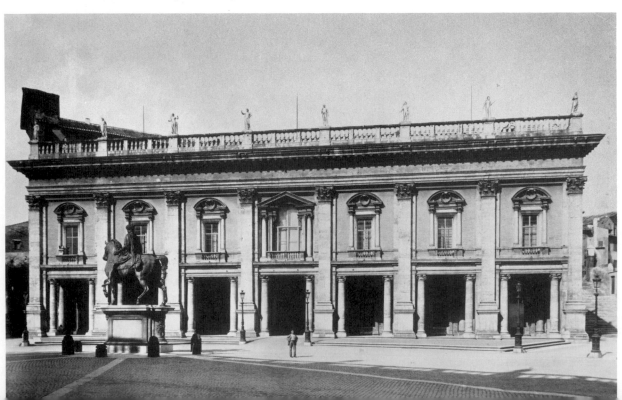

of the third building on the piazza, the three-storied Palazzo dei Senatori, uses the same design elements as the other two palazzi, but in a less plastic fashion. The axial building, with its greater height, thus becomes a distinctive and commanding accent for the ensemble, providing variety within the design without disrupting its unity.

The piazza might have become a room-like enclosure, as Renaissance squares often were and as Alberti, in his treatise, had advised that they be. But again Michelangelo parts with tradition and points to the future. Instead of enclosing his piazza with four walls with entrances leading through their centers, as a room-like enclosure would seem to demand, he left the fourth side open. A fourth wall is merely suggested by a balustrade and a thin screen of Classical statuary that effectively defines the limits of the piazza without obstructing a panoramic view across the city's roofs toward the Vatican. The accidental symbolism of this axis must have pleased the pope just as much as the piazza's dynamic design, and the sweeping vista must have pleased later Baroque planners.

Michelangelo took over the supervision of the building of the new St. Peter's a few years after he had designed the Capitoline Hill; neither project was finished at the time of his death. His work on St. Peter's—after efforts by a succession of architects following the death of Bramante—apparently became a show of dedication, thankless and without pay, on his own decision. Writing in May 1557 to his friend Giorgio Vasari, Michelangelo complains:

> God is my witness how much against my will it was that Pope Paul forced me into this work on St. Peter's in Rome ten years ago. If the work had been continued from that time forward as it was begun, it would by now have been as far advanced as I had reason to hope . . . .*

Among Michelangelo's difficulties had been his struggle to preserve and carry through (with modifications) Bramante's original plan (FIG. 17-7), which he praised even as he changed it:

> It cannot be denied that Bramante was a skillful architect and the equal of any one from the time of the ancients until now. It was he who drew up the original plan of St. Peter's, not full of confusion but clear and straightforward . . . . It was considered to be a fine design, and there is still evidence that it was so: indeed, every architect who has departed from Bramante's plan . . . has departed from the right way . . . .†

*In Robert J. Clements, ed., *Michelangelo: A Self-Portrait* (Englewood Cliffs, N.J.: Prentice-Hall, 1964), p. 57.

†In E.G. Holt, ed., *Literary Sources of Art History* (Princeton, N.J.: Princeton University Press, 1947), p. 195.

We have already seen Michelangelo's respect for a good plan in his carrying out of Sangallo's Farnese Palace design with only minor modifications (FIG. 17-14). With Bramante's plan for St Peter's, Michelangelo managed a major concentration, reducing the central fabric from a number of interlocking crosses to a domed Greek cross inscribed in a square and fronting the whole with a Pantheon-like, double-columned portico (FIG. 17-32). Without destroying the centralizing features of Bramante's plan (the nave was lengthened after Michelangelo's death), Michelangelo, with a few strokes of the pen, converted its snowflake complexity into massive, cohesive unity.

The same striving for a unified and cohesive design can be seen in Michelangelo's treatment of the building's exterior. As the front of the church was changed later, his style and intention are best seen on the west (apse) end (FIG. 17-33). The colossal order again serves him nobly, as the giant pilasters march around the undulating wall surfaces, confining the movement without interrupting it. The architectural sculpturing, which Michelangelo began in the Laurentian Library (FIG. 17-28), here extends itself up from the ground through the attic stories and moves on into the drum and the dome, pulling the whole building together into a unity from base to summit. The Baroque architects will learn much from this kind of integral design, which is ultimately based on Michelangelo's conviction that architecture is one with the organic beauty of the human form. The domed west end—as majestic as it is today and as influential as it

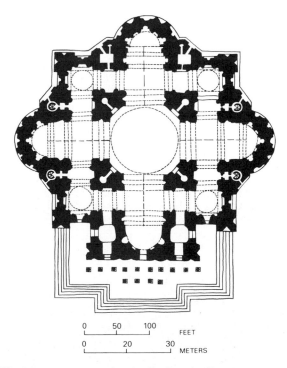

| 0 | 50 | 100 | FEET |
| 0 | 20 | 30 | METERS |

17-32 MICHELANGELO, plan for St. Peter's, Rome.

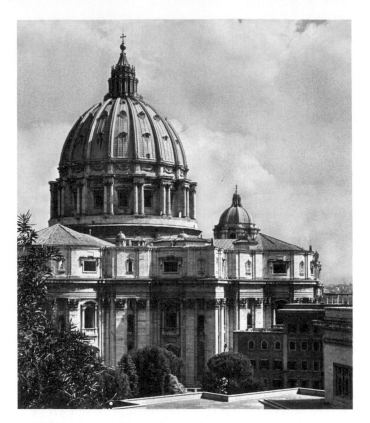

17-33 MICHELANGELO, St. Peter's, Rome, 1546–1564 (view from the northwest). Dome completed by GIACOMO DELLA PORTA in 1590.

has been on architecture throughout the centuries—is not quite as it was intended to be. Originally, Michelangelo had planned a dome with a raised silhouette, like that of the Florence Cathedral. But in his final version he decided on a hemispheric dome (FIG. 17-34), to moderate the verticality of the design of the lower stories and to establish a balance between dynamic and static elements. However, when GIACOMO DELLA PORTA executed the dome after Michelangelo's death, he restored the earlier high design, ignoring Michelangelo's later version. Giacomo's reasons were probably the same ones that had impelled Brunelleschi to use an ogival section for his Florentine dome (FIG. 16-15): greater stability and ease of construction. The result is that the dome seems to be rising from its base, rather than resting firmly on it—an effect that Michelangelo might not have approved. Nevertheless, the dome of St. Peter's is probably the most impressive and beautiful in the world and has served as model to generations of architects down to our own time.

While Michelangelo endured the tribulations of age and the long frustrations of art, his soul was further oppressed by the events that had been erupting around him from the time he fled Florence as a young

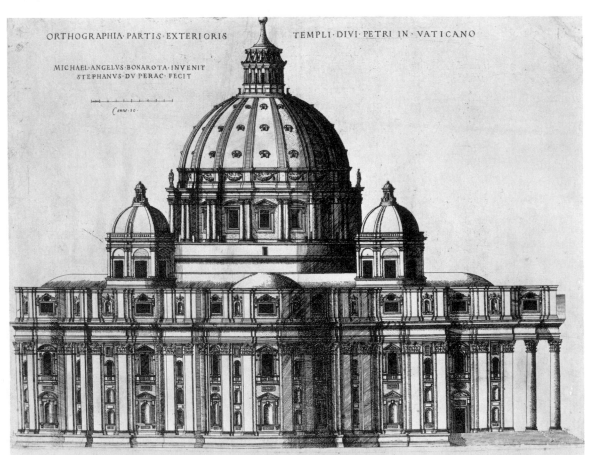

17-34 MICHELANGELO, south elevation of St. Peter's, Rome. (Engraving by ÉTIENNE DUPÉRAC, c. 1569.)

man after the fall of the Medici. The liberties of Florence were destroyed; the Medici had returned as tyrants, and Michelangelo felt himself an exile, even while he worked for them. Italy was laid waste by the French and Spanish invasions, and the Protestant Reformation divided Christendom into warring camps. The Catholic Counter-Reformation gained, and Europe was to be racked by religious war for more than a century. The glories of the High Renaissance faded, and the philosophy of Humanism retreated before the resurgence of a religious spirit that was often pessimistic, moralizing, and grimly fanatical, whether Protestant or Catholic. Michelangelo himself turned from his Humanist beginnings to a deep religious preoccupation with the fate of man and of his own soul. His sense that the world had gone mad and that man, forsaking God, was doomed

must have been sharpened by his still vivid memory of Savonarola's foreboding summons of sinners to repent and by his reading of Dante, in whom he was expert. In this spirit, Michelangelo undertook the great *Last Judgment* fresco on the altar wall of the Sistine Chapel (FIG. 17-35). The change from the mood of the ceiling paintings of 20 years before is radical. Fallen man was to have been exalted by the coming of the Redeemer, everywhere announced in the thronging figures of the ceiling. Now, on the altar wall, Christ indeed has come, but as the Medieval judge of the world—a giant whose mighty right arm is lifted in a gesture of damnation so broad and universal as to suggest he will destroy all creation, Heaven and earth alike. The choirs of Heaven surrounding him pulse with anxiety and awe. The spaces below are crowded with trumpeting angels, the ascending just,

17-35 MICHELANGELO, *The Last Judgment*, fresco on the altar wall of the Sistine Chapel, 1534–1541. The Vatican, Rome.

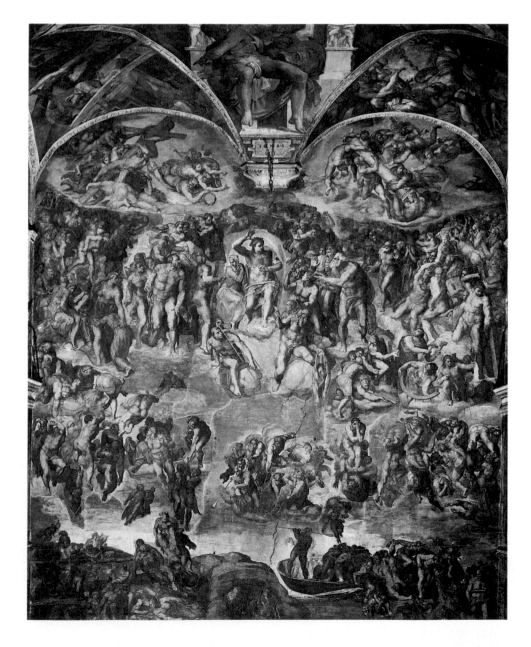

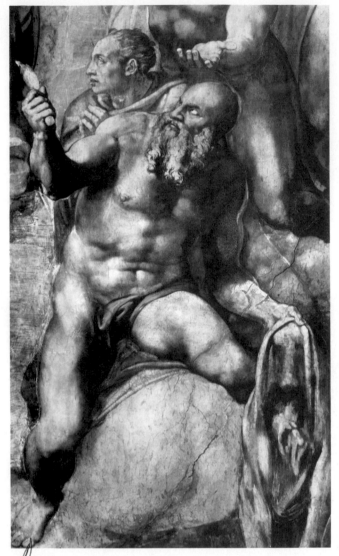

17-36 MICHELANGELO, *St. Bartholomew and "Self-Portrait"* (detail of FIG. 17-35).

and the downward-hurtling damned. On the left, the dead awake and assume flesh; on the right, the damned are tormented by demons whose gargoyle masks and burning eyes revive the demons of the Romanesque tympana (FIG. 9-31). Martyrs who suffered especially agonizing deaths crouch below the Judge. One of them, St. Bartholomew, who was skinned alive, holds the flaying knife and the skin, in which hangs a grotesque self-portrait of Michelangelo (FIG. 17-36). In all this, there is no trace of the old Neo-Platonic aspiration to beauty. The figures are grotesquely huge, violently twisted, with small heads and contorted features. The expressive power of ugliness and terror in the service of a terrible message reigns throughout the composition.

Michelangelo's art began in the manner of the fifteenth century, rose to an idealizing height in the

High Renaissance, and, at the end, moved toward the Baroque. Like a colossus, he bestrides three centuries. He became the archetype of the supreme genius who transcends the rules by making his own. Few artists could escape his influence, and variations on Michelangelo's style will constitute much of artistic experiment for centuries.

Andrea del Sarto and Correggio

The towering achievements of Raphael and Michelangelo in Rome tend to obscure everything else that was done during their time. Nevertheless, aside from the flourishing Venetian School, some excellent artists were active in other parts of Italy during the first part of the sixteenth century. One of these, the Florentine ANDREA DEL SARTO (1486–1531), expresses, in his early paintings, the ideals of the High Renaissance with almost as much clarity and distinction as Raphael. Andrea's *Madonna of the Harpies* (FIG. 17-37) shows the Madonna standing majestically on an altar-like base decorated with sphinxes (misidentified as harpies by Vasari; hence, the name of the painting). The composition is based on a massive and imposing figure pyramid, the static qualities of which are relieved by the opposing contrapposto poses of the flanking saints—a favorite and effective High Renaissance device to introduce variety into symmetry. The potentially rigid pyramid is further softened by the skillful coordination of the figures' poses into an organic movement that leads from St. Francis, on the left, to the Virgin, to St. John the Evangelist, and downward from him toward the observer. This main movement is either echoed or countered by numerous secondary movements brought into perfect formal balance in a faultless compositional performance. The soft modeling of the forms is based on Leonardo but does not affect the colors, which are rich and warm. Andrea's sense of and ability to handle color set him well apart from his central Italian contemporaries; he is perhaps the only Renaissance artist to transpose his rich color schemes from panels into frescoes. Andrea's later compositions tend to be less firmly knit and his color schemes move toward the cool harshness that will become typical of Mannerist painting. Although he was greatly admired in the sixteenth and seventeenth centuries, Andrea's fame has waned; today, he seems to be remembered primarily as the teacher of Jacopo da Pontormo, Rosso Fiorentino, and Vasari and, thus, as one of the forerunners of Mannerism.

Andrea del Sarto may still be firmly placed in the High Renaissance, but his north Italian contemporary, CORREGGIO (Antonio Allegri da Correggio, *c.* 1489–1534), of Parma, is almost impossible to classify.

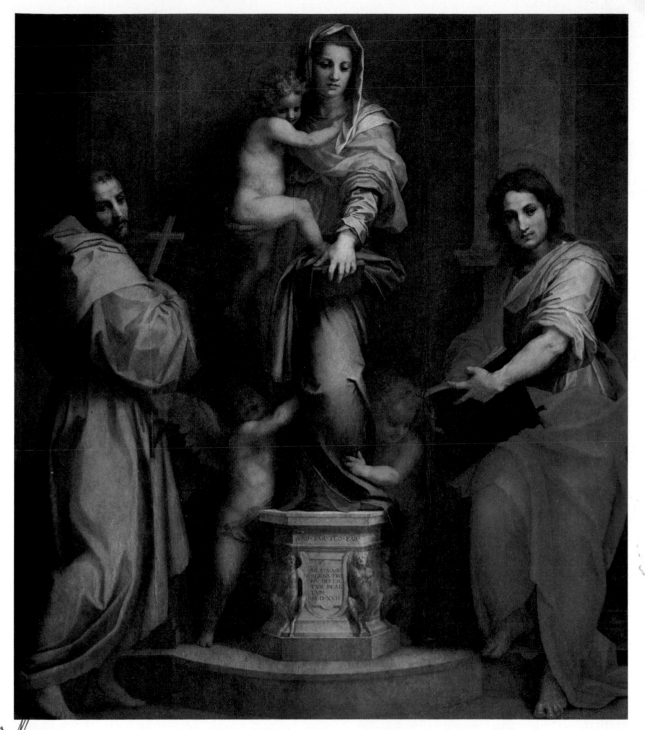

17-37 ANDREA DEL SARTO, *Madonna of the Harpies*, 1517. Oil on wood, approx. 6' 9" × 5' 10". Galleria degli Uffizi, Florence.

A solitary genius, Correggio brings together many stylistic trends, including those of Leonardo, Raphael, and the Venetians; yet he developed a unique personal style, which, if it must be labeled, might best be called "proto-Baroque." Historically, his most enduring contribution was the development of illusionistic ceiling perspectives to a point seldom sur-

passed by his Baroque emulators. At Mantua, Mantegna had painted a hole into the ceiling of the Camera degli Sposi (FIG. 16-65); some 50 years later, Correggio painted away the entire dome of the cathedral of Parma (FIGS. 17-38 and 17-39). Opening up the cupola, the artist shows his audience a view of the sky, with concentric rings of clouds among which hun-

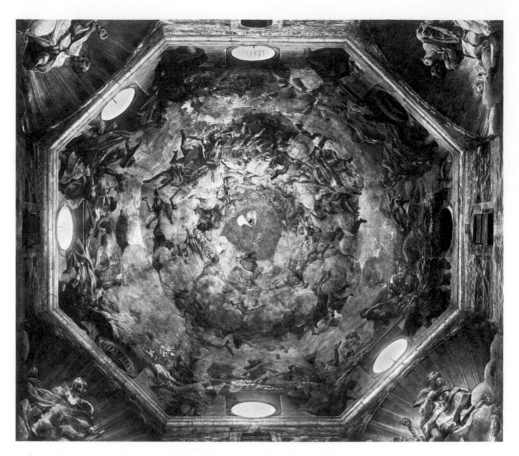

17-38 CORREGGIO, *The Assumption of the Virgin*, 1526–1530. Fresco. Dome of Parma Cathedral, Italy.

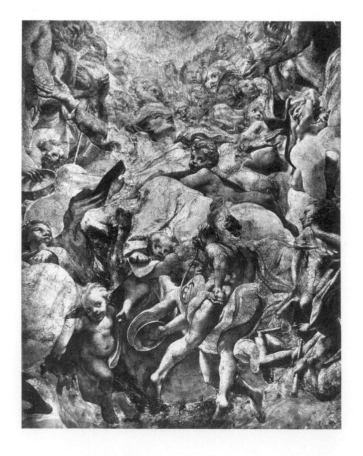

dreds of soaring figures perform a wildly pirouetting dance in celebration of *The Assumption of the Virgin*. These angelic creatures, twinkling their rosy toes at the spectators below, will become permanent tenants of numerous Baroque churches in later centuries. Correggio was also an influential painter of religious panels, in which he forecast many other Baroque compositional devices. As a painter of erotic mythological subjects, he had few equals. *Jupiter and Io* (FIG. 17-40) depicts a suavely sensual vision out of the pagan past. The painting is one of a series on the loves of Jupiter that Correggio painted for the Duke of Mantua, Federigo Gonzaga. The god, who assumed many disguises to hide his numerous liaisons from his wife, Juno, here appears as a cloud that embraces the willing nymph. The soft, smoky modeling *(sfumato)*, derived from Leonardo, is fused with glowing color and renders the voluptuous moment with exquisite subtlety. Even Titian, in his mythological paintings, was rarely able to match the sensuous quality expressed here by Correggio. Unlike Andrea del Sarto, Correggio was little appreciated by his contemporaries; only during the seventeenth century did Baroque painters recognize him as spiritual kin.

17-39 CORREGGIO (detail of FIG. 17-38).

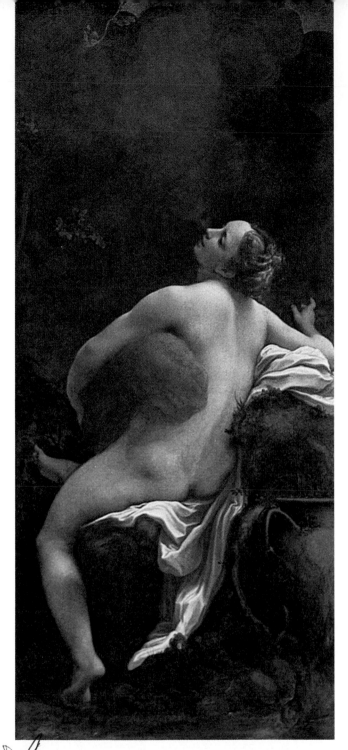

17-40 CORREGGIO, *Jupiter and Io, c.* 1532. Oil on canvas, approx. 64½″ × 29¾″. Kunsthistorisches Museum, Vienna.

MANNERISM

The term "Mannerism" refers to certain tendencies in the art of the Late Renaissance—the period from the death of Raphael (1520) to the end of the sixteenth century. In its broadest sense, the word means excessive or affected adherence to a distinctive manner, especially in art and literature. In its early application to these tendencies, it also carried the pejorative connotation of the term when applied to a description of individual behavior. Today, we view these styles more objectively and appreciate much that is excellent in them.

The Early Renaissance and the High Renaissance developed their characteristic styles from the studious observation of nature and the formulation of a pictorial science. By the time Mannerism matured (after 1520), all the representational problems had been solved; a vast learning was there to be drawn on. In addition, an age of antiquarianism and archeology was now bringing to light thousands of remnants of ancient Roman art. The Mannerists, instead of continuing the former research into nature and natural appearance, turned for their models to the masters of the High Renaissance, especially Michelangelo, and to Roman sculpture, especially relief sculpture. Instead of nature as their teacher, they took art. One could say that whereas their predecessors sought nature and found their style, the Mannerists looked first for a style and found a manner.

Following Michelangelo's example in one respect, the Mannerists declared the artist's right to his own interpretation of the rules, looking for inspiration to the Platonic Idea—referred to by them as the *disegno interno*—which fired their creative fervor. They saw a roughness in nature that needed refining, and they turned to where it had already been refined in art. From the antique and the High Renaissance, each artist, to the limit of his own ingenuity and skill, abstracted forms that he further idealized, so that the typical Manneristic picture or statue looks like an original essay in human form somewhat removed from nature. As *maniera* (as the style was called by Mannerist theorists) is an art of the human figure almost exclusively, its commonest expression is in paintings of numerous figures performing what appears to be a complicated dance and pantomime, in which the compositions, as well as the fanciful gestures and attitudes, are deliberately intricate. The movements are so studied and artificial that they remind us not of the great stage dramatics of the High Renaissance but of an involved choreography for interpretive dancers. Where the art of the High Renaissance strives for balance, Mannerism seeks instability. The calm equilibrium of the former is replaced by a restlessness that leads to distortions, exaggerations, and bizarre posturings on the one hand and sinuously graceful, often athletic attitudes on the other. The positions and actions of the figures often have little to do with the subject. The Mannerist requirement of "invention" leads its practitioner to the *maniera*, a self-conscious stylization involving complexity, caprice, bizarre fantasy (the "conceit"), elegance, preciosity, and polish. This is an art made for aristocratic patrons by artists who sense that their profession is worthy of honor and the admiration of kings. It is an age when monarchs and grandees may plead for anything from the hands of Raphael and Michelangelo, if only a sketch. The concepts of "classic" and "old master" are abroad, and artists are being called *divino*. The artist becomes conscious of his own personality, powers of imagination, and technical skill; he acquires learning and aims at virtuosity. He cultivates not the knowledge of nature but the intricacies of art.

In Painting

The Descent from the Cross (FIG. 17-41) by JACOPO DA PONTORMO (1494–1556) exhibits almost all the stylistic features characteristic of the early phase of Mannerism in painting. The figures crowd the composition, pushing into the front plane and almost completely blotting out the setting. The figure masses are disposed around the frame of the picture, leaving a void in the center, where the High Renaissance artists had concentrated their masses. The composition has no focal point, and the figures swing around the edges of the painting without coming to rest. The representation of space is as strange as the representation of

17-41 JACOPO DA PONTORMO, *The Descent from the Cross*, 1525–1528. Oil on wood, approx. 10' 3" × 6' 6". Capponi Chapel, Santa Felicità, Florence.

the figure. Mannerist space is ambiguous; we are never quite sure where it is going or just where the figures are in it. We do not know how far back the depicted space extends, although its limit is defined by the figure at the top. But we do know that the space is really too shallow for what is taking place in it. For example, there is no room in Pontormo's work for the body belonging to the head that appears immediately over Christ's. The centrifugal effect of the positions of the figures is strengthened by the curiously anxious glances that the actors cast out of the picture in all directions. There is an athletic bending and twisting, with distortions (a torso cannot bend at the point at which the foreground figure's does), an elastic elongation of the limbs, and a rendering of the heads as uniformly small and oval. The composition is further jarred by clashing colors, which are unnatural and as dissimilar as possible to the sonorous primary color chords used by painters of the High Renaissance. The mood of the painting is hard to describe; it seems the vision of an inordinately sensitive soul, perhaps itself driven, as are the actors, by nervous terrors. The psychic dissonance of the composition would indeed appear out of tune to a Classical artist.

ROSSO FIORENTINO (1494–1540)—like Pontormo, a pupil of Andrea del Sarto—compresses space in a manner similar to Pontormo but fills it with turbulent

17-42 ROSSO FIORENTINO, *Moses Defending the Daughters of Jethro*, 1523. Oil on canvas, approx. 63" × 46". Galleria degli Uffizi, Florence.

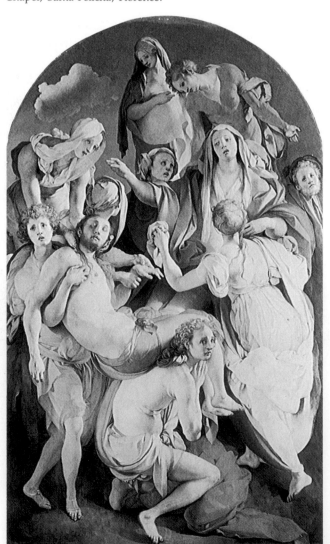

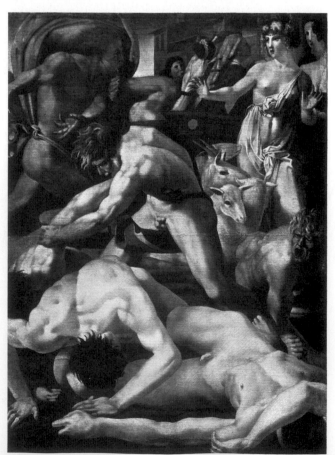

action. Rosso's painting of *Moses Defending the Daughters of Jethro* (FIG. 17-42) recalls the titanic struggles and powerful musculature of Michelangelo's figures on the Sistine Chapel ceiling, but his purpose is not so much expressive as it is inventive of athletic poses. At the same time, although the figures are modeled for three-dimensional effect, they are compressed within a limited space, so that surface is emphasized as a two-dimensional pattern. By 1530, when Francis I of France called him to decorate the palace at Fontainebleau, Rosso had all but forsaken this early furor for more graceful, elongated forms (FIG. 18-51).

Correggio's pupil PARMIGIANINO (Girolamo Francesco Maria Mazzola, 1503–1540), in his best-known work, *Madonna with the Long Neck* (FIG. 17-43), achieves the elegance that is a principal aim of Mannerism. He smoothly combines the influences of his master and of Raphael in a picture of exquisite grace and precious sweetness. The small, oval head of the Madonna, her long, slender neck, the unbelievable length and delicacy of the hand, and the sinuous, swaying elongation of her frame—all are marks of

the aristocratic, gorgeously artificial taste of a later phase of Mannerism. Here is Leonardo distilled through Correggio. To the left is a bevy of angelic creatures, melting with emotions as soft and smooth as their limbs (the left side of the composition is quite in the manner of Correggio). To the right is a line of columns without capitals: an enigmatic setting for an enigmatic figure with a scroll, whose distance from the foreground is immeasurable and ambiguous.

The Mannerists sought a generally beautiful style that had its rules—but rules, as we have seen, that still permitted the artist the free play of his powers of invention. Thus, although all Mannerist paintings have common factors, each artist, as it were, has his recognizable signature. All the points made thus far about Mannerist composition are recognizable in *Venus, Cupid, Folly, and Time,* (or *The Exposure of Luxury,* FIG. 17-44) by BRONZINO (Agnolo di Cosimo, 1503–1572). A pupil of Pontormo, Bronzino was a Florentine and painter to Cosimo I, first Grand Duke of Tuscany. In this painting, he manifests the Mannerist fondness for extremely learned and intricate

17-43   PARMIGIANINO, *Madonna with the Long Neck, c.* 1535. Oil on wood, approx. 7′ 1″ × 4′ 4″. Galleria degli Uffizi, Florence.

17-44   BRONZINO, *Venus, Cupid, Folly, and Time (The Exposure of Luxury), c.* 1546. Oil on wood, approx. 61″ × 56¾″. Reproduced by courtesy of the Trustees of the National Gallery, London.

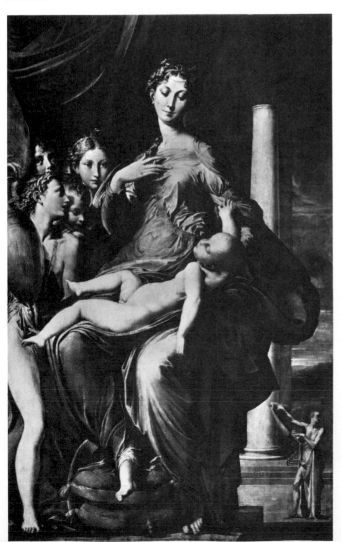

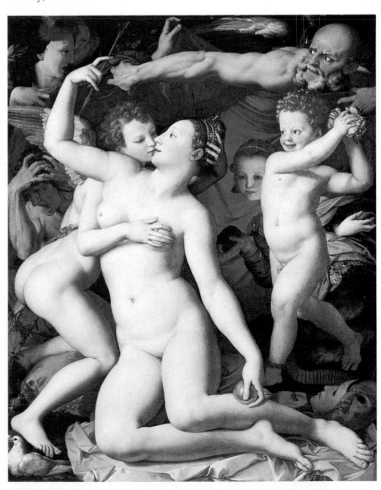

allegories that often have lascivious undertones; here, we are far from the simple and monumental statements and forms of the High Renaissance. Venus, fondled by her son Cupid, is uncovered by Time, while Folly bombards them with roses; other figures represent Hatred and Inconstancy. The masks, a favorite device of the Mannerists, symbolize falseness. The picture seems to convey that love—accompanied by its opposite, hatred, and plagued by inconstancy—is foolish, and its folly will be discovered in time. But, as in many Mannerist paintings, the meaning is ambiguous, and interpretations vary. The figures are drawn around the front plane and almost entirely block the space, although there really is no space. The contours are strong and sculptural; the surfaces, of enamel smoothness. Of special interest are the heads, hands, and feet, for the Mannerists considered the extremities to be the carriers of grace and the clever depiction of them evidence of skill in *maniera*.

The sophisticated elegance sought by the Mannerist painter was most often achieved in portraiture, in which the Mannerists excel. Bronzino's *Portrait of a Young Man* (FIG. 17-45) is exemplary of Mannerist portraiture. The subject is a proud youth—a man of

17-45 BRONZINO, *Portrait of a Young Man, c.* 1550. Oil on wood, approx. 37⅝" × 29½". Metropolitan Museum of Art, New York (H.O. Havemeyer Collection, bequest of Mrs. H.O. Havemeyer, 1929).

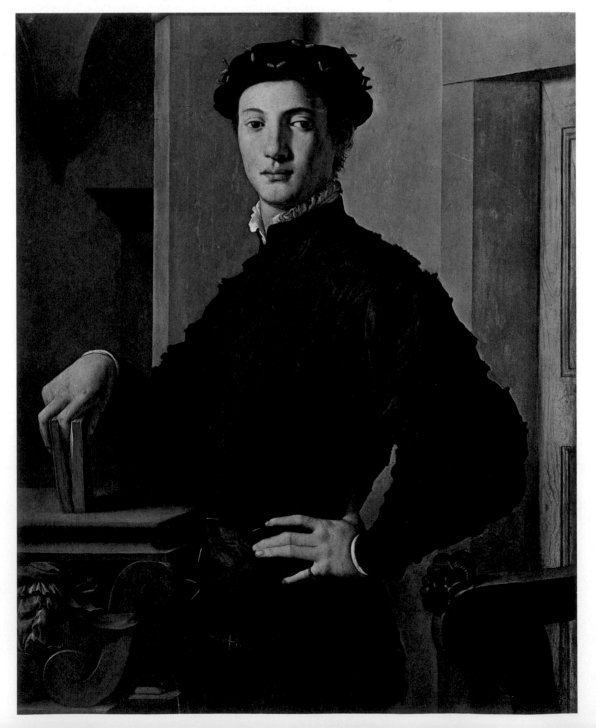

books and intellectual society, rather than a man of action or a merchant. His cool demeanor is carefully affected, a calculated attitude of nonchalance toward the observing world. This austere and incommunicative formality is standard for the Mannerist portrait. It asserts the rank and station of the subject, but not his personality. The haughty poise, the graceful, long-fingered hands, the book, the masks, the severe architecture—all suggest the traits and environment of the high-bred, disdainful patrician. The somber Spanish black of the young man's doublet and cap (this is the century of Spanish etiquette) and the slightly acid olive green walls of the room make for a deeply restrained color scheme—a muted background for the sharply defined, impassive silhouette.

In Sculpture

With Bronzino, Florentine Mannerism in painting passed its high-water mark. But a remarkable person, as Mannerist in his action as in his art, has left us, in his sculpture, the mark of the prevailing style. BENVENUTO CELLINI (1500–1571), perhaps best known for his *Autobiography*, had, to judge by that fascinating work, an awesome proficiency as an artist, statesman, soldier, lover, and many other things. He was, first of all, a goldsmith. The influence of Michelangelo led him to attempt larger works, and, in the service of Francis I, he cast in bronze the *Diana of Fontainebleau* (FIG. 17-46), which sums up Italian and French Mannerism. The figure is derived from the reclining tomb figures in the Medici Chapel (FIG. 17-27), but it exaggerates their characteristics. The head is remarkably small, the torso stretched out, and the limbs elongated. The contrapposto is more apparent than real, for it is flattened out almost into the forward plane, as Mannerist design sense dictates. This

almost abstract figure, along with Mannerist works in paintings by Rosso and others, considerably influenced the development of French Renaissance art, particularly in the school of Fontainebleau.

Italian influence, working its way into France, had strength enough to draw a brilliant, young French sculptor, Jean de Boulogne to Italy, where he practiced his art under the Italian cognomen GIOVANNI DA BOLOGNA (1529–1608). Although his quality and importance have not always been recognized, he is the most important sculptor in Italy after Michelangelo and is the stylistic link between that great master and the Baroque sculptor Gianlorenzo Bernini. Giovanni's *Rape of the Sabine Women* (FIG. 17-47) wonderfully exemplifies the Mannerist principles of figure composition and, at the same time, shows an impulse to break out of the Mannerist formulas of representation. The title was given to the group after it was raised (Giovanni probably intended to present only an interesting figure composition involving an old man, a young man, and a woman). The story, derived from mythic Roman history, tells how the Romans took wives for themselves from the neighboring Sabines. The amateurs, critics, and scholars who flocked around works of art in this age of Mannerism, naming groups in any way they found appropriate, serve to indicate how important and how valued the visual arts had become. The artist himself is learned in his sources; here, Giovanni twice adapts the *Laocoön* (FIG. 5-80) discovered early in the century—once in the figure of the crouching old man and again in the gesture of the woman with one arm flung up. The three bodies interlock on an axis, along which a spiral movement runs; significantly, the figures do not break out of this vortex but remain as if contained within a cylinder. It is necessary to walk around the sculpture to appreci-

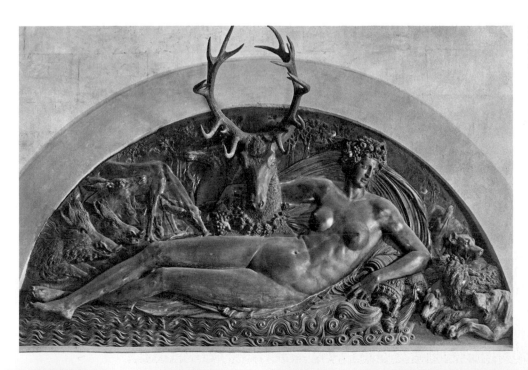

17-46 BENVENUTO CELLINI,
Diana of Fontainebleau,
1543–1544. Bronze,
over life-size. Louvre, Paris.

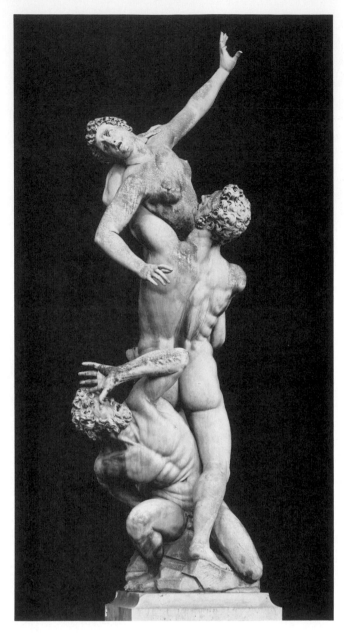

17-47 GIOVANNI DA BOLOGNA, *Rape of the Sabine Women*,
completed 1583. Marble, approx. 13′ 6″ high. Loggia dei
Lanzi, Florence.

ate that, despite its confinement, the aspect of the
group changes radically according to the point from
which it is viewed. One reason is that the open
spaces that pass through the masses (for example, the
space between an arm and a body) have as great an
effect as the solids. This is the first large-scale group
composed to be seen from multiple points of view
since Hellenistic sculpture, which it recalls. But, as
yet, the figures do not freely reach out into space and
relate to the environment. The fact that they remain
"enclosed" prevents our calling them Baroque. Yet
the Michelangelesque potential for action and the
athletic flexibility of the figures are there. The Baroque period will see the release of the sculptured
figure into full action.

In Architecture

Mannerism in painting and sculpture has been studied fairly extensively since the early decades of this
century. But only in the 1930s was it discovered that
the term could also be applied to much of sixteenth-
century architecture. However, the corpus of Mannerist architecture that has been compiled since then
is far from homogeneous and includes many works
that do not really seem to fit the term "Mannerism."
The fact that Michelangelo was using Classical architectural elements in a highly personal and unorthodox manner does not necessarily make him a Mannerist architect. In his designs for St. Peter's he was
certainly striving for those effects of mass, balance,
order, and stability that are the very hallmarks of
High Renaissance design, and even some of the most
unusual features in the Laurentian Library (FIG. 17-
28) were dictated by structural necessity. Michelangelo never really aimed to baffle or to confuse, but
this was the precise goal of GIULIO ROMANO when he
designed the Palazzo del Tè, in Mantua (FIGS. 17-48
and 17-49) and, with it, formulated almost the entire
architectural vocabulary of Mannerism.

Giulio Romano was born either in 1492, if we accept Vasari's suggestion, or in 1499, if we disallow the
possibility of error in a document that states that he
died in Mantua in 1546 at the age of 47. If we give
credence to the latter birthdate, however, Giulio must
have been one of the most precocious young prodigies in the history of world art, as he could then have
been little more than 16 when he became Raphael's
chief assistant in the decoration of the Vatican stanze.
After Raphael's premature death in 1520, Giulio became his master's artistic executor by completing
Raphael's unfinished frescoes and panel paintings. In
1524, Giulio went to Mantua, where he found a patron in Federigo Gonzaga, for whom he built and
decorated the Palazzo del Tè between 1525 and 1535.

The Palazzo del Tè was intended to combine the
functions of a suburban summer palace with those of
a stud farm for the duke's famous stables. Originally
planned as a relatively modest country villa, Giulio's
building so pleased the duke that he soon commissioned his architect to enlarge the structure. In a second building campaign, the villa was expanded to a
palatial scale by the addition of three wings, which
were placed around a square central court. This once-
paved court, which serves both as a passage and as
the focal point of the design, has a near-urban character and, with its surrounding buildings, forms a self-
enclosed unit to which a large, stable-flanked garden
has been attached on the east side. The first impression of the north façade (FIG. 17-48) is that of a fairly
standard Renaissance structure with rusticated walls
that have been articulated with smooth Doric pilas-

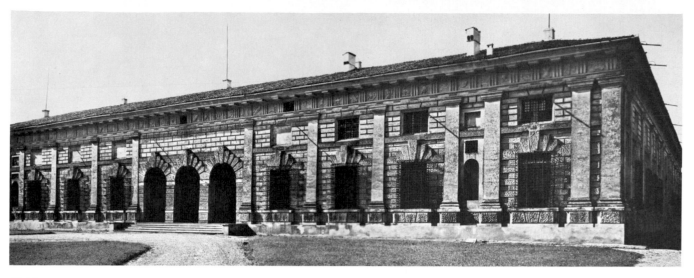

17-48 GIULIO ROMANO, north façade of the Palazzo del Tè, Mantua, Italy.

ters. Closer study reveals a number of startling departures from the Renaissance norm. Most immediately noticeable is the ambiguity of the elevation, which can be read either as a one-story or a two-story system. Other discrepancies gradually reveal themselves. The distances from the central loggia to the corners of the building are unequal; the windows are located eccentrically between pilasters; the pilasters are paired at varying distances from each other; and the voussoirs above the windows and portals are handled in a way that makes them seem to tumble outward from the building. These divergences from convention serve as an overture to a building so laden with structural surprises and contradictions that the whole becomes an enormous parody on the Classical style of Bramante. To be sure, the appreciation of the joke required a highly sophisticated audience, and the recognition of some quite subtle departures from the norm presupposed a thorough familiarity with the established rules of Classical architecture. It speaks well for the duke's sophistication that he accepted Giulio's form of architectural humor.

It has recently been claimed that the irregularities of the north façade were forced on Giulio by the need to adjust its design to the features of the already completed villa behind it. Such impediments, however, rarely kept Renaissance architects from designing regular and symmetrical façades (compare Alberti's Palazzo Rucellai; FIG. 16-39). In any case, Giulio's intent seems to be expressed clearly enough in the palace's garden façade, where the irregularly spaced arches do not have to conform to any preexisting conditions. Even more chaotic is the design of the façades that face the interior courtyard (FIG. 17-49), where keystones (central voussoirs) either have not fully settled or seem to be slipping from the arches. There, massive Tuscan columns carry incongruously narrow architraves; the latter's structural insufficiency is stressed by the fact that they break midway between the columns, evidently unable to support the weight of the triglyphs above. And if this architectural chaos does not suffice to shock the visitor, Giulio delivers the *coup de grace* in the Sala dei Giganti (FIG. 17-50). In a panoramic sequence that covers the

17-49 GIULIO ROMANO, court façade of the Palazzo del Tè.

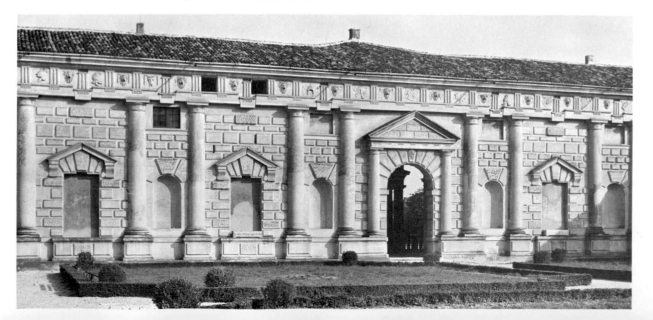

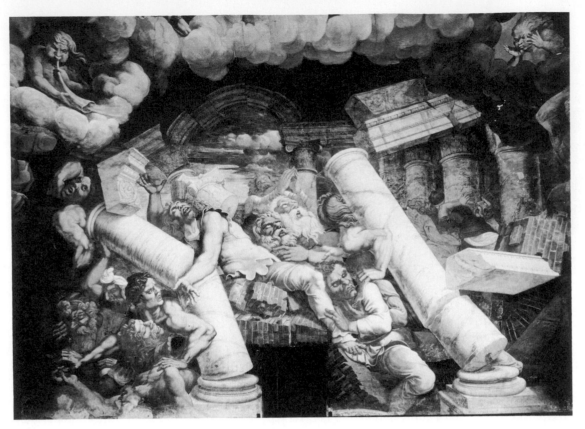

17-50 GIULIO ROMANO, *The Fall of the Giants* (detail), 1532–1534. Fresco. Sala dei Giganti, Palazzo del Tè.

ceiling and all the walls of this room, Giulio has represented the destruction of the palaces of the rebellious giants by the thunder-bolt-hurling Jupiter, from which visitors cringe involuntarily as the entire universe appears to be collapsing around them in a *tour de force* of pictorial illusionism and wild Mannerist convulsion.

In short, in the Palazzo del Tè, most of the Classical rules of order, stability, and symmetry have been deliberately flouted, and every effort has been made to startle and shock the beholder. This desire to create ambiguities and tensions is as typical of Mannerist architecture as it is of Mannerist painting, and many of the devices invented by Giulio Romano for the Palazzo del Tè will become standard features in the formal repertoire of later Mannerist building.

VENICE

In the sixteenth century, Venetian art became a strong, independent, and influential school in its own right, touched, if at all, only very slightly by the fashions of Mannerism sweeping Western Europe. Venice had long been the proud maritime mistress of the Mediterranean and its coasts; as the gateway to the Orient, it "held the gorgeous east in fee; and was the safeguard of the west." At the height of its commercial and political power during the fifteenth century, Venice saw its fortunes decline in the sixteenth.

Even so, Venice and the papal state were the only Italian sovereignties to retain their independence during the century of strife; all others were reduced to dependency on either France or Spain. Although the fundamental reasons for the decline of Venice were the discoveries in the New World and the economic shift from Italy to the Hapsburg Germanies and Netherlands, other even more immediate and pressing events drained her wealth and power. Venice was constantly embattled by the Turks, who, after their conquest of Constantinople, began to contest with Venice over control of the eastern Mediterranean. Early in the century, Venice also found itself attacked by the European powers of the League of Cambrai, formed and led by Julius II, who coveted Venetian holdings on the mainland. Although this wearing, two-front war sapped its strength, Venice's vitality endured, at least long enough to overwhelm the Turks in the great sea battle of Lepanto in 1571. This time, Europe was on Venice's side.

Architecture: Sansovino and Palladio

Venice was introduced to the High Renaissance style of architecture by a Florentine called JACOPO SANSOVINO (Jacopo Tatti, 1486–1570). Originally trained as a sculptor under ANDREA SANSOVINO, whose name he adopted, Jacopo went to Rome in 1518, where, under the influence of Bramante's circle, he increasingly turned toward architecture. When he arrived in Venice as a refugee from the Sack of Rome in 1527, he soon established himself as that city's leading and most admired architect; his buildings frequently inspired the architectural settings of the most prominent Venetian painters, including Titian and Veronese (FIG. 17-68).

Sansovino's largest and most rewarding public commissions were the Zecca (Mint) and the adjoining State Library (FIG. 17-51) in the heart of the island city. The Zecca, begun in 1535, faces the Canale San Marco with a stern and forbidding three-story façade; its heavy rustication gives it an intended air of strength and impregnability. This fortress-like look is emphasized by a boldly projecting, bracket-supported cornice reminiscent of the machicolated galleries of Medieval castles.

A very different spirit is expressed by the neighboring State Library of San Marco, begun a year after the Zecca, which Palladio referred to as "probably the richest and most ornate edifice since ancient times." With 21 bays (only 16 of which were completed during Sansovino's lifetime), it faces the Gothic Doge's Palace (FIG. 10-64) across the Piazzetta, a lateral extension of Venice's central Piazza San Marco. The relatively plain ground-story arcade has Doric columns attached to the arch-supporting piers in the manner of the Roman Colosseum (FIG. 6-46). It serves as a sturdy support for the higher, lighter, and much more decorative Ionic second story, which housed the reading room, with its treasure of manuscripts, safe from not-uncommon flooding. On this second level, the stern system of the ground story has been softened by the introduction of Ionic colonnettes that flank the piers and are paired in depth, rather than in the plane of the façade. Two-thirds the height of the main columns, they rise to support the springing of arches, the spans of which are two-thirds those of the lower arcade. The main columns carry an entablature with a richly decorated frieze on which, in strongly projecting relief, putti support garlands. This favorite decorative motif of the ancient Romans is punctuated by the oval windows of an attic story. Perhaps the most striking feature of the building is its roofline, where Sansovino replaces the traditional straight and unbroken cornice with a ballustrade (reminiscent of the one on Bramante's Tempietto, FIG. 17-6) interrupted by statue-bearing pedestals. The spacing of the latter corresponds to that of the orders below, so that the sculptures become the sky-piercing finials of the building's vertical design elements. The deft application of sculpture to the massive framework of the building (there are no visible walls) mitigates the potential severity of its design and gives its aspect an extraordinary plastic richness.

One feature rarely mentioned is the subtlety with which the library echoes the design of the lower two stories of the Doge's Palace (FIG. 10-64) opposite it. Although using a vastly different architectural vocabulary, Sansovino manages to adjust his building to the older one. Correspondences include the almost identical spacing of the lower arcades, the rich and decorative treatment of the second stories (including their balustrades), and the dissolution of the rooflines (by use of decorative battlements in the palace and a statue-surmounted balustrade in the library). It is almost as if Sansovino set out to translate the Gothic architecture of the Doge's Palace into a "modern" Renaissance idiom. If so, he was eminently success-

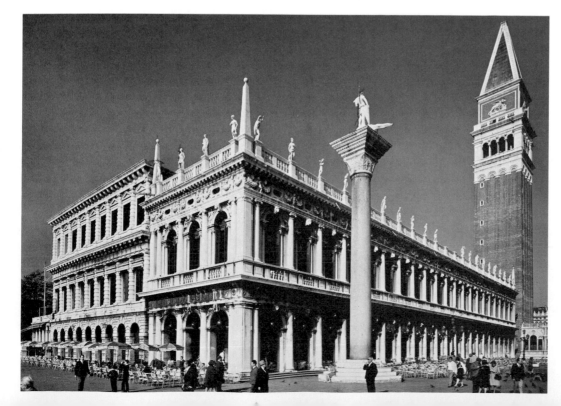

17-51 JACOPO SANSOVINO, La Zecca (Mint), 1535–1545 (left) and State Library, begun 1536, San Marco, Venice.

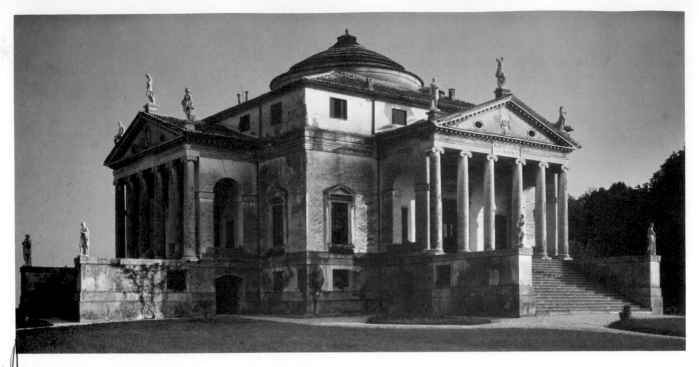

17-52 ANDREA PALLADIO, Villa Rotonda, near Vicenza, Italy, c. 1566–1570.

ful; the two buildings, although of different spiritual and stylistic worlds, mesh and combine to make the Piazzetta one of the most elegantly framed urban units in Europe.

When Jacopo Sansovino died he was succeeded as chief architect of the Venetian Republic by ANDREA PALLADIO (1508–1580). Beginning as a stonemason and decorative sculptor, Palladio, at 30, turned to architecture, the ancient literature on architecture, engineering, topography, and military science. Unlike the universal scholar, Alberti, Palladio became more of a specialist. He made several trips to Rome to study the ancient buildings at first hand. He illustrated Daniele Barbaro's edition of *Vitruvius* (1556), and he wrote his own treatise on architecture, *I quattro libri dell' architettura (Four Books on Architecture)*, originally published in 1570, which had a wide-ranging influence on succeeding generations of architects throughout Europe. Palladio's influence outside Italy, most significantly in England and in colonial America, was stronger and more lasting than that of any other architect.

Palladio is best known for his numerous villas built on the Venetian mainland, of which 19 still stand; the villas were especially influential on later architects. The same Arcadian spirit that prompted the ancient Romans to build villas in the countryside and that will be expressed so eloquently in the art of the Venetian painter Giorgione, motivated a similar villa-building boom in the sixteenth century. One can imagine that Venice, with its very limited space, must have been more congested than any ancient city. But a longing for the countryside was not the only mo-

tive; declining fortunes prompted the Venetians to develop their mainland possessions with new land investment and reclamation projects. Citizens who could afford it were encouraged to set themselves up as gentlemen farmers and to develop swamps into productive agricultural land. Wealthy families could look on their villas as providential investments. The villas were thus gentleman farms (like the much later American plantations, which were architecturally in-

17–53 ANDREA PALLADIO, plan of the Villa Rotonda, near Vicenza.

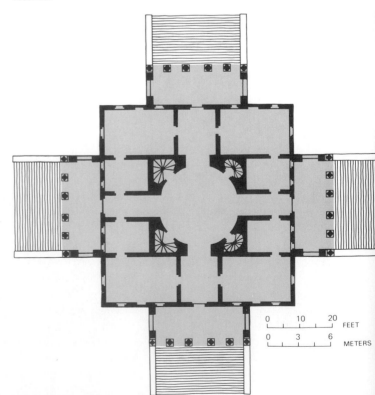

fluenced by Palladio) surrounded by service out-buildings that Palladio generally arranged in long, low wings branching out from the main building and enclosing a large, rectangular court area.

Although it is the most famous, Villa Rotonda (FIG. 17-52), near Vicenza, is not really typical of Palladio's villa style; it was not built for an aspiring gentleman farmer, but for a retired monsignor who wanted a villa for social events. Located on a hilltop, Villa Rotonda was planned and designed as a kind of belvedere, without the usual wings of secondary buildings. Its central plan (FIG. 17-53), with four identical façades and projecting porches, is therefore both sensible and functional; each of the porches can be used as a platform from which to enjoy a different view of the surrounding landscape. In this design, the central dome-covered rotunda logically functions as a kind of revolving platform, from which the visitor can turn in any direction for the preferred view. The result is a building with parts that are functional and systematically related to one another in terms of calculated mathematical relationships. Villa Rotonda, like Santa Maria della Consolazione at Todi (FIG. 17-9), thus embodies all the qualities of self-sufficiency and formal completeness of which most Renaissance architects dreamed. In his formative years, Palladio was influenced by Alberti, by Bramante, and, briefly, by Giulio Romano. By 1550, however, he had developed his own personal style, which, in its clarity and lack of ambiguity, was as different from contemporary Mannerism as it was—in its static qualities and rather dry, ''correct'' Classicism—different from the dynamic style of Michelangelo.

San Giorgio Maggiore (FIG. 17-54), directly across a broad canal from the Piazza San Marco, is one of the most dramatically placed buildings in Venice. Dissatisfied with earlier solutions to the problem of integrating a high central nave and lower aisles into a unified façade design, Palladio solved it by superimposing a tall, narrow, Classical porch on a low, broad one. This not only reflects the interior arrangement of the building, but also introduces the illusion of three-dimensional depth—an effect that is intensified by the strong projection of the central columns and the shadows they cast. Although at first the result seems to be a rigid formalism, the play of shadow across the building's surfaces, its reflection in the water, and its gleaming white against sea and sky create a remarkably colorful effect. The interior of the church (FIG. 17-55) is flooded with light, which crisply defines the contours of the rich wall articulations (pedestals, bases, shafts, capitals, entablatures), all beautifully and ''correctly'' profiled—the exemplar of what Classical architectural theory means by ''rational'' organization.

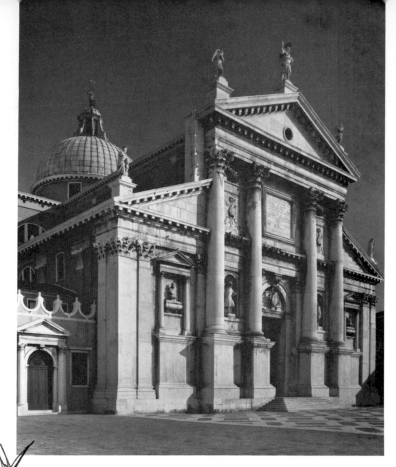

17-54 ANDREA PALLADIO, west façade of San Giorgio Maggiore, Venice, 1565.

17-55 ANDREA PALLADIO, interior of San Giorgio Maggiore (view facing east).

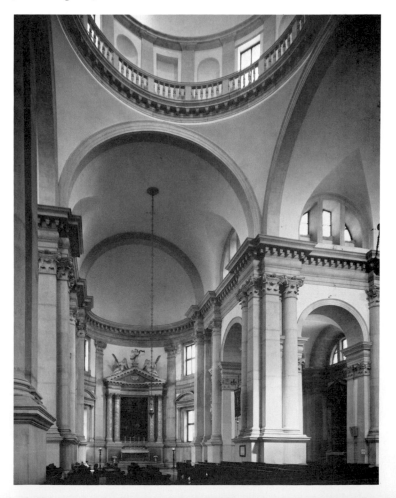

Painting: Giovanni Bellini and Giorgione

The soft, colored light of Venice, which relaxes the severe lines of Palladio's architecture, lives at its fullest in Venetian painting. In the career of GIOVANNI BELLINI (c. 1430–1516), we find the history of that style. In his long productive life, Bellini, always alert to what was new, never ceased to develop artistically and, almost by himself, created what is known as the Venetian style, which will be so important to the subsequent course of painting. Trained in the tradition of the International style by his father, a student of Gentile da Fabriano, Bellini worked in the family shop and did not develop his own style until after his father's death in 1470. His early independent works show him to be under the dominant influence of his brother-in-law, Andrea Mantegna. But in the late 1470s, impressed by the possibilities offered by the new oil technique that Antonello da Messina (FIG. 16-67) introduced during a visit to Venice, Bellini abandoned the Paduan's harsh, linear style and developed a sensuous, coloristic manner that was to become characteristic of Venetian painting.

Bellini is best known for his many Madonnas, which he painted both in half-length (with or without accompanying saints) on small devotional panels and on large, monumental altarpieces of the *sacra conversazione* type (FIG. 16-32). Judging by what appears to have been an unending string of commissions, his half-length Madonnas were especially popular. More than 80 of these are still extant, and, if arranged chronologically, they provide an almost gapless overview of the painter's artistic development. Our example, *Madonna of the Trees* (FIG. 17-56) dates from 1487 (a year or two after Bellini's adoption of the oil technique) and stands about halfway between his early linear, Mantegnesque approach and the fully developed, painterly style of his later years.* Placed before a wide strip of green satin, the grave and pensive Madonna steadies her child's uneasy pose, her somber expression suggesting foreknowledge of the infant's eventual fate. Although firmly modeled, the forms are softly rounded and, combined with warm and luminous colors, instill the painting with a quality of subdued voluptuousness that will become a trademark of much of later Venetian painting.

Despite the large number of similar works he painted, Bellini never repeated himself and always found some new variation on his Madonna theme. In most of his versions, the Madonna is placed behind a low parapet and, quite often, before a hanging drapery—devices that detach without completely isolat-

*The painting suffered some damage during restoration in 1902, when the Madonna's veil was repainted in a style that does not conform with that of the rest of the painting.

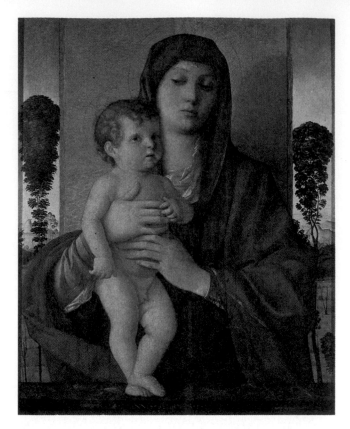

17–56   GIOVANNI BELLINI , *Madonna of the Trees, c.* 1487. Oil on wood, 29″ × 22″. Galleria dell' Accademia, Venice.

ing the sacred subject from its worldly surroundings. The Christ child is shown standing or sitting on the parapet, cradled in the Madonna's arms, or seated on her lap; he is shown facing his mother or the viewer. At times, the drapery in back of the figures is moved off-center and its width is varied to show more or less of the background landscape. The drapery may extend into the picture from either the left or the right frame to permit a view into the distance on one side only, creating the kind of asymmetrical composition that will enjoy great favor with Bellini's most illustrious student, Titian. After 1500, the landscape backgrounds become more and more important, to the point that the artist often omits the middle-ground drapery and sometimes changes his format from vertical to horizontal to show a greater expanse of landscape behind his Madonnas—landscapes that take on an increasingly Arcadian character.

If the long series of Bellini's half-length Madonnas reveals the gradual change in his painting style, two of his large altarpieces—the *San Giobbe Altarpiece, c.* 1490 (FIG. 17-57), and the *San Zaccaria Altarpiece,* 1505 (FIG. 17-58)—illustrate not only two stages in the artist's stunning development but also the essential differences between the Early and the High Renaissance treatments of the same subject. In the earlier work, The *San Giobbe Altarpiece* (FIG. 17-57), although the space is large, airy, and clearly defined, the figures seem to be crowded; they cling to the foreground plane and are seen in a slightly forced, Man-

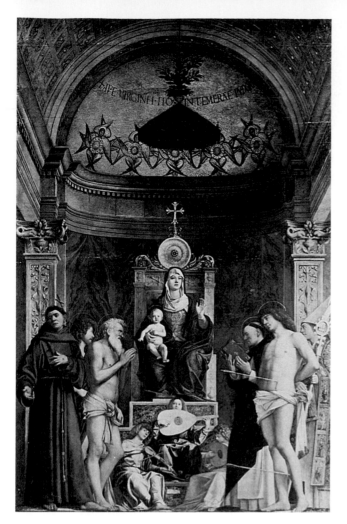

17-57 GIOVANNI BELLINI, *San Giobbe Altarpiece*, c. 1490. Oil on wood, 15' 4" × 8' 4". Galleria dell' Accademia, Venice.

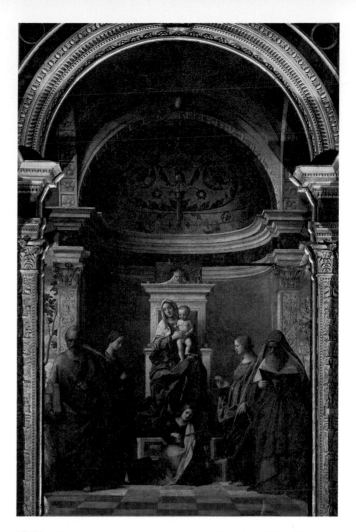

17-58 GIOVANNI BELLINI, *San Zaccaria Altarpiece*, 1505. Oil on wood transferred to canvas, approx. 16' 5" × 7' 9". San Zaccaria, Venice.

tegnesque, "worm's eye" perspective. The drawing remains sharp and precise, particularly in that charming Venetian trademark, the group of angel–musicians at the foot of the Madonna's throne. The figures are already arranged in the pyramidal grouping preferred by the High Renaissance, but they tend to exist as individuals rather than as parts of an integrated whole. Seen by itself, the *San Giobbe Altarpiece* is an orderly, well-balanced painting that can hold its own with any produced during the Early Renaissance. But side by side with the subsequent *San Zaccaria Altarpiece* (FIG. 17-58), it suddenly seems cluttered and overly busy. By adding simplicity to the order, balance, and clarity of the earlier painting, Bellini takes the long step into the High Renaissance.

In the *San Zaccaria Altarpiece*, in contrast to his earlier treatment of the theme, Bellini raises the observer's viewpoint and deemphasizes the perspective. The number of figures is reduced, and they are more closely integrated with each other and with the space that surrounds them. Combined into a single, cohesive group, the figures no longer cling to the front of the painting; disposed in depth, they now move in

and out of the apse instead of standing before it. Their attitudes produce a rhythmic movement within the group, but all obvious gestures have been eliminated and former busyness has changed to serene calm. In addition, Bellini's method of painting has become softer and more luminous. Line is no longer the chief agent of form but has been submerged in a sea of glowing color—a soft radiance that envelops the forms with an atmospheric haze and enhances their majestic serenity.

The San Zaccaria Madonna is the mature work of an old man who, in a single lifetime, spanned the development that took three generations in Florence. Departing from the Gothic, Bellini moved through the Early Renaissance and arrived in the High Renaissance even before Raphael and Michelangelo. And, at the very end of his long life, this astonishingly apt artist was still willing and able to make changes in his style and approach to keep himself abreast of his times; he began to deal with pagan subjects.

The Feast of the Gods (FIG. 17-59) represents a feedback of influence from one of Bellini's own students, Giorgione, who developed his master's landscape

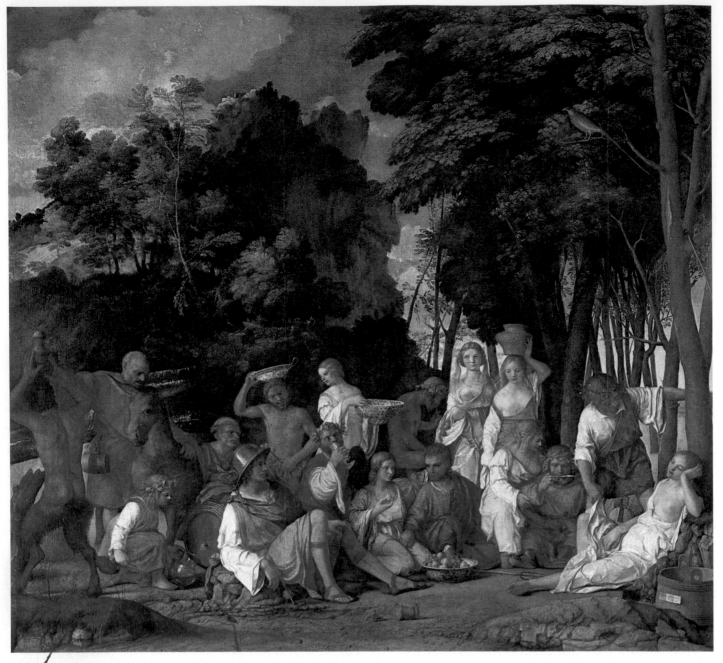

17-59 GIOVANNI BELLINI (and TITIAN ?), *The Feast of the Gods*, 1514. Oil on canvas, approx. 5′ 7″ × 6′ 2″. National Gallery of Art, Washington, D.C. (Widener Collection).

backgrounds into poetic, Arcadian reveries. (In this case, Titian, another of Bellini's pupils, probably completed the right background.) After Giorgione's premature death, Bellini embraced his student's interests and, in *The Feast of the Gods*, developed a new kind of mythology in which the Olympian gods appear as peasants enjoying a heavenly picnic in a shady northern Italian glade. His source is Ovid's *Fasti*, which describes a banquet of the gods. The figures are spread across the foreground. Satyrs attend the gods, nymphs bring jugs of wine, a child draws from a keg, couples engage in love play, and the sleeping nymph at the right receives amorous atten-

tion. The mellow light of a long afternoon glows softly around the gathering, touching the surfaces of colorful draperies, smooth flesh, and polished metal. Here, Bellini announces the delight the Venetian School will take in the beauty of texture revealed by the full resources of gently and subtly harmonized color. Behind the warm, lush tones of the figures, a background of cool, green, tree-filled glades reaches into the distance; at the right, a screen of trees makes a verdant shelter. The atmosphere is idyllic, a floral countryside making a setting for the never-ending pleasure of the immortal gods. The poetry of Greece and Rome, as well as that of the Renaissance, is filled with this pastoral mood, and the Venetians make a specialty of its representation. Its elements include the smiling landscape, eternal youth, and song and revelry, always with a touch of the sensual.

Thus, with Bellini, Venetian art becomes the great complement of the schools of Florence and Rome. The Venetians' instrument is color; that of the Florentines and Romans, sculpturesque form. These two schools run parallel—sometimes touching and engaging—through the history of Western art from the Renaissance on. Their themes are different. Venice paints the poetry of the senses and delights in the beauty of nature and the pleasures of mankind. Florence and Rome attempt the sterner, intellectual themes—the epic of man, the masculine virtues, the grandeur of the ideal, the lofty conceptions of religion as they involve the heroic and the sublime. The history of later Western art can be broadly understood as a dialogue between these two traditions.

The inspiration for Bellini's late Arcadianism is to be found in paintings like the so-called *Pastoral Sym-*

phony (FIG. 17-60) by his illustrious student GIORGIONE (Giorgione da Castelfranco, 1478–1510), a work held by some to be an early Titian. Out of dense color shadow emerge the soft forms of figures and landscape. The theme is as mysterious as the light. Two nude females, accompanied by two clothed young men, occupy the rich, abundant landscape through which a shepherd passes; in the distance, a villa crowns a hill. The pastoral mood is so eloquently evoked here that we need not know (as we do not) the precise meaning of the picture; the mood is enough. The shepherd is symbolic of the poet; the pipes and the lute, of his poetry. The two nymphs accompanying the young men may be thought of as their invisible inspiration, their muses; one turns to lift water from the sacred well of poetic inspiration. The great, golden bodies of the nymphs, softly modulated by the smoky shadow, become the standard Venetian type. It is the Venetian School that resurrects the Venus figure from antiquity, making her the fecund goddess of nature and of love. The full opu-

17-60   GIORGIONE (and/or TITIAN ?), *Pastoral Symphony, c.* 1508. Oil on canvas, approx. 43″ × 54″. Louvre, Paris.

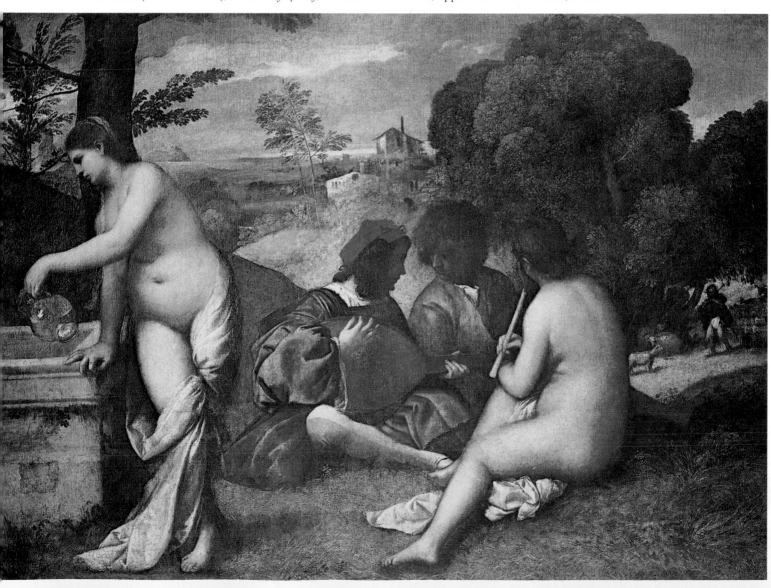

lence of the figures should, of course, not be read according to modern preferences in womanly physique but as poetic personifications of the abundance of nature. Giorgione—himself a pastoral poet in the pictorial medium and one of the greatest masters in the handling of light and color—praises the beauty of nature, music, woman, and pleasure. Vasari reports that Giorgione was an accomplished lutist and singer, and adjectives from poetry and music seem best suited to describe the pastoral air and muted chords of his painting. He casts a mood of tranquil revery and dreaminess over the whole scene, evoking the landscape of a lost but never forgotten paradise. Arcadia and its happy creatures persist in the subconscious memory and longing of mankind. Among the Italians, the Venetians were the first to express a love of nature and a realization of its potentialities for the painter, although they never represent it except as inhabited by man. The ancient spirits, the deities of field and woodland, still inhabit it too, and landscape—manifesting the bounty of Venus and sanctified by her beauty—as yet simply provides the inspiring setting for the poet, without whom it would be incomplete.

Titian

Giorgione's Arcadianism passed not only to his much older yet constantly learning master, Bellini, but also to Tiziano Vecelli, whose name we anglicize into TITIAN (c. 1490–1576). Titian is the most prodigious and prolific of the great Venetian painters. He is among the very greatest painters of the Western world—a supreme colorist and, in a broad sense, the father of the modern mode of painting. An important change that took place in Titian's time was the almost universal adoption of canvas, with its rough-textured surface, in place of wood panels for paintings. It is the painting of Titian that establishes oil color on canvas as the typical medium of our pictorial tradition.

According to a contemporary of Titian, Palma Giovane:

. . . Titian [employed] a great mass of colors, which served . . . as a base for whatever he was going to paint over it . . . I myself have seen his determined brushstrokes laden with color, sometimes a streak of pure earth-red which served him (one might say) as a half-tone, other times with a brushstroke of white lead; and with the same brush colored with a red, black, and yellow, he formed a highlight; and with these rules of technique made the promise of an excellent figure appear in four brushstrokes.

After having laid these important foundations, he then used to turn the pictures to the wall, and leave them—sometimes for as long as several months—without looking at them; and when he wanted to apply his brush to them again, he [examined] them most rigorously . . . whether he could find any defects in them or discover anything which would not be in harmony with the delicacy of his intentions. . . . Working thus, and redesigning his figures, Titian brought them into a perfect symmetry which could represent the beauty of Art as well as of Nature. After this was done, he put his hand to some other picture until the first was dry, working in the same way with this other; thus gradually he covered those quintessential outlines of his figures with living flesh . . . . He never painted a figure all at once, and used to say that he who improvises his song can form neither learned nor well-turned verses. But the final polish . . . was to unite now and then by a touch of his fingers the extremes of the light areas, so that they became almost half-tints . . . at other times, with a stroke he would place a dark streak in a corner; to reinforce it he would add a streak of red, like a drop of blood. . . . in the final phase [he] painted more with his fingers than with his brushes.

Trained by both Bellini and Giorgione, Titian learned so well from them that there is still no general agreement as to the degree of his participation in their later works. He completed several of Bellini's and Giorgione's unfinished works. One of his own

17-61 TITIAN, *Sacred and Profane Love*, c. 1515. Oil on canvas, approx. 3′ 11″ × 9′ 2″. Galleria Borghese, Rome.

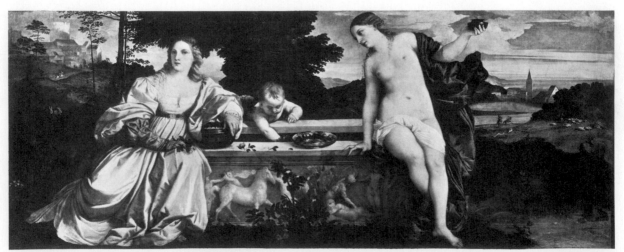

early works, *Sacred and Profane Love* (FIG. 17-61), is very much in the manner of Giorgione, with its Arcadian setting, its allegory, and its complex and enigmatic meaning. Two young women—one draped, the other nude—flank a sarcophagus into which a cupid reaches. Immediately behind them is a screen of trees and, to left and right, deep vistas into different landscapes. The two figures may represent the different levels of Neo-Platonic love: the sumptuously draped woman, a kind of allegory of vanity and the love of this world; the nude who holds aloft her lamp, the highest level of love that can be reached (love of the divine, nudity being symbolic of truth). Titian's figures are not suffused with Giorgione's glowing, mysterious tones; they are firmly drawn and boldly and brilliantly colored, and the artist manifests his chief interest in the play of light over the

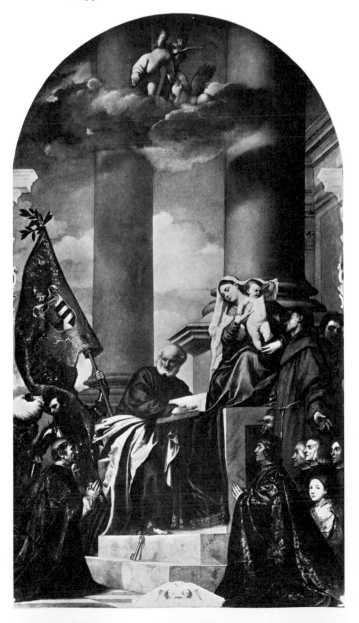

17-62 TITIAN, *Madonna of the Pesaro Family*, 1519–1526. Oil on canvas, approx. 16' × 9'. Santa Maria dei Frari, Venice.

rich satins and the smooth volumes of the body and glossy flesh. The world given to the eye is a world of color before it is a world of solid forms. And it is this truth that the Venetians were the first to grasp.

On the death of Giovanni Bellini in 1516, Titian was appointed painter to the republic of Venice. Shortly thereafter, he painted the *Madonna of the Pesaro Family* (FIG. 17-62) for the church of the Frari. This great work, which furthered the reputation and established the personal style of Titian, was presented to the church by Jacopo Pesaro, Bishop of Paphos in Cyprus and commander of the papal fleet, in thanksgiving for a successful expedition in 1502 against the Turks during the Venetian–Turkish war. In a stately, sunlit setting, the Madonna receives the commander, who kneels at the foot of her throne. A soldier (St. George?) behind the commander carries a banner with the arms of the Borgia (Pope Alexander VI); behind him is a turbaned Turk, a captive of the Christian forces. St. Peter occupies the steps of the throne, and St. Francis introduces other members of the Pesaro family, who kneel solemnly in the right foreground. The massing of monumental figures, singly and in groups, within a weighty and majestic architecture is, as we have seen, characteristic of the High Renaissance. But Titian does not compose a horizontal and symmetrical arrangement, as does Leonardo in *The Last Supper* (FIG. 17-3) or Raphael in *The School of Athens* (FIG. 17-17). Rather, he places the figures in occult balance on a steep diagonal, positioning the Madonna, the focus of the composition, well off the central axis. Attention is directed to her by the perspective lines, by the inclination of the figures, and by the directional lines of gaze and gesture. The design is beautifully brought into poise by the banner that inclines toward the left, balancing the rightward and upward tendencies of the main direction. This kind of composition is more dynamic than what we have seen so far in the High Renaissance. The forces already moving in it promise a new kind of pictorial design—one built on movement rather than rest. In his rendering of the rich surface textures, Titian gives a dazzling display of color in all its nuances. The human—especially the Venetian—scene is one with the heavenly, as the Madonna and saints find themselves honoring the achievements of particular men in this particular world. A quite worldly transaction is taking place between a queen, her court, and her loyal servants; the tableau is constructed in terms of Renaissance protocol and courtly splendor.

As Praxiteles brought the motif of the feminine nude into ancient Greek art, so Giorgione and Titian re-create it for the art of the modern West. In 1538, at the height of his powers, Titian painted for the Duke of Urbino the *Venus of Urbino* (FIG. 17-63), which gives us the compositional essentials for the representation

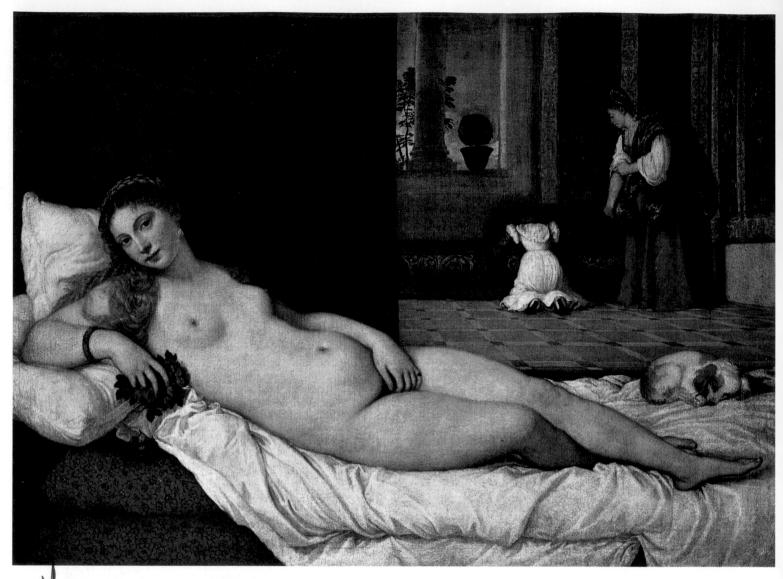

17-63   TITIAN, *Venus of Urbino*, 1538. Oil on canvas, approx. 48" × 66". Galleria degli Uffizi, Florence.

of a theme that will be popular for centuries. His version, based on an earlier and pioneering one painted by Giorgione, was to become official for paintings of the reclining nude, no matter how many variations would ensue. Venus reclines on a gentle slope made by her luxurious, pillowed couch, the linear play of the draperies contrasting with the sleek, continuous volume of her body. At her feet is a pendant (balancing) figure—in this case, a slumbering lapdog. Behind her, a simple drape serves both to place her figure emphatically in the foreground and to press a vista into the background at the right half of the picture. In the vista, two servants bend over a chest; beyond them, a smaller vista opens into a landscape. The steps backward into space and the division of the space into progressively smaller units are beautifully contrived. All of the resources of pictorial representation are in Titian's hands, and he uses them here to create original and exquisite effects.

Deep Venetian reds set off against the pale, neutral whites of the linen and the warm ivory–gold of the flesh are echoed in the red tones of the matron's skirt, the muted reds of the tapestries, and the neutral whites of the matron's sleeves and the gown of the kneeling girl. One must study the picture carefully to realize what subtlety of color planning is responsible, for example, for the placing of the two deep reds (in the foreground cushions and in the background skirt) that function so importantly in the composition as a gauge of distance and as terminals of an implied diagonal opposed to the real one of the reclining figure. Here, color is used not simply for the tinting of preexisting forms but as a means of organization that determines the placement of forms.

Titian could paint a Virgin Mary or a nude Venus with equal zeal. Neither he nor the connoisseurs of his time were aware of any contradiction. Yet it is significant that the female nude reappears in Western art as Venus, the great goddess of the ancient world, whom Medieval Christianity had especially feared

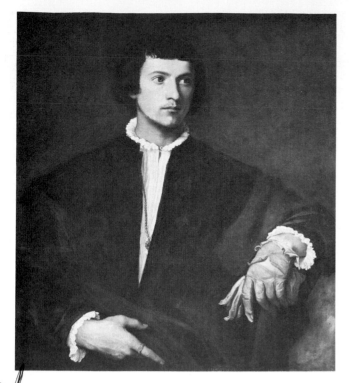

17-64 TITIAN, *Man with the Glove*, c. 1519. Oil on canvas, approx. 39″ × 35″. Louvre, Paris.

particular individual. It is the meditative, poetic youth, who is at the same time Baldassare Castiglione's ideal courtier, perfectly poised and self-assured, handsome, gallant, debonair, the "glass of fashion and the mold of form." No portrait gives us so much of the Renaissance manner in a single individual, unless it be Raphael's *Castiglione* (FIG. 17-19).

Honor and glory attached to Titian as he grew older. He was known to and sought after by all the great of Europe. He was painter to and close friend of Emperor Charles V, who made him a knight of the Holy Roman Empire; afterward, he painted numerous pictures for Charles's son, Philip II of Spain. The great Hapsburg painting collections centered around Titian's works, and his fame and wealth recall the success of Raphael. Toward the end of his life, his work became increasingly introspective, and a religious picture like the *Christ Crowned with Thorns* (FIG. 17-65) seems to be a sincerely devotional theme repudiating the paganism of the artist's prime. In this picture, Titian shows Christ tormented by the soldiers of Pilate, who twist a wreath of thorns around his head. The drama is achieved by the limited num-

17-65 TITIAN, *Christ Crowned with Thorns*, c. 1573–1575. Oil on canvas, approx. 9′ × 6′. Alte Pinakothek, Munich.

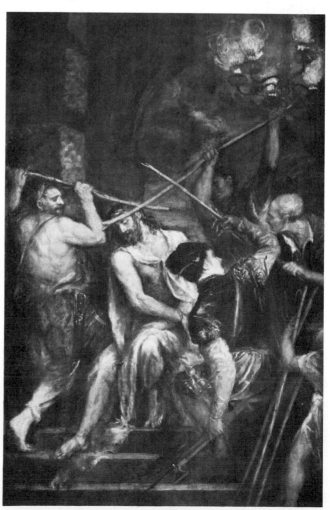

and whom it damned in exalting virginity and chastity as virtues. Now Venus returns, and the great Venetian paintings of her almost constitute pagan altarpieces. The Venetian Renaissance resurrects a formidable competitor for the saints.

Titian was not only a prolific painter of mythological and religious subjects but also a highly esteemed portraitist, and one of the very best. Of the well over 50 portraits by his hand to survive, an early example, *Man with the Glove* (FIG. 17-64), must suffice to illustrate his style. The portrait is a trifle more than half-length. The head is turned slightly away from the observer; the right hand gathers the drapery of a mantle, and the gloved left hand holds another glove. The blade-shaped shirt-front directs attention to the right hand; the subject's gaze controls the left. These dexterous compositional arrangements, creating a kind of "three-spot" relationship among head and hands, had already been made by Leonardo in his *Mona Lisa* (FIG. 17-4). A Titian portrait, as well as many of the Venetian and subsequent schools, generally makes much of the psychological reading of the most expressive parts of the body—the head and the hands. We are not immediately aware that these subtle placements influence our response to the portrait subject. In fact, a portrait must be as skillfully composed as a great figure composition. The mood of this portrait is Giorgionesque—one of dreamy preoccupation. The eyes turn away from us, as if, in conversation, the subject has recalled something that sets him musing in silence. Titian's *Man with the Glove* is as much the portrait of a cultivated state of mind as of a

ber of figures, the concentration on the figure of Christ, and the muted, flickering light that centers the action. The color scheme is almost monochromatic; the light and color play freely within and beyond the contours, making a patchy, confused mixture of lights and darks, in which it is difficult to read the forms with precision. But this only enhances the mystery, the gloomy environment, and the mood of torment. Titian's intention is not so much to stage the event as to present his religious and personal response to it. His very brushstroke—broad, thick, and freely applied—bespeaks the directness of his approach. It melts and scatters solid form to produce the wavering, supernatural glow that encircles spiritual vision. Here Titian's art looks forward to the painting of Rembrandt in the next century.

Tintoretto and Veronese

TINTORETTO (Jacopo Robusti, 1518–1594), claimed to be a student of Titian and aspired to combine the color of Titian with the drawing of Michelangelo. He is usually referred to as the outstanding Venetian representative of Mannerism. He adopts many Mannerist pictorial devices, but his dramatic power, depth of spiritual vision, and glowing Venetian color schemes do not seem to fit the Mannerist mold. We need not settle here the question of whether or not Tintoretto is a Mannerist; we need only mention that he shares some common characteristics with central Italian Mannerism and that, in other respects, he really looks forward to the Baroque. The art of Tintoretto is always extremely dramatic. In his *Miracle of the Slave* (FIG. 17-66), we find some of his typical stageplay. St. Mark hurtles downward to the assistance of a Christian slave, who is about to be martyred for the faith, and shatters the instruments of torture. These are held up by the executioner to the startled judge as the throng around the central action stares. The dynamism of Titian is greatly accelerated, and the composition is made up of contrary and opposing motions; for any figure leaning in one direction, there is another to counter it. At the extreme left a group—two men, a woman, and a child—winds contrapuntally about a column, resembling the later Mannerist twisting of Giovanni da Bologna's *Rape of the Sabine Women* (FIG. 17-47). The main group curves deeply back into space. But the most dynamic touch of all is made by the central trio of the slave, the executioner, and the inverted St. Mark. The three figures sweep together in a great, upward, serpentine curve, the motion of which is checked by the plunging figure of St. Mark, moving in the opposite direction. The entire composition is a kind of counterpoint of motion characteris-

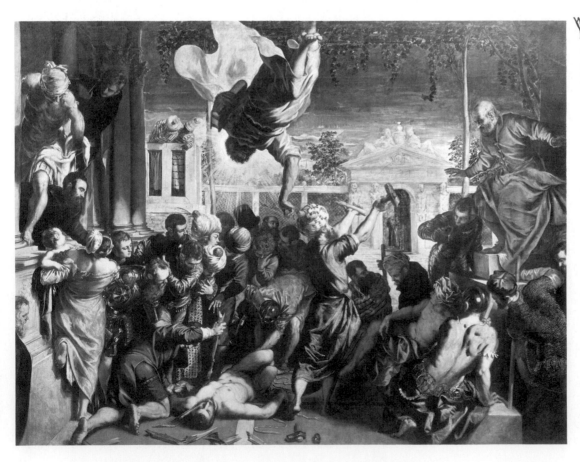

17-66 TINTORETTO, *The Miracle of the Slave*, 1548. Oil on canvas, approx. 14′ × 18′. Galleria dell' Accademia, Venice.

tic of Mannerism. The motion, however, is firmly contained within the picture frame, and the robustness of the figures, their solid structure and firm movement, the clearly composed space, and the coherent action have little that is Manneristic. There is nothing hesitant or ambiguous in the depiction of the miraculous event, which is dramatized forcefully and with conviction. Tintoretto's skillful theatricality and sweeping power of execution set him apart from the Mannerists and make him a forerunner of the Baroque, the age of theater and opera. And the tonality—the deep golds, reds, and greens—is purely Venetian.

Toward the end of his life, Tintoretto's art, like Titian's, becomes spiritual, even visionary, as solid forms melt away into swirling clouds of dark, shot through with fitful light. In Tintoretto's *Last Supper* (FIG. 17-67), painted for Palladio's church of San Giorgio Maggiore (FIG. 17-55), the actors take part in a ghostly drama; they are as insubstantial as the shadows cast by the faint glow of their halos and the flame of a single lamp that seems to breed phosphorescent spirits. All are moved by an intense, psychic commotion. The space speeds away into an unearthly darkness peopled by phantoms. Only the incandescent nimbus around his head identifies Jesus as he administers the Sacrament to his disciples. The contrast with Leonardo's *Last Supper* (FIG. 17-3) is both extreme and instructive. Leonardo's composition, balanced and symmetrical, parallels the picture plane in a geometrically organized and closed space; Christ's figure is the tranquil center of the drama and the focus of the perspective. In Tintoretto's painting, Christ is above and beyond the converging perspective lines that race diagonally away from the picture surface, creating disturbing effects of limitless depth and motion. Tintoretto's Christ is located by light flaring beacon-like out of darkness; Leonardo's, by geometric and perspectival centralization. The contrast of the two expresses the direction Renaissance painting takes in the sixteenth century, as it moves away from architectonic clarity of space and neutral lighting toward the dynamic perspectives and dramatic chiaroscuro of the coming Baroque.

17-67 TINTORETTO, *The Last Supper*, 1594. Oil on canvas, 12′ × 18′ 8″. San Giorgio Maggiore, Venice.

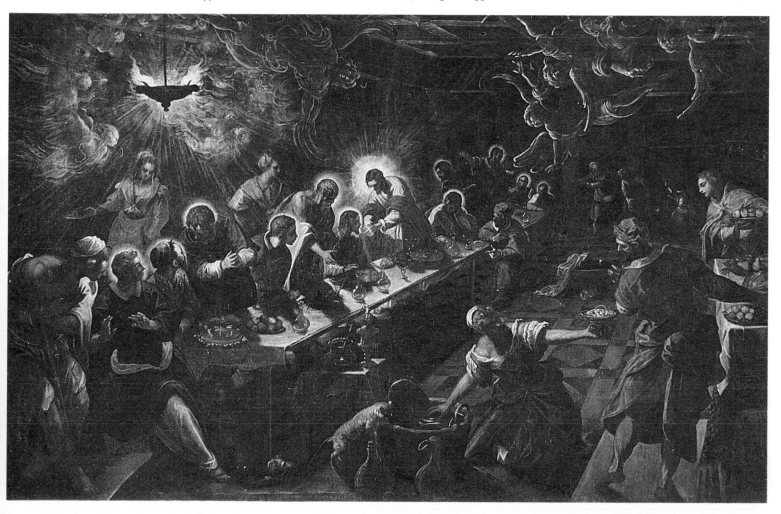

The last of the great Venetian masters was VERONESE (Paolo Cagliari, 1528–1588). Where Tintoretto glories in monumental drama and deep perspectives, Veronese specializes in splendid pageantry painted in superb color and set within a majestic, Classical architecture. Like Tintoretto, Veronese painted on a huge scale, with canvases often as large as 20 by 30 feet. His usual subjects, painted for the refectories of wealthy monasteries, afforded him an opportunity to display magnificent companies at table. *Christ in the House of Levi* (FIG. 17-68), originally called *The Last Supper*, is a good example. Here, in a great open loggia framed by three monumental arches (the style of the architecture closely resembles the upper arcades of Jacopo Sansovino's library; FIG. 17-51), Christ is seen seated at the center of splendidly garbed grandees of Venice, while with a courtly gesture, the very image of gracious grandeur, the chief steward welcomes guests. The spacious loggia is crowded not only with robed magnificoes but with their colorful retainers, clowns, dogs, and dwarfs. The Holy Office of the Inquisition accused Veronese of impiety in painting such creatures so close to the Lord, and he was ordered to make changes at his own expense. Reluctant to do so, he simply changed the painting's title, converting the subject to a less solemn one. As Palladio looks to the example of the Classical architecture of the High Renaissance, so Veronese returns to High Renaissance composition, its symmetrical balance, and its ordered architectonics. His shimmering color is drawn from the whole spectrum, although he avoids solid colors for half shades (light blues, sea greens, lemon yellows, roses, and violets), creating veritable flower beds of tone.

Tintoretto and Veronese were employed by the republic of Venice to decorate the grand chambers and council rooms of the Doge's Palace. A great and popular decorator, Veronese shows himself to be a master of imposing, illusionistic ceiling compositions like *The Triumph of Venice* (FIG. 17-69), where within an oval frame, he presents Venice, crowned by Fame, enthroned between two great, twisted columns in a balustraded loggia, garlanded with clouds, and attended by figures symbolic of her glories. This work represents one of the very first modern, pictorial glorifications of a state—a subject that will become very popular during the Baroque period. Veronese's perspective is not, like Mantegna's or Correggio's, projected directly up from below; rather, it is a projection of the scene at a 45° angle to the spectator, a technique that will be used by many later Baroque decorators, particularly the Venetian Tiepolo in the eighteenth century.

It is fitting that we close our discussion of Italian art in the sixteenth century with a scene of triumph, for indeed the century witnessed the triumph of architecture, sculpture, and painting. They achieve the status of fine arts, and a tradition is established by these masters of prodigious genius, whose works inspire all artists who follow but never surpass them.

17-68 VERONESE, *Christ in the House of Levi*, 1573. Oil on canvas, approx. 18' 6" × 42' 6". Galleria dell' Accademia, Venice.

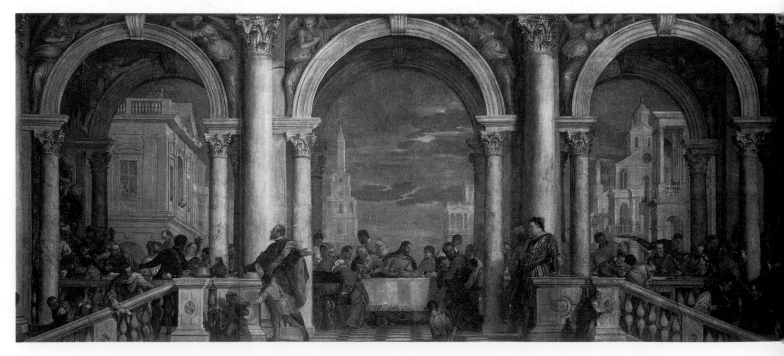

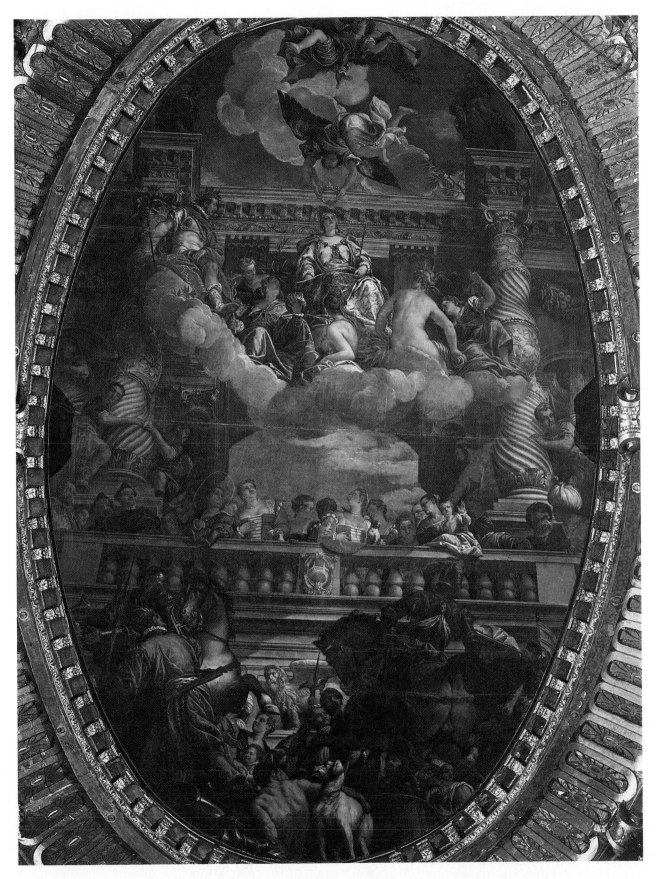

17-69   VERONESE, *The Triumph of Venice, c.* 1585. Oil on canvas. Ceiling of the Doge's Palace, Venice.

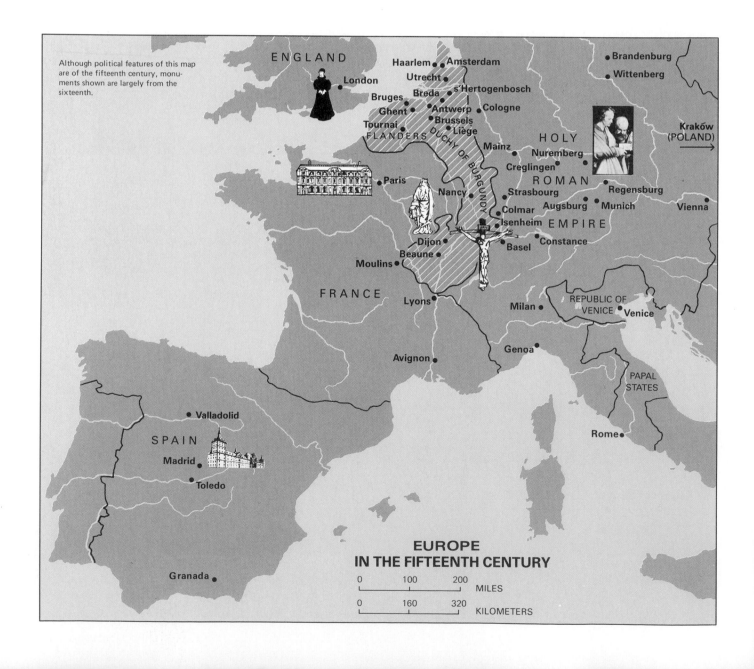

18

Although political features of this map are of the fifteenth century, monuments shown are largely from the sixteenth.

ENGLAND

London

Haarlem • Amsterdam
Utrecht
Bruges • Breda • s'Hertogenbosch
Ghent • Antwerp • Cologne
Tournai • Brussels
Liège
FLANDERS

DUCHY OF BURGUNDY

• Brandenburg
• Wittenberg

Kraków
(POLAND) →

HOLY

Paris

Nancy

Mainz
Nuremberg
Creglingen

ROMAN

Regensburg

Strasbourg
Colmar
Isenheim

Augsburg • Munich
Constance
Basel

Vienna

EMPIRE

Dijon
Beaune
Moulins

FRANCE

Lyons

Avignon

Milan

Genoa

REPUBLIC OF
VENICE • Venice

PAPAL
STATES

Valladolid

SPAIN

Madrid
Toledo

Rome •

Granada •

**EUROPE
IN THE FIFTEENTH CENTURY**

0   100   200
                          MILES

0   160   320
                          KILOMETERS

THE RENAISSANCE OUTSIDE OF ITALY

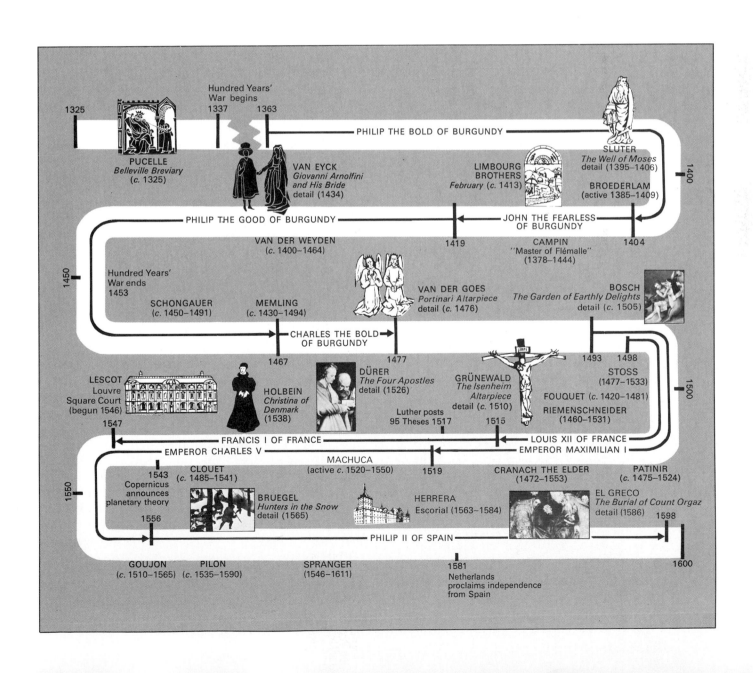

1325

Hundred Years'
War begins
1337   1363

PHILIP THE BOLD OF BURGUNDY

PUCELLE
Belleville Breviary
(c. 1325)

VAN EYCK
*Giovanni Arnolfini
and His Bride*
detail (1434)

LIMBOURG
BROTHERS
February (c. 1413)

SLUTER
The Well of Moses
detail (1395–1406)

BROEDERLAM
(active 1385–1409)

1400

PHILIP THE GOOD OF BURGUNDY

JOHN THE FEARLESS
OF BURGUNDY

VAN DER WEYDEN
(c. 1400–1464)

1419

CAMPIN
"Master of Flémalle"
(1378–1444)

1404

1450

Hundred Years'
War ends
1453

SCHONGAUER
(c. 1450–1491)

MEMLING
(c. 1430–1494)

VAN DER GOES
Portinari Altarpiece
detail (c. 1476)

BOSCH
The Garden of Earthly Delights
detail (c. 1505)

CHARLES THE BOLD
OF BURGUNDY

1467   1477   1493   1498

LESCOT
Louvre
Square Court
(begun 1546)

HOLBEIN
*Christina of
Denmark*
(1538)

DÜRER
The Four Apostles
detail (1526)

GRÜNEWALD
*The Isenheim
Altarpiece*
detail (c. 1510)

Luther posts
95 Theses 1517   1515

STOSS
(1477–1533)

FOUQUET (c. 1420–1481)

RIEMENSCHNEIDER
(1460–1531)

1500

1547

FRANCIS I OF FRANCE

LOUIS XII OF FRANCE

EMPEROR CHARLES V

EMPEROR MAXIMILIAN I

MACHUCA
(active c. 1520–1550)

1519

CLOUET
(c. 1485–1541)

1543
Copernicus
announces
planetary theory

CRANACH THE ELDER
(1472–1553)

PATINIR
(c. 1475–1524)

1550

BRUEGEL
Hunters in the Snow
detail (1565)

HERRERA
Escorial (1563–1584)

EL GRECO
The Burial of Count Orgaz
detail (1586)

1556

1598

PHILIP II OF SPAIN

1600

GOUJON
(c. 1510–1565)

PILON
(c. 1535–1590)

SPRANGER
(1546–1611)

1581
Netherlands
proclaims independence
from Spain

WHILE THE GREAT artistic events were happening in Renaissance Italy, the lands beyond the Alps were still immersed in the Gothic style that Italy had never really accepted as its own.* Gothicism in architecture persisted well into the sixteenth century in the north, although in the fifteenth century we find the stirring of new artistic forces in sculpture and painting. The north never knew Classical antiquity as the Italians knew it. In Italy, the remains of the Classical world were everywhere, and the Italians believed themselves to be descendants of the ancient Romans. The Gothic International style of the fourteenth century was, for the Italians, only a passing fashion; coming between Giotto and Masaccio, it hardly constitutes more than a brief interruption of a new stylistic movement that will carry along with it the future of European art. In the north, too, the International style will pass, giving way to a powerful realism, which, even without the inspiration of the Classical antique style, will break with the past and point directions of its own.

The northern painter, evolving out of the illuminator, finds, as did the artist in Italy, a new prestige and place. Although coexisting with a development of commerce and wealth almost modern in tone, the social structure of the north in the fifteenth century adhered to the hierarchies of the Middle Ages. The nobles and clergy continued to rule, although the true source of wealth and power was the bourgeoisie. This large middle class, in turn, was still organized and controlled by the guild system that had taken form in the Middle Ages. In the north, the guild dominated the life of the average man to an even greater extent than in Italy. To pursue a craft, a man had to belong to the guild controlling that craft—the painter, for example, to the Guild of St. Luke, which included the saddlers, glassworkers, and mirror-workers as well. To secure membership in the guild, the aspiring painter was apprenticed in boyhood to a master, with whom he lived as a son and who taught him the fundamentals of his craft: how to make implements; how to prepare panels with gesso (plaster mixed with a binding material); and how to mix colors, oils, and varnishes. Once the youth mastered these procedures and learned to work in the traditional manner of his master, he usually spent several years working as a journeyman in various cities, observing and gaining ideas from other masters.

He was then eligible to become a master and was admitted to the guild. Through the guild, he obtained commissions; the guild inspected his painting for honest materials and workmanship and secured him adequate payment. The result was the solid craftsmanship that characterizes the best work of Flanders as well as of Italy.

This craftsmanship involved mastery of the new oil medium, which had such great influence on Venetian painters at the end of the fifteenth century; we have spoken of Titian's management of it (p. 646). Traditionally, Jan van Eyck is credited with the invention of oil painting a century before Titian, although the facts surrounding its early history still remain mysterious. Flemish painters built up their pictures by superimposing translucent paint layers, called *glazes*, on a layer of opaque monochrome underpainting, which in turn had been built up from a carefully planned drawing made on a white-grounded panel of wood. The base of the binding medium for the pigments was a fast-drying oil that had been known and used by certain painters in the Late Middle Ages. The secret of the new technique appears to have been an unidentified supplement to the usual composition of the glazes. With the new medium, painters were able to create richer colors, seemingly lit from within, than had previously been possible. As a result, northern painting of the fifteenth century is characterized by a deep, intense tonality, glowing light, and hard, enamel-like surfaces, quite unlike the high-keyed color, sharp light, and rather matte surfaces of Italian tempera.

The brilliant and versatile new medium was exactly right for the formal intentions of the northern painters, who aimed for sharply focused, hard-edged, sparkling clarity of detail in the representation of thousands of objects ranging in scale from large to almost invisible. The Italians were interested primarily in the *structure* behind the appearances given to the eye—that is, in perspective, composition, anatomy, the mechanics of bodily motion, and proportion through measure. The northern painters were intent on rendering the *appearances* themselves—the bright, colored surfaces of things touched by light. Their tradition of stained glass and miniatures made their realism one of radiant, decorative color rather than of sculpturesque form. The differences between the painting of Italy and of northern Europe are emphasized by the fact that, when oil painting spread to Italy after the mid-century, it did not radically affect Italian sensibility to form. Although the color of Italian painting became richer, particularly in Venice, the new medium—which, in time, completely replaced tempera—was exploited in the service of the structural purposes of Italian art. On the whole, until the early sixteenth century, artistic communication between northern and southern Europe seems to have

---

*Strictly speaking, the term "Renaissance" refers to the revival of ancient Roman ideals and forms in Italian art of the fifteenth century and later and really does not apply to the still Gothic European art outside Italy, where no such revival took place. Nevertheless, strikingly new and promising developments in the Late Gothic centuries contemporaneous with classicizing Italian art invite the use of the term, and it now has wide currency.

been limited to a relatively few individuals, and both areas tended to develop independently of each other.

The political background against which the development of northern art took place in the fifteenth century was not unlike that of Italy. The commercial free cities that dominated the political scene at the beginning of the fifteenth century gradually fell under the rule of princes until the beginning of the sixteenth century, which saw the emergence of powerful states—France, England, and the Hapsburg empire, comprising Spain, the Germanies, and the Netherlands. As in Italy, the wealth and leisure necessary to encourage the growth of the arts was based on commerce and on the patronage of the powerful princes and rich merchants who controlled it.

THE FIFTEENTH CENTURY

Flanders

The most important of the prosperous commercial cities of the north was Bruges, which, like Florence, derived its wealth from the wool trade and from banking. Until late in the fifteenth century, an arm of the North Sea, now silted up, reached inland to Bruges. Here, ships brought raw wool from England and Spain and carried away the fine manufactured woolen cloth that became famous throughout Europe. The wool trade brought bankers, among them representatives of the House of Medici, and Bruges became the financial clearinghouse for all of northern Europe. In its streets, merchants from Italy and the Near East rubbed shoulders with traders from Russia and Spain. Despite the flourishing economies of its sister cities—Ghent, Louvain, and Ypres—Bruges so dominated Flanders that the Duke of Burgundy chose to make the city his capital and moved his court there from Dijon in the early fifteenth century.

The dukes of Burgundy were probably the most powerful rulers in northern Europe during the first three quarters of the fifteenth century. Although cousins of the French kings, they usually supported England (on which they relied for the raw materials for their wool industry) during the Hundred Years' War and, at times, were in control of much of northern France, including Paris. Through intermarriage with the House of Flanders, they annexed the Low Countries, and, during the height of their power, their lands stretched from the Rhône River to the North Sea. Only the rash policies of the last of their line, Charles the Bold, and his death at the battle of Nancy in 1477 brought to an end the Burgundian dream of forming a strong middle kingdom between France and the Holy Roman Empire. After Charles's death, the southern Burgundian lands were reabsorbed by France, and the Netherlands passed to the

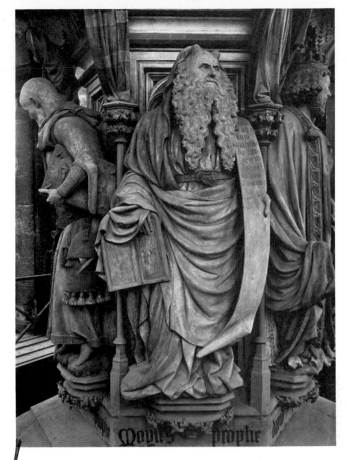

18-1 CLAUS SLUTER, *The Well of Moses*, 1395–1406. Figures approx. 6' high. Chartreuse de Champmol, Dijon, France.

Holy Roman Empire by virtue of the dynastic marriage of Charles's daughter, Mary of Burgundy, to Maximilian of Hapsburg.

Philip the Bold of Burgundy, who ruled from 1364 to 1404, and his brother John, Duke of Berry, were the greatest sponsors of the arts of their time in northern Europe. Their interests centered on illuminated manuscripts, Arras tapestries, and rich furnishings for their numerous castles and town houses throughout their duchies. Philip's largest artistic enterprise was the foundation of the Chartreuse de Champmol, near Dijon. Intended to receive the tombs of the family, its magnificent endowment attracted artists from all parts of northern Europe. The outstanding representative of this short-lived Burgundian School was the sculptor CLAUS SLUTER (active *c.* 1380–1406).

For the cloister of the Chartreuse de Champmol, Sluter designed a symbolic well in which Moses and five other prophets surround a base that once supported a Crucifixion group. The six prophets of *The Well of Moses* (FIG. 18-1) recall the jamb figures of the Gothic portals, but they far surpass even the most realistic of those (FIG. 10-33) in their intense observation and rendering of minute detail and in their bulk, which manages to contain a wealth of detail that might otherwise be distracting. The life-size figures are swathed in heavy draperies with voluminous folds, characteristic of Sluter's style, and the artist manages to make their difficult, complex surfaces seem remarkably lifelike. This effect is enhanced by the skillful differentiation of textures, from coarse drapery to smooth flesh and silky hair, and by the paint, which is still partly preserved. This fascination with the specific and tangible in the visible world will be one of the chief characteristics of fifteenth-century Flemish painting. But despite its realism, Sluter's *Moses* (FIG. 18-1), compared with Donatello's *St. Mark* (FIG. 16-5), reveals what is still missing in the northern concept of the figure: the principle of interior movement, or weight shift.

The Chartreuse de Champmol must have been furnished with numerous altarpieces, but only a carved altarpiece representing the Adoration of the Magi survives. The odd-shaped wings for this altarpiece were painted by MELCHIOR BROEDERLAM (active 1385–1409), a Flemish painter who had been drawn to Dijon. On the left wing are *The Annunciation* and *The Visitation*; on the right wing (FIG. 18-2), <u>*The Presentation* and *The Flight into Egypt*</u>. The paintings show that Broederlam was a major northern exponent of the International style. His compositional devices—the uptilted plane of the landscape in the *Flight* scene, with its high horizon topped by a castle; the serpentine recession into the background; the elegant silhouettes of the figures, reminiscent of Sienese art—

18-2 MELCHIOR BROEDERLAM, *The Presentation* and *The Flight into Egypt*, 1394–1399. Tempera and oil on wood, approx. 64″ × 51″. Musée des Beaux-Arts, Dijon.

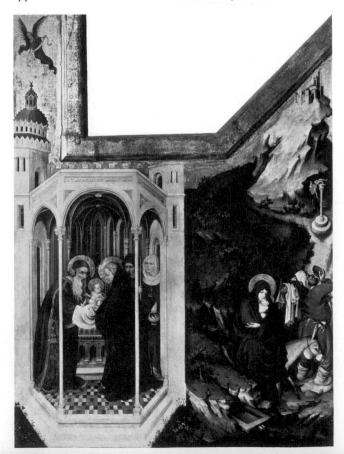

have already been seen in such southern works as Gentile da Fabriano's *Adoration of the Magi* (FIG. 16-25). Also pointing back to Sienese art is Broederlam's modest essay into perspective and the delicate architectural enframement of the *Presentation* scene. All this has been combined with the minutest observation and rendering of realistic details. That Broederlam was not immune to the influence of Sluter is seen in the handling of the voluminous drapery and, near the panel's right border, the strikingly massive figure of Joseph, planted like a tree stump, taking a draft from his cup—and looking like a figure from a painting by Pieter Bruegel some 150 years later.

It is sometimes pointed out that Broederlam's miniaturistic style is ill-suited for the size of the panels, which are some 5 feet high. The reason for this disproportion lies in the fact that, being among the earliest surviving examples of northern panel paintings, these works still reflect some of the long-standing northern painting traditions from which they are a revolutionary departure. For centuries, the characteristic painted surface in the north had been either stained glass or the illuminated manuscript page. Gothic architecture in northern Europe had successfully eliminated solid walls and had left few continuous, blank surfaces that invited painted decorations, contrary to the case in Italy, where climate and architecture favored mural painting in fresco. The northern artist was accustomed to working not only in miniature but with rich, jewel-like color, which, especially in stained glass, has a profound luminosity, the light seeming to irradiate the forms. Thus, he came into the fifteenth century habituated to deep color worked into exquisitely tiny and intricate shapes and patterns. When the northern miniaturist became acquainted, through the International style, with Italian forms and ideas, he saw himself forced to reduce to page size, or smaller, the inventions used in large compositions by Italian wall and panel painters like Duccio, Giotto, Simone Martini, and others. This development, which led to a kind of "perspective naturalism," was inconsistent with the basic function of book illumination—to decorate a page and illustrate part of the written text. Toward the end of the fourteenth century, illuminations began to take on the character of independent paintings, expanding on the page until they occupied it completely. By about 1400, these new forces generated in miniatures seemed to demand larger surfaces, and the shift was made to panel painting.

The first steps toward the illumination's expansion within the text appear in the work of JEAN PUCELLE (active *c.* 1320–1370), a Parisian illuminator who revitalized the stagnating Gothic manner of the Paris School. A page from the so-called *Belleville Breviary*, *c.* 1325 (FIG. 18-3), shows how the entire page has

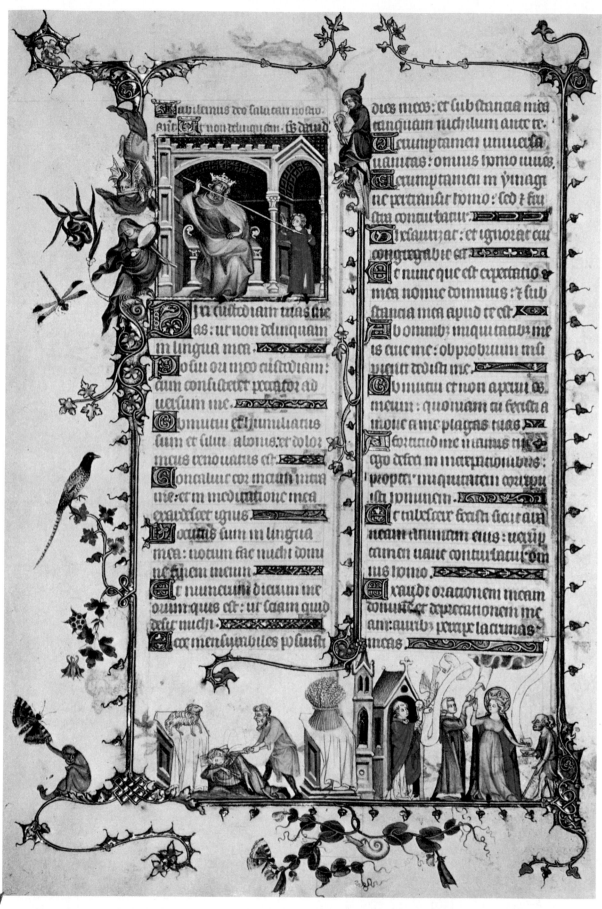

18-3 JEAN PUCELLE, page from the *Belleville Breviary*, c. 1325. Illumination, approx. 9½" × 6¾". Bibliothèque Nationale, Paris.

become the province of the illuminator. The borders, extended to invade the margins, include not only decorative tendrils and a profusion of spiky ivy and floral ornaments, but also a myriad of insects, small animals, and grotesques. In addition, three narrative scenes encroach on the columns of the next, the graceful postures and flowing draperies of the figures reflecting Sienese influence. One feels that any of these narratives could have been expanded into a full-page illustration or even a panel painting.

Such an expansion has occurred in the calendar pages of a gorgeously illustrated ''Book of Hours,'' made for the Duke of Berry, brother of the king of France and of Philip the Bold of Burgundy. The manuscript, *Les Très Riches Heures du Duc de Berry* (FIGS. 18-4 and 18-5), was completed in 1416 by the three LIMBOURG BROTHERS—Pol, Hennequin, and Herman. Such books became favorite possessions of the northern aristocracy during the fourteenth and fifteenth centuries. As prayer books, they replaced the traditional psalters, which had been the only liturgical books in private hands until the mid-thirteenth century. The heart of the ''Book of Hours'' is the ''Office of the Blessed Virgin,'' which contains liturgical passages to be read privately at eight set points during the day, from Matins to Compline. This part is usually preceded by an illustrated calendar containing local religious feast days; it is followed by penitential psalms, devotional prayers, litanies to the saints, and other offices, including that of the Dead and of the Holy Cross.

The calendar pictures of *Les Très Riches Heures* are perhaps the most famous in the history of manuscript illumination. They represent the 12 months of the year in terms of the associated seasonal tasks, alternating the occupations of nobility and peasantry. Above each picture is a lunette representing the chariot of the sun as it makes its yearly round through the 12 months and signs of the zodiac; numerical notations designate the zodiacal degree passed through in the course of the year. The picture for the month of *February* (FIG. 18-4), under the signs of Aquarius and of Pisces, displays a snowy landscape, bare trees, a woodsman at work, another driving a donkey laden with faggots to the distant village. A woman blowing on her fingers moves through a farmyard toward the house, where the red-capped master of the domicile and his womenfolk warm themselves before a fire. The high horizon and steep, carefully laid-out landscape, in which the details of the ordinary environment are carefully enumerated and authentically depicted, recall the landscape of Ambrogio Lorenzetti's *Good Government* fresco in Siena (FIG. 15-24); it is possible that one of the Limbourg brothers had seen these works or ones like them. In any event, *February* exemplifies the International style in its northern flowering. Even more representative, perhaps, is the

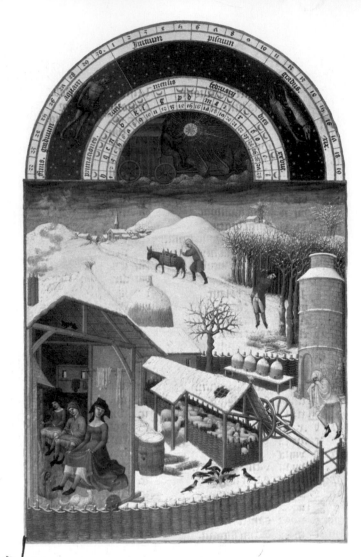

18-4 THE LIMBOURG BROTHERS, *February*, from *Les Très Riches Heures du Duc de Berry*, 1413–1416. Illumination, approx. 8¾" × 5½". Musée Condé, Chantilly.

colorful *May* from the same series (FIG. 18-5). Here, a cavalcade of patrician ladies and gentlemen, preceded by trumpeters, rides out to celebrate the first day of May, a spring festival observed by the courts throughout Europe. They are clad in springtime green, garlanded with fresh leaves, and sparkle with ornate finery. Behind them is a woodland and the château of Riom. These great country seats, most of which belonged to the Duke of Berry, loom in the backgrounds of most of the calendar pictures and are so faithfully represented that those surviving today are easily recognized. The spirit of the picture is Chaucerian (*The Canterbury Tales* is hardly a generation older)—lightsome, artificial, chivalric, pleasure-loving, and, of course, much in contrast with the peasant mood. The elegant silhouettes, rich colors, and decorative linear effects again recall Sienese art. *February* and *May* were evidently painted by different artists (note especially the differences in figure representation), but it has never been possible to assign specific pictures to the various Limbourg brothers. Nevertheless, although their styles may differ, their

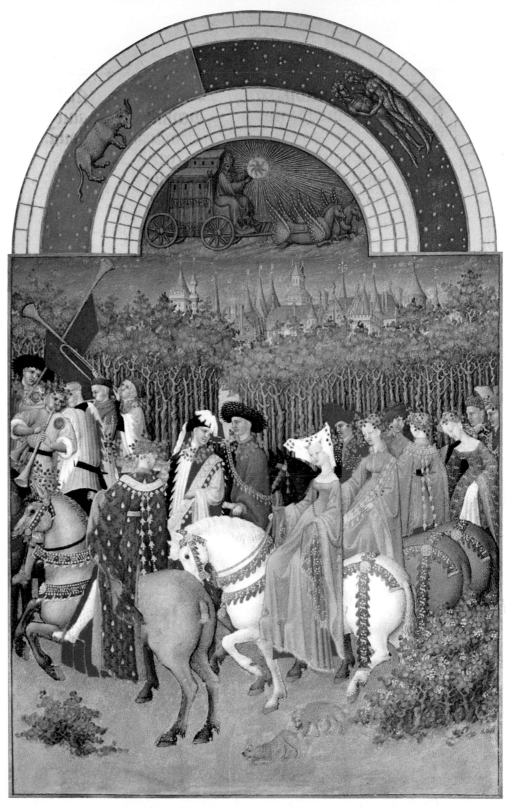

18-5 The Limbourg Brothers, *May*, from *Les Très Riches Heures du Duc de Berry*, 1413–1416. Illumination, approx. 8½″ × 5½″. Musée Condé, Chantilly.

main interests were the same. Within the confines of the International style, they represented as accurately as possible the actual world of appearances and the activities of man, peasant or aristocrat, in his natural surroundings at specific times of the year. Thus, the traditional field of subject matter has been expanded to include genre subjects; they are given a prominent place, even in a religious book. Secular and religious subjects remain neatly separated, but they will increasingly encroach on each other during the course of the fifteenth century to produce as thorough a humanization of religious subject matter as we saw in Italy.

Hardly a decade after *Les Très Riches Heures*, an example of the International style at its peak, we have a work of quite different and novel conception, *The Mérode Altarpiece* (FIG. 18-6) by the Master of Flémalle, now identified as ROBERT CAMPIN (c. 1378–1444), the

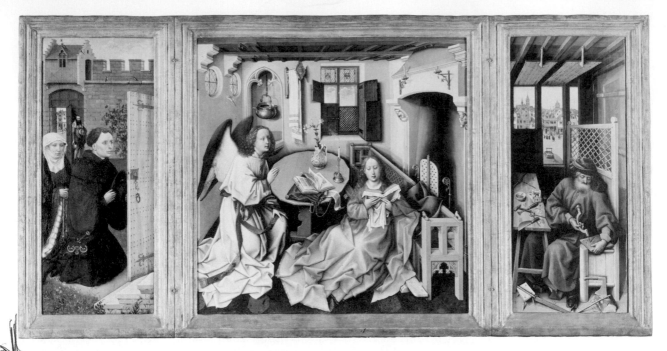

18-6 ROBERT CAMPIN (Master of Flémalle), *The Mérode Altarpiece, c.* 1425–1428. Tempera and oil on wood, center panel approx. 25″ × 25″, wings approx. 25″ × 11″. Metropolitan Museum of Art, New York (Cloisters Collection).

leading painter of the city of Tournai. Here, the aristocratic taste, romantic mood, and ornamental style of the International painters are replaced with a relatively blunt, sober realism in setting and characterization. The old theme of the Annunciation occupies the central panel of the tripytych, and something of Internationalism remains in its decorative line play. But the donors, depicted in the left panel, set the tone. Man and wife, they are of the grave and sedate middle class; unostentatiously prosperous, quietly dressed, they kneel in a little courtyard, the man peering through the door at the mystery taking place. Discreetly set apart from it, they take the mystery as a fact, and factualness determines the artist's whole approach. All the objects in the Annunciation scene are rendered with careful attention to their actual appearance, and the event takes place in an everyday, middle-class Flemish interior, in which all accessories, furniture, and utensils are indicated, lest the setting be incomplete. But the objects represented are not merely that; book, candle, flowers, sink (in the corner niche), fire screen, polished pot, towels, and bench symbolize, in different ways, the Virgin's purity and her divine mission. In the right panel, Joseph has made a mousetrap, symbolic of the theological tradition that Christ is bait set in the trap of the world to catch the Devil. The carpenter's shop is completely inventoried by the painter, down to the vista into a distant city street. Thus, we have a thorough humanizing of a traditional religious theme—a transformation of it in terms of a particular time and place: a middle-class house, courtyard, and shop in a fifteenth-century city of Flanders. So close is the status of the sacred actors to the human level that they are even represented without halos; this does not happen in Italy until the end of the fifteenth century.

We have been tracing the humanization of art from the thirteenth century. The distance between the sacred and the secular has now narrowed to such a degree that they become intermixed. As Johan Huizinga, renowned modern student of the fifteenth century, describes it:

> Individual and social life, in all their manifestations, are imbued with the conception of faith. There is not an object nor an action, however trivial, that is not constantly correlated with Christ or salvation. . . . All life was saturated with religion to such an extent that the people were in constant danger of losing sight of the distinction between things spiritual and things temporal. If, on the one hand, all details of ordinary life may be raised to a sacred level, on the other hand, all that is holy sinks to the commonplace, by the fact of being blended with everyday life . . . the demarcation of the spheres of religious thought and that of worldly concerns was nearly obliterated.*

Hence, the realistically rendered, commonplace objects in a Flemish painting become suffused with religious significance and, as such, take on the nature of sacramental things. With this justification for their existence in art, the ordinary things that surround man—and man himself—share the realm of the saints; conversely, the saints now occupy the realm of man. But man, as well as the things of man, will remain when, with the secularization of art, the saints and sanctity have disappeared.

*Johan A. Huizinga, *The Waning of the Middle Ages* (Garden City, N.Y.: Doubleday, 1954), p. 156.

JAN VAN EYCK

One of the largest and most admired Flemish altarpieces of the fifteenth century is *The Ghent Altarpiece* in the church of St. Bavo in Ghent (FIGS. 18-7, 18-8, 18-9). It has also been one of the most controversial ever since the discovery, in 1832, of a partly damaged, four-line Latin poem on the frame of one of the outside panels which, in part, translates: "The painter Hubert van Eyck, greater than whom no one was found, began [this work]; Jan, second in art, completed it at the expense of Jodocus Vyt. . . ." The last line of the quatrain gives the date of 1432.

For more than a century after the discovery of this inscription under a coat of greenish paint, the altarpiece was believed to be the product of a collaboration between JAN VAN EYCK (*c.* 1390–1441) and his older brother HUBERT. But none of the numerous attempts to assign different parts of the many-paneled work to one or the other brother found more than partial acceptance among art historians. Even Erwin Panofsky's tightly argued conclusion that the present altarpiece is the result of an artful combination of

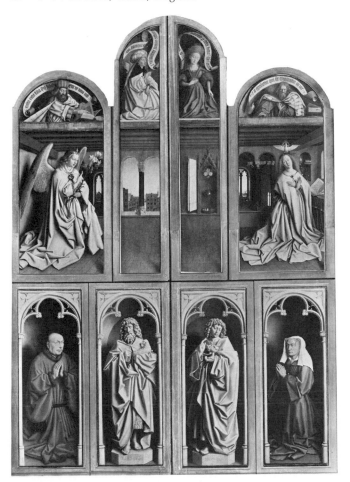

18-7   HUBERT and JAN VAN EYCK, *The Ghent Altarpiece* (closed), completed 1432. Tempera and oil on wood, approx. 11′ × 7′ 3″. St. Bavo, Ghent, Belgium.

three independent works, begun by Hubert and finished by Jan, that originally were not meant to be seen together, left considerable room for doubt and argument.*

An entirely new light was thrown on the controversy with the more recent suggestion that Hubert may not have been a painter at all, but rather a sculptor, who carved an elaborate, now-lost framework for the painted panels. Lotte Brand Philip points out that the damaged word "-ictor" in the inscription, which precedes Hubert's name and had been restored to read "pictor" (painter), could also be read "fictor" (sculptor).† "Second in art" would then not mean that Jan was a less accomplished painter than his brother; instead, it would be a chronological reference to the fact that Jan worked on the altar *after* Hubert. Judging from surviving contracts and commissions of the period, it seems to have been fairly common practice for a painter to begin work on panels after their frames had been completed.

In 1566, the panels were removed from the original frame and hidden, to protect them from Protestant iconoclasts who probably destroyed the frame. The panels were reinstalled in 1587, but without the original framework, which Lotte Brand Philip envisions to have been in the form of a richly carved, two-storied, Gothic reliquary front. Her ingenious theory and imaginative reconstruction would give sole authorship of the paintings to Jan van Eyck and solve the problem of attribution that has vexed art historians for almost a century and a half. It would also tend to explain the disparity of the scale used on the inner panels, which has disturbed some modern observers. If, indeed, the panels were originally more widely spaced and separated by richly carved, Gothic architectural elements, the formal unity of the altarpiece may have been stronger and more cohesive, especially if perspective devices in the lower level created the illusion that the smaller-scale scenes receded and were seen through—and at some distance behind— the architectural screen. On the other hand, it may well be that fifteenth-century viewers paid much less attention to formal unity than we do today and that the spiritual unity of the work was their real concern.

The Ghent polyptych remains an outstanding example of the large, folding altarpiece, typical of the north, that discloses new meanings to the observer as the unfolding panels reveal new subjects in sequence. The very form of the folding altarpiece expresses the Medieval tendency to uncover truth behind natural appearances, to clothe thought in

*Erwin Panofsky, *Early Netherlandish Painting* (Cambridge, MA: Harvard University Press, 1953).

†Lotte Brand Philip, *The Ghent Altarpiece and the Art of Jan van Eyck* (Princeton, N.J.: Princeton University Press, 1972).

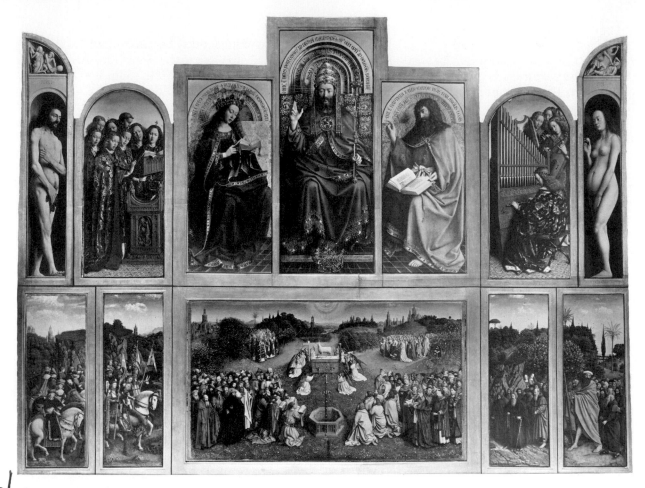

18-8   HUBERT and JAN VAN EYCK, *The Ghent Altarpiece* (open). Approx. 11' × 15' 1".

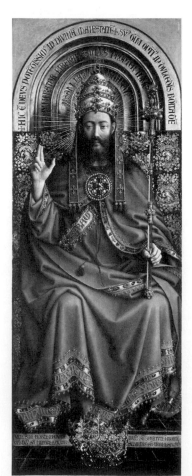

18-9   HUBERT and JAN
VAN EYCK, *God the Father*
(detail of FIG. 18-8).

allegory, to find "essential" meaning hidden beneath layers of secondary meanings. When closed (FIG. 18-7), *The Ghent Altarpiece* shows the Annunciation and simulated statues of St. John the Baptist and St. John the Evangelist, flanked by the donors, Jodoc Vyt and his wife; above, in the lunettes, are the Prophet Zechariah with the Erythraean sibyl and the Prophet Micah with the Cumaean sibyl. All these are symbolic references to the Coming of Christ. The Annunciation figures are set in a raftered room in which there are both Romanesque and Gothic architectural elements that may symbolize the Old and the New Testaments, respectively. As it does in *The Mérode Altarpiece* (FIG. 18-6), a vista opens on a distant street. The angel and the Virgin are bundled in the heavy flannel draperies of the Burgundian School, resembling those of Sluter's Moses (FIG. 18-1). Although the architecture is spacious, the figures are in ambiguous relation to it and quite out of scale; as yet, there is little concern for a proportioned space adjusted to the human figure.

When opened (FIG. 18-8), the altarpiece reveals a sumptuous, superbly colored representation of the Medieval conception of the redemption of man. In the upper register, God (FIG. 18-9)—wearing the triple tiara of the papacy, with a worldly crown at his feet and resplendent in a deep-scarlet mantle—is flanked on the left by the Virgin, represented as Queen of Heaven, with a "crown of twelve stars upon her head," and on the right by St. John the Baptist. To either side is a choir of angels and, on the right, St. Cecilia at her organ. Adam and Eve are in the far panels. The inscriptions in the arches above the Virgin and St. John extol the virtue and purity of the former and the greatness of the latter as the forerunner of Christ. The particularly significant inscription above the head of the Lord (FIG. 18-9) translates: "This is God, all-powerful in his divine majesty; of all the best, by the gentleness of his goodness; the most liberal giver, because of his infinite generosity." The step behind the crown at the Lord's feet bears the inscription: "On his head, life without death. On his brow, youth without age. On his right, joy without sadness. On his left, security without fear." This is a most concise and beautiful statement of the change from the concept of God as a stern, Medieval judge of mankind to the benevolent Franciscan father of the human race. This Franciscan concept of the benevolent nature of God is reinforced by the pelicans embroidered on the tapestry draped over the back of his throne, for pelicans—then thought to tear open their breasts to feed their starving young with their own blood—were symbols of self-sacrificing love. The entire altarpiece amplifies this central theme; though man is sinful—symbolized by Adam and Eve—he will be saved because God, in his infinite love, will sacrifice his own son for this purpose.

The figures are rendered in a shimmering splendor of color that defies reproduction. Both Hubert and Jan van Eyck were trained miniaturists, and not the smallest detail has escaped their eyes; they amplify the beauty of the most insignificant object as if it were a work of piety as much as a work of art. The soft texture of hair, the glitter of gold in the heavy brocades, the luster of pearls, the flashing of gems—all are given with tireless fidelity to appearance (FIG. 18-9). The new medium of oil paint—here in its very beginning—shows its marvelous magic.

The panels of the lower register extend the symbolism of the upper. In the central panel, the community of saints comes from the four corners of the earth through an opulent, flower-spangled landscape. They move toward the altar of the Lamb, from whose heart blood flows into a chalice, and toward the octagonal fountain of life into which spills the "pure river of water of life, clear as crystal, proceeding out of the throne of God and of the Lamb" (Revelation 22:1). On the right, the Twelve Apostles and a group of martyrs in red robes advance; on the left, with minor prophets, the Four Evangelists arrive carrying their Gospels. In the right background come the holy virgins; in the left background, the holy confessors.

On the lower wings, other approaching groups symbolize the four cardinal virtues: the hermits, Temperance; the pilgrims, Prudence; the knights, Fortitude; the judges, Justice. The altarpiece celebrates the whole Christian cycle from the fall to the redemption, presenting the Church triumphant in heavenly Jerusalem. The uncanny naturalism and the precise rendering, in the miniaturist tradition, make the great event as concrete and credible as possible to the observer. The realism is so saturated with symbolism that we almost think of it as a kind of superreality or "surrealism," as what is given to the eye is more than the eye alone can report.

Jan van Eyck's matchless color craft is evident in *The Virgin with the Canon van der Paele* (FIG. 18-10), painted in 1436. The figures are grouped in a manner reminiscent of the *sacra conversazione* paintings that appear in Florence about the same time (FIG. 16-32). The architecture, the elaborately ornamented rug, and the figures all lead the eye to the Madonna and Child, who sit in the apse of a church. The rich texture of the Virgin's red robes strongly contrasts with the white surplice of the kneeling Canon van der Paele. A similar contrast plays across the space between the dull glint from the armor of St. George, the patron saint of the canon, and the rich brocades of St. Donatian, the patron of the church for which the painting was commissioned. The incredibly brilliant profusion of color is carefully controlled, so that the forms are clearly distinguished in all detail. The symbolism is as profuse and controlled as the color, incorporating again the complete cycle of the fall and the promise of redemption. The arms of the Virgin's throne and the historiated capitals of the pilasters behind her make reference to the Old Testament prefiguration of the Coming of Christ, so well known in the Middle Ages.

There is evidence in the picture of Van Eyck's use of perspective—not a single perspective that would consistently unify the space, but several. His intention here appears once again to be indirect, the multiple perspectives directing attention to the principal figures. For example, a projection of the line of the column base at the far right leads to the head of the canon; the orthogonals of the floor tiles converge on the midpoint of the figure of the Virgin; and the base of the throne can be projected to the infant Christ. Thus, there is no real spatial unification. The figures do not interrelate as we might expect; each fills its own space with, as it were, its own perspective. Although St. George lifts his helmet to the Virgin, the direction of his gaze goes well beyond her; this disorientation is also true of the other figures. Jan van Eyck and his generation still essentially conceive the organization of the two-dimensional picture surface in terms of shape, color, and symbol; they have not yet

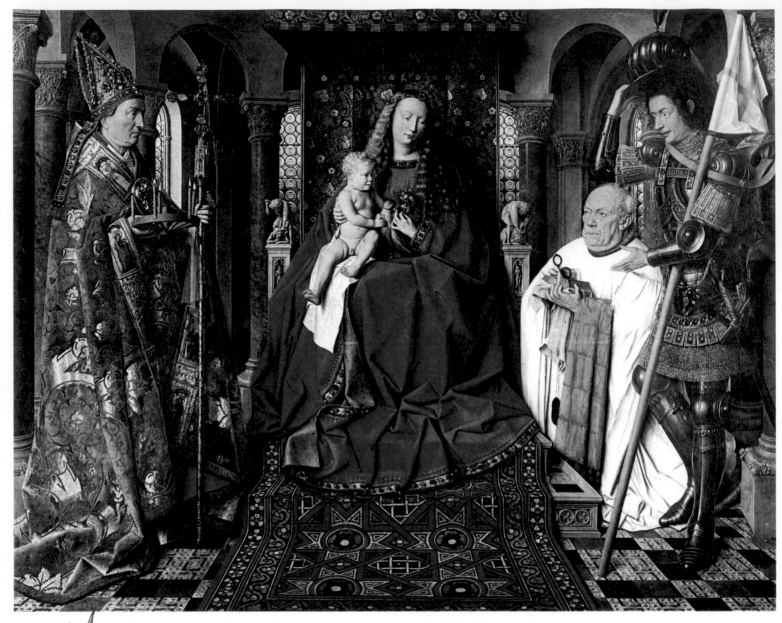

18-10 Jan van Eyck, *The Virgin with the Canon van der Paele*, 1436. Tempera and oil on wood, approx. 48″ × 62″. Musées Communaux, Bruges.

thought of it as a window into a constructed illusion of the third dimension, as the painters of the later Flemish schools will.

The portrait head of Canon van der Paele shows the same nonstructural approach. The heavy, wrinkled visage of the canon is recorded in precise detail, almost to the pores; the artist makes a relief map of his subject, delineating every minute change of the facial surface. Unlike the Italian portraitists, who think first of the structure of the head and then draw the likeness over it, Jan van Eyck works from the outside inward, beginning with the likeness and shaping the head incidentally. This is what gives the mask-like aspect to the canon's face, despite the portrait's fidelity to physiognomy; the surface is all there, but the illusion of three-dimensional mass is only implied.

We have seen three works that included painted portraits of their donors: *The Mérode Altarpiece* (FIG. 18-6), *The Ghent Altarpiece* (FIG. 18-8), and *The Virgin with Canon van der Paele* (FIG. 18-10). These portraits mark a significant revival of a genre unknown since antiquity. A fourth portrait, Jan van Eyck's *Man in a Red Turban* (FIG. 18-11) marks another step in the humanization process. In the Mérode and Ghent altarpieces, the donors were depicted apart from the saints; in the Canon van der Paele portrait, the donor associates with the saints at the throne of the Virgin. In this portrait (possibly of the artist himself) the image of a living individual apparently needs no religious purpose for being—only a personal one; the portrait is simply a record of one's features interesting to oneself or another. These private portraits now begin to multiply, as both artist and patron become

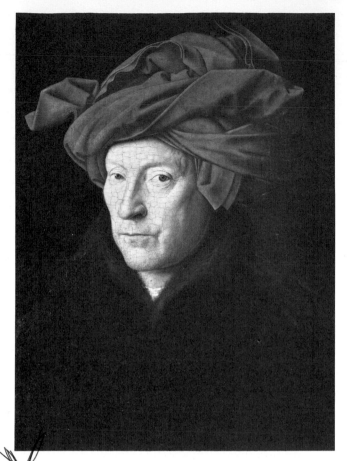

18-11 JAN VAN EYCK, *Man in a Red Turban (Self-Portrait?)*, 1433. Tempera and oil on wood, approx. 10¼″ × 7½″. Reproduced by courtesy of the Trustees of the National Gallery, London.

interested in the reality they reveal, for the painter's close observation of the lineaments of a human face is as revealing of the real world as his observation of objects in general. As man confronts himself in the painted portrait, he objectifies himself as a self, as a person. In this confrontation, the otherworldly anonymity of the Middle Ages must fade away. The *Man in a Red Turban* looks directly at us, or perhaps at himself in a mirror. So far as is known, this is the first painted portrait in a thousand years to do so. The level, composed gaze, directed from a true three-quarter pose of the head, must have impressed observers deeply. There is the illusion that from whatever angle we observe the face, the eyes still fix us. A painting of this kind by the great Rogier van der Weyden must have inspired the writing of *The Vision of God* (1453) by Nicholas of Cusa, who says, in the preface to that work:

> To transport you to things divine, I must needs use a comparison of some kind. Now among men's works I have found no image better suited to our purpose than that of an image which is *omnivoyant* [all-seeing]— its face, by the painter's cunning art, being made to appear as though looking on all around it—for example . . . that by the eminent painter, Roger, in his

priceless picture in the governor's house at Brussels. . . . this I call the icon of God.

Nicholas goes on with a praise of sight and vision that amounts to a sanctification of it:

> Thou, Lord . . . lovest me because Thine eyes are so attentively upon me . . . where the eye is, there is love. . . . I exist in that measure in which Thou art with me, and since Thy look is Thy being, I am because Thou dost look at me, and if Thou didst turn Thy glance from me I should cease to be.

> Apart from Thee, Lord, naught can exist. If, then, Thine essence pervade all things, so also does Thy sight, which is Thine essence. . . . Thou Lord, seest all things and each thing at one and the same time. . . .

Nicholas of Cusa is a contemporary of the great Flemish painters, and it is likely that he spoke in a sense they could understand and in a mood they could share. The exaltation of sight to divine status and the astonishing assertion that the essence of God is sight—not being, as St. Thomas tells us—are entirely in harmony with the new vision in painting. As sight and being in God are essentially the same, so the painter's sight, which is instrumental in making likenesses, brings them into being. As the contemplative man achieves union with God by making himself like God, the imitation of objects in the sight of (hence, caused by) God must be a holy act on the part of the painter: seeing what God sees, he achieves the reality of God's vision and reveals it to others. In the light of Nicholas' doctrine, the minute realism of the Flemish painters can be understood. God sees everything, great and small alike, and Nicholas' fundamental doctrine that all opposites and contradictions are resolved and harmonized in God makes God present in the greatest and in the smallest, in the macrocosm and in the microcosm, in the whole earth and in a drop of water. In the whole world of vision *caused* by God's sight, everything is worthwhile because it is seen by God—even the "meanest flower that blows." Nicholas' sanctification of the faculty of sight provides Flemish painters with a religious warrant to apply sight in the investigation of the given world; painters in the north will continue the investigation long after the original religious motive is gone.

Above all, an age had begun in both the Netherlands and Italy in which men gloried in the faculty of sight for what it could reveal of the world around them. The artist now began to show Western man "what things look like," and he took extreme pleasure in recognizing a revelation. The level gaze of the *Man in a Red Turban*, in all its quiet objectivity, is not only the omnivoyant "icon of God"; in its historical destiny, it is the impartial, eternally observant face of science. It is also, significantly, man beginning to confront nature in terms of himself. This is the climax of the slow but mighty process that will bring man's eyes down from the supernatural to the natural world—a process that is expressed with just as much conviction and vigor in the north as it is in Italy.

The humanization of pictorial themes advances another step in Jan van Eyck's double portrait of *Giovanni Arnolfini and His Bride* (FIG. 18-12). The Lucca financier, who had established himself in Bruges, and his lady occupy a scene that is empty of saints but charged with the spiritual. Almost every object depicted is in some way symbolic of the holiness of matrimony. The persons themselves, hand in hand, take the marriage vows. Their shoes have been removed, for the sacrament of matrimony makes the room a holy place. The little dog symbolizes fidelity (the origin of the common canine name, "Fido"). Behind the pair, the curtains of the marriage bed have been opened. The finial of the bedpost is a tiny statue of St. Margaret, patron saint of childbirth; from the finial hangs a whisk broom, symbolic of domestic care (FIG. 18-13). The oranges on the chest below the window may refer to the golden apples of the Hesperides, representing the conquest of death. And the presence of the omnivoyant eye of God seems to be referred to

twice: once in the single candle burning in the ornate chandelier and again in the mirror, in which the entire room is reflected (FIG. 18-13). The small medallions set into the mirror's frame show tiny scenes from the Passion of Christ and represent Van Eyck's ever-present promise of salvation for the figures reflected on the mirror's convex surface. These figures include not only the principals, Arnolfini and his wife, but two persons who look into the room through the door. One of these must be the artist himself, as the florid inscription above the mirror, *Johannes de Eyck fuit hic*, announces that he was present. The purpose of the picture, then, is to document and sanctify the marriage of two particular persons. In this context, man comes to the fore of his own setting; the spiritual is present—but in terms of symbol, not image.

The paintings of Jan van Eyck have a weighty formality that banishes movement and action. His symmetrical groupings have the stillness and rigidity of the symbol-laden ceremony of the Mass; each person and thing has its prescribed place and is adorned as befits the sacred occasion. The long tradition of manuscript illumination accepted that the Holy Book must be as precious as the words it contains; Jan van

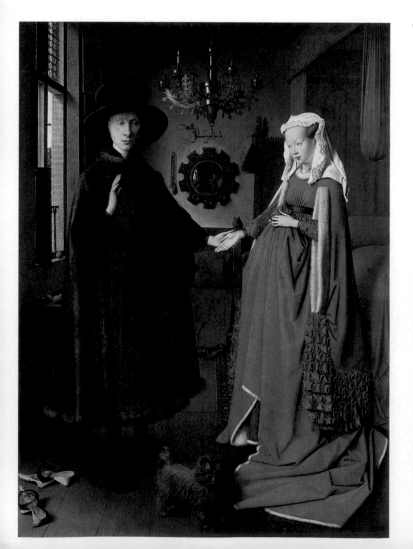

18-12 JAN VAN EYCK, *Giovanni Arnolfini and His Bride*, 1434. Tempera and oil on wood, approx. 32″ × 22″. Reproduced by courtesy of the Trustees of the National Gallery, London.

18-13 JAN VAN EYCK, *Mirror and Chandelier* (detail of FIG. 18-12).

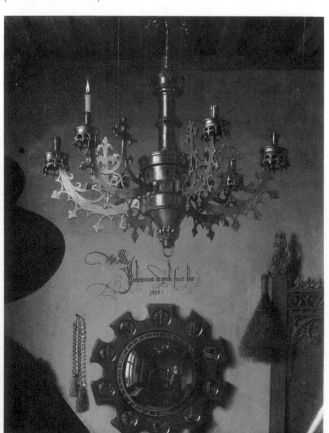

Eyck, himself a miniaturist and illuminator, instinctively created a rich and ornamental style in which to proclaim his optimistic message of human salvation. In their own way, the paintings of Jan van Eyck are perfect and impossible to surpass. After him, Flemish painting looked for new approaches, and Van Eyck had few, if any, emulators.

VAN DER WEYDEN, CHRISTUS, AND BOUTS

The art of ROGIER VAN DER WEYDEN (c. 1400–1464) had a much greater impact on northern painting of the fifteenth century. A student of Robert Campin, Rogier evidently recognized the limitations of Van Eyck's style, although it had not been without influence on his early work. By sweeping most of the secondary symbolism from his paintings, Rogier cleared his pictorial stage for fluid and dynamic compositions stressing human action and drama. He concentrates on themes like the Crucifixion and the Pietà, in which

he moves the observer by relating the sufferings of Christ. For Van Eyck's symbolic bleeding lamb, Rogier substitutes the tortured body of the Redeemer and his anguished mother. His paintings are filled with deep religiosity and powerful emotion, for he conceived his themes as expressions of a mystic yearning to share in the Passion of Jesus.

The great *Escorial Deposition* (FIG. 18-14) sums up Rogier's early style and content. Instead of creating a deep landscape setting, as Jan van Eyck might have, he compresses the figures and action onto a shallow stage to concentrate the observer's attention. Here, Rogier imitates the large, sculptured shrines so popular in the fifteenth century, especially in Germany, and the device well serves his purpose of expressing maximum action within disciplined structure. The painting resembles a stratified relief carving in the crisp drawing and precise modeling of its forms. A series of lateral, undulating movements gives the

18-14 ROGIER VAN DER WEYDEN, *The Escorial Deposition*, c. 1435. Tempera and oil on wood, approx. 7′ 3″ × 8′ 7″. Museo del Prado, Madrid.

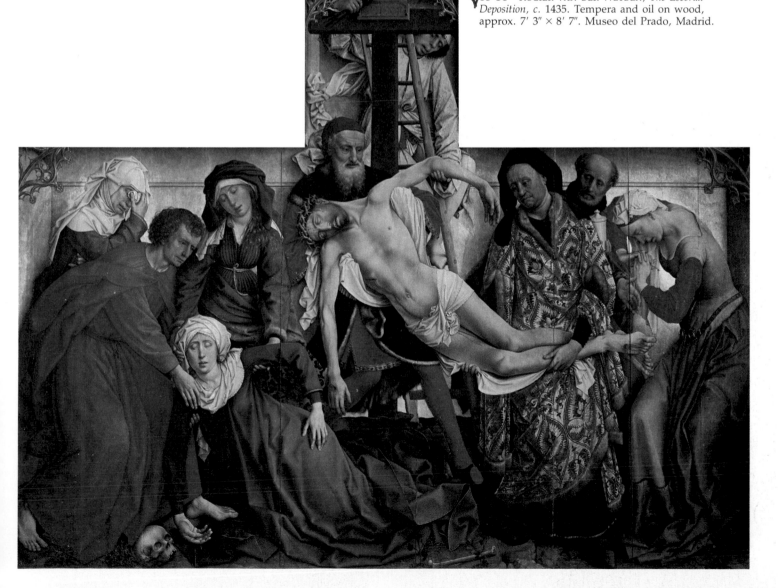

group a unity, a formal cohesion, that is underlined by psychological means—by the desolating anguish common to all the figures. Few painters have equaled Rogier in the rendering of passionate sorrow as it vibrates through a figure or distorts a tear-stained face. His depiction of the agony of loss is the most authentic in religious art; in a painting as bare of secondary symbolism as the *Deposition*, the emotional impact on the observer is immediate and direct. From this single example, we can understand why Rogier's art became authoritative for the whole fifteenth century outside of Italy.

His portraits were no less important than his altarpieces. With Campin, Van Eyck had established portraiture among the artist's principal tasks. Great patrons were ready to have their likenesses painted—and for many reasons: to memorialize themselves in their dynastic lines; to establish their identity, rank, and station by an image far more concrete than a heraldic coat of arms; to represent themselves at occasions of state when they could not be present—even as a kind of photograph, with the families who had arranged their children's marriages exchanging portraits of the betrothed. Royalty, nobility, and the very rich might send painters to "take" the likeness of a prospective bride or groom. It is reported that when a bride was sought for young King Charles VI of France, a painter was sent to three different royal courts to make portraits of the candidates, on the basis of which the king then made his choice.

We are not sure for what specific purpose Rogier's portrait of an unknown young lady (FIG. 18-15) was painted. From her dress and bearing, she was probably of noble rank. The artist is at pains to realize not only a faithful likeness of the somewhat plain features, but to read, with his uncommon perception, her individual character. Her lowered eyes, tightly locked, thin fingers, and fragile physique bespeak a personality reserved, introverted, devout. The unflattering honesty and directness, typical in the Flemish artist's approach, reveals much, despite the formality of pose and demeanor. This style contrasts with the formality of the Italian approach (FIG. 16-58) derived from the profiles common to coins and medallions, which is more stern and admits little revelation of personality. The Italian patron and portraitist will prefer the profile view throughout most of the century, rather than the full-face and three-quarter views favored by the Flemish. Rogier is perhaps chief among the Flemish in his penetrating readings of his subjects, and—great pictorial composer that he is—he makes beautiful use here of flat, sharply pointed angular shapes that themselves so powerfully suggest an "angularity" of this subject's personality. Unlike Jan van Eyck, Rogier lays little stress on minute description of surface detail. Instead, he defines

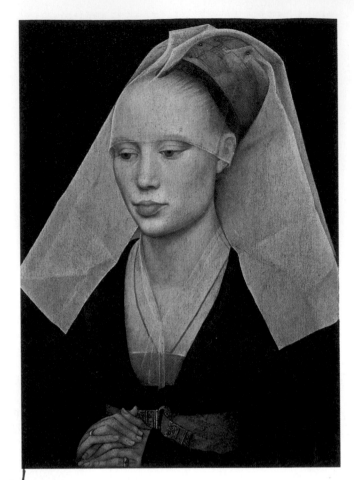

18-15   ROGIER VAN DER WEYDEN, *Portrait of a Lady*, c. 1460. Oil on wood, 14½″ × 10¾″. National Gallery, Washington, D.C. (Andrew W. Mellon Collection).

large, simple planes and volumes, achieving an almost "abstract" effect, in the modern sense, of dignity and elegance characteristic of his portraiture.

Although evidence that Rogier traveled to Italy is not unequivocal, some of his paintings clearly show his acquaintance with Italian pictorial devices; his religious sincerity and concern with sin and guilt, however, remained undimmed by them. The appearance of these mid-century Italian influences in Rogier's paintings was not an isolated instance in Flemish art. The work of PETRUS CHRISTUS (c. 1410–1472) shows so marked an interest in the depiction of space and cubic form that, although the idea is now largely discounted, it was often felt that he too traveled to Italy. Little is known of Christus' life, except that he may have been Van Eyck's student and that he settled and worked in Bruges. Christus' style vacillates between Van Eyck's and Rogier's. Still, his interests are quite different from those of his models. His painting of *The Legend of Saints Eligius and Godeberta* (FIG. 18-16) seems, at first glance, to exhibit all of Van Eyck's miniaturistic traits—from the stitching on the lady's gown to the carefully enumerated attributes that identify the seated saint as a patron of the goldsmith's guild. Even the convex mirror seems to have

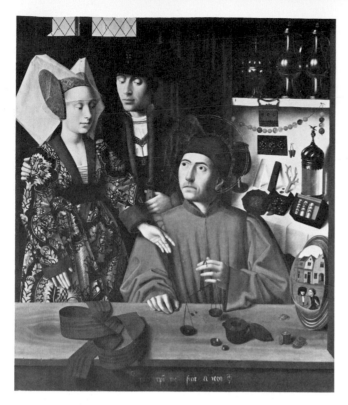

18-16 PETRUS CHRISTUS, *The Legend of Saints Eligius and Godeberta*, 1449. Tempera and oil on wood, approx. 39″ × 34″. Metropolitan Museum of Art, New York (the Lehman Collection).

been extracted from Van Eyck's portrait of Arnolfini and his bride (FIG. 18-12), and the two "witnesses" reflected in it suggest that this may also be a wedding picture. But Christus' concept of reality and his approach to it are quite different from Van Eyck's; he is much more concerned with the underlying structure of an object's appearance and, in this respect, is more closely related to the Italian than to the northern approach. The three solidly constructed figures within the cubic void defined by the desk and the room corner represent an essentially southern essay in pictorial form that has been overlaid with Van Eyck's surface realism. Curiously, in his effort to make the structure of his picture clear, Christus resorts to the same kind of simplification of forms seen in the paintings of Paolo Uccello and Piero della Francesca (FIGS. 16-29 and 16-33). Even more striking, perhaps, is the similarity of Christus' "volumetric" portrait heads to those by Antonello da Messina (FIG. 16-67). The speculation that these two artists may have met, either in Flanders or in Italy, remains tempting, despite the lack of solid documentation.

A slightly younger artist with similar temperament and interests, who may have had some contact with Christus, is DIRK BOUTS (c. 1415–1475). Rogier may have known about the Italian science of linear perspective, although he apparently did not use it in his paintings. For a long time, the central panel of *The Altarpiece of the Holy Sacrament* by Bouts was believed to be the first northern painting in which the use of a

single vanishing point for the construction of an interior could actually be demonstrated. More recent studies tend to give precedence in this field to Petrus Christus, from whom, in fact, Bouts may have acquired his knowledge. The setting for the altarpiece's *Last Supper* (FIG. 18-17) is probably the refectory of the headquarters of the Louvain Confraternity of the Holy Sacrament, by which the painting was commissioned. All orthogonals of the depicted room lead to a single vanishing point in the center of the mantelpiece above the head of Christ. This is not only the most successful northern fifteenth-century representation of an interior; it is also the first in which the scale of the figures has been realistically adjusted to the space they occupy. So far, however, the perspective unity is confined to single units of space only; the small side room has its own vanishing point, and neither it nor the vanishing point of the main room falls on the horizon of the landscape seen through the windows. The tentative manner with which Bouts solves his spatial problems suggests that he arrived at his solution independently and that the Italian science of perspective had not yet reached the north, except perhaps in fragments. Nevertheless, the works of Christus and Bouts clearly show that, by mid-century, northern artists had become involved with the same scientific, formal problems that occu-

18-17 DIRK BOUTS, *The Last Supper*, 1464–1468. Tempera and oil on wood, approx. 6′ × 5′. St. Peter's, Louvain, Belgium.

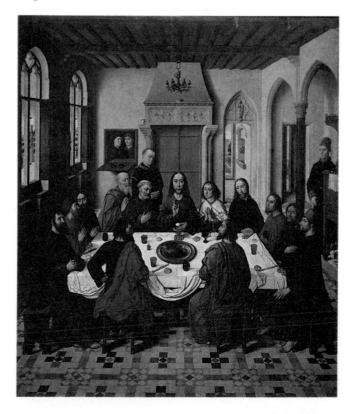

pied Italian artists during most of the fifteenth century.

The mood of Bout's *Last Supper* is neutral. The gathering is solemn enough, but it lacks all pathos and dramatic tension—almost as if the artist was more concerned with the solution of a difficult formal problem than with the pictorial interpretation, either personal or traditional, of the sacred event.

VAN DER GOES AND MEMLING

The highly subjective and introspective paintings of HUGO VAN DER GOES (*c.* 1440–1482) seem to express a discontent with the impersonal quality that the artist must have felt was a loss of religious meaning in the paintings of his older contemporaries. Hugo was dean of the painter's guild of Ghent from 1468 to 1475 and an extremely popular painter. At the height of his success and fame, he entered a monastery as a lay brother. While there, he suffered a mental breakdown in 1481 and died a year later. His retirement to the monastery did not immediately interrupt Hugo's career as a painter; he continued to receive commissions and probably completed his most famous work, *The Portinari Altarpiece* (FIG. 18-18), within the monastery's walls. Hugo painted the triptych for Tommaso Portinari, an agent of the Medici, who appears on the wings of the altarpiece with his family and their patron saints. The central panel represents *The Adoration of the Shepherds* (FIG. 18-19). There, on a large surface, Hugo displays a scene of solemn grandeur, muted by the artist's introspective nature. The high drama of the joyous occasion is stilled; the Virgin, Joseph, and the angels seem to brood on the suffering that is to come rather than to meditate on the miracle of the Nativity. On a tilted ground that has the expressive function of centering the main actors, the Virgin kneels, somber and monumental. From the right

enter three shepherds, represented with powerful realism in attitudes of wonder, piety, and gaping curiosity. Their lined, plebeian faces, work-worn hands, and uncouth dress and manner are so sharply characterized as to make us think of the characters in such literature of the poor as *Piers Plowman* and the *Second Shepherd's Play*. The three panels (FIG. 18-19) are unified by the symbolic architecture and a continuous, wintry, northern landscape. Symbols are scattered plentifully throughout the altarpiece: iris and columbine symbolize the Sorrows of the Virgin; the fifteen angels represent the Fifteen Joys of Mary; a sheaf of wheat stands for Bethlehem (the "house of bread" in Hebrew), a reference to the Eucharist; and the harp of David, emblazoned over the portal of the far building, signifies the ancestry of Christ. To further stress the meaning and significance of the depicted event, Hugo revives Medieval pictorial devices and casts aside the unities of time and action so treasured by other Renaissance artists, wherein a single episode in time is confined to a single framed piece. Small scenes shown in the background of the altarpiece represent (from left to right across the three panels) the Flight into Egypt, the Annunciation to the Shepherds, and the Arrival of the Magi—the "prelude and epilogue to the Nativity." Also out of the past is the manner in which Hugo varies the scale of his figures to differentiate them according to their importance in relation to the central event. At the same time, he puts a vigorous, penetrating realism to work in a new direction, characterizing human beings according to their social level while showing their common humanity, and the painting becomes a plea for all men to join the Brotherhood of Man.

Portinari placed his altarpiece in the church of Sant' Egidio in Florence, where it created a considerable stir among Florentine artists. Although the painting

18-18   HUGO VAN DER GOES, *The Portinari Altarpiece* (open), *c.* 1476. Oil on wood, center panel 8' 3½" × 10'. Galleria degli Uffizi, Florence.

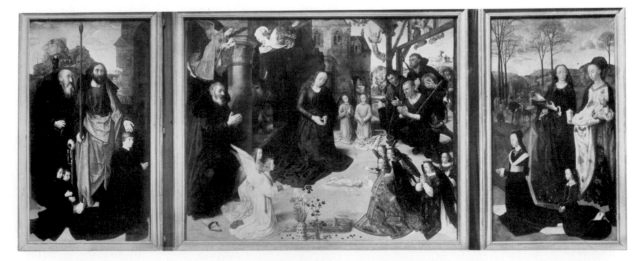

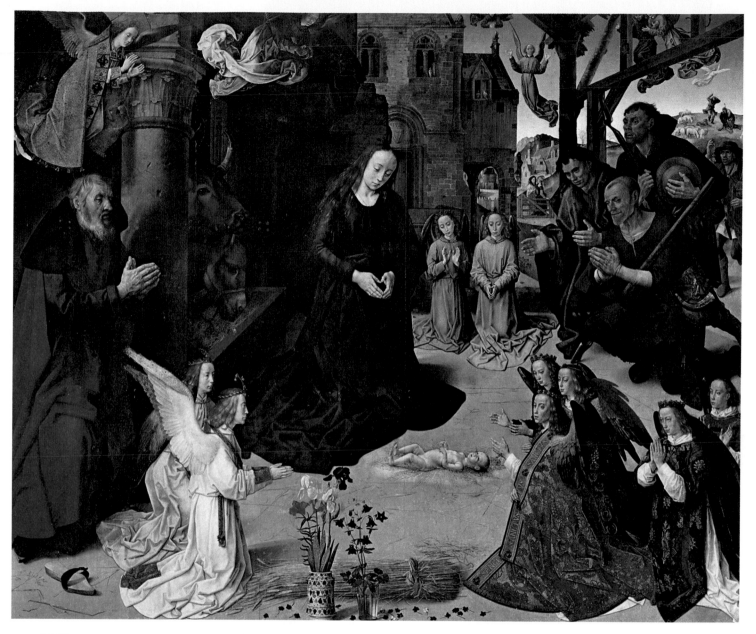

18-19   HUGO VAN DER GOES, *The Adoration of the Shepherds*, center panel of *The Portinari Altarpiece* (FIG. 18-18).

as a whole must have seemed unstructured to them, Hugo's brilliant technique and what they thought of as incredible realism in representing drapery, flowers, animals, and, above all, human character and emotion made a deep impression on them. At least one Florentine artist, Domenico Ghirlandaio, paid tribute to the northern master by using his most striking motif, the adoring shepherds, in one of his own Nativity paintings a few years later.

Hugo's contemporary, HANS MEMLING (c. 1430–1494)—although, like him, esteemed by all, and called, at his death, the "best painter in all Christendom"—was of a very different temperament. Gentle and genial, he avoided the ambitious, dramatic compositions of Rogier and Hugo, and his sweet, slightly

melancholy style fits well into the twilight of the waning fifteenth century. Memling's speciality is the Madonna, of which he has left many. They are slight, pretty, young princesses; the infant Christ, a doll. A good example of his work is the center panel of a triptych, representing *The Mystic Marriage of St. Catherine* (FIG. 18-20). The composition is balanced and serene; the color, sparkling and luminous; the execution, of the highest technical quality (Memling's paintings are among the best preserved from the fifteenth century). The prevailing sense of isolation and the frail, spiritual human types contrast not only with Hugo's monumental and somber forms but also with Van Eyck's robust and splendid ones. The century began, with Van Eyck's sumptuous art, on a note of

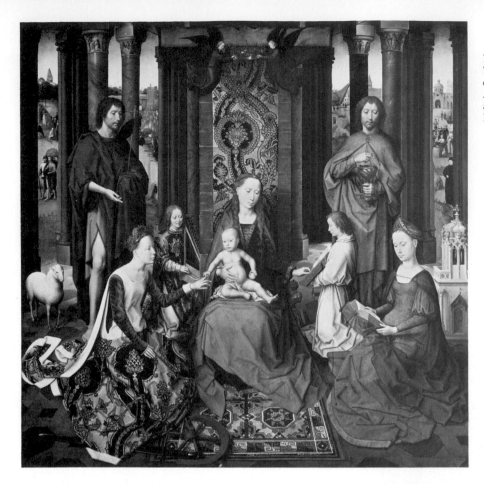

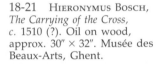

18-20 HANS MEMLING, *The Mystic Marriage of St. Catherine*, center panel of *The St. John Altarpiece*, 1479. Oil on wood, approx. 69″ × 69″. Hospitaal Sint Jan, Bruges, Belgium.

18-21 HIERONYMUS BOSCH, *The Carrying of the Cross*, c. 1510 (?). Oil on wood, approx. 30″ × 32″. Musée des Beaux-Arts, Ghent.

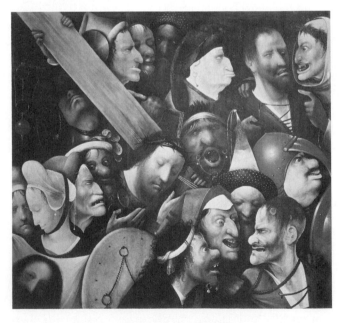

humanistic optimism. It ends with a waning strength of spirit, an erosion of confidence in the moral and religious authority of the Church. Contemporary poetry is filled with dreary pessimism and foreboding, almost in anticipation of another fall of man and the disasters that will lie ahead for Christendom in the Reformation.

HIERONYMUS BOSCH

This time of pessimistic transition finds its supreme artist in one of the most fascinating and puzzling painters in history, HIERONYMUS BOSCH (c. 1450–1516). Interpretations of Bosch differ widely. Was he a satirist, an irreligious mocker, or a pornographer? Was he a heretic or an orthodox fanatic like Girolamo Savonarola? Was he obsessed by guilt and the universal reign of sin and death? Certainly, his art is born from the dark pessimism of his age, burdened with the fear of human fate—with the conviction that man's doom is approaching. A contemporary poet, Eustache Deschamps, writes:

> Now the world is cowardly, decayed and weak,
> Old, covetous, confused of speech:
> I see only female and male fools. . . .
> The end approaches . . .
> All goes badly.

In a much copied and imitated series of small panels with half-length figures, Bosch describes the Passion of Christ. *The Carrying of the Cross* (FIG. 18-21) from this group is a bitter judgment of humanity. Christ is surrounded by hate and evil; his executioners show a sadistic delight in the suffering of their victim. Heedless of spatial effects, Bosch packs the entire surface of his panel with hate-distorted faces. In the upper right corner, a grinning scoundrel in monk's habit exhorts the repentant thief; in the lower right corner, the unrepentant thief grimaces at two leering comrades, forming with them a triad of stupidity, bestiality, and hate. On the lower left, St. Veronica, representing the Church, turns away from Christ and becomes a symbol of vanity. No further interpretation of this panel seems needed; Bosch not only makes his meaning clear but expresses it with unrivaled ferocity.

Much more difficult to understand are Bosch's large altarpieces, which are packed with obscure meaning and symbolism. But even if we may not fully understand his teeming fantasies, we can appreciate the incredible scope of an imagination that makes him the poet of the nightmarish subconscious. The dreaming and waking worlds are one in Bosch, as he draws on the tradition of beast and monster that we have followed from Mesopotamia to the Gothic gargoyle.

His most famous work, the so-called *Garden of Earthly Delights* (FIGS. 18-22 and 18-23), is also his most puzzling, and no interpretation of it is universally accepted. The left wing of the triptych (FIG. 18-22) shows the *Creation of Eve* in the Garden of Eden. However, here Eve is not the mother of mankind, as she is in Van Eyck's *Ghent Altarpiece* (FIG. 18-8), but rather the seductress whose temptation of Adam resulted in the original sin, the central theme of the main panel. Evil lurks even in Bosch's paradise; a central fountain of life is surrounded by ravens, the traditional symbols for nonbelievers and magicians; an owl, hiding in the dark hole in the center of the fountain, represents witchcraft and sorcery. The central panel, *The Garden of Earthly Delights* (FIG. 18-22), swarms with the frail nude figures of men and women sporting licentiously in a panoramic landscape that is studded with fantastic growths of a quasisexual form. Bosch seems to show erotic temptation and sensual gratification as a universal disaster and the human race, as a consequence of original sin, succumbing to its naturally base disposition. The subjects are derived in part from three major sources: Medieval bestiaries, Flemish proverbs, and the then very popular dream books, all mixed in the melting pot of Bosch's astoundingly inventive imagination. In addition, there are frequent allusions to magic and alchemy, and animal and vegetable forms are mingled in the most absurd combinations. Symbols are scattered plentifully throughout the panel: fruit for carnal pleasure, eggs for alchemy and sex, the rat for falsehood and lies, dead fish for memories of past joys. A couple in a glass globe may illustrate the proverb "Good fortune, like glass, is easily broken." We have lost the key to many of Bosch's symbols, but it may be assumed that they were well enough known to his contemporaries. In the right wing, the fruits of license are gathered in *Hell* (FIG. 18-22). There, sinful mankind undergoes hideous torments to diabolic music, while the hellish landscape burns. This symphony of damnation apparently comments on the wickedness of music, with which the Devil lures souls away from God. In this context, the ears and the musical instruments would represent the erotic, soul-destroying thoughts engendered by music. A man is crucified on a harp; another is shut up in a drum. A gambler is nailed to his own table. A girl is embraced by a spidery monster and bitten by toads. The observer must search through the hideous enclosure of Bosch's hell to take in its fascinating though repulsive details. The great modern poet Charles Baudelaire catches the mood in his *Flowers of Evil*:

Who but the Devil pulls our walking-strings!
Abominations lure us to their side;
Each day we take another step to hell,
Descending through the stench, unhorrified . . .

Packed in our brains incestuous as worms
Our demons celebrate in drunken gangs . . .

. . . in this den of jackals, monkeys, curs,
Scorpions, buzzards, snakes . . . this paradise
Of filthy beasts that screech, howl, grovel, grunt—
In this menagerie of mankind's vice. . . .

The triptych as a whole may represent the false paradise of this world between Eden and Hell, but this is only one interpretation. Another has it that Bosch belonged to a secret, heretical sect, the Adamites, and that the central panel was thought of as a kind of altarpiece symbolically celebrating its rites and practices. Recently, a fairly strong case has been made for an interpretation in terms of contemporaneous alchemical knowledge and practice.* In this connection, it should be pointed out that alchemy, in Bosch's time, was not an illegal and occult art but a practical and legitimate science practiced to make artist's paints, women's cosmetics, herbal cooking preparations, and healing potions. The alchemical science of distillation is basic to modern chemistry, and Philippus Aureolus Paracelsus, an early sixteenth-century physician, stated emphatically that the true and only purpose of alchemy is to heal the sick, not to make gold.

Numerous alchemical treatises circulated during Bosch's time, and some of them may well have been known to our artist. It has long been noted that the triptych is punctuated by forms and shapes similar to diagrams found in distillation texts. Most striking, perhaps, is the beaker-shaped "fountain of life,"

*See Laurinda S. Dixon, "Bosch's *Garden of Delights* Triptych: Remnants of a 'Fossil' Science," *The Art Bulletin*, Vol. LXIII, No. 1 (March 1981), pp. 96–113.

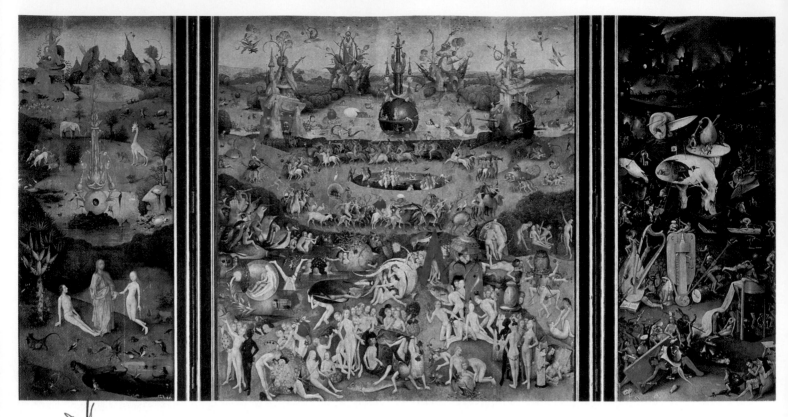

18-22　Hieronymus Bosch, *Creation of Eve* (left wing), *The Garden of Earthly Delights* (center panel), *Hell* (right wing), 1505–1510. Triptych, oil on wood, center panel 7′ 2″ × 6′ 5″. Museo del Prado, Madrid.

which appears twice (once in the center of the left wing, and again in the background of the central panel) and which, in form, strongly resembles an alchemical mixing retort. Many other distillation appa-

18-23　Hieronymus Bosch, *The Garden of Earthly Delights*, exterior of closed wings representing *The Third Day of Creation* (?).

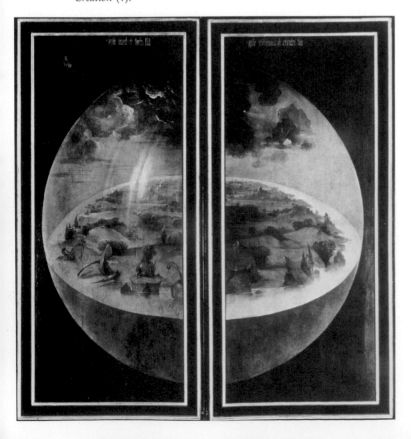

ratus appear, especially in the central panel, including glass pipes and lids and transparent globes and funnels. Numerous egg shapes seem to refer to the ovoid mixing vessels in which ingredients were combined to produce the hoped-for transmutations. These vessels, called "eggs" in the symbolic language of alchemy, were considered microcosmic models of the world, which contained all the qualities of life and in which "the four elements [earth, air, fire, water] were perfectly conjoined." Egg shapes appear on all three panels of Bosch's altarpiece; the most prominent one, on the right panel (FIG. 18-22), forms the body of a grotesque, human-headed monster. This creature has been called the "alchemical man," and the tiny figures inside his eggshell torso—usually interpreted as embodying the sins of gluttony and lust—are seen as gathered around a table to watch the glow of an alchemical furnace hidden by the broken shell of the egg man's body.

According to this interpretation, the subject and organization of the triptych correspond to the basic (and, at the time, current) alchemical allegory, in which the distillation process—seen as the cyclical and self-perpetuating creation, destruction, and rebirth of the world and its inhabitants—takes place in four stages: "conjunction" (the marriage of opposites); "coagulation" (the multiplication of Adam and Eve into the peoples of the earth); "putrification" (the separation of the opposing elements previously joined in "matrimony"); and "cleansing" (the washing and purifying of the separated ingredients, a process compared to the Christian resurrection and purification of the soul). The final outcome of this entire allegorical distillation—union with God—is symbolized by the circle and the globe.

If interpreted in these terms, the first three stages of the distillation process are symbolically represented in sequence from left to right on the interior of the three altarpiece panels. The fourth and final stage appears on the outside of the closed wings (FIG. 18-23), where a transparent globe containing earth, water, and clouds—painted in *grisaille* (tones of gray)—represents God's creation of the earth, which the alchemists tried to imitate in their operations.

In keeping with the cyclical and self-perpetuating process of distillation, the exterior of the altarpiece can be read either as the beginning or as the end of the cycle depicted on the interior. Placed at the end, it would provide the altarpiece with a comforting conclusion—a consolatory postscript promising that the sufferings of Hell may not be the end of everything after all. Most scholars, however, place the outside panels at the beginning of the sequence. To them, the grisaille represents *The Third Day of Creation,* when dark, light, water, land, and flora—but not the fauna—had been created. The outside thus becomes the natural prelude to the altarpiece's interior, where the remainder of Genesis is recorded on the left wing. On the central panel, the descendants of the first parents abandon themselves to the delights of the flesh, oblivious to the eventual but inevitable consequences recorded on the right wing—the apocalyptic results of the Last Judgement in the form of the fearsome destruction and tortures suffered in Hell. And if we realize how far God—a tiny figure in the upper left corner of the left exterior panel—has been removed from his creation, then Bosch's message seems to become quite clear: humanity, left to its own devices, is destined for damnation. Although far from being universally accepted, this last interpretation of *The Garden of Earthly Delights* appears to conform best with the remainder of the artist's oeuvre. Neither in this, nor in Bosch's other works, does humankind appear to advantage. Abandoned to evil by the fall, humanity merits Hell.

Bosch was a supreme narrative painter, and the visions of his bubbling imagination demanded quick release. His technique is more rapid and spontaneous than the labored traditional Flemish manner. He seemed to have had no time for the customary monochrome underpaintings or careful modeling of figures. His method forecasts the *alla prima* technique of the seventeenth and eighteenth centuries, as he puts down with quick and precise strokes the myriad creatures that populate his panels. His use of *impasto,* which did not require the traditional laborious application of numerous glazes, was ideally suited to the spinning of his mordant fantasies. And if he extends

no hope of salvation for man, he only anticipates Michelangelo, who, in his *Last Judgment* fresco (FIG. 17-35), came to the same conclusion some 30 years later.

France and Germany

The bourgeoisie in France, unlike that in the Netherlands, was not wealthy, localized in strong towns, nor interested in fostering the arts. In France, the Hundred Years' War had wrecked economic enterprise and prevented stability. During the fifteenth century, the anarchy of war and the weakness of the kings resulted in a group of rival duchies. The strongest of these, as we have seen, was the duchy of Burgundy; through marriage and political alliance, it occupied the Netherlands and became essentially Flemish, particularly in art commissioned by the court. In France, artists joined the retinues of the wealthier nobility—the dukes of Berry, Bourbon, and Nemours—and sometimes the royal court, where they were able to continue to develop an art that is typically French despite its regional variations. But no artist of the fifteenth century north of the Alps could escape the influence of the great artists of Flanders; French art accepted it, and works of high quality were produced, although only one really major figure emerged. JEAN FOUQUET (*c.* 1420–1481) is the outstanding French artist of the fifteenth century. During his career, he worked for the king, Charles VII, for the Duke of Nemours, and for Étienne Chevalier, the king's minister of finance. Fouquet's portrait of Chevalier with his patron, St. Stephen (FIG. 18-24), shows, in addition to Flemish influence, the effect of the two years he spent in Italy, between 1445 and

18-24 JEAN FOUQUET, *Étienne Chevalier and St. Stephen,* *c.* 1450. Tempera on wood, $36\frac{1}{2}'' \times 33\frac{1}{2}''$. Gemäldegalerie, Staatliche Museen, Berlin-Dahlem.

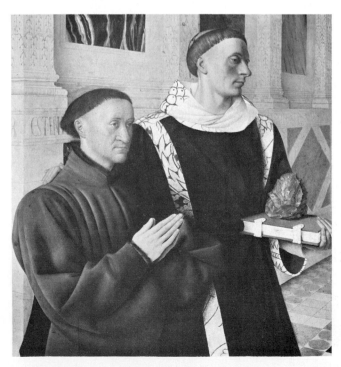

1447. The kneeling donor with his standing saint is familiar in Flemish art, as are the three-quarter stances and the sharp, clear focus of the portraits. The reading of the surfaces, however, is less particular than in the Flemish practice; the artist is trying to represent the forms underneath the surfaces, in the Italian manner. Also of Italian inspiration are the architectural background and its rendering in perspective. The secularizing tendency advancing so rapidly in the fifteenth century shows in the familiar, comradely demeanor of the two men; nothing whatever distinguishes them as being of different worlds, except possibly that St. Stephen, who holds the stone of his martyrdom, is dressed as a priest.

An isolated masterpiece of great power, painted in the extreme south of France by an anonymous artist, is *The Avignon Pietà** (FIG. 18-25), which has both Flemish and Italian elements. Rogier van der Weyden's great *Escorial Deposition* (FIG. 18-14) comes to mind at once when we see the Avignon work, although the balanced, almost symmetrical massing is of the Italian Renaissance. (The subdued color scheme has also suggested Iberian influence to some writers.) The donor, now familiarly present at the sacred event, kneels at the left. His is a strikingly characteristic portrait—the face gnarled, oaken, ascetic. The group of Christ and saints is united by the splendidly painted figure of Christ and by the angu-

lar shapes that seem deliberately simplified for graphic emphasis. As in Italian art, surface ornament is suppressed in the interest of monumental form. The luminous gold background, against which the figures are silhouetted and into which the halos are incised, is a strangely conservative feature, contrasting with the detailed background landscape reminiscent of Flemish paintings. No matter what his sources, the painter is deeply sensitive to his theme. Along with Rogier's version, *The Avignon Pietà* is one of the most memorable in the history of religious art.

To an even greater extent than in France, the development of German painting in the fifteenth century was strongly colored by the achievements of Flemish painting. In northern Germany, the influence of Jan van Eyck joined the tradition of the International style to produce the gentle, pictorially ornate world of delicacy and charm of STEPHAN LOCHNER (c. 1400–1451), the leading master of the school of Cologne. Lochner is noted for his compositions on the idyllic theme of the *Madonna in the Rose Garden* (FIG. 18-26), which seems particularly well suited to his sophisticated and refined sensibilities. Sometimes referred to as the "soft" style because of its feminine suavity and curvilinear rhythm, Lochner's manner was very different from the sculptural, blocky, "hard" style of southern Germany as we find it in the work of the Swiss painter CONRAD WITZ (c. 1400–1447). Although *The Miraculous Draught of Fish* (FIG. 18-27) by this remarkable painter also shows Flemish influence, par-

---

*Now attributed to ENGUERRAND QUARTON (c. 1410–1466), a French artist active in Provence in the south of France.

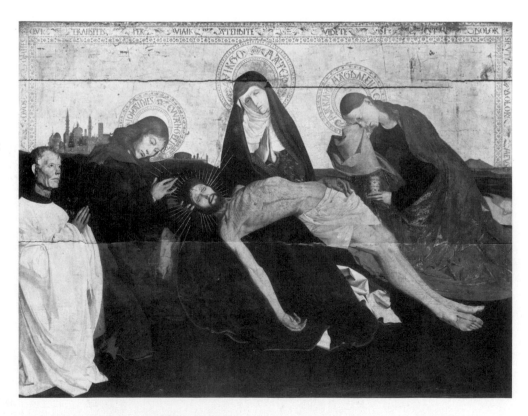

18-25 Attributed to ENGUERRAND QUARTON, *The Avignon Pietà*, c. 1455. Tempera on wood, approx. 5' 4" × 7' 2". Louvre, Paris.

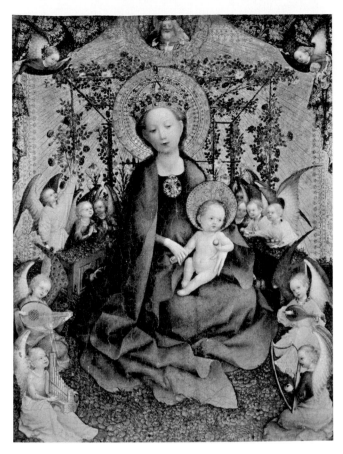

18-26 STEPHAN LOCHNER, *Madonna in the Rose Garden,*
c. 1430–1435. Tempera on wood, approx. 20″ × 16″.
Wallraf-Richartz-Museum, Cologne.

ticularly that of Van Eyck, the painting demonstrates Witz's powerful and original sense of realism. Witz shows precocious skill in the study of water effects: the sky-glaze on the slowly moving lake surface, the mirrored reflections of the figures in the boat, the transparency of the shallow water in the foreground. This is one of the first Renaissance pictures in which the landscape not only predominates over the figures but is also the representation of a specific place—the shores of Lake Geneva, with the town of Geneva on the right and the ranges of the Alps in the distance.

The Late Gothic style is seen to best advantage in the works of German artists, who specialized in the carving of large retables (altar screens) in wood. The sculptor VEIT STOSS (1447–1533) carved a great altar for the church of St. Mary in Kraków, Poland (FIG. 18-28), no element of which is recognizable as Italian Renaissance. Typically, the altar consists of a central, box-like space; the shrine is flanked by hinged, movable wings—an inner pair (shown here) and an outer pair. In the shrine, a composition of huge figures (some 9 feet high) represent *The Death and Assumption of the Virgin* and, in the wings, scenes from the lives of Christ and the Virgin. The altar expresses the intense piety of Gothic culture in its late phase, when every resource of figural and ornamental design from the vocabulary of Gothic art is drawn on to heighten the emotion and to glorify the apparition of the sacred event. The disciples of Christ are gathered about the Virgin, who sinks down in death. One of them

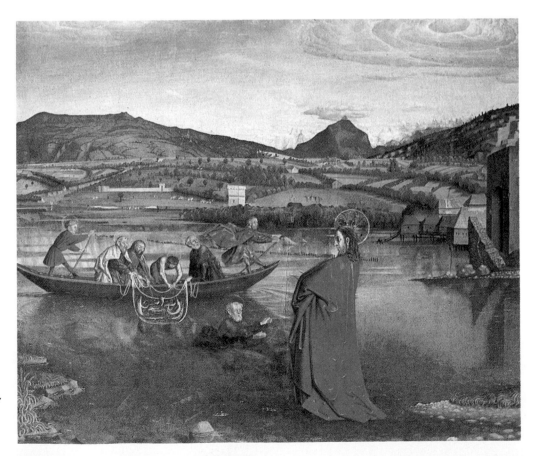

18-27 CONRAD WITZ,
The Miraculous Draught
of Fish, 1444. Tempera on
wood, approx. 51″ × 61″.
Musée d'Art et d'Histoire,
Geneva.

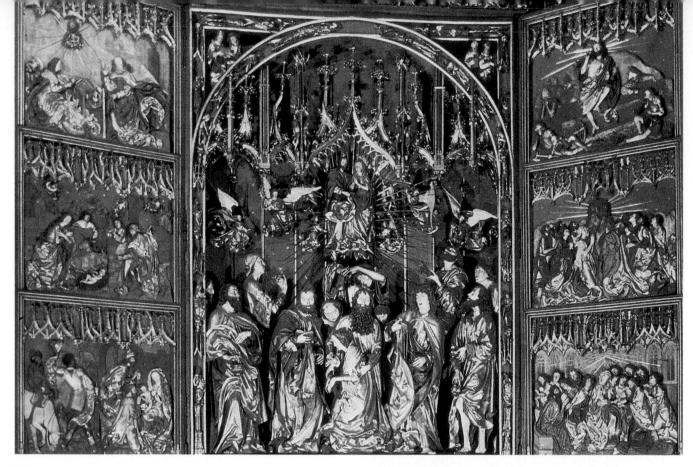

18-28 VEIT STOSS, *The Death and Assumption of the Virgin,* from the Altar of the Virgin Mary, 1477–1489. Painted and gilded wood, triptych (wings open) 43′ high, 35′ wide. Church of St. Mary, Kraków, Poland.

supports her; another, just above her, wrings his hands in grief; others are posed in attitudes of woe and psychic shock. The sculptor strives for minute realism in every detail. At the same time, he enwraps the figures in an almost abstract pattern of restless, twisting, curving swaths of drapery, which, by their broken and writhing lines, unite the whole tableau in a vision of agitated emotion. The massing of sharp, broken, and pierced forms, which dart flame-like through the composition—at once unifying and animating it—recalls the design principles of Late Gothic, "flamboyant" architecture (FIG. 10-39). Indeed, in the Kraków altarpiece, sculpture and architecture are amalgamated, and their union is enhanced by painting and gilding. The distinction of the different media, familiar in Italian Renaissance art and furthered by it, is as yet unknown to this Late Gothic artist, even though, like the Italian artist, his eye focuses ever more sharply on natural appearance.

In the work of TILMAN RIEMENSCHNEIDER (1460–1531), we find, as we do in the work of Veit Stoss, scarcely a trace of the Italian Renaissance. The canopy of Tilman's *Creglingen Altarpiece* (FIG. 18-29) is an intri-

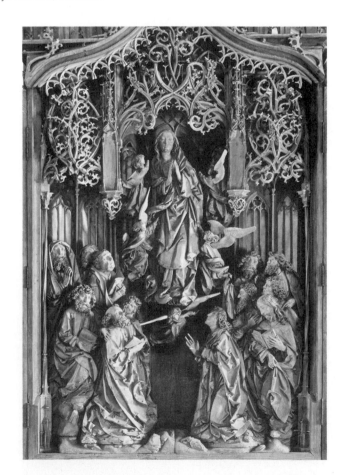

18-29 TILMAN RIEMENSCHNEIDER, *The Assumption of the Virgin,* center panel of *The Creglingen Altarpiece,* *c.* 1495–1499. Carved lindenwood, 6′ 1″ wide. Parish church, Creglingen, West Germany.

cate weaving of flamboyant Gothic forms, and the endless and restless line is communicated to the draperies of the figures. The whole design is thus in motion and complication, and no element functions without the rest. The draperies float and flow around bodies lost within them, serving not as descriptions but as design elements that tie the figures to each other and to the framework. The spirituality of the figures, immaterial and weightless as they appear, is heightened by a facial expression common to Tilman's figures and consonant with the age of troubles that is coming—a look of psychic strain. They brood in pensive melancholy, their brows often furrowed in anxiety. A favorite theme in Late Gothic German sculpture was the *Schmerzensmann* (man of sorrows); for Tilman, all his actors were men of sorrow—weary, grave, unsmiling.

With the sculptor–painter MICHAEL PACHER (*c.* 1435–1498), we come to the first important meeting of German art with the Italian Renaissance. Pacher, a Tyrolean, must have journeyed down the Po valley and become familiar with the style of Andrea Mantegna and his school. In his painting *St. Wolfgang Forces the Devil to Hold His Prayerbook* (FIG. 18-30), we find the hard, wiry linearity of Mantegna and a combination of Late Gothic and Mantegna's drapery style. The figure of St. Wolfgang now has the monumental solidity of Italian form. The whole setting is Italian Renaissance. Familiar in northern Italian and Venetian compositions are a perspective down a street—the plunging orthogonals remind us of Mantegna's architecture

in the *St. James Led to Martyrdom* fresco (FIG. 16-63)— and the figures standing on a fretted balcony, which slow the swift recession of the perspective to the horizon. But the gargoylish Devil tells us that the Gothic is still very much in the northern environment.

In Germany, where printing with movable type was developed, we would expect the graphic arts to be well represented by competent masters. And indeed, MARTIN SCHONGAUER (*c.* 1450–14901) was the century's most skilled and subtle northern master of the new metal engraving technique. Printing pictures from woodblocks was developed in Europe around 1400 (the Chinese had known the technique centuries before) and remained popular, especially for book illustration, well into the 1500s. But engraving on metal surfaces—begun, as we have seen, in the 1430s and well developed by 1450—proved a much more flexible technique and, in the second half of the century, widely replaced the woodcut. Schongauer's *St. Anthony Tormented by the Demons* (FIG. 18-31) shows both the versatility of the medium and the artist's mastery of it. Although better known for his gentle Madonnas in a style based on that of Rogier van der Weyden, here Schongauer displays almost the same taste for the diabolical as Hieronymus Bosch; his stoic saint is caught in a revolving thornbush of spiky demons, who claw and tear at him furiously. With unsurpassed skill and subtlety, the artist makes mar-

18-31 MARTIN SCHONGAUER, *St. Anthony Tormented by the Demons,* c. 1480–1490. Engraving, approx. 13″ × 11″. Metropolitan Museum of Art, New York (Rogers Fund, 1920).

18-30 MICHAEL PACHER, *St. Wolfgang Forces the Devil to Hold His Prayerbook,* panel from the Altar of the Fathers of the Church, *c.* 1481. Tempera and oil on wood, approx. 40″ × 37″. Alte Pinakothek, Munich.

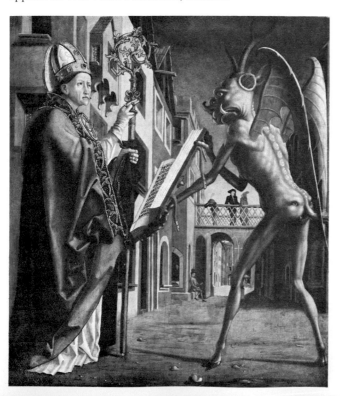

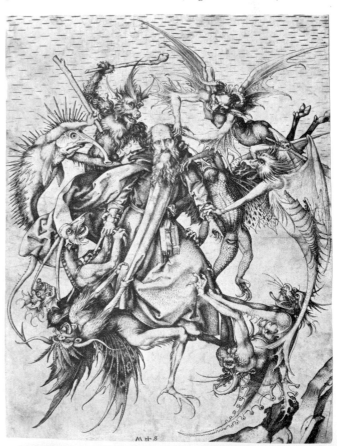

velous distinctions of tonal values and textures—from smooth skin to rough cloth, from the furry and feathery to the hairy and scaly. The method of describing forms with hatching that follows the forms, probably developed by Schongauer, became standard with German graphic artists. The Italians preferred parallel hatching (compare Antonio Pollaiuolo's engraving, FIG. 16-55) and rarely adopted this method, which, in keeping with the general northern approach to art, tends to describe the surfaces of things rather than their underlying structures.

THE SIXTEENTH CENTURY

Germany

The art of northern Europe during the sixteenth century is characterized by a sudden awareness of the advances made by the Italian Renaissance and by a desire to assimilate this new style as rapidly as possible. Many artists traveled to Italy to study the new art first hand; others met it either directly, in the form of Italian artists who came to the north, or indirectly, through the numerous Italian engravings that circulated throughout northern Europe. One of the most prolific Italian engravers, MARCANTONIO RAIMONDI, rarely invented his own compositions but copied those of other artists, particularly Raphael. In this way, many panel paintings and frescoes by Italian Renaissance artists became the common property of all Europe. Naturally, the impact of Italian art varied widely, according to the artist, the time, and the place. Many artists never abandoned existing local traditions; others were frequently content to borrow only single motifs or the general form of a composition. In Germany, the wealthy merchant class maintained close commercial relations with Venice, and German Humanists were in contact with the Neo-Platonic academy of Florence. As a result, Albrecht Dürer frequently illustrated Florentine thought clothed in Venetian and German forms.

During the fifteenth century, painting in the wealthy towns of southern Germany developed along its own expressionistic lines under the dominant influences of Flemish art. Around the turn of the century, it suddenly burst into full bloom. By 1528, with the death of its two greatest exponents, Dürer and Matthias Grünewald, it had spent itself. Thus, its most brilliant period corresponds almost exactly to the High Renaissance in Italy. Its decline around 1530 was just as abrupt as its rise, and the reason for this is uncertain. The almost incessant religious wars devastated the German lands, and puritanism, accompanying the triumph of Protestantism in the north, may

have opposed Humanistic paganism in the figurative arts. With the exception of Hans Holbein the Younger, the main representatives of the German School were born within 10 years of one another and were contemporaries of Michelangelo, Raphael, Giorgione, and Titian.

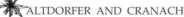

ALTDORFER AND CRANACH

ALBRECHT ALTDORFER (c. 1480–1538) is the primary representative of the *Donaustil* (Danube style), which flourished along the Danube River from Regensburg (Altdorfer's hometown) eastward into Austria. The style is formed around the depiction of landscape and stresses mood, sometimes heightened to passion. Altdorfer's own style is highly personal and only occasionally modified by the influence of Dürer. He was a gifted colorist and observer of atmospheric and light effects. He loved forests and ruins, in which his figure groups are half-submerged. He painted at least one landscape without figures, making *Danube Landscape, Near Regensburg,* (c. 1522, not shown) perhaps the first landscape in Western art painted entirely for its own sake.

His most renowned work, *The Battle of Issus* (FIG. 18-32), bears little resemblance to a Danube setting, although it does give a bird's-eye view of an Alpine landscape. Here, Altdorfer spreads out in awesome detail the battle in which Alexander the Great overthrew the Persian king, Darius (FIG. 6-38); a huge inscription hanging in the clouds relates this. Swarms of warriors from both sides contest on a plain backed by cities, mountains, seas, and the opposed forces of nature: the sun and the moon in an illuminated sky. This sudden opening up of space, with its subordination of the human figure to the cosmic landscape, bespeaks a new view of nature—a view that will see man as an insignificant mote in an infinite universe. We need not suppose that German artists knew of the work of the contemporary astronomer, Copernicus, who was about to revise the age-old view that the earth is fixed and to suggest instead that the earth and the other "fixed" planets revolve about the sun. It is interesting that such high-horizoned, "topographical" landscapes (we might better call them "cosmographical") anticipate the coming cosmic view that the sciences of physics and physical astronomy will open to the Western world. Altdorfer's technique is still that of the miniaturist, yet his setting is no longer a page but a world—one in which his insect-like combatants are all but lost. In this first vision of the immense space and power of the cosmos, Altdorfer seems to suggest what all subsequent philosophers, scientists, and churchmen, as well as artists, will confront—the fact of the littleness of man.

The early works of LUCAS CRANACH THE ELDER (1472–1553) are close to the *Donaustil*, which im-

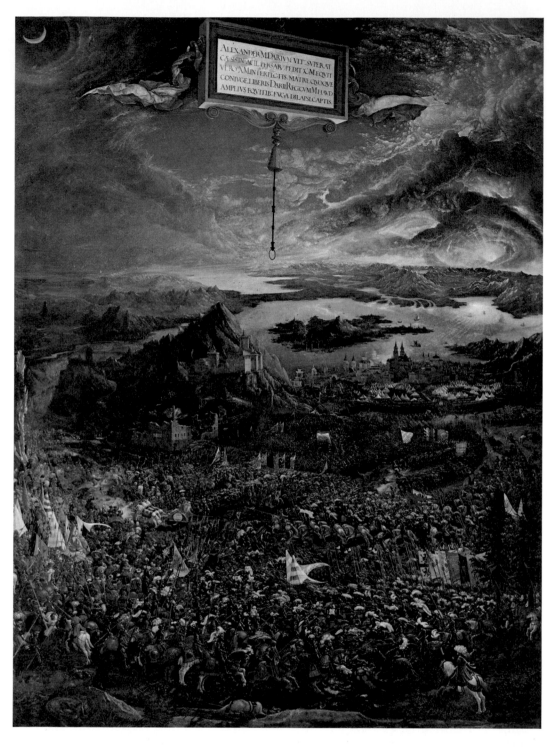

18-32 ALBRECHT ALTDORFER, *The Battle of Issus*, 1529. Oil on wood, 63″ × 46″. Alte Pinakothek, Munich.

merses man in the breadth of nature. At Wittenberg, where he was summoned by the elector of Saxony, Cranach became a friend and follower of Luther, and he has been called the outstanding representative of German Protestant painting. His later works are marked by a shift from religious to humanistic subject matter: mythology, history, and portraits. Best known are his figure compositions featuring the nude, which he renders with a charming, provincial naïveté. A good example is *The Judgment of Paris* (FIG.

18-33). Here, Paris and Mercury consult, while three spindly little goddesses show off their pretty contours. One of them bashfully stands on one foot; another coquettishly calls attention to her charms; the third stands by, wearing a fashionable hat. Cranach makes no effort to dress his gods after the antique manner; they wear the functional armor of German knights attached to provincial courts. Doughty and square-faced, they could have just come in from the field of honor. The background landscape reflects

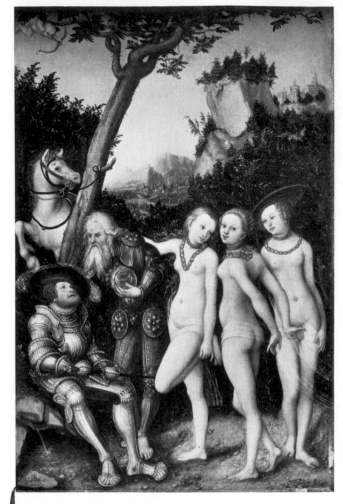

18-33 LUCAS CRANACH THE ELDER, *The Judgment of Paris*, 1530. Oil on wood, approx. 14″ × 9″. Staatliche Kunsthalle, Karlsruhe.

Cranach's earlier *Donaustil* in its meticulous description of foliage. And so far, only Dürer's approach to the nude (FIG. 18-37) is tutored by Italian art.

MATTHIAS GRÜNEWALD

One of the greatest individualists of the Renaissance and an artist of highly original genius is Matthias Neithardt, known conventionally as MATTHIAS GRÜNEWALD (*c.* 1480–1528). Forgotten until our time, he appears to have had the wide interests of the individualistic Renaissance artists. Working for the archbishops of Mainz from 1511 on as court painter and decorator, he also served them as architect, hydraulic engineer, and superintendent of works. Undoubtedly, he had Lutheran sympathies. He participated in the Peasant Revolt in 1525, and, after its collapse, had to flee to northern Germany, where he settled at Halle in Saxony. The sources of Grünewald's style are not certain. He may have been to Italy, but there is little of Renaissance Classicism in his art. He knew the work of Dürer and perhaps of Bosch. A brilliant colorist, he is not interested in the construction of the monumental, idealized figure in the Italian manner.

His color is characterized by subtle tones and soft harmonies on the one hand and shocking dissonance on the other. Uninterested in natural landscape, Grünewald shows us either the celestial or the infernal.

In his appalling *Crucifixion* from *The Isenheim Altarpiece* (FIG. 18-34), Grünewald gives us perhaps the most memorable interpretation of the theme in the history of art. The altar is composed of a carved wooden shrine with two pairs of movable panels, one directly in back of the other. Painted by Grünewald between 1510 and 1515 for the monastic hospital order of St. Anthony of Isenheim, the panels show three scenes, with the *Crucifixion* outermost, when the altar is closed. The dreadful aspect of the painting may be due in part to its placement in a house of the sick, where it may have admonished the inmate that another had suffered more. It may also have had a therapeutic function, in that it offered some hope to the afflicted. Two saints are represented on the wings flanking the central panels: on the left, St. Sebastian, whose intercession was invoked to ward off disease (especially the plague); on the right, St. Anthony, the patron saint of the order, who was identified with miraculous cure. Together, the saints establish the theme of disease and healing that is reinforced by the paintings on the inner wings.

One of the main illnesses treated at the hospital was ergotism (called "St. Anthony's Fire"), a disease caused by ergot, a fungus that grows especially on rye. Although its cause was not discovered until about 1600, its symptoms (convulsion and gangrene) were well known. The gangrene often compelled amputation, and it has been noted in this connection that the two movable halves of the predella of the altarpiece, if slid apart, make it appear as if the legs of the body of Christ have been amputated. The same observation can be made of the two main panels. Due to the off-center placement of the cross, the opening of the left center panel would "sever" one arm from the crucified figure.

Much of this symbolism may have been dictated by his patrons, but Grünewald's own inflamed imagination produced the terrible image of the suffering Christ. Against the pall of darkness lowered on the earth, the devasted body looms—dead, the flesh already discolored by decomposition and studded with the thorns of the lash. In death, the strains of the superhuman agony twist the blackening feet, tear at the arms, wrench the head to one side, and turn the fingers into crooked spikes. One has only to tense one's fingers in the position of Christ's to experience the shuddering tautness of nerves expressed in every line of the figure. No other artist has produced such an image of the dreadful ugliness of pain. The sharp, angular shapes of anguish appear in the figures of the

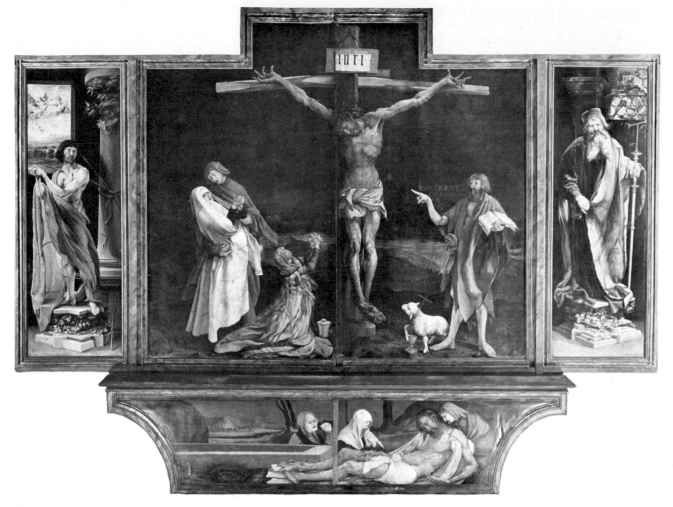

18-34 MATTHIAS GRÜNEWALD, *Crucifixion* from *The Isenheim Altarpiece* (closed), *c.* 1510–1515. Oil on wood, center panel approx. 8′ 10″ × 10′ 1″. Musée Unterlinden, Colmar.

swooning Virgin and St. John and in the shrill delirium of the Magdalene. To the other side, the gaunt, spectral form of John the Baptist stands in ungainly pose, pointing with a finger sharp as a bird's beak to the dead Christ and indicating in a Latin inscription Christ's destiny as Redeemer and his own as mere precursor: "It is fitting that he increase and I diminish." The bright, harsh, dissonant colors—black, blood-red, acid-yellow, and the dreadful green of death—suit the flat, angular shapes. Placed in a wilderness of dark mountains, the scene is relieved by a flood of glaring light that holds the figures in a tableau of awful impact.

Death and suffering seem to be the dominant themes shown by the altarpiece in its closed state. Yet they are combined with symbols offering hope and comfort to the viewer. Behind St. John is a body of water (the river Jordan?), which signifies baptism— the healing action of water, which symbolically washes away sin. (It may also refer to the growing contemporary interest in hydrotherapy, as numerous handbooks advertising local thermal and mineral baths were being published around the turn of the century.) The wine-red sky behind the cross evokes

the blood of Christ and may symbolize the Eucharist. These references to the sacraments of baptism and the Eucharist offer the viewer the hope of salvation through the sacrifice of Christ, should earthly cures fail.

When we turn from the Good Friday of the *Crucifixion* to the Easter Sunday of the *Resurrection* (FIG. 18-35), an inner panel of *The Isenheim Altarpiece*, the mood changes from disaster to triumph. Christ, in a blazing aureole of light so incandescent that it dissolves his form and overwhelms the guards, rises like a great flame into the starlit heavens. The fluttering Gothic line prevails in the ascending Christ, and something of the awkward angularity of the *Crucifixion* scene shapes the fallen soldiers. The highly expressive light in both scenes is supernatural, not the light of common day. It is certainly not the even, flat light that models Piero della Francesca's *Resurrection* fresco (FIG. 16-36). Indeed, in these two pictures, we find the fundamental differences that set the German School apart from the Italian School in the Renaissance. Piero's *Resurrection* typically represents the event in terms of a static grouping of solidly rendered figures in a completely balanced, measured composi-

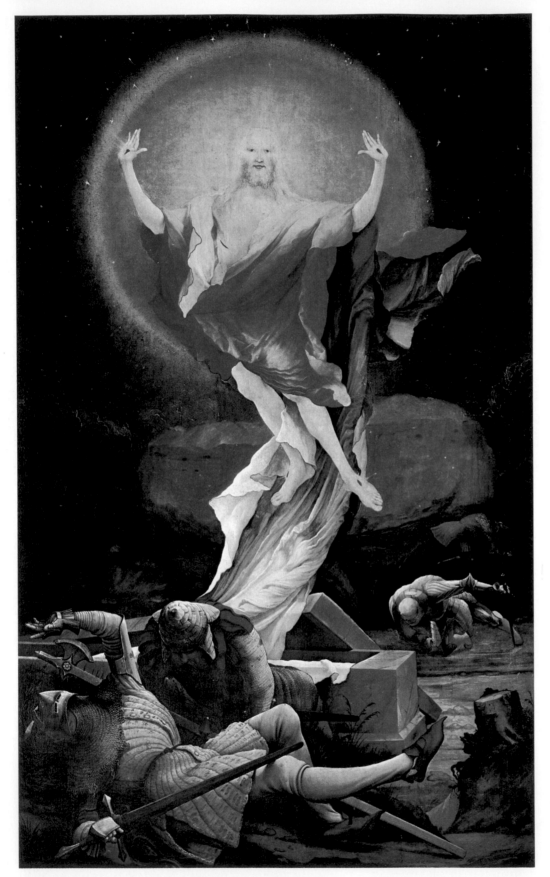

18-35 MATTHIAS GRÜNEWALD, *Resurrection*, detail of the inner right panel of *The Isenheim Altarpiece* (open). Approx. 8′ 10″ × 5′.

tion; the central figure of Christ stands solid as a column, one foot placed weightily on the edge of the sarcophagus. Grünewald converts everything into flowing motion; his Christ is disembodied, almost formless, and the composition has the irregularity and free form of a flaming cloud. Color determines everything here—not sculpturesque form and geometric composition, as with Piero. Moreover, Grünewald's intention is to render the supernatural in a bodiless way appropriate to it; Piero makes Christ as massive and corporeal as the stone sarcophagus on which he stands. From the Italian point of view, the visionary flashing and flickering of Grünewald's *Resurrection* must have appeared crude, formless, and utterly devoid of the order that theory, based on the study of nature and measurement, could confer.

ALBRECHT DÜRER

We know that Grünewald's great contemporary ALBRECHT DÜRER (1471–1528) felt this way about much of the art of the north and that, in comparison with Italian art, it appeared to him old-fashioned, clumsy, and without knowledge. In the introduction to an unfinished and unpublished treatise on painting, Dürer writes:

> Now, I know that in our German nation, at the present time, are many painters who stand in need of instruction, for they lack all real art theory. . . . For as much as they are so numerous, it is very needful for them to learn to better their work. He that works in ignorance works more painfully than he who works in understanding; therefore let all learn to understand art aright.

While still a journeyman, Dürer became acquainted with, and began to copy, prints by Mantegna and Pollaiuolo. Fascinated with Classical ideas, as transmitted through Italian Renaissance artists, Dürer became the first northern artist to travel to Italy expressly to study Italian art and its underlying theories at their source. After his first journey in 1495 (he made a second trip in 1505–1506), it became his life mission to bring the modern—the Italian Renaissance—style north and establish it there. Although Dürer did not always succeed in fusing his own native German style with the Italian manner, he was the first northern artist who fully understood the basic aims of the southern Renaissance.

Dürer was also the first artist outside of Italy to become an international art celebrity. Well-traveled and widely admired, he knew many of the leading Humanists and artists of his time, among them Erasmus of Rotterdam and Giovanni Bellini. A man of wide talents and tremendous energy, he became the "Leonardo of the North," achieving fabulous fame in his own time and a firm reputation ever since. Like Leonardo da Vinci, Dürer wrote theoretical treatises on a variety of subjects, such as perspective, fortification, and the ideal in human proportions. Through his prints, he exerted strong influence throughout Europe, especially in Flanders, but also in Italy. Moreover, he was the first northern artist to make himself known to posterity through several excellent self-portraits, through his correspondence, and through a carefully kept, quite detailed and readable diary.

In his own time, Dürer's fame and influence depended on his mastery of the graphic arts, and we

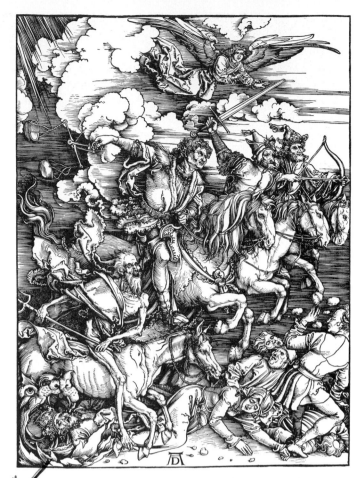

18-36 ALBRECHT DÜRER, *The Four Horsemen of the Apocalypse, c.* 1498. Woodcut, approx. 15¼″ × 11″. Metropolitan Museum of Art, New York (gift of Junius S. Morgan, 1919).

still think that his greatest contribution to Western art lies in this field. Trained as a goldsmith before he took up painting and printmaking, he developed an extraordinary proficiency in the handling of the burin, the engraving tool. This technical ability, combined with a feeling for the form-creating possibilities of line, enabled him to create a corpus of graphic work in woodcut and engraving that has seldom been rivaled for quantity and quality. In addition to illustrations for books, Dürer circulated and sold prints in single sheets, which people of ordinary means could buy and which made him a "people's artist" quite as much as a model for professionals. It also made him a rich man.

An early and very successful series of woodblock prints on 14 large sheets illustrates the Apocalypse, or the Revelation of St. John, the last book of the Bible. With great force and inventiveness, Dürer represents terrifying visions of doomsday, and of the omens preceding it. The fourth print of the series, *The Four Horsemen of the Apocalypse* (FIG. 18-36), represents, from foreground to background, Death trampling a bishop, Famine swinging scales, War wielding a sword, and Pestilence drawing his bow. The human race, in the last days of the world, is trampled by the Terrible Four. Technically, the virtuosity of Dürer's woodcuts has never been surpassed. By adapting to the woodcut the form-following hatching from Schongauer's engravings (FIG. 18-31), Dürer converts the former's primitive contrasts of black and white into a gliding scale of light and shade, achieving a quality of luminosity never before seen in woodblock prints. This dynamic composition retains some Late Gothic characteristics in the angularity of shapes and the tendency of forms to merge one into the other. On the other hand, Mantegna's influence can be found in the plastic and foreshortened poses of the trampled victims in the right foreground and in the head of Famine. But despite such Italicisms, the dramatic complexity of the composition remains essentially northern.

From 1500 on, Dürer became increasingly interested in the theoretical foundations of Italian Renaissance art; an engraving of *Adam and Eve* (FIG. 18-37) represents the first distillation of his studies of the Vitruvian theory of human proportions. Clearly outlined against the dark background of a northern forest, the two idealized figures of Adam and Eve stand in poses reminiscent of the *Apollo Belvedere* and the *Medici Venus*—two Hellenistic statues probably known to Dürer through graphic representations. Preceded by numerous geometric drawings, in which he tried to systematize sets of ideal human propor-

18-37 ALBRECHT DÜRER, *Adam and Eve* (*The Fall of Man*), 1504. Engraving, approx. 10″ × 7⅜″. Centennial Gift of Landon T. Clay. Courtesy of Museum of Fine Arts, Boston.

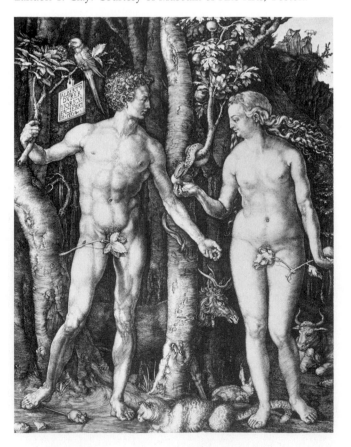

tions in balanced contrapposto poses, the final print presents Dürer's 1504 concept of the "perfect" male and female figures. Adam does, in fact, approach the southern ideal quite closely, but the fleshy Eve remains a German matron, her individualized features suggesting the use of a model. Northern also is the elaborate symbolism of the background "accessories" to the main figures. The choleric cat, the melancholic elk, the sanguine rabbit, and the phlegmatic ox represent the four humors of man, and the relation between Adam and Eve at the crucial moment of *The Fall of Man* is symbolized by the tension between cat and mouse in the foreground.

Dürer's *Adam and Eve* shows idealized forms and strongly naturalistic ones in a close combination that, depending on the viewer's attitude, may be regarded as complementing or as conflicting—closely allied ingredients in most of Dürer's works. For he agreed with Aristotle (and the new critics of the Renaissance) that "sight is the noblest faculty of man" and that "every form brought before our vision falls upon it as upon a mirror." "We regard," says Dürer, "a form and figure out of nature with more pleasure than any other, though the thing itself is not necessarily altogether better or worse." This is a new and important idea for artists. Nature holds the beautiful, says Dürer, for him who has the insight to extract it. Thus, beauty lies even in humble, perhaps ugly things, and the ideal, which bypasses or improves on nature, may not be the truly beautiful in the end. There is the hint here that uncomposed and ordinary nature might be a reasonable object of the artist's interest, quite as much as its composed and measured aspect. With an extremely precise watercolor study of a piece of turf (FIG. 18-38), Dürer allies himself to the scientific studies of Leonardo; for both artists, observation yields truth. Sight—sanctified by mystics like Nicholas of Cusa and artists like Jan van Eyck—becomes the secularized instrument of modern knowledge. The "mirror" that is our "vision" will later become telescope, microscope, and television screen. The remarkable *Great Piece of Turf* is as scientifically accurate as it is poetic; the botanist can distinguish each springing plant and variety of grass: dandelions, great plantain, yarrow, meadow grass, heath rush. "Depart not from nature in your opinions," says Dürer, "neither imagine that you can invent anything better. . . . for art stands firmly fixed in nature, and he who can find it there, he has it." The exquisite still life one finds in the northern paintings of the fifteenth century is irradiated with religious symbolism. Dürer's still life is of and for itself; he has found it in nature, and its representation no longer requires religious justification.

As Dürer closely studies floral nature, so he makes his portraits readings of character. The fifteenth-century portrait, like Van Eyck's *Man in a Red Turban* (FIG.

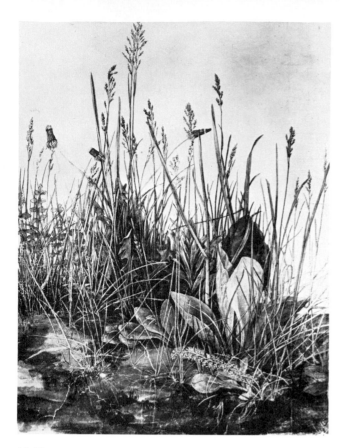

18-38 ALBRECHT DÜRER, *The Great Piece of Turf*, 1503. Watercolor, approx. 16″ × 12½″. Graphische Sammlung Albertina, Vienna.

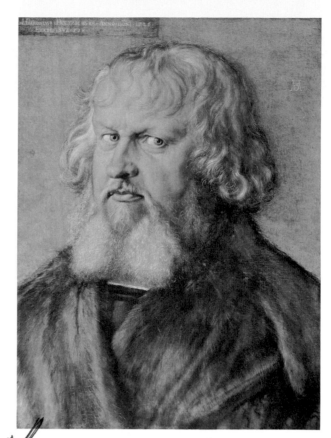

18-39 ALBRECHT DÜRER, *Hieronymus Holzschuher*, 1526. Oil on wood, approx. 19″ × 14″. Gemäldegalerie, Staatliche Museen, Berlin-Dahlem.

18-40 ALBRECHT DÜRER, *Melencolia I*, 1514. Engraving, approx. 9½″ × 7½″. Fogg Museum of Art, Harvard University, Cambridge, Massachusetts (bequest of Francis Calley Gray).

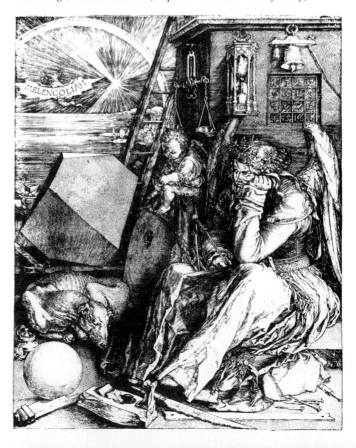

18-11) or his *Canon van der Paele* (FIG. 18-10), is a graphic description of features; Dürer's portraits, like that of *Hieronymus Holzschuher* (FIG. 18-39), are interpretations of personality. It may be, however, that they are as much projections of Dürer's own personality as they are readings of his subjects', for his portraits of men all show the subject as bold and virile, square-jawed, flashing-eyed, and truculent. All the subjects appear intense and intently aware of the observer. This strong psychic relationship to the external world, when the features are precisely particularized, makes for an extremely vivid presence. Holzschuher, a friend of Dürer's and town councilor of Nuremberg, fairly bristles with choleric energy and the burly belligerence of Nuremberg citizens, who, on many an occasion, had defended the city against all comers, including the Emperor himself. Leaving the background blank, except for an inscription, the artist achieves a remarkable concentration on the forceful personality of his subject. The portrait in Italy never really brings the subject into such a tense personal relationship to the observer.

Dürer always found it quite difficult to reconcile his northern penchant for precise naturalism with his intellectual, theoretical pursuits and with the demands of southern High Renaissance art for simplified monumentality. This life-long dilemma seems to be expressed in *Melencolia I* (FIG. 18-40), one of three so-called "master prints" Dürer made between 1513 and 1514. These works (the other two are *Knight, Death, and the Devil* and *St. Jerome in His Study*)—probably intended to symbolize the moral, theological, and intellectual virtues—carry the art of engraving to the highest degree of excellence. Dürer used his burin to render differences in texture and tonal values that would be difficult to match even in the much more flexible medium of etching, which was developed later in the century. The complex symbolism of *Melencolia I* is based primarily on concepts derived from Florentine Neo-Platonism. About the seated, winged figure of Melancholy, the instruments of the arts and sciences lie strewn in idle confusion; she is the personification of knowledge that, without divine inspiration, lacks the ability to act. Also, according to then current astrological theory, the artist, or any man engaged in creative activity, is the subject of Saturn. As such, he is characterized by a melancholia bordering on madness that either plunges him into despondency or raises him to the heights of creative fury; Michelangelo was regarded as subject to this humor. Like Michelangelo also, Dürer conceived of the artist (and thus of himself) as a genius who struggles to translate the pure Idea in his mind into gross but visible matter. Thus, the monumental image of the winged genius, with burning eyes in a shaded face and wings that do not fly, becomes the symbol for divine aspirations defeated by human frailty and, in a way, a "spiritual self-portrait of Albrecht Dürer."

Only toward the very end of his life, and in one of his very last paintings, was Dürer finally able to reconcile the two opposed tendencies—northern naturalism and southern monumentality—that had struggled for dominance in his entire oeuvre. He painted *The Four Apostles* (FIG. 18-41) without commission and presented the two panels to the city fathers of Nuremberg in 1526 to be hung in the city hall. The work has been called Dürer's religious and political testament, in which he expresses his sympathies for the Protestant cause and warns against the dangerous times, when religion, truth, justice, and the virtues will all be threatened. The four apostles (John and Peter on the left panel; Mark and Paul on the right) stand on guard for the city. Quotations from each of their books, in the German of Luther's translation of the New Testament, are written on the frames. They warn against the coming of perilous times and the preaching of false prophets who will distort the word of God. The figures of the apostles summarize Dürer's whole craft and learning. Representing the four temperaments, or humors, of the human soul—as well as the four ages of man and other quaternities—these portrait-like characterizations of the apostles have no equal in the idealized representations of Italian saints. At the same time, the art of the Italian Renaissance is felt in the monumental grandeur and majesty of the figures, which are heightened by a vivid color and sharp lighting. Here, Dürer unites the northern sense of minute realism with the Italian tradition of balanced forms, massive and simple. The result is a vindication of the artist's striving toward a new understanding—a work that stands with the greatest of the masterpieces of Italian art.

HANS HOLBEIN THE YOUNGER

What Dürer had struggled all his life to formulate and construct was achieved almost effortlessly by his younger contemporary, HANS HOLBEIN THE YOUNGER (1497–1543). Holbein's speciality was portraiture, in which he displayed a thorough assimilation of all that Italy had to teach of monumental composition, bodily structure, and sculpturesque form. He retains the northern traditions of close realism elaborated in fifteenth-century Flemish art. The color surfaces of his paintings are as lustrous as enamel; his detail, exact and exquisitely drawn; and his contrasts of light and dark, never heavy.

Holbein knew Erasmus of Rotterdam in Basel, where Holbein was first active. Because a religious civil war was imminent in Basel, Erasmus suggested that Holbein leave for England and gave him a recommendation to Thomas More, chancellor of Eng-

18-41   ALBRECHT DÜRER, *The Four Apostles,* 1526. Oil on wood, each panel 7' 1" × 2' 6". Alte Pinakothek Munich.

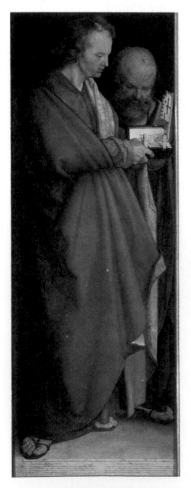
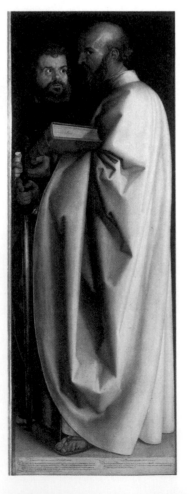

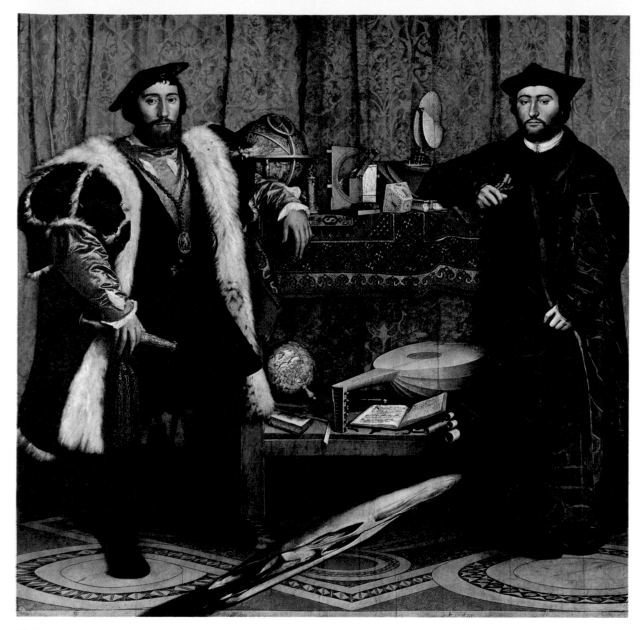

18-42   HANS HOLBEIN THE YOUNGER, *The French Ambassadors*, 1533. Oil and tempera on wood, approx. 6′ 8″ × 6′ 9½″. Reproduced by courtesy of the Trustees of the National Gallery, London.

land under Henry VIII. Holbein did leave and became painter to the English court. While there, he painted a superb double portrait of the French ambassadors to England, Jean de Dinteville and Georges de Selve (FIG. 18-42). The two men, both ardent Humanists, stand at either end of a side table covered with an oriental rug and a collection of objects reflective of their interests: mathematical and astronomical models and implements, a lute with a broken string, compasses, a sundial, flutes, globes, and an open hymnbook with Luther's translation of *Veni, Creator Spiritus* and of the Ten Commandments. The still-life objects are rendered with the same meticulous care as are the men themselves, the woven design of the deep emerald curtain behind them, and the floor tiles constructed in faultless perspective; not a figure is missing from the astronomical instruments. The

stable, balanced, serene composition is interrupted only by a long, gray shape that slashes diagonally across the picture plane. This is an *anamorphic* image that needs to be viewed by some special means (for example, reflected in a cylindrical mirror) if it is to be recognizable. In this case, the image is of a death's-head, for, like Dürer, Holbein was interested in symbolism as well as in radical perspectives. The color harmonies are adjusted in symphonic complexity and richness. The grave, even somber portraits indicate that Holbein follows the Italian portrait tradition, which gives the face a neutral expression, rather than Dürer's practice of giving it an expression of keen intensity. *The French Ambassadors* exhibits the peculiar talents of Holbein—his strong sense of composition, his subtle linear patterning, his gift for portraiture, his marvelous sensitivity to color, his faultlessly firm technique. This painting may have been Holbein's favorite; it is the only one signed with his full name.

In his later works, Holbein's style underwent a gradual change. He eliminated inventories of objects, confining himself to a simple neutral ground behind the subject. In the portrait of *Christina of Denmark* (FIG. 18-43), his simplification is carried over to the figure itself, to the costume, and to the face. The handsome young widow (of Duke Francesco Maria Sforza), with whom Henry VIII tried unsuccessfully to arrange a marriage, is shown at full length, a format reserved for the most eminent personages (bust portraits or half-lengths sufficed for Holbein's numerous portraits of merchants and court officials). Nothing is shown that might detract from the subject. With flawless draftsmanship, Holbein renders the figure firm and solid; his descriptive line is subtly reinforced

18-43 HANS HOLBEIN THE YOUNGER, *Christina of Denmark,* 1538. Oil on wood, approx. 70″ × 32″. Reproduced by courtesy of the Trustees of the National Gallery, London.

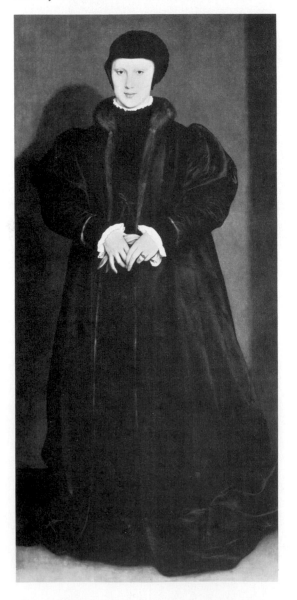

with flat modeling. The complete lack of perspective space may make us think of Mannerism, but we do not feel any ambiguity here; the volume of the figure itself clearly defines the space it occupies. Thus, with utmost restraint and simplicity, Holbein, in his later portraits, is able to achieve the monumental effects of the High Renaissance.

Holbein died prematurely in 1543 and, with him, the great German School of the Renaissance. But in 1532, when he left Basel for England, he had already taken the Renaissance with him. There were no significant successors. German art faded in the uproar of a century of religious war.

The Netherlands

The resurgence of France and the eclipse of the House of Burgundy robbed the Flemish schools of their precedence. The tremendous acclaim of Albrecht Dürer when he visited Antwerp in 1520 indicates a reverse for Flanders; Germany, which had followed, now led developments in the north. The decay of the old Flemish tradition, both in form and content, left a void that was filled by the confusing appearance of Italian ideas, received secondhand through Dürer. As with any new, inspiring, but ill-understood fashion, a number of conflicting mannerisms arose, which, if anything, had in common only their misunderstanding of the principles behind the novel forms. This period is characterized by a great delight in decorative extravagance, in which pedantic allusion to the classics is combined with exotic settings made of piled-up fragments of Italianate ornament. For a generation or so, the north, as it has been said, "simply could not get its Renaissance on straight."

But from all this confusion, new and confident movements could begin. For one thing, remnants of the Medieval tradition had to be swept away, and this happened. The dominance of religious conventions yielded to experiments in subject matter and form; although religious material persisted, it no longer prevailed in art. We have seen how it had been modified by humanization for over a century; now it had to share the artist's interest in portraiture, mythology, landscape, and genre. The structural basis for a new, Humanistic realism had been introduced by the great German painters. It was on this basis that an international, European art, dealing primarily with human interests, had to be built.

Changing views and attitudes were accompanied by a geographical shift in the region's commercial center. Partly due to the silting-up of the Bruges estuary, traffic was diverted to Antwerp, which became the hub of economic activity in the Low Countries after 1510. By mid-century, a jealous Venetian envoy had to admit that more business was transacted in

Antwerp in a few weeks than in a year in Venice. As many as 500 ships a day passed through Antwerp's harbor, and large trading colonies from England and Germany and from Italy, Portugal, and Spain established themselves in the city.

QUENTIN METSYS

Antwerp's growth and prosperity, along with the propensity of its wealthy merchants for collecting and purchasing art, attracted artists to the city—among them, QUENTIN METSYS (c. 1465–1530), who became Antwerp's leading master after 1510. Son of a Louvain blacksmith, Metsys may have been largely self-taught, which would explain, in part, his susceptibility to outside influences and his willingness to explore the styles and modes of a variety of models,

from Van Eyck to Bosch, and from Van der Weyden to Dürer and Leonardo. Yet his eclecticism was subtle and discriminating and enriched by an inventiveness that gave a personal stamp to his paintings and made him a popular as well as important artist. Quentin Metsys represents both the bad and the good aspects of early sixteenth-century Flemish art in its struggle to shed fifteenth-century traditions in favor of a more "modern" Renaissance mode of expression.

Metsys painted *The St. Anne Altarpiece* for the Louvain Brotherhood of St. Anne between 1507 and 1509. Its central panel (FIG. 18-44) shows a stable and orderly grouping of figures before a triple-vaulted loggia, through which a finely painted distant landscape can be seen. The round-arched architecture, complete with tie-rods and a central dome, seems

18-44   QUENTIN METSYS, *The St. Anne Altarpiece,* center panel, 1507–1509. Oil on wood, 7' 4½" × 7' 2¼". Musées Royaux des Beaux-Arts de Belgique, Brussels.

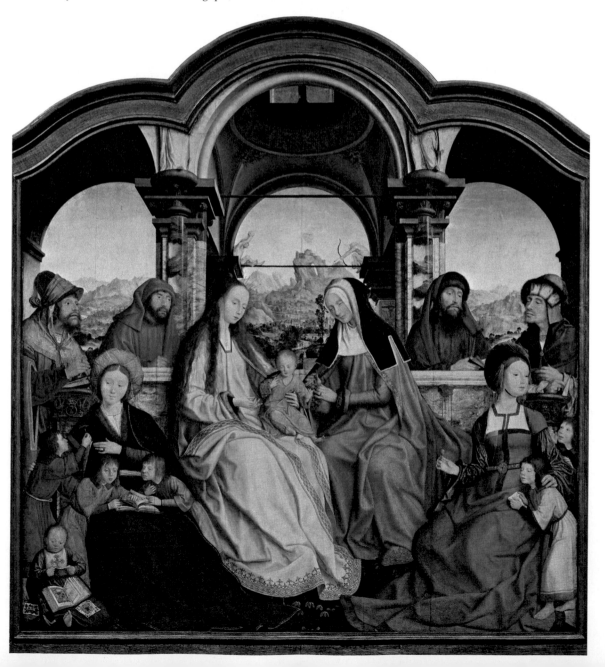

functional enough (except for the rectangular window, which intrudes illogically into the hemispheric dome), but it has little to do with Italian Renaissance architecture, which Metsys evidently tried to emulate. In this respect, he was no more successful than his Romanist contemporaries, whose attempts to provide their paintings with "modern" (Italian Renaissance) settings produced little more than architectural fantasies. On the other hand, the triple loggia effectively unifies the solemn, softly draped figures, whose heads are grouped in three inverted triangles. The compression of the composition may have been inspired by one of the late paintings of Hugo van der Goes, and the calm serenity of the scene evokes memories of Hans Memling's paintings (FIG. 18-20). But these and other possible sources of inspiration are thoroughly assimilated and synthesized by Metsys into a personal style. The regularized composition and the light coloration of his forms produce a tapestry-like effect that is both decorative and memorable.

Metsys' explorations of the past are liberally mixed with forward-looking genre and moralizing subjects to give his oeuvre a highly diversified aspect. The variety of his inventions provides a bridge from the fifteenth into the sixteenth century and makes him an influential inspiration to many of his contemporaries.

JAN GOSSAERT

More single-minded, although no more successful than Metsys in his exploration of Italian Renaissance art, is JAN GOSSAERT (c. 1478–1535), who worked for the later Philip of Burgundy, associated with Humanist scholars, and visited Italy. There, Gossaert (who adopted the name MABUSE, after his birthplace of Maubeuge) became fascinated with the antique and its mythological subject matter. Giorgio Vasari—Italian historian and Gossaert's contemporary—wrote that "Gossaert was almost the first to bring the true method of representing nude figures and mythologies from Italy to the Netherlands," although it is obvious that he derived much of his Classicism from Dürer. The composition and poses in his *Neptune and Amphitrite* (FIG. 18-45) are borrowed from Dürer's *Adam and Eve* (FIG. 18-37), although Gossaert's figures have been inflated, giving an impression of ungainly weight. The artist approximates the Classical stance, but Gossaert seems to have been more interested in nudity than in a Classical, ideal canon of proportions. The setting for the figures is a carefully painted architectural fantasy that illustrates a complete lack of understanding of the Classical style. Yet the painting is executed with traditional Flemish polish, and the figures are skillfully drawn and modeled. Although Gossaert also painted religious subjects in the traditional style, attempting unsuccessfully to outshine the fifteenth-century Flemish masters, his *Neptune*

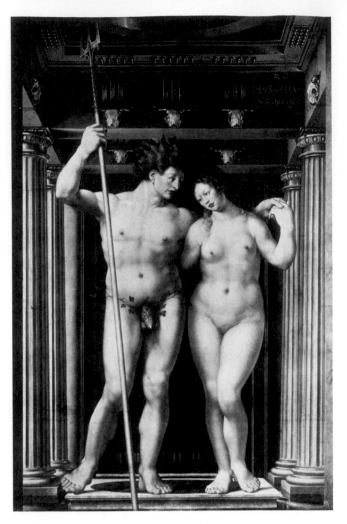

18-45 JAN GOSSAERT (MABUSE), *Neptune and Amphitrite*, c. 1516. Oil on wood, 7' 2" × 4' 1". Gemäldegalerie, Staatliche Museen, Berlin-Dahlem.

and Amphitrite aligns him firmly with the so-called Romanists, in whose art Italian Mannerism joins with fanciful native interpretations of the Classical style to form a highly artificial, sometimes decorative, often bizarre and chaotic style.

BARTHOLOMEUS SPRANGER

Much more the Romanist than Gossaert, the Netherlandish painter BARTHOLOMEUS SPRANGER (1546–1611) exaggerates the stylistic peculiarities of Italian Mannerism almost to the point of caricature. Spranger traveled widely in Italy and France, studying a variety of pictorial styles from Jacopo da Pontormo and Parmigianino to the painters of the School of Fontainebleau (FIG. 18-51). What he learned from them merged with his earlier training in the Netherlands to form a highly sophisticated and imaginative style. For the connoisseur Emperor Rudolph II, whose court painter he became at Prague, he fashioned such classically learned, intricately composed, and suggestively erotic pictures as *Hercules and Omphale* (FIG. 18-46), much to the taste of his bachelor patron. Hercules was enslaved by the beautiful Om-

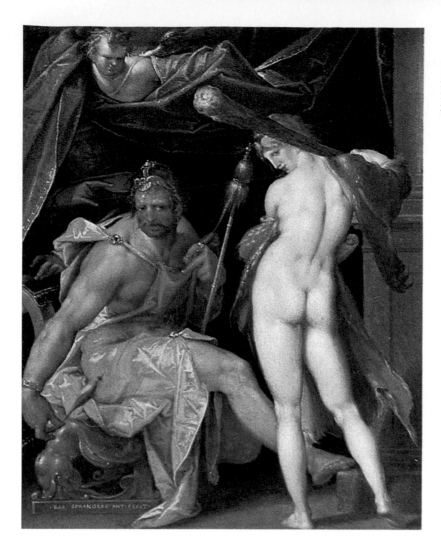

18-46 BARTHOLOMEUS SPRANGER,
Hercules and Omphale, c. 1598.
Paint on copper, 9¼″ × 7½″.
Kunsthistorisches Museum,
Vienna.

phale, who garbed him in the attributes of woman-
hood. Here, he wears women's satins and jewels and
does women's work, spinning with distaff and spin-
dle. His massive wrist is braceleted, and his hand is
bent in an effeminate gesture. Behind him, an ugly
hag makes the gesture of cuckoldry. The nude Omphale, her form androgynous (the emperor had a
penchant for the epicene), smiles coquettishly over
her shoulder. She carries Hercules' club and wears
his lion's skin teasingly. Spranger's themes, lascivious and pagan, find their appropriate vehicle of expression in Italian Mannerism. The Manneristic traits
are all here: the gliding, bending, turning poses; the
constricted space; the crowded surface; the bright,
decorative colors. Worldly, sensuous and ornamental, his pictures express a luxurious, courtly taste that
contrasts markedly with the reverent art of the bourgeois towns in which the Netherlandish master
painters worked.

JOACHIM PATINIR

An outstanding representative of a very different
trend in sixteenth-century Flemish art is JOACHIM
PATINIR (1475–1524)—the first Netherlandish landscape painter and the counterpart of the German Al-

brecht Altdorfer. A highly valued specialist in this
field, Patinir often collaborated with other artists, letting them paint figures into his landscapes. Little is
known of his background, and, although no definite
links can be established between the two artists,
Bosch may well have provided the initial inspiration
for Patinir's panoramic vistas. Significantly, however,
the landscapes in Bosch's paintings are of secondary
importance and serve only as broad stages on which
his figures perform their fantastic frolics; in Patinir's
works, the landscapes take on primary importance,
and the figures become mere accessories. In his
Landscape with St. Jerome (FIG. 18-47), the insignificant
figure of Patinir's title saint is almost hidden in the
left middle ground. The vast panorama is seen from a
mountaintop, and the artist works like a cartogra-
pher, building up his landscape in strips or layers
parallel to the picture plane. The effect of recession is
achieved by the careful diminution of familiar things
(houses, trees, figures) and by the emphatic use of
aerial perspective, in which the generally warm foreground colors shift to greens in the middle distance
and to cool blues in the far distance. Realism is confined to the description of details. Plants are painted
with botanical accuracy, and trees and rock forma-

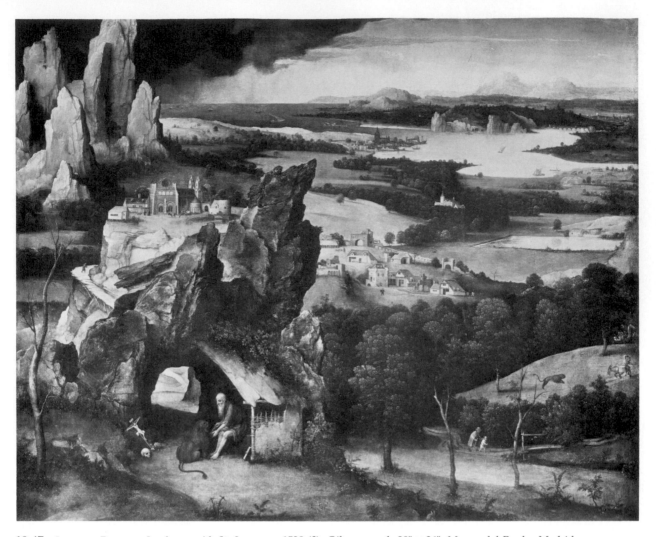

18-47 JOACHIM PATINIR, *Landscape with St. Jerome, c.* 1520 (?). Oil on wood, 30" × 36". Museo del Prado, Madrid.

tions are rendered with great feeling for their textural differences. The rich multiplicity of Patinir's paintings, with activity almost everywhere, is drawn together by a strong design and an extremely effective dark–light pattern. The tiny figures scattered throughout his landscape effectively contrast human frailty and the power of nature.

PIETER BRUEGEL THE ELDER

A similar interest in the interrelationship of man and nature is expressed in the works of the greatest and most original Flemish painter of the sixteenth century, PIETER BRUEGEL THE ELDER (*c.* 1525–1569), whose early, high-horizoned, "cosmographical" landscapes were probably influenced by Patinir. But in Bruegel's paintings, no matter how huge a slice of this world he may show, the activities of man remain the dominant theme. Bruegel was apprenticed to a "Romanist," PIETER COECKE, and, like many of his contemporaries, traveled to Italy, where he seems to have spent almost two years, going as far south as Sicily. But unlike his contemporaries, Bruegel was not overwhelmed by Classical art, and his Italian experiences are only incidentally reflected in his paint-

ings, usually in the form of Italian or Alpine landscape features that he recorded in numerous drawings during his journey. On his return from Italy, Bruegel was exposed to the works of Bosch, and the influence of that strange master, strongly felt in Bruegel's early paintings, must have swept aside any Romanist inclinations he may have had.

Hunters in the Snow (FIG. 18-48) is one of five surviving paintings of a series of six in which Bruegel illustrated seasonal changes in the year. It shows man and landscape locked in winter cold. The weary hunters return with their hounds, wives build fires, skaters skim the frozen pond, the town and its church huddle in their mantle of snow; and beyond the typically Flemish winter scene lies a bit of Alpine landscape. Aside from this trace of fantasy, however, the landscape is realistic and quite unlike Patinir's; it develops smoothly from foreground to background and draws the viewer diagonally into its depths. The artist's consummate skill in the use of line and shape and his subtlety in tonal harmony make this one of the great landscape paintings in history and an Occidental counterpart of the masterworks of classical Chinese landscape.

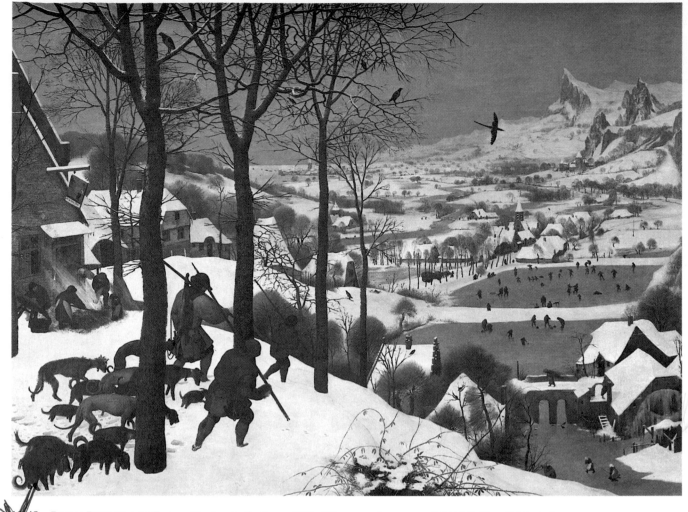

18-48 Pieter Bruegel the Elder, *Hunters in the Snow*, 1565. Oil on wood, approx. 46″ × 64″. Kunsthistorisches Museum, Vienna.

Bruegel, of course, is not simply a landscapist. In his series of the months, he presents—in a fairly detached manner, occasionally touched with humor—the activities of man at different times of the year. And he chooses for his purpose the social class that is most directly affected by seasonal changes, the peasantry. But usually Bruegel is much more personal as he makes satirical comments on the dubious condition of man. His meaning in specific cases is often as obscure as Bosch's, and he seems to delight in leading us into his pictures through devious paths and confronting us sometimes with mystery, sometimes with an appalling revelation. As a vehicle for his sarcasm, he again chooses the peasant, whom he sees as an uncomplicated representative of humanity—a member of society whose actions and behavior are open, direct, and unspoiled by the artificial cultural gloss that disguises but does not altar the city dweller's natural inclinations. These good countryfolk are shown enjoying themselves in *The Peasant Dance* (FIG. 18-49), which is no mincing quadrille, but a boisterous, whirling, hoedown in which plenty of sweat is shed. One can almost hear the feet stomping to the rhythm of the bagpipe. With an eye much more inci-

sive than any camera lens, the artist grasps the entire scene in its most characteristic aspect and records it in a broad technique that discards most of the traditional Flemish concern for detail. Strong but simplified modeling emphasizes the active, solidly drawn silhouettes, which, combined with strong local colors, give the painting the popular robustness so suited to its subject. From the hilltop that he shared with the *Hunters,* Bruegel descends into the village to look more closely at its life and amusements—and he finds that all is not well in this rustic paradise. A fight is brewing at the table on the left; everyone is turning his back to the church in the background; nobody is paying the least attention to the small picture of a Madonna tacked to the tree on the right; and the man next to the bagpiper is wearing the feather of a peacock—a symbol of vanity—in his cap. And what about the young couple kissing unashamedly in public in the left middle ground? Is Bruegel telling us, like Bosch in his *Hell* (FIG. 18-22), that music is an instrument of the Devil and a perverter of morals? A closer inspection of the painting reveals that Bruegel is telling much more than the simple story of a country festivity. He is showing that a *kermess,* a festival cele-

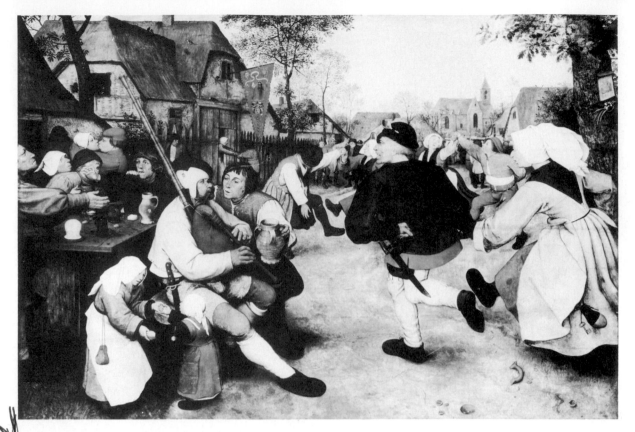

18-49   PIETER BRUEGEL THE ELDER, *The Peasant Dance, c.* 1567. Oil on wood, approx. 45″ × 65″. Kunsthistorisches Museum, Vienna.

brating a saint, has become a mere pretext for man to indulge his lust, anger, and gluttony.

Toward the end of his life, Bruegel's commentary on man takes on an increasingly bitter edge. The Netherlands, racked by religious conflict, had become the seat of cruel atrocities, made even more cruel by the coming of the power of Catholic Spain to put down the Reformation. We do not know whether Bruegel took sides; like the great satirist he was, he may have preferred to make all mankind, not just partisans, the object of his commentary. His secret meanings may partly be explained by the danger of too much outspokenness. His biographer, Karel van Mander* (1548–1606), writes:

> Many of Bruegel's strange compositions and comical subjects one may see in his copper engravings . . . he supplied them with inscriptions which, at the time, were too biting and too sharp, and which he had his wife burn during his last illness, because of . . . fear that most disagreeable consequences might grow out of them.

Bruegel knew well how to disguise his intent—so well that in his day he was called "Peter the Droll," because, as Van Mander writes, "there are very few works from his hand that the beholder can look at seriously, without laughing."

*Karel van Mander's *Het Schilderboeck (The Painter's Book)* was published in Haarlem in 1604. It contains a section with biographies of Netherlandish and German painters that is the northern equivalent of Giorgio Vasari's *Vite.*

France

Divided and harried during the fifteenth century, France, reorganized under decisive kings, was strong enough to undertake an aggressive policy toward her neighbors by the end of the century. Under the rule of Francis I, the French held a firm foothold in Milan and its environs. The king eagerly imported the Renaissance into France, bringing Leonardo da Vinci and Andrea del Sarto to his court, but they left no permanent mark on French art. It was Florentine Mannerists like Rosso Fiorentino and Benvenuto Cellini who implanted the Italianate style that replaced the Gothic. Francis' attempt to glorify the state and himself meant that the religious art of the Middle Ages was finally superseded, for it was the king and not the Church who now held power. A portrait of *Francis I* by JEAN CLOUET (*c.* 1485–1541), in the Franco–Italian manner, shows a worldly prince magnificently bedizened in silks and brocades, wearing a gold chain, and caressing the pommel of a dagger (FIG. 18-50). One would not expect the king's talents to be directed to spiritual matters, and legend has it that the "merry monarch" was a great lover and the hero of hundreds of "gallant" situations. The flat light and suppression of modeling give equal emphasis to head and costume, so that the king's finery and his face enter equally into the effect of royal splendor. Yet, despite this Mannerist formula for portraiture, the features are not entirely immobile; there is the faint-

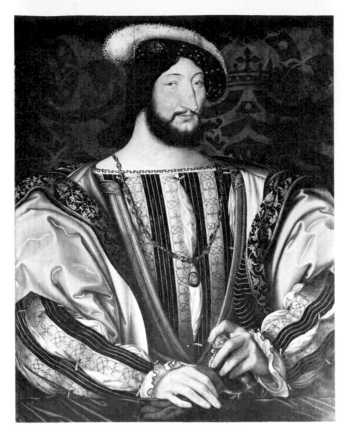

18-50 JEAN CLOUET, *Francis I, c.* 1525–1530. Tempera and oil on wood, approx. 38″ × 29″. Louvre, Paris.

est flicker of an expression that we might read as "knowing."

The personal tastes of Francis and his court must have run to an art at once suave, artificial, elegant, and erotic. The sculptors and painters working to-

gether on the decoration of the new royal palace at Fontainebleau, under the direction of Florentines Rosso and FRANCESCO PRIMATICCIO (1504–1570), are known as the School of Fontainebleau. Rosso became the court painter of Francis I shortly after 1530. In France, his style no longer showed the turbulent harshness of *Moses Defending the Daughters of Jethro* (FIG. 17-42), but became consistently more elegant and graceful. When Rosso and Primaticcio decorated the Gallery of Francis I at Fontainebleau, they combined painting, fresco, imitation mosaic, and stucco sculpture in low and high relief (FIG. 18-51). The abrupt changes in scale and texture are typically Mannerist, as is the composition of the central painting, which shows *Venus Reproving Love* in compressed Mannerist space with elongated grace and mannered poses. The same artificial grace can be seen in the flanking caryatids, and the viewer is jarred by the shift in scale between the painted and the stucco figures. However, the combination of painted and stucco relief decorations became extremely popular from this time on and remained a favorite decorative technique throughout the Baroque and Rococo periods.

It has been said of Francis I that, besides women, his one obsession was building. During his reign, which lasted from 1515 to 1547, several large-scale châteaux were begun—among them the Château de Chambord in 1519 (FIG. 18-52). Reflecting the more peaceful times, these châteaux, developments from the old countryside fortresses, served as country houses for royalty and were usually built near a for-

18-51 ROSSO FIORENTINO and FRANCESCO PRIMATICCIO, *Venus Reproving Love, c.* 1530–1540. Gallery of Francis I, Fontainebleau, France.

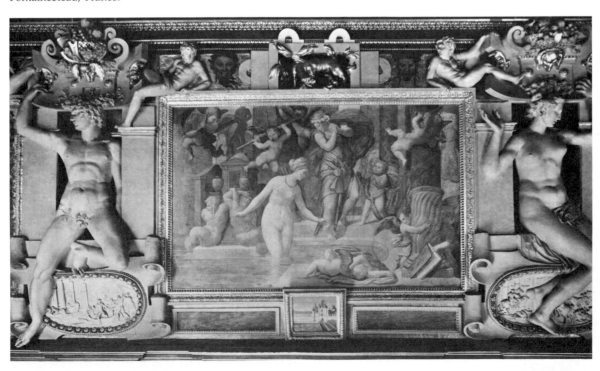

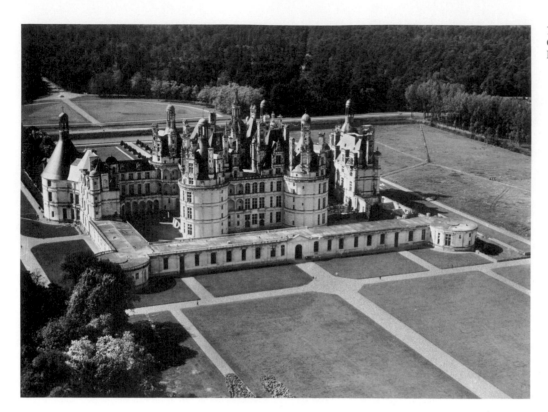

18-52 Aerial view of the Château de Chambord, France, begun 1519.

est, for use as hunting lodges. The plan of Chambord, originally drawn by a pupil of Giuliano da Sangallo, imposes Italian concepts of symmetry and balance on the irregularity of the old French fortress. There is a central square block with four corridors, in the shape of a cross, leading to a broad, central staircase that gives access to groups of rooms—ancestors of the modern suite of rooms or apartments. The square plan is punctuated at each of the four corners by a round tower, and the whole is surrounded by a moat. From the exterior, Chambord presents a carefully contrived horizontal accent on three levels, its floors separated by continuous moldings. Windows are placed exactly over one another. This matching of horizontal and vertical features is, of course, derived from the Italian palazzo. But above the third level, the lines of the structure break chaotically into a jumble of high dormers, chimneys, and lanterns that recall soaring, ragged, Gothic silhouettes on the skyline.

The architecture of Chambord is still French at heart. During the reign of Francis' successor, Henry II (1547–1559), however, treatises by Italian architects were translated and Italian architects came to work in France; at the same time, the French turned to Italy for study and travel. This interchange brought about a more thoroughgoing revolution in style, although it never eliminated certain French elements that persisted from the Gothic tradition. Francis began the enlargement of the Louvre in Paris (FIG. 18-53) to make a new royal palace, but died before the work was well begun. His architect, PIERRE LESCOT (1510–

1578), continued under Henry II and, with the aid of the sculptor JEAN GOUJON (c. 1510–1565), produced the Classical style of the French Renaissance. Although Chambord incorporated the formal vocabulary of the Early Renaissance, particularly from Lombardy, Lescot and his associates were familiar with the High Renaissance of Bramante and his school. Each story of the Louvre forms a complete order, and the cornices project enough to furnish a strong horizontal accent. The arcading on the ground story reflects the ancient Roman arch-order and is recessed enough to produce more shadow than in the upper stories, strengthening the visual base of the design. On the second story, the pilasters rising from bases and the alternating curved and angular pediments supported by consoles have direct antecedents in several Roman High Renaissance palaces. On the other hand, the decreased height of the stories, the proportionately much larger windows (given the French weather!), and the steep roof are northern. Especially French are the pavilions that jut from the wall. These are punctuated by a feature that the French will long favor—the double columns framing a niche. The vertical lines of the building remain strong; the wall is deeply penetrated by openings and (in un-Italian fashion) profusely sculptured. This French Classical manner—double-columned pavilions, tall and wide windows, profuse statuary, and steep roofs—will be widely imitated in other northern countries, with local variations. The mannered Classicism produced by the French will be the *only*

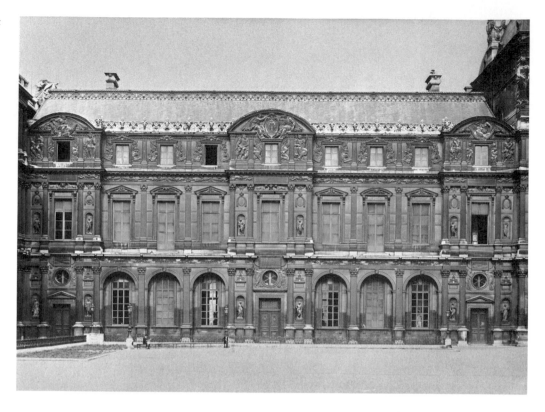

18-53 PIERRE LESCOT, west façade of the Square Court of the Louvre, Paris, begun 1546.

Classicism to serve as a model for northern architects through most of the sixteenth century. The west courtyard façade of the Louvre is the best of French Renaissance architecture; eventually, the French will develop a quite native Classicism of their own, cleared of Italian Mannerist features.

The statues of the Louvre courtyard façade, now much restored, are the work of Goujon. We can best appreciate the quality of Goujon's style from his *Nymphs* reliefs from the Fountain of the Innocents in Paris (FIG. 18-54). Like the architecture of the Louvre, Goujon's nymphs are intelligent and sensitive French adaptations of the Italian Mannerist canon of figure design. Certainly, they are Mannerist in their ballet-like contrapposto and in their flowing, clinging drapery, which recalls the ancient "wet" drapery of Hellenic sculpture—for example, the figures on the parapet of the Temple of Athena Nike (FIG. 5-59). The slender, sinuous figures perform their steps within the structure of Mannerist space, and it is interesting that they appear to make one continuous motion—an illusion produced by reversing the gestures, as they might be seen in a mirror. The style of Fontainebleau, and ultimately of Primaticcio and Cellini, guides the sculptor here, but Goujon has learned the manner so well that he can create originally within it. The nymphs are truly French masterpieces, with lightness, ease, grace, and something of a native French chic that saves them from being mere lame derivatives of the Italian Mannerist norm.

In France, as in all Europe in the sixteenth century,

the influence of Italian art was direct and overpowering. But as the century progressed, native French artists adapted the new elements to the strong Gothic traditions and created a distinctively French expression. An example of this maturing style is seen in the works of the sculptor GERMAIN PILON (c. 1535–1590), who made his reputation with monumental tomb sculpture, especially for the monument of Henry II and Catherine de' Medici in St. Denis, Paris. Like Goujon and other French sculptors, Pilon began in the Fontainebleau style, emphasizing artifice in pose

18-54 JEAN GOUJON, *Nymphs,* reliefs from the Fountain of the Innocents, Paris, 1548–1549.

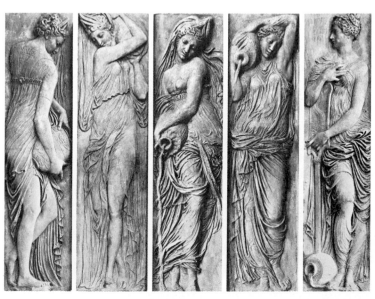

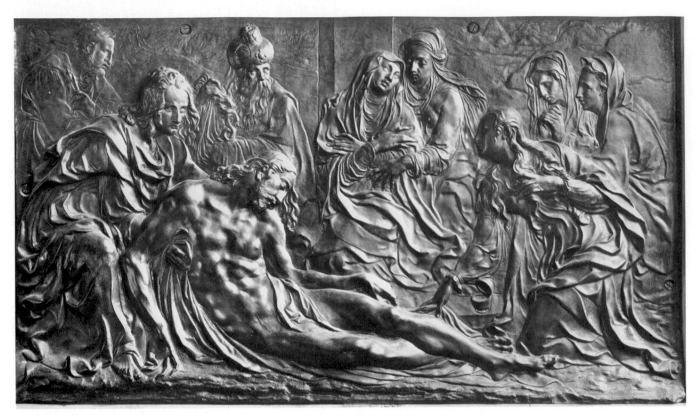

18-55 GERMAIN PILON, *Descent from the Cross*, 1583. Bronze relief, 19″ × 32½″. Louvre, Paris.

and gesture and graceful, sinuous contour. Gradually, his style changed as he made contact with the still strong tradition of Late Gothic realism. A bronze relief, *Descent from the Cross* (FIG. 18-55), recalls monumental compositions of Rogier van der Weyden (FIG. 18-14) and the master of *The Avignon Pietà* (FIG. 18-25). Unlike them, Pilon shows the influence of Mannerism in the great, elongated, muscular Christ; like them, he expresses a quiet yet profound pathos that Mannerism could not sincerely convey. The realistic element appears in the very staging of the drama. The Virgin, consoled by a holy woman, is removed from the center of the action; those in authority are at the head and feet of Christ. There is a curiously steady, almost serene reading of the emotions of those present. The curving lines of the draperies have lost the angularity of the Gothic but are not arranged in the contrived patterns of Mannerism. Pilon, from a fusion of the old tradition with the new fashion, has risen to a bold statement of his own—a statement making use of both while transcending them in a moving, personal interpretation of the Medieval theme.

Spain

In some respects, the sixteenth century is the Spanish century. Under Charles V of Hapsburg and his son, Philip II, the Spanish empire dominated a territory greater in extent than any ever known: a large part of Europe, the western Mediterranean, a strip of North Africa, and vast expanses in the newly discovered Western Hemisphere. The Hapsburg empire, enriched by the plunder of the New World, supported the most powerful military force in Europe, which everywhere backed the ambitions and the adventures of the "Most Catholic Kings." Spain defended and then advanced the interests of the Catholic Church in its struggle against the inroads of the Protestant Reformation. What we call the Catholic Counter-Reformation was funded, directed, fought for, and enforced by Spain. By force and influence—by the preaching and the propaganda of the newly founded Spanish order of the Society of Jesus (the Jesuits)— Spain drove Protestantism from a large part of Europe and sponsored the internal reform of the Catholic Church at the great Council of Trent. She humbled France; trampled the Netherlands; reclaimed much of Germany, Poland, and Hungary for Catholicism; and held England at bay (until the end of the century), while she converted the Indian empires of the New World to the Catholic faith and destroyed them in a relentless search for treasure. The material and the spiritual exertions of Spain—the fanatical courage of her soldiers and the incandescent fervor of her great mystical saints—went together. The former became the terror of the Protestant and pagan worlds; the latter, the inspiration of the Catholic. The crusading spirit of Spain, nourished by centuries of war with Islam, engaged body and soul in the formation of the most Catholic civilization of Europe and the Americas. In the sixteenth century, for good or for ill, Spain left the mark of her power, religion, language, and culture on two hemispheres.

Yet Spain, like all of Europe at this time, came under the spell of Renaissance Italy; her architecture especially shows that influence, but not all at once. During the fifteenth century and well into the sixteenth, a Late Gothic style of architecture, the Plateresque, prevailed side by side with buildings influenced by Italy. ("Plateresque" is derived from the Spanish *platero*, meaning silversmith, and is applied to the style because of the delicate execution of its ornament.) The Collegio di San Gregorio in the Castilian city of Valladolid handsomely exemplifies the Plateresque manner (FIG. 18-56). The Spanish were particularly fond of great carved retables, like the German altar screens that influenced them (FIGS. 18-28 and 18-29)—so much so that they made them a conspicuous decorative feature of their exterior architecture, dramatizing a portal set into an otherwise blank wall. The Plateresque entrance of San Gregorio is a lofty, sculptured stone screen that bears no functional relation to the architecture behind it. On the entrance level, ogival, flamboyant arches are hemmed with lace-like tracery reminiscent of Moorish design. Above rises a great screen, paneled into sculptured compartments; in the center, the coat of arms of Ferdinand and Isabella is wreathed by the branches of a huge pomegranate tree (symbolizing "Grenada," the Moorish capital of Spain just recently captured by the "Catholic Kings"). Cupids play among the tree branches, and, flanking the central panel, niches enframe armed pages of the court, heraldic wildmen, and armored soldiers, attesting to the new, proud militancy of the united kingdom of Spain. In typical Plateresque and Late Gothic fashion, the whole design is unified by the activity of a thousand intertwined motifs, which, in sum, create an exquisitely carved panel greatly expanded in scale.

A sudden and surprising Italianate Classicism makes its appearance in the unfinished palace of Charles V in the Alhambra in Granada (FIG. 18-57), the work of the painter–architect PEDRO MACHUCA (active 1520–1550). The circular central courtyard is ringed with superposed Doric and Ionic orders, with continuous horizontal entablatures rather than arches. Ornament consists only of the details of the orders themselves, which are rendered with the simplicity, clarity, and authority we find in the work of Bramante and his school. The lower story recalls the ring colonnade of the Tempietto (FIG. 17-6), although here, of course, the curve is reversed. This pure Classicism, entirely exceptional in Spain at this time, may

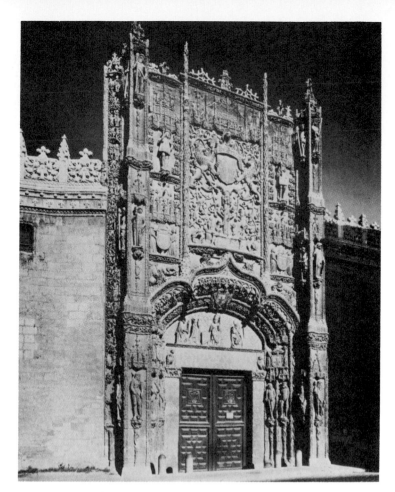

18-56 Portal, Collegio di San Gregorio, Valladolid, Spain, *c.* 1498.

18-57 PEDRO MACHUCA, courtyard of the palace of Charles V, Alhambra, Granada, Spain, *c.* 1526–1568.

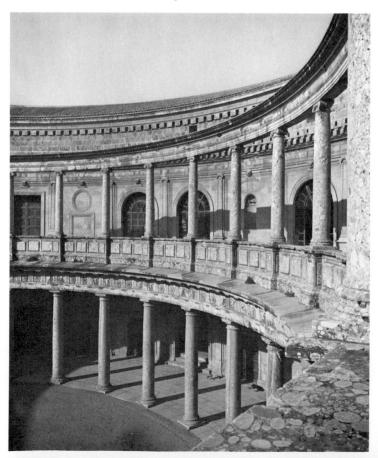

be a reflection of Charles V's personal taste acquired on one of his journeys to Italy. (It should be remembered that the emperor was an enthusiastic patron of Titian.) Machuca himself had sojourned in Italy, and the courtyard may be the consequence of his endeavor to revive this feature of the ancient Classical palace.

But the Spanish spirit of the time would seem to disdain the ideal purity of feature and correctness of proportion sought in Classical design. Something different must be done with what is received from Italy. What could be done is visible in the great fortress–palace–mausoleum–monastery–church complex called the Escorial (FIGS. 18-58, 18-59, 18-60), which was constructed for Philip II by JUAN BAUTISTA DE TOLEDO (?–1567) and JUAN DE HERRERA (1530–1597)—principally the latter. The king, perhaps the greatest in Spanish history, must have had much to do with the design. Certainly, there was close collaboration between Philip and his architects. The whole vast structure is in keeping with his austere and conscientious character, his passionate Catholic religiosity, his proud reverence for his dynasty, and his stern determination to impose his will worldwide.

Philip wrote to Herrera what he expected from him: "Above all, do not forget what I have told you—simplicity of form, severity in the whole, nobility without arrogance, majesty without ostentation." The result is a Classicism of Doric severity, ultimately derived from Italian architecture and with the grandeur of St. Peter's implicit in the scheme, but unique in Spanish and European architecture—a style inimitably of itself, even though later structures will reflect it.

In his will, Charles V stipulated that a "dynastic pantheon" be built to house the remains of past and future monarchs of Spain. Philip II, obedient to his father's wishes, chose a site some 30 miles northwest of Madrid, a rugged terrain with barren mountains. Here, he built not only the royal mausoleum, but a church, a monastery, and a palace above and around it. Legend has it that the grid-like plan for the enormous complex, 625 feet wide and 520 feet deep, was meant to symbolize the gridiron on which St. Lawrence, patron of the Escorial, was martyred.

The long sweep of the severely plain walls is broken only by the three entrances, with the dominant central portal framed by superposed orders topped

18-58 JUAN DE HERRERA, the Escorial (aerial view), near Madrid, Spain, *c.* 1563–1584.

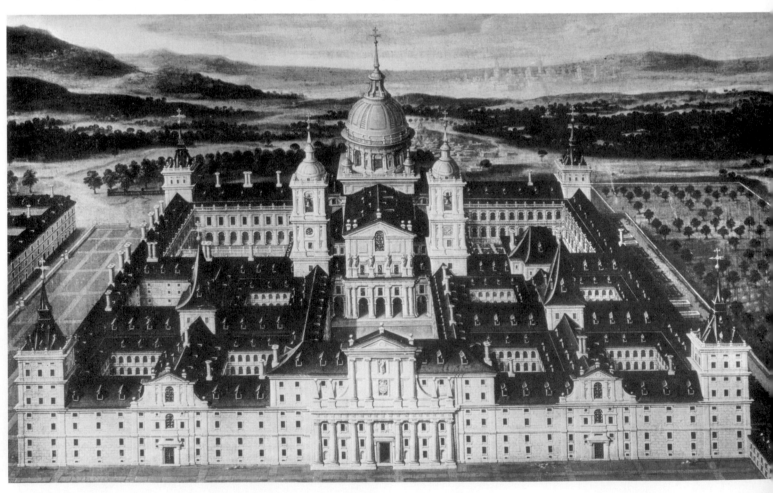

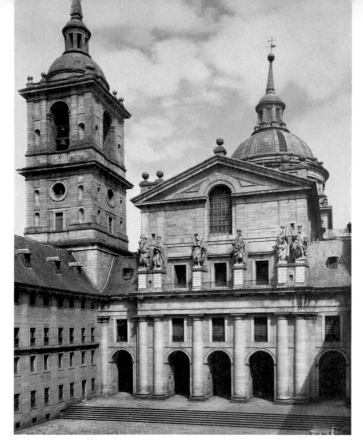

18-59 JUAN DE HERRERA, the Escorial, façade of church.

18-60 JUAN DE HERRERA, the Escorial, interior of church.

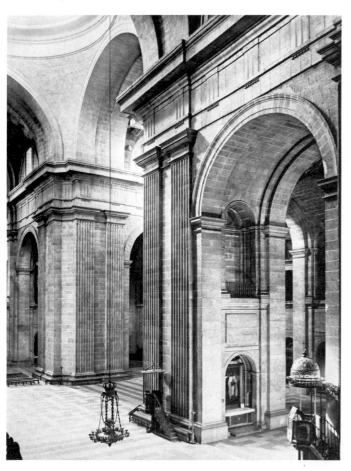

by a pediment in the Italian fashion. The corners of the wall are punctuated by massive square towers. The stress on the central axis, with its subdued echoes in the two flanking portals, forecasts the three-part organization of later Baroque palace façades. Like the whole complex of buildings, the domed-cross church, with similarly heavy towers, is constructed of granite, expressing, in its grim starkness of mass, the obdurate quality of a material most difficult to work. The massive façade of the church (FIG. 18-59) and the austere geometry of its interior, the blocky walls and ponderous arches (FIG. 18-60), dominate the Classical forms, producing an effect of overwhelming strength and weight that contradicts the grace and elegance we associate with much of the Renaissance architecture of Italy.

The Escorial is a monument to the collaboration of a great king and a remarkably understanding architect, who made of it an original expression of a unique idea and personality—the embodiment of the stern virtues of a monarch, a realm, and an age conscious of their peculiar power and purpose. The visitor to the Escorial is awed by the overpowering architectural expression of the spirit of Spain in its heroic epoch and of the character of Philip II, who directed it.

There appear to be two sides to the Spanish genius in the period of the Counter-Reformation: fervent religious faith and ardent mysticism on the one hand and an iron realism on the other. St. Theresa of Avila and St. John of the Cross can be considered representative of the first; the practical St. Ignatius of Loyola, founder of the Jesuit order, of the latter. It is possible for the two tempers to be found in the same persons and works of art, but it is more common to find them apart. Interestingly enough, a painter of foreign extraction was able to combine them in a single picture. Kyriakos Theotokopoulos (c. 1547–1614), called EL GRECO, was born in Crete but emigrated to Italy as a young man. In his youth, he was trained in the traditions of Late Byzantine frescoes and mosaics. While still young, El Greco went to Venice, where he was connected with the shop of Titian, although Tintoretto's painting seems to have made a stronger impression on him. A brief trip to Rome explains the influences of Roman and Florentine Mannerism on his work. By 1577, he had left for Spain to spend the rest of his life in Toledo. El Greco's art is a strong, personal blending of Late Byzantine and Late Italian Mannerist elements. The intense emotionalism of his paintings, which naturally appealed to the pious fervor of the Spanish, the dematerialization of form, and a great reliance on color bind him to sixteenth-century Venetian art and to Mannerism. His strong sense of movement and use of light, however, prefigure the Baroque. El Greco's art is not strictly Spanish, although it appealed to certain sectors of that society,

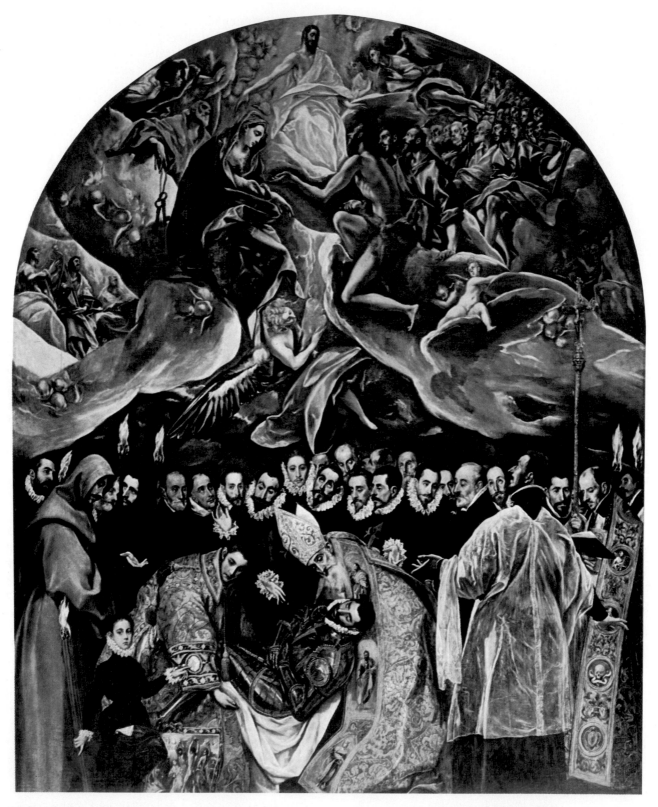

18-61　EL GRECO, *The Burial of Count Orgaz*, 1586. Oil on canvas, approx. 16′ × 12′. Santo Tomé, Toledo, Spain.

for it had no Spanish antecedents and had little effect on future Spanish painting.

Nevertheless, the paintings of this hybrid genius interpret Spain for us in its Catholic zeal and yearning spirituality. This is true of his masterpiece, *The Burial of Count Orgaz* (FIG. 18-61), painted in 1586 for the church of Santo Tomé in Toledo. The theme illustrates the legend that the Count of Orgaz, who had died some three centuries before and who had been a great benefactor of the church of Santo Tomé, was buried in the church by Saints Stephen and Augustine, who miraculously descended from heaven to lower the count's body into its sepulcher. The earthly scene is irradiated by the brilliant heaven that opens above it, as El Greco carefully distinguishes the terrestrial and celestial spheres. The terrestrial is represented with a firm realism; the celestial, in his quite personal manner, with elongated, undulant figures, fluttering draperies, cold highlights, and a peculiar kind of ectoplasmic, swimming cloud. Below, the two saints lovingly lower the count's armor-clad body, the armor and heavy draperies painted with all the rich sensuousness of the Venetian School. The background is filled with a solemn chorus of black-clad Spanish grandees, in whose carefully individualized features El Greco shows us that he was also a great portraitist. These are the faces that looked on the greatness and glory of Spain when she was the leading power of Europe—the faces of the *conquistadores,* who brought her the New World and who, two years after this picture was completed, would lead the Great Armada against Protestant England and Holland.

The lower and upper spheres of the painting are linked by the upward glances of the figures below and by the flight of an angel above, who carries the soul of the count in his arms as St. John and the Virgin intercede for it before the throne of Christ. El Greco's deliberate change in style to distinguish between the two levels of reality gives the viewer the opportunity to see the artist's early and late manners in the same work, one above the other. The relatively sumptuous and realistic presentation of the earthly sphere shows a still strong root in Venetian art. But the abstractions and distortions that El Greco uses to show the immaterial nature of the heavenly realm will become characteristic of his later style. Pulling heaven down to earth, he will paint worldly inhabitants in the same abstract manner as celestial ones. His elongated figures will exist in undefined spaces, bathed in a cool light of uncertain origin. For this, El Greco has been called the last and greatest of the Mannerists, but it is difficult to apply that label to him without reservations. Although using Manneristic formal devices, El Greco was not a rebel, nor was he aiming for elegance in his work; he was concerned primarily with emotion and with the effort to express his own religious fervor or to arouse the observer's. To make the inner meaning of his paintings forceful, he developed a highly personal style in which his attenuated forms become etherealized in dynamic swirls of unearthly light and color. There may be some ambiguity in El Greco's forms, but there is none

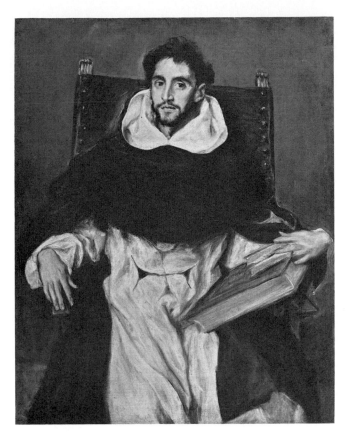

18-62   EL GRECO, *Fray Félix Hortensio Paravicino,* 1609. Oil on canvas, 44½″ × 33¾″. Isaac Sweetser Fund, Museum of Fine Arts, Boston.

in his meaning—mystical, spiritual, ecstatic devotion.

Toward the end of his life, El Greco painted a portrait of his friend, the theologian, poet, and Trinitarian priest, *Fray Félix Hortensio Paravicino* (FIG. 18-62). It is one of the most distinguished portraits of the age. Father Hortensio, clad in the black-and-white vesture of his order, is represented seated, which, since the time of Raphael, was customary for portraits of ecclesiastics of high rank. He holds books, attributes of intellectual dedication and accomplishment. The vividly contrasting black and white of his canonicals and the square-backed leather chair, with its gilt bronze studs and finials, magnificently set off the pale, ascetic face, accented by the dark hair, eyebrows, and beard. El Greco renders the character of a man, given wholly to other-worldly concerns, as a kind of apparition not quite of this world. The likeness fades into the image of a typical El Greco saint. As is often the case when a great painter makes the likeness of a great-souled subject, the latter becomes more than an individual person. He becomes, as here, generalized into a type, that of the spiritually exalted priest—protagonist in the drama of Spanish history in its great century.

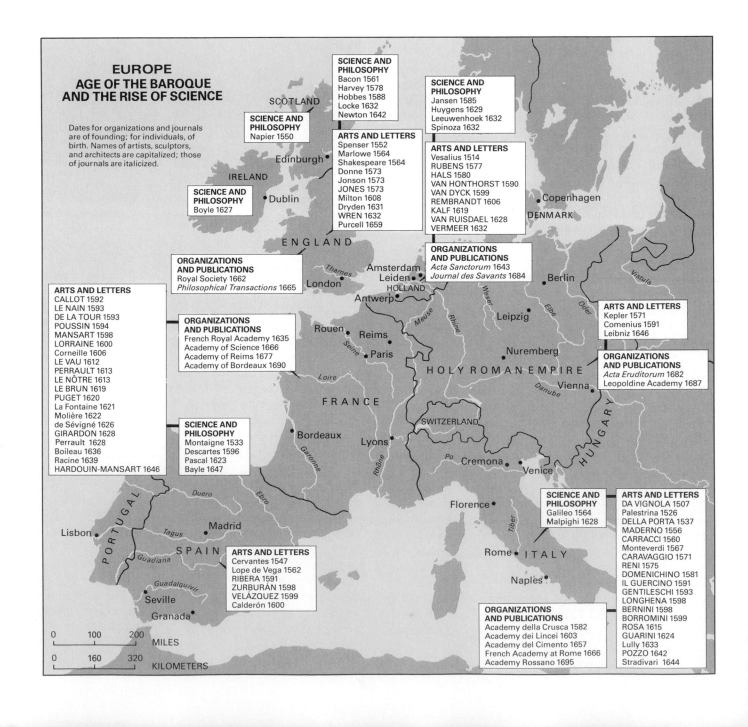

19

**EUROPE
AGE OF THE BAROQUE
AND THE RISE OF SCIENCE**

Dates for organizations and journals
are of founding; for individuals, of
birth. Names of artists, sculptors,
and architects are capitalized; those
of journals are italicized.

SCOTLAND

**SCIENCE AND
PHILOSOPHY**
Napier 1550

IRELAND

• Edinburgh

• Dublin

**SCIENCE AND
PHILOSOPHY**
Boyle 1627

**SCIENCE AND
PHILOSOPHY**
Bacon 1561
Harvey 1578
Hobbes 1588
Locke 1632
Newton 1642

ARTS AND LETTERS
Spenser 1552
Marlowe 1564
Shakespeare 1564
Donne 1573
Jonson 1573
JONES 1573
Milton 1608
Dryden 1631
WREN 1632
Purcell 1659

**SCIENCE AND
PHILOSOPHY**
Jansen 1585
Huygens 1629
Leeuwenhoek 1632
Spinoza 1632

ARTS AND LETTERS
Vesalius 1514
RUBENS 1577
HALS 1580
VAN HONTHORST 1590
VAN DYCK 1599
REMBRANDT 1606
KALF 1619
VAN RUISDAEL 1628
VERMEER 1632

ENGLAND

**ORGANIZATIONS
AND PUBLICATIONS**
Royal Society 1662
Philosophical Transactions 1665

Thames
Amsterdam •
London • Leiden •
HOLLAND
Antwerp •

• Copenhagen
DENMARK

**ORGANIZATIONS
AND PUBLICATIONS**
Acta Sanctorum 1643
Journal des Savants 1684

• Berlin

Vistula

Weser
Elbe
Oder

ARTS AND LETTERS
CALLOT 1592
LE NAIN 1593
DE LA TOUR 1593
POUSSIN 1594
MANSART 1598
LORRAINE 1600
Corneille 1606
LE VAU 1612
PERRAULT 1613
LE NÔTRE 1613
LE BRUN 1619
PUGET 1620
La Fontaine 1621
Molière 1622
de Sévigné 1626
GIRARDON 1628
Perrault 1628
Boileau 1636
Racine 1639
HARDOUIN-MANSART 1646

**ORGANIZATIONS
AND PUBLICATIONS**
French Royal Academy 1635
Academy of Science 1666
Academy of Reims 1677
Academy of Bordeaux 1690

Rouen • Reims •
Meuse
Rhine
Leipzig •
Nuremberg •

ARTS AND LETTERS
Kepler 1571
Comenius 1591
Leibniz 1646

Seine
• Paris

HOLY ROMAN EMPIRE

**ORGANIZATIONS
AND PUBLICATIONS**
Acta Eruditorum 1682
Leopoldine Academy 1687

**SCIENCE AND
PHILOSOPHY**
Montaigne 1533
Descartes 1596
Pascal 1623
Bayle 1647

Loire
FRANCE
SWITZERLAND

• Bordeaux
Lyons •
Garonne
Rhône
Danube
Vienna •

Po
Cremona •
Venice •
HUNGARY

PORTUGAL
Duero
Ebro

Tagus
Madrid •
SPAIN

Guadiana

Guadalquivir

Lisbon •

Seville •
Granada •

ARTS AND LETTERS
Cervantes 1547
Lope de Vega 1562
RIBERA 1591
ZURBURÁN 1598
VELÁZQUEZ 1599
Calderón 1600

Florence •

Tiber

Rome • ITALY

Naples •

**SCIENCE AND
PHILOSOPHY**
Galileo 1564
Malpighi 1628

ARTS AND LETTERS
DA VIGNOLA 1507
Palestrina 1526
DELLA PORTA 1537
MADERNO 1556
CARRACCI 1560
Monteverdi 1567
CARAVAGGIO 1571
RENI 1575
DOMENICHINO 1581
IL GUERCINO 1591
GENTILESCHI 1593
LONGHENA 1598
BERNINI 1598
BORROMINI 1599
ROSA 1615
GUARINI 1624
Lully 1633
POZZO 1642
Stradivari 1644

**ORGANIZATIONS
AND PUBLICATIONS**
Academy della Crusca 1582
Academy dei Lincei 1603
Academy del Cimento 1657
French Academy at Rome 1666
Academy Rossano 1695

0   100   200
MILES

0   160   320
KILOMETERS

BAROQUE ART

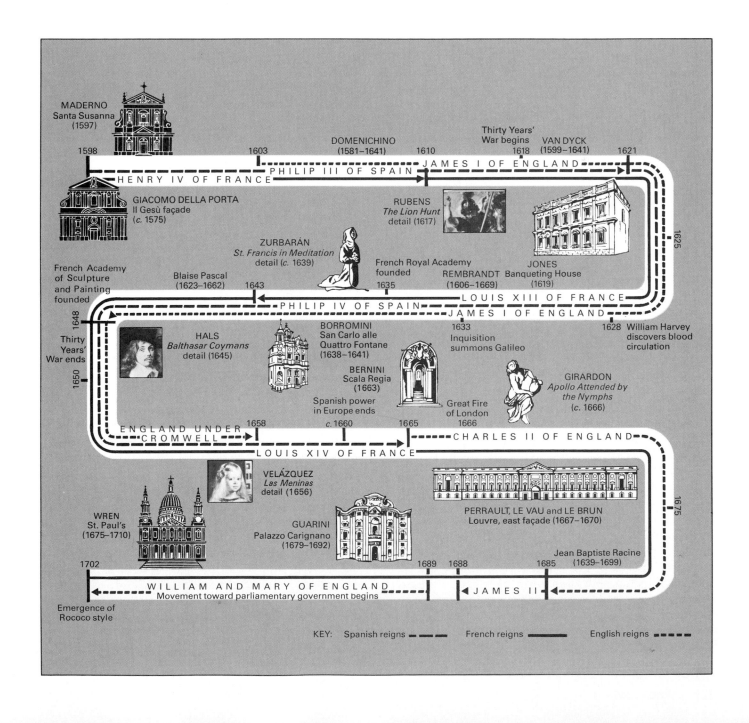

MADERNO
Santa Susanna
(1597)

1598 — 1603

HENRY IV OF FRANCE

GIACOMO DELLA PORTA
Il Gesù façade
(c. 1575)

DOMENICHINO
(1581–1641)

1610

PHILIP III OF SPAIN

Thirty Years'
War begins
1618

JAMES I OF ENGLAND

VAN DYCK
(1599–1641)

1621

1625

ZURBARÁN
St. Francis in Meditation
detail (c. 1639)

RUBENS
The Lion Hunt
detail (1617)

JONES
Banqueting House
(1619)

French Academy
of Sculpture
and Painting
founded

Blaise Pascal
(1623–1662)

1643

French Royal Academy
founded

1635

REMBRANDT
(1606–1669)

PHILIP IV OF SPAIN

LOUIS XIII OF FRANCE

JAMES I OF ENGLAND

1648

Thirty
Years'
War ends

1650

HALS
Balthasar Coymans
detail (1645)

BORROMINI
San Carlo alle
Quattro Fontane
(1638–1641)

BERNINI
Scala Regia
(1663)

Spanish power
in Europe ends

1633
Inquisition
summons Galileo

1628 William Harvey
discovers blood
circulation

GIRARDON
Apollo Attended by
the Nymphs
(c. 1666)

Great Fire
of London
1666

ENGLAND UNDER
CROMWELL

1658

c. 1660

1665

CHARLES II OF ENGLAND

LOUIS XIV OF FRANCE

VELÁZQUEZ
Las Meninas
detail (1656)

WREN
St. Paul's
(1675–1710)

GUARINI
Palazzo Carignano
(1679–1692)

PERRAULT, LE VAU and LE BRUN
Louvre, east façade (1667–1670)

1675

Jean Baptiste Racine
(1639–1699)

1702

1689 1688

1685

WILLIAM AND MARY OF ENGLAND
Movement toward parliamentary government begins

◄ JAMES II ◄

Emergence of
Rococo style

KEY: Spanish reigns - - - - -   French reigns ——————   English reigns ▬ ▬ ▬ ▬

THE GENERAL PERIOD we have labeled "Renaissance" continues without any sharp stylistic break, unless it be the interrupting episode of Mannerism, into the seventeenth and eighteenth centuries. The art of this later period we call "Baroque," although there is no one Baroque style or set of stylistic principles. The origin of the word is not clear. It may come from the Portuguese word *barroco*, meaning an irregularly shaped pearl. Certainly, the term was originally used in a disparaging sense, especially of post-Renaissance architecture, which nineteenth-century critics regarded as decadent Classical: unstructural, overornamented, theatrical, and grotesque. But the use of "Baroque" as a pejorative has faded, and the term has long been current in art-historical vocabulary as a blanket designation for the art of the period roughly covering 1600 to 1750. Scholars gradually came to see that the Baroque styles were quite different from those of the Renaissance. The Baroque, for example, looks dynamic; the Renaissance, relatively static. This led to the claim that the two are fundamentally in opposition; there is still disagreement about the historical and formal relation of the two stylistic periods, especially since it is clear that the Classicism of the High Renaissance is restored and flourishes in the Baroque. The historical reality lies in the flow of stylistic change, and "Baroque" is a classification useful in isolating the tendencies and products of stylistic change for examination. Traits that the styles of the seventeenth and earlier eighteenth centuries seem to have in common we shall designate as Baroque.

Like the art it produced, the Baroque era was manifold—spacious and dynamic, brilliant and colorful, theatrical and passionate, sensual and ecstatic, opulent and extravagant, versatile and *virtuoso*. It was an age of expansion following on an age of discovery, and its expansion led to still further discovery. The rising national powers colonized the globe. Wars between Renaissance cities were supplanted by wars between continental empires, and the history of Europe could be influenced by battles fought in the North American wilderness and in India.

Baroque expansiveness extended well beyond earth in the conceptions of the new astronomy and physics of Galileo, Kepler, and Newton. The same laws of mechanics were found to govern a celestial body moving at great velocity and a falling apple. Man's optical range was expanding to embrace the macroscopic spaces of the celestial world and the microscopic spaces of the cellular. There is in the Baroque almost an obsession with the space of the unfolding universe. Descartes makes extension (space and what occupies it) the sole physical attribute of being; there exist only mind and extension, the former proving the reality of the latter in Descartes'

famous phrase, *Cogito, ergo sum* ("I think, therefore I am"). Pascal confesses in awe that "the silence of these infinite spaces frightens me." Milton expresses the Baroque image of space in a phrase—"the vast and boundless deep."

The Baroque scientist comes to see physical nature as matter in motion through space and time; the latter two are thought of as the conditions of the first. The measurement of motion is made possible by the new mathematics of analytical geometry and the infinitesimal calculus, and experiment comes to be accepted as the prime method for getting at the truth of physical nature. Time, like space and motion, is a preoccupation of the creative Baroque mind—in art as well as in science. The age-old sense of time, rich with religious, philosophical, psychological, and poetic import, persists alongside the new concept of it as a measurable property of nature. Time—"the subtle thief of youth" that steals away the lives of all of us; that, in the end, reveals the truth, vindicates goodness, and rescues innocence; that demolishes the memory of great empires; and that points to the ultimate judgment of humankind by God—this sense of time pervades the art and literature of the Baroque. The sonnets of Shakespeare dwell on the mutability and brevity of life and on time's destruction of beauty ("that time will come/and take my love away"). The great landscapes of Van Ruisdael suggest the passage of time in hurrying clouds, restless sea, and everchanging light. Painters and sculptors, eager to make action explicit and convincing, depict it at the very moment it is taking place, as in Bernini's *David* (FIG. 19-10). There are countless allegorical representations of time as the fierce old man carrying his scythe or devouring his children. For the Baroque artist, then, time has acquired its new "scientific" connotations of the instantaneous and the infinite, yet without any loss of its significance for each human life.

Scarcely less fascinating to the Baroque mind is light. Light—for thousands of years thought of and worshiped as the god-like sun or the truth of the Holy Spirit—now becomes a physical entity, propagated in waves (or corpuscles) through Pascal's "infinite spaces," capable of being refracted into color by a prism. But, as with time, the new-found materiality of light by no means diminishes its ancient association with spirituality in the religion, poetry, and art of the Baroque. It still stands for inspiration, truth of dogma, the mystical vision of the transcendental world, the presence of the Divine, the "inner light" (page 520). And it can have these associations in a commonplace setting or in one of splendor and magnificence (FIG. 19-9). Yet the age of the new science, adapting the old metaphor of light to the dawn of a new day, would be called the "Enlightenment," signifying that the old, dark, mythical way of reading the world has been given up and that the light of knowledge brings a new day. Alexander Pope, expressing the enthusiasm of his day for the discoveries of Newton, makes them out to be a kind of second revelation:

Nature, and Nature's laws lay hid in night.
God said: "Let Newton be!" and all was Light!

The elements of perception in naturalistic Baroque art are the elements of nature described by Baroque science: matter in motion through space, time, and light. And the ingredients of an increasingly precise method for the scientific study of nature—observation and measurement, representation and experimental testing—are analogous to the naturalistic artist's careful reproduction of natural appearances.

Although the exclusive and exacting report of these elements is a most important enterprise in the age of the Baroque, the mechanical simulation of appearances for its own sake is by no means the naturalistic artist's intention. Although he obviously delights in the achievement of astonishing illusion, his images embody spiritual and metaphysical meanings of nature so persuasively real and present that their significance and truth are strongly reinforced. In this way, he brings before us the reality of the unseen world by means of the seen—the visible objects he regards as symbolic or emblematic of invisible and unchanging truth. Baroque naturalism remains largely religious in content.

While naturalism thrived in Baroque art, Classicism was revised and further developed, and the two styles divided the taste of the age with a third—the dynamic, colorful, sensuous style characteristic of Rubens and Bernini. The differences among these three styles were not so definitive as to disallow exchanges of influence or even occasional collaboration, although the esthetic doctrines or presuppositions of naturalism were fundamentally opposed to those of the other two, and the French Academy could debate the virtues of the Classical (formalistic) Poussin over the coloristic Rubens. Art theory flourished, and most of it was on the side of Classicism. The cause of Classicism was also favored by an increasing antiquarian literature—the fruit of an expanding enthusiasm for ancient civilization and art and an increasingly sophisticated and systematic study of it. The Classical masters of the Baroque took as their models the great artists of the High Renaissance, antique statuary, and nature; artists of whatever stylistic bent were often learned in Classical literature and antiquities. Although the Classical masters' philosophy of art proclaimed the ideal rather than the real as the only worthy subject and form for painting and sculpture, they believed that study of nature was essential to the full and valid realization of the idea in its purity and perfection. This was manifest in their insistence on the careful observation and depiction of the human figure from life.

Nevertheless, the opposition of Classicism to the dramatic dynamism of painters like Rubens becomes conscious and fixed in the Baroque. This dualism will hold well into the nineteenth and even the twentieth century. Indeed, it reaches through the entire Western tradition, exclusive of the Middle Ages; an ancient statement of this dualism may be seen in the art of Greece and Rome (compare FIGS. 5-52 and 5-79). Classicism in art and thought amounts to calm rationality; we see it in the landscapes of Poussin (FIG. 19-62). Its opposite—turbulent action stirred by powerful passions—(later, we shall call it "Romanticism") appears in the painting of Rubens (FIG. 19-40) and in the sculpture of Bernini (page 520). A central theme of Baroque art and literature is the conflict of reason with passion. The representation of that conflict is, of course, as ancient as Plato and survives as a great dualism in Western thinking about human nature.

Accompanying, quite consistently, the exploration of the elementary structure of physical nature is the exploration of human nature, the realm of the senses and the emotions. The function of the representational arts is to open that realm to full view. The throwing open of the two physical universes of macrocosm and microcosm to human scrutiny did not distract Baroque humanity from the age-old curiosity about the nature of humankind. After all, it was now perceived that if we are one with nature, the knowledge of ourselves must be part of the knowledge of nature. The new resources given to the Baroque artist allow him to render, with new accuracy and authority, the appearances of the world and of the beings that people it. Painting and sculpture, equipped with every device of sensuous illusion now available, provide a stage for the enactment of the drama of human life in all its variety. For Baroque is preeminently the age of theater. Art shares with the actor's stage the purpose (as Shakespeare puts it in *Hamlet*)

To hold, as 'twere, the mirror up to nature, to show virtue her own feature, scorn her own image, and the very age and body of the time his form and pressure. (III:2)

This means to present and analyze the spectrum of human actions and passions in all its degrees of lightness, darkness, and intensity. In this great era of the stage, tragedy and comedy are reborn. At the same time, the resources of music greatly expand, creating the opera and refining the instruments of the modern orchestra. All the arts approve the things of the senses and the delights of sensuous experience. Although here and there the guilty fear of pleasure lingers from the times of Hieronymus Bosch, poetry and literature in all countries acquire a richly expressive language capable of rendering themes that involve the description, presentation, conflict, and resolution of human emotions. In the Catholic countries, every device of art is used to stimulate pious emotions—sometimes, it might be thought, to the pitch of ecstasy. Luxurious display and unlimited magnificence and splendor frame the extravagant life of the courts, cost notwithstanding; the modes of furniture and dress are perhaps the most ornate ever designed. Even in externals, a dramatic, sensuous elaborateness is the rule. However, what people wear and what they do must approach perfection, with the added flourish of seeming effortlessness. Not only courtiers, at one end of Baroque society, and brigands and pirates at the other, but also the men who fashion the arts and the sciences are brilliant performers. They are virtuosi, proud of their technique and capable of astonishing quantities of work.

ITALY

The age of the Baroque has been identified with the Catholic reaction to the advance of Protestantism. Although it extends much more widely in time and place than seventeenth-century Italy and is by no means only a manifestation of religious change, there can be little doubt that Baroque art had papal Rome as its birthplace. Between the pontificates of Paul III (Farnese) from 1534 to 1549 and of Sixtus V (Peretti) in the 1580s, the popes led a successful military, diplomatic and theological campaign against Protestantism, wiping out many of its gains in central and southern Europe. The great Council of Trent, which met in the early 1540s and again in the early 1560s, was sponsored by the papacy in an effort to systematize and harden orthodox Catholic doctrine against the threat of Protestant persuasion. The Council strongly resisted Protestant objection to the use of images in religious worship, insisting on their necessity in the teaching of the laity. This implied separation of the priest from an unsophisticated congregation was to be reflected in architecture as well, the central type of church plan being rejected in favor of the long church and of other plans that maintained the distinction between clergy and laity; an example is the addition of the nave to the central plan of Bramante and Michelangelo for St. Peter's (FIGS. 19-3 and 19-6).

Interrupted for a while, the building program begun under Paul III (with Michelangelo's Capitoline Hill design) was taken up again by Sixtus V, who had greatly augmented the papal treasury and who intended to construct a new and more magnificent Rome, an "imperial city that had been subdued to Christ and purged of paganism." Sixtus was succeeded by a number of strong and ambitious popes—Paul V (Borghese), Urban VIII (Barberini), Innocent X (Pamfili), and Alexander VII (Chigi)—the patrons of Bernini and Borromini and the builders of the modern city of Rome, on which they left their Baroque mark everywhere. The energy of the Catholic Counter-Reformation, transformed into art, radiated throughout Catholic countries and even into Protestant lands, which found a response to it in their own art.

Architecture and Sculpture

The Jesuit order, newly founded (in 1534, in the pontificate of Paul III), needed an impressive building for its mother church. Because Michelangelo was dilatory in providing the plans, the church, called Il Gesù (Church of Jesus), was designed and built between 1568 and 1584 (FIG. 19-1) by GIACOMO DA VIGNOLA (1507–1573), who designed the ground plan, and GIACOMO DELLA PORTA (1537–1602), who is responsible for the façade. Although the church dates from the sixteenth century and stylistically is Late Renaissance, it is transitional to Baroque architecture. Its façade is an important model and point of departure for the façades of Roman Baroque churches for two

19-1 GIACOMO DELLA PORTA, façade of Il Gesù, Rome, c. 1575–1584. Interior by GIACOMO DA VIGNOLA, 1568. (Engraving by JOACHIM VON SANDRART.)

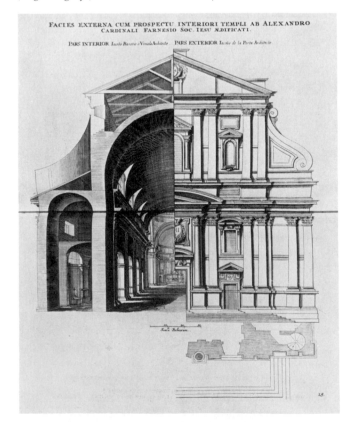

centuries, and its basic scheme is echoed and reechoed throughout the Catholic countries, especially Latin America. It is not entirely original; the union of the lower and upper stories, effected by scroll buttresses, goes back to Leon Battista Alberti's Santa Maria Novella in Florence (FIG. 16-40); its Classical pediment is familiar in Alberti and Andrea Palladio; and its paired pilasters appear in Michelangelo's design for St. Peter's. But the façade is a skillful synthesis of these already existing motifs; the two stories are well unified, the horizontal march of the pilasters and columns builds to a dramatic climax at the central bay, and the bays of the façade snugly fit the nave-chapel system behind them. The many dramatic Baroque façades of Rome will be architectural variations on this basic theme. In plan (FIG. 19-2), a monumental expansion of Alberti's scheme for Sant' Andrea in Mantua (FIG. 16-43), the nave takes over the main volume of space, so that the structure becomes a great hall with side chapels; the approach to the altar is emphasized by a dome. The wide acceptance of the Gesù plan in the Catholic world, even until modern times, seems to attest that it is ritually satisfactory. The opening of the church building into a single great hall provides an almost theatrical setting for large promenades and processions (that seemed to com-

19-2   GIACOMO DA VIGNOLA, plan of Il Gesù, Rome.

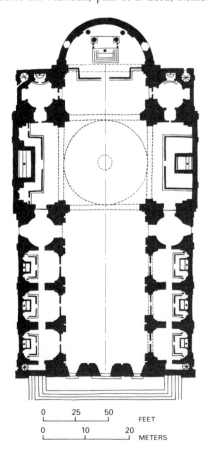

bine social with sacerdotal functions) and, above all, a space adequate to accommodate the great crowds that gathered to hear the eloquent preaching of the Jesuits. The Jesuits had a strong, indirect influence on art and architecture through the teachings of Saint Ignatius of Loyola, their Spanish founder. Loyola, in his *Spiritual Exercises*, advocated that the spiritual experience of the mysteries of the Catholic faith be intensely imagined, so much so as to be visible to the eye. The content of faith was to be visualized, and the sacred objects of the Church were to be venerated as defenses against false doctrine and the powers of Hell. This is still the function and warranty of religious art throughout the Roman Catholic world.

The great Baroque project in Rome was the completion of St. Peter's (FIG. 19-3). Bramante's and Michelangelo's central plan was unsatisfactory to the clergy of the seventeenth century, who thought it smacked of paganism and who felt it was inconvenient for the ever-growing assemblies. Under Paul V, CARLO MADERNO (1556–1629) was commissioned to add three bays of a nave to the earlier nucleus and to provide the building with a façade (FIG. 19-4). Before he received the St. Peter's commission, Maderno had designed the façade of Santa Susanna (FIG. 19-5), concentrating and dramatizing in it the major features of the façade of Il Gesù. Strong shadows cast by the vigorously projecting columns and pilasters of Santa Susanna mount dramatically toward the emphatically stressed central axis; the sculptural effect is enhanced by the recessed niches, which contain statues.

The façade of St. Peter's (FIG. 19-4) is a gigantic expansion of the elements of Santa Susanna's first level. But Maderno overextends his theme, and the compactness of Santa Susanna's façade is lost. The elements are spread too wide, and the quickening rhythm of pilasters and columns from the sides toward the center becomes slack. The role of the central pediment is reduced to insignificance by the façade's excessive width. In fairness to Maderno, it must be pointed out that his design for the façade was never completely executed. The two outside bays are the first stages of two flanking towers, which were never built; their vertical accents might well have visually compressed the central part of the façade. As it stands, this unfinished, watered-down frontispiece is almost universally criticized by artists and historians and has, unfortunately, become the dominant feature of the church's exterior. Lengthening the nave moves the façade outward and away from the dome, and the effect that Michelangelo had planned—a structure pulled together and dominated by its dome—is seriously impeded. When viewed at close range, the dome hardly emerges above the soaring cliff of the façade; seen from farther back, it appears to have no drum. One must go back beyond the piazza to see the

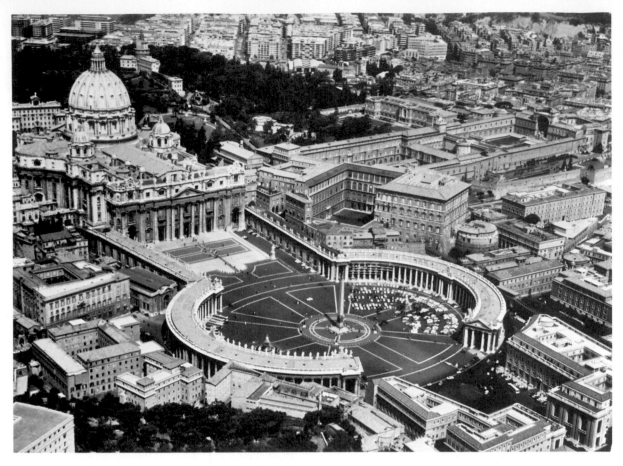

19-3   Aerial view of St. Peter's, Rome.

19-4   Carlo Maderno, façade of St. Peter's, 1606–1612.

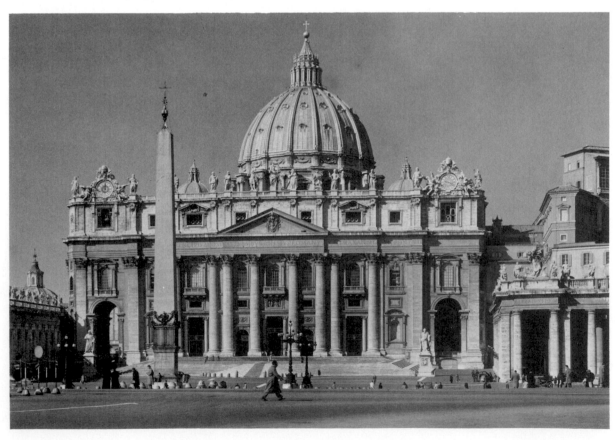

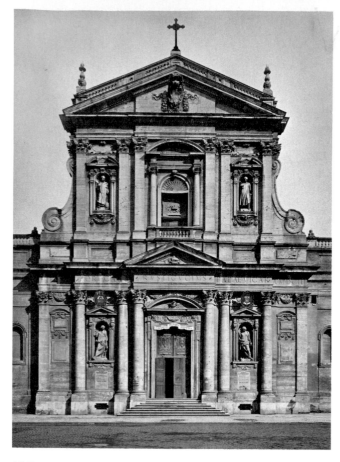

19-5 CARLO MADERNO, Santa Susanna, Rome, 1597–1603.

dome and drum together and to experience the effect that Michelangelo intended. Today, to see the structure as it was originally planned, it must be viewed from the back (FIG. 17-33).

BERNINI AND BORROMINI

The design of St. Peter's, which had been evolving since the days of Bramante and Michelangelo and had engaged all of the leading architects of the Renaissance and Baroque periods, was completed (except for details) by GIANLORENZO BERNINI (1598–1680). Bernini was architect, painter, and sculptor—one of the most brilliant and imaginative artists of the Baroque era and, if not the originator of the Baroque style, probably its most characteristic and sustaining spirit. Bernini's largest and most impressive single project was the design for a monumental piazza in front of St. Peter's (FIGS. 19-3 and 19-6). Like Michelangelo in the case of the Capitoline Hill, Bernini had to adjust his design to some preexisting structures on the site: an ancient obelisk brought from Egypt and a fountain designed by Maderno. He used these features to define the long axis of a vast oval embraced by colonnades that are joined to the façade of St. Peter's by two diverging wings. Four files of huge Tuscan columns make up the two colonnades, which terminate in severely Classical temple fronts. The dramatic gesture of embrace made by the colonnades

(FIG. 19-3) symbolizes the welcome given its communicants by the Roman Catholic Church. Thus, the compact, central designs of Bramante and Michelangelo are expanded by a Baroque transformation into a dynamic complex of axially ordered elements that reach out and enclose spaces of vast dimension. Where the Renaissance building stood in self-sufficient isolation, the Baroque design expansively relates it to its environment.

The wings that connect St. Peter's façade with the oval piazza flank a trapezoidal space also reminiscent of the Capitoline Hill. But here the latter's visual effect is reversed; as seen from the piazza, the diverging wings counteract the natural perspective and tend to bring the façade closer to the observer. Emphasizing the façade's height in this manner, Bernini subtly and effectively compensates for its excessive width.

The Baroque delight in illusionistic devices is expressed again in the Vatican in the Scala Regia (FIG. 19-7), a monumental stairway connecting the papal apartments and the portico and narthex of the church. Because the original passageway was irregular, dark, and dangerous to descend, Pope Alexander VII commissioned Bernini to replace it. Bernini, like Michelangelo at the Campidoglio, here makes architectural virtue of necessity by using illusionistic techniques characteristic of stagecraft. The stairway, its entrance crowned by a sculptural group of trumpeting angels and the papal arms, is covered by a barrel vault (in two stages) carried on columns that form aisles flanking the central corridor. By gradually reducing the distance between columns and walls as the stairway ascends, Bernini actually eliminates the aisles on the upper levels, while creating an illusion of uniformity of width and continuity of aisle for the whole stairway. At the same time, the space between the colonnades also narrows with ascent, reinforcing the natural perspective and making the stairs appear to be longer than they actually are. To minimize this effect, Bernini made the lighting at the top of the stairs brighter, exploiting the natural human inclination to move from darkness toward light. To make the

19-6 Plan of St. Peter's, Rome, with adjoining piazza designed by GIANLORENZO BERNINI.

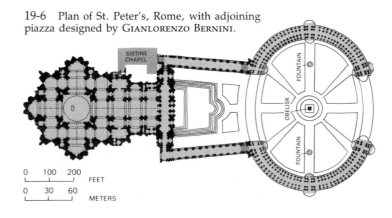

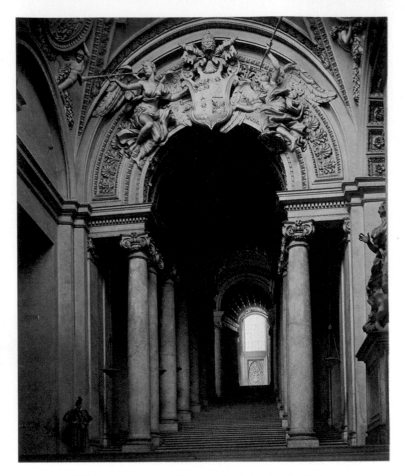

19-7 GIANLORENZO BERNINI, Scala Regia, the Vatican, Rome, 1663–1666.

Indeed, it is this theme of triumph that dictates the architectural as well as sculptural symbolism both inside and outside St. Peter's. Suggesting a great and solemn procession, the main axis of the complex traverses the piazza, slowed by the central obelisk, and enters Maderno's nave. It comes to a temporary halt at the altar beneath the baldacchino, but it continues on toward its climactic destination at another great altar in the apse, the Cathedra Petri (FIG. 19-9), also the work of Bernini. In this explosively dramatic composition, the Chair of St. Peter is exalted in a burst of light, in which the Dove of the Holy Ghost appears amidst flights of angels and billowing clouds. Four colossal figures in gilt bronze seem to support the chair miraculously, for they scarcely touch it. The two in the foreground represent two fathers of the Latin Church, Saints Ambrose and Augustine. Behind them, and less conspicuously, stand Saints Athanasius and Chrysostom, representing the Greek Church. The grouping of the figures constitutes an appeal for unity within Christianity and, at the same time, suggests the subservience of the Eastern Church to the Western. The Cathedra Petri is the quintessence of Baroque composition. Its forms are generated and grouped not by clear lines of structure but by forces that unfold from a center of violent en-

19-8 GIANLORENZO BERNINI, baldacchino for St. Peter's, Rome, 1624–1633.

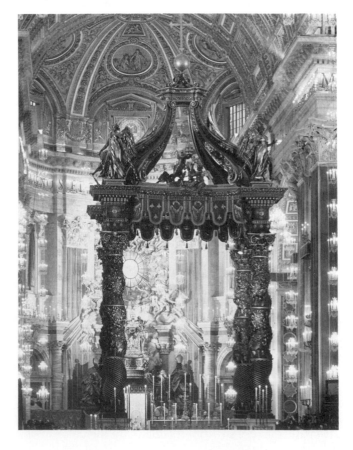

long ascent more tolerable, he provided an intermediate goal in the form of an illuminated landing that promises a midway resting point. The result is a highly sophisticated design, both dynamic and dramatic, which repeats on a smaller scale, but perhaps even more effectively, the processional sequence found inside St. Peter's.

Long before the planning of the piazza and the completion of the Scala Regia, Bernini had been at work decorating the interior of St. Peter's. His first commission called for the design and erection of the gigantic bronze *baldacchino* above the main altar under the cathedral's dome (FIG. 19-8) to mark and memorialize the tomb of St. Peter. Almost 100 feet high (the height of an average eight-story building), this canopy is in harmony with the tremendous proportions of the new church and is a focus of its splendor. Its four spiral columns recall those of the ancient baldacchino over the same spot in Old St. Peter's. Partially fluted and wreathed with vines, they seem to deny the mass and weight of the tons of bronze resting on them. At the same time, they communicate their Baroque energy to the four colossal angels standing guard at the upper corners and to the four serpentine brackets that elevate the orb and the cross, symbols of the triumph of the Church.

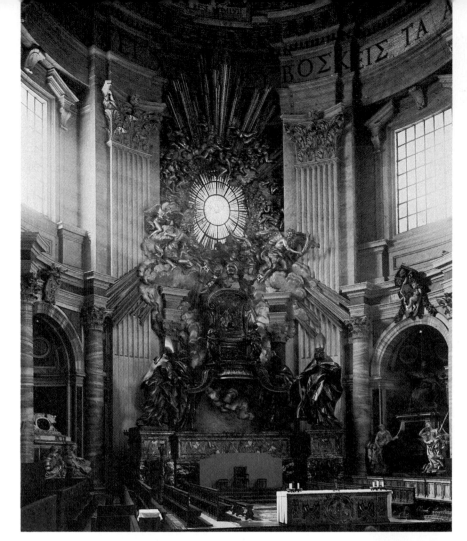

19-9 GIANLORENZO BERNINI, Cathedra Petri, 1656–1666. Gilt bronze, marble, and stucco. St. Peter's, Rome.

19-10 GIANLORENZO BERNINI, *David*, 1623. Marble, life-size. Galleria Borghese, Rome.

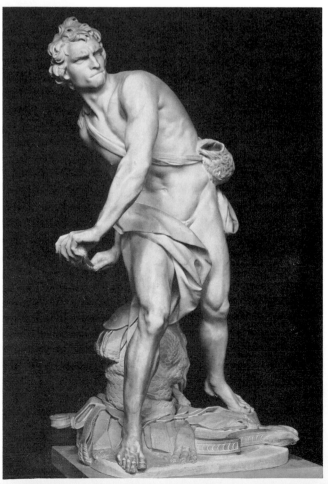

ergy. Everything moves, nothing is distinct, light dissolves firmness, and the effect is visionary. The vision asserts the triumph of Christianity and the papal claim to doctrinal supremacy.

Much of Bernini's prolific career was given to the adornment of St. Peter's, where his works combine sculpture with architecture. Although Bernini was a great and influential architect, his fame rests primarily on his sculpture, which, like his architecture, expresses the Baroque spirit to perfection. It is expansive and dramatic, and the element of time usually plays an important role in it. Unlike the states of rest or tension that one finds in the *Davids* of Donatello (FIG. 16-12), Verrocchio (FIG. 16-52), and Michelangelo (FIG. 17-20), Bernini's version (FIG. 19-10) aims at catching the split-second action. His muscular legs widely and firmly planted, *David* is beginning the violent, pivoting motion that will launch the stone from his sling. A moment before, his body was in one position; the next moment, it will be in a completely different one. Bernini selects the most dramatic of an implied sequence of poses, so that the observer has to think simultaneously of the continuum and of this tiny fraction of it. The implied continuum imparts a dynamic quality to the statue that suggests a bursting forth of the energy one sees pent in Michelangelo's

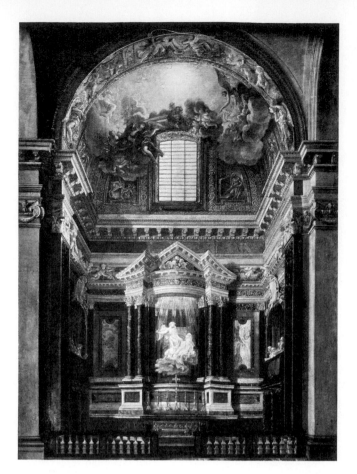

figures (FIGS. 17-20 and 17-21). And as the statue seems to be moving through time, so it does through space. This is not the kind of statue that can be inscribed in a cylinder or confined to a niche; its implied action demands space around it. Nor is it self-sufficient in the Renaissance sense, as its pose and attitude direct the observer's attention beyond itself and to its surroundings (in this case, toward an unseen Goliath). For the first time since the Hellenistic era (FIG. 5-76) a sculptured figure moves out into and partakes of the physical space that surrounds it and the observer.

The expansive quality of Baroque art and its disdain to limit itself to firmly defined spatial settings are encountered again in *The Ecstasy of St. Theresa* in the Cornaro Chapel of the church of Santa Maria della Vittoria (FIG. 19-11). In this chapel, Bernini draws on the full resources of architecture, sculpture, and painting to charge the entire area with crosscurrents of dramatic tension. St. Theresa was a nun of the Carmelite order and one of the great mystical saints of the Spanish Counter-Reformation. Her conversion took place after the death of her father, when she fell into a series of trances, saw visions, and heard voices. Feeling a persistent pain in her side, she came to believe that its cause was the fire-tipped dart of Divine love, which an angel had thrust into her bosom and which she described as making her swoon in delightful anguish. The whole chapel becomes a theater for the production of this mystical drama. The niche in which it takes place is a proscenium crowned with a

19-11 GIANLORENZO BERNINI, interior of the Cornaro Chapel, 1645–1652, Santa Maria della Vittoria, Rome. Eighteenth-century painting, Staatliches Museum, Schwerin.

broken Baroque pediment and ornamented with polychrome marble (FIG. 19-11). On either side of the chapel, portraits of the Cornaro family in sculptured opera boxes represent an audience watching the denouement of the heavenly drama with intent piety. Bernini shows the saint in ecstasy, unmistakably a mingling of spiritual and physical passion, swooning back on a cloud, while the smiling angel aims his arrow (page 520). The group is of white marble, and the artist goes to extremes of virtuosity in his management of textures: the clouds, rough monk's cloth, gauzy material, smooth flesh, feathery wings—all are carefully differentiated , yet harmonized in visual and visionary effect. Light from a hidden window pours down bronze rays that are meant to be seen as bursting forth from a painting of Heaven in the vault (FIG. 19-11). Several tons of marble seem to float in a haze of light, the winds of heaven buoying draperies as the cloud ascends. The remote mysteries of religion, taking on recognizable form, descend to meet the world of man halfway, within the conventions of Baroque

19-12 GIANLORENZO BERNINI, Triton Fountain, 1642–1643. Travertine. Piazza Barberini, Rome.

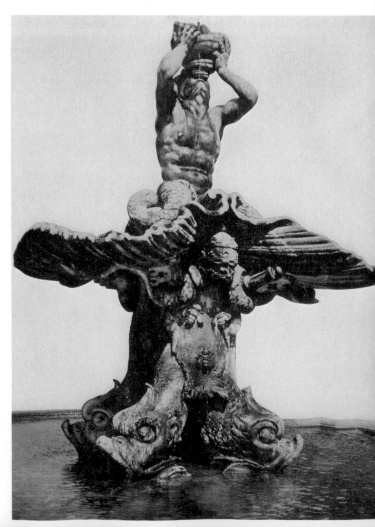

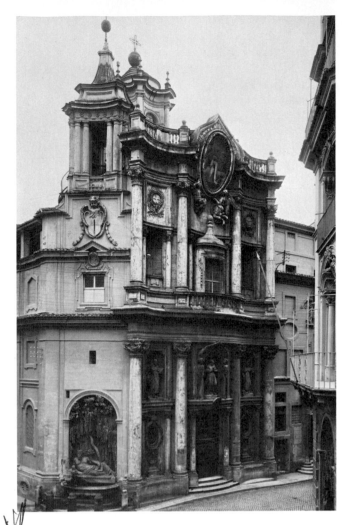

19-13 FRANCESCO BORROMINI, façade of San Carlo alle Quattro Fontane, Rome, 1665–1676.

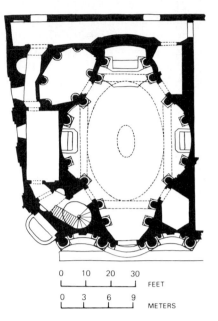

19-14 FRANCESCO BORROMINI, plan of San Carlo alle Quattro Fontane, Rome, 1638–1641.

art and theater. Bernini had much to do with the establishment of the principles of visual illusion that guided both.

The evident desire of the time to instill designs with dynamic qualities finds expressive release in the design of monumental fountains. The challenge of working with an element that actually *is* in motion fascinated Baroque artists, and it may not be too surprising to find that Bernini was one of the most inventive and most widely imitated designers in this field. It is largely his doing that Rome is a city of fountains. One of his most charming inventions is the Triton Fountain (FIG. 19-12), in which Bernini shows the male counterpart of the mermaid, seated on a shell supported by dolphins, blowing a jet of water toward the sky. The jet falls back into the shell, and the water dribbles in thin rivulets from its corrugated edges into the collecting basin below. The maritime group, risen from the depths of the ocean, is enveloped in rising and falling sprays of water. Sunlight reflected from the constantly agitated surface of the collecting pool around the base of the monument ripples across the stone surfaces of the sculptured group in ever-changing patterns that make the Triton seem alive, his bel-

lows-like chest heaving with the effort of blowing into his shell. For centuries, he has performed his task for Urban VIII, the Barberini Pope, whose emblems (the bees) decorate the fountain's base.

It seems curious that Bernini, whose sculpture expresses the very essence of the Baroque spirit, should remain relatively conservative in his architecture. Frequently planning on a vast scale and employing striking illusionistic devices, Bernini tends to use the Classical orders in a fairly sober and traditional manner, obvious exceptions being his baldacchino in St. Peter's and the St. Theresa altar (FIGS. 19-8 and 19-11). One might call his architectural style academic, in comparison with the unorthodox and quite revolutionary manner of his contemporary FRANCESCO BORROMINI (1599–1667). A new dynamism appears in the little church of San Carlo alle Quattro Fontane (FIGS. 19-13 and 19-14), where Borromini goes well beyond any of his predecessors or contemporaries in the plastic handling of a building. Maderno's façades of St. Peter's and Santa Susanna (FIGS. 19-4 and 19-5) are deeply sculptured, but they develop along straight, lateral planes. Borromini, perhaps thinking of Michelangelo's apse wall in St. Peter's (FIG. 17-33), sets his whole façade in serpentine motion forward and back, making a counterpoint of concave and convex on two levels (note the sway of the cornices), and emphasizes the sculptured effect by deeply recessed niches. This is no longer the traditional, flat frontispiece that defines a building's outer limits; it is a pulsating membrane inserted between interior and exterior space, designed not to separate but to provide a fluid transition between the two. This functional interrelation of the building and its environment is underlined by the curious fact that it has not one but two façades; the second—a narrow bay crowned with its own small tower—turns away from the main façade and, following the curve of the street, faces an intersection. (The upper façade was completed seven years after Borromini's death, and we cannot be sure to what degree the present structure reflects his original intention.)

The interior is a provocative variation on the theme of the centrally planned church. In plan (FIG. 19-14) it looks like a hybrid of a Greek cross and an oval, with a long axis between entrance and apse. The side walls move in an undulating flow that reverses the motion of the façade. Vigorously projecting columns articulate the space into which they protrude just as much as they do the walls to which they are attached. This molded interior space is capped by a deeply coffered, oval dome that seems to float on the light entering through windows hidden in its base. Rich variations on the basic theme of the oval, dynamic relative to the static circle, create an interior that appears to flow from entrance to altar, unimpeded by the segmentation so characteristic of Renaissance buildings.

The unification of interior space is carried even further in Borromini's Chapel of St. Ivo in the courtyard of the College of the Sapienza (Wisdom) in Rome (FIG. 19-15). In his characteristic manner, Borromini

19-15 FRANCESCO BORROMINI, St. Ivo, begun 1642. College of the Sapienza, Rome.

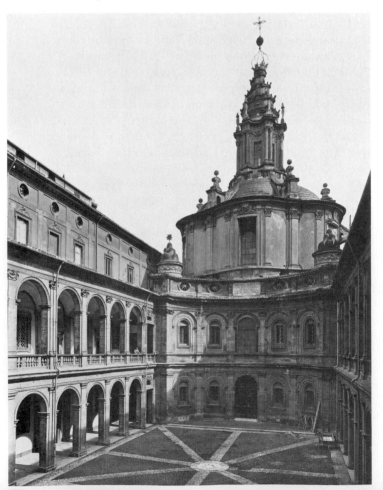

plays concave off against convex forms on the upper level of the exterior of his chapel. The lower stories of the court, which frame the bottom façade, were already there when Borromini began work. Above the inward curve of the façade—its design adjusted to the earlier arcades of the court—rises a convex, drum-like structure that supports the lower parts of the dome. Powerful pilasters restrain the forces that seem to push the bulging forms outward. Buttresses above the angle pilasters curve upward to brace a tall, plastic lantern topped by a spiral that seems to fasten the structure, screw-like, to the sky. The centralized plan (FIG. 19-16) is that of a star, having rounded-off points and apses on all three sides. Indentations and projections along the angled, curving walls create a highly complex plan, all the elements of which are fully reflected in the interior elevation. From floor to lantern, the wall panels rise in a continuously tapering sweep that is halted only momentarily by a single, horizontal cornice (FIG. 19-17). The dome is thus not, as in the Renaissance, a separate unit placed on the supporting block of a building; rather it is an organic part that evolves out of and shares the qualities of the supporting walls, from which it cannot be separated. The complex, horizontal motion of the walls is transferred fully into the elevation, creating a dynamic and cohesive shell that encloses and energetically molds a scalloped fragment of universal space. Few architects have matched Borromini's ability to translate extremely complicated designs into such masterfully unified and cohesive structures as that of St. Ivo.

The heir to Borromini's sculptured architectural style was GUARINO GUARINI (1624–1683), a priest,

19-16 FRANCESCO BORROMINI, plan of St. Ivo, Rome.

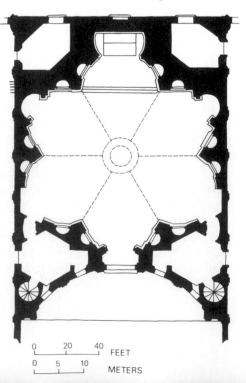

0 20 40 FEET
0 5 10 METERS

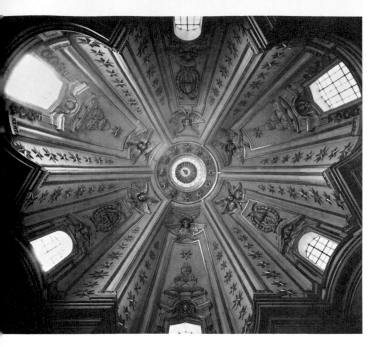

19-17 View into the dome of St. Ivo.

mathematician, and architect who spent the last 17 years of his life in Turin, converting that provincial Italian town into a fountainhead of architectural theories that would sweep much of Europe. In his Palazzo Carignano (FIG. 19-18), Guarini effectively applies Borromini's principle of undulating façades. He divides his long façade into three units, the central one of which curves much like the façade of San Carlo alle Quattro Fontane (FIG. 19-13) and is flanked by two block-like wings. This lateral, three-part division of façades, characteristic of most Baroque palazzi, is probably based on the observation that the average human can instinctively recognize up to three objects as a unit; a greater number will require the observer to count each object individually. A three-part organization of extended surfaces thus gives the artist the opportunity to introduce variety into his design without destroying its unity. It also permits him to place added emphasis on the central axis, which Guarini has done here most effectively by punching out deep cavities in the middle of his convex central block. The variety of his design is enhanced by richly textured surfaces (all executed in brick) and by pilasters, which further subdivide his units into three bays each. High and low reliefs create shadows of different intensities and add to the decorative effect a dramatic one that makes this one of the finest façades of the late seventeenth century.

Guarini's mathematical talents must have been guiding him when he designed the extraordinarily complex dome of the Chapel of the Santa Sindone (Holy Shroud), a small, central-plan building attached to the cathedral of Turin. A view into this dome (FIG. 19-19) reveals a bewildering display of geometric figures that appear to wheel slowly around a circular focus that contains the bright Dove of the Holy Ghost. Here, the traditional dome has been dematerialized into a series of figures that seem to revolve around each other in contrary motion; they ·

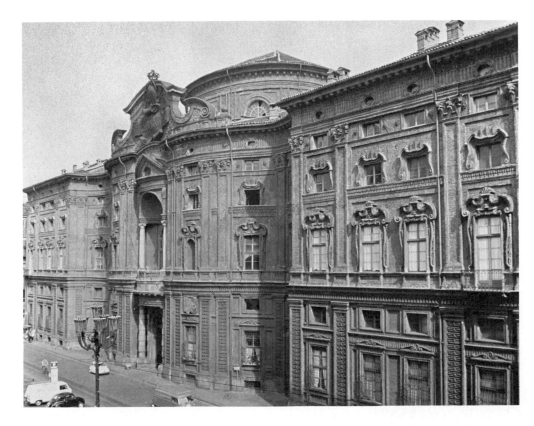

19-18 GUARINO GUARINI, Palazzo Carignano, Turin, Italy, 1679–1692.

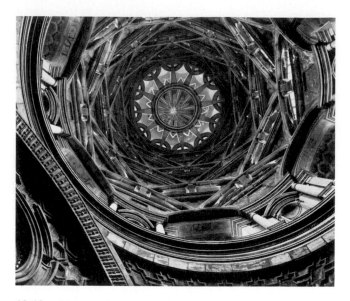

19-19 GUARINO GUARINI, Chapel of the Santa Sindone, Turin, Italy, 1667–1694 (view into dome).

define it, but they no longer limit the interior space. A comparison of Guarini's dome with that of the church of Sant' Eligio degli Orifici in Rome (FIG. 19-20), attributed both to Bramante and to Raphael and reconstructed about 1600, indicates that a fundamental change has taken place. The static "dome of heaven" of architecture and philosophy has been converted into the dynamic apparition of a mathematical heaven of calculable motions.

The style of Borromini and Guarini will move across the Alps to inspire architecture in Austria and South Germany in the late seventeenth and early eighteenth centuries. Popular in the Catholic regions

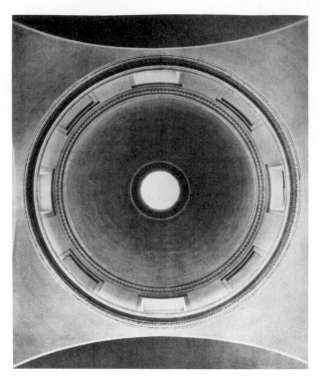

19-20 Attributed to BRAMANTE and RAPHAEL, Sant' Eligio degli Orifici, Rome, c. 1509 (reconstructed c. 1600; view into dome).

in Europe and the New World (especially in Brazil), it will exert little influence in France, where the more conservative style of Bernini will be favored.

In Venice, something of the Late Renaissance Classicism of Andrea Palladio survives, paradoxically, in the very Baroque church of Santa Maria della Salute (FIGS. 19-21 and 19-22), often called simply the "Salute" ("health"). Built by BALDASSARE LONGHENA (1598–1682), the church was commissioned by the

19-21 BALDASSARE LONGHENA, Santa Maria della Salute, Venice, 1631–1648 (consecrated 1687).

19-22 BALDASSARE LONGHENA, plan of Santa Maria della Salute, Venice.

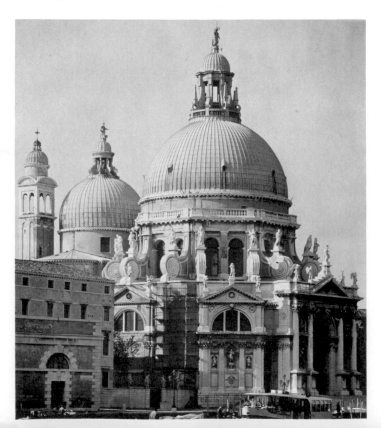

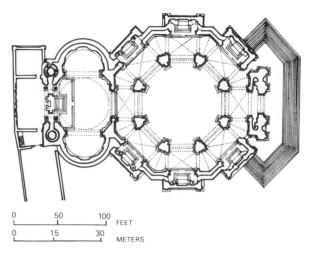

republic in thanksgiving to the Virgin Mary for ridding the city of plague. At the head of the Grand Canal, the main thoroughfare of Venice, the Salute has for centuries dominated it like a gorgeous crown, the admiration of generations of travelers and artists. Longhena knew well the architectural value of the site; the two domes of the Salute harmonize with the family of domes in its vicinity, among them those of St. Mark's (FIG. 7-49) and of the Palladian churches of San Giorgio Maggiore (FIG. 17-54) and Il Redentore ("The Redeemer"). Together, they make a skyline of surpassing beauty, floating above the city or reflected in its waters in ever-changing groupings as the admiring visitor moves.

Central plans were largely foreign to Venice, and it may be that the domes and central plan of St. Mark's suggested the design of the Salute, although Longhena insisted his design had not been done before. The plan of the building (FIG. 19-22) is an octagon with an auxiliary choir. The greater of the two domes is over the octagon; the lesser is over the choir and is flanked by campaniles. Both in plan and elevation, the grouping of the masses and spaces is essentially Renaissance, without the intricacies of Bernini, Borromini, or Guarini. This is especially true of the interior, which has the clear arrangement, the correct orders, and the steady gray–white color of Palladio's wall-and-column features, as in San Giorgio Maggiore (FIG. 17-55). But the exterior elevation is dramatic. The façade-like faces of the octagon play counterpoint with the main façade, and there is the highest excitement of Baroque invention in the great scroll buttresses that seem to open organically from the main body and to sprout statuary (FIG. 19-21). The Salute is a splendid example of an architecture rooted in a native (Venetian) tradition, yet flowering successfully in a new stylistic climate.

The style of Palladio and the Venetian Renaissance could be and was transplanted into a widely different environment. While Longhena was building the Salute, the Palladian style was already being naturalized in the distant north, in England (FIG. 19-76).

Painting

Italian painters of the seventeenth century, with the possible exception of Caravaggio and the later decorators, were somewhat less adventurous than the sculptors and architects. The painters of the High Renaissance had bequeathed to them an authoritative tradition as great as that of Classical antiquity. After the sixteenth century, the artists of Europe drew from both, and the history of painting well into the nineteenth century—that is, well into modern times—is an account of the interpretation, development, and modification of these two great traditions. The three most influential stylistic bequests of the High Renais-

sance were the styles of Raphael, of Michelangelo, and of Titian, with an additional subdominant trend inspired by Correggio. Baroque painting is the consequence of many and varied interchanges among these styles, with the antique sometimes supplementing them and sometimes appealed to against them. Outside the traditions of the antique and of the Renaissance, there rises what might be called "native naturalism"—a style that seems hostile to both authorities and that is based on the assumption that the artist should paint what he sees, without regard for either the antique or the Renaissance masters. This native naturalism appears as a minority style in Italy and France but plays an important role in Spain and a predominant one in the Dutch School.

The Baroque gets well under way in Italian painting around the year 1600, with the decoration of the gallery of the Farnese Palace by ANNIBALE CARRACCI (1560–1609). His generation, weary of the strained artifice of Mannerism, returned for a fresh view of nature, but only after they had carefully studied the Renaissance masters. Annibale had attended an academy of art in his native city of Bologna. Founded cooperatively by members of his family, among them LODOVICO and AGOSTINO CARRACCI, the Bolognese academy is the first significant institution of its kind in the history of Western art. It was founded on the premises that art can be taught—the basis of any academic philosophy of art—and that the materials of instruction must include the antique and the Renaissance traditions, in addition to the study of anatomy and drawing from life. The Bolognese painters were long called academics, and sometimes eclectics, for they appeared to assume that the development of a correct style in painting is learned and synthetic. In any event, we can tell from the gallery of the Farnese Palace that Annibale was familiar with Michelangelo, Raphael, and Titian, and that he could also make clever, illusionistic paintings. The Farnese ceiling (FIG. 19-23) is a brilliant and widely influential revision of High Renaissance painting—restoring its interest in human themes and emotions, renouncing the artificialities of Mannerism to return to the study of nature, and forming a firm bridge between the Renaissance and the Baroque. The style is a vigorous, sensuous, and adroit naturalism, modified by the Classical form inherited from the masters.

The iconographical program of the ceiling is the *Loves of the Gods*, interpretations of the subtle and various stages and degrees of earthly and Divine love (see Titian's treatment of the theme in *Sacred and Profane Love*, FIG. 17-61). Despite the apparent paganism of the subjects, they are found to have Christian overtones. The principal motif is the human nude, as it is in Michelangelo's frescoes and in much of Venetian art. Luxuriantly pagan images from Classical literature, especially Ovid's *Metamorphoses*, throng the

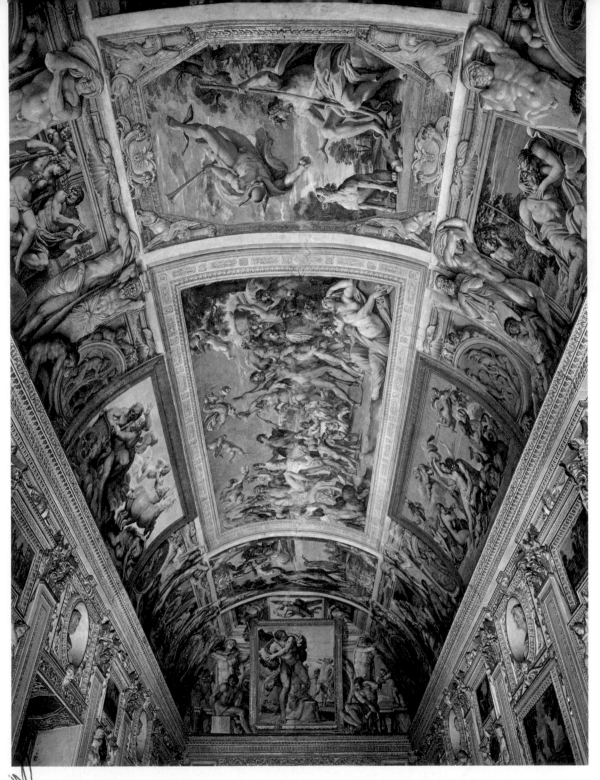

19-23   ANNIBALE CARRACCI, ceiling frescoes in the Farnese Gallery, 1597–1601. Farnese Palace, Rome.

vault, binding together and filling the composition with exuberant and passionate life (FIG. 19-23).

The scenes are arranged in panels resembling framed paintings on a wall, but here they are on the surfaces of a shallow, curved vault; the Sistine Ceiling (FIG. 17-25), of course, comes to mind, although it is not an exact source. This type of simulation of wall painting for ceiling design is called *quadro riportato*. The great influence of the Carracci will make it fash-

ionable for more than a century. The framed pictures are flanked by seated, nude youths, who turn their heads to gaze at the scenes above them, and by standing giants—motifs taken directly from Michelangelo's Sistine Ceiling. It is noteworthy that the chiaroscuro is not the same for both the pictures and the painted figures surrounding them. The figures inside the pictures are modeled in an even, sculptured light; the outside figures are lit from beneath, as if they

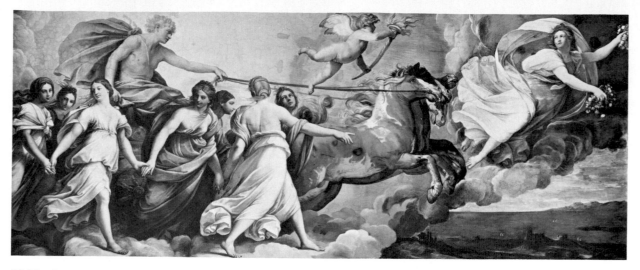

19-24 GUIDO RENI, *Aurora*, 1613–1614. Ceiling fresco in the Casino Rospigliosi, Rome.

were three-dimensional statues illuminated by torches in the gallery below. This interest in illusion, already manifest in the Renaissance, will continue in the grand ceiling compositions of the seventeenth century. In the crown of the vault, a long panel representing the Triumph of Bacchus is a quite ingenious crossing of Raphael and Titian and represents Annibale's adroitness in adjusting their authoritative styles to make something of his own.

Another artist trained in the Bolognese academy, GUIDO RENI (1575–1642), selected Raphael for his inspiration, as we see in his *Aurora* (FIG. 19-24), a ceiling painting conceived in *quadro riportato. Aurora*, the dawn, leads the chariot of Apollo, while the Hours dance about it. The fresco exhibits a suave, almost swimming motion, soft modeling, and sure composition, without Raphael's sculpturesque strength. It is an intelligent interpretation of the master's style, but in every sense learned, or "academic." However,

"academic" should not be burdened here with the bad sense it will later acquire as art that is mechanical, imitative, dull, and uninspired. The *Aurora* is a masterpiece of the Bolognese style and of its age. Guido was so much admired in his own day and well into the nineteenth century that he was known as "the divine Guido."

Like Guido, Giovanni Francesco Barbieri, called IL GUERCINO (1591–1666), another member of the Bolognese School, painted a ceiling *Aurora*, but with a very different effect (FIG. 19-25). Guercino abandons the method of *quadro riportato* for that of Veronese, in which the figures are seen from below at a 45° angle (FIG. 17-69). By this method, the subject of the picture is painted as if happening above our heads and seen from beneath; it is not simply a transfer of a painting from wall to ceiling. Taking his cue from the illusionistic figures in the Farnese Gallery and from its central ceiling panel (FIG. 19-23), Guercino converts the ceil-

19-25 IL GUERCINO, *Aurora*, 1621–1623. Ceiling fresco in the Villa Ludovisi, Rome.

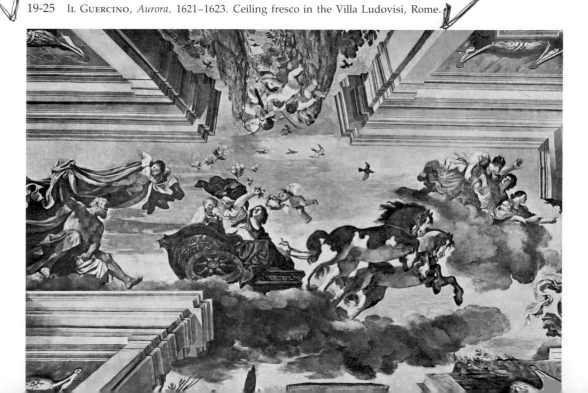

ing into a limitless space, through which the procession sweeps past. The observer's eye is led toward the celestial parade by converging, painted extensions of the room's architecture. While the perspective may seem a little forced, Guercino's *Aurora* inspired a new wave of enthusiasm for illusionistic ceiling paintings that culminated in some of history's most stupendous decorations.

Although the Bolognese painters were willing enough to imitate nature as directly as possible, they believed that the Renaissance and the antique masters had already captured much of its essence and that their works would prepare them for the study of nature. Michelangelo Merisi (1571–1610), called CARAVAGGIO after the northern Italian town from which he came, thought very much otherwise. His outspoken disdain for the Classical masters (probably more vocal than real) drew bitter criticism from many painters, one of whom denounced him as the "anti-Christ of painting." Yet many paid him the genuine compliment of borrowing from his innovations.

The unconventional life of this great painter was consistent with the defiant individualism of his art. We know almost as much about Caravaggio from police records as from other documents. Violent offenses and assaults reaching to murder trace his antisocial, tragic career through restless, tormented wanderings, which, nevertheless, did not prevent him from producing a large number of astonishing works. His very association with lowlifes and outcasts may help to account for his unglorified and unfashionable view of the great themes of religion, as well as his indifference to the Renaissance ideals of beauty and decorum. In his art, he secularizes both religion and the Classics, reducing them to human dramas that might be played out in the harsh and dingy settings of his time and place. He employs a cast of unflattering characters selected from the fields and the streets; these, he was proud to declare, were his only teachers—meaning that to paint from them gave him sufficient knowledge of nature.

We can appreciate how startling Caravaggio's methods must have been for his contemporaries when we look at *The Conversion of St. Paul* (FIG. 19-26), which he painted for the Roman church of Santa Maria del Popolo. The scene illustrates the conversion of the Pharisee Saul by a light and a voice from Heaven (Acts 9: 3–9). The saint-to-be is represented flat on his back, his arms thrown up, while an old ostler appears to maneuver the horse away from its fallen master. At first inspection, there is little here to suggest the awful grandeur of the spiritual event that is taking place. We seem to be witnessing a mere stable accident, not a great saint overcome by a great miracle. The saint is not specifically identified; he could be anyone. The ostler is a swarthy, bearded old man, who looks well-acquainted with stables. The horse fills the picture as if it were the hero, and its explicitness and the angle from which it is viewed might betray an irreverence on the part of the artist for this subject. Although Caravaggio found numerous sympathetic patrons in both church and state, some of his works were refused on the ground that they lacked propriety (that is to say, decorum). He sometimes appears to pay no attention to the usual dignity appointed to scenes from scripture and to go too far in dismissing the formal graces of Renaissance figure composition and color.

The fact is that, above all, Caravaggio seeks to create a convincing copy of the optical world as a vehicle of spiritual meanings; his intention in this respect is like Bernini's in the *St. Theresa* (page 520). To this end, he uses a perspective and a chiaroscuro designed to bring viewers as close as possible to the space and action of the scene, almost as if they were participating in it. *The Conversion of St. Paul* is placed on the chapel wall and is composed with an extremely low horizon or eye level, to be on the viewers' line of sight as they stand at the entrance of the chapel. The sharply lighted figures are meant to be seen as emerging from the dark of the background; the actual light from windows outside the chapel functions as a kind of stage lighting for the production of a vision, analogous to the rays in Bernini's *St. Theresa*. Thus, Caravaggio, like Bernini, makes use of the world of optical experience to stage the visionary one. In *The Conversion of St. Paul*, what we see first as merely commonplace is in fact the elevation of the commonplace to the miraculous.

The stark contrast of light and dark was the feature of Caravaggio's style that first shocked and then fascinated his contemporaries. The sharp and sudden relief it gives to the forms and the details of form emphasizes their reality in a way that an even or subtly modulated light could never do. Dark next to light is naturally dramatic; we do not need a director of stage lighting to tell us this. Caravaggio's device—a profound influence on European art—has been called *tenebroso*, or the "dark manner." It goes quite well with material that is realistic. It is another mode of Baroque illusionism by which the eye is almost forced to acknowledge the visual reality of what it sees. Although tenebrism is widespread in Baroque art, it will have its greatest consequences in Spain and the Netherlands.

A contemporary of Caravaggio observed that he had "abandoned beauty and was interested in depicting reality"; and Giovanni Pietro Bellori, the most influential critic of the age and an admirer of the Carracci, wrote: "Caravaggio deserves great praise, as he was the only one who attempted to imitate nature as opposed to the general trend in which painters imi-

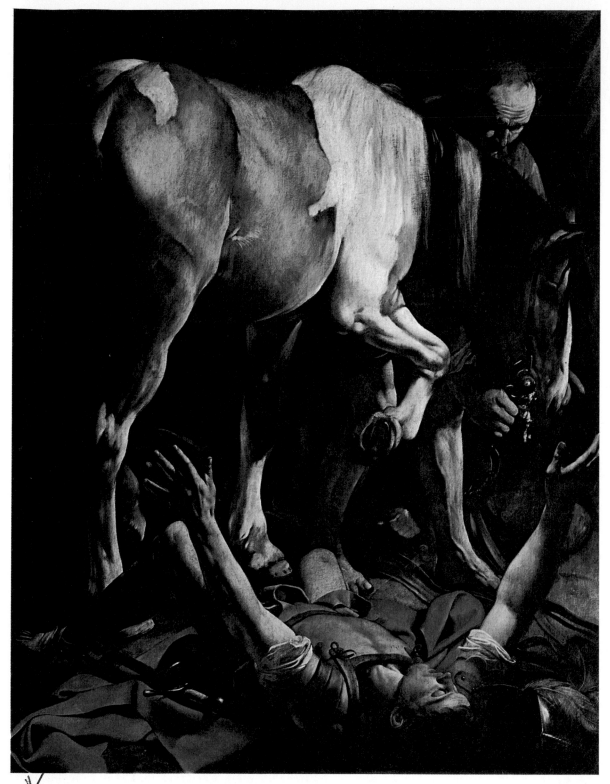

19-26 CARAVAGGIO, *The Conversion of St. Paul,* c. 1601. Oil on canvas,* approx. 7′ 6″ × 5′ 9″. Santa Maria del Popolo, Rome.

*Unless stated otherwise, all subsequent paintings are in oil on canvas.

tated other painters.'' The instrumentalities of this unorthodox realism find full orchestration in Caravaggio's *Death of the Virgin* (FIG. 19-27). The painting, refused (on the grounds of irreverence) as an altarpiece for Santa Maria della Scala in Rome, rep-

resents the Virgin Mary dead, mourned by the disciples and friends of Christ. The Virgin is indeed unceremoniously laid out in the awkward stiffness of death—her body swollen, limbs uncomposed, and feet uncovered (the last feature considered indecent

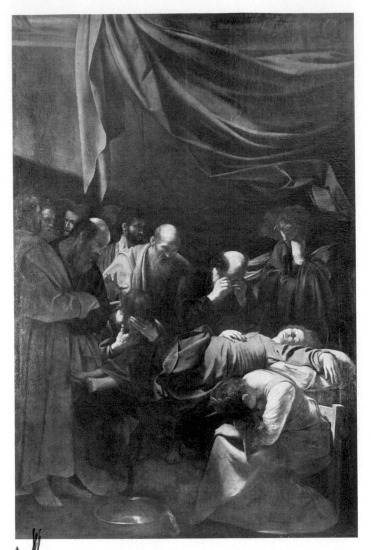

19-27 CARAVAGGIO, *Death of the Virgin*, 1605–1606. Approx. 12′ × 8′, Louvre, Paris.

at the time). Contemporaries complained that Caravaggio had used the corpse of a young woman who had drowned as his model for the mother of Christ. Around the dead woman, in attitudes of genuine if uncouth grief, without rhetoric or declamation, are the customary plebeian types that Caravaggio casts in his pictorial dramas of reality. The drawn curtain emphasizes the stage-like setting, into which the grouping of the figures invites the viewer as participant. The harsh light plunges into the space from a single source, shattering the darks into broken areas of illumination that reveal the coarse materialities of the scene. But again—as in *The Conversion of St. Paul*, but in a different way—we can read the artist's interpretation not as diminishing the spiritual import of the theme but rather as informing it with a simple, honest, unadorned piety that is entirely sincere, the very piety that moves the humble watchers of the dead to tears.

One would think that Annibale and Ludovico Carracci and their colleagues at the Bolognese academy would have carefully avoided the dangerous art of

Caravaggio. To the contrary, many borrowed from it (some more than others), unconsciously integrating it into the tradition and into their own work. A painting so typical of the Catholic Baroque—so expressive of the Counter-Reformation and its ideals that we can hardly find its equal as a document of the times—is *The Last Communion of St. Jerome* (FIG. 19-28), painted by another Bolognese disciple, DOMENICHINO (Domenico Zampieri, 1581–1641). In a Renaissance loggia that opens into a Venetian landscape background, St. Jerome, propped up to receive the viaticum (Eucharist), is surrounded by sorrowing friends. The realism of Caravaggio stamps the old man's sagging features, his weakened, once rugged body, and the faces of at least three of his attendants and of the grave old priest. The sharpened darks and lights are also out of Caravaggio; the general composition, the architecture, the floating putti, and the turbaned spectator echo Titian, Correggio, and the mood of the High Renaissance. A painting like this would seem to be, of necessity, an academic pastiche, but all of its borrowed elements are successfully synthesized in a rare, effective unity. Domenichino's *St. Jerome* is a

19-28 DOMENICHINO, *The Last Communion of St. Jerome*, 1614. Approx. 13′ 9″ × 8′ 5″. Vatican Museums, Rome.

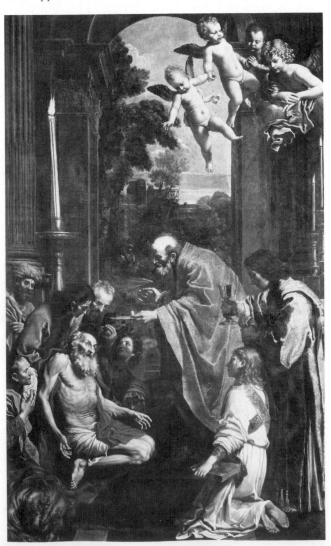

successful "school" picture, nourished as it is by all the sources, traditional and contemporary, available to him.

We have already mentioned the spread of Caravaggio's style outside Italy. Of course, he had many followers within its borders also, and they were artists more directly in tune with his message than eclectics like Domenichino. One of the best, whose work is increasingly appreciated by modern critics, is ARTEMISIA GENTILESCHI (1593–1653). Although we have knowledge of women who were painters as far back as the thirteenth century and although they came into their own in the sixteenth, they were few and not prominent. Social conventions, restricted education, and guild rules tended to exclude women from training and practice in the arts. Artemisia Gentileschi was instructed by her artist father, ORAZIO, who was himself strongly influenced by Caravaggio. Her successful career, pursued in Florence, Venice, Naples, and Rome, helped to propagate Caravaggio's manner throughout the peninsula. In her *Judith and Maidservant with the Head of Holofernes* (FIG. 19-29), we find the dark manner (*tenebroso*) and what might be called the "dark" subject matter favored by the *Caravaggisti*, the painters of "night" pictures. The heroism of Judith, often a subject in Italian painting and sculpture, is depicted here. The story, told in an Apocryphal work of the Old Testament, the Book of Judith, relates the delivery of Israel from its enemy Holofernes. Succumbing to the charms of Judith,

19-29 ARTEMISIA GENTILESCHI, *Judith and Maidservant with the Head of Holofernes*, c. 1625. Approx. 6' × 4' 8". Detroit Institute of the Arts (gift of Leslie H. Green).

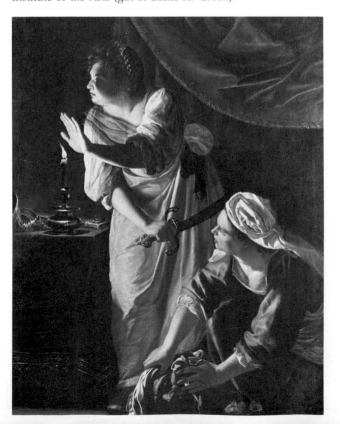

Holofernes invites her to his tent for the night. When he has fallen asleep, Judith cuts off his head. Here, the act performed, her maidservant is putting the severed head in a sack. The action takes place in a curtained, oppressively closed space. The atmosphere of menace and horror is thickened by the heavy darks, scarcely relieved by the feeble candle, the sole source of light. Yet the light falls on the courtly splendor of the women's raiment and exhibits forms and characters intended by the artist to be convincingly real. The light is interrupted dramatically by Judith's hand, which casts a shadow on her face. This is a favorite device of the night painters: a single source of illumination within the painting—partly or wholly concealed by an object in front of it or, as in this case, intercepted by an object—casting an abrupt shadow. The effect is like opening the shutter of a lantern for a brief moment in a pitch-black cellar where unspeakable things are happening.

The Carracci and Caravaggio powerfully influenced the art of figure painting for two centuries, but the Carracci largely determined the dominant course taken by landscape painting over the same period. In his *Flight into Egypt* (FIG. 19-30), Annibale Carracci created the "ideal" or "classical" landscape. Adopted and developed in France by Nicolas Poussin and Claude Lorraine (FIGS. 19-62 and 19-63), this kind of landscape would come to prevail as the accepted pictorial representation of nature ordered by Divine law and human reason. The roots of the style are in the landscape backgrounds of Venetian paintings of the Renaissance (compare FIGS. 19-30 and 17-60). Tranquil hills and fields, quietly gliding streams, serene skies, unruffled foliage, shepherds with their flocks—all the props of the pastoral scene and mood—expand to fill the picture space. They are regularly introduced by a screen of trees in the foreground, dark against the even light of the sky. Attenuated streams or terraces, carefully placed one above the other, make a compositional direction left or right through the terrain. In the middle ground, there generally appear (as in FIG. 19-30) compositions of architecture, walled towns or citadels, towers, temples, monumental tombs, villas—the constructed environment of idealized antiquity and the idyllic life, undisturbed by the passions. The subjects are drawn from religious or heroic story; here, Mary, with the Christ Child, and St. Joseph wend their slow way to Egypt, after having been ferried across a stream (Matthew 2:13–14). The figures, relative to the landscape, shrink in scale and importance, and are sometimes simply its excuse. For now, in the seventeenth century, landscape comes fully into its own as a major subject for the painter.

But there are landscape types other than the Classical. In dramatic contrast with *Flight into Egypt* is a landscape by SALVATOR ROSA (1615–1673), *St. John the*

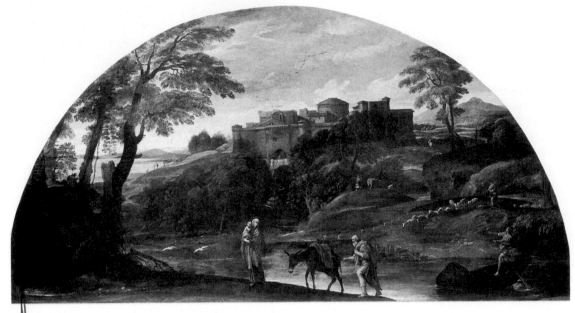

19-30 ANNIBALE CARRACCI, *Flight into Egypt*, 1603–1604. Approx. 4' × 7' 6". Galleria Doria Pamphili, Rome.

Baptist in the Wilderness (FIG. 19-31). Rosa's painting, like Annibale Carracci's, has a sacred theme, and the figures in it are subordinate to the landscape; otherwise, the two paintings obviously have nothing in common. Instead of the calm of idealized nature in Annibale's landscape, we have nature in a violent mood, a savage wilderness abandoned by Heaven. A ragged tree, blasted by generations of thunderbolts, writhes before a chaos of barren rocks. For Rosa, nature appears malevolent, the home only of wild beasts, of holy or of desperate men. The broken surfaces, jagged contours, and harsh textures in confused arrangement here should be compared with the smooth volumes and contours and regular placement of forms that characterize the Classical landscape. The alternative style of Rosa will greatly influence the next century's taste for the "picturesque"—sublime and awesome scenes, filled with terror and foreboding, which will indulge the Romantic temperament and fuel its enthusiasm.

The development of landscape painting was contemporary with that of ceiling painting, the latter being stimulated anew by the large, new churches of Baroque Rome. The problems associated with ceiling painting are, of course, special. Looking *up* at a painting is different from simply looking *at* a painting, for there is an element of awe in the experience of looking at what is above us, particularly when it is at con-

19-31 SALVATOR ROSA, *St. John the Baptist in the Wilderness, c.* 1640. Approx. 5' 8" × 8' 6". Glasgow Art Gallery and Museum.

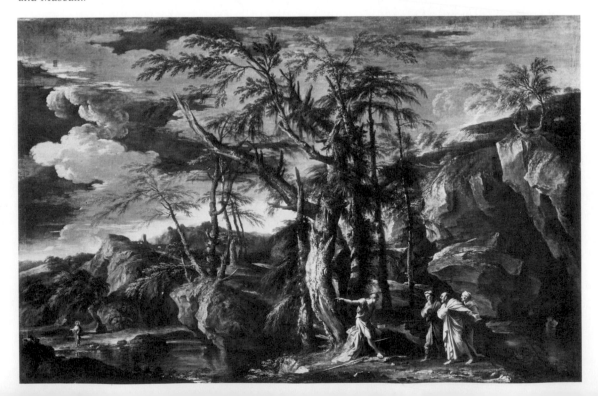

siderable height. Guercino saw this in his *Aurora* (FIG. 19-25), but apparently Guido Reni did not in his (FIG. 19-24)—or, rather, preferred or was required to use the *quadro riportato* method. The Baroque artist found a ceiling surface high above the ground a natural field for the projection of visual illusion. The devout Christian, thinking of Heaven as "up," must be overwhelmed with emotion when, looking up, he sees its image before his eyes. In the Sistine Ceiling, Michelangelo made no attempt to project an image of the skies opening into heaven; rather, he represented an epic narrative of events of no physical place or time that could be read almost as well from walls as from ceilings. The *illusion* of bodies actually soaring above was of no interest to him; the truth of certain events in the history of Genesis was, and these events and figures could be shut off in their own compartments, self-contained. It is quite otherwise with a Baroque master of ceiling decoration like FRA ANDREA POZZO (1642–1709). A lay brother of the Jesuit order and a master of perspective, on which he wrote an influential treatise, Pozzo designed and executed the vast ceiling fresco depicting *The Glorification of St. Ignatius* (FIG. 19-32) for the church of Sant' Ignazio in Rome. This is indeed the culmination of the *di sotto in sù* experiments of Mantegna (FIG. 16-65) and Correggio (FIG. 17-38). The artist intends to create the illusion that Heaven is opening up above the heads of the congregation—indeed, of the very congregation that fills this church of Sant' Ignazio. For, in painted illusion, Pozzo continues the actual architecture of the church into the vault, so that the roof seems to be lifted off, as Heaven and Earth commingle and St. Ignatius is carried to the waiting Christ in the presence of the four corners of the world. A metal plate in the nave floor marks the standpoint for the whole perspective illusion. Looking up from this point, the observer takes in the celestial–terrestrial scene as one, for the two are meant to fuse in Pozzo's design without the interruption of a boundary. To achieve his visionary effects, the artist employs all means offered by architecture, sculpture, and painting and unites them in a fusion that surpasses even the Gothic effects of total integration.

Sound, as well as light, is a vehicle of ecstasy and vision in the Baroque experience. We know that churches were designed with acoustical effect in mind and can imagine how, in a Baroque church filled with Baroque music, the power of both light and sound would be vastly augmented. Through simultaneous stimulation of both the visual and auditory senses, the faithful might be transported into a trance-like state that would indeed, in the words of Milton, "bring all Heaven before [their] eyes." But this transport would always have to be effected by physical means, for although in the Middle Ages men

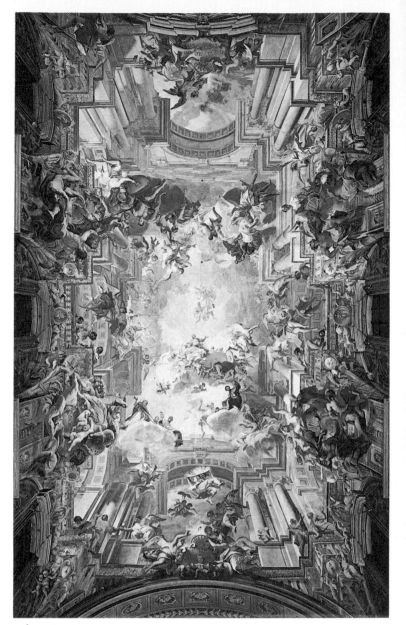

19-32 FRA ANDREA POZZO, *The Glorification of St. Ignatius,* 1691–1694. Ceiling fresco in the nave of Sant' Ignazio, Rome.

were able to find the vision within, in the Baroque period they demanded that that mystery be made visible to the outward sight. Thus, to be credible, Heaven must more and more visually resemble the domain of earth; Dante could see Heaven in a dream, but Pozzo wanted to see it unfold above him while he was awake and walking in a church. Medieval man aspired to Heaven; Baroque man wanted Heaven to come down to his station, where he might see it—even inspect it. Vision is the supreme faculty in seventeenth-century art and science.

Baroque expansiveness is expressed not only in the characteristic movement toward the infinite horizontal but in an emphasis on the vertical as well. The heavens are more and more within reach; Galileo and Newton will penetrate them to find the laws of their movement. The clouds of Heaven are not simply the seat of angels; the seventeenth century discovers that they are water vapor. The bright air through which light is propagated has density and weight. As the heavens become physical, so man may dream of taking possession of them someday by flight—not the flight of the soul, but the flight of the body. The Baroque period transforms spirit into matter in motion, as Pozzo's ceiling relates.

SPAIN

In Spain, as in the other countries of Europe, Italianate Mannerism was adopted in the sixteenth century and cast off in the Baroque period. But along with Mannerism, Spain seemed to reject most of what the Italian Renaissance stood for, just as it would reject, for a long time, the scientific revolution and the Enlightenment. Since the Middle Ages, Spain had maintained a proud isolation from the events of Europe—an isolation that has not entirely ended today.

In the art of El Greco, we have seen the mystical side of the Spanish character (FIG. 18-61). The hard, unsentimental realism that is the other side appears in the painting of JOSÉ DE RIBERA (1591–1652), who, because he emigrated to Naples early and settled there, is sometimes called by his Italian nickname, Lo Spagnoletto, "the little Spaniard." The realism of his style—a mixture of a native Spanish strain and the "dark manner" of Caravaggio—gives shock value to his often brutal themes, which express at once the harsh times of the Counter-Reformation and a Spanish taste for the representation of courageous resistance to pain. His *Martyrdom of St. Bartholomew* (FIG. 19-33) is grim and dark in subject and form. St. Bartholomew, who suffered the torture of being skinned alive, is being hoisted into position by his executioners. The saint's rough, heavy body and swarthy, plebeian features express a kinship between him and his tormentors, who compose the same cast of characters we found in the painting of Caravaggio and the Neapolitan School. In this painting, Ribera scorns idealization of any kind, and we have the uncomfortable feeling that he is recording rather than imagining the grueling scene. In that age of merciless religious fanaticism on both sides, torture, as a means of saving stubborn souls, was a common and public spectacle.

FRANCISCO DE ZURBARÁN (1598–1664) softens realism with an admixture of the mystical. His principal subjects are austere saints, represented singly in devotional attitudes and usually sharply lighted from the side. He shows us *St. Francis in Meditation* (FIG. 19-34), his uplifted face almost completely shadowed by his cowl, clutching to his body a skull—the *memento mori*, the constant reminder to the contemplative of his own mortality. The bare, unfurnished set-

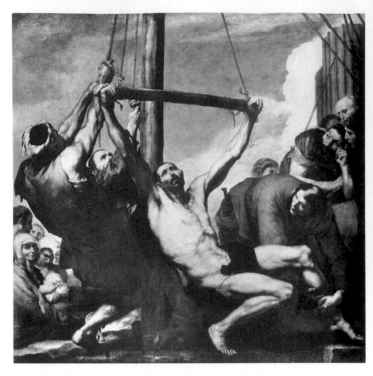

19-33   JOSÉ DE RIBERA, *The Martyrdom of St. Bartholomew,* c. 1639. Approx. 6' × 6' 6". Museo del Prado, Madrid.

19-34   FRANCISCO DE ZURBARÁN, *St. Francis in Meditation,* c. 1639. Approx. 60" × 39". Reproduced by courtesy of the Trustees of the National Gallery, London.

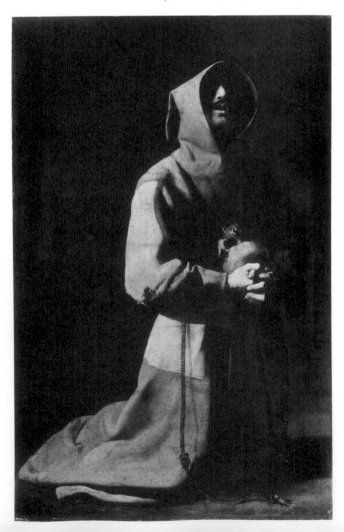

ting and the stark light and somber dark are the bleak environment of this entranced soul. We see enough to read this as an image of rapt meditation—the parted lips, the tensely locked fingers, the rigid attitude of a devotee utterly unaware of his surroundings and mystically in contact with God. Here, Zurbarán gives us a personification of the fierce devotion of Catholic Spain.

In the Baroque age, visions and the visual go together. It may be that DIEGO VELÁZQUEZ (1599–1660)—an artist who set aside visions in the interest of what is given to the eye in the optical world—stands among the great masters of visual realism of all time. Although he painted religious pictures, he was incapable of idealism or high-flown rhetoric, and his sacred subjects are bluntly real. Velázquez, trained in Seville, early came to the attention of the king, Philip IV, and became the court painter at Madrid, where, save for two extended trips to Italy and a few excursions, he remained for the rest of his life. His close personal relationship with Philip and his high office of marshal of the palace gave him prestige and a rare opportunity to fulfill the promise of his genius with a variety of artistic assignments. In an early work, *Los Borrachos* ("The Drinkers," FIG. 19-35), Velázquez shows his cool independence of the ideals of Renaissance and Baroque Italy in a native naturalism that has the strength and something of the look of Caravaggio. Commissioned to paint Bacchus among his followers, Velázquez makes mock of Classical conventions in both theme and form. He bur-

lesques the stately, Classical Bacchic scenes—making the god a mischievous young *bravo*, stripped to the waist, crowning a wobbly tippler who kneels before him. The rest of the company is of the same type: weather-beaten, shabby roisterers of the tavern crowd, who grin and jape at the event uncouthly, enjoying the game for what it is. Painting the crude figures in strong light and dark that is evenly distributed so as not to obscure them, Velázquez makes sharp characterizations of each person, showing not only his instinct for portraiture but a Baroque interest in human "types." And, typically Spanish, he caricatures, through realism, an Italianate subject that ordinarily would be idealized. Enrique Lafuente, a modern critic, states the Spanish attitude:

> Spain refuses to accept the basic ideas which inspire the Italian Renaissance because they are repugnant to its sense of the life of the Spanish man. The Spaniard knows that reality is not Idea but Life. . . . The supreme value of life is linked with experience and the moral values that are based on personality. Idea, beauty, formal perfection, are abstractions and nothing more. Art, in its turn, is bound to concern itself with realities and not with dreams.*

To Velázquez, as to many Spanish artists, the academic styles of Baroque Italy must have seemed pretentious and insincere, not to say pagan. He turned away from them to the world before his eyes.

*Enrique Lafuente, *Velázquez* (New York: Oxford University Press, 1943), p. 6.

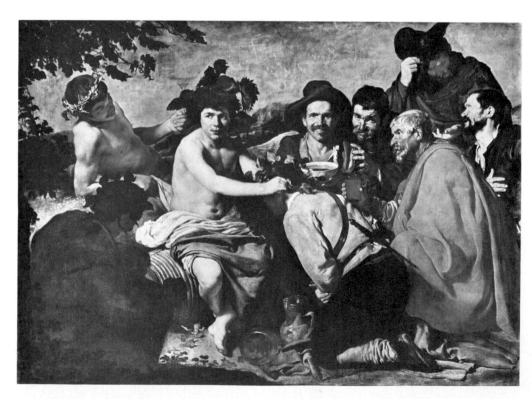

19-35 DIEGO VELÁZQUEZ, *Los Borrachos*, c. 1628. Approx. 5' 6" × 7' 6". Museo del Prado, Madrid.

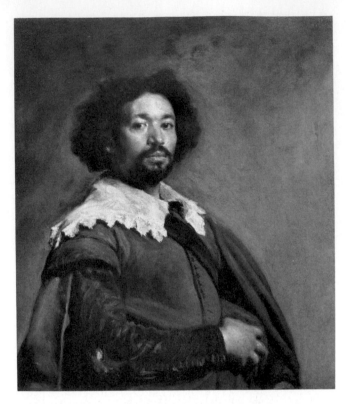

19-36 Diego Velázquez, *Juan de Pareja*, 1649–1650. Approx. 33″ × 28″. Metropolitan Museum of Art, New York.

One could hardly find in art a better example of Lafuente's dictum that "reality is not Idea, but Life" than Velázquez's portrait of *Juan de Pareja* (FIG. 19-36). At the height of his powers, Velázquez painted his assistant when they were in Rome together in 1650. He was intending to paint a portrait of Pope Innocent X, a patron of Bernini, and he did the study of Pareja as a kind of trial run. Today, we would probably agree that it is a masterpiece in its own right.

The work was exhibited in the Pantheon and drew the admiration of the many artists in Rome, Italian and foreign alike. They perceived in it an almost incredible knowledge of the structure of appearance, a matchless technique of execution, and an eloquent simplicity of composition that rejected conventional Baroque props and rhetoric. The apparent simplicity of the formal means matches the simplicity of presentation. Placed before an entirely neutral ground, Pareja looks directly at us with a calm dignity and quiet pride, a man perfectly self-contained. His character gives him a natural poise, utterly without arrogance or affectation. His level gaze, the easy gesture of arm and hand, and his erect carriage place him directly in front of us, and Velázquez introduces him.

Velázquez's uncanny power of penetration of the form and meaning before him, though in some ways unique, was not entirely untaught. He had carefully studied the works of other artists and was fully aware of the achievements of the great masters like Michelangelo and the Venetians. He knew the latter from the king's collections, of which he had charge, and he studied them further in Italy, where he journeyed at the suggestion of the great Flemish painter Peter Paul Rubens, whom he met when the older Rubens was copying the Venetians in the collections at the Madrid court. But his studies in Italy did not make a "Romanist" of Velázquez. Their most notable effects were a softening of his earlier, somewhat heavy-handed realism (seen in *Los Borrachos*) and a lighter palette, which gave his paintings brighter and subtler tonality.

Looking at his masterpiece, *Las Meninas* ("The Maids in Waiting," FIG. 19-37), with our experience of his portrait of *Juan de Pareja*, we must view Velázquez as a master of a brilliant optical realism that has seldom been approached and has never been surpassed. The painter represents himself in his studio before a large canvas, on which he may be painting this very picture or, perhaps, the portraits of the king and queen, whose reflections appear in the mirror on the far wall. The little infanta, Margarita, appears in the foreground with her two maids in waiting, her favorite dwarfs, and a large dog. In the middle ground are a duenna and a male escort; in the background, a gentleman is framed in a brightly lit open doorway. The personages present have been identified. On the wall above the doorway and mirror, two faintly recognizable pictures represent the immortal gods as the source of art. Our first impression of *Las Meninas* is of an informal family group (it was long called "The Family" by the Austrian kings of Spain), casually arranged and miraculously lifelike; one could think of it as a genre painting—"A Visit to the Artist's Studio"—rather than as a group portrait.

As first painter to the king and as chief steward of the palace, Velázquez was conscious not only of the importance of his court office but of the honor and dignity belonging to his profession as painter. In this painting, he appears to bring the roles together, asserting their equivalent value. A number of pictures from the seventeenth century show painters with their royal patrons, for painters of the time continued to seek to aggrandize their profession among the arts and to achieve by it appropriate rank and respect. Throughout his career, Velázquez hoped to be ennobled by royal appointment to membership in the ancient and illustrious Order of Santiago, from which, he must have expected, his profession as painter would not disqualify him. Because some of the required patents of nobility were lacking in his background, he achieved this only with difficulty at the very end of his life, and then only through a dispensation from the pope. In the painting, he wears the red cross of the order on his doublet, which was painted there, legend tells us, by the king himself; the truth is that the artist painted it. In Velázquez's mind, *Las Meninas* might have embodied the idea of the

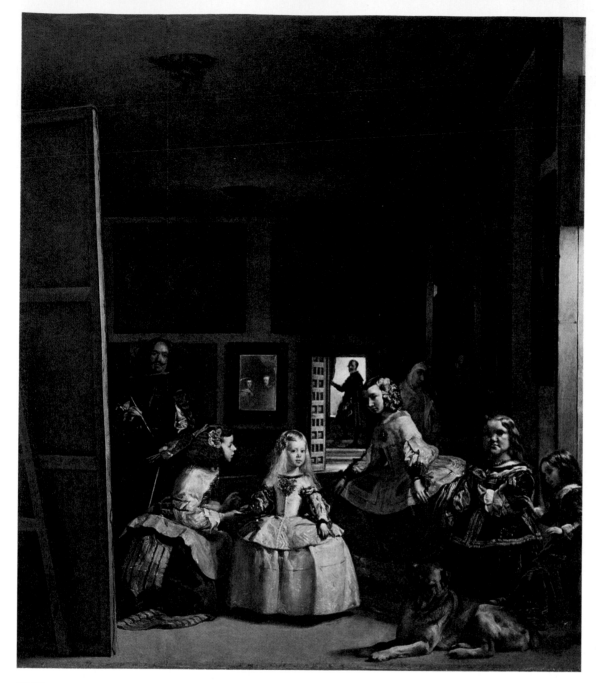

19-37 Diego Velázquez, *Las Meninas*, 1656. Approx. 10′ 5″ × 9′. Museo del Prado, Madrid.

great king visiting his artist's studio, as Alexander the Great visited the studio of Apelles in ancient times.

Although Velázquez intends an optical report of the event, authentic in every detail, he also seems to intend a pictorial summary of the various kinds of images in their different levels and degrees of "reality"—the "reality" of canvas image, of mirror image, of optical image, and of the two imaged paintings. The work—with its cunning contrasts of mirrored spaces, "real" spaces, picture spaces, and pictures within pictures—itself appears to have been taken from a large mirror reflecting the whole scene, which would mean the artist has not painted the princess and her suite, but himself in the process of painting

them. In the Baroque period, when artists were taking Leonardo's dictum that "the mirror is our master" very seriously, it is not surprising to find mirrors and primitive camera-like devices used to achieve optimum visual fidelity in painting. *Las Meninas* is a pictorial summary as well as a commentary on the essential mystery of the visual world and on the ambiguity that results when we confuse its different states or levels.

How does Velázquez achieve this stunning illusion? He opens the spectrum of light and the tones that compose it. Instead of putting lights abruptly beside darks—as Caravaggio, Ribera, and Zurbarán would do or as he himself, in earlier works like *Los*

Borrachos (FIG. 19-35), had done—he allows a great number of intermediate values of gray to come between the two extremes. Thus, he carefully observes and records the subtle gradations of tone, matching with graded glazes what he sees in the visible spread of light and dark, using strokes of deep dark and touches of highlight to enliven the neutral tones in the middle of the value scale. This essentially cool, middle register of tones is what gives the marvelous effect of daylight and atmosphere to the painting. Velázquez's matching of tonal gradations approaches effects that the age of the photograph will later discover. His method is an extreme refinement of Titian's. No longer does Velázquez think of figures as first drawn, then modeled into sculptural effects, and then colored. He thinks of light and tone as the whole substance of painting—the solid forms being only *suggested,* never really constructed. Observing this reduction of the solid world to purely optical sensations in a floating, fugitive skein of color tones, one could say that the old, sculpturesque form has disappeared. The extreme thinness of Velázquez's paint and the light, almost accidental touches of thick pigment here and there destroy all visible structure; we examine his canvas closely, and everything dissolves to a random flow of paint. As a wondering Italian painter exclaimed of a Velázquez painting: "It is made of nothing, but there it is!" Painters 300 years later will realize that Velázquez's optical realism constitutes a limit. Their attempts to analyze it and to take it further will lead in an opposite direction to the one taken by the great Spanish master—to the abstract art of our own time.

FLANDERS

In the sixteenth century, the Netherlands came under the crown of Hapsburg Spain when the emperor Charles V retired, leaving the Spanish throne and his Netherlandish provinces to his only son, Philip II. Philip's repressive measures against the Protestants led to the breaking away of the northern provinces from Spain and the setting up of the Dutch republic under the House of Orange. The southern provinces remained with Spain, and their official religion continued to be Catholic. The political distinction between modern Holland and Belgium more or less reflects this original separation, which, in the Baroque period, signalized not only religious but also artistic differences. The Baroque art of Flanders (the Spanish Netherlands) remained in close contact with the Baroque art of the Catholic countries, while the Dutch schools of painting developed their own subjects and styles, consonant with their reformed religion and the new political, social, and economic structure of the middle-class Dutch republic.

The brilliant Flemish master PETER PAUL RUBENS (1577–1640) preceded Bernini in the development and dissemination of the Baroque style. Rubens' influence was international; he drew together the main contributions of the masters of the Renaissance (Michelangelo and Titian) and of the Baroque (the Carracci and Caravaggio) to synthesize in his own style the first truly European manner. Thus, Rubens completes the work begun by Albrecht Dürer in the previous century. The art of Rubens, even though it is the consequence of his wide study of many masters, is no weak eclecticism but an original and powerful synthesis. From the beginning, his instinct was to break away from the provincialism of the old Flemish Mannerists and to seek new ideas and methods abroad. His aristocratic education, his courtier's manner, diplomacy, and tact, as well as his Classical learning early made him the associate of princes and scholars. He became court painter to the dukes of Mantua (descended from the patrons of Mantegna), friend of the King of Spain and his adviser on art collecting, painter to Charles I of England and Maria de' Medici, queen of France, and permanent court painter to the Spanish governors of Flanders. Rubens also won the confidence of his royal patrons in matters of state, being entrusted often with diplomatic missions of the highest importance. In the practice of his art, he was assisted by scores of associates and apprentices, turning out large numbers of paintings for an international clientele. In addition, he functioned as an art dealer, buying and selling works of contemporary art and Classical antiquities. His numerous enterprises made him a rich man, with a magnificent town house and a château in the countryside. Wealth and honors, however, did not spoil his amiable, sober, self-disciplined character. We have in Rubens, as in Raphael, the image of the successful, renowned artist, the consort of kings, and the shrewd man of the world, who is at the same time the balanced philosopher. Rubens more than makes good the Renaissance claim for the preeminence of the artist in society.

Rubens became a master in 1598 and went to Italy two years later, where he remained until 1608. During these years, he formed the foundations of his style. Shortly after his return from Italy, he painted *The Elevation of the Cross* (FIG. 19-38) for Antwerp Cathedral. This work shows the result of his long study of Italian art, especially of Michelangelo, Tintoretto, and Caravaggio. The scene is a focus of tremendous, straining forces and counterforces, as heavily muscled giants strain to lift the cross. Here, the artist has the opportunity to show foreshortened anatomy and the contortions of violent action—not the bound action of Mannerism, but the tension of strong bodies meeting resistance outside themselves. The body of Christ is a great, illuminated diagonal that cuts dy-

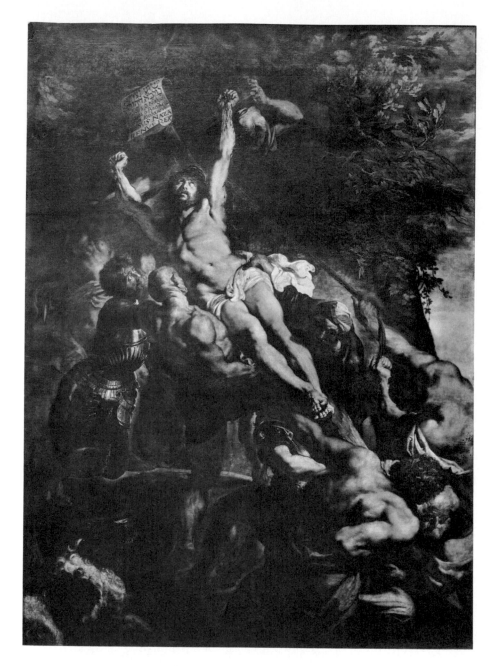

19-38 PETER PAUL RUBENS, *The Elevation of the Cross*, 1610. 15' 2" × 11' 2". Antwerp Cathedral, Belgium.

namically across the picture and, at the same time, inclines back into it. The whole composition seethes with a power that we feel comes from genuine exertion, from elastic human sinew taut with effort. Strong modeling in dark and light marks Rubens' work at this stage of his career; it will gradually give way to a much subtler, coloristic style.

The vigor and passion of Rubens' early manner never leaves his painting, although its vitality is modified into less strained and more subtle forms, depending on the theme. Yet Rubens has one general theme—the human body, draped or undraped, male or female, freely acting or free to act in an environment of physical forces and other interacting bodies. There is nothing profoundly tragic in Rubens' con-

ception of the human scene, nor is there anything manneristically intellectual, enigmatic, or complex. His forte is the strong animal body described in the joyful, exuberant motion natural to it. His *Rape of the Daughters of Leucippus* (FIG. 19-39) describes the abduction of two young mortals by the gods Castor and Pollux, who have fallen in love with them. The amorous theme permits departures from realism, especially in the representation of movement and exerted strength. The gods do not labor at the task of sweeping up the massive maidens—descendants of the opulent Venuses of Giorgione and Titian (FIGS. 17-60 and 17-63)—nor do the maidens energetically resist. The figures are part of a highly dynamic, slowly revolving composition that seems to turn on an axis—a

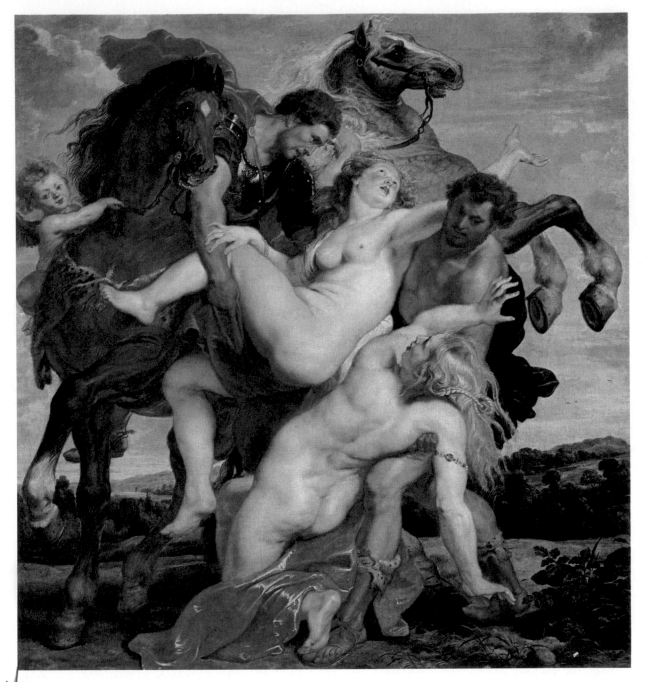

19-39 PETER PAUL RUBENS, *The Rape of the Daughters of Leucippus*, 1617. Approx. 7′ 3″ × 6′ 10″. Alte Pinakothek, Munich.

diamond-shaped group that defies stability and the logic of statics. The surface pattern, organized by intersecting diagonals and verticals, consists of areas of rich, contrasting textures: the soft luminous flesh of the women, the bronzed tan of the muscular men, lustrous satins, glinting armor, and the taut, shimmering hides of the horses. And around this surface pattern, a tight massing of volumes moves in space; the solid forms are no longer described simply in terms of the dark–light values of Florentine draftsmanship but are now built up in color and defined by light, as in Venetian painting.

The impact of Rubens' hunting pictures lies in their depiction of ferocious action and vitality. In *The Lion Hunt* (FIG. 19-40), a cornered lion, three lances meeting in his body, tears a Berber hunter from his horse. A fallen man still grips his sword, while another, in a reversed position, stabs at a snarling cat. Horsemen plunge in and out of the picture space, and the falling Berber makes a powerful, diagonal cut across the composition. The wild melee of thrusting, hacking, rearing, and plunging is almost an allegory of the bound tensions of Mannerism exploding into the extravagant activity of the Baroque.

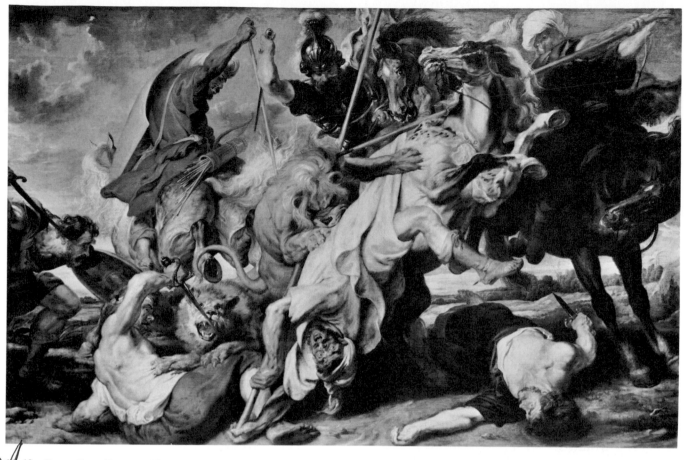

19-40 PETER PAUL RUBENS, *The Lion Hunt*, 1617–1618. Approx. 8′ 2″ × 12′ 5″. Alte Pinakothek, Munich.

Rubens shared heartily in the Baroque love of magnificent pomp, especially as it set off the majesty of royalty, in which Rubens, born courtier that he was, heartily believed. The Baroque age saw endless, extravagant pageants and festivals produced whenever the great or even lesser dynasts moved. Their authority and right to rule was forever being demonstrated by lavish display; we have seen that the popes themselves, the princes of the Church, made of St. Peter's a permanently festive monument to papal supremacy. And Maria de' Medici, a member of the famous Florentine House of Medici, commissioned Rubens to paint a cycle memorializing and glorifying her career and that of her late husband, the first of the Bourbon kings, Henry IV.

Rubens' imposing, vigorous figure compositions were not his only achievement; he also produced rich landscapes and perceptive portraits. A painting of singular power is Rubens' portrait of *Thomas Howard, Earl of Arundel* (FIG. 19-41). This great nobleman played a leading role in the complicated diplomacy and statecraft of the age of Charles I, when England was verging on the tragic civil war between the Stuart king and the Parliament. He is best remembered, however, as a lover of art, who built a collection of ancient statuary and other works of art unsurpassed in the Europe of his time. Rubens was a friend of Arundel and an admirer of his taste and learning. Rubens' admiration for the man himself, regarded by contemporaries as the bringer of "true virtu"— knightly gallantry and magnanimity—to England, is clearly expressed in the portrait. The earl is posed in an attitude of regal majesty. He directs a sharp, stern, haughty glance over his shoulder, creating instant distance between *his* rank and that of the observer. The look given by the aquiline features is that of a commander of armies silencing a subordinate; it is full of an authority not to be questioned. Rubens gives us not the sensitive lover of art but the fearless captain; we realize that the earl himself must have stipulated that this aspect of his character and career be shown. To this end, Rubens has garbed him in magnificent ceremonial armor. His gauntleted hand rests on the commander's staff; his plumed helmet, on a table at his side. Behind him, a curtain is drawn aside, showing a severe Classical architecture that echoes his mood. Rubens lavishes all of his rich resources of color tone in the rendering of the splendid accoutrements of high rank and latter-day chivalry. This imperious image speaks for an autocratic age—

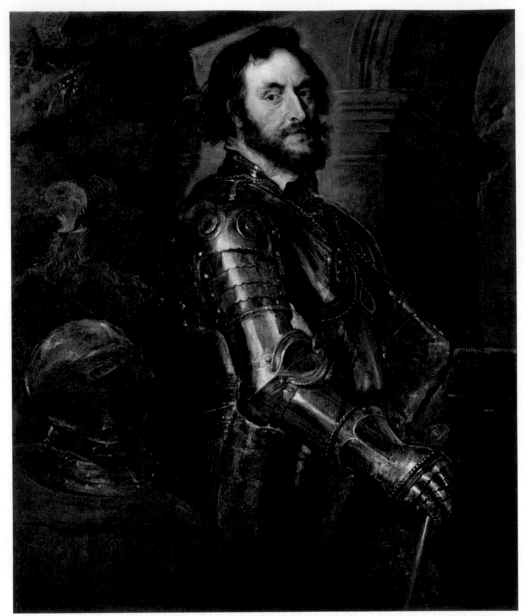

19-41 PETER PAUL RUBENS, *Thomas Howard, Earl of Arundel*, c. 1630. Approx. 54" × 45". Isabella Stewart Gardner Museum, Boston.

for the great dynasts of the Baroque, whom Rubens knew well and who were his patrons.

Most of Rubens' successors in Flanders had been his assistants. The most famous, ANTHONY VAN DYCK (1599–1641), probably worked with his master on the canvas of *The Rape of the Daughters of Leucippus*. Quite early, the younger man, unwilling to be overshadowed by the undisputed stature of Rubens, left his native Antwerp for Genoa and then London, where he became court portraitist to Charles I. Although Van Dyck created dramatic compositions of high quality, his specialty became the portrait, and he developed a courtly manner of great elegance that would be internationally influential. His style is felt in English portrait painting down to the nineteenth century. In one of his finest works, *Charles I Dismounted*

(FIG. 19-42), he shows the ill-fated Stuart king standing in a Venetian landscape (with the river Thames in the background!), attended by an equerry and a page. Although the king personates a nobleman out for a casual ride in his park, there is no mistaking the regal poise and the air of absolute authority that his Parliament resented and was soon to rise against. The composition is exceedingly artful in the placement of the king—off-center, but balancing the picture with a single keen glance at the observer. The full-length portraits by Titian and the cool composure of the Mannerists alike contribute to Van Dyck's sense of pose and arrangement of detail. For centuries, artists who make portraits of the great will keep Van Dyck very much in mind—Thomas Gainsborough, Joshua Reynolds, and John Singer Sargent, among them.

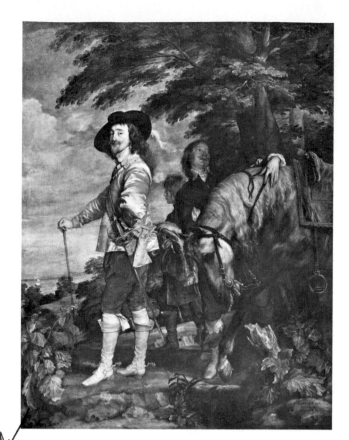

19-42 Anthony van Dyck, *Charles I Dismounted*, c. 1635.
Approx. 9′ × 7′. Louvre, Paris.

HOLLAND

For all intents and purposes, the style of Peter Paul
Rubens is the style of Baroque Flanders; he had few
rivals of significance and a monopoly on commissions. The situation is so completely different in Holland that it is difficult to imagine how, within such a
tiny area, two such opposite artistic cultures could
flourish. The Dutch Protestants and the Flemish
Catholics went their separate ways after the later sixteenth century. Although closer in outlook to the
Germans, the Dutch were ethnically the same as the
Flemish, who were, in turn, closer in viewpoint to
their neighbors to the south—the French. A Catholic,
aristocratic, and traditional culture reigned in the
Flanders of Rubens. In Holland, severe, Calvinistic
Protestantism was puritanical toward religious art,
sculptural or pictorial, although there were many
Dutch Catholics, including painters. The churches
were swept clean of images, and any recollection of
the pagan myths, the material of Classicism, or even
historical subjects was proscribed in art. During the
Middles Ages and the Renaissance, religious subjects
and, later, Classical and historical subjects had been
the major stimuli for artistic activity. Divested of
these sources, what remained to enrich the lives of

wealthy Hollanders? For they *were* wealthy! During
the early part of the Spanish rule, the Dutch, like the
Flemish, prospered. The East India Company was
formed, and the discovery of the New World opened
up further opportunities for trade and colonization.
The wars of independence from Spain made Holland
the major maritime country of Europe; its closest rival
was England, another Protestant power in the times
of the Spanish decline. The great Dutch commercial
cities, such as Haarlem and Amsterdam, had been
stimulated and enriched, and civic pride was strong.
Although it was not internationally recognized until
the Peace of Westphalia in 1648, Holland had been
independent from Spain in fact since about 1580 and
was extremely proud of its hard-won freedom. Under
these circumstances, writes the nineteenth-century
French painter Eugène Fromentin

> Dutch painting . . . was and could be only the por-
> trait of Holland, its exterior image, faithful, exact,
> complete, with no embellishments. Portraits of men
> and places, citizen habits, squares, streets, country-
> places, the sea and the sky—such was to be . . . the
> program followed by the Dutch School, and such it
> was from its first day to the day of its decline.*

Thus, it came about that the Dutch painters pried into
the pictorial possibilities of everyday life and kept an
eye on their customers, the middle-class burghers,
who wanted paintings to hang on their walls as evidence of their growing wealth and social position.

We have followed the secularization and humanization of religious art since the thirteenth century. In
the Dutch School of the seventeenth century, the
process is completed. A thousand years and more of
religious iconography is dismissed by a European
people who ask for a view of the world from which
angels, saints, and deities have been banished. The
old Netherlandish realism remains, but it no longer
serves religious purposes. The Dutch artists rise to
the occasion, matching the open, competitive, Dutch
society, which is thoroughly middle-class, with an
equally open arrangement of their own, in which the
painter works not for a patron but for the market. He
becomes a specialist in any one of a number of subjects—genre, landscape, seascape, cattle and horses,
table still life, flower still life, interiors, and so on. In
short, he paints subjects that he feels will appeal to
his public and therefore be marketable. This independence from the patron gives the Dutch painter a certain amount of freedom, even if it is only the freedom
to starve on the free-picture market. With respect to
the artist–market relationship, the contrast between

*Eugène Fromentin, *The Masters of Past Time: Dutch and Flemish
Painting from Van Eyck to Rembrandt*, trans. A. Boyle (London:
Phaidon, 1948), p. 130.

Flanders and Holland in the seventeenth century is poignantly reflected in the careers of Rubens and Rembrandt. The former *is* the market in Flanders; his genius determines it. The latter, after finding a place in the market, is rejected by it when his genius is no longer marketable.

The realism of Dutch art is made up of the old tradition, which goes back to Hubert and Jan van Eyck, and of the new "realism of light and dark," brought back to Holland by Dutch painters who had studied Caravaggio in Italy. One of these "night painters" (as they were called), GERARD VAN HONTHORST (1590–1656) of Utrecht, spent several years in Italy absorbing Caravaggio's style. He is best known for merry genre scenes like *The Supper Party* (FIG. 19-43), in which unidealized, human figures are shown in an informal gathering. Although these "merry companies," naturalistically rendered in night settings, were popular and widely produced in the Baroque period, they were not necessarily taken simply as pictures of people enjoying themselves. We must remember the Baroque mental habit of allegorizing and symbolizing even the most realistic images. Here, for example, we may be expected to witness the loose companions of the Prodigal Son (Luke 15:13)—panders and prostitutes, drinking, singing, strumming, laughing. Perhaps, at the same time, we have an allegory of the Five Senses through which sin can enter the soul: taste, touch, sight, sound, scent. Fascinated by nocturnal effects, Van Honthorst frequently places a hidden light source (two, in this case) in his pictures and uses it as a pretext to work

with dramatic and violently contrasted dark–light effects. Without the incisive vision of Caravaggio, Van Honthorst is nevertheless able to match, and sometimes to surpass, the former's tenebristic effects.

The Dutch schools were as various as their cities (Utrecht, Haarlem, Leiden, Amsterdam), but all had in common the lesson of Caravaggio interpreted by Dutch "Caravaggisti" like Van Honthorst. FRANS HALS (c. 1580–1666)—the leading painter of the Haarlem School and one of the great realistic painters of the Western tradition—appropriates what he needs from the new lighting to make portraiture (his specialty) an art of acute psychological perception as well as a kind of comic genre. The way light floats across the face and meets shadow can be arranged by the artist, as can the pose and the details of costume and facial expression. Hals shows himself to be a master of all the devices open to a portraitist who no longer need keep the distance required by the strictly formal portrait. The relaxed relationship between the portraitist and his subject is apparent in the engaging portrait of *Balthasar Coymans* (FIG. 19-44), dated 1645. Although the subject is a young man of some importance, the artist seems to be taking a great deal of liberties with his portrait. The young man leans on one arm with a jaunty air of insolence, his hat cocked at a challenging angle, a look of contemptuous drollery in his eyes. The illusion of life is such that we take cues from the subject's expression as if we were face-to-face with him. Hals' genius lies in this capture of the minute, expressional movements by which, in everyday life, we appraise the man across from us. Until now, this

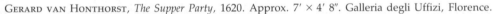

19-43 GERARD VAN HONTHORST, *The Supper Party*, 1620. Approx. 7′ × 4′ 8″. Galleria degli Uffizi, Florence.

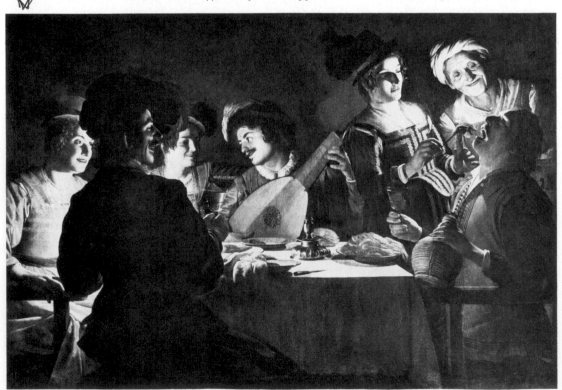

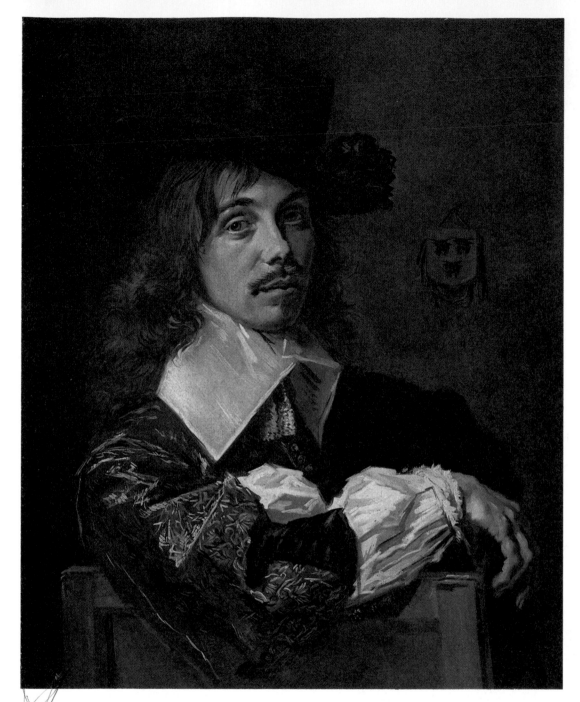

19-44 FRANS HALS, *Balthasar Coymans*, 1645. Approx. 30¼″ × 25″. National Gallery of Art, Washington, D.C. (Andrew W. Mellon Collection).

kind of intimate confrontation had rarely been seen in painting. It is a kind of contradiction of the masks of formal portraiture created in the Renaissance. We are in the presence of an individual without formal introduction; the gap between us and the subject is reduced until we are almost part of his physical and psychological environment. The casualness, immediacy, and intimacy are intensified by the manner in which the painting is executed. The touch of the painter's brush is as light and fleeting as the moment in which the pose is caught; the pose of the figure, the highlights on the sleeve, the reflected lights within face and hand, the lift of the eyebrow—all are

the instant prey of time. Thus, the evanescence of time that Bernini caught in his *David* (FIG. 19-10) is recorded far to the north a few years later in a different subject and a different medium. Both are Baroque.

Frans Hals is a genius of the comic. He had precedents in the gargoylism and grotesquerie of the northern Middle Ages and, in later times, in Hieronymus Bosch and Pieter Bruegel. But Hals' comedy is that of character, rather than situation. He shows us—as Aristotle would demand of comedy—people as they are and somewhat less than they are; this puts us at ease, out of superiority, so that we can laugh at

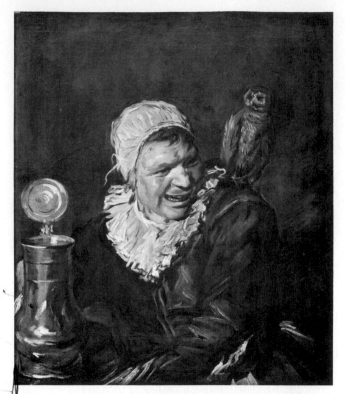

19-45′ FRANS HALS, *Malle Babbe*, c. 1650 (?). Approx.
30″ × 25″. Gemäldegalerie, Staatliche Museen, Berlin-Dahlem.

others and ourselves. Hals takes his comic characters, as did Shakespeare, his contemporary, from the depths of society. The *Malle Babbe* ("Mad Babbe," FIG. 19-45), with her owl and her shiny pewter tankard, holds her cackling own in a verbal exchange, doubtless in some cellar tavern. In the Baroque era, as the heavens descend to earth, so Hell rises and becomes familiar in human forms; all the spheres tend to meet. Hals' dashing, *alla prima* brushwork (perhaps more studied than it appears) seems to catch the quick outburst in almost the moment it would take it to be heard. This instant reportage is a development inspired out of the deliberate, almost static method of Caravaggio. No painter, not even among the Impressionists, wanted more than Hals to bring the instantaneous image of life before us.

Good-humored stageplay brightens Hals' great canvases of units of the Dutch civic guard, which played an important part in the liberation of Holland. These companies of archers and musketeers met on their saints' days in dress uniform for an uproarious banquet, giving Hals an opportunity to attack the problem of adequately representing each subject of a group portrait while retaining action and variety in the composition. Earlier group portraits in the Netherlands represent the sitters as so many jugs on a shelf; Hals undertakes to correct this and, in the process, produces dramatic solutions to the problem, like that found in his *Archers of St. Adrian* (FIG. 19-46). Here, the troopers have finished their banquet, the wine has already gone to their heads, and each in his own way is sharing the abundant high spirits. As a

stage director Hals has few equals. In quite Baroque fashion, he balances direction of glance, pose, and gesture, making compositional devices of the white ruffs, broad-brimmed black hats, and banners. Although the instantaneous effect—the preservation of every detail and facial expression—is, of course, the result of careful planning, Hals' vivacious brush seems to have moved spontaneously, directed by a plan in the artist's mind but not traceable in any preparatory scheme on the canvas. The bright optimism of this early period of Dutch freedom is caught in the swaggering bonhomie of the personalities, each of whom plays his particular part within the general unity of mood. This is the gregariousness that goes with the new democracy, as well as the fellowship that grows from a common experience of danger.

With Hals, Baroque realism concentrates on the human subject so intimately that we are forced to relate it to ourselves. We and the subject look at each other, as if in a sharing of mood; there is a confrontation of personalities. Yet it is still mostly a public image that the subject is willing to present; in this respect, Hals has not entirely broken away from the tradition of formal portraiture that goes back to the fifteenth century. The first deep look into the *private* man will be made by Hals' younger contemporary, REMBRANDT VAN RIJN (1606–1669).

Rembrandt's way was prepared spiritually by the Protestant Reformation and the Dutch aspiration to freedom and formally by the Venetian painters, by Rubens, and by Caravaggio and his Dutch imitators. The richness of this heritage, however, cannot alone account for the extraordinary achievement of this artist, one of the very greatest among those geniuses who excel in revealing Western man to himself. Rembrandt used painting as a method for probing the states of the human soul, both in portraiture and in his uniquely personal and authentic illustrations of the Scriptures. The abolition of religious art by the Reformed Church in Holland did not prevent him from making a series of religious paintings and prints that synopsize the Bible from a single point of view— that of a believing Christian, a poet of the spiritual, convinced that the biblical message must be interpreted in human terms for human beings. In Rembrandt, the humanization of Medieval religion is now completed in the vision of a single believer. In the Baroque age, this is roughly parallel to the sighting of a new planet by some single "watcher of the skies."

Rembrandt's pictorial method involves refining light and shade into finer and finer nuances, until they blend with one another. (Caravaggio's "absolute" light has, in fact, many shadows; his "absolute" dark, many lights.) We have seen that Velázquez renders optical reality as a series of values—a number of degrees of lightness and darkness. Thus, the use of abrupt lights and darks gives way in the works of

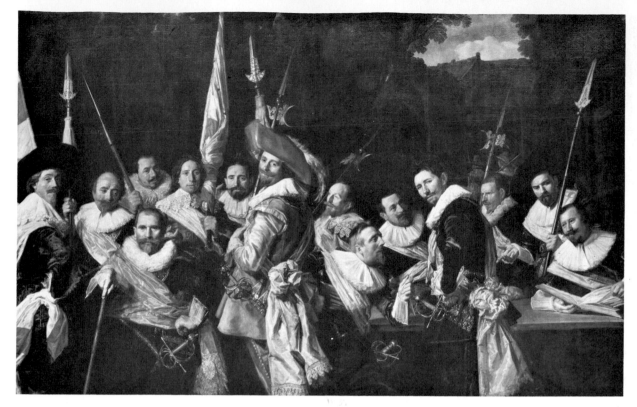

19-46 FRANS HALS, *Archers of St. Adrian* (*Assembly of Officers and Subalterns of the Civic Guard*), c. 1633. Approx. 6′ 9″ × 11′. Frans Halsmuseum, Haarlem.

men like Rembrandt and Velázquez to gradation, and, although the dramatic effects of violent chiaroscuro may be sacrificed, the artist gains much of the truth of actual appearances—for, to the eye, light and dark are not static but are always subtly changing. Changing light and dark can suggest changing human moods; we might say that the *motion* of light through a space and across human features can express *emotion*, the changing states of the psyche.

The Renaissance represents forms and faces in a flat, neutral, modeling light (even Leonardo da Vinci's shading is of a standard kind), just as it represents action in a series of standard poses. The Renaissance painter represents the *idea* of light and the *idea* of action, rather than the actual *look* of either. Light, atmosphere, change, and motion are all concerns of Baroque art, as well as of Baroque mathematics and physics. The difference from what went before lies largely in the new desire to *measure* these physical forces. For example, as the physicist in the seventeenth century is concerned not just with motion, but with acceleration and velocity—degrees of motion— so the Baroque painter discovers degrees of light and dark, of differences in pose, in the movements of facial features, and in psychic states. He arrives at these differences *optically*, not conceptually or in terms of some ideal. Rembrandt found that by manipulating light and shadow in terms of direction, intensity, distance, and texture of surface, he could render the most subtle nuances of character and mood, of persons, or of whole scenes. Rembrandt discovers for

the modern world that differences of light and shade, subtly modulated, can be read as emotional differences. In the visible world, light, dark, and the wide spectrum of values between the two are charged with meanings and feelings that are sometimes independent of the shapes and figures they modify. The lighted stage and the photographic arts have long accepted this as the first assumption behind all their productions. What Masaccio and Leonardo began, the age of Rembrandt completes.

In his early career in Amsterdam, Rembrandt's work was influenced by Rubens and by Dutch Caravaggesque painters like Van Honthorst. Thus, in a work like *Supper at Emmaus*, dating from about 1630 (FIG. 19-47), he represents the subject with high drama—in sharp light and dark contrast—even using the device, familiar among his contemporaries, of placing the source of illumination behind an obstructing form (in this case, the head of Christ). This puts the darkest shadow in front of the brightest light, creating an emphatic, if obvious, dramatic effect. The poses of the two alarmed disciples to whom the risen Christ reveals himself are likewise a studied stage maneuver. Some 18 years later, in another painting of the same subject (FIG. 19-48), the mature Rembrandt forsakes the earlier melodramatic means for a serene and untroubled setting. Here, with his highly developed instinct for light and shade, he gives us no explosive contrasts; rather, a gentle diffusion of light mellows the whole interior, condensing just slightly to make an aureole behind the head of

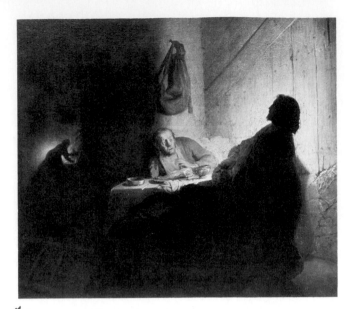

19-47 REMBRANDT VAN RIJN, *Supper at Emmaus,*
c. 1628–1630. 14½″ × 16⅛″. Musée Jacquemart-André, Paris.

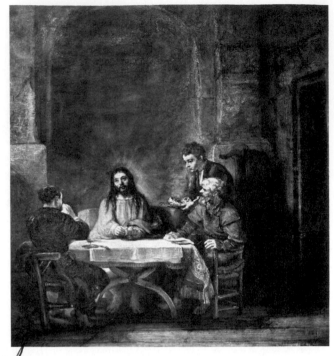

19-48 REMBRANDT VAN RIJN, *Supper at Emmaus, c.* 1648.
Approx. 27″ × 26″. Louvre, Paris.

19-49 REMBRANDT VAN RIJN, *The Return of the Prodigal Son,*
c. 1665. Approx. 8′ 8″ × 6′ 8¾″. Hermitage Museum,
Leningrad.

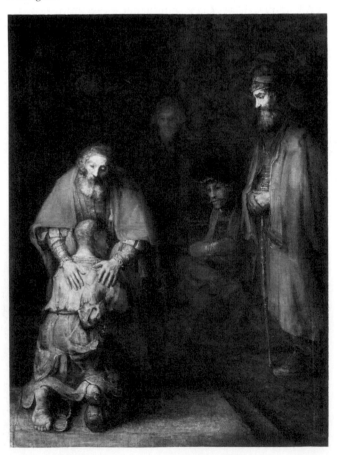

Christ. The disciples only begin to understand what
is happening; the servant is unaware. The Christ is
Rembrandt's own interpretation of the biblical picture
of the humble Nazarene—gentle, with an expression
both loving and melancholy.

The spiritual stillness of Rembrandt's religious
painting is that of inward-turning contemplation, far
from the choirs and trumpets and the heavenly tu-
mult of Bernini or Pozzo. Rembrandt gives us not the
celestial triumph of the Church, but the humanity
and humility of Jesus. His psychological insight and
his profound sympathy for human affliction produce,
at the very end of his life, one of the most moving
pictures in all religious art, *The Return of the Prodigal
Son* (FIG. 19-49). Tenderly embraced by his forgiving
father, the son crouches before him in weeping con-
trition while three figures, immersed in varying degrees in the soft shadows, note the lesson of mercy.
The scene is wholly determined by the artist's inward
vision of its meaning. The light, everywhere mingled
with shadow, controls the arrangement of the figures—illuminating father and son, largely veiling the
witnesses. Its focus is the beautiful, spiritual face of
the old man; secondarily, it touches the contrasting,
stern face of the foremost witness. There is no flash or
glitter of light or color; the raiment is as sober as the
characters are grave. Rembrandt, one feels, has put
the official Baroque style far behind him and has developed a personal style completely in tune with the
simple eloquence of the biblical passage. One could
not help but read the Bible differently, given the authority of Rembrandt's pictorial interpretations of it.

Rembrandt carries over the spiritual quality of his
religious works into his later portraits by the same
means—what we might call the "psychology" of
light. Light and dark are not in conflict in his por-

traits; they are reconciled, merging softly and subtly to produce the visual equivalent of quietness. The prevailing mood is that of tranquil meditation, of philosophical resignation, of musing recollection—indeed, a whole cluster of emotional tones heard only in silence. He records the calamities of his own life and the age-old ones of the Jewish people (he had many friends in the Jewish quarter of Amsterdam) in the worn faces of aged and silent men. His study of the influence of time on the human features was one with his study of light; the mood of reflection conveyed by the slow movement of lights and darks complements the appearance of the aged face in slanting light: a sunken terrain crisscrossed with deep lines. In a long series of self-portraits, Rembrandt preserved his own psychic history from the bright alert optimism of youth to the worn resignation of his declining years. These last years, when he was at the height of his artistic powers, cost him much physically if we are to judge from two portraits only eight years apart. The earlier (FIG. 19-50) shows the artist in his maturity—confident, even challenging, confronting the observer as if he would like to see his creden-

19-50 REMBRANDT VAN RIJN, *Self-Portrait*, 1652. Approx. 45″ × 32″. Kunsthistorisches Museum, Vienna.

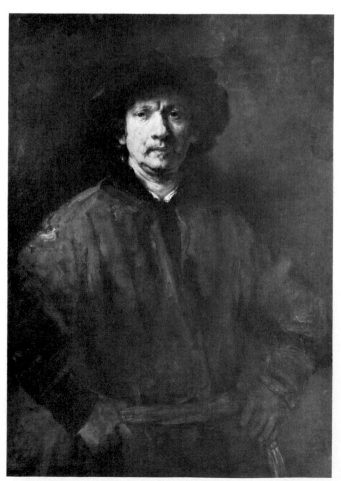

tials. Rembrandt hooks his thumbs into the belt of his studio smock, stands on no formality, waits for the observer to declare himself. In its familiarity and lack of formality, the portrait is a radical departure from the Renaissance tradition still alive in Van Dyck. The later portrait is an almost shocking contrast (FIG. 19-51). The light from above and from the artist's left pitilessly reveals a face ravaged by anxiety and care. The pose is that of Raphael's *Baldassare Castiglione* (FIG. 17-19), which Rembrandt had seen in Holland and copied in an earlier self-portrait. The difference between Raphael's and Rembrandt's portraits tells us much about the difference between the approaches of the artists and between the philosophies of their times. In Raphael's subject, the ideal has modified the real; Rembrandt shows himself as he appears to his own searching and unflattering gaze. Here, an elderly man is not idealized into the image of the courtly philosopher; he is shown merely as he is, a human being in the process of dwindling away. For some, the portrait and the self-portrait, which began as a medium for the recording of likeness, came to be painted out of motives of vanity; with Rembrandt, they are the history of Everyman's painful journey through the world.

19-51 REMBRANDT VAN RIJN, *Self-Portrait*, c. 1659. Approx. 33″ × 26″. National Gallery of Art, Washington, D.C. (Andrew W. Mellon Collection).

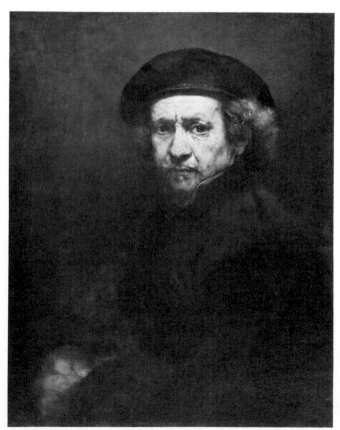

In the group portrait, an area of painting in which Frans Hals excelled, Rembrandt shows himself to be the supreme master. In *Syndics of the Cloth Guild* (FIG. 19-52), representing an archetypal image of the new businessmen, Rembrandt applied all that he knew of the dynamics and the psychology of light, the visual suggestion of time, and the art of pose and facial expression. The syndics, or board of directors, are going over the books of the corporation. It would appear that someone has entered the room and they are just at the moment of becoming aware of him, each head turning in his direction. Rembrandt gives us the lively reality of a business conference as it is interrupted; yet he renders each portrait with equal care and with a studied attention to personality one would expect to be possible only from a long studio sitting for each man. Although we do not know how Rembrandt proceeded, this harmonizing of the instantaneous action with the permanent likeness seems a work of superb stage direction that must have needed long rehearsal. The astonishing harmonies of light, color, movement, time, and pose have few rivals in the history of painting.

Rembrandt's virtuosity also extends to the graphic media—in particular, etching. Here again, he ranks at the summit, alongside the original master, Dürer, who was actually an engraver. Etching, perfected early in the seventeenth century, was rapidly taken up; it was far more manageable than engraving and allowed greater freedom in drawing the design. In etching, a copper plate is covered with a layer of wax or varnish in which the design is drawn with an etching needle or any pointed tool, exposing the metal below but not cutting into its surface. The plate is then immersed in acid, which etches, or eats away, the exposed parts of the metal, acting in the same capacity as the burin in engraving. The softness of the medium gives the etcher greater freedom than the woodcutter and the engraver, who work directly in their more resistant media of wood and metal. Thus, prior to the invention of the lithograph in the nineteenth century, etching was the most facile of the graphic arts and the one that offered the greatest subtlety of line and tone.

If Rembrandt had never painted, he would still be renowned, as he principally was in his lifetime, for his prints. Prints were a major source of income for him, and he often reworked the plates so that they could be used to produce a new issue or edition. The illustration here shows the fourth state, or version, of his *Three Crosses* (FIG. 19-53). In the earlier states, he represents the hill of Calvary in a quite pictorial, historical way, with crowds of soldiers and spectators, all descriptively and painstakingly rendered. In this last state, not the historical but the symbolic significance of the scene comes to the fore. As if impatient

19-52   REMBRANDT VAN RIJN, *Syndics of the Cloth Guild*, 1662. Approx. 6' 2" × 9' 2". Rijksmuseum, Amsterdam.

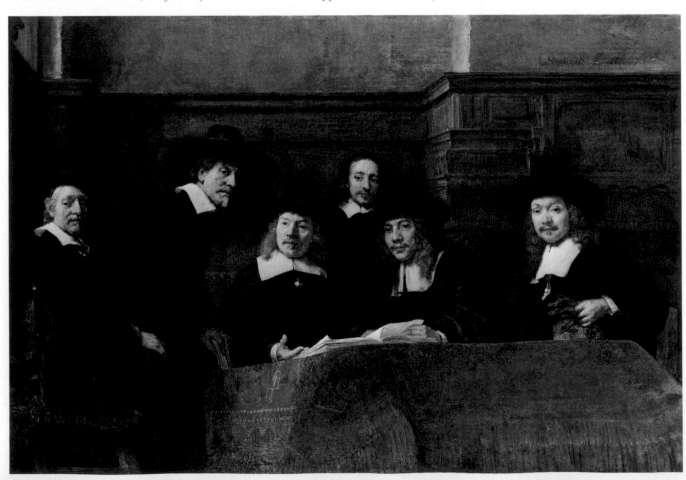

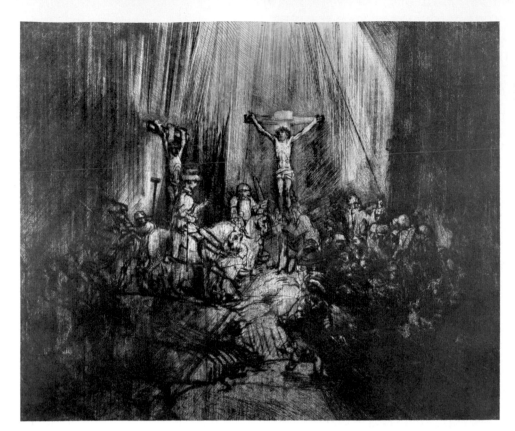

19-53 REMBRANDT VAN RIJN, *The Three Crosses*, 1653. Fourth-state etching, approx. 15″ × 18″. British Museum, London.

with the earlier detail, Rembrandt furiously eliminates most of it with hard, downward strokes of the needle, until what appears like a storm of dark lines pours down from Heaven, leaving a zone of light on the lonely figure of the crucified. Here, Rembrandt seems clearly to show that, in the words of theologian William Vischer-T'Hooft, "the entire biblical story is meant to lead us to the cross."

The art of his later years was not really acceptable to Rembrandt's contemporaries (although he occasionally got important commissions, like that for *Syndics of the Cloth Guild*). It was too personal, too eccentric; many, like the Italian biographer Filippo Baldinucci, thought Rembrandt was a tasteless painter, concerned with the ugly and ignorant of color. This prejudice lasted well into the nineteenth century, when his genius was finally acknowledged. We see him now as one of the great masters of the whole tradition, an artist of great versatility, and the unique interpreter of the Protestant conception of scripture. For our time, he stands as the archetype of the modern artist—the isolated and courageous master who finds his own way to new heights of expression, no matter the barriers of misunderstanding raised against him.

The "Little Dutch Masters"

The pictorial genius of the Dutch masters of the seventeenth century surpassed all others in its comprehensiveness of subject, taking all that is given to the eye as its province. The whole world of sight is explored, but especially the things of man in their ordinary use and aspect. In some ways, the old Netherlandish tradition of Jan van Eyck lives on in the rendering of things in the optical environment with a loving and scrupulous fidelity to their appearances. Dutch painters came to specialize in portraiture, genre, interiors, still life, landscape and seascape, and even in more specialized subdivisions of these. With many, the restriction of their professional interest is all to the good; they may not create works of grand conception, but, within their small compass, they produce exquisite art.

The best-known and most highly regarded of these painters, once referred to as the "little Dutch masters," is JAN VERMEER (1632–1675) of Delft, who was rediscovered in the nineteenth century. Vermeer's pictures are small, few, and perfect within their scope. While the fifteenth-century Flemish artists painted interiors of houses occupied with persons who were usually of sacred significance, Vermeer and his contemporaries composed neat, quietly opulent interiors of Dutch middle-class dwellings, in which they placed men, women, and children engaged in household tasks or some little recreation—actions totally commonplace, yet reflective of the values of a comfortable domesticity that has a simple beauty. Vermeer usually composes with a single figure, but sometimes with two or more. His *Young Woman with a Water Jug* (FIG. 19-54) can be considered typical, although we cannot be sure of the precise action or the

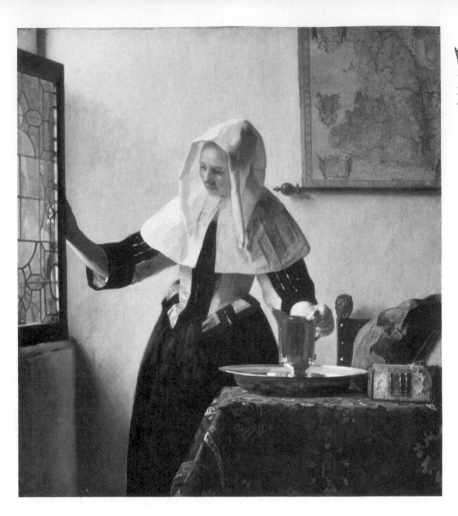

19-54 JAN VERMEER, *Young Woman with a Water Jug*, c. 1665. Approx. 18″ × 16″. Metropolitan Museum of Art, New York (gift of Henry G. Marquand, 1889).

19-55 JAN VERMEER, detail of *Young Woman with a Water Jug* (FIG. 19-54).

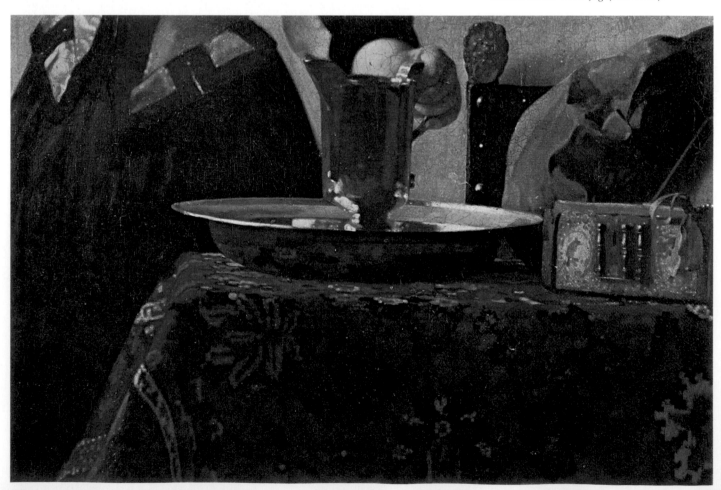

moment of action. The girl may be opening the window to water flowers in a window box outside. This action is insignificant in itself and only one of hundreds performed in the course of a domestic day. Yet Vermeer, in his lighting and composing of the scene, raises it to the level of some holy, sacramental act. The old Netherlandish symbolism that made every ordinary object a religious sign is gone; but this girl's slow, gentle gesture is almost liturgical. The beauty of humble piety, which Rembrandt finds in human faces, is here extended to a quite different context. The Protestant world, renouncing magnificent churches, finds a sanctuary in a modest room illuminated by an afternoon sun. Yet the light is not the mysterious, spiritual light that falls on the face in a Rembrandt portrait, an outward manifestation of the "inner light" of grace stressed in Protestant mysticism; it is ordinary daylight, observed with a keenness of vision unparalleled—unless we think of Velázquez—in the history of art.

Vermeer is master of pictorial light and so comprehends its functions that it is completely in the service of the artist's intention, which is to render a lighted depth so faithfully that the picture surface is but an invisible glass through which we look immediately into the constructed illusion. We know that Vermeer made use of mirrors and of the *camera obscura*—an ancestor of the modern camera in which a tiny pinhole, acting as a lens, projected an image on a screen or the wall of a room (or, in later versions, on a ground-glass wall of a box, the opposite wall of which contained the pinhole). This does not mean Vermeer merely copied the image; these aids helped him to obtain results that he reworked compositionally, arranging his figures and the furniture of the room in a beautiful stability of quadrilateral shapes that gives his designs a matchless Classical calm and serenity. This quality is enhanced by a color so true to the optical facts and so subtly modulated that it suggests Vermeer was far ahead of his time in color science. A detail of the picture (FIG. 19-55) shows, for one thing, that Vermeer realized that shadows are not colorless and dark, that adjoining colors affect one another,* and that light is composed of colors. Thus, the blue drape is caught as a dark blue on the side of the brass pitcher, and the red of the carpet is modified in the low-intensity gold hue of the basin. It has been recently suggested that Vermeer also perceived the phenomenon photographers call *circles of confusion*, which appear on out-of-focus films; Vermeer could have seen them in images projected by the primitive

lenses of the *camera obscura*. These he approximates in light dabs and touches that, in close view, give the impression of an image slightly "out of focus"; when we draw back a step, however, as if adjusting the lens, the color spots cohere, giving an astonishingly accurate illusion of a third dimension. All of these technical considerations reflect the scientific spirit of the age, but they do not explain the exquisite poetry of form and surface, of color and light, that could come only from the sensitivity of a great artist. In Marcel Proust's *Swann's Way*, the connoisseur hero, trying unsuccessfully to write a monograph on Vermeer, admits that no words could ever do justice to a single patch of sunlight on one of Vermeer's walls.

The "little Dutch masters" treat the humblest objects, which receive their meaning by their association with human uses, as reverently as if they were sacramentals. The Dutch painters of still life isolate these objects as profoundly interesting in themselves, making of their representation both scientific and poetic exercises in the revelation of the functions and the beauties of light. There are many fine examples of Dutch still life, all of which are done with the expertness of the specialist in analytical seeing. A still life by WILLEM KALF (1619–1693) can serve as exemplary of the school (FIG. 19-56). Here, against a dark ground, the artist arranges glass goblets, fruit, a silver salver, and a Turkish carpet, making a rich, luminous counterpoint of absorptive and reflective textures. The glossy, transparent shells of the goblets gleam like night skies with galaxies of sparklets and light filaments, contrasting with the duller highlights that edge the rim of the salver. There is a textural gradation from the glass to the silver, from a lemon to a pomegranate to the muted glow of the light-absorbing Turkish carpet. The luminous flesh of the peeled lemon gleams as if lighted from within. (Oranges, emblem of the ruling House of Orange, occur more frequently in Dutch still life than do lemons.) This little masterpiece shows how this age of seeing must have taken pleasure in the infinite variety of the play of light in the small universe as well as the large. This is not dull imitation; it is revelation of what can be seen if the eye will learn to see it.

The Baroque world discovers the infinite, whether it is the infinitely small or the infinitely great. The spark of light that lifts the rim of a glass out of darkness becomes, when expanded, the sunlit heavens. The globule of dew on a leaf in a Dutch flower painting becomes the aqueous globe of Earth itself. The space that began to open behind the figures of Giotto (FIG. 15-15) now, in Dutch landscape, takes flight into limitless distance, and man dwindles to insignificance—"his time a moment, and a point his place." In some of the works of JACOB VAN RUISDAEL (1628–1682), the human figure does not appear or appears

---

*Due to the phenomenon of *complementary afterimage*, in which, for example, the eye retains briefly a red image of a green stimulus; thus, a white area adjoining a green will appear "warm" (slightly pink), and a blue adjoining the same green will shift toward violet (blue plus the afterimage red).

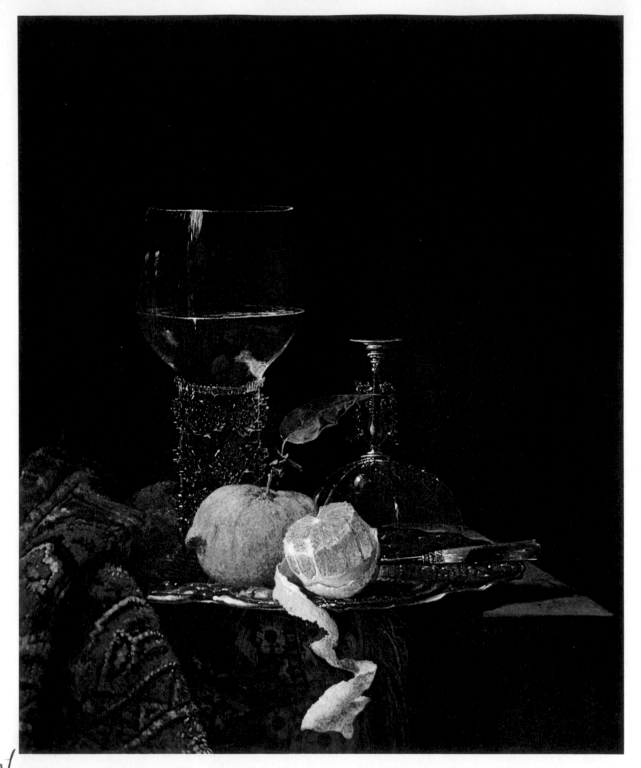

19-56 WILLEM KALF, *Still Life*, 1659. Approx. 20″ × 17″. Royal Picture Gallery (Mauritshuis), the Hague.

only minutely. In *View of Haarlem from the Dunes at Overveen* (FIG. 19-57), he gives us almost a portrait of the newly discovered, infinite universe, allowing the sky to take up two-thirds of the picture space. One of the great landscape painters of all time, Van Ruisdael turns to the vast and moody heavens that loom above the flat dunelands of Holland. His sullen clouds, in great droves never quite scattered by the sun, are herded by the winds that blew the fortunes of Hol-

land's fleets as well as the disasters of the invading sea. Storms are always breaking up or gathering; the earth is always drenched, or about to be. As Rembrandt reads the souls of men in their faces, so Van Ruisdael reads the somber depths of the heavens. No angels swoop through his skies or recline on his clouds, for clouds now are simply water vapor. Like Rembrandt's, his is a "Protestant" reading of nature. The difference between northern and southern Ba-

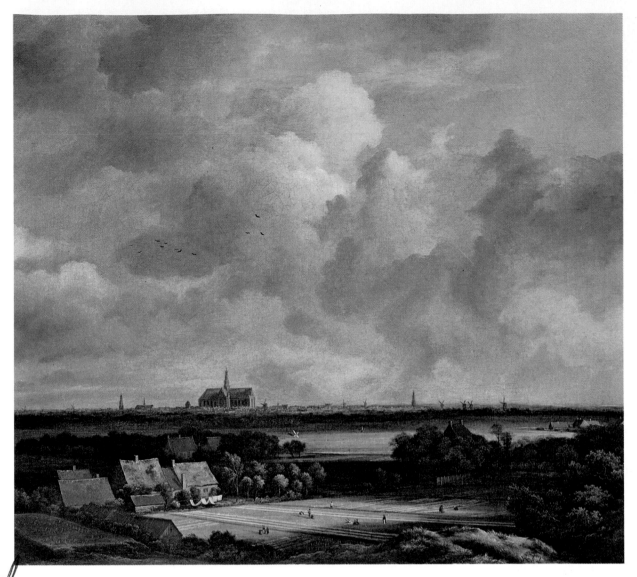

19-57   JACOB VAN RUISDAEL, *View of Haarlem from the Dunes at Overveen,* c. 1670. Approx. 22″ × 25″. Royal Picture Gallery (Mauritshuis), the Hague.

roque is evident at once and completely in a comparison of Pozzo's *Glorification of St. Ignatius* (FIG. 19-32) and Van Ruisdael's *View of Haarlem.* It is the difference between the heavens of Jesuit vision and the heavens of Newton and Leibniz.

FRANCE

In the second half of the seventeenth century, the fortunes of both Holland and Spain sank before those of France, whose "Sun King," Louis XIV, dominated the period of European history between 1660 and 1715. The age of Louis XIV saw the ascendancy of French power in Europe, politically and culturally, and the achievement of an international influence in taste that France has still not entirely lost. The French regard this period as their "golden age"—when Paris began to replace Rome as the art center of Europe; when the French language became the polished instrument of discourse in diplomacy and in the courts of all countries; and when French art and criticism, fashion and etiquette, were imitated universally. Art and architecture came into the service of the king, as once they had been in the service of the Church, and the unity of style so conspicuous in them is the result of the taste of Louis XIV himself—imposed on the whole nation through his able minister Jean Baptiste Colbert and through the new academies Colbert set up to regularize style in all the arts.

The king's taste and, therefore, the taste of France favored a stately and reserved Classicism in place of the lavish and emotional Baroque of Italy and most of the rest of Europe. The severe Classical regularity of form—in the plays of Pierre Corneille and Jean Baptiste Racine, in the Corinthian colonnade of the Louvre (FIG. 19-65), and in the paintings of Nicolas Poussin (FIGS. 19-61 and 19-62)—is exceptional in the age of the Baroque. Even though we can find much that is Baroque in the "Classical" art produced in the time of *le Roi Soleil*, Classicism came to be thought of as standard by the French, and continued to be so for centuries.

Painting

The earlier part of the seventeenth century saw the slow recovery of France from the anarchy of the religious wars. While Cardinals Richelieu and Mazarin painfully rebuilt the power and prestige of the French throne, French art remained under the influence of Italy and Flanders. Even so, artists of originality emerged—for example, GEORGES DE LA TOUR (1593–1652), a painter who learned of Caravaggio possibly through the Dutch School of Utrecht. Much as De la Tour uses the devices of the northern "Caravaggisti," his effects are strikingly different from theirs. His *Lamentation Over St. Sebastian* (FIG. 19-58) shows us the type of night scene favored by that school, as we have seen it in Honthorst (FIG. 19-43). However, De la Tour places the source of illumination (the flaming torch) within the picture and does not shield it. His strong light falls on greatly simplified, almost abstract forms, with no complication of surface, drapery, or texture to deflect or splinter the light and shade. This geometric simplicity of light falling on smooth volumes gives a kind of Classical stability and a calm stillness that—in another place and time—belongs especially to the art of Piero della Francesca (FIG. 16-34). In the *St. Sebastian*, only the light is dramatic; the gestures and attitudes of the figures are coolly understated.

LOUIS LE NAIN (*c.* 1593–1648) bears, with his contemporary, De la Tour, comparison with the Dutch. Subjects that in Dutch painting are an opportunity for boisterous good humor are managed by the French

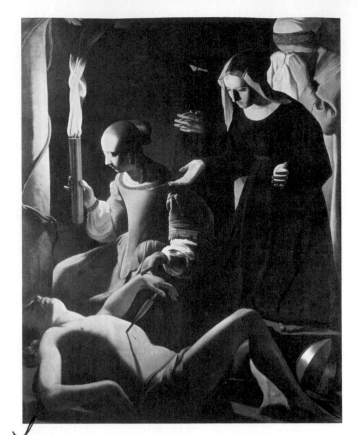

19-58 GEORGES DE LA TOUR, *The Lamentation Over St. Sebastian, c.* 1630 (copy?). Approx. 63″ × 51″. Gemäldegalerie, Staatliche Museen, Berlin-Dahlem.

with a cool stillness. *Family of Country People* (FIG. 19-59) expresses the grave dignity of a family close to the soil, one made stoic and resigned by hardship. Obviously, Le Nain sympathizes with his subjects and seems here to want to emphasize their rustic virtue, far from the gorgeous artificiality of the courts. Stress on the honesty, integrity, and even innocence of un-

19-59 LOUIS LE NAIN, *Family of Country People, c.* 1640. Approx. 44″ × 62″. Louvre, Paris.

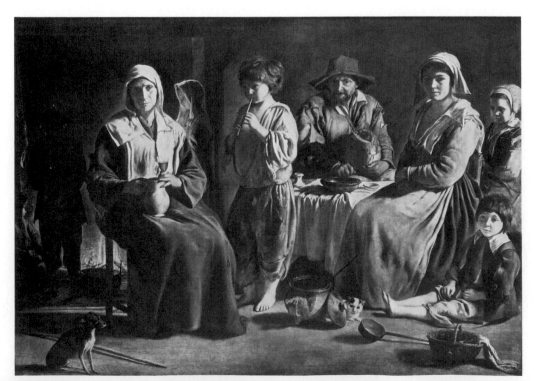

corrupted country folk in the following century will become sentimentality. However, Le Nain's objectivity permits him to record a group of such genuine human beings that the picture rises above anecdote and the picturesqueness of genre. These still, sombre country folk could have had little reason for merriment. The lot of the peasant, never easy, was miserable during the time Le Nain painted. The terrible conflict we call the Thirty Years' War (1618–1648) was raging. The last and most devastating of the wars of religion between Protestants and Catholics, which had begun a century before, spread atrocity and ruin throughout France, Italy, and the Germanies. The anguish and frustration of the peasantry, suffering from the cruel depredations of unruly armies living off the country, often broke out in savage revolts that were savagely put down.

A record of the times appears in a series of etchings by Jacques Callot (1592–1635) called *Miseries of War*. Callot, the first great master of the art of etching, a medium to which he almost exclusively confined himself, was widely influential in his own time and since; Rembrandt was among those who knew and learned from his work. Callot perfected the medium and the technique of etching, developing a very hard surface for the copper plate, to permit fine and precise delineation with the needle. In one small print, he may assemble as many as 1,200 figures, which only close scrutiny can discriminate. His quick, vivid touch and faultless drawing produce a panorama sparkling with sharp details of life—and death. In the *Miseries,* he observes these coolly, presenting without comment things Callot himself must have seen of the wars in his own country, Lorraine. In one etching, he depicts a mass execution by hanging (FIG. 19-60). The unfortunates may be war prisoners, or defeated peasant rebels. The event takes place in the presence of a disciplined army, drawn up on parade, with banners, muskets, and lances, their tents in the right background. Hanged men sway in clusters from the branches of a huge, cross-shaped tree. A monk climbs a ladder, holding up a crucifix to a man, around whose neck the noose is being adjusted. At the foot of the ladder, another victim kneels to receive absolution. Under the tree, men roll dice on a drumhead for the belongings of the executed. (This may be an allusion, in the Baroque manner, to the soldiers who cast lots for the garments of the crucified Christ.) In the right foreground, a bound man is consoled by a hooded priest. Callot's *Miseries* are the first realistic, pictorial record of the human disaster of war. They look ahead to Goya's great prints on the same theme (FIG. 21-11).

The brisk animation of Callot's manner contrasts with the quiet composure in the art of De la Tour and Le Nain, his exact contemporaries. Yet although there is calm simplicity and restraint in the latter two, in comparison with other northern painters inspired by Caravaggio, and although these qualities suggest the Classical, it remains for another contemporary, Nicolas Poussin (1594–1665), to establish Classical painting as peculiarly expressive of French taste and genius in the seventeenth century. Poussin, born in Normandy, spent most of his life in Rome. There, inspired by its monuments and the landscape of the Campagna, he produced his grandly severe and regular canvases and carefully worked out a theoretical explanation of his method. He worked for a while under Domenichino but shunned the exuberant Italian Baroque; Titian and Raphael were the models that he set for himself. Of his two versions of a single theme—titled *Et in Arcadia Ego* ("I, too, in Arcadia" or

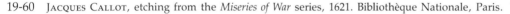

19-60 Jacques Callot, etching from the *Miseries of War* series, 1621. Bibliothèque Nationale, Paris.

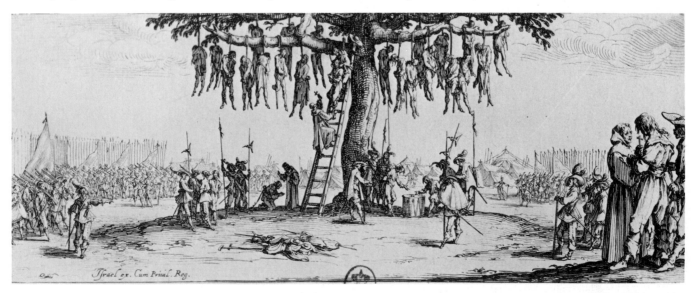

"Even in Arcadia, I [am present]")—the earlier is strikingly Titianesque, with all the warm, rich tonality of the Venetian master and the figure types familiar in Titian's idyllic "bacchanals." But, in the end, the rational order and stability of Raphael proved most appealing to Poussin. His second version of *Et in Arcadia Ego* (FIG. 19-61) shows what he learned from Raphael, as well as directly from antique statuary; landscape, of which Poussin became increasingly fond, expands in the picture, reminiscent of Titian but also indicative of Poussin's own study of nature. The theme is somewhat obscure and of interest to modern scholars. As three shepherds living in the idyllic land of Arcadia spell out an enigmatic inscription on a tomb, a stately female figure quietly places her hand on the shoulder of one of them. She may be the spirit of death, reminding these mortals, as does the inscription, that death is found even in Arcadia, where naught but perfect happiness is supposed to reign. The compact, balanced grouping of the figures, the even light, and the thoughtful, reserved, elegiac mood set the tone for Poussin's art in its later, Classical phase.

In notes for an intended treatise on painting, Poussin outlines the "grand manner" of Classicism, of which he became the leading exponent in Rome. One must first of all choose great subjects: " . . . the first requirement, fundamental to all others, is that the subject and the narrative be grandiose, such as bat-tles, heroic actions, and religious themes." Minute details should be avoided, as well as all "low" subjects, like genre ("Those who choose base subjects find refuge in them because of the feebleness of their talents"). This rules out a good deal of both the decorative and realistic art of the Baroque, and will lead to a doctrinaire limitation on artistic enterprise and experiment in the rules of the French Royal Academy, which, under Charles le Brun in the 1660s, will take Poussin as its greatest modern authority. Although Poussin can create with ease and grandeur within the scope of his rather severe maxims, his method can become wooden and artificial in the hands of academic followers.

Poussin represents that theoretical tradition in Western art that goes back to the Early Renaissance and that asserts that all good art must be the result of good judgment—a judgment based on sure knowledge. In this way, art can achieve correctness and propriety, two of the favorite categories of the classicizing artist or architect. Poussin praises the ancient Greeks for their musical "modes," by which, he says, "they produced marvelous effects." He observes that "this word 'mode' means actually the rule or the measure and form which serves us in our production. This rule constrains us not to exaggerate by making us act in all things with a certain restraint and moderation." "Restraint" and "moderation" are the very essence of French Classical doctrine; in the age of

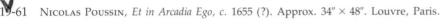

19-61 NICOLAS POUSSIN, *Et in Arcadia Ego*, c. 1655 (?). Approx. 34″ × 48″. Louvre, Paris.

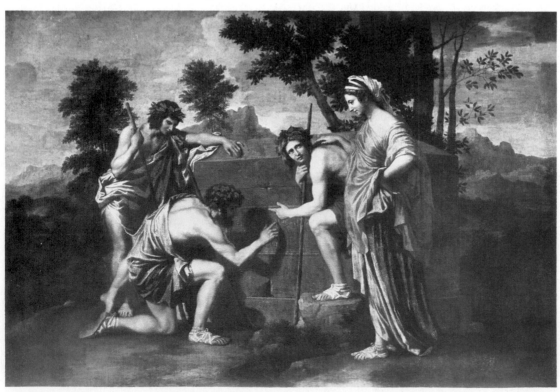

Louis XIV, we find it preached as much for literature and music as for art and architecture. Poussin tells us further that

> The Modes of the ancients were a combination of several things . . . in such a proportion that it was made possible to arouse the soul of the spectator to various passions. . . . the ancient sages attributed to each style its own effects. Because of this they called the Dorian Mode stable, grave, and severe, and applied it to subjects which are grave and severe and full of wisdom.*

Poussin's finest works, like *The Burial of Phocion* (FIG. 19-62), are instances of his obvious preference for the "Dorian Mode." His subjects are chosen carefully from the literature of antiquity, where his age would naturally look for the "grandiose," and it is with Poussin that the visual arts draw closer to literature than ever before. Here, he takes his theme from Plutarch's life of Phocion, an Athenian hero who was unjustly put to death by his countrymen but then given a public funeral and memorialized by the state. In the foreground, Poussin represents the body of the hero being taken away, his burial on Athenian soil having at first been forbidden. The two massive bearers and the bier are starkly isolated in a great landscape that throws them into solitary relief, eloquently

*In E.G. Holt, ed., *Literary Sources of Art History* (Princeton: Princeton University Press, 1947), p. 380.

expressive of the hero abandoned in death. The landscape is composed of interlocking planes that slope upward to the lighted sky at the left, carefully arranged terraces that bear slowly moving streams, shepherds and their flocks, and, in the distance, whole assemblies of solid geometric structures (temples, towers, walls, villas). The skies are untroubled; the light, even and form-revealing. The trees are few and carefully arranged, like curtains lightly drawn back to reveal a nature carefully cultivated as a setting for a single human action. For, unlike Van Ruisdael's *View of Haarlem* (FIG. 19-57), this is not the scene of a particular place and time; it is the construction of an *idea* of a noble landscape to frame a noble theme, as we have seen it in Annibale Carracci's Classical landscape (FIG. 19-30). The *Phocion* landscape is nature subordinated to a rational plan, much like the gardens of Versailles (FIG. 19-67); it is eminently of the "age of reason."

The disciplined, rational art of Poussin, with its sophisticated revelation of the geometry of landscape, is modulated in the softer style of Claude Gellée, called CLAUDE LORRAINE (1600–1682) and sometimes only Claude. Unlike Poussin's pictures, Claude's are not "Dorian." The figures in his landscapes tell no story, point out no moral, praise no hero; indeed, they often appear added as mere excuses for the radiant landscape itself (FIG. 19-63). For Claude, there is essentially one theme: the beauty of a

19-62 NICOLAS POUSSIN, *The Burial of Phocion*, 1648. Approx. 47″ × 70″. Louvre, Paris.

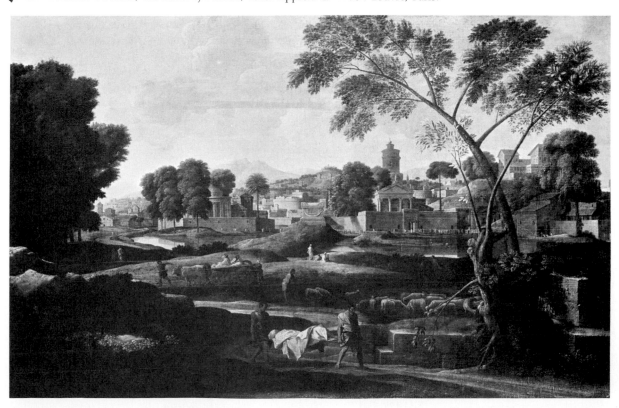

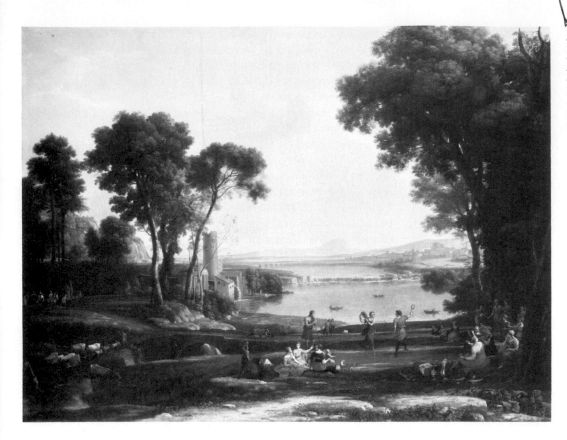

broad sky suffused with the golden light of dawn or sunset that makes its glowing way through a hazy atmosphere. The setting may be a seaport, a wooded dell, watered plains; generally, there are screens of dark trees to the left or right and sometimes at the center, making stage-like wings that intensify the central light. Occasionally, a Classical temple will appear in the cool shadows, and some little idyll will play itself out inconspicuously in the foreground. In essence, Claude seeks to capture the mood of the Italian landscape; like Poussin, he was a French expatriate in Italy and a lover of the broad Campagna, with its romantic ruins. Claude's own pensive and nostalgic mood blends with his setting, and it is his stress on the subjective side of nature that will make his work so popular with the early Romantics at the end of the eighteenth century.

The softening of Poussin's manner (FIG. 19-62) in Claude (FIG. 19-63) is similar to what appears in the work of other painters of the time, who reacted against the severe rules and regulations of the French Royal Academy, under the dictatorial administration of Le Brun. Established in 1648, the Academy had been intended to free artists from the constraints of the old guild system of art training, to improve the social status of painters and sculptors as more than mere handicraftsmen, to regularize instruction in the arts, and to centralize art production in the interest of the absolute monarchy. Above all, the institution of the Academy was to develop and propagate a Classi-

cal taste, based on the study and imitation of ancient works of art and such classicizing modern masters as Raphael, the Carracci, and Poussin himself. Students were taught the supremacy of drawing over coloring, of sculpturesque form over painterly tonality, of symmetrical and closed composition over the dynamic and open—in short, the superiority of Poussin over Rubens. Yet well before the end of the century, the painting of Rubens was increasingly admired, and his influence would weaken the doctrine of the Academy and shape the taste of eighteenth-century Rococo.

Architecture and Sculpture

In architecture, as in painting, France maintained an attitude of cautious selectivity toward the Italian Baroque. The Classical bent early asserted itself in the work of FRANÇOIS MANSART (1598–1666), as seen in the Orléans wing of the Château de Blois (FIG. 19-64), built between 1635 and 1638. Here are the polished dignity and sobriety that will become the hallmarks of French "classical-baroque," in contrast with the more daring, excited, and fanciful styles of the Baroque in Italy and elsewhere. The strong, rectilinear organization and a tendency to design in terms of repeated units remind us of Italian Renaissance architecture, as does the insistence on the purity of line and sharp relief of the wall articulations. Yet the emphasis on a focal point—achieved through the curving colonnades, the changing planes of the walls, and the

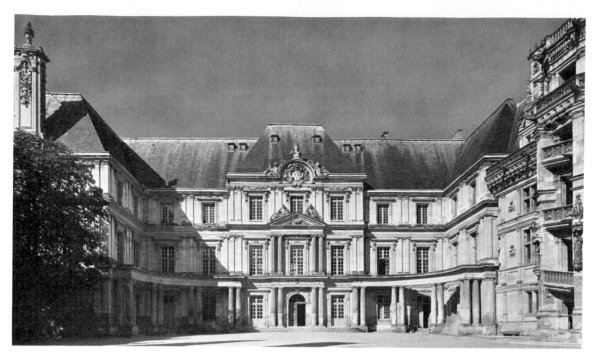

19-64 FRANÇOIS MANSART, Orléans wing of the Château de Blois, France, 1635–1638.

concentration of ornament around the portal—is characteristic of Baroque architectural thinking in general.

The formation of the French Classical style accelerated with the foundation of the Royal Academy of Painting and Sculpture in 1648, of which Poussin was a director, and with the determination of Louis XIV and Colbert to organize art and architecture in service of the state. No pains were spared to raise great symbols and monuments to the king's absolute power and to regularize taste under the academies. The first project undertaken by the young king and Colbert was the closing of the east side of the Louvre court, left incomplete by Lescot in the sixteenth century. Bernini, as the most renowned architect of his day, was summoned from Rome to submit plans, but he envisioned an Italian palace on a monumental scale that would have involved the demolition of all previous work. His plan rejected, Bernini returned to Rome in high indignation. The east façade of the Louvre (FIG. 19-65) is the result of a collaboration between CLAUDE PERRAULT (1613–1688), LOUIS LE VAU (1612–1670), and CHARLES LE BRUN (1619–1690), with Le Vau probably taking a preponderant part, and is a

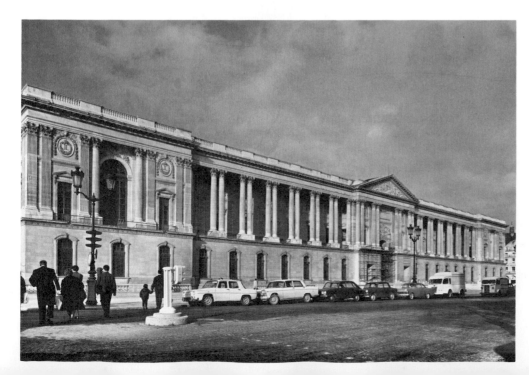

19-65 CLAUDE PERRAULT, LOUIS LE VAU, and CHARLES LE BRUN, east façade of the Louvre, Paris, 1667–1670.

brilliant adjustment of French and Italian Classical elements, culminating in a new and definitive formula. The French pavilion system is retained; the central pavilion is in the form of a Classical temple front, and a giant colonnade of paired columns, resembling the columned flanks of a temple folded out like wings, is contained by the two salient pavilions at either end. The whole is mounted on a stately basement, or podium; an even roof line, balustraded and broken only by the central pediment, replaces the traditional French pyramidal roof. All memory of Gothic verticality is brushed aside in the emphatically horizontal sweep of this façade. Its stately proportions and monumentality are both an expression of the new official French taste and a symbol for centrally organized authority.

Work on the Louvre had hardly begun when Louis XIV decided to convert a royal hunting lodge at Versailles, a few miles outside Paris, into a great palace. A veritable army of architects, decorators, sculptors, painters, and landscape architects was assembled under the general management of former Poussin student Le Brun, the king's impresario of art and dictator of the Royal Academy. In their hands, the conversion of a simple hunting lodge into the Palace of Versailles became the greatest architectural project of the age (FIGS. 19-66 and 19-67).

Planned on a gigantic scale, the project called not only for a large palace facing a vast park but also for the construction of a satellite city to house court and government officials, military and guard detachments, courtiers, and servants. This town is laid out to the east of the palace along three radial avenues that converge on the palace; their axes, in a symbolic assertion of the ruler's absolute power over his domains, intersect in the king's bedroom. (As the site of the king's morning levée, this bedroom was actually an audience room, a state chamber.) The palace itself, over a quarter of a mile long, is placed at right angles to the dominant east–west axis that runs through city and park. Its most impressive feature is the garden façade (FIG. 19-68), begun by Le Vau and continued in his style by JULES HARDOUIN-MANSART (1646–1708), a great-nephew of François who took over the project after Le Vau's death in 1670. In typical Baroque fashion, the vast lateral extension of the façade has been broken up into units and subunits of threes, an effective organizational device even on this scale.

Careful attention has been paid to every detail of the extremely rich decoration of the palace's interior; everything from wall paintings to doorknobs was designed in keeping with the whole and executed with the very finest sense of craftsmanship. Of the literally hundreds of rooms within the palace, the most famous is the Galerie des Glaces, or Hall of Mirrors (FIG. 19-69), which overlooks the park from the second floor and extends along most of the width of the central block. Although deprived of its original sumptuous furniture, which included gold and silver chairs and bejeweled trees, it retains much of its

19-66 Aerial view of the Palace of Versailles and a small portion of the surrounding park. The white trapezoid in the lower part of the plan (FIG. 19-67) outlines the area shown here.

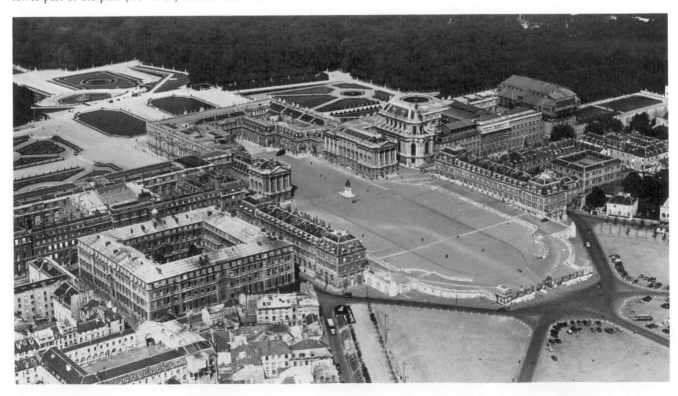

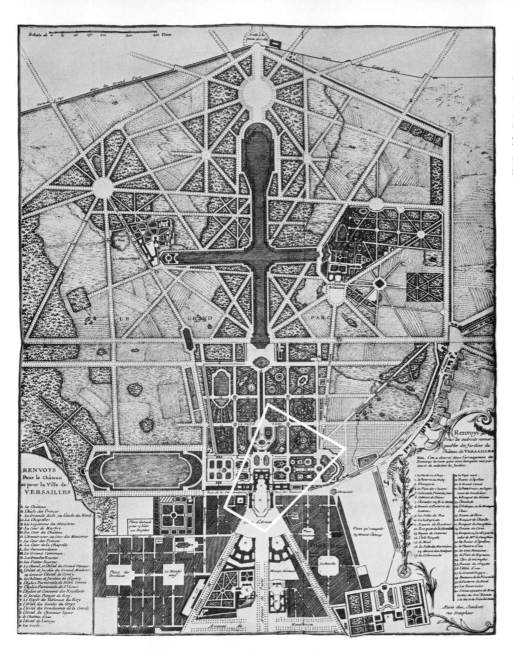

19-67 Plan (after a seventeenth-century engraving by FRANÇOIS BLONDEL) of the Palace of Versailles and related buildings, ANDRÉ LE NÔTRE's vast surrounding park (1661–1668), and a portion of the town of Versailles. The area outlined in the white trapezoid (lower center) is shown in FIG. 19-66.

19-68 LOUIS LE VAU and JULES HARDOUIN-MANSART, garden façade of the Palace of Versailles, France, 1669–1685.

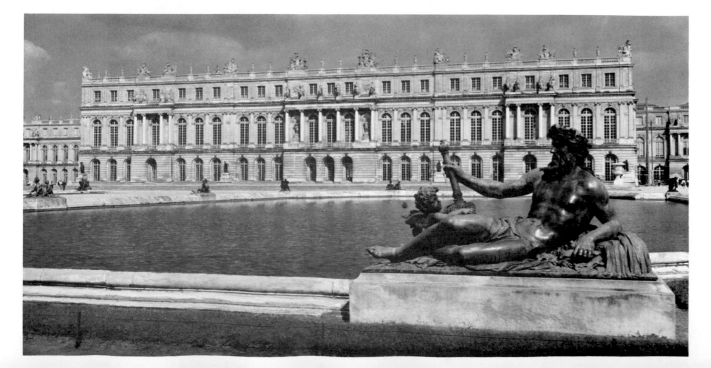

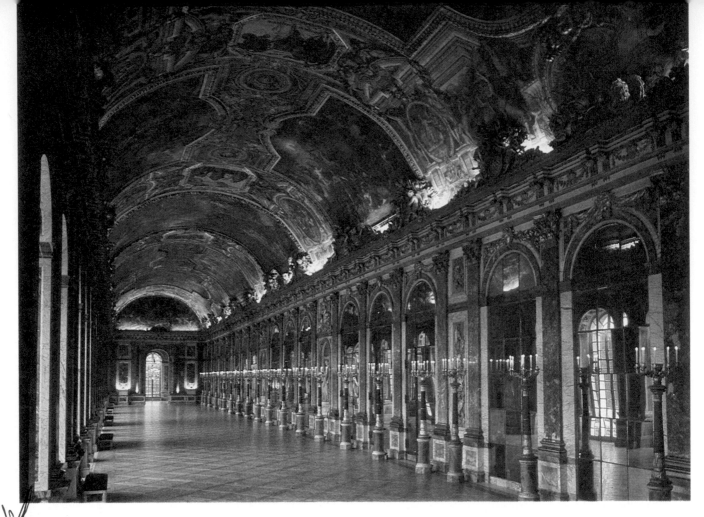

19-69 JULES HARDOUIN-MANSART and CHARLES LE BRUN, Galerie des Glaces, Palace of Versailles, *c.* 1680.

splendor today. Its tunnel-like quality is alleviated by hundreds of mirrors, which, set into the wall opposite the windows, illusionistically extend the width of the room. The mirror, that ultimate source of illusion, was a favorite element of Baroque interior design; here, it must have harmonized as it augmented the flashing splendors of the great festivals of which Louis XIV was so fond.

The enormous palace might appear unbearably ostentatious, were it not for its extraordinary setting in the vast park to which it becomes almost an adjunct. The Galerie des Glaces, itself a giant perspective, is dwarfed by the sweeping vista (seen from its windows) down the park's tree-lined central axis and across terraces, lawns, pools, and lakes toward the horizon. The park of Versailles (FIG. 19-67), designed by ANDRÉ LE NÔTRE (1613–1700), must rank as one of man's greatest works of art—not only in size, but also in concept. Here, an entire forest has been transformed into a park. Although the geometric plan may appear stiff and formal, the park, in fact, offers an almost unlimited variety of vistas, as Le Nôtre utilized not only the multiplicity of natural forms but also the slightly rolling contours of the terrain with

19-70 JULES HARDOUIN-MANSART, Royal Chapel of the Palace of Versailles, 1698–1710. (Ceiling decorations by ANTOINE COYPEL.)

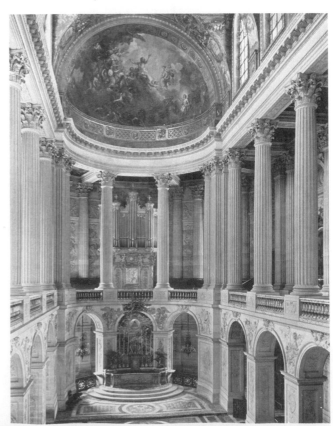

stunning effectiveness. A rational transition from the frozen forms of the architecture to the living ones of nature is provided by the formal gardens near the palace. Here, tightly designed geometric units are defined by the elegant forms of trimmed shrubs and hedges, each one different from its neighbor and having a focal point in the form of a sculptured group, a pavilion, a reflecting pool, or perhaps a fountain. Farther away from the palace, the design becomes looser as trees, in shadowy masses, screen or frame views into bits of open countryside. All vistas are carefully composed for maximum effect. Dark and light, formal and informal, dense growth and open meadows—all are played off against each other in unending combinations and variations. No photograph or series of photographs can reveal the full richness of the design; the park unfolds itself only to the person who actually walks through it. In this respect, it is a temporal work of art; its aspects change with time and with the relative position of the observer.

As a symbol of the power of absolutism, Versailles is unsurpassed. It also expresses, in the most monumental terms of its age, the rationalistic creed, based on the mathematical philosophy of Descartes, that all knowledge must be systematic and all science must be the consequence of the imposition of the intellect on matter. The whole stupendous design of Versailles proudly proclaims the mastery of human intelligence over the disorderliness of nature.

On the garden façade of Versailles, Hardouin-Mansart follows the style of his predecessor, Le Vau. When commissioned to add a Royal Chapel to the palace in 1698, he was in a position to give full play to his talents. The interior of the chapel (FIG. 19-70) is a masterful synthesis of Classical and Baroque elements. It is essentially a rectangular building with an apse as high as the nave, which gives the fluid central space a curved Baroque quality. But the light entering through the large clerestory windows lacks the directed, dramatic effect of the Italian Baroque and illuminates the precisely chiseled details of the interior brightly and evenly. Pier-supported arcades carry a majestic row of Corinthian columns that define the royal gallery, the back of which is occupied by the royal pew, accessible directly from the king's apartments. The decoration is restrained and, in fact, only the illusionistic ceiling decorations, added in 1708–1709 by ANTOINE COYPEL, can be called Baroque without reservation. Throughout the architecture, Baroque tendencies are severely checked by Classicism.

Although checked, they are not entirely suppressed in Hardouin-Mansart's masterwork, the Église de Dôme, Church of the Invalides in Paris (FIGS. 19-71 and 19-72). An intricately composed domed square of great scale, it is attached to the veterans' hospital set

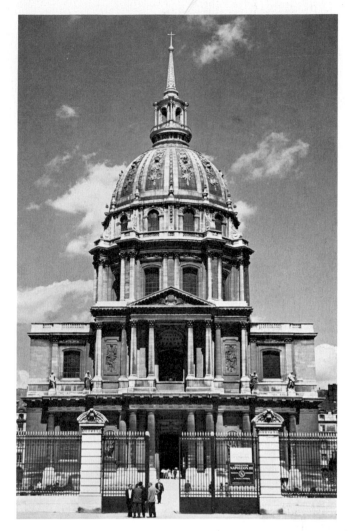

19-71 JULES HARDOUIN-MANSART, Église de Dôme, Church of the Invalides, Paris, 1676–1706.

up by Louis XIV for the disabled soldiers of his many wars. The frontispiece is composed of two firmly separated levels, the upper pedimented; the grouping of the orders and the bays they frame is not unlike that in Italian Baroque. The compact façade is low and narrow in relation to the vast drum and dome, for which it seems to serve simply as a base. The overpowering dome, conspicuous on the skyline of Paris, is itself expressive of the Baroque love for dramatic magnitude. The way that its design aims for theatrical effects of light and space is especially Baroque. The dome is built of three shells, the lowest cut off so that the visitor looks up through it to the next above, which is painted illusionistically with an apotheosis of St. Louis, patron of France. This second dome—filled with light from hidden windows in the third, outermost dome—creates an impression of the open, limitless space and brightness of the heavens. Below, the building is only dimly illuminated and is de-

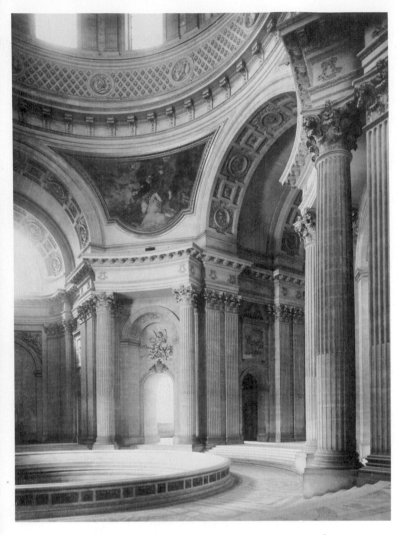

19-72 JULES HARDOUIN-MANSART, interior of the Église de Dôme, Church of the Invalides.

signed in a Classicism only less severe than that of the Escorial (FIG. 18-58). The rapid vertical gradation from the austerely membered masses below to the ethereal light and space above is Baroque through and through. Yet we feel here the dominance of the Classical style in substance, despite the soaring illusion for which it serves as a setting.

The stylistic dialogue between Classicism and the Italian Baroque in seventeenth-century French sculpture also ends with the former's victory. The strained dramatic and emotional qualities in the work of PIERRE PUGET (1620–1694) were not at all to the taste of the court. His *Milo of Crotona* (FIG. 19-73) represents the powerful ancient hero, his hand trapped in a split stump, helpless before the attacking lion. There is nothing here of heroic idealism; with physical and psychic realism, Puget presents a study of immediate and excruciating agony. This ran counter to the official taste dictated by the king and Le Brun, and, although Puget was very briefly in vogue, the most original French sculptor of his time never found acceptance at the court.

Much more fortunate was FRANÇOIS GIRARDON (1628–1715), who admirably adjusted his style to the taste of his sponsors. His *Apollo Attended by the Nymphs* (FIG. 19-74) was designed as a tableau group for the Grotto of Thetis in the gardens of Versailles. (The arrangement of the figures was slightly altered when the group was moved to a different grotto in the eighteenth century.) Both stately and graceful, the nymphs have a compelling charm as they minister to the god–king at the end of the day. The style of the figures is heavily conditioned by the artist's close study of Hellenistic sculpture, the central figure imitating the ancient Apollo Belvedere in the Vatican; the arrangement is inspired by Poussin's figure compositions (FIG. 19-61). And if this combination did not suffice, the group's rather florid reference to Louis XIV as the "god of the sun" was bound to assure its success at the court. Girardon's style and symbolism were found to be ideally suited to the glorification of royal majesty.

19-73 PIERRE PUGET, *Milo of Crotona*, 1671–1682. Marble, approx. 8' 10" high. Louvre, Paris.

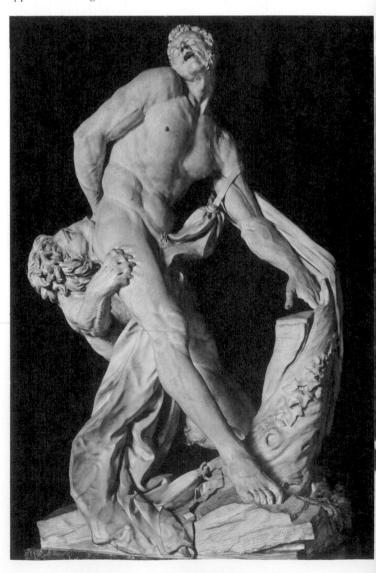

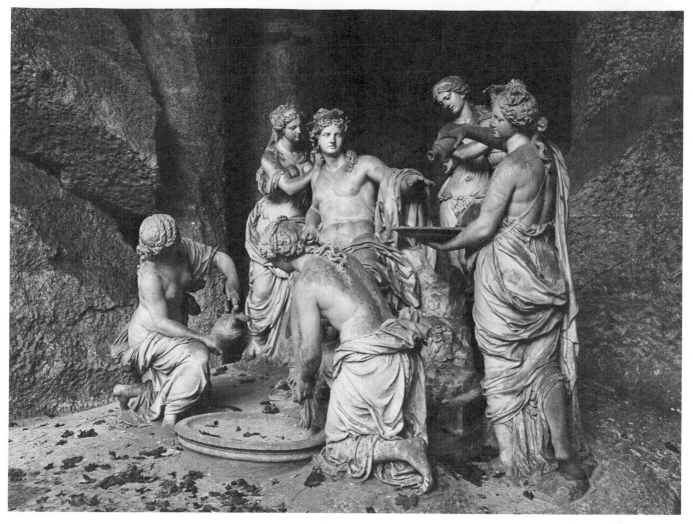

19-74   FRANÇOIS GIRARDON, *Apollo Attended by the Nymphs, c.* 1666–1672. Marble, life-size. Park of Versailles, France.

ENGLAND

English art has been mentioned little since the Middle Ages because, except for its architecture, England is outside the main artistic streams of the Renaissance and the Baroque periods. It is as if the English genius were occupied enough with its prodigious creation in dramatic literature, lyric poetry, and music, and not, after all, particularly suited to the purely visual arts. Not until the eighteenth century does England develop an important native school of painting and extend its distinguished architectural tradition.

Gothic practices lived on in English, as in French, building, long after Renaissance architects in Italy struck out in new directions. During the sixteenth century, the English made minor concessions to Italian architectural ideas. Classical ornament appeared frequently in the decoration of buildings, and there was a distinct trend toward more regular and symmetrical planning. But not until the early seventeenth century did England wholeheartedly accept the prin-

ciples that govern Italian architectural thinking. The revolution in English building was primarily the work of one man, INIGO JONES (1573–1652), surveyor (architect) to James I and Charles I. Jones spent considerable time in Italy. He disliked Michelangelo's work as intensely as he admired Palladio's, whose treatise on architecture he studied with great care. From the stately palaces and villas of Palladio, Jones selected certain motifs and systems of proportions to use as the basis of his own architectural designs. The nature of his achievement is evident in the Banqueting House at Whitehall (FIG. 19-75). The structure, a symmetrical block of great clarity and dignity, superimposes two orders in the form of columns in the center and pilasters near the ends. The balustraded roof line, uninterrupted in its horizontal sweep, anticipates the Louvre façade (FIG. 19-65) by more than 40 years. There is almost nothing here that Palladio would not have recognized and approved, but the

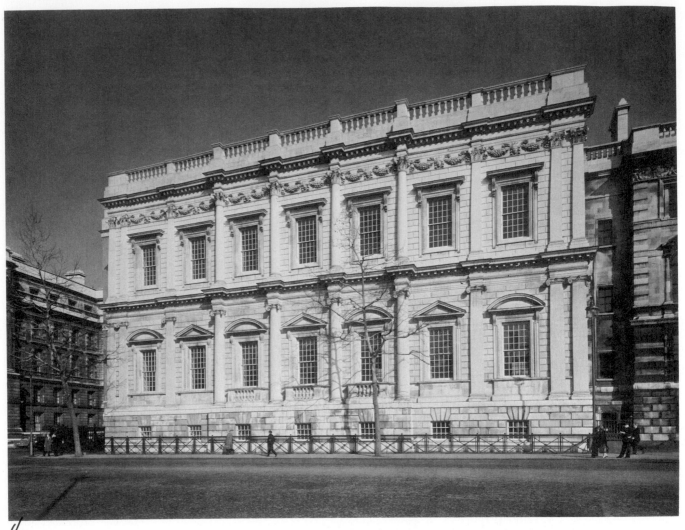

19-75   INIGO JONES, Banqueting House at Whitehall, London, 1619–1622. British Crown Copyright.

building as a whole is no copy. While working within the architectural vocabulary and syntax of the revered Italian, Jones retains his own independence as a designer, and, for two centuries, his influence will be almost as authoritative in English architecture as Palladio's. It is noteworthy that Jones' interior at Whitehall is adorned with paintings by Rubens, in a fruitful collaboration recalling the combination of painting by Veronese and architecture by Palladio in northern Italian villas.

Until almost the present day, the dominant feature of the London skyline has been the majestic dome of St. Paul's (FIG. 19-76), the work of England's most renowned architect, CHRISTOPHER WREN (1632–1723). A mathematical genius and skilled engineer, whose work won the praise of Isaac Newton, Wren began as a professor of astronomy and took an amateur's interest in architecture. Asked by Charles II to prepare a plan for the restoration of the old Gothic church of St. Paul, he proposed to remodel the building "after a good Roman manner" rather than "to follow the

Gothic rudeness of the old design." Within a few months, the Great Fire of London in 1666, which destroyed the old structure and many churches in the city, gave Wren his opportunity. He built not only the new St. Paul's but numerous other churches as well. Wren was a Baroque virtuoso of many talents, the archetype of whom we see in Bernini. He was strongly influenced by the work of Jones, but he also traveled in France, where he must have been much impressed by the splendid palaces and state buildings being created in and around Paris at the time of the competition for the Louvre design. Wren must also have closely studied prints illustrating Baroque architecture in Italy, for Palladian, French, and Italian Baroque features are harmonized in St. Paul's. In view of its size, the cathedral was built with remarkable speed—in a little over 30 years—and Wren lived to see it completed. The form of the building was constantly refined as it went up, and the final appearance of the towers was not determined until after 1700. The splendid skyline composition, with the two fore-

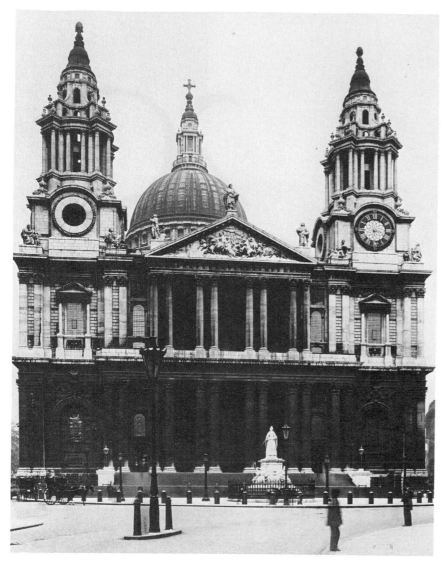

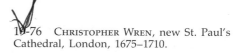

ground towers acting so effectively as foils to the great dome, must have been suggested to Wren by similar schemes devised by Italian architects to solve the problem of the façade–dome relation of St. Peter's in Rome (FIGS. 17-34 and 19-4). Perhaps Borromini's solution at Sant' Agnese in Piazza Navona influenced him. Certainly, the upper levels and lanterns of the towers are Borrominesque, the lower levels are Palladian, and the superposed, paired columnar porticoes remind us of the Louvre façade. Wren's skillful eclecticism brings all of these foreign features into a monumental unity.

Wren's designs for the city churches are masterpieces of Baroque planning ingenuity. His task was never easy, for the churches often had to be fitted into small, irregular areas. Wren worked out a rich variety of schemes to meet awkward circumstances. In designing the exteriors of the churches, he concentrated his attention on the towers—the one element of the structure that would set the building apart from its crowding neighbors. The skyline of London, as left by Wren, is punctuated with such towers, which will serve as prototypes for later buildings both in England and in colonial America.

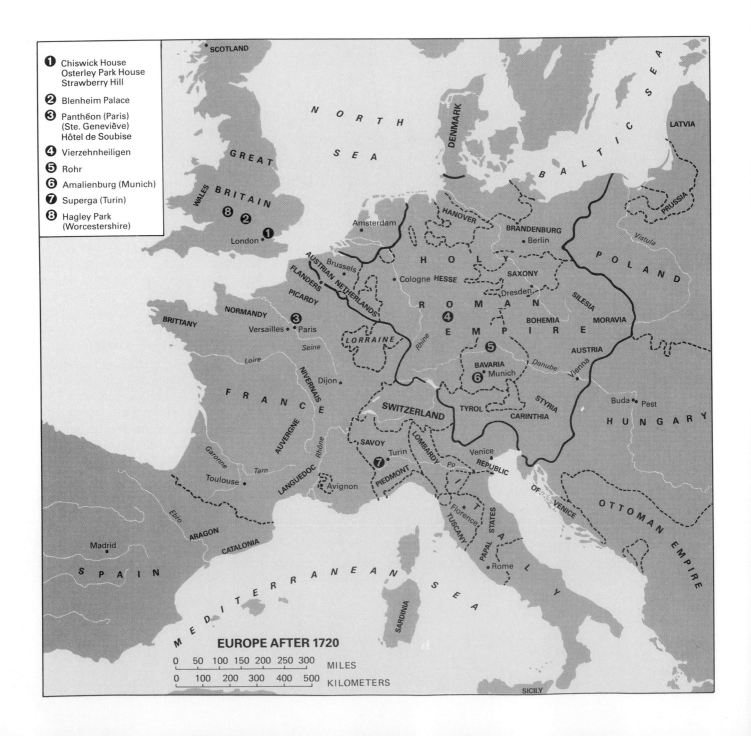

1 Chiswick House
Osterley Park House
Strawberry Hill

2 Blenheim Palace

3 Panthéon (Paris)
(Ste. Geneviève)
Hôtel de Soubise

4 Vierzehnheiligen

5 Rohr

6 Amalienburg (Munich)

7 Superga (Turin)

8 Hagley Park
(Worcestershire)

SCOTLAND

NORTH SEA

DENMARK

BALTIC SEA

LATVIA

GREAT BRITAIN

WALES

PRUSSIA

Vistula

POLAND

HANOVER

BRANDENBURG

Amsterdam

Berlin

HOLY

SAXONY

AUSTRIAN NETHERLANDS

Brussels

Cologne HESSE

Dresden

FLANDERS

PICARDY

ROMAN

SILESIA

MORAVIA

BOHEMIA

NORMANDY

BRITTANY

LORRAINE

Rhine

EMPIRE

AUSTRIA

3

Versailles Paris

4

5

Seine

BAVARIA

Munich

Danube

Vienna

Loire

6

NIVERNAIS

Dijon

STYRIA

Buda Pest

FRANCE

AUVERGNE

Rhône

SWITZERLAND

TYROL

CARINTHIA

HUNGARY

SAVOY

LOMBARDY

Venice

Garonne

Tarn

7

Turin

Po

REPUBLIC

OF VENICE

LANGUEDOC

Toulouse

Avignon

PIEDMONT

OTTOMAN EMPIRE

I

Ebro

Florence

T

Madrid

ARAGON

TUSCANY

PAPAL STATES

A

CATALONIA

L

Y

Rome

SPAIN

MEDITERRANEAN SEA

SARDINIA

EUROPE AFTER 1720

| 0 | 50 | 100 | 150 | 200 | 250 | 300 | | MILES |

| 0 | 100 | 200 | 300 | 400 | 500 | KILOMETERS |

SICILY

THE EIGHTEENTH CENTURY: ROCOCO AND THE RISE OF ROMANTICISM

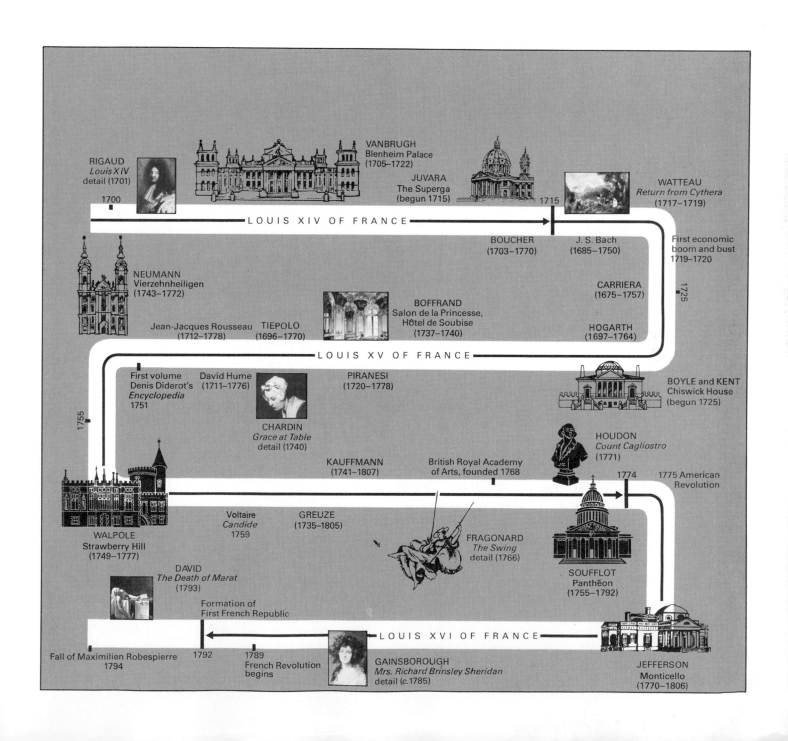

RIGAUD
Louis XIV
detail (1701)

1700

VANBRUGH
Blenheim Palace
(1705–1722)

JUVARA
The Superga
(begun 1715)

1715

WATTEAU
Return from Cythera
(1717–1719)

LOUIS XIV OF FRANCE

BOUCHER
(1703–1770)

J. S. Bach
(1685–1750)

First economic
boom and bust
1719–1720

NEUMANN
Vierzehnheiligen
(1743–1772)

CARRIERA
(1675–1757)

1725

Jean-Jacques Rousseau
(1712–1778)

TIEPOLO
(1696–1770)

BOFFRAND
Salon de la Princesse,
Hôtel de Soubise
(1737–1740)

HOGARTH
(1697–1764)

LOUIS XV OF FRANCE

First volume
Denis Diderot's
Encyclopedia
1751

David Hume
(1711–1776)

PIRANESI
(1720–1778)

BOYLE and KENT
Chiswick House
(begun 1725)

1755

CHARDIN
Grace at Table
detail (1740)

KAUFFMANN
(1741–1807)

British Royal Academy
of Arts, founded 1768

HOUDON
Count Cagliostro
(1771)

1774

1775 American
Revolution

Voltaire
Candide
1759

GREUZE
(1735–1805)

FRAGONARD
The Swing
detail (1766)

WALPOLE
Strawberry Hill
(1749–1777)

SOUFFLOT
Panthéon
(1755–1792)

DAVID
The Death of Marat
(1793)

Formation of
First French Republic

LOUIS XVI OF FRANCE

Fall of Maximilien Robespierre
1794

1792

1789
French Revolution
begins

GAINSBOROUGH
Mrs. Richard Brinsley Sheridan
detail (c. 1785)

JEFFERSON
Monticello
(1770–1806)

THE EIGHTEENTH CENTURY has a dual character; its two parts correspond chronologically to an earlier and a later stage. The earlier is a simple continuation of the Baroque seventeenth century, with a number of distinctive differences; the later, a more-or-less abrupt break onto a new scene. The new scene belongs to the modern world and may be regarded as a kind of overture to it. The present chapter, in its title and arrangement, reflects this division. However, a brief view of the century as a whole can be useful.

The political world takes new shapes in the eighteenth century. This is the century of the rise to great power of the maritime British empire and its disputes with France over the continent of North America and the subcontinent of India. Against the awkward and shaky Holy Roman (later Austrian) Empire rises the small but aggressive state of Prussia, soon to become a significant military power. Farther to the east looms the unsuspected might of half-Asiatic Russia, accelerating its slow turn toward the West under Peter the Great. Spain is sunk in decadence; Italy, a jumble of properties owned by the great powers. The real domain of the once-universal Church is confined to a narrow strip of territory in Italy called the "States of the Church"; elsewhere the State controls, and the Church is subordinate to the sovereign.

New ideas are being propagated that will attack both Church and State—democratic ideas of the freedom and equality of all men. "Enlightened" monarchs cultivate outspoken men like Voltaire, who call for reforms of old abuses and for limitations on the privileges of monarchy, aristocracy, and clergy. Reason and common sense are put forth as the real remedies of human ills; progress, as a law of human development. In France, Diderot and the "philosophes" publish an *Encyclopedia* of human knowledge to instruct all mankind. In the eighteenth century, it is as if all Europe is waiting breathlessly for the tremendous revolutions to come. For the great changes that will make the modern world are in preparation—not only the political, social, and economic revolutions, but, perhaps of even greater importance for the entire globe, the technological and industrial revolutions. Following rapidly on the Newtonian laws that reinterpret physical nature as mechanically (rather than spiritually or organically) constituted, come important advances from the emerging natural sciences concerning the nature of such phenomena as electricity, combustion (and, as a concomitant, oxygen), and living matter. But most important (for its immediate application) is the development of steam power and its enormous significance as a substitute for human labor. The invention of steam engines for production and, later, for transportation begins in England, the scene of the primitive phase of the still-expanding machine age. The environment of England, and then of Europe, will be utterly transformed in this age of steam, of coal and oil, of iron and steel.

The political, economic, and social consequences will be tremendous. The era of industrial capital and labor will be born. The system of production in factories, where the new steam engines are housed, will create an urban working class and, with it, the social antagonisms of the nineteenth century. The merchant rich will become the captains of industry, demanding production and trade free of government regulation, as well as participation in the fiscal decisions of government. Later in the century, democracy and free trade will be the animating principles of political revolutions. Ideas and institutions originating at this time (around 1750) are still with us; the era we call "modern" begins.

While these great forces of change are gathering momentum, older patterns of life and society are obscuring their emergence. Between the death of Louis XIV (1715) and about 1750 is a period of relative relaxation after the exhausting "world" wars waged by the great kings; although wars continue to be fought, they are of the nature of balancing maneuvers among the various states and are waged by professionals with a kind of chessboard formality. The ruling aristocracies, as if conscious of their waning historical significance, gradually abandon their administrative—even executive—functions to men of the ambitious "third estate"—the increasingly wealthy and influential middle class. Without fully realizing it, royalty and nobility are slowly becoming obsolete, although the latter, stubbornly insisting on their ancient privileges, will help to precipitate the French Revolution. Still, in this time, they remain the patrons of the arts, and the arts express to a remarkable degree the philosophy of the aristocracy in decline. Life for the aristocracy is simply the pursuit of pleasure, the escape from boredom. Art is luxurious, frivolous, sensual, clever; the great religious and Classical themes of the Baroque, presented in the grand manner of the masters, are forgotten. Intricate and witty artifice is the objective in all the arts—drama, music, painting, sculpture.

EARLY EIGHTEENTH CENTURY: LATE BAROQUE AND ROCOCO

All Europe breathed a sigh of relief at the death of Louis XIV in 1715. The court of Versailles was at once abandoned for the pleasures of town society, and the *hôtels* (town houses) of Paris became the centers of the style we call Rococo—the reaction to the style of

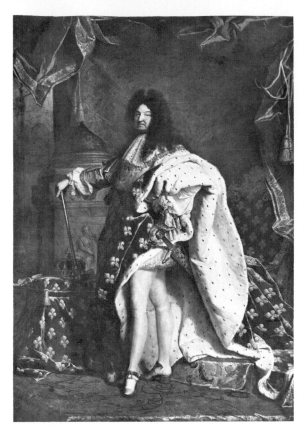

20-1 HYACINTHE RIGAUD, *Louis XIV*, 1701. Approx. 9′ 2″ × 6′ 3″. Louvre, Paris.

20-2 ANTOINE WATTEAU, *L'Indifférent*, c. 1716. Approx. 10″ × 7″. Louvre, Paris.

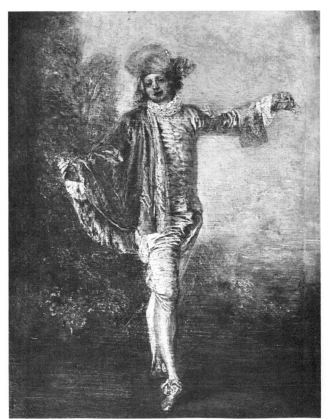

Louis XIV. With respect to this change, it has been well said that the seventeenth century ends with a portrait of a king and the eighteenth century begins with a portrait of a clown. HYACINTHE RIGAUD's portrait of *Louis XIV* (FIG. 20-1) set side by side with ANTOINE WATTEAU's *L'Indifférent* (FIG. 20-2) illustrates the contrast of the periods exactly. On the one hand is pompous majesty in slow and stately promenade, as if reviewing throngs of bowing courtiers at Versailles; on the other is a languid, gliding dancer, whose mincing minuet might also mimic the monarch's solemn pacing. In the first, stout architecture, banner-like curtains, flowing ermine, and fleur-de-lis exalt the king, while fanfares of trumpets blast; in the second, the dancer, to the silken sound of strings, moves in a rainbow shimmer of color from the wings onto the stage of the comic opera. The portrait of the king is very large, the "portrait" of the "clown," quite small. The first is Baroque; the second, Rococo.

Architecture

Late Baroque and Rococo overlap and interpenetrate in the early decades of the century, although Rococo has distinctive features of its own. The scale and grandeur of Baroque architecture, its spatial dynamism, persisted in an age when the grandees of Europe were emulating Versailles in palace architecture and when splendid churches continued to be built and dedicated by royalty. One of the finest of these, the Superga, near Turin in northwestern Italy (FIG. 20-3), was built by FILIPPO JUVARA (1678–1736) for Victor Amadeus II, king of Savoy, to commemorate his victory over the French in 1706. This was during

20-3 FILIPPO JUVARA, the Superga, near Turin, Italy, 1715–1731.

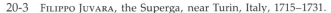

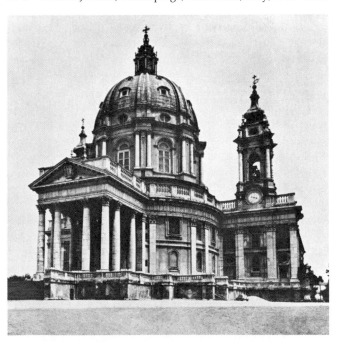

the War of the Spanish Succession, when the "Sun King," Louis XIV of France, suffered his final eclipse. Juvara, the royal architect, began his career in the lavish Baroque manner of his predecessor at Turin, Guarino Guarini (FIGS. 19-18 and 19-19), but study at Rome turned him toward the enduring Classical style. Even so, the setting of the Superga, in itself, is entirely Baroque. Placed on a lofty hill some 2,000 feet above the city of Turin, the church and the monastery, of which it is the frontispiece (an arrangement similar to that of the Church of the Invalides in Paris, FIG. 19-71), command a sweeping view of the city and the surrounding countryside. Close to the dimensions of the Invalides, the great dome and drum of the Superga may reflect Juvara's knowledge of that building. At the same time, there is a Palladian Classicism in the deep, four-columned portico surmounted by a balustrade, which continues around the building, and the relation of the portico to the rotunda-like structure behind it recalls the ancient Pantheon. The severity of the portico and of the colossal orders that articulate the walls is offset by the light, fanciful bell towers that flank the dome. In its adroit adjustment of Classical feature and Baroque grouping, the building is an impressive example of Juvara's intelligent eclecticism.

The victory that occasioned the building of the Superga was won by a great general of the time, Prince Eugene of Savoy. Victories over the forces of Louis XIV, won by Eugene's famous partner in arms, John Churchill, Duke of Marlborough, were also commemorated. In his honor, the government of Great Britain commissioned the building of the vast palace of Blenheim for his residence (FIG. 20-4). Blenheim is not a unique instance of English building, but it is of uncommon scale. Beginning with England's prosperous expansion into the New World, most particularly in the latter half of the seventeenth century, a demand arose for fine mansions on great estates, and the country houses of England in the eighteenth century, both in number and quality of design, are outstanding in European architecture. In the hands of a small group of architects associated with the aging Wren, the Baroque briefly triumphs over the accepted Palladian Classicism of Inigo Jones. The best known of this group, and the designer of Blenheim, was JOHN VANBRUGH (1664–1726), who began as a writer of witty and popular comedies and as the builder of a theater in which to produce them. Certainly, his architecture tends toward the theatrical on a mighty and extravagant scale. The picturesque silhouette of Blenheim, its massing, and its inventive architectural detail are all thoroughly Baroque. The design shows a love of variety and contrast, tempered by a desire for focus found so frequently in the architecture of the seventeenth century. The tremendous forecourt,

hugely projecting pavilions, and extended colonnades simultaneously recall St. Peter's and Versailles. Vanbrugh was not the only Baroque artist to sacrifice convenience to dramatic effect (as, for example, in placing the kitchen at Blenheim some 400 yards from the dining salon), but even in his own time, his piling up of colossal masses of masonry was ridiculed. Great as Blenheim is as scenic art, Voltaire could remark that if the rooms had only been as wide as the walls were thick, the palace would have been convenient enough. Vanbrugh's Baroque architecture did not please his patrons long; before Blenheim was completed, there was criticism of what contemporaries considered its ponderous and bizarre qualities.

This criticism, as it sharpened, came to extend to Baroque architecture as such. For English taste in the eighteenth century, the exaggerations of Blenheim came to be thought of as the general defects of Baroque style. Pomp and magnificence, great space-dominating scale, theatrical effects, irregular forms, exuberant details, grandiose rhetoric—all should be banished as irrational, unnatural, and artificial. "Good sense" should reign instead in simplicity, harmony, and utility of design. Doubtless Baroque was also thought to be the obnoxious art of absolute monarchical pride and display—something to be played down in parliamentary England. In English architecture, the instinct for an unostentatious and common-sensical style led straight to the authority of Vitruvius, Andrea Palladio (FIG. 17-52) and Inigo Jones (FIG. 19-75). Alexander Pope, in his "Fourth Moral Epistle" (1731), addresses his friend, the statesman and architectural amateur RICHARD BOYLE, Earl of Burlington (1695–1753):

> You, too, proceed! make falling arts your care,
> Erect new wonders, and the old repair;
> Jones and Palladio to themselves restore
> And be whate'er Vitruvius was before.

Lord Burlington strongly restated the Palladian doctrine of Inigo Jones and generously endowed the new style that resulted. With the talented professional WILLIAM KENT (1685–1748), Burlington built Chiswick House (FIG. 20-5) on the outskirts of London. The way had been paved for Burlington by, among others, the influential esthetic philosophy (succinctly echoed in Pope's epistle) of the third Earl of Shaftesbury and by Colin Campbell's *Virtuvius Britannicus* (1715), three volumes of engravings of ancient buildings in Britain prefaced by a denunciation of Italian Baroque and praise of Palladio and Inigo Jones.

Chiswick House is a free variation on the theme of Palladio's Villa Rotonda (FIG. 17-52). It was doubtless intended to be a "rational" answer to the colorful splendors of Versailles. Although, in its simple symmetry, unadorned planes, right angles, and stiffly

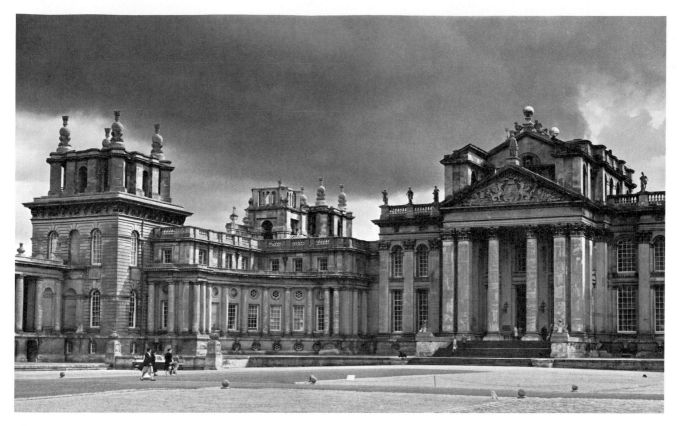

20-4 JOHN VANBRUGH, Blenheim Palace, Oxfordshire, England, 1705–1722.

20-5 RICHARD BOYLE (Earl of Burlington) and WILLIAM KENT, Chiswick House, near London, begun 1725.
British Crown Copyright.

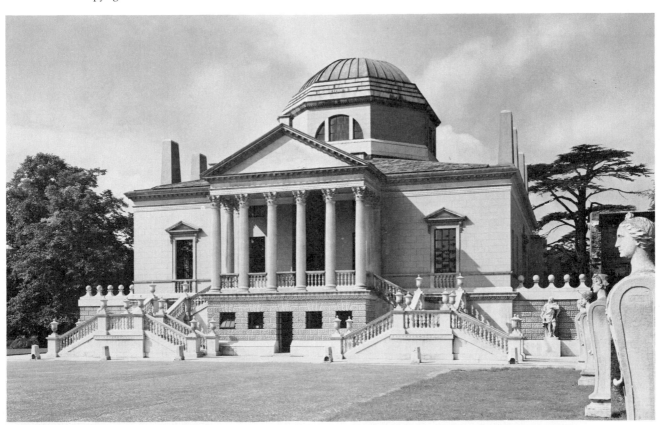

wrought proportions, Chiswick looks very Classical and "rational," it, like so many Palladian villas in England, is set within informal gardens, where a charming irregularity of layout and freely growing, uncropped foliage dominate the scene. The development of the "English garden" as a rival to the formality of the continental garden is an important chapter in the history of eighteenth-century taste, and we shall return to it. As irregularity was cultivated in landscaping surrounding the Palladian villa, so the interior of the villa was sometimes ornamented in a more-or-less reserved version of the Rococo style fashionable on the continent, belying the severity of the Classical exterior. At Chiswick, the Late Baroque of Kent's interior design is a luxurious foil to the stern symmetry of the exterior and the plan. But, in general, Rococo was never widely known or accepted in England.

Palladian Classicism prevails in English architecture until about 1760, when it begins to merge into what we will call Neoclassicism. This is quite different from what happens on the continent, where, during the same period (roughly 1710–1760), the Rococo style flourishes.

Rococo, in its French manifestation, appears around 1710 as a style primarily of interior design. As with English architecture, the French exterior is most often simple, even plain; Rococo takes over the interior. The sparkling gaiety cultivated by the new age, associated with the regency that followed on Louis XIV's death and with the reign of Louis XV, finds perfectly harmonious expression in Rococo. The word "Rococo" comes from the French *rocaille,* which literally means "pebble," but which refers especially to the small stones and shells used to decorate the interiors of grottoes. Such shells or shell forms are the principal motifs in Rococo ornament. The Rococo is a style preeminently of small art; furniture, utensils, accessories—objects of all sorts, useful and otherwise—are exquisitely wrought in the characteristically delicate, undulating Rococo line. A typically Rococo room is the Salon de la Princesse (FIG. 20-6) in the Hôtel de Soubise in Paris, decorated by GERMAIN BOFFRAND (1667–1754). If we compare it with the Galerie des Glaces at Versailles (FIG. 19-69), we see the fundamental difference at once. The strong architectural lines and panels of the earlier style are softened here into flexible, sinuous curves. The walls melt into

20-6 Salon de la Princesse, Hôtel de Soubise, Paris, 1737–1740. Decorations by GERMAIN BOFFRAND. British Crown Copyright.

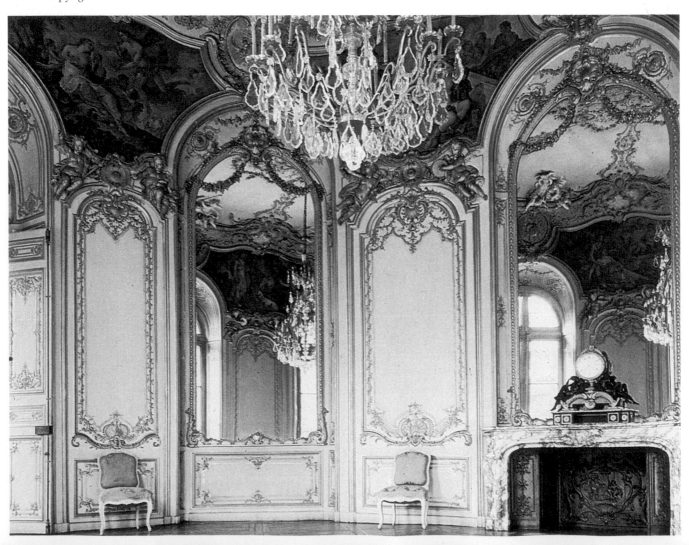

the vault; the cornices are replaced by irregular shapes that are painted, surmounted by sculpture, and separated by the typical shells of *rocaille*. Painting, architecture, and sculpture make a single ensemble. The profusion of curving tendrils and sprays of foliage combine with the shell forms to give an effect of freely growing nature and to suggest that the Rococo room is permanently decked for a festival. Such rooms, with their alternating gilded moldings, vivacious relief sculpture, and daintily colored ornament of flowers and garlands, must have harmonized with the chamber music played in them, with the elegant and elaborate costumes of lustrous satins and brocades, and with the equally elegant etiquette and sparkling wit of the people who graced them.

The Rococo salon was the locale of Parisian society, and Paris was the social capital of Europe in the eighteenth century. Wealthy, ambitious, and clever society women vied with one another to attract the most famous, the wittiest, and most accomplished people to their salons. The medium of social intercourse was conversation spiced with wit, repartee as quick and deft as a fencing match. The feminine look of the Rococo style suggests that the age was dominated by the taste and the social initiative of women—and, to a large extent, it was. Women held the highest places in Europe—Madame de Pompadour in France, Maria Theresa in Austria, Elizabeth and Catherine in Russia—and female influence was felt in any number of smaller courts. The masculine heroics and rhetoric of

the Baroque were replaced by dainty gallantries and pointed sallies of wit. Artifice reigned supreme, and it was considered in bad taste to be "original" or "enthusiastic," eccentric or sincere. The spirit of the age is expressed perfectly in Lord Chesterfield's *Letters to His Son,* instructing him in the manners of the Rococo salon. The honest Dr. Johnson, when he complained that the letters taught "the manners of a dancing master and the morals of a whore," may have been indicting the whole age.

The Rococo in architecture quickly became an international style during the early eighteenth century. There had been indications throughout late-seventeenth-century Europe of a general shift toward a lighter, gayer, more decorative type of expression, and the great prestige enjoyed by France gave impetus to this development.

A brilliant example of French Rococo abroad is the Amalienburg (FIGS. 20-7 and 20-8), a small lodge built by FRANÇOIS DE CUVILLIÉS (1698–1768) in the park of the Nymphenburg Palace in Munich. Although we think of Rococo as essentially interior design, the Amalienburg beautifully harmonizes the interior and the exterior elevations, the curving flow of their lines and planes cohering in a plastic unity of great elegance. The *bombé* (outward-bowed) shape of the central bay commonly occurs in Rococo furniture design; indeed, in its compactness, diminutive scale, graceful lines, and exquisite detail, Amalienburg is a kind of precious furnishing set down on the greens-

20-7 FRANÇOIS DE CUVILLIÉS, the Amalienburg, Nymphenburg Park, Munich, West Germany, 1734–1739.

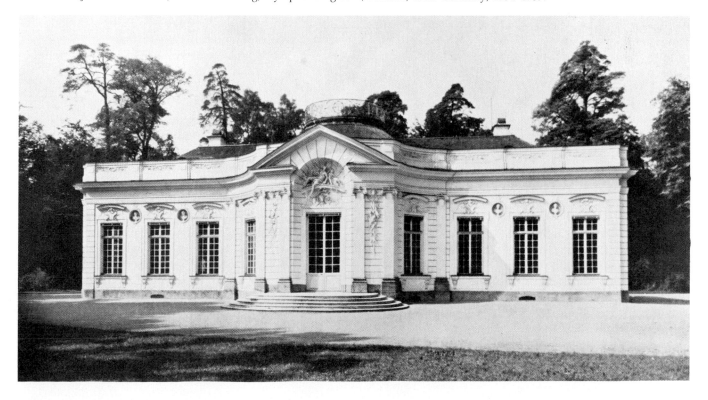

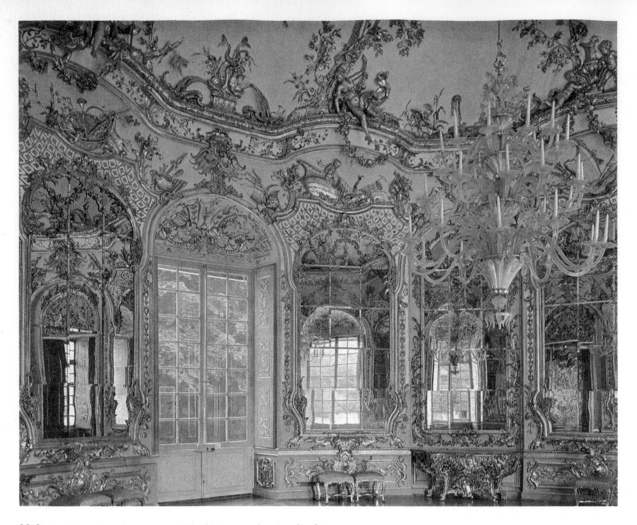

20-8　FRANÇOIS DE CUVILLIÉS, Hall of Mirrors, the Amalienburg.

ward of the park. Within the structure, the circular Hall of Mirrors (FIG. 20-8)—a silver and blue ensemble of architecture, stucco relief, silvered-bronze mirrors, and crystal—dazzles the sight with myriad scintillating motifs, forms, and figurations from the full Rococo repertory of ornament. This is the "high noon" of the style. Facets of silvery light, multiplied by windows and mirrors, sharply or softly delineate the endlessly proliferating shapes and contours that weave rhythmically around the upper walls and the coves of the ceiling. Everything seems organic, growing and in motion, an ultimate rarefaction of illusion. And everything is created with virtuoso flourishes by artists magically in command of all the resources of their media.

One of the most distinctive variants of Rococo architecture developed, side-by-side with French designs like that of Cuvilliés, in an area of southern Germany and Austria that had lain dormant artistically during the seventeenth century. Here, in a great wave of church building in the eighteenth century, the new style is not confined to interiors but appears in exteriors and plans as well. The chief influence, moreover, is not French but stems from the architecture of Francesco Borromini and Guarini, so that it is

perhaps more accurate to think of it as Late Baroque with strong stylistic affinities to Rococo. One of the most splendid of the German buildings is the pilgrimage church of Vierzehnheiligen (Fourteen Saints) by BALTHASAR NEUMANN (1687–1753). The rounded corners and the undulating center of the façade (FIG. 20-9) recall Borromini without approaching his dramatic intensity. Numerous large windows in the richly articulated but continuous walls flood the interior with an even, bright, and cheerful light. The interior (FIG. 20-10) exhibits a vivacious play of architectural fantasy that retains the dynamic but banishes all the dramatic qualities of Italian Baroque. The features pulse, flow, and commingle as if they were plastic ceaselessly in the process of being molded. The fluency of line, the floating and hovering surfaces, make us reach for the analogy of music; indeed, in this great age of music, the intricacy of the voices in a Bach fugue are brought to mind by the interwoven spaces and dematerialized masses of a structure that is the image of "frozen music." The complexity of Vierzehnheiligen is readable in its ground plan (FIG. 20-11), which has been called "one of the most ingenious pieces of architectural design ever conceived." The straight line seems to have been deliberately ban-

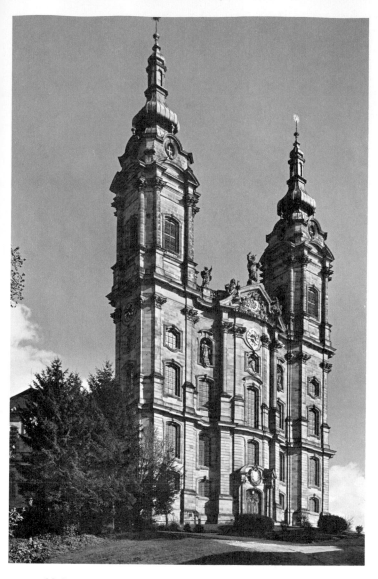

20-9 BALTHASAR NEUMANN, façade of the pilgrimage church of Vierzehnheiligen, near Bamberg, West Germany, 1743–1772.

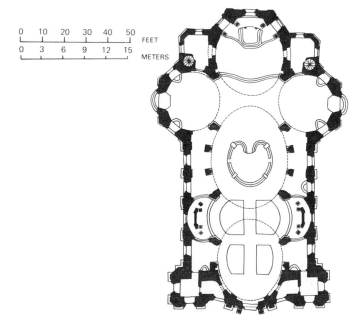

20-11 BALTHASAR NEUMANN, plan of Vierzehnheiligen, near Bamberg.

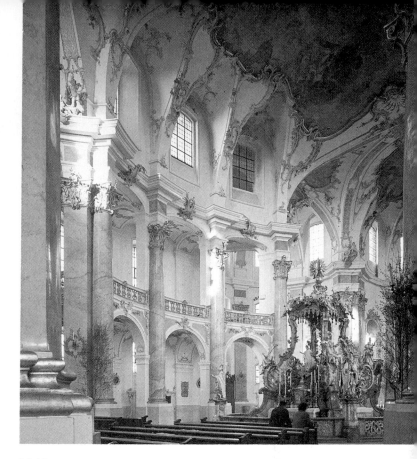

20-10 Interior of Vierzehnheiligen.

ished. The composition is made up of tangent ovals and circles, so that, within the essential outlines of the traditional Gothic church (apse, transept, nave, and western towers), a quite different interior effect is achieved—an undulating space in continuous motion, creating unlimited vistas bewildering in their variety and surprise effects. We must think of this kind of church as a brilliant ensemble of architecture, sculpture, music, and painting, in which the boundaries of the arts dissolve in visionary unity.

Painting and Sculpture

The ceiling decorations of Vierzehnheiligen, like those of most German Rococo churches, are inspired by the last great Italian painter to have an international impact, GIAMBATTISTA TIEPOLO (1696–1770). Of Venetian origin, Tiepolo worked for patrons in Austria, Germany, and Spain, as well as in Italy, leaving a strong impression wherever he went. His bright, cheerful colors and his relaxed compositions are ideally suited to Rococo architecture. *The Apotheosis of the Pisani Family* (FIG. 20-12), a ceiling fresco in the Villa Pisani at Stra in northern Italy, shows airy populations fluttering through vast sunlit skies and fleecy clouds, their figures making dark accents against the brilliant light of high noon. While retaining the illu-

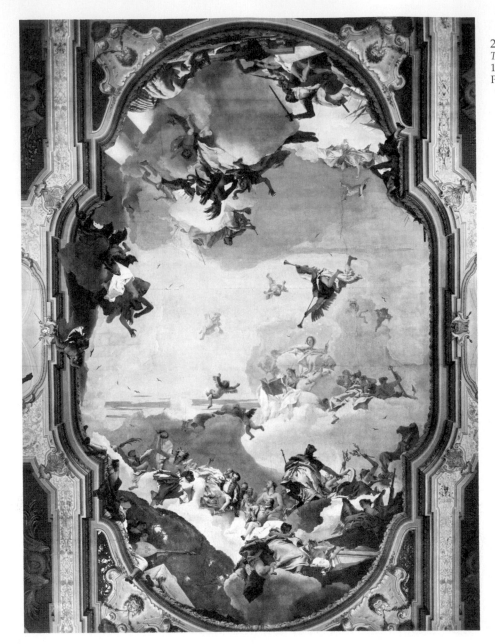

20-12 GIAMBATTISTA TIEPOLO, *The Apotheosis of the Pisani Family,* 1761–1762. Ceiling fresco in the Villa Pisani, Stra, Italy.

sionistic tendencies of the seventeenth century, Tiepolo discards all rhetoric to create gay and brightly colored pictorial schemes of great elegance and grace, which, for sheer effectiveness as decor, are unsurpassed.

Pictorial embellishment of the churches of the Germanies and Austria, whether by Italian or native painters, was supplemented by sculpture often contrived to produce entirely pictorial effects. In the group of the *Assumption of the Virgin* (FIG. 20-13) above the altar in the monastery church at Rohr, EGID QUIRIN ASAM (1692–1750) carries Baroque illusionism to its limit. Here, as in Bernini's *St. Theresa* (page 520), the miraculous is made real before our eyes, a spiritual vision materially visible. The Virgin, effortlessly borne aloft by angels, soars to the glowing paradise above her while the apostolic witnesses below gestic-

ulate in astonishment around her vacant tomb. The figures are colored to simulate life. The setting is a luxuriously ornamented theater; the scene itself, pure opera—an art that was perfected and became very popular in the eighteenth century. One can imagine the Virgin as protagonist in an operatic production: singing the climactic aria with all appropriate gestures, an excited chorus in accompaniment, while a virtuoso designer directs the stagecraft. Sculpture dissolves into painting, theater, and music—its mass rendered weightless, its natural compactness of composition broken up and diffuse. Here, the art of the sculptor is, paradoxically, to disguise its substance and function, its weight and tactility, in the interest of eye-deceiving illusion. Baroque sculpture could go no further, and the later eighteenth century will experience a strong reaction to it in Neoclassicism.

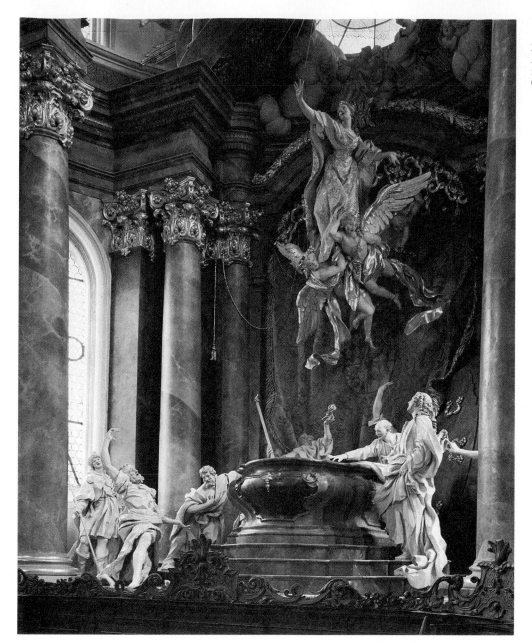

The painters of France in the eighteenth century give the Rococo its earthly setting (the salon, the theater, and the boudoir) and create its sensuous moods and luxuriant intimacy. The painter above all others whom we associate with the Rococo is ANTOINE WATTEAU (1684–1721), whose *L'Indifférent* (FIG. 20-2) we have already cited to exhibit what is typical of the Rococo in painting. His masterpiece (he made two versions of it) is *Return from Cythera* (FIG. 20-14), which he painted between 1717 and 1719 as his acceptance piece for admission to the French Royal Academy. Watteau was Flemish, and his style is a beautiful derivative from that of Rubens—a kind of rarefaction and refinement of it. At the turn of the century, the Academy was rather sharply divided between two doctrines. One stated what Le Brun had derived from the art and writings of Nicolas Poussin—

that form is the most important element in painting and that, as Poussin asserts, "the colors in paintings are, as it were, blandishments to lure the eyes," merely something added for effect, and not really essential. The other doctrine, with Rubens as its apostle, proclaimed the supremacy of color as natural and the coloristic style as the proper guide to the artist. Depending on which side they took, members of the Academy were "Poussinistes" or "Rubénistes." With Watteau, the latter carried the day, and the Rococo style in painting was established on the colorism of Rubens and the Venetians.

Return from Cythera represents a group of lovers preparing to depart from the island of eternal youth and love, sacred to Aphrodite. Young and luxuriously costumed, they perform, as it were, an elegant, tender, graceful ballet, moving from the protective

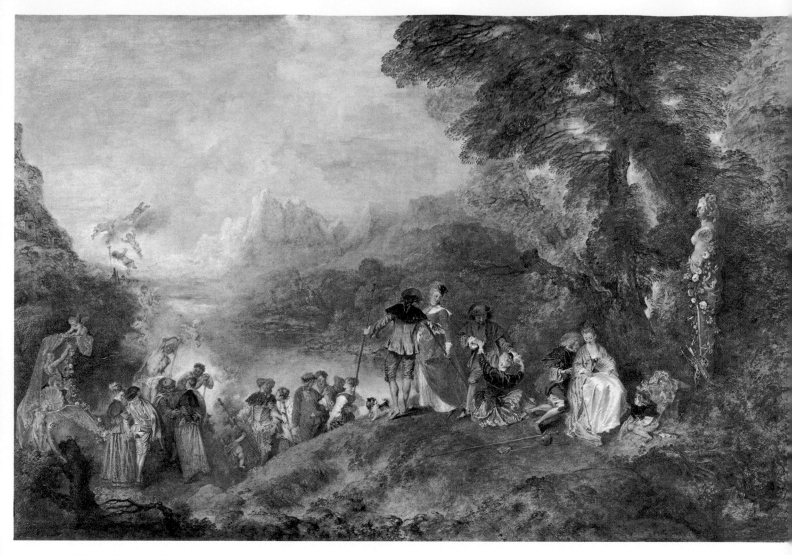

20-14 ANTOINE WATTEAU, *Return from Cythera*, 1717–1719. Approx. 4' 3" × 6' 4". Louvre, Paris.

shade of a woodland park, peopled with amorous cupids and voluptuous statuary, down a grassy slope to an awaiting golden barge. The attitudes of the figures are carefully studied; Watteau has never been equaled for his distinctive poses, which so beautifully combine elegance and sweetness. He composed his generally quite small paintings from albums of superb drawings, which are still preserved and in fine condition. In these, we find him observing slow movement from difficult and unusual angles, obviously with the intention of finding the smoothest, most poised, and most refined attitudes. As he seeks nuances of bodily poise and movement, so Watteau strives for the most exquisite shades of color difference, defining in a single stroke the shimmer of silk at a bent knee or the iridescence that touches a glossy surface as it emerges from shadow. Here, the color craft of the Venetians and Rubens is exquisitely specialized in the hands of a master of the nuance. It has long been noted that the theme of love and Arcadian happiness in Watteau's pictures (which we have seen since Giorgione and which Watteau may have seen in

works by Rubens) is slightly shadowed with wistfulness, even melancholy, as if Watteau, despite his own short life, had opportunity to meditate on the swift passage of youth and pleasure. Although his mood is never easily described, it is caught in a contemporary work, not of painting but of poetry—Alexander Pope's *Rape of the Lock*. This extraordinary passage from that work shows how widespread the Rococo was in the arts:

> But now secure the painted vessel glides,
> The sunbeams trembling on the floating tides;
> While melting music steals upon the sky,
> And softened sounds along the waters die . . . .
> The lucid squadrons round the sails repair:
> Soft o'er the shrouds aërial whispers breathe,
> That seemed but zephyrs to the train beneath.
> Some to the sun their insect wings unfold,
> Waft on the breeze, or sink in clouds of gold;
> Transparent forms, too fine for mortal sight,
> Their fluid bodies half dissolved in light,
> Loose to the wind their airy garments flew,
> Thin glittering textures of the filmy dew,

Dipped in the richest tincture of the skies,
Where light disports in ever-mingling dyes,
While every beam new transient colors flings,
Colors that change whene'er they wave their wings.

The poet's and the painter's language are in perfect harmony. The haze of color, the subtly modeled shapes, the gliding motion, the air of suave gentility—all are the objective and achievement of the Rococo artist and all are to the taste of his aristocratic patronage in its last age. The unifying power of that taste draws the arts together. The titles as well as the mood of many musical compositions by Watteau's exact contemporary, Jean Philippe Rameau, are perfectly suited to Watteau's pictures.

20-15 FRANÇOIS BOUCHER, *Cupid a Captive,* 1754. Approx. 66″ × 34″. Reproduced by permission of the Trustees of the Wallace Collection, London.

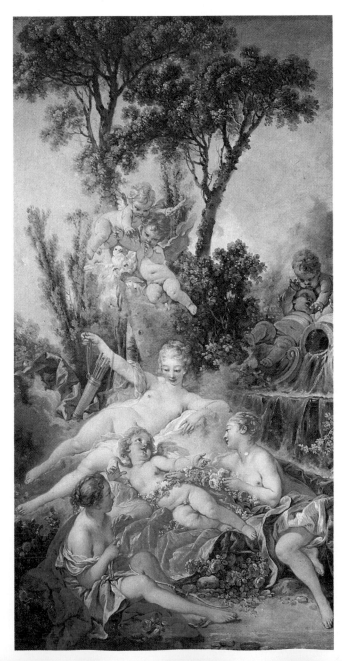

The successors of Watteau never quite match his taste and subtlety. Their themes concern love artfully and archly pursued, erotic frivolity, and playful intrigue. After Watteau's untimely death, his follower FRANÇOIS BOUCHER (1703–1770), painter to Madame de Pompadour, rose to the dominant position in French painting. Although he was also an excellent portraitist, Boucher's fame rests primarily on his gay and graceful allegories, in which Arcadian shepherds, nymphs, and goddesses cavort in shady glens, engulfed in pink and sky-blue light. The *Cupid a Captive* (FIG. 20-15) presents the viewer with a rosy pyramid of infant and female flesh, set off against a cool, leafy background, the figures' nudity both hidden and revealed by fluttering draperies. Boucher uses all of the Baroque devices to create his masterly composition: the dynamic play of crisscrossing diagonals, curvilinear forms, and slanting recessions. But powerful Baroque curves are dissected into a multiplicity of decorative arabesques, and Baroque drama dissipates into sensual playfulness. Gay and superficial, Boucher's artful fantasies were the mirrors in which his patrons, the French aristocracy, saw the cherished reflections of their own ornamental decadence.

Boucher's student JEAN HONORÉ FRAGONARD (1732–1806) was a first-rate colorist whose decorative skill almost surpassed his master's. An example of his manner can stand as characteristic not only of him, but of the later Rococo in general. *The Swing* (FIG. 20-16) is a typical "intrigue" picture. A young gentleman has managed an arrangement by which an unknowing, friendly old bishop swings the gentleman's pretty sweetheart higher and higher, while he himself, strategically placed, ardently admires her. The young lady is quite aware of his presence and boldly kicks off her shoe at the little statue of the god of discretion, who holds his finger to his lips. The landscape setting is out of Watteau—a luxuriant perfumed bower in a park that very much resembles a stage scene for the comic opera. The glowing pastel colors and soft light convey, almost by themselves, the sensuality of the theme.

The medium of pastel is especially associated with the art of the Rococo, although it will be popular again with the Impressionists of the late nineteenth century. Pastels are chalk-like crayons, made of ground color pigments mixed with water and a binding medium. They lend themselves to quick execution, particularly of portraits, and provide the artist with a very wide range of colors and subtle variations of tone, suitable for rendering nuances of value and fleeting expressions of feature. The Venetian painter ROSALBA CARRIERA (1675–1757), working almost exclusively with pastels, pioneered the medium, and, in the 1720s and 1730s, made an international reputation for herself with pastel portraits of the gentry, nobility, and royalty of Europe. Her art became the

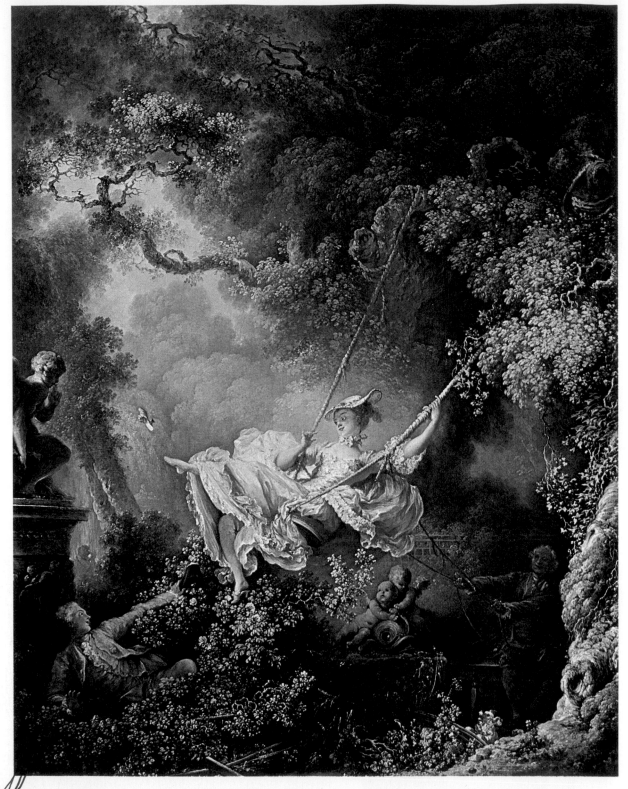

20-16   JEAN HONORÉ FRAGONARD, *The Swing*, 1766. Approx. 35″ × 32″. Reproduced by permission of the Trustees of the Wallace Collection, London.

fashion in Paris, and she had more commissions than she could handle. Her pastel of *Cardinal de Polignac* (FIG. 20-17), diplomat and collector of ancient art, shows her new portrait method. Essentially informal, the composition includes only the head and bust, eliminating all details not needed to record the features and status of the subject. The design is simple; the pose and presentation, forthright and unpretentious. The pomp and rhetorical flourishes of the Baroque (FIG. 20-1) are missing. Typically for the pastel medium, the colors are high-keyed and luminous, shading is minimal, and the cardinal's grave features are modulated by a slightly hazed, soft focus, suggestive of sunlit atmosphere.

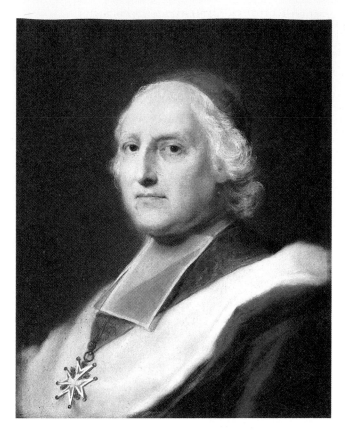

20-17 ROSALBA CARRIERA, *Cardinal de Polignac*, 1732. Pastel. Gallerie dell' Accademia, Venice.

A host of pastelists followed Carriera's example. One of the best of them, QUENTIN DE LA TOUR (1704–1788), gives us, in his *Self-Portrait*, the very type of the Enlightenment personality (FIG. 20-18). In his own features and expression, in the sidelong glance and

20-18 QUENTIN DE LA TOUR, *Self-Portrait, c.* 1751. Pastel, approx. 25″ × 21″. Musée de Picardie, Amiens.

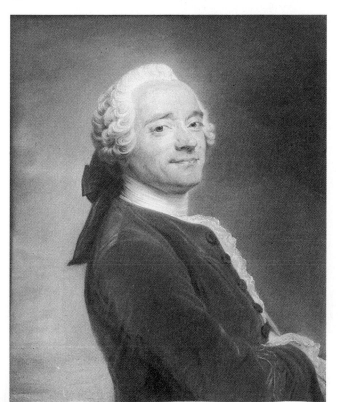

almost jaunty pose, we find the kind of poise and suave elegance characteristic of the age—the *esprit* of Enlightenment society. In striking contrast with the solemn portrait of the Cardinal, the face is open and lively, with a bright look of amiable and active intelligence. Here is the optimistic (if slightly sardonic) believer in human progress—a man of good sense and good taste, conversant with the ideas of the "age of reason." He is critical of ancient privilege, prejudice, and superstition, a reader of Locke, Montesquieu, Voltaire, Rousseau, and the other "philosophes," whose principles will rationalize the American and French Revolutions. The smile on his face, familiar in many portraits of the time, has been called "the smile of the eighteenth century"—confident, interested, amused, slightly mocking. It is the face one wears to the salon to confront the brilliant society of the *beau monde*.

Along with the sensuous style of the Rococo, patronized by such "first ladies" of Louis XV as Madame de Pompadour and Madame du Barry, a different taste developed—one much more likely to appeal to the middle classes of Paris, who disapproved of the licentious gallantries of Fragonard. JEAN BAPTISTE SIMÉON CHARDIN (1699–1779), briefly Fragonard's teacher, made a specialty of simple interiors and still life, which he painted masterfully in his own mode, rivaling the Dutch masters of the previous century. In *Grace at Table* (FIG. 20-19), Chardin gives us an unpre-

20-19 JEAN BAPTISTE SIMÉON CHARDIN, *Grace at Table*, 1740. 19″ × 15″. Louvre, Paris.

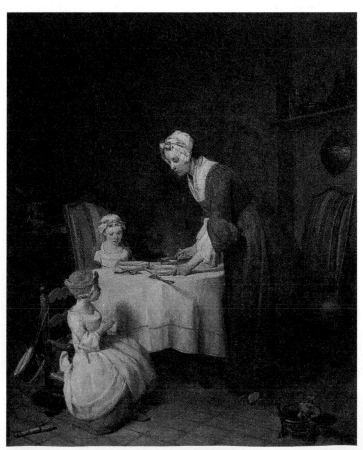

tentious room in which a mother and her small daughters are about to dine. The mood of quiet attention is at one with the hushed lighting and mellow color and the closely studied still-life accessories, with worn surfaces that tell their own humble domestic history. In his own way, Chardin is the poet of the commonplace and the master of its nuances. A gentle sentiment prevails in all his pictures—not contrived and artificial, but born of the painter's honesty, insight, and sympathy.

The taste of the newly prosperous and confident middle classes of England found expression in the art of WILLIAM HOGARTH (1697–1764), who satirized contemporary life with comic zest and with only a modicum of Rococo "indecency." With Hogarth, a truly English style of painting emerges. England had had no painters or sculptors to match its architects; traditionally, painters were imported from the continent (Holbein, Rubens, Van Dyck). Hogarth waged a lively campaign throughout his career against the English feeling of dependence on and inferiority to continental art. Although Hogarth himself would have been the last to admit it, his own painting owes

much to the work of his contemporaries across the channel in France, the artists of the Rococo. He uses the same bright, opaque colors, applied with dash and virtuosity. Yet his subject matter, frequently moral in tone, is distinctively English. It was the great age of English satirical writing, and Hogarth—who knew and admired this genre and included Henry Fielding, author of *Tom Jones*, among his closest friends—clearly saw himself as translating it into the visual arts:

> I therefore turned my thoughts to . . . painting and engraving modern moral subjects. . . . I have endeavored to treat my subjects as a dramatic writer; my picture is my stage, and men and women my players, who by means of certain actions and gestures, are to exhibit a dumb show. . . .

Hogarth's favorite device was to make a series of narrative paintings and prints, in a serial sequence like chapters in a book or scenes in a play, that follow a character or group of characters in their encounters with some social evil. He is at his best in pictures such as the *Breakfast Scene* (FIG. 20-20) from the *Marriage à la*

20-20   WILLIAM HOGARTH, *Breakfast Scene*, from *Marriage à la Mode, c.* 1745. Approx. 28″ × 36″. Reproduced by courtesy of the Trustees of the National Gallery, London.

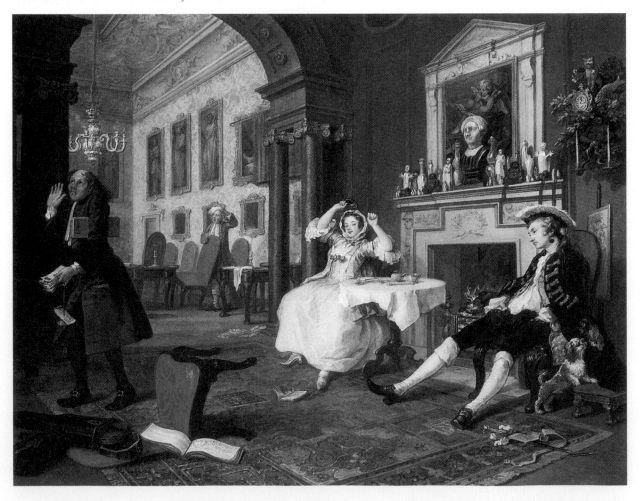

Mode, in which the marriage of the young viscount, arranged through the social aspirations of one parent and the need for money of the other, is just beginning to founder. The bright, gay character of the anglicized Rococo style is admirably suited to the situation. The situation, however, must be read completely from its large inventory of detail if we are to enjoy it fully. It is past noon. Husband and wife are very tired after a long night spent in other company. The young nobleman keeps his hat on in his wife's presence. His hands are sunk deep in his pockets, emptied by gambling, and the little dog sniffs suspiciously at a lace cap that protrudes from a pocket. The broken sword suggests that the master has been in a fight; an overturned chair signifies that the previous evening has been somewhat spirited. A steward, his hands full of unpaid bills, raises his eyes to heaven in despair at what this family is coming to. The setting is overly grand. Hogarth pokes fun at the style of interior decoration and mocks the Classical taste in the bust on the mantelpiece. There is a great deal more; typically, Hogarth proceeds as a novelist would, elaborating on his subject with carefully chosen detail, which, as we continue to discover it, heightens the comedy.

LATE EIGHTEENTH CENTURY: THE RISE OF ROMANTICISM

The second half of the century quickens in tempo and changes in mood as the course of history sweeps toward the climax of the revolutions that will open the modern epoch. An uneasiness and then an impatience with the status quo breeds a new and restless spirit of criticism that, here and there, edges toward rebellion. Against what was thought to be the wanton lavishness and profligacy of the Rococo, an impulse toward the simple, the earnest, and the moral begins to rise. It is the time of Rousseau, the "age of sensibility," that preaches sincere feeling and natural human sympathy over artful reason and the cold calculations of courtly societies. The slogan of Sensibility is "Trust your heart rather than your head," or, as Goethe puts it, "Feeling is all!" Werther, the young Goethe's archetype of Romantic sensibility, cries: "We desire to surrender our whole being, that it may be filled with the perfect bliss of one glorious emotion!" All that is false and artificial must be banished as the enemy of honest emotion.

Sensibility is swiftly overtaken by the heroic emotions of the revolutionary age. Models of self-sacrificing virtue are summoned from the Greek and Roman past and from the rebellious present—heroes like Cato and Washington, Regulus and Marat—to inspire thoughts and deeds of civic idealism. And contemporary with both the sentimental and the heroic comes the taste for the sublime in art and nature. The sublime inspires feelings of awe mixed with terror, what is felt when we look on vast, impassable mountain peaks or great storms at sea. Accompanying the taste for the sublime is the "gothick" taste for the fantastic, the occult, the grotesque, the macabre—for the adventures of the soul voyaging into the dangerous reaches of consciousness.

Whatever moves the artist and the audience in this period—the sentimental, the heroic, the sublime, the "gothick," or combinations of them, there is a marked shift in emphasis from reason to feeling, from calculation to intuition, from objective nature to subjective emotion. Here, that attitude of the modern mind we call Romanticism first emerges.

For almost two centuries, scholars have debated the definition and the historical scope of Romanticism; neither the scholarship nor the controversy has ended. The very widest definition—say, Baudelaire's—would equate Romanticism and Modernism, making Romanticism the mood of the modern world and coextensive with its history. More narrowly, Romanticism is a phenomenon beginning around 1750 and ending about 1850. Still more narrowly, Romanticism is just another of a miscellany of styles that rise and decline in the course of modern art. In this view, Romanticism flourishes from about 1800 to 1840, coming between Neoclassicism and Realism.

The term itself originated toward the end of the eighteenth century among German literary critics, who aimed to distinguish peculiarly "modern" traits from the "Classical" traits that had advanced once more against the Baroque and Rococo. "Romance," which can refer as much to the novel, with its sentimental hero, as it does to the old Medieval tales of fantastic adventure written in the "romance" languages, has never quite fitted with the broader term "romantic," nor has "romantic" ever covered snugly all we seem to understand by it. J.P. Eckermann's *Conversations with Goethe* throws a strong, revealing light on Romanticism, especially on its supposed opposition to Classicism. There, Goethe is recorded as declaring:

> The distinction between Classical and Romantic poetry, which is now spread over the whole world and occasions so many quarrels and divisions, came originally from Schiller and myself. [Goethe is recalling some 40 years after the time.] I laid down the maxim of objective treatment in poetry, and would allow no other; but Schiller, who worked quite in the subjective way, deemed his own fashion right, and to defend himself against me, wrote the treatise upon *Naive and Sentimental Poetry.* He proved to me that I, against my

will, was romantic, and that my *Iphigenia,* through the predominance of sentiment, was by no means so much in the antique spirit as some people supposed. The Schlegels took up this idea, and carried it further, so that it has now been diffused over the whole world; and everybody talks about Classicism and Romanticism—of which nobody thought 50 years ago.*

It will be seen that Goethe wants his play to be in the antique spirit and, "against his will," discovers that he has been romantic all the time. This is probably the case with artists throughout the era of Romanticism. The break with tradition forces the artist to look at tradition historically; if he prefers Classical art, then he will have to assume or *affect* a "classic" bent of mind—but he will be *representing* Classical form, not *creating* it. In the end, it is his response to Classical form that counts, and that response is emotional; the emotional response to Classical form will be precisely Romantic!

We treat Romanticism here as a broad generality, finding that it comprehends a number of styles, including Neoclassicism, prevalent throughout the late eighteenth and the nineteenth centuries. Although these styles differ formally, the artists and architects who work within them share a common Romantic attitude. The underlying attitude broadens, deepens, and clarifies in the nineteenth century, and we shall consider it further then. For the moment, it is only necessary to point out that renewed interest in the historical styles (Classic, Gothic, Egyptian, and Chinese among them), as part of a rising eclecticism of taste, is all part of the new Romantic view of nature and of art.

Architecture

In England, where Romanticism was born, the revolt against the "regularity" of Classical architecture stirred early. The late seventeenth century witnessed the beginning of an enthusiasm for Chinese art—in particular, the Chinese garden. An English critic of the time, Sir William Temple, comparing the Chinese garden with the symmetry and uniformity of the European garden, described the beauty of the former as "without . . . order or disposition of parts that shall be commonly or easily observed. . . ." The Chinese term for this quality is defined as "being impressive or surprising through careless or unorderly grace." Within a generation of Temple's observation, English gardens were being designed along Oriental lines. In the eighteenth century, the English garden became a vogue throughout Europe, and the formality of such gardens as those at Versailles was thought unnatural.

Thus, "naturalness," rather than formal order, in architecture came to be the quality in demand, and

"natural" styles like Gothic, which had never entirely died out in England, became very popular. In 1718, John Vanbrugh, the architect of the Baroque Blenheim Palace (FIG. 20-4), designed his country house to look like a Gothic castle to give it a "masculine" (an unaffected or "natural") appearance. The picturesque qualities of the Gothic style had already begun to be appreciated when the Earl of Burlington was building Chiswick House (FIG. 20-5).

The contradiction between the formal villa and its informal gardens was apparently not felt at once; for one thing, the meaning of "nature" had not yet been agreed on in the early eighteenth century. Was it, in the Classical sense, a regularity of proportion, or, in the newer sense, the irregularity of growing things, with their wildness and accidents—in a word, their picturesqueness, or even their primitiveness? In the end, it would be decided that *all* historical styles are "natural," as they evolve historically from the artistic instinct of peoples, who are, after all, part of nature.

Thus, we see a number of "revivals" of styles almost simultaneously parading the romantic past before the eyes and imaginations of the romantically inclined public. Lord Burlington's Palladian revival was on course, having been made current and popular by the designs of William Kent, who was also a pioneer of the picturesque garden. HORACE WALPOLE (1717–1797) a wealthy architectural dilettante, renovated his villa at Twickenham in the rising "gothick" fashion, converting it into a sprawling "castle" with turrets, towers, battlements, galleries, and corridors, "whose fretted roofs, carved panels, and illuminated windows," as Sir Walter Scott describes, "were garnished with the appropriate furniture of escutcheons, armorial bearings, shields, tilting lances, and all the panoply of chivalry." Indeed, at Strawberry Hill (FIG. 20-21), Walpole's villa in Twickenham, the master could enjoy his favorite pastime, which was "to gaze on Gothic toys through Gothic glass." The features of the structure are, of course, pseudo-Gothic, the kind of fairy-tale vision raised in our own times by the late Walt Disney. But Walpole's trifling with Gothic architecture will be as influential as his Gothic novels.

The thrill produced by contemplation of the vanished past was cultivated by garden designers in England, who, when the opportunity offered, decorated the irregularities of random copses of trees, little rustic bridges, and winding streams with replicas of period architecture. Sometimes a single garden would boast four or five different styles. Typical are the gardens at Hagley Park, where a sham Gothic ruin of 1747 (FIG. 20-22) stands near a Doric portico built in 1758 (FIG. 20-23). The latter is of special interest as the work of JAMES STUART (1713–1788), who, with Nicholas Revett, introduced to Europe the splendor and originality of Greek art in the enormously influential *Antiquities of Athens,* the first volume of which was

*John Oxenford, trans., and J.K. Moorehead, ed., *Conversations of Goethe with Eckermann,* (New York: Dutton, 1935), p. 366.

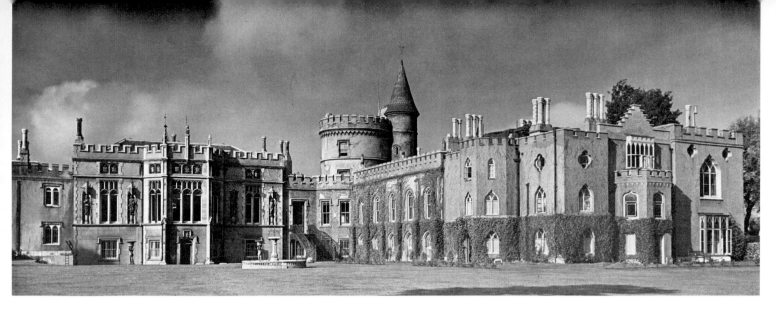

20-21   Horace Walpole, Strawberry Hill, Twickenham, near London, 1749–1777.

published in 1762. These volumes firmly distinguished Greek art from the "derivative" Roman, which had served as the model of Classicism since the Renaissance. Stuart's efforts were greeted with enthusiasm by those who had no use for the Rococo, the Chinese, the Gothic, or any of the "irregular" manners in art. A contemporary journal hoped that Stuart's writings and Robert Wood's magnificently illustrated *Ruins of Palmyra* (1753) and *Ruins of Baalbek* (1757) would "expel the littleness and ugliness of the Chinese, and the barbarity of the Goths, that we may see no more useless and expensive trifles; no more dungeons instead of summer houses."

By mid-century, the rediscovery of Greek art and architecture had turned the romanticizing taste of Europe in a new direction and inaugurated the style we call Neoclassicism, which reembraces the idea of a changeless generality that supposedly transcends the accidents of time. Neoclassicism, once thought of as in opposition to Romanticism, is now understood as simply one of the many fashions within that general movement but in opposition to the "irregularity" of Romantic styles, like Neo-Gothic and Chinese. By 1763, the German critic Friedrich Grimm could write that "everything is being done today in the Greek mode." Earlier, in 1755, Johann Winckelmann, the first modern historian of art, published his *Thoughts on the Imitation of Greek Art in Painting and Sculpture*, in which he uncompromisingly designated Greek art as the most perfect from the hands of man and the only model to be followed, for doing so would confer "assurance in conceiving and designing works of art, since they [the Greeks] have marked for us the utmost limits of human and divine beauty."

Winckelmann characterizes Greek sculpture as manifesting a "noble simplicity and quiet grandeur," and, in his *History of Ancient Art* (1763), he undertook to describe each monument as an element in the de-

20-22   Sanderson Miller, sham Gothic ruin, Hagley Park, Worcestershire, England, 1747. Copyright, *Country Life,* London.

20-23   James Stuart, Doric portico, Hagley Park, Worcestershire, England, 1758. Copyright, *Country Life,* London.

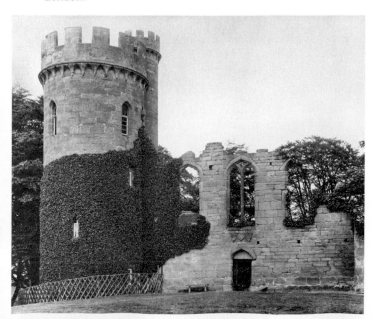

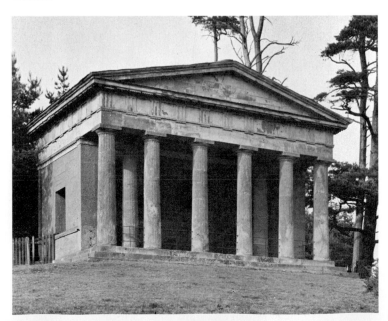

velopment of a single grand style. Before Winckelmann, the history of art had been a matter of biography, as with Giorgio Vasari; Winckelmann initiates the modern method of classification and description on the basis of general stylistic traits that change over time. Winckelmann, strangely enough, did not know much about original Greek art—at least not much beyond the *Laocoön* group (FIG. 5-80) and other late Greek works in the Vatican collections, of which he was custodian. For the most part, he had only late Roman copies for study, and he never visited Greece, where he might have seen the genuine thing. Despite the obvious defects of his work, however, its pioneering character cannot be overlooked. Winckelmann had wide influence, and his writings laid a theoretical and historical foundation for Neoclassicism.

Within Neoclassicism's admiration for the art of Greece, sentiment for the art of Rome arose again; "the glory that was Greece / And the grandeur that was Rome" summarized the conception of a noble Classical world. The first great archeological event of modern times—the discovery and initial excavations of the ancient buried Roman cities of Pompeii (FIG. 6-21) and Herculaneum in the 1730s and 1740s—

startled and thrilled all Europe. This was the veritable resurrection of the ancient world, not simply a dim vision of it inspired by a few moldering ruins; historical reality could now replace fancy with fact. The wall paintings and other artifacts of Pompeii (FIGS. 6-23, 6-25, 6-27) inspired the slim, straight-lined, elegant "Pompeian" style that, after mid-century, almost entirely displaced the curvilinear Rococo. In France, the new manner was associated with Louis XVI; in England, it took the name of its most artful practitioner, ROBERT ADAM (1728–1792), whose interior architecture was as influential in Europe as the English garden. The Etruscan Room in Osterley Park House (FIG. 20-24), begun in 1761, compared with the Rococo salon of the Hôtel de Soubise (FIG. 20-6) and the Amalienburg (FIG. 20-8), shows how completely symmetry and rectilinearity have returned, but with great delicacy and none of the massive splendor of the style of Louis XIV. The decorative motifs (medallions, urns, vine scrolls, paterae, sphinxes, and tripods) are taken from Roman art and, as in Roman stucco work, are arranged sparsely within broad, neutral spaces and slender margins.

Adam was an archeologist as well as an architect

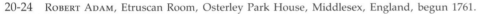

20-24 ROBERT ADAM, Etruscan Room, Osterley Park House, Middlesex, England, begun 1761.

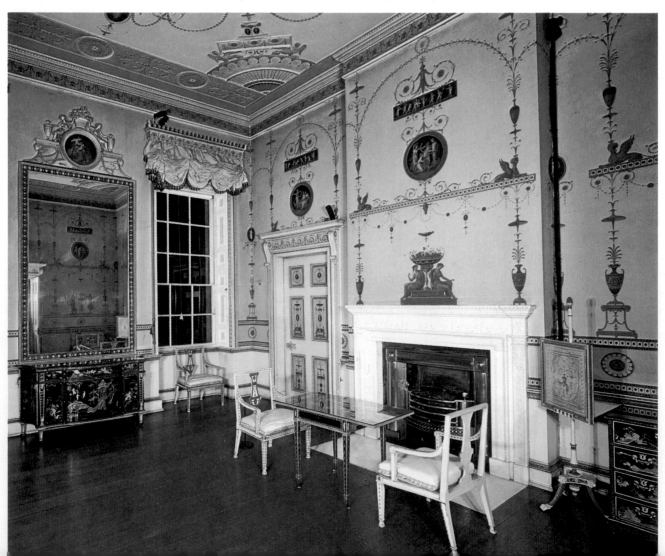

and had explored and written accounts of the ruins of the palace of Diocletian at Spalatum (FIG. 6-77). His Kedleston House in Derbyshire, Adelphi Terrace in London, and many other structures show the influence of Spalatum on his work.

The Romantic fascination with ruins is blended with archeological curiosity about the facts. In Rome, in the late 1740s, Giovanni Battista Piranesi began his *Views of Rome* (FIG. 7-5)—some 135 prints that romantically present the eternal city's majestic ruins and that have served for generations as the standard image of Roman grandeur. Edward Gibbon wrote his monumental *Decline and Fall of the Roman Empire,* which matches in words the stately and august subjects of Piranesi's *Views.* The Roman ruins at Baalbek in Syria, especially a titanic colonnade, inspired the Neoclassical portico of the church of Ste. Geneviève (FIG. 20-25), now the Panthéon, in Paris, designed by JACQUES GERMAIN SOUFFLOT (1713–1780). The columns, reproduced with studied archeological exactitude, are the first revelation of Roman grandeur in France. The walls are severely blank, except for a repeated garland motif in the attic level. The colonnaded dome—a Neoclassical version of the domes of St. Peter's in Rome, the Church of the Invalides in Paris, and St. Paul's in London (FIGS. 17-34, 19-71, 19-76)—rises above a Greek-cross plan, and both vaults and dome rest on an interior grid of splendid, freestanding Corinthian columns, as if the colonnade of the portico were continued within. Although the whole effect—inside and out—is Roman, the structural principles employed are essentially Gothic. Soufflot early maintained that Gothic engineering was highly functional structurally and could be applied

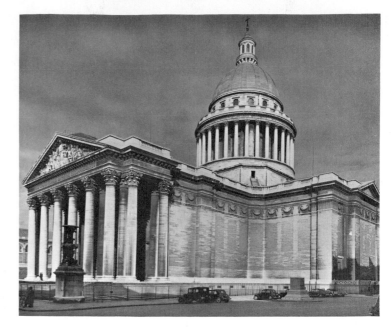

20-25 JACQUES GERMAIN SOUFFLOT, the Panthéon (Ste. Geneviève), Paris, 1755–1792.

in modern building. In Soufflot, we have the curious, but not unreasonable conjunction of Gothic and Classical—not in mere decorative juxtaposition, as they appear at Hagley Park (FIGS. 20-22 and 20-23), but in structural integration. Thus, Soufflot anticipates the nineteenth-century admiration of Gothic engineering that will result in a firmer and more authentic Gothic manner than the stage sets favored by Walpole.

International Neoclassicism will extend across continent and ocean, from the Russia of Catherine the Great to the new American republic. THOMAS JEFFERSON (1743–1826), a gifted amateur, shows in his design for his country house at Monticello (FIG. 20-26) how well acquainted he was with Palladio and his

20-26 THOMAS JEFFERSON, Monticello, Charlottesville, Virginia, 1770–1806.

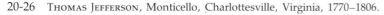

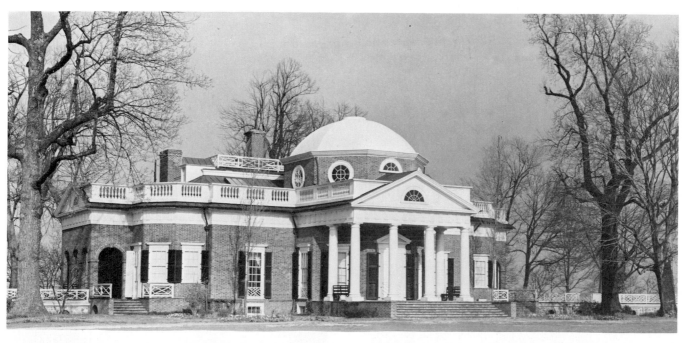

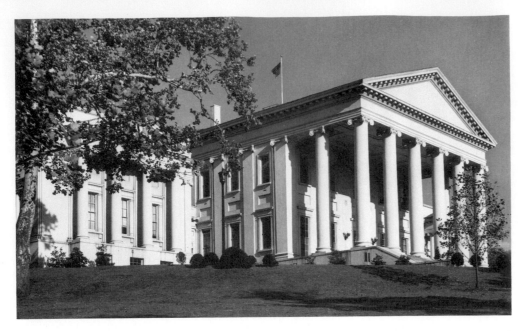

eighteenth-century English adherents. Monticello is a kind of Villa Rotonda (FIG. 17-52) or Chiswick House (FIG. 20-5)—developed out of the pleasant provincial architecture of Virginia, with the setting of green lawns and the red brick walls and white facings of American Colonial architecture. Even before it was finished (Monticello was built in two stages), Jefferson's experience of Classical art in Europe convinced him that a strictly Classical manner, if not always appropriate for private dwellings, was certainly so for public buildings. He showed his feeling for the Classical past by going beyond those architects who incorporated only elements of ancient architecture in their buildings and taking the complete Roman temple form as his model for the Virginia statehouse at Richmond (FIG. 20-27). He had seen the Roman temple at Nîmes called the Maison Carrée (which resembles the Temple of "Fortuna Virilis," FIG. 6-16) while serving in France as American ambassador. Jefferson's choice was based on the admiration he felt for the original, both as an embodiment of the pure beauty of antiquity and as a symbol of idealized Roman Republican government.

Thus, in a single career, we witness the passage from Palladian Classicism to the stricter Neoclassicism of the end of the eighteenth century. Selection of the Roman model reflects as well the attempt, also found in the thought of Jefferson's contemporary French revolutionaries, to rediscover in antiquity certain lofty principles of life that had presumably been distorted during the intervening centuries. The young United States adopted many Roman symbols: the eagle; the lictor's ax and rods; "Columbia," the allegorical figure of the nation (as a kind of new "Roma"). Its national motto was in Latin: *e pluribus unum*; Washington was honored as a new Cincinnatus, who, after liberating his country, retired to his farm when he could have been king; the upper house

of Congress was named after the Roman Senate. The official architecture of Washington has long been Neoclassical, and the Capitol itself is named after the ancient Roman hill.

Sculpture and Painting

In sculpture, as in the architecture of Jefferson, we can find a similar passage from the less to the more formal—in this case, from the Rococo to the threshold of Neoclassicism. The small group *Nymph and Satyr* (FIG. 20-28) by CLODION (Claude Michel, 1738–

20-28 CLODION, *Nymph and Satyr, c.* 1775. Terra cotta, approx. 23" high. The Metropolitan Museum of Art, New York (bequest of Benjamin Altman, 1913).

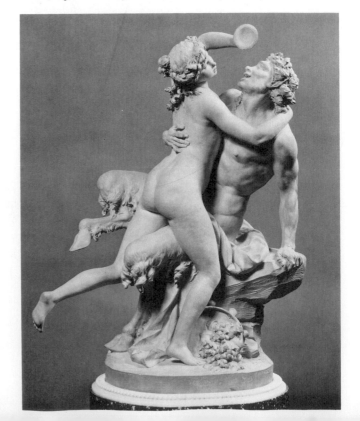

1814) is witness to the fact that the Rococo taste is not altogether passé in the later eighteenth century. The erotic playfulness of Boucher and Fragonard, in an open and vivid composition faintly echoing Gianlorenzo Bernini, energizes the eager nymph and the laughing satyr, into whom she pours a cup of wine. The sensual exhilaration of the Rococo is caught in diminutive scale and fragile terra cotta; as with so many of its artifacts, and most of Clodion's best works, the group is designed for a tabletop.

In sharp contrast, the *Diana* (FIG. 20-29) of JEAN ANTOINE HOUDON (1744–1828) is a bronze statue almost 7 feet high. The fleet goddess of the hunt is caught in one swift moment, elegantly poised. The suavely modeled volumes, the supple contours, and the compact silhouette contribute to her cool simplicity and dignity. All traces of Rococo complexity,

asymmetry, and restlessness have vanished. We cannot yet call the *Diana* Neoclassical (it reflects something of the French Mannerism of the sixteenth century), but it surely represents a *détente* of the Rococo and anticipates Neoclassical formalism.

Houdon was not only a master sculptor of the figure, but the greatest and most successful portraitist of his time. Throughout his long life, Houdon had the opportunity to have as his subjects some of the greatest men of the age: Voltaire, Rousseau, Franklin, Washington, Jefferson, Lafayette. His art comes between the mannered Rococo and the mannered Neoclassicism of the Napoleonic period. Houdon's strong, perceptive realism penetrates at once to personality, catching its most subtle shade. For his *Count Cagliostro* (FIG. 20-30), Houdon had a subject not so much great as notorious. Cagliostro (the name was an alias)—one of the most successful confidence men in history, a brilliant fake, mountebank, quack, and impostor—charmed European society (especially the ladies) even as he swindled it. Houdon renders him in open-necked, romantic *déshabillé*, turning a large-eyed, innocent gaze heavenward, as if in protestation of the purity of his motives and of his love and sympathy for credulous mankind. Houdon's *Cagliostro*, like Molière's earlier *Tartuffe*, presents with exquisite acuteness the character of the sanctimonious fraud.

20-29 JEAN ANTOINE HOUDON, *Diana*, 1790. Bronze, 6′ 11″ high. Louvre, Paris.

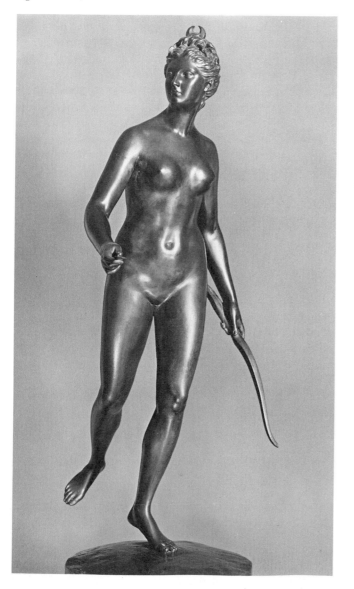

20-30 JEAN ANTOINE HOUDON, *Count Cagliostro* (Giuseppe Balsamo), 1771–1789. Marble, approx. 25″ high (without base). National Gallery of Art, Washington, D.C. (Samuel H. Kress Collection).

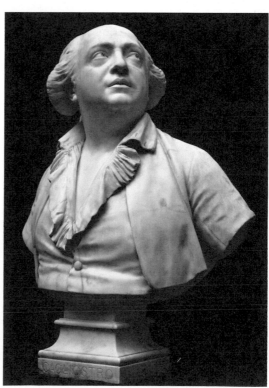

Hogarth believed that portraiture, rather than his own genre, was the forte of the English School of painting. The accumulating fortunes of both the English nobility and merchants in the eighteenth century led, in the first days of the British empire, to the demand not only for fine buildings but also for fine portraits. The tradition of Van Dyck still flourished and was taken up again by a whole school of painters, who gradually modified it for the more modern taste. THOMAS GAINSBOROUGH (1727–1788)—who began as a landscape painter and always preferred landscape to portrait—gives us, in *The Honourable Mrs. Graham* (FIG. 20-31), the very essence of the early preferred Van-Dyckian manner. Dressed in the Rococo flamboyance of feathers and brocade, silver and crimson, the young gentlewoman poses haughtily by a great column and against a deep Venetian background of dark russet. The pride of birth and station is announced in every detail. Full-length, life-sized canvases like this were intended to decorate the grand

20-31 THOMAS GAINSBOROUGH, *The Honourable Mrs. Graham*, 1775. 7′ 9½″ × 5′ ¾″. National Gallery of Scotland, Edinburgh.

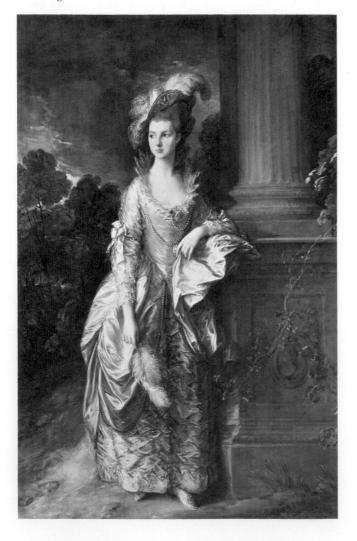

stairways of the great country houses of affluent England. But there is a different intention and result in Gainsborough's portrait of *Mrs. Richard Brinsley Sheridan* (FIG. 20-32). The lovely lady, dressed informally, is seated in a rustic landscape faintly reminiscent of Watteau in its soft-hued light and feathery brushwork. (The artist had intended to give the picture "an air more pastoral than it at present possesses" by the addition of sheep, which he did not live to paint in.) Gainsborough intends to match the unspoiled beauty of natural landscape with the natural beauty of the subject, whose dark brown hair blows freely in the slight wind and whose clear, unassisted "English" complexion and air of ingenuous sweetness are in sharp contrast with the pert sophistication of continental Rococo portraits. The Romantic view of life and nature, already manifest in the transitional "age of sensibility," as we have seen, is pretty much the creation of England. That view is rooted in the concept of naturalness, against the artificiality of the Baroque and the Rococo, at least in their official guise.

The vogue of naturalness easily crosses the channel. The ingenuous, quite charming *Self-Portrait* (FIG. 20-33) by ÉLISABETH LOUISE VIGÉE-LEBRUN (1755–1842), a fashionable portraitist for whom Marie Antoinette, queen of France, sat on several occasions, shows us the new, more natural manner, freed of the frills of the Rococo. The lady—dressed simply in the "Republican" mode and proud of her profession of artist—poses with palette and brushes in the act of painting the portrait of the queen. With a slightly coy, quite excusable vanity, she represents herself younger than she was at the time. In her memoirs, written toward the end of a long and productive life, she cannot help recording how well this portrait was received by the art world of Florence. The vivacious subject renders her likeness with a naïve, unaffected enthusiasm that is quite compelling. One of the finest portraits of the eighteenth century, it expresses all we can mean by "naturalness."

For a type of realistic and revealing portrait of participants in the great events that usher in modern times, we turn to SIR JOSHUA REYNOLDS (1723–1792)—rival of Gainsborough and president of the British Royal Academy of Arts from its foundation in 1768—who, in theory, kept very close to the academic Baroque, as we can read in his *Discourses*. There he expounds a doctrine from which, luckily, he often deviated in practice—that "general" nature, as represented by the Carracci and others, is always superior to "particular" nature, as rendered by the Dutch. Yet he showed himself capable of sturdy, characterful portraits, like that of *Lord Heathfield* (FIG. 20-34). Accustomed to highly formal portraits in the tradition of Van Dyck, Reynolds seems almost relieved when he can turn to a subject like this burly,

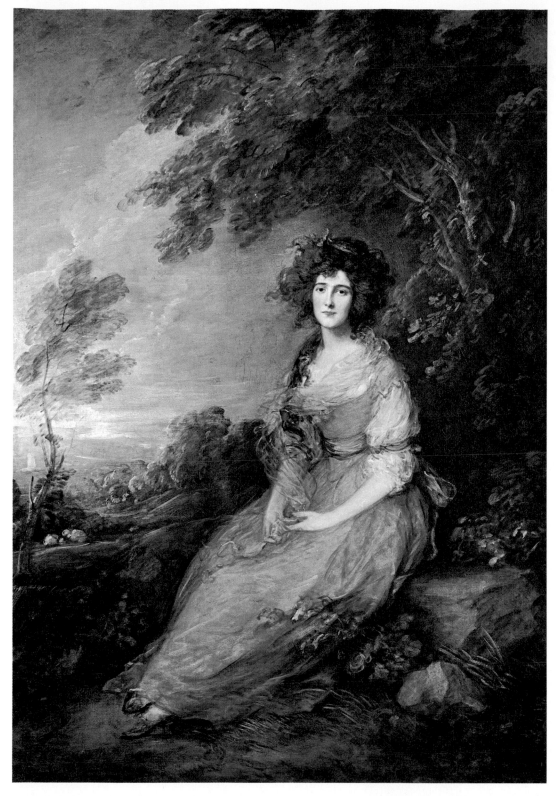

20-32 THOMAS
GAINSBOROUGH,
*Mrs. Richard Brinsley
Sheridan*, c. 1785.
Approx. 7' 2" × 5'.
National Gallery of Art,
Washington, D.C.
(Andrew W. Mellon
Collection).

brandy-flushed English officer, commandant of the
fortress of Gibralter during the American Revolution.
Lord Heathfield doggedly defended the great rock
against the Spanish, and his victory is symbolized by
the key of the fortress, which he holds so casually.
The heavy, honest, unidealized face belongs to a different world from that of Quentin de la Tour (FIG.
20-18). This is a world of camps, battles, and wars

and of revolutions now taking shape in deadly earnest, as the old regime, with all its esthetic artifice,
fades into the past.

The commotion attendant on the emerging modern
world is dramatized by the American painter
BENJAMIN WEST (1738–1820) in a work pioneering a
type of painting based on particular historical events.
Born in Pennsylvania, on what was then the colonial

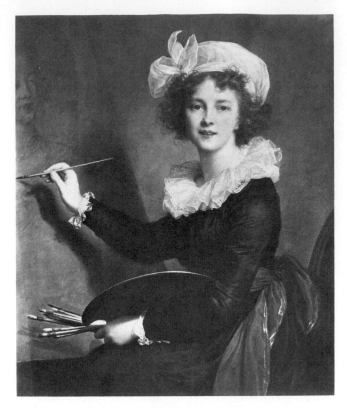

20-33 ÉLISABETH LOUISE VIGÉE-LEBRUN, *Self-Portrait*, 1790. 8′ 4″ × 6′ 9″. Galleria degli Uffizi, Florence.

20-34 SIR JOSHUA REYNOLDS, *Lord Heathfield*, 1787. Approx. 56″ × 45″. Reproduced by courtesy of the Trustees of the National Gallery, London.

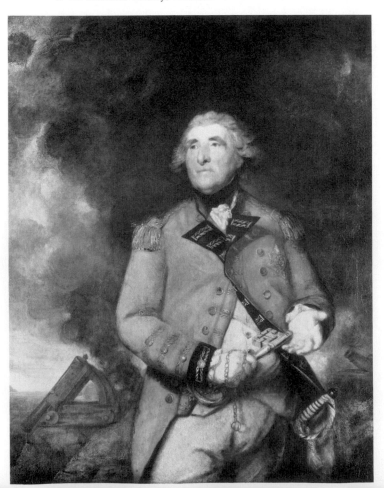

frontier, West was sent to Europe early in life to study art, and then to England, where he had almost immediate success. He was a cofounder of the Royal Academy, and succeeded Sir Joshua Reynolds as its president. He became painter to George III and remained so during the strains of the American Revolution. In *The Death of General Wolfe* (FIG. 20-35), West depicts the mortally wounded young English commander, who has just defeated the French under Montcalm in the decisive battle of Quebec (1759), which gave Canada to Great Britain. Recalling the traditional Pietà theme (FIG. 18-25) in religious painting, the composition, still essentially Baroque, replaces Christ with the modern hero, who swoons to death among his grieving officers on the field of victorious battle. The figures are represented in contemporary military garb (not entirely accurately), rather than in the conventional Classical draperies—a startling innovation that would catch on and last through the nineteenth century. The Anglo-American School of history painting is the leader in the development of the genre.

Born of a general enthusiasm for a new, moral seriousness, the later eighteenth century is preoccupied with themes of heroism and virtuous action sharply antagonistic to the hedonism and escapism of the Rococo style. The sober telling of stories with a moral comes suddenly into fashion in the 1760s. The work of JEAN BAPTISTE GREUZE (1735–1805) became widely popular as the Rococo style faded. Greuze's art expresses perfectly the transition of taste from the Rococo to nineteenth-century Romanticism—his vogue coming in the interim period, the "age of sensibility." Almost overnight, France—and Europe—abandoned the wanton frivolity and luxuriance of the Rococo and became not only serious and moralistic but especially "sensible" and "feeling," which is to say *emotional*. Against what he saw as the cold, heartless, selfish culture of courts, Jean Jacques Rousseau, one of the most influential writers of modern times, called for the sincere expression of sympathetic and tender emotions. He exalted the simple life of the peasant as the most "natural" and set it up as a model to be imitated. The joys and sorrows of uncorrupted "natural" people, now described everywhere in novels, soon drowned Europe in a flood of tears; it became fashionable to weep, to fall on one's knees, to swoon, and to languish in hopeless love. This kind of contrived and melodramatic emotion, this *sentimentality*, has been a fundamental ingredient of popular art from the time of its appearance in the eighteenth century until the present. Greuze won wide acclaim with paintings entitled the *Father of the Family Reading the Bible to His Children*, the *Village Bride*, and the *Father's Curse*, in all of which he pointed a moral and sentimentalized his characters. In his *Return of the Prodigal Son* (FIG. 20-36) the theme is plain enough and the action is rather crudely obvious. Yet his moralizing

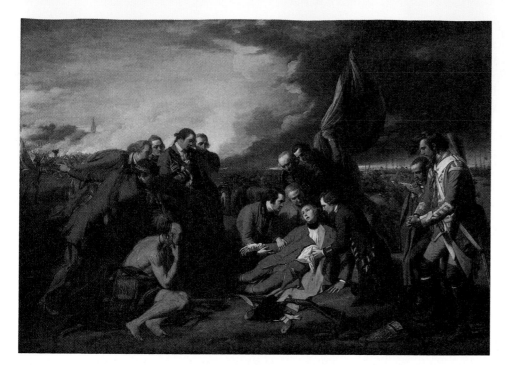

20-35 BENJAMIN WEST, *The Death of General Wolfe*, 1771. Approx. 5' × 7'. National Gallery of Canada, Ottawa (gift of the Duke of Westminster, 1918).

does look forward to that of Jacques Louis David and Neoclassicism, and we may credit Greuze with a kind of pioneer work in a type of subject and expression that meets with more general acceptance at present, when his reputation, suffering from later criticism, has been restored to a degree.

It is noteworthy that Denis Diderot, the great philosophe and scholar, advanced the cause of Greuze for a while but afterward acknowledged his artificiality. In *Salon of 1765*, Diderot describes a sketch for *The Return of the Prodigal Son*:

This is the sight which meets the eyes of the ungrateful son. He comes forward, he is on the threshold. . . . His mother meets him at his entrance; she is silent, but with her hand points to the corpse as if to say: "See what you have done."

The ungrateful son is struck with amazement; his head falls forward, and he strikes his forehead with his hand. What a lesson is here depicted for fathers and children! . . . I do not know what effect this short and simple description . . . will produce on others, but for my own part I could not write it without emotion.*

We feel today that the attitudes and gestures of Greuze's figures are somewhat inauthentic and forced; in fact, they are drawn from the stock vocabu-

*See E.G. Holt, *A Documentary History of Art* (Princeton, N.J.: Princeton University Press, 1958), Vol. 2, p. 319.

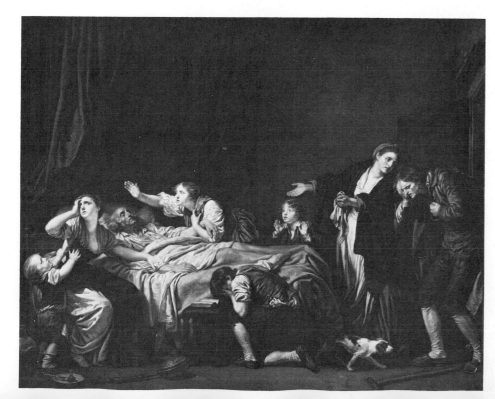

20-36 JEAN BAPTISTE GREUZE, *The Return of the Prodigal Son*, 1777–1778. Approx. 51" × 65". Louvre, Paris.

lary of the academic tradition and will be repeated even more provincially in melodramatic stageplays throughout the nineteenth century.

With the approaching French Revolution, the temper of the times becomes more severe and the type and quality of emotion changes. Following the "age of sensibility," the values of moral virtue, civic dedication, heroism, and self-sacrifice, rather than gentleness and tenderness, now demand expression. The change of interest is from the private to the public theater of action, where the *naturally* noble attributes of human nature are supposed to emerge, cleansed of those past and present corruptions denounced by Rosseau. Naturalness—formerly associated, whether by Rosseau or by Greuze, with the simple people of the French countryside—comes to be identified with the heroes of Classical Greece and Rome, who are understood as the paragons of all goodness, truth, and beauty. "Natural" and "Classical" are identical in Neoclassical thinking.

In the art of ANGELICA KAUFFMANN (1741–1807), the "naturalness" of Greuze's figure types, situations, and contemporary settings is replaced by a Neoclassicism still suggestive of the Rococo. Born in Switzerland and trained in Italy, Kauffmann spent many of her productive years in England. A protégée of Sir Joshua Reynolds and a decorator of the interiors of houses built by Robert Adam, she was a founding member of the British Royal Academy of Arts, and enjoyed a fashionable reputation. Her *Cornelia, Mother of the Gracchi* (FIG. 20-37) is a kind of "set piece" of early Neoclassicism; its subject is an *exemplum virtutis* (example or model of virtue) of the didactic kind, drawn from the history and literature of Greece and Rome. This turning away from the frivolous and sensuous subjects of the Rococo to themes thought to be noble and elevating becomes general in the late eighteenth century. Greuze's moralizing pictures already mark a change in taste; but whereas he stages idealized rustics in peasant cottages, Kauffmann clothes her actors in ancient Roman garb, poses them in classicizing Roman attitudes, and places them in Roman interiors. Her theme here is the virtue of Cornelia, mother of the future political leaders Tiberius and Gaius Gracchus, who, in the second century B.C., attempted to reform the Roman republic. When a lady visitor, boasting of her fine jewels, asks Cornelia to show hers, Cornelia—praised for her gentle and wise education of her children—brings them forward, saying "*These* are my jewels!" The architecture is severely Roman, with not a Rococo motif in evidence, and the composition and drawing have the simplicity and firmness of bas-relief. Yet the charm and grace of Rococo lingers, moderated by Kauffmann's own bland, tranquil manner.

Greuze's philosophy of sentiment and Kauffmann's sentimental Neoclassicism harden into the public, programmatic stoicism of JACQUES LOUIS DAVID (1748–1825), the painter—ideologist of the Neoclassical art of the French Revolution and the Napoleonic empire.

20-37 ANGELICA KAUFFMANN, *Cornelia, Mother of the Gracchi, c.* 1785. 40″ × 50″. Museum of Fine Arts, Richmond, Virginia.

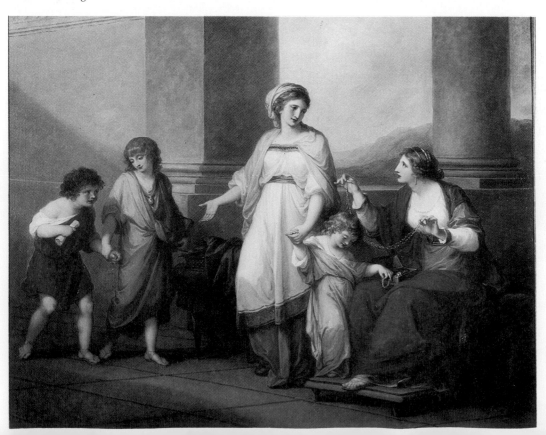

We have noted that Neoclassicism is only one of the revival styles of Romanticism. The fact is, too, that Classical art had a long tradition in Europe and France before the time of David and that academies had long based their existence on the principle that the elements of art can be taught according to rules taken from the ancients and the great masters of the Renaissance. In his own quite individual and often non-Classical style, David reworks the Classical and academic traditions. He rebels against the Rococo as an "artificial taste" and exalts Classical art as, in his own words, "the imitation of nature in her most beautiful and perfect form." He praises Greek art enthusiastically, although he, like Winckelmann, knew almost nothing about it firsthand: "I want to work in a pure Greek style. I feed my eyes on ancient statues; I even have the intention of imitating some of them. . . ." But David's doctrine of the superiority of Classical art is not based on an isolated esthetic; believing, as he writes, that "the arts must . . . contribute forcefully to the education of the public," he was prepared both as artist and politician when the French Revolution offered the opportunity to create a public art, an art of propaganda.

David was active in the French Revolution as a Jacobin friend of the radical Maximilien Robespierre, as a member of the National Convention that voted for the death of the king, Louis XVI, and as quasi-dictator of the Committee on Public Education, where he directed the art programs of the new republic. He joined scholars and artists in soliciting the revolutionary government to abolish the old French Royal Academy and to establish in its place panels of experts to guide the reformation of taste. His position of power made him dominant in the transformation of style, and his own manner was the official model for many years.

Although painted in 1784, before the French Revolution, David's *Oath of the Horatii* (FIG. 20-38) reflects his politically didactic purpose and his doctrine of the educational power of Classical form, as well as his method of composing the Neoclassical picture. Most important of all to David, as artistic descendant of the old Academy, is the choice of subject matter: It must have grandeur and a moral. If effectively presented, David writes, the "marks of heroism and civic virtue offered the eyes of the people will electrify its soul, and plant the seeds of glory and devotion to the fatherland." For this *Oath*, David selected a story from pre-Republican Rome—the heroic phase of Roman history that had been pushed to the foreground of public interest by the sensational archeological discoveries made at the time at Herculaneum and Pompeii. The subject, a conflict between love and patriotism, is based on a play by Pierre Corneille that had been performed in Paris several years earlier and thus was known to the Parisian public. According to the story, first told by Livy, the leaders of the Roman and Alban armies, poised for battle, decide to resolve their conflicts in triple combat among three representatives from each side. The Roman choice falls on the three Horatius brothers; that of the Albans, on the three sons of the Curatius family. A sister of the Horatii, Camilla, is the bride-to-be of one of the Curatius sons.

David's painting shows the Horatii as they swear on their swords to win or die for Rome, oblivious to the anguish and sorrow of their sisters. The theme is

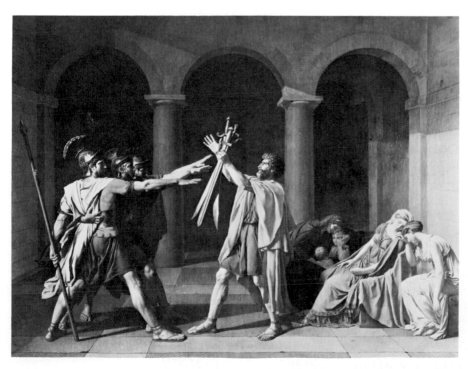

20-38 Jacques Louis David, *Oath of the Horatii*, 1784. Approx. 11' × 14'. Louvre, Paris.

stated with admirable force and clarity. The rigid and virile forms of the men effectively eclipse the soft, curvilinear shape of the mourning women in the right background. Such manly virtues as courage, patriotism, and unwavering loyalty to a cause are emphasized over the less heroic emotions of love, sorrow, and despair symbolized by the women. The message is clear and of a type with which the prerevolutionary French public could readily identify. The picture created a sensation when it was exhibited in Paris in 1785, and although it had been painted under royal patronage and was not at all revolutionary in intent, its Neoclassical style became the semiofficial voice of the revolution. David may have been painting in the academic tradition, but he makes of it something new—a program for arousing an audience to patriotic zeal. From David's *Oath* onward, art will become political—if not often in the sense of serving a state or party, then in its division into trends, movements, and ideologies.

In its form, *Oath of the Horatii* is a paragon of Neoclassical academicism. In a shallow picture box, defined by a severely simple architectural framework, statuesque and carefully modeled figures are deployed laterally and close to the foreground in a manner reminiscent of ancient relief sculpture. But caught up in the general mid-eighteenth-century enthusiasm for the archeological recovery and study of great civilizations, David's goal is the precise description of the monuments and personages of the historical past. This almost pedantic dedication to historical reality (he once complained that Raphael, that paragon of Classicism, erred by putting people of different periods into the same picture) compels David to modify his Neoclassical formula. In later work, he seeks to avoid such changes in formula and even stiffens his style in keeping with his concept of the antique manner, but in a painting like *The Death of Marat* (FIG. 20-39), the Classical elements of closed outline and compact composition, though present, are made to serve the ends of a dramatic realism of strong, psychic impact. The cold, neutral space above the densely organized figure composition makes for a chilling oppressiveness. Here, the scene is shaped by historical fact, not Neoclassical theory; and the "stele"-like composition reveals that David has closely studied Michelangelo, especially the Christ of the *Pietà* in St. Peter's. Marat, a personal friend of David and a revolutionary radical, was stabbed to death in his bath by Charlotte Corday, a political enemy. Narrative details—the knife, the wound, the blood, the letter by which the young woman gained entrance—are vividly placed to sharpen the sense of pain and outrage, but above all to confront the viewer with the scene itself. *Marat*, given David's personal involvement, is a poignantly felt theme, realized with almost painful sincerity. It is convincingly *real*, yet it

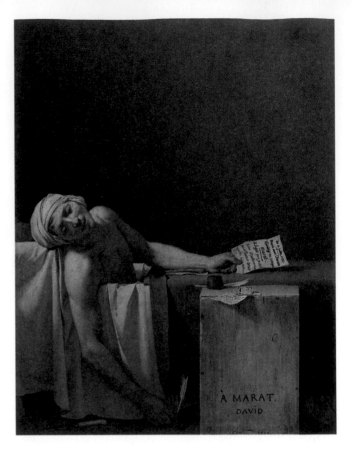

20-39 JACQUES LOUIS DAVID, *The Death of Marat*, 1793. Approx. 63″ × 49″. Musées Royaux des Beaux-Arts de Belgique, Brussels.

loses nothing of pose, composition, and rendering of light and shadow in David's astonishingly calm execution.

From modernizing Classical antiquity in the quasi-Realism of the *Oath of the Horatii*, David eventually moves to the point where he is classicizing the modern, as in his *Madame Récamier*, in which a Parisian socialite, dressed and coiffed *à la greque*, reclines on a Pompeian couch in a severely formal setting. The corner is turned, and we are now exposed to the staged, rather than the real, Classicism—much like a modern motion picture concerned with historical events. This is the consequence of David's mobilization of the Classical manner in the service of contemporary political struggles. However, even before David's time, it had been discovered that Classical philosophy and art *were* historical and that they did, after all, belong to a particular time and place.

Thus, for all his loyalty to Classical theory, David turns out not to be a Classicist at all, and his pupils will either drop his program altogether or change Classicism into a decorative, contour manner valued not for its idealism or truth but for its purely visual qualities. David's avowed purpose was to "electrify the soul," but he believed that art must be "of the reason, and rise above the passions." This contradiction—symptomatic of the turbulent change from the "age of reason" to the "age of revolution"—makes

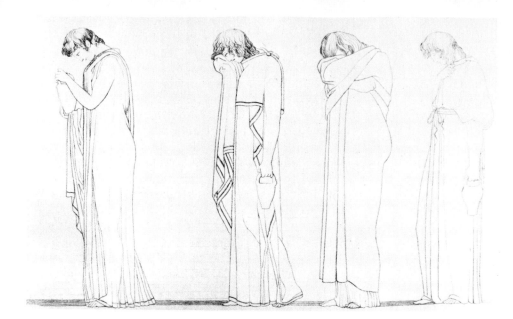

20-40 John Flaxman, *Electra Leading the Procession to Agamemnon's Tomb* (from the *Choephoroe*), 1795. Engraving.

his art inconsistent. His followers, although they will agree with the romantic aim to "electrify the soul," will break it into different combinations and directions, using a variety of stylistic means—for all the styles of past times and distant places are now becoming available to the artist.

Neoclassicism, treated in a confused and ambivalent fashion by David and his school, finds clear and simple expression in the influential art of the sculptor and draughtsman, John Flaxman (1755–1826), whose style inspired Ingres, David's greatest pupil. Flaxman, creating the extreme limit of withdrawal from the intricacy and sensuality of the Rococo, which he loathed, reduces his forms to bare, linear outlines, without color or chiaroscuro, and his content to themes of an almost ascetic purity and severity (FIG. 20-40). His models were taken from Greek and Etruscan vase painting (FIGS. 5-8, 5-9, 5-10, 5-11) and Greek sculpture (FIGS. 5-52 and 5-57). He chose his subjects from Homer, Hesiod, Aeschylus, Dante, and other great classics of the West, and his illustrations of them were immensely popular, both in Europe and America. Shown here is the opening scene of the *Choephoroe* of Aeschylus, in which Electra and her mourning women move slowly to the tomb of her murdered father, Agamemnon. There, she will meet her brother Orestes and swear with him to revenge their father's death on their hated mother, Clytemnestra, his murderer. Flaxman renders the procession with epic spareness; indeed, his interpretations of the Classical themes were thought worthy of Homer. The drooping figures of the sorrowing women lose nothing of majesty; they have a columnar strength reminiscent of the caryatids of the Erechtheum (FIG. 5-57). At the same time, there is a slow, steady, rhythmic motion, as of some solemn dance interpretive of grief. The disciplined delineation in pure, unaccented line loses nothing of this sense of movement; it does not become immobilized into rigidity. For more than

a generation, Flaxman's style was considered the perfection of the Neoclassical ideal.

The contrast between Flaxman and his older contemporary, Henry Fuseli (1741–1825), could not be a more startling illustration of the abrupt conflict and contradiction between styles within the same time and place, even within an artist's own development. The stylistic pluralism, the multiplicity of stylistic options characteristic of the nineteenth century, is manifest here. Fuseli, Swiss by birth, settled in England and eventually became a member of the Royal Academy and an instructor there. Largely self-taught, he contrived a distinctive manner, compounded of Michelangelo, the antique style, and his own extravagant invention. He specializes in night moods of horror and in "gothic" fantasies—in the demonic, the macabre, often the sadistic. The twisted poses and frantic gestures of his figures go well beyond exaggeration and often suggest the influence of Italian Mannerism. *The Nightmare* (FIG. 20-41) is the first of four versions of this terrifying theme. The beautiful young woman, tormented by some terrible dream and still not awake, has thrown herself partly from her couch. Her attitude shows her helpless beneath the incubus that squats malignantly on her body, as a horse with flaming eyes bursts into the scene from beyond the curtain. The Romantic vein of violent emotion and of perverse and tragic action will be heavily mined in the nineteenth century. Fuseli's art is near the start of an enterprise that will lead to the uncovering of the dark terrain of the human subconscious.

The later eighteenth century sees the calm weather of romantic Neoclassicism alternate with the storm and stress of emotional Romanticism. This alternation appears almost randomly in the art of William Blake (1757–1827), the visionary poet and engraver. A friend of both Flaxman and Fuseli, Blake can manage their contradictory moods as if he were merely

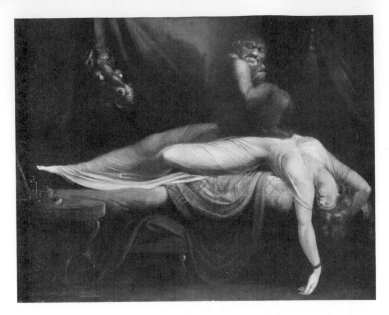

20-41 HENRY FUSELI, *The Nightmare*, 1781. Approx. 40" × 51". The Detroit Institute of the Arts (gift of Mr. and Mrs. Bert L. Smokler and Mr. and Mrs. Lawrence A. Fleishman).

changing the content of his own dreams. He draws on Flaxman for Neoclassical effects, and exchanges subjects with Fuseli. There is a curious thematic and compositional resemblance between Blake's *Pity* (FIG. 20-42) and Fuseli's *Nightmare* (FIG. 20-41), but the mood and atmosphere are completely different. Blake's is serene; Fuseli's, dark and tormented. In Blake's picture, the soul of the dying woman is snatched up by angels of death, who sweep by on spectral white horses. The gesture of the near angel is benign, almost loving, in contrast with the malignancy of the incubus in Fuseli's picture. The sculptural relief and linearity, as well as the almost total

suppression of color, relate, at some distance, to the manner of Flaxman.

In the work of a great master in the art of etching, GIOVANNI BATTISTA PIRANESI (1720–1778), the Classical world and a world of pure, romantic fantasy coexist, reconciled in a single mood, style, and technique. We have already met Piranesi as the artist whose etched prints spread the monuments of ancient Rome before the eyes of Europe and who took a leading part in stimulating the enthusiasm for the Classical style. But he could also take an utterly different tack—his powerful imagination conjuring up awe-inspiring visions of bafflingly complicated architectural masses, piled up and spread out through gloomy spaces. In such pictures, vistas are multiplied and broken by a seeming infinity of massive arches, vaults, piers and stairways, through which move human figures small as insects. Despite wandering, soaring perspectives, there is a suffocating sense of enclosure; the spaces are locked in, and there is no exit. These grim places are, in fact, prisons (*carceri*), filled with brooding menace and hopelessness. Piranesi etched a series of them, often darkening subsequent editions to make them even more sinister. Our picture (FIG. 20-43) is one of these. In a different way from Fuseli and Blake, Piranesi creates oppressive dreams, and his *Carceri 14* will haunt the night imaginings of many a Romantic poet.

The eighteenth century, as the "age of reason," seems to have found the rational ideal in Neoclassical art (Romantic Classicism)—for example, in a Jefferson or a Flaxman. But Fuseli and Blake and Piranesi show that the equation of reason and nature in Neo-

20-42 WILLIAM BLAKE, *Pity, c.* 1795. Watercolor, approx. 17" × 21". Tate Gallery, London.

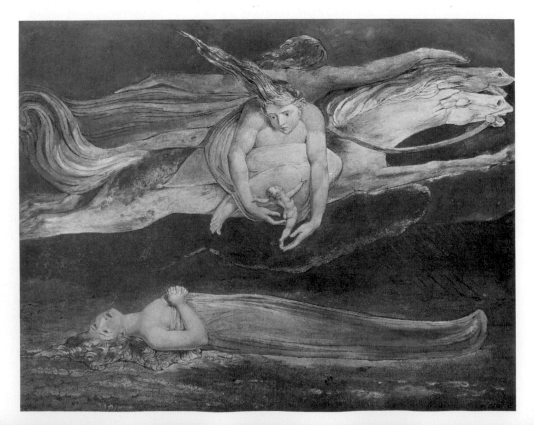

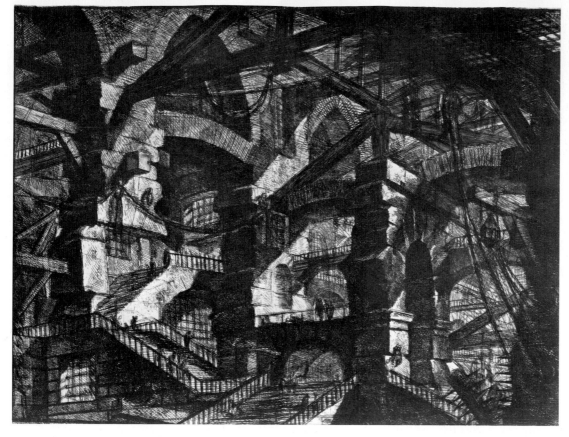

20-43 GIOVANNI BATTISTA PIRANESI, *Carceri 14, c.* 1750. Etching, second state, approx. 16″ × 21″. Ashmolean Museum, Oxford.

classicism can be false, or at least insufficient to do justice to the human reality. Imagination may reach farther than reason and find, by suprarational intuition and enkindled emotion, a higher and a deeper experience. The worlds of dream and vision may provide more valid materials for the soul of the artist liberated from the rules of reason; Blake writes: "I will not reason and compare, my business is to create." Feeling, emotion, and passion at full intensity may be surer guides than reason in the quest for meaning; Blake again: "The road of excess leads to the palace of wisdom." Yet there are grave risks. Raw feeling could lead the soul astray, perhaps beyond the limits of sanity. The "age of reason" leaves a warning for the "age of romanticism" and its offspring, the modern world, in a print by the Spanish master FRANCISCO GOYA, whom we shall soon consider in some detail. In a print from a series called *Los Caprichos* (FIG. 20-44), Goya depicts the artist asleep, while around him throng winged monsters and demons—the nightmare brood that peoples his dreams (again, the nightmare!). Goya captions the print: "The Dream of Reason Produces Monsters."

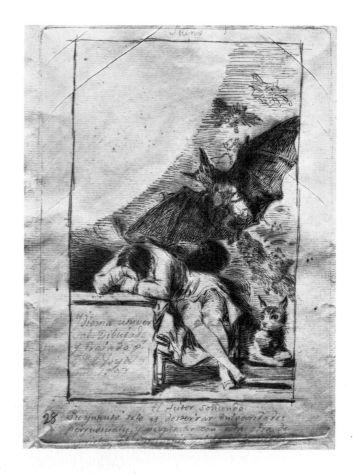

20-44 FRANCISCO GOYA, *"The Dream of Reason,"* from *Los Caprichos, c.* 1794–1799. Pen-and-sepia drawing, approx. 8″ × 5″. Museo del Prado, Madrid.

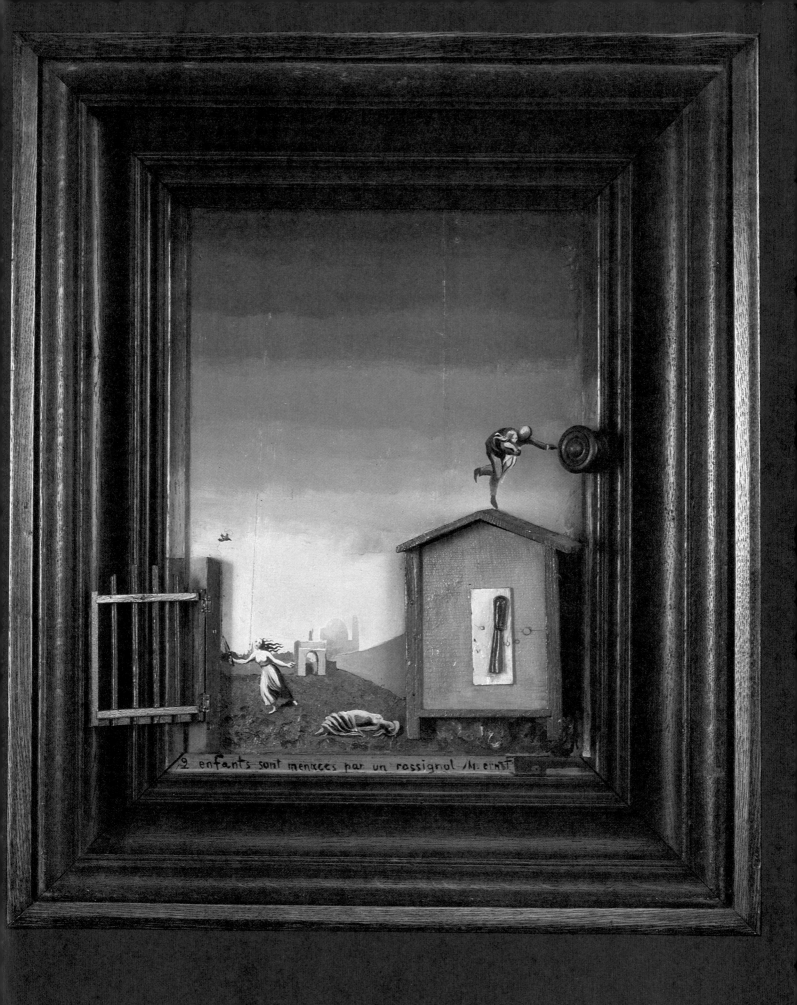

V

THE MODERN WORLD

Our era, the "modern" era, differs from the past as a result of several fundamental revolutions that have radically changed—and are continuing to change—the world. Least dramatic in its arrival, but by far the most fateful for mankind, was the Industrial Revolution: the revolution that introduced the age of the machine. To match the importance of the Industrial Revolution, we would have to go back thousands of years to the development of agriculture. For, in two centuries (an extremely short span of historical time), we have

Max Ernst, *Two Children Are Threatened by a Nightingale*, 1924. Oil on wood with wood construction, 27½″ high, 22½″ wide, 4½″ deep. Museum of Modern Art, New York (purchase).

created a universe of machines that replaces physical labor and extends the powers of the brain enormously, bringing changes in the conditions of life with such speed that we find it difficult to adjust to them. Human knowledge, dawning in the Old Stone Age, reaches "high noon" in our own times. Control of nature is now widespread and tenacious; science has become our most authoritative source of natural knowledge, and the application of it in technology and industry has become the characteristic activity or ambition of modern societies.

As science and technology challenged old views of the physical world, so political revolution, beginning in the late eighteenth century, challenged the old absolutisms of Church and Realm, setting up such new aims and values as democracy, nationalism, and social justice. Subsequent revolutions have transformed the social and economic organization of vast areas of the world; regions colonized by Europe since the Renaissance have risen against her to the call of her own revolutionary slogans. As Europeans conquered and colonized the non-European world, they unwittingly began an exchange not only of goods, but of ideas and cultures. In the twentieth century, European colonial empires decline or vanish, and non-European nations rise in their place. The trend appears to be away from separate civilizations and toward a *world* civilization, and the peculiarly European traits that took form in the Renaissance lose their distinctive character. In all sectors of Western culture, the Humanist's image of man, created in the Renaissance, is being blurred and, here and there, effaced. In the modern view, man has been displaced from the commanding position the Renaissance assigned him as master of the Nature that God created for him. Now, though man holds greater control than ever before over his environment, he is seen to be as much the despoiler and victim of it as he is its master. Within Western nations, established values and institutions are being challenged on all sides. In fear and mistrust of what the West has created—great evil that seems to outweigh great good—many are turning to non-Western cultures to find fresh and alternative interpretations of life. For many thoughtful persons, there is the poignant feeling that the West has had its day and that its fundamental assumptions about human values have been discredited. They hear, with André Malraux, voices clamoring for the abdication of the West.

The revolutionary changes of the modern world on all fronts—scientific, technological-industrial, political, social, economic, and cultural—make for the characteristic temper of our age: a mixture of restlessness, obsession with progress and novelty, and a ceaseless questioning, testing, and challenging of authority. Old certainties give place to new, and the new give place to still newer. Scarcely a traditional value, system, institution, or rule in the modern world has escaped relentless critical analysis. At the same time, discovery and invention, proceeding at an always accelerating pace, are making the once impossible both possible and actual; today's "nonsense," as Alfred North Whitehead puts it, may be demonstrated truth tomorrow. The rapid obsolescence of ideas and things gives life a tentative and temporary quality and makes confusion a constant in its ever-changing patterns.

It is little wonder, then, that art in this period is a sequence and medley of competing "movements"—each seeking to establish its authority, each having its own ideology, and each subject to displacement in the bewilderingly rapid process of stylistic turnover. We describe these movements in terms (rarely precise) that aim to define their artistic content, form, and intention: "Romanticism," "Realism," "Impressionism," and the like.* Implicit in such words is the notion of doctrine; certainly, the principles and issues of these movements, hotly and widely argued in their time, ultimately spread beyond territorial and national boundaries. Appropriately enough for an age that sees the making of a world civilization, modern art, in all its component movements, tends to be international, like modern science, technology, industry, and politics.

*Terms like these, which we will now encounter more frequently, designate stylistic trends, movements, philosophies, and periods. Where they are so used, we will capitalize them as nouns and also as adjectives. When such terms are used in their broader senses, they will not be capitalized. Realism, for example, can be, on the one hand, the narrower, specific reference to the nineteenth-century movement of that name and, on the other, the wider, more general reference to art that emphasizes the literal reproduction of the facts of appearance, no matter the period, as in the painting of Velázquez, Vermeer, and many others (in the latter case, our choice is "realism" and "realistic.") Any rule for capitalization is arbitrary and sometimes inconsistent; it can, however, be useful in defining trends and influences and as a mnemonic device.

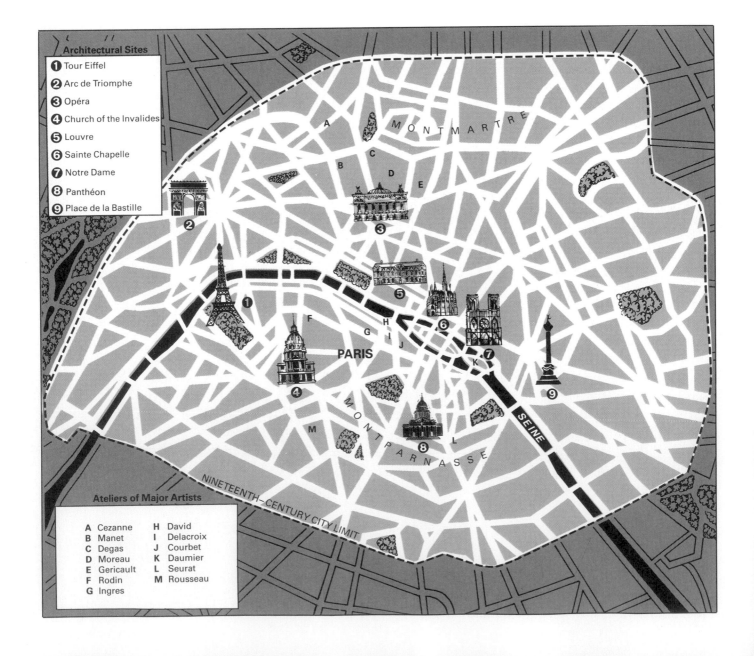

Architectural Sites

1. Tour Eiffel
2. Arc de Triomphe
3. Opéra
4. Church of the Invalides
5. Louvre
6. Sainte Chapelle
7. Notre Dame
8. Panthéon
9. Place de la Bastille

MONTMARTRE

PARIS

MONTPARNASSE

SEINE

NINETEENTH–CENTURY CITY LIMIT

Ateliers of Major Artists

A	Cezanne	H	David
B	Manet	I	Delacroix
C	Degas	J	Courbet
D	Moreau	K	Daumier
E	Gericault	L	Seurat
F	Rodin	M	Rousseau
G	Ingres		

21

THE NINETEENTH CENTURY: PLURALISM OF STYLE

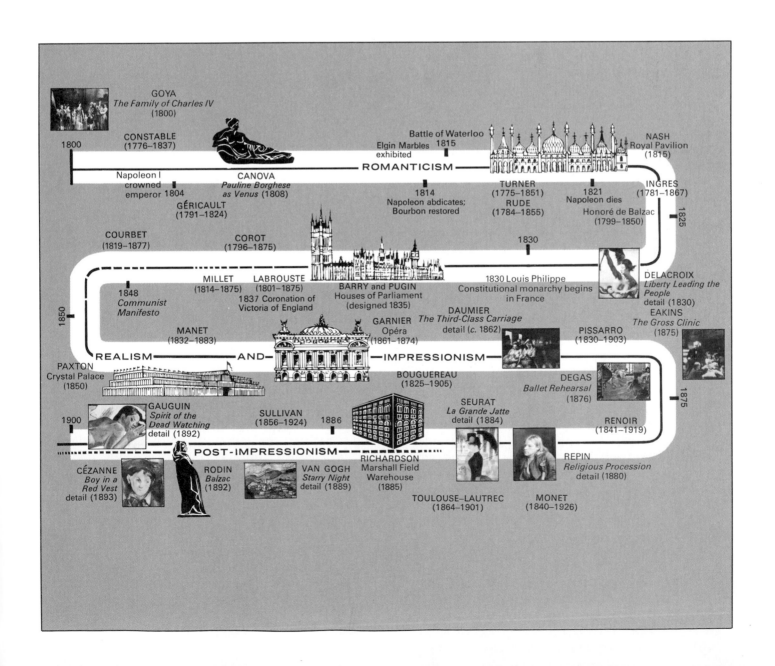

GOYA
The Family of Charles IV
(1800)

CONSTABLE
(1776–1837)

1800

Battle of Waterloo
Elgin Marbles 1815
exhibited

NASH
Royal Pavilion
(1815)

Napoleon I
crowned
emperor 1804

CANOVA
*Pauline Borghese
as Venus* (1808)

ROMANTICISM

TURNER
(1775–1851)
RUDE
(1784–1855)

1821
Napoleon dies

INGRES
(1781–1867)

1825

GÉRICAULT
(1791–1824)

1814
Napoleon abdicates;
Bourbon restored

Honoré de Balzac
(1799–1850)

COURBET
(1819–1877)

COROT
(1796–1875)

1830

DELACROIX
*Liberty Leading the
People*
detail (1830)

MILLET
(1814–1875)

LABROUSTE
(1801–1875)

BARRY and PUGIN
Houses of Parliament
(designed 1835)

1830 Louis Philippe
Constitutional monarchy begins
in France

1848
*Communist
Manifesto*

1837 Coronation of
Victoria of England

EAKINS
The Gross Clinic
(1875)

1850

MANET
(1832–1883)

GARNIER
Opéra
(1861–1874)

DAUMIER
The Third-Class Carriage
detail (c. 1862)

PISSARRO
(1830–1903)

REALISM

AND

IMPRESSIONISM

PAXTON
Crystal Palace
(1850)

BOUGUEREAU
(1825–1905)

DEGAS
Ballet Rehearsal
(1876)

1875

GAUGUIN
*Spirit of the
Dead Watching*
detail (1892)

SULLIVAN
(1856–1924)

1886

SEURAT
La Grande Jatte
detail (1884)

RENOIR
(1841–1919)

1900

POST-IMPRESSIONISM

RICHARDSON
Marshall Field
Warehouse
(1885)

REPIN
Religious Procession
detail (1880)

CÉZANNE
*Boy in a
Red Vest*
detail (1893)

RODIN
Balzac
(1892)

VAN GOGH
Starry Night
detail (1889)

TOULOUSE–LAUTREC
(1864–1901)

MONET
(1840–1926)

FOR EUROPE, the nineteenth century was an age of radical change during which the modern world took shape. In a world experiencing a population explosion of unprecedented magnitude, revolution followed on revolution, punctuated by counterrevolution and conservative reaction. Authority was ceaselessly challenged and reaffirmed in all areas of experience. In the political world, democratic governments were demanded, and the demand was resisted. Social and economic struggle pitted industrial capitalism and the bourgeoisie against the teeming and widely impoverished industrial masses. Reform was everywhere urged and often adopted. The technological transformation of the environment that began in the eighteenth century pushed forward with immense speed and made possible European colonization of the globe. The formation of empires abroad was backed by the enthusiasm of popular nationalism at home, and patriotism and imperialism went hand in hand. Improvements in transportation and communication quickened the exchange of ideas and the dissemination of information, propaganda, and opinion. These, in turn, incited competition and conflict among interests and values, theories and practices, programs and policies in all spheres of action—not the least in the arts.

A profound sense of history pervaded the century. The past was rapidly receding, and a unique present was asserting its originality—as decisively as the Early Christian world asserted *its* new value against the defeated and devalued pagan past. The new age, created by the great revolutions, was *modern,* and modern, for many, was good. What was not modern was rejected, for what was to come would be better. This was the doctrine of Progress, which maintained the permanency of change for the better. As early as 1750, Turgot had predicted that the doctrine of Progress would replace that of the will of God.

Many in the nineteenth century did not accept the doctrine of Progress, or did so with reservations—often with grave misgivings. They saw much of value being lost through change and feared for the traditions, institutions, customs, and mores that knit society together and gave meaning to life. They could accept neither the depreciation of human value implicit in scientific explanations of human nature nor the alienation and degradation of human beings by a mechanized and impersonal industry. They had special distaste for the type of modern society built by new wealth, with all its ostentatious materialism. Many who objected to the vulgarity and banality of taste of that society were artists—some of them, the best artists of the century. In a moment, we shall describe their predicament.

The liberal belief in progress is a belief that the course of history can be changed by thought and action, as long as people are not impeded by authority. The great debate of the nineteenth century was about authority: what should be believed, respected, defended, conformed to? Revolutionary shake-ups of authority reverberated throughout the century, carrying the hope of peoples for something newer, better, truer, and purer. Humanity was thought to be perfectible, and the principle of utility—calling for the greatest good of the greatest number—was advocated for law, government, and economic life. But confusion arose over the means to these ends, a confusion that produced a wide multiplicity of philosophies rationalizing change and the reactions to change. These ideologies, which provided the maxims and slogans of the countless movements that agitated the century and remain current, are the "isms": liberalism, radicalism, socialism, communism, conservatism, nationalism—all coinages of the nineteenth century. We will presently meet their counterparts in the world of art: Romanticism, Realism, Naturalism, Impressionism, and the rest.

What all of these ideologies have in common is dissatisfaction with a status quo, in which the past lingers, and disagreement about how it should be corrected—that is, modernized. For the arts, this means continuing debate over the relative values of the "traditional" and the "modern"—a debate restimulated as each new style is itself rapidly superseded by yet a newer one. This rapid appearance and obsolescence of a variety of artistic styles (analogous to the concurrent rapid turnover in types of mechanically produced commodities and to the quick progression of scientific and technological discoveries and inventions) transforms painting, the graphic arts, sculpture, and architecture so radically that the transformations amount to a dismantling of tradition altogether and the appearance of something utterly novel. This is the reverse of the development of science, which builds on its tradition in largely unbroken continuity within the expanding language of mathematics.

The nineteenth-century artist had to face formidable changes on all sides. As sources of artists' commissions, the Church and the secular nobility were replaced by the triumphant middle class (the bourgeoisie), the national state, and national academies. The new, uncultivated taste of large publics—concerned, above all, with money and property and guided and manipulated by the new profession of public critics writing in the press—created an uncertain and risky market for the artist working alone, like a preindustrial handicraftsman. Competition (their number had more than doubled since the end of the previous century) forced crowds of artists, influenced by the fluctuations of fashion and by their natural desire for success, to bid for the public's attention by flattering its taste. Like small, independent capitalists with their own stocks and stores, artists took chances in the market, aiming to please. Where they did not, they risked the suspicion and the hostility of the public. Thus, the century witnessed the gradual alienation of the artists and the emergence of their problematic situation in modern society.

Artists who were dissatisfied with standards of public taste and the professional performances designed to satisfy it protested, in their own work and through that of friendly critics, what they called the degeneration of art into shallow entertainment. Highly individualistic and imbued with the romantic ideals of self-expression, they called for a new vision— original and sincere, free from the sentimentalities, trivialities, and hypocrisies of conventional taste. Rejecting the authority of prevailing taste and of the institutions backing it, they claimed the right to an authority of their own, often with a sense of mission not unlike that of the seer and prophet: to restore or re-create art. These artists tended to group or be grouped into parties or ''movements,'' analogous to those in political life and recognizable by their opposition to the status quo. Whichever side they occupied in the complex, stylistic dialogues that took place, they were, in fact, debating in a new way the very nature of art and the function of the artist. As it turns out, they were dealing with the question of a *modern* art, one fundamentally different from that of the past even though it might be constructed out of the ''tradition'' to greater or lesser degree.

The Tradition, as we will refer to it, was the whole corpus of art acknowledged to be good or great: the art of Greece and Rome, of the Renaissance, and of the Baroque. These occupied a stylistic spectrum from ''classical idealism'' to ''optical realism'' that seemed to exhaust the physical possibilities of the media as well as their thematic content. The Tradition was first challenged and, by the end of the century, rejected for an art ''of our own times,'' a *modern* art. In the course of the century, challenge was met by response, and response by new challenge, so that the modes of traditional and modern were interwoven, combined, recombined, and separated by independent artists, producing a bewildering plurality of individual styles that are not easily categorized. Although we will use the conventional categories of art history—''Romanticism,'' ''Realism,'' ''Impressionism,'' and so on—as markers, these terms cannot help but be indefinite and often misleading. What we *do* perceive by mid-century is a bifurcation of the pictorial arts not heretofore seen. It is a bifurcation of specialty and purpose: one branch, optical realism, leading to the photograph and the motion picture; the other, imaginative figuration, leading to the abstract art of the twentieth century. The former is directed to the public and popular taste; the latter, for the most part, to a select, specially trained audience.

It is necessary, finally, to point out the factors that contributed to this historical division. Painters in the nineteenth century were confronted by three innovations that fatefully affected their craft: the camera, the mass-produced print, and the printed reproduction. The almost infinite proliferation of the products of these new media flooded the world with images that became formidable rivals of the unique picture made by hand. In a way, the nineteenth-century artist was technologically displaced, as the manuscript illuminator was by the printer in the sixteenth century. Moreover, the collective techniques of an industrial age forced the artists, as individual craftsmen, to analyze their function and to study closely the physical nature of their medium—paint on a flat surface. Mechanically produced images sap the iconic function of painting insofar as painting replicates, through tone-matching, the optical world of human experience. Toward the end of the century, artists will find themselves with canvas and paint, using the elements of line, shape, and color to represent their private world, the realm of imagination and feeling. The functions of the artist and of the artist's medium will be decisively transformed by the modern world, and the art of that world is sundered from the Tradition.

THE FIRST HALF OF THE NINETEENTH CENTURY: THE PREDOMINANCE OF ROMANTICISM

The revolutions that usher in the modern world are accompanied by a widespread agitation of spirit—a kind of collective *mental* revolution, the emotional response to accelerating change. We have already met Romanticism in the eighteenth century, noting its rise and the problems of its definition and its period. It continues and sharpens the eighteenth-century concern for human freedom and equality, for liberty of thought and expression, for the abrogation of traditions, institutions, and privileges that have held back human progress. Romanticism as a view of life, as well as a state of mind, inherits the Enlightenment's admiration of nature and the natural, over convention and artifice, and continues to uncover history as a store of natural lessons for correcting the defects of the present.

The emphasis on human rights in the public sphere is accompanied by the assertion of the value of feeling and emotion in private experience. Truth can be sought and found inwardly more surely than in doctrines of religion or rules of reason; for Romanticism's orientation is subjective, and the intensity of the religious and mystical emotions associated with traditional Christianity could live on in the individual, with or without reference to specific creeds. The ardor of Romanticism is religious, as is its soul-searching and truth-seeking through feeling and vision. The pantheistic union of the soul with nature—nature, for many, replacing the Christian God—is part of the Romantic ritual and excitement. T.E. Hulme defines Romanticism as "spilled religion": the old doctrinal vessels are broken, and their volatile contents spread widely and indefinitely.

Indefinitely—because there are really no fixed doctrines for Romanticism; in a world of critical change, where all that is fixed, dogmatic, and categorical is challenged, how could there be? On issues of the day, we can find Romantic spirits on opposing sides: progressive and conservative, democratic and monarchist, religious and agnostic, hoping and despairing, satanic and angelic. The world of history, for example, now being systematically recovered, could be valued as serving the hopes of new nations by showing them the heroic past, by supplying them with an identity. Or it could be regarded as a nightmare from which the present is trying to wake; "The world," wrote Percy Bysshe Shelley, "is weary of the past / O might it die, or rest at last!"

Romanticism—protean as the modern world it reflects and, like the modern mind, incorrigibly romantic—has one firm conviction at its center: the identity of reality is rooted in the self, not in the external, man-made world. The search for this identity—the revelation and expression of it in art and life—is the objective and meaning of personal existence. Jean Jacques Rousseau preaches the religion of the value of the individual in a single assertion: "I may be no better than anyone else; at least I am different." For the Romantic, it is the difference that counts.

Despite the plurality of styles in the nineteenth century, the artist's claim of autonomy is a constant, and this individualism can sometimes result in alienation. The right to be an individual authority justifies this procedure, even when an artist chooses to accept the authority of, say, the academies. The broad right to choose a mode of expression is then matched by the broad range of materials supplied by the Tradition—from which the artist chooses, or chooses to turn aside. The artist's motives may be various: to stir an audience with drama or melodrama; to reconstruct historical incident; to exhibit the beauty of the human figure, landscape, still life, and other traditional subjects; to present the genre of modern life; to paint the inventions of a fertile imagination; to externalize dreams as images, private and strange. The subjects, modes of representation, and techniques of the artists of the nineteenth century, various as they may be, are

all derived from a common attitude and claim of autonomy.

In this earlier century of the modern era, then, the subject matter of art is predominantly "romantic," in that the artist stresses dramatic emotion or ideal beauty, or combinations of these with other material. "Romantic" artists will discover their themes in history, literature, religion—the exotic and the esoteric—and draw on the pictorial modes of the Tradition, the Classical, the Renaissance, and the Baroque. "Romantic" architects will recover the historical styles of Western architecture and the non-European world and parade them dramatically. Historical and literary material, often produced with a photographic realism, will predominate. It is this retrospective subject matter, seeming apart or escaping from the specifically modern scene, that, in part, invites the use of the term "romanticism." Yet we shall see that Romanticism is a vital principle that survives into the twentieth century and that much of contemporary art is also, in essence, subjective—an intellectual and emotional reflection of always accelerating and demanding change.

Architecture

The Romantic Neoclassical taste for the more-or-less exact replication of Greek and Roman buildings, as we have seen it expressed in Thomas Jefferson's statehouse (FIG. 20-27), spread throughout Europe and America. From Virginia to Munich, from Paris to St. Petersburg, Neoclassicism could be romantically associated with revolutionary aspirations to primitive democratic purity or with imperial ambitions for unshakable authority. Begun in 1808, at the zenith of Napoleon's power, La Madeleine in Paris (FIG. 21-1) was intended to be a temple of honor for Napoleon's armies and a monument to the newly won glory of France; it was converted to a church before its completion in 1842. Designed by PIERRE VIGNON (1763–1828) as an octastyle peripteral temple, its high podium and the broad flight of stairs leading to a deep porch simulate the buildings of the time of the first caesars, making La Madeleine a symbolic link between the Napoleonic and Roman empires. A curious feature of the building is the fact that its Classical shell surrounds an interior that is covered by a sequence of three domes; a feature found in Byzantine or Aquitanian Romanesque churches has been clothed in the costume of Pagan Rome.

While Romantic Neoclassicism flourished, the Romantic Gothic taste by no means died; it paralleled the former and took on new significance, a religious and national one. In 1802, Chateaubriand published his influential *Genius of Christianity*—a defense of religion (against the skeptical rationalism of the Enlight-

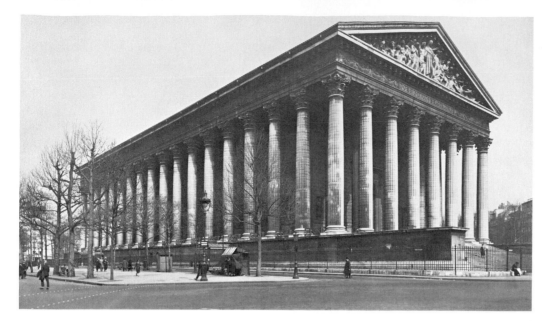

21-1 Pierre Vignon, La Madeleine, Paris, begun 1808.

enment and the French Revolution) on the grounds, not of its truth, but of its beauty and mystery. "There is nothing," Chateaubriand says, "of beauty, sweetness, or greatness in life that does not partake in mystery." This is a significant contradiction of "Be thou clear!"—the classical injunction from the "age of reason." Christian ritual and Christian art, born of mystery, move adherents by their strange and ancient beauty. Gothic cathedrals, according to Chateaubriand, are translations into stone of the sacred groves of the Druidical Gauls and must be cherished as manifestations of France's holy history. In his view, the history of Christianity and that of France merged in the Middle Ages. As the nineteenth century gathered the documentary materials of European history in a stupendous historiographic enterprise, each nation came to value its past as evidence of the validity of its ambitions and claims to greatness. The art of the remote past was now appreciated as a product of racial and national genius. In 1773, Goethe, praising the Gothic cathedral of Strasbourg in *Of German Architecture*, declares that the German art scholar "should thank God to be able to proclaim aloud that it is German architecture, our architecture . . ."; he bids the observer "approach and recognize the deepest feeling of truth and beauty of proportion emanating from a strong, vigorous German soul . . . ." This was at a time when Gothic architecture, even though enjoyed as picturesque, was generally disparaged as a style inferior to Classical architecture.

Modern nationalism thus brought about a new evaluation of the art in each country's past. In London, when the old Houses of Parliament burned in 1834, the Parliamentary Commission decreed that designs for the new building should be either "Gothic or Elizabethan." Charles Barry (1795–1860), with the assistance of A.W.N. Pugin (1812–1852), submitted the winning design in 1835, and the work was carried on from the 1840s into the 1860s (FIG. 21-2). By this time, style had become a matter of selection from

21-2 Charles Barry and A.W.N. Pugin, Houses of Parliament, London, designed 1835.

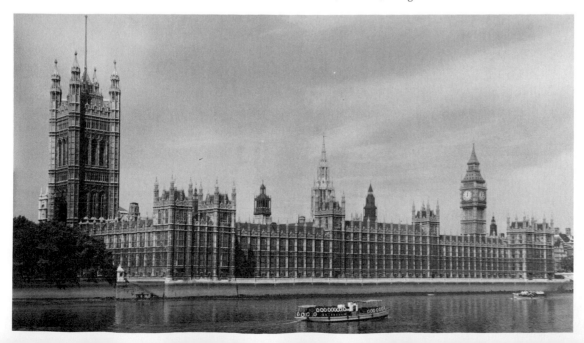

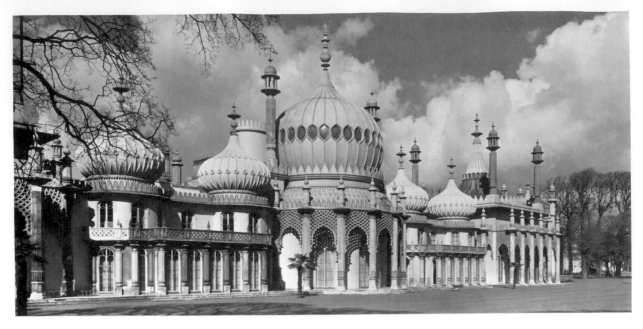

21-3 JOHN NASH, Royal Pavilion, Brighton, England, 1815–1818.

the historical supply. Barry preferred the Classical, but Pugin influenced him successfully in the direction of English Late Gothic. Pugin was one of a group of English artists and critics that included WILLIAM MORRIS and John Ruskin, who saw moral purity and spiritual authenticity in the religious architecture of the Middle Ages and glorified the careful Medieval craftsmen who had produced it. The Industrial Revolution was now flooding the market with cheaply made and ill-designed commodities; handicraft had been replaced by the machine, and men like Pugin believed in the necessity of restoring the old craftsmanship, which had honesty and quality. The design of the Houses of Parliament, however, is not genuinely Gothic, despite its picturesque tower group-

ings. It has a formal axial plan and a kind of Palladian regularity beneath its Tudor detail. Pugin himself is reported to have said of it: "All Grecian, sir, Tudor details on a classic body."*

Neoclassical and Gothic architecture dominate the early nineteenth century, but exotic styles of all sorts, with fancifully mixed ingredients borrowed from the East, began to appear, especially in connection with places of recreation. At Brighton, England—the shore resort fashionable during the reign of the prince regent, later George IV—JOHN NASH (1752–1835) built the Royal Pavilion (FIG. 21-3) from 1815 to 1818. A confection of Islamic domes, minarets, and

*In Nikolaus Pevsner, *An Outline of European Architecture* (Baltimore: Penguin, 1960), p. 627.

21-4 J.L. CHARLES GARNIER, the Opéra, Paris, 1861–1874.

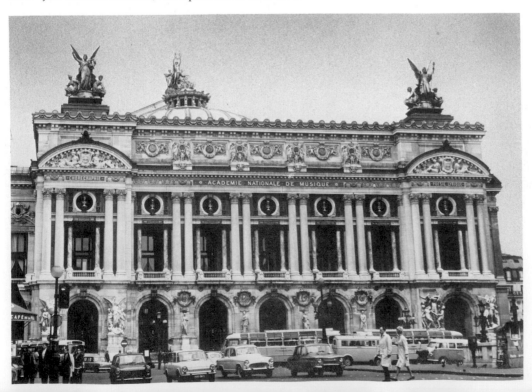

screens, this "Indian Gothic" structure, an appropriate enough backdrop for gala throngs pursuing pleasure by the seaside, served as the prototype of any number of playful architectural exaggerations that can still be found at European and American resorts.

By mid-century, Renaissance and Baroque had been added to the stylistic repertory. France under Napoleon III, the "Second Empire," expanded its vast holdings in Africa and Asia, and its businessmen obeyed the statesman Guizot's patriotic admonition—made early in the previous reign of Louis Philippe—to get rich. The opulence of the period is mirrored in the Paris Opéra (FIG. 21-4), designed by J.L. CHARLES GARNIER (1825–1898). Built between 1861 and 1874, the Opéra parades a festive and spectacularly theatrical front that should be compared with the façade of the Louvre (FIG. 19-65), which it mimics to a degree. The interior is ingeniously planned for the convenience of human traffic. Intricate arrangements of corridors, vestibules, stairways, balconies, alcoves, entrances, and exits facilitate easy passage throughout and provide space for entertainment and socializing at intermissions. The Baroque grandeur of the layout and of the ornamental appointments of the opera house proclaim and enhance its function as a gathering place for glittering audiences in an age of conspicuous wealth. Until the First World War, theaters and opera houses will reflect the Paris Opéra design.

Sculpture

As in architecture, there are several Romantic styles in nineteenth-century sculpture, but their sequence and character are naturally closer to those of painting. A Romantic Classicism is strongly determinative of the work of ANTONIO CANOVA (1757–1822). His reclining portrait-figure of *Pauline Borghese as Venus* (FIG. 21-5) shows him to be learned in the traits of Classicism—drapery, pose, form, and feature. That he adroitly draws the likeness of his subject within the

21-5 ANTONIO CANOVA, *Pauline Borghese as Venus*, 1808. Marble, life-size. Galleria Borghese, Rome.

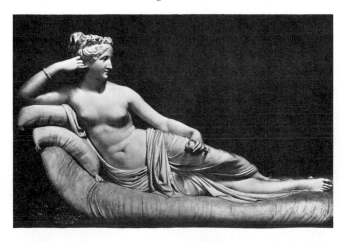

almost standard outlines of a Classical statue shows that he is not slavishly bound by Neoclassical doctrine. At the same time, with quite remarkable discretion, Canova creates a daring image of seductive charm that is generalized enough to personify the goddess of love rather than to exhibit the living person. Both the voluptuousness and the tact with which he veils it recall the earlier Rococo, when esteemed ladies were often represented as seminude goddesses. The realism of the couch and its drapery, however, almost betray Canova into a too graphic presentation. Despite a lingering Rococo charm and realistic accessories, Canova is firmly Neoclassical in his approach. Considered the greatest sculptor of his time, he has suffered greatly in reputation since. Present criticism has restored him a little, although he still carries, as the most typical of Neoclassicists, something of the burden of negative criticism laid on that often doctrinaire and artificial style. Its defects can be seen well enough in a statue of *George Washington* (FIG. 21-6) by the American sculptor HORATIO GREENOUGH (1805–1852). Here the sculptor aims at monumental majesty, perhaps with a Classical Zeus in mind; but whether his subject was not susceptible of deification or whether the Realistic temper of the period simply could not bring the concepts of ancient god and modern man together, the statue was considered a failure in Greenough's time; today, it is

21-6 HORATIO GREENOUGH, *George Washington*, 1832–1841. Marble, approx. 11' 4" high. Smithsonian Institution, Washington, D.C.

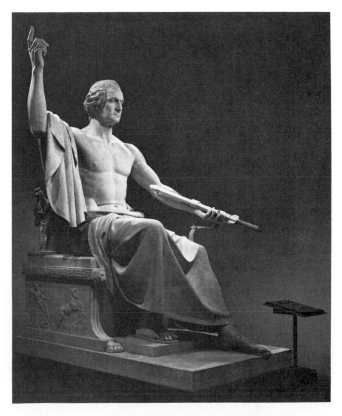

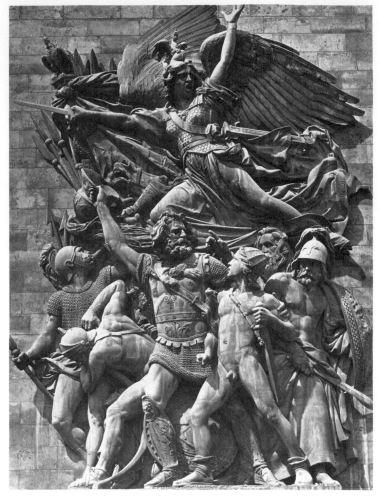

21-7 FRANÇOIS RUDE, *"La Marseillaise,"* Arc de Triomphe, Paris, 1833–1836. Approx. 42' × 26'.

more highly regarded. The father of his country, wearing his eighteenth-century wig and with ancient drapery and nude torso, approximates the period's image of a majestic law-giver. The statue manifests, more than many of its Neoclassical age, the contradictions that sometimes develop when idealization and realistic illusionism meet. Canova appears to harmonize these two trends; Greenough puts them in opposition. Most nineteenth-century monumental sculpture, especially in the Neoclassical mode, seems stiff, cold, or simply unconvincing. Nevertheless,

Greenough's statue has an imperious majesty appropriate to the national memory of its subject.

One monumental group, however, done between 1833 and 1836 and recalling the Baroque, still moves us—the so-called *"La Marseillaise"* (FIG. 21-7) by FRANÇOIS RUDE (1784–1855). The colossal figures, in bold relief against the Arc de Triomphe in Paris, represent French volunteers leaving to defend the borders of France against the foreign enemies of the revolution in 1792. They are dressed in Classical armor, and the Roman war goddess, Bellona (who may be thought of here as La Marseillaise, or the Goddess of Liberty), shouts the battle cry as she rallies the militia forward. The Classical accessories do not disguise the essentially Baroque qualities of the group—the densely packed masses, jagged contours, violence of motion. If we were to think here of the Classical at all, it would be of the "post-classical baroque" of Hellenistic works like the great frieze at Pergamon (FIG. 5-79).

This explosive style, here effective enough in sculpture, finds its natural medium in Romantic painting. Stormy emotion and untamed nature, those obsessions of Romanticism, require a style full of movement and color; and, to make them sharply convincing to the spectator, they require as realistic a representation as possible. Animal ferocity, which nineteenth-century taste generally does not permit to be shown at full in human beings, Romanticism describes in brute beasts. ANTOINE LOUIS BARYE (1795–1875) was a specialist in such depiction. His *Jaguar Devouring a Hare* (FIG. 21-8), painful as the subject is, draws us irresistibly to it by its fidelity to brute nature; the belly-crouching cat's swelling muscles, hunched shoulders, and tense spine—even the switch of the tail—tell of Barye's long sessions of observing the beasts in the Jardin des Plantes in Paris. The work tells, too, of the influence of the vast, exotic world of animal life—a geography opening before the naturalistic eyes and temper of the nineteenth century, from which artists, novelists, and poets, as well as scientists, would draw increasing knowledge and inspiration.

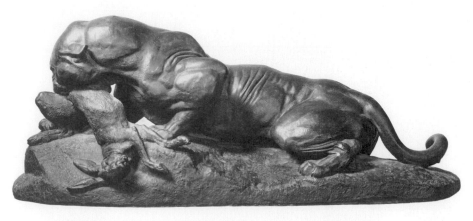

21-8 ANTOINE LOUIS BARYE, *Jaguar Devouring a Hare*, 1850–1851. Bronze, approx. 16" × 37". Louvre, Paris.

Painting

GOYA

Painting in the nineteenth century, touched strongly by the spirit of Romanticism, proves to be a far more sensitive medium for the kind of personal expression we would expect from the Romantic subjectivity of the time. At the very beginning of the modern period stands the imposing figure of FRANCISCO GOYA (1746–1828), the great independent painter of Spain. Founder of no school and acknowledging indebtedness to Diego Velázquez, Rembrandt van Rijn, and "nature," Goya takes his place as a giant of the Romantic age. He ranges from the Late Venetian Baroque of Giambattista Tiepolo through a brilliant Impressionistic Realism of his own, to a Late Expressionism in which dark and powerful distortions anticipate much of the violence, pain, and psychic upheaval in the art of the twentieth century. Goya is a great transitional figure, who changes the tradition while he manifests the present and prophesies the future of pictorial art. From a much higher vantage point than most of his contemporaries, he often depicts, in a bitter and unsparing revelation, the capacity of man for evil. Great Spanish painting is rarely sentimental; it insists, often with ruthless honesty, on the cruel facts of life. The art of Goya is no exception; it is for the strong-minded and the strong-nerved.

Little of the grim account of humanity foreshadowed in "The Dream of Reason" (FIG. 20-44) can be seen in Goya's early, vivacious manner, brilliantly adapted from Tiepolo. At the royal court in Madrid, where his precocious talent had brought him early in his career, Goya produced a series of genre paintings designed to serve as models for tapestries. Their prevailing mood of gaiety is the mood of the Rococo. But the noonday blitheness of Goya's early style soon wanes.

His experiences as painter to Charles IV, at whose sensationally corrupt court he lived, must have fostered his unsentimental, hard-eyed realism. In his large painting of *The Family of Charles IV* (FIG. 21-9), probably inspired by Velázquez's *Las Meninas* (FIG. 19-37), Goya presents, with a straight face, a menagerie of human grotesques who, critics have long been convinced, must not have had the intelligence to realize that the artist was caricaturing them. This superb revelation of stupidity, pomposity, and vulgarity, painted in 1800, led a later critic to summarize the subject as the "grocer and his family who have just won the big lottery prize." The painter, by his canvas, is dimly discernible at the left; his features impassively ironical, he looks beyond his subjects to the observer. Here, Goya exhibits his extraordinary skill as a colorist and manager of the oil medium. The colors float with a quiet iridescence across the surface, and the paint is applied with deft economy. Great solidity is suggested by the most transparent tones. A magician of optical pictorialism, Goya uses the methods of his great predecessor Velázquez.

Goya sharpened his criticisms of human vanity and vice in a series of satirical paintings and prints done between 1794 and 1799 called *Los Caprichos*, "The Caprices" (FIG. 20-44), in which monsters, grotesques, and caricatured men and women represent the repulsiveness of stupidity and folly. But the intervention of Napoleon Bonaparte in Spain in 1808 and the ensuing conflict gave Goya a new subject: not the foolishness of human ways, but the horror of war. In paintings and etchings, without national bias (although he was a patriot) and without mercy for the viewers' sensitivities, Goya exhibits the atrocities men visit on one another—no matter the issues, no matter the persons involved. His is a peculiarly modern vision; Picasso, in his *Guernica* (FIG. 22-16), which

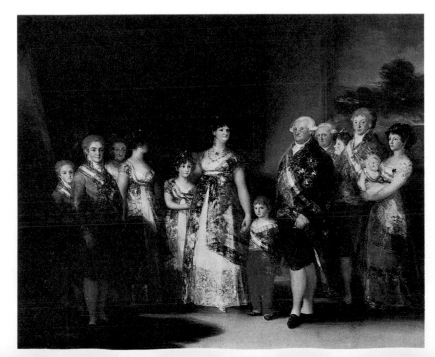

21-9 FRANCISCO GOYA, *The Family of Charles IV*, 1800. Approx. 9' 2" × 11'. Museo del Prado, Madrid.

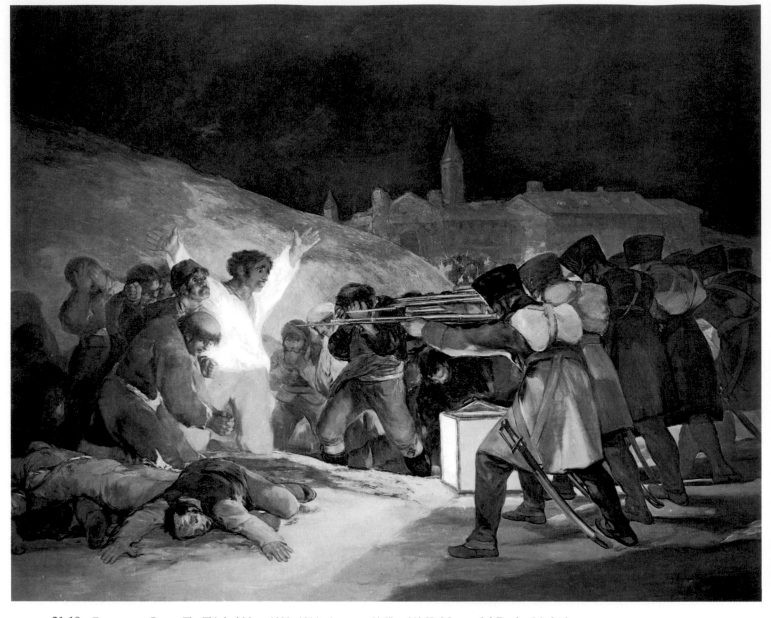

21-10   FRANCISCO GOYA, *The Third of May, 1808*, 1814. Approx. 8' 8" × 11' 3". Museo del Prado, Madrid.

he calls "brutality and darkness," gives us Goya's vision once again, translating his truth into a different formal language.

In *The Third of May, 1808* (FIG. 21-10) a French firing squad butchers citizens of Madrid by lamplight after the fall of the city. Unlike the subtle, even suave, realism of *The Family of Charles IV*, Goya's method here is coarse and extreme in its departure from optical fact. The postures and gestures of the figures are shockingly distorted to signal defiance, hatred, and terror. In keeping with the distortions of the figures, the color is acid and harsh, wrenched out of any normal harmony. Violent suffering and death can be rendered only in painful dissonances of shape and color. It is recorded that Goya visited the site of the event and made sketches.

Goya's perception of the insignificance of human life, of death and suffering in war, and of the obscen-ity of human wreckage is vented bitterly in a series of aquatint etchings entitled *The Disasters of War*. A print in that series, *Tampoco*, or "Neither Nor" (FIG. 21-11),

21-11   FRANCISCO GOYA, *Tampoco*, 1810. Aquatint etching, from *The Disasters of War*. Courtesy of The New York Public Library (Astor, Lenox, and Tilden Foundations).

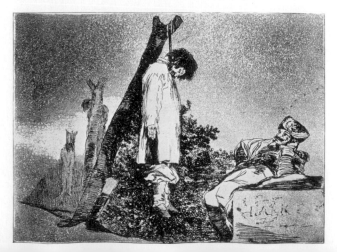

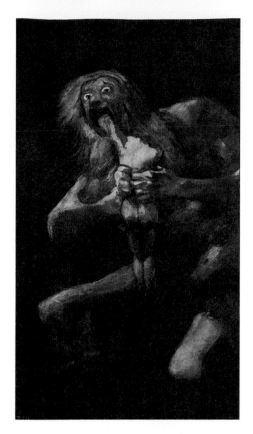

21-12 FRANCISCO GOYA, *Saturn Devouring His Children*, 1819–1823. Detail of a detached fresco on canvas, full size approx. 57" × 32". Museo del Prado, Madrid.

Employing an overriding irony and ingenious compositions, his refined art serves as a scourge of human complacency. Goya's strength as a graphic artist lies in his astonishing economy of means. Like a master of pantomime, he gives us only a few cues, strengthening the force and meaning of gestures by abbreviating and simplifying them. He reduces all to the essential. It is this that recommends Goya to the painters and graphic artists who follow him, like Honoré Daumier.

The folly and brutalities he witnessed and his own increasing infirmities, including deafness, combined to depress Goya's outlook and led to his late "dark style." In ominous midnight colors, he creates a whole population of subhuman monsters who worship the devil and swarm in nightmares. *Saturn Devouring His Children* (FIG. 21-12) is one product of this pessimistic and misanthropic style. Saturn (Time), glaring in lunatic frenzy, is devouring part of a small body clutched in his hands. The forms are torn and jagged; the colors, raw. Life is in time, and time devours us all. Goya's horror is not merely of man's inhumanity to man, but of life itself. This appalling work came from a supreme artist who had evidently become convinced that "The Dream of Reason Produces Monsters" (FIG. 20-44).

GIRODET, BARON GROS, GÉRICAULT

In France, Jacques Louis David demanded that his pupils select their subjects from Plutarch, ancient author of the *Lives of the Great Greeks and Romans* and principal source of standard Classical subject matter. But often they found their subjects elsewhere. ANNE LOUIS GIRODET-TRIOSON (1767–1824) turned to a popular novel by Chateaubriand, *Atala*, to produce his *Burial of Atala* (FIG. 21-13), a picture that could be a set

shows a French soldier brutalized by his profession to the point of utter indifference to the death of others, lounging in a grove of hanged Spanish peasants and gazing with vague boredom at a miscellaneous victim. Goya, one of the greatest masters of the graphic arts, is at his very best in the *Disasters* series, as he sets out—in the most striking simplicity of sharp shapes, light and dark—the ghastly tableau of death.

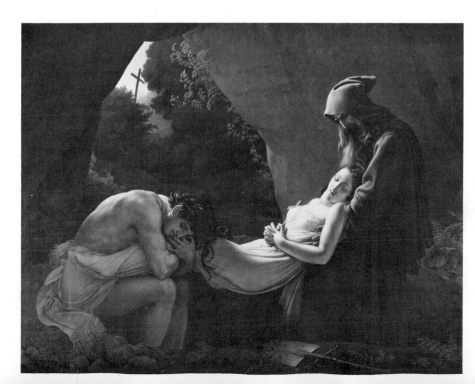

21-13 ANNE LOUIS GIRODET-TRIOSON, *The Burial of Atala*, 1808. Approx. 6' 11" × 8' 9". Louvre, Paris.

817

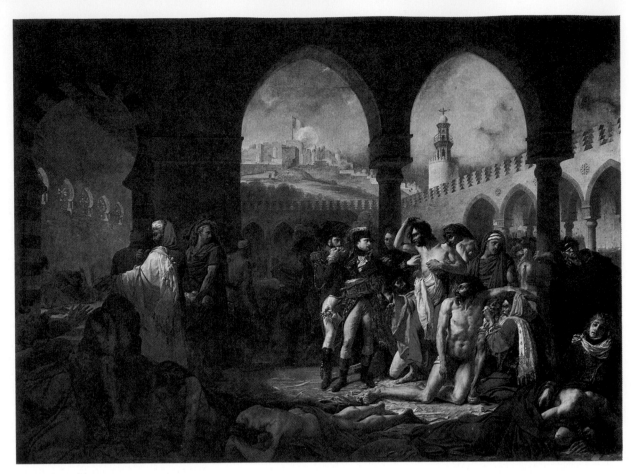

21-14 Antoine Jean Gros, *Pest House at Jaffa*, 1804. Approx. 17′ 5″ × 23′ 7″. Louvre, Paris.

piece for Romanticism. Atala, sworn to lifelong virginity, falls passionately in love with a wild, young savage of the Carolina wilderness. Rather than break her oath, she commits suicide and is buried in the shadow of the cross by her distracted lover; the Holy Church is represented in the person of a gentle priest. Thus, Girodet daringly puts religion and sexual passion side by side, binding them with the theme of death and burial. Hopeless love, perished beauty, the grave, the consolation of religion, the purity of primitive life—these are some of the thematic constants of Romanticism that Girodet successfully interweaves. The picture's composite style combines classicizing contours and modeling with a dash of the erotic sweetness of the Rococo and the dramatic illumination of the Baroque. The appeal is to the viewer's private world of fantasy and emotion, unlike David's appeal to the feelings that manifest themselves in public action. If David's purpose is to "electrify the soul," Girodet's is, in the language of Rousseau, to "wring the heart." In either case, the artist speaks to our emotions, rather than inviting philosophical meditation or revealing some grand order of nature and form. The Romantic artist, whether David, Girodet, or any other, wants to excite his audience.

Another pupil of David, the Baron Antoine Jean Gros (1771–1835), deviates from his master's teachings quite as much as—and much more influentially

than—Girodet. In his *Pest House at Jaffa* (FIG. 21-14), painted in 1804, he takes a radically independent tack, sorting through and selecting numerous Baroque pictorial devices of light, shade, and perspective to stage, as dramatically as possible, a tableau testifying to the superhuman power and glory of Napoleon Bonaparte. A comparison of the *Oath of the Horatii* (FIG. 20-38) with the *Pest House* illustrates Gros' departure from David. The works are similar in that they stage an action within an architectural enframement, the figures being deployed before an arcade; but David's arcade is Roman and Gros' is Moorish, and the vista through Gros' arcade is of a distant landscape, a fortress, and the tricolor flag of the revolution. Time has changed the setting, and the painter's means have changed to suit the present. Gros, using every device to focus the viewer's attention on the central figure of the hero, dismisses most theoretical considerations of Classical balance and modeling and poses Napoleon as a stage director would, making the fullest use of stage lights and dramatic darkness to center the figure of the chief protagonist. His purpose is to elevate a historical event to an act of almost religious significance and solemnity, in which Napoleon, the messiah of democracy, plays simultaneously the roles of Alexander, Christ, and Louis XIV. Bonaparte, the First Consul, not yet Emperor Napoleon I, at the end of the disastrous Egyptian campaign, has retreated up the coast of Palestine (modern Israel). His army is stricken with the plague, and he is shown visiting his sick and dying soldiers in a hospital in the ancient city of Jaffa. There in the midst of the dead and dying, the fearless genius of the New Order touches the plague sores of a sick soldier, who stares at him in awe, as if he were the miracle-working Christ. The staff officers stop their noses against the stench of the place, but the general is calm and unperturbed, like the king curing by the King's Touch. In the left foreground, men brood, crouch, and sprawl in a gloom of misery and anguish; these figures will be of special interest to later Romantic artists, like Théodore Géricault and Eugène Delacroix. The whole scene is wrapped in the glamor of its Near Eastern setting: the turbaned Moslem physician and his assistants, the Moorish arches, the exotic landscape. As with Girodet, we have identifiable, if not identical, themes: suffering and death, faith and personal heroism, the lure of distant places, patriotism—all that can appeal to the modern need for emotional stimulation; in a word, Romanticism.

With THÉODORE GÉRICAULT (1791–1824), the programed Classicism of the Davidian school fades and David's sharp light and shade and his insistent accuracy in rendering from nature come to the fore. This maturing of the naturalistic element present in David and his successors is, in Géricault's masterpiece, *Raft of the Medusa* (FIG. 21-15), quickened by the catalytic influences of Michelangelo and Peter Paul Rubens. David and Gros have already initiated the trend to-

ward the dramatic presentation of contemporary events on huge canvases. Géricault takes for his theme the ordeal of the survivors of the French ship Medusa, which foundered off the west coast of Africa, laden with Algerian immigrants. The incident, a result of tragic mismanagement, caused a scandal, and Géricault's depiction of the anguish of the survivors on the raft was construed by the government as a political attack. Géricault chooses the most dramatic moment of the episode, when the frantic castaways attempt to attract the attention of a distant ship. The figures are piled on one another in every attitude of suffering, despair, and death, recalling the foreground figures in Gros' *Pest House at Jaffa* (FIG. 21-14). Powerful light and dark contrasts suit the violence of the twisting and writhing bodies. Although Baroque devices are everywhere present, Géricault's use of shock tactics that stun the viewer's sensibilities amounts to something new—a new tone and intention that distinguish the second and "high" phase of Romanticism. In this phase, an instinct for the sublime and the terrible—qualities already celebrated by the esthetic theory of the mid-eighteenth century—finds sharpest expression in the method of reportorial accuracy already noted in certain pictures by David (FIG. 20-39). Géricault, like a painstaking reporter out to "get the facts," interviewed survivors of the Medusa and made careful studies of dying men and dead bodies in preparation for his work.

His *Mounted Officer of the Imperial Guard* (FIG. 21-16), painted in 1812, shows the Romantic's admiration for

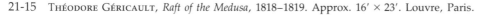

21-15 THÉODORE GÉRICAULT, *Raft of the Medusa*, 1818–1819. Approx. 16′ × 23′. Louvre, Paris.

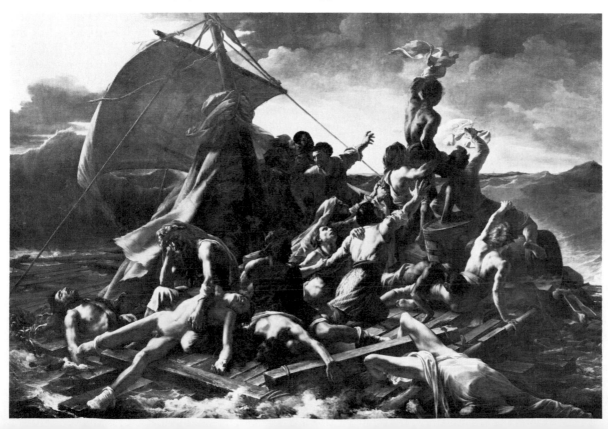

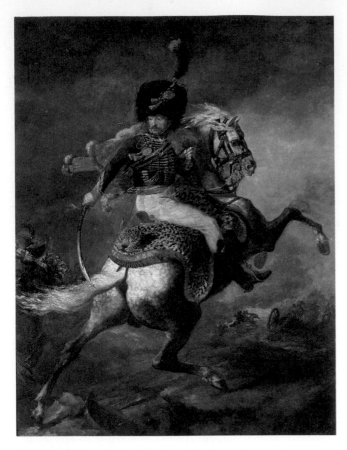

21-16 THÉODORE GÉRICAULT, *Mounted Officer of the Imperial Guard*, 1812. Approx. 9′ 7″ × 6′ 4″. Louvre, Paris.

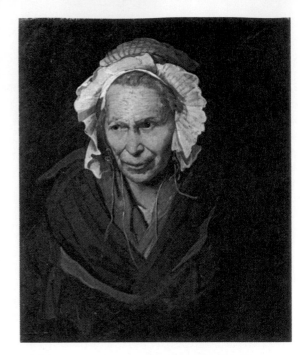

21-17 THÉODORE GÉRICAULT, *Insane Woman* (*Envy*), 1822–1823. Approx. 28″ × 21″. Musée des Beaux-Arts, Lyons.

fierce power. Géricault's generation is born of the French Revolution and the Napoleonic Wars, in the midst of the thunder of cannon and cavalry. Military splendor, the glamor and pomp of war, its valor and terror—all are natural themes of the times; and pictures by Géricault and his contemporaries celebrate war's furious excitement rather than its horror and degradation. In his *Officer*, man and horse are as if one—part man, part beast. The Romantic obsession with the forces of nature extends to the subhuman in man and the "innocent cruelty" of beasts of prey. Here, Géricault throws his horse and rider into exaggerated gyrations in an effort to create an illusion of explosive action. His color and "open" form recall Rubens, but his intent is to thrill the viewer with the contemporary apparition of fury as he exalts the idea of the Napoleonic hero.

An interest in mental aberration, which contributed to the development of modern psychopathology later in the nineteenth century, is part of the Romantic fascination with the irregular and the abandoned. The inner storms that overthrow rationality could hardly fail to be of interest to the rebels against the "age of reason." Géricault, like many of his contemporaries, studied the influence of mental states on the human face and believed, as they did, that a man's face accurately reveals his character, especially in madness and at the instant of death. He made many studies of inmates of hospitals and institutions for the criminally insane (indeed, he spent some time as a patient in such places) and he studied the severed heads of victims of the guillotine. Scientific and artistic curiosity are not easily separated from the morbidity of the Romantic interest in derangement and death. Géricault's *Insane Woman* (*Envy*) (FIG. 21-17)— her face twisted, her eyes red-rimmed—leers with paranoid hatred in one of several "portraits" of insane subjects that have a peculiar hypnotic power and present the psychic facts with astonishing authenticity. The *Insane Woman* is only another example of the increasingly realistic core of Romantic painting. The closer the Romantics become involved with nature, sane or mad, the more they hope to get at the truth. For painting, this will increasingly come to mean the *optical* truth, as well as the truth to "the way things are." Meanwhile, for the Romantic, the real is nature, wild and untamed. In Géricault's paintings, suffering and death, battle frenzy, and madness amount to nature itself—for nature, in the end, is formless and destructive.

DELACROIX

It is evident that nature cares very little whether man has a mind or not. The real man is the savage; he is in accord with nature as she is. As soon as man sharpens his intelligence, increases his ideas and the way of expressing them, and acquires need, nature runs counter to him in everything.*

In these words EUGÈNE DELACROIX (1798–1863) succinctly gives us a clause from the Romantic's testament of nature and of man in nature.

*See *The Journal of Eugène Delacroix*, Walter Pach, trans. (New York: Grove Press, 1937, 1948).

We have seen that the qualities of the sublime and the terrible, and the emotions of awe and admiring wonder they produce, are most sought after by the Romantic poet and artist. As Delacroix writes in his famous journal: "Baudelaire* . . . says that I bring back to painting . . . the feeling which delights in the terrible. He is right. . . ." Delacroix, who knew and admired Géricault, greatly expands the expressive possibilities of Romantic art, developing its themes and elaborating its forms in the direction of ever-greater emotional power—in Romantic parlance, "sublimity." Literature of like power supplied him his subjects, and, as Baudelaire remarks in this regard, he "inherited from the great Republican and Imperial school [of David] a love of the poets and a strangely impulsive spirit of rivalry with the written word. David, Guérin, and Géricault kindled their minds at the brazier of Homer, Vergil, Racine, and Ossian. Delacroix was the soul-stirring translator of Shakespeare, Dante, Byron, and Ariosto. . . ." Since David, literature and art had been developing an ever-more intimate association. Their relation had already been established in the Renaissance. But in the Romantic age, much painting could almost be said to be "programed" by literature, as could most music (for example, Berlioz's *Harold in Italy,* after Lord Byron's *Childe Harold*). As we speak of "program" music, we can also speak of "program" art, and it is the "story picture" produced by this art that will evolve into the genre of the motion picture—a

*Charles Baudelaire (1821–1867), one of the nineteenth century's finest and most influential poets, was also a perceptive art critic.

composite of drama, narrative, sound, and pictures. In Delacroix, what starts with David culminates in the literature-inspired staging of exciting and disturbing human events, real or imaginary, and in a concern for the most accurate visual means of conveying them. From David to Delacroix, and in their lesser followers, the belief is that the purpose of pictorial art is to stir, to "electrify," and to render accurately and sympathetically the modern spirit in a modern look. This art is aimed at large publics—to move and to appeal to the new, populous democratic society. With the great, programmatic pictorialism of the Romantic period, we begin the truly modern and familiar experience of public spectacular drama—the production of thrilling stories, thrillingly staged.

Although the faculty of mind most valued by the Romantic is imagination, Delacroix realized that skill and restraint must go along with it. "In his eyes," Baudelaire writes of Delacroix, "imagination was the most precious gift, the most important faculty, but [he believed] that this faculty remained impotent and sterile if it was not served by a resourceful skill which could follow it in its restless and tyrannical whims." Delacroix's picture dramas are products of his view that the power of imagination—nourished and continually kindled by great literature, art, and music—will synthesize works that will catch and inflame the imagination of the observer. To be intensely imaginative is to be intensely alive.

An example of pictorial grand opera on a colossal scale is *The Death of Sardanapalus* (FIG. 21-18), which he painted in 1826. Undoubtedly, Delacroix was in-

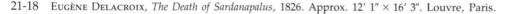

21-18 EUGÈNE DELACROIX, *The Death of Sardanapalus*, 1826. Approx. 12′ 1″ × 16′ 3″. Louvre, Paris.

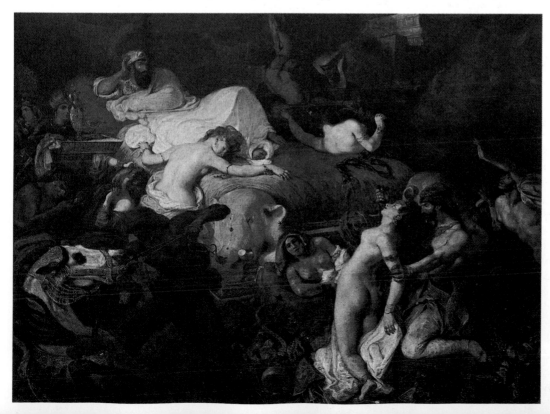

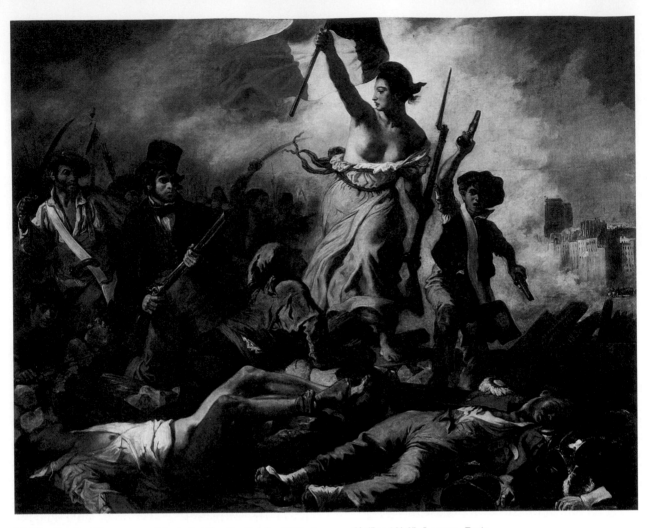

21-19   Eugène Delacroix, *Liberty Leading the People*, 1830. Approx. 8′ 6″ × 10′ 8″. Louvre, Paris.

spired by Lord Byron's narrative poem *Sardanapalus* and perhaps by other ancient sources, but here he relates the last hour of the ancient king in a much more tempestuous and crowded setting than Byron describes. Hearing of the defeat of his armies and the enemies' entry into his city, the king orders all of his most precious possessions—his women, slaves, horses, and treasure—destroyed in his sight while he watches gloomily from his funeral pyre, soon to be set alight. The king presides like a genius of evil over the panorama of destruction, most conspicuous in which are the tortured and dying bodies of his Rubenesque women; the one in the foreground is dispatched by an ecstatically murderous slave. This carnival of suffering and death is glorified by superb drawing and color, the most daringly difficult and tortuous poses, and the richest intensities of hues and contrasts of light and dark. The king is the center of the calamity, the quiet eye of a hurricane of form and color. It testifies to Delacroix's art that his center of meaning is placed away from the central action yet entirely controls it.

Generally, Delacroix chose his stories from either pre- or post-Classical periods and literature, but sometimes he dealt with a Greek subject that moved him. Other sources of subjects were the events of his own time, notably popular struggles for freedom: the ill-fated revolt of the Greeks against Turkish rule in the 1820s; the Parisian revolution of 1830, which overthrew the restored Bourbons and placed Louis Philippe on the throne of France. In *Liberty Leading the People* (FIG. 21-19), done in 1830, Delacroix makes no attempt to represent a specific incident seen in actuality. Instead, he gives us an allegory of revolution itself. Liberty—a partly nude, majestic woman, whose beautiful features wear an expression of noble dignity—waves the people forward to the barricades, the familiar revolutionary apparatus of Paris streets. She carries the tricolor banner of the republic and a musket with a bayonet and wears the cap of Liberty. Her advance is over the dead and dying of both parties—the people, and the royal troops. Arrayed around her are bold Parisian types: the street boy brandishing his pistols, the menacing *prolétaire* with a cutlass, the intellectual dandy in plug hat and with sawed-off musket. The towers of Notre Dame rise through the smoke and clamor, witnessing the ancient tradition of liberty cherished by the people of Paris throughout the centuries. The *Liberty*, a document of the intimate union of revolution and Roman-

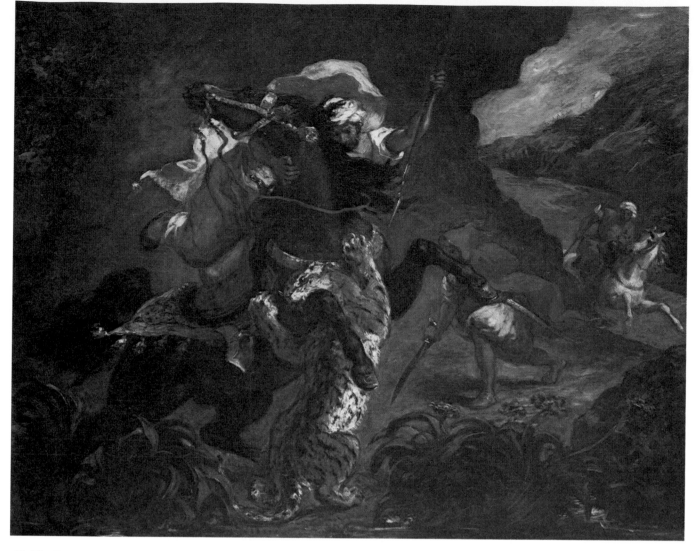

21-20 Eugène Delacroix, *Tiger Hunt*, 1854. Approx. 29″ × 36″. Louvre, Paris.

ticism, conveys the political temper of revolutionary Europe more powerfully than any other early nineteenth-century painting.

In terms of form, the *Liberty* still reflects the strong impression made on Delacroix by the art of Géricault, especially *Raft of the Medusa* (FIG. 21-15); the fact that Delacroix makes an allegory of *Liberty* shows that he was familiar with traditional conventions. The clutter of sprawling bodies in the foreground provides a kind of base to support the pyramiding figures in the central ground, building up to frantic energy from the heavy and the inert. The light flashes like the fire of guns, and the darks mingle freely with the lights, like drifting smoke roiled by cannon fire. The forms are generated from the Baroque, as they are in Géricault, but Delacroix's sharp agitation of them creates his own special brand of tumultuous excitement.

Delacroix, who could assert that "style can result only from great research," was ever studying the problems of his craft and ever searching for fresh materials to supply his imagination. He was able to visit North Africa in 1832, and what he found there shocked his imagination with impressions that would

last throughout his life. He discovered, in the sun-drenched landscape and in the hardy and colorful Arabs dressed in robes reminiscent of the Roman toga, new insights into a culture built on proud virtues—one that he believed to be more Classical than anything European Neoclassicism could conceive. "The Greeks and the Romans," he writes to a friend, "they are here, within my reach. I had to laugh heartily about the Greeks of David." Their gallantry, hardihood, valor, and fierce love of liberty made them, in Delacroix's eyes, "nature's noblemen"—unspoiled heroes, uninfected by European decadence.

The Moroccan journey renewed Delacroix's Romantic conviction that there is beauty in the fierceness of nature, natural processes, and natural beings, especially animals. After Morocco, more and more of Delacroix's subjects involved combats between beasts, and men and beasts (FIG. 21-20). He painted snarling tangles of lions and tigers, battles between horses, and clashes of Arabs with great cats in swirling hunting scenes. In these, what he had learned from the hunting pictures of Rubens (FIG. 19-40) mingles in explosive combination with his own visions, reinforced by his memories of the North African scene.

What Delacroix learned about color he passed on to later painters of the nineteenth century, most particularly to the Impressionists. He observed that pure colors are as rare in nature as lines, that color appears only in an infinitely varied scale of different tones, shadings, and reflections, which he tried to re-create in his paintings. He recorded his observations in his *Journal*, which became a veritable corpus of pre-Impressionistic color theory, acclaimed as such by the Neo-Impressionist painter PAUL SIGNAC in 1898–1899. Delacroix anticipates the later development of Impressionist color science, but that science had to await the discoveries by Michel Eugène Chevreul and Hermann von Helmholtz of the laws of light decomposition and the properties of complementary colors before its problems could be properly formulated. Nevertheless, Delacroix's observations are significant: "It is advisable not to fuse the brushstrokes," he writes, "as they will [appear to] fuse naturally at [a] . . . distance. In this manner, color gains in energy and freshness." This observation, suggested to him by his examination of a group of landscapes by John Constable, the great English landscape painter (FIG. 21-30), had strongly impressed Delacroix even before his color experiences in Morocco. He writes:

> Constable said that the superiority of the green he uses for his landscapes derives from the fact that it is composed of a multitude of different greens. What causes the lack of intensity and of life in verdure as it is painted by the common run of landscapists is that they ordinarily do it with a uniform tint. What he said about the green of meadows can be applied to all other tones.

Although these are primarily matters of technique and execution, Delacroix expresses his radical colorism most forcibly in the following statement: "Speaking radically, there are neither lights nor shades. There is only a color mass for each object, having different reflections on all sides." These observations were stimulated by Delacroix's Moroccan visit and do not consistently apply to his early works done under the influence of Géricault. This conception of the optical world as planes of color will find a new realization in the art of Paul Cézanne, who will make color planes serve a structural purpose in locking the composition together.

No other painter of the time explores the domain of Romantic subject and mood as thoroughly and definitively as Delacroix, and none matches his style and content. Delacroix's technique—impetuous, improvisational, instinctive, rather than deliberate, studious, and cold—epitomizes Romantic painting, catching the impression at the very beginning and developing it in the process of execution. We know how furiously Delacroix worked once he had an idea, keeping the whole painting progressing at once. The fury of his attack matches the fury of his imagination and his subjects. He is indeed the artist of passion. Baudelaire sums him up as "passionately in love with passion . . . an immense passion, reinforced with a formidable will—such was the man." In the end, his friend Silvestre, in the language of Romanticism, delivered a eulogy that amounts to a definition of the Romantic artist:

> Thus died, almost with a smile on August 13, 1863, that painter of great race, Ferdinand Victor Eugène Delacroix, who had a sun in his head and storms in his heart; who for forty years played upon the keyboard of human passions and whose brush—grandiose, terrible, or suave—passed from saints to warriors, from warriors to lovers, from lovers to tigers, and from tigers to flowers.

INGRES

The history of nineteenth-century painting in its first 60 years has often been interpreted as a contest between Delacroix, the colorist, and Ingres, the draftsman. They reach back to the end of the seventeenth century to revive the quarrel between "Poussinistes" and "Rubénistes," which pitted the conservative defenders of academicism, who held that drawing was superior to color, against the "Rubénistes," who proclaimed that color was not only more important to a painting than drawing, but had wider appeal than the more intellectual, and thus restrictive, quality of line. Even so, in the art of Delacroix and of his great rival Ingres, we must see the two as complementary rather than contradictory. They are part of the Romantic dialogue.

JEAN AUGUSTE DOMINIQUE INGRES (1781–1867) came to David's studio after Gros and Girodet had left to establish themselves as independent artists. But he did not stay very long, for he broke with David on matters of style. Ingres, feeling that David's art relied too heavily on nature, adopted a manner based on what he believed to be the true and pure Greek style: flat and linear figures approximating those in Greek vase paintings. This early manner was severely criticized as "primitive," even "Gothic," and one critic ridiculed Ingres' work as being the vision of "a Chinaman wandering through the ruins of Athens." Ingres' departure, both in form and content, from David and the French Royal Academy made him a kind of rebel, and the critics did not cease their attacks until the mid-1820s, when an even greater enemy of the official style, Delacroix, appeared. The critics then suddenly perceived that Ingres' art, despite its innovations and deviations, contained many elements that adhered to the official Classicism; he

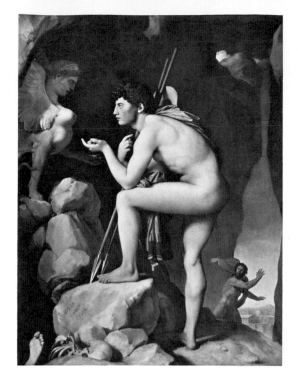

21-21　Jean Auguste Dominique Ingres, *Oedipus and the Sphinx*, 1808. 6′ 2″ × 4′ 8″. Louvre, Paris.

was soon to become the leader of the academic forces in their battle against the "barbarism" of Géricault, Delacroix, and their party. Gradually, Ingres warmed to the role in which he was cast by the critics and came to believe himself to be the conservator of good and true art, protecting its principles from those advanced by the "destroyers" of art.

Ingres' *Oedipus and the Sphinx* (FIG. 21-21), painted in 1808, shows his avowed attempt to get at the reality of Greek art instead of the academic myth. He gives us the wise hero, Oedipus, answering the three fatal questions of the Sphinx—a winged, taloned

female monster who terrified the city of Thebes, killing all passersby who could not answer her questions. Oedipus answered, slew the Sphinx, delivered the city, and was made king of Thebes by the grateful citizens; his subsequent tragic history is related in one of the most magnificent dramatic works of ancient Greece, Sophocles' *Oedipus the King.* In Ingres' work, the figure is placed in the foreground, like a piece of low-relief sculpture. The pose is stable, even rigid; the gestures, a kind of pantomime of asking and answering. The value Ingres places on the flow of the contours is characteristic, not only in his early period, but for the rest of his career. For contour, which is simply shaded line, is all there is for Ingres, and drawing is the means of creating contour. Ingres has been credited with the famous slogan, the battle cry of his school, "Drawing is the probity of art," as well as with the statement—which places him squarely against Delacroix and resolutely for the view that the past must provide the model for the present— "Never a color too warm! It is antihistorical!" But Ingres is not always consistent in following his own doctrine—that is, to improve on nature as the Greeks did. Some years after painting the *Oedipus,* he angrily denied that he had "idealized" his model, insisting that the figure was the very image of his model, whom he had copied as faithfully as he could; Ingres is not always sure whether he is following the Greeks or his own often quite naturalistic bent in his search for beautiful form.

Although the *Grande Odalisque* (FIG. 21-22), painted in 1814, drew acid criticisms ("she has three vertebrae too many," "no bone, no muscle, no life"), it seems today to sum up Ingres' artistic intentions. But it also illustrates the rather strange mixture of Ingres' artistic

21-22　Jean Auguste Dominique Ingres, *Grande Odalisque*, 1814. Approx. 35″ × 64″. Louvre, Paris.

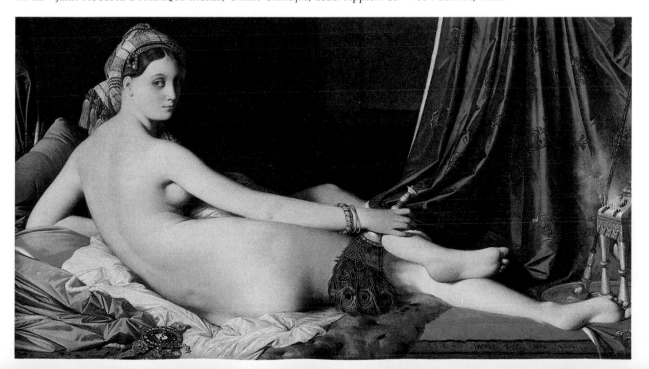

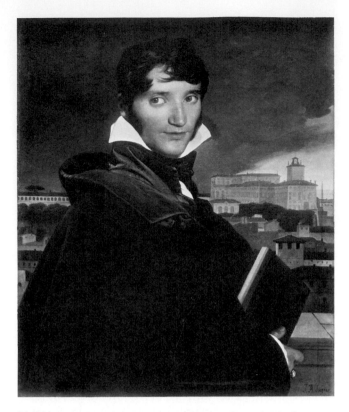

21-23 JEAN AUGUSTE DOMINIQUE INGRES, *François Marius Granet*, 1807. Approx. 28″ × 24″. Musée Granet, Aix-en-Provence.

allegiances. His subject, the reclining nude figure, is traditional, going back to Giorgione and Titian; but by converting her into an odalisque (an inhabitant of a Turkish harem), he makes a strong concession to the contemporary Romantic taste for the exotic. Ingres treats the figure in his own "sculpturesque" style: polished surfaces and simple rounded volumes controlled by rhythmically flowing contours. The smoothness of the planes of the body is complemented by the broken, busy shapes of the drapery. His admiration for Raphael is shown in the borrowing of that master's type of female head and headdress and in the inclination of the head, as seen in Raphael's *Madonna of the Chair* (not shown) in the Pitti Palace in Florence. But Ingres is drawing not only from the High Renaissance; his figure's languid pose and her proportions (small head, elongated limbs) betray his debt to such Mannerists as Parmigianino (FIG. 17-43), as does the generally cool color scheme.

Often criticized for not being a colorist, Ingres, in fact, had a superb color sense. It is true that he did not seem to think of his paintings primarily in terms of their color, as did Delacroix, but he did far more than simply tint his drawings for emphasis, as recommended by the Academy. In his best paintings, Ingres creates color and tonal relationships so tasteful and subtle as to render them unforgettable.

Although he always aspired to become a history painter in the academic sense, Ingres never really was successful with multifigured compositions. He is at

his best when he paints single figures and portraits; as a portraitist, he must be ranked among the greatest masters—one of the last in a field that will soon be dominated by the camera. Although the portrait of *François Marius Granet* (FIG. 21-23) is not, by itself, sufficient to demonstrate Ingres' great distinction in this field, it does show the artist's stagecraft in arranging the pose and adjusting the costume to bring out Granet's amiability, self-confident poise, and ever-so-slight swagger. Never insisting on likeness for its own sake, Ingres rarely fails to produce a striking characterization and—analogously to the smooth, formal treatment he gives his nudes—never fails to impart to both characterization and setting an air of suave elegance. In his portraits, as with his nudes, Ingres contrasts the simple and regular volume of the head with the broken, irregular, and complicated folds of the drapery and costume. His apparently cool detachment from his models and his search for "pure form" commend him to the twentieth-century taste for the "abstract."

A comparison of Ingres' pencil portrait of the great violin virtuoso Nicolò Paganini (FIG. 21-24) with Delacroix's version of the same personality (FIG. 21-25) discloses the difference in approach that separates the two artists. Both painters were passionately fond of music, and Ingres was a creditable violin amateur who knew Paganini personally. His version, executed with that marvelously crisp precision of descriptive line that we find in his pencil portraits, is quite literal, relative to Delacroix's. He gives us the man's appearance and public deportment—one

21-24 JEAN AUGUSTE DOMINIQUE INGRES, *Paganini*, 1819. Pencil drawing, approx. 12″ × 8½″. Louvre, Paris.

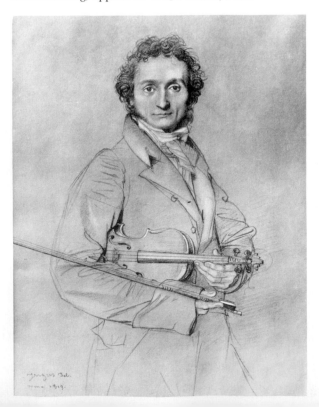

might say his official likeness—enhanced by Ingres' powers of suggestive characterization and sense of setting. Paganini, sharing with violin and bow a certain delicacy—both being fragile and supple—seems about to make his introductory obeisance to his audience. Above all, Ingres' portrait is *formal,* as is his subject, face-to-face with the public world; but it is a graceful, not a stiff formality. Delacroix's *Paganini* presents a likeness not of the virtuoso's *form* but of his *performance.* Forgetting his audience, no longer in formal confrontation with his listeners, Paganini yields himself completely to the whirlwind of his own inspiration, which envelopes his reed-like frame, making it vibrate in tune to the quivering strings of his instrument. Delacroix tries to give us the portrait, as it were, of Paganini's music, as it plays to his own ear and spirit. Ingres gives us the outward aspect of his subject; Delacroix, the inner substance. With Delacroix, the musician is transformed by his music, as is Delacroix himself. Ingres tries to perfect the form as given to the eye; Delacroix, to realize the truth as given to the imagination.

Critics now regard both masters as equally great, but, in the end, Delacroix may have been more generously endowed with imagination—that faculty of supraperception that catches the essential in experience and unifies its multiplicity of particulars, giving it a force and coherence that mundane experience

21-25 EUGÈNE DELACROIX, *Paganini,* c. 1832. Approx. 17″ × 11½″. The Phillips Collection, Washington, D.C.

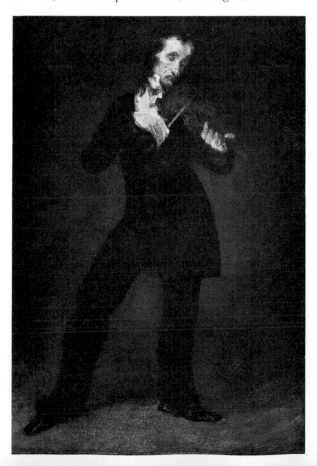

cannot have. Delacroix called the art of Ingres "the complete expression of an incomplete intellect." Yet he found much to admire in Ingres, especially in his drawings, and although it was necessary that they go their separate ways in theory and practice, it is pleasant to hear that their personal antagonism eventually may have softened. The painter PAUL JOSEPH CHENAVARD relates how he and Delacroix accidentally encountered Ingres on the steps of the French Institute, at a time late in the lives of both great artists. Although Ingres had been instrumental in preventing Delacroix's election to the Académie des Beaux Arts until 1857, he, after an awkward pause, impulsively extended his hand to Delacroix, who shook it sincerely.

SOME EPIGONES: CHASSÉRIAU, COUTURE, GÉRÔME
"Epigones" are artists of a succeeding and less distinguished generation. Although the artists named above are contemporaneous with Ingres and Delacroix, they follow them at some distance. Paul Delaroche and Jean Léon Gérôme were regarded by nineteenth-century critics as the last great painters of the Tradition—the line of the masters of the Renaissance and Baroque. Aware of an ever-deepening and widening rift separating the past from the present, the Tradition from modern times, the most intelligent critics sensed the necessity of coming to grips with "modernity" and the problem of creating an art "for one's own time." The issue will become serious and urgent by mid-century. A leading critic, Théophile Gautier, could exclaim: "It is well known that something must be done, but what?" And Charles Baudelaire, reviewing the Paris Salon (an annual, government-sponsored exhibition) of 1846, wrote: "It is true that the great tradition has been lost, and that the new one is not yet established. But what *was* this great tradition . . . ?" Almost in answer to this question, the "great tradition" will be analyzed away and replaced with the art we call "modern."

The epigones of Ingres and Delacroix studied with them or were strongly influenced by them; they can be said to have carried on the Tradition, with often unintentional revisions. THÉODORE CHASSÉRIAU (1819–1856), Ingres' favorite pupil, was irresistibly drawn to the style of Delacroix, so much so that he was accused of plagiarizing him. That, in fact, he made his own quite original—if not deliberate—synthesis of Ingres and Delacroix is evident in *Esther Adorning Herself* (FIG. 21-26). Esther (like Judith, a heroine of Israel), adorns herself for King Ahasuerus, through whom she will save her people (Book of Esther, 2:8–17). She is represented seminude, attended by the women sent to serve her. Her torso and upraised arms recall poses of figures by Ingres, and Chassériau certainly learned his faultless drawing from that master. But the softer, more coloristic tonal-

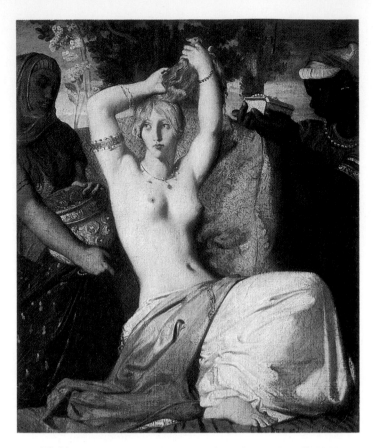

21-26 THÉODORE CHASSÉRIAU, *Esther Adorning Herself*, 1841. 18″ × 14″. Louvre, Paris.

ity indicates that he looked carefully, too, at the painting of Delacroix. The compression of the space puts the figures into the forward plane, so that they compose gracefully ornamental shapes, creating a kind of surface arabesque that will appear in the designs of artists like Pierre Puvis de Chavannes and Gustave Moreau later in the century and, ultimately, in Art Nouveau. Esther's pensiveness and an atmosphere of gentle mystery are characteristic features of the intensely personal style of Chassériau, itself distinctive in the art of his times.

An early specimen of the kind of art that will be called "academic," which had the admiration of the public and the support of the government, is the so-called *Romans of the Decadence* (FIG. 21-27) by THOMAS COUTURE (1815–1879), a pupil of both Gros and Delaroche. Later on, we shall say more about the "academic" style and the Academy. In fact, Couture was not an Academician and loathed the institution. Yet this vast picture is of the kind praised and patronized by the Academy. It marks a stage in Romanticism's revitalization of pictorial drama, and its type flourishes throughout the nineteenth century. Couture's *Romans* directly solicits the public's attention with its historical references (vague, to be sure), its sensational setting, and its somewhat sardonic moralism. It is, in fact, an allegory of the decadence of the July Monarchy of 1830; the picture is dated 1847 and was

exhibited just a year before the fall of that government in the Europe-wide revolutions of 1848. We are shown a drunken orgy of Romans of the late empire who have strayed from the severe morality of their forefathers, whose stern statues here frown their disapproval. How this painting differs from David's heroic *Oath of the Horatii* (FIG. 20-38) or the epic stance of Napoleon in Gros' *Pest House at Jaffa* (FIG. 21-14)! Couture knew both pictures well enough; but for his different purpose, he looks back to the huge banquet pieces of Veronese (FIG. 17-68). Taking many cues from the Venetian master, but not his religious content, Couture constructs a luxurious, architecturally strengthened setting for a multitude of figures, nude and draped, posed in attitudes of sensual indulgence and indolence.

Couture's painting is a fanciful reconstruction of the Roman past—significantly, in its decadence rather than in its primitive heroism. Moreover, its disparagement of Rome would seem in defiance of the proprieties of the Tradition, which insisted on the nobility of the ancients. Nevertheless, the design of the *Romans* is certainly traditional; sculptural figures are arranged horizontally in balancing groups, and the setting is so generalized that time and place are not specified. "History painting," as it had been known since the Renaissance, was supposed to depict elevating scenes from Christian and Classical story, with settings, costumes, poses, and accessories left in a more-or-less indefinite and conventional mode. Although actual historical events have been depicted before, notably by Velázquez, it is Benjamin West's *Death of General Wolfe* (FIG. 20-35) that heads a series of history paintings that, unlike those of the Tradition, aim at reporting actual historical events in more-or-less authentic circumstances of time and place.

This new kind of history painting matures in the nineteenth century, at a time when the foundations are being laid and the materials are being gathered for the modern science of historiography. The aim of historical scholarship is to recover and present the past in all accurate detail. Not only the scholars, but poets, artists, and the educated public began to read history; the period became obsessed with it. We have already seen this in architecture; and, as in architecture, so also in art and literature (this is the century of the historical novel) can the reconstruction of the past be imaginary, arbitrary, often inaccurate, often simply wrong. For example, Couture's *Romans* can hardly be taken as evidence that the great empire fell because its citizens became orgiastic.

On the other hand, painters can be as careful as scholars about the truth of the historical events they describe (although, being concerned with the dramatic essence of an event, painters may exaggerate in

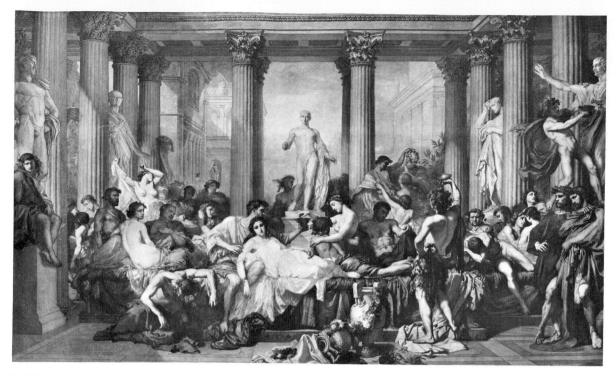

21-27 THOMAS COUTURE, *Romans of the Decadence*, 1847. Approx. 15′ 1″ × 25′ 4″. Louvre, Paris.

the interest of excitement). For it now becomes the history painter's function to produce, as on a stage, a convincing reenactment of an incident out of the past that will appeal both to his audience's sense of drama and to its knowledge of history. His goal is to neutralize the intrusion of his personality to produce effects entirely independent of it. He is after an illusion so objective, complete, and immediate that the spectator will think: "It might have looked this way, it might not have looked this way, but it *could* have looked this way." The value of the history painter's picture lies in its presumptive truth—not simply to life, but to life at

a particular time and place, and *as once lived*. This is a new genre, unknown to the Tradition, born of the age of West and David, that will develop well beyond the limits they may have appeared to set for it.

With PAUL (Hippolyte) DELAROCHE (1797–1856)—a pupil of Delacroix, who himself painted many historical pictures—traditional subject matter begins to take on a more and more photographic appearance. This can be seen in the work of Delaroche's pupil JEAN LÉON GÉRÔME (1824–1904). In his painting *Thumbs Down! (Pollice Verso)* (FIG. 21-28), Gérôme moves far from Couture and the Tradition; the inher-

21-28 JEAN LÉON GÉRÔME, *Thumbs Down! (Pollice Verso)*, c. 1874. 40″ × 69″. Phoenix Art Museum purchase.

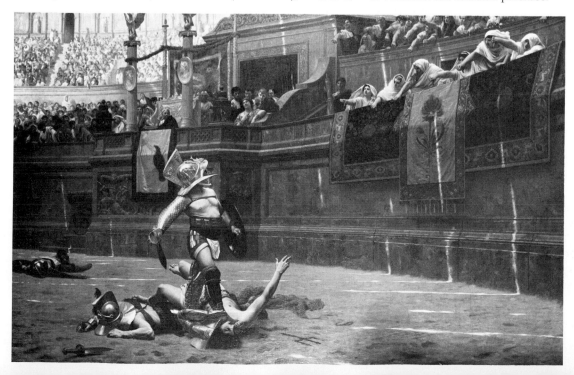

ited formulas have been almost entirely transformed. The time and place specifications are as exact as they can be. Although we do not know the day, month, and year of the event, nor the names of the principals involved, we recognize it for what it is and where it is happening; we can even guess the time of day. Gladiatorial combats were part of the Roman imperial games held regularly in great arenas or amphitheaters like the one pictured—the Colosseum at Rome (FIG. 6-45). The incident represented must have happened countless times, and its very ordinariness makes it dramatic and factual. A triumphant gladiator bestrides his fallen opponent and looks toward the box where the Vestal Virgins are seated. The fallen man gestures for mercy. The Vestals deny his appeal by turning their thumbs down; he will be killed on the spot.

Gérôme authenticates the scene to the last detail: the Vestals, the emperor's party (in the box fronted with columns and trophies), the streaks of light (clue to the time of day) thrown on the tapestried barrier walls by chinks in the great awnings overhead, the texture of the bloodstained sand, and, conspicuously, the fantastic garb of the gladiators, their splendid helmets replicating originals found at Pompeii. The scenic illusion is produced by a smooth continuum of tone that runs through the whole scale of values. There is scrupulous fidelity to optical fact. Evidence of brush strokes is suppressed in an exquisitely finished glassy surface. The effect is photographic; the brush stroke is intended to be invisible. In this way, the artist reduces to the barest minimum interference by his own imagination or feeling, or even by the agent of that feeling—his "hand." Like a director in the theater, he expects to be judged on his interpretation—manifest in the characterizations he elicits, in the species of action, scene design, and authenticity of detail. Gérôme makes use of an off-centered, dynamic placement of his figures, to make us spectators at a *real* event, which we witness from *within* the framed space of the action. The curving wall sweeps toward us, and we can feel that our own vantage point is continuous with that of the Vestal Virgins. Gérôme thus brings us onto the stage; with Couture and the Tradition, we are still out in front of it. This radical narrowing of the space between the spectator and the event being watched is a device of great importance in nineteenth-century pictorial technique.

What we are seeing here is an instance of the century's increasing appetite for the optically real in art. Real events (in the cases presented thus far, events verified by history) become subjects for artists who are willing to report or to reconstruct them in visual modes faithful to appearance. These artists paint, for receptive audiences, images that invite comparison with everyday optical experience in life. This criterion of simple recognition is appealed to in paintings like that of Gérôme, with subjects taken from the historical past. But how does one represent the historical present? Will the same modes be as suitable for representations of current events, in which one is a participant, as they are for past events, which must be reconstructed and of which one can only be a spectator?

At this moment in time, a technological device of immense consequence for modern experience was invented: the camera, with its attendant art of photography. We are all familiar with what the camera equips us to do—report and record optical experience at will. We assume that there is a very close correspondence between the photographic image and the fragment of our visual world that it records. The evidence of the photograph is evidence that what we think we see is really there. In other words, the camera report can be a check of what is "real," "true," or "fact" in our visual experience. Naturally, the invention of the first practical photographic process by Louis J.M. Daguerre in 1839 must have suggested answers to the great debate about what is real and how to represent the real in art. The improvement of the process through daguerreotype, calotype, wet plate, dry plate, and film to snapshot and motion picture is a story that properly belongs to the history of photography. But from its beginnings, the new medium was celebrated as embodying a kind of revelation of visible things. We already find, in the paintings by Delaroche and Gérôme, just such astonishing, cohering aggregations of optical information. Here, then, was a mechanism that could displace the painstaking artist who busied himself with such matters in the interest of truth to his subject. Delaroche is said to have exclaimed, on hearing of Daguerre's invention, "From this day, painting is dead!" And at the end of the century (in 1900), the Fauve-painter-to-be Maurice de Vlaminck declares: "We [painters] hate everything that has to do with the photograph." Yet, as a helpful auxiliary to painting, the photograph was welcomed by Ingres, Delacroix, Gustave Courbet, Edgar Degas and many other leading masters. It is doubtful they could have foreseen the enormous monopoly photography would win in the modern enterprises of image-making and the accumulation of visual information.

Ingres and Delacroix were still living while the Tradition, especially in the hands of Delaroche and Gérôme, was being changed—in substance and direction, in subject matter, in form and technique—to a new concern for the optically real. In the interest of what is real, painting and photography, whether in collaboration or opposition, were destined to replace the Tradition altogether.

Landscape Painting: England and America

Romanticism lifts landscape painting to the level of first importance—the level once occupied exclusively by figure painting. It encourages the expression of moods and feelings animated by experiences of nature undominated by man, experiences into which one can release oneself and with which one can join one's life. In England, as early as the 1740s, a school of poetry began that would reach its height in the early 1800s; its practitioners are the contemporaries of the early Romantics we have seen in architecture and art. These poets, absorbed in describing the look and temper of nature in all its variations, read the landscape closely and sympathetically, from the sublime to the familiarly beautiful. They came to see it almost as the projection of themselves. In a word, they subjectivized it.

There is no better introduction to the English school of landscape painting, so widely influential in the Romantic movement, than the works of these poets. Nature, emotionalized in both its grand and minute manifestations, lives in the canvases of the English School. As literature and history are keys to the art of the French Romantics, so is poetry to the English landscapists.

In the works of JOSEPH MALLORD WILLIAM TURNER (1775–1851), we find readings of nature in its terror and grandeur somewhat more often than in its peace and serenity, although Turner was capable of realizing all of nature's emotions. The brilliant and influential critic, John Ruskin, the first to really understand and call attention to the art of Turner, wrote, in his *Modern Painters* (1846), of the work illustrated here (FIG. 21-29):

> But I think the noblest sea that Turner has ever painted, and if so, the noblest certainly ever painted by man, is that of *The Slave Ship*, the chief Academy picture of the exhibition of 1840. . . . I believe, if I were reduced to rest Turner's immortality upon any single work, I should choose this.

Turner began in the Tradition, an admirer of Claude Lorraine, whose glowing, tranquil, idyllic landscapes (FIG. 19-63) never ceased to move him. But he powerfully wrenches the Tradition in *The Slave Ship*, where he transforms a Claudian sun into an incandescent comet amid flying, scarlet clouds that burst above a sea choked with the bodies of slaves

21-29 JOSEPH MALLORD WILLIAM TURNER, *The Slave Ship*, 1840. 36″ × 48″. Museum of Fine Arts, Boston.

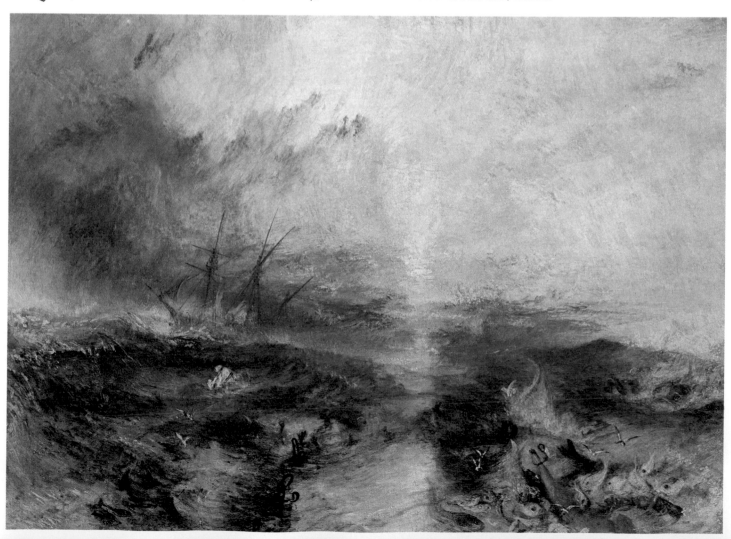

jettisoned from the ship by a ruthless master. Ruskin's masterly prose describes it:

> Between [these] two ridges the fire of the sunset falls along the trough of the sea, dyeing it with an awful but glorious light, the intense and lurid splendor of which burns like gold and bathes like blood. Along this fiery path and valley the tossing waves by which the swell of the sea is restlessly divided lift themselves in dark, indefinite, fantastic forms, each casting a faint and ghastly shadow behind it along the illumined foam. They do not rise everywhere, but three or four together in wild groups, fitfully and furiously, as the under-strength of the swell compels or permits them; leaving between them treacherous spaces of level and whirling water, now lighted with green and lamp-like fire, now flashing back the gold of the declining sun, now fearfully dyed from above with the undistinguishable images of the burning clouds, which fall upon them in flakes of crimson and scarlet and give to the reckless waves the added motion of their own fiery flying. Purple and blue, the lurid shadows of the hollow breakers are cast upon the mist of night, which gathers cold and low, advancing like the shadow of death upon the guilty ship as it labors amidst the lightening of the sea, its thin masts written upon the sky in lines of blood, girded with condemnation in that fearful hue which signs the sky with horror and mixes its flaming flood with the sunlight, and, cast far along the desolate heave of the sepulchral waves, incarnadines the multitudinous sea.

Ruskin's impassioned language matches Turner's turbulent emotion. It is important to note that the particulars of the incident are almost lost in the boiling colors—just as they are almost eliminated from Ruskin's description, which itself is all color. Turner is a great innovator, who releases color from defining outlines to express its nature, as well as the painter's emotion, in storms and calms of its own. The reality of color is one with the reality of feeling. Turner's painting will have an incalculable influence on the development of modern art. His discovery of the esthetic and emotive power of pure color (the most fundamental element of the painting medium), as well as his pushing of the fluidity of the medium to a point at which the subject is almost manifest through the paint itself, points the way to an art that could dispense with shape and form altogether—and the Tradition along with them.

JOHN CONSTABLE (1776–1837), Turner's great contemporary, takes a different route away from the Tradition in his quest for the real. His landscapes—for the most part, placid, untroubled views of the English (Suffolk) countryside—are careful studies of nature in the local colors of woodland, meadow, pond and stream, hill and sky, interspersed with the architecture of mill, cottage, and country church. All these, Constable's favorite subjects, he observes as lighted by a mild sun or shadowed briefly by a changing cloud, bathed in an atmosphere fresh with dew or rain, moved by soft winds. There is no heroic action, nor is the landscape constructed to stage it. In *The Haywain* (FIG. 21-30)—a great success at the Paris Salon of 1824—a farmer in a cart fords a stream. Living nature includes him as it does the dog, the cottage, the stream, the copse, the distant park, the scudding clouds. Here is the oneness with nature sought by the Romantic poets; man is not the observer, but a participant in the landscape's being. But this is not the creation of a dream vision. Constable insists on the reality of the landscape as given to the eye and rendered with the brush: "I hope to show that our profession as painters is *scientific* as well as *poetic;* that imagination never did, and never can, produce works that are to stand by comparison with *realities*" (emphasis added). The reality of the landscape is especially the texture given it by atmosphere (the climate, the weather, which delicately veils what we see) and that atmosphere—constantly *changing* through the hours of the day, the shifts of the weather, and the seasons of the year—is shown by Constable to be the ultimate semblance of nature in its ceaseless process. His use of tiny dabs of local color, stippled with white, creates a sparkling shimmer of light and hue across the surface of the canvas, the vibration itself suggestive of movement and process. The word "fresh" peculiarly denotes Constable's technique and its effects. In speaking of the qualities he intended in his pictures, he mentions: "light—dews—breezes—bloom—and freshness, not one of which . . . has yet been perfected on the canvas of any painter in the world." These are the qualities that we sense in the fleeting states of changing nature—the qualities that startled the young Delacroix when he saw *The Haywain* in the Paris Salon of 1824. In his search for the reality of landscape, Constable studied it like a meteorologist (which he was by avocation). His certainty that the painting of nature partakes of science was his challenge and bequest to Delacroix and the Impressionists.

Less concerned than either Turner or Constable with pioneering advances in color and technique, the American painter THOMAS COLE (1801–1848) typifies the landscape of reflection and mood so romantically appealing to the public, especially in the English-speaking world. Although best known as the leading painter of the Hudson River School, whose members drew their subjects from the still uncultivated regions of the Hudson Valley and the Adirondacks, Cole himself favored more heroic subjects, like *The Course of Empire: Desolation* (FIG. 21-31). The picture describes the final episode in the presumed cycle of the rise, decline, and fall of all the empires of this world. In a setting and atmosphere reminiscent of Claude Lor-

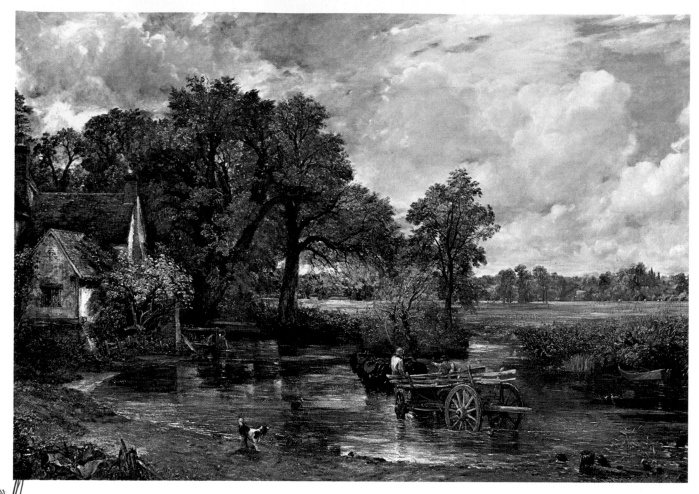

21-30 JOHN CONSTABLE, *The Haywain*, 1821. 4′ 3″ × 6′ 2″. National Gallery, London.

raine, Cole places a giant column embraced by rough vines—all that remains of some colossal temple—in the left foreground. Vegetation runs wild around the silent ruins; the desolation is only partly revealed by a sad moon. Here is the mood of nostalgic moralizing on the fate of empires that dominates Lord Byron's *Childe Harold's Pilgrimage*, the Romantic work that made him famous throughout Europe. Here, as in the poem, we presume that some melancholy, "self-exiled" outcast has stumbled on the scene and somberly

21-31 THOMAS COLE, *The Course of Empire: Desolation*, 1836. Approx. 39″ × 63″. New York Historical Society.

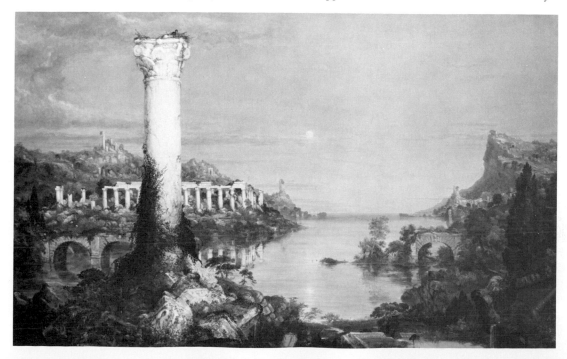

contemplates its meaning for human history. From his viewing point, we see that

> . . . some solitary column mourns
> Above its prostrate brethren of the cave.
> . . . far and wide
> Temple and tower went down, nor left a site:—
> Chaos of Ruins! who shall trace the void,
> O'er the dim fragments cast a lunar light,
> And say, "here was, or is," where all is doubly night?

The tone of Cole's painting is exactly the tone of Byron's lines, and a wide public praised the feelings elicited by both. Indeed, we have in the two works an almost standard blend of familiar Romantic feelings—the melancholy, loneliness, and proud isolation of the contemplative wayfarer, sensitive to the pathos of the distant past and the never-again, to the overtones of the sublime and the flourishes of the picturesque.

Cole may have been thinking that the decay of Europe would be followed by the new promise of youthful America, and that—through its unspoiled experience and pristine virtue—his adopted country (Cole was English-born) might avoid the fateful cycle that dooms great empires. The thoroughly Romantic myth of the innocence of America in contrast to the corruptions of Europe was widely believed on both sides of the Atlantic in the nineteenth century; Cole's colleague, ASHER DURAND, declares America innocent of European "pollution."

Landscape Painting in Germany

Most landscape painting and poetry in the earlier nineteenth century to some degree expresses the Romantic, pantheistic view of nature as a "being" that includes the totality of things in organic unity and harmony; in Goethe's phrase, nature is "the living garment of God." Within nature, man is a sensitive corpuscle that can, by mystical intuition and creative power, reveal the truth of nature, of which humanity is the highest form. In Germany in particular, this view is enspirited with religion. As we saw with Chateaubriand in France, against the materialism, mechanism, and rationalism of the Enlightenment and the Revolution, religion rises once again to regain its lost prestige. But it is not the older, dogmatic, orthodox and institutional religion that returns; rather, it is a religion of nature—Wordsworth's "natural piety," a profoundly personal religion of esthetic emotion. In the thought of the Idealist philosopher Schelling, who made a great impression on the philosophy of art, the artist is a kind of priest; in the act of esthetic creation, he duplicates—or becomes one with—the creative power of nature itself and resolves the contradictions of the inner (subjective) and the outer (objective) worlds. The landscape reveals the divine being of nature to the artist who is prepared by innocence, sincerity, and intuitive insight to

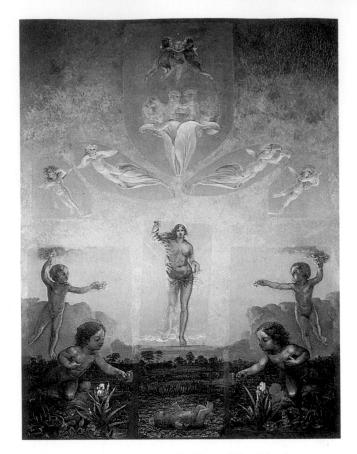

21-32   PHILIPP OTTO RUNGE, *The Times of Day: Morning* (large version), 1809. Approx. 60″ × 45″. Kunsthalle, Hamburg.

receive the revelation. As all nature is mysteriously permeated by "being," the landscape painter has the task of interpreting the signs, symbols, and emblems of universal "spirit" disguised as the material things he sees. He is no longer a beholder of natural landscape, but a participant in its "spirit"; he no longer paints mere things, but the transcendent meaning of them arrived at through his own inspired feelings.

In the art of PHILIPP OTTO RUNGE (1777–1810) landscape becomes religious revelation. Runge declares that true art can be understood only through the deepest mystical experience of religion. In words, as well as images, he celebrates

> . . . the feeling of the whole universe with us; this united chord which in its vibrations touches every string of our heart; the love which keeps us and carries us through life. . . . each leaf and each blade of grass teems with life and stirs beneath me, all resounds together in a single chord. . . . I hear and feel the living breath of God who holds and carries the world, in whom all lives and works; here is the highest that we divine—God!*

Nature is so much a part of God, and we of nature, that, Runge says, "Once we see in all of nature only our own life, then it follows clearly, the right land-

*From letters translated in R.M. Bisanz, *German Romanticism and Philipp Otto Runge* (Dekalb: Northern Illinios University Press, 1970), pp. 48–51.

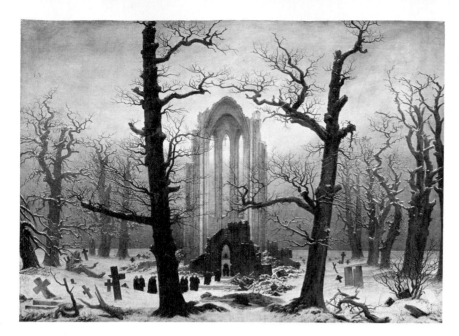

21-33 CASPAR DAVID FRIEDRICH, *Cloister Graveyard in the Snow*, 1810. Approx. 47" × 70". (Painting destroyed during World War II.)

scape can come about." In *Morning* (FIG. 21-32), from his four-part series *The Times of Day*, Runge gives us an allegory of dawn enriched with his personal flower and color symbolism. All plants descend from Paradise and are emblematic of the states of the human soul, as are colors and musical harmonies. The image of the great lily floating in the sky is the floral manifestation of light and the symbol of Divine knowledge and purity. The morning star, Venus, glows above, under the arc of the earth; below it, on the central axis, is the graceful figure of the goddess herself in the guise of Aurora. On the ground below, the supine figure of an infant is an allusion to the Christ child, as well as a symbol of regeneration and redemption and all the promise of the newborn day. The composition has the symmetry and formality of traditional religious painting and the mood of supernatural mystery. But the careful, quite objective study of color tone—the actual hues of dawn, with its tincture of rose turning to radiance—shows Runge's concern for the truth of appearance as the vehicle of symbolic truth. Crossing the empirical world with the transcendental, he gives us an apparition of the supernatural in a natural sky. Like Blake, whose work he must have known, Runge was a religious visionary who believed in angels; unlike Blake, he revered nature as given to the eye. It is interesting that *The Times of Day* were designed as sacred pictures for a chapel dedicated to a new religion of nature.

It is believed that the ideas of Runge influenced the art of his great contemporary, CASPAR DAVID FRIEDRICH (1774–1840); in the work of both, as Robert Rosenblum remarks, "the experience of the supernatural has . . . been transposed from traditional religious imagery to nature."* Nature, as immanent

God, requires no personifications, other than its organic and inorganic subjects and objects—its things visible to the eye, which symbolically express through their forms the truth of nature, which is to say, Divine truth. For Friedrich, landscapes are temples; his paintings themselves, altarpieces. His reverential mood demands the silence appropriate to sacred places filled with the Divine presence. In *Cloister Graveyard in the Snow* (FIG. 21-33) Friedrich gives us a solemn requiem. Under a winter sky, through the leafless oaks of a snow-covered cemetery, a funeral procession bears a coffin into the ruins of a Gothic chapel. The emblems of death are everywhere: the desolation of the season, leaning crosses and tombstones, the black of mourning worn by the grieving and by the skeletal trees, the destruction wrought by time on the chapel. The painting is a kind of meditation on human morality, as Friedrich himself remarks: "Why, it has often occurred to me to ask myself, do I so frequently choose death, transience, and the grave as subjects for my paintings? One must submit oneself many times to death in order some day to attain life everlasting."* Yet the sharply focused rendering demonstrate's the artist's keen perception of the physical environment in all the detail relevant to his message. In Friedrich, we find a balance of inner and outer experience. "The artist," he writes "should paint not only what he sees before him, but also what he sees within him. If, however, he sees nothing within him, then he should also refrain from painting that which he sees before him." It is interesting that these landscapists, whether a Turner or a Friedrich, insist on the necessity of feeling and of truth to appearance simultaneously, even if their means and emphases seem to differ widely.

*Robert Rosenblum, *Modern Painting and the Northern Romantic Tradition: Friedrich to Rothko* (New York: Harper & Row, 1975), p. 22.

*In H. Börsch-Supan, *Caspar David Friedrich* (New York: Braziller, 1974), p. 7.

THE SECOND HALF OF
THE NINETEENTH CENTURY:
THE PREDOMINANCE
OF REALISM

We have already seen realism in the first half of the century, particularly in the art of Delaroche and Gérôme, and we have seen realistic images mechanically produced by the camera. For that matter, realism, in different degrees of focus, has been ingredient in Western art for centuries, from Van Eyck to Velázquez and Vermeer and beyond. The nineteenth-century kind of realism can be described technically and iconographically—technically, as replication of an optical field by matching its color tones on a flat surface, whether or not the subject matter has or could have been seen by the artist; iconographically, as the subject matter of everyday, contemporary life as seen or seeable by the artist, whether recorded photographically or by other modes of visual report. The quarrel between Realism and Romanticism at mid-century is primarily over subject matter. Realism disapproves of traditional and fictional subjects on the grounds that they are not real and visible and are not of the present world. Realism argues that only the things of one's own times, the things one can see, are "real." The Realist vision and report make for a *modern* style—one, by definition, cut off from the past.

The Realist position in art and literature was strengthened by the scientific and technological achievements of the century. Scientific positivism asserted that only scientifically verified fact was "real" and that the "scientific method" was the only legitimate means of gaining knowledge; the others—religion, revelation, intuition, imagination—produced only fictions and illusions. Writing in 1892, Karl Pearson insists confidently that "science claims for its heritage the whole domain to which the word knowledge can be legitimately applied. . . . It refuses to admit any coheirs to its possession." Modern science was indeed the most prestigious of all nineteenth-century intellectual enterprises; its authority rose from its triumphs. Its rigorous practicality, its search for the facts, necessarily served as an example to artists searching for a modern truth and a modern style free from fable and fantasy.

Numerous Realist artists—foremost among them, Gustave Courbet and Édouard Manet—record the life of their times in factual images of it; yet their styles have little in common. At the same time, many artists embody imaginative subject matter in strikingly realistic forms. Indeed, there is a dialogue throughout the century between Realism and Romanticism, and, although technical Realism seems predominant during the latter half of the century, Romantic subject matter and arbitrary formal experiment persist—and, by the end of the century, appear to carry the day for pure artistic subjectivity.

The realism of Manet, which became the realism of the Impressionists, reveals a striking paradox of Realism. To catch the entire optical field spread before him, the artist must paint it just as he sees it. But to record this instantaneous impression, the artist must work swiftly in a sketch-like execution that blurs the visual field as it increasingly emphasizes the brush stroke and the blot of color. The wholeness of the field disintegrates into a plurality of color functions. The scientist would say that the artist is not painting the world, but only his visual sensations of it. As his sensations belong to his private world, the Realist artist finds that the external reality he has sought is *really* only his own inescapable subjectivity.

Transition: Corot, Millet, Daumier

An early turn toward Realism is made in France by the most prominent landscape painter before the Impressionists, JEAN BAPTISTE CAMILLE COROT (1796–1875). In his *Harbor of La Rochelle* (FIG. 21-34), we can see the artist's interest in the full tonal spread, the careful arrangement of dark and light values, which the new device of photography was automatically achieving. Corot's method is to be as faithful as possible to the scale of light to dark. His procedure is interesting. He writes in his notebooks:

> The first two things to study are form and values. For me, these are the bases of what is serious in art. Color and finish put charm into one's work. In preparing a study or a picture, it seems to me very important to begin by an indication of the darkest values . . . and continue in order to the lightest value. From the darkest to the lightest I would establish twenty shades. . . .

In *La Rochelle*, we can appreciate these careful gradations of tone. At the same time, the composition is not the random one of a snapshot; the forms are carefully placed, and the general ordering of them recalls the Classical landscape tradition of Nicolas Poussin (FIG. 19-62). Indeed, there is such firm definition of the forms and such gradation of the half-tones that Corot was said to "Ingres-ize" the landscape. Both

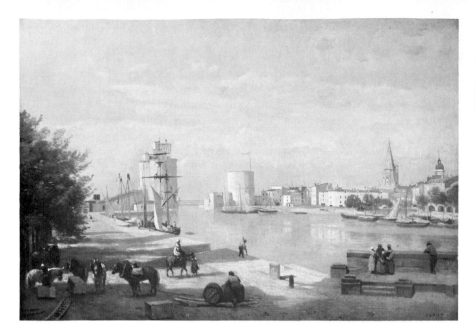

Constable and Corot point toward the Impressionists, but in different ways: Constable, in his brilliant freshness of color and divided brush stroke; Corot, in his concerns for the rendering of outdoor light and atmosphere in terms of values.

Corot painted in close association with members of the "Barbizon School," a group of landscape and figure painters who settled near the village of Barbizon in the forest of Fontainebleau. Chief among these was Jean François Millet (1814–1875). Of peasant stock, Millet undertook to glorify the humble country folk of France. In *The Gleaners* (fig. 21-35), done in 1857, he characteristically poses his peasants as monumental figures against the flat, dull land and sky. The quiet design of Millet's paintings accents his scrupulous truth of detail and contributes to the dignity he gives to even the simplest rural tasks. The solemn grandeur with which Millet invests the poor causes him to be identified with a kind of socialism that was prevalent

in his lifetime. Actually, it is a late echo of the Romantic intuition, held by such men as Wordsworth, which found a touch of nobility in the humblest lives. The objective, carefully realistic landscapes of other painters of the Barbizon School, like Théodore Rousseau, Charles François Daubigny, and Narcisse Virgile Diaz, will powerfully influence the Impressionists and Post-Impressionists.

Corot and his friends in Barbizon were little concerned with the course of events in Paris, where the rapid development of an urban industrial civilization was creating acute political and social unrest. But in a Parisian studio only a few steps from Notre Dame, the lithographer and painter Honoré Daumier (1808–1879) was in close touch with this social ferment. For 40 years, from the July Monarchy of 1830 through the Second Empire, he contributed satirical lithographs to the leading humor journals. In this prodigious output of some 4,000 prints, Daumier's keen insight,

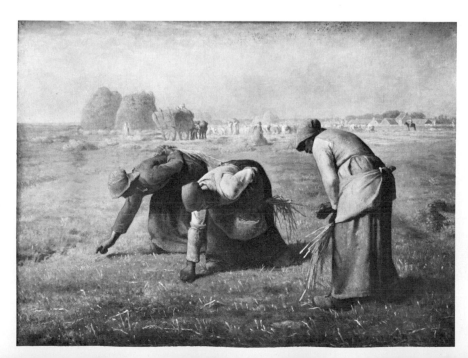

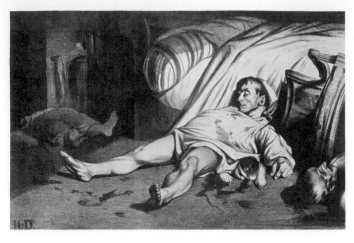

21-36 HONORÉ DAUMIER, *Rue Transnonain*, 1834.
Lithograph, approx. 12″ × 17½″. Philadelphia Museum of Art.

coupled with his sympathy for human beings, was constantly expressed in superb draftsmanship. The sharpness of his political criticism often put him into conflict with the government, as one would expect in view of such prints as *Rue Transnonain* (FIG. 21-36). Soldiers, fired on from a building on the Rue Transnonain in the working quarter of Paris, entered the building and massacred the inhabitants. Daumier, with the power of Goya, gives us a view of the atrocity from a sharp, realistic angle of vision, almost as if we ourselves are among the felled victims. The broken, scattered forms, lying in the midst of violent disorder, are reported as they were found; Daumier uses every available device of his skill to make the situation real. Long before the age of the police photographer, a great artist snaps the picture of a brutal crime committed at a certain place at a certain time. The harsh fact speaks for itself; the artist does not

have to interpret it for us. The print's significance lies in its *factualness;* the artist is becoming concerned with fact as his subject and with the optical realization of fact as his method. Not that Daumier uses the tonal realism of the new medium of photography; he does not. His manner is rough and spontaneous and carries the strong mark of caricature, exaggeration, and dash; this is part of its remarkable force. Thus, Daumier is true to life in content, but his style is uniquely personal.

Although known principally for his lithographs during his lifetime, Daumier was also a very powerful painter and, after 1848, was acclaimed as such. His unfinished *Third-Class Carriage* (FIG. 21-37) gives us a glimpse into the rude railway compartment of the 1860s, in which sit the poor, who can afford only third-class tickets. The disinherited masses of nineteenth-century industrialism were Daumier's indignant concern, and he makes them his subject over and over again. He does not set them off with the sometimes Romantic idealism of Millet; he simply shows them to us in the unposed attitudes and unplanned arrangements of the millions thronging through the modern city—anonymous, insignificant, dumbly patient with a lot they cannot change. Not only is Daumier's subject real, but so is his view of it; he sees people as they ordinarily appear, their faces vague, impersonal, blank—unprepared for any observer. The artist, in a novel approach, tries to achieve the real by isolating from the continuum of ordinary vision an entirely unrehearsed collection of random aspects of human existence. This is prophetic of the candor that will be introduced into the visual arts by use of the modern surreptitious camera.

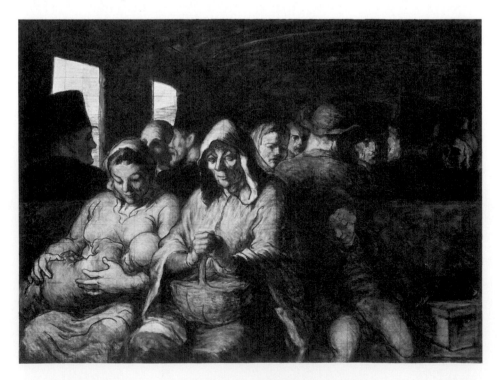

21-37 HONORÉ DAUMIER, *The Third-Class Carriage*, c. 1862. 25¾″ × 35½″. Metropolitan Museum of Art, New York (Havemeyer Collection, bequest of Mrs. H.O. Havemeyer, 1929).

Realism—The Theme: Courbet and Manet

To be able to translate the customs, ideas, and appearances of my time as I see them—in a word, to create a living art—this has been my aim. . . . The art of painting can consist only in the representation of objects visible and tangible to the painter . . . , [who must apply] his personal faculties to the ideas and the things of the period in which he lives. . . . I hold also that painting is an essentially *concrete* art, and can consist only of the representation of things both *real* and *existing*. . . . An *abstract* object, invisible or nonexistent, does not belong to the domain of painting. . . . Show me an angel, and I'll paint one. . . . *

From fragmentary observations like these, made by GUSTAVE COURBET (1819–1877), we get some general idea of Realism as the Realists and their friendly critics understood it. Courbet has long been regarded as the father of the Realist movement in nineteenth-century art; certainly, he used the term "realism" in exhibiting his own works, even though he shunned labels. "The title of Realist," he insists, "was thrust upon me, just as the title of Romantic was imposed upon the men of 1830. Titles have never given a true idea of things." In and since Courbet's time, there has been confusion about what Realism *is*. Writing in 1857, Champfleury, one of the first critics to recognize and appreciate Courbet's work, declares: "I will not define Realism. . . . I do not know where it comes from, where it goes, what it is. . . . The name horrifies me by its pedantic ending; . . . there is enough confusion already about that famous word." There still is confusion, or at least disagreement, about Realism among historians of nineteenth- and, for that matter, twentieth-century art. Yet from Courbet's own brief statements, we gather that he wishes to be only of his own time and to paint only what it makes visible to him. Although Courbet himself started as a painter more or less in the manner of the Barbizon School, there is here a sharp iconographical break with Romanticism and the Tradition; all mythological, religious, fantastic, purely imaginative subjects are ruled out as they are not visible to the modern eye. The critic Jules Antoine Castagnary, writing in 1863, says of Courbet: "[His] great claim is to represent what he sees. It is, in fact, one of his favorite axioms that everything that does not appear upon the retina is outside the domain of painting." But what of pictures like those of Delaroche and Gérôme (FIG. 21-28)? The Realist would reply that Delaroche and Gérôme never saw these events, that they are documenting only illusions, no matter how eye-fooling—for the eye can see only what is present, and what we cannot see, we cannot paint. The modern painter, if

he is free, sincere, and honest, rejects fictions and refuses to create them. What is *real*, then, is *modern*; and the true modern style is Realism. Champfleury writes in 1857: "M. Courbet is a Realist. . . . M. Courbet is a new man." Critics looking for an expressly modern art could find their hero in Courbet.

A man of powerful personality, Courbet was indeed cut out to be the truculent champion of the Realist cause, defying alike public taste and the art juries that rejected two of his major works for the Paris International Exhibition in 1855 on the grounds that his subjects and figures were too coarsely materialistic (so much so as to be plainly "socialistic") and too large. Plain people of the kind Courbet shows us in *Burial at Ornans* (FIG. 21-38) were considered (by the public) unsuitable for artistic representation and were linked in the middle-class mind with the dangerous, newly defined working class, which was finding outspoken champions in men like Marx, Engels, and Proudhon and in the work of novelists like Balzac, Flaubert, Zola, Dickens, and others. Courbet, rejected by the exhibition jury, set up his own gallery outside the grounds, calling it the Pavilion of Realism.

Courbet's Pavilion and his utterances amounted to the manifestoes of the new movement. Although he maintained that he founded no school and was of no school, he did, as the name of his Pavilion suggests, accept the term "realism" as descriptive of his art. With the unplanned collaboration of Millet and Daumier, Courbet challenged the whole iconographic stock of the Tradition and summoned public attention to what Baudelaire calls the "heroism of modern life," which he felt should replace all the heroism of traditional subject matter. For the public, it was a contest between the painters of the "ugly" (Courbet) and the painters of the "beautiful" (those who opposed Courbet)—as the public understood those qualities.

But Courbet's bold, somber palette is essentially traditional—even though his subject is "new"—and certainly in harmony with his subject matter. Lights and darks converge abruptly along the edges of simplified planes, and a surface richness results from the way in which he used his pigments. To Courbet's contemporaries, his intentionally simple and direct methods of expression, in composition as well as in technique, seemed unbearably crude, and he was called a primitive. Courbet made much use of the palette knife, with which large daubs of paint could be quickly placed and unified, producing a roughly wrought surface. His example inspired the young men who worked with him (later Impressionists like Édouard Manet, Claude Monet, and Auguste Renoir), but the public accused him of carelessness and the critics wrote of his "brutalities." Courbet insisted that he wished to paint only the life of his own times

*Robert Goldwater and Marco Treves, eds., *Artists on Art,* 3rd ed. (New York: Pantheon, 1958), pp. 295–97.

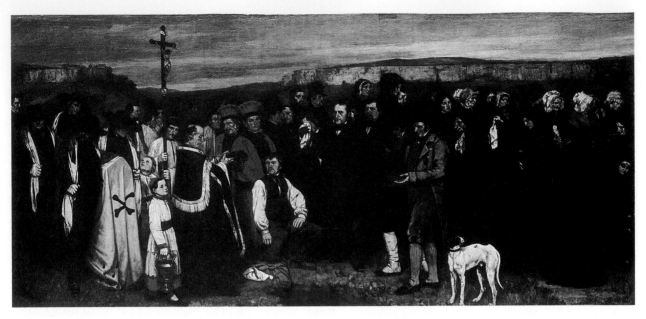

21-38 GUSTAVE COURBET, *Burial at Ornans*, 1849. Approx. 10′ × 22′. Louvre, Paris.

in the costumes of the day, and, toward this end, he "studied without prejudice the art of the old and modern masters." But to the public, which believed that only the ideal or imaginary subject was suitable for major paintings, Courbet's assertion that he could not paint an angel because he had never seen one sounded blasphemous.

Burial at Ornans represents a funeral in a bleak, provincial landscape, attended by obscure persons "of no importance," the kind of people presented by Balzac and Flaubert. Garbed in rusty black, they cluster dumbly around the excavation, while the officious clergyman reads the Office of the Dead. Their faces register all degrees of response to the situation, a gallery of funereal expressions and faithful portraits of the poor—some of them sat for by friends of the artist. Courbet monumentalizes a theme that could hardly have been of less concern to the Salon-going public of Paris but that promises to show full and wide development in all avenues of nineteenth-century life and art: humanitarianism and concern for social reform. The heroic, the sublime, and the terrible are not here—only the drab fact of undramatized life and death. In 1857, Champfluery writes of *Burial at Ornans* ". . . it represents a small-town funeral and yet reproduces the funerals of *all* small towns." What the artist now finds interesting is in his own environment; it is people—not as superhuman or subhuman actors on a grand stage, but as themselves, moved by the ordinary rhythms of modern life.

Although Courbet was often embattled with the critics over the spirit and the form of Realism, he had secure official backing from 1855 onward, and, in his later years, he painted with greater intention to please the public. Indeed, the mode of these later pic-

tures recalls the Baroque, with dark underpainting, heavy chiaroscuro, and subject matter familiar in the popular Salon. This conservatism disappointed the younger artists, who had come to rely strongly on Courbet's vigorous style and technique and on his courageous individualism. Most of the Impressionists had associated and exhibited with him in their early years, but Courbet failed to catch the drift of the new style that was emerging in their work. He spoke disparagingly of Manet's *Olympia*, a reclining nude, as "flat"—that is, without a strong chiaroscuro. He still used dark underpainting after Manet and Monet began to paint on a white surface for greater luminosity. As close to the new generation of painters as he had been, he could say of Manet, in 1867, when the curtain had already risen on a new act: "I myself shouldn't like to meet this young man . . . I should be obliged to tell him that I don't understand anything about his paintings, and I don't want to be disagreeable to him." But the Impressionists could not deny, nor could history itself, the impetus that Courbet's art had given the movement toward a modern style based on observation of the modern environment.

Courbet's art had hardly established one kind of realism before a different version, leading away from Courbet, took its place. In the fall of 1864, the English painter DANTE GABRIEL ROSSETTI wrote home about French Realism, as he had seen it in visits to the studios of Courbet and Manet: "There is a man named Manet . . . whose pictures are for the most part mere scrawls, and who seems to be one of the lights of the Realist School. Courbet, the head of it, is not much better." This comment, though a priggish dismissal of them, does link the two great Realists (who, as we have seen, had little use for one another's work).

With ÉDOUARD MANET (1832–1883), the course of modern painting shifts into a new phase, accelerating its move toward that point at the end of the century when the major transformation of the great tradition that began with Giotto will occur.

In 1863, following the protests of angry artists, an exhibition—the Salon des Refusés—was held to accommodate the exceptionally numerous works rejected by the jury for the Salon that year. (The Salons were government-subsidized "warehouses," as Zola called them, where, yearly, the artists of France exhibited canvases by the thousands. Prizes or recognition at the Salon could ensure professional success; refusal or rejection, neglect and failure. In the nineteenth century, at least until the 1880s, the Salon was the field of intense professional competition among artists and the battleground of "modern" versus "traditional.") It was at the Salon des Refusés that Manet shocked the public with his *Déjeuner sur l'herbe*, "Luncheon on the Grass" (FIG. 21-39)—originally titled simply "The Bath." Manet may have been "a child of the century," as Zola called him in praise of his daring modernity, but he did not care to isolate himself as such. He wished to shine in the Salon with

a work as strong as the masterpieces of the Tradition, preferably a figure painting. We know that at first he had Giorgione's (and Titian's?) *Pastoral Symphony* (FIG. 17-60) in mind as a source, but that, for the actual composition, he used an engraving by Marcantonio Raimondi, a pupil of Raphael. Manet must also have been mindful of Baudelaire's observation (made as early as 1845): "We are surrounded by the heroism of modern life, [but there is as yet no painter] . . . who will know how to tear out of actual life its epic side and make us see, with color or drawing, how grand we are in our neckties and varnished boots!" Baudelaire may have been smiling ironically when he wrote that; nevertheless, the age, or at least thoughtful artists like Manet, took it seriously—or could have. We have already noted Gautier's query: "It is well known that something must be done [in art], but what?"—an especially urgent question for those who believed, with historian Hippolyte Taine, that the age of heroism was past, or, with Eugène Fromentin, that "Great painting is dead. That is understood." In the *Déjeuner*, Manet does not attempt to revive "great painting," but to speak in a new voice and with an authority equal to his celebrated predecessors. He

21-39 ÉDOUARD MANET, *Le Déjeuner sur l'herbe*, 1863. Approx. 7' × 8' 10". Galerie du Jeu de Paume, Paris.

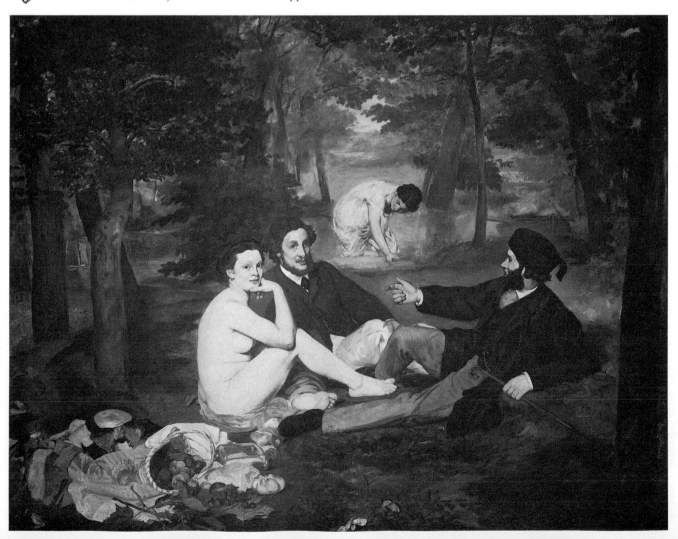

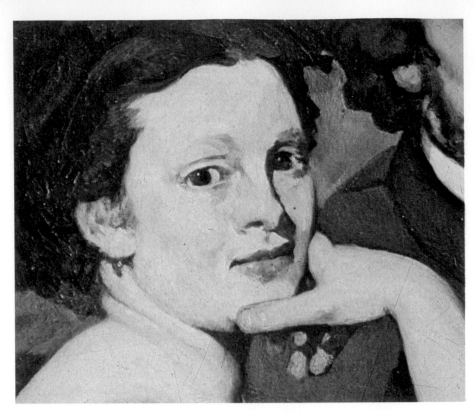

21-40   Detail of *Le Déjeuner sur l'herbe* (FIG. 21-39).

takes the theme of a pastoral paradise, familiar in painting from Giorgione to Antoine Watteau, and embodies it in living, identifiable people: his model Victorine Meurend, his brother Gustave (with cane), and the sculptor Leenhof. This is what outraged the public; the pastoral brought up to date—the promiscuous present in a Paris park—was more the concern of the police than of lovers of art. It is worth quoting a hostile critic of the painting—the voice, no doubt, of public opinion:

> A commonplace woman of the *demi-monde,* as naked as can be, shamelessly lolls between two dandies dressed to the teeth. These latter look like schoolboys on a holiday, perpetrating an outrage to play the man. . . . This is a young man's practical joke—a shameful, open sore.*

Manet's work would have been accepted had he shown men and women as nymphs and satyrs in Classical dress or undress, as did his contemporary, the Academician Adolphe William Bouguereau (FIG. 21-52), ten years later, or as did Giorgione (and Titian?) in *Pastoral Symphony* (FIG. 17-60). But here Manet raises the veils of allusion and reverie and bluntly confronts the public with reality (demonstrating, incidentally, the incompatibility of myth and realism). This masterpiece has the force of tradition without its form; the *Déjeuner* is the valedictory of the world of present fact to the world of the mythic past. The public expected the latter world and was overwhelmed by the former; defeated expectation is part

of the shock tactics of modern art in its unceasing effort to force the public to face a reality that modern art defines for it.

Throughout almost his entire career, Manet suffered the hostility of the critics as surrogates of the public. He never understood their animosity and most often sought their approval, but the doses of the real that he administered were too harsh. His contemporary, the philosopher and historian Ernest Renan, may have been expressing what the public feared from the new realism in art when he said:

> It is possible, then, that the ruin of idealistic beliefs is destined to follow the destruction of supernatural beliefs, and that a real abasement of human morality dates from *the day it saw the reality of things.* [emphasis added.]*

Hardly less than the subject, the public and the critics disliked the new method Manet used to present his figures. His light is photographic, but in a novel way, throwing a harsh, strong illumination directly on the figures to produce a kind of flashbulb effect, similar to that seen in newspaper photographs of night scenes. The middle values, so carefully observed and recorded by Corot, are blotted out; there is a "crowding of the lights" and a compensating "crowding of the darks," whereby many values are summed up in one or two lights or darks. The effect is both to flatten the form and to give it a hard, snapping presence. A detail (FIG. 21-40) shows Manet's procedure, learned partly from Couture, under

*In G.H. Hamilton, *Manet and His Critics* (New Haven: Yale University Press, 1954), p. 45.

*In J.C. Sloane, *French Painting Between the Past and the Present* (Princeton, N.J.: Princeton University Press, 1951), p. 57.

whom he studied, but mostly from Velázquez and Frans Hals. A single high tonality for the flesh is brushed boldly in strokes that create the form. Into this bright tone Manet places abruptly, and without transitions, the strong darks of the eyes and the shadow accents of nose and fingers. The closeup effect is of a blocked-out first or second sketch, but, at a distance, the roughly juxtaposed light and dark cohere. The paint directly reports what is given to the eye, without any presuppositions of form, structure, or contour. Henri Matisse, himself a master of modern art, said of Manet: "He was the first to act by reflex and thus to simplify the painter's task . . . expressing only what immediately touched his senses." He could have added that Manet thereby eliminates painting based on form drawing and sculpture. Form, no longer a matter of line, is only a function of paint and light. Manet himself declared that the chief actor in the painting is the light; *what* the light reveals becomes incidental. The public and the critics, guardians of public taste, knew nothing of this. They saw only a crude sketch without the customary "finish."

One of the byproducts of Manet's new technique is impersonality. The artist, reflexively recording with trained eye and hand, is more or less indifferent to his subject matter, except as it gives him an opportunity to arrange his light sensations in a new way; he creates pictures in which his feelings seem utterly uninvolved. Manet offers the same impersonality and "scientific" detachment in works reporting contemporary events, although we are coming to realize that his subjects meant more to him than was first thought. Without perhaps realizing it, he has given us a representation of man the automaton and man

the disposable object—not the rational animal, the immortal soul, the hero, the darling of nature and the universe, but an ever-changing physical datum whose value is primarily statistical. In this product of the nineteenth-century successes of the biological and social sciences, man is a mere adaptive mechanism, an insignificant unit that blends its biological, political, and social backgrounds. Manet's masterpiece, *Bar at the Folies-Bergère* (FIG. 21-41), painted in 1882, reflects an analogous absorption of the human figure into the pictorial context. The surface of the canvas vibrates with the reflections of light spilling from the gas globes onto the figures and the brilliant still life of fruit and bottles on the counter. In this study of artificial light, both direct and reflected in the mirror background, the subject matter has lost its earlier importance. Manet tells us little about the barmaid and less about her customers, but much about his optical experience of this momentary pattern of light, in which the barmaid is only another *motif*— a larger still life amid the glittering bottles. There is no story, no moral, no plot or stage direction; there is simply an optical event, an arrested moment, in which lighted shapes of one kind or another participate. One is reminded of the novels of Manet's friend Zola, especially of *Nana*, whose heroine is nothing but a meaningless human consequence of an intersection of social forces that create and destroy her. The barmaid in Manet's painting is nothing more than a compositional device—automatic and nonpersonal.

The *Folies-Bergère* illustrates another quality that was to loom with increasing importance in the works of later painters, and that first made its appearance in *Le Déjeuner sur l'herbe*. Although the effect was per-

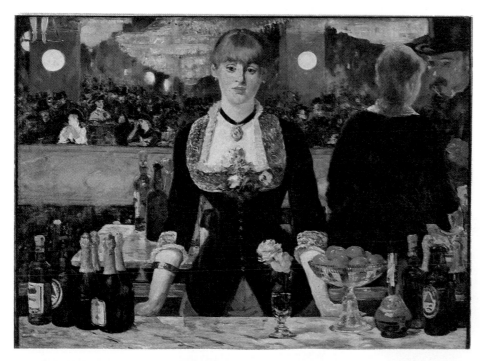

21-41 ÉDOUARD MANET, *Bar at the Folies-Bergère*, 1882. Approx. 37" × 51". Courtauld Institute Galleries, London.

haps unplanned, Manet's painting made a radical break with tradition by redefining the function of the picture surface. Ever since the Renaissance, the picture had been conceived as a "window" and the viewer as looking *through* the painting's surface at an illusory space developed behind it. Manet, by minimizing the effects of modeling and perspective, forces the viewer to look *at* the surface and to recognize it once more as a flat plane covered with patches of paint. This "revolution of the color patch," combined with Manet's cool, objective approach, points painting in the direction of abstraction, with its indifference to subject matter and its emphasis on optical sensations and the problem of organizing them into form. In the twentieth century, not only the subject matter, but even its supposed visual manifestation in the external world, will disappear.

As we have seen in the cases of Courbet and Manet, the modern movement called Realism met powerful resistance. The public found it "ugly," and the critics who explained art to the public in the press mostly agreed, as did many artists; Couture represented the Realist seated on a fragment of Classical statuary, painting the portrait of a pig. Although the government, the greatest patron of art, was often quite tolerant, the Academy (composed of recognized "official" artists who were members of the Institute of France) was largely hostile; so were the juries of the annual Salons and the instructors of the École des Beaux-Arts, the official art school. The conflicts of the Salon are reflected in the ideological wars fought in the newspapers and in reviews, where strident journalistic criticism exhorted the public to admire or despise this or that artist exhibited at the Salon.

It is noteworthy that the press had (and has today) a fundamental role in shaping and sustaining modern movements in art. Whether attacking or defending new movements, the art press, through its heated polemics, has often made esthetic controversy into something resembling the strife of parties in political life, and artistic dogmas have been labeled with the essentially political suffix "-ism": Realism, Romanticism, Impressionism, and so on. The polemics entailed a rhetoric of value opposites—good and bad, right and wrong, true and false. With the triumph of Realism, the defeated opposition (the defenders of the Tradition) came to be disparaged as "academic"— meaning at best, reactionary; at worst, the makers of false art or non-art. Fortunately, contemporary art-historical scholarship has mitigated the harshness and distortions of long-standing partisan criticism, which—although it may have been historically necessary to promote the advance and the reception of modern art—was indiscriminate and misleading in its destruction of artists' reputations and in its devaluation of works that may have both a place in history and quality as art.

In what follows, as well as what has already been said, the reader should keep in mind the intensely competitive and contentious environment in which new art has appeared in the West during the last century and a half. This environment has all the temper of the great revolutions that encompass it and shares the prevailing instinct for restless, impatient, often intemperate controversy. Yet an objective account must attempt to show the personalities and the developments involved, without recourse to any scenario of heroes and villains struggling for the honor or dishonor of art. Painters like the epigones of Ingres and Delacroix need no longer be dismissed as the enemies of artistic progress or the producers of inferior or tasteless works. They, and others like them whom we have yet to study, have made contributions, greater or smaller, to the history of modern art, which it is our business to trace and to fill in without old prejudice and special pleading.

Some Variations on the Theme of Realism

Independent Realism was not exclusively French. In the second half of the century, it is international, although French artists and writers take the lead in promoting it—especially the idea that Realism is and should be the depiction of scenes of modern life. Realistic painting of historical and literary anecdote, as in the work of Delaroche, Gérôme, and many others, continued to be official and popular, while "modern" Realism mostly was not. Yet the latter appeared in all countries and was taken for granted by the end of the century.

Manet had been the pupil of the history painter Couture. The American painter THOMAS EAKINS (1844–1916) studied under Gérôme in the École des Beaux Arts for three years. The generational descent of modern Realism from what might be called Romantic Realism can be seen in the sequences of Delaroche–Gérôme–Eakins, and, much more abruptly, of Couture–Manet, the latter's break with his predecessor being far more marked than Eakins' with his. Eakins, along with Winslow Homer (FIG. 21-47), was a leader of the American School. Like Manet, Eakins had difficulty with the public and the critics. His early masterpiece, *The Gross Clinic* (FIG. 21-42), rejected by the art jury for the exhibition in Philadelphia that celebrated the first century of American independence, was denounced as brutally realistic. It represents the renowned surgeon Dr. Samuel Gross in the operating amphitheater of the Jefferson Medical College in Philadelphia, where the painting now hangs. The surgeon is accompanied by colleagues, all of whom have been identified, and by the patient's mother, who covers her face. Dr. Gross, with bloody fingers and scalpel, lectures on his procedure. It is indeed an unsparing description of a contemporary event, with a good deal more reality than many could endure: "It is a picture," according to one critic, "that even strong men find it difficult to look at long, if they can look at it at all." True to the program of "scenes from modern life," Eakins puts the modern surgeon in the context of his business, as Manet puts the bargirl in the context of hers (FIG. 21-41) and as Courbet, in his *Atelier* (not illustrated), shows himself at work in his studio. Although Eakins' surgeon is certainly of his time and particular place, the subject and its form recall the great group portraits of surgeons painted by Rembrandt—which doubtless were Eakins' inspiration. The lighting is Rembrandtesque, as is something of the feeling. And in his manipulation of the traditional form and technique, Eakins is closer to Courbet than he is to his own master, Gérôme.

He is also much closer to Courbet than he is to Manet. Instead of the quick, "reflexive" report of visual impressions, Eakins preferred a slower, more deliberate method, with long conceptual preparation and the cooperation of visual memory. Knowledge was a prerequisite always—and, where relevant, *scientific* knowledge. Eakins was an expert in mathematics and perspective and taught human anatomy at the Jefferson Medical College. His concern for anatomical correctness led him to investigate human motion with the camera; a skillful and inventive photographer, he made what is thought to be the first rapid-exposure sequence of photographs (with a single camera) of a continuous action. His collaboration with Eadweard Muybridge in the photographic study of human action drew favorable attention in France, especially from Degas, and anticipated the motion picture.

This is not the place to do more than state the vast importance of the photograph as a record of the modern environment. The medium, of considerable value to many painters and especially admired in America, went far beyond the function of a simple auxiliary to painting. Its challenge, historically and technologically, amounted to an expropriation of the realistic image, the property of painting for many centuries. Within three generations or less from the invention of photography, painting was to lose the realistic image to abstraction. This fact is too often disregarded by the historian of art. The reader should keep in mind the steady presence of the camera in the modern environment and its overpowering influence on the way we modern beings see. Although we cannot here do justice to the subject, we can assert that photogra-

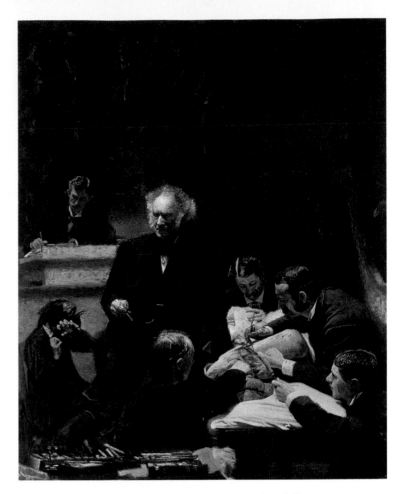

21-42 THOMAS EAKINS, *The Gross Clinic*, 1875. 8' × 6' 6".
Jefferson Medical College, Philadelphia.

phy seems to capture the essence of what Realism calls for—objective representation of modern life.

To represent modern life authentically and in all its variety, artists of Realist bent expanded and diversified their subject matter to embrace all classes and levels of society, all types of people and of environment: the working class, urban and rural, the denizens of the big city, the burghers of the small town, the leisure class at its resorts, the rustics of the provinces. Added to the social sympathies we find in Millet, Daumier, and Courbet were other motives—of an anthropological kind, reflecting interest in national and regional characteristics, folk customs and culture, the quaintness and picturesqueness of local color. WILHELM LEIBL (1844–1900), perhaps the most important Realist painter of Germany in the later nineteenth century, is a master of this latter kind of subject. Influenced by Courbet, but lacking his breadth and depth, Leibl exemplifies the Realist credo. His masterpiece, *Three Women in a Village Church* (FIG. 21-43), is the record of a moment sacred in the life of these country women of three generations—the moment of prayer. Dressed in rustic costume, their Sunday best, they pursue their devotions unselfconsciously, their prayer books held in big

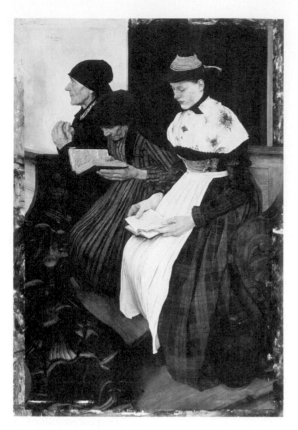

21-43 WILHELM LEIBL, *Three Women in a Village Church*, 1878–1881. Approx. 29″ × 25″. Kunsthalle, Hamburg.

21-44 JAMES TISSOT, *The Ball on Shipboard*, 1874. Approx. 33″ × 51″. Tate Gallery, London.

hands roughened by work. Their manners and their dress proclaim them innocent of the affectations and refinements of the metropolis, which they have probably never seen. Leibl chooses to show their natural virtues: simplicity, honesty, steadfastness, patience. He could subscribe, doubtless, to the words of a poet from another country and another time: ''Far from the madding crowd's ignoble strife / they kept the noiseless tenor of their way.''* Leibl himself writes in a letter: ''Here in the open country and among those who live close to nature, one can paint naturally.'' For three years, he worked from his peasant models in the little church, often under impossible conditions of lighting and temperature.

The light in the picture is hard and neutral, without cast shadows and with only the slightest modeling. The focus is sharp, the forms and space flattening out into pattern. We are aware of the documentary power of the photograph-like approach. Yet, for all its objectivity, the picture is a moving expression of the artist's intelligent sympathy with his subjects, a reading of character without a trace of sentimentality, rare for a subject like this.

One could hardly find more different subjects or better examples of the anthropologizing interests of Realism than the earlier work of JAMES TISSOT (1836–1902), who was born in France but worked for many years in England. His *Ball on Shipboard* (FIG. 21-44) is a

*Thomas Gray, from *Elegy Written in a Country Churchyard*.

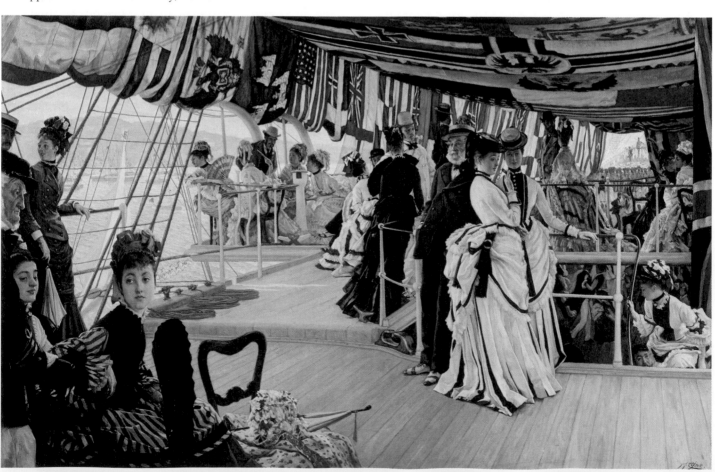

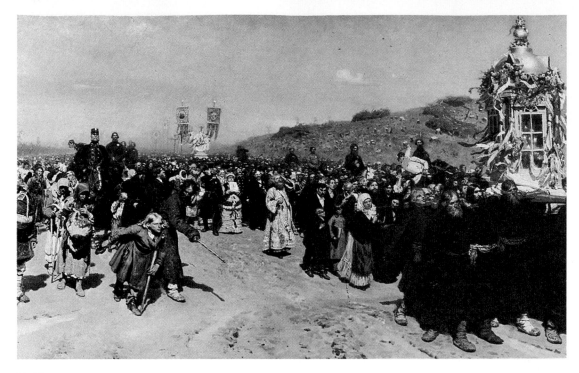

21-45   ILYA REPIN, *A Religious Procession in the Kursk District*, c. 1880. Tretyakov Gallery, Moscow.

pageant of Victorian high society in an age of great opulence, when the yachts of millionaires served as stages for the exhibition of leisured wealth. The setting is a splendid private cruiser anchored on the Thames, probably downstream at Greenwich. The upper, promenade deck, canopied with flags of the great nations and abloom with the brilliant gowns of society belles, is apparently intended for relaxing and socializing; the companionway at the right leads to the main event on the deck below.

The painter carefully observes the lighting peculiar to the scene; it comes from either side of the ship and from far astern, leaving bright areas left and right, with the center zone shaded by the flag canopy. This obliqueness of light direction makes for a most complex tonality. The dominant shade permits no cast shadows, rather a subtle halftone with subdued hues. A tonal neutrality prevails, setting off the sharply contrasting blacks and whites of the gowns, flattening form into pattern, as in Leibl's painting. In both paintings, the artist intends not only to represent the human types objectively in their characteristic environment, but also to light that environment characteristically, whether it be a country church or a rich man's yacht. Moreover, in Tissot's painting particularly, the perspective space progresses beyond the cropping limit of the frame to include the observer and his viewpoint. And the off-center (eccentric) arrangements of figures, with numerous overlappings and directions of glance, show that the painter is concerned above all with rendering the scene as if it is occurring at an instant in time—spontaneous, unposed, natural. The effect is photographic, as John Ruskin recognized.

The literature of nineteenth-century Russia has long received the attention it deserves; not so its art. We need not argue the value of Russian art of that time, but only recognize the achievement of ILYA REPIN (1844–1930), a master too often passed over in histories of modern art. His painting *A Religious Procession in the Kursk District* (FIG. 21-45), simultaneously drama and document, is a Realistic work of extraordinary power. From the viewing point of the artist, we are witness to a dense throng of people in slow, straggling march behind shrines carried on the shoulders of monks. There are priests, peasants, burghers, provincial officials and bureaucrats, students, soldiers, police—all rallying to the bunting-bedecked shrines and the icon banners of some saint on his feast day. It is a multitude that, in itself, characterizes the society of "Holy Russia" as it was before the revolutions of the twentieth century. The throng tramps along a country road, raising clouds of dust in the heat of noon, in a featureless Russian landscape where trees have been recently hacked down. Closer inspection reveals two files of mounted riders—some in uniform, some priestly in appearance—coming slowly forward through the crowd, their way being cleared by men who savagely ply whips and cudgels to open a path. In the left foreground a boy on a crutch has just been struck heavily by a staff in the hands of a priest. We can read in the crowded details of Repin's *Procession* the sullen poverty and misery, the dogged, almost primitive religion, the officious arrogance, the pitiless harshness of the old Russian scene, almost exactly as in the novels of Dostoevsky (*Procession* and *The Brothers Karamazov* are contemporary). One need suspect no interinfluence; painter and novelist are simply confronting the same realities. In a way, moreover, the *Procession* is a kind of

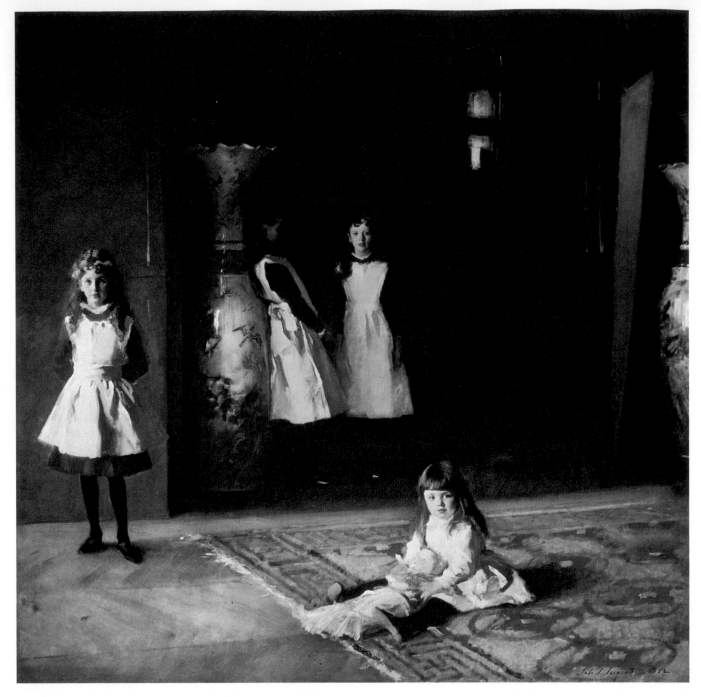

21-46 JOHN SINGER SARGENT, *The Daughters of Edward Darley Boit*, 1882. 7′ 3″ × 7′ 3″. Museum of Fine Arts, Boston.

Russian *Burial at Ornans* (FIG. 21-38); both Repin and Courbet reveal a society through real images of its people.

Repin's painting expands the program of Realism formulated in his time. It is a scene directly from modern life, at a particular place and time, objectively recorded without Romantic tone and with little of the artist's comment, unless a touch of sad irony or protest. The artist, using his acute visual memory, reconstructs the scene, perhaps from sketches but certainly close to the way he saw it—similar to Eakins' method. The space is fluent and is assumed to continue, along with the action, beyond the frame. The light is out-of-doors, rather than of the studio, and

the color—with its myriad modulations and accents— is suited to the time of day and the local color of landscape and dress. A motion-picture camera set up at the artist's viewpoint would probably record the scene much as we see it here. Indeed, in Repin's *Procession*, we are not far, either in subject or form, from the work of the great directors of the Russian cinema.

The versatility of the Realist approach and the diversity of style it allows are evident when we move across the world from Repin to the work of the American painter JOHN SINGER SARGENT (1856–1925), a younger contemporary of Repin and also of Eakins, Leibl, and Tissot. Sargent was born in Florence of expatriate Bostonians, studied art in Paris, and eventually settled in London—a polished cosmopolitan in culture and a facile and fashionable painter of portraits. His remarkably easy brushing of paint in thin films and his effortless achievement of quick and lively illusion are learned from his study of Velázquez. Sargent may have had in mind the latter's masterpiece, *Las Meninas* (FIG. 19-37), when he painted his own version of a family group portrait, *The Daughters of Edward Darley Boit* (FIG. 21-46). Sargent paints the girls (children of a close friend) in their Paris home, their natural environment, grouped casually within a hall and small drawing room. The informal, eccentric arrangement of their slight figures suggest how much at ease they are within this familiar space and with objects like the monumental Japanese vases, the red screen, and the fringed rug. (The size of the objects, moreover, subtly emphasizes the girls' diminutive stature.) Sargent must have known the Boit children well, and liked them; certainly, they seem comfortable in his presence, being on home ground and not in a studio. Relaxed and trustful, they give Sargent an opportunity to record sensitively a gradation of young innocence—from the naive, wondering openness of the little girl in the foreground, to the grave artlessness of the ten-year-old, to the slightly self-conscious poise of the adolescents. From the positioning of the figures and the continuity of the space of hall and room (made so by the lighting), we sense how spontaneously they move through their element. They seem to be attending momentarily to an adult who has asked them to interrupt their activity and "look this way." Here is a most effective embodiment of the Realist belief that the business of the artist is to record the modern being in modern context. In this case, the persons and their environment are sharply specified. The Realist painter increasingly moves into the space of the painting, regulating the distance of his standpoint from the objects he is representing, so that he seems to share the space with them and to participate in the action or in the environment of the action.

The Realist's manipulation of distance, whereby the artist is placed in the locale of the subject's action, is evident in a painting by WINSLOW HOMER (1836–1910), who, with Eakins, was a leading representative of the American School. As if equipped with a modern telephoto lens, Homer, in *The Fox Hunt* (FIG. 21-47), witnesses and reports a poignant event in the nonhuman world of nature. A fox, bogged down in heavy winter snow, is attacked by crows made fierce by starvation; trapped, its fate is sure. The double irony of the title is clear. A fox is hunted for sport by the mounted hunter, who has no intention of devouring it; it is not normally hunted by crows. In this case, the swift and elusive fox is caught by a shift of circumstances, and the hungry crows find unaccustomed prey. The fox once hunted birds; now birds hunt the fox. Homer expresses the impersonal, cruel competition of natural species—asserted as a rule of life in the Darwinian–Spencerian theory of the survival of the fittest and appearing in the writers of the time, notably in Jack London's *Call of the Wild*. The Realist factually conveys the Romantic mood of struggle and death in nature. Homer's method is objective

21-47 WINSLOW HOMER, *The Fox Hunt*, 1893. 38″ × 68½″. The Pennsylvania Academy of the Fine Arts, Philadelphia (Temple Fund Purchase).

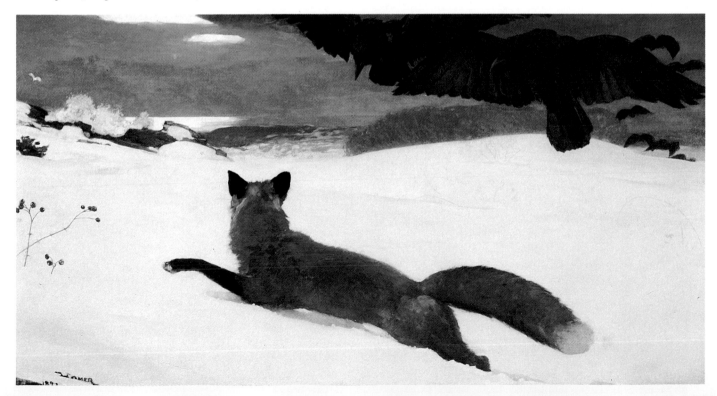

and simple. The figure of the fox is silhouetted against the flat white of the snowy ground; above, the dark shapes of the crows fill the dark sky, overshadowing and overwhelming the fox. The color areas are sharp-edged and icy cold, except for the faintly warm tonality of the fox's vulnerable coat. Form and color convey the grim mood of the scene in reinforcement of what the images literally present. The artist is "present" but powerless to intervene. In any event, this is a fact of nature.

Romantic Responses to Realism

Realism stands for what the eye can see in the modern world—for actuality in all subject matter and verisimilitude in all images. Works of imagination based on subjects from myth and history are believed false. About art, the philosopher Friedrich Nietzsche, reflecting the Realist credo, writes: "We do not demand beautiful, illusory lies from it. . . . Brutal positivism reigns, recognizing facts without becoming excited." The Realist artists, then, confine their subject to what is optically present in the contemporary environment. (Yet, by the end of the century, the realistic recording of modern life will seem hopelessly trivial and will be largely abandoned for wholly subjective, nonrealistic styles.) Like the positivists of science, the Realists believe in the supremacy of cold fact,

the enemy of all fictions and illusions, and make it the basis of esthetic truth and personal honesty.

But wasn't this doctrine arbitrary and severely restrictive of that play of artistic imagination long honored in the Tradition? Some artists who subscribed to this view refused to be restricted to the contemporary scene; they painted fictional, fanciful, and historical subjects—realistically. In England, JOHN EVERETT MILLAIS (1829–1896), whom Baudelaire called "the poet of meticulous detail," used the Realistic technique to render religious, historical, and literary subjects. Painstakingly careful in his study of visual fact closely observed from nature, he was a founder of the so-called Pre-Raphaelite Brotherhood in 1848, a group of young English artists who wished to create an art fresh, sincere, and free from what they considered to be the tired and artificial manner propagated by the successors of Raphael in the academies. Millais' method is seen to advantage in his *Ophelia* (FIG. 21-48), which he exhibited in the Universal Exposition in Paris in 1855, where Courbet set up his Pavilion of Realism. The subject, from Shakespeare's *Hamlet*, is the drowning of Ophelia, who, in her madness, is unaware of her plight:

> Her clothes spread wide,
> And mermaid-like awhile they bore her up;
> Which time she chanted snatches of old tunes.
>
> (IV:3)

21-48   JOHN EVERETT MILLAIS, *Ophelia*, 1852. 30" × 44". Tate Gallery, London.

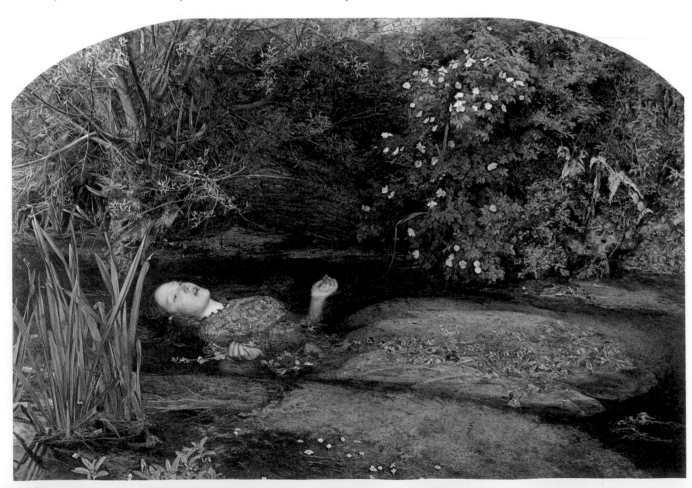

Concerned to make the pathos of the scene visible, Millais becomes a faithful and feeling witness of it in every detail, as if it were indeed before his eyes, reconstructing it with a circumstantial stagecraft worthy of the original poetry.

Millais' technique is Realistic, but the orthodox Realist would complain that the subject is not—that it is playacting. Yet it is unlikely that an impartial observer of the painting who is also familiar with *Hamlet* will object that, as the subject is not from the artist's time and place, it is, of necessity, deficient in truth—certainly not deficient in truth to appearance. It may be that this conflict between the *seen* (in everyday experience) and the *seeable* (in plausible reconstructions of past events or fictions) is resolved in modern cinema. The kind of picture drama we have in *Ophelia*—in bringing before our eyes with all optical fidelity the fictive action of a nonpictorial medium, literature—is an anticipation of the motion picture, in which fictions and facts are presented to the eye as equally real. Nineteenth-century Realists like Courbet and Manet might have objected that the picture-drama was not painting, but stage production, and could only be judged as such. The German painter HANS THOMA remarked that many history paintings looked as though they had been made by theater directors, and they were often referred to disparagingly as "costume pieces."

In any event, there were also many painters during this period who did not accept Realism either in terms of subject or technique. Among them was EDWARD BURNE-JONES (1833–1898), a friend and protégé of John Ruskin and (in a later circle of the Pre-Raphaelite Brotherhood) an associate of William Morris and Dante Gabriel Rossetti, who, earlier, had slurred the work of Courbet. Burne-Jones agreed with their distaste for the materialism and ugliness of the contemporary, industrializing world and with their appreciation of the spirituality and idealism, as well as the art and craftsmanship, of past times, especially the Middle Ages and the Early Renaissance. Burne-Jones drew his subjects from literature and depicted them in a soft, languid style much influenced by Sandro Botticelli (FIG. 16-59). His *King Cophetua and the Beggar Maid* (FIG. 21-49) illustrates a little poem of that name written by Alfred Tennyson in 1842, a modern reworking of an ancient and popular ballad. The situation is given in the last lines:

So sweet a face, such angel grace
  In all that land had never been.
Cophetua sware a royal oath:
  "This beggar maid shall be my queen!"

The king, in grave reverie, contemplates the maiden, who sits serenely above him, like some pedestaled perfection oblivious to mortal presence. Burne-Jones

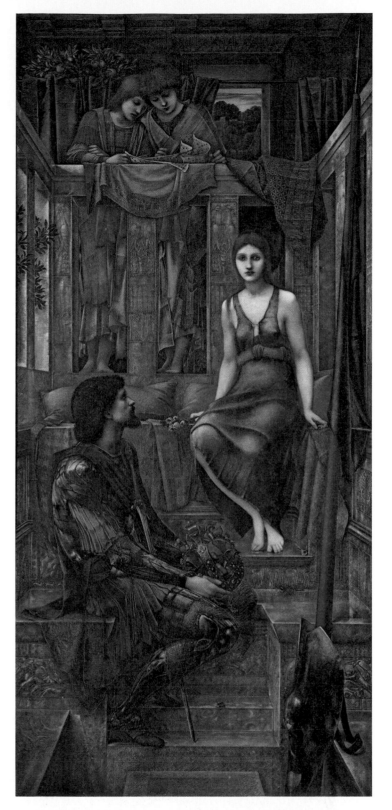

21-49 EDWARD BURNE-JONES, *King Cophetua and the Beggar Maid*, 1884. Approx. 9' 7" × 4' 5". Tate Gallery, London.

is certainly no Realist; although he insisted he wanted the maiden to look like a beggar, she looks anything but. Like the atmosphere, she belongs to the world of trance and dream, in which images arise from some lost age of beauty and innocence. The composition, planar and still, recalls the mural tableaux of the Ren-

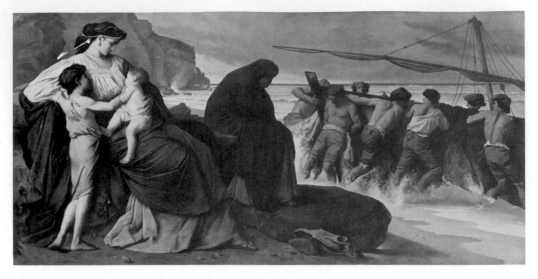

21-50 ANSELM FEUERBACH, *Medea*, 1870. 6′ 6″ × 13′. Bayerische Staatsgemäldesammlungen, Munich.

aissance, the suspended action of stained glass and tapestry. (For the manufacture of works in the latter two media, in fact, Burne-Jones supplied the shop of William Morris with many designs.) His dreamy, abstract, decorative manner perfectly suits the somewhat precious, estheticizing taste of the later nineteenth century. We can appreciate how far we are here from Realism, as well as the great diversity of style at the time, if we compare Burne-Jones' beggar maid with Manet's barmaid (FIG. 21-41). Only two years separate the dates of the paintings.

In the age of Courbet and Manet, the authority of the Tradition could still command artistic obedience. Only slightly touched by the influence of Courbet in Paris, ANSELM FEUERBACH (1829–1880) found in Italy, as did so many of his German compatriots, the age-old inspiration of the Renaissance and Classical antiquity. A long resident of Rome, he was under the spell of Raphael when he painted the *Medea* (FIG. 21-50). Here, Feuerbach gives us not the climax of the tragedy, but its quiet prologue. Jason and his argonauts

set out to find the Golden Fleece, while Medea, not foreseeing his faithlessness, embraces the children whom she will later kill. The grieving nurse has a premonition of the disaster to come. Yet nothing disturbs the calm of the composition, in which the Classicism of Raphael is enhanced by Feuerbach's study of ancient sculpture. The conception of the figure of Medea is in the spirit of the reclining goddess from the east pediment of the Parthenon (FIG. 5-48). In this picture, more than in any of his others, Feuerbach realizes his stated ideal: a "truly majestic, forbidding tranquility," a Classicism aristocratic and aloof.

This altogether turning away from Realism and, indeed, the modern world that called for it, is also to be seen in the work of PIERRE PUVIS DE CHAVANNES (1824–1898). Again it is Classical mood and form that the artist seeks to adapt to his own esthetic ends—an art ornamental and reflective, removed from the noisy world of Realism. Puvis had been a pupil of Chassériau, who, early on, pointed the way of retreat into an art of beauty for its own sake, an art uncom-

21-51 PIERRE PUVIS DE CHAVANNES, *The Sacred Grove*, 1884. 2′ 11½″ × 6′ 10″. (Potter Palmer Collection)

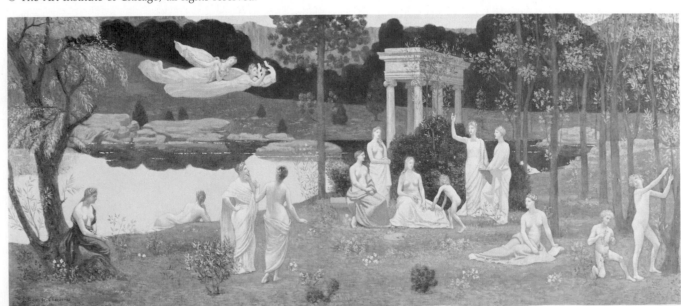

pelled by the dictates of Realism and of modern pragmatism. In his *Sacred Grove* (FIG. 21-51), Puvis deploys statuesque figures in a tranquil landscape with a Classical shrine—their motion suspended in timeless poses, their contours simple and sharp, their modeling as shallow as bas-relief. Puvis, primarily a mural painter, is obedient to the requirements of the wall surface, neutralizing and restraining color, banishing pictorial illusionism with its perspective and tone matching. The calm, almost bland atmosphere suggests some consecrated place, where all movements and gestures, undisturbed by the busyness of life, have a perpetual, ritual significance. The stillness and simplicity of the forms, the linear patterns created by their rhythmic contours, and the suggestion of their symbolic import amount to a kind of program of anti-Realism that impressed younger painters like Paul Gauguin and the Symbolists, who saw in Puvis the prophet of a new style that would replace Realism. Puvis had a double reputation: he was accepted by the Academy and the government for his Classicism, and he was revered by the avant-garde for his vindication of imagination and artistic independence from the world of materialism and the machine. Puvis asks a question significant for artists of his time and later: "What will become of us artists in the face of this invasion of engineers and mechanics?"

In the painting of ADOLPHE WILLIAM BOUGUEREAU (1825–1905), we find a point of view diametrically opposed to that of Puvis. Although he uses a Classical, mythological subject, as Puvis commonly does, Bouguereau renders his *Nymphs and Satyr* (FIG. 21-52) with an optical realism of high finish—scrupulously matching and blending values to achieve, through tonal gradation and continuity, a startling illusion. A painting like this presses the question: Can the subjects of myth, fancy, and fiction be painted with the modern tonal simulation we associate with the camera, without evoking incredulity and, perhaps, a sense of absurdity in the observer? We have raised the question earlier; it is the Realist's. Here, Bouguereau gives us not the tranquil, disassociated vision of Puvis, which is rendered in an almost abstract form, but a heated, orgiastic struggle, which, were it not veiled by Classical allusion, would make us think of those similar, but openly titillating tableaux produced in certain photographers' studios in the later years of the century. What is at question is the appropriateness of the subject in relation to the technique of representation. Do they belong together? *Can* they appear together without contradiction that promotes disbelief? For the Classicist, this picture would fail to fulfill a longing "for nothing more than the moment in which conception and representation will flow together." The Realist, would find the picture false, due to the incongruence of its form and content and the unrealistic nature of its subject.

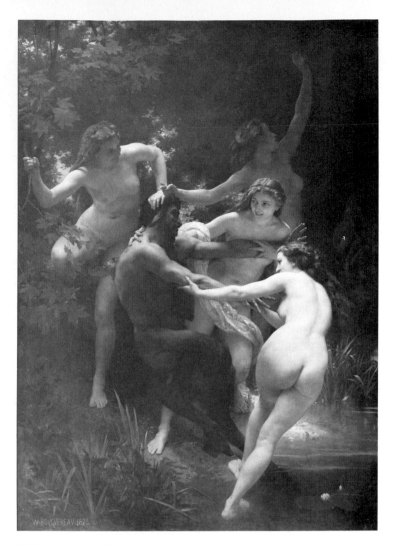

21-52   ADOLPHE WILLIAM BOUGUEREAU, *Nymphs and Satyr*, 1873. Approx. 8′ 6″ high. Clark Institute, Williamstown, Massachusetts.

The obvious conflict of conception and representation in many of Bouguereau's pictures, as well as in those of other recognized artists of the time, did not displease the public. Bouguereau was immensely popular, enjoying the favor of state patronage throughout his career. His reputation has fluctuated violently; the moderns of his century damned him as the very archetype of the official painter, but critics of our own day acknowledge his love of beauty and his undeniable painterly skills, if not always his esthetic wisdom and taste.

Much of the reputation of the popular, "official," "academic" art of the century stood, fell, and rose again—rehabilitated with Bouguereau and his colleague Gérôme, considered earlier. There were painters, touched lightly or heavily by Realism, who borrowed from it or compromised with it but remained independent of its principal dogma—that the artist must see and represent modern life in a modern way. We need mention only two of a very large number of these to exemplify further the stylistic pluralism of the age.

ROSA BONHEUR (1822–1899), a winner of many

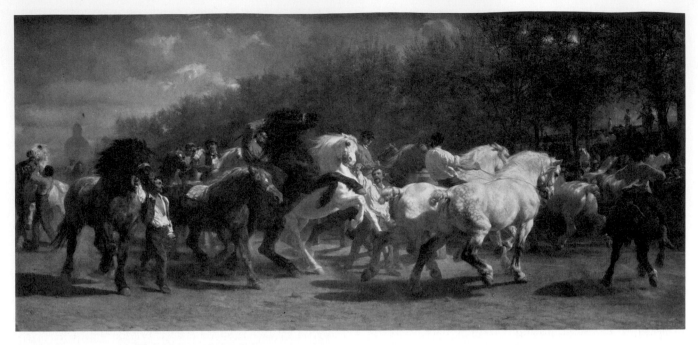

21-53 ROSA BONHEUR, *The Horse Fair*, 1853. 8′ ¼″ × 16′ 7½″. Metropolitan Museum of Art, New York (gift of Cornelius Vanderbilt, 1887).

prizes at the Paris Salon, was very popular in England. Her monumental canvas *The Horse Fair* (FIG. 21-53) displays a scientific naturalist's knowledge of equine anatomy and motion, in combination with an honest love of and admiration for brute beauty and strength. To pictorialize her theme, she makes use of the results of her own sure observation of horses, but a familiarity with Rubens, and especially the compositions of Gericault and Delacroix, also seems likely to have been a factor. The horses and their grooms make the circuit of the exhibition ring of the fair; the excitement of the action generates tensions among men and animals. Horses, some not quite broken, rear up; others plod or trot, guided on foot or ridden by their brawny keepers. The uneven line of march, the tread and tramp, the thunderous pounding of the heavy-weight percherons, the overwhelming power partly breaking out—all are orchestrated by the artist visually, yet almost aurally as well. The great Baroque arc of the painting's space, across which roll and

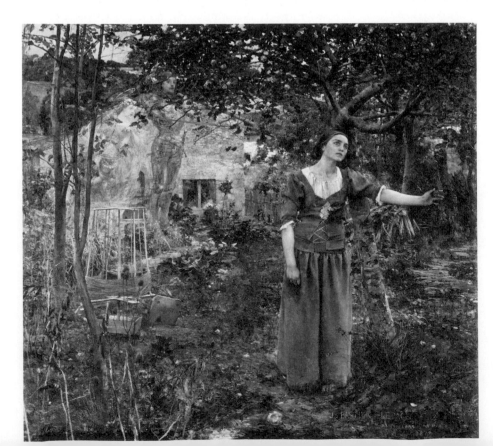

21-54 JULES BASTIEN-LEPAGE, *Joan of Arc*, 1880. 8′ 4″ × 9′ 2″. Metropolitan Museum of Art, New York (gift of Erwin Davis, 1889).

surge the curving, muscular forms, determines the whole composition. Although she had in mind the horses of the Parthenon frieze (FIG. 5-51), the artist seems to have settled on this structure, quite instinctively, as the shape of the motion of powerful masses. Without deliberate intention, Bonheur strongly restates the Baroque in a painting that is, nevertheless, one of the most original of the nineteenth century.

In a balance of Realist style and Romantic subject, JULES BASTIEN-LEPAGE (1848–1884) makes the perfect compromise. His *Joan of Arc* (FIG. 21-54) represents the inspired heroine of France in the garden of her parents' humble cottage. She hearkens, entranced, to her hovering saints—Michael, Catherine, and Margaret—who announce her mission to save her country from the English enemy. The saints appear as dim apparitions in the trees at the upper left; Joan is off-center at the right. The informal arrangement—the continuing, inclusive space cropped accidentally by the frame—is, as we shall presently see, characteristic of Impressionist composition, which seeks to catch the casual, the informal, the unposed "snapshot." It is as if we have come on the saint suddenly and unannounced. Although the figure is farther away from us and the optical manifold (all the details within the frame) is more sharply focused than in Manet's *Bar at the Folies-Bergère* (FIG. 21-41), the profusion of evenly stressed detail, spread flatly across the picture plane, is closely comparable. If the saints were eliminated and the situation and dress made contemporary, the Realist would have little to complain of. In Bastien-Lepage's *Joan of Arc*, the stylistic paths of Romanticism and Realism run together; the disagreement could only be about the subject: is it "modern" or not? Here, the dialogue-like exchanges between Romanticism and Realism seem to end, at least, in an agreement about form. But do they? We have seen that many artists rejected Realism altogether, and some compromised with it. Still others will follow the Realist premise to its conclusion. These are the Impressionists, and their point of departure is the art of Manet.

Impressionism

Although the term "Impressionism" was first used in 1874 (by a journalist ridiculing a landscape by Monet called *Impression—Sunrise*), the controversy that raged for 20 years over the merits of Impressionism began 11 years earlier with Manet's *Le Déjeuner sur l'herbe* (FIG. 21-39).

From the middle of the 1860s, such Impressionist painters as Monet, Camille Pissarro, Renoir, and Degas followed Manet's lead in depicting scenes of contemporary life and landscape. Their desire for a more modern expression led them to prize the imme-diacy of visual impression and persuaded the landscapists, especially Monet and Pissarro, to work out of doors. From this custom of painting directly from nature came the spontaneous revelation of atmosphere and climate so characteristic of Impressionist painting. Their rejection of idealistic interpretation and literary anecdote was paralleled by their scrutiny of color and light. Scientific studies of light and the invention of chemical pigments increased their sensitivity to the multiplicity of colors in nature and gave them new colors with which to work. Most of their eight cooperative exhibitions, held between 1874 and 1886, irritated the public. But their technique was actually less radical than it seemed at the time; in certain respects, they were simply developing the color theories of Leonardo and the actual practice of Rubens, Constable, Turner, and Delacroix.

The Impressionists sought to create the illusion of forms bathed in light and atmosphere. This required an intensive study of outdoor light as the source of our experience of color, which revealed the important truth that local color—the actual color of an object—is usually modified by the quality of the light in which it is seen, by reflections from other objects, and by the effects produced by juxtaposed colors. Complementary colors, for example, if used side by side over large enough areas, intensify each other. In small quantities or mixed, though, they fuse into neutral tone. Shadows do not appear gray or black, as many earlier painters had thought, but seem to be composed of colors modified by reflections or other conditions. (Jan Vermeer evidently observed this.) Furthermore, the juxtaposition of colors on the canvas for the eye to fuse at a distance produces a more intense hue than the mixing of the same colors on the palette. Although it is not strictly true that the Impressionists used only primary hues, juxtaposing them to create secondary colors (blue and yellow, for example, to produce green), they did achieve remarkably brilliant effects with their characteristically short, choppy brush strokes, which so accurately caught the vibrating quality of light. The fact that the surfaces of their canvases look unintelligible at close range and their forms and objects appear only when the eye fuses the strokes at a certain distance accounts for much of the early adverse criticism—such as the conjecture that the Impressionists fired their paint at the canvas with a pistol.

Of the Impressionists, CLAUDE MONET (1840–1926), whose *Impression—Sunrise* we just mentioned, carries the method furthest, especially in a series of paintings of the same subject. He painted 16 views of Waterloo Bridge in London and some 40 views of Rouen Cathedral (Introduction FIG. 5 and FIG. 21-55). In each case, the cathedral is observed from the same point of view, but at different times of day and under various

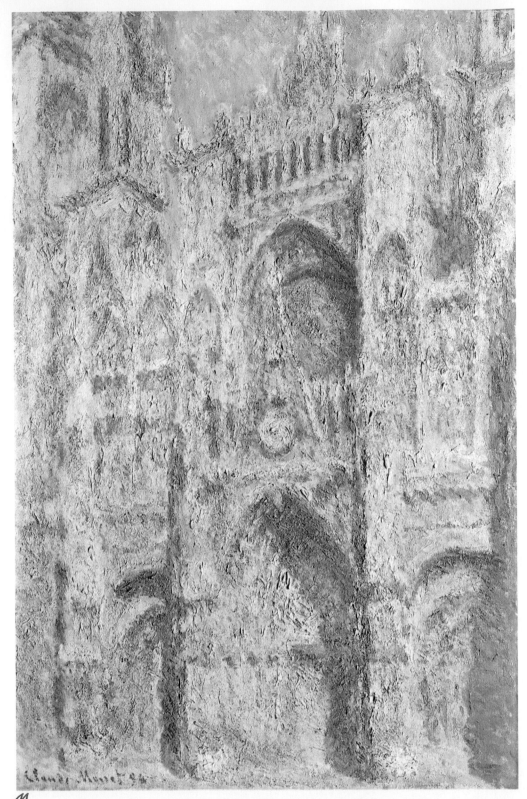

21-55 CLAUDE MONET, *Rouen Cathedral* (façade), 1894. Approx. 39″ × 26″. Metropolitan Museum of Art, New York (Theodore M. Davis Collection, bequest of Theodore M. Davis, 1915).

climatic and atmospheric conditions. Monet, with a scientific precision, gives us an unparalleled and unexcelled record of the passing of time as seen in the movement of light over identical forms. Later critics accused Monet and his companions of destroying form and order for the sake of fleeting atmospheric effects. But we may feel that light is properly the "form" of Monet's finest paintings, rather than accept the narrower definition that recognizes "formal" properties only in firm, geometric shapes. The Impressionist artist does not paint the world we presumably "see"—the world of Corot's "values," of graduated tones of lights and darks; rather, he records his own sensations of color, and the outlines and solidities of the world interpreted by common sense melt away.

The *Place du Théâtre Français* (FIG. 21-56) by CAMILLE PISSARRO (1830–1903) shows the same qualities. The artist's visual sensations of a crowded Paris square, viewed from several stories above street level, yield a panorama of blurred, dark accents against a light ground. Like Monet, Pissarro is after the most fugitive effects of movement; but, unlike Monet, the movements are not so much of light as of the life of the street. He achieves a deliberate casualness in the arrangement of his figures—the effect a single glance from a window would provide if it were prolonged only a few seconds. Ceaseless change of position and ceaseless change of color are the new order of the painter's experience. There is no longer a standard of unchanging optical truth, just as there is no longer a standard way of seeing. The artist's subjective experience is all he has to deal with, and, for him, "nature" is simply the source of his sensations. When Pissarro writes, in a letter to his son Lucien, "we have to approach nature sincerely, with our own modern sensibilities," we should understand him to mean not the "nature" of the great landscape tradition but "nature" precisely as it is revealed to our modern senses. For the Impressionist, the modern sensibility gets at what is *real* in nature—namely the color stimuli it reveals to the analytic eye of the modern painter.

In the later nineteenth century, artists are not alone in emphasizing the prime reality of sensation in the process of apprehending nature or the world. Scientists, philosophers of science, and psychologists in great number begin to assert that reality *is* sensation, or that knowledge can be based only on the analysis of our sensations. Indeed, the Austrian physicist Ernst Mach could hold that the *sole* reality is sensation and that all the laws and principles of physics are only a kind of shorthand referring to complex linkages of the data of sense. And modern experimental psychology, of course, begins with the measurement of sense experience.

What we might call "color sensationism" and fugitive effects of light and motion are what link the Impressionist artists; for on closer view, each has very much his own manner, despite the more-or-less fundamental agreements. For example, AUGUSTE RENOIR (1841–1919) is a specialist in the human figure, a sympathetic admirer of what is beautiful in the body and what is pleasurable in the simple round of human life. The bright gaiety of *Le Moulin de la Galette* (FIG. 21-57), where a Sunday throng enjoys a popular Paris dance hall, is a characteristically Renoir celebration of vivacious charm. People crowd the tables and chatter, while others dance energetically. The whole scene is dappled by sunlight and shade, artfully blurred into the figures themselves to produce just that effect of floating and fleeting light so cultivated by the Impressionists. The casual, unposed place-

21-56   CAMILLE PISSARRO, *Place du Théâtre Français*, 1895. Approx. 28½″ × 36½″. Los Angeles County Museum of Art (the Mr. and Mrs. George Gard De Sylva Collection).

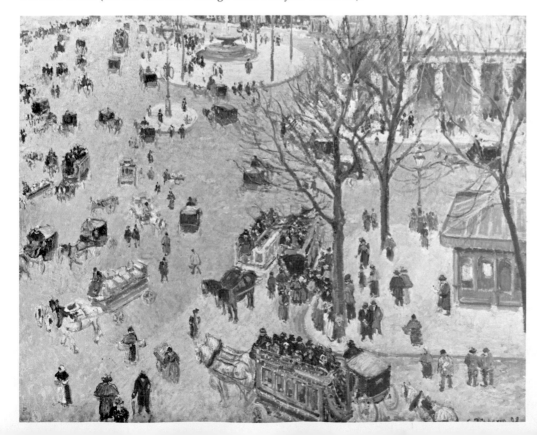

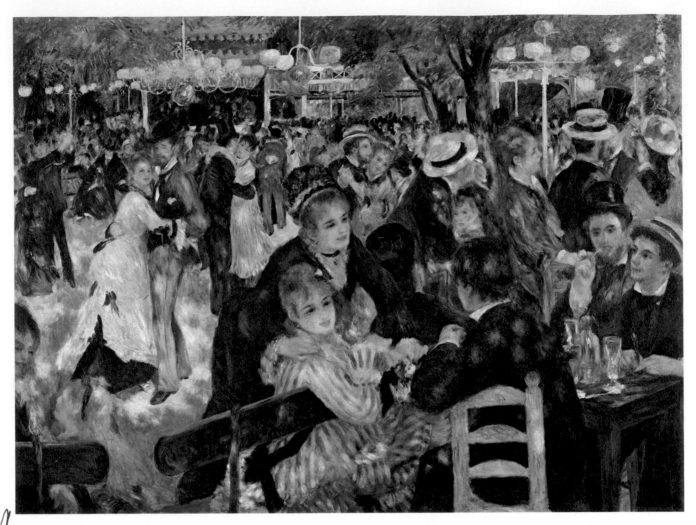

21-57   AUGUSTE RENOIR, *Le Moulin de la Galette*, 1876. Approx. 51″ × 68″. Louvre, Paris.

ment of the figures, and the suggested continuity of space spreading in all directions and only accidentally limited by the frame introduce us, as observers, into the very scene. We are not, as with the Tradition, observing a performance on a stage set; rather, we ourselves are part of the action. Renoir's subjects are quite unconscious of the presence of an observer; they do not pose but merely go about the business of the moment. In his search for the real, Renoir not only analyzes his own visual sensations but attempts to capture the process of events, to catch nature utterly unawares, to find some unique and particular aspect of it that will never recur in quite the same way. As Classical art seeks the universal and typical, Realistic art seeks just the opposite—the incidental, momentary, and passing.

EDGAR DEGAS (1834–1917) is usually included in any discussion of Impressionism. Although actively sympathetic with the Impressionists, he stood somewhat apart from them, an independent talent of great power. In his earlier work, he shares the Realist intentions of Manet, BERTHE MORISOT (1841–1895), and

other Realists not connected with the Impressionist movement. As a Realist, Degas observes and records modern life in its modern settings, whether at a distance or immediately at hand.

A painting of his early middle period, *Intérieur (Le Viol)* (FIG. 21-58), exhibits a penetrating Realism that invades the very bedroom of a newly married couple already in unhappy conflict. This is a time when literature and the stage, as well as art, sought to analyze and present the peculiarly modern problems of human relationships, especially the tensions between the sexes; we think of the plays of Ibsen and the novels of Flaubert, De Maupassant, and Zola, among many others. A novel by Zola, *Thérèse Raquin* (1867), is believed to have provided the program of the picture. The positions and attitudes of man and woman, the latter's gown, the accessories of the room, the play of shadows cast by the fireside and lamp—all are noted by Degas as they appear in the novel. Like Manet, Degas was a cultivated man of the world, conversant with the ideas of the day; like both Manet and Zola, he would be interested in the influences

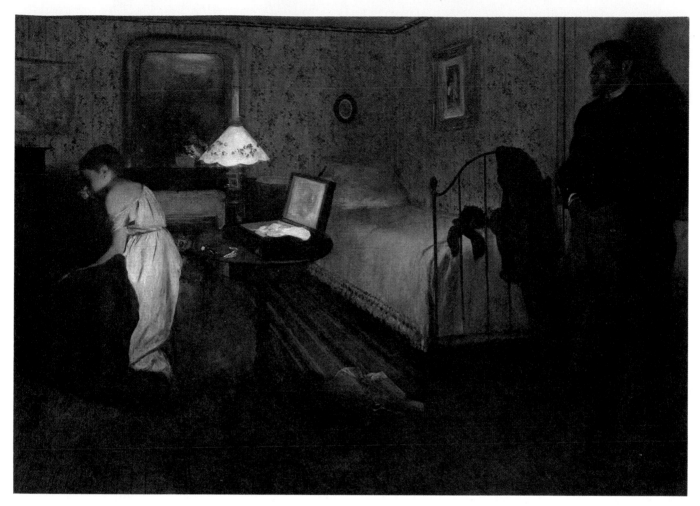

21-58 EDGAR DEGAS, *Intérieur* (*Le Viol*), c. 1868–1870. Approx. 32″ × 46″. Collection of Henry P. McIlhenny, Philadelphia; photo: Philadelphia Museum of Art.

that positive science now saw as determining human behavior—biological, sociological, and psychological forces active in the heredity and environment of every human individual. Human emotions, in Zola's and, presumably, Degas' views, are akin to physiological or even pathological symptoms; love, hate, desire, anxiety, frustration, alienation, and despair are the results of hidden, psychic mechanisms of an irrational or subrational nature. In light of these concepts, which foreshadow the epoch-making teachings of Sigmund Freud, the Realist studies human subjects dispassionately, like a clinician in a laboratory, seeking to describe and interpret their actions in terms of their hidden motivations. The persons in *Intérieur* are entirely unaware that they are being observed. This is the case in almost all of Degas' works.

In this painting, Degas explores the pictorial values of artificial light; later, in association with the Impressionists, he will brighten his palette to daylight hues, although he would never approve of out-of-doors (*plein-air*) painting. He abandons staged space and paused action for cropped spaces produced by acci-

dental or unusual angles of sight. Figures move swiftly into, within, and out of these irregular spaces.

More than any of his contemporaries, Degas studied the infinite variety of particular movements that make up continuous motion. Ballerinas in arrested movements—a split-second pose cut from the sequence of their dance—are one of his favorite subjects. In *Ballet Rehearsal (Adagio)* (FIG. 21-59), Degas uses several devices to bring the observer to the pictorial space. The frame cuts off the spiral stair, the windows in the background, and the group of figures in the right foreground; the rapid diagonals of the wall bases and floorboards carry us into and along the directional lines of the swift dancers; the figures are uncentered and "accidental" in arrangement; and, as is customary in Degas' ballet pictures, a large, off-center, empty space creates the illusion of a continuous floor that connects us with the pictured figures. By standing on the "same" surface with them, we seem to be drawn into their space. This cunning spatial projection derives from careful observation and may have been inspired by hints from Japanese prints

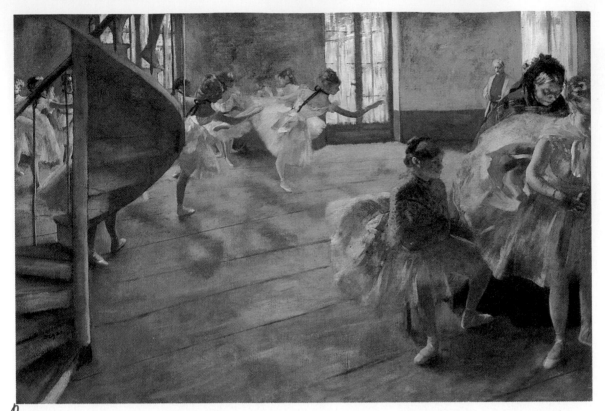

21-59   EDGAR DEGAS, *Ballet Rehearsal* (*Adagio*), 1876. 23″ × 33″. Glasgow Art Galleries and Museum (Burrell Collection).

21-60   SUZUKI HARUNOBU, *The Evening Glow of the Andon*, 1765. 11¼″ × 8½″. (Clarence Buckingham Collection)
© The Art Institute of Chicago, all rights reserved.

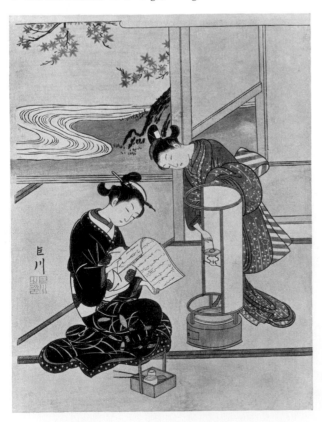

(FIG. 21-60), in which diverging lines not only organize the flat shapes of the figures but function as lines directing the viewer's attention into the picture space. The Impressionists, familiar with these prints as early as the 1860s, greatly admired their spatial organization, the familiar and intimate themes, and the flat, unmodeled color areas and drew much instruction from them. It is the popular Japanese print of the eighteenth century, "discovered" by European artists in the mid-nineteenth, that has the first definitive non-European influence on European pictorial design. Earlier borrowings from China, India, and Arabia had been superficial.

Degas' *Viscount Lepic and His Daughters* (FIG. 21-61), painted in 1873, summarizes what he learned from his own painstaking research and what his generation in general learned from the Japanese print: the clear, flat pattern; the unusual point of view; the informal glimpse of contemporary life. Whatever his subject, Degas—mindful of Ingres, whose work he greatly admired—sees it as a clear line and pattern, observed from a new and unexpected angle. In the divergent movement of the father and his small daughters, of the man entering the picture at the left, and of the horse and carriage passing across the background, we have a vivid pictorial account of a moment in time at a particular position in space, much as Monet, in his own way, defines such space and time in landscape painting. In another instant, there would be no picture, for each of the figures would move in a different direction, and the group would

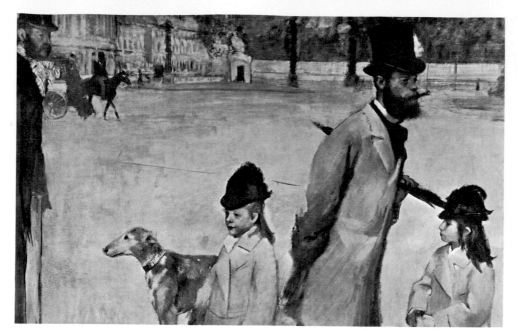

21-61 EDGAR DEGAS, *Viscount Lepic and His Daughters*, 1873. Approx. 32″ × 47″. Location unknown.

dissolve. Here again, Degas makes clever use of the empty space of the street to integrate the viewer into the space containing the figures. Actually, the painter seems to be taking into account the range of the sweep of our glance—what we would see in a single split-second inspection; indeed, the picture resembles a snapshot made with a hastily aimed camera.

When Degas was a very young man and about to enter on a career as painter, he met Ingres, who advised him: "Draw lines, young man, many lines, from memory or from nature; it is this way that you will become a good painter." Degas, faithful to the old linearist's advice, became a superb master of line, so much so that his identification as an Impressionist—in the sense that Monet, Pissarro, and Renoir are Impressionists—often seems mistaken to many critics. Certainly, his designs do not cling to the surface of the canvas, as do Manet's and Monet's; they are developed in depth and take the viewer well behind the picture plane; and we are always aware of the elastic strength of his firmly drawn contours. However, Degas does specialize in studies of figures in rapid and informal movement, recording the quick impression of arrested motion, and he does use the spectral color—the fresh, divided hues of the Impressionists—especially when he works in his favorite medium, pastel. These dry sticks of powdered pigment cannot be "muddied" by mixing them on a palette, so that they produce, almost automatically, those fresh and bright colors so favored by the Impressionists. All this is seen in *The Morning Bath* (FIG. 21-62), which is like Renoir's treatment of the same subject in its informality and intimacy but totally unlike Renoir in the indifference to either formal or physical beauty. Degas' concern is with the unplanned realism of the purely accidental attitude of the human figure, seen in an awkward yet natural enough moment. The broken volume of the nude

body twists across "Japanese" angles, flat planes, and patterns. It is the verity of motion that Degas seeks above all. Mingling the method of Ingres with that of the Impressionists, Degas makes an entirely un-"academic" picture that is appropriate to and consistent with the dawning age of the motion picture.

In the Paris Salon of 1874, Degas admired a painting by a young American artist, MARY CASSATT (1845–1926), the wealthy daughter of a Philadelphia banker.

21-62 EDGAR DEGAS, *The Morning Bath*, c. 1883. Pastel on paper, 27¾″ × 17″. (Potter Palmer Collection)
© The Art Institute of Chicago, all rights reserved.

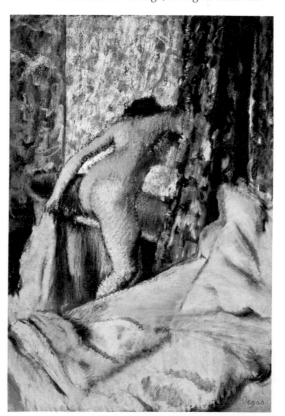

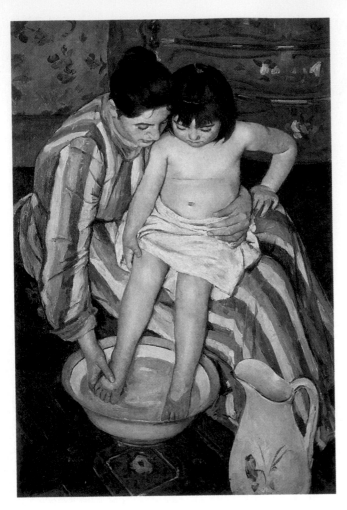

21-63 MARY CASSATT, *The Bath*, c. 1892. 39" × 26". The Art Institute of Chicago.

their purely visual sensations. The world out there is no longer a given order of masses in space. Rather, it is the source of sensations of light and color with no fixed order whatsoever; the only order is the one artists create from their own optical experience, the record of the stimulation of the optic nerve by light.

Thus, there is a paradox in Impressionism. Seeking, through realism, to capture the look of the modern, public world, Impressionist artists rely on an increasingly private vision of it. They do not render the optical world so much as they record their visual sensations of it. They analyze the tonal continuum away and replace it with discontinuous spots of color, the quality and placement of which depend on their *personal choice* in the technical process of painting. The public world is only a stimulus for the reflexive, unreflecting Impressionist response. The way the world looks is not given; it becomes the decision—in a way, the invention—of the artist. Searching for reality, the artist comes to find it in himself. Nothing could be more romantic!

In what follows, we trace the astonishing artistic sequences that complete the transformation of the old pictorial Tradition and produce the prevailing anti-Realism of the first 50 years of twentieth-century art.

Responses to Impressionism

By 1886, the Impressionists were accepted as serious artists by most critics and by a large segment of the public. But just at the time when their gay and colorful studies of contemporary life no longer seemed crude and unfinished, the painters themselves and a group of young followers came to feel that too many of the traditional elements of picture-making were being neglected in the search for momentary sensations of light and color. A more systematic examination of the properties of three-dimensional space, of the expressive qualities of line, pattern, and color, and of the symbolic character of subject matter was undertaken by four men in particular: Georges Seurat, Paul Cézanne, Vincent van Gogh, and Paul Gauguin. Because their art diverges so markedly from earlier Impressionism, although each painter at first accepted the Impressionist methods and never rejected the new and brighter palette, they and others sharing their views have come to be known as the Post-Impressionists—a classification that simply signifies their chronological position in nineteenth-century French painting. A sound understanding of their individual styles and achievements is necessary to comprehend twentieth-century art fully.

SEURAT

At the eighth and last Impressionist exhibition in 1886, GEORGES SEURAT (1859–1891) showed his *Sunday Afternoon on the Island of La Grande Jatte* (FIG. 21-64), which set forth the Impressionist interest in holi-

"There," he remarked, "is a person who feels as I do." Cassatt was befriended and influenced by Degas and exhibited regularly with the Impressionists. The compositional devices of Degas and of the Japanese print are equally evident in paintings like *The Bath* (FIG. 21-63), but they do not impair Cassatt's own strong originality and firmness of design. Degas is said to have observed that it was impossible for a woman to draw that well, but he seemed satisfied enough to be proven wrong. Cassatt's subjects are principally women and children, whom she presents with a quite inimitable conjunction of cool objectivity and genuine sentiment. Gauguin's estimate hits it exactly: "Mary Cassatt has charm, but she also has force."

Almost at the moment when the Realists began to discard Romantic subject matter to represent what they saw around them, Manet, in his later works, and the Impressionists seemed to raise the question of whether *what* we see is not ultimately a matter of *how* we see it. What is more "real"—a world of solid objects moving in space, or one's optical sensations of light and color in fleeting patterns? In a sense, Realistic Impressionism continues the Romantic preoccupation with the *self* of the artist, except that artists now consult not so much their feelings and imagination as

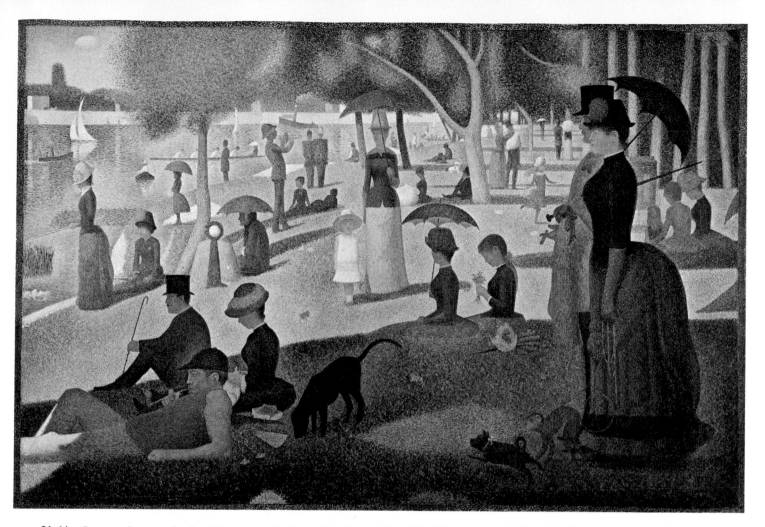

21-64 GEORGES SEURAT, *Sunday Afternoon on the Island of La Grande Jatte*, 1884–1886. Approx. 6' 9" × 10'. (Helen Birch Bartlett Memorial Collection) © The Art Institute of Chicago, all rights reserved.

day themes and the analysis of light in a new and monumental synthesis that seemed strangely rigid and remote. Seurat's system of painting in small dots that stand in relation to each other was based on the color theories of Delacroix and the color scientists Helmholtz and Chevreul. (The method, called "divisionism" by Seurat, was often confused with "pointillism," in which dots of color are distributed systematically on a white ground that remains partially exposed and hence visually functional.) It was a difficult procedure, as disciplined and painstaking as the Impressionist method had been spontaneous and exuberant.

Seurat is less concerned with the recording of his immediate color sensations than he is with their careful and systematic organization into a new kind of pictorial order. The free and fluent play of color is disciplined into a calculated arrangement by prior rules of design accepted and imposed by the artist. The effect is ambiguous, as it produces both a surface pattern and a perspective depth. The apparent formlessness of Impressionism hardens into severe regularity. The pattern in *La Grande Jatte* is based on the verticals of the figures and trees, the horizontals in the shadows and the distant embankment, and the

diagonals in the shadows and shoreline, each of which contributes to the pictorial effect. At the same time, by the use of meticulously calculated values, the painter carves out a deep rectangular space. In creating both pattern and suggested space, he plays on repeated motifs: the profile of the lady, the parasol, and the cylindrical forms of the figures, each so placed in space as to set up a rhythmic movement in depth as well as from side to side. The picture is filled with sunshine, but not broken into transient patches of color. Light, air, people, and landscape are fixed in an abstract design in which line, color, value, and shape cohere in an organization as precise as a machine.

This is a severely intellectual art, of which Seurat himself said: "They see poetry in what I have done. No, I apply my method, and that is all there is to it." There is in this statement something of the scientific attitude we have found manifesting itself throughout nineteenth-century painting. On the other hand, there is something of Renaissance geometric formalism also; the stately stage space, with its perspective and careful placement of figures, is reminiscent of an art, descended from Paolo Uccello and Piero della Francesca, that moves us by its serene monumentality. Manet, in *Le Déjeuner* (FIG. 21-39), uses a Renaissance composition to manifest new techniques; Seurat, in *La Grande Jatte*, turns traditional pictorial stage space into pattern by applying a color formula of which space is only a fairly unimportant variable. For our optical experience of space can only be a function of color. Whereas, in the tradition of Giotto and Raphael, the reality was space, with color something superadded, now with Seurat (and, as we shall see, with Cézanne), color is the reality and spaces and solids are merely figments. Having found the formula of color relationships, the artist need no longer rely on the dubious evidence of his impressions. Paul Signac, Seurat's friend and collaborator in the design of the "neo-impressionist" method, describes it with bland confidence:

> By the elimination of all muddy mixtures, by the exclusive use of the optical mixture of pure colors, by a methodical divisionism and a strict observation of the scientific theory of colors, the Neo-Impressionist ensures a maximum of luminosity, of color intensity, and of harmony—a result that has never yet been obtained.*

We remember Constable's assertion that landscape painting is a natural science! We also remember that the formulas of optical science of the nineteenth century develop into those of the twentieth century and that what is scientific can have technological application. In one respect—the breaking of mass into discrete particles (and color into dots of component colors)—Seurat's *Grande Jatte* may be said to have been the forerunner of the modern techniques of photoengraving and color reproduction.

CÉZANNE

In a conversation with the influential art dealer Ambroise Vollard about 1883, Renoir said: "I had wrung Impressionism dry, and I finally came to the conclusion that I knew neither how to paint nor how to draw. In a word, Impressionism was a blind alley, as far as I was concerned. . . ." This conviction had probably come to other Impressionists; certainly, it must have come early to PAUL CÉZANNE (1839–1906). Although a lifelong admirer of Delacroix, he allied himself with the Impressionists, especially Pissarro, and at first accepted their theories of color and their faith in subjects chosen from everyday life. Yet his own studies of the old masters in the Louvre persuaded him that Impressionism lacked form and structure. As he said: "I want to make of Impressionism something solid and lasting like the art in the museums."

The basis of Cézanne's art is his new way of studying nature (FIG. 21-66). Of course, this could be said of all nineteenth-century landscapists from Constable on; however, each artist's concept of what *is* is different. Cézanne's aim is not truth to appearance, especially not photographic truth, nor is it the "truth" of Impressionism. Rather, he searches for a lasting *structure* behind the formless and fleeting screens of color the eye takes in. If all that we see is color, then color must fulfill the structural purposes of the old perspective and the old light and shade; color alone must give depth and distance, shape and solidity. But if color is only optical sensation, as the Impressionists show, then the structure sought in the optical world is, after all, the structure of one's own sensation. Face-to-face with nature, Cézanne attempts to bring an intellectual order, rather than the random approach of the Impressionists, into his sensations of it, constantly and painfully checking with that part of the scene—he calls it the "motif"—that he is studying. When he says, "We must do Poussin over again, this time according to nature," he apparently means that Poussin's effects of distance, depth, and solidity must be achieved not by perspective and chiaroscuro but entirely in terms of the color-relief maps provided by our analysis of nature.

The old tonal coherence lost, Cézanne sets out to find a new one. Although he never reduces natural objects to geometric abstractions—this will be the work of the Cubists—the monumentality of his forms suggests that they have been stripped of the accidental variations of individual appearance. In this sense, we can read his famous remark to a young follower—that the painter should "treat nature in terms of the cylinder, and the sphere, and the cone"—as an injunction to present natural forms in terms of their simplest and broadest dimensions, rather than to replace them with geometric constructions.

Cézanne's method is to use his intense powers of visual concentration to observe the motif, sustaining the process of minute inspection through days, months, and even years. He resembles the contemporary scientist who proves his hypothesis with repeated tests. With special care, he explores the properties of line, plane, and color, and their interrelationships: the effect of every kind of linear direction, the capacity of planes to create the sensation of depth, the intrinsic qualities of color, and the power of colors to modify the direction and depth of lines and planes. Through the recession of cool colors and the advance of warm ones, he controls volume and depth. Having observed that saturation (or the highest intensity of a color) produces the greatest effect of fullness of form, he would paint an object chiefly in one hue—apples, for example, in green—achieving convincing solidity by the control of color intensity alone, in place of the traditional method of modeling in light and dark.

*Robert Goldwater and Marco Treves, eds., *Artists on Art*, 3rd ed. (New York: Pantheon, 1958). p. 378.

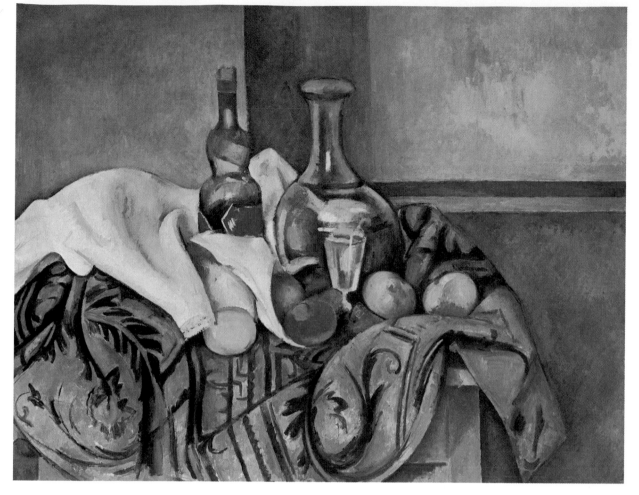

21-65 PAUL CÉZANNE, *Still Life*, c. 1894. Approx. 26″ × 32″. National Gallery of Art, Washington, D.C. (Chester Dale Collection, 1962).

In *Still Life,* painted in 1890 (FIG. 21-65), Cézanne's method may be seen at its best. The individual forms have lost something of their private character as bottles and fruit and approach the condition of cylinders and spheres. A sharp clarity of planes and the edges of planes sets forth the objects as if they had been sculptured. Even the highlights of the glassware are as sharply defined as the solids. The floating color of the Impressionists has been arrested, held, and analyzed into interlocking planes. Cézanne gives us here what might be called, paradoxically, an architecture of color.

The still life was the ideal vehicle for Cézanne's experiments, as a limited number of selected objects can be arranged by the artist to provide a well-ordered point of departure. The landscape does not afford the artist this advantage; the problems of representation are complicated by the need to select from the multiplicity of disorganized natural forms those that seem most significant and to order them into pictorial structure that will have cohesive unity. To apply his methods to the painting of landscapes was one of Cézanne's greatest challenges. Thus, just as landscape had been the principal mode of Impressionist theory and experiment, so it became the sub-

ject for Cézanne's most complete transformation of Impressionism.

La Montagne Sainte-Victoire (FIG. 21-66), done around 1886, is one of the many views that Cézanne painted of the mountain near his home in Aix-en-Provence. In it, we can see how the transitory effects of changing atmospheric conditions, effects that occupied Monet, have been replaced by a more concentrated, lengthier analysis of large, lighted spaces. This space stretches out behind and beyond the plane of the canvas (emphasized by the pattern of the pine tree in the foreground) and is made up of numerous small elements, such as roads, fields, houses, and the aqueduct at the far right, each seen from a slightly different point of view. Above this shifting, receding perspective rises the largest mass of all, the mountain, with an effect—achieved by stressing background and foreground contours equally—of being simultaneously near and far away. This is close to the actual experience a person observing such a view might have when the forms of the landscape are apprehended piecemeal and the relative proportions of objects vary, rather than being fixed once and for all by a strict one- or two-point perspective, as a photograph normally shows. Cézanne immoblizes the

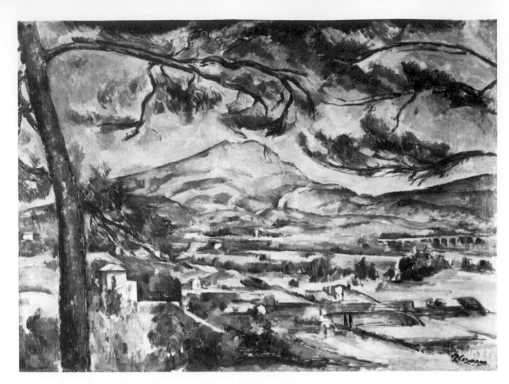

21-66 PAUL CÉZANNE, *La Montagne Sainte-Victoire*, c. 1886–1888. Approx. 26″ × 35½″. Courtauld Institute Galleries, London.

shifting colors of Impressionism, creating a kind of façade of color that is divided into an array of clearly defined planes. Further analyses of these color planes by the Cubists will give them an independent existence, in which there is little reference to the full optical range of nature.

The *Boy in a Red Vest* (FIG. 21-67) shows Cézanne's application of his method to the human figure. Here, the breaking up of the pictorial space, the volumes of the figure, and the drapery into emphatic planes is so advanced that the planes almost begin to take over the picture surface. The geometric character of the color area pushes to the fore, and we at once become aware of the egg-like shape of the head and the flexible, almost metallic shapes of the prominent planes of the body and drapery. The disproportionally long left arm is obvious, for the distortions and rearrangement of natural forms that may go unnoticed in landscape and still-life paintings are immediately apparent in the human figure and often disturbing to the viewer. Still, we may be sure that Cézanne's distortions—and they occur in most of his figure paintings—are not accidental. What Cézanne does, in effect, is to rearrange the parts of his figure, shortening and lengthening, them in such a way as to make the pattern of their representation in two dimensions conform to the proportions of his picture surface. Thus, Cézanne draws the first conclusion from the Impressionists: deemphasis of subject matter. However, although the depicted object is primarily a light-reflecting surface to the Impressionists, to Cézanne it becomes a secondary aid in the organization of the picture plane. By further reducing the importance of subject matter, Cézanne automatically enhances the value of the object he is making—the picture, which has its

own independent existence and must be judged entirely in terms of its own inherent pictorial qualities. In Cézanne's works, the simplification of the shapes and their sculpture-like relief and weight give that peculiar look of stable calm and dignity that reminds one of the art of the fifteenth-century Renaissance and that has led modern criticism to find in Cézanne some vestige of that ancient Mediterranean sense of

21-67 PAUL CÉZANNE, *Boy in a Red Vest*, 1893–1895. 35¼″ × 28½″. National Gallery, Washington, D.C. (collection of Mr. and Mrs. Paul Mellon).

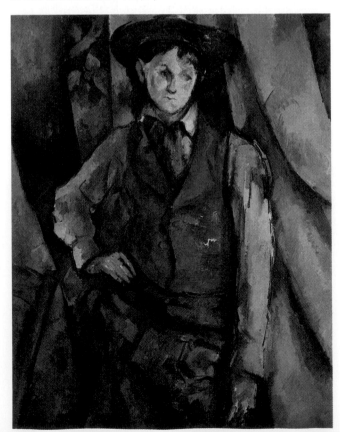

monumental and unchanging simplicity of form that produced Classical art.

VAN GOGH

Unlike Seurat and Cézanne—who, in different ways, sought, by almost scientific investigation, new rules for the ordering of the experience of color—VINCENT VAN GOGH (1853–1890) impetuously and arbitrarily exploits the new color to express his emotions as he is confronted by nature. A Hollander by birth, son of a Protestant pastor, Van Gogh believed that he had a religious calling and did missionary work in the slums of London and in the mining districts of Belgium. Repeated failures exhausted his body and brought him close to despair. Only after he turned to painting and mastered the Impressionist technique did he find a means to communicate his experience of the sun-illuminated world of so many of his landscapes, which he represented pictorially in terms of his favorite color, yellow. His insistence on the expressive values of color led him to develop a corresponding expressiveness in his very application of the paint. The thickness, shape, and direction of his brushstrokes create a tactile counterpart to his intense color schemes. Now a thickly loaded brush moves vehemently back and forth or at right angles, giving a textile-like effect; now the tube squeezes dots or streaks on the canvas. This bold, almost slapdash attack might have led to disaster had it not been controlled by Van Gogh's sensibility.

A rich source of Van Gogh's thought on his art is left in the letters he wrote to his brother, Theo. In one of these, he says: "Instead of trying to reproduce exactly what I have before my eyes, I use color more arbitrarily so as to express myself forcibly. . . ." In another letter, he explains that the color in one of his paintings is "not locally true from the point of view of the stereoscopic Realist, but color to suggest any emotion of an ardent temperament." This sounds like Delacroix, and indeed Van Gogh writes: "And I should not be surprised if the Impressionists soon find fault with my way of working, for it has been fertilized by the ideas of Delacroix rather than by theirs," by which he seems to mean that he took his color method from Delacroix directly rather than from the Impressionists.

The Night Café (FIG. 21-68), as Van Gogh writes, is meant to convey an oppressive atmosphere of evil, through every possible distortion of color. The scene, a café interior in a dreary provincial town, is supposed to be felt, not simply observed. The slumped denizens are the very color of the mood in which they

21-68 VINCENT VAN GOGH, *The Night Café*, 1888. Approx. 28½" × 36". Yale University Art Gallery, New Haven, Connecticut (bequest of Stephen Carlton Clark, B.A., 1903).

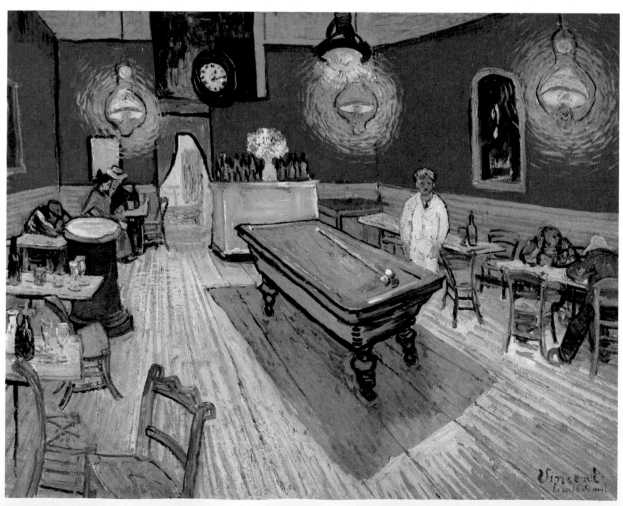

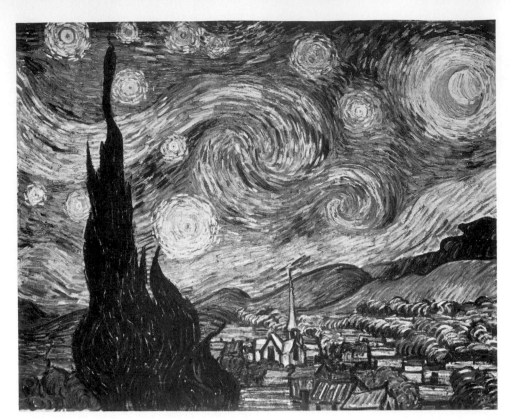

21-69 VINCENT VAN GOGH, *Starry Night*, 1889. Approx. 29" × 36". Collection, Museum of Modern Art, New York (bequest of Lillie P. Bliss).

drown—a melancholy green. The ceiling is a poisonous green, in dizzying contrast with the febrile red walls. The floor is an acid yellow; the shadow of the billiard table, green. The yellow halos of light are like accumulations of mephitic gases. The proprietor, the pale demon that rules over the place, rises like a specter from the edge of the billiard table, itself in a steeply tilted perspective that suggests the spinning, vertiginous world of nausea.

Even more illustrative of this "expressionist" method is *Starry Night* (FIG. 21-69), painted in 1889. In it, Van Gogh does not envision the sky as we see it when we look up on a clear dark night—as a spangling of twinkling pinpoints of light against a deep curtain of blue. Rather, he feels the vastness of the universe, filled with whirling and exploding stars and galaxies of stars, beneath which the earth and men's habitations huddle in anticipation of cosmic disaster. Mysteriously, a great cypress is in the process of rapid growth far above the earth's surface and into the combustion of the sky. The artist does not seek or analyze the harmony of nature here. Instead, he transforms it by projecting on it a vision that is entirely his own.

GAUGUIN

A similar rejection of objective representation in favor of subjective expression is found in the work of PAUL GAUGUIN (1843–1903). Gauguin writes disparagingly of Impressionism:

The Impressionists study color exclusively, but without freedom, always shackled by the need of probabil-ity. For them the ideal landscape, created from many different entities, does not exist. Their edifice rests upon no solid base and ignores the nature of the sensations perceived by means of color. They heed only the eye and neglect the mysterious centers of thought, so falling into merely scientific reasoning. When they speak of their art, what is it? A purely superficial thing, full of affectations and only material. In it thought does not exist.*

Gauguin also uses color in new and unexpected combinations, but his art is very different from Van Gogh's. It is no less tormented, perhaps, but more learned in its combination of rare and exotic elements and more broadly decorative. Gauguin had painted as an amateur, but after taking lessons with Pissarro, he resigned from his prosperous brokerage business in 1883 to devote his time entirely to painting. Although his work did not sell and he and his family were reduced to poverty, he did not abandon his art, for he felt that, despite ridicule and neglect, he was called to be a great artist. In his search for provocative subjects, as well as for an economical place to live, he stayed for some time in small villages in Brittany and visited the tropics (Martinique). Thus, even before he settled in Tahiti in 1891, tropical color and subjects drawn from primitive life had entered his art. In his attitude toward color, Gauguin broke with the Impressionist studies of minutely contrasted hues. As he says: "A meter of green is greener than a centimeter if you wish to express greenness. . . . How does

*Robert Goldwater and Marco Treves, eds., *Artists on Art*, 3rd ed. (New York: Pantheon, 1958), p. 373.

that tree look to you? Green? All right, then use green, the greenest on your palette. And that shadow, a little bluish? Don't be afraid. Paint it as blue as you can." His influence was especially felt by members of the younger generation, such as Parisian artist MAURICE DENIS, who writes in *Definition of Neo-Traditionalism* in 1890:

Gauguin freed us from all the restraints which the idea of copying nature had placed upon us. For instance, if it was permissible to use vermilion in painting a tree which seemed reddish . . . why not stress even to the point of deformation the curve of a beautiful shoulder or conventionalize the symmetry of a bough . . . ?

Gauguin's art, too, can be understood as a complex mixture of Eastern and Western elements, of themes common to the great masters of the European Renaissance treated in a manner based on his study of earlier arts and of non-European cultures. In Tahiti and the Marquesas, where he spent the last 10 years of his life, he expressed his love of primitive life and brilliant color in a series of magnificent, decorative canvases. The design is often based, although indirectly, on native motifs, and the color owes its peculiar har-

monies of lilac, pink, and lemon to the tropical flora of the islands. But the mood of such works is that of a sophisticated, modern man interpreting an ancient and innocent way of life already threatened by European colonization. Although the figure and setting in *Spirit of the Dead Watching* (FIG. 21-70) are Tahitian, the theme of a reclining nude with a pendant, watching figure—that is, a matching or balancing figure—belongs to the Renaissance and after. The simplified linear pattern and broad areas of flat color recall Byzantine enamels and Medieval stained glass, which Gauguin admired, and the slight distortion of the flattened forms is not unlike similar effects in Egyptian sculpture. Romantic art began with the admiration of "exotic" lands (and peoples) peripheral to Europe; with Gauguin, a kind of adaptation of their very style begins. He represents a new rebelliousness—not only against the artistic tradition, but against the whole of European civilization. According to Gaugin, "civilization is what makes you sick." The search for vitality in new peoples and new life styles, begun in the eighteenth century, now quickens. The twentieth century will draw artistic inspiration from Japan, from the Pacific islands, and from much of the non-European world.

21-70   PAUL GAUGUIN, *Spirit of the Dead Watching*, 1892. Oil on burlap mounted on canvas, 28½" × 36⅜". Albright-Knox Art Gallery, Buffalo (A. Conger Goodyear Collection, 1965).

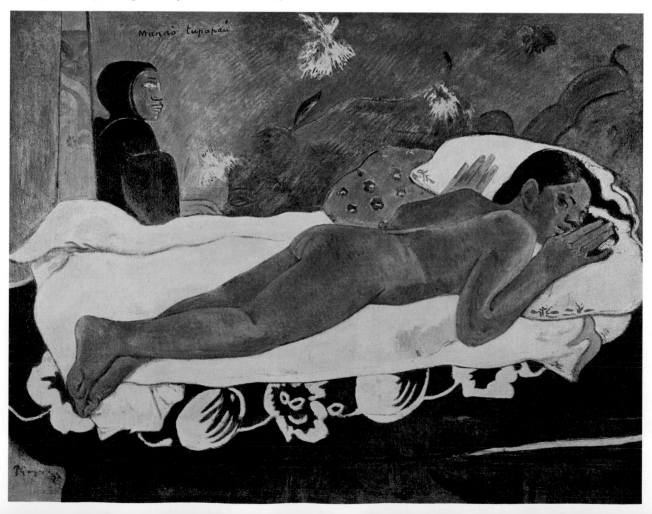

TOULOUSE-LAUTREC

A dissatisfaction with civilization, an anxious awareness of the psychic strains it imposes, and a perception of the banality and degradation it can bring with it color the mood of the artist toward the end of the century and during the years before the First World War. This is the period of the *fin de siècle*, ''the end of the century,'' when art and literature languish in a kind of malaise compounded of despondency, boredom, morbidity, and hypersensitivity to the esthetic. From recording the contemporary scene, with all its variety and human interest, as the Impressionists had done, painters influenced by Gauguin and Van Gogh now often interpreted it in bitter commentary communicated in harsh distortion—both of form and of color. In the work of HENRI DE TOULOUSE-LAUTREC (1864–1901), who deeply admired Degas, the old master's cool scrutiny of contemporary life is transformed into grim satire and mordant caricature. Lautrec's art is, to a degree, the expression of his life.

He was a dwarf, self-exiled from the high society that his ancient, aristocratic name would have entitled him to enter. He became a denizen of the night world of Paris, consorting with a tawdry population of entertainers, prostitutes, and other social outcasts. His natural environment became the din and nocturnal colors of cheap music halls, cafés, and bordellos. In his *At the Moulin Rouge* (FIG. 21-71), the influence of Degas and the Japanese print can be seen in the oblique and asymmetrical composition, the spatial diagonals, and the strong patterns of line to which Lautrec added dissonant color. But each element, although closely studied in actual life and already familiar to us in the work of the older Impressionists, has been so emphasized or exaggerated that the tone is new. Compare, for instance, the mood of this painting with the relaxed and casual atmosphere of Renoir's *Moulin de la Galette* (FIG. 21-57). Lautrec's scene is night life, with its glaring artificial light, brassy music, and assortment of corrupt, cruel, and

21-71 HENRI DE TOULOUSE-LAUTREC, *At the Moulin Rouge*, 1892–1895. Approx. 48″ × 55″. (Helen Birch Bartlett Memorial Collection) © The Art Institute of Chicago, all rights reserved.

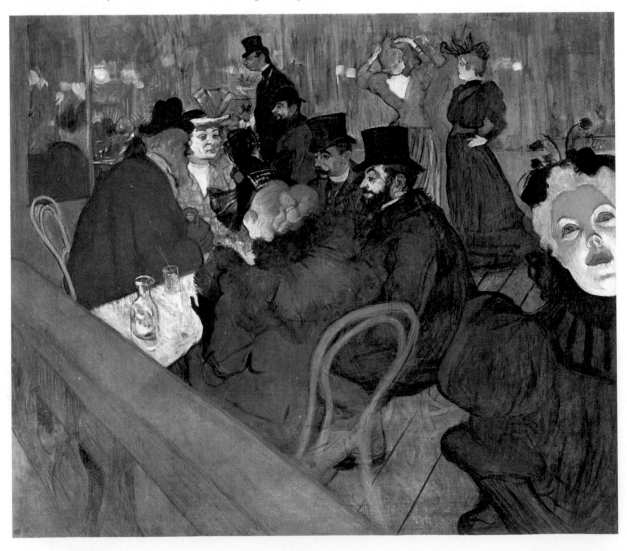

mask-like faces. (He includes himself in the background: the tiny man with the derby accompanying the very tall man, his cousin.) Such distortions by simplification of the figures and faces anticipate the later Expressionism, when artists will become ever more arbitrary in altering what they see (in translation onto canvas) to increase its impact on the observer. Lautrec and his contemporaries are transitional from Impressionism to a highly subjective strain in twentieth-century art.

Persisting Romanticism: Symbolism, Estheticism, Primitivism

That subjective strain is, precisely, Romantic and persists throughout the whole of the nineteenth century and into the twentieth. It could be argued that what seem to be antagonistic movements—like Realism Impressionism, and Post-Impressionism—are only so many permutations of Romanticism, changing its earlier iconography, but always putting artistic autonomy at the center of the argument, no matter the subject or the technique. Artistic freedom remains all-in-all. Nature as given to the eye was early transformed by the artist's emotion and sensation and, in the end, comes to be completely subjectivized, to the point that the artist does not *imitate* nature but *creates* it by free interpretations of it. The optical world as "given" is rejected in favor of a world of fantasy, of forms conjured up and produced by the artist's free imagination, with or without reference to things conventionally seen. His technique comes to be his own, as well as his ideas. Color, line, and shape, separated from conformity to the optical image, may be used as he pleases, as symbols of his emotions in transaction with the world. He recognizes no requirement other than that he express himself in sincere accord with his spirit and intuition. If he is often not understood, that is because he chooses to stand outside of conventional meanings, as he does outside of conventional images, and speak, like a seer or prophet, in signs and symbols. In the words of the critic Konrad Fiedler, writing in 1876:

> The artist is called upon to create another world beside and above the real one, a world freed from earthly conditions, a world in keeping with his own discretion. This realm of art opposes the realm of nature. . . . Artistic activity begins when man finds himself face-to-face with the visible world as with something immensely enigmatical. . . . What art creates is the world, made by and for the artistic consciousness. . . . It is not the artist who has need of nature; nature much more has need of the artist. . . . By comprehending and manifesting nature in a certain sense, the artist does not comprehend and manifest anything which could exist apart from his activity. . . .

Only through artistic activity does man comprehend the visible world.*

Thus the unceasingly romantic artist, becomes not an imitator of nature, but an arbitrary interpreter of it, trusting absolutely to his own vision. Romanticism, in fostering this view of the artist, presides over the proliferation of individual styles, which, within the broad realm of their variation, can be thought of as Romantic in intention, method, and effect.

We have already met artists, often referred to as "Post-Impressionists," who revised or broke entirely away from Realism and Impressionism. Many others adopted an approach to subject matter and form that associates them with a general European movement called "Symbolism." The term has application to both art and literature, which, as critics in both fields noted, were in especially close relation at this time. A manifesto of literary Symbolism appeared in Paris in 1886, and, in 1891, the critic Albert Aurier applied the term to the painting of Gauguin and Van Gogh. Symbolism disdains the "mere fact" of Realism as trivial and asserts that fact must be transformed into a symbol of the inner experience of that fact. Fact is thus nothing in itself; mentally transformed, it is the utterance of a sensitized temperament responding in its own way to the world. In Symbolism, the subjectivity of Romanticism becomes radical; it will continue to be so in the art of the twentieth century. The artist's task is not to *see* things but to see *through* them to a significance and reality far deeper than what is given in superficial appearance. In this function, the artist, as the poet Arthur Rimbaud insists, becomes a seer, a being of extraordinary insight. (One group of Symbolist painters, influenced by Gauguin, called itself *Nabis*, the Hebrew word for prophet.) Rimbaud, whose poems had great influence on the artistic community, goes so far as to say, in his *Lettre du Voyant*, that to achieve the seer's insight, the artist must become deranged or, in effect, must systematically unhinge and confuse the everyday faculties of sense and of reason, which serve only to blur his vision. The objects given us in our commonsense world must be converted by the artist's mystical vision into symbols of a reality beyond it, and, ultimately, a reality from within himself.

The extreme subjectivism of the Symbolists led them to cultivate all the resources of fantasy, all the regions of imagination, no matter how recondite and occult. Moreover, it led them to urge the exclusiveness, not to say the elitism, of the artist against the vulgar materialism and conventional mores of industrial and middle-class society. Above all, by their phi-

*Linda Nochlin, *Realism and Tradition in Art* (Englewood Cliffs, N.J.: Prentice-Hall, 1966), pp. 168–76.

losophy of *estheticism*, the Symbolists wished to purge art of anything utilitarian, to cultivate an exquisite esthetic sensitivity, and to make the slogan "art for art's sake" into a doctrine and a way of life. As early as 1856, Gautier writes:

> We believe in the autonomy of art; art for us is not the means but the end; any artist who has in view anything but the beautiful is not an artist in our eyes. . . .

And Walter Pater, an English scholar and esthete, advances the same point of view in 1868 in the conclusion to his work *The Renaissance:*

> Our one chance lies in expanding that interval [of our life], in getting as many pulsations as possible into the given time. Great passions may give us this quickened sense of life. . . . Only be sure it *is* passion—that it does yield you this fruit of a quickened, multiplied consciousness. Of such wisdom, the poetic passion, the desire of beauty, the love of art for its own sake has most. For art comes to you proposing frankly to give nothing but the highest quality to your moments as they pass, and simply for those moments' sake.

The subject matter of the Symbolists, determined by this worshipfulness toward art and exaggerated esthetic sensation, becomes increasingly esoteric and exotic, weird, mysterious, visionary, dream-like, fantastic. (It is noteworthy that, contemporary with the Symbolists, Sigmund Freud, the founder of psychoanalysis, begins the new century and the age of psychiatry with his *Interpretation of Dreams,* and introduction to the concept and the world of unconscious experience.)

GUSTAVE MOREAU (1826–1898) seeks a form to suit the content of his fantasies, but not disdaining reference to the facts of the optical world when he needs them. A pupil of Chassériau and influential teacher of Henri Matisse and Georges Rouault, Moreau expanded his master's love of sensuous design to embrace gorgeous color, intricate line, and richly detailed shape. Like Chassériau also, Moreau preferred subjects arising from dreaming solitude, remote as possible from waking commonplaces—subjects that could be submerged in all the glittering splendor that imagination could envision and painterly ingenuity could supply. His *Jupiter and Semele* (FIG. 21-72), one of his rare finished works, demonstrates the full orchestration of his instruments in an opera-like setting. (Moreau was a lover of the music of Wagner and, like him, dreamed of a grand synthesis of the arts.) The grandiose theme is presented within an architecture of towering opulence, the royal hall of Olympus, shimmering in iridescent color, with tiers and tabernacles filled with the glowing and flashing shapes that enclose the icon of Jupiter like encrusta-

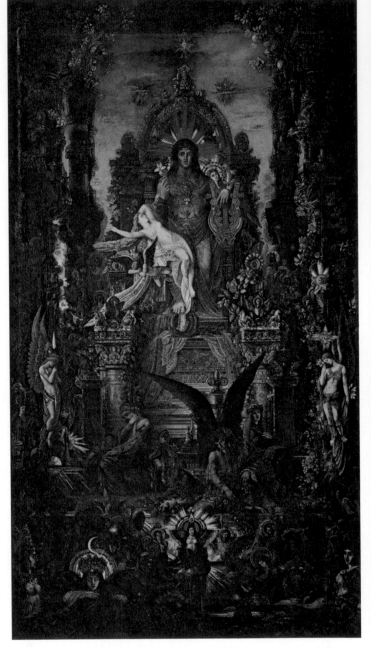

21-72 GUSTAVE MOREAU, *Jupiter and Semele*, c. 1875. Approx. 7' × 3' 4". Musée Gustave Moreau, Paris.

tions of gems. The color of Delacroix is harmonized with the exotic hues of Medieval enamels, Indian miniatures, Byzantine mosaics, and the designs of exotic wares now coming into the ornamental repertories of modern artists. Semele, in the lap of Jupiter, is overwhelmed by the apparition of the god, crowned with a halo of thunderbolts. Her languorous swoon and the suspended motion of all the entranced figures show that "beautiful inertia" which Moreau said he wished to render with all "necessary richness." His cherishing of the enigmas of fable, myth, vision, and dream caused Manet to remark of him: "I have a lively sympathy for him, but he is taking a bad road. . . . He takes us back to the incomprehensible,

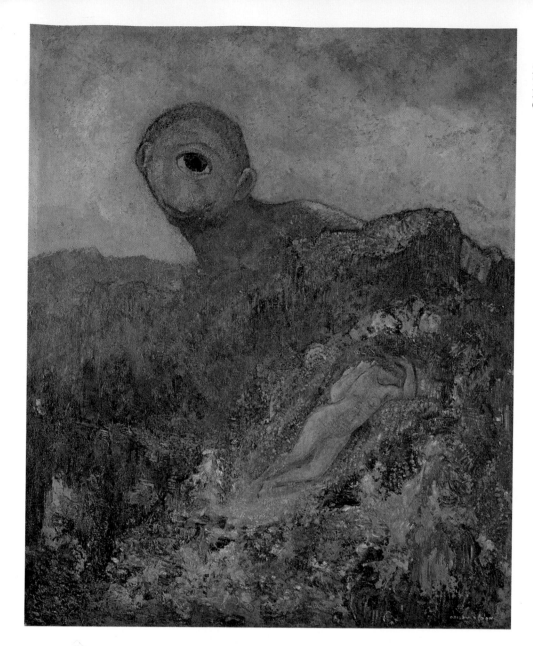

21-73 ODILON REDON,
The Cyclops, 1898. 25" × 20".
Kroeller–Moeller Rijksmuseum,
Otterloo, Netherlands.

while we wish that everything be understood." And Degas said, unsympathetically, "He puts watch chains on the gods." Two Realists confronting Symbolism!

The sharp difference of artistic intention expressed in these comments is even more striking in any comparison of the work of ODILON REDON (1840–1916) and of Monet, who were born in the same year. Redon, the foremost Symbolist painter, uses the Impressionist palette and stippling brush stroke for a very different purpose. In *The Cyclops* (FIG. 21-73), he does not record a fleeting impression of a one-eyed giant in love; rather, he projects a figment of the imagination as if it were seeable, coloring it whimsically—in fresh hues, in full saturation, and in rich profusion—in harmony with the mood he feels befits the subject. The fetal head of the shy, simpering Polyphemus, with its huge, loving eye, rises balloon-like above the sleeping Galatea. The image born of

the dreaming world and the color analyzed and disassociated from the waking world here come together at the will of the artist. As Redon himself observes: "My originality consists in bringing to life, in a human way, improbable beings and making them live according to the laws of probability, by putting—as far as possible—the logic of the visible at the service of the invisible." In the poetry of Redon's friend and contemporary, the Symbolist Stéphane Mallarmé, words and their meanings often lose contact, drift apart, and enter into mystifying relationships with other words and other meanings.

Symbolism had a wide appeal for the so-called "decadents" of the *fin de siècle*, who shunned action for esthetic passivity and who sought escape in art from the ugliness and brutality of a materialistic world on its way to war. Although not strictly speaking a Symbolist, AUBREY BEARDSLEY (1872–1898) was one of a circle of English esthetes that included the

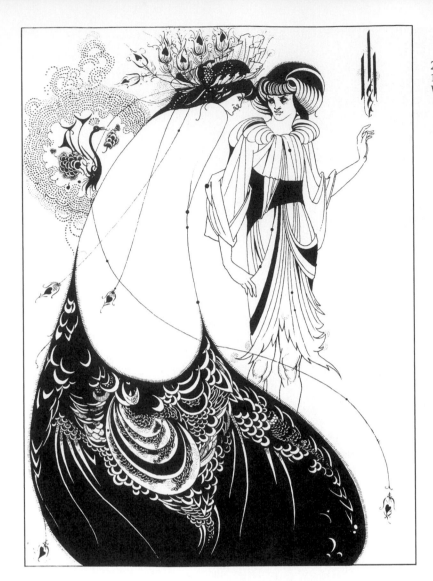

21-74 AUBREY BEARDSLEY, *The Peacock Skirt*, 1894. Pen-and-ink illustration for Oscar Wilde's *Salomé*.

brilliant wit, Oscar Wilde, whose close friend he was and whose controversial books and plays he illustrated. For one of them, *Salomé,* Beardsley drew *The Peacock Skirt* (FIG. 21-74), a dazzlingly decorative composition perfectly characteristic of his influential style. The influence of the Japanese print is obvious, although Beardsley has assimilated it into his own unique manner. Banishing Realism, he confines himself to line and to patterns of black and white, eliminating all shading. His tense, elastic line encloses sweeping, curvilinear shapes that lie flat on the surface—some left almost vacant, others filled with swirling complexes of mostly organic motifs. His mastery of calligraphic line is supported by his unfailing sense of linear rhythms and harmonies. In his short lifetime—he died at 26—he expressed in both his life and art the esthete's ideal of "art for art's sake." Beardsley's work exhibits its own beauty; it has no other message. It reflects and will strongly influence the design principles of Art Nouveau (FIG. 21-91).

Symbolism, although suitable to the withdrawn fancy of artist–esthetes, could also provide the means for a telling criticism of the workaday world they scorned. To produce his corrosive pictures of the declassed denizens of Paris (FIG. 21-71), Lautrec still worked with his human models in their actual setting, having them always before his eyes, in the manner of the Realist. Given the permissiveness of Symbolism, the Belgian painter JAMES ENSOR (1860–1949) creates a spectral and macabre world in which grotesques, masked skeletons, and hanged men populate sideshows, carnivals, and city streets. His best-known work, severely criticized at the time for blasphemy, is *Christ's Entry into Brussels* (FIG. 21-75). In spirit, it recalls the demonizing, moralizing pictures of Hieronymus Bosch (FIG. 18-21) and Pieter Bruegel that represent Christ surrounded by false and ugly creatures utterly unworthy of his mission. But here, in modern fashion, the human creatures are masked "hollow men" who have no real substance, no genuine identity, but are only "images." This is a theme often sounded in modern criticism of modern civilization. Ensor's color is hard, strident, and spotted—a tonal cacophony that matches the sound of the repulsive crowd.

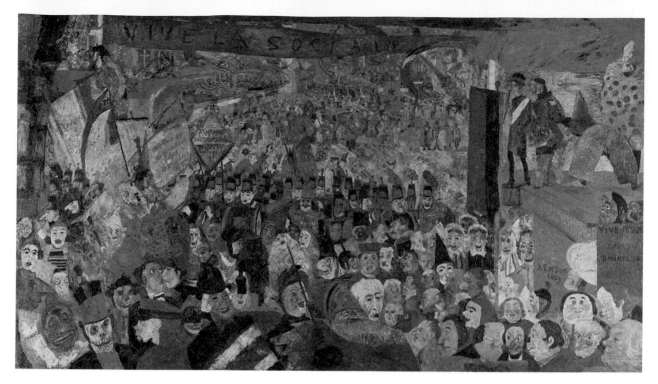

21-75   JAMES ENSOR, *Christ's Entry into Brussels*, 1888. Approx. 8′ 5″ × 14′ 1″. Kunsthaus Zurich.

Linked in spirit to Ensor is the Norwegian painter and graphic artist EDVARD MUNCH (1863–1944), also a moralizing critic of modern man. Munch's chief themes are pain, death, and perverse love. In *The Scream* (FIG. 21-76), he gives us quite a disturbing vision of neurotic panic breaking forth in a dreadful but silent scream—the scream heard within the mind cracking under prolonged anxiety. Like his friend,

21-76   EDVARD MUNCH, *The Scream*, 1893. Approx. 36″ × 29″. Oslo Kommunes Kunstsamlinger Munch-Museet.

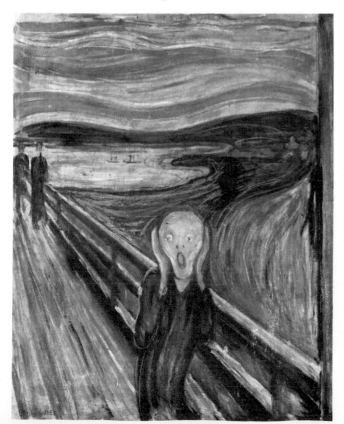

the dramatist August Strindberg, Munch presents almost unbearable pictures of the tensions and psychic anguish that beset modern men and the ultimate loneliness that, according to the modern philosophy of existentialism, is the inescapable lot of us all. Influenced by the strong patterns and color of Gauguin, as well as by Gauguin's use of the print medium, Munch transmitted the influence through his own work to the German Expressionists of the early twentieth century.

Protest against the disease of civilization sent Gauguin to the South Seas in search of primitive innocence. HENRI ROUSSEAU (1844–1910) was a "primitive" without leaving Paris—an untrained amateur painter who held a post as customs collector (hence, his sobriquet, *le douanier*). Rousseau produces an art of dream and fantasy in a style that has its own sophistication and makes its own departure from the artistic currency of the *fin de siècle*. His apparent visual, conceptual, and technical naïveté are compensated by a natural talent for design and an imagination teeming with exotic images of mysterious, tropical landscapes. In perhaps his best-known work, *The Sleeping Gypsy* (FIG. 21-77), a desert world, silent and secret, dreams beneath a pale, perfectly round moon. In the foreground, a lion—like a stuffed but somehow menacing animal doll—sniffs at the gypsy. A critical encounter impends, one that is not possible for most of us in the waking world but that is all too common when our vulnerable, subconscious selves are menaced in uneasy sleep. Rousseau early mirrors the landscape of the subconscious, and we may regard him as the forerunner of the Surrealists in the

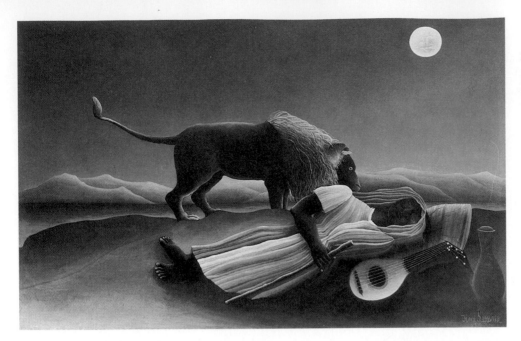

21-77 HENRI ROUSSEAU, *The Sleeping Gypsy*, 1897. 4' 3" × 6' 7". Museum of Modern Art, New York (gift of Mrs. Simon Guggenheim).

twentieth century, who will attempt to represent the ambiguity and contradiction of waking and dreaming experiences taken together.

The art of the American painter ALBERT PINKHAM RYDER (1847–1917) is made up of dream that never wakes. It is the very essence of Romantic inwardness and is witness to the persistence of Romanticism and its seemingly endless variety of utterance. A recluse, shut away by choice from the world, Ryder found a depthless reservoir of subject solely in his own imagination, from which arose images uniquely private yet often universal. Such is his *Death on a Pale Horse* (FIG. 21-78). The scythe-bearing specter speeds on its ceaseless round through a dead landscape that bears only a withered stalk of a tree. In the foreground, a malignant cobra with glowing eyes undulates. No

21-78 ALBERT PINKHAM RYDER, *Death on a Pale Horse*, c. 1910. Approx. 28" × 35". The Cleveland Museum of Art (purchased from the J.H. Wade Fund).

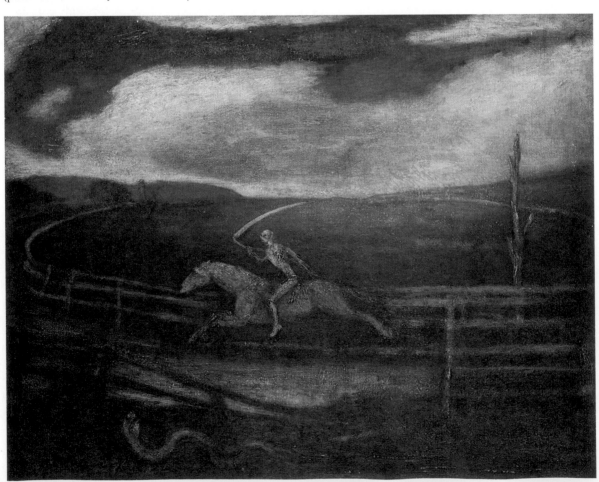

one remains on earth but Death and the serpent, the symbol of primordial evil. The utter simplicity of the conception and the execution require none but the barest reference to things outside the mind. Blank zones of dark and sombre light are traced through by the faint streaks of the rails, which remain undisturbed by the passage of the phosphorescent wraith. Ryder's indifference to the material world unfortunately extended to his material medium and technique. He painted in thick layers with badly prepared or nonfunctional pigments, and many of his works have suffered serious deterioration.

By the end of the nineteenth century, the Western artist's vision of reality had changed. Attitudes stemming from the rise of experimental science could not help but stimulate the artist's interest in the distinction between *what* is seen and *how* it is seen. A curiosity about and a taste for experiment with the tools of the artist's trade—new pigments and new theories of light and color—was aroused, which markedly influenced the procedure of Impressionists and Post-Impressionists alike. At the same time, the invention of photography profoundly affected the pictorial mode and the artist's manner of expression, offering a mechanical means of recording the spectrum of values of light and shade and of achieving the utmost fidelity to appearance. The pictorial artist—until then the sole maker of flat images and revealer of the structure of appearance—seemed suddenly to be technologically displaced, much as the Medieval scribe was displaced by the invention of the printing press. Artist's then, had to look for new purposes and new means for their craft. These searches would ultimately lead them to break altogether with the long tradition of imitative painting based on the optical check of nature. In the twentieth century, the separation between art and natural appearance is stated by Pablo Picasso: "Nature and art, being two different things, cannot be the same thing. Through art we express our conception of what nature is not."

By mid-century, the nineteenth-century painter was replacing the thematic material of Romanticism with scenes from the modern public world. This new interest paralleled widespread scientific curiosity about human society and group behavior. The artist's method, like the photographer's or the sociologist's, was at first descriptive; but, in the latter part of the century, this was gradually replaced by analysis and expression, and the artist came to realize that his activity is a function of his tools and materials. He discovered that his canvas is not a transparent window opening onto the optical world of nature, but a tangible surface on which pigments are arranged in a variety of ways. This is now the reality he confronts. Whether the artist, like Cézanne, examines color sensations to devise a system of color use or, like Van Gogh, regards the surface and colors simply as means for expressing emotional states, the artist is finally separated from the pictorial tradition that began with Giotto.

The testament of Seurat and Cézanne, Van Gogh and Gauguin is presented to the twentieth-century artist by Denis, in his famous positivist definition of painting: "Remember that a picture—before being a war horse, a nude woman, or some anecdote—is essentially a plane surface covered with colors assembled in a certain order."

In the Romantic painter's long search for the real, he discovers reality in himself and in the physical medium with which he works. But the long relied on optical world of common experience, lost in the radical transformation of traditional art, is rediscovered and preserved in the domain of the photograph and the motion picture. At the turn of the century, the current of art history in the West is divided sharply and fatefully around the problems of reality and of the nature and function of art in relation to it.

Sculpture in the Later Nineteenth Century

The three-dimensional art of sculpture is not readily adaptable to the optical realism favored by many painters and the public in the nineteenth century. Its very nature requires the sense of its permanence as an enduring form, a palpable mass sufficient unto itself. The timeless ideal, not the evanescent real, best suits it. The space it occupies is abstract, not descriptive of some particular locale it does not occupy; certainly, sculpture is not the apt medium for representing the passing season or time of day, fleetingly observed and fleetingly recorded. Thus, sculpture is not really suitable for the description either of historical events or of scenes from contemporary life, although it was often required to do both in the nineteenth century.

Classical or Baroque form limits optical realism; it does not break into the modern scene with the dissembling illusionism of the stage or the trivialities of the street. AUGUSTUS SAINT-GAUDENS (1848–1907), an American sculptor trained in France, used realism efficiently in a number of his portraits, where realism is most appropriate. For the design of a memorial monument of Mrs. Henry Adams, wife of the historian (FIG. 21-79), he chose a Classical mode of representation, which he freely modified, as Puvis had done in painting (FIG. 21-51). Of course, he had no need to specify a particular character; he wanted to represent a generality outside of time and place. A woman of majestic bearing sits in mourning, her classically beautiful face partly shadowed by a sepulchral

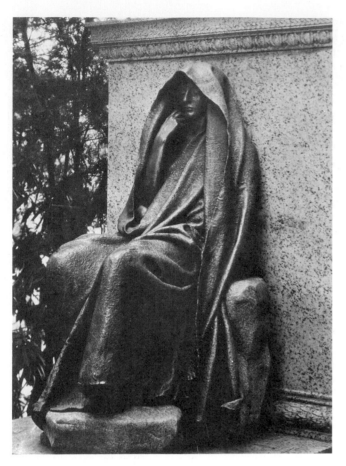

21-79 AUGUSTUS SAINT-GAUDENS, Adams Memorial, 1891.
Bronze, 70″ high. Rock Creek Cemetery, Washington, D.C.

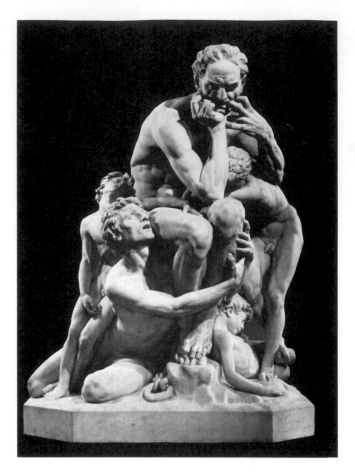

21-80 JEAN BAPTISTE CARPEAUX, *Ugolino and His Children*,
1865–1867. Marble, 6′ 5″ high. Metropolitan Museum of Art,
New York (Josephine Bay Paul and C. Michael Paul
Foundation, Inc., and the Charles Ulrick and Josephine Bay
Foundation, Inc., gifts, 1967).

drapery that voluminously enfolds her body. The
immobility of her form, set in an attitude of eternal
vigilance, is only slightly stirred by a natural, yet
mysterious and exquisite gesture. Saint-Gaudens'
masterpiece is a work worthy of the grave steles of
Classical Athens (FIG. 5-58).

The inspiration of the Baroque and of Michelangelo, both in form and content, show in the art of
JEAN BAPTISTE CARPEAUX (1827–1875), a precursor of
Auguste Rodin. The theme of his group *Ugolino and
His Children* (FIG. 21-80) is grim, even repulsive. Based
on a passage in Dante's *Inferno* (xxxiii, 58–75), it
shows Count Ugolino with his four sons shut up in a
tower to starve to death. In Hell, Ugolino relates to
Dante how:

> I bit both hands for grief. And
> they, thinking I did it for hunger,
> suddenly rose up and said, "Father" . . .

and offered him their own flesh as food. The powerful forms—twisted, intertwined, and densely concentrated—suggest the self-devouring torment of
frustration and despair that wracks the unfortunate
Ugolino. A careful student of the male figures of Mi-

chelangelo, Carpeaux also said that he had the
Laocoön group (FIG. 5-80) in mind—presumably not so
much the precise image, as the predicament, mood,
and action. Certainly, the storm and stress of the *Ugolino* would recall the Hellenistic "baroque" not only of
that group but of others, like the battle of the gods
and giants on the frieze of the Pergamon altar (FIG.
5-79).

For the leading sculptors of the nineteenth century,
the influence of Michelangelo was decisive. ANTOINE
AUGUSTE PRÉAULT (1810–1879) supplemented his
study of that great artist with close reference to sculptors of the French Renaissance. Baudelaire heard him
say: "I am a connoisseur of Michelangelo, of Jean
Goujon, of Germain Pilon . . ." (see FIGS. 18-54 and
18-55). Certainly, the influences of the latter two are
visibly commingled in Préault's superb *Ophelia* (FIG.
21-81). Taking the same Shakespearean theme that
Millais did for his painting (FIG. 21-48), Préault creates
a pattern of swirling, rippling line that simulates both
the clinging, drenched drapery and the rushing
water. The body of the drowning heroine makes a

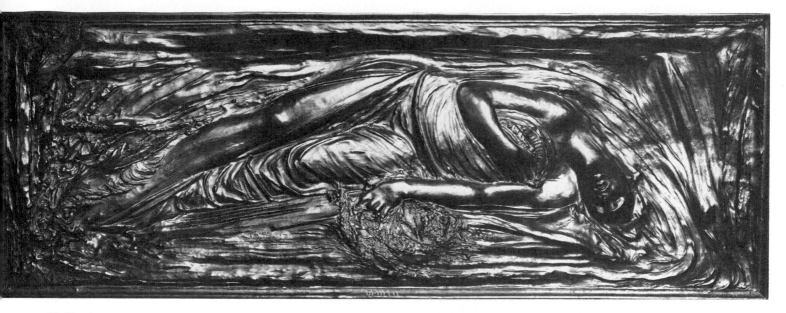

21-81 Antoine Auguste Préault, *Ophelia*, 1876 (original 1843). Bronze, 6′ 7″ long. Musée de Longchamps, Marseille.

beautiful, buoyant curve, expressive of the undulating current in which she is suspended and which is sucking her down. She is one of Goujon's fountain nymphs, tragically overwhelmed by the flooding waters she has poured. The sweep and play of curving line are both passionate and decorative; they look forward to the intricate, abstract style of Art Nouveau and its esthetic ideal of graceful, curvilinear ornament.

It is in the art of Auguste Rodin (1840–1917) that sculpture regains the artistic preeminence it had lost to the pictorial media in the nineteenth century. Rodin ably assimilates and manages the century's concurrent esthetic forces and forms—Romanticism, Realism, Impressionism, and Symbolism—and generates in the process a unique personal style that anticipates the Expressionism of the next century. He studied sculpture from the start, as it were, investigating the peculiarities of its materials and form. Avoiding the stilted formulas of the Academy, he studied—as Carpeaux had done—the sculpture of Michelangelo and of Pierre Puget (FIG. 19-73) as well, learning from them to appreciate the unique possibilities of the art for expressive bodily pose and gesture. As a contemporary of the Impressionists, Rodin embraces an esthetic based on a similar acceptance of the world of appearances revealed through light on surface. A modeler of soft material rather than a carver of hard, Rodin could work his surfaces with fingers sensitive to the subtlest variations of plane, catching the fugitive play of living motion as it changes fluidly under light. His touch is analogous to that of the deft Impressionist brush stroke. But, although Rodin's technique and formal sense aligned him with Impres-

sionism, his subjects were still in the Romantic vein, and his Realism bent strongly toward Expressionism as he searched for new forms in which to cast his Romantic themes. Without resorting to the repertory of historical styles, he found fitting and powerful forms for his subjects out of his own exercise of a kind of "impressionist realism." A splendid example is the group of life-size figures, *Burghers of Calais* (FIG. 21-82), commemorating a heroic episode of the Hundred Years' War, when the leading citizens of Calais, which had been taken by the English, offered their lives in return for those of all their fellow citizens. Each of the individual figures is a convincing study of despair, resignation, or quiet defiance. The psychic effects, the result of the technical management, are achieved through the movement of a few simplified planes, the rugged surfaces of which catch and disperse the light. But moving though the work is, it is difficult to believe that Rodin visualized the group as a unit; indeed, the separate figures were conceived as individual pieces and then shifted about until their relationship was considered satisfactory.

Rodin's mastery of dramatic gesture, so evident in the eloquent pantomime of *Burghers,* finds expression in a very different theme in *The Kiss* (FIG. 21-83). Intended to be only one of a number of groups composing the monumental Gates of Hell (including the famous *Thinker;* Introduction, FIG. 2), which was never finished, *The Kiss* is a subtle, if explicit, essay in a contrast of ardent approach and clumsily shy response, the attitude of the figures suiting the artist's poetic conception of the event perfectly. The group was meant to represent sensual love absorbed in self and rooted in matter. The artist may have carried in

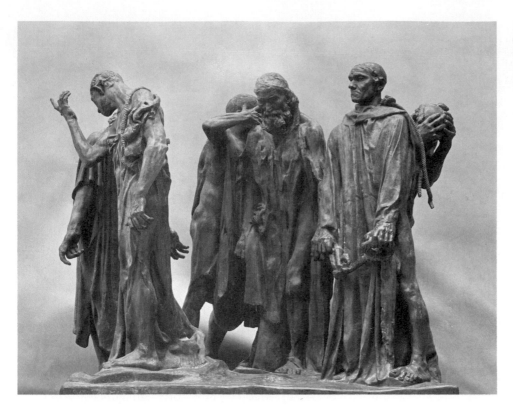

21-83 AUGUSTE RODIN, *The Kiss*, 1886–1898. Marble, over life-size. Musée Rodin, Paris.

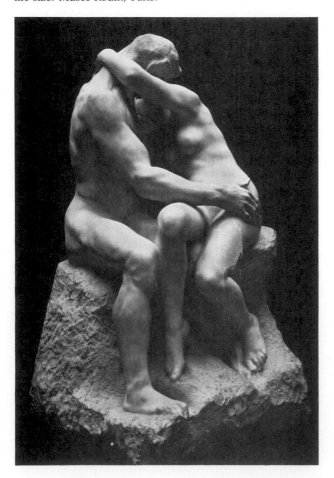

his mind a memory of Michelango's *Temptation of Adam and Eve*, one of the masterpieces of the Sistine Ceiling. Rodin, who declared that his encounter with the art of Michelangelo had been decisive in the formation of his style, was struck by that master's many uncompleted sculptures and admired the half-finished figures left in the rough block, as here (see Introduction, FIG. 10). The lovers' figures are modeled to a smoothness that suggests the supple surfaces and texture of living bodies. We recall the *sfumato* of Correggio (FIG. 17-40), which melts all harshness and angularity and which here contrasts with the rugged stone from which the figures emerge.

Incompleteness of figure becomes both a means and an end for Rodin. Most of his projects remain unfinished, or are deliberate fragments. Seeing the esthetic and expressive virtue of it, modern sculpture has taken this mannerism from Rodin. The half-completed, the fragment, the vignette lifted out of context, the sketch—all have the power of suggestion and understatement. Rodin's *Balzac* (FIG. 21-84) reveals the method most successfully. Features are not carved but are only suggested by indefinite surfaces that variegate the light and dark in deft blurs and smudges, producing a sketch-like effect. Contours melt away; volumes are not permitted to assert themselves. The great novelist, who surveyed mankind in his *La Comédie Humaine (The Human Comedy)*, draws himself up to a towering height. Wrapped in what seems to be an enormous cloak, he surveys again, from the lofty standpoint of immortality, the little-

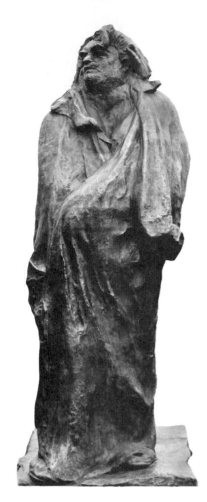

21-84 AUGUSTE RODIN, *Balzac*, 1892–1897. Plaster, approx. 9′ 10″ high. Musée Rodin, Paris.

ness of man. It is characteristic of Rodin's art that, though we feel its power, we cannot quite describe what traits make us feel it. His Impressionist methods, through daring emphasis and distortions, achieve an overwhelmingly Expressionist effect.

Rodin's personal passage from Impressionism to Expressionism was a historical one. While he was still living, sculpture was firmly set on the base he had constructed.

Architecture: The Beginnings of a New Style

The epoch-making development in international architecture that paralleled pictorial Realism could well be called Realistic—or just as well, rational, practical, or functional. For the nineteenth-century architect gradually comes to abandon sentimental and Romantic designs from the historical past in the interest of an honest expression of the building's purpose. Since the eighteenth century, inconspicuous utility architecture—factories, warehouses, dockyard structures, mills, and the like—had often been built simply and without historical ornament, sometimes out of the new, convenient material, cast iron. Iron, along with

other materials of the Industrial Revolution, permitted engineering advancements in the construction of larger, stronger, and more fire-resistant structures. The tensile strength of iron (and especially of steel, available after 1860) allowed new designs involving vast enclosed or spanned spaces, as in the great train sheds of railroad stations and in exposition halls.

The Bibliothèque Ste. Geneviève (1843–1850), built by HENRI LABROUSTE (1801–1875), shows an interesting adjustment of the revived Romantic style—in this case, Renaissance—to a Realistic interior, the skeletal elements of which are cast iron (FIG. 21-85). The row of arched windows in the façade recalls the flank of Alberti's San Francesco at Rimini (FIG. 16-41), yet the division of its stories distinguishes the levels of the interior—the lower, reserved for stack space; the upper, for the reading rooms. The latter consist essentially of two tunnel-roofed halls, roofed in terra cotta, separated by a row of slender cast-iron columns on concrete pedestals. The iron columns, recognizably Corinthian, support the iron roof arches, which are pierced with intricate vine-scroll ornament out of the Renaissance architectural vocabulary. One could scarcely find a better example of how the forms of traditional masonry architecture are esthetically transformed by the peculiarities of the new structural material. Nor could one find a better example of how reluctant the nineteenth-century architect was to surrender traditional forms even when fully aware of the new possibilities for design and construction. For many years, architects would scoff at "engineer's ar-

21-85 HENRI LABROUSTE, reading room of the Bibliothèque Ste. Geneviève, Paris, 1843–1850.

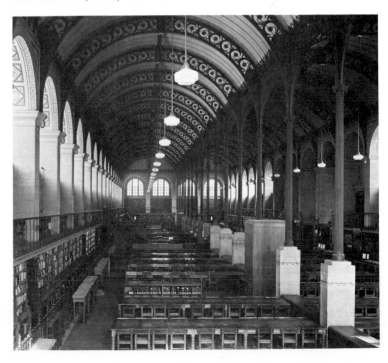

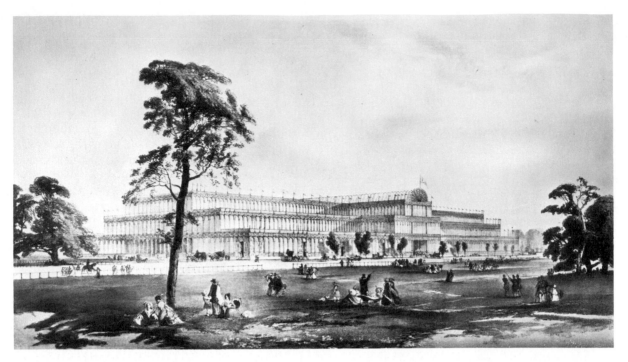

21-86   JOSEPH PAXTON, Crystal Palace, London, 1850–1851. Iron and glass. (Contemporary print.)

chitecture" and clothe their steel and concrete structures in the Romantic "drapery" of a historical style. Many great railroad stations juxtaposed the Romantic with practical, "undraped" construction in steel—historically decorated ticket concourses contrasting with open steel sheds just behind them.

Standardization and prefabrication of structural members permitted JOSEPH PAXTON (1801–1865) to construct the exposition building in London called the Crystal Palace (FIG. 21-86), a work almost wholly of iron and glass, in the unheard-of time of six months from 1850 to 1851. But the climax of nineteenth-century enterprise in wide-span construction was the 375-foot span of the 1,365-foot-long Galerie des Machines (FIG. 21-87), erected at the Paris Exhibition of 1889. The building had no encumbering inte-

21-87   Galerie des Machines, Paris International Exhibition, 1889. Steel and glass.

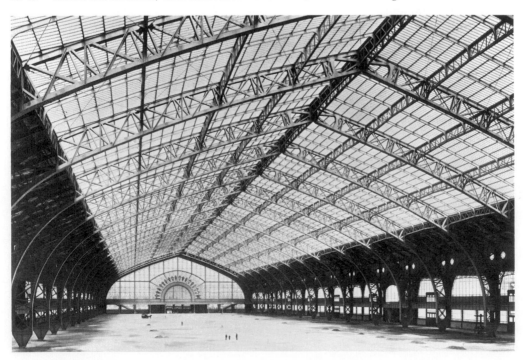

rior supports, so that as many as 100,000 visitors could circulate daily through its vast interior, their movement facilitated by a great rolling bridge from which they could look down at the panorama of operating machines far below. The structural scheme was composed of hinged (at apex and bases), nearly parabolic metal arches that supported a framework on which broad sheets of glass rested. Alexander Eiffel's daring tower, symbol of modern Paris, was also built at this time, and these two feats of engineering jolted some of the architectural profession into a realization that the new materials and new processes might contain the germ of a completely new style—something that picturesque, historical Romanticism had failed to produce.

The desire for greater speed and economy in building, as well as a reduction in fire hazards, encouraged the use of cast and wrought iron for many other building programs, especially commercial ones. Both England and America enthusiastically developed cast-iron architecture until a series of disastrous fires in the early 1870s in New York, Boston, and Chicago demonstrated that cast iron by itself was far from impervious to fire. This led to the practice of encasing the metal in masonry, combining the strength of the first with the fire-resistance of the second.

In cities, convenience required buildings to be closely grouped, and increased property values forced architects literally to raise the roof. Even attics could command high rentals if the newly invented elevator was also provided, as it was for the first time in the Equitable Building in New York (1868–1871). Metal could support such tall structures, and the American skyscraper was born. It was with rare exceptions, however, as in the work of Louis Sullivan (FIGS. 21-89 and 21-90), that this original type of building was treated successfully and produced distinguished architecture.

Sullivan's predecessor, HENRY HOBSON RICHARDSON (1838–1886), frequently used heavy round arches and massive masonry walls, and because he was particularly fond of the Romanesque architecture of the Auvergne in France, his work was sometimes thought of as a Romanesque revival. This designation does not do credit to the originality and quality of most of the buildings Richardson designed during the brief 18 years of his practice. Although Trinity Church in Boston and his smaller public libraries, residences, railroad stations, and court houses in New England and elsewhere best demonstrate his vivid imagination and the solidity—the sense of enclosure and permanence—so characteristic of his style, his most important and influential building was the Marshall Field Warehouse (now demolished) in Chicago (FIG. 21-88), which was begun in 1885. The vast building, occupying a city block and designed for the most

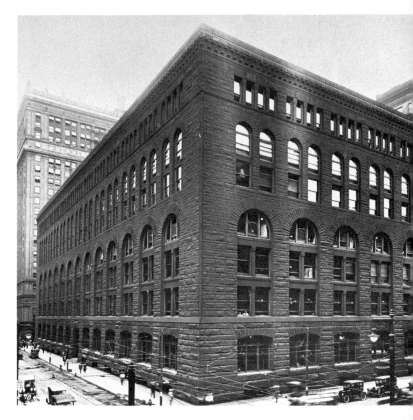

21-88   HENRY HOBSON RICHARDSON, Marshall Field Warehouse, Chicago, Illinois, 1885–1887.

practical of purposes (storage) recalls historical styles without being at all in mere imitation of them. The tripartite elevation of a Renaissance palace or of the aqueduct near Nîmes (FIG. 6-43) may have been close to Richardson's mind, but he uses no Classical ornament, makes much of the massive courses of masonry, and—in the strong horizontality of the window sills and in the interrupted courses that define the levels—stresses the long sweep of the building's lines as well as its ponderous weight.

Although the structural frame still lies behind and in conjunction with the masonry screen of the Marshall Field Warehouse, the great glazed arcades, in opening up the walls of a large-scale building, point the way to the modern, total penetration of the wall and the transformation of it into a mere screen or curtain that serves to express the structural grid and protect it from the weather.

LOUIS SULLIVAN (1856–1924), who has been called the first truly modern architect, recognized Richardson's architectural suggestions early in his career and worked forward from them to his new "tall buildings," especially in the Guaranty (Prudential) Building in Buffalo, New York, built between 1894 and 1895 (FIG. 21-89). Here, the subdivision of the interior is expressed on the exterior, as is the skeletal (as opposed to the bearing-wall) nature of the supporting structure, with nothing more substantial than

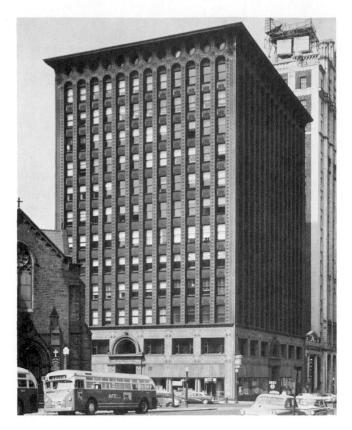

21-89 Louis Sullivan, Guaranty (Prudential) Building, Buffalo, New York, 1894–1895.

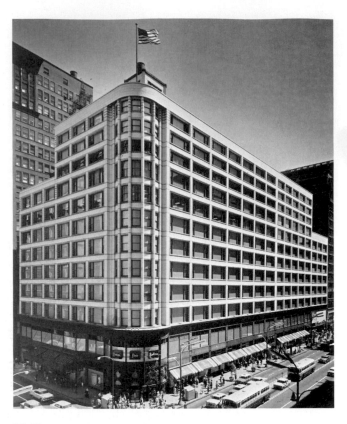

21-90 Louis Sullivan, Carson, Pirie, Scott Building, Chicago, Illinois, 1899–1904.

windows occupying most of the space between the terra-cotta-clad vertical members. In Sullivan's designs, one can be sure of an equivalence of interior and exterior design, as one cannot in Richardson's warehouse (FIG. 21-88) or in Labrouste's library (FIG. 21-85). Yet something of old habits of thought hangs on; the Guaranty Building has a base and cornice. The base, however, is penetrated in such a way as to suggest the later free supports of modern architecture.

The form of the building, then, is beginning to express its function, and Sullivan's famous "form follows function"—long the slogan of early twentieth-century architects—finds its illustration here. It is important to note that Sullivan did not mean by this slogan that functional building is automatically beautiful; nor did he advocate a rigid and doctrinaire correspondence between external and interior design. Rather, he espoused a free and flexible relationship—one that his great pupil Frank Lloyd Wright will later describe as like that between the bones and tissue of the hand.

Sullivan takes a further step in the unification of exterior and interior design in his Carson, Pirie, Scott Building in Chicago, Illinois (FIG. 21-90), built between 1899 and 1904. A department store, this building required broadly open, well illuminated display spaces. The structural steel skeleton, being minimal, permits the singular achievement of this goal. The relation of spaces and solids here is so logical that nothing in the way of facing need be added, and the skeleton is clearly revealed in the exterior. The deck-like stories, faced in white ceramic slabs, seem to sweep freely around the building and show several irregularities (notably the stressed bays of the corner entrance) that help the design to break out of the cubical formula of Sullivan's older buildings. In the general search for a new style at the end of the century, Sullivan was a leader. He gave as much attention to finding new directions in architectural ornament as in architecture itself. In this respect, he is an important figure in the movement called Art Nouveau, which will seek an end to all traditional ornamental styles—indeed, to the whole preoccupation with historical style that has been postponing the true advent of a modern method in the arts of form. The lower two levels of the Carson, Pirie, Scott Building are given over to an ornament (of Sullivan's invention) made of wildly fantastic motifs that bear little resemblance to anything traditional architecture could show.

Yet designs of interiors in the later century could still exhibit taste for the historical and the exotic—an eclectic estheticism that would linger on until finally purged by the puritanism of an austere new architec-

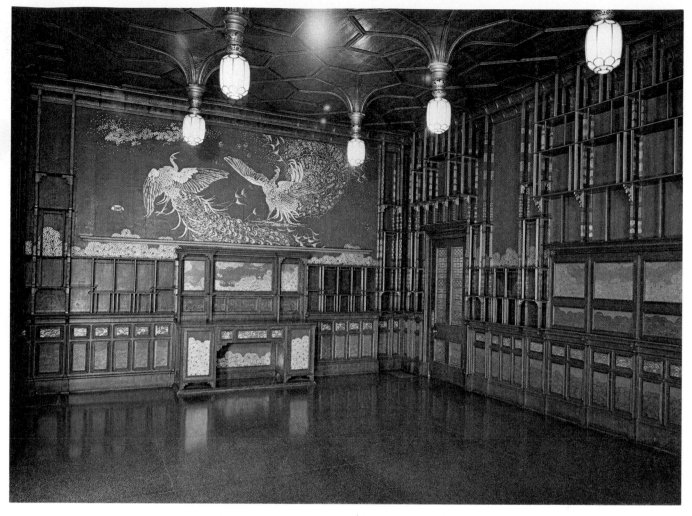

21-91   JAMES A. MCNEILL WHISTLER, Peacock Room from the home of F.R. Leyland, 1876–1877. Freer Gallery of Art, Washington, D.C.

tural style. The renowned Peacock Room (FIG. 21-91) is a superb example of architectural "art for art's sake." Designed as a dining room for F.R. Leyland of London by THOMAS JECKYL, it was decorated by JAMES A. MCNEILL WHISTLER (1834–1903), an American artist who exhibited with the Impressionists and who was strongly influenced by Japanese decorative art, as was Aubrey Beardsley (FIG. 21-74). The room was intended as a showcase for Leyland's collection of Japanese porcelain, as well as for Whistler's own "Japanified" painting, *The Princess of Porcelain Land.*

Although Whistler painted peacocks in blue and gold to heighten the "Japanese" atmosphere, the general design and its details are more Tudor English than Japanese. In their deft elegance, the painted and hand-crafted elements and accessories of the ensemble constitute a kind of manifest transition to Art Nouveau. Although experiment with ornament will have its brief vogue in Art Nouveau, it is the twentieth century that will sweep away the traditional systems and discover its own ornament, as it will discover its own principles of design.

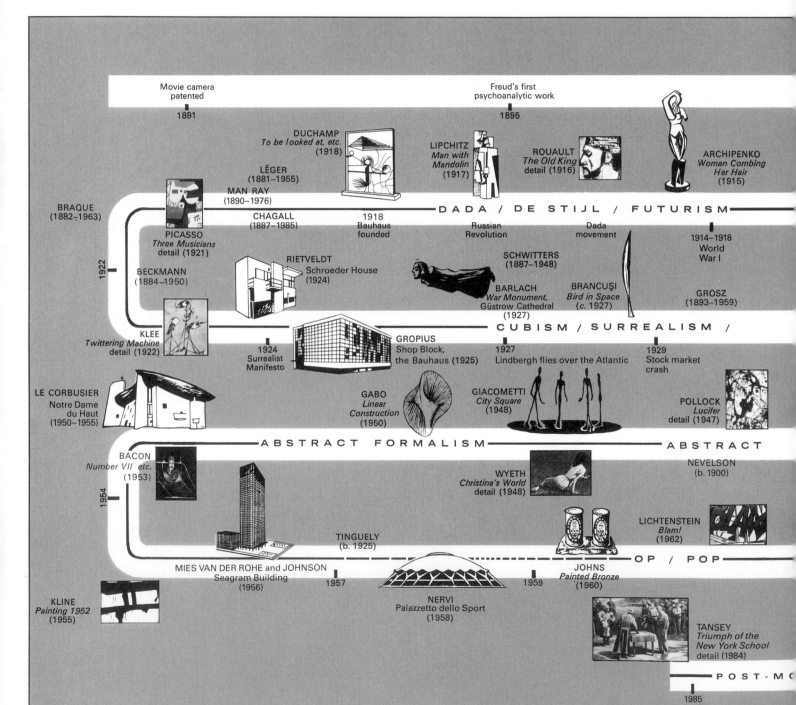

22

Movie camera
patented
1891

Freud's first
psychoanalytic work
1895

ARCHIPENKO
*Woman Combing
Her Hair*
(1915)

DUCHAMP
To be looked at, etc.
(1918)

LIPCHITZ
*Man with
Mandolin*
(1917)

ROUAULT
The Old King
detail (1916)

LÉGER
(1881–1955)

MAN RAY
(1890–1976)

BRAQUE
(1882–1963)

CHAGALL
(1887–1985)

1918
Bauhaus
founded

DADA / DE STIJL / FUTURISM

PICASSO
Three Musicians
detail (1921)

Russian
Revolution

Dada
movement

1914–1918
World
War I

1922

BECKMANN
(1884–1950)

RIETVELDT
Schroeder House
(1924)

SCHWITTERS
(1887–1948)

BARLACH
War Monument,
Güstrow Cathedral
(1927)

BRANCUŞI
Bird in Space
(c. 1927)

GROSZ
(1893–1959)

KLEE
Twittering Machine
detail (1922)

CUBISM / SURREALISM /

1924
Surrealist
Manifesto

GROPIUS
Shop Block,
the Bauhaus (1925)

1927
Lindbergh flies over the Atlantic

1929
Stock market
crash

LE CORBUSIER
Notre Dame
du Haut
(1950–1955)

GABO
*Linear
Construction*
(1950)

GIACOMETTI
City Square
(1948)

POLLOCK
Lucifer
detail (1947)

ABSTRACT FORMALISM

ABSTRACT

BACON
Number VII etc.
(1953)

WYETH
Christina's World
detail (1948)

NEVELSON
(b. 1900)

1954

LICHTENSTEIN
Blam!
(1962)

TINGUELY
(b. 1925)

JOHNS
Painted Bronze
(1960)

OP / POP

MIES VAN DER ROHE and JOHNSON
Seagram Building
(1956)

1957

1959

NERVI
Palazzetto dello Sport
(1958)

KLINE
Painting 1952
(1955)

TANSEY
*Triumph of the
New York School*
detail (1984)

POST-MO

1985

THE TWENTIETH CENTURY

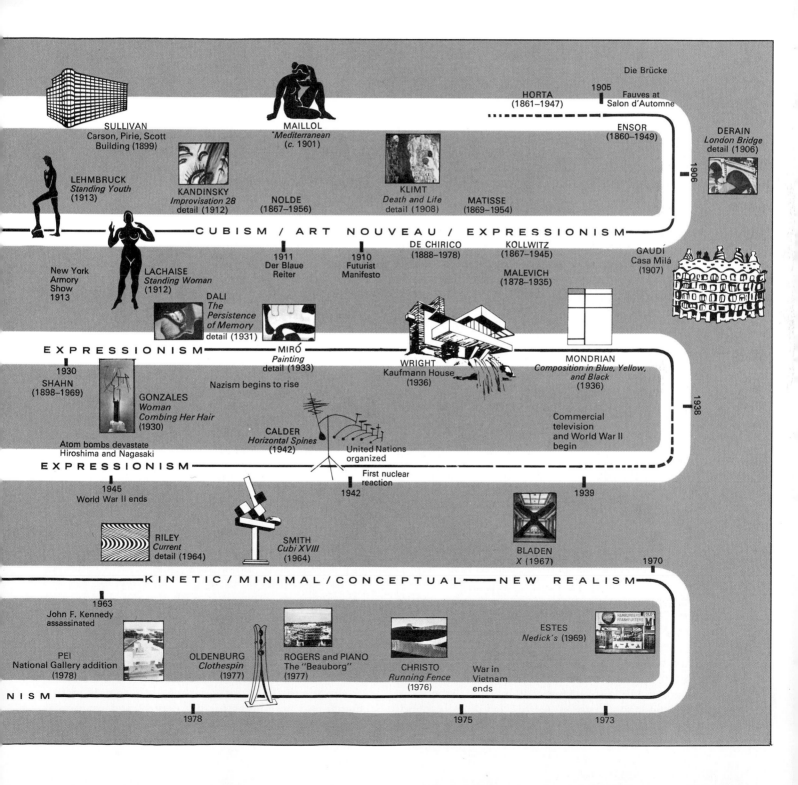

Die Brücke

HORTA
(1861–1947)

1905

Fauves at
Salon d'Automne

SULLIVAN
Carson, Pirie, Scott
Building (1899)

MAILLOL
Mediterranean
(c. 1901)

ENSOR
(1860–1949)

DERAIN
London Bridge
detail (1906)

LEHMBRUCK
Standing Youth
(1913)

KANDINSKY
Improvisation 28
detail (1912)

NOLDE
(1867–1956)

KLIMT
Death and Life
detail (1908)

MATISSE
(1869–1954)

1906

CUBISM / ART NOUVEAU / EXPRESSIONISM

DE CHIRICO
(1888–1978)

KOLLWITZ
(1867–1945)

GAUDÍ
Casa Milá
(1907)

New York
Armory
Show
1913

LACHAISE
Standing Woman
(1912)

1911
Der Blaue
Reiter

1910
Futurist
Manifesto

MALEVICH
(1878–1935)

DALI
*The
Persistence
of Memory*
detail (1931)

EXPRESSIONISM

MIRÓ
Painting
detail (1933)

WRIGHT
Kaufmann House
(1936)

MONDRIAN
*Composition in Blue, Yellow,
and Black*
(1936)

1938

1930

SHAHN
(1898–1969)

GONZALES
*Woman
Combing Her Hair*
(1930)

Nazism begins to rise

Commercial
television
and World War II
begin

Atom bombs devastate
Hiroshima and Nagasaki

CALDER
Horizontal Spines
(1942)

United Nations
organized

EXPRESSIONISM

First nuclear
reaction

1942

1939

1945
World War II ends

RILEY
Current
detail (1964)

SMITH
Cubi XVIII
(1964)

BLADEN
X (1967)

1970

KINETIC / MINIMAL / CONCEPTUAL — NEW REALISM

1963
John F. Kennedy
assassinated

ESTES
Nedick's (1969)

PEI
National Gallery addition
(1978)

OLDENBURG
Clothespin
(1977)

ROGERS and PIANO
The "Beauborg"
(1977)

CHRISTO
Running Fence
(1976)

War in
Vietnam
ends

NISM

1978

1975

1973

BECAUSE we are in the midst of it and, hence, still being shaped by it, the twentieth century is perhaps more difficult to characterize than any in history. It has been said that the Renaissance died finally in the holocaust of World War I; it is certain that this century has brought to a close an epoch of a thousand years—from the dim time in the Romanesque era, when Europe began a new life, until now, when European civilization is blending into a world civilization. This century is in a continuing crisis; we are making ourselves into something different from what we have been, at a cost we cannot yet estimate and with consequences we cannot guess. Our historical knowledge has already placed our abandoned traditions an unbridgeable distance behind us and left us self-conscious and isolated in the stream of time, confronted with tremendous possibility or appalling disaster. Science has utterly changed our picture of the physical world and of ourselves. Our technology has provided unique experiences: high-speed flight, instantaneous communication over great distances, expanded ranges of sensory perception, and—for a minority, as yet—conditions of physical ease never before imaginable. But the new patterns of life that are separating us so decisively from the past are also confronting us with new and difficult problems of adjustment. The passing of old traditions and beliefs has robbed us of assurances and securities; we are often doubtful of the meaning and purpose of life and of the very source and nature of our own identity. We hear much of modern man's "alienation," his sense of strangeness and loneliness in the world, where he is, like the figures in Alberto Giacometti's *City Square* (FIG. 22–54), only an aimless unit in a "lonely crowd."

This problematic quality of modern life is the result of the constantly shifting grounds of our beliefs; an axiom for our time could well be "where nothing is certain, everything is a question," the fundamental question being: What is "real"? The twentieth century seems chronically and constitutionally skeptical about all answers to this question, especially the traditional ones. But of one thing it appears to be certain: "reality" is infinitely complex, perhaps ultimately elusive, and by no means given to us in our everyday, conventional, commonsensical experience. "Seeing" is certainly no longer ground for "believing." The world of common sense is simply not what it seems. The quantum theory and the theory of relativity—new theories in physics set forth at the beginning of the century—describe subsensible and suprasensible universes of electrical fields in which there is no absolute space or time and in which all motion is relative to systems themselves in motion. There is no stable "center" in this headlong, expanding universe swarming with electronic and galactic events—no absolute standpoint that can certify our measurements of space and time. A principle of "indeterminacy" reigns in the world of the electron and of outer space, where the speeds of events approach the speed of light. The world of familiar solids and spaces thus dissolves, on physical analysis, into a "dance of atoms"; their configurations apparently have little relation to what we see and feel as "real." In such a world picture, the stature of man, so elevated in the Renaissance, shrinks to infinitesimal dimensions.

If physical science's picture of the world drastically reduces our central role in the old, classical Christian cosmos, modern biology has done little to restore it. In the nineteenth century, the privileged status of human beings in nature had been questioned by the hypothesis that we evolved from lower forms of life. In the newly developed social sciences, biological concepts were adapted to explanations of human culture and of individual differences, and the human individual came to be seen as a resultant of the interacting factors of heredity and environment. Thus, life may be determined rather than free—and man, in the collective, comes to be studied statistically, like the subatomic particles of physics.

A further blow to age-old beliefs was delivered in the twentieth century by the new psychology, associated in its early development with Freud. Although it is deeply rooted in Romanticism, this restatement of our essential irrationality struck at a thousand years of explanations of human conduct and may be seen as a modern revision of the theme of original sin. In the new view, our actions are seen as largely determined by motives operating beneath consciousness at an unconscious or "subconscious" level.

A further modern development, which we might call the information–communication crisis, contributes to uncertainty and the uneasiness that accompanies it. Literacy has been widespread in the Western world since the end of the nineteenth century, and printing has been supplemented by radio, television, and electronic telecommunication. The resulting expansion in communication services has been accompanied by a diminution in credibility and belief; thus, although technical competence has increased, its application may have little relevance to deeper human concerns. From about 1950, a new technological revolution, associated with the development of computer science, has been converting the data of our experience into the language of number. Such "artificial intelligence" augments and may even replace natural intelligence in many of its functions, and this may lead to the automation of the human environment. The consequences of these new instruments and languages for the control and manipulation of our lives can only be imagined. They aim at rigorous solutions to problems and unambiguous definitions; but life and art are rich in ambiguity, and to eliminate it could impoverish and trivialize both.

In our time, "meaning" and "truth" join "reality" as problematic and relative terms. The reduction of truth from absolute, transcendental, and eternal to public, relative, and debatable makes our acquisition of it conditional on language. And ordinary verbal language is ambiguous.

The success of experimental science has had everything to do with making meaning and truth into functions of instruments and languages. Our knowledge of the physical world is obtained by the manipulation of instruments, and the specialized language of mathematics mediates that knowledge. Thus, the meaning, truth, and reality of scientific experience—that is, scientific knowledge—are contained in its media and inseparable from them. This is true also of the arts in this age of science and mechanism. As we saw in Chapter 21, Maurice Denis insists that before a picture is *of* anything it is simply a flat surface covered with colors arranged in a certain way. By a similar reduction, a poem is only a sequence of words or word-images, and a piece of music is only a sequence of sounds. A dominant modern view defines art as consisting of the free manipulation of such elements in arrangements that need not refer to anything outside themselves—that need not *represent* anything. The arrangement is complete and self-contained; one cannot find its message by demanding that it point to something recognizable beyond itself. The modern artist, like the scientist, "experiments" with his medium, investigates its possibilities, and discovers or invents new forms. But unlike the scientist, who searches for new uniformities and regularities, most modern artists seek the singular and the unique; JUAN GRIS, one of the best Cubist painters, remarks: "My aim is to create new objects which cannot be compared to any object in actuality." The task of projecting the optical order of the world onto a flat surface—the task of generations of painters since Giotto—is given up. For, given the new view of the world, the optical "look" of it is problematic and to make pictures that copy it is futile or trivial. New forms must be discovered or created out of the possibilities of the physical medium itself so that new and profound reality can be expressed. Paul Klee, one of the great masters of modern art, puts it this way:

> We used to represent things visible on earth. . . . Now we reveal the reality of visible things, and thereby express the belief that visible reality is merely an isolated phenomenon latently outnumbered by other realities. Things take on a broader and more varied meaning, often in seeming contradiction to the rational experience of yesterday. . . . In the end, a formal cosmos will be created out of purely abstract

elements of form quite independent of their configurations as objects, beings, or abstract things like letters or numbers.*

In other words, the reality of visible things is now no longer merely their visibility. The visible state of a thing, given in a single perspective as in traditional art, is an extremely limited account of it; the reality is much more than that. Klee provides an example: "An apple tree in bloom is in effect a complex of stages of growth, its roots, the rising sap, its trunk, the cross section with the annual rings, the blossom, its structure, its sexual function, the fruit, the core with its seeds." Klee wants to express this complexity of parts as a whole that is, in effect, more than the sum of its parts—as a whole that has a meaning that cannot be apprehended by the analysis of the apple tree into parts and phenomena. Thus, the ambiguity that scientists try to eliminate from their procedures, findings, and communicated information is the very essence of the reality the artist deals with. Klee continues:

> In the highest sense, an ultimate mystery lies behind the ambiguity which the light of the intellect fails miserably to penetrate. Yet one can to a certain extent speak reasonably of the salutary effect which art exerts through fantasy and symbols. Fantasy, kindled by instinct-born excitements, creates illusory conditions which can rouse or stimulate us more than familiar, natural, or supernatural ones. Symbols reassure the mind that we need not depend exclusively upon mundane experience. . . .†

The mystery that modern science tries to dispel, modern art cultivates as if it were at the heart of our human experience of reality. The union of art and science in the Renaissance, made on the basis of Humanistic reason, is dissolved in the twentieth century. Even though the arts in one respect—the experiment with forms and materials—have paralleled modern logic and mathematics and have often been close to technology, their intention and their results have led them in the precisely opposite direction. The artist–experimenter is at the same time the artist–prophet. Working ceaselessly at the possibilities of his physical medium, he seeks a reality behind the screen of the conventional world. His search depends not on a general, public agreement about reality or on a general pictorial language for communicating it, but on his own instincts, insight, inner experience, which he expresses as a kind of personal vision—strange, ambiguous, mystifying, impossible to communicate in words. It is little wonder that, as modern art has

---

*In Margaret Miller, ed., *Paul Klee* (New York: Museum of Modern Art, 1946), p. 12.

†*Ibid.*, p. 13.

developed in its many movements, the general public has been most often hostile to it. Undoubtedly, the artist most often invites that hostility, for almost from the beginning it has been his intention to *épater le bourgeois*—to shake up stodgy citizens and make them see and think in a new way. Picasso insists that art, in this respect, must be subversive, essentially revolutionary. The modern artist, in this view, must live in the avant-garde of society, and his very life must be a model of defiant freedom from spirit-destroying convention.

What has been said by way of background to the ensuing discussion of the art of the twentieth century is, of course, a simplification and it should be viewed only as a partial and uncertain explanation of the central fact—that modern art looks very different from the art of the past. We have generalized modern art and the modern artist, and particular cases escape generalization; what remains unequivocal is the picture of the artist in a dangerous, confused world, experimenting to find a free means of expression of his insights. The modern-artist's task is to reconstruct reality from private experience.

PAINTING BEFORE WORLD WAR II

Symbolism and Art Nouveau

Two movements discussed or anticipated in Chapter 21, continue from the late nineteenth century: Symbolism and Art Nouveau. We have seen that the Symbolists carried the subjectivity of Romanticism to new extremes. In doing so, they turned from the common nineteenth-century stock of historical, mythological, and anecdotal themes to the relatively unfamiliar ones of the Orient, Oceania, Byzantium, Persia, the Early Middle Ages, and the Early Renaissance.

It is in these uncommon sources that the Symbolists search for new forms. The picture-box of the pictorial tradition is replaced by flat surfaces, decoratively embellished with figures that are not modeled or, if modeled, that are often contrasted with flat patterns. An example of this experimental adjustment of planar shapes and plastic forms is the painting *Death and Life* (FIG. 22-1) by the Viennese artist GUSTAV

22-1   GUSTAV KLIMT, *Death and Life*, 1908 and 1911. 5' 10" × 6' 6". Collection of Marietta Preleuthner, Salzburg.

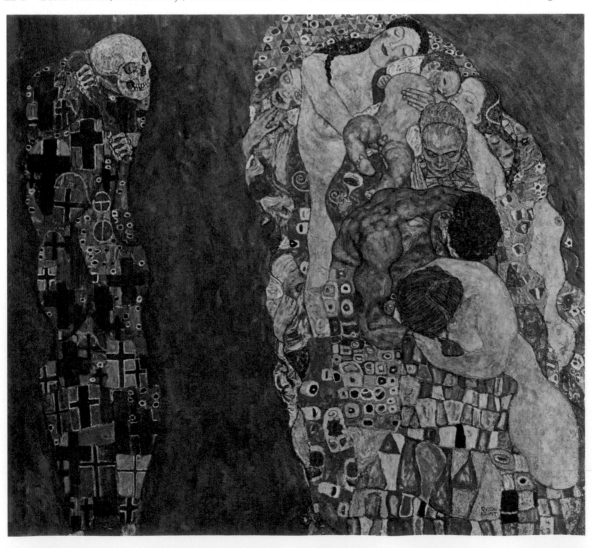

KLIMT (1862–1918). In 1903, Klimt visited Ravenna and saw its great mosaics. Although Byzantine art had begun to be appreciated in the early nineteenth century, Klimt approaches it here not as critic, historian, or connoisseur, but as an artist open to fresh inspiration, ready and competent to assimilate form from outside his own tradition to express a modern mood. The painting is quite typically Symbolist in both content and form. Bright colors, mosaic-like or enamel-like, stud the surfaces that enwrap the voluptuously somnolent figures in the *Life* group, in which intertwined images of infancy, youth, maturity, and old age celebrate life as bound up with love. Outlined shapes are modeled to the extent needed to show the softness of flesh and the firmness of sinew. It is characteristic of Klimt to contrast often quite realistically modeled forms with flat patterns. The tableau of defenseless sleep is set off against the specter of Death, the nocturnal assassin, who advances threateningly upon it. The shroud of the fleshless Death is appropriately dark as night, only dimly decked with funereal black crosses and chiromantic symbols. While Life, sated with love, sleeps, its enemy, Death, wakes. The grim interval between Life and Death will soon be crossed.

In this and other Symbolist works, the ornamental flatness of the drapery, the organic, undulating contours, and the arbitrary placement of the figures, so that they seem to float and hover as they would in a dream, contradict the presuppositions of realistic representation. From this contradiction and from the example of art outside the Western tradition arose new possibilities of form independent of pictorial Realism that produced an international style, Art Nouveau, which dominated the arts from 1890 to World War I. Art Nouveau, primarily an ornamental style, was a protest not simply against a sterile Realism, but against the whole drift toward industrialization and mechanization and the unnatural artifacts they produced. The forms of nature—growing, sinuous, and graceful—were set against the blunt, ugly masses of the encroaching machine. Art Nouveau called for the renovation of a taste corrupted by mass-produced objects and cluttered urban environments, which seemed to be assuming dominance in the name of unesthetic utility.

The sources of Art Nouveau, as of Symbolism, lay in the arts and crafts of other cultures and times and in the exotic styles cultivated by innovative artists like Paul Gauguin (FIG. 21-70), Vincent Van Gogh (FIG. 21-69), and their contemporaries. The Japanese print played an important part (FIGS. 13-29 and 21-60), as did the movement led by John Ruskin and William Morris, who, as we have seen, extolled careful craftsmanship in all the arts, stressing the moral as well as the esthetic value of honest, individual craft. Art

Nouveau, especially effective in architecture and the handicrafts (FIG. 22-55) decisively influenced the figural arts; and most of the great modern painters of the early twentieth century participated in or were touched by the movement at the beginning of their careers.

The Fauves and Expressionism

The first signs of a new and specifically twentieth-century movement in painting appeared in Paris in 1905. In that year, at the third Salon d'Automne, a group of younger painters, independent of the French Royal Academy and the "official" Salon and under the leadership of Henri Matisse, exhibited canvases so simplified in design and so shockingly brilliant in color that a startled critic described the artists as *fauves* ("wild beasts"). The influence of the non-European cultures of the new colonial dominions was everywhere apparent. The "Fauves" were encouraged by the newly discovered exotic arts to seek more personal forms of expression than had been known in the West. In African fetishes, in Polynesian decorative wood carvings, and in the sculptures and textiles from the ancient cultures of Central and South America, they saw unexpected shapes and colors that suggested new ways of communicating emotion. This led them individually into various paths of free invention and took them once and for all out of the traditions of the Renaissance. Deft, spirited painters, they produced canvases of great spontaneity and verve, with a rich surface texture, lively linear patterns, and boldly clashing effects of primary colors. Their subject matter was as varied as their methods of painting, although many subjects familiar in Impressionist and Post-Impressionist painting—such as landscapes, still lifes, and nude figures—still appeared. Thus, the Fauves carried on and expanded the trends begun by Van Gogh and Gauguin, whose works had become better known through extensive retrospective exhibitions held in Paris in 1901 and 1903.

The Fauves brought color to a new intensity with startling discords of vermilion and emerald green, cerulean blue and vivid orange held together by sweeping brush strokes and bold patterns. Relationships to the past and contributions to the present can be seen in a painting like the one exhibited in the 1905 Salon d'Automne entitled *London Bridge* (FIG. 22-2) by ANDRÉ DERAIN (1880–1954), whose Fauve work remains among his finest. We can judge how thoroughly the Fauve painters have broken with most of the art of the late nineteenth century when we recall that Claude Monet had completed his series of views of Waterloo Bridge in London only three years before. Derain entirely rejects the subtle harmonies of Im-

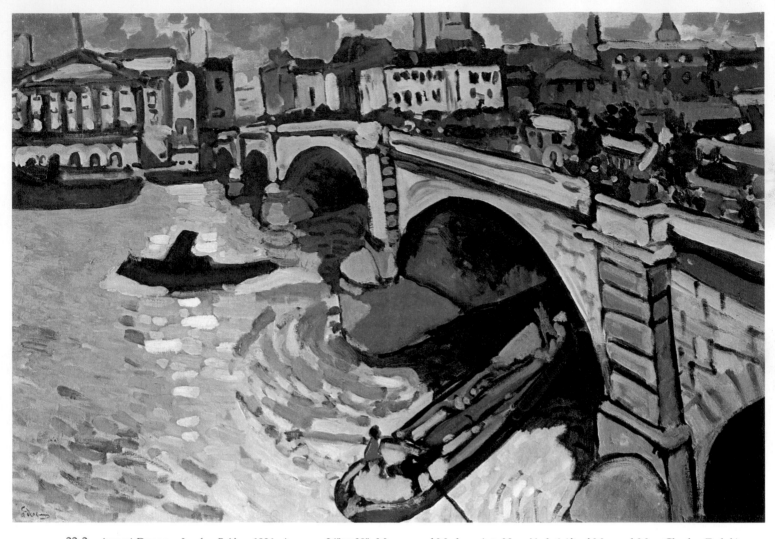

22-2 ANDRÉ DERAIN, *London Bridge*, 1906. Approx. 26″ × 39″. Museum of Modern Art, New York (gift of Mr. and Mrs. Charles Zadok).

pressionism, so expressive of atmospheric and climatic conditions, in favor of a distorted perspective emphasized by clashing yellows, blues, greens, and reds against the black accents of the arches. Implicit in such work is the philosophy already adopted by Van Gogh and Gauguin (pages 867–69) and fundamental to Expressionism: the artist's presentation of his emotional reaction to the subject in the boldest color and strongest linear pattern is more important than any attempts at objective representation. In this way, the Fauves freed color from its traditional role as the description of the local tone of an object and helped to prepare both artists and public for the use of color as an expressive end in itself. In a sense, color became the "subject" of the picture.

The Fauve movement, never an official organization of painters, was short-lived; within five years, most of the artists had modified their violent colors and found their own more personal treatment of the medium.

The artist who remains most faithful to the Fauve principles yet, through his extraordinary sensitivity for color, transforms them into one of the strongest

and most influential personal expressions in modern art is HENRI MATISSE (1869–1954). Throughout his long life, his gift for combining colors in unsuspected ways and for inventing new combinations never flagged. He preferred working in two dimensions but, by the subtlest of color accents, his surfaces, no matter how apparently flat, convey effects of three-dimensional space.

Studying his *Red Room (Harmony in Red)*, shown in FIG. 22-3, we find that Matisse uses the color craft of Gauguin and Paul Cézanne for his own decorative–expressive purpose. The composition is an essay in the contrast of warm and cool colors and curving and straight lines. Although the planes of the picture seem to resolve into a single, flat spread, directional lines and the variation in the strength of color suggest a front and back, but in a kind of contrived spatial ambiguity. Matisse himself tells us that his procedure is one of continuous adjustment of color to color, shape to shape, and color to shape until the exactly right "feel" is achieved and the painting is completed. He puts the matter of Expressionism very succinctly:

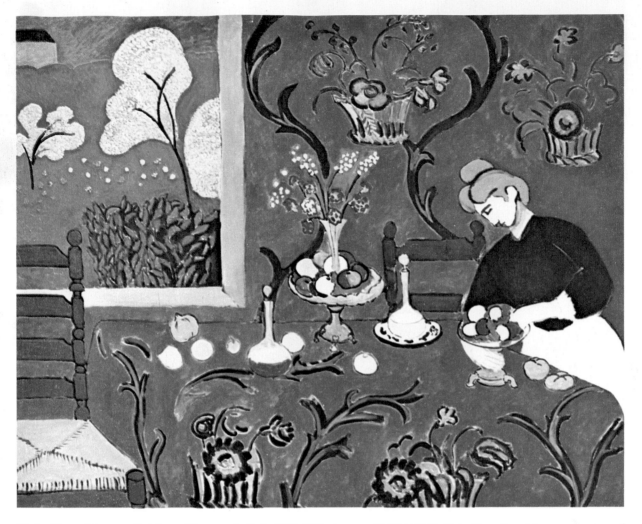

22-3　Henri Matisse, *Red Room (Harmony in Red)*, 1908–1909. Approx. 5′ 11″ × 8′ 1″. State Hermitage Museum, Leningrad.

What I am after, above all, is expression. . . . I am unable to distinguish between the feeling I have for life and my way of expressing it. . . . The whole arrangement of my picture is expressive . . . everything plays a part. Composition is the art of arranging in a decorative manner the various elements at the painter's disposal for the expression of his feelings. . . . All that is not useful in the picture is detrimental.*

This way of letting the picture "emerge" out of deep, even unconscious, feeling, letting one's artistic sensitivity and instinct be one's guide, is common in the practice not only of Expressionism but of modern art in general.

Much modern art is based on severely intellectual doctrines (frequently proclaimed in manifestos) and, to be enjoyed, may require some understanding of the artist's relation to contemporary currents of thought. Although Matisse intellectualizes painting, as his *Notes of a Painter* reveals, his art reflects a great love of nature, of color, and of joyous subjects. He

*In Robert Goldwater and Marco Treves, eds., *Artists on Art* (New York: Pantheon, 1945), pp. 409–10.

once observed that he did not care for weighty themes and moods and that art should be as restful as a comfortable chair after a hard day. For this reason, his art is sometimes disparaged as too decorative and lacking in profundity. But this is to overlook its very special and very French qualities, those that an early critic of Matisse expresses as "simplicity, serenity, and clarity." It is significant that these qualities, so evident in Classicism, are manifest in Matisse's subjects as well as his forms; he concerned himself almost exclusively with figure painting.

In a vein very different from that of Matisse, Georges Rouault (1871–1958) treats themes of grave social and religious import. His studies of sad clowns and broken prostitutes and his long series of religious paintings are Fauve in their simplified designs. They are constructed with black outlines like the leads in Medieval stained glass, which Rouault, who had worked as a glassmaker's apprentice in his youth, had always admired. These strongly effective black bar-like divisions and the somber tonalities he preferred—the glowing reds, greens, and midnight blues of stained glass—are harmonized in Rouault's

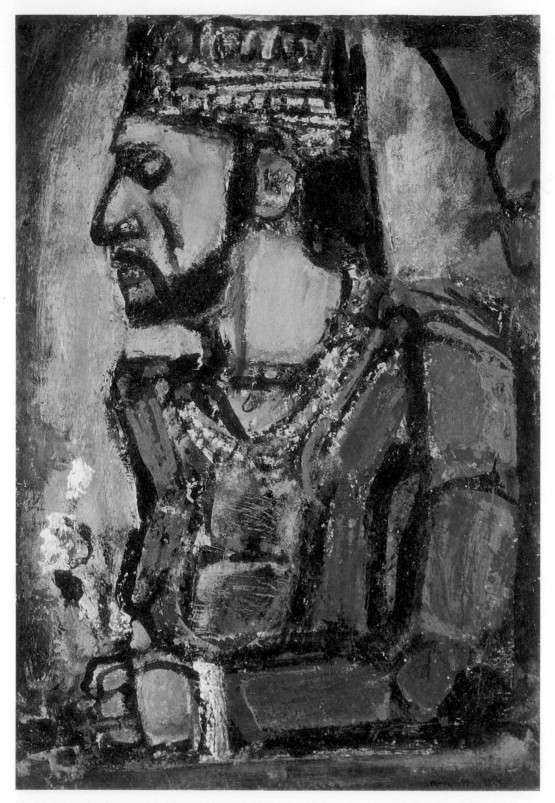

22-4   GEORGES ROUAULT, *The Old King*, 1916–1938. Approx. 30″ × 21″. Museum of Art, Carnegie Institute, Pittsburgh (Patrons Art Fund).

powerful evocation of *The Old King* (FIG. 22-4). The fierce aquiline features, dark complexion, and thick black hair and beard recall some ancient Assyrian despot in brooding reverie, almost an icon of absolute and pitiless authority. The sharp and rugged simplification of the forms and the harsh, hacked-out edges convey, with blunt force, an aspect of monarchic vengefulness.

The influence of the Fauves was almost immediately felt outside of France, coalescing with that of James Ensor (FIG. 21-75) and Edvard Munch (FIG. 21-76) in the German schools of the early twentieth cen-

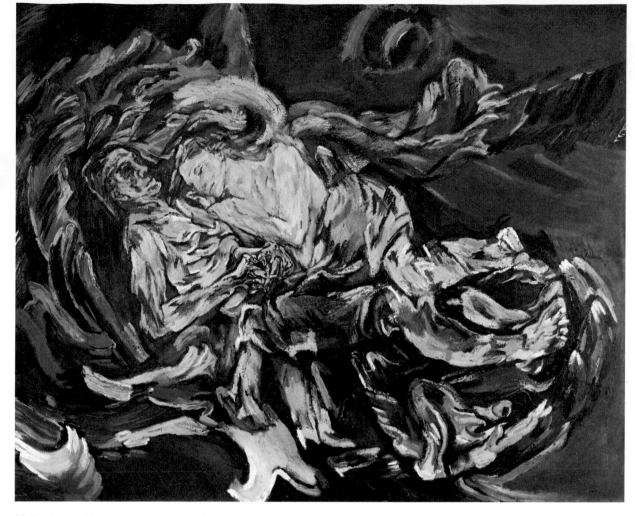

22-5   OSKAR KOKOSCHKA, *The Bride of the Wind*, 1914. 5' 11½" × 7' 2½". Kunstmuseum, Basel.

tury. Here, the element of immediate personal expression, especially characteristic of Fauve painting,
appealed to groups of German painters who had organized into movements: *Die Brücke* ("the Bridge,"
symbolizing the unity of nature and emotion) in
Dresden and *Der Blaue Reiter* ("the Blue Rider," after
a picture of that name by Vasily Kandinsky) in Munich. These painters carried the tendencies in the
work of Derain and Matisse even further. In Germany, there was less concentration than in France on
purely formal problems. German Expressionism was
a manifestation of subjective feeling toward objective
reality and the world of imagination. With bold, vigorous brushwork, emphatic lines, and bright color,
the German painters produced splendid, almost savagely powerful canvases, particularly expressive of
intense human feeling. A striking example is *The
Bride of the Wind* (FIG. 22-5) by OSKAR KOKOSCHKA
(1886–1980), a Viennese painter early influenced by
Klimt. The theme of the painting has its roots far back
in the peak of the Romantic period and (even farther
back) in the pathetic story of Paolo and Francesca told
by Dante in his *Inferno* (V, 73–142), although it may
also be Kokoschka's response to a poignant love af-

fair. Two lovers are swept by turbulent winds
through a nightmare landscape, neither they nor the
winds ever to be at rest. The anguish of love—its lac-
erating power, not its delight and ecstasy—is expressed in the violence of shredded contours, alternating cold and lurid color, and painfully agitated
brushwork. The painting is a passionate expression
of the state of two souls who embrace not in joy but in
unmitigated sorrow. Here, Kokoschka gives us a
clear instance of the transition from Symbolism to
Expressionism.

German Expressionism is in the direct line of descent from earlier German painting and engraving,
especially in its strong color, linear pattern, emphasis
on subject matter of a highly emotional character, and
frequent transcendental overtones. These elements
appear most effectively in the work of EMIL NOLDE
(1867–1956), and an especially good example is *St.
Mary of Egypt Among Sinners* (FIG. 22-6). Although he
learned much from the masks of Ensor and the color
of Matisse, Nolde's painting has an original force of
its own, reminiscent of Matthias Grünewald (FIG. 18-
35) and Hieronymus Bosch (FIG. 18-21) in its expressive violence. Mary, before her conversion, entertains

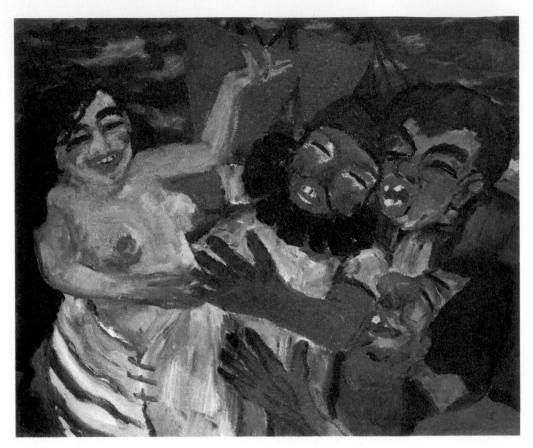

22-6   EMIL NOLDE, *St. Mary of Egypt Among Sinners*, 1912. Left panel of a triptych, approx. 34″ × 39″. Kunsthalle, Hamburg.

22-7   MAX BECKMANN, *Departure*, 1932–1935. Triptych, center panel 7′ ¾″ × 3′ 9⅜″. Museum of Modern Art, New York (given anonymously).

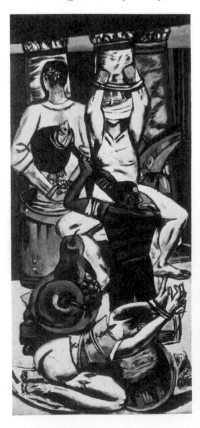

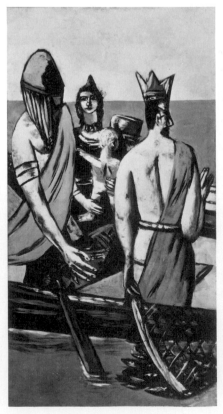

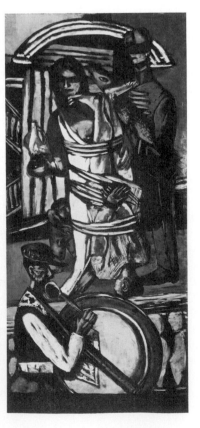

lechers whose brutal ugliness is magnified by their lust. The distortions of form and color (especially the jarring juxtapositions of red and green) work to the same end—an appalling tableau of subhuman and depraved passion in which evil wreaks its visible consequence in the repulsive faces and gestures.

MAX BECKMANN (1884–1950), an independent and forceful Expressionist, has left some of the most memorable works of the German schools. His art was elicited by some of the darkest moments of the twentieth century, when Nazi tyranny threatened European civilization. While his message is bitter, its reference is not specific to one time or place but concerns human cruelty and suffering in general. In perhaps his best-known painting, a triptych entitled *Departure* (FIG. 22-7), he organizes figures rendered in caricature-like distortion and simplification, their sculptural relief accentuated by hard, black line. In the left panel is a scene of torture prophetic of the death camps: a bound man stands in a barrel of water; another's hands have been severed; a trussed woman crouches in the foreground; the executioner wields his ax. The horror is continued in the right panel, partly staged as a mad carnival. In striking contrast, the central panel represents a royal family in calm daylight, the figures resigned and serene, departing the terrors of night in what may be an allusion to Beckmann's own flight from Nazi Germany after his work, along with that of most of the Expressionists, had been condemned and banned by Hitler as "degenerate." The hard, bright color, beautifully harmonized, carries in itself a large burden of the meaning.

Beckmann's visions of human disaster were shared by many artists of his generation who had witnessed at first hand the carnage of the battlefields of France and the shattered and corrupted society of postwar Germany. Sensitized by their experience, they often made works that were in an almost prophetic strain. *Punishment* (FIG. 22-8) by GEORGE GROSZ (1893–1959) is both a recollection of the destruction of Sodom and Gomorrah and a premonition of the apocalyptic obliteration of the world by bombs. A wildly free brush configures blazing explosions, thunderclouds of smoke, and the cascading debris of buildings in a furious image of man-made hell where no figure of man survives. Curiously, Grosz's picture is but a step from the total nonobjectivity of Kandinsky's *Improvisations* (FIG. 22-10), in which coherent images are lost in an apparent chaos of shape and color.

The emotional range of German Expressionism varies greatly—from the terror and indignation of artists like Nolde, Beckmann, and Grosz to the poignantly expressed pity for the poor in the moving prints of KÄTHE KOLLWITZ (1867–1945). The graphic art of Gauguin and Munch stimulated a revival of the print medium in Germany, especially the woodcut,

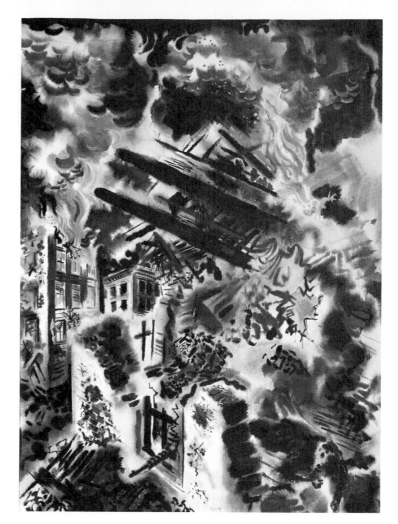

22-8 GEORGE GROSZ, *Punishment*, 1934. Watercolor, approx. 27½″ × 20½″. Museum of Modern Art, New York (gift of Mr. and Mrs. Erich Cohn).

and the forceful block prints cut in the days of the German Reformation proved inspiring models. The harsh, black, splintered lines of the woodblock print were ideal for the stark forms and blunt emphasis of message prized by the German Expressionists. In her *Memorial to Karl Liebknecht* (FIG. 22-9), Kollwitz produces a classic of the Expressionist print. The compo-

22-9 KÄTHE KOLLWITZ, *Memorial to Karl Liebknecht*, 1919. Woodcut. (Location unknown.)

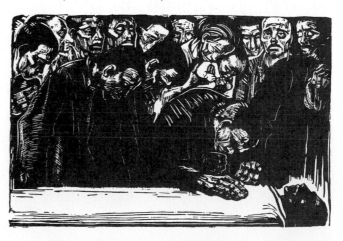

sition is both a masterful presentation of mute sorrow at the bier of a lost leader and a strong political protest. We have seen to what effective political use Honoré Daumier put the graphic medium. Regrettably, modern methods of reproduction have largely usurped the public role of the graphic arts.

The emphasis on color by the Fauves and the German Expressionists made it almost logical that color by itself, without any figurative material, could come to constitute the full "content" of a picture. In the Blue Rider group, the Russian painter VASILY KANDINSKY (1866–1944) carried his research into the emotional and psychological properties of color, line, and shape to the point that subject matter and even representational elements were entirely eliminated. Now that abstract art has become so much a part of our experience, we tend to forget the courage such a step required and the creative imagination needed to undertake such a completely new direction in the art of painting. By 1914, Kandinsky had perfected his methods and established, in two groups of works, two principal kinds of painting. He called one kind *Compositions*, the title for this group implying that

such arrangements of geometric shapes were consciously planned and intellectually ordered; on the other hand, in his *Improvisations* (an example of which is shown in FIG. 22-10), he approached the canvas with no preconceived theme but allowed the colors to come as they would, prompted by subconscious feelings. In these works, the brilliant colors flow across the canvas with as little conscious order or control as possible on the artist's part. In utilizing subconscious sensations, Kandinsky uncovered an area soon to be exploited by other artists, notably the Surrealists. Kandinsky describes his methods and the philosophical connotations of his art in his influential treatise *Concerning the Spiritual in Art* (1912),* in which he proclaims the independence of color and the spiritual value inherent in it. In Kandinsky's view, colors have deep-seated, psychic correlations and the artist's being is revealed in the prerational, utterly uninhibited expression of them. The "rational" world, given to ordinary vision, is hopelessly deceptive, and we must set aside reasoned "seeing" and planning so

*M.T. Saddler, trans., *Concerning the Spiritual in Art* (Mineola, N.Y.: Dover, 1977).

22-10 VASILY KANDINSKY, *Improvisation 28*, 1912. Approx. 44″ × 63¾″. Solomon R. Guggenheim Museum, New York.

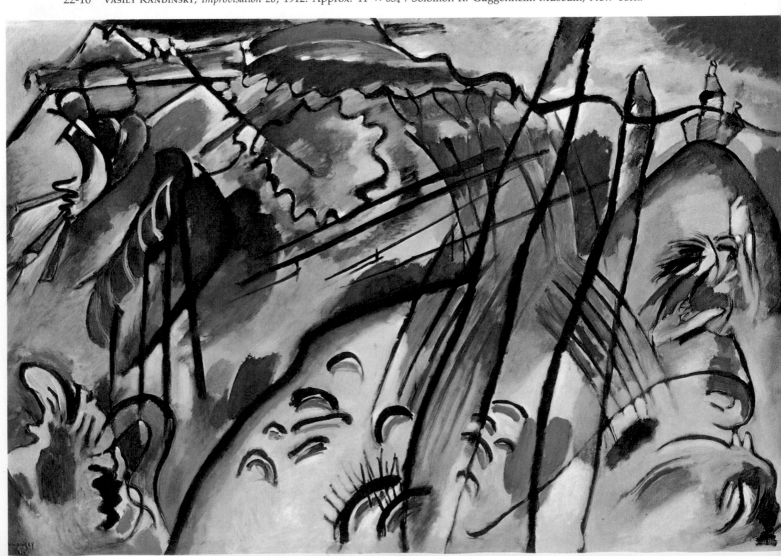

that the deeper reality of ourselves, living in the instinctual world of the subconscious, may rise into sight. This view harmonizes with Freud's conclusions concerning the subconscious and with Arthur Rimbaud's claim that the true artist is a visionary.

Cubism and Its Derivatives

Just as Expressionism, with its emphasis on subjective experience, can be traced back through all its branches to Van Gogh and Gauguin, so two other important currents in modern art—Cubism and Constructivism—can be shown to have vital connections with the Post-Impressionist, Paul Cézanne. Although Matisse and other members of the Fauve group were familiar with Cézanne's work, they admired it chiefly for the color and expressive linear distortions. Cézanne's death in 1906, the retrospective exhibition of his work (held the following year at the Salon d'Automne), and especially the publication by Émile Bernard that year of Cézanne's famous letter, in which he wrote of treating nature in terms of the cylinder, sphere, and cone, enabled the younger painters for the first time to recognize Cézanne's principal intention—to establish substantial forms within a space in which the actual properties of the two-dimensional picture surface and the illusionary effects of three dimensions are consciously and subtly adjusted. Beginning with Cézanne, this adjustment of new sensations of color and form to the physical medium became the common task.

This aspect of Cézanne's practice and theory became the chief concern of a group of younger French painters soon to be known as the Cubists. They drew encouragement from the remarkable personality and achievements of the Spanish painter Pablo Picasso (1881–1973), whose adult life was spent in France and whose works are inseparably connected with the history of modern French art. From his earliest studies in the Barcelona Academy of Art, Picasso showed precocious ability. At an age when others have learned only the rudiments of their art, Picasso had already mastered all aspects of late nineteenth-century Realist techniques. For one so greatly gifted, not only in manual dexterity but also in powers of pictorial visualization, there was no question of quietly following conventional methods of painting, and it is not surprising that Picasso investigated more than one aspect of picture-making. Even so, the public was ill prepared for the astonishing variety of his "styles" and "periods." Picasso is characteristic of the modern age in his constant experimentation, in his sudden shifts from one kind of painting to another, and in his startling innovations in painting and even sculpture. He is said to have been amused at the attempts of critics and historians to "explain" him and to follow the bewildering turns of his development. But it is a fact that his work over such a long lifetime manifested most of the significant modern trends in art that have prevailed from the beginning of the period through World War II.

When Picasso settled permanently in Paris in 1904, his work had evolved from the sober Realism of Spanish painting, through a brightening of color in an Impressionistic manner (for a while he was influenced by the early works of Toulouse-Lautrec), and into the so-called Blue Period (1901-1905), in which he painted worn, pathetic, alienated figures in the pessimistic mood of the *fin de siècle*—a "blue" mood conveyed, appropriately, in a predominantly blue tonality. Around 1905 or 1906, Picasso became aware almost simultaneously of the importance of the art of Cézanne, of the primitive art of Africa and Oceania, and especially of the sculpture of ancient Iberia. He detected in them a way of organizing formal elements that differed from anything in Western tradition—a way of giving them esthetic independence from pictorial Realism and a new and vivid value of their own. In *Portrait of Gertrude Stein* (FIG. 22-11), Picasso approximates Cézanne's method, carefully analyzing forms into simple planes, making contours strong and precise, and, particularly in the face, assuming different viewpoints, which makes for an ambiguous

22-11 PABLO PICASSO, *Portrait of Gertrude Stein*, 1906. 39⅜" × 32". Metropolitan Museum of Art, New York (bequest of Gertrude Stein, 1946).

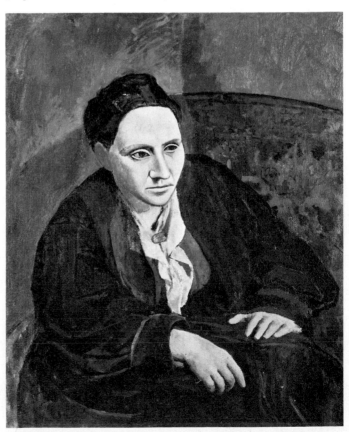

perspective. The two sides of the mask-like face do not fit; the near side reads almost as a profile (a favorite trick of Picasso's). This breaking-up of smoothly continuous volumes into separate but interlocking planes leads sharply away from Realism toward a concept of design independent of nature. African works like the mask shown in FIG. 14-53 must have given Picasso many a lead as to the direction his abstraction from nature could take. A painting that shows the painter well on the path of the reduction of visual fact to abstract form is the startling *Les Demoiselles d'Avignon* (FIG. 22-12), "Avignon" being the name of a street in Barcelona's red-light district. Instead of representing his figures as continuous volumes in motion, the volumes in *Les Demoiselles* are fractured and the jagged planes that result are slipping well beyond the bodies' contours. The images are disintegrating into their planes. Picasso takes this process, begun in the landscape and figures of Cézanne, to the threshold of a radically new kind of painting. Not only does he challenge the traditional concept of an orderly, constructed, unified pictorial space that mirrors the world, but he also dismisses the idea of the human figure as a dynamic unity and, especially in the two figures at the right, twists and breaks it into grotesque dislocations. Three of the heads are adaptations of African masks. Indeed, it was in the abrupt dislocations of African and Iberian sculpture, as well as in the art of Cézanne, that Picasso found a hint of how to dissect natural forms into their essential planes and volumes—a task that was to occupy him for the next few years.

By 1910, Picasso and his experimenting colleague Georges Braque had laid the basis for this new kind of painting, which was soon nicknamed "Cubism" by a critic who was amused by the approximately geometric forms in many of their works.* The name was soon accepted by the painters and their critics, but it suggests very little of the seriousness and originality of the Cubist achievement. Very simply, this consists of the discovery of a new kind of pictorial space, which replaces the one that had been developing since the time of Giotto. Like Cézanne's, this space is based on the principle of basic, simplified forms and a shifting point of view, but the viewpoint is expanded to the point that the Cubists present an object as if from several markedly different angles.

From the time of Masaccio, painting had been assumed to give, in one- or two-point perspective, a fixed and complete "view," in which everything in one plane appears simultaneously with everything

*At present, historians of twentieth-century art are crediting Braque with the first stylistic transformations that produced Cubism. By 1908, working directly from the principles of design found in the late paintings of Cézanne, Braque had produced work that led directly—almost logically—from Cézanne's premises to Cubism. Almost at once, Picasso perceived the importance of Braque's discovery, changed his own direction, and worked concordantly with Braque to develop the new style.

22-12   PABLO PICASSO, *Les Demoiselles d'Avignon*, 1907. 8′ × 7′ 8″. Museum of Modern Art, New York (bequest of Lillie P. Bliss).

22-13   PABLO PICASSO, *Accordionist*, 1911. Approx. 51″ × 35″. Solomon R. Guggenheim Museum, New York.

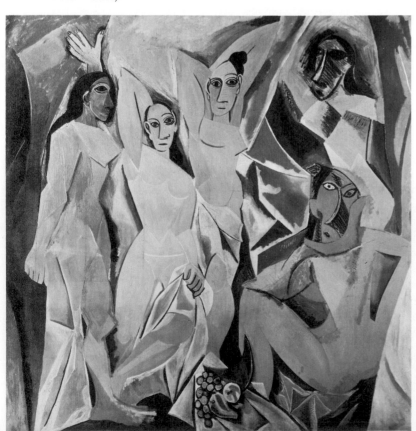

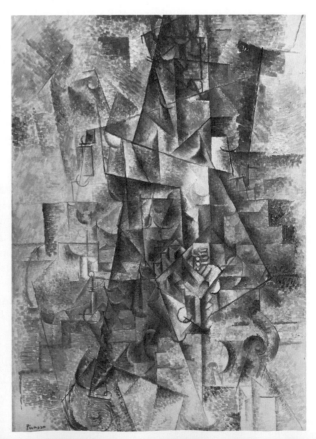

else. But this is neither true to visual fact (the fact of seeing the objects rendered) nor to the way we see the picture of these objects, our view of the picture being the result of a great number of eye movements that we make as we take it in. In essence, this is the basis of Cézanne's innovation with respect to a shifting viewpoint. The Cubists, however, go beyond this purely optical reason for using multiple viewpoints. They wish to present the total essential reality of forms in space, and because objects do not appear only as they are seen from one viewpoint at one time, it becomes necessary to introduce multiple angles of vision and simultaneous presentations of discontinuous planes. This, of course, shatters the old continuity of single-viewpoint composition imposed by the Renaissance. The Cubist painter believes that "in order to discover one true relationship it is necessary to sacrifice a thousand surface appearances."*

The concept of reality thus becomes separated from that of appearance, and the resemblance of essential form to ordinary vision is no longer important. The assumption, beginning in the Renaissance, that what we see in nature should find correspondence in the forms that the artist paints is given up, and the epoch that began with Giotto and Masaccio comes to an end in the twentieth century.

Cubism's break with the world of ordinary vision was not simply a matter of esthetic fashion, random experiment, or quixotic exhibitionism, although it has been denounced as all these things and worse: "Cubists," claimed the *New York Times* on the occasion of the 1913 Armory show in that city, "are making insanity pay." However, affinities of thought and imagination give a certain coherence to historical periods; seen within the context of the new Einsteinian vision of the physical world, the new art seems less strange. It has been said that Cubist pictorial space suggests the addition of the dimension of time to spatial dimensions, because objects are represented in temporal sequence, not as they are seen at any one moment. To perceive the many views of the object as given would require movement by the viewer (or at least the viewer's eyes) through some temporally sequential positions. In Einstein's description of the physical world, there is a similar merger of space and time. Time is "assimilated" to the three dimensions of space in such a way that measurements of space and time, especially when astronomical distances are involved, are functions of each other and are never independent. This is decisively different from the Baroque, Newtonian concept of space and time, where both are absolute and independent and where, no matter the distance between two events, it is possible for them to be simultaneous. By extension, simultaneous events presuppose a continuous space that is invariant with respect to them. But in the space–time of Einstein's relativity, it is impossible to prove that two physical events at an astronomical distance are actually simultaneous, because time elapses in the very process of their measurement.

Perspective space in Western painting since Masaccio assumes a continuous, unbroken space fixed from a single point of view. We can say of this rigid, geometric space that all the represented objects in it are *simultaneous*; the single *scene* constitutes a single *event*. Cubism, with its new kind of simultaneity—the simultaneity of different viewpoints—destroys consistency of image and appearance and replaces it with "abstract" form. This process is well begun in Picasso's *Les Demoiselles d'Avignon.*

Thus, the recognition and involvement of time in the very pictorial process destroys the structure of appearance constructed over centuries. It replaces appearances with the unlimited possibilities of form. No longer restricted to a single viewpoint, the artist may see any given object in the world not as a fixed appearance or shape, but as a universe of possible lines, planes, and colors. The world of appearance can be analyzed into a world of patterns that is open to endless exploration and adjustment. The shattering of the rigid Renaissance structure of appearance comes to be regarded as a means by which art can be returned to its fundamental functions.

Analysis of these functions is a process that gives its name to the earlier phase of Cubism—the "analytic" phase. A striking example of this style, Picasso's *Accordionist* (FIG. 22-13), is a construction of large, intersecting planes that suggests the forms of the man and his instrument. Hosts of smaller shapes—each probably a simplification of some aspect of the original subject—hover in and interpenetrate the large planes. The total effect is that of a new kind of pictorial reality. We are no longer obliged to contemplate merely a man playing an accordion; we can let our eyes set out on another kind of adventure as they probe the manifold aspects of an object that has been disintegrated, so to speak, and then reintegrated to offer us a great variety of views from different angles.

Picasso's experiments work a still more radical change in what can be called pictorial "reality." From 1908 on, he occasionally attached extraneous materials to the canvas in a technique called *collage*. In his *Still Life with Chair-Caning* (FIG. 22-14), Picasso combines an oilcloth replica of a caned chair seat with elements recovered from disintegrations of pictorial form such as we see in *Accordionist*. This produces a startling confrontation—or juxtaposition—of a commonplace, manufactured surface familiar in everyday experience and the painted abstract shapes. The composition not only introduces violent contrasts of texture but presupposes the painting surface in itself to

*Albert Gleizes and Jean Metzinger, "Cubism," in R.L. Herbert, *Modern Artists on Art* (Englewood Cliffs, N.J.: Prentice-Hall, 1964), p. 3.

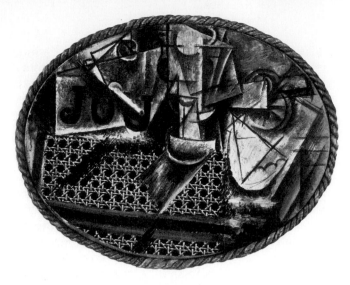

22-14 PABLO PICASSO, *Still Life with Chair-Caning*, 1911–1912. Oil and pasted paper simulating chair-caning on canvas, 10⅝″ × 13¾″. Musée Picasso, Paris.

serts that the painting is not a "picture," as it were, but a flat area that can receive almost any kind of application of apparently unrelated substances. Here, pictorial art takes a step toward becoming relief sculpture—an effect intensified by the rope frame. Collage has great importance for later Russian Constructivism and Dada, as well as for various movements today, in which there is a studied ambiguity in the relation of sculpture and painting. Picasso's and Braque's experiments with this new medium marked the end of the "analytic" phase of Cubism.

The premises of "analytic" Cubism are so rational, and the artists' application of their theories so intellectual and logical, that the styles of different painters in the "school" began to become almost indistinguishable. The similarity of the products of "analytic" Cubism became even more apparent when the artists, in their excessive concern with matters of pure form, began to neglect color, so that their paintings became almost monochrome. When the artists recognized this defect—and the fact that they had placed a stylistic straitjacket on themselves—"analytic" Cub-

be an object given to touch as well as sight, a plane surface on which materials other than paint can be placed. This texturing of the surface is new and as-

22-15 PABLO PICASSO, *Three Musicians*, 1921. Approx. 6′ 7″ × 7′ 3¾″. Museum of Modern Art, New York (Mrs. Simon Guggenheim Fund).

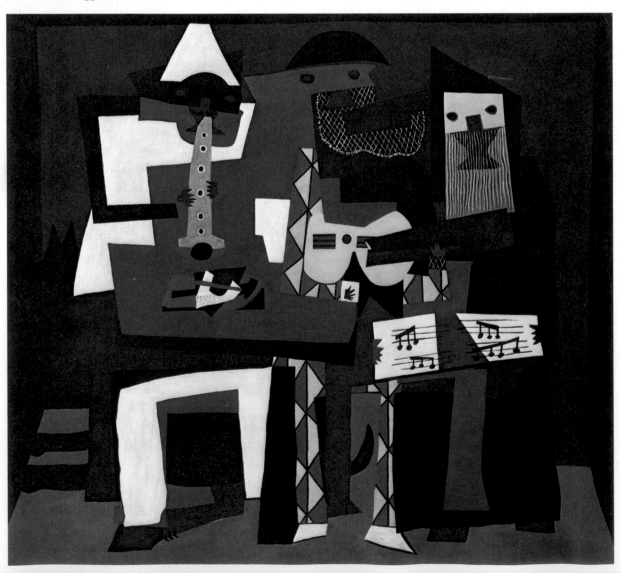

ism yielded to "synthetic" Cubism, which uses stronger colors and allows greater freedom of expression. Again, Picasso led the way by developing a style in which a more limited number of views of an object are selected for their decorative rather than their exclusively spatial significance. The mingling of forms became more spontaneous, their colors stronger, their textures more varied. In an early and superbly decorative example of this aspect of Picasso's work, *Three Musicians* (FIG. 22-15), the space is much flatter, scarcely deeper than a series of planes laid like playing cards one on another, as if different parts, the consequence of multiple views, have been reassembled before a single viewpoint. There is a strong tendency to reduce each form to a simple rectangular shape, but for all that, the figures of the clown, the Harlequin, and the monk, their instruments and music, and the table at which they are sitting can be detected without effort. The broken shapes, filled with flat, bright color against dark tonal variations, move with a syncopated rhythm and vivid dissonance analogous to those of modern music.

Although the development of Cubism must be considered one of Picasso's greatest achievements, he was never content to work for long in any one mode. While still painting "synthetic" Cubist pictures, he also made "Ingres-like" drawings and painted figure subjects in a broadly Realistic manner often influenced by Antique sculpture. In the late 1920s, he created, with heavy swirling lines and rich color, visual distortions that seemed related to contemporary Expressionism. The climax of this personal style came in

1937 in his large mural *Guernica* (FIG. 22-16), painted for the Spanish pavilion of the Paris International Exposition of that year to protest the bombing of the open town Guernica during the Spanish Civil War. In this allegorical presentation of the plight of his native country, where brute force seems momentarily triumphant, Picasso uses all the resources of his Cubist experience. The severe colors—the blacks, whites, and grays—emphasize the marvelously complex design of interpenetrating planes; unexpected and violent linear distortions communicate the horror of the event. In the figures of the dead warrior, the dying horse, and the bellowing bull, Picasso creates impressive and public symbols for the plight of his native country; in his own words, he expresses here an age of "brutality and darkness." The contention that modern forms of expression in art are unequal to the task of interpreting the humanistic values of modern society is contradicted by this painting, for in it Picasso sets forth in masterly terms an indictment of the evils of modern totalitarianism and his conviction that art is the most effective means of affirming the preeminent worth of individual human beings.

In contrast to Picasso's violence of form as well as of expression, GEORGES BRAQUE (1882–1963), the pioneer and master of Cubism per se, works in a more lyrical and even, one might say, more French manner. The rhythmic effect of *The Table* (FIG. 22-17) reveals his admiration for the great masters of French decorative painting; such a work, although entirely contemporary, would not be out of place in an eighteenth-century drawing room. Much of the effect of

22-16 PABLO PICASSO, *Guernica*, 1937. Mural, approx. 11′ 6″ × 25′ 8″. Museo del Prado, Madrid.

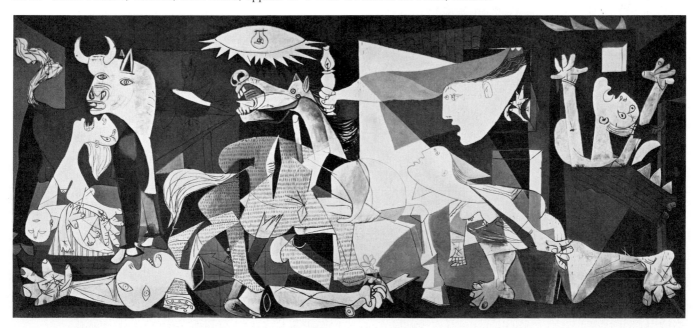

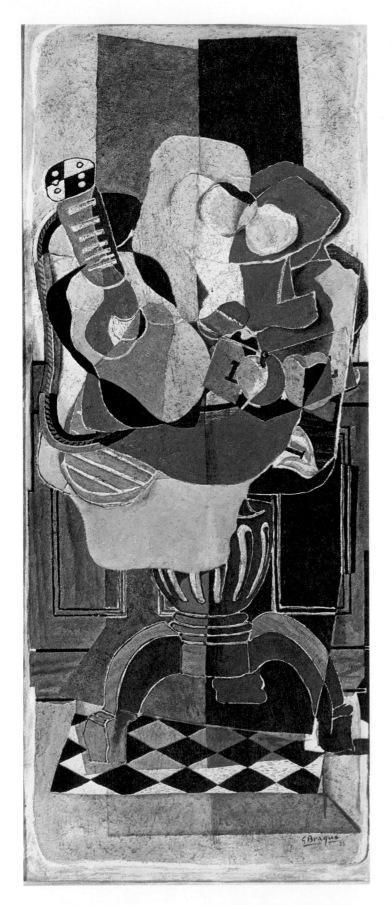

Braque's work depends on his mastery of two-dimensional design, for he maintained that a painting is a flat surface and should remain a flat surface, animated by line, color, and texture. He works within a narrow range of restrained but subtly related colors, often using grays and whites to advantage, with frequent unexpected passages of modulated textures. According to Braque:

> The aim of painting . . . is not to reconstruct an anecdotic fact, but to constitute a pictorial fact. . . . We must not imitate what we want to create. The aspect of things is not to be imitated, for the aspect of things is the result of them.*

FERNAND LÉGER (1881–1955) was a friend to and, in his approach to painting, derives from the original Cubists. His works have the sharp precision of the machine, the beauty and quality of which Léger was one of the first to discover. A modern composer, George Antheil, composed a score for a Léger film, *Ballet Méchanique;* it is significant that the work included the sound of an airplane engine. Léger is preeminently the painter of modern urban life, incorporating into his work the massive effects of modern posters and billboard advertisements, the harsh flashing of electric lights, the noise of traffic, the robot-like movements of mechanized people. An early work in which these effects appear—modulated, however, by the esthetic of "synthetic" Cubism—is *The City* (FIG. 22-18). Its monumental scale proves that Léger, had he been given the opportunity, would have been one of the great mural painters of our age. In a definitive way, he presents the mechanical commotion of the contemporary city.

Outside of France, Cubism received its most significant reception in the Italian school of Futurism, inaugurated in 1909 by the manifesto of the poet Filippo Marinetti. Enraptured by the machine age, Marinetti proclaimed a new art of "violence, energy, and boldness," which went along with an extreme dislike of all traditional art and an uncompromising demand for modernism. In the words of the Futurist Umberto Boccioni:

> We propose . . . to sweep from the field of art all motifs and subjects that have already been exploited . . . to destroy the cult of the past . . . to despise utterly every form of imitation . . . to extol every form of originality . . . to render and glorify the life of today, unceasingly and violently transformed by victorious science.†

In principle, the Futurist painters attempt to present aspects of modern mechanized society seen in

22-17 GEORGES BRAQUE, *The Table*, 1928. Approx. 70¾" × 28¾". Museum of Modern Art, New York (bequest of Lillie P. Bliss).

*In Maurice Raynal, *Modern French Painting,* trans. Ralph Roeder (New York: Brentano's, 1928), pp. 51–52.

†In Robert Goldwater and Marco Treves, eds., *Artists on Art* (New York: Pantheon, 1945), pp. 409–10.

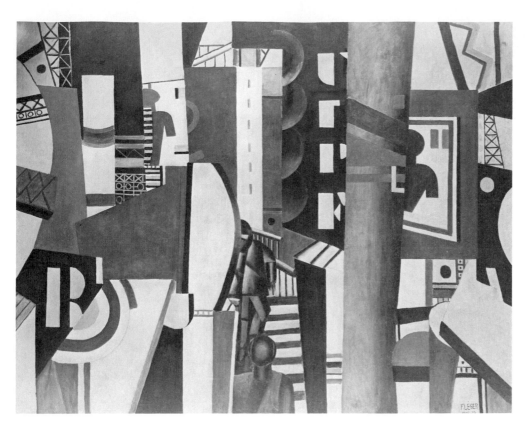

22-18 FERNAND LÉGER, *The City*, 1919. Approx. 7' 7" × 9' 9½". Philadelphia Museum of Art
(A.E. Gallatin Collection).

moments of violently energetic movement. In practice, they adopt the Cubist analysis of space; but by repetition of forms across the plane of the canvas, they attempt to impart movement to the static Cubist compositions. Movement and time obsessed the Futurists. Boccioni's manifesto of 1910 rings with a new recognition of universal process:

> Everything moves, everything runs, everything turns swiftly. The figure in front of us never is still, but ceaselessly appears and disappears. Owing to the persistence of images on the retina, objects in motion are multiplied and distorted, following one another like waves through space. Thus, a galloping horse has not four legs; it has twenty, and their movements are triangular.*

A method accommodating observations like these was devised from the example of photography by the French painter MARCEL DUCHAMP (1887–1968) in his *Nude Descending a Staircase #2* (FIG. 22-19). The effect is that of a closely spaced series of "still" photographs of an action, although Duchamp analyzed the figure first into planes in the manner of Cubism (which was natural enough, considering that Duchamp and his brother, the sculptor RAYMOND DUCHAMP-VILLON, experimented early with Cubist analysis, perhaps

*In Robert Goldwater and Marco Treves, eds., *Artists on Art* (New York: Pantheon, 1945), pp. 409–10.

even before Picasso and Braque). About this time, of course, the motion picture was being developed; this would give the illusion of movement not through the analysis of forms within a single framed space, but through the rapid (relative to the eye's ability to retain an image briefly) projection of a sequence of still photographs (or "frames") of an action. Futurism reaches the limits of the traditional static picture's ability to yield a visual impression of motion. The best Futuristic work is done in sculpture, notably that of Boccioni (FIG. 22-44).

It seems inevitable, once Cubism had broken the Renaissance structure of fixed appearance into a limitless world of forms, that the questions should repeatedly arise: How may these forms be recognized, invented, appropriated, arranged? Assuming the need for completely new principles of pictorial design (or restoration of the old, fundamental ones), how is this to be achieved? The many answers to these questions have produced the many schools and "isms" of modern art. Cubism had hardly made its crucial point when criticisms of it were voiced by artists who wanted to go beyond it to an even more abstract, "purer" formalism. The special effect of Cubist painting is found in the balance maintained between the appearance of the original object or figure, as the viewer may remember it, and the degree of abstraction with which it has been transformed into a work of art. That Cubist technique would almost inevitably

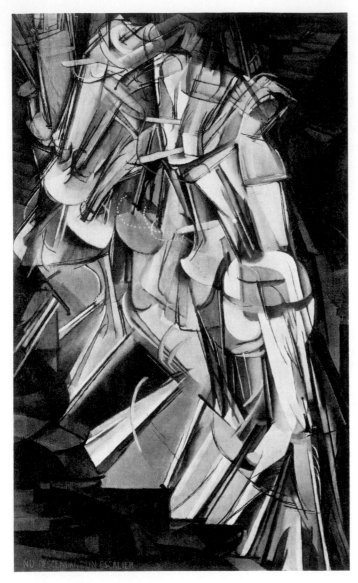

22-19 MARCEL DUCHAMP, *Nude Descending a Staircase #2*, 1912. Approx. 58″ × 35″. Philadelphia Museum of Art (Louise and Walter Arensberg Collection).

lead to a greater and finally to an absolute degree of abstraction is implicit in Juan Gris's remark:

> Cézanne turns a bottle into a cylinder, but I begin with a cylinder and create an individual of a special type: I make a bottle—a particular bottle—out of a cylinder. Cézanne tends towards architecture; I tend away from it. That is why I compose with abstractions (colors) and make my adjustments when these colors have assumed the form of objects.*

But what would happen if one started with the geometric shape and did not develop the resemblance, no matter how remote, to any actual object? Such was the proposal of the Dutch painter PIET MONDRIAN (1872–1944), who felt that "Cubism did not accept the

logical consequences of its own discoveries; it was not developing abstraction toward its ultimate goal, the expression of pure reality."

Mondrian himself, influenced by his most famous countryman, Van Gogh, began painting as an Expressionist. But after studying in Paris, just before World War I, he turned toward a stricter conception of pictorial design. When hostilities began, he was obliged to return to Holland, where he remained during the war, meditating on the theories of Cubist painting and continuing his own research into the absolute properties of artistic order. His investigations led him to renounce all representational elements and to concentrate on a severely limited vocabulary of colors and shapes: black, white, and the primaries (red, yellow, and blue) and straight lines, squares, and rectangles. With these elements, Mondrian constructed two-dimensional designs arranged in such subtle asymmetrical balances of line, color, and area that even slight changes destroy the composition. His rectilinear purism is closely related to the architecture of the De Stijl movement (a group of Dutch artists, essentially disciples of Mondrian), as is evident in Gerrit Rietveldt's Schroeder House in Utrecht (FIG. 22-60). In his *Composition in Blue, Yellow, and Black* (FIG. 22-20), Mondrian has adjusted the design so carefully that no single portion of the surface is more important than any other; the tension between the rectangles is maintained to the very edges. The power of the colors to hold the viewer's attention is subtly equivalent to the attraction exercised by the much larger blank areas, and the proportions of each of these areas are cunningly varied to avoid a mechanical uniformity of the general equilibrium. Mondrian held the firm belief that

> true reality is attained through dynamic movement in equilibrium. Plastic art affirms that equilibrium can only be established through the balance of unequal but equivalent oppositions. The clarification of equilibrium through plastic art is of great importance for humanity. . . . It is the task of art to express a clear vision of reality.*

To compare Mondrian with the Kandinsky of the *Improvisations* (FIG. 22-10) is to become aware of the range of experimentation within which the search for a new basis for the arts of design took place (although it must be acknowledged that Kandinsky's *Compositions* have much of the "hard-edge" quality of Mondrian's work).

The resources of abstraction opened up by Cubism could be drawn on by artists not directly influenced by it. The American painter GEORGIA O'KEEFFE (b. 1887), in place of reductive analysis of form into frac-

---

*In D.H. Kahnweiler, *Juan Gris, His Life and Work,* trans. Douglas Cooper (New York: Valentin, 1947), p. 138.

*Piet Mondrian, *Plastic Art and Pure Plastic Art* (New York: Wittenborn, 1951), p. 10.

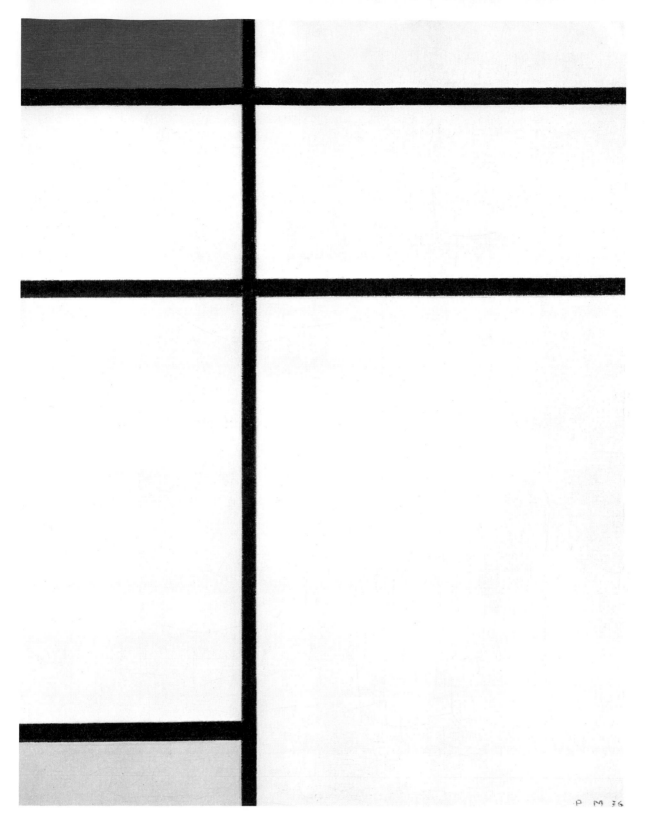

22-20 PIET MONDRIAN, *Composition in Blue, Yellow, and Black*, 1936. Approx. 17″ × 13″. Kunstmuseum, Basel (Emmanuel Hoffman-Stiftung).

tured shapes, gives us, in *Jack-in-the-Pulpit IV* (FIG. 22-21), an expanded, sharply focused close-up view of the handsome plant. Exhibiting the natural flow of curved plane and contour, she takes the abstraction almost to the limit of the flower's identity; it might, at first sight, be something exfoliating on some unknown planet or in the cellular world of our bodies. The fluid planes unfold like undulant petals from a subtly placed axis—the white, jet-like streak—in a vision of the slow, controlled motion of growing life.

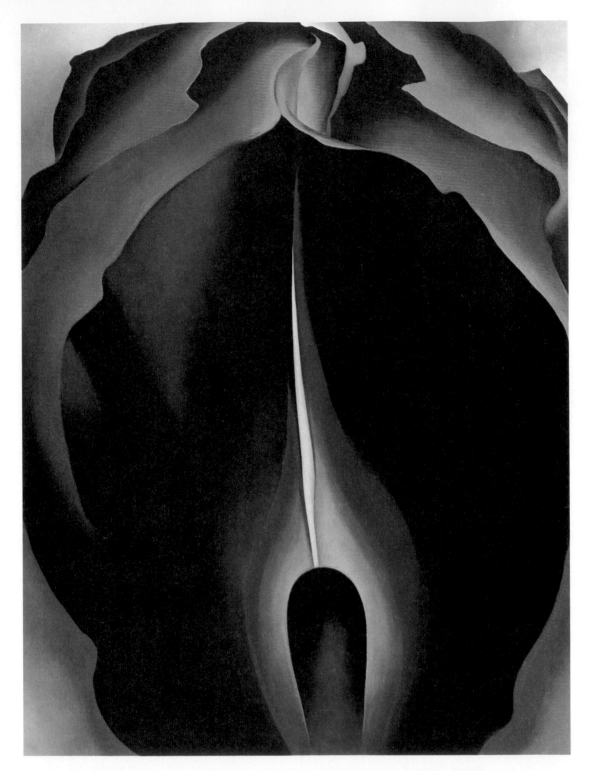

22-21 GEORGIA O'KEEFFE, *Jack-in-the-Pulpit IV*, 1930. 40″ × 30″. Collection of Georgia O'Keeffe.

O'Keeffe's painting, in its graceful, quiet poetry, reveals the organic reality of the object by abstracting and strengthening its characteristic forms, in striking contrast with either Kandinsky's explosions or Mondrian's rectilinear absolutes.

In Russia, the influence of Cubist painting led to a somewhat similar concern with basic design elements. Before 1914, Cubist and even Futurist paintings were exhibited in Moscow and St. Petersburg, and Russian artists of the younger generation were anxious to contribute to the modern movement. KASIMIR MALEVICH (1878–1935), after working in the Cubist and Futurist manners, created what he called Suprematist paintings, in which his intention was the expression of nonobjectivity—a form of expression removed as far as possible from the world of natural forms. In this way, he arrived at what he calls "the supremacy of pure feeling or perception," for "the essential thing [in pictorial art] is feeling—in itself and completely independent of the context in which

22-22 KASIMIR MALEVICH, *Suprematist Composition: White on White*, c. 1918. Approx. 31¼″ × 31¼″. Museum of Modern Art, New York.

it has been evoked." The most nonobjective of Malevich's works is his famous *Suprematist Composition: White on White* (FIG. 22-22). Here, color, shape, and line are reduced to the elements of an off-white square superimposed on a larger off-white square. The two shapes are differentiated only by their size, their angle of inclination, and slight modulations in texture and "color" (one is cool in tone; one, warm).

The other important movement descending, with Cubism, from Cézanne's "geometric" view of nature is Constructivism. Its principles, as stated by the Russian artist Antoine Pevsner and his brother, Naum Gabo (see p. 923), are manifested in painting by a lithe austerity of line and a formal geometricity. Pevsner's belief that art must express contemporary culture led to the use of "modern" materials (sheet metal, plastics, wire), which were particularly suited to the expression of the dynamic character of the emerging industrial culture of the time. Constructivist artists strove for an effect of interpenetration and simultaneity, which was more readily achieved in "constructions" and sculpture. Emotion—apart from a purely esthetic one—was largely secondary in their work.

Dada to Surrealism

The purist artists, Constructivist and Suprematist, tried to create a new art of clarity and order; elsewhere other attitudes toward the times led to a basically destructive artistic expression. In several places and at nearly the same time—in Zurich, Barcelona, and New York in 1916 and 1917—a number of artists independently stated their disgust with the war and life in general by making works of nonart. This movement was early christened Dada, a nonsense or baby-talk term indicative of the conviction that European culture had lost any real meaning. Those who professed to respect the art of the past had been unable

to prevent the outbreak of the holocaust and were now eagerly destroying one another. The artists, refugees from the war, set out in their bitterness to mock all the values of what they believed to be a culture gone mad. "Dada," said one of its historians, "was born from what it hated." Because the Dadaists' intentions were fundamentally nihilistic, Dada works are difficult to interpret and are best approached with their creators' avowed spirit of nonart, or even antiart, in mind: "Dada is against everything, even Dada"—that is, against all that has become organized and formalized. In this sense, the works may be considered destructive criticisms of artistic expression of the present and recent past. Such a critical attitude appears in Duchamp's famous photograph of the *Mona Lisa*, on which he drew a mustache as if defacing a billboard. The public was shocked—as Duchamp intended it to be—and interpreted the defacement as an outrage on the *Mona Lisa* itself. However, we can now see that Duchamp's intention was rather an indirect and witty attack on those he felt had betrayed the Humanistic ideals of the Renaissance, of which the *Mona Lisa* remains one of the noblest expressions. Modern artists did not escape; in 1920, a Dadaist, FRANCIS PICABIA, exhibited a toy monkey nailed to a door and called it *Portrait of Cézanne*. After 1918, Dada spread quickly through Europe, especially France and Germany, where it appealed to the respective national moods of disillusion in the Pyrrhic victory and despair in defeat.

Since the Dadaists claimed that they were not creating art, it is perhaps unfair to examine their works in a critical spirit. Nevertheless, certain positive contributions emerged from their intentionally negative attitude. Among these are the collage compositions by the German artist KURT SCHWITTERS (1887–1948), which he called by the meaningless name of *Merz Pictures*. Although put together from the contents of the gutter and the trash basket (*merz*, a syllable of the German word for "commercial," caught Schwitters' fancy while he was cutting the word into pieces), the *Merz Pictures* always show Schwitters' sensitivity to texture and design (FIG. 22-23). The typical Dada disdain for conventional techniques accounts for the materials used, but truly artistic feeling for color and form endows these works with appeal beyond their historical significance.

In Duchamp, whom we have already seen as a Futurist, the Dada movement found its most provocative and witty champion, as well as its most eloquent philosopher. Duchamp's philosophy and influence continued in the 1970s and 1980s until he has become almost a legend among younger artists. Dada, according to Duchamp, was "a metaphysical attitude . . . a sort of nihilism . . . a way to get out of a state of mind—to avoid being influenced by one's immediate environment, or by the past: to get away from *clichés*—

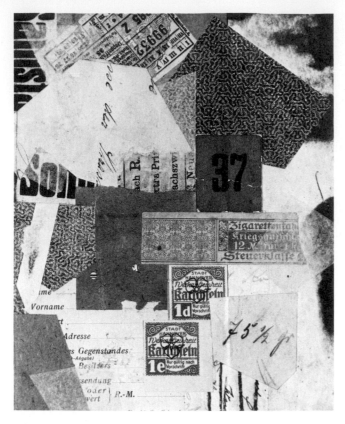

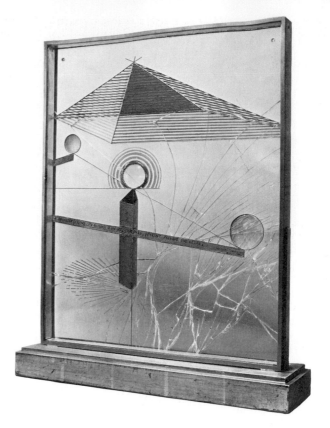

22-23 KURT SCHWITTERS, *Merz Picture 19*, 1920. Collage, approx. 7¼″ × 5⅝″. Yale University Art Gallery, New Haven, Connecticut (Collection, Société Anonyme).

22-24 MARCEL DUCHAMP, *To be looked at (from the other side of the glass), with one eye, close to, for almost an hour*, 1918. Framed double-glass panel, with oil paint, collage of paper, lens, etc., 20⅛″ high, 16⅝″ wide, 1⅜″ deep. Museum of Modern Art, New York (bequest of Katherine S. Dreier).

to get free.'' This escape from conventional forms and modes of expression can be seen in Duchamp's glass constructions. Unlike the painting and sculpture of the Russian Constructivists, who had a proud sense of public responsibility, Duchamp's painted glass is his own private jest about the world and art. And if its meaning is inseparable from its nonmeaning—as in the title of *To be looked at (from the other side of the glass), with one eye, close to, for almost an hour* (FIG. 22-24)—at least we can admire the perfection with which he has designed and painted the geometric shapes in such irrational perspective on the sheet of plate glass. Not the least perplexing aspect of Duchamp's work is his scrupulous regard for craftsmanship combined with apparently quite irrelevant subject matter. When, at a later date, this and other glass objects by Duchamp were accidentally cracked, Duchamp insisted that the unexpected pattern of fractures completed his original design.

Although much Dada work is intentionally ephemeral (the movement came to a sudden end in 1922), it has important consequences for later art—reinforcing a trend away from the reasoned, formal aim and cool disciplinary requirements of Cubism and abstract art toward a spontaneous, intuitive expression of the whimsical, fantastic, humorous, sardonic, and absurd. Those aspects of experience, expressed in earlier art, were neglected by Cubism and Constructivism. Now a whole new realm of artistic possibility opens, in which the remnants of the optical world,

shattered by compositional analysis, can return in whole and in part to play new, expressive roles. Without the demand that they function in exactly the old context, perspective and chiaroscuro reappear, and their purposes are entirely at the command of the artist. The artist's free imagination now draws on materials lying deep in his consciousness, and his act of expression is the proclamation of new realities that are no less real because they are psychic. In the psychoanalytic view of Freud and others, developing contemporaneously, art is a powerfully practical means of self-revelation and catharsis, and the images that rise out of the subconscious have a truth of their own that is independent of the world of conventional vision. Dreaming fancy demands its own stage and its own means of production in the new, fantastic painting that arises almost at the same time as Cubism but that diverges from it. The historical past as well as the dynamic present can provide inspiration. In the early work of the Greco–Italian painter GIORGIO DE CHIRICO (1888–1978), the squares and palaces of Roman and Renaissance Italy are visualized in a mood of intense and mysterious melancholy. In *The Delights of a Poet* (FIG. 22-25), De Chirico gives us a strange, tilted perspective of a street with arcades, a fountain, a wraith, a distant train, a clock, a blank sky. The hard light fills the emptiness with sharp shadows; there is a foreboding sense of depar-

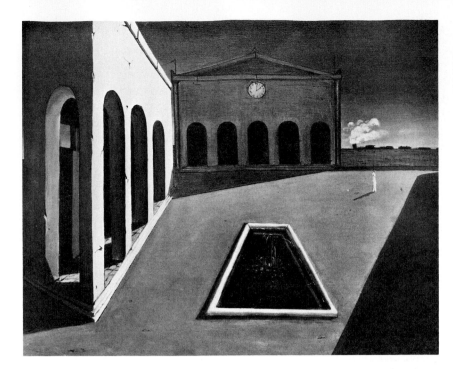

22-25 GIORGIO DE CHIRICO, *The Delights of a Poet*, c. 1913. Approx. 27⅞″ × 34″. Collection of Helen and Leonard Yaseen, New York.

ture and of a time long past yet always present, as in T. S. Eliot's "The Hollow Men":

In death's dream kingdom

. . . .

There, the eyes are
Sunlight on a broken column
There, is a tree swinging
And voices are
in the wind's singing
More distant and more solemn
Than a fading star.

Delights is not only visually disturbing, with its sharp inclinations of space and shadow, but so philosophically puzzling that De Chirico's works between 1911 and 1919 are considered to belong to the short-lived school of the *pittura metafisica* in modern Italian art. De Chirico himself has supplied some evidence for a philosophical interpretation by remarking that he was inspired to paint such architectural scenes by Nietzsche's poetic interpretation of autumn afternoons in northern Italian cities. Although such "metaphysical painting" does not, strictly speaking, introduce supernatural elements, it does communicate a feeling of reality very different from our ordinary experience. For this reason, De Chirico is considered to have been a source of inspiration for those artists who created the Surrealist movement in the early 1920s.

The Surrealists' intention is to discover and explore the "more real than real world behind the real"—in other words, the world of psychic experience as revealed by psychoanalytic research, especially that of Freud. In 1924, in his *Surrealist Manifesto*, the French poet André Breton formulated this intention to resolve "conscious" and "subconscious" reality into a new and absolute reality—a superreality (*surréalité*)—

and so "to reestablish man as psychology instead of anatomy." Thus, the dominant motivation of Surrealist painting and construction is to bring together into a single composition aspects of outer and inner "reality," in much the same way that seemingly unrelated fragments of life combine in the vivid world of dreams. The projection in visible form of this new conception required new techniques of pictorial construction. At first, the Surrealists adopted some Dadaist devices, but with new purposes. They used automatic writing and various types of planned "accidents" not so much to reveal a world without meaning as to provoke reactions closely related to subconscious experience. And as Surrealism appeared so soon after the formulations of the principles of abstract and nonobjective art,* the techniques of the latter and even some of its adherents were enlisted in the cause.

Originally a Dada activist in Cologne, MAX ERNST (1891–1976), became one of the early adherents of the Surrealist circle around André Breton, the formulator of the manifesto of Surrealism. The chance association of things and events, the dislocation of images and meanings, the scrambling of conventional contexts, the exploration of the subconscious, the radical freedom of artistic choice, which together make up the creative bases of Surrealism, are all manifest in Ernst's *Two Children Are Threatened by a Nightingale* (page 802 and FIG. 22-26). The heavy frame and the house and gate in actual relief give a concreteness to the dream-like vision while forcing a shock of contrast between representation and the actual. Ernst

---

*An *abstract* work has been "abstracted" from natural appearance, and vestiges of figures or objects may still be detected in it, as in Cubist paintings. A *nonobjective* work has no reference, in conception or execution, to natural appearance, as in the later paintings of Kandinsky and Mondrian.

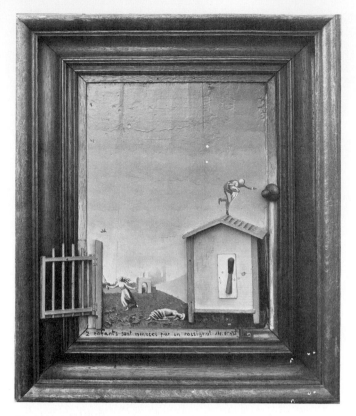

22-26 MAX ERNST, *Two Children Are Threatened by a Nightingale*, 1924. Oil on wood with wood construction, 27½" high, 22½" wide, 4½" deep. Museum of Modern Art, New York (purchase).

himself writes revealingly of the Surrealist artist's management of subject matter: ''He never imposes a title on a painting. He waits until a title imposes itself.

Here however the title existed *before* the picture was painted.'' A line from an earlier poem written by the artist provided the title. Its subject found, the picture simply happened. In Ernst's later work, he experimented with the texture of the picture surface, leaving surface effects much to the laws of chance. His procedures were widely adopted and influential.

Loosely related or allied to Surrealism, the abstract paintings of Spaniard JOAN MIRÓ (1893–1983) incorporate aspects of organic imagery that lend them a weird and disturbing humor. Intensive work in collage in various mediums led Miró to a greater simplification of shapes, with stress on curved lines and amoeba-like organisms that seem to float in an immaterial space. In *Painting* (FIG. 22-27), black shapes— solid or in outline and with dramatic accents of white and vermilion—appear against a dark background of closely related reds, blues, and greens. These elements give the canvas, which is quite large, a handsome, decorative quality. Several figures are recognizable, including a dog and an ox. But as Miró often attempted to work automatically, moving his brush over the surface with as little direction as possible from his conscious mind (as in automatic writing), he himself could not always explain the meanings of his pictures. They are, in the truest sense, spontaneous and intuitive expressions of the little-understood, submerged, unconscious life.

A new interest in subject matter was perhaps the most important contribution of the Surrealists to modern painting. Miró has said:

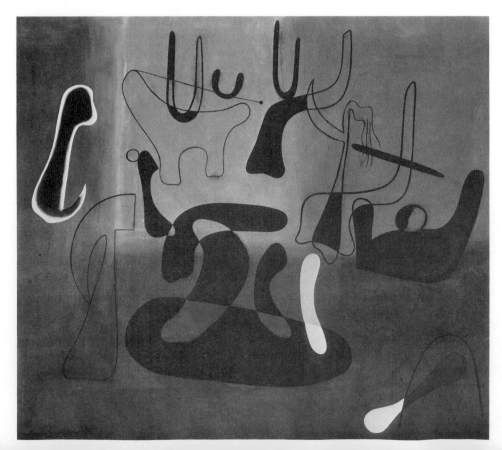

22-27 JOAN MIRÓ, *Painting*, 1933. Approx. 5' 8½" × 6' 5¼". Museum of Modern Art, New York (gift of the Advisory Committee).

I am attaching more and more importance to the subject matter of my work. To me it seems vital that a rich and robust theme should be present to give the spectator an immediate blow between the eyes before a second thought can intervene. In this way, poetry pictorially expressed speaks its own language.*

It is important to note that the title announcing the subject matter often plays an important role in modern art. Most often, it is ambiguous and seems to have little relation to what the spectator sees; there may be an apparent conflict between it and the picture's meaning, which the spectator must struggle to resolve. Indeed, this sense of contradiction of title and picture is like an "immediate blow between the eyes," and the spectator is knocked off balance, expectations defeated and preconceptions challenged. Much of the impact of a work of modern art begins with the viewer's sudden intuition of the incongruous and the absurd.

Nowhere is the tension of divergent title and image so evident as in Surrealist works using dream imagery. Of all forms of nonconscious experience, dream imagery is the most common and the most vivid, but its presentation requires more than a mastery of abstract design. To project the world of dreams as convincingly as possible, the Catalan painter SALVADOR DALI (b. 1904) restudied the masters of seventeenth-century realism, especially the Dutch masters of genre. As, in dreams, objects and situations collide and interpenetrate in ceaseless metamorphoses, Dali uses multiple images of multiple symbolic meanings to suggest evocations from his subconscious. He has also developed a fundamental

*In James T. Soby, *Joan Miró* (New York: Museum of Modern Art, 1959), p. 13.

Surrealist method—the juxtaposition of seemingly irrelevant and certainly unrelated objects in unexpected situations. This method was suggested to the Surrealists by a metaphor originated by one of their spiritual predecessors, the somewhat obscure nineteenth-century French poet Isidore Ducasse (known as the Comte de Lautréamont), who, in his *Maldoror*, speaks of a situation as "beautiful as the encounter of an umbrella and a sewing machine on a dissecting table." The surprise effect of Dali's work depends on his presentation of such incongruities in a meticulous, miniature-like technique.

All of these aspects of Dali's style can be seen in perhaps his most familiar work, *The Persistence of Memory* (FIG. 22-28). Here, he creates his most haunting allegory of empty space in which time is at an end. The barren landscape, without horizon, drifts to infinity, lit by some eerie, never-setting sun. An amorphous creature sleeps in the foreground, draped with a limp watch. Another such watch hangs from the branch of a dead tree; yet another hangs half over the edge of a rectangular form. The watches are visited by ants and a fly, as if they were decaying, organic life, soft and viscous. Here is the impact of contradiction at its sharpest. The watch—a metallic, intricate, and precise instrument—is metamorphosed into an object devourable by busy ants. We recognize the impossible landscape and its impossible contents as perfectly possible in the dream world.

In painting dream images, the artist is handicapped by the fact that each dream is the experience of a single individual and depends for its meaning on the events in the private life of that one person; the clearer and more detailed its description, the less likely that it will be comprehensible to others. Thus, Surrealist art almost inevitably presents feelings so

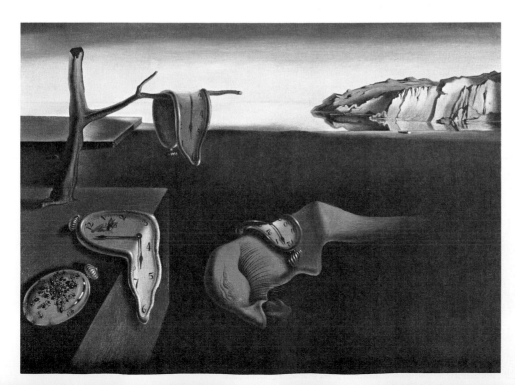

22-28 SALVADOR DALI, *The Persistence of Memory*, 1931. 9½" × 13". Museum of Modern Art, New York (given anonymously).

private that communication with an audience of any appreciable size is difficult, if not impossible, except when the artist, through the choice of familiar symbols, describes experiences common to groups of people. Such a broadened use of symbol and fantasy occurs in the work of MARC CHAGALL (1887–1985), who was born in Russia and studied and worked in Paris, Berlin, and New York. Although he accepted many aspects of the most sophisticated theories and practices of the times—Expressionism, Cubism, Fauvist color—Chagall never forgot his early life in an obscure Russian village. Themes from his childhood return as if in dreams and memories. Some, gay and fanciful, suggest the simpler pleasures of folk life; others, somber and even tragic, recall the trials and persecutions of the Jewish people. In his *Crucifixion* (FIG. 22-29), the terror of wars and pogroms is suggested by the pitiful little figures and the village in the background, while resignation and hope are expressed in the flying angel, the Torah scroll, and the rabbi–Christ figure on the cross. The work is a moving portrayal of the artist's feeling that faith is important in a world of war and brutality. Although the very free, floating composition—with unexpected juxtapositions of the actual and the unearthly—is Surrealist in the sense that it perpetuates the fantastic content of a dream, the individual symbols refer to much more than Chagall's personal psychic life. A

comparison of Chagall's interpretation of war with Picasso's (FIG. 22-16) illuminates the broad scale of expressive emotion on which art can play.

The most subtle and one of the most influential of all the masters of fantasy was the German–Swiss artist PAUL KLEE (1879–1940). In his contempt for illusionistic art, which (as a member of the Blue Rider School) he believed to be superseded, he turned to the art of children and primitives for a new kind of brevity, simplicity, and primeval significance unknown to civilized conventions and rational modes of thought. With this inspiration, Klee was able to make, in exquisite line and color, pictorial records of his own sensitive and perceptive reaction to the modern world. His wry whimsy uses strangely delineated figures of men, animals, and fantastic creatures as commentary on human weakness and folly, but his tone is almost always gentle and his irony subdued. Although his paintings and drawings are usually very small and seem at first to be the most private of visual communications, they are charged with meaning that gradually becomes clearer to the imaginative spectator. His *Twittering Machine* (FIG. 22-30), in its title and execution, at first compels a smile. Primitive, flimsy bird "mechanisms" stand on or are attached to an equally flimsy crankshaft. We assume that the shaft can be turned and that, when it is, the "birds" twitter. Here, most effectively, is the cooperative tension of title and design. We do not usually think of machines and birds in association, or of machines as ludicrous, hand-driven works made of bent picture wire. Out of these forced associations and distortions, a new entity seems to emerge that slyly spoofs

22-29 MARC CHAGALL, *Crucifixion*, 1943. 55⅛″ × 39¾″. Collection of the artist, Pierre Matisse Gallery, New York.

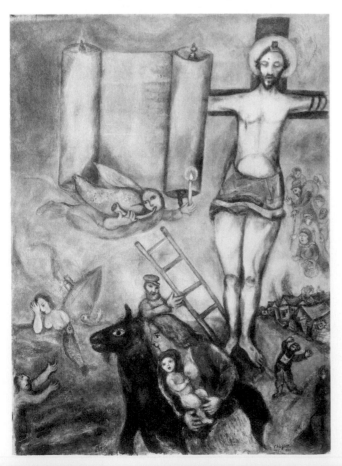

22-30 PAUL KLEE, *Twittering Machine*, 1922. Watercolor and pen and ink, approx. 16¼″ × 12″. Museum of Modern Art, New York (purchase).

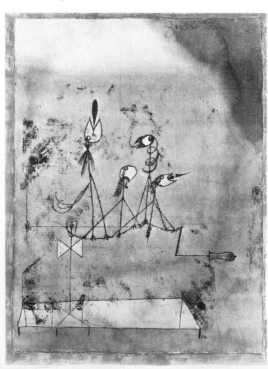

the "machine age"; although the device "works," it has no real purpose, unless it is to twitter, and birds do this much better. It has recently been suggested that the sly humor of the work may conceal a mordant comment on man's mortality. The heads of the creatures, each carefully distinguished as one of the four temperaments, resemble metallic lures capable of trapping real birds. Below them is a rectangular trough on short legs—perhaps a death trap. The lures and death trap could symbolize the entrapment of all of us by existence. Perhaps no other artist of the twentieth century matches the subtlety of Klee as he adroitly plays with sense, making an artistic means of ambiguity and understatement.

Klee shared the widespread modern apprehension concerning the rationalism behind a technological civilization that could be as destructive as it was constructive. As do some psychologists, he sought clues to man's deeper nature in primitive shapes and symbols. Like his compatriot, the psychologist Carl Jung, Klee seems to have accepted the existence of a collective unconscious that reveals itself in archaic signs and patterns going back to prehistoric times and is everywhere evident in the art of primitive peoples. His *Death and Fire* (FIG. 22-31) manifests his interest in the ideogram—the simple, picture-like sign filled with implicit meaning. A white death's-head, heavily outlined, dominates the work and seems to rise toward a glowing sun. A figure moving left is preceded by three bars of color. The features of the skull could be letters perhaps *tod* ("death"). It has been suggested that the pale green, so definitely harmonized

22-31 PAUL KLEE, *Death and Fire*, 1940. Approx. 18″ × 17″. Paul Klee-Stiftung, Bern.

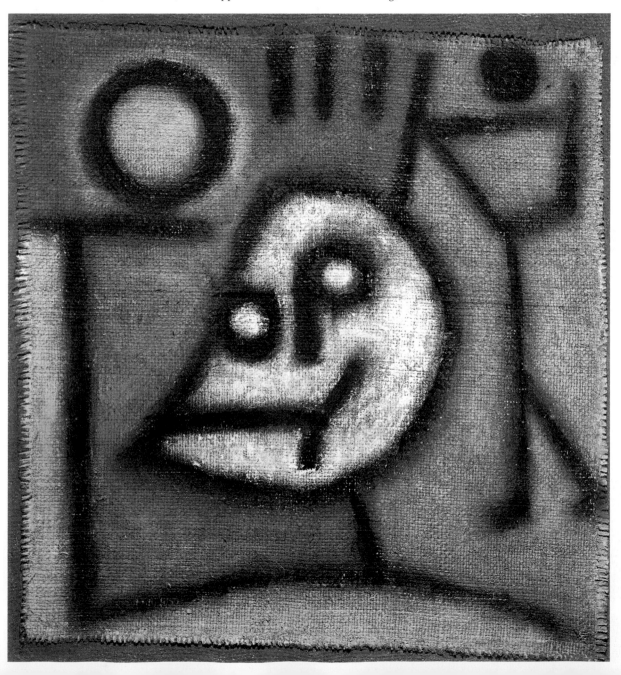

with the chords of red, could suggest the element of water reconciled with fire in the ever-changing alternation of life and death. The eerie color, the primitive starkness of the images, and the mysterious arrangement convey an almost religious sense of awe, as if one were in the presence of a totem having magical powers. Enigmatic as the subject is, we feel its sources in the religious experience—an experience probably as old as human history.

Social Realism and Commentary

It is noteworthy that a conservative Realism—a Realism most often enlisted in the service of social and political movements—persisted alongside the busy experimentalism in Western art and was only slightly affected by it. This "Social Realism," as it may be called, is an international phenomenon—a genre in which the environment, the labors, and the struggles of the working classes are sympathetically described and exalted. In the West, this kind of art flourished in the 1930s—especially in Mexico and the United States, frequently with overtones critical of "the Establishment."

In the influential Mexican School, JOSÉ CLEMENTE OROZCO (1883–1949) excelled in mural painting dynamically expressive of the spirit of social criticism and revolution that agitated both hemispheres in the earlier twentieth century. Although not himself an ideologue urging a particular political program, his powerful, graphically blunt art sufficiently declares his sympathies. Orozco lived in the United States between 1927 and 1932, during which time he completed several important commissions. In one of his finest mural cycles at Dartmouth College, he depicts the history of ancient and modern Mexico (FIG. 22-

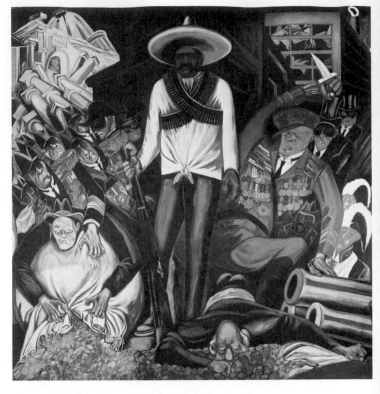

22-32 JOSÉ CLEMENTE OROZCO, *Hispano–America, c.* 1933. Mural. Baker Memorial Library, Dartmouth College, Hanover, New Hampshire.

32). Here, he shows the dauntless Mexican peasant of the revolutionary days, armed and resolute, pressed on all sides by bankers and soldiers—the enemies, as Orozco sees them, of the common people. Money-grubbers pour hoards of gold before the incorruptible *peón*, cannon threaten him, and a bemedalled general raises a dagger to stab him in the back. The allegory is easy to read, for Orozco's training as a maker of political prints and as a newspaper artist taught him the rhetorical strength of graphic brevity and simplicity. At the same time, his training as an architect gave

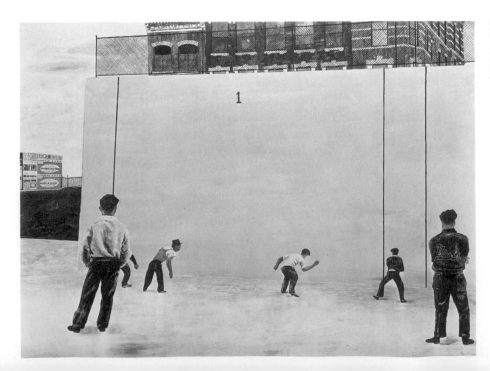

22-33 BEN SHAHN, *Handball,* 1939. Tempera on paper mounted on composition board, approx. 22¾″ × 31¼″. Museum of Modern Art, New York (Abby Aldrich Rockefeller Fund).

him a sense of the framed wall surface, which he easily commands, projecting these quickly grasped figurations of the newspaper cartoon onto the solid mural plane in monumental scale. Thus, he combines the effects of the graphic and mural media to give his work an originality and force rarely seen in mural painting after the Renaissance and Baroque periods.

Like Orozco, the American painter BEN SHAHN (1898–1969) was a trained graphic artist and muralist. A political and social commentator of great force, Shahn came to attention with his unforgettable series of 23 prints on the controversial Sacco and Vanzetti case of the 1920s, in which, using flat intense color, he denounces injustice in a sharp, dry, angular manner. Shahn adapted and developed the visual idioms of commercial art, at which he worked throughout his life, using its concise and abrupt method to convey his own highly individual messages. He was engaged to do numerous murals in public buildings, and worked with Mexican painter DIEGO RIVERA on the never completed murals of Rockefeller Center in New York. The loneliness of city streets fascinated him, and he made numerous photographic studies of them. *Handball* (FIG. 22-33), although obviously checked with the photographic record, is a skillfully eclectic work. It at once recalls the geometry of Cubism, the haunted space of Surrealism, with its weird vacancy, the still perspectives of Italian painting in the fifteenth century, and the quick, accidental poses and changes of scale of the candid photograph.

Another painter of the American scene, EDWARD HOPPER (1882–1967) shows it through a very personal brand of realism, untouched by the experiments in abstraction carried on by his generation. His cross sections of city life are curiously muted, still, often empty; motion is stopped and time is suspended, as if the artist is recording a completed and unalterable memory to the last detail in all the original poignancy of the scene remembered. His *Eleven A.M.* (FIG. 22-34) combines precise inventory and delineation with ambiguity of situation to create a mood of unmitigated loneliness. The nude, young woman is seated staring out of a hotel window (we see its sign partly blocked by the stone courses of the outer wall), her face concealed by long, luxuriant hair that falls below her shoulders. She is the forlorn heroine of many a naturalistic American novel and short story. The cold light of one more common day falls without luster on the plain, hard, architectural features and nondescript furnishings of the dismal room. In *Preludes, II*, written a few years before Hopper's painting, the poet T. S. Eliot might have been setting the scene:

The morning comes to consciousness
. . . .
With the other masquerades that time resumes,
One thinks of all the hands
That are raising dingy shades
In a thousand furnished rooms.

Hopper's woman is even more anonymous than Édouard Manet's bargirl (FIG. 21-41) or Edgar Degas' bather (FIG. 21-62), to whom she should be compared (Hopper greatly admired Degas); and a comparison with Titian's *Venus of Urbino* (FIG. 17-63) should remind us of the mighty changes in the interpretation of the nude that have taken place since the Renaissance. In any event, with Hopper, the Realism of the nineteenth century, European and American, is brought up to date and vindicated by an original and sensitive vision.

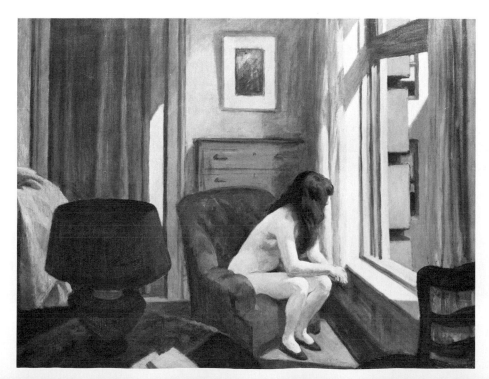

22-34 EDWARD HOPPER, *Eleven A.M.*, 1926. 28″ × 36″. Hirshhorn Museum and Sculpture Garden, Washington, D.C.

917

SCULPTURE BEFORE WORLD WAR II

Auguste Rodin (FIGS. 2, 21-82, 21-83, 21-84) was the greatest sculptor of the nineteenth century, an artist whose international reputation rivaled that of Michelangelo and Gianlorenzo Bernini; he was also a great teacher. His reputation brought to his studio in Paris, as pupils or as admirers, many members of the younger generation who would develop new kinds of sculpture, either under Rodin's influence or in reaction against him.

The French sculptor ARISTIDE MAILLOL (1861–1944) turned away from Rodin's evanescent effects of light and broken planes toward a simple and weighty style. He began his career as a painter, executing broadly decorative designs in the manner of Gauguin, and was also known as a graphic artist through his book illustrations. About 1900, Maillol turned to sculpture and, until the end of his life, scarcely deviated from his chosen subject—the female figure—which he interpreted in massive planes and volumes devoid of historical stylization or literary anecdote. One of his first and most important works, the seated figure *Mediterranean* (FIG. 22-35), is conceived as an organization of almost abstract volumes simplified from the endless complexities of the human figure. It has weight and solidity, and the largely unbroken surfaces of the smoothly modeled masses take the light evenly and quietly. The pose itself, familiar in several Tahitian figures by Gauguin, whose art Maillol greatly admired, also has in its tranquil closure,

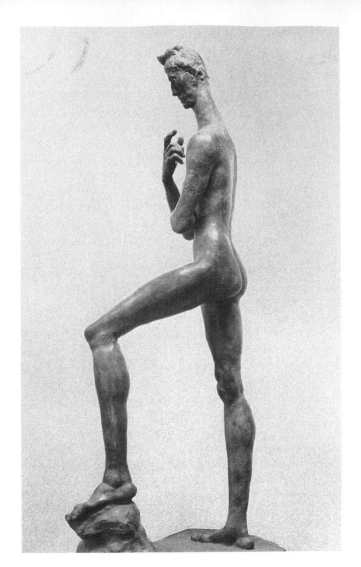

22-36 WILHELM LEHMBRUCK, *Standing Youth*, 1913. Cast stone, approx. 7' 8" high. Museum of Modern Art, New York (gift of Abby Aldrich Rockefeller).

22-35 ARISTIDE MAILLOL, *Mediterranean, c.* 1901. Bronze, approx. 41" high, base 45" × 24¾". Museum of Modern Art, New York (gift of Stephen C. Clark).

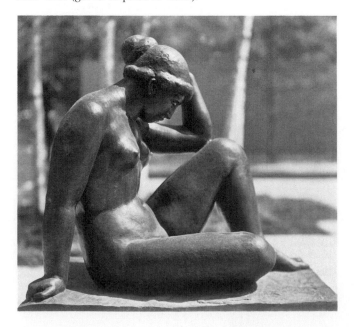

monumentality, and dignity more than a little of the Early Classical sculpture of Greece. The figure carries its own meaning (it refers to nothing outside itself; the title "Mediterranean" was added later). The form alone is sufficient to the artist's purpose.

The Expressionistic element in Rodin proved most sympathetic to the young German sculptor WILHELM LEHMBRUCK (1881–1919). Perceiving in Rodin's later work the possibilities of distortion, Lehmbruck developed an impressive style of his own based on the elongation and attenuation of human proportions. His *Standing Youth* (FIG. 22-36)—we have already seen his *Seated Youth* (FIG. 1)—elegantly slender and tall, poses in solemn reverie, making a slow, deliberate, and eloquent gesture, as if participating in some grave ritual. Without specific subject or historical reference, Lehmbruck's figure "tells" by pose and gesture alone; its mood is entirely a function of its form. The extreme proportions recall Medieval (FIG. 9-36) and even Mannerist (FIG. 17-43) attenuation and announce a new freedom to interpret the human figure

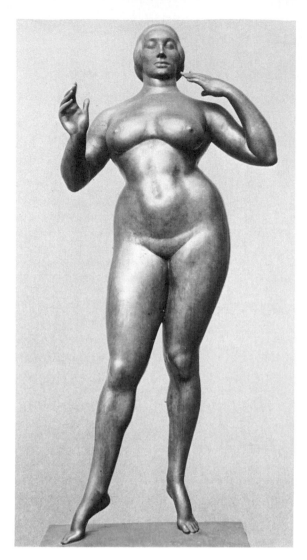

22-37 GASTON LACHAISE, *Standing Woman*, 1912–1918. Bronze, 6' 7" high, 2' 5" wide. Albright-Knox Gallery, Buffalo (James A. Forsyth Fund, 1938).

quite without regard for the measure of it established in antiquity and in the Renaissance.

GASTON LACHAISE (1882–1935), of French descent but active most of his life in the United States, specialized, like Maillol, in sculpture of the female figure and, like Lehmbruck, dealt freely with the proportions of the human body. His life-size *Standing Woman* (FIG. 22-37) is as broadly modeled as Maillol's, but with a more sensuous treatment of the anatomy. The strongly felt movement swells rapidly upward from the lightly poised, delicate feet to the large rounding hips; after a sharp accent in the angle of the waist, it again swells into the broad shoulders and bent arms. There is an elastic, abstract rhythm of both volume and contour and a union of weight and grace. Bronze is an ideal medium for this beautifully contrived equilibrium of opulent mass with delicate supporting strength. If we compare Lehmbruck's *Standing Youth* with Lachaise's figure, we can appreciate the wide variation in the formal and expressive results when the sculptor experiments with noncanonical proportions.

Symbolism and Art Nouveau opened the stylistic troves of other ages and cultures to the modern artist. Thus, the Expressionist sculptor could find in Medieval art both unsophisticated and intense spirituality and abstract forms as yet uncomplicated by Realism. Although the sculptors discovered Romanesque and Gothic art much later than the architects did, they made of their borrowing from it something far more genuine. The works of ERNST BARLACH (1870–1938), a German sculptor much influenced by Medieval carving, combine sharp, smoothly planed forms with intense action and keen expression. His *War Monument* for Güstrow Cathedral (FIGS. 22-38 and 22-39) is one

22-38 ERNST BARLACH, *War Monument*, Güstrow Cathedral, 1927. Bronze. Schildergasse Antoniterkirche, Cologne.

22-39 ERNST BARLACH, *Head*, detail of FIG. 22-38, separately cast. Approx. 13½" high. Museum of Modern Art, New York (gift of Edward M.M. Warburg).

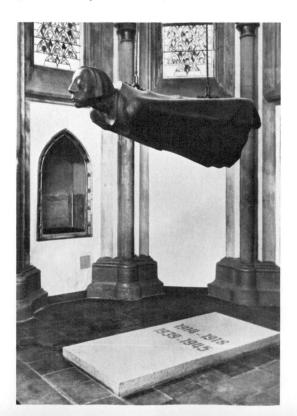

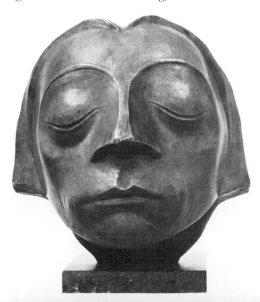

of the most poignant memorials of World War I. The sculptor depicts a dying soul at the moment when it is about to awaken to everlasting life—the theme of death and transfiguration; the rigid economy of surfaces concentrates attention on the superb head. The spiritual anguish evoked by the disaster of war and the release from that anguish through the hope of salvation are rarely expressed as movingly as they are in this work.

Cubism to Constructivism

Although sculpture does not register the major stylistic groupings—Expressionism, Cubism, and Surrealism—as clearly as painting does, we still may discern them. On the other hand, sculpture, the three-dimensional art, is perhaps more at home in the age of metals and industrially produced artifacts; later in the century, it is sculpture in particular that achieves the inevitable linkage of art and technology. The Expressionism of Lehmbruck and Lachaise overlaps the new experience of Cubism, which, in its concern for the creation of the effects of three-dimensional space on a flat surface, was not easily adapted to the sculptural mode. Nevertheless, we can see a development from the Rodinesque mode to total Cubist abstraction in two figures (FIGS. 22-40 and 22-41) by Henri Matisse, who was a sculptor as well as a painter (FIG. 22-3). Although these figures—the first and last of a series of four made between 1909 and 1929—are not in the more characteristic linear mode (or ''arabesque,'' as Matisse called it) preferred by the artist, they reveal with great force a profound change in sculptural vision. *Back I* (FIG. 22-40), the first of these representations of back views of the female nude, is a believable anatomy not far removed from the roughly modeled surfaces of Rodin's sculptures. *Back II* and *Back III* (not illustrated here), made in quick succession in 1913 and 1914, show a rapid breaking up—an abstraction—of the main bodily shapes. *Back IV* (FIG. 22-41), the final version, made in 1929, is the last stage of the disintegration and embodies the emergence of a totally different concept and procedure—the geometrizing, radical simplifications of Cubism.

Matisse's ''exercise in the progressive reduction and concentration of form'' took place as an exclusively sculptural enterprise, independent of painting. On the other hand, the earlier works of JACQUES LIPCHITZ (1891–1973), born in Poland but long resident in France and the United States, are among the most successful solutions to the problem of developing the spatial feeling of Cubist painting in three dimensions. In *Man with Mandolin* (FIG. 22-42), the continuous form is broken down into planes that, no matter the direction of the light, can be read as flat, shaded surfaces. As with Cubist painting, there is now no single point of view, no continuity or simul-

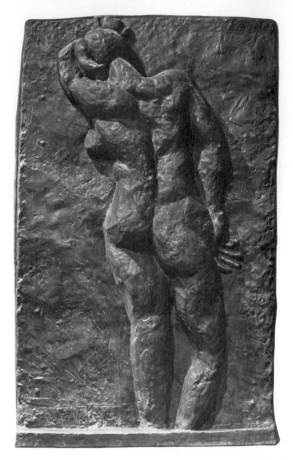

22-40   HENRI MATISSE, *Back I*, 1909. Bronze, 6' 2¾" high, 3' 10" wide, 7¼" deep. Tate Gallery, London.

22-41   HENRI MATISSE, *Back IV*, 1929. Bronze, 6' 2½" high, 3' 8½" wide, 6¼" deep. Tate Gallery, London.

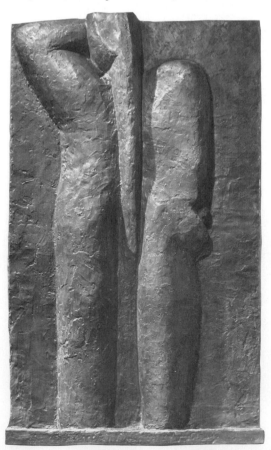

taneity of image contour. But an even more decisive break with the long tradition of Western sculpture than this analysis of mass into planes is the piercing of the mass. An early example of this new turn can be seen in *Woman Combing Her Hair* (FIG. 22–43) by Russian sculptor ALEXANDER ARCHIPENKO (1887–1964). This statuette, recalling in its graceful contrapposto something of Renaissance Mannerism, introduces in place of the head a void with a shape of its own that figures importantly in the whole design. Enclosed spaces have always existed in figure sculpture—for example, the space between the arm and the body when the hand rests on the hip, as in Verrocchio's *David* (FIG. 16-52). But here there is penetration of the continuous mass of the figure, and shaped space (often referred to as "negative space") occurs with shaped mass in the same design. Archipenko's figure shows the same slipping of the planes that we have seen in pictorial Cubism, and the relation of the planes to each other is similarly complex. Thus, in painting and sculpture, the traditional limits are broken through and the media transformed.

Archipenko's figure is still quasi-representational, but sculpture (like painting) executed within the Cub-

ist orbit tends to cast off the last vestiges of representation. By 1913, UMBERTO BOCCIONI (1882–1916), already mentioned as a Futurist and both painter and sculptor, pushes his forms so far toward abstraction that the title of his *Unique Forms of Continuity in Space* (FIG. 22-44) calls attention to the formal and spatial effects rather than to the fact that the source for these is the striding human figure. The "figure" is so expanded, interrupted, or broken in plane and contour that it disappears, as it were, behind the blur of its movement; only the blur remains. Boccioni's search for plastic means with which to express dynamic movement reaches a monumental expression here. In its power and sense of vital activity, this sculpture surpasses similar efforts in painting (by Boccioni and his Futurist companions) to create images symbolic of the dynamic quality of modern life. To be convinced by it, we need only reflect on how details of an adjacent landscape appear in our peripheral vision when we are traveling at great speed on a highway or in a low-flying airplane. Although Boccioni's figure bears a curious resemblance to the ancient *Nike of Samothrace* (FIG. 5-76), a cursory comparison reveals how the modern work departs from the ancient one.

22-42 *Left:* JACQUES LIPCHITZ, *Man with Mandolin*, 1917. Stone, approx. 29¾" high. Yale University Art Gallery, New Haven, Connecticut (Collection, Société Anonyme).

22-43 *Right:* ALEXANDER ARCHIPENKO, *Woman Combing Her Hair*, 1915. Bronze, approx. 13¾" high. Museum of Modern Art, New York (bequest of Lillie P. Bliss).

22-44 UMBERTO BOCCIONI, *Unique Forms of Continuity in Space*, 1913. Bronze, approx. 43½" high. Museum of Modern Art, New York (bequest of Lillie P. Bliss).

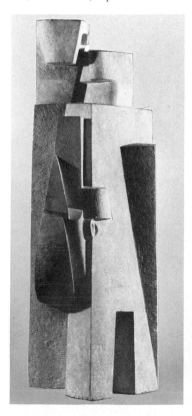
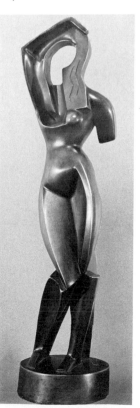
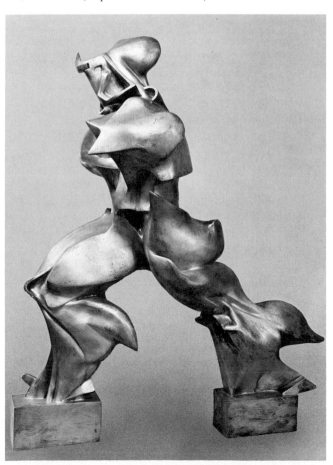

The Romanian sculptor CONSTANTIN BRANCUŞI (1876–1957) carries abstraction to the limit beyond which the representational element is lost entirely. At the same time, he extracts from the material—whether marble, metal, or wood—its maximum effect. It may be that it is with Brancuşi's scrupulous attention to the nature of his materials that the pervading doctrine and mystique of modern art—"truth to the material"—arises. This doctrine demands that the artist respect the material, that formal intentions never abuse its peculiar nature. What is appropriate for bronze is not so for marble; what is appropriate for marble is not so for wood; and so on. Respect for the function of the material is a necessity in industrial production. This truth to material goes along with the modern quest for purity or "reality" of form. As the painter Mondrian finds rectilinear form to be most "real," so Brancuşi visualizes an extended ovoid shape as the most "natural" shape, and simplifies the most complex natural forms and even natural movements to variations on this fundamental shape. In his famous *Bird in Space* (FIG. 22-45) everything accidental is eliminated or compressed into the most direct and economical expression, yet the form as a whole suggests the essence of a bird's sudden upward movement through air. Even more, there is a remarkable suggestion of airflow, as delineated by modern aerodynamics, and Brancuşi's means of conveying flight are not unrelated to those the modern engineer generally uses in designing "streamlined" industrial forms. There is the same study of the nature of the material—the same meticulous attention to proportions, contour, and surface finish. Thus, even at this early stage, the coming together of art and technology is predictable. At the same time, there appears what might be considered a contradiction of the technological connection—namely, *biomorphic abstraction*, in which the artist derives forms from living and growing things.

A friend of Brancuşi and Picasso, JULIO GONZALEZ (1876–1942), shared their interest in the artistic possibilities of new materials and new methods borrowed from both industrial technology and traditional metalworking. Constructed or "direct" shapes (using ready-made bars, sheets, rods, or the like) of welded or wrought iron and bronze can produce, in effect, simple or incredibly complex sculptured *spaces* in a kind of fluent openwork, in which the solids function only as contours, boundaries, or dividing planes. In *Woman Combing Her Hair* (FIG. 22-46) by Gonzalez (compare with Archipenko's version of the same subject; FIG. 22-43), fantasy is restrained by no traditional convention of representation, and the actual constructive process is unimpeded by the more demanding methods of carving and casting. Sculptors in the 1960s and 1970s would fully exploit the advantages of this method: linear effects impossible for other

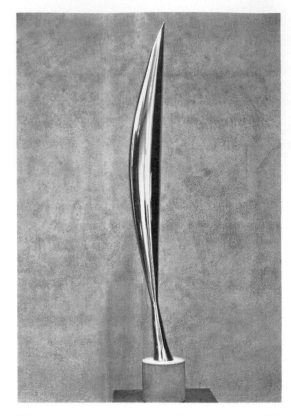

22-45   CONSTANTIN BRANCUŞI, *Bird in Space, c.* 1927. Bronze, unique cast, approx. 54" high. Museum of Modern Art, New York.

22-46   JULIO GONZALEZ, *Woman Combing Her Hair, c.* 1930–1933. Iron, 57" high. Moderna Museet, Stockholm.

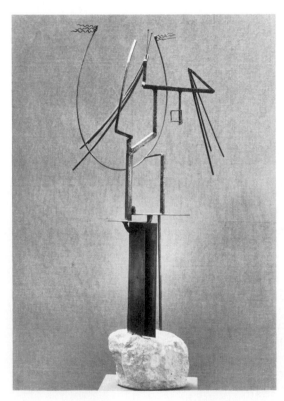

modes, flexibility in construction, speed of execution, and easy correction of errors or changes in intention. The direct-metal method in the hands of contemporary sculptors parallels the methods used by the so-called "abstract expressionist" painters. It should be noted that although Gonzalez innovates in material and method, he still thinks (as the title of this piece indicates) of the human figure as a point of departure for abstraction, even though the forms could, like Brancuşi's, stand without external reference to the natural world. After years as an unsuccessful painter, Gonzalez was asked by Picasso for technical help in constructing metal sculpture. From that time, his influence has been continuous, with a special impact on today's sculptors.

Unlike Gonzalez or Brancuşi, De Stijl and Constructivist artists prefer to work with forms that refer not to the natural world but to the worlds of mathematics and mechanism. The search for pure form led naturally to mathematics; its abstract and impersonal beauty could be projected into three dimensions. But it also reflected the sculptor's impulse toward the "engineering" and machining of forms "to specification"—as with the use of a blueprint or plan. Early in the development of Synthetic Cubism, a group of Russian artists working in Moscow became interested in applying industrial engineering techniques to sculpture. Their point of departure was provided by some of the more three-dimensional collages of Picasso, which contained miscellaneous, recognizable objects taken from the environment, such as bottles, pipes, guitars. VLADIMIR TATLIN (1885–1953) saw some of these collages when he visited Picasso in Paris in 1913. On his return to Moscow, he made similar collage reliefs that significantly excluded all representational motifs and recognizable objects. Tatlin's compositions were completely abstract—the first of their kind. He called them "constructions," giving a name to the very influential movement, Constructivism. Tatlin was the moving spirit among a group of progressive Constructivists whose experiments were eventually banned by the new Soviet regime in 1922; some left Russia and spread their ideas and practices through the West.

Shortly before Constructivism was banned in Russia, Tatlin designed a prodigious monument; it was never built, but the model survives (FIG. 22-47). A tower called *Monument to the Third International, 1919–1920,* and intended to be about 1,300 feet high, it was to be a spiraling, leaning, openwork structure composed of steel, wood, and glass and was to contain three vast, moving, geometric elements. A cube, a pyramid, and a cylinder, designed to house facilities for cultural, political, administrative, and scientific activities, would have revolved on their axes at different speeds, ranging from one revolution per year to one per day.

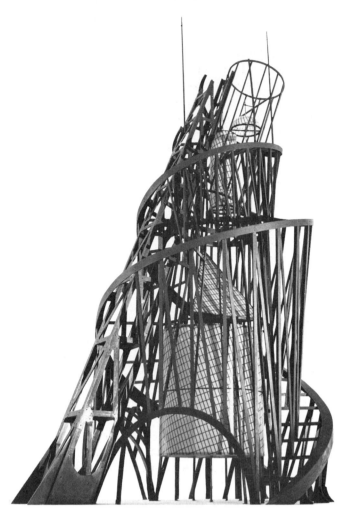

22-47 VLADIMIR TATLIN, *Monument to the Third International,* 1919–1920. Model in wood, iron, and glass. Re-created in 1968 for exhibition at the Moderna Museet, Stockholm.

In 1920, the Constructivists divided and Tatlin allied himself with the so-called Productivists, who renounced art altogether in favor of productive, collective engineering. The Productivist position was rejected by the brothers ANTOINE PEVSNER (1886–1962) and NAUM GABO (1890–1977), who championed the individual freedom of the artist and the right to free experimentation. In 1920, they issued their *Realist Manifesto,* in which they called for the representation of a "new reality":

In order to interpret the reality of life, art must be based upon two fundamental elements: space and time. Volume is not the only concept of space. Kinetic and dynamic elements must be used to express the true nature of time. The static rhythms are no longer sufficient. Art must not be more imitative, but seek new forms.

We have seen something of this last statement already explicit in Brancuşi and Gonzalez, and the rotating elements of Tatlin's *Monument* anticipate the expression of time in space. In their placing of mass to make, enframe, and divide spaces, as we have seen in Gonzalez especially, we have the essential procedure laid down by Pevsner and Gabo in their *Manifesto:*

> Mass and space are two concrete and measurable things. We consider and use space as a new and absolutely sculptural element, a material substance which really enters into construction.

Architecture had always implicitly admitted the reality of space. For sculpture to admit space was a triumph, already announced in Archipenko's "pierced" figure (FIG. 22-43). It now appeared that space could be "sculptured" as well as mass. In their concern with the properties of space, Pevsner and Gabo created objects in which voids acted as forcefully as the elements of solid mass, conceding that, for sculpture, mass and void could be made esthetically equivalent—a radical position indeed in view of the fact that the essence of sculpture had been commonly thought of as pure mass. Gabo turned to the new synthetic plastic materials, as many younger sculptors have since. He used celluloid first and later nylon and lucite for constructions in which space seems to flow through as well as around the transparent materials. His prewar experiments culminated in some of his most subtle postwar compositions. In his *Linear Construction* (FIG. 22-48) space is caught and held in suspension, as it were, by the most delicate combination of hovering planes. In the "fields of force" of physics, conventional "solids" and "voids" alike are only mathematical expressions; in the subatomic universe, solids and voids are always in am-

biguous relation and never definitely one or the other. Like the mathematician, the artist may express his conception of this undecidable relation of space and mass. Like Mondrian, Gabo believed that indeed "such artfully constructed images are the very essence of the reality of the world which we are searching for." In our time, science and art alike make their models of the reality of the physical world.

From the "transparency" of mass and the consequent creation of interior spaces, it seems but a step to the attempt to create actual movement in space. Yet movement must come as a reality in which the positions of the work or of the spectator, or both, are constantly changing. Anticipating today's kinetic sculptors, the American sculptor ALEXANDER CALDER (1898–1976) was the first to set his works in continuous and "natural" (unmotorized) motion. His "mobiles," as they are appropriately called, are made of rods, wires, and sheet-metal forms so balanced that the slightest current of air moves the parts within a carefully planned pattern, creating a constantly shifting "definition" of space. Traditionally, sculpture has had very few standards of space and these have demanded its fixity and sometimes the fixity of the spectator. A remark of Salvador Dali's expresses our traditional view of the sculptural mode: ". . . the least one can expect of sculpture is that it stand still." Calder's work, most often nonrepresentational, is sprightly and witty and contains many unexpected felicities of line and shape. In this respect, it often reminds us of the paintings of Miró (FIG. 22-27). In *Horizontal Spines* (FIG. 22-49), the delicate grace and precision of pure line in the fine steel wires contrast and combine in constantly changing relationships with the sharp accents of the flat shapes.

22-48 NAUM GABO, *Linear Construction*, 1950. Plastic and nylon thread. Private collection.

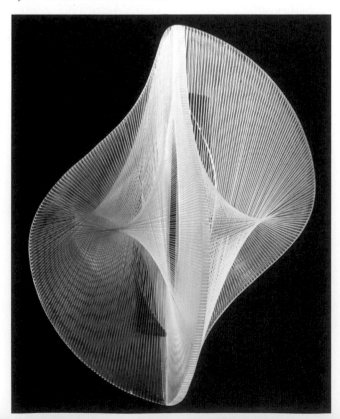

22-49 ALEXANDER CALDER, *Horizontal Spines*, 1942. Approx. 54" high. Addison Gallery of American Art, Phillips Academy, Andover, Massachusetts.

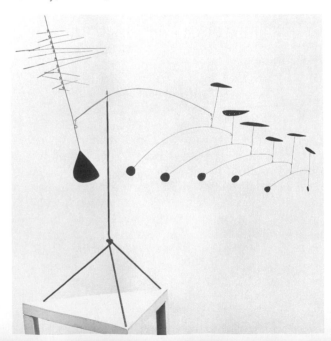

Dada and the Fantastic

The biting Dadaist critique of modern life cuts across the whole development of formalizing, abstract sculpture, bringing with it a new permissiveness. Objects out of the ordinary environment of modern life were selected and exhibited in the Dada shows as works of art. Duchamp, with serene impudence, mocked serious artistic intention with chance selections of objects like a bicycle wheel (FIG. 22-50), bottle washer, urinal, corkscrew, and other "ready-made," commonplace things. These André Breton called "manufactured objects promoted to the dignity of objects of art through the choice of the artist." According to Duchamp—and for a generation of artists after him who were profoundly influenced by his art and especially by his attitude—life and art are a matter of chance and arbitrary choice; the essence of the artistic act is willful selection, and each act is individual and unique: "Your chance is not the same as mine, just as your throw of the dice will rarely be the same as mine." This philosophy of utter freedom for the artist is fundamental to the history of art in the twentieth century, and Duchamp can stand as perhaps the shrewdest and most perceptive theorist of

the modern movement. The freedom he granted himself to set up a bicycle wheel (with its fork) on a kitchen stool, he granted to the visitor in allowing him to spin the wheel as he chose.

The "ready-mades" of Duchamp led to "found objects" like the random junk that Schwitters used in his *Merz Pictures* (FIG. 22-23); the collages of Cubism had pointed the way. Interest in "found objects" spread to the public, which began to collect such oddments as rocks, driftwood, and fragments of manufactured objects. A happy conjunction of two ordinary objects, never appearing together in this way, makes up Picasso's *Bull's Head* (FIG. 22-51). The never-failing ingenuity of this modern master turns the handle bars and seat of a bicycle into an image of a bull, beautifully stylized. The work, which might seem only a clever trick, illustrates an important method in modern art—the unexpected unity that two objects can make when taken out of their usual context and brought into a radically new relationship. We have seen this phenomenon of new meanings arising out of uncommon juxtapositions in the case of the seemingly opposed caption and image in painting. Much of the pungency and surprise—the impact—of modern painting and sculpture is the result of such strenuous feats of conjunctive imagination.

Ordinary manufactured objects and utensils can be modified just enough to create a startling paradox. MAN RAY (1890–1976), Duchamp's collaborator in his brief reintroduction of Dada to the United States in 1921, equips a laundry iron with a row of wicked-looking spikes, contravening its proper function of smoothing and pressing (FIG. 22-52). The malicious

22-50 MARCEL DUCHAMP, *Bicycle Wheel*, 1951 (third version after lost original of 1913). Metal wheel mounted on painted wooden stool, 50½" high, 25½" wide, 16⅝" deep. Museum of Modern Art, New York (gift of the Sidney and Harriet Janis Collection).

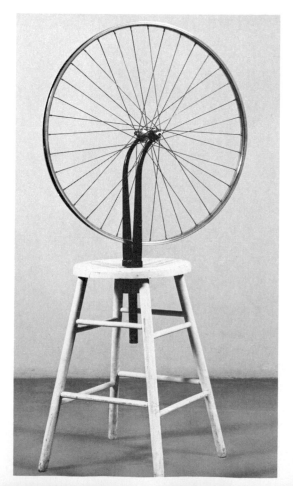

22-51 PABLO PICASSO, *Bull's Head*, 1943. Handlebars and seat of a bicycle. Galerie Louise Leiris, Paris.

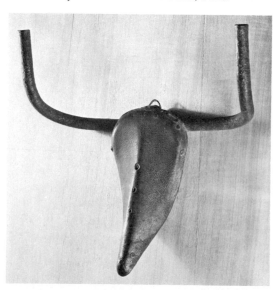

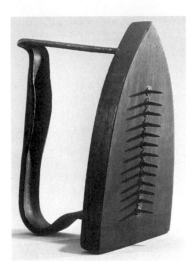

22-52 MAN RAY, *Gift*, c. 1958 (replica after destroyed original of 1921). Painted flatiron with metal tacks, 6¼" high, 3⅝" wide, 4½" deep. Museum of Modern Art, New York (James Thrall Soby Fund).

humor of *Gift*—seen throughout Dada and, indeed, in much of contemporary art—gives it a characteristic edge that can cut the unwary. Contradiction, paradox, irony, even blasphemy are the bequest of Dada. They are, in the view of Dada and its successors, the free and defiant artist's weapons in what has been called the "hundred years' war with the public."

In these later years of that "war," sculptors, like painters, have explored numerous avenues of possibility. Where human reference would seem to have been once and for all expelled from the sculptor's interest by exclusively formal concerns, it insistently reappears. The English sculptor HENRY MOORE (b. 1898) has created many variations on the human figure; some are more abstract than others, but all reflect an instinctive feeling for the dignity of the human form. Moore also often disregards the human form in favor of pure biomorphic abstraction and, like his colleague BARBARA HEPWORTH (1903–1975), shows a profound love for and knowledge of natural forms and materials. In such a work as *Reclining Figure* (FIG. 22-53), the massive, interlocking shapes reflect the discipline of abstract art, particularly the architectonic counterpoint of mass and void; but their total visual reality relates the human being to the enduring world of natural experience, even as the smooth, polished wooden surfaces suggest the action of wind and water on natural materials. Quite another treatment of the human figure is found in the works of ALBERTO GIACOMETTI (1901–1966)—a Swiss sculptor, long a resident of Paris, who participated in both the Cubist and Surrealist movements and contributed significant works in each mode. In 1947, however, he turned to representational sculpture to produce unexpectedly poignant figures that seem to be immediate projections of the modern experiences of bewilderment, loss, alienation. At the beginning of this chapter, we referred to Giacometti's *City Square* (FIG. 22-54) as a peculiar projection of the image of the modern, isolated individual in the "lonely crowd." It is noteworthy that Giacometti disapproved of any such classification of his work and believed that he was simply trying to render the effect of great space as it presses around a figure—and nothing more. But this is precisely the point: The lone, modern man is only too aware of the vastness of the space that separates him from his neighbor by only a few feet. The artist's ver-

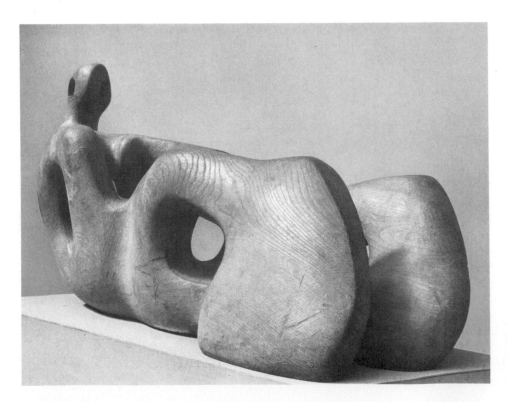

22-53 HENRY MOORE, *Reclining Figure*, 1939. Elmwood, 6' 9" long. Detroit Institute of the Arts (gift of the Dexter M. Ferry, Jr., Trustee Corporation).

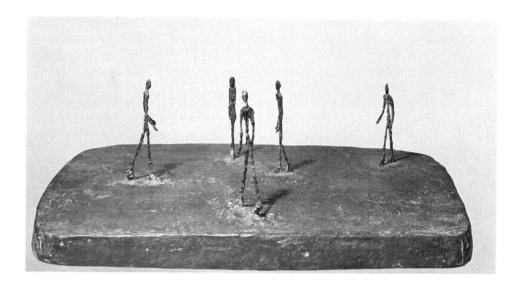

22-54 ALBERTO GIACOMETTI, *City Square* (*La Place*), 1948. Bronze, approx. 6¾" high, 23½" wide, 16" deep. Museum of Modern Art, New York (purchase).

bally expressed intention and our own verbally expressed interpretation may seem to differ, as is the case so often in modern art; yet we recognize when he is speaking for his age through his art. Giacometti's pencil-thin, elongated figures stride abstractedly through endless space; they never meet and never can. At certain angles, the forms are so attenuated that they almost disappear, as, often in the human condition, people fade noiselessly out of sight. If we compare Giacometti's figures with those in Rodin's *Burghers of Calais* (FIG. 21-82), we can readily appreciate the changes wrought by half a century of revolution in the interpretation of the human being in art.

ARCHITECTURE BEFORE WORLD WAR II

The structural promise of steel and concrete, only partly recognized in the later nineteenth century, finds its fulfillment in the twentieth. Like painting and sculpture, architecture has been revolutionized by industrial materials and by the example of the pure functionalism of machines. Radical contradictions and reversals of tradition, analogous to what we have seen in the figurative arts, have produced architectural styles with no precedent in the past. Architecture, with all the other arts, has been brought within the domain of modern technology. In the words of the critic Siegfried Giedion, "Mechanization takes command!" This does not mean that individual talent became submerged in collective production; rather, architects of genius welcomed the machine and its potential for inspiring new form. Indeed, architecture and engineering were drawn closer and were embodied in one person.

Technology, if not altogether taking the initiative in inspiring modern architecture, is always implicit in it.

It is intriguing that the old Renaissance ideal of the union of theory and practice seems to find its full realization in a style fundamentally different from that of the Renaissance. In any event, we find in the history of modern architecture—more conspicuously than in the past—a kind of tension between the individual architect's impulse toward personal expression and the demand for vast, public, impersonal projects that impose their uniformity on whole cities. Within the titanic scale of modern, collective, public design, the old individualism of a Michelangelo or a Bernini would be likely to lose some of its distinctiveness. The modern architect is more like the Medieval master of works than the isolated Renaissance genius imposing his will on the whole form. To a degree, although modern architecture has its heroes, architects of our time tend, like modern sculptors and painters, to take their characters from the broad, collective movements of style, rather than to create them. Architects like Frank Lloyd Wright seem to be the rule-proving exceptions.

We have seen in "exhibition" architecture (FIGS. 21-86 and 21-87) and in the mercantile buildings of Henry Hobson Richardson (FIG. 21-88) and Louis Sullivan (FIGS. 21-89 and 21-90) the move toward a utilitarian architecture of a large enough scale to accommodate the traffic of thousands of people. The metal frames of the Americans' buildings, like that of Henri Labrouste's Bibliothèque Ste.-Geneviève (FIG. 21-85), are clothed in a fabric reminiscent of traditional styles, although Sullivan was deeply interested in devising an architectural ornament independent of tradition. In this respect, he was the leading American representative of Art Nouveau, which exhibits the typical architectural motif of an undulant, sweeping, serpentine line that wraps about or rises from structural members, its weaving spirals ending in tense scrolls. Easily adaptable to light metal construction, the Art Nouveau style is seen primarily in private houses, although many of the Paris Metro entrances are also decorated with Art Nouveau motifs. A good example of the style is the staircase in the Hotel van Eetvelde (FIG. 22-55), built in Brussels in 1895 by VICTOR HORTA (1861–1947), whose name is particularly associated with the Art Nouveau style in architecture. This decorative experiment was hailed enthusiastically as a truly modern style, although in fact it is the last appearance of the old "craftsman" style of the nineteenth century. A number of influences can be identified in Art Nouveau; they range from the rich, foliated, two-dimensional ornament and craftsman's respect for materials of William Morris' Arts and Crafts movement in nineteenth-century England to the free, sinuous, whiplash curve of Japanese designs. The boldness of Horta's use of metal may also be seen in the light supports, the ductile, curvilinear ornamentation, and the candor with which design and structure are integrated.

In Horta's hands, Art Nouveau was most effective as interior design, although all the arts were under its sway—from architecture to book illustration. On a monumental architectural scale, the style may be

22-55 VICTOR HORTA, staircase in the Hotel van Eetvelde, Brussels, Belgium, 1895.

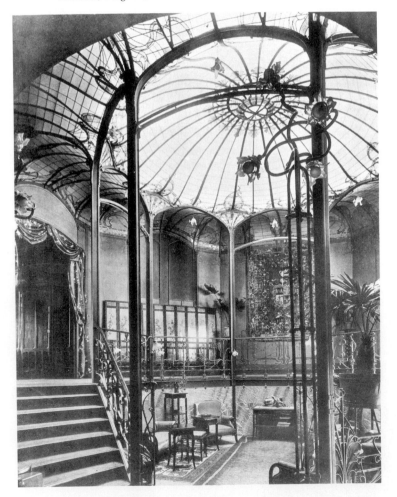

seen in the Casa Milá apartment house (FIG. 22-56), erected in Barcelona in 1907 by ANTONIO GAUDÍ (1852–1926), an inventive architect who strove mightily to create forms utterly divorced from tradition and as close as possible to the randomness of nature. Here, Gaudí superposes bulky layers of cut stone in restless undulation, banishing the straight line altogether. The surfaces of the stone are left in the rough, suggesting naturally worn rock; entrance portals look like eroded sea caves. Passionate naturalism, seeking to escape from all regularity of artifice into the formless dynamism of nature, has never had more striking expression. Gaudí's work is the spiritual kin of Expressionist painting and sculpture.

The work of Horta and Gaudí provided components for a new and deeply searching art: a declaration of independence from all tradition, a profound respect for nature and the nature of materials, and the expectation of an entirely new architecture. As with painting and sculpture, an age of experiment opened for architecture at the turn of the century. The most striking and original personality in the development of a "modern" architecture is unquestionably FRANK LLOYD WRIGHT (1867–1959), whose experimental projects still startle the world. Always a believer in architecture as "natural" and "organic", Wright sees it in the service of free individuals who have the right to move within a "free" space—that is, as an asymmetrical design in natural surroundings. He seeks to develop an organic unity of planning, structure, materials, and site. He identifies the principle of *continuity* as fundamental to the understanding of his view of organic unity:

> Classic architecture was all fixation. . . . Now why not let walls, ceilings, floors become seen as component parts of each other, their surfaces flowing into each other? . . . You may see the appearance in the surface of your hand contrasted with the articulation of the bony structure itself. This ideal, profound in its architectural implications . . . I called . . . continuity.*

The concept of flux, of constant change, of evolution and progress is inherent in this principle, as it is in the views of Walt Whitman, also a prophet of continuity. It appears, too, in the work of the then greatly influential philosopher Henri Bergson, a contemporary of Wright, who stresses the reality of vitalism, of living process, above any other.

A pupil of Sullivan, Wright could well understand the former's long-debated slogan "form follows function" as the difference between the surface of the hand and its bony structure—the relation being dynamic and necessary, determined yet flexible. His

*Frank Lloyd Wright, *American Architecture*, ed. Edgar Kaufmann (New York: Horizon, 1955), pp. 205, 208.

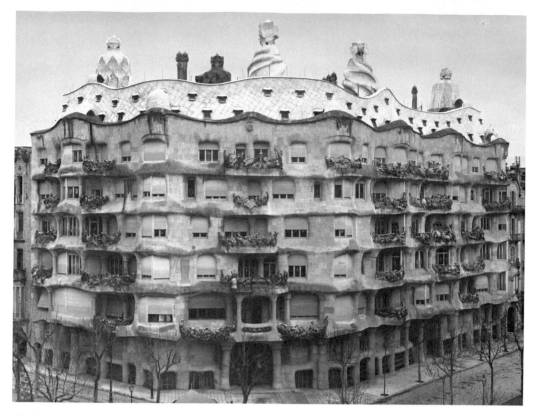

22-56 ANTONIO GAUDÍ, Casa Milá, Barcelona, Spain, 1907.

vigorous originality was manifested early and, by 1900, he had arrived at a style entirely his own; in his work during the first decade of this century, his cross-axial plan and his fabric of continuous roof planes and screens (derived from Richardson's "shingle-plan" resort houses) defined a new domestic architecture. Although the skeleton frame makes its significant appearance in the works of Sullivan and others, Wright attacks the concept in his studies of other systems. His demand: "no posts, no columns. . . . In my work, the idea of plasticity may now be seen as the element of continuity." He acclaims "the new reality that is space *instead* of matter." As for architectural interiors, he declares: "I came to realize that the reality of a building was not the container but the space within."

These elements and concepts are fully expressed in Wright's Robie House in Chicago (FIG. 22-57), built between 1907 and 1909. This building, like others of his houses at the time, was called a "prairie house." The long, sweeping, ground-hugging lines, unconfined by abrupt limits of wall, seem to reach out toward and to express the great flatlands of the Middle West. This is a good example of Wright's "naturalism" in the adjustment of building to site, although, in this particular case, the confines of the city lot provide less opportunity than do the sites of some of Wright's more expansive suburban villas. In the "wandering" plan of the Robie House (FIG. 22-58), intricately articulated spaces (some, large and open; others, closed) are grouped freely around a great central fireplace. (Wright felt strongly the age-old domestic significance of the hearth.) Wright's new and fundamental spatial arrangement of the interior is matched in his treatment of the exterior. Symmetry is disposed of, the façade disappears, the roofs extend

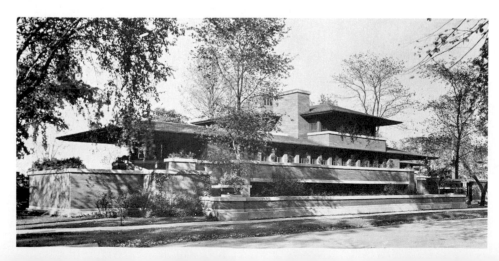

22-57 FRANK LLOYD WRIGHT, Robie House, Chicago, Illinois, 1907–1909.

929

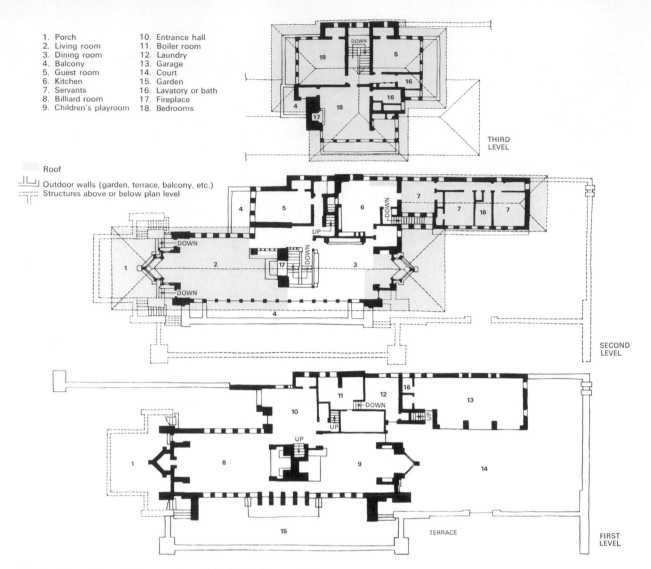

1. Porch
2. Living room
3. Dining room
4. Balcony
5. Guest room
6. Kitchen
7. Servants
8. Billiard room
9. Children's playroom
10. Entrance hall
11. Boiler room
12. Laundry
13. Garage
14. Court
15. Garden
16. Lavatory or bath
17. Fireplace
18. Bedrooms

Roof

Outdoor walls (garden, terrace, balcony, etc.)

Structures above or below plan level

THIRD LEVEL

SECOND LEVEL

FIRST LEVEL

TERRACE

22-58   FRANK LLOYD WRIGHT, plan of the Robie House, Chicago.

far beyond the walls, the windows are in continuous strips, and the entrance is all but concealed. Masses and voids have come into equilibrium; the flow of space determines the placement of the walls. The "Cubist" aspect of the exterior, with its sharp, angular planes meeting at apparently odd angles, matches the complex play of interior solids, where the solids function not as inert, containing surfaces but as equivalent in role to the spaces in the design.

The implied message of this new architecture is *space*, not *mass*—a space that fits the life of the patron and that is simply enclosed and divided as required. Wright took special pains to meet the requirements of his clients, often designing the accessories of the house himself (including, in at least one case, the gowns of his client's wife!). Discerning clients commissioned his works, but his reputation grew more rapidly in Europe, especially in Holland and Germany, than in America. The publication in Berlin in 1910 of a portfolio of Wright's work hastened the death of Art Nouveau and stimulated younger archi-

tects to turn in the new direction. Had Wright died at that time, his work would still have a revolutionary significance. In 1940, Ludwig Mies van der Rohe, himself a great modern architect, wrote:

> At this moment [1911], so critical for us, the exhibition of the work of Frank Lloyd Wright came to Berlin. . . . The encounter was destined to prove of great significance to the European development. . . . The dynamic impulse from his work invigorated a whole generation. His influence was strongly felt even when it was not actually visible.*

The International Style

World War I was the dividing line for European architecture, eliminating the blind alley of Art Nouveau and bringing Wright's ideas into broad acceptance and eager expansion. Even until after World War II, American and European architects would practice

*In Philip Johnson, *Mies van der Rohe*, rev. ed. (New York: Museum of Modern Art, 1954), pp. 200–201.

what could be called an International style, so closely did they agree on fundamental principles including the new principle of *structure.* In the modern building, the great tensile strength of steel and the great crushing (or compression) strength of concrete are employed together to support enormous loads. The steel framework obviates the historical necessity of bracing thrust pressures with resisting mass and makes heavy bearing walls unnecessary, so that the walls become mere screens or "curtains." The long cantilever, another product of the use of steel, can reach out into space with support at only one end; and with the development of prestressed concrete, load and support become one.* Thus, the demands of stability and support can be subordinated to the concerns of utility and esthetics as never before in the history of architecture.

Another principle basic to the International style deals with a radically different approach to the *plan.* The enormous strength of the new building materials now at the architect's disposal permits an unprecedented flexibility in the planning of the interiors of buildings. With steel and concrete, spans without interior supports can be constructed on a scale that goes far beyond the wildest dreams of earlier builders. The resultant interior space can be arranged and rearranged with movable, nonbearing partitions or thrown open completely for an "open plan." Glass "walls" often make interior and exterior ambiguous. "Out" and "in" become relative terms, like "forward" and "back" in Cubist art. New demands are

*In *reinforced concrete,* steel bars are embedded in concrete and the resulting member combines the respective *tensile* and *compressive* strengths of the two materials. In *prestressed concrete,* the embedded bars are fastened at the ends of the member in such a way that they are kept under tension, thus increasing tensile strength.

placed on the viewer, who now must move through the interior to comprehend its "wandering" space-flow.

The third principle animating the International School, the architectural philosophy of *functionalism,* is naturally related to the new approaches to structure and design. In this view, the function of the building is considered first and determines the building's form. Thus, there is no given form into which a function can be made to fit; a building cannot be made that will function just as well as an art school, a hospital, or a warehouse. The functions to be enclosed must be particularized; a building is then designed to enclose and esthetically express those functions. Just as the plan is determined first by the space, so the function of the building—the activities that are to take place in it—must dictate its form. The parts of the building should visually distinguish its functions; for example, its servant (utility) spaces should be distinct from its primary spaces.

The structural essentials of the International style are graphically shown in the 1914 drawing (FIG. 22-59) by Swiss architect Charles Édouard Jeanneret-Gris (1887–1965), called LE CORBUSIER. A Cubist painter as well as an influential writer on modern architecture, Le Corbusier applied himself principally to the design of the "functional" house, which he describes, in a phrase that has acquired wide currency, as a "machine for living." The drawing shows the skeleton of a dwelling in which the properties of reinforced concrete have been utilized with maximum efficiency. Reinforced concrete slabs, serving the double function of ceiling (for the lower story) and floor (for the upper), are supported by steel posts that rise freely through the interior space of the structure. Exterior walls can be suspended from the projecting edges of

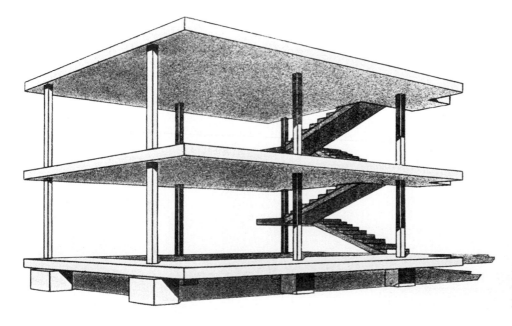

22-59 LE CORBUSIER, perspective drawing for Domino House Project, Marseilles, France, 1914.

the concrete slabs like free-hanging curtains. Because the skeleton is self-supporting, the architect has complete freedom to subdivide the interior as desired with nonbearing walls. Furthermore, the unit shown can be repeated almost indefinitely (as a kind of module), both horizontally and vertically, as indeed it is in most modern office buildings and skyscrapers (see FIGS. 22-66 and 22-67). Although Le Corbusier did not invent the system shown (it had been anticipated about half a decade earlier by PETER BEHRENS, with whom Le Corbusier worked in his early career, and by Walter Gropius), the drawing clearly states the basic structural principles on which much of twentieth-century architecture is based.

Early examples of the International style show its very close relationship to Cubist and Formalist developments in painting. The Schroeder House at Utrecht in Holland (FIG. 22-60), built in 1924 by GERRIT RIETVELDT (1888–1964), shows the influence of the De Stijl purists and—in its sweeping planes and overhanging roofs—of Frank Lloyd Wright. A severe and doctrinaire insistence on the rectilinearity of the planes, which seem to slide across each other like movable panels, makes Rietveldt's house a kind of three-dimensional projection of the rigid but carefully proportioned flat planes in Mondrian's paintings (FIG. 22-20). Ornament is, of course, entirely banished; ADOLPH LOOS, a forerunner of this kind of purist trend, equates ornament with "crime." A triumph of International purism is the Villa Savoye (FIG. 22-61) at Poissy-sur-Seine, near Paris, designed by Le Corbusier. The building is a cube of lightly enclosed and deeply penetrated space, supported, at least visually, on thin columns (*pilotis*)—a seemingly deliberate analogy with the isolated, "machined" space of an ocean liner; the flat roof-terrace may appropriately be called a "deck," as the modern flat roof commonly is now. There is no façade; the approach does not define an entrance, and one must walk around and through the building to comprehend its layout. Spaces and masses interpenetrate so fluently that there is the familiar Internationalist ambiguity of "inside" and "outside." The machine-planed smoothness of the surfaces, entirely without adornment, the slender "ribbons" of continuous windows, the buoyant lightness of the whole fabric—all present a total effect that is the very reverse of the traditional country house (compare Andrea Palladio's Villa Rotunda and John Vanbrugh's Blenheim; FIGS. 17-52 and 20-4). There are no basement walls of masonry; the "load" hovers lightly on its slender supports, the inverse of the traditional design, which places the light elements above and the heavy ones below. Le Corbusier's use of color—dark-green base, cream walls, and rose and blue superstructure (a windscreen)—is a deliberate analogy with contemporary painting, in which he was actively engaged.

The Villa Savoye is set conspicuously within its site, tending to dominate it, and has a broad view of the landscape. In this way, it *does* resemble the Palladian villa and contrasts sharply with Frank Lloyd Wright's dwellings, which hug and adjust to the landscape, almost as if they were intended to be part of it and concealed by it. Wright's Kaufmann House (FIG. 22-62), built at Bear Run, Pennsylvania, in 1939, crouches within its isolated woodland site, reaching

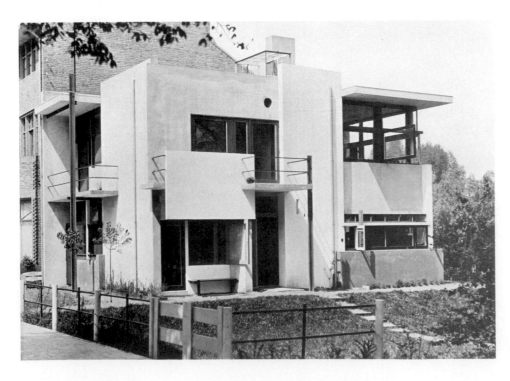

22-60 GERRIT RIETVELDT, Schroeder House, Utrecht, Netherlands, 1924.

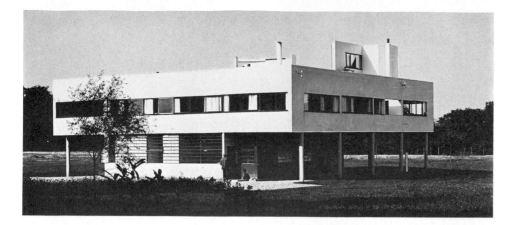

22-61 LE CORBUSIER,
Villa Savoye,
Poissy-sur-Seine, France, 1929.

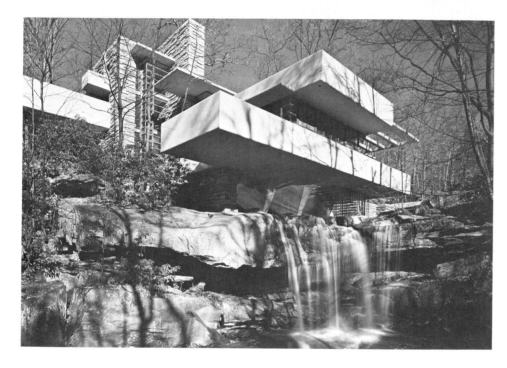

22-62 FRANK LLOYD WRIGHT,
Kaufmann House ("Falling Water"),
Bear Run, Pennsylvania,
1936–1939.

out almost protectively over a little waterfall. The machine-planed decks of the International style function like the broad overhanging roofs of the Robie House (FIG. 22-57), meeting and intersecting dramatically. Although he disliked the cubic regularity of the International style, here Wright makes a virtue of the contrast between the sharp, clean lines and planes of the International deck and the rockwork and freely falling water of the natural site. Thus, Wright's customary naturalism—his love of free and irregular forms, the "organic" in its unspoiled setting—is beautifully adjusted to the severe regularity of the European designs, as if he were editorializing on the International style.

Wright accepted the machine as a challenge to be met, but he warned against being overcome by it. In Europe, architecture was long dominated by what might be called the "romanticism of the machine." Le Corbusier's vision of the house as a "machine for living" expresses this, and we have seen the broad influence of machine design and dynamics on painting

and sculpture. German architecture, particularly the factories and industrial buildings designed by Gropius (FIG. 22-63), reveals a deep respect for the machine, with its parts precisely tooled, seemingly unrelated, and functioning only as parts of a whole. This may be seen in the Bauhaus in Dessau, West Germany, originally founded in 1906 as the Weimar School of Arts and Crafts by the Dutch architect–designer HENRY VAN DE VELDE (1863–1957). He was an outstanding representative of Art Nouveau, and his educational program emphasized craftsmanship along with free creativity and experimentation. When Van de Velde left Weimar at the outbreak of World War I, he recommended a young German architect, WALTER GROPIUS (1883–1969), as his successor. Gropius assumed the directorship of the school in 1919; he reorganized the various departments of the original school under the new name of Das Staatliche Bauhaus, Weimar, and moved it to the newly built quarters in Dessau in 1925. The redesigned curriculum stressed the search for solutions to contemporary

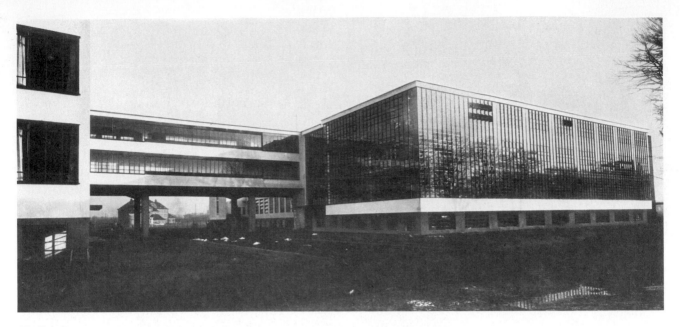

22-63 WALTER GROPIUS, shop block, the Bauhaus, Dessau, West Germany, 1925–1926.

problems in such areas as housing, urban planning, and high-quality, utilitarian mass production—all vital needs in impoverished post-World War I Germany. Under the guidance of Lyonel Feininger, Kandinsky, and Klee, The Bauhaus, which takes its name from the German word for building *(bau)*, offered courses not only in architecture, but also in music, drama, and, in particular, painting. In design, handicraft was considered the natural training device for mass production and the natural basis for experimental models leading to industrial products. In these respects, and in the minimizing of philosophy and other "verbal" disciplines, the Bauhaus was the earliest working example of much that is still sought in design education. Its training was rooted in the Arts and Crafts movement of earlier generations and in the work of Friedrich Froebel, a German educator, and others' work with children's art, but its vision was firmly fixed on the requirements and potentialities of its day.

Gropius' design for the Bauhaus buildings, which included a workshop, a studio, a school, and an administrative office, firmly established the principles of the International style—an expression of the "machine age" as the Europeans of the 1920s wished to see it. Planned as a series of cells, each with its own specific function, it is the direct expression, in glass, steel, and thin concrete veneer, of the technical program (that is, the function) of the building. The forms are clear, cubic units—the epitome of classicizing purity. The workshop block (FIG. 22-63) is a cage of glass that extends beyond and encloses its steel supports in a realization of Le Corbusier's early schematic sketch (FIG. 22-59). Here, the new concept of flexible structure triumphs. The transparent block makes an equilibrium of inner and outer space.

In the work of LUDWIG MIES VAN DER ROHE (1886–1969), the International style found its most imaginative solutions and perhaps a new order. His German Pavilion (FIG. 22-64), built for the International Exposition at Barcelona in 1929, has a program—an information center and rest house—so simple that the architect was able to concentrate almost exclusively (as is the case for many exposition buildings) on the dramatic principles of the new style. Fine stone and marble, chromium and glass, water and sculpture mold the space and subtly lead the visitor through a succession of areas that vary in degree of enclosure—now open on several sides, now enclosed by two, three, or four walls. Grace and elegance, refined and subtle harmonies, are realized to a degree comparable to that in such eighteenth-century masterpieces as the Hôtel de Soubise (FIG. 20-6) and Robert Adam's Osterley Park House (FIG. 20-24), but in this instance in a language and spirit wholly of the twentieth century.

Although American architecture did not keep up with the progressive International style during the 1920s, the example of its mighty skyscrapers stimulated the imagination of European architects. For a time, the typical American skyscraper was clothed in traditional stylistic features, but something of the new International manner began to appear just at the end of the skyscraper age in the early 1930s. In the Philadelphia Savings Fund Society Building (FIG. 22-65), designed by GEORGE HOWE (1886–1955) and WILLIAM E. LESCAZE (1896–1969), the horizontal banding, ribbon windows, and clean geometric planes of the International style appear on the soaring scale of the American urban office building. Mies van der Rohe had been inspired by the skyscraper as early as 1920, when he made a startlingly beautiful

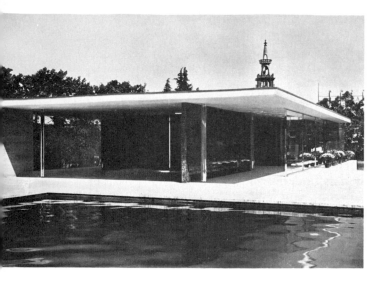

22-64 LUDWIG MIES VAN DER ROHE, German Pavilion, Barcelona International Exhibition, Spain, 1929.

22-65 GEORGE HOWE and WILLIAM E. LESCAZE, Philadelphia Savings Fund Society Building, Philadelphia, Pennsylvania, 1931–1932.

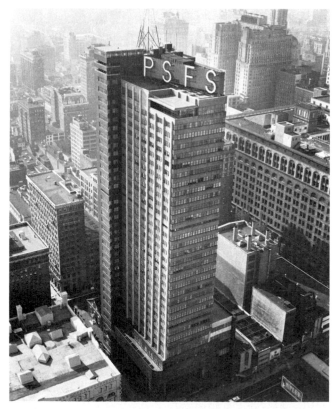

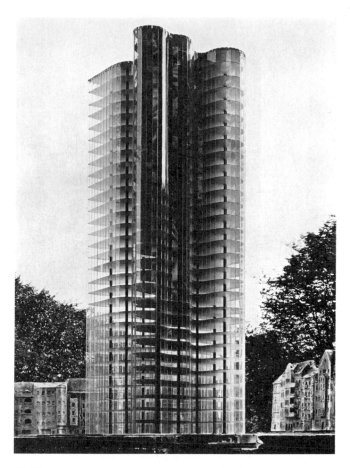

22-66 LUDWIG MIES VAN DER ROHE, model for a glass skyscraper, 1920–1921. Present location of model unknown.

model for a glass building (FIG. 22-66)—a work that was never carried out but showed a profound under-standing of the technical and esthetic possibilities of steel, glass, and concrete in symphonic relationship. The structure's transparency, which may have influ-enced Gropius' Bauhaus design (FIG. 22-63), the web-like delicacy of its lines, its radiance, and the illusion of movement created by reflection and by light changes seen through it prefigure the contemporary glass skyscraper slabs of our major cities. Indeed, the model anticipates by 30 years Mies van der Rohe's design—carried out in collaboration with PHILIP JOHNSON (b. 1906)—of the Seagram Building (FIG. 22-67), built in New York City from 1956 to 1958. This towering, prismatic block, raised on piers, is meas-ured out in modular units, each detail of surface and silhouette dictated by Mies van der Rohe's sense for the purity of straight line and uncomplicated, rectilin-ear shape. Here, the evolution of function–form is completed. The myriad operations performed by thousands of human beings are revealed in a lumi-nous cage of glass that, at the same time, serves as a vast, almost pictorial, reflective surface that mirrors the titanic city. Enclosure and disclosure are simulta-neous; the building is the perfect expression of an anonymous public world articulated by innumerable impersonal functions. Yet Mies van der Rohe—no matter his belief that architectural beauty may be as impersonal as its function—spared no pains in his attention to detail, for "God," he said, "dwells in the details."

To the three principles of structure, plan, and func-tionalism that guide the architect working in the In-ternational style should be added a fourth—one deci-

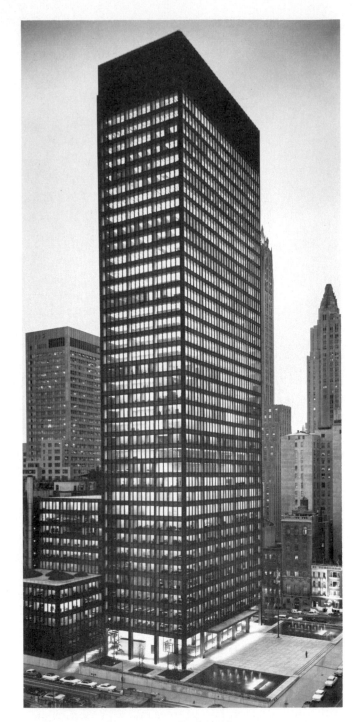

22-67 LUDWIG MIES VAN DER ROHE and PHILIP JOHNSON, Seagram Building, New York, 1956–1958.

sive for the characteristic look of the style: *mechanical control of the interior environment.* If the elevator made the development of the high-rise building possible, so air conditioning has made design according to the new principles possible without respect to geographical location or climatic conditions. Thus, true to their name, International style buildings resemble one another, whether they rise in Canada or Brazil, in Tokyo, New York, Capetown, or Calcutta.

PAINTING AND SCULPTURE AFTER WORLD WAR II

Since World War II, brilliant variations have been made on the great central themes stated in the "classical age" of modern art, when most of our contemporary artists were born. The shock of the war and its "cold" aftermath, the persisting threat of nuclear annihilation, the widening recognition of human suffering in a large part of the world, and a haunting fear among many that life has no meaning or value have sharpened the protest of highly sensitive artists against a mechanized culture that often appears to have no place in it for the nonconforming individual. Expressionism becomes harsher, more defiant and rebellious; Dadaistic satire, more bitter; and Formalistic art insists on an ever-more-radical abstraction from the world of appearance. As European–American civilization broadens into world civilization, a crisis of values is taking place—or, rather, continues to take place. Traditional values and the values of organized modern life are criticized mercilessly and declared to be largely false. It is almost as if the only value left is the belief in the artistic process itself on the grounds that in creativity alone resides true humanity. The artist's way of life has become a possible model for all human life, with its religion of free expression, its pursuit of identity and self-knowledge through art, and its overtones of prophetic mysticism. On the other hand, neither art nor artist has escaped the peculiar dynamics of modern society. Art has become a big business, and the artist might sometimes be thought of as a kind of piecework employee of ambitious and commercially minded galleries. The work of art is a commodity on the art "market," and methods familiar to modern advertising promote it. The old divisions between the arts are vanishing. Painting, sculpture, and architecture interfuse, and all are increasingly bound to developments in technology. The revolution that began even before the century itself continues at an ever-more-rapid pace.

It is of course impossible to do historical justice to contemporary events, especially when the men and women who create them are still living. The selection and presentation of certain contemporary monuments suggests that a judgment of their superiority has already been made by history. This is not the case; historical judgment moves slowly, and its selection of the touchstone masterpieces of the epoch has scarcely begun for the twentieth century.

At first glance, developments in painting and sculpture after World War II seem all confusion, with bewildering overlaps and intersections of tendencies and influences. Yet closer study reveals a certain order susceptible of at least rough classification. This

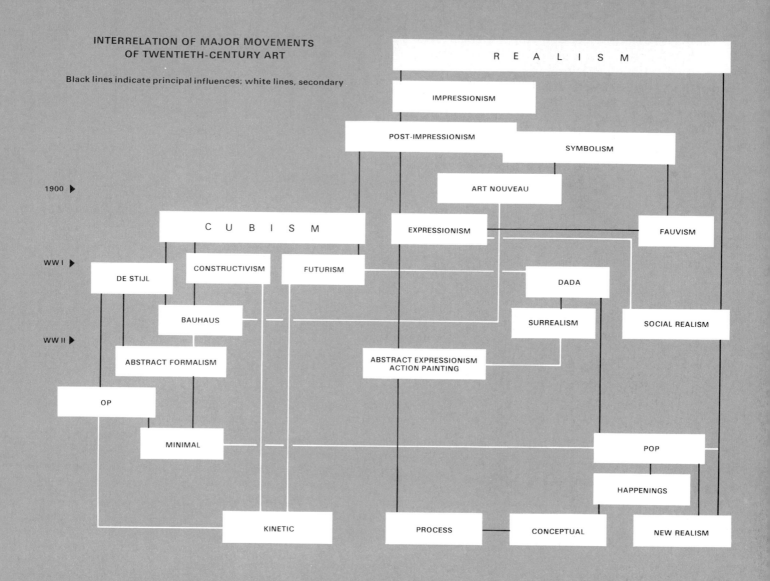

INTERRELATION OF MAJOR MOVEMENTS
OF TWENTIETH-CENTURY ART

Black lines indicate principal influences; white lines, secondary

1900 ▶

WW I ▶

WW II ▶

REALISM

IMPRESSIONISM

POST-IMPRESSIONISM

SYMBOLISM

ART NOUVEAU

CUBISM

EXPRESSIONISM

FAUVISM

DE STIJL

CONSTRUCTIVISM

FUTURISM

DADA

BAUHAUS

SURREALISM

SOCIAL REALISM

ABSTRACT FORMALISM

ABSTRACT EXPRESSIONISM
ACTION PAINTING

OP

MINIMAL

POP

HAPPENINGS

KINETIC

PROCESS

CONCEPTUAL

NEW REALISM

order appears as a fundamental (though by no means clear-cut) dualism that seems to arise in the work of the fathers of modern art—Cézanne on the one hand, Gauguin and Van Gogh on the other. One can believe it is the old familiar dualism in Western art between "classicizing formalism" directed by intellect and "baroque–romantic expressivism" prompted by sensation and feeling.

As indicated in the chart of twentieth-century art (see above), Cubism and Expressionism and the styles derivative from them dominate the art of the first half of the century (the period before World War II). Some semblance of order can be brought into the seemingly chaotic profusion of postwar trends and styles by grouping them on the basis of artists' approaches to their mediums, which can be either predominantly rational–formalistic or emotional–expressive. Accordingly, most of the postwar trends are grouped as

descendants of either Cubism or Expressionism (although we are aware of the crosscurrents and interchanges of influence) under the generic headings Abstract Formalism and Abstract Expressionism. Admittedly, the organization is rough, oversimplified, and undoubtedly subject to future modifications as increasing distance from contemporaneous events allows us to view them with greater detachment.

Expressionism: Figural and Abstract

Against the Constructivist depersonalization of the work of art and against the prevailing Social Realism, Expressionists after World War II strenuously assert the artist's personality, individuality, identity, even pathology. In this, they can follow the example and the precepts of the distinguished tradition of Expressionism that reaches back to Gauguin, Van Gogh,

Kandinsky, and their contemporaries and successors. But among the later artists, the Expressionist conviction and method seem stronger. Basically, what sets them apart from the earlier Expressionists is the question of whether to retain the human figure and related images or to banish them altogether from painting. The Expressionists accept the first alternative and can be conveniently designated "figural"; the others are "abstract."

The distortion of the human figure in painting for the purpose of the expression of strong emotion is, as we have seen, a very old practice in Western art and by no means solely a modern invention. That distortion works strongly in many works of the British painter FRANCIS BACON (b. 1910), which express an excruciating crisis of nerves that goes well beyond Munch (FIG. 21-76), for example, in its emphasis. A subject that Bacon often returns to is the human being locked in a box-like space by a malignant, glittering mesh of spectral light rays. His 1953 *Number VII from Eight Studies for a Portrait* (FIG. 22-68), painted in 1953, shows us Pope Innocent X (from a Velázquez portrait) as if restrained by a straitjacket and capable of no action but a continuing, dreadful scream. The picture is an almost unbearable image of insane terror. Our age—the "age of psychology"—is obsessed as perhaps no other age before it with the fear and the fact of mental illness.

22-68 FRANCIS BACON, *Number VII from Eight Studies for a Portrait*, 1953. Approx. 60" × 46". Museum of Modern Art, New York (gift of Mr. and Mrs. William A.M. Burden).

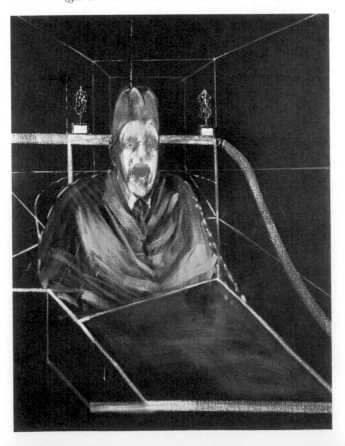

The construction of the new art seems almost to require the destruction of the ideals of the old; thus destructiveness, as Gertrude Stein recognized, plays a large role in the new art's vitality: "everything destroys itself in the twentieth century, and nothing continues. . . ." (Compare Jean Tinguely's *Homage to New York*, FIG. 22-86.) This wide destruction involves not only the Cubist shattering of perspective and the denial that there is only one perspective; it also dismisses the traditional notion (both Greek and Renaissance) of beauty in art as being a reflection of human beauty, for, as Gauguin thought, beauty in this sense is nothing but a lie. The Expressionist artist is only too aware of pain and suffering in his age.

Although his intuitive manner of painting seems related to the methods of the Abstract Expressionist painters, Bacon is largely independent of international Abstract Expressionism and provides a kind of figural reaction against the movement's more abstract tendencies. Abstract Expressionism carries all before it after World War II, especially in America, to which the artistic center of gravity appears to shift from Europe. The style—or, rather, method—has its roots in Kandinsky's automatic and spontaneous nonobjectivity and his mystical interpretations of color and line (FIG. 22-10). (The label "abstract expressionism" was attached to Kandinsky's art as early as 1919.) It also owes much to Surrealists like Ernst (FIG. 22-26), who experimented with chance effects of manipulating paint and surface in ways other than by the brush. Most immigrant European artists in the 1930s and 1940s were Constructivists like Mondrian (FIG. 22-20). On the other hand, HANS HOFMANN (1880–1966) developed an expressionistic method of painting in his later years in America that directly preceded the native American school of Abstract Expressionism and had a deep influence on it. Hofmann's double career as artist and art teacher spanned two generations and two continents. As a young man, he was the associate and friend of the founders of abstract art—Matisse, Braque, Picasso. Later, in America, he became an influential teacher and expressed his new ideas in a vigorous, almost violent method of painterly attack. Hofmann charges his surfaces with primary colors of unparalleled richness in jolting contrasts and conflicts—painting impastos densely and with dashing spontaneity, leaving each stroke or splash unmodified. The painted surface becomes only that: a record of the artist's intense experience of paint and of color, of the process of painting—arbitrary, accidental, unthinking, automatic, direct. In *Effervescence, 1944* (FIG. 22-69), Hofmann mixes media (oil, India ink, casein, enamel), a method common in Abstract Expressionist painting. Colors explode in a chaos controlled only by the picture frame—a chaos that seems to have sucked the artist into its swirl and to have painted itself.

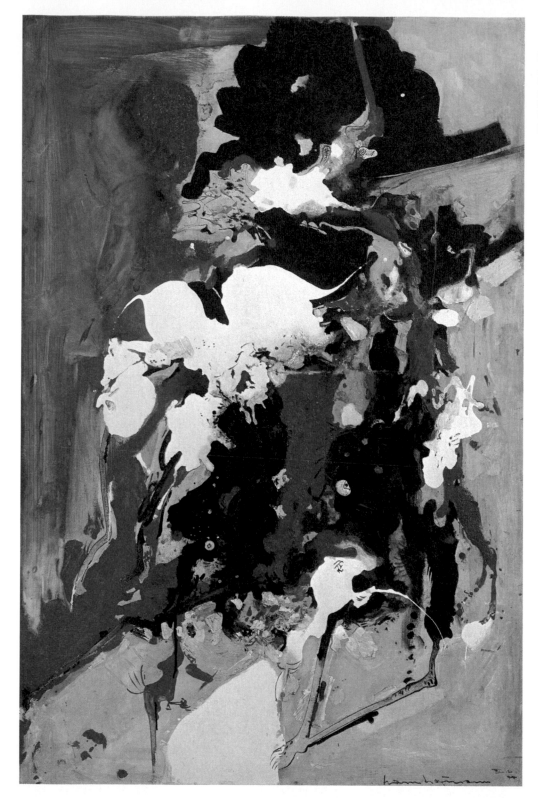

22-69 HANS HOFMANN, *Effervescence*, 1944. Oil, India ink, casein, and enamel on plywood, 54½″ × 36″. University Art Museum, Berkeley, California.

Hofmann's method in effect produces painting that is a record of the producing action, that is almost a *picture* of that action. This is the rationale behind the designation "action painting" attached to many Abstract Expressionist works. Painting is thus a largely uncontrolled, prerational action or event; the process of painting becomes more real than the painted surface.

An artist who certainly must have subscribed to this "action" view and who was the central figure of the New York School in the 1940s and 1950s was JACKSON POLLOCK (1912–1956). Pollock once practiced Social Realism; his abrupt turnabout to Abstract Expressionism typifies the postwar situation in the arts. At the height of his powers, in the years just before his untimely death in 1956, Pollock shared with his brilliant colleagues in New York a collective achievement that has been called the most original and distinctive in the history of American art. The principal method in American Abstract Expressionism (for there were other methods) was the painting-action revealed through the brush gesture and the signature left by the fall and touch of the paint. Pollock would roll out a large canvas on the floor and drip and splatter paint on it while he himself was in energetic motion along its edge or sometimes within it. For him, the expression of the artist's whole content, which is inward, is directed by mysterious psychic forces; hence, in his view, to label the look of such painting "accidental" would be misleading. Yet there is something of the mystique of the materials that we saw in Brancuși motivating the action painter; the random fall and scatter of the paint emphasizes the liquid nature of the medium itself, which enters into the sum of the painting's qualities. The jarring dynamism of Pollock's large-scale paintings, in turn, echoes the restless, perhaps rootless life style of the postwar years. It manifests too, in its extremely personal nature, the interest of many Expressionist artists in Existentialism, the widely adopted philosophy of the postwar years that stresses absolute freedom of choice in life and art as a human commitment.

In an early (1947) example of Pollock's art, his *Lucifer* (FIG. 22-70), the materials—oil, aluminum paint, and enamel—are dragged, dripped, and splattered from well above the surface in a process of excited movement that has in its tracing and retracing a remarkable coherence of direction and pattern. The painter strives for unplanned immediacy and directness and for an effect of unstudied, spontaneous freshness of statement. As Pollock says ". . . it doesn't make much difference how the paint is put on as long as something has been said. Technique is just a means of arriving at a statement." The state-

ment arrived at is at the same time the record—the signature, as it were—of the creating process itself, which *arrives* at something rather that aims at it intentionally. Modern philosophy, when it is influenced by the views of modern biology, often stresses the reality of process over structure, and if Pollock's painting is an image of anything, it is of process itself in its never-ending, never-wearying creation of nature. Action painting completes, moreover, that introduction of time and motion into the static arts of form that began in Futurism. Now the artist himself is truly in motion; his viewpoint is constantly changing. It is significant that the easel picture is inappropriate for his creative "dance"; as he moves, he looks not out (as from a viewpoint) but *down*, seeing his "landscape" unfold somewhat as we see the earth from an airplane moving through the air some 10,000 feet up. Thus, although action painting may seem strange and formless at first, we need only reflect on the vast new vocabulary of forms that the surface of the earth itself yields to modern eyes and imaginations. To these, add the marvelous, formal complexities of the microcosm and the macrocosm revealed by microphotography and our probing of outer space. The macroscopic and microscopic worlds—where endless and intricate processes weave endless and intricate relationships of living forms—are given a visual presence in the dense, entangled skeins of lines and colors in Pollock's art.

Abstract Expressionism had many possible methods of approach. In the work of FRANZ KLINE (1910–1962), it is a vehicle of very personal psychic revelation, possibly as mysterious to the artist as to the observer. Kline himself admitted that there was no

22-70 JACKSON POLLOCK, *Lucifer*, 1947. Oil, aluminum paint, and enamel on canvas, approx. 3' 5" × 8' 9". Collection of Mr. and Mrs. Harry W. Anderson.

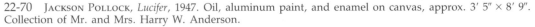

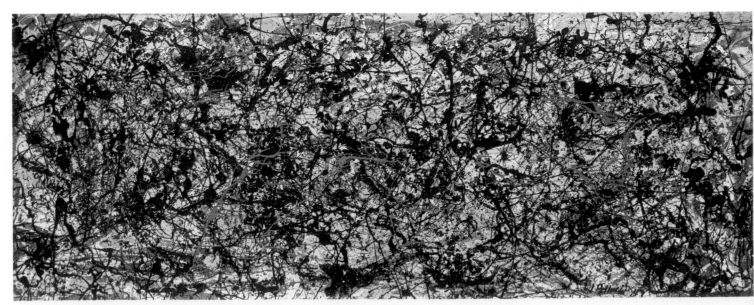

22-71 Franz Kline, *Painting 1952*, 1955–1956. Approx. 6' 5" × 8' 4". Present location unknown.

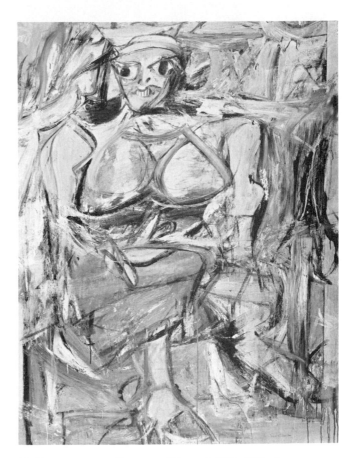

22-72 Willem de Kooning, *Woman I*, 1950–1952. Approx. 6' 4" × 4' 10". Museum of Modern Art, New York (purchase).

way to find a verbal equivalent or sometimes even a caption, to express his meaning. He painted, in black and white on large canvases, ragged bars and stripes of black enclosing (or overlapped by) rectilinear white areas as sharp-edged as broken planes of glass (FIG. 22-71). These configurations suggest Chinese characters boldly brushed and greatly magnified, a kind of ideogram of the artist's psychic states. As hieratic and quasi-magical shapes, they can be interpreted as the observer pleases; as purely nonobjective forms in a wide variety of arrangements, they appeal through their blunt esthetic force and bold, free execution.

Of the New York action painters, WILLEM DE KOONING (b. 1904), a native of Holland who began as a figure and portrait painter, practices a quick alternation between abstract and figural painting. The tension between the two approaches is itself expressive of De Kooning's attitude; he has been called an "artist who makes ambiguity a hypothesis on which to build."* Ambiguity prevails in an art and in an age where nothing, as De Kooning himself says, is certain but self-consciousness. Shapes and colors play through, over, and across one another with no definable order, with no completeness of decision. De Kooning's best-known works, his series of paintings of female nudes on large canvases, comprise a gallery of sometimes harsh and biting, sometimes sinister and menacing, sometimes jovial and sensuous caricatures. In *Woman I* (FIG. 22-72), the attack is carried out with manic excitement, the figure slashed out with brush at arm's length and at full speed. There is a curious effect, typically ambiguous, of simultaneous delineation and defacement, of construction and cancellation—a conflict between sketch and finished pic-

*Thomas B. Hess, *Willem de Kooning* (New York: Museum of Modern Art, 1968), p. 25.

ture. The brazen and baleful mask mixes the toothpaste smile with the grimace of the death's head. The enormous sketch is carried through by the compulsive drive that marks the action painter.

That Abstract Expressionism is a good deal less homogeneous in style than once seemed to be the case is particularly apparent in the work of MARK ROTHKO (1903–1973). Although he was a friend and contemporary of Pollock, Kline, and De Kooning, Rothko's paintings exhibit none of their aggressive attack or slashing brushwork. *Four Darks on Red* (FIG. 22-73) dismisses the usual *brio* of "action painting" for a calm and contemplative mood. Subtle tonal variations transcend the essentially monochromatic theme and create a mysterious effect of forms or images hovering in an ambiguously defined space. Where the dynamics of the other Abstract Expressionists might be taken as visual metaphors of the hostility and alienation implicit in contemporary Existential philosophy, Rothko's work seems more in tune with a Zen viewpoint—the one, a call to action; the other, an invitation to meditate. Yet, despite the profound differences, all these painters share a primary interest in the painterly problem of painting—that is, a concern with the actual process of applying paint to canvas rather than with questions of narrative content.

22-73　Mark Rothko, *Four Darks on Red*, 1958. 8′ 6″ × 9′ 8″. Collection of the Whitney Museum of American Art (gift of the Friends of the Whitney Museum of American Art, Mr. and Mrs. Eugene Schwartz, Mrs. Samuel A. Seaver, Charles Simon, and purchase).

Realism

It is indicative of the diversity of modern trends that, at the height of its vogue, Abstract Expressionism was by no means universally adopted. It was possible in the general debate about styles and the purposes of art for voices old and new to be heard—and in many stylistic accents. The painting of Andrew Wyeth (b. 1917) is still the subject of considerable disagreement among critics. Contemporaneous with the vivid action painting of the New York School, Wyeth treats the American scene with a meticulous Realism in a muted poetic way that has something of the dreaming detachment of Surrealism without Surrealism's fantasy. At first glance, Wyeth's spirit seems utterly untouched by the storms of twentieth-century artistic revolution; but the odd angles of his compositions and his carefully selected perspectives and vignettes show that he is no stranger to experimentation in

modern design. His quiet appeal to the long-established taste of America for realism speaks in pictures like *Christina's World* (FIG. 22-74), a work almost exactly contemporary with Pollock's *Lucifer* (FIG. 22-70). Here, his skilled representation of the optical world does not intrude on the genuinely felt human situation and its gentle pathos. The title, in the modern fashion, seems askew from the theme, and the subject is not given literally but only alluded to, in familiar modern ambiguity. In its own way, the picture is as personal and introspective as the works of the Abstract Expressionists.

Realism in both painting and sculpture has been the prevailing mode of artistic representation in the countries altered or affected by the great revolutions of the twentieth century. In the Soviet Union, as well as in the People's Republic of China (FIG. 12-29), it has become the official style of the state; and in Marxist Socialist movements and regimes throughout the

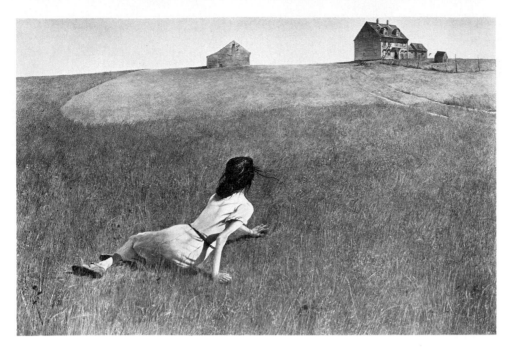

22-74 ANDREW WYETH, *Christina's World*, 1948. Tempera on gesso panel, approx. 32¼″ × 47¾″. Museum of Modern Art, New York (purchase).

world, Social Realism advertises the merits of revolutionary socialism. Ironically, similar elements are manifest in the official art of Germany and Italy in the 1930s and early 1940s, although their Fascist political philosophy is generally held to be diametrically opposed to that of Soviet Marxism. It would appear that the highly centralized twentieth-century dictatorship not only favors conservative Realism in art but also uses art to achieve propagandistic ends, denying the "art for art's sake" orientation of much modern art. Much the same could be said of many government-subsidized WPA (Works Projects Administration) art projects in the United States during the Great Depression of the 1930s.

Abstract Formalism

An early phase of the Formalist approach is epitomized by the work of the productive and influential American painter STUART DAVIS (1894–1964), the first artist to assimilate French Cubism and naturalize it in the American setting. His long career extends from his exhibit in New York at the Armory show of 1913 (which introduced modern art to the general public in this country) to the 1960s. Beginning with the collage, Davis gradually eliminated all representational and associative forms from his compositions. (There are some exceptions; for example, Davis occasionally introduced advertising signs into his work, anticipating Pop Art.) This process of elimination and the achievement of a total abstraction can be followed in his famous series of "egg-beater" paintings, wherein, beginning with an image of that ordinary kitchen utensil, Davis gradually evolves an organization of line, shape, and color that shows no trace of the original image. But Davis was not merely a foreign member of the French school of abstract art. He was an original master who developed his own style, expressive of the vivid syncopation of the American scene; and he was at least partly responsible for raising the level of competence of American painting to that of the European schools. Throughout his career, Davis yielded little to the pressures of new vogues, maintaining with astonishing consistency the principles of Cubist art as he had reinterpreted them to suit his purpose. At the same time, he retained the respect of modern innovators, who acknowledged him as the dean of American abstract painters. In *Colonial Cubism* (FIG. 22-75), Davis shows, in a densely organized composition, the play of angular and rectilinear shapes and flat, hard colors in the characteristic Cubist ambiguity of figure and ground, where "forward" and "backward" alternate rapidly. Here, the "subject" of the painting is nothing but the carefully adjusted elements of a purely formal, two-dimensional order. The whole visual field is a lively vibration of colors and shapes in combination and contrast.

The Formalistic interest represented by Davis withstood the powerful competition of America's original postwar style—Abstract Expressionism or "action painting," with its subjectivity and painterly extravagance. We must keep in mind the context of these movements and countermovements. Restless experimentation, the rapid successions of inventions and obsolescences of stylistic conventions, and the fluctuations of a highly sensitive art market kept producing almost violent reversals of interest and tendency in contemporary art. In the Formalistic reaction to Abstract Expressionism—generally called Post-Painterly Abstraction (a phrase of the critic Clement Greenberg), a movement with such allied manifestations as

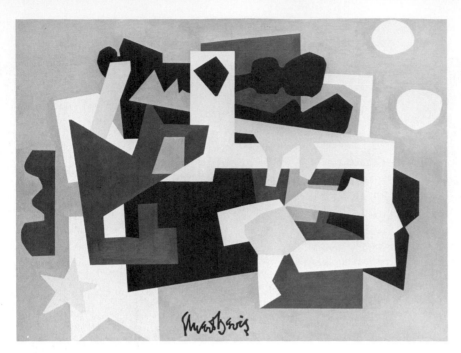

22-75 STUART DAVIS, *Colonial Cubism*, 1954. 45″ × 60″. Collection, Walker Art Center, Minneapolis.

Op Art and Hard-Edge and Color-Field painting— the disciplined line favored by the tradition of Cubism, Constructivism, and De Stijl comes to be appreciated once again, and the painter aims at radical simplicity and purity of shape and color. While Abstract Expressionism was fulminating, BARNETT NEWMAN (1905—1970) was experimenting with the condensation rather than the explosion of forms, searching, as it were, for the still center of shape and color function—rigid linearity and primary color at full intensity. Returning to these elements of painting, Newman seeks their elemental drama in the division, contrast, opposition, advance, and retreat of planes ambiguously spaced but marked off with the authority of lines on a spectrum. His attachment of a caption to his huge painting *Vir Heroicus Sublimis* (FIG. 22-76) provides a cue for reading the colossal scale, the blood red, and the spare verticals as metaphors of heroism as well as essays in pure color, proportion, and nonperspective space. Thus, unlike more puristic Formalists, Newman does not exclude meaning; he simply finds a new way to embody it. His influence carried beyond the days of Abstract Expressionism into the later 1960s, when its ostensible purism and radical abstraction guided both painters and sculptors.

An extension of the field of Newman's interest can be found in the work of ELLSWORTH KELLY (b. 1923). His *Red, Blue, Green* (FIG. 22-77)—an example of Color-Field painting, in which subject is excluded

22-76 BARNETT NEWMAN, *Vir Heroicus Sublimis*, 1950–1951. 8′ × 17′ 10″. Museum of Modern Art, New York (gift of Mr. and Mrs. Ben Heller).

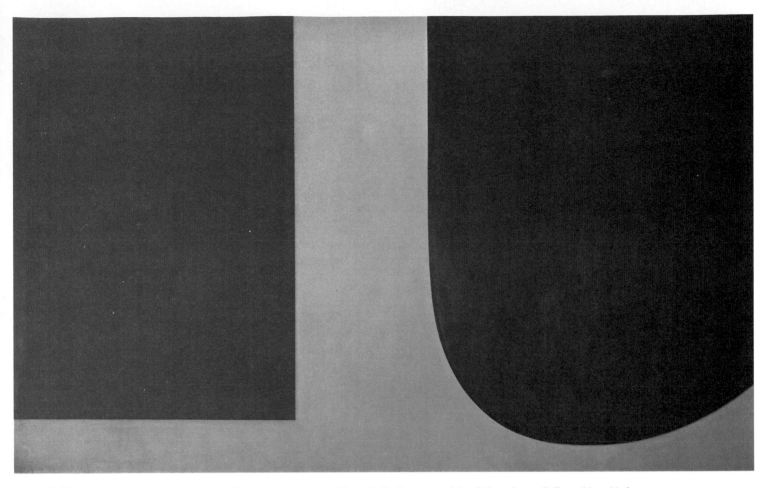

22-77 ELLSWORTH KELLY, *Red, Blue, Green*, 1963. Approx. 7' × 11' 4". Courtesy of the Sidney Janis Gallery, New York.

absolutely—shows a scrupulous management of pure color for its own sake and a knife-edge clarity in the contours that contain it. The title declares clearly enough what the artist considers to be the painting's exclusive meaning. The fundamental modern Formalist and Constructivist claim that the "subject" of the painting should be its form and nothing else is here powerfully stressed.

It is but a slight step from an interest in the elementary properties of line, shape, and color to an interest in our mode of perceiving them. Here is the reverse of the whole traditional process of seeing a picture. Originally, we "looked through" the picture "window" of a constructed perspective space; then, with modern art, the canvas itself became the perceptual object, with its arrangement of lines, shapes, and colors. Now, in Perceptual Abstraction, or Op Art, the optical "illusion," which has its seat in the brain, is the object. Thus, the picture is meant to reach out and stimulate, even disturb, our actual seeing. *Current* (FIG. 22-78), painted in 1964 by BRIDGET RILEY (b. 1931), seems to swim in contrary motions. If we stare at it long enough, its vibrations seem to penetrate the eye and cause some discomfort.

It is noteworthy that the elements of the patterns in

22-78 BRIDGET RILEY, *Current*, 1964. Synthetic-resin paint on composition board, approx. $53\frac{3}{8}$" × $58\frac{7}{8}$". Museum of Modern Art, New York (Philip Johnson Fund).

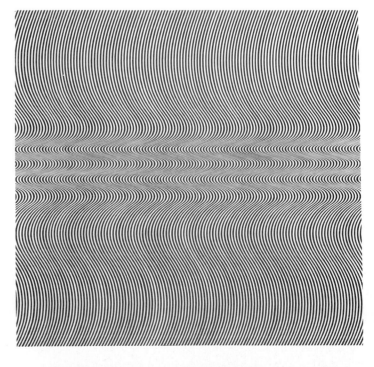

Current stand in a definable, mathematical relation to one another, and patterns like this can be generated by computer. Technologically created forms such as this can produce an esthetic response; for example, the pattern of a sinusoidal wave, with a linearly increasing period, gives an overwhelming impression of motion. Technology has had a most powerful influence on the arts throughout the era since the French Revolution—that era that has no name as yet but "modern." A whole new world of materials and instruments, beginning with the camera (in 1840) and the example of the machine in general, have stimulated—even forced—the arts into radical innovation.

At the same time, much of modern art, as we have seen, is made of reaction *against* the mechanization and standardization of human life imposed by technology. Yet any kind of making—and the artist is engaged in *making* art—inevitably has to acknowledge, adapt to, even yield to the irresistible presence, example, and power of technology. This is especially true of the art of sculpture, which, since World War II, has changed profoundly as it adopted new technological materials and procedures and has come to command as wide a field of action and interest as contemporary painting.

We have already observed in sculpture before World War I and between the world wars the rapid advance of Formalism in the guise of Cubism and Constructivism; the availability of industrial materials and technical procedures accelerated that advance. Gonzalez taught Picasso the method of "direct-metal sculpture," the quasi-industrial procedure of welding together pieces of basic metal "stock" (rod, tube, sheet)—an early instance of the application of modern metalworking techniques to art. This involved the shaping and assembling of metal elements by the artist more or less from the start. EDUARDO PAOLOZZI (b. 1924) went a step farther, welding together (and rendering immobile) elements already machined to perform mechanical functions. This separation of machined elements from their functions is all-important here, both as a kind of reaction against the growing presence in human life of the functioning machine and as an opportunity for the creation of an utterly new medium and Constructivist style. For one thing, the Formalist–Structuralist artist has, in the found object or engine component, a starting point—a "pure" form, already produced, that has no meaning other than its own form. However, Paolozzi can and does arrange these components in unconventional, bizarre ways—as biomorphic constructions, for example. His *Medea* (FIG. 22-79), with its welded aluminum slab and writhing, pipe-like tubules, imposes organic shape on the inorganic material and, at the same time, sets the shapes of the slab and tubules in inorganic–organic opposition. The title is a kind of

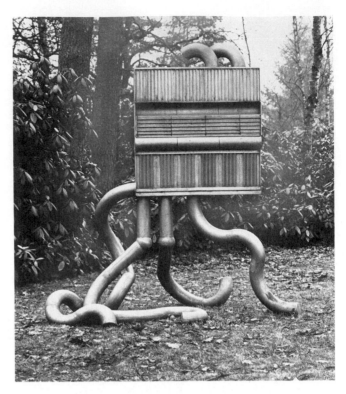

22-79 EDUARDO PAOLOZZI, *Medea*, 1964. Welded aluminum, 6' 9" high, 6' wide, 3' 9" deep. National Museum Kröller-Müller, Otterlo, Netherlands.

Dadaist reinforcement of the ambiguity of the piece—a literary reference without images to illustrate it.

Paolozzi's enthusiasm for machine elements not only foreshadows Pop Art, but is itself partly responsible—along with the efforts of his older contemporary DAVID SMITH (1906–1965)—for recent sculptors' fascination with metal sculpture and the simplicity of machined surface. A master of this material and mode, a master of what one might call the "personality" of steel, Smith worked earlier in a delicate, linear, open style. His late *Cubi* compositions (FIG. 22-80), done in the 1960s, are monumental constructions in stainless steel, in which he arranged solid, geometric masses in remarkable equilibriums of strength and buoyancy. Smith, like his Structuralist contemporaries, was at ease in the age of the machine; he declared that machinery was in his nature. "His ambition," writes Barbara Rose

> was to turn his studio into a factory, where he could produce sculpture whose forms were as impressive, monumental, and contemporary as the locomotive. He preferred to work in iron and steel because it "possesses little art history. What associations it possesses are those of this century: power, structure, movement, progress, suspension, destruction, brutality."*

Thus, we find in the art of Smith, and in his charac-

*Barbara Rose, *American Art Since 1900* (New York: Praeger, 1967), pp. 253–54.

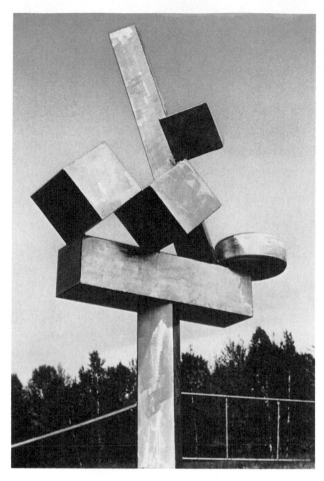

22-80 DAVID SMITH, *Cubi XVIII*, 1964.
Stainless steel, 9' 7¾" high. Courtesy of the Museum of
Fine Arts, Boston (gift of Stephen D. Paine) and of the
Estate of David Smith and the Marlborough-Gerson
Gallery, New York.

terization of it, the aim of the Formalist–Structuralist to eliminate the human element from art altogether— almost as a source of impurity?—and to present blunt metal in its unmitigated "power . . . brutality."

It is instructive to turn for the moment from Smith to the art of LOUISE NEVELSON (b. 1900) to get a sense of the stylistic diversity and disagreement within contemporary art. (Of course we have witnessed it since the nineteenth century!) Working in wood—though, recently, also in metal—Nevelson's style is so markedly different from Smith's that it is hard to believe they are contemporaries. She uses the easily worked medium of wood, a favorite of the later Middle Ages (FIG. 18-29), to create a multiplicity of detail, almost to confusion, and clusters of reference and association to things both familiar and mysterious in human experience. Her work appears to be a skillful joinery that assembles shelves, cupboards, closets, chests, cabinets, boxes crammed with oddments and fragments of furnishings, and accessories of all periods, picked up at random. Painted black, white, and gold (FIG. 22-81), these assemblages of objects and nonobjects evoke the apprehensive curiosity we experience when confronted by unfamiliar, cased collections of things not inventoried and liable to be puzzling. Nevelson *intends* her compositions to signify, even if ambiguously; Smith would banish meaning from form altogether. The influence of Smith, Paolozzi, and the great tradition of Constructivism to which they belong is widely accepted by modern metal sculptors—even, perhaps, by Nevelson in her later, monumental work.

In the interest of a sculpture that banishes all refer-

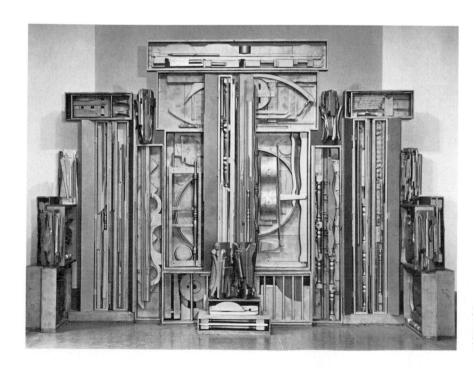

22-81 LOUISE NEVELSON, *An American Tribute to the British People*, 1960–1965. Painted wood, 10' 2" × 14' 3". Tate Gallery, London.

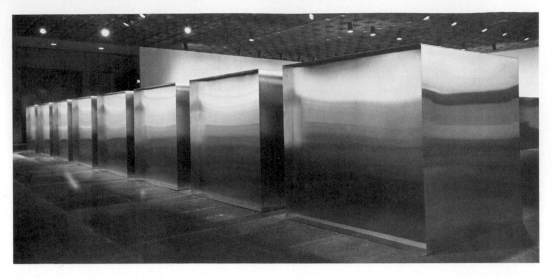

22-82 DONALD JUDD, *Untitled*, 1968. Stainless steel, each box is 4′ square. Collection of Miles Fiterman, Minneapolis, Minnesota.

ence beyond itself, DONALD JUDD (b. 1928)—widely influential as artist and critic, especially in the 1960s—asserts a doctrine of ultimate purity of three-dimensional form, manifest in figures of solid geometry like the cube (FIG. 22-82). Against all two-dimensional space that invites illusionistic figuration, including even Mondrian's paintings (FIG. 22-20), Judd insists that such treatment is a distortion of space, and that only the spatial wholeness of the third dimension in the ultimate reduction of geometry bears the truth of art. Here, he aligns eight brightly machined, identical cubes so that they multiply the reflections of their neighbors and the environment, exhibiting, in their superhuman precision and exactitude, the depersonalized technological order that produces them.

The forms preferred by Judd and many of his contemporaries have been called "minimal" or "primary"; hence, the work of this school is labeled Minimal Art or Primary Art. Typically, RONALD BLADEN (b. 1918), like Judd, reacts against romantic subjectivism (particularly that of Abstract Expressionism and welded metal), personal signature or touch, allusive association—anything extraneous to the form itself. He seeks a purism of simplicity so austere as to remove any trace of the artist's self from his work. The elimination of every vestige of personality amounts to the elimination of the artist himself; the artist seeks to achieve the impersonal, anonymous aspect of the machine. (Few people even wonder who built a particular machine.) Works like Bladen's are often constructed on a great scale, asserting their severity of outline, economy of means, and domination of the environment; above all, they emphasize their isolation from human personality and affects. They are a new kind of object that silently commands the environment, natural or artificial. Bladen's *X* (FIG. 22-83) manifests the Structuralist's credo; a stark, tremendous form, painted black, it confronts the observer with an overpowering weight and awesome blankness. It should be noted that *X* is made of wood, a

full-scale model of the metal object it is designed to become. But metal on this scale is extremely expensive, and the artist must await a patron. Here, the ambition of the metal Structuralist may take him beyond the possibility of realizing his design in his chosen medium, the properties of which inspired the design in the first place.

The great scale of much Minimal Art naturally brought to the fore the problems of the relation of the piece to its site or environment. Concerned that sculpture too emphatically separates its reality from the reality of its site, a number of sculptors trained in Minimal Art, ROBERT SMITHSON (1938–1973) among them, sought a solution to the problem of sculptural site in an entirely new context for their art, the unbounded spread of the earth itself. Their method and results, although widely differing in look, have been

22-83 RONALD BLADEN, *X*, 1967. Painted wood, 22′ high, 26′ wide, 14′ deep. Fischbach Gallery, New York.

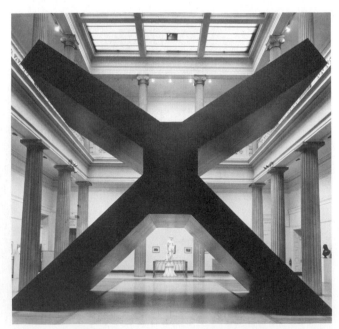

called Earth Art, which consists of manipulating vast quantities of earth and rock (usually in desolate terrains in the American West) with earth-moving equipment to produce a new unity of sculpture, site, and context. One Smithson work, *Spiral Jetty* (FIG. 22-84) in Great Salt Lake, Utah, the making of which he filmed, is a vast spiral of earth and stone built out from a shore of the lake that expresses monumentally, although in open form (unlike the closed shapes of Minimal Art), the reality of time, which is missing from sculpture—Minimal or traditional. Smithson's movie carefully describes the forms and life of the whole site, even the difficult approach to it, as he builds within it; he shows both the work and the context in reciprocal relation, sharing the same reality. Against the boundedness and closure of sculpture and its architectural sites, as well as the limits of "differentiated" thinking, Smithson tries for an indissoluble unity of art and nature, much like the suspension of the boundaries between "self" and "nonself" that he asks of the critic. (Smithson was killed when the airplane in which he was surveying a site for a new earth sculpture crashed.) The Earth Artist's work thus is neither imitation of nor flight from physical nature; rather, it asserts the unity of the physical reality of the world. The prodigious energy that goes into this reshaping of physical nature, embodied in the great earth-movers and the masses of earth they lift

and place, represents in itself the shaping forces of the physical world in which the artist shares.

Earth Art differs only in method and matter from the Structuralist search for formal truth and purity that leads to the Minimal or Primary constructions inspired by the hard, clean, precisely machined surfaces of industrial metal. But ingredient in the model of machinery (and, indeed, in all nature) is also the fact of motion. Early Constructivists like Tatlin and Gabo perceived this, and the Futurists made it central to their philosophy. Pevsner and Gabo, in their *Realist Manifesto* of 1920, included time with space as a prime reality for the modern experience; and the combination of time and space makes for motion. Motion then must be a reality for modern art, as for modern life, and the construction of forms in motion, powered by some form of motor energy, has come to be called Kinetic Art.

Paolozzi, Smith, Judd, and Bladen all express the power of static form. Artists like POL BURY (b. 1922) say in effect that, for art, motion is as real and as interesting as stasis and is the very model of industrial process. The motion that Bury and his associates in the international movement of Kinetic Art experiment with is not at all like the freely disposed, "air-sketching" of Calder (FIG. 22-49), in which delicately cut and poised filaments and fins move buoyantly on natural currents of air. Rather, it is motion produced

22-84 ROBERT SMITHSON, *Spiral Jetty*, April 1970. Black rocks, salt crystal, earth, red water, algae, 1,500' long, 15' wide. Great Salt Lake, Utah.

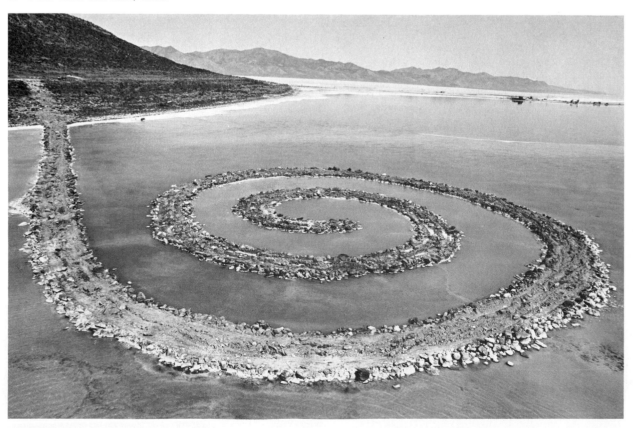

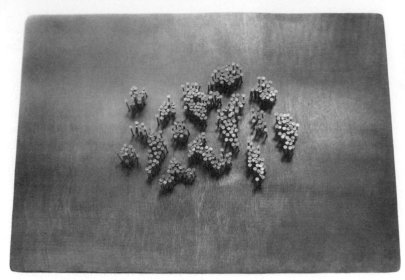

22-85 POL BURY, *Broad Flatheads*, 1964.
Wood and nails, approx. 39½″ × 29½″.
Collection of Mr. and Mrs. Frank M. Titelman,
Altoona, Pennsylvania.

by a mechanical drive—the difference between it and Calder's art being somewhat like the difference between a glider and an airplane. Although it is, of course, impossible to represent the kinetic object in a still picture, some sense of it may be had in Bury's *Broad Flatheads* (FIG. 22-85) from the blur caused by the movement of the nails. The movements are very slow and subtle and must be observed carefully over a considerable period of time, much of the work's appeal being derived from the changing relationships of the moving parts. Of course, all sorts and degrees of movement can be made by varying speed, rate of variation, and interval; and these are often augmented by accompanying sound and light effects. Kinetic Art enjoys great currency in the area of pop entertainment, bringing together plastic art, sound, and light into sometimes overpowering orchestration.

Constructivism, in its search for ultimate form and a consistent logic of procedure, can lead to contradictions. It may lead to forms, motions, spaces, and times that are already complete in themselves and do not need the artist's hand (for example, the machined parts and fixed motions of an existing machine). Or, as artists strive to eliminate themselves from the form they have produced, so the form might be made to eliminate itself—that is, to "self-destruct." Or, again, artists might have to concede their own replacement by, say, the machine. Still further, they might intrude meaning on their nonobjective forms by bestowing titles on them. JEAN TINGUELY (b. 1925) seems to have pondered all of these possibilities. At ease with paradox—one of his own being "the only stable thing is movement"—Tinguely builds Kinetic sculptures somewhat in the satiric, Dadaist spirit of Duchamp (FIG. 22-24), often with the droll import of Klee's *Twittering Machine* (FIG. 22-30). Tinguely's art manifests a kind of dangerous playfulness and a gusto for the absurd. His *Homage to New York* (FIG. 22-86)—a giant, motorized, explosive "junk sculpture" crowned with a weather balloon—was designed to destroy itself, which it resolutely did in the garden of the Museum

of Modern Art in New York in 1960. The gesture may have been of profounder historical significance than was first supposed. Earlier, as a spoof of Abstract Expressionism, which held—almost alone—the international art stage of the late 1940s and 1950s, a painting machine designed by Tinguely, called *Metamatic-Automobile-Odorante et Sonore*, produced 40,000 "Abstract Expressionist" paintings during the first Biennial of Paris in 1959. Here, indeed, might be the ultimate elimination of the painter.

22-86 JEAN TINGUELY, *Homage to New York*, 1960, just prior to its self-destruction in the garden of the Museum of Modern Art, New York.

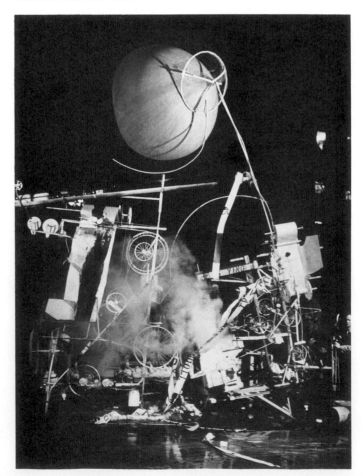

Pop Art and Other Trends

In the later 1950s, the tendencies to total "inwardness" had hardly been established by the mode of Abstract Expressionism before it received a jarring reversal from the rise of a movement—called, among many things, Neo-Dada, but now Pop (for *popular* art)—that has striking resemblances, in both attitude and method, to Dada (although there are important differences). The English critic Lawrence Alloway, who is generally credited with inventing the label "Pop Art," asserts that it refers not so much to the art as to the new attitudes that led to it—principally an acceptance of the prevalence of mass art media, including advertising, industrial design, photography, and cinema. The Pop artist turns outward to his environment—not the natural environment, but the artificial one of mass popular culture—finding material in the manipulated and programed folkways and the mass-produced commodities of modern urban and suburban life. Pop Art challenges the tradition of the "fine arts," insisting that the common culture in its multitudinous forms is as valid as, and indeed continuous with, the fine arts. The tone of Pop Art is for the most part sympathetic with mass culture, although it can range from sympathetic to neutral to hostile. Against the extremely personal and private symbolic utterances of Abstract Expressionism, Pop seeks a hard, tough, impersonal objectivity in the mood of composer John Cage's remark: "Object is *fact*, not symbol." The Pop fact is as visibly in front of us as the cans of soup on our shelves and the billboards along our highways. Its appearance commands our responses daily. It is one of billions of shapes and images that continually rain on us in the visual explosion of the twentieth century. The Pop fact is an expendable object—due in part to its immediacy in our experience and to its significance for that experience. We are continually confronted with the expendable products of Hollywood, Detroit, and Madison Avenue. Taken together, Pop facts make a vast universe of fascinating images, which can, like any "facts," become the source of new fantasies.

The origins of Pop Art are not precisely traceable. It had an early start in London in the mid-1950s, and was restated in New York and Los Angeles in 1960 and for some time after. In London, the influence of Paolozzi (FIG. 22-79) was strong, especially his conviction of the importance of the interaction of the individual and technology, his sincerely cultivated taste for popular culture, and his sense of the presence of a new universe of images with manifold possibilities of significance. Paolozzi was a member of the pioneering Independent Group, which shared his interest in mass culture. Among the members were architects, critics, designers, painters, and sculptors who were especially aware of the lessons of Duchamp's "an-

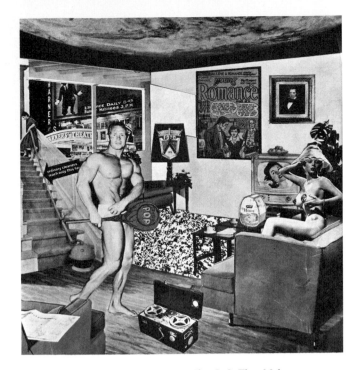

22-87   RICHARD HAMILTON, *Just What Is It That Makes Today's Homes So Different, So Appealing?*, 1956. Collage, 10¼" × 9¾". Kunsthalle Tübingen, West Germany.

tiart," the collages of Schwitters, and the work of Picasso, much of which owes something to the hard facts of the street culture of Paris. In a small collage (FIG. 22-87), later turned into a photo-mural, RICHARD HAMILTON (b. 1922), a display artist and member of the Independent Group, shows us an interior laden with the images of mass culture—in effect, the contents of a mass mind: muscle man, magazine female, fetish figure, television ad, canned ham, tape recorder, posters, automobile logo, and so on. This is a collage or montage of images lifted from specific contexts and brought together with almost sardonic effect, whether or not the artist intends to make a pointed comment. The images have a kind of realism, while the composition and context repudiate traditional Realism altogether.

Pop Art developed slightly later in America than in England—and differently. The influence of Duchamp's philosophy of art and life was active, as was, to a degree, the influence of Léger's art with its acceptance of the machine culture. Further, the examples of the so-called "cool" Abstract Expressionists like Rothko (FIG. 22-73) and of the Post-Painterly Abstraction or Color-Field painters like Kelly (FIG. 22-77) provided the formal means. In 1955, ROBERT RAUSCHENBERG (b. 1925), whose work bridges Abstract Expressionism and the American Pop movement, began working with collages, which he called "combine painting," composed of photographs, news clippings, prints, and the like. Unlike the collages of Schwitters (FIG. 22-23) and the Dadaists (FIG. 22-24), Rauschenberg's compositions are topical, with reference to events of the day or to commonly seen objects used in the mass environment; they are,

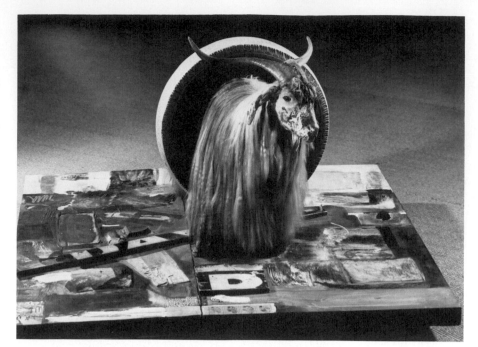

22-88 ROBERT RAUSCHENBERG, *Monogram*, 1959. Construction, 4' high, 6' wide, 6' deep. Collection, Moderna Museet, Stockholm.

moreover, of far greater scale. The evanescence of the referent events and objects is expressed in the ordinariness and expendability of the items chosen by Rauschenberg, which led him naturally to collages or constructions in three dimensions composed of perishable or throwaway materials. In *Monogram* (FIG. 22-88), a stuffed ram wearing an automobile tire is mounted on a collage base, with dense passages of free-brush painting pulling the whole together in a *tour de force* of mixed-media procedure. Dada, Surrealism, and Abstract Expressionism meet here in ambiguous equilibrium.

It is noteworthy that Rauschenberg originally was part of the Abstract Expressionist movement. It is symbolic of his personal rebellion against it— symbolic, perhaps, of the whole reaction of Pop against action painting—that he obtained a drawing from De Kooning, erased it, and then exhibited it as *Erased de Kooning by Robert Rauschenberg*. The gestures of modern artists have much in common, no matter the diversity of their styles.

An early associate of Rauschenberg and of the influential musician John Cage, JASPER JOHNS (b. 1930), like Duchamp, takes the commonplace out of context and makes us *look* at it—not simply use it and throw it away. In *Painted Bronze* (FIG. 22-89), part of the modern cultural landscape—the beer can—is reconstituted as an object not to be discarded but to exist for our attention. Johns goes beyond Duchamp in solemnly exalting the banal by casting it in bronze, faithfully reproducing its label, and placing it firmly on a base, so that the flimsy and disposable container, intended to be used and forgotten, is monumentalized and made permanent as a profoundly symbolic twentieth-century artifact. As has been the case with so many ancient cultures, it is by our manufactured products—at least, by the less perishable ones—that

we are and will be known. The irony of Johns and Duchamp echoes T. S. Eliot's prediction that nothing will survive us but a thousand lost golf balls.

The ephemeral and the banal in popular art naturally attracted the attention of the Pop artist, although we must remember that the Pop philosophy accepts and approves the art (such as illustration and comic strips) and artifacts of mass culture as entirely valid art in themselves. To reconstruct on a giant scale the thudding clichés and earsplitting rhetoric of certain comic strips devoured daily by millions is to comment wordlessly on the taste and fantasy life of the public. A good example of this punishing presentation of what can be forgotten quite as easily as an empty beer can is *Blam!* (FIG. 22-90), painted in 1962 by ROY LICHTENSTEIN (b. 1923). Familiar as the form and iconography are, they create a powerful effect when

22-89 JASPER JOHNS, *Painted Bronze*, 1960. Approx. 5½" high, 8" wide, 4¾" deep. Wallraf-Richartz-Museum, Cologne (Sammlung Ludwig).

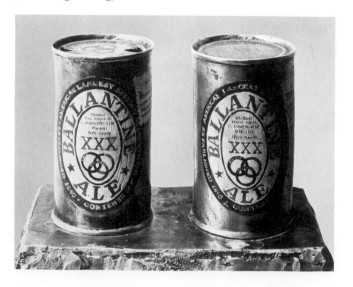

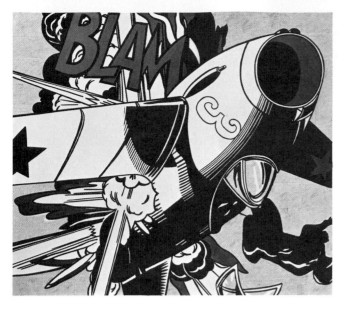

22-90 Roy Lichtenstein, *Blam!*, 1962. Approx. 5' × 6' 8".
Collection of Richard Brown Baker, New York.

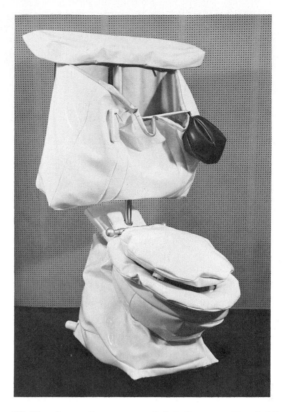

22-91 Claes Oldenburg, *Soft Toilet*, 1966. Vinyl, plexiglass, and kapok, 55" high, 28" wide, 33" deep. Collection of Mr. and Mrs. Victor W. Ganz, New York.

written large and out of context. The new landscape and still life of Pop replace the Traditional; they offer a view of a world in which we are surrounded by garish artifice that only too clearly reflects ourselves.

The new universe of shapes and colors produced by mass culture and its visual explosion supplied Pop Art with its material—its new fact. But, as Rauschenberg shows us (FIG. 22-88), instant fact can be made fantasy simply by shattering factual contexts and realigning and regrouping the elements that compose conventional aggregates of facts. The effect of this process is to surprise and to defeat expectation—the old Dada aim to shake up (*épater*) the observer. The sympathetic neutrality of the Pop attitude toward mass culture could, under the impact of this mischievous Dada impulse, very quickly yield to mockery of that culture through fantastic exaggeration and paradox. This is the case in the art of CLAES OLDENBURG (b. 1929), in which, once more, the example of the good-humoredly cynical Duchamp seems to be influential. Oldenburg's *Soft Toilet* (FIG. 22-91) gives us a shock by knocking our perceptions (categories) of "hard" and "soft" sharply together and confusing our responses. What is conventionally hard, rigid, and prophylactic is shown as soft, sagging, and positively unsanitary. The artist makes fun of our modern dependence on our prized household appliances, which, for the masses, can be the ultimate expressions of civilized living.

The flat, severe planes and hard edges of much modern design find satirical reversal in Pop forms that are soft or that simulate softness. An early example of this whimsical opposition of soft to hard appears, in spirit, in Salvador Dali's reply to Le Corbusier's query concerning how Dali envisioned the architect's future buildings: "soft and hairy." EDWARD KIENHOLZ (b. 1927) uses soft and unresist-

ant materials of almost every kind, made or found, to produce his realistic–fantastic tableaux—three-dimensional constructs that combine theater (stage sets), sculpture, architecture, furniture, and mannequins and recall the grotesquerie of Surrealism while mirroring the tawdry aspects of modern life. His *Birthday* (FIG. 22-92) depicts a hospital maternity room with draped patient and hospital accessories. The pangs of childbirth are represented as great, transparent, plastic arrows rising and branching out from the patient's body. Hard reality and eerie fantasy mingle in this emphatic restatement of the Pop absorption in the forms and events of the mass scene.

The world of fancy that hovers above Pop Art seems to win a place of its own in what has been called Psychedelic Art, presumably because it approximates the visions produced by "mind-expanding" drugs. Its formal roots are in Art Nouveau, Odilon Redon, Kandinsky, Klee, and others of the extremely subjective Expressionist camp. Although worldwide in extent, Psychedelic Art has belonged mostly to the American Pop scene since the late 1960s. Its primary media are the poster and the underground comic strip—the area of Pop already explored by the young. Seemingly a contradiction of Pop factualism, Psychedelic Art presents simply another kind of fact—induced by the drugs that widely circulate among the youthful consumers of Pop Art and culture.

In the study of the art of the twentieth century, we become used to the shock of stylistic contrast. We

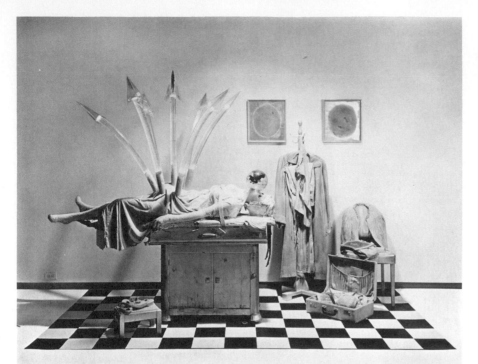

find yet another contrast in works of the Pop-born school of New Realism or Photo Realism. In *Nedick's* (FIG. 22-93), RICHARD ESTES (b. 1936) gives us the portrait of a familiar, fast-food restaurant and fountain with all the glassy fidelity of a photograph taken through a pristine, plate-glass window with the latest refinement in cameras. We have already seen (FIG. 22-87) the importance of the camera in supplying Pop Art with unlimited images for collages made of fragments taken out of their visual contexts. But here all the images are back in context, pulled together by the habit of a long tradition of Realism and brought into sharp focus by the camera in a single scene in an infinitesimal interval of time. The last gives a peculiar stillness to the picture, arresting all action and concentrating the viewer's attention on the wide range of "information" given. By projecting a photograph onto a canvas and then painting over it, as if it were a cartoon (in the traditional sense of a full-sized, preparatory drawing), the artist uses the camera as a

22-93 RICHARD ESTES, *Nedick's*, 1969–1970. Oil, 48" × 66". Collection of Mrs. Donald Pritzker.

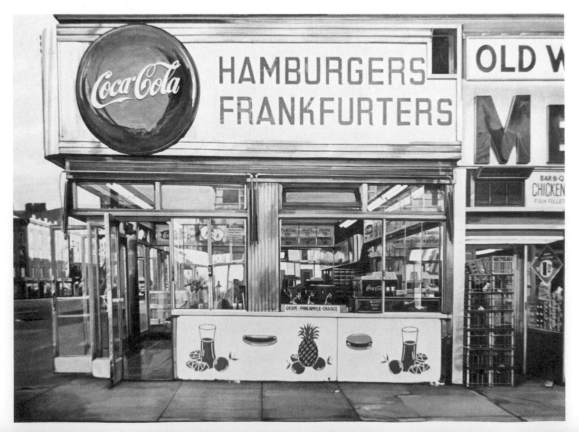

means to the picture—not the photograph as an end in itself. Yet the photograph from which the artist renders is his new "nature," replacing both the natural and artificial environments that traditional Realism draws on or that Pop exhibits without transformation.

Two terms that have come into currency latterly—Process Art and Conceptual Art—seem to be the product of a search for some unifying agent among the widely diverging trends of Post-Pop Art. In a literal sense, the Process artist claims that the act of making an object is more important than the eventual product. If such is the case, the product will have meaning primarily to the artist and to those participating in the "process." This attitude is similar to that of the "action painters" of the Abstract Expressionist movement. In Conceptual Art, in which this notion is seemingly carried one step further, the artistic concept—the creative thought—is more important than either the process or the product. Although based on different premises, Process Art and Conceptual Art tend to differ little in actual practice.

The aim of both Process and Conceptual artists is to eliminate the isolated art object or product as such and to arrange "environments" composed of both objects and audiences. The process of creation and the concepts directing it thereby become superior to any made form. The audience is introduced into a setting that is automated, sometimes in such a way that the audience itself becomes an element of the circuitry—functioning, via "feedback," like a component of some modern electronic system. Objects and audience are the shifting foci of relationships of interdependent events: process is reality, and reality is process—as some modern physicists understand the way of things.* Light, sound, color, and automata (among numerous devices), and materials adapted from industrial technology all function together to saturate audiences with intensified and continually varying sensory experiences. Or, latterly, environments are constructed to reduce sense stimuli and produce an effect of soundless isolation. This extreme "systemic" art supplies "information" that directs audience response, creating a programed situation much like that experienced by astronauts in their spacecraft or, for that matter, by anyone operating a machine (as the latter, if it is not totally automated, compels responses from the former). As receptors of the informational output, audience members need not deal with the images and appearances that stay to be evaluated; they need only react to them. This means that the artist is a node in such a network of

*Cf. the fundamental work of the philosopher Alfred North Whitehead, *Process and Reality*.

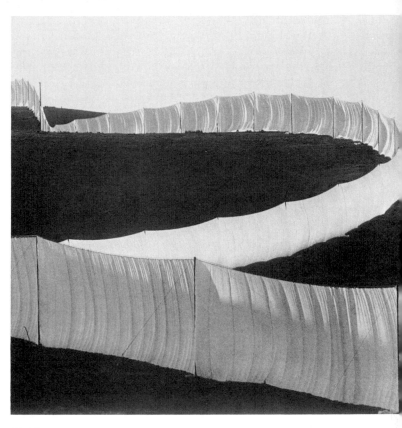

22-94　Christo, *Running Fence*, 1976. Steel posts and nylon sheeting, approx. 20' high, 24 miles long. Petaluma, California (now dismantled).

informational relationships, rather than an isolated system. In the transactions between himself and the environment—which includes the audience—the artist becomes part of an unlimited, ceaselessly varying process.

The idea and the event engaged in the creative act, along with the recording of them, are the preoccupation of Christo Javacheff, called Christo (b. 1935). Like the Earth artists (in some respects, he can be considered one) Christo is attracted to the natural environment as a medium. He has, among other projects, wrapped over 1,000,000 square feet of Australian coast in plastic and curtained a canyon at Rifle Gap, Colorado. In 1976, Christo constructed *Running Fence* (FIG. 22-94) across the California hills north of Petaluma to the Pacific Coast. Made of nylon panels (some 20 feet high) fastened to 2,050 steel poles, the fence was 24 miles long; until it was dismantled (it stood two weeks), it was the largest work created by an artist. Christo's objective was the harmonious relation of art and nature. The architecture of the piece articulated—rather than destroyed—the rhythms of the landscape in precisely effected perspectives; their fluid sequences, with fortuitous foreshortenings, made the interplay of the shapes of the hills readable.

The innovative character of the work lay not so much in its esthetic inventiveness and audacious scale as in the wide employment of a variety of hands, resources, decisions, and media that made the process of realization even more of a social than an artistic enterprise. During two years of preparation, permissions had to be gained, court decisions sought, workers assembled, and over $2 million raised (largely through the sale of preliminary drawings by Christo, an excellent draftsman and graphic artist). Of greater significance than the finished product was the fact that two years of preparation and six months of actual work were required for a project that stood for only 14 days! During its limited existence, however, it became the focus of the public media's power to publicize and promote. Innumerable photographs, two movies, three books, a documentary exhibition, reproductions, and postcards—all guaranteeing the familiarity and the permanency of *Running Fence*—it has become perhaps the widest known monument of contemporary art, and pieces of it have been contracted for and sold widely. Here again, the record of an artistic concept and process preserves and validates it in a mode of existence and identity other than its own.

In retrospect, we can note a process in modern art in which the role of the artist is undergoing permutation, as are the once-understood media of painting and sculpture. The artist may now be painter, printmaker, or sculptor; the artist can also be prophet, seer, entrepreneur, producer, performer, entertainer, photographer, filmmaker, ceramist, glassblower, electrician. In schools, colleges, and exhibitions, the title "artist" includes all of these activities and many others; the forms of modern design they share draw them closely together. It may be that we see here the withering away of the special status given by the Renaissance to the "fine arts" and a return to the craft collectivization and, ultimately, to the anonymity of the Middle Ages, or the anonymity of the industrial designer in the modern world.

The media are similarly permuted. The materials of sculpture range from traditional marble and bronze through plastics and nylon to junk. Forms are carved, cast, welded, wired, sewn, glued, painted, and lighted. They are pierced with space, reduced to filaments, set in motion by air currents or electrical means. The framed picture loses its illusionistic picture-perspective space and becomes a painted, two-dimensional object. The frame itself is discarded, the wall takes its place, and, eventually, the gallery or the spaces of physical nature become the setting for the object. The relation of the artist to the viewer through the object becomes problematical, as does the status of the object within the space it occupies with the viewer. Finally, focus moves from the object to the process of its production and to the idea of the object

as conceived, described, recorded. The making of the object, an incomplete and temporary process, is followed by its elimination and by the elimination of the artist as the determiner of its effect on audience or environment. The physical media are replaced by act, performance, and then, by the record of these. Like vapor trails, the arts leave an ephemeral trace.

The art of the twentieth century (commencing in the 1880s!) can perhaps be understood as simultaneously the brilliant debris of a great tradition and an aggregate of elements for new languages of design, in dependence on or rejection of the machine forms of an industrialized world.

Post-Modernism—The Art of the 1970s and 1980s

At present, in some quarters, the art we have been describing as "Modern" is being renamed "Modernist," and its ideology, the set of ideas by which it explains itself, is now called Modernism. This indicates an important shift of historical and critical points of view. The complex of "Modernist" styles originating at the end of the nineteenth century is beginning to be identified as a distinct period; its art-historical development seems to be reaching a conclusion or, at least, a bewildered pause—perhaps a transition to something new. Modernist art and ideology are being revised and reacted against. The revision and reaction go by the name Post-Modernism.

In the previous sections of this chapter, we have sorted out the Modernist styles and traced their development; in passing, we have touched on some of the ideas behind them. In simple summation, the most important axioms of Modernism will be examined here.

Modern art is the consequence of a successful and continuing revolution led by an *avant-garde* of artists and critics who overthrew the Tradition that began in the Renaissance and exhausted itself in the nineteenth century. Their formal method is *abstraction*, by which images referring to objects in the world of sight are progressively distorted or eliminated, leaving the particular painting or sculpture to refer only to itself as a unique thing. The mission and triumph of the *avant-garde* is the "liberation" of the pictorial and sculptural object from any obligation to mean something other than itself. This liberation of the plastic media from all but self-reference makes for a "purification" of visual art, which had been corrupted by its bondage to subject matter drawn from myth, religion, history, literature. The only "truth" for art is to be found not in something extraneous to it, like the forms of nature, but in its own materials, techniques, and forms. All reference otherwise is a lie; the truth of the object is simply *that*, and *what*, it is. The main avenue, up which the *avant-garde* march forever, is abstraction. The truly modern styles all branch from abstraction; all others run counter to it in anachronistic, retrograde reaction. Abstract art and its relatives constitute the only authentic art for our times; this art is always revolutionary and progressive—in a word, "modern." In the search for truth of statement, the Modern artist strives for the ever-more abstractive reduction of the art object, until nothing is left but its minimal elements and the *process* of composing them.

This Modernist ideology, hardened into inflexible doctrine, has exercised considerable control over both artistic procedure and critical judgment. (We are reminded of the influence of the French Royal Academy in the time of Louis XIV; see Chapter 19.) Against this Modernism, Post-Modernism now seems to be in uncertain revolt.

The value and method of abstraction are still acknowledged, even as its absolute claims are being rejected; indeed, it seems still dominant at the very moment it is being sharply challenged. For the referential, mediating function of art—its age-old purpose—is being appealed to once again. The importance of content and meaning is being reaffirmed, and traditional subject matter is being reintroduced: report of optical fact, the human figure, the human environment, narrative, social commentary, imaginative transformation of the commonplace. Increasingly, the world of the photograph is yielding vast quantities of materials for the expression and representation of human experience. One thing is certain; artists, searching in all directions for fresh inspiration, feel that abstraction has reached its limit of invention, that it is a dead end, and that they wish to escape from a stern and doctrinaire formalism that

has narrowed into academic precept. But thus far, the revisionism is incoherent; it has no central theme, no certain direction.

Meanwhile, the play of the art market, with its urgent demands for novelty, stimulates the feverish exploration for innovation at any cost and the rapid turnover of fads and fashions—adding to the confusion of the scene. Old paths are being sought out once more, and old modes are being restored with superficial changes. We find Neo-Primitivism, Neo-Symbolism, Neo-Abstract Expressionism, Neo-Formalism, Neo-Social Realism, even Neo-Impressionism—and hybrids of all of them. Side-by-side with these persist elements of Pop, Op, Minimalism, Conceptualism, Photo Realism, and the like.

It is difficult for us to find a way through what, at present, seems to be both the recapitulation and the deconstruction of Modernism to locate firm evidence of an emerging style that could replace it. Nevertheless, some description can be made of the present situation by pointing to a small selection of artists whose work is Post-Modern by date, if by no agreed-on definition. Many characteristics of art after 1945 remain in evidence: the pieces are very large; the broad, monochrome areas of Color-Field painting persist; the pictorial and sculptural media are combined; "installations" continue to be popular; experiment with both Formalistic and Expressionistic modes goes on.

JULIAN SCHNABEL (b. 1951) who disclaims that he is Post-Modernist, makes a powerful restatement of Expressionism, experimenting widely with materials and supports—from broken plates bonded to wood to paint on velvet. *The Walk Home* (FIG. 22-95) is a vast

22-95 JULIAN SCHNABEL, *The Walk Home*, 1984–1985. Oil, plates, copper, bronze, fiberglass, and bondo on wood, 9′ 3″ × 19′ 4″. Collection of Aaron Katz.

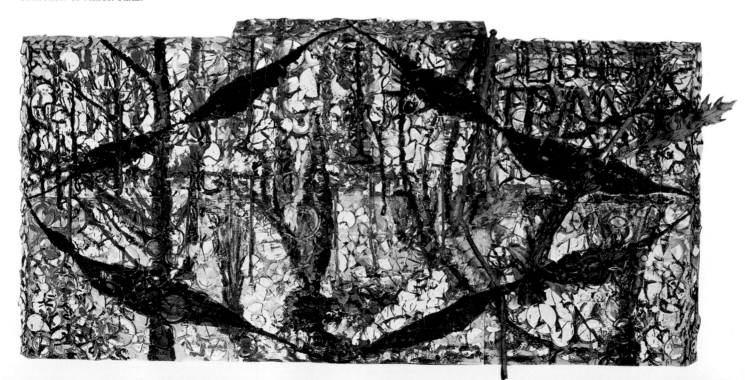

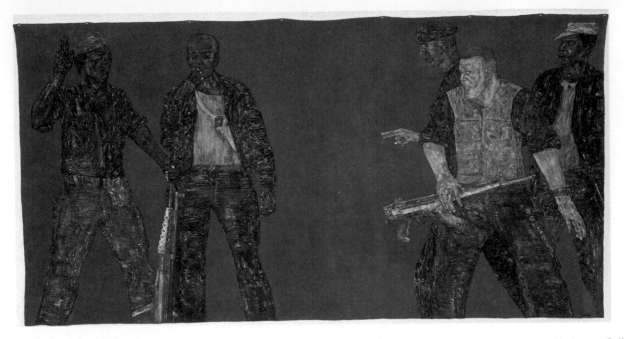

22-96 LEON GOLUB, *Mercenaries (IV)*, 1980. Oil on canvas, figures life-size. Susan Caldwell Gallery/Barbara Gladstone Gallery.

mosaic of broken crockery, painted and glued to a wooden support. Its origin in the Abstract Expressionism of the New York School is clear, recalling the stippling of Jackson Pollock (FIG. 22-70) and the black slashes of Franz Kline (FIG. 22-71). But the artist amalgamates these techniques in a new and distinctive medium of his own—glazed, tesselated relief. In effect, Schnabel reclaims the great tradition of Medieval mosaic.

The abstractions of Schnabel contrast with works that reaffirm the referential and mediating importance of the human figure in art. The figures in the paintings of LEON GOLUB (b. 1923), usually well over life-size, fiercely express the brutalities of our time—its street violence, terrorism, torture, death squads. In *Mercenaries (IV)* (FIG. 22-96), one of a series on this theme, Golub presents an unforgettable gathering of soldiers of fortune—tough, merciless men who kill for pay and seem here to have just come back from a

mission. In stark relief from the flat ground of monochromatic red, the figures project from a kind of Color-Field painting charged with meaning; it is the color of fire and blood, crime and cruelty. Gnarled, wrinkled, and sweaty, their miscellaneous field garb clings to their hard bodies. Their weapons, bright and ready, are modeled in full tone and contrast with the harshly scraped, flattened surfaces of the bodies. The viewer, part of the space they occupy, cannot help but feel their menacing presence. Here and in his other works, Golub has reference to the news photograph and greatly augments the shock of its often atrocious report.

Drawing fully on the resources of photography, especially as it is found in newspapers and magazines, MARK TANSEY (b. 1949) makes oil paintings that comment wryly and wittily on the contemporary world. His method is to bring persons, things, times, places, and events that are not usually—if ever—

22-97 MARK TANSEY, *Triumph of the New York School*, 1984. Oil on canvas, 6' 2" × 10'. Grace Borgenicht Gallery, New York.

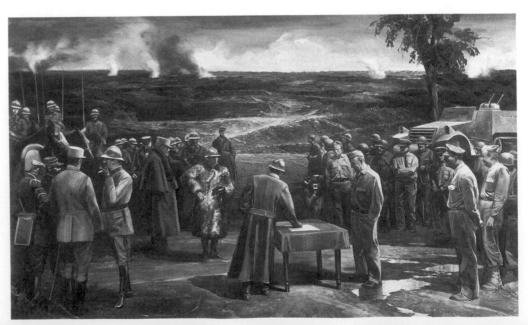

associated into new and surprising conjunctions and to render them in fully pictorial tonalities reminiscent of on-the-spot news photography. He prefers monochromatic sepias and gray–greens, recalling the color of old rotogravure pictures printed decades ago in Sunday newspaper supplements. Disparates, incongruities, and contradictories invite the viewer to search out the artist's meaning, to solve the iconographic problems he deliberately sets up. Tansey makes frequent references and allusions to the history of art, one of which, *Triumph of the New York School* (FIG. 22-97), takes for its subject the historical shift of the artistic fulcrum from Paris to New York after 1945. The event is dramatized as a surrender of the French army, clad in the uniforms of World War I on the left, to the American army, in the garb and with the motorized armor of World War II on the right. This, of course, is an event that never happened and, given the pictured circumstances, that could never have happened in this way. We are confronted with a large group portrait of artists and critics, all identifiable. Among the French are Pablo Picasso, Henri Matisse, Guillaume Apollinaire, and André Breton; among the Americans, Clement Greenberg, Jackson Pollock, Robert Motherwell, Harold Rosenberg, and others associated with the New York School. The trig elegance of the French and the firm ground they stand on are metaphors for Abstract Formalism; the slouchiness of the GIs and the puddles beneath their feet stand for the "drip" and "spatter" techniques of "action painting." The surrender theme—with the central officers, the balancing armies, the smoking landscape and the lancers—alludes to Velázquez's great painting *The Surrender of Breda* ("The Lances"), but the allusion is checked by the anachronistic uniforms and the modern armor. The kneeling news photographer signalizes the paradoxicality of the message: this is a veritable photograph of nothing that in fact happened, but the shift of focus of the art world from Paris to New York *did* happen.

Without the domination and push of *avant-garde* abstractionism, artists in the 1970s and 1980s have felt free to wander through and to take second looks at the art-historical past—borrowing, where they are interested, or working old mines for new ores. *Deep Pool* (FIG. 22-98) by NEIL WELLIVER (b. 1929) recalls certain traits of Impressionism—for example, the early water studies of Monet and the rugged rocks in landscapes by Gustave Courbet—but they have been rethought and reinforced by close attention to the optical facts. Welliver's patient analysis and firm technical command recover in a new synthesis features of later nineteenth-century landscape painting, as it passes from Realism to Impressionism.

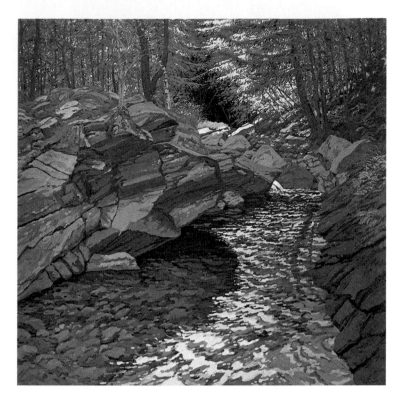

22-98   NEIL WELLIVER, *Deep Pool*, 1983. Oil on canvas, 8′ × 8′. The Collection of Exxon Corporation.

Young European artists from France, Germany, Italy, and Britain, like their American contemporaries, are producing abundantly in a great variety of styles and substyles—and, like the Americans, they aim at the New York galleries, but not exclusively. In the Soviet Union, painting is dominated by a rather heavy-handed kind of Social Realism, which is only occasionally softened by the influence of Western modes. Under the watchful supervision of the authorities, subject matter continues to be an advertisement of the heroism of the Soviet worker. But despite such strictures, a few artists are able to create works that are impressive by any standard of criticism. In one such work, *Construction Workers* (FIG. 22-99) by BORIS MALUEV (b. 1929), the principal figure is an epic hero of labor, fashioned in steel, his towering frame interlocked with the girders he commands. Man and girders almost fuse in a heavy framework of dark, vertical shapes, which, with abstraction of detail, could reduce to a Formalist—even Constructivist—expression of the attributes of brute power.

Ambiguities, conundrums, stretched metaphors, paradoxes, puns, and puzzlements are all part of the ideational equipment of artists working in three dimensions, as well as in two. Viewers of three-dimensional art are also put off-balance and forced to find their own equilibrium. More and more, they are required to complete the meaning of the pieces that

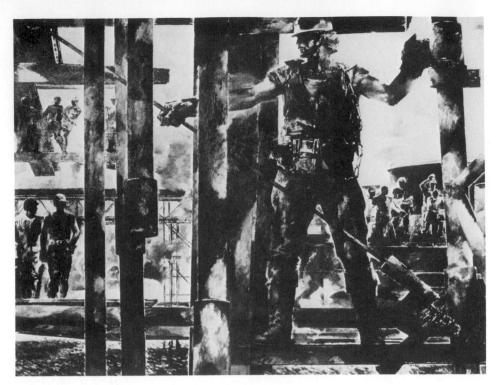

22-99 BORIS MALUEV, *Construction Workers*, 1975. Oil on canvas, approx. 5' 2" × 6' 6". Union of Artists of the USSR.

confront them and to come to terms with the viewing predicament. The esthetic experience—once thought restfully contemplative—now entails surprise and perplexity, requiring the viewer to figure out riddles and to get the point of jokes (when there is a point). There are no rules of interpretation; the viewer is meant to feel uneasy and to be left dangling, or at sea.

Claes Oldenburg, whom we have seen as a leader in the Pop movement (FIG. 22-91), lifts his utilitarian motifs to the giant scale characteristic of much Minimal sculpture. His colossal *Clothespin* (FIG. 22-100) dominates a city square in Philadelphia, as if it were a pedestaled obelisk in a Roman piazza (FIG. 19-4) or in the Place de la Concorde in Paris.The insignificant, domestic utensil takes on the proportions of a civic monument, mocking the pretentious, official architecture that is now merely a foil for it. It is as if Bach were to write an oratorio in honor of a square nail. The incongruity of scale and significance of Oldenburg's *Clothespin* is matched by incongruity of another sort in *Brick Knot* (FIG. 22-101) by WENDY TAYLOR (b. 1945) a British sculptor. The mixed-media construction appears to be a heavy brick pier tied in a knot. The factually impossible is made visibly "real"— we should almost say "sur-real." The impact of the piece derives from our visual association of the contraries "hard" and "soft," "brick" and "rope." The simplicity of form and the large scale are of the Minimal sort, but the imitation of the texture of brick and the referential joke give a quite independent twist to that approach.

A popular and prevalent type of construction, the gallery "installation," brings into a single composition gallery walls, gallery spaces, light, color, form, and illusion, in an endless variety of materials and

shapes; or—at the other extreme—creates neutral blankness of unencumbered space. The installation is impermanent and meant to be dismantled; like

22-100 CLAES OLDENBURG, *Clothespin*, 1976. Steel, 45' high, 18 tons. Centre Square, Philadelphia, Pennsylvania.

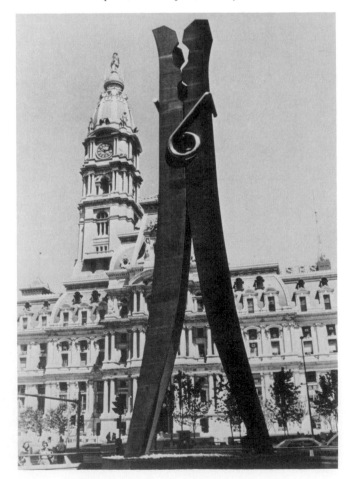

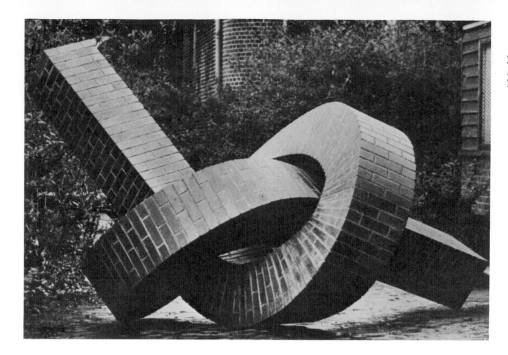

22-101 WENDY TAYLOR, *Brick Knot*, 1978. Mixed media, 7' high, 11' 9" wide, 7' 7" deep.

booths after a carnival, it is taken down, but is not likely to be set up again in another place. In this respect, the installation is like Christo's *Running Fence* (FIG. 22-94)—an evanescent phenomenon deliberately created for the moment and sacrificed to time, the only record of it being the photographs made of it. The exuberant clutter of the installation *Rock/Paper/Scissors* (FIG. 22-102) by JUDY PFAFF (b. 1946) suggests the sights and sounds of a New Year's Eve or of a giant kaleidoscope wired for sound. The "subject," of course, is the variety and impact of the materials, shapes, and colors.

22-102 JUDY PFAFF, *Rock/Paper/Scissors*, September 24, 1982–January 9, 1983. Installation. Albright-Knox Art Gallery, Buffalo.

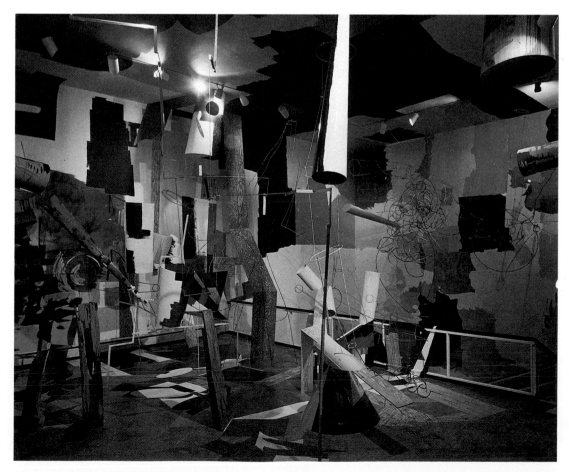

Most of the art we have studied in this book was produced, we may believe, with the intention that it would last. The installation is not expected to last and is not intended to last. In this respect, an installation is analogous to the commodities of industrial manufacture; in the end, all are disposable. Judd—in calling for the permanent installation of his own works, which are not "installations" (FIG. 22-82), and those of masters like Rothko, Kline, De Kooning, Pollock, and Newman—seems to sense that the *avant-garde* period (1945–1975) has ended and to believe that the public should be given the opportunity to view the art of that period in appropriate and lasting settings. The implication can be drawn that the *impermanent* installation, of the kind we have described, marks the end of an era—and is, in any case, perishable and inconsequent.

As the traditional boundaries of the media of painting and sculpture are being erased and as artists work more and more in "multi-media," objects are being produced out of whatever materials suit the artist's esthetic and expressive purposes. At the same time, science and technology are providing new materials and techniques that may or may not be thought of as "art" (unless we wish to define "art" as "what artists do") and that may or may not be the media of the future. We have video art, reporting on magnetic tape a continuum of images that can be instantly combined, recombined, and replayed in an infinite variety of ways; computer-generated art, programing abstract or figural shapes and colors to appear on a display terminal, as on a television screen; light "sculpture" and projection and reflection, having a purity and intensity comparable to laser beams; and holograms, producing perfect illusions of objects in three dimensions, so that they can be "walked around." We can only speculate whether these essentially impermanent media, and others like them, will displace once and for all the more permanent media of painting and sculpture, which, with architecture, have been the subjects of this book.

Much of contemporary art may seem ephemeral and made for the day, but the scientific *conservation* of historical art is being swiftly advanced and is contributing greatly to art-historical knowledge. Since the 1960s, highly refined techniques adapted from industrial, nuclear, space, and medical science, luminescent dating, infrared spectroscopy, infrared reflectography, to name some—represent vast improvements over the older X-ray methods formerly used to get at the physical facts of a work of art. They probe beneath picture surfaces, make cross sections of pigments, detect underpainting and underdrawing, and recover signatures and inscriptions. At the same time, computer science is revolutionizing our methods of the storage and retrieval of art-historical information, making it accessible to research scholarship as never before. Computers organize collections of museums, libraries, slide and photographic archives, and catalogs of shows, sales, and auctions; they index iconographic themes and provenances, as well as compose lexicons and thesauri of artists, artworks, and art terminology. In a new collaboration of scientist and scholar, the full resources of "high-technology" are being placed at the service of conservation and of the history of art. If developments and trends of artistic activity presently seem to be in disarray, our historical knowledge of art is permitting us to discover more secure methods of procedure and ever-more-reliable tests of the data they yield.

ARCHITECTURE AFTER WORLD WAR II

The first 25 years after World War II saw the rapid spread of the International style over the Western world. While Mies van der Rohe was still refining his style, the building type pioneered by him and other members of the CIAM (Congrès Internationale d' Architecture Moderne, founded in 1928) began to dominate the skylines of most major Western cities. Appealing in its structural logic and clarity, the style, although often vulgarized, was easily emulated and quickly became the norm for postwar, commercial, high-rise buildings. We have seen a 1958 example of the type in the Seagram Building of New York (FIG. 22-67).

As early as 1949, Mies van der Rohe demonstrated the flexibility of his style by applying it to domestic architecture. The Lakeshore Drive Apartments (FIG. 22-103) are two of several high-rise apartments which he built along the Chicago waterfront. Some 250 apartments are suspended within the steel frames of the two towers, which are placed and oriented so that a majority of tenants have a view of Lake Michigan. In their appearance—quite similar to the Seagram Building and based on the same structural principles—these apartment blocks seem to bring to full realization Le Corbusier's concept of dwellings as "machines for living." They also prove that the design principles of the International style can be applied equally to commercial and domestic building.

While Mies van der Rohe was bringing his translucent style to ultimate refinement, Le Corbusier was moving in another direction—toward more sculptural, architectural forms. In answer to one of the most insistent contemporary needs—a functional design for urban living—he designed the Unité d' Habitation in Marseilles (FIG. 22-104). Mighty piers (so different from the slender stilts of the Villa Savoye, shown in FIG. 22-61) support the framework

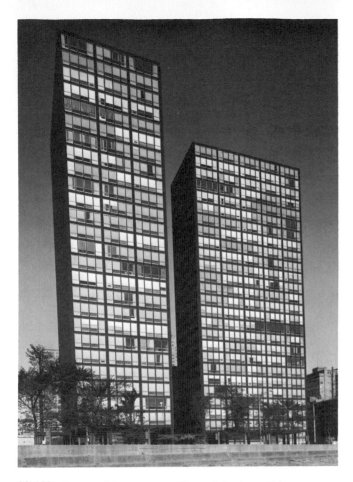

22-103 LUDWIG MIES VAN DER ROHE, Lakeshore Drive Apartments, Chicago, Illinois, 1949–1951.

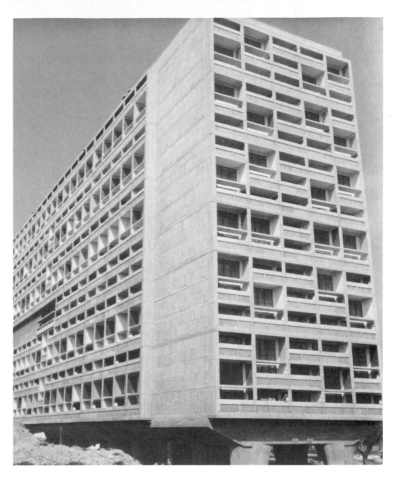

22-104 LE CORBUSIER, Unité d'Habitation, Marseilles, France, 1946–1952.

that contains 337 apartments of 23 different types. Most of them are two-storied and extend through the entire width of the building, permitting cross ventilation and admitting light from two sides. The apartments are designed as integral, self-contained units that offer maximum privacy, or, as Le Corbusier describes it, "give freedom to the individual within a collective organization," as demanded by our civilization. Recessed porches, each with a sunbreak, are hollowed out of the massive block, so that the building exists neither as a skeletal frame enclosed by a membrane nor as a solid mass. Solids and voids are carefully balanced, as in Greek temples, which, to Le Corbusier, sounded "clear and tragic, like brazen trumpets." Every effort has been made to provide residents with all of the conveniences and some of the luxuries of modern life: the seventh and ninth floors of the 17-story structure contain shopping malls, hotel rooms, restaurants, drug stores, and a post office; the roof has been converted into a park, complete with swimming pool and gymnasium. In short, all of the demands of an entire subdivision of small townhouses are met within a single building block. All of this seems somewhat removed from the rather spartan concept of the "machine for living" advocated by Le Corbusier in the 1920s.

The startling forms of Le Corbusier's Notre Dame du Haut (FIG. 22-105) built at Ronchamp, France, in 1955, challenge us in their fusion of architecture and sculpture in a single expression. Here, in Le Corbusier's own terms, is a "vessel" on a "high place," intended to respond to a "psychology–physiology of the senses" and to "a reverberating landscape, holding the four horizons as witness." (Could the architect have been thinking of the first temple after man's first cataclysm—the ark of Noah stranded on Mount Ararat by the receding waters of the Flood? It is noteworthy that we speculate, as with a work of figurative art, on the architect's possible meaning.) In these powerful, surging masses, these sculptural solids and voids, is a new environment in which man may find new values—new interpretations of his sacred beliefs and of his natural environment. The interior of Notre Dame du Haut (FIG. 22-106) is illuminated fitfully and mysteriously by deeply recessed windows, placed almost randomly. The absence of ornament reminds us not so much of Internationalist purism as of the chaste severity of the Cistercian architecture of the twelfth century. Ronchamp is a unique work that could not possibly find membership in a movement. The extremely personal touch is that of a sculptor who has made a unique masterwork.

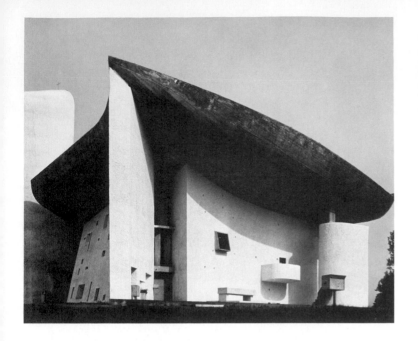

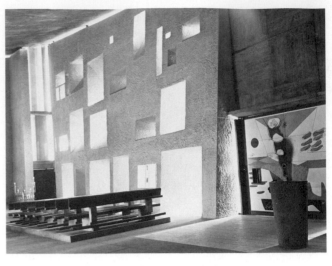

22-105 *Left:* Le Corbusier, Notre Dame du Haut, Ronchamp, France, 1950–1955.

22-106 *Above:* Le Corbusier, interior of Notre Dame du Haut.

The long, incredibly productive career of Frank Lloyd Wright, meanwhile, ends with a testament to art itself—the Guggenheim Museum (figs. 22-107 and 22-108), built in New York between 1943 and 1959. The principle of dynamic continuity that guided Wright through his life is triumphantly stated here. The immense structure is boldly composed essentially as a cylinder expanding with height, its floors expressed on the exterior as a spiraling strip of skylight, in levels marked by shadow by day and by light at night. The cantilevered decks of Wright's Kaufmann House (fig. 22-62) are here drawn around an immense circle, determined by the function of circulation. Visitors are brought by elevator to the top of the building and walk down the gently inclined spiral ramp, viewing the pictures displayed on its outer wall. The bold, monumental design, the assertion of a powerful personality, merges space and void without remainder and, despite its overwhelming strength, subtly sets off the pictures on exhibition. Wright's humanism directs him here, as ever, to serve human needs. In this case, one of the highest experiences given to modern urbanites—delighting in the works of their gifted fellows—is facilitated and honored in a building that itself must be regarded as an enduring contribution. Yet here, Wright—the great Jeffersonian, agrarian democrat—seems to turn his back on the city. The rounded, closed form, like a visitor from outer space, is entirely at odds with the rectilinear urban pattern and fabric. The building

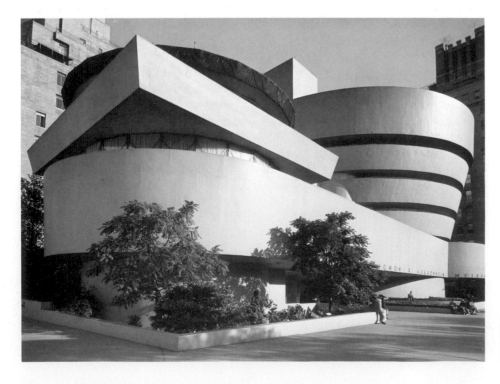

22-107 Frank Lloyd Wright, Solomon R. Guggenheim Museum, New York, 1943–1959 (exterior view from the north).

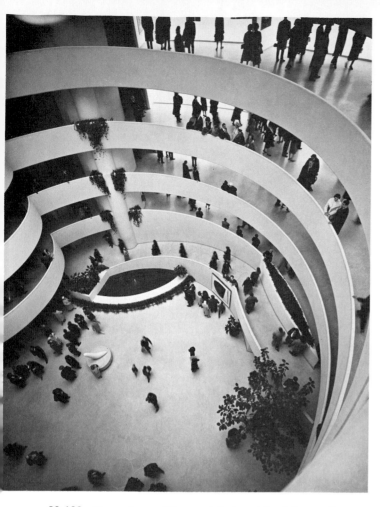

22-108 FRANK LLOYD WRIGHT, interior of the Solomon R. Guggenheim Museum (view from the dome).

turns in on itself, the long gallery area opening onto a 90-foot well of space that seems to provide an environment secure from the hostile city.

The later works of Le Corbusier and Wright illustrate the postwar movement away from the Formalistic rigidity of the International style, with its insistence on a purely rectilinear frame of reference. At the same time, new developments in building technology increasingly became a part of the expressive vocabulary of the Modern movement. The engineer PIER LUIGI NERVI (1891–1978), using the remarkable tensile strength of prestressed concrete, covers huge spaces with designs that offer dazzling geometric beauty as well as great economy of materials. His method and material make it possible to omit the steel columns of the International style—as in the Palazzetto dello Sport in Rome (FIG. 22-109), built in 1958—and his vast roofs seem to soar daringly with a grace and crispness of detail that leave severe rectilinearity behind and bring a new vision of architectural form, an organic rather than a mechanical one. Yet, despite his more personal statement, Nervi shows keen interest and insight concerning one of the ongoing themes of modern architectural theory: the rational expression of structural elements. With the grace and surety of a Gothic flying buttress (FIGS. 10-10 and 10-19), Nervi's structural members make the force lines of the building visible and carry, with a technical elegance, the lateral thrust of the vault to the ground.

Only four years later, EERO SAARINEN (1910–1961) exploits the malleable nature of concrete to its very limits. We are reminded of the ancient Roman architects who built Nero's Domus Aurea (FIG. 6-50) and the Pantheon (FIG. 6-51) some 1900 years ago and who, without structural steel and with concrete of greatly inferior quality, had similar aspirations. In his design for the Trans World Airlines Terminal at John F. Kennedy International Airport in New York (FIGS. 22-110 and 22-111), Saarinen covers the functional nucleus of the huge layout with four doubly curved concrete shells that rest on massive Y-shaped piers. Two concrete tubes, each 328 feet long, channel the passengers from the check-in counters to the waiting rooms and the finger-docks, through which they board the planes. Even if the layout does not present the final solution, it provides a satisfactory answer to

22-109 PIER LUIGI NERVI, Palazzetto dello Sport, Rome, 1958.

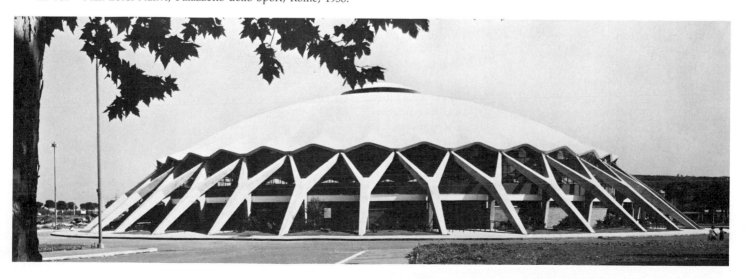

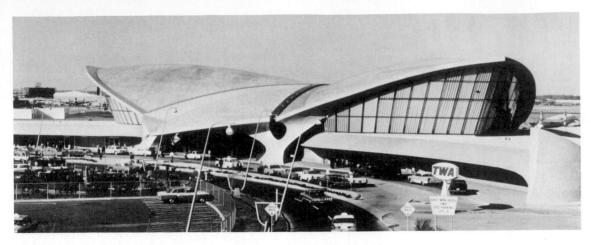

22-110 EERO SAARINEN, Trans World Airlines Terminal, John F. Kennedy International Airport, New York, 1956–1962.

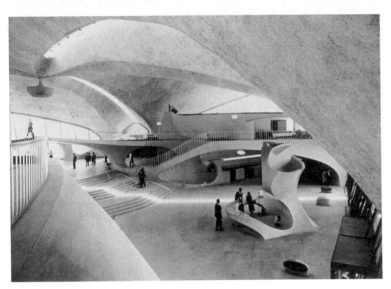

22-111 EERO SAARINEN, interior of the Trans World Airlines Terminal, John F. Kennedy International Airport.

the complex problems of sheltering large crowds of people and of moving them in time-coordinated flows to and from multiple flight departures and arrivals. But Saarinen goes beyond the purely logistical problems, which might well have been solved with the by-now-traditional rectilinear and cubical forms of the International style. Like a sculptor working with steel and concrete on a monumental scale, the architect creates a huge, three-dimensional symbol that stands for "Flight." From a distance, the rooflines of the structure resemble the outstretched wings of a soaring bird. Like arteries, arched bridges transect the building's interior space and echo the forms of plan and ceiling. In sum, Saarinen's forms combine to create the impression of a living organism and they realize to perfection his stated aim—to express the excitement of air travel.

Our summary of trends in modern architecture, of necessity, stresses the contributions of those architects who, in our foreshortened historical perspective, appear to be pioneers in the creation of an archi-

22-112 FREI OTTO, model for the roof of the Olympic Stadium, Munich, West Germany, 1971–1972.

tecture free of reference to earlier architectural styles. It seems certain that Wright, Mies van der Rohe, and Le Corbusier will be recognized by future generations; their work continues to inspire younger architects even as they experiment to expand the horizons of both building form and building technology. The rapid development and exploitation of new engineering possibilities can be seen in a comparison of Nervi's Olympic Palazzetto (FIG. 22-109) with the buildings constructed in Munich by FREI OTTO (b. 1925) for the 1972 Olympic Games (FIG. 22-112). Nervi's structure, light and graceful as it is, seems massive and dense next to Otto's airy, transparent, tent-like enclosures. Part of the difference is due to Otto's revolutionary approach to structure; Nervi, for all his experiments with prestressed concrete, still conceives of structure in traditional terms of *compression*—the principle that underlies all architecture studied in this history, from the Egyptians onward. Otto, on the other hand, exploits the tensile strength of steel to create a structural system based on *tension*, the same engineering principle that permits the construction of the light-appearing but remarkably strong free spans of suspension bridges. No less up-to-date is Otto's selection of a kind of gossamer plastic membrane to sheathe the building—a sheathing that provides shelter without confinement, just as his radical struc-

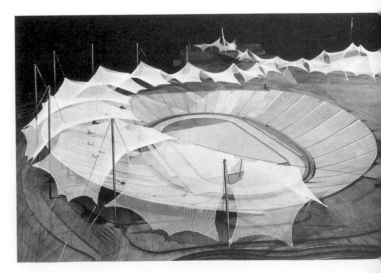

tural system provides vast enclosures without the interruption of interior supports.

The soaring, graceful forms of Otto's giant tent may appear limited in their application to the solution of more common architectural problems; but just as the Crystal Palace (FIG. 21-86), believed to be a building of limited potential about a century and a half ago, proved to be the prototype of a dominant structural form of our time, so perhaps tension structures will revolutionize architectural concepts of the future. In any case, the same principles can be seen at work in an office building designed by GUNNAR BIRKERTS (b. 1925) in Minneapolis. His Federal Reserve Bank Building (FIG. 22-113) combines the tension of great cables strung in a catenary curve between massive end towers with more traditional compression members that support the stack of floors above the cables. The floors below the catenary are also carried by the cables, but this time in suspension. The result of this extremely complex system is a free-span structure of 330 feet between the supporting towers, which contain service facilities, elevators, fire stairs, and so forth. Le Corbusier's original idea of raising a building on slender columns (pilotis) to free the site for other uses is here carried a step further; Birkert's structure leaves an open, virtually unobstructed urban space of over 100,000 square feet, framed and articulated by the office block. The principal functional elements of the bank—the vaults and other high-security facilities—are tucked away beneath the huge "piazza" that becomes a gift to the city and a fine urban amenity.

The increasing urbanization of the world population, a byproduct of the Industrial Revolution, has brought into focus one of the critical building problems of our time—the provision of adequate housing for an ever-expanding urban population. With land

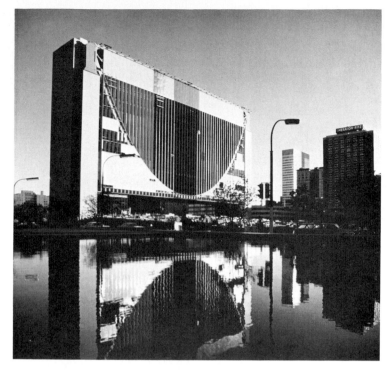

22-113 GUNNAR BIRKERTS, Federal Reserve Bank Building, Minneapolis, Minnesota, 1972–1973.

becoming more and more precious in cities, the single-family house is increasingly being considered an inefficient use of a dwindling resource, and architects have responded with a variety of proposals for mass housing. We have already examined Le Corbusier's contribution in his Marseilles apartment block (FIG. 22-104), with its clear attempt to return a sense of dignity to the urban dwelling by running each apartment the width of the building to approximate the characteristics of a free-standing house. This idea is carried a step further by the young Israeli architect MOSHE SAFDIE (b. 1938) in his Habitat (FIG. 22-114), a demonstration building constructed for Montreal's Expo '67. An experiment in the application of mass

22-114 MOSHE SAFDIE, Habitat, Montreal, Canada, 1967–1968.

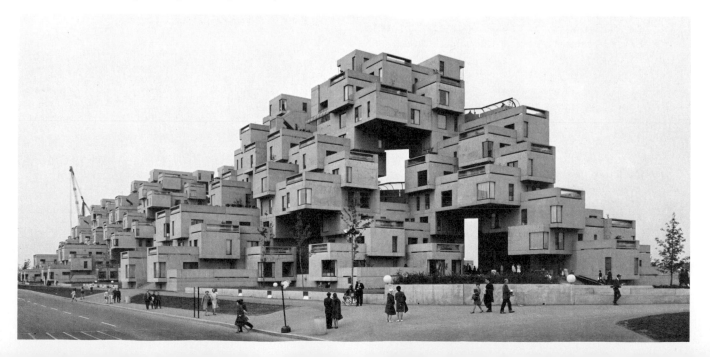

production and complete prefabrication to the building industry, Habitat carries Le Corbusier's handling of each apartment as a hypothetically independent unit to its logical realization; here, each apartment is reduced to a single, box-like, precast concrete module made at a plant and trucked to the site. Like outsized children's building blocks, the units were then lifted into their appropriate slots in the matrix of the building by a huge crane. The heroic scale of the undertaking, with its implication of a kind of fully industrialized architecture, seems to fulfill the Crystal Palace's promise of prefabrication (FIG. 21-86). Visually, the building has a boldly sculptured look that appeals both to contemporary sensibilities and to the rational insistence on structural clarity while providing an appropriate setting for modern urban living.

In the later half of the century an ever-broadening public interest in art has fundamentally changed the concept of the museum. No longer the exclusive repository of artistic treasure—administered by curatorial experts and visited only by scholars, connoisseurs, and an educated minority of art lovers—the museum, whether the Guggenheim in New York (FIG. 22-107) or the ''Beaubourg'' in Paris (FIG. 22-117), invites and receives a general public numbering in the millions. Curatorial and exhibition functions have been expanded and widely diversified to include popular as well as scholarly study of the arts. The traditional halls and galleries are supplemented by libraries, lecture halls, study rooms, motion-picture theaters, and shops that sell audio-visual materials, slides, prints, postcards, reproductions, and imitations. Facilities aimed at enhancing the circulation, comfort, convenience, and even the amusement of

large crowds of visitors place art increasingly in a context of entertainment.

The museums of the nineteenth and earlier twentieth centuries are vast, converted palaces like the Louvre—buildings of palatial scale that overwhelm the artworks or obscure them in ill-lighted, crowded galleries or darkened halls laid out in monotonous, rectilinear plans. In the later twentieth century, the expansionary function that has transformed the museum into a great community center has presented contemporary architecture with one of its major challenges. In a variety of ways, modern architects are addressing the problem of combining the marginal services that encourage large public attendance with the still-primary function of exhibiting works of art effectively.

IEOH MING PEI (b. 1917), an American architect born in China, solves the problem with conspicuous success in his East Building of the National Gallery in Washington, D.C. (FIG. 22-115), for which he won the Gold Medal of the American Institute of Architects in 1978. In Pei's hands, the awkward building site becomes a virtue made from necessity, somewhat as the Campidoglio (FIG. 17-29) did in the hands of Michelangelo. The irregular, trapezoidal site had been set aside in 1937 for expansion of the main building—a handsome, domed, Neoclassical structure of the Jeffersonian type, built in 1941. Bisecting the trapezoid into a larger isosceles triangle and a smaller right triangle, Pei ingeniously maximized his use of the difficult site, producing an esthetically and functionally impressive aggregation of angular masses unified by a vast, faceted skylight 80 feet above a spacious courtyard six levels high. The larger triangle, with its dia-

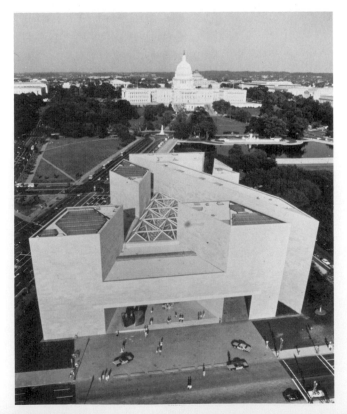

22-115 IEOH MING PEI, National Gallery Addition (East Building), Washington D.C., 1978.
Below: IEOH MING PEI, site plan of the National Gallery Addition.

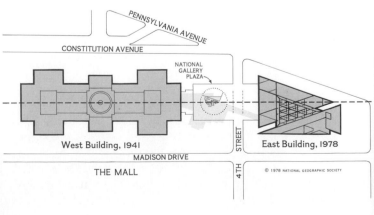

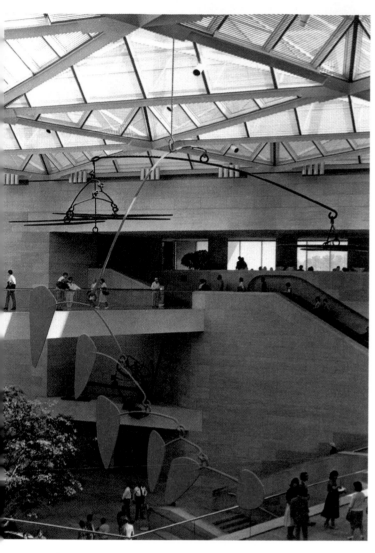

22-116 IOEH MING PEI, interior of the National Gallery Addition. (The mobile shown in the foreground is by ALEXANDER CALDER.)

shapes as one moves. The experience of fluid space and transformation of form is intensified by the mobile by Alexander Calder that majestically commands the scene. Bridges, escalators, and stairways casually connect the central space with numerous irregularly shaped and randomly placed galleries of varying dimensions—"houses" diminutive and intimate enough to show very small pictures or ample enough to accommodate the largest canvases of the New York School.

Despite the rich variety of its forms, the whole structure is a marvel of coherence and order and a triumph of craftsmanship down to the least detail; the last is creditable to the donor, who stipulated that no expense be spared in bringing the building to perfection. This collaboration of patron and architect is reminiscent of that of the Medici or the artistic geniuses of the Renaissance. It is significant, moreover, that the building, itself a masterpiece, has been designed to house masterpieces and that it occupies a site continuous with monuments visited and revered by the public as national shrines. The National Gallery—completing the original, Classical design of Pierre Charles L' Enfant, the city planner of Washington, D.C.—has become an unforgettable part of this great ensemble.

In Paris, another new museum—the Georges Pompidou National Center of Art and Culture, known as the "Beaubourg" (FIG. 22-117), opened in 1977—recalls in many ways the spirit, intention, and structure of the Crystal Palace (FIG. 21-86) and of the Galerie des Machines of the Paris International Exhibition of 1889 (FIG. 21-87). This spirit of making the fruits of the arts and sciences accessible to as wide a public as possible is evident throughout the "Beaubourg." The anatomy of this six-level building designed by RICHARD ROGERS (b. 1933) and RENZO PIANO (b. 1937) is fully exposed. So is its "metabolism"—the actual movements and processes it produces, directs, and surrounds. Pipes, ducts, tubes, and corridors are coded in color according to function (red, for the movement of people; green, for water; blue, for air conditioning; yellow, for electricity)—much as in a sophisticated industrial plant. This total "archigraphic" revelation of the structural body is, at the same time, a self-revelation for the public, for the great crowds that flow through the building (some 4,000 visitors a day) can readily perceive its functions, including those that serve their own needs and interests. In addition to art galleries, the building houses a center for industrial design, a library (described as "the first truly open library in France"), science and music centers, conference rooms, research and archival facilities, projection rooms, rest areas, and a restaurant that looks down and through the building to sculptured terraces outside. The meaning and

mond-shaped towers, provides exhibition space; the smaller, with its dramatic wedge shape (the walls meet in a sharp 19° angle) provides space for art-historical research.

The East Building artfully compliments the West Building by aligning with its axis (it is connected with it by an underground, moving walkway) and by wearing a facing of the same pink Tennessee marble that adorns the older building. The centerpiece of a skillful urban composition, the East Building makes the most of the angularity of the site (especially the lines of convergence of the avenues and the great Mall), reflecting in its many contradictory planes and lesser axes the directional sweep and pattern of the adjacent traffic.

The interior (FIG. 22-116) is illuminated by a great skylight made up of glass tetrahedra, set in a complex tracery, that seem to change, multiply, and create

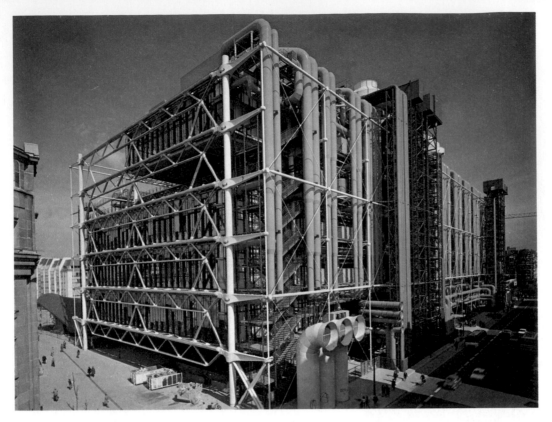

22-117 RICHARD ROGERS and RENZO PIANO, Georges Pompidou National Center of Art and Culture (the "Beaubourg"), Paris, 1977.

function of the "Beaubourg" is stated simply in the words of a director of the museum, Pontus Hulten:

> If the hallowed, cult-like calm of the traditional museum has been lost, so much the better. . . . We are moving toward a society where art will play a great role, which is why this museum is open to disciplines that were once excluded by museums and which is why it is open to the largest possible public.*

Of course, the building is not without its critics. Detractors have called it a "cultural supermarket" and have pointed out that its exposed entrails require excessive maintenance to protect them from the elements.

Architecture of the last 25 years has shown a growing departure from the doctrines, forms, and practices of the International style; this phase has been called Post-Modern. A new freedom of conception has set in, expressing itself in an almost Baroque inventiveness and elaboration of design. For inspiration, architects range through all the resources provided by the history of architecture; or they may indulge in fanciful, even quixotic experiments in search of novel forms and significance, making use of an ever-richer technology of materials and methods of construction. Not least among their opportunities for inventiveness are those offered by new problems related to environment, energy, and the changing patterns of public and private life. It is little wonder

*Architectural Record (February 1978), p. 103.

that the bewildering diversity of design that has resulted makes identification of a dominant contemporary trend close to impossible. This diversity extends to architectural types. Buildings designed for similar functions can differ so widely in appearance that they seem to have little in common or to be suited for any number of not necessarily consistent uses. The museums we have considered are cases in point. The Guggenheim, the National Gallery Addition, and the "Beaubourg" are all markedly individualistic, unique, and anything but representative of a type.

A familiar architectural type that characterizes the International style in the cities of the world is the concrete, steel, and glass tower—the skyscraper reduced to a sheer, vertical grid. We have seen the perfection of the skyscraper type—a respected formula for more than 20 years—in the Seagram Building in New York (FIG. 22-67). Philip Johnson, who collaborated with Mies van der Rohe on that structure and who, for most of his career, has been close to the International style, has departed from the strictness of the "Miesian" scheme into geometric adventures similar to Pei's in the National Gallery Addition. Like many of his younger contemporaries, Johnson has moved away from the severity of the elementary, solid, geometric figures to much more complex ones. In the Pennzoil Place, in Houston, Texas, Johnson modifies and complicates the skyscraper type, greatly reducing its height and articulating its plan and elevation for dramatic effect (FIG. 22-118). In collaboration with

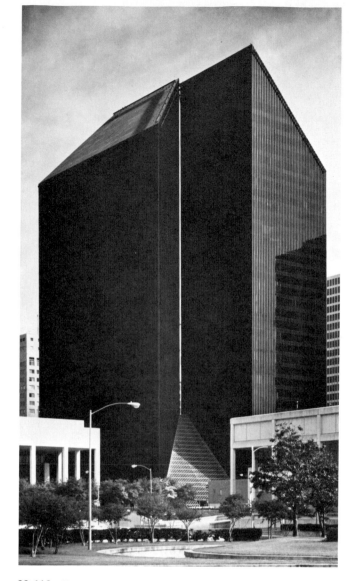

22-118 Philip Johnson, John Burgee, and Associates, Pennzoil Place, Houston, Texas, 1977.

John Burgee and associates, he has erected twin, trapezoidal, dark towers of steel and anodized aluminum, 36 stories high. Angled toward one another, and separated by a 10-foot slot of space, they appear as mirror images. Within the slot, repeating its angle, a glazed atrium rises eight stories from the street.

Johnson's departures belong to a general shifting of Post-Modern design and taste. Criticism of the International style reaches back into the 1940s, when the philosopher and architectural critic Ernst Bloch denounced "modernity" in architecture as "polished death offered as morning-glow," or as "chrome-covered misery." A somewhat less severe critic, architect Robert Venturi (b. 1925), remarks "on the richness and ambiguity of modern experience." In *Complexity and Contradiction in Architecture*, published by the Museum of Modern Art in 1966, Venturi declares:

. . . architects can no longer afford to be intimidated by the puritanically moral language of orthodox

Modern architecture. . . . A valid architecture evokes many levels of meaning and combinations of focus; its space and its elements become readable and workable in several ways at once.

True to form, Venturi, a leader in the Post-Modern movement, has produced work that reflects his words. At Vail, Colorado, Venturi and associates built a four-story vacation lodge (FIG. 22-119), set into a steep slope that, in its elevation reverses the traditional distribution of functions. Here, the private rooms are on the two lower stories; the public rooms, on the two upper. The exterior of the building suggests the rustic mountain cabin, with the flavor of the chalet; Venturi declares it "romantic," in its evocation of a tower among trees. The massive, peaked roof—pulled tightly down—contrasts with the large, lunette-shaped dormers; the abrupt contrast of exterior with interior and the free proportions, asymmetries, and almost random placement of the features certainly avoid all formulas. In frank eclecticism, both outside and inside, borrowings are evident from sources widely separated in time and tone: Palladio, Art Nouveau, the "romantic" Internationalist Alvar Aalto, Le Corbusier. The material throughout is wood (cedar siding and shingles, oak stairs, maple counters), scrupulously handcrafted. The fourth floor dramatically caps the design, in all its "complexity and contradiction," with a vaulted parlor, luminous with outdoor light from the lunette dormers and the sheen of cedar (FIG. 22-120). The building is an expression of a self-conscious manner that deliberately looks away from the conventional wisdoms of the International style.

The multiple aspects of Post-Modern architecture, in all their diversity, share a common rejection of the machined and frigid monotony of the International style. In reaction to the straight-edged, antiseptic forms of the "Miesian" style, a fascination with curvilinear forms, both in plan and elevation, can be observed. The dome, the arch, and the vault are being resurrected—sometimes with whimsical and, occasionally, even humorous results, reminiscent of the Manneristic style of Giulio Romano's Palazzo del Tè (FIGS. 17-48 and 17-49). In Europe, a shift of focus can be discerned—away from a building's efficiency and toward a greater concern for the well-being of its occupants. Although only an undercurrent in architectural thought, the slogan "humanization of the workplace" is gaining currency. Here and there, the science-fiction settings of glass-encased, high-rise office silos are being replaced with three- and four-story buildings, grouped around landscaped courts, to provide workers with a home-like atmosphere in which they can feel like inhabitants rather than robots. The self-glorification of financial and industrial

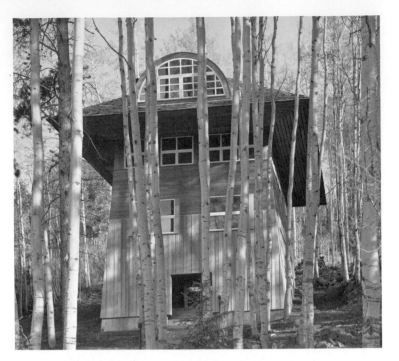

22-119   ROBERT VENTURI and Associates, Brant–Johnson house, Vail, Colorado, 1977.

22-120   ROBERT VENTURI and Associates, interior of the Brant–Johnson house.

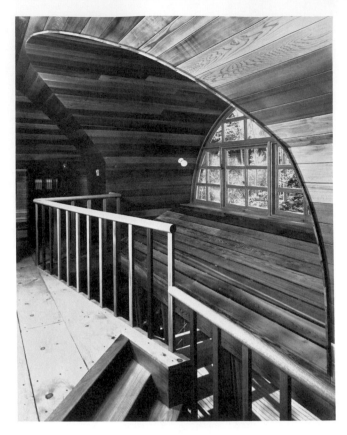

giants, with their ever-higher and more daring skyscrapers, may one day come to an end. At present, however, elephantine high-rises are still sprouting from urban centers, and the revolution of office planning lies in the future.

The great shift in architectural style is accompanied by considerable confusion about the architect's role and purpose, as well as about the nature and goal of the Post-Modern movement itself. In reporting a conference on architectural design, Robert Gutman observes that the members of the conference "expressed dramatically opposite points of view" and that all were applauded to the same degree:

> Architecture, as it shakes off Modernism and the International style, is slouching toward a new architectural order through a chaos of styles that many find alarming and others delight in. . . . Design in architecture, as that pluralism unfolds, is swinging toward humanism; or it is growing more and more victimized by a technocratic society; or it is managing to reconcile the two.*

However historians may interpret these stylistic events, they agree that, as we have already suggested, the function of the architect is often blurred or shared among other persons or agencies. A design is no longer the product of the individual architect, or even of the architectural firm, but reflects the additional influences of a group that includes regulatory

agencies, zoning boards, financiers, ecologists, and—not least—the energy-conscious.

A new and pressing demand is that architecture be energy-efficient. A premise of the International style—that the interior environment of a building can be totally controlled by elaborate heating, cooling, and ventilation systems, installed with little effect on the design—presupposes an inexhaustible supply of relatively inexpensive energy to fuel these systems. The rise in cost of energy in the 1970s and the recognition of the finite character of fossil fuels has increasingly elicited the demand that energy consumption be considered at the very beginning of the design process—a fact that could make the principles as well as the look of the International style largely obsolete. Concerning the energy-wasteful building, Richard Stein observes:

> . . . the hope for the future lies in the fundamental reversal in our present commitment to the sealed building, with its massive plant for manufacturing the air and delivering it at predetermined temperatures and velocities and its large lighting apparatus that substitutes a universal switch for selectivity. If these helped cause our problem, their reversal can help solve it.*

With new sources of energy being sought, solar energy has become an attractive field for recent experiment—as the many new residential and commer-

*Journal of the American Institute of Architects, Vol. 67, No. 1 (January 1978), p. 49.

*Architecture and Energy (New York: Doubleday, Anchor Press, 1977), p. 292.

cial buildings using solar techniques testify. In 1978, a design competition for a state office building in Sacramento, California, was won by BUFORD DUKE for an energy-efficient design that combines "maximum exposure for solar generation with minimum exposure for energy conservation." Most of the building's office space is underground, arranged around a great, sunken courtyard, with lightwells providing natural light. Overhead, an urban park provides insulation. At one end of the complex, a six-story tower contains additional office space, but its main purpose is to serve as support for some 12,000 square feet of solar collectors that generate the energy for heating and cooling the building.

Related to the need for energy conservation is the problem of urban sprawl. In keeping with the progressing trend toward specialization, urbanism—once part of the architect's sphere of activity—has become the problem child of a new specialist, the city planner. For a little more than a century (since about 1850), the modern city has been attracting a rural population that has lost its livelihood in the country. Ironically, the explosive growth of cities largely has been a consequence of the enormous rise in agricultural producivity. (If only 5 percent of a population can feed the rest, then the other 95 percent must move to cities and industrial centers to find work.) But yesterday's panacea has lost its charm today, and Aristotle's vision of the "good life" in the city has evaporated in smog, noise, and pollution. Since World War II, metropolitan centers have become increasingly deserted, as people move, if not all the way back, at least closer to the rural surroundings from which their parents and grandparents emigrated. Today, we find the once-bustling, metropolitan cores surrounded by satellite residential towns, complete with shopping and recreational centers, to which disenchanted city workers rush back each evening, fleeing their dehumanized workday surroundings. As a result of this flight back to the country, many urban centers stand dark and deserted for some 14 hours a day five days a week and 24 hours a day on weekends. All this has placed an enormous strain on transportation systems (primarily on highways in the United States), which must move millions of people to and from their jobs, at the cost of commensurate amounts of fuel. And the specter of yet another "doomsday" arises to threaten us not with the Last Judgement or a nuclear holocaust, but with the inevitable depletion of the earth's energy resources.

Thus, one of the most urgent issues confronting the contemporary city planner is how to revitalize urban centers and make them attractive again, so that people will no longer feel the need to vacate them at 5 P.M. each evening. Under the general heading of "urban renewal," numerous solutions have been attempted, but none yet have proved to be entirely successful. Partial answers have been provided: shopping malls, high-rise (!) hotels, convention centers, museums, and occasional designs for public squares.

An interesting example of a public square is the Piazza d' Italia in New Orleans (FIGS. 22-121 and 22-122), which incidentally, also is a fascinating specimen of Post-Modern design. Created by CHARLES MOORE (b. 1925), it illustrates still another of the many facets of Post-Modern architecture—unabashed eclecticism—which here, however, serves a specific purpose. The piazza is dedicated to the Italian colony of New Orleans, and Moore's use of Classical models for its design is meaningful in its direct reference to the Mediterranean origin of Italians and to a region, strewn with Greek and Roman ruins, that evokes ancient cultural reminiscences.

Backed up against a contemporary high-rise and set off from urban traffic patterns, the Piazza d' Italia can be reached on foot from three sides, through gateways of varied design. The approaches lead to an open, circular area—partially framed by short segments of colonnades arranged in staggered, concentric arcs—and direct the eye to the composition's focal point: an exedra (a semicircular, walled space, like an apse) on a raised platform that serves as rostrum during the annual festivities of St. Joseph's Day. The piazza's pavement is inlaid with the map of Italy, in which Sicily, the place of origin of the Italian colony's majority, is centrally placed. From there, the Italian boot moves in the direction of the steps that ascend the rostrum and that, geographically, correspond to the Alps. The piazza's most immediate historical reference is to the Greek agora or the Roman forum; on the other hand, its circular form refers to the ideal geometric figure of the Renaissance. The irregular placement of the concentrically arranged colonnade fragments inserts a note of instability into the design that is reminiscent of Mannerism; and illusionistic devices, like the continuation of the piazza's pavement design (apparently through a building and out into the street), are Baroque in character. All of the Classical orders are represented—some with whimsical modifications: fluting defined by rising jets of water; water falling from metopes (Moore calls these "wetopes") and spouting from the mouths of the architect's relief portraits that have been set into spandrels. Twentieth-century touches are provided in the form of stainless-steel columns and capitals, neon collars around the necks of columns, and the framing of various features of the exedra with neon lights.

In sum, the design of the Piazza d' Italia is a complex conglomerate of symbolic, historical, and geographical allusions—some overt, others hidden—

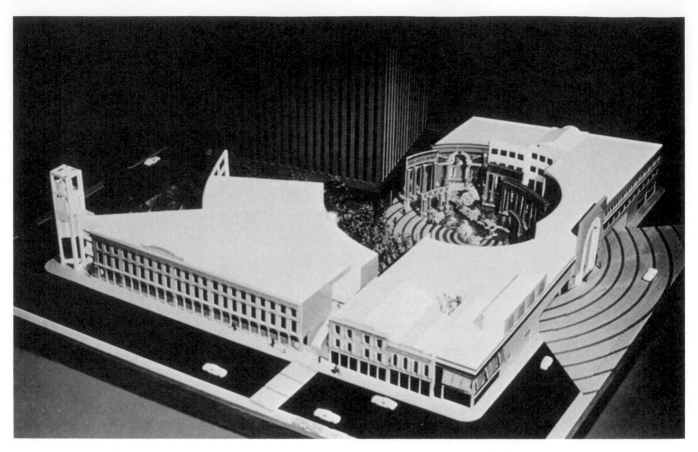

22-121   CHARLES MOORE, model of the Piazza d'Italia, New Orleans, Louisiana, 1976–1980.

22-122   CHARLES MOORE, Piazza d'Italia, view of the exedra (detail of FIG. 22-121).

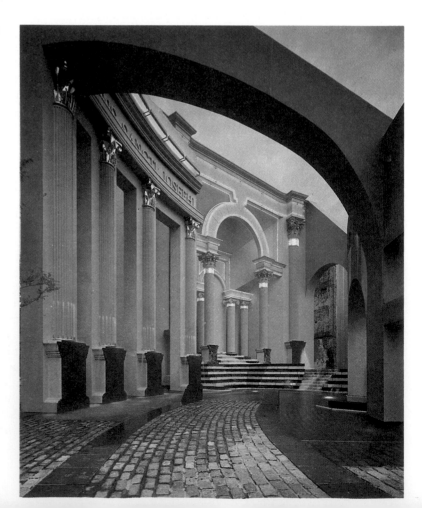

assembled for visual effect and not without humor. The piazza's specific purpose is to give identity (or, to use a favorite Post-Modern expression, a "heart") to the Italian community of New Orleans. Its more general purpose is to revitalize an urban area by becoming a focal point and an architectural setting for the social activities of the neighborhood residents. It remains to be seen if it can fulfill this expectation, or if it will become just another curiosity and tourist attraction.

Great works, as we have seen, transcend the stature of any one architect. What philosopher–historian Stephen Toulmin writes of scientific work in this century could well apply to architecture now: "Ours is not so much a century of *genius* as a century of *scale* and *organization*." The International style, developed in the early years of the twentieth century, provided the elements of an architectural language that is recognized and understood throughout the world. It remains the dominant trend in today's building. Its further sophistication and consolidation—however edited, revised, and transformed—will be the work of great collaborations rather than of isolated genius, resembling, as Mies van der Rohe predicted, the corporate architectural creativity of the Gothic world.

EPILOGUE

The transformation of the world by science and technology is the signal fact that separates the modern epoch from all of the past. The influence on architecture is obvious enough; in painting and sculpture, it is perhaps less obvious but certainly just as decisive. The image-making function of the figurative arts, insofar as they simulate appearance, has been largely displaced by the making of objects with or without reference to the public world as we see it. These are the products of the artist's private vision and vocabulary. The ironic, mythic, and social functions of representation have been monopolized by mechanical media—photography, motion pictures, television, and computers. By these means, images can be produced and reproduced in countless millions. The art object itself, through sophisticated means of reproduction, loses its uniqueness and its "space," like the original sound of an orchestral performance reproduced in high-fidelity recording. Reproductions of art and artifacts in special collections are offered for sale as exact duplications. This is analogous to biological cloning or to the standardization and mass production of industrial commodities; the processes employed are quite different from the ones that made the original object. At the same time, there is a multiplication of hands involved—a collectivization of the agents and the agencies of creation. The independent role of the artist as hand craftsman could not help but be fundamentally affected by the fact and the method of mechanized production. And the esthetic values of nonobjective sculpture and painting cannot help but be shared and exchanged with, or even transferred to, the esthetic values we appreciate in the best industrial design.

Meanwhile the Tradition has been dismantled. Has a new one appeared? The triumph of modern art is at the same time its crisis. At the heart of the crisis is a paradox. Modernism, created by the break with tradition, has itself become a "tradition"; we have seen that Post-Modernism is precisely a reaction against the "tradition" of Modernism. Everything now becomes problematical: the purpose of art, the function of the artist, the nature of the media with which the artist works or should work, the artist's relationship to patron and public. Questions abound: What is wanted? What is needed? What is to be done? How is it to be done? This pervasive disagreement is explicit in the very plurality of works and styles, programs and processes, interpretations and assessments.

In the marketplace, where artists compete fiercely, there is unrelenting pressure for novelty, uniqueness, and variety of expression. For economics, as well as science and technology, has touched the art of today and influenced it definitively. The old, direct relationship of artist and patron has been replaced by "the system"—an unregulated art market managed (sometimes manipulated in concert) by critics, dealers, collectors, gallery owners, museum directors, art schools, and other agencies and institutions. The estimate of the intrinsic value of a work of art is often directly related to its value on the market, and conflicts of interest can render critical and art-historical judgments suspect. As the critic Robert Hughes observes:

> The flight of speculative capital to the art market has done more to alter and distort the way we experience painting and sculpture in the last twenty years than any style, movement, or polemic. . . . The subversion of esthetic experience by monetary value is by now as pervasive and visible as the alteration of unique objects by mass reproduction. Colossal sums of money are exchanged every day on the art market.

Thus, the industrial and the economic worlds have had their way with art and artist—with their integrity and with their independence. But there is no reason to believe that creative power has been sapped, even if it has often been confused and frustrated. As the West has lost its tradition, the non-Western sectors of humanity have lost or modified theirs. To judge by style, an international—a world—art is emerging. As traditional differences disappear and as art gains a wholeness never before known, it may promise spiritual and esthetic experiences of incalculable worth for all the human race.

GLOSSARY

Italicized terms are also defined in the Glossary.

abacus (ab'a·kus) The uppermost portion of the *capital* of a *column,* usually a thin slab.

abstract In painting and sculpture, emphasizing a derived, essential character having little visual reference to objects in nature.

academy A place of study, derived from the name of the grove where Plato held his philosophical seminars. Giorgio Vasari founded the first academy of fine arts, properly speaking, with his Accademia di Disegno in Florence in 1563.

Achaea (a·ka'ya) An ancient section of the northern Peloponnesos; loosely, Greece in general.

Achaean (a·kee'an) Of or pertaining to *Achaea.*

acroterium or **acroterion** (ak·roh·tee' ri·um) In Classical buildings, a figure or ornament usually at the apex of the *pediment.*

addorsed Set back-to-back, especially as in heraldic design.

adobe (a·do'bee) The clay used to make a kind of sun-dried brick of the same name; a building made of such brick.

aerial perspective See *perspective.*

agora (ag'o·ra) An open square or space used for public meetings or business in ancient Greek cities.

aisle The portion of a church flanking the *nave* and separated from it by a row of *columns* or *piers.*

alabaster A variety of gypsum or calcite of dense, fine texture, usually white, but also red, yellow, gray, and sometimes banded.

alla prima (a'la pree'ma) A painting technique in which pigments are laid on in one application, with little or no drawing or underpainting.

altarpiece A panel, painted or sculptured, situated above and behind an altar. See also *retable.*

ambulatory A covered walkway, outdoors (as in a *cloister*) or indoors, especially the passageway around the *apse* and the *choir* of a church.

amphora (am'fo·ra) A two-handled, egg-shaped jar used for general storage purposes.

anamorphic image An image that must be viewed by some special means (such as a mirror) to be recognized.

apadana (ap·a·dan'a) The great audience hall in ancient Persian palaces.

apse A recess, usually singular and semicircular, in the wall of a Roman *basilica* or at the east end of a Christian church.

arabesque Literally, "Arabian-like." A flowing, intricate pattern derived from stylized organic motifs, usually floral, often arranged in symmetrical *palmette* designs; generally, an Islamic decorative motif.

arcade A series of *arches* supported by *piers* or *columns.*

arcading An uninterrupted series of *arches.*

arch A curved structural member that spans an opening and is generally composed of wedge-shaped blocks (*voussoirs*) that transmit the downward pressure laterally. A **diaphragm arch** is a transverse, wall-bearing arch that divides a *vault* or a ceiling into compartments, providing a kind of firebreak. See also *thrust.*

architectonic Having structural or architectural qualities, usually as elements of a nonarchitectural object.

architrave (ark'i·trayv) The *lintel* or lowest division of the *entablature;* sometimes called the *epistyle.*

archivolt (ark'i·volt) One of a series of concentric *moldings* on a Romanesque or a Gothic arch.

arcuated (ar'kew·ate·id) Of *arch–column* construction.

armature In sculpture, a skeleton-like framework to support material being modeled.

aspara In India, a nymph of the sky or air; in Chinese Buddhism, a heavenly maiden.

atlantes (at·lan'teez; *sing.* **atlas**) Male figures that function as supporting columns. See also *caryatid.*

atmospheric perspective See *perspective.*

atrium (ay'tree·um) The court of a Roman house that is near the entrance and partly open to the sky. Also, the open, colonnaded court in front of and attached to a Christian *basilica.*

avant-garde (a·vahn·gard') Artists whose work is in (or work that reflects) the latest stylistic direction.

avatar (ah'vah·tar) In Hinduism, an incarnation of a god.

axial plan See *plan.*

axis An imaginary line or lines about which a work, a group of works, or a part of a work is visually or structurally organized, often symmetrically.

baldacchino (bal·da·kee'no) A canopy on columns, frequently built over an altar.

barrel vault See *vault.*

bas (bah) **relief** See *relief.*

basilica (ba·sil'i·ka) In Roman architecture, a public building for assemblies (especially tribunals), that is rectangular in plan with an entrance on a long side. In Christian architecture, an early church somewhat resembling the Roman basilica, usually entered from one end and with an *apse* at the other, creating an *axial plan.*

batter To slope inward, often almost imperceptibly, or such an inward slope of a wall.

bay A subdivision of the interior space of a building. In Romanesque and Gothic

churches, the transverse *arches* and *piers* of the *arcade* divide the building into bays.

beehive tomb A beehive-shaped type of subterranean tomb constructed as a *corbeled vault* and found on pre-Archaic Greek sites.

belvedere (bell·vuh·dare'eh) An open, roofed story built to provide a scenic view.

ben-ben A pyramidal stone; a *fetish* of the Egyptian god Re.

benizuri-e (ben'i·zur'i-ee) A two-color method of Japanese printing in pink and green that produces strong color vibration.

bevel See *chamfer.*

bhakti (buh·hock'tee) In Hinduism, the devote, selfless direction of all tasks and activities of life to the service of one god; the adoration of a personalized deity.

black-figure technique In early Greek pottery, the silhouetting of dark figures against a light background of natural, reddish clay.

blind arcade (wall arcade) An *arcade* having no actual openings, applied as decoration to a wall surface.

Bodhisattva (bo·dee·sot'va) In Buddhism, a being who is a potential *Buddha.*

bottega (but·tay'ga) A shop; the studio-shop of an Italian artist.

bouleuterion (boo·loo·tee'ri·on) In ancient Greece, an assembly hall or council chamber.

broken color A painting technique using short, thick strokes laid over a ground color to create rich textures and vibrant effects of light.

broken pediment A *pediment* in which the *cornice* is discontinuous at the apex or the base.

Buddha The supreme enlightened being of Buddhism, an embodiment of divine wisdom and virtue. **Buddhist** (*adj.*)

burin (byoor'in) A pointed steel tool for *engraving* or *incising.*

buttress An exterior masonry structure that opposes the lateral thrust of an *arch* or a *vault.* A **pier buttress** is a solid mass of masonry; a **flying buttress** consists typically of an inclined member carried on an arch or a series of arches and a solid buttress to which it transmits lateral *thrust.*

calidarium The hot-bath section of a Roman bathing establishment.

calligraphy Handwriting or penmanship, especially elegant or "beautiful" writing as a decorative art.

camera obscura An ancestor of the modern camera in which a tiny pinhole, acting as a lens, projects an image on a screen, the wall of a room, or the ground-glass wall of a box; used by seventeenth- and eighteenth-century artists as an aid in compositional arrangement.

campanile (kam·pa·neel'eh) A bell tower, usually freestanding.

capital The upper member of a *column*, serving as a transition from the *shaft* to the *lintel*.

Caravaggisti (kara·va·gee'stee) Artists influenced by Caravaggio's dramatically contrasting dark–light effects; painters of "night" pictures in the "dark manner" (*tenebroso*).

cardo The north–south road in Etruscan and Roman towns, intersecting the *decumanus* at right angles.

carrier The material support for a painting (wood, canvas, wall, etc.).

cartoon In painting, a full-size drawing from which a painting is made. Cartoons were usually worked out in complete detail; the design was then transferred to the working surface by coating the back with chalk and going over the lines with a *stylus*, or by pricking the lines and "pouncing" charcoal dust through the resulting holes.

cartouche (kar·toosh') A scroll-like design or medallion, purely decorative or containing an inscription or heraldic device. In ancient Egypt, an oval device containing such elements as *hieroglyphic* names of Egyptian kings.

caryatid (kar'ee·at'id) A female figure that functions as a supporting *column*. See also *atlantes*.

casting In sculpture, duplication of a clay original in plaster or metal by use of a mold.

cella (sel'a) An enclosed chamber (Greek, *naos*); the essential feature of a Classical temple, in which the cult statue usually stood.

centering A wooden framework to support an *arch* or a *vault* during its construction.

central plan See *plan*.

ceramics The art of making objects such as pottery out of clay; also, the objects themselves.

chaitya (chight'yuh) An Indian shrine, especially a Buddhist assembly hall having a votive *stupa* at one end.

chalice A cup or goblet, especially that used in the sacraments of the Christian Church.

chamfer The surface formed by cutting off a corner of a board or post; a *bevel*.

champlevé (shahn·le·vay') A process of enameling in which a design is cut into a metal plate in such a way as to leave thin, raised lines that create compartments to hold the enamel.

chandi A Javanese temple.

chatra See *parasol*.

chevet (sheh·vay') The eastern end of a Gothic church, including *choir*, *ambulatory*, and radiating chapels.

chevron A zigzag or V-shaped motif of decoration.

chiaroscuro (kee·ar'o·skoor'o) In painting or drawing, the treatment and use of light and dark, especially the gradations of light that produce the effect of *modeling*.

chinoiserie (shee·nwaz·eh·ree') Chinese motifs used as decorations for furniture, in wallpaper, etc., applied largely to eighteenth-century Rococo style.

chiton (kite'on) A Greek tunic, the essential (and often only) garment of both men and women, the other being the *himation* or *mantle*.

choir The space reserved for the clergy in the church, usually east of the *transept* but, in some instances, extending into the *nave*.

ciborium (sih·bor'ee·um) A canopy, often freestanding and supported by four columns, erected over an altar; also, a covered cup used in the sacraments of the Christian Church. See *baldacchino*.

cinquecento (cheenk·way·chain'toh) The sixteenth century in Italian art.

cire perdue (seer pair·dew') The **lost-wax process.** A bronze-casting method in which a figure is modeled in wax and covered with clay; the whole is fired, melting away the wax and hardening the clay, which then becomes a mold for molten metal.

clerestory (kleer'sto·ry) The *fenestrated* part of a building that rises above the roofs of the other parts.

cloison (klwa·zohn') Literally, a partition. A cell made of metal wire or a narrow metal strip (usually gold) that is soldered edge-down to a metal base to hold enamel or other decorative materials.

cloisonné (klwa·zoh·nay') A process of enameling employing *cloisons*.

cloister A court, usually with covered walks or *ambulatories* along its sides.

closed form A *form*, especially in painting, with a contour that is not broken or blurred.

cluster pier See *compound pier*.

codex Separate pages of *vellum* or *parchment* bound together at one side and having a cover; the predecessor of the modern book.

coffer A sunken panel in a *soffit*, a *vault*, or a ceiling, often ornamental.

collage (kul·lahzh') A composition made by pasting together on a flat surface various materials such as newspaper, wallpaper, printed text and illustrations, photographs, and cloth. See also *montage*.

colonnade A series or row of *columns*, usually spanned by *lintels*.

colonnette A small *column*.

color See *hue*, *saturation*, and *value*.

color-field painting A style of painting characterized by radical simplicity (disciplined line) and purity of shape and color.

column A vertical, weight-carrying architectural member, circular in cross section and consisting of a base (sometimes omitted), a *shaft*, and a *capital*.

complementary afterimage The image (in a *complementary color*) that is retained briefly by the eye after the stimulus is removed.

complementary colors Those pairs of colors, such as red and green, that together embrace the entire spectrum. The complement of one of the three *primary colors* is a mixture of the other two. In pigments, they produce a neutral gray when mixed in the right proportions.

compluvium An opening in the center of the roof of a Roman *atrium* to admit light.

compound or **cluster pier** A *pier* composed of a group or cluster of members, especially characteristic of Gothic architecture.

connoisseur (kon·nuh·ser') An expert on works of art and the individual styles of artists.

contour A visible border of a *mass* in space; a *line* that creates the illusion of *mass* and *volume* in space.

contrapposto (kon·tra·poh'stoh) The disposition of the human figure in which one part is turned in opposition to another part (usually hips and legs one way, shoulders and chest another), creating a counter-positioning of the body about its central *axis*. Sometimes called **weight shift** because the weight of the body tends to be thrown to one foot, creating tension on one side and relaxation on the other.

cool color Blue, green, or violet. Psychologically, cool colors are calming, unemphatic, depressive; optically, they generally appear to recede. See also *warm color*.

corbel (kor'bel) A projecting wall member used as a support for some element in the superstructure. Also, courses of stone or brick in which each course projects beyond the one beneath it. Two such structures, meeting at the topmost course, create an arch.

cornice The projecting, crowning member of the *entablature*; also, any crowning projection.

cosmati (koz·ma'tee) Cut-stone *mosaic* inlay decoration in geometric patterns.

cramp or **clamp** A device, usually metal, to hold together blocks of stone of the same course. See also *dowel*.

crenelated (kren'el·ate·id) Notched or indented, usually with respect to tops of walls, as in battlements.

crocket A projecting, foliate ornament of a *capital*, *pinnacle*, *gable*, *buttress*, or spire.

Cro-Magnon (kro-mag'non) Of or pertaining to the *homo sapiens* whose remains, dating from the Aurignacian period, were found in the Cro-Magnon caves in Dordogne, France.

cromlech (krom'lek) A circle of *monoliths*.

crossing The space in a cruciform church formed by the intersection of the *nave* and the *transept*.

crossing square The area in a church that is formed by the intersection (crossing) of a *nave* and a *transept* of equal width.

crown The topmost part of an *arch*, including the *keystone*; also, an open *finial* of a tower.

cruciform (kroo'suh·form) Cross-shaped

crypt A *vaulted* space under part of a building, wholly or partly underground; in Medieval churches, normally the portion under an *apse* or a *chevet*.

cubiculum A small room constructed in the wall of an Early Christian catacomb to serve as a mortuary chapel.

cuneiform (kyoo·nee'ih·form) Literally, "wedge-shaped." A system of writing used in ancient Mesopotamia, the characters of which were wedge-shaped.

Cyclopean (sike·lo·pee'an) Gigantic; vast

and rough; massive. **Cyclopean architecture** is a method of stone construction using large, irregular blocks without mortar.

dado (day'doh) A horizontal band, often decorated, at the base or lower part of a wall or a pedestal.

daguerreotype (dah·gair'oh·type) A photograph made by an early method on a plate of chemically treated metal or glass; developed by Louis J.M. Daguerre.

decumanus (dek·yoo·man'us) The east–west road in an Etruscan or Roman town, intersecting the *cardo* at right angles.

diptych (dip'tik) A two-paneled *altarpiece*; also, an ancient Roman and Early Christian two-hinged writing tablet, or two ivory memorial panels.

dolmen (dohl'men) Several large stones (*megaliths*) capped with a covering slab, erected in prehistoric times.

dome A hemispheric *vault*; theoretically, an *arch* rotated on its vertical *axis*.

dowel In ancient architecture, a wooden or metal pin placed between stones of different courses to prevent shifting. See also *cramp*.

dromos The passage to a *beehive tomb*.

drum The circular wall that supports a *dome*; also, one of the cylindrical stones of which a non-monolithic *shaft* of a *column* is made.

dry point An engraving in which the design, instead of being cut into the plate with a *burin*, is scratched into the surface with a hard steel "pencil." The process is quicker and more spontaneous than standard engraving and lends itself to the creation of painterly effects. Its disadvantage is the fact that the plate wears out very quickly. See also *engraving, etching, intaglio*.

duecento (doo·ay·chain'toh) The thirteenth century in Italian art.

earth colors Pigments, such as yellow ochre and umber, that are obtained by mining; usually compounds of metals.

echinus (eh·ky'nus) In architecture, the convex element of a *capital* directly below the *abacus*.

eclecticism (eh·klek'ti·sism) The practice of selecting from various sources, sometimes to form a new system or style.

écorché (ay·kor·shay') A figure painted or sculptured to show the muscles of the body without skin.

elevation In drawing and architecture, a geometric projection of a building on a plane perpendicular to the horizon; a vertical projection.

embrasure A *splayed* opening in a wall that enframes a doorway or a window.

enamel A vitreous, colored paste that solidifies when fired. See also *champlevé, cloisonné*.

encaustic An ancient method of painting with colored, molten wax in which the wax is fused with the surface by the application of hot irons.

engaged column A column-like, nonfunctional form projecting from a wall and articulating it visually. See also *pilaster*.

engobe (en·gohb') A slip of finely sifted clay used by Greek potters; applied to a pot, it would form a black *glaze* in firing.

engraving The process of *incising* a design in hard material, often a metal plate (usually copper); also, the print or impression made from such a plate. See also *dry point, etching, intaglio*.

entablature The part of a building above the *capitals* of *columns* and below the roof or the upper story.

entasis (en'·tah·sis) An almost imperceptible convex tapering (an apparent swelling) in the *shaft* of a *column*.

epigone An artist of a succeeding and less distinguished generation.

epistyle See *architrave*.

esthetic The distinctive vocabulary and theory of a given *style*.

etching A kind of *engraving* in which the design is *incised* in a layer of wax or varnish on a copper plate. The parts of the plate left exposed are then **etched** (slightly eaten away) by the acid in which the plate is immersed after incising. Etching is one of the most facile of the graphic arts and the one most capable of subtleties of line and tone. See also *dry point, engraving, intaglio*.

extrados (eks·trah'dohs) The upper or outer surface of an *arch*.

façade Usually, the front of a building; also, the other sides when they are emphasized architecturally.

faïence (feye·ahnce') Pottery (except *porcelain*) glazed with compounds of tin; also, any *glazed* earthenware.

fan vault See *vault*.

fenestration The arrangement of the windows of a building.

ferroconcrete See *reinforced concrete*.

fête galante (fet ga·lahnt') An elegant and graceful celebration; often represented in the works of Antoine Watteau and other Rococo painters.

fetish An object believed to possess magical powers, especially one capable of bringing to fruition its owner's plans; sometimes regarded as the abode of a supernatural power or spirit.

fibula A decorative pin, usually used to fasten garments.

figure-ground The visual unity, yet separability, of a form and its background.

filigree A delicate, lace-like, intertwined, ornamental work or design.

fin de siècle (fan·duh·see'akl) Characteristic of the progressive ideas and customs of the last years of the nineteenth century.

finial A knob-like ornament (usually with a foliate design) in which a vertical member, such as a *pinnacle*, terminates.

flamboyant Flame-like, flaming; applied to aspects of Late Gothic style, especially architectural tracery.

flute or **fluting** Vertical channeling, roughly semicircular in cross section and used principally on *columns* and *pilasters*.

flying buttress See *buttress*.

foreshortening The apparent visual contraction of an object viewed as extended in a plane that is not perpendicular to the

line of sight; also, the representation of this phenomenon.

form In its widest sense, total structure; a synthesis of all the elements of that structure and of the manner in which they are united to create its distinctive character. The *form* of a work is what enables us to apprehend it. See also *closed form* and *open form*.

formalism Strict adherence to, or dependence on, prescribed forms of execution.

forum The public square or marketplace of an ancient Roman city.

fresco Painting on plaster, either dry **(dry fresco** or **fresco secco)** or wet **(wet** or **true fresco).** In the latter method, the pigments are mixed with water and become chemically bound to the plaster. Also, a painting executed in either method.

fret or **meander** An ornament, usually in bands but also covering broad surfaces, consisting of interlocking geometric motifs.

frieze (freez) The part of the *entablature* between the *architrave* and the *cornice*; also, any sculptured or ornamented band in a building, on furniture, etc.

full round Sculpture in full and completely rounded form (not in *relief*).

gable See *pediment*.

gallery The second story of an *ambulatory* or *aisle*.

garbha griha The *cella* or inner sanctum of the Hindu temple.

gargoyle In architecture, a waterspout (usually carved), often in the form of a *grotesque*.

genre (zhahn'reh) A style or category of art; also, a kind of painting realistically depicting scenes from everyday life.

gesso (jess'oh) Plaster mixed with a binding material and used for *reliefs* and as a *ground* for painting.

glaze A vitreous coating applied to pottery to seal the surface and as decoration; it may be colored, transparent, or opaque, and glossy or *matte*. In oil painting, a thin, transparent, or semitransparent layer put over a color to alter it slightly.

glory See *nimbus*.

golden mean or **golden section** A proportional relation obtained by dividing a line so that the shorter part is to the longer part as the longer part is to the whole. The *esthetic* appeal of these proportions has led artists of varying periods and cultures to employ them in determining basic dimensions.

gopuram (go'poor·am) The massive, ornamented entrance structure of South Indian temples.

gouache (goo·ahsh') *Watercolor* rendered opaque by the addition of a filler, such as gum. It has more body and dries more slowly than the transparent watercolor and lends itself to bright color effects and meticulous detail. Also, a picture painted in this medium.

granulation In jewelry, a method of ornamenting in which small grains of metal (usually gold) are soldered to a flat surface.

graphic arts Visual arts that are linear in character, such as drawing and *engraving*; also, generally, visual arts that involve impression (printing and printmaking).

graver A cutting tool used by engravers and sculptors.

Greek cross A cross in which all the arms are the same length.

grisaille (greez·eye') A monochrome painting done mainly in neutral grays to simulate sculpture.

groin The edge formed by the intersection of two *vaults*.

groin vault See *vault*.

grotesque In art, a kind of ornament used in antiquity—and sometimes called (imprecisely) *arabesque*—consisting of representations of medallions, sphinxes, foliage, and imaginary creatures.

ground A coating applied to a canvas or some other surface to prepare that surface for painting; also, background.

guilloche (gee·u͞sh) An ornament consisting of interlaced, curving bands.

hallenkirche (holl'en·keer·sheh) A hall church. In this variety of Gothic church, especially popular in Germany, the *aisles* are as high as the *nave*.

haniwa Sculptured pottery tubes placed around early (archaic) Japanese burial mounds.

harmika A square enclosure atop the *dome* of a *stupa* from which the *yasti* arises.

hatching A technique used in drawing, engraving, etc., in which fine lines are cut or drawn close together to achieve an effect of shading.

haunch The part of an *arch* (roughly midway between the *springing* and the *crown*) at which the lateral *thrust* is strongest.

herringbone perspective See *perspective*.

hieratic (higher·at'tic) The priestly supernaturalism disparaging matter and material values that prevailed throughout the Christian Middle Ages, especially in Orthodox Byzantium.

hieroglyphic (high·roh·glif'ic) A system of writing using symbols or pictures; also, one of the symbols.

himation (him·mat'ee·on) A Greek *mantle* worn by men and women over the tunic and draped in various ways.

historiated Ornamented with representations, such as plants, animals, or human figures, that have a narrative—as distinct from a purely decorative—function. Historiated initial letters were a popular form of manuscript decoration in the Middle Ages.

horror vacui (vack'ui) Literally, "fear of empty space"; crowded design.

hue The name of a color. The *primary colors* (blue, red, and yellow) together with the *secondary colors* (green, orange, and violet) form the chief colors of the spectrum. See also *complementary colors, cool color, saturation, value, warm color*.

hydria (high'dree·a) An ancient Greek three-handled water jar.

hypostyle hall A hall with a roof supported by columns; applied to the colonnaded hall of the Egyptian *pylon* temple.

icon (eye'con) A portrait or image; especially in the Greek church, a panel with a painting of sacred personages that are objects of veneration. In the visual arts, a painting, a piece of sculpture, or even a building regarded as an object of veneration.

iconography (eye·con·og'ra·fee) The study dealing with the symbolic, often religious, meaning of objects, persons, or events depicted in works of art.

iconostasis (eye·con·os'ta·sis) In eastern Christian churches, a screen or a partition, with doors and many *tiers* of *icons*, that separates the sanctuary from the main body of the church.

idealization The representation of things according to a preconception of ideal *form* or type; a kind of *esthetic* distortion to produce idealized forms. See also *realism*.

illumination Decoration with drawings (usually in gold, silver, and bright colors), especially the initial letters of a manuscript.

imagines (i·maj'i·nees; *sing.* **imago**) In ancient Rome, wax portraits of ancestors.

imam (eye·mahm') One who leads worshipers in prayer in Moslem services.

impasto (im·pah'stoh) A style of painting in which the pigment is applied thickly or in heavy lumps, as in many of Rembrandt's paintings.

impluvium A depression in the floor of a Roman *atrium* to collect rainwater.

impost block A stone with the shape of a truncated, inverted pyramid, placed between a *capital* and the *arch* that springs from it.

incising Cutting into a surface with a sharp instrument; also, a method of decoration, especially on metal and pottery.

in situ (si'too) In place; in original position.

insula A multi-storied Roman apartment block.

intaglio (in·tal'yoh) A category of graphic technique in which the design is *incised*, so that the impression made is in *relief*. Used especially on gems, seals, and dies for coins, but also in the kinds of printing or printmaking in which the ink-bearing surface is depressed. Also, an object so decorated. See also *dry point, engraving, etching*.

intarsia (in·tahr'sya) Inlay work, primarily in wood and sometimes in mother-of-pearl, marble, etc.

intercolumniation The space or the system of spacing between *columns* in a *colonnade*.

intrados (in·trah'dohs) The underside of an *arch* or a *vault*.

isocephaly (eye·soh·sef'ah·lee) The arrangement of figures so that the heads are at the same height.

jataka (jah'tah·kah) Tales of the lives of the *Buddha*.

ka (kah) In ancient Egypt, immortal human substance; the concept approximates the Western idea of soul.

kagle A rough, highly abstracted African (Don) mask.

kakemono (kah'keh·moh·noh) A Japanese hanging or scroll.

karma (kar'muh) In Buddhist and Hindu belief, the ethical consequences of a person's life, which determine his or her fate.

keystone The central, uppermost *voussoir* in an *arch*.

khutbah (koot'bah) In Moslem worship, a sermon and a declaration of allegiance to a community leader.

kiln A large stove or oven in which pottery is fired.

kore (kor'ay) Greek for "girl."

kouros (coor'aus) Greek for "young man."

krater/crater (kray'ter) An ancient Greek wide-mouthed bowl for mixing wine and water.

kuang (gwahng) A Chinese covered libation vessel.

kylix/cylix (kye'liks) An ancient Greek drinking cup, shallow and having two handles and a stem.

lacquer A resinous spirit varnish, such as shellac, often colored.

lantern In architecture, a small, often decorative structure with openings for lighting that crowns a *dome*, *turret*, or roof.

lapis lazuli (la'pis la'zyoo·lye) A rich, ultramarine, semiprecious stone used for carving and as a source of *pigment*.

Latin cross A cross in which the vertical member is longer than the horizontal member.

lectionary A list, often illustrated, of **lections,** selections from the Scriptures that are read in church services.

lierne (lee·ern) A short *rib* that runs from one main rib of a *vault* to another.

line The mark made by a moving point and having psychological impact according to its direction and weight. In art, a line defines space and may create a silhouette or define a *contour*, creating the illusion of *mass* and *volume*.

linear perspective See *perspective*.

lintel A beam of any material used to span an opening.

lithography In graphic arts, a printmaking process in which the printing surface is a polished stone on which the design is drawn with a greasy material. Greasy ink, applied to the moistened stone, is repelled by all surfaces except the lines of the drawing. The process permits linear and tonal *values* of great range and subtlety.

local color In painting, the actual *color* of an object.

loggia (luh'jee·uh) A gallery that has an open *arcade* or a *colonnade* on one or both sides.

lost-wax process See *cire perdue*.

lotiform In the form of a lotus petal.

lunette A semicircular opening (with the flat side down) in a wall over a door, a niche, or a window.

luster A thin *glaze* (usually metallic) sometimes used on pottery to produce a rich, often iridescent color. Used particularly in Persian pottery and in *majolica*.

machicolation (mah·chik'oh·lay·shun) An opening (in the floor of an overhanging gallery) through which the defenders of a castle dropped stones and boiling liquids on attackers.

madrasah (muh·drah'suh) A combined Moslem school and *mosque*.

magazine A room or building designed for storage.

majolica (ma·jo'lik·ah) A kind of Italian Renaissance pottery coated with a whitish tin-compound enamel, brilliantly painted and often *lustered*.

makimono (mah'kee·moh'noh) A Japanese horizontal scroll.

malanggan (mah·lohng'gahn) Intricately carved Melanesian ceremonial masks.

mandala (man'duh·luh) In Hinduism and Buddhism, a magical, geometric symbol of the cosmos.

mandapa (man·dop'ah) A Hindu assembly hall, part of a temple.

mandorla An almond-shaped *nimbus*, or *glory*, surrounding the figure of Christ.

maniera greca (man·yera'greka) A formal Byzantine style that dominated Italian painting in the twelfth and thirteenth centuries; characterized by shallow space and linear flatness.

mantle See *himation*.

mass The effect and degree of bulk, density, and weight of matter in space. As opposed to plane and area (**volume**), mass is three-dimensional.

mastaba (mah'sta·bah) A bench-shaped ancient Egyptian tomb.

matte (mat) In painting, pottery, and photography, a dull finish.

mbari Ceremonial houses filled with clay sculptures, honoring community deities of the Ibo tribe in Africa.

meander See *fret*.

medium The substance or agency in which an artist works; also, in painting, the vehicle (usually liquid) that carries the *pigment*.

megalith Literally, "great stone"; a large, roughly hewn stone used in the construction of monumental, prehistoric structures. **megalithic** (*adj.*). See also, *cromlech, dolmen, menhir*.

megaron (meh'ga·ron) A rectangular hall, fronted by an open, two-columned porch, traditional in Greece since Mycenaean times.

menhir (men'heer) A prehistoric *monolith*, uncut or roughly cut, standing singly or with others in rows or circles.

merlon The solid part of a battlement.

metope (met'a·pee) The space between *triglyphs* in a Doric *frieze*.

mihrab (mee'rahb) In the wall of a *mosque*, the niche that indicates the direction of Mecca.

minbar (meen'bar) The pulpit in a *mosque*.

miniature A small picture illustrating a manuscript; also, any small portrait, often on ivory or *porcelain*.

modeling The shaping of three-dimensional forms in a soft material, such as clay; also, the gradations of light and shade reflected from the surfaces of matter in space, or the illusion of such gradations produced by alterations of *value* in a drawing or a painting.

module (mod'yool) A basic unit of which the dimensions of the major parts of a work are multiples. The principle is used in sculpture and other art forms, but it is most often employed in architecture, where the module may be the dimensions of an important part of a building, such as a *column*, or simply some commonly accepted unit of measurement (the centimeter or the inch, or, as with Le Corbusier, the average dimensions of the human figure).

molding In architecture, a continuous, narrow surface (projecting or recessed, plain or ornamented) designed to break up a surface, to accent, or to decorate.

monochrome A painting in one color; also, the technique of making such a painting.

monolith A column that is all in one piece (not built up); a large, single block or piece of stone used in *megalithic* structures.

montage (mohn'tahzh) A composition made by fitting together pictures or parts of pictures; also, motion-picture effects produced by superimposing images or showing them in rapid sequence. See also *collage*.

monumental In art criticism, any work of art of unpretentious grandeur and simplicity, regardless of its size.

mortice See *tenon*.

mosaic Patterns or pictures made by embedding small pieces of stone or glass (*tesserae*) in cement on surfaces such as walls and floors; also, the technique of making such works.

mosque A Moslem place of worship.

mudra (muh·drah') A stylized gesture of mystical significance, usually in representations of Hindu deities.

mullion A vertical member that divides a window or that separates one window from another.

mural A wall painting; a *fresco* is a type of mural medium and technique.

naos See *cella*.

narthex A porch or vestibule of a church, generally colonnaded or arcaded and preceding the *nave*.

Naturalism The doctrine that art should adhere as closely as possible to the appearance of the natural world. Naturalism, with varying degrees of fidelity to appearance, recurs in the history of Western art.

nave The part of a church between the chief entrance and the *choir*, demarcated from *aisles* by *piers* or *columns*.

necking A groove at the bottom of the Greek Doric *capital* between the *echinus* and the *flutes* that masks the junction of *capital* and *shaft*.

necropolis (neh·krop'o·lis) A large burial area; literally, a city of the dead.

niello (nee·el'o) Inlay in a metal of an alloy of sulfur and such metals as gold or silver. Also, a work made by this process, or the alloy itself.

nimbus A halo, aureole, or **glory** appearing around the head of a holy figure to signify divinity.

nirvana (neer·vah'nah) In Buddhism and Hinduism, a blissful state brought about by absorption of the individual soul or consciousness into the supreme spirit.

objet d'art (objay·dar') A relatively small object (figurine, vase, etc.) of artistic value.

obverse On coins or medals, the side that bears the principal type or inscription. See also *reverse*.

oculus A round, central opening or "eye" in a *dome*.

odalisque (oh'dah·lisk) An Oriental slave girl or concubine, a favorite subject of such artists as Ingres and Matisse.

oenochoe (eh·nuk'oh·ee) An ancient Greek wine pitcher.

oeuvre (uh'vreh) The whole of an artist's output; literally, the artist's "work."

ogee (oh'jee) A *molding* having in profile a double or S-shaped curve. Also, an *arch*, each side of which has this *form*.

ogive The diagonal *rib* of a Gothic *vault*; a pointed, or Gothic, *arch*. **ogival** (*adj.*).

oil color *Pigment* ground with oil.

open form A *mass* penetrated or treated in such a way that space acts as its environment rather than as its limit. See also *closed form*.

order In Classical architecture, a style represented by a characteristic design of the *column* and its *entablature*. See also *superimposed order*.

orthogonal A line imagined to be behind and perpendicular to the *picture plane*; the *orthogonals* in a painting appear to recede toward a *vanishing point* on the horizon.

pagoda A Buddhist tower with a multiplicity of winged eaves; derived from the Indian *stupa*.

palestra A Roman exercise room.

palette (pal'it) A thin board with a thumb hole at one end on which an artist lays and mixes colors; any surface so used. Also, the colors or kinds of colors characteristically used by an artist.

palmette (pal·met') A conventional, decorative ornament of ancient origin composed of radiating petals springing from a cup-like base.

Panathenaea (pan'a·then·ee'a) The most ancient and important festival of Athens, held in honor of the goddess Athena.

Pantheon (Pan'thee·on) All the gods of a people, or a temple dedicated to all such gods; especially, the Pantheon in Rome (although it is not certain that this was its function).

papyrus (pah·pye'rus) A plant native to Egypt and adjacent lands used to make a paper-like writing material; also, the material or any writing on it.

parasol An umbrella atop a Chinese *pagoda*; a vestige of the **chatra** on an Indian *stupa*.

parchment Lambskin prepared as a surface for writing or painting.

passage grave A burial chamber entered through a long, tunnel-like passage.

pastel Finely ground *pigments* compressed into chalk-like sticks. Also, work done in this *medium,* or its characteristic paleness.

pastiche (pas·teesh') An artistic hodge-podge that imitates or ridicules another artist's style.

patina (pa·teen'a) The green, oxidized layer that forms on bronze and copper.

pediment (ped'i·ment) In Classical architecture, the triangular space (**gable**) at the end of a building, formed by the ends of the sloping roof and the *cornice;* also, an ornamental feature having this shape.

pendentive (pen·den'tiv) A concave, triangular piece of masonry (a triangular section of a hemisphere), four of which provide the transition from a square area to the circular base of a covering *dome.* Although they appear to be hanging (**pendent**) from the dome, they in fact support it.

peripteral (per·ip'ter·al) A style of building in which the main structure is surrounded by a *colonnade.*

peristyle (pair'i·stile) A *colonnade* surrounding a building or a court.

perspective A formula for projecting an illusion of the three-dimensional world onto a two-dimensional surface. In **linear perspective,** the most common type, all parallel lines or lines of projection seem to converge on a single point on the horizon, known as the *vanishing point,* and associated objects are rendered smaller the further from the viewer they are intended to seem. **Atmospheric** or **aerial perspective** creates the illusion of distance by the greater diminution of *color* intensity, the shift in color toward an almost neutral blue, and the blurring of *contours* as the intended distance between eye and object increases. In **herringbone perspective,** the lines of projection converge not on a vanishing point, but on a vertical *axis* at the center of the picture as in Roman paintings.

pi (bee) The Chinese symbol of Heaven, a jade disk.

piano nobile (peea'no no'bee·lay) The principal story, usually the second, in Renaissance buildings.

pictograph A picture, usually stylized, that represents an idea; also, writing using such means. See also *hieroglyphic.*

picture plane The surface of a picture.

pier A vertical, unattached masonry support.

Pietà (peeay·ta') A work of art depicting the Virgin mourning over the body of Christ.

pigment Finely powdered coloring matter mixed or ground with various vehicles to form paint, crayon, etc.

pilaster (pi·las'ter) A flat, rectangular, vertical member projecting from a wall of which it forms a part. It usually has a base and a *capital* and is often *fluted.*

pillar Usually a weight-carrying member, such as a *pier* or a *column;* sometimes an isolated, freestanding structure used for commemorative purposes.

pinnacle A tower, primarily ornamental, that also functions in Gothic architecture to give additional weight to a *buttress* or a *pier.* See also *finial.*

pithos (pith'oss; *pl.* **pithoi**) A large, clay storage vessel frequently set into the earth and therefore possessing no flat base.

plan The horizontal arrangement of the parts of a building, or a drawing or a diagram showing such an arrangement as a horizontal *section.* In **axial plan,** the parts of a building are organized longitudinally, or along a given *axis;* in a **central plan,** the parts radiate from a central point.

plasticity In art, the three-dimensionality of an object. **plastic** (*adj.*)

plein-air painting (plen·air) The representation of the observed effects of outdoor light and atmosphere practiced by some late nineteenth-century Impressionists.

plinth The lowest member of a base; also, a block serving as a base for a statue.

pointillism The method of painting of some French Impressionists in which a white ground is covered with tiny dots of color, which, when viewed at a distance, blend together to produce a luminous effect.

polychrome Done in several colors.

polyptych (pol'ip·tik) An *altarpiece* made up of more than three sections.

porcelain Translucent, impervious, resonant *pottery* made in a base of **kaolin,** a fine white clay; sometimes any pottery that is translucent, whether or not it is made of kaolin.

porphyry (pour'feary) An Egyptian rock containing large crystals in a purplish groundmass.

portico A porch with a roof supported by *columns;* an entrance porch.

post-and-lintel system A *trabeated* system of construction in which two posts support a *lintel.*

potsherds Broken pottery, discarded by earlier civilizations, that settles into firmly stratified mounds over time and provides archeological chronologies.

pottery Objects (usually vessels) made of clay and hardened by firing.

predella The narrow ledge on which an *altarpiece* rests at the back of an altar.

primary colors The *hues* red, yellow, and blue. From these three colors, with the addition of white, it is theoretically possible to mix the full color spectrum. The primary colors cannot be produced by mixing other colors together.

program The architect's formulation of a design problem with respect to considerations of site, function, materials, and aims of the client; also, in painting and sculpture, the conceptual basis of a work.

pronaos (pro·nay'os) The space in front of the *cella* or *naos* of a Greek temple.

propylaeum (prah·pi·lay'um; *pl.* **propylaea**) A gateway building leading to an open court preceding a Greek or Roman temple.

proscenium (pro·seen'i·um) The stage of an ancient Greek or Roman theater.

prostyle A style of Greek temple in which the *columns* stand in front of the *naos* and extend to its width.

provenance Origin; source.

psalter A book containing the Psalms of the Bible.

putto (*pl.* **putti**) A young child, a favorite subject in Italian painting and sculpture.

pylon (pie'lon) The *monumental* entrance of an Egyptian temple.

qiblah (keeb'lah) The direction (toward Mecca) in which Moslems face in prayer. (Often *kibla.*)

quadro-riportato (kwahd·roh·ree·por·tah'toh) The simulation of a wall painting for a ceiling design in which painted scenes are arranged in panels resembling frames on the surface of a shallow, curved *vault.*

quatrefoil (kat're·foyl) An architectural ornament having four lobes or **foils.** See also *trefoil.*

quattrocento (kwat'tro·chain'toh) The fifteenth century in Italian art.

quoin (koin) Large, sometimes *rusticated,* usually slightly projecting stone (or stones) that often form the corners of the exterior walls of masonry buildings.

raking cornice The *cornice* on the sloping sides of a *pediment.*

Ramayana A Sanskrit epic telling of Rama, an incarnation of the Hindu god Vishnu.

rathas Small, freestanding Hindu temples, perhaps sculptured as architectural models.

rayonnant The "radiant" style in thirteenth-century architecture that is associated with the royal Paris court of Louis IX.

realism The representation of things according to nature (without *idealization*).

red-figure technique In later Greek pottery, the silhouetting of red figures against a black background; the reverse of the *black-figure technique.*

reinforced concrete (ferroconcrete) Concrete with increased tensile strength produced by iron or steel mesh or bars embedded in it.

relief In sculpture, figures projecting from a background of which they are part. The degree of relief is designated high, low (**bas**), or sunken (hollow). In the last, the backgrounds are not cut back and the points in highest relief are level with the original surface of the material being carved. A kind of low relief that is hardly more than a scratching of the surface, originated by Donatello, is termed **stiacciata** or **sciacciata.** See also *repoussé.*

reliquary A small receptacle for a sacred relic, usually of a richly decorated, precious material.

repoussé (ruh·poo·say') Formed in *relief* by beating a metal plate from the back, leaving the impression on the face. The metal is hammered into a hollow mold of wood or some other pliable material and finished with a *graver.* See also *relief.*

reserve column In Egyptian rock-cut tombs, a *column* that is hewn from the living rock and serves no supporting function.

respond An engaged *column, pilaster,* or similar structure that either projects from a *compound pier* or some other supporting device or is bonded to a wall and carries one end of an *arch,* often at the end of an *arcade*. A **nave arcade,** for example, may have nine *pillars* and two responds.

retable (ruh·tay'bl) An architectural screen or wall above and behind an altar, usually containing painting, sculpture, carving, or other decorations. See also *altarpiece*.

reverse On coins or medals, the side opposite the *obverse*.

rhyton (right'on) An ancient Greek ceremonial drinking vessel with a base usually in the form of the head of an animal, a woman, or a mythological creature.

rib A relatively slender, molded masonry *arch* that projects from a surface. In Gothic architecture, the *ribs* form the framework of the *vaulting*.

ribbed vault See *vault*.

ridgepole The horizontal beam at the ridge of a roof, to which the upper ends of the rafters attach.

rinceau (ran·so') An ornamental design composed of undulating foliate vine motifs.

Romanitas (Roh·man'ee·tahs) The religion of the Holy Roman Empire; its ritual and practice was based on imperial dominion.

rose or **wheel window** The large, circular window with *tracery* and stained glass frequently used in the *façades* of Gothic churches.

rotulus A long manuscript scroll used by the Egyptians, Greeks, and Romans; predecessor of the *codex*.

rusticate To give a rustic appearance by *beveling* the edges of stone blocks to emphasize the joints between them. A technique popular during the Renaissance, especially for stone courses at the ground-floor level.

sacra conversazione (sah'krah·cone·ver·sotz·ee·ohn'ee) In Italian, literally "holy conversation"; a grouping of the Madonna, Child, and Saints in the same spatial setting, so that they appear to be conversing with one another.

sacral-idyllic scene A landscape depicting country life and idealized nature.

Salon The government-sponsored exhibition of works by living artists held in Paris, first biennially and (since the mid-eighteenth century) annually.

samsara (som·sah'rah) In Hindu belief, the rebirth of the soul into a succession of lives.

sarcophagus (sar·kof'a·gus) A stone coffin.

saturation The purity of a *hue;* the higher the *saturation,* the purer the hue. *Value* and saturation are not constantly related. For example, high-saturation yellow tends to have a high value, but high-saturation violet tends to have a low value.

satyr (sat'er) In Greek mythology, a kind of demi-god or deity, a follower of Dionysos, wanton and lascivious and often represented with goat-like ears and legs and a short tail.

scale The dimensions of the parts or the totality of a building or an object in relation to its use or function. In architectural

plans, the relation of the actual size of a structure to its representative size.

scriptorium A Medieval writing room in which scrolls were also housed.

sculpture in the round Freestanding figures, carved or modeled in three dimensions.

secondary colors The colors (green, orange, and purple) that result from mixture of pairs of *primary colors*.

section In architecture, a diagram or representation of a part of a structure or building along an imaginary plane that passes through it vertically.

seicento (say·chain'toh) The seventeenth century in Italian art.

serdab A small, concealed chamber in an Egyptian tomb for the statue of the deceased.

severe style An early, pre-Classical, transitional style of mid-fifth-century Greek statuary that is formal but not rigid in pose and emphasizes the principle of weight distribution; a liberation from the Archaic limitations of frontal rigidity found in Egyptian portrait statues.

sfumato (sfoo·ma'toh) A smoke-like haziness that subtly softens outlines in painting, particularly applied to the painting of Leonardo and Correggio.

sgraffito (zgra·fee'toh) Decoration produced by scratching through a surface layer of plaster, *glazing,* etc., to reveal a different colored *ground;* also, pottery or other ware so decorated.

shaft The part of a *column* between the *capital* and the base.

shaft grave A grave in the form of a deep pit, the actual burial spot being at the base of the shaft or in a niche at the base.

shaman (shah'mon) A priest or medicine man who can influence good and evil spirits; the religion of some American Indians and Eskimos. **shamanism** (*adj.*)

shoji (show'jee) A rice-paper-covered sliding screen that serves as a room divider in traditional Japanese houses.

sikhara (shih'ka·rah) In Hindu temples of Vishnu, the tower above the shrine.

silver point A drawing technique involving the use of a silver-tipped "pencil" on a paper with a white *matte* coating; also, the delicate drawings so made.

sinopia or **sinopie** Reddish-brown earth color; also, the *cartoon* or underpainting for a *fresco*.

sistrum An instrument of metal rods loosely held in a metal frame, which jingle when shaken. Peculiarly Egyptian, it was used especially in the worship of Isis and is still used in Nubia.

Siva or **Shiva** (shee'vuh) Hindu god of destruction and creation.

slip Potter's clay dispersed in a liquid and used for *casting,* decoration, and to attach parts of clay vessels, such as handles.

smalto The colored glass or enamel used in *mosaics*.

socle (soh'kel) A molded projection at the bottom of a wall or a *pier,* or beneath a pedestal or a *column* base.

soffit The underside of an architectural member such as an *arch, lintel, cornice,* or stairway. See also *intrados*.

spandrel The roughly triangular space enclosed by the curves of adjacent *arches* and a horizontal member connecting their vertexes; also, the space enclosed by the curve of an *arch* and an enclosing right angle.

splay A large *bevel* or *chamfer*.

splayed opening An opening (as in a wall) that is cut away diagonally so that the outer edges are farther apart then the inner edges. See also *embrasure*.

springing The lowest stone of an *arch,* resting on the *impost block*.

square schematism A church *plan* in which the *crossing square* is used as the *module* for all parts of the design.

squinch An architectural device used to make a transition from a square to a polygonal or circular base for a *dome*. It may be composed of *lintels, corbels,* or *arches*.

stave A wedge-shaped timber; vertically placed staves embellish the architectural features of a building.

stele (stee'lee) A carved stone slab or *pillar* used especially by the ancient Greeks as grave or site markers and for similar purposes.

still life A painting representing inanimate objects, such as flowers, fruit, or household articles.

stoa (stoh'a) In ancient Greek architecture, an open building with a roof supported by a row of *columns* parallel to the back wall.

stringcourse A horizontal *molding* or band in masonry, ornamental but usually reflecting interior structure.

stucco Fine plaster or cement used as a coating for walls or for decoration.

stupa (stoo'puh) A large, mound-shaped Buddhist shrine.

style A manner of treatment or execution of works of art that is characteristic of a civilization, a people, or an individual; also, a special and superior quality in a work of art.

stylobate (sty'loh·bate) The upper step of the base of a Greek temple, which forms a platform for the *columns*.

stylus A needle-like tool used in *engraving* and *incising*.

superimposed orders *Orders* of architecture that are placed one above another in an *arcaded* or *colonnaded* building, usually in the following sequence: **Doric** (the first story), **Ionic,** and **Corinthian.** Superimposed orders are found in Greek *stoas* and were used widely by Roman and Renaissance builders.

sutra (soo'truh) In Buddhism, an account of a sermon by or a dialogue involving the *Buddha*.

swag A kind of decoration for walls, furniture, etc., done in *relief* and resembling garlands and gathered drapery, that was particularly popular in the eighteenth century.

symmetry *Esthetic* balance that is usually achieved by disposing *forms* about a real or an imaginary *axis* so that those on one side more-or-less correspond with those on the other. The correspondence may be in terms of shape, *color,* texture, etc.

tablinum A room behind the *atrium* in a Roman house in which family archives and statues were kept.

tectiforms Shapes resembling man-made structures found painted on the walls of Paleolithic caves.

tell In Near Eastern archeology, a hill or a mound, usually an ancient site of habitation.

tempera A technique of painting using *pigment* mixed with egg yolk, glue, or casein; also, the *medium* itself.

Tenebrists (Ten'i·brists) A group of seventeenth-century European painters who used violent contrasts of light and dark.

tenebroso Painting in the "dark manner"; a technique of the *Caravagisti*.

tenon A projection on the end of a piece of wood that is inserted into a corresponding hole (**mortice**) in another piece of wood to form a joint.

terra cotta Hard-baked clay, used for sculpture and as a building material, that may be *glazed* or painted.

tesserae (tess'er·ee) Small, shaped pieces of glass or stone used in making *mosaics*.

tholos (thoh'los) A circular structure, generally in Classical Greek style; also, an ancient, circular tomb.

thrust The outward force exerted by an *arch* or a *vault* that must be counterbalanced by *buttresses*.

tier A series of architectural rows, layers, or ranks arranged above or behind one another.

tondo A circular painting or *relief* sculpture.

torano (tor'uh·nuh) Gateways in the stone fence around a *stupa*, located at the cardinal points of the compass.

torus A convex *molding* or part of a molding, usually the lowest in the base of a *column*.

totem An animal or object and its representation or image, considered to be a symbol of a given family or clan.

trabeated (tray'bee·ate·id) Of *post-and-lintel* construction.

tracery Branching, ornamental stonework, generally in a window, where it supports the glass; particularly characteristic of Gothic architecture.

transept The part of a *cruciform* church with an *axis* that crosses the main axis at right angles.

trecento (tray·chain'toh) The fourteenth century in Italian art.

trefoil An architectural ornament having three lobes or *foils*. See also *quatrefoil*.

triforium In a Gothic cathedral, the blind, *arcaded* gallery below the *clerestory*.

triglyph A projecting, grooved member of a *Doric frieze* that alternates with *metopes*.

trilithon A pair of *monoliths* topped with a *lintel*; found in *megalithic* structures.

triptych (trip'tik) A three-paneled *altarpiece*.

trompe l'oeil (trohmp loy') A form of illusionistic painting that attempts to represent an object as if it exists in three dimensions at the surface of the painting; literally, "eye-fooling."

trumeau (troo·moh') A *pillar* in the center of a Romanesque or Gothic portal.

turret A small, often ornamental tower projecting from a building, usually at a corner.

tympanum The space enclosed by a *lintel* and an *arch* over a doorway; also, the recessed face of a *pediment*.

ukiyo-e (oo'kee·oh·ee) A style of Japanese *genre* painting ("pictures of the floating world") that influenced nineteenth-century Western art.

Upanishads (oo·pan'i·shads) A series of late Vedic metaphysical treatises dealing with man in relation to the universe.

urna The whorl of hair, represented as a dot, between the brows of a Hindu diety.

ushnisha (ush·nish'uh) Stylized protuberance of the *Buddha*'s forehead, emblematic of his superhuman consciousness.

value The amount of light reflected by a *hue*; the greater the amount of light, the higher the value. See also *saturation*.

vanishing point In *linear perspective*, that point on the horizon toward which parallel lines appear to converge and at which they seem to vanish.

vault A masonry roof or ceiling constructed on the *arch* principle. A **barrel** or **tunnel vault**, semicylindrical in cross section, is in effect a deep arch or an uninterrupted series of arches, one behind the other, over an oblong space. In a **cross-barrel vault**, the main barrel (tunnel) vault is intersected at right angles with other barrel (tunnel) vaults at regular intervals. A **quadrant vault** is a half-barrel (tunnel) vault. A **sexpartite vault** is a rib vault with six panels. A **fan vault** is a development of *lierne* vaulting characteristic of English Perpendicular Gothic, in which radiating *ribs* form a fan-like pattern. A **groin** or **cross vault** is formed at the point at which two *barrel (tunnel) vaults* intersect at right angles. In a **ribbed vault,** there is a framework of ribs or arches under the intersections of the vaulting sections.

vellum Calfskin prepared as a surface for writing or painting.

vignette Originally, a decorative element of vine leaves and tendrils; any decorative design in a book or manuscript that is rather small and that has no definite boundaries or frame.

vihara (vee·hah'rah) A Buddhist monastery, often cut into a hill.

vimana (vih·mah'nuh) In Hindu and Buddhist temples, the pyramidal tower above the shrine (composed of the *garbha griha* and the *sikhara*).

Vishnu Hindu god, called "The Preserver," one of whose incarnations is Krishna.

volume See *mass*.

volute A spiral, scroll-like form characteristic of the Greek Ionic *capital*.

voussoir (voo·swahr') A wedge-shaped block used in the construction of a true *arch*. The central voussoir, which sets the arch, is the *keystone*.

warm color Red, orange, or yellow. Psychologically, warm colors tend to be exciting, emphatic, and affirmative; optically, they generally seem to advance or to project. See also *cool color*.

wash In *watercolor* painting especially, a thin, transparent film of color.

watercolor A painting technique using *pigment* (usually prepared with gum) mixed with water and applied to an absorbent surface; also, the *medium* itself. The painting is transparent, with the white of the paper furnishing the lights. See also *gouache*.

weight shift See *contrapposto*.

westwork A multi-storied *mass*, including the *façade* and usually surmounted by towers, at the western end of a Medieval church.

woodcut A wooden block on the surface of which those parts not intended to print are cut away to a slight depth, leaving the design raised; also, the printed impression made with such a block.

yaksha (yak'shah) A divinity in the Hindu and Buddhist pantheon. (*f.* **yakshi**)

yamato-e (yah·mah'toh·ee) A purely Japanese style of sophisticated and depersonalized painting created for the Fujiwara nobility.

yasti (yahs'tee) The mast surmounting the *dome* of a *stupa*.

yu A covered Chinese libation vessel.

Zen A Buddhist sect and its doctrine, emphasizing enlightenment through intuition and introspection rather than the study of scripture. In Chinese, *Ch'an*.

ziggurat (zig'oor·at) A roughly pyramidal structure, built in ancient Mesopotamia, consisting of stages; each succeeding stage is stepped back from the one beneath.

zoomorphism The representation of gods in the form or with the attributes of animals; the use of animal forms in art or symbolism.

BIBLIOGRAPHY

This bibliography lists the basic general books in the field and contains a few entries for monographs and museum exhibition catalogs. There are no entries for periodical articles; for reference to these, consult your library.

Reference Books

Arntzen, Etta, and Rainwater, Robert. *Guide to the Literature of Art History.* Chicago: American Library Association/Art Book Company, 1980.

Bator, Paul M. *The International Trade in Art.* Chicago: University of Chicago Press, 1983.

Broude, Norma, and Garrard, May D., eds. *Feminism and Art History.* New York: Harper & Row, 1982.

Encyclopedia of World Art. 15 vols. New York: McGraw-Hill, 1959–1968, revised 1972.

Feilden, Bernard B. *Conservation of Historic Buildings.* London: Butterworth Scientific Books, 1982.

Fielding, Mantle. *Dictionary of American Painters, Sculptors and Engravers.* New York: James F. Carr, 1965.

Fleming, John; Honour, Hugh; and Pevsner, Nikolaus. *Penguin Dictionary of Architecture.* Baltimore: Penguin, 1980.

Fletcher, Sir Banister. *A History of Architecture.* 18th rev. ed. New York: Scribner, 1975.

Giedion, Siegfried. *The Beginnings of Architecture.* Princeton: Princeton University Press, 1981.

————*Space, Time and Architecture.* 5th ed., rev. and enl. Cambridge: Harvard University Press, 1982.

Gombrich, Ernst Hans Josef. *Art and Illusion.* 5th ed. London: Phaidon, 1977.

Hall, James. *Dictionary of Subjects and Symbols in Art.* Rev. ed. London: J. Murray, 1977.

Hauser, Arnold. *The Sociology of Art.* Chicago: University of Chicago Press, 1982.

Hind, Arthur M. *A History of Engraving and Etching from the Fifteenth Century to the Year 1914.* 3rd rev. ed. New York: Dover, 1963.

Holt, Elizabeth B. *A Documentary History of Art.* 2nd ed. 2 vols. Garden City, N.Y.: Doubleday, 1981.

Huyghe, René, ed. *Larousse Encyclopedia of Byzantine and Medieval Art.* New York: Prometheus Press, 1963; New York: Hamlyn/American (paperbound), 1976.

————*Larousse Encyclopedia of Renaissance and Baroque Art.* New York: Prometheus Press, 1964; Hamlyn/American (paperbound), 1976.

Kostof, Spiro. *A History of Architecture.* Oxford: Oxford University Press, 1985.

Kronenberger, Louis. *Atlantic Brief Lives: A Biographical Companion to the Arts.* Boston: Little, Brown, 1971.

Murray, Peter, and Murray, Linda. *A Dictionary of Art and Artists.* New York: Penguin, 1976.

Myers, Bernard Samuel, ed. *Encyclopedia of Painting: Painters and Painting of the World from Prehistoric Times to the Present Day.* 4th rev. ed. New York: Crown, 1979.

————*Encyclopedia of World Art,* Suppl. vol. 16. Palatine, Ill.: McGraw-Hill/The Publishers Guild, 1983.

Myers, Bernard S., and Myers, Shirley D., eds. *Dictionary of 20th Century Art.* New York: McGraw-Hill, 1974.

Pevsner, Nikolaus. *An Outline of European Architecture.* 8th rev. ed. Baltimore: Penguin, 1974.

Pierson, William H., and Davidson, Martha. *Arts of the United States, A Pictorial Survey.*

1960. Reprint. Athens: University of Georgia Press, 1975.

Placzik, A. K., ed. *Macmillan Encyclopedia of Architects.* 4 vols. New York: Macmillan/Free Press, 1982.

Podro, Michael. *The Critical Historians of Art.* New Haven: Yale University Press, 1982.

Quick, John. *Artists' and Illustrators' Encyclopedia.* New York: McGraw-Hill, 1977.

Rubenstein, Charlotte Streifer. *American Women Artists from Early Indian Times to the Present.* Boston: G.K. Hall/Avon Books, 1982.

Smith, G. E. Kidder. *The Architecture of the United States: An Illustrated Guide to Buildings Open to the Public.* 3 vols. Garden City, N.Y.: Doubleday/Anchor, 1981.

Stierlin, Henri. *Encyclopedia of World Architecture 1978.* 1978. Reprint. New York: Van Nostrand, Reinhold, 1983.

Tufts, Eleanor. *American Women Artists, Past and Present, A Selected Bibliographic Guide.* New York: Garland Publishers, 1984.

————*Our Hidden Heritage, Five Centuries of Women Artists.* London: Paddington Press, 1974.

Waterhouse, Ellis. *The Dictionary of British 18th Century Painters in Oils and Crayons.* Woodbridge, England: Antique Collectors' Club, 1981.

Wittkower, Rudolf. *Sculpture Processes and Principles.* New York: Harper & Row, 1977.

Wölfflin, Heinrich. *The Sense of Form in Art.* New York: Chelsea, 1958.

Young, William, ed. *A Dictionary of American Artists, Sculptors, and Engravers.* Cambridge, Mass.: W. Young, 1968.

chapter 1 The Birth of Art

Bandi, Hans; Breuil, Henri; et al. *The Art of the Stone Age: Forty Thousand Years of Rock Art.* 2nd ed. London: Methuen, 1970.

Bataille, Georges. *Lascaux: Prehistoric Painting or the Birth of Art.* Lausanne: Skira, 1980.

Breuil, Henri. *Four Hundred Centuries of Cave Art.* New York: Hacker, 1979.

Graziosi, Paolo. *Paleolithic Art.* New York: McGraw-Hill, 1960.

Leroi-Gourhan, Andre. *The Dawn of European Art, and Introduction to Paleolithic Cave Painting.* Cambridge: Cambridge University Press, 1982.

————*Treasurers of Prehistoric Art.* New York: Abrams, 1967.

Megaw, J. V. S. *The Art of the European Iron Age.* New York: Harper & Row, 1970.

Renfrew, Colin, ed. *British Prehistory.* London: Duckworth, 1974.

Sandars, Nancy K. *Prehistoric Art in Europe.* Harmondsworth, England: Penguin, 1969.

Trump, David H. *The Prehistory of the Mediterranean.* New Haven: Yale University Press, 1980.

Windels, Fernand. *The Lascaux Cave Paintings.* New York: Viking, 1950.

chapter 2 The Ancient Near East

Culican, William. *The Medes and Persians.* London: Thames & Hudson, 1965; New York: Praeger, 1965.

Frankfort, Henri. *The Art and Architecture of the Ancient Orient.* Baltimore: Penguin, 1971.

Garbini, Giovanni. *The Ancient World.* London: Hamlyn, 1976.

Ghirshman, Roman. *Iran from Earliest Times to the Islamic Conquest.* New York: Penguin, 1978.

Hinz, Walther. *The Lost World of Elam.* New York: New York University Press, 1973.

Kenyon, Kathleen M. *Digging Up Jericho.* New York: Praeger, 1974.

Kramer, Samuel N. *The Sumerians: Their History, Culture, and Character.* Chicago: University of Chicago Press, 1963.

Lloyd, Seton. *The Archaeology of Mesopotamia from the Old Stone Age to the Persian Conquest.* London: Thames & Hudson, 1978.

————*The Art of the Ancient Near East.* New York: Praeger, 1969.

Lloyd, S. H.; Muller, H. W.; and Martin, R. *Ancient Architecture: Mesopotamia, Egypt, Crete, Greece.* New York: Abrams, 1974.

Mellaart, James. *Çatal Hüyük: a Neolithic Town in Anatolia.* New York: McGraw-Hill, 1967.

————*The Earliest Civilizations of the Near East.* New York: McGraw-Hill, 1965.

————*The Neolithic of the Near East.* New York: Scribner, 1975.

Oppenheim, A. Leo. *Ancient Mesopotamia.* Rev. ed. Chicago: University of Chicago Press, 1977.

Parrot, André. *The Arts of Assyria.* New York: Golden Press, 1961.

————*Sumer: The Dawn of Art.* New York: Golden Press, 1961.

Perkins, Ann Louise. *The Art of Dura-Europos.* Oxford: Clarendon Press, 1973.

Porada, Edith, and Dyson, R. H. *The Art of Ancient Iran: Islamic Cultures.* Rev. ed. New York: Greystone Press, 1969.

Woolley, Charles L. *The Art of the Middle East, Including Persia, Mesopotamia and Palestine.* New York: Crown, 1961.

————*The Development of Sumerian Art.* Westport, Conn.: Greenwood Press, 1981.

chapter 3 The Art of Egypt

Aldred, Cyril. *The Development of Ancient Egyptian Art from 3200 to 1315 B.C.* 3 vols. London: Academy Edition, 1973.

Badawy, Alexander. *A History of Egyptian Architecture.* 3 vols. Berkeley: University of California Press, 1973.

Breasted, James. *History of Egypt.* 1909. Reprint. New York: Scribner's, 1964.

Emery, Walter B. *Archaic Egypt.* Baltimore: Penguin, 1972.

Gardiner, Sir Alan Henderson. *Egypt of the Pharaohs.* London: Oxford University Press, 1978.

Lange, Kurt, with Hirmer, Max. *Egypt: Architecture, Sculpture and Painting in Three Thousand Years.* 4th ed. London: Phaidon, 1968.

Lurker, Manfred. *The Gods and Symbols of Ancient Egypt: an Illustrated Dictionary.* New York: Thames & Hudson, 1980.

Mekhitarian, Arpag. *Egyptian Painting.* New York: Skira, 1978.

Smith, E. Baldwin. *Egyptian Architecture as*

Cultural Expression. Watkins Glen, N.Y.: American Life Foundation, 1968.

Smith, William Stevenson, and Simpson, W. *The Art and Architecture of Ancient Egypt*. Rev. ed. New York: Viking, 1981.

Woldering, Irmgard. *Gods, Men and Pharaohs: The Glory of Egyptian Art*. New York: Abrams, 1967.

chapter 4   The Art of the Aegean

Demargne, Pierre. *Aegean Art: The Origins of Greek Art*. London: Thames & Hudson, 1964.

Evans, Arthur. *The Palace of Minos*. 4 vols. 1921–1935. Reprint. New York: Biblo & Tannen, 1964.

Graham, James W. *The Palaces of Crete*. Princeton: Princeton University Press, 1969.

Marinatos, Spyridon, with Hirmer, Max. *Crete and Mycenae*. London: Thames & Hudson, 1960.

Matz, Friedrich. *The Art of Crete and Early Greece*. New York: Crown, 1965.

Pendlebury, John. *The Archeology of Crete*. London: Methuen, 1967.

Schliemann, Heinrich. *Ilios*. 1881. Reprint. New York: B. Blom, 1968. (Other reprints available.)

——— *Mycenae*. 1880. Reprint. New York: Arno Press, 1976.

——— *Tiryns*. 1885. Reprint. New York: Arno Press, 1976.

Vermeule Emily. *Greece in the Bronze Age*. Chicago: University of Chicago Press, 1972.

Wace, Alan. *Mycenae, an Archeological History and Guide*. New York: Biblo & Tannen, 1964.

Warren, Peter M. *The Aegean Civilizations*. London: Elsevier/Phaidon, 1970.

Willetts, R. F. *The Civilization of Ancient Crete*. Berkeley: University of California Press, 1978.

chapter 5   The Art of Greece

Arias, Paolo. *A History of One Thousand Years of Greek Vase Painting*. New York: Abrams, 1962.

Ashmole, Bernard. *Architect and Sculptor in Classical Greece*. New York: New York University Press, 1972.

Beazley, John D. *Attic Red-Figure Vase-Painters*. 3 vols. 1963. Reprint. New York: Hacker, 1984.

——— *The Development of Attic Black-Figure*. Berkeley: University of California Press, 1964.

Beazley, John D., and Ashmole, Bernard. *Greek Sculpture and Painting to the End of the Hellenistic Period*. Cambridge: Cambridge University Press, 1932, 1966.

Berve, Helmut. *Greek Temples, Theatres, and Shrines*. New York: Abrams, 1963.

Blumel, Carl. *Greek Sculptors at Work*. London: Phaidon, 1969.

Brilliant, Richard. *Arts of the Ancient Greeks*. New York: McGraw-Hill, 1973.

Buschor, Ernst. *Greek Vase Painting*. New York: Hacker, 1978.

Carpenter, Rhys. *Greek Sculpture: A Critical Review*. Chicago: University of Chicago Press, 1960.

Charbonneaux, Jean. *Archaic Greek Art*. New York: Braziller, 1971.

Charbonneaux, Jean; Martin, Roland; and Villard, François. *Hellenistic Art*. New York: Braziller, 1973.

Cook, Robert M. *Greek Art: Its Development, Character and Influence*. Harmondsworth, England: Penguin, 1976.

Coulton, J. J. *Ancient Greek Architects at Work*. Ithaca, N.Y.: Cornell University Press, 1977.

Dinsmoor, W. B. *The Architecture of Ancient Greece*. 3rd ed. New York: Norton, 1975.

Havelock, Christine Mitchell. *Hellenistic Art:*

The Art of the Classical World. 2nd ed., rev. New York: W. W. Norton, 1981.

Lawrence, Arnold W. *Greek Architecture*. 2nd ed. Baltimore: Penguin, 1967.

Lullies, Reinhard, and Hirmer, Max. *Greek Sculpture*. Rev. ed. New York: Abrams, 1960.

Pfuhl, Ernst. *Masterpieces of Greek Drawing and Painting*. 2nd ed. Chicago: Argonaut, 1967.

Pollitt, Jerome J. *The Ancient View of Greek Art*. New Haven: Yale University Press, 1974.

——— *Art and Experience in Classical Greece*. Cambridge: Cambridge University Press, 1972.

——— *The Art of Greece 1400–31 B.C*. Englewood Cliffs, N.J.: Prentice-Hall, 1965.

Richter, Gisela M. *Attic Red-Figure Vases: A Survey*. New Haven: Yale University Press, 1958.

——— *A Handbook of Greek Art*. 6th ed. New York: Phaidon, 1969.

——— *The Sculpture and Sculptors of the Greeks*. 4th ed. New Haven: Yale University Press, 1970.

Ridgway, Brunilde Sismondo. *Fifth Century Styles in Greek Sculpture*. Princeton: Princeton University Press, 1981.

Robertson, Donald S. *Greek and Roman Architecture*. 2nd ed. Cambridge: Cambridge University Press, 1969.

Robertson, Martin. *Greek Painting*. New York: Rizzoli, 1979.

——— *A History of Greek Art*. 2 vols. Cambridge: Cambridge University Press, 1976.

——— *A Shorter History of Greek Art*. Cambridge: Cambridge University Press, 1981.

Scranton, Robert L. *Greek Architecture*. New York: Braziller, 1962.

Scully, Vincent J. *The Earth, the Temple and the Gods: Greek Sacred Architecture*. Rev. ed. New York: Praeger, 1969.

Swindler, Mary H. *Ancient Painting*. New Haven: Yale University Press, 1929.

Vermeule, Cornelius C. *Greek and Roman Sculpture in America: Masterpieces in Public Collections*. Berkeley: University of California Press, 1981.

chapter 6   Etruscan and Roman Art

Andreae, Bernard. *The Art of Rome*. New York: Abrams, 1977.

Bianchi Bandinelli, Ranuccio. *Rome, the Late Empire*. New York: Braziller, 1971.

Boethius, Axel. *The Golden House of Nero*. Ann Arbor: University of Michigan Press, 1960.

Brilliant, Richard. *Roman Art, from the Republic to Constantine*. New York: Praeger, 1974.

Brown, Frank Edward. *Roman Architecture*. New York: Braziller, 1961.

Buchthal, Hugo. *Art of the Mediterranean World, A.D. 100 to 1400*. Art History Series 5. Washington, D.C.: Decatur House Press, 1983.

Goldscheider, Ludwig. *Roman Portraits*. London: Phaidon, 1940.

Hanfmann, George. *Roman Art*. Greenwich, Conn.: New York Graphic Society, 1964.

Kraus, Theodor. *Pompeii and Herculaneum: The Living Cities of the Dead*. New York: Abrams, 1975.

MacDonald, William L. *The Architecture of the Roman Empire*. Rev. ed. New Haven: Yale University Press, 1982.

McKay, Alexander G. *Houses, Villas, and Palaces in the Roman World*. Ithaca, N.Y.: Cornell University Press, 1975.

Maiuri, Amedeo. *Pompeii*. 14th ed. Rome: Istituto poligrafico dello Stato, 1970.

——— *Roman Painting*. Geneva: Skira, 1953.

Mansuelli, Guido. *The Art of Etruria and Early Rome*. New York: Crown, 1965.

Nash, Ernest. *Pictorial Dictionary of Ancient Rome*. 2nd ed. 2 vols. New York: Praeger, 1968.

Pollitt, Jerome J. *The Art of Rome, 753 B.C.– A.D. 337*. Englewood Cliffs, N.J.: Prentice-Hall, 1966.

Richardson, Emeline. *The Etruscans: Their Art and Civilization*. Chicago: University of Chicago Press, 1976.

Rivoira, Giovanni. *Roman Architecture and Its Principles of Construction Under the Empire*. New York: Hacker, 1972.

Robertson, Donald S. *Greek and Roman Architecture*. 2nd ed. Cambridge: Cambridge University Press, 1969.

Strong, Donald. *Roman Art*. Harmondsworth, England: Penguin, 1980.

Strong, Eugenie. *Art in Ancient Rome*. Ann Arbor, Michigan: University Microfilms, 1979.

Ward-Perkins, John. *Roman Architecture*. New York: Abrams, 1977.

Ward-Perkins, John, and Boethius, Axel. *Etruscan and Roman Architecture*. Harmondsworth, England: Penguin, 1970.

chapter 7   Early Christian, Byzantine, and Islamic Art

Anthony, Edgar W. *A History of Mosaics*. New York: Hacker, 1968.

Arnold, Thomas W. *Painting in Islam*. New York: Dover, 1965.

Aslanapa, Oktay. *Turkish Art and Architecture*. London: Faber & Faber, 1971.

Atil, Esin. *Renaissance of Islam: Art of the Mamluks*. Washington, D.C.: Smithsonian Institution Press, 1981.

Baynes, Norman, and Moss, Henry, eds. *Byzantium*. Oxford: Clarendon Press, 1969.

Beckwith, John. *The Art of Constantinople: An Introduction to Byzantine Art (330–1453)*. New York: Phaidon, 1968.

——— *Early Christian and Byzantine Art*. New York: Penguin, 1979.

Chatzidakis, Manolis. *Byzantine and Early Medieval Painting*. New York: Viking, 1965.

Creswell, K. A. C., and van Berchem, Marguerite. *Early Muslim Architecture*. 2nd ed. Oxford: Clarendon Press, 1969.

Dalton, Ormonde M. *Byzantine Art and Archaeology*. New York: Dover, 1961.

Demus, Otto. *Byzantine Art in the West*. New York: New York University Press, 1970.

Ettinghausen, Richard. *Arab Painting*. Geneva: Skira, 1977.

——— *From Byzantium to Sasanian Iran and the Islamic World*. Leiden: Brill, 1972.

Goodwin, Godfrey. *A History of Ottoman Architecture*. Baltimore: Johns Hopkins University Press, 1971.

Gough, Michael. *The Origins of Christian Art*. New York: Praeger, 1973.

Grabar, André. *The Beginnings of Christian Art, 200–395*. London: Thames & Hudson, 1967.

——— *Byzantine Painting*. Geneva: Skira, 1953.

——— *The Golden Age of Justinian: From the Death of Theodosius to the Rise of Islam*. New York: Odyssey Press, 1967.

Grabar, André, and Chatzidakis, Manolis. *Greek Mosaics of the Byzantine Period*. New York: New American Library, 1964.

Grabar, Oleg. *The Formation of Islamic Art*. New Haven: Yale University Press, 1973.

Grunebaum, Gustave von. *Classical Islam: A History, 600–1258*. Chicago: Aldine, 1970.

Hamilton, George H. *The Art and Architecture of Russia*. 2nd ed. New York: Viking, 1975.

Hamilton, John A. *Byzantine Architecture and Decoration*. 1933. Freeport, N.Y.: Books for Libraries/Arno, 1972.

Hawley, Walter A. *Oriental Rugs, Antique and Modern*. 1936. Reprint. New York: Dover, 1970.

Hoag, John D. *Islamic Architecture*. New York: Abrams, 1977.

Huyghe, René, ed. *Larousse Encyclopedia of Byzantine and Medieval Art.* See **Reference Books.**

Kitzinger, Ernst. *The Art of Byzantium and the Medieval Ages.* Bloomington: Indiana University Press, 1976.

——— *Early Medieval Art in the British Museum.* London: British Museum, 1983.

Krautheimer, Richard. *Early Christian and Byzantine Architecture.* Harmondsworth, England: Penguin, 1975.

Kühnel, Ernst. *Islamic Art and Architecture.* London: Bell, 1966.

Lane, Arthur. *Early Islamic Pottery, Mesopotamia, Egypt and Persia.* New York: Faber & Faber, 1965.

Levey, Michael. *The World of Ottoman Art.* New York: Scribner, 1975.

Lowrie, Walter S. *Art in the Early Church.* New York: Norton, 1969.

MacDonald, William L. *Early Christian and Byzantine Architecture.* New York: Braziller, 1962.

Maguire, Henry. *Art and Eloquence in Byzantium.* Princeton: Princeton University Press, 1981.

Mango, Cyril A. *Byzantine Architecture.* New York: Abrams, 1975.

Meyer, Peter. *Byzantine Mosaics: Torcello, Venice, Monreale, Palermo.* London: Batsford, 1952.

Morey, Charles R. *Early Christian Art.* Princeton: Princeton University Press, 1953.

Pope, Arthur, and Ackerman, Phyllis. *A Survey of Persian Art from Prehistoric Times to the Present.* London: Oxford University Press, 1977.

Rice, David T. *The Appreciation of Byzantine Art.* London: Oxford University Press, 1972.

——— *The Art of Byzantium.* New York: Abrams, 1959.

——— *Byzantine Art.* London: Variorum Reprints, 1973.

——— *Islamic Art.* London: Thames & Hudson, 1975.

Simson, Otto von. *Sacred Fortress: Byzantine Art and Stagecraft in Ravenna.* Chicago: University of Chicago Press, 1976.

Smith, Earl Baldwin. *Architectural Symbolism of Imperial Rome and the Middle Ages.* Princeton: Princeton University Press, 1956.

——— *The Dome, a Study in the History of Ideas.* Princeton: Princeton University Press, 1971.

Swift, Emerson H. *Hagia Sophia.* New York: Columbia University Press, 1980.

Volbach, Wolfgang. *Early Christian Mosaics, from the Fourth to the Seventh Centuries.* New York: Oxford University Press, 1946.

Volbach, Wolfgang, and Hirmer, Max. *Early Christian Art.* New York: Abrams, 1962.

Weitzmann, Kurt. *Ancient Book Illumination.* Cambridge: Harvard University Press, 1959.

——— *Illustrations in Roll and Codex.* Princeton: Princeton University Press, 1970.

Weitzmann, Kurt, et al. *The Icon.* New York: Knopf, 1982.

chapter 8 Early Medieval Art

Arnold, Bruce. *A Concise History of Irish Art.* Rev. ed. London: Thames & Hudson, 1977.

Beckwith, John. *Early Medieval Art: Carolingian, Ottonian, Romanesque.* New York: Oxford University Press, 1974.

Calkins, Robert G. *Illuminated Books of the Middle Ages.* Ithaca, N.Y.: Cornell University Press, 1983.

Conant, Kenneth. *Carolingian and Romanesque Architecture 800–1200.* 2nd integrated rev. ed. Harmondsworth, England: Penguin, 1978.

Dodwell, C. R. *Anglo-Saxon Art: A New Perspective.* Ithaca, N.Y.: Cornell University Press, 1982.

Finlay, Ian. *Celtic Art, an Introduction.* London: Faber & Faber, 1973.

Goldschmidt, Adolf. *German Illumination.* New York: Hacker, 1970.

Grabar, André, and Nordenfalk, Carl. *Early Medieval Painting from the Fourth to the Eleventh Century.* New York: Skira, 1967.

Harbison, Peter, et al. *Irish Art and Architecture from Prehistory to the Present.* London: Thames & Hudson, 1978.

Henderson, George. *Early Medieval.* Pelican Style and Civilization Series. New York: Penguin, 1972.

Henry, Françoise. *Irish Art During the Viking Invasions, 900–1200 A.D.* Ithaca, N.Y.: Cornell University Press, 1970.

——— *Irish Art in the Early Christian Period, to 800 A.D.* Rev. ed. London: Methuen, 1965.

Hinks, Roger P. *Carolingian Art.* Ann Arbor: University of Michigan Press, 1974.

Laszlo, Gyula. *The Art of the Migration Period.* London: Allen Lane, 1974.

Leeds, Edward T. *Early Anglo-Saxon Art and Archaeology.* Westport, Conn.: Greenwood Press, 1970.

Mütherich, Florentine, and Gaehde, J. E. *Carolingian Painting.* New York: Braziller, 1976.

Nordenfalk, Carl. *Celtic and Anglo-Saxon Painting: Book Illumination in the British Isles 600–800.* New York: Braziller, 1977.

Simons, Gerald. *Barbarian Europe.* New York: Time-Life Books, 1979.

Taylor, Harold M., and Taylor, Joan. *Anglo-Saxon Architecture.* 2 vols. Cambridge: Cambridge University Press, 1978.

Wilson, David M., and Klindt-Jensen, Ole. *Viking Art.* London: Allen & Unwin, 1980.

Zarnecki, George. *Art of the Medieval World.* New York: Abrams, 1975.

chapter 9 Romanesque Art

Anthony, Edgar W. *Romanesque Frescoes.* Princeton: Princeton University Press, Westport, Conn.: Greenwood Press, 1971.

Baum, Julius. *Romanesque Architecture in France.* 2nd ed. London: Country Life, 1928.

Bevan, Bernard. *History of Spanish Architecture.* London: Batsford, 1938.

Brooke, Christopher. *The Monastic World, 1000–1300.* London: Elek, 1974.

Clapham, Alfred W. *English Romanesque Architecture After the Conquest.* Oxford: Clarendon Press, 1964.

——— *Romanesque Architecture in Western Europe.* Oxford: Clarendon Press, 1959.

Conant, Kenneth. *Carolingian and Romanesque Architecture 800–1200.* Baltimore: Penguin, 1979.

Crichton, George H. *Romanesque Sculpture in Italy.* London: Routledge & Paul, 1954.

Decker, Heinrich. *Romanesque Art in Italy.* New York: Abrams, 1959.

Demus, Otto. *Romanesque Mural Painting.* New York: Abrams, 1970.

Deschamps, Paul. *French Sculpture of the Romanesque Period—Eleventh and Twelfth Centuries.* 1930. Reprint. New York: Hacker, 1972.

Dodwell, C. R. *Painting in Europe 800–1200.* Harmondsworth, England: Penguin, 1971.

Evans, Joan. *Art in Medieval France 987–1498.* Oxford: Clarendon Press, 1969.

Focillon, Henri. *The Art of the West in the Middle Ages.* 2nd ed. London: Phaidon, 1969.

Gantner, Joseph; Pobé, Marcel; and Roubier, Jean. *Romanesque Art in France.* London: Thames & Hudson, 1956.

Gibbs-Smith, Charles H. *The Bayeux Tapestry.* London: Phaidon, 1973.

Grabar, André, and Nordenfalk, Carl. *Romanesque Painting.* New York: Skira, 1958.

Hearn, Millard F. *Romanesque Sculpture in the Eleventh and Twelfth Centuries.* Ithaca, N.Y.: Cornell University Press/Phaidon, 1981.

Holt, Elizabeth Filmore, ed. *A Documentary History of Art, I: The Middle Ages.* Princeton: Princeton University Press, 1981.

Kuback, Hans E. *Romanesque Architecture.* New York: Abrams, 1975.

Kuenstler, Gustav, ed. *Romanesque Art in Europe.* New York: Norton, 1973.

Leisinger, Hermann. *Romanesque Bronzes: Church Portals in Mediaeval Europe.* New York: Praeger, 1957.

Michel, Paul H. *Romanesque Wall Paintings in France.* Paris: Éditions Chêne, 1949.

Morey, Charles R. *Medieval Art.* New York: Norton, 1970.

Pickering, Frederick P. *Literature and Art in the Middle Ages.* Coral Gables: University of Miami Press, 1970.

Porter, Arthur K. *Medieval Architecture.* 2 vols. 1909. Reprint. New York: Hacker, 1969.

——— *Romanesque Sculpture of the Pilgrimage Roads.* 1923. Reprint. New York: Hacker, 1969.

Ricci, Corrado. *Romanesque Architecture in Italy.* London: W. Heinemann, 1925.

Rickert, Margaret. *Painting in Britain: The Middle Ages.* 2nd ed. Harmondsworth, England: Penguin, 1965.

Rivoira, Giovanni. *Lombardic Architecture: Its Origin, Development, and Derivatives.* 1933. Reprint. New York: Hacker, 1975.

Saalman, Howard. *Medieval Architecture: European Architecture 600–1200.* New York: Braziller, 1962.

Schapiro, Meyer. *Romanesque Art: Selected Papers.* London: Chatto & Windus, 1977; New York: Braziller, 1976.

Stoddard, Whitney. *Art and Architecture in Medieval France.* New York: Harper & Row, 1972.

——— *Monastery and Cathedral in France.* New York: Harper & Row, 1972.

Stone, Lawrence. *Sculpture in Britain in the Middle Ages.* Baltimore: Penguin, 1972.

Swarzenski, Hanns. *Monuments of Romanesque Art.* Chicago: University of Chicago Press, 1974.

Webb, Geoffrey F. *Architecture in Britain: The Middle Ages.* Harmondsworth, England: Penguin, 1965.

Zarnecki, George. *Romanesque Art.* New York: Universe Books, 1971.

——— *Studies in Romanesque Sculpture.* London: Darian Press, 1979.

chapter 10 Gothic Art

Adams, Henry. *Mont-Saint-Michel and Chartres.* New York: Doubleday/Anchor, 1959.

Arnold, Hugh. *Stained Glass of the Middle Ages in England and France.* London: A. & C. Black, 1956.

Arslan, Edoardo. *Gothic Architecture in Venice.* London: Phaidon, 1971.

Aubert, Marcel. *The Art of the High Gothic Era.* New York: Crown, 1965.

——— *Gothic Cathedrals of France and Their Treasures.* London: N. Kay, 1959.

Bony, Jean. *French Gothic Architecture of the XII and XIII Centuries.* Berkeley: University of California Press, 1983.

Branner, Robert. *Chartres Cathedral.* New York: Norton, 1969.

——— *Gothic Architecture.* New York: Braziller, 1961.

Duby, George. *The Age of the Cathedrals.* Chicago: University of Chicago Press, 1981.

Dupont, Jacques, and Gnudi, Cesare. *Gothic Painting.* New York: Rizzoli, 1979.

Evans, Joan. *Art in Medieval France 987–1498.* Oxford: Clarendon Press, 1969.

——— *The Flowering of the Middle Ages.* London: Thames & Hudson, 1985.

Fitchen, John. *The Construction of Gothic Cathedrals.* Chicago: University of Chicago Press, 1977.

Focillon, Henri. *The Art of the West in the Middle*

Ages. Vol. 2. Ithaca, N.Y.: Cornell University Press, 1980.

Foster, Richard. *Discovering English Churches.* New York: Oxford University Press, 1982.

Frankl, Paul. *Gothic Architecture.* Baltimore: Penguin, 1963.

————*The Gothic Literary Sources and Interpretations.* Princeton: Princeton University Press, 1960.

Grodecki, Louis, et al. *Gothic Architecture.* New York: Abrams, 1977.

Harvey, John H. *The Gothic World.* New York: Harper & Row, 1969.

Huizinga, Johan. *The Waning of the Middle Ages.* London: E. Arnold, 1970.

Jantzen, Hans. *The High Gothic: The Classic Cathedrals of Chartres, Reims, and Amiens.* New York: Pantheon, 1962.

Johnson, James. *The Radiance of Chartres.* New York: Random House, 1965.

Johnson, Paul. *British Cathedrals.* New York: William Morrow, 1980.

Katzenellenbogen, Adolf. *The Sculptural Programs of Chartres Cathedral.* Baltimore: Johns Hopkins Press, 1959.

Male, Émile. *The Gothic Image: Religious Art in France of the Thirteenth Century.* New York: Harper & Row, 1958.

————*The Gothic Image: Religious Art in the Twelfth Century.* Rev. ed. Princeton: Princeton University Press, 1978.

Mark, Robert. *Experiments in Gothic Structure.* Cambridge: MIT Press, 1982.

Martindale, Andrew. *Gothic Art.* London: Thames & Hudson, 1967.

————*The Rise of the Artist in the Middle Ages and Early Renaissance.* New York: McGraw-Hill, 1972.

Panofsky, Erwin. *Abbot Suger on the Abbey Church of St. Denis and Its Art Treasures.* 2nd ed. Princeton: Princeton University Press, 1979.

————*Gothic Architecture and Scholasticism.* New York: Meridian Books, 1963.

Pevsner, Nikolaus. *The Buildings of England.* 46 vols. Harmondsworth, England: Penguin, 1951–1974.

Robb, David M. *The Art of the Illuminated Manuscript.* Cranbury, N.J.: A. S. Barnes, 1973.

Sauerlander, Willibald, and Hirmer, Max. *Gothic Sculpture in France 1140–1270.* New York: Abrams, 1973.

Sheridan, Ronald, and Ross, Anne. *Gargoyles and Grotesques: Paganism in the Medieval Church.* Boston: New York Graphic Society, 1975.

Simson, Otto von. *The Gothic Cathedral.* 2nd rev. ed. Princeton: Princeton University Press, 1974.

Stoddard, Whitney. *Monastery and Cathedral in France.* Middletown, Conn.: Wesleyan University Press, 1966.

Swaan, Wim. *The Late Middle Ages: Art and Architecture from 1350 to the Advent of the Renaissance.* Ithaca, N.Y.: Cornell University Press, 1977.

Thompson, Daniel. *The Materials and Techniques of Medieval Painting.* New York: Dover, 1956.

Ward, Clarence. *Medieval Church Vaulting.* 1915. Reprint. New York: AMS Press, 1973.

Zarnecki, George. *Art of the Medieval World.* New York: Abrams, 1975.

chapter 11   The Art of India

Archer, William G. *Indian Miniatures.* Greenwich, Conn.: New York Graphic Society, 1960.

————*Indian Paintings from the Punjab Hills.* 2 vols. London: Sotheby Parke Bernet, 1973.

Bachhofer, Ludwig. *Early Indian Sculpture.* 1929. Reprint. New York: Hacker, 1972.

Balasubrahmanyan, S. R. *Early Chola Art—*

Part I. New York: Asia Publishing House, 1966.

————*Early Chola Temples: Parantakat to Rajaraja I, A.D. 907–985.* Bombay: Orient Longman, 1971.

Barrett, Douglas E. *Early Cola Bronzes.* Bombay: Bhulabhai Memorial Institute, 1965.

Barrett, Douglas E., and Gray, Basil. *Painting of India.* Geneva: Skira, 1963.

Basham, Arthur L. *The Wonder That Was India.* 3rd rev. ed. Paris: Arthaud, 1976.

Bhattacharji, Sukumari. *The Indian Theogony, a Comparative Study of Indian Mythology.* London: Cambridge University Press, 1970.

Coomaraswamy, Ananda K. *History of Indian and Indonesian Art.* New Delhi: Munshiram Manaharlal, 1972.

————*Yaksas.* New Delhi: Munshiram Manaharlal, 1971.

Dehijia, Vidya. *Early Buddhist Rock Temples.* Ithaca, N.Y.: Cornell University Press, 1972.

Ghosh, Amalananda. *Ajanta Murals.* New Delhi: Archaeological Survey of India, 1967.

Gopinatha Rao, T. A. *Elements of Hindu Iconography.* 2nd ed. 4 vols. New York: Paragon, 1968.

Gray, Basil, ed. *The Arts of India.* Ithaca, N.Y.: Cornell University Press/Phaidon, 1981.

Groslier, Philippe, and Arthaud, Jacques. *The Arts and Civilization of Angkor.* New York: Praeger, 1957.

Harle, James C. *Gupta Sculpture: Indian Sculpture of the Fourth to the Sixth Centuries A.D.* Oxford: Clarendon Press, 1974.

Kramrisch, Stella. *The Art of India.* 3rd ed. London: Phaidon, 1965.

————*The Hindu Temple.* 2 vols. Delhi: Motilal Banarsidass, 1976.

————*Indian Sculpture.* The Heritage of India Series. London: Oxford University Press, 1933.

Krishna Deva. *Temples of North India.* New Delhi: National Book Trust, 1969.

Lee, Sherman E. *Ancient Cambodian Sculpture.* New York: Intercultural Arts Press, 1970.

Rawson, Philip. *The Art of Southeast Asia.* New York: Praeger, 1967.

Rosenfield, John. *Dynastic Arts of the Kushan.* Berkeley: University of California Press, 1967.

Rowland, Benjamin. *The Art and Architecture of India: Buddhist, Hindu, Jain.* Harmondsworth, England: Penguin, 1977.

Sivaramamurti, C. *South Indian Bronzes.* New Delhi: Lalit Kala Akademi, 1963.

————*South Indian Paintings.* New Delhi: National Museum, 1968.

Srinivasan, K. R. *Temples of South India.* New Delhi: National Book Trust, 1972.

Williams, Joanna Gottfried. *The Art of Gupta India: Empire and Province.* Princeton: Princeton University Press, 1982.

Zimmer, Heinrich, and Campbell, Joseph, eds. *The Art of Indian Asia; Its Mythology.* Bollingen Series 39. 2 vols. Princeton: Princeton University Press, 1983.

chapter 12   The Art of China

Cahill, James. *Chinese Painting.* New ed. Geneva: Skira, 1977; New York: Rizzoli, 1977.

Davidson, J. Leroy. *The Lotus Sutra in Chinese Art: A Study in Buddhist Art to the Year 1880.* New Haven: Yale University Press, 1954.

Gray, Basil, and Vincent, John B. *Buddhist Cave Paintings at Tun-Huang.* Chicago: University of Chicago Press, 1959.

Honey, William B. *The Ceramic Art of China and Other Countries of the Far East.* New York: Beechhurst Press, 1954.

Lee, Sherman E. *Chinese Landscape Painting.* 2nd ed. Cleveland: Cleveland Museum of Art, 1962.

————*Past, Present, East and West.* New York: Braziller, 1983.

Loehr, Max. *The Great Painters of China.* New York: Harper & Row, 1980.

————*Ritual Vessels of Bronze Age China.* New York: Asia Society, 1968.

Mizuno, Seiichi. *Bronzes and Jades of Ancient China.* Tokyo: Nihon Keizai, 1959.

Mizuno, Seiichi, and Nagahiro, Toshio. *A Study of the Buddhist Cave Temples at Lung-Men, Honan.* Tokyo: Zanho Press, 1941.

Munsterberg, Hugo. *Dictionary of Chinese and Japanese Art.* New York: Hacker, 1981.

Rudolph, Richard. *Han Tomb Art of West China.* Berkeley: University of California Press, 1951.

Sickman, Lawrence C., and Soper, Alexander. *The Art and Architecture of China.* Baltimore: Penguin, 1956.

Siren, Oswald. *Chinese Painting: Leading Masters and Principles.* New York: Hacker, 1973.

————*Chinese Sculpture from the Fifth to the Fourteenth Centuries.* 4 vols. 1925. Reprint. New York: Hacker, 1970.

————*A History of Later Chinese Painting.* 1938. Reprint. London: Medici Society, 1978.

Sullivan, Michael. *The Birth of Landscape Painting in China.* Berkeley: University of California Press, 1962.

————*A Short History of Chinese Art.* Berkeley: University of California Press, 1970.

Sullivan, Michael, and Darbois, Dominique. *The Cave Temples of Maichishan.* London: Faber & Faber, 1969.

Weber, Charles D. *Chinese Pictorial Bronze Vessels of the Late Chou Period.* Ascona: Artibus Asiae, 1968.

Willetts, William. *Foundations of Chinese Art.* New York: McGraw-Hill, 1965.

chapter 13   The Art of Japan

Akiyama, Terukazu. *Japanese Painting.* Geneva: Skira; New York: Rizzoli, 1977.

Cahill, James F. *Scholar Painters of Japan: The Nanga School.* New York: Arno Press, 1976.

Drexler, Arthur. *The Architecture of Japan.* New York: Arno Press, 1966.

Fontein, Jan, and Hickman, M. C., eds. *Zen Painting and Calligraphy.* Greenwich, Conn.: New York Graphic Society, 1970.

Hirano, Chie. *Kiyonaga: A Study of His Life and Works.* Cambridge: Harvard University Press, 1939.

Kidder, J. Edward. *Early Japanese Art.* London: Thames & Hudson, 1969.

————*Japanese Temples: Sculpture, Painting, and Architecture.* Tokyo: Bijutsu Shuppansha, 1964.

Lee, Sherman E. *A History of Far Eastern Art.* London: Thames & Hudson, 1975.

————*Japanese Decorative Style.* New York: Harper & Row, 1972.

Paine, Robert, and Soper, Alexander. *The Art and Architecture of Japan.* Baltimore: Penguin, 1955.

Rosenfield, John M. *Japanese Art of the Heian Period, 749–1185.* New York: Asia Society, 1967.

Rosenfield, John M., and Shimada, Shujiro. *Traditions of Japanese Art.* Cambridge: Fogg Art Museum, Harvard University, 1970.

Soper, Alexander. *The Evolution of Buddhist Architecture in Japan.* 1942. Reprint. New York: Hacker, 1978.

Stern, Harold P. *Master Prints of Japan: Ukiyo-e Hanga.* New York: Abrams, 1969.

chapter 14   The Native Arts of the Americas, Africa, and the South Pacific

PRE-COLUMBIAN ART

Bennett, Wendell C. *Ancient Arts of the Andes.* New York: Museum of Modern Art/Arno Press, 1966.

Bernal, Ignacio. *The Olmec World.* Berkeley: University of California Press, 1977.

Bushnell, G. H. S. *Peru*. Rev. ed. New York: Praeger, 1963.

Coe, Michael D. *The Maya*. London: Thames & Hudson, 1980.

Coe, Michael D., and Diehl, R. A. *In the Land of the Olmec*. 2 vols. Austin: University of Texas Press, 1980.

Coe, William R. *Tikal: A Handbook of the Ancient Maya Ruins*. 3rd ed. Philadelphia: University Museum, University of Pennsylvania, 1970.

Emmerich, André. *Sweat of the Sun and Tears of the Moon: Gold and Silver in Pre-Columbian Art*. New York: Hacker, 1977.

Grider, Terence. *Origins of Pre-Columbian Art*. Austin: University of Texas Press, 1982.

Heyden, Doris, and Gendrop, Paul. *Pre-Columbian Architecture of Mesoamerica*. New York: Abrams, 1975.

Kubler, George. *The Art and Architecture of Ancient America: The Mexican, Maya, and Andean Peoples*. 2nd ed. Harmondsworth, England: Penguin, 1975.

Lapiner, Alan C. *Pre-Columbian Art of South America*. New York: Abrams, 1976.

Lehmann, Walter, with Heinrich Doering. *The Art of Old Peru*. New York: Hacker, 1975.

Los Angeles County Museum of Art. *Sculpture of Ancient West Mexico: Nayarit*. Los Angeles: Los Angeles County Museum of Art, 1970.

Mason, John Alden. *The Ancient Civilizations of Peru*. Rev. ed. Harmondsworth, England: Penguin, 1975.

Morley, Sylvanus G. *The Ancient Maya*. 3rd rev. ed. Stanford: Stanford University Press, 1973.

Paddock, John, ed. *Ancient Oaxaca: Discoveries in Mexican Archeology and History*. Stanford: Stanford University Press, 1970.

Pasztory, Esther. *Aztec Art*. New York: Abrams, 1983.

Peterson, Frederick. *Ancient Mexico*. New York: Capricorn Books, 1962.

Pettersen, Carmen L. *The Maya of Guatemala: Their Life and Dress*. Guatemala City: University of Washington Press, 1976.

Proskouriakoff, Tatiana Avenirovna. *A Study of Classic Maya Sculpture*. Washington, D.C.: Carnegie Institute of Washington, 1950.

Robertson, Donald. *Pre-Columbian Architecture*. New York: Braziller, 1963.

Robertson, Merle G.; Rands, Robert L.; and Graham, John A. *Maya Sculpture from the Southern Lowlands*. Berkeley: Lederer, Street & Zeus, 1972.

Rowe, John H. *Chavín Art: An Inquiry into Its Form and Meaning*. New York: Museum of Primitive Art, 1962.

Steward, Julian H. *Handbook of the South American Indians*. 7 vols. New York: Cooper Square Publishers, 1963.

Stierlin, Henri. *Art of the Aztecs, and Its Origins*. New York: Rizzoli, 1982.

Thompson, John E. S. *Maya History and Religion*. Norman: University of Oklahoma Press, 1972.

Wauchope, Robert, ed. *Handbook of Middle American Indians*. 16 vols. Austin: University of Texas Press, 1964–1976.

Weaver, Muriel Porter. *The Aztecs, Maya, and their Predecessors: The Archaeology of Mesoamerica*. 2nd ed. New York: Academic Press, 1981.

NORTH AMERICAN INDIAN AND ESKIMO ART

Boas, Franz. *Primitive Art*. 1927. Reprint. Magnolia, Mass.: Peter Smith, 1962.

Collins, Henry, et al. *The Far North: Two Thousand Years of American Eskimo and Indian Art*. Bloomington, Ind.: Indiana University Press in association with the National Gallery of Art, Washington, D.C., 1977.

Curtis, Edward S. *The North American Indian*. 30 vols. Cambridge: Cambridge University Press, 1907–1930.

Dockstader, Frederick. *Indian Art in America: The Arts and Crafts of the North American Indian*. Greenwich, Conn.: New York Graphic Society.

——— *Indian Art of the Americas*. New York: Museum of the American Indian, Heye Foundation, 1973.

Ewers, John C. *Plains Indian Painting*. Stanford: Stanford University Press, 1939.

Feder, Norman. *Two Hundred Years of North American Art*. New York: Praeger, 1972.

Fraser, Douglas. *The Many Faces of Primitive Art*. Englewood Cliffs, N.J.: Prentice-Hall, 1966.

Grant, Campbell. *Rock Art of the American Indian*. 1967. Reprint. New York: Promontory Press, 1974.

Gunther, Erna. *Art in the Life of the Northwest Coast Indians*. Portland, Ore.: Portland Art Museum, 1966.

Harding, Anne D., and Boling, Patricia. *Bibliography of Articles and Papers on North American Indian Arts*. 1938. Reprint. New York: Kraus, 1969.

Murdock, George P., and O'Leary, Timothy. *Ethnographic Bibliography of North America*. 4th ed. New Haven: Human Relations Area Files Press, 1972.

Ray, Dorothy J. *Artists of the Tundra and the Sea*. Seattle: University of Washington Press, 1961.

Ritchie, Carson I. A. *The Eskimo and His Art*. New York: St. Martin's Press, 1976.

Snow, Dean. *The Archaeology of North America/American Indians*. New York: Thames & Hudson, 1980.

Whiteford, Andrew H. *North American Indian Arts*. New York: Golden Press, 1973.

AFRICAN ART

Allison, Philip. *African Stone Sculpture*. New York: Praeger, 1968.

Bascom, William R. *African Art in Cultural Perspective: An Introduction*. New York: Norton, 1973.

Ben-Amos, Paula. *The Art of Benin*. New York: Thames & Hudson, 1980.

Brentjes, Burchard. *African Rock Art*. London: Dent, 1967.

Cornet, Joseph. *Art of Africa: Treasures from the Congo*. London: Phaidon, 1971.

D'Azevedo, Warren L., ed. *The Traditional Artist in African Societies*. Bloomington: Indiana University Press, 1973.

Delange, Jacqueline. *Art and Peoples of Black Africa*. New York: Dutton, 1974.

Elisofon, Eliot, and Fagg, William. *The Sculpture of Africa*. New York: Hacker, 1978.

Eyo, Ekpo, and Willett, Frank. *Treasures of Ancient Nigeria*. New York: Knopf, 1980.

Fagg, William B. *Nigerian Images: The Splendor of African Sculpture*. New York: Praeger, 1963.

Forman, Werner. *Benin Art*. London: Hamlyn, 1960.

Fraser, Douglas F., and Cole, H. M., eds. *African Art and Leadership*. Madison: University of Wisconsin Press, 1972.

Gaskin, L. J. P. *A Bibliography of African Art*. London: International African Institute, 1965.

Laude, Jean. *The Arts of Black Africa*. Berkeley: University of California Press, 1973.

Lieris, Michel, and Delange, Jacqueline. *African Art*. New York: Golden Press, 1968.

Thompson, Robert F. *Black Gods and Kings: Yoruba Art at U.C.L.A.* Bloomington: Indiana University Press, 1976.

——— *Flash of the Spirit: African and Afro-American Art and Philosophy*. New York: Random House, 1983.

Trowell, Kathleen M. *Classical African Sculpture*. London: Faber & Faber, 1970.

Walker Art Center. *Art of the Congo*. Minneapolis: Walker Art Center, 1967.

Wassing, René S. *African Art: Its Background and Traditions*. New York: Abrams, 1968.

Willett, Frank. *African Art: An Introduction*. London: Thames & Hudkson, 1971.

——— *Ife in the History of West African Sculpture*. New York: McGraw-Hill, 1967.

OCEANIC ART

Barrow, Tui T. *Art and Life in Polynesia*. Rutland, Vt.: Charles E. Tuttle, 1973.

——— *Maori Wood Sculpture of New Zealand*. Rutland, Vt.: Charles E. Tuttle, 1970.

Batterberry, Michael, and Ruskin, Ariane. *Primitive Art*. New York: McGraw-Hill, 1973.

Bernot, Ronald M. *Australian Aboriginal Art*. New York: Macmillan, 1964.

Buck, Peter H. *Arts and Crafts of Hawaii*. Honolulu: Bishop Museum Press, 1964.

Dodd, Edward H. *Polynesian Art*. New York: Dodd, Mead, 1967.

Firth, Raymond. *Art and Life in New Guinea*. 1936. Reprint. New York: AMS Press, 1977.

Fraser, Douglas. *Primitive Art*. London: Thames & Hudson, 1962.

Guiart, Jean. *Arts of the South Pacific*. New York: Golden Press, 1963.

Kooijman, S. *The Art of Lake Sentani*. New York: Museum of Primitive Art, 1959.

Linton, Ralph, and Wingert, Paul. *Arts of the South Seas*. 1946. Reprint. New York: Arno Press, 1972.

Newton, Douglas. *Art Styles of the Papuan Gulf*. New York: Museum of Primitive Art, 1961.

Rockefeller, Michael C. *The Asmat of New Guinea: The Journal of Michael Clark Rockefeller*. Greenwich, Conn.: New York Graphic Society, 1967.

Schmitz, Carl A. *Oceanic Art; Myth, Man and Image in the South Seas*. New York: Abrams, 1971.

Stubbs, Dacre. *Prehistoric Art of Australia*. New York: Scribner, 1975.

Taylor, Clyde R. H. *A Pacific Bibliography: Printed Matter Relating to the Native People of Polynesia, Melanesia, and Micronesia*. 2nd ed. Oxford: Clarendon Press, 1965.

Wingert, Paul. *Primitive Art: Its Traditions and Styles*. Cleveland: World Publishing, 1970.

chapter 15 The "Proto-Renaissance" in Italy

Antal, Frederick, *Florentine Painting and Its Social Background*. London: Kegan Paul, 1948.

Cole, Bruce. *Sienese Painting: From Its Origin to the Fifteenth Century*. Bloomington: Indiana University Press, 1985.

De Wald, Ernest T. *Italian Painting: 1200–1600*. New York: Holt, Rinehart & Winston, 1961.

Fremantle, Richard. *Florentine Gothic Painters from Giotto to Masaccio: A Guide to Painting in and near Florence*. London: Secker & Warburg, 1975.

Marle, Raimond van. *The Development of the Italian Schools of Painting*. 19 vols. 1923–1938. Reprint. New York: Hacker, 1970.

Meiss, Millard. *Painting in Florence and Siena After the Black Death*. New York: Harper & Row, 1973.

Panofsky, Erwin. *Renaissance and Renascences in Western Art*. New York: Harper & Row, 1969.

Pope-Hennessy, John. *Introduction to Italian Sculpture*. 2nd ed. 3 vols. New York: Phaidon, 1970–1972.

Schevill, Ferdinand. *The Medici*. New York: Harper & Row, 1960.

Smart, Alastair. *The Dawn of Italian Painting*. Ithaca, N.Y.: Cornell University Press, 1978.

Stubblebine, James, ed. *Giotto: The Arena Chapel Frescoes*. New York: Norton, 1969.

Venturi, Lionello, and Skira-Venturi, Rosabianca. *Italian Painting: The Creators of the Renaissance*. 3 vols. Geneva; Skira, 1950–1952.

White, John. *Art and Architecture in Italy, 1250 to 1400*. Baltimore: Penguin, 1966.

chapter 16 Fifteenth-Century Italian Art

Baxandall, Michael. *Painting and Experience in Fifteenth Century Italy*. New York: Oxford University Press, 1983.

Berenson, Bernard. *The Italian Painters of the Renaissance*. Ithaca, N.Y.: Phaidon/Cornell University Press, 1980.

———*Italian Pictures of the Renaissance*. Ithaca, N.Y.: Phaidon/Cornell University Press, 1980.

Borsook, Eve. *The Mural Painters of Tuscany*. New York: Oxford University Press, 1981.

Burckhardt, Jacob. *The Civilization of the Renaissance in Italy*. 4th ed. 1867. Reprint. London: Phaidon, 1960.

Chastel, André. *The Age of Humanism*. New York: McGraw-Hill, 1964.

———*Studios and Styles of the Italian Renaissance*. New York: Braziller, 1971.

Cole, Bruce. *Masaccio and the Art of Early Renaissance Florence*. Bloomington: Indiana University Press, 1980.

Decker, Heinrich. *The Renaissance in Italy: Architecture, Sculpture, Frescoes*. New York: Viking, 1969.

De Wald, Ernest T. *Italian Painting, 1200–1600*. New York: Holt, Rinehart & Winston, 1961.

Edgerton, Samuel Y., Jr. *The Renaissance Rediscovery of Linear Perspective*. New York: Harper & Row, 1976.

Ferguson, Wallace K., et al. *The Renaissance*. New York: Henry Holt, 1940.

Gadol, Joan. *Leon Battista Alberti: Universal Man of the Early Renaissance*. Chicago: University of Chicago Press, 1969.

Gilbert, Creighton. *History of Renaissance Art throughout Europe*. New York: Abrams, 1973.

———*Italian Art 1400–1500: Sources and Documents*. Englewood Cliffs, N.J.: Prentice-Hall, 1970.

Godfrey, F. M. *Early Venetian Painters, 1415–1495*. London: Tiranti, 1954.

Hale, John R. *Italian Renaissance Painting from Masaccio to Titian*. New York: Dutton, 1977.

Hartt, Frederick. *History of Italian Renaissance Art*. New York: Abrams, 1979.

Helton, Tinsley, ed. *The Renaissance: A Reconsideration of the Theories and Interpretations of the Age*. Madison: University of Wisconsin Press, 1964.

Heydenreich, Ludwig H., and Lotz, Wolfgang. *Architecture in Italy 1400–1600*. Harmondsworth, England: Penguin, 1974.

Holt, Elizabeth B. *A Documentary History of Art*. 2nd ed. Vol. 1. Garden City, N.Y.: Doubleday, 1957.

Huyghe, René. *Larousse Encyclopedia of Renaissance and Baroque Art*. See **Reference Books.**

Janson, Horst W. *The Sculpture of Donatello*. 2 vols. Princeton, N.J.: Princeton University Press, 1957.

Krautheimer, Richard, and Krautheimer-Hess, Trude. *Lorenzo Ghiberti*. Princeton, N.J.: Princeton University Press, 1956.

Lieberman, Ralph. *Renaissance Architecture in Venice*. New York: Abbeville, 1982.

Lowry, Bates. *Renaissance Architecture*. New York: Braziller, 1962.

McAndrew, John. *Venetian Architecture of the Early Renaissance*. Cambridge: MIT Press, 1980.

Marle, Raimond van. *The Development of the Italian Schools of Painting*. 19 vols. 1923–1938. Reprint. New York: Hacker, 1970.

Meiss, Millard. *The Painter's Choice, Problems in the Interpretation of Renaissance Art*. New York: Harper & Row, 1976.

Murray, Peter. *The Architecture of the Italian Renaissance*. London: Secker & Warburg, 1985.

Murray, Peter, and Murray, Linda. *The Art of the Renaissance*. London: Thames & Hudson, 1981.

Panofsky, Erwin. *Renaissance and Renascences in Western Art*. New York: Harper & Row, 1969.

Pater, Walter. *The Renaissance: Studies in Art and Poetry*. Edited by D. L. Hill. Berkeley: University of California Press, 1980.

Pope-Hennessy, John. *An Introduction to Italian Sculpture*. 2nd ed. 3 vols. New York: Phaidon, 1970–1971.

———*Sienese Quattrocento Painting*. New York: Oxford University Press, 1947.

Schevill, Ferdinand. *The Medici*. New York: Harper & Row, 1960.

Seymour, Charles. *Sculpture in Italy, 1400–1500*. Baltimore: Penguin, 1966.

Symonds, John Addington. *The Renaissance in Italy*. 7 vols. 1875–1886. Reprint. New York: Modern Library, 1935. (Other reprints available.)

Vasari, Giorgio. *The Lives of the Most Eminent Painters, Sculptors, and Architects, 1550–1568*. 3 vols. New York: Abrams, 1979.

Werkmeister, William H., ed. Ferguson, Wallace, et al. *Facets of the Renaissance*. New York: Harper & Row, 1963.

Wittkower, Rudolf. *Architectural Principles in the Age of Humanism*. 4th ed. London: Academy, 1973.

chapter 17 Sixteenth-Century Italian Art

Ackerman, James S. *The Architecture of Michelangelo*. London: Zwemmer, 1966.

———*Palladio*. New York: Penguin, 1978.

Bialostocki, Jan. *The Art of the Renaissance in Eastern Europe*. Ithaca, N.Y.: Cornell University Press, 1976.

Blunt, Anthony. *Artistic Theory in Italy, 1450–1600*. London: Oxford University Press, 1975.

Briganti, Giuliano. *Italian Mannerism*. London: Thames & Hudson, 1962.

Castiglione, Baldassare. *The Courtier*. 1528. Reprint. New York: National Alumni, 1907. (Other reprints available.)

Cellini, Benvenuto. *Autobiography*. Reprint. New York: Grolier, 1969. (Other reprints available.)

Einem, Herbert von. *Michelangelo*. London: Methuen, 1976.

Freedberg, Sydney F. *Painting in Italy: 1500–1600*. Harmondsworth, England: Penguin, 1983.

———*Painting of the High Renaissance in Rome and Florence*. 1st rev. New York: Harper & Row, 1975.

Friedlaender, Walter. *Mannerism and Anti-Mannerism in Italian Painting*. New York: Schocken Books, 1965.

Holt, Elizabeth Gilmore, ed. *A Documentary History of Art*. Vol. 2, *Michelangelo and the Mannerists*. Rev. ed. Princeton: Princeton University Press, 1982.

Levey, Michael. *High Renaissance*. Harmondsworth, England: Penguin, 1975.

Murray, Linda. *The High Renaissance and Mannerism*. New York: Oxford University Press, 1977.

Partner, Peter. *Renaissance Rome, 1500–1559: A Portrait of a Society*. Berkeley: University of California Press, 1977.

Pope-Hennessy, John. *Italian High Renaissance and Baroque Sculpture*. 3 vols. Greenwich, Conn.: Phaidon, 1963.

Shearman, John K. G. *Mannerism*. Baltimore: Penguin, 1978.

Venturi, Lionello. *The Sixteenth Century: From Leonardo to El Greco*. New York: Skira, 1956.

Wölfflin, Heinrich. *The Art of the Italian Renaissance*. New York: Schocken Books, 1963.

———*Classic Art*. London: Phaidon, 1968.

Würtenberger, Franzsepp. *Mannerism: The European Style of the Sixteenth Century*. New York: Holt, Rinehart & Winston, 1963.

chapter 18 The Renaissance Outside of Italy

Alpers, Svetlana. *The Art of Describing: Dutch Art in the Seventeenth Century*. Chicago: University of Chicago Press, 1983.

Benesch, Otto. *Art of the Renaissance in Northern Europe*. Rev. ed. London: Phaidon, 1965.

———*German Painting from Dürer to Holbein*. Geneva: Skira, 1966.

Blunt, Anthony. *Art and Architecture in France 1500–1700*. 4th ed. Baltimore: Penguin, 1982.

Chatelet, Albert. *Early Dutch Painting*. New York: Rizzoli, 1981.

Conway, William M. *The Van Eycks and Their Followers*. 1921. Reprint. New York: AMS Press, 1979.

Cuttler, Charles P. *Northern Painting from Pucelle to Bruegel*. New York: Holt, Rinehart & Winston, 1968.

Evans, Joan. *Monastic Architecture in France from the Renaissance to the Revolution*. New York: Hacker, 1980.

Friedlander, Max J. *Early Netherlandish Painting*. New York: Praeger/Phaidon, 1967–1976.

———*From Van Eyck to Bruegel*. 3rd ed. Ithaca, N.Y.: Cornell University Press, 1981.

Fuchs, Rudolph H. *Dutch Painting*. London: Thames & Hudson, 1978.

Hind, Arthur M. *History of Engraving and Etching from the Fifteenth Century to the Year 1914*. 3rd rev. ed. New York: Dover, 1963.

———*An Introduction to a History of Woodcut*. New York: Dover, 1963.

Hitchcock, Henry-Russell. *German Renaissance Architecture*. Princeton: Princeton University Press. 1981.

Huizinga, Johan. *The Waning of the Middle Ages*. 1924. Reprint. New York: Doubleday/Anchor, 1970.

Lassaigne, Jacques, and Delevoy, Robert. *Flemish Painting*. New York: Skira, 1957.

Mather, Frank J. *Western European Painting of the Renaissance*. New York: Cooper Square Publishers, 1966.

Meiss, Millard. *French Painting in the Time of Jean de Berry*. New York: Braziller, 1974.

Panofsky, Erwin. *Early Netherlandish Painting*. Cambridge: Harvard University Press, 1953.

———*The Life and Art of Albrecht Dürer*. 4th ed. Princeton: Princeton University Press, 1971.

Puyvelde, Leo van. *The Flemish Primitives*. London: Collins, 1948.

Réau, Louis. *French Painting in the Fourteenth, Fifteenth, and Sixteenth Centuries*. New York: Hyperion Press, 1939.

Snyder, James. *Northern Renaissance Art*. New York: Abrams, 1985.

Stechow, Wolfgang, ed. *Northern Renaissance Art, 1400–1600*. Englewood Cliffs, N.J.: Prentice-Hall, 1966.

Waetzold, Wilhelm. *Dürer and His Time*. Enl. ed. London: Phaidon, 1955.

Whinney, Margaret. *Early Flemish Painting*. London: Faber & Faber, 1968.

Wilenski, Reginald H. *Flemish Painters, 1430–1830*. 2 vols. London: Faber & Faber, 1960.

chapter 19 Baroque Art

Bazin, Germain. *Baroque and Rococo Art*. New York: Praeger, 1974.

Blunt, Anthony, ed. *Baroque and Rococo: Architecture and Decoration*. Cambridge: Harper & Row, 1982.

Chatelet, Albert, and Thuillier, Jacques. *French Painting from Fouquet to Poussin*. Geneva: Skira, 1963.

Fokker, Timon H. *Roman Baroque Art: The History of a Style*. London: Oxford University Press, 1938.

Freedberg, Sydney J. *Circa 1600: A Revolution of Style in Italian Painting*. Cambridge: Harvard University Press, 1983.

Gerson, Horst, and ter Kuile, E. H. *Art and*

Architecture in Belgium 1600–1800. Baltimore: Penguin, 1960.

Haak, Bob. *The Golden Age: Dutch Painters of the Seventeenth Century.* London: Thames & Hudson, 1984.

Held, Julius, and Posner, Donald. *17th and 18th Century Art.* New York: Abrams, 1974.

Hempel, Eberhard. *Baroque Art and Architecture in Central Europe.* Baltimore: Penguin, 1965.

Hibbard, Howard. *Bernini.* Harmondsworth, England: Penguin, 1976.

————*Caravaggio.* New York: Thames & Hudson, 1983.

————*Carlo Maderno and Roman Architecture, 1580–1630.* London: Zwemmer, 1971.

Hinks, Roger P. *Michelangelo Merisi da Caravaggio.* London: Faber & Faber, 1953.

Howard, Deborah. *The Architectural History of Venice.* London: B. T. Batsford, 1981.

Kahr, Madlyn Millner. *Dutch Painting in the Seventeenth Century.* New York: Harper & Row, 1978.

————*Velázquez: The Art of Painting.* New York: Harper & Row, 1976.

Kitson, Michael. *The Age of Baroque.* London: Hamlyn, 1976.

Lees-Milne, James. *Baroque in Italy.* New York: Macmillan, 1960.

Martin, John R. *Baroque.* New York: Harper & Row, 1977.

Millon, Henry A. *Baroque and Rococo Architecture.* New York: Braziller, 1965.

Norberg-Schulz, Christian. *Baroque Architecture.* New York: Rizzoli, 1985.

Pope-Hennessy, Sir John. *The Study and Criticism of Italian Sculpture.* New York: Metropolitan Museum, 1981.

Portoghesi, Paolo. *The Rome of Borromini.* London: Phaidon, 1972.

Powell, Nicolas. *From Baroque to Rococo: An Introduction to Austrian and German Architecture from 1580 to 1790.* London: Faber & Faber, 1959.

Rosenberg, Jakob; Slive, Seymour; and ter Kuile, E. H. *Dutch Art and Architecture, 1600–1800.* Baltimore: Penguin, 1979.

Spear, Richard E. *Caravaggio and His Followers.* New York: Harper & Row, 1975.

Stechow, Wolfgang. *Dutch Landscape Painting of the 17th Century.* Oxford: Phaidon, 1981.

Summerson, Sir John. *Architecture in Britain: 1530–1830.* 7th rev. and enl. ed. Baltimore: Penguin, 1983.

Tapie, Victor-Lucien. *The Age of Grandeur: Baroque Art and Architecture.* New York: Praeger, 1966.

Waterhouse, Ellis Kirkham. *Baroque Painting in Rome.* London: Phaidon, 1976.

————*Italian Baroque Painting.* 2nd ed. London: Phaidon, 1969.

————*Painting in Britain, 1530–1790.* 4th ed. New York: Penguin, 1978.

Wittkower, Rudolf. *Gian Lorenzo Bernini: The Sculptor of the Roman Baroque.* 3rd ed. rev. Oxford: Phaidon, 1981.

Wölfflin, Heinrich. *Principles of Art History.* 7th ed. New York: Dover, 1950.

chapter 20   The Eighteenth Century: Rococo and the Rise of Romanticism

Bacou, Roseline, *Piranesi: Etchings and Drawings.* Boston: New York Graphic Society, 1975.

Blunt, Anthony. *Art and Architecture in France, 1500–1700.* 2nd ed. Harmondsworth, England: Penguin, 1970.

Braham, Allan. *The Architecture of the French Enlightenment.* Berkeley: University of California Press, 1980.

Chatelet, Albert, and Thuillier, Jacques. *French Painting from Le Nain to Fragonard.* Geneva: Skira, 1964.

Conisbee, Philip. *Painting in Eighteenth-Century France.* Ithaca, N.Y.: Phaidon/Cornell University Press, 1981.

Hayes, John T. *Gainsborough: Paintings and Drawings.* London: Phaidon, 1975.

Herrmann, Luke. *British Landscape Painting of the Eighteenth Century.* New York: Oxford University Press, 1974.

Hitchcock, Henry Russell. *Rococo Architecture in Southern Germany.* London: Phaidon, 1968.

Irwin, David. *English Neoclassical Art.* London: Faber & Faber, 1966.

Kalnein, Wend Graf, and Levey, Michael. *Art and Architecture of the Eighteenth Century in France.* New York: Viking/Pelican, 1973.

Kimball, Sidney F. *The Creation of the Rococo.* New York: Norton, 1964.

Levey, Michael. *Painting in Eighteenth-Century Venice.* Ithaca, N.Y.: Phaidon/Cornell University Press, 1980.

Millon, Henry A. *Baroque and Rococo Architecture.* New York: Braziller, 1961.

Norberg-Schulz, Christian. *Late Baroque and Rococo Architecture.* New York: Abrams, 1974.

Pierson, William. *American Buildings and Their Architects: The Colonial and Neo-Classical Style.* Vol. 1. Garden City, N.Y.: Doubleday, 1970.

Pignatti, Terisio. *The Age of Rococo.* New York: Hamlyn, 1969.

Rosenblum, Robert. *Transformations in Late Eighteenth Century Art.* Princeton: Princeton University Press, 1970.

Waterhouse, Ellis K. *Painting in Britain, 1530–1790.* 4th ed. New York: Penguin, 1978.

Whinney, Margaret Dickens. *English Art, 1625–1714.* Oxford: Clarendon Press, 1957.

————*Sculpture in Britain, 1530–1830.* Baltimore: Penguin, 1964.

Whinney, Margaret D., and Millar, Oliver. *English Art, 1720–1830.* London: H. M. Stationery Office, 1971.

Wittkower, Rudolf. *Art and Architecture in Italy, 1600–1750.* New York: Penguin, 1980.

chapter 21   The Nineteenth Century: Pluralism of Style

Arnason, H. *The Sculptures of Houdon.* New York: Oxford University Press, 1975.

Aslin, Elizabeth. *The Aesthetic Movement: Prelude to Art Nouveau.* New York: Praeger, 1969.

Baudelaire, Charles. *The Mirror of Art, Critical Studies.* Garden City, N.Y.: Doubleday, 1956.

Boime, A. *The Academy and French Painting in the 19th Century.* London: Phaidon, 1971.

Brion, Marcel. *Art of the Romantic Era: Romanticism, Classicism, Realism.* New York: Praeger, 1966.

Brown, Milton. *American Art to 1900.* New York: Abrams, 1977.

Brunhammer, Yvonne, et al. *Art Nouveau—Belgium, France: Catalogue of an Exhibition.* Houston: Institute for the Arts, Rice University, 1976.

Canaday, John. *Mainstreams of Modern Art.* New York: Holt, 1959.

Clark, Kenneth. *The Gothic Revival: An Essay in the History of Taste.* New York: Humanities Press, 1970.

Clay, Jean. *Romanticism.* New York: Phaidon, 1981.

Courthion, Pierre. *Romanticism.* Geneva: Skira, 1961.

Delacroix, Eugène. *The Journals of Eugène Delacroix.* New York: Phaidon, 1951.

Dixon, Roger, and Muthesius, Stefan. *Victorian Architecture.* London: Thames & Hudson, 1978.

Eitner, Lorenz. *Neo-Classicism and Romanticism, 1750–1850: Sources and Documents on the History of Art.* 2 vols. Englewood Cliffs, N.J.: Prentice-Hall, 1970.

Flexner, James Thomas. *America's Old Masters.* New York: McGraw-Hill, 1982.

Friedlaender, Walter. *From David to Delacroix.* New York: Schocken Books, 1968.

Gernsheim, Helmut, and Gernsheim, Alison. *The History of Photography from the Camera Obscura to the Beginning of the Modern Era.* London: Thames & Hudson, 1969.

Hamilton, George H. *Nineteenth and Twentieth Century Art.* Englewood Cliffs, N.J.: Prentice-Hall, 1972.

Hanson, Anne Coffin. *Manet and the Modern Tradition.* New Haven: Yale University Press, 1977.

Hawley, Henry. *Neo-Classicism, Style and Motif.* Cleveland: Cleveland Museum of Art, 1964.

Hilton, Timothy. *The Pre-Raphaelites.* New York: Praeger, 1974.

Hitchcock, Henry-Russell. *Architecture: Nineteenth and Twentieth Centuries.* 4th ed. Baltimore: Penguin, 1977.

Holt, Elizabeth B. *From the Classicists to the Impressionists: Art and Architecture in the Nineteenth Century.* Garden City, N.Y.: Doubleday/Anchor, 1966.

Honour, Hugh. *Neo-Classicism.* New York: Harper & Row, 1979.

————*Romanticism.* New York: Harper & Row, 1979.

Janson, Horst W. *19th Century Sculpture.* New York: Abrams, 1985.

Leymarie, Jean. *French Painting in the Nineteenth Century.* Geneva: Skira, 1962.

Licht, Fred. *Sculpture—Nineteenth and Twentieth Centuries.* Greenwich, Conn.: New York Graphic Society, 1967.

Loyer, Francois. *Architecture of the Industrial Age.* New York: Rizzoli, 1983.

Macaulay, James. *The Gothic Revival, 1745–1845.* Glasgow: Blackie, 1975.

Martinell, César. *Gaudi: His Life, His Theories, His Work.* Cambridge: MIT Press, 1975.

Middleton, Robin, ed. *The Beaux-Arts and Nineteenth Century French Architecture.* Cambridge: MIT Press, 1982.

Newton, Eric. *The Romantic Rebellion.* New York: Schocken Books, 1964.

Nochlin, Linda. *Gustave Courbet: A Study of Style and Society.* New York: Garland, 1976.

————*Impressionism and Post-Impressionism 1874–1904: Sources and Documents.* Englewood Cliffs, N.J.: Prentice-Hall, 1966.

————*Realism and Tradition in Art.* New York: Penguin, 1976.

Novak, Barbara. *American Painting of the Nineteenth Century.* New York: Praeger, 1969.

Novotny, Fritz. *Painting and Sculpture in Europe 1780–1880.* 2nd ed. Harmondsworth, England: Penguin, 1978.

Pelles, Geraldine. *Art, Artists and Society: Origins of a Modern Dilemma, Painting in England and France 1750–1850.* Englewood Cliffs, N.J.: Prentice-Hall, 1963.

Pevsner, Nikolaus. *Pioneers of Modern Design.* Harmondsworth, England: Penguin, 1964.

Rewald, John. *The History of Impressionism.* New York: Museum of Modern Art, 1973.

Roberts, Keith. *The Impressionists and Post-Impressionists.* New York: Dutton, 1977.

Rosenblum, Robert. *Modern Painting and the Northern Romantic Tradition.* New York: Harper & Row, 1975.

Rosenblum, Robert, and Janson, Horst W. *19th Century Art.* New York: Abrams, 1984.

Sambrook, James, ed. *Pre-Raphaelitism: A Collection of Critical Essays.* Chicago: University of Chicago Press, 1974.

Schapiro, Meyer. *Modern Art: 19th and 20th Centuries.* New York: Braziller, 1980.

Sloane, Joseph C. *French Painting Between the Past and the Present: Artists, Critics, and Traditions from 1848 to 1870.* Princeton: Princeton University Press, 1973.

Sypher, Wylie. *Rococo to Cubism in Art and Literature.* New York: Random House, 1960.

Vaughan, William. *German Romantic Painting.* New Haven: Yale University Press, 1980.

Weisberg, Gabriel P. *The Realist Tradition: French Painting and Drawing, 1830–1900.* Cleveland: Cleveland Museum/Indiana University Press, 1980.

Whiffen, Marcus, and Koeper, Frederick. *American Architecture, 1607–1976.* Cambridge: MIT Press, 1983.

Wood, Christopher. *The Pre-Raphaelites.* New York: Viking Press, 1981.

chapter 22   The Twentieth Century

Amaya, Mario. *Pop Art and After.* New York: Viking, 1972.

Andersen, Wayne. *American Sculpture in Process 1930/1970.* Boston: New York Graphic Society, 1975.

Apollinaire, Guillaume. *The Cubist Painters: Aesthetic Meditations, 1913.* New York: Wittenborn, 1970.

Arnason, H. Harvard. *History of Modern Art: Painting, Sculpture, Architecture.* 2nd rev. and enl. ed. Englewood Cliffs, N.J.: Prentice-Hall, 1977.

Ashton, Dore. *American Art Since 1945.* New York: Oxford University Press, 1982.

Banham, Reyner. *Guide to Modern Architecture.* Princeton: D. Van Nostrand, 1962.

Battcock, Gregory. *Minimal Art: A Critical Anthology.* New York: Studio Vista, 1969.

Battcock, Gregory, ed. *The New Art: A Critical Anthology.* New York: Dutton, 1973.

Benevolo, Leonardo. *History of Modern Architecture.* 2 vols. Cambridge: MIT Press, 1977.

Blake, Peter. *The Master Builder.* New York: Norton, 1976.

Breton, André. *Surrealism and Painting.* New York: Harper & Row, 1972.

Brown, Milton; Hunter, Sam; and Jacobus, John. *American Art: Painting, Sculpture, Architecture, Decorative Arts, Photography.* New York: Abrams, 1979.

Canaday, John. *Mainstreams of Modern Art.* New York: Holt, 1959.

Carter, Peter. *Mies van der Rohe at Work.* London: Pall Mall Press, 1974.

Cassou, Jean, and Pevsner, Nikolaus. *Gateway to the Twentieth Century.* New York: McGraw-Hill, 1962.

Collins, Peter. *Changing Ideals in Modern Architecture, 1750–1950.* London: Faber & Faber, 1971.

Condit, Carl W. *The Rise of the Skyscraper: Portrait of the Times and Career of Influential Architects.* Chicago: University of Chicago Press. 1952.

Cummings, Paul. *Dictionary of Contemporary American Artists.* 3rd ed. New York: St. Martin's Press, 1977.

Curtis, William J. R. *Modern Architecture Since 1900.* Englewood Cliffs, N.J.: Prentice-Hall, 1982.

Diehl, Gaston. *The Moderns: A Treasury of Painting Throughout the World.* Milan: Uffizi, 1961.

Duthuit, Georges. *The Fauvist Painters.* New York: Wittenborn, Schultz, 1950.

Elderfield, John. *The "Wild Beasts": Fauvism and Its Affinities.* New York: The Museum of Modern Art/Oxford University Press, 1976.

Elsen, Albert. *Origins of Modern Sculpture.* New York: Braziller, 1974.

Frampton, Kenneth. *Modern Architecture: A Critical History.* New York: Oxford University Press, 1980.

Giedion-Welcker, Carola. *Contemporary Sculpture: An Evaluation in Volume and Space.* New York: Wittenborn, 1961.

Golding, John. *Cubism: A History and an Analysis, 1907–1914.* Rev. ed. Boston: Boston Book & Art Shop, 1968.

Goodyear, Frank H., Jr. *Contemporary American Realism Since 1960.* Boston: New York Graphic Society, 1981.

Gray, Christopher. *Cubist Aesthetic Theories.* Baltimore: Johns Hopkins University Press, 1953.

Haftmann, Werner. *Painting in the Twentieth Century: A Pictorial Survey.* London: Lund Humphries, 1965.

Hamilton, George Heard. *Painting and Sculpture in Europe.* New York: Penguin, 1983.

Hamlin, Talbot F., ed. *Forms and Functions of Twentieth-Century Architecture.* 4 vols. New York: Columbia University Press, 1952.

Hitchcock, Henry-Russell. *Architecture—Nineteenth and Twentieth Centuries.* New York: Penguin, 1977.

Hunter, Sam. *American Art of the Twentieth Century.* New York: Abrams, 1973.

——*Modern French Painting, 1855–1956.* New York: Dell, 1966.

Hunter, Sam, and Jacobus, John. *Modern Art: Painting, Sculpture, and Architecture.* New York: Abrams, 1985.

Jacobus, John. *Twentieth-Century Architecture: The Middle Years, 1940–1964.* New York: Praeger, 1966.

Janis, Sidney. *Abstract and Surrealist Art in America.* 1944. Reprint. New York: Arno Press, 1969.

Kahnweiler, Daniel H. *The Rise of Cubism.* New York: Wittenborn, Schultz, 1949.

Kaprow, Allan. *Assemblage, Environments, and Happenings.* New York: Abrams, 1966.

Kepes, Gyorgy. *The Visual Arts Today.* Middletown, Conn.: Wesleyan University Press, 1960.

Kraus, Rosalind, E. *Passages in Modern Sculpture.* Cambridge: MIT Press, 1981.

Lake, Carlton, and Maillard, Roger, eds. *Dictionary of Modern Painting.* 3rd rev. enl. ed. New York: Tudor, 1964.

Licht, Fred. *Sculpture of the Nineteenth and Twentieth Centuries.* Greenwich, Conn.: New York Graphic Society, 1967.

Lippard, Lucy R. *Pop Art.* New York: Praeger, 1966.

Lucie-Smith, Edward. *Art in the Seventies.* Ithaca, N.Y.: Cornell University Press, 1980.

——*Art Now: From Abstract Expressionism to Superrealism.* New York: Morrow, 1981.

——*Symbolist Art.* New York: Oxford University Press, 1972.

Lynton, Norbert. *The Modern World.* New York: McGraw-Hill, 1965.

McShine, Kynaston. *An International Survey of Recent Painting and Sculpture.* New York: Museum of Modern Art, 1984.

Martin, Marianne W. *Futurist Art and Theory.* Oxford: Clarendon Press, 1968.

Meyer, Ursula. *Conceptual Art.* New York: Dutton, 1972.

Mondrian, Pieter Cornelius. *Plastic Art and Pure Plastic Art.* 3rd ed. New York: Wittenborn, Schultz, 1952.

Motherwell, Robert, ed. *The Dada Painters and Poets.* New York: Wittenborn, Schultz, 1951.

Nochlin, Linda. *Realism.* Baltimore: Penguin, 1976.

Pehnt, Wolfgang. *Encyclopedia of Modern Architecture.* New York: Abrams, 1964.

Pierson, William. *American Buildings and Their Architects: Technology and the Picturesque.* Vol. 2. Garden City, N.Y.: Doubleday, 1978.

Raymond, Marcel. *From Baudelaire to Surrealism.* London: Methuen, 1970.

Raynal, Maurice. *History of Modern Painting.* 3 vols. Geneva: Skira, 1949–1950.

Read, Herbert. *A Concise History of Modern Painting.* 3rd ed. New York: Praeger, 1975.

——*A Concise History of Modern Sculpture.* Rev. and enl. ed. New York: Praeger, 1964.

Read, Herbert, ed. *Surrealism.* New York: Praeger, 1971.

Riseboro, Bill. *Modern Architecture and Design: An Alternative History.* Cambridge: MIT Press, 1983.

Ritchie, Andrew C. *Abstract Painting and Sculpture in America.* New York: Arno Press, 1969.

——*Sculpture of the Twentieth Century.* New York: Arno Press, 1972.

Rose, Barbara. *American Art Since 1900.* Rev. ed. New York: Praeger, 1975.

Rosenblum, Robert. *Cubism and Twentieth-Century Art.* New York: Abrams, 1976.

Rubin, William S. *Dada, Surrealism and Their Heritage.* New York: Museum of Modern Art, 1977.

Russell, John. *The Meanings of Modern Art.* New York: Museum of Modern Art/Thames & Hudson, 1981.

Schiee, Gert, ed. *Picasso in Perspective.* Englewood Cliffs, N.J.: Prentice-Hall, 1976.

Schlenoff, Norman. *Art in the Modern World.* New York: Bantam, 1965.

Schneede, Uwe M. *Surrealism.* New York: Abrams, 1974.

Schwarz, Arturo. *Marcel Duchamp.* New York: Abrams, 1974.

Scully, Vincent. *American Architecture and Urbanism.* New York: Praeger, 1969.

——*Modern Architecture.* Rev. ed. New York: Braziller, 1974.

Selz, Peter. *German Expressionist Painting.* 1957. Reprint. Berkeley: University of California Press, 1974.

Sotriffer, Kristian. *Expressionism and Fauvism.* New York: McGraw-Hill, 1972.

Tuchman, Maurice. *American Sculpture of the Sixties.* Los Angeles: Los Angeles County Museum of Art, 1967.

Vogt, Paul. *Expressionism: German Painting 1905–1920.* New York: Abrams, 1980.

Whittick, Arnold. *European Architecture in the Twentieth Century.* Aylesbury, England: Leonard Hill Books, 1974.

Wilmerding, John. *American Art.* Harmondsworth, England: Penguin, 1976.

——*The Genius of American Painting.* London: Weidenfeld & Nicolson, 1973.

PICTURE CREDITS

The authors and publisher are grateful to the proprietors and custodians of various works of art for photographs of these works and permission to reproduce them in this book. Sources not included in the captions are listed below.

KEY TO ABBREVIATIONS

ACL	Copyright A.C.L., Brussels
AMNH	American Museum of Natural History, New York
AR	Art Resource, New York
Al	Fratelli Alinari
Bulloz	J.E. Bulloz, Paris
Caisse	Caisse Nationale, Paris
Fototeca	Fototeca Unione, Rome
Gab	Gabinetto Fotografico Nazionale, Rome
Gir	Giraudon
Harding	Robert Harding Picture Library, London
Hir	Hirmer Fotoarchiv, Munich
Mansell	The Mansell Collection, London
Mar	Bildarchiv Foto Marburg
MAS	Ampliaciones y Reproducciones MAS, Barcelona
MN	Cliché des Musées Nationaux, Paris
NYPL	New York Public Library
OI	Courtesy of The Oriental Institute of the University of Chicago
PRI	Photo Researchers, Inc., New York
Scala	Scala Fine Art Publishers

Note: All references in the following credits are to figure numbers.

Paperbound covers Volume I: Scala-AR; Volume II: Museum of Modern Art, New York

Introduction Opening illustration: The British Museum, London; Drawing by Alain, © 1955, 1983 The New Yorker Magazine, Inc.: 11; Al-AR: 9a, 10; Josef Albers: 6, 7; Dr. Thomas Brachert, Courtesy of *Art Bulletin*, Dec. 1971, LIII, 4: 4; Giacomo Brogi-AR: 9b; Hir: 12; Walter Steinkopf: 14.

Part I Opening illustration: Shostal Associates, Inc.

Chapter 1 Aerofilms, Ltd., London: 15; AMNH: 9, 10, 13; Caisse: 7, 8; Colorphoto Hans Hinz, Basel: 1, 4, 6; MAS: 14; © 1982 Scientific American, Inc.: 2, 3; Edwin Smith: 16; Studio Laboric, Bergerac: 5, 12.

Chapter 2 Al-AR: 40; British School of Archeology in Jerusalem: 1, 2; Hir: 10, 12, 19, 24, 27, 31; Arlette Mellaart: 5, 6, 7, 8; James Mellaart: 3, 4; Mansell: 28, 29; MN: 21, 22, 23, 34, 37; OI: 13, 14, 18, 35, 38, 39.

Chapter 3 The Bettmann Archive/BBC Hulton: 11; © Lee Boltin: 39; Reproduced by courtesy of the Trustees of the British Museum: 35, 43; Egyptian Antiquities Organization: 22, 44; Egyptian Expedition, Metropolitan Museum of Art: 18, 20, 34; George Gerster/PRI: 7; Harding: 6, 29, 40, 41; HBJ Collection: 1; Hir: 2, 3, 12, 13, 14, 15, 16, 17, 23, 31, 36; Holle Bildarchiv, Baden-Baden: 27; Mar-AR: 25; MN: 42; OI: 21; © John G. Ross/Harding: 10; © Jim Walston/Taurus Photos, Inc.: 24.

Chapter 4 AR: 14, 15, 16; © Alison Frantz: 25; Courtauld Institute Galleries, London University: 27; Harding: 12; Hir: 4, 5, 7, 8, 9, 11, 13, 17, 18, 19, 20, 21, 24, 28, 29, 30, 31; TAP Service: 10; From Christian Zervos, *L'Art des Cyclades*, Éditions Cahiers d'Art, Paris: 1, 2, 3.

Chapter 5 Al-AR: 14, 25, 61, 67, 68, 70, 77, 87; Frederick Ayer III/PRI: 89; Deutsches Archäologisches Institut, Rome: 12; © Robert Ellis/Harding: 57; © Alison Frantz: 39, 40, 41, 53, 54; Gir-AR: 2; Walter Hege: 46; HBJ Collection: 64; Hir: 4, 8, 17, 18, 19, 22, 28, 31, 32, 37, 38, 45, 48, 49, 50, 51, 52, 55, 58, 59, 65, 66, 69, 76, 83, 88; Colorphoto Hans Hinz, Basel: 10; © C.H. Krüger-Moessner: 7, 60; Photo by Herschel Levit: 23; Mar-AR: 73, 74; Ministero Beni Culturali e Ambientali, Rome. Photo: Barbara Malter: 85; MN: 9, 63; Photophile: 42; Josephine Powell, Rome: 62; Courtesy of the Royal Ontario Museum, Toronto, Canada: 44; Scala-AR: 6, 33, 34, 35, 36, 72, 80; Photo: R. Schoder, SJ: 98; Dr. Franz Stoedtner: 27; TAP Service: 16.

Chapter 6 Al-AR: 6, 10, 11, 17, 25, 35, 38, 39, 42, 59, 62, 63, 66, 69, 75, 90, 91; Anderson-AR: 60; Photograph by Bruno Balestrini by courtesy of Electa Editrice, Milan: 50; Frank Brown/Fototeca: 15; Deutsches Archäologisches Institut, Rome: 8, 14, 68, 70, 87, 89; Walter Drayer: 2, 9, 12; Fototeca: 7, 16, 18, 19, 20, 21, 47, 52, 55, 58; Gab: 3, 71; M. Grimoldi: 40, 92; Photo Andre Held: 30; John Johnston: 88; G.E. Kidder-Smith: 85; Foto KLM: 46; Photo by Herschel Levit: 61; From Amedeo Maiuri, *Roman Painting*, Éditions d'Art, Albert Skira: 26; Rhenisches Landesmuseum, Trier: 80, 81; H. Roger-Viollet: 43; Charles Rotkin/PFI: 45; Oscar Savio: 33; Scala-AR: 5, 23, 28, 32, 34, 36, 51, 83, 84; Photo: R. Schoder, SJ: 4; Leonard von Matt/PRI: 64, 65, 72; Courtesy of the Yugoslav National Tourist Office, New York: 77; Zefa: 79.

Chapter 7 © Aerofilms, Ltd.: 67; AR: 43; Al-AR: 11, 35, 36, 37, 51, 65; Anderson-AR: 17, 22, 25, 68; From K.A.C. Creswell, *Early Muslim Architecture*, Clarendon Press: 74; Courtesy of © 1985 Dumbarton Oaks, Trustees for Harvard University, Washington, D.C.: 42; Enrico Ferorelli/DOT: 57; © Alison Frantz: 45, 48; HBJ Collection: 5, 52, 53, 54; Photo Andre Held: 10, 19, 60; Hir: 7, 9, 16, 18, 20, 21, 24, 29, 32, 34, 41; Werner Kalber (from a color proof by Kurt Weitzmann, Princeton): 40; A.F. Kersting, London: 86; G.E. Kidder-Smith: 80; Irving Trust, New York: 72; Linares, Yale University Photo Collection: 78; MAS: 70, 71; Novosti Press Agency: 62; OI: 23; Pontifica Commissione Centrale per l'Arte Sacra in Italia: 3; Josephine Powell, Rome: 55, 56, 77; Ekkehard Ritter: 58, 59; Salmer: 79; Scala-AR: 12, 26, 27, 28, 30, 31, 38, 39; Sergio Sostegni/Fotocielo: 49; Sovfoto: 63; State of Israel, Department of Antiquities and Museums, Jerusalem: 76; Tiers/Monkmeyer: 82; Turkish Culture and Information Office: 83; By courtesy of the Board of Trustees of the Victoria and Albert Museum, London: 64; Leonard von Matt/PRI: 2; Plan drawn by Christopher Woodward: 84.

Part II Opening illustration: Scala-AR.

Chapter 8 Dr. Harald Busch: 17; De Antonis: 5; HBJ Collection: 19, 20; Hir: 13, 18, 28; Mar-AR: 26; © University Museum of National Antiquities, Oslo, Norway: 3, 4; Wagner Göttingen, Germany: 22; Hermann Wehmeyer: 24, 25.

Chapter 9 Al-AR: 11, 13, 20, 26; © Arch. Phot. Paris/S.P.A.D.E.M.: 33; Bulloz: 27, 31; The Master and Fellows of Corpus Christi College, Cambridge: 39, 41; Caisse: 28; Jean Dieuzaide: 4, 24; Gir-AR: 34, 37, 38; J. Guidol/Archive Photographiques, Paris: 29; Hir: 9; HBJ Collection: 10; Evelyn Hofer: 21; A.F. Kersting, London: 17; © Erich Lessing Culture and Fine Art Archives: 35; Jean Roubier, Paris: 1, 6, 14, 23, 25, 30; Scala-AR: 22, 32, 36; Sergio Sostegni/Fotocielo: 19; W.S. Stoddard: 15.

Chapter 10 © Aerofilms, Ltd.: 28; Aero-Photo, Paris: 15; Al-AR: 38, 61, 62, 63; Anderson-AR: 60; Pierre Berger/PRI: 8; Dr. Harald Busch: 52; Electa Editrice: 17; Theo Felton: 57; Gir-AR: 26, 31, 33; HBJ Collection: 1, 3; George Holton/PRI: 58, 64; Mar-AR: 30, 32, 49, 51, 53, 59; National Monuments Record, London: 40, 46; Rapho Agence/PRI: 35, 39; Revue Française de l'Électricité: 34; Rheinisches Bildarchiv, Cologne: 56; H. Roger-Viollet: 13, 27; Jean Roubier, Paris: 9, 12, 14; Royal Commission on the Historical Monuments of England: 44, 45; Scala-AR: 28; Helga Schmidt-Glassner: 54; Edwin Smith: 42, 47; W.S. Stoddard: 10, 19; Clarence Ward: 24, 25; Clarence Ward Collection, Photographic Archives, National Gallery of Art, Washington, D.C.: 7, 21, 22, 24, 25, 48.

Part III Opening illustration: Shostal Associates, Inc.

Chapter 11 © Black Star: 32; © J. LeRoy Davidson: 13, 16, 18, 19, 22, 24, 27; © Eliot Elisofon/Time Inc.: 28; Government of India, Archeological Survey of India: 1, 2, 3, 4, 5, 6, 7, 9, 11, 12, 14, 15, 17, 20; HBJ Collection: 26; The Indian Government Tourist Office, New York: 21; Elizabeth Lyons: 33; I. Job Thomas: 23.

Chapter 12 Harry N. Abrams, Inc.: 4; Chavannes: 6; © Joan Lebold Cohen: 30; Courtesy of the Cultural Relics Bureau, Beijing and the Metropolitan Museum of Art, New York: 5; Gir-AR: 27; Harding: 24; HBJ Collection: 15; Magnum: 7, 8; MN: 11; Scala-AR: 10; Audrey R. Topping: 29; Charles Uht: 13; C.C. Wang Family Collection: 26; Langdon Warner's Family: 14.

Chapter 13 Japan National Tourist Organization: 31; National Commission for Protection of Cultural Properties, Tokyo, Japan: 3, 4, 9, 11, 13; From *A History of Far Eastern Art* by Sherman E. Lee, Harry N. Abrams, Inc., Publisher: 6, 10, 27, 28; International Society for Educational Information: 20; Sakamoto Photo Research Laboratory: 5, 8, 12; Shashinka Photo: 16, 17, 18, 23, 24, 25; Spaulding Collection, Museum of Fine Arts, Boston: 30; Yoshi Watanabe: 7; Zauho Press: 26.

Chapter 14 Archaeological Institute of America, reproduced from *Art and Archaeology*, IV, 6, © 1916: 6, 22; Photograph © copyright 1986 by The Barnes Foundation: 55; Chicago Natural History Museum: 15a; Herbert M. Cole: 49; Field photo by Dr. George A. Corbin, Oct. 1972: 62; From H.S. and C.B. Cosgrove, *The Swarts Ruin: A Typical Mimbres Site in Southwestern New Mexico*. Peabody Museum Papers, Vol. 15, No. 1. Reprinted with the permission of the Peabody Museum, Harvard University, Cambridge, Massachusetts: 25; David Gebhard, The Art Galleries, University of California, Santa Barbara: 24; From Campbell Grant, *Rock Art of the American Indian*: 23; Abraham Guillen M.: 17; HBJ Collection: 9; Dr. George Kennedy, University of California, Los Angeles: 64; From J.D. Lajoux, *The Rock Painting of Tassili*: 40; Archive of Hispanic Culture, Library of Congress: 15b; Courtesy of Museum of the American Indian, Heye Foundation, New York: 21, 30; © National Geographic: 1; National Museum, Lagos, Nigeria: 43; National Park Service, U.S. Department of the Interior: 26, 27; New Mexico State Monuments: 28; Frances Pratt: 2; Photo: Jerry Thompson: 56; From Karl von den Steinen, *Die Marquesaner und ihre Kunst I*: 60; The Wheelwright Museum of the American Indian, Santa Fe: 29; Frank Willett: 41, 42, 46.

Part IV Opening illustration: Scala-AR.

Chapter 15 Al-AR: 2, 4, 5, 9, 12, 13, 15, 16, 17, 18; Anderson-AR: 7, 10, 22, 25; Giacomo Brogi-AR: 3, 20; Gab: 11; Scala-AR: 1, 6, 8, 14, 19, 21, 23, 24.

Chapter 16 Al-AR: 4, 5, 6, 8, 9, 11, 12, 13, 14, 15, 16, 19, 21, 26, 27, 28, 36, 38, 42, 45, 47, 48, 49, 54, 57, 62, 63, 66; Anderson-AR: 17, 24, 30, 31, 39, 41, 53; Marcello Bertoni: 1, 2; Giacomo Brogi-AR: 3, 23, 51; Farbenfotografie: 67; HBJ Collection: 7; La Photothèque: 59; Rollie McKenna/PRI: 40, 44; Scala-AR: 10, 25, 32, 33, 34, 35, 37, 52, 60, 61, 64, 65.

Chapter 17 Harry N. Abrams: 10, 51; Al-AR: 1, 3, 15, 16, 18, 20, 23, 24, 27, 28, 36, 42, 43, 46, 47, 61, 62, 64, 66; Anderson-AR: 4, 31, 38, 39, 48; AR: 50, 56; Harvey J. Barad/PRI: 21; British Architectural Library, London: 11; Caisse: 19; Fototeca: 30, 33; Gir-AR: 22; M. Grimoldi: 6, 9, 12, 14; Phyllis Dearborn Massar: 52, 54, 55; The Metropolitan Museum of Art: 34; Charles Rotkin/PFI: 29; Scala-AR: 17, 25, 26, 35, 37, 41, 57, 58, 60, 63, 67, 68, 69; Edwin Smith: 49.

Chapter 18 ACL: 7, 8, 9, 20, 21; Al-AR: 18, 55; Artothek, Munich: 41; Giacomo Brogi-AR: 33; Bulloz: 54; Caisse: 1, 51; Gir-AR: 4, 5, 35, 50, 53; L. Gundermann/Photo-Verlag: 29; HBJ Collection: 49; Colorphoto Hans Hinz, Basel: 23; MAS: 22, 56, 57, 58, 59, 60; MN: 25; Rapho Agence/PRI: 61; Studio Remy: 2; Rheinisches Bildarchiv, Cologne: 26; Charles Rotkin/PFI: 52; Scala-AR: 19; Sovfoto: 28; Stedelijke Musea, Louvain: 17; Walter Steinkopf: 24, 39.

Chapter 19 Harry N. Abrams, Inc.: 21; Aero-Photo, Paris: 66; Al-AR: 8, 10, 12, 13, 15, 18, 24, 25, 28, 42, 43, 73; Anderson-AR: 5, 33, 35; © Arch. Phot., Paris/S.P.A.D.E.M.: 72; Avery Library, Columbia University, New York: 1; British Crown Copyright, Reproduced with permission of the Controller of Her Brittanic Majesty's Stationery Office: 75; Giacomo Brogi-AR: 38; © 1966, Henri Dauman. All rights reserved: 69; Gab: 20; Gir-AR: 62, 66; Gene Heil/PRI: 68; A.F. Kersting, London: 4, 65, 76; G.E. Kidder-Smith: 17, 19; Frank Lerner, photo: 55; Mansell: 61; MAS: 37; MN: 27, 48, 59; Courtesy of NYPL (Astor, Lenox and Tilden Foundations): 67; Photo Henrot: 70; H. Roger-Viollet: 71; Charles Rotkin/PFI: 3; Scala-AR: 7, 9, 23, 26, 30, 32, 34; Helga Schmidt-Glassner: 64; Walter Steinkopf: 58.

Chapter 20 ACL: 39; Al-AR: 1, 2, 7, 12; Bulloz: 36; J. Allan Cash/PRI: 4; British Crown Copyright, Reproduced with permission of the Controller of Her Britannic Majesty's Stationery Office: 5; Caisse: 19; By kind permission of Country Life Magazine: 22, 23; H.B. Fleming & Co.: 24; Gir-AR: 18, 29, 38; Hir: 13; A.F. Kersting, London: 10, 21, 25; Library of Congress: 26; Merisio, Pepi, Bergano, courtesy Art and Architecture Div., NYPL (Astor, Lenox and Tilden Foundations): 3; Erich Muller: 9; Courtesy of the NYPL (Astor, Lenox and Tilden Foundations): 40; Scala: 14, 17; Virginia Chamber of Commerce: 27; Virginia Museum of Fine Arts, Richmond: 37.

Part V Opening illustration: Collection of The Museum of Modern Art, New York.

Chapter 21 Al-AR: 5, 8, 21, 24, 27, 83; AR: 39, 40; Bridgeman-AR: 41; John R. Brownlie/PRI: 2; Bulloz: 7, 20, 23, 35; Caisse: 1; Gir-AR: 15, 16, 57, 81; HBJ Collection: 61, 85, 86, 88, 89, 90; Hedrich-Blessing: 87; A.F. Kersting, London: 3; Photo Kleinhempel: 43; Library of Congress: 79; Mar-AR: 82; MN: 13, 14, 17, 19, 22, 26, 38; Neue Pinakothek, Munich: 50; Novosti: 45; Collection Phoenix Art Museum: 28; H. Roger-Viollet: 4; Scala-AR: 9, 12, 18; Photo courtesy of National-Galerie, Staatliche Museen, Berlin: 33.

Chapter 22 Albright-Knox Art Gallery, Buffalo: 102; Photo by Rudolph Burckhardt, New York: 82; Photo Courtesy of Leo Castelli Gallery, New York: 88, 90; Geoffrey Clements: 91; John Donat: 101; David Gahr: 86; Barbara Gladstone Gallery, New York: 96; © Gianfranco Gorgoni/Contact Press Images: 84; Photo by Carmelo Guadagno: 9; Solomon R. Guggenheim Museum, New York. Photo by Robert E. Mates: 107, 108; HBJ Collection: 55, 57, 58, 71; Photo by David Heald: 13; Lucien Hervé: 59, 61, 104, 105, 106; Colorphoto Hans Hinz, Basel: 5, 20; Institut für Leichte Flachentragwerke, Stuttgart: 112; Photo Kleinhempel: 6; William Lescaze Associates: 65; Courtesy of Marlborough Gallery Inc., New York: 98; MAS: 56; © Norman McGrath: 122; Museum of Modern Art, New York: 63, 66; Office du Film du Québec: 114; Courtesy of The Pace Gallery and Julian Schnabel. Photographed by Phillips/Schwab: 95; Courtesy of the Philadelphia Convention and Visitors Bureau: 100; Robert Phillips for Fortune Magazine: 113; Musée Picasso, Paris: 14; © Margaret K. Porter: 116; Photo: Michel Proulx, *Architectural Record*: 117; Oscar Savio: 109; © foto Stedelijk Museum, Amsterdam: 60; Dr. Franz Stoedtner: 64; © 1956 Ezra Stoller, ESTO: 103; Ezra Stoller, © ESTO: 67; Photo by Don Sudnik, *AIA Journal*: 118; Photo by James A. Sugar © National Geographic Society: 115; Tiofoto: 47; Trans World Airlines: 110, 111; Courtesy of the Union of Artists of the USSR: 99; Malcolm Varon, New York: 21; Venturi and Rauch: 119, 120; Wolfgang Volz, Essen: 94; Galerie Welz: 1; Collection of the Whitney Museum, Gift of Robert and Nancy Kaye: 97.

© S.P.A.D.E.M., Paris/V.A.G.A., New York, 1985: 19-72; 20-25; Part V Opening illustration; 21-1, 75; 22-3, 4, 5, 8, 10, 11, 12, 14, 15, 17, 18, 20, 23, 25, 26, 30, 31, 33, 35, 40, 41, 51, 59, 60, 61, 80, 88, 90, 104, 105, 106.

© A.D.A.G.P., Paris/V.A.G.A., New York, 1985: 22-8, 14, 17, 29, 46, 49, 52, 58.

Illustration Credits

FIG. 3-4 Adapted from the "Later Canon" of Egyptian Art, figure 1 in Erwin Panofsky, *Meaning in the Visual Arts*. Copyright © 1955 by Erwin Panofsky. Used by permission of Doubleday and Company, Inc.

FIGS. 3-19, 28; 5-26; 6-24, 48, 52a, 56; 7-50; 10-59 From Sir Banister Fletcher, *A History of Architecture on the Comparative Method*, 17th ed., rev. by R.A. Cordingly, 1961. Used by permission of the Athlone Press of the University of London.

FIGS. 4-6; 7-1, 8, 33 Hirmer Fotoarchiv, Munich.

FIGS. 5-92, 93, 95 From Richard Brilliant, *Arts of the Ancient Greeks*, 1973. Adapted by permission of McGraw-Hill Book Co.

FIG. 5-96 From J. Charbonneaux, et al., *Hellenistic Art 330–50 B.C.*, 1973. Adapted by permission of George Braziller, Inc.

FIG. 6-49 From J.B. Ward-Perkins, *Roman Architecture*, 1977. Adapted by permission of Electa Editrice.

FIG. 6-54 From Robert Furneaux Jordan, *A Concise History of Western Architecture*, © 1969 by Harcourt Brace Jovanovich, Inc. Reproduced by permission of the publisher.

FIG. 6-76 Deutsches Archäologisches Institut, Rome.

FIG. 6-78 From Fiske Kimball, M. Arch, and G.H. Edgell, *A History of Architecture*, 1918. Used by permission of Harper & Row, Inc., publishers.

FIG. 6-82 From George M.A. Hanfmann, *Roman Art: A Survey of the Art of Imperial Rome*, A New York Graphic Society Book. By permission of Little, Brown and Company.

FIG. 7-6 From Kenneth J. Conant, *Early Medieval Church Architecture*. Used by permission of The Johns Hopkins Press.

FIGS. 7-66, 73 From K.A.C. Creswell, *Early Muslim Architecture*. Adapted by permission of Clarendon Press.

FIG. 7-69 From G. Marçais, *L'Architecture Musulmane d'Occident*. By permission of Arts et Métiers Graphiques, Paris.

FIG. 7-75 Staatliche Museen, Berlin.

FIG. 7-85 From "Sinan" by D. Kuban from *Macmillan Encyclopedia of Architects*, Adolf K. Placzek, Editor-in-Chief, Vol. 4, p. 68. © 1982 by the Free Press, a Division of Macmillan, Inc.

FIG. 9-3 From H. Stierlin, *Die Architektur der Welt*, Vol. 1, p. 147. © 1977 by Hirmer Verlag, Munich.

FIGS. 10-4, 5, 6 From Ernst Gall, *Gotische Kathedralen*, 1925. Used by permission of Klinkhardt & Biermann, publishers.

FIG. 10-18 Used by permission of Umschau Verlag, Frankfort.

FIG. 11-8 From Benjamin Rowland, *The Art and Architectural India*, 1953, Penguin Books.

FIG. 11-29 From Madeleine Giteau, *The Civilization of Angkor*. Adapted by permission of Rizzoli International Publications.

FIG. 14-4 Field Museum of Natural History, Chicago.

FIG. 14-22 From "The Serpent Mound of Adams County, Ohio" by Charles C. Willoughby from *American Anthropologist* 21 (2): 156, 1919. Reproduced by permission of The American Anthropological Association.

FIG. 16-43 From Nikolaus Pevsner, *An Outline of European Architecture*, 6th ed., 1960, Penguin Books, Ltd., © Nikolaus Pevsner, 1943, 1960, 1963.

INDEX

Page numbers in italics indicate illustrations.

A

Aalto, Alvar, 971
Abelam cult art, 516, *516*
Abelard, Peter, 374, 531
Abraham and the Three Angels, from the *Psalter of St. Louis,* 396, *397*
Abstract art, 906–909, 911 n, 912–13, 920, 921, 922, 938–41, 943–50, 956
Abstract Expressionism, 938–41
Abstract Formalism, 943–50
Abu Simbel, Temple of Ramses II at, 87–88, *88,* 91
Accordionist (Picasso), *900,* 901–902
Achaemenid Persia, 64–69
Acropolis, Athens, 150–58, *150, 151;* Geometric bronze warrior, 133, *134;* Kore figures, 136–37; *Kritios Boy,* 138, *138;* Temple of Athena Nike, *139*
Acropolis, Pergamon, 179–80, *179, 180*
Action painting, 939–41
Adam, Robert, 788–89; Etruscan Room, Osterley Park House, 788, *788*
Adam and Eve (The Fall of Man) (Dürer), 688, *688*
Adam and Eve Reproached by the Lord, St. Michael's, Hildesheim, 335–36, *335*
Adams Memorial, Washington, D.C. (Saint-Gaudens), 877–78, *878*
Additive technique, in sculpture, 15
Adena art, 496–97
Adena pipe, 496, *496*
Admonitions of the Instructress to the Court Ladies (Ku K'ai-chih), 448, *449*
Adoration of the Magi, The (Gentile da Fabriano), 564–65, *564*
Adoration of the Magi, Santa Maria, Tahull, 364–66, *365*
Adoration of the Shepherds, from *The Portinari Altarpiece* (Hugo van der Goes), 672, *673*
Aegean art, 104–23; architecture, 117–20; craft art, 121–22; Cycladic, 104, 105–106; Minoan, 104, 105–17; Mycenaen, 117–23; painting, 109–14; pottery, 106–107; 115–16, 122–23; sculpture, 116–17
Aelius Spartianus, 233 n
Aeschylus, 146
African art, 504–12, 900
Agesander (with Athenodorus and Polydorus): *Head of Odysseus,* 173, *173; Laocoön* group, 172, *172,* 173; *Odysseus' Helmsman Falling,* 173, *173*
Agnellus, 267
Agora: of Athens, 127; in Hellenistic cities, 177
Ajanta, cave painting at, 429–30, *430*
Akbar, 430
Akhenaton, 94–97, 99; pillar statue of, from the Temple of Amen-Re at Karnak, 75, *94,* 95
Akkadian art, 53–55
Alain: drawing, *17*
Albers, Josef, *12*
Alberti, Leon Battista, 524, 525, 557, 569, 575, 576–78, 579, 624, 625; Palazzo Rucellai, Florence, 576–77, *576;* San Francesco, Rimini, 577–78, *577;* Sant' Andrea, Mantua, 578–79, *578,* 624, 625; Santa Maria Novella, Florence, 577, *577*
Alcuin of York, 324
Alexander VI (pope), 604
Alexander the Great, 64, 166, 169, 180, 414
Alhambra palace, Granada, 300–301, *301*
Al-Khazneh (the "Treasury"), Petra, 237, *237*
Allegory of Africa, Piazza Armerina, 240, *240*
Altamira cave art, 26
Altar of the Hand, Benin, *505,* 506
Altar of Zeus and Athena, Pergamon, 170–71, *171*
Altdorfer, Albrecht, 682; *Battle of Isis, The,* 682, *683*

Amalienburg, the, Munich (Cuvilliés), 775–76, *775, 776*
Amaravati, India, relief sculpture from, 427, *427*
Amarna period, Egypt, 94–101
Amenemhet, tomb of, Beni Hasan, 84–85, *85*
Amen-Mut-Khonsu, Temple of, Luxor, 91–92, *91*
Amenophis IV. *See* Akhenaton
Amen-Re, Temple of, Karnak, 89–91, *90, 91,* 95
American art, 789–90, 793; architecture, 789–90, 928–30, 934–36, 964–65; painting, 793–94, 832–34, 844–45, 848–50, 861–62, 876–77, 906–908, 917, 938–41; sculpture, 877–78, 924; twentieth-century, 906–908, 917, 924, 928–30, 934–36, 938–41, 964–65. *See also* North American Indian art; Pre-Columbian art
American Indian art. *See* North American Indian art
American Tribute to the British People, An (Nevelson), 947, *947*
Amida (Jocho), from Byodoin temple, 470–71, *470*
Amida Triad, from *Shrine of Lady Tachibana,* 465–66, *466*
Amiens Cathedral, France, 385–88, *386, 387, 388*
Ammianus Marcellinus, 242 n
Amphiprostyle temple, 139, *139*
Amphoras, 128, *130; The Blinding of Polyphemus and Gorgons,* 129–30, *129; Dipylon Vase,* 128–29, *129; Herakles and Apollo Struggling for the Tripod* (Andokides Painter), 132, *132;* Proto-Geometric, 128, *129; Revelers* (Euthymides), 132–33, *133*
Anatolian art, 41–43, 56, *57*
Ancestral poles, Asmat, 516, *517*
Andokides Painter, 132, 144, 163; *Herakles and Apollo Struggling for the Tripod,* 132, *132*
Andrea del Castagno, 568–69, 584, 593; *Last Supper, The,* 568; *Pippo Spano,* 569, *569*
Andrea del Sarto, 628, 698; *Madonna of the Harpies,* 628, *629*
Andrea del Verrocchio. *See* Verrocchio, Andrea del
Andrea Pisano. *See* Pisano, Andrea
Angel Appearing to Joseph, The, Santa Maria de Castelseprio, Italy, 285, *286*
Angelico, Fra, 573; *Annunciation,* 573–74, *574*
Angilbert II, 328
Angkor temples, 434–37, *435;* Angkor Thom, Kampuchea, 434, 436–37, *436, 437;* Angkor Wat, Kampuchea, 434–36, *435, 436*
Annunciation (Fra Angelico), 573–74, *574*
Annunciation (Piero della Francesca), 571–72, *572*
Annunciation, The, Reims Cathedral, *392, 393*
Annunciation, The (Simone Martini), 543, *544*
Annunciation and the Nativity, The (Giovanni Pisano), 533–34, *533*
Annunciation and the Nativity, The (Nicola Pisano), 533
Annunciation of the Death of Mary, The, from the *Maestà Altarpiece* (Duccio), 536–37, *536*
Annunciation to the Shepherds, The, from the *Lectionary of Henry II,* 336–39, *337*
Antheil, George, 904
Anthemius of Tralles, 279
Antikythera Youth, 166–67, *167*
Antonello da Messina, 596, 642, 671; *The Martyrdom of St. Sebastian,* 596, *597*
Antonines, 214
Antoninus Pius, 230–31
Antonio da Sangallo the Younger, 608; Farnese Palace, Rome, 608–10, *609*
Antonio Rossellino. *See* Rosellino, Antonio
Aphaia, Temple of, Aegina, *139,* 142; pedimental sculptures of, 145–46, *145, 146*
Aphrodite of Cyrene, 164–65, *165,* 173

Aphrodite of Melos, 173–74, *174*
Apocalypse of Saint Sever, 368, *368*
Apollo, from the Temple of Zeus, Olympia, 6, 149, *149*
Apollo, from Veii, 189, *189,* 190
Apollo, Temple of, Bassae, 168
Apollo, Temple of, Didyma, *139,* 176, *176*
Apollodorus, 229; Column of Trajan, Rome, 229–30, *229*
Apollonius: *Seated Boxer,* 175, *175*
Apotheosis of the Pisani Family, The (Tiepolo), 777–78, *778*
Apoxyomenos (Lysippos), 166, *166,* 169
Apuleius, 175
Aqa Mirak, 307; *Laila and Majnun in Love at School,* 308, *309*
Aqueducts, Roman, 214–15, *214*
Aquinas. *See* St. Thomas Aquinas
Aquitanian churches, 355
Ara Pacis Augustae, Rome, 225–26, *226,* 230
Arch of Constantine, Rome, 227, 243, *243,* 260, 261; relief sculpture from, 243–45, *244, 249*
Arch of Titus, Rome, 227–29, *227, 228,* 230
Archaic period, Greece, 128, 129–33, *134–46*
Archers of St. Adrian (Hals), 744, *745*
Arches: Islamic, 295–96; Roman, 223–24, *223, 227; Romanesque,* 354
Archipenko, Alexander, 921; *Woman Combing Her Hair,* 921, *921,* 924
Architectural wall painting, 203–206, *203, 204,* 205
Architecture, 13–14; African, 509; American, 789–90, 928–30, 934–36, 964–65; Anatolian, 40–42; arcuated, 236, *237;* Assyrian, 57–59; Babylonian, 62–63; Baroque, 712–17, 719–23, 758–67, 771–74; Byzantine, 265–66, 269, 271–73, 279–81, 282–85; Chinese, 461; Early Christian, 252–55; Early Medieval, 328–35; Egyptian, 45, 76–81, 86–92, 93–94, 222; English, 765–67, 786–87; Etruscan, 184–86; French, 5, 699–701, 758–64, 789; Gothic, 5, 373–80, 383–91, 400–405, 407–11, 656, 703; Greek, 14, 91, 138–46, 150–58, 168–69, 176–80, 222; Indian, 420–23, 432–33, 434–37; International style, 930–36, 965, 970, 971, 972; Islamic, 294–305; Italian, 5, 559–64, 576–80, 605–10, 620–26, 712–17, 719–23; Japanese, 465, 473–74, 483; Mannerist, 636–38; Mesopotamian, 46–48, 222; Minoan, 107–12; Mycenaean, 117–20; nineteenth-century, 881–85; North American Indian, 498–99; Ottoman, 303–305; Persian, 64–66; Plateresque, 703; Post-Modern, 970–72; pre-Columbian, 488–89, 490–91, 494, 495; Renaissance, 14, 559–64, 576–80, 605–10, 620–26, 636–41, 699–701, 703–705; Rococo, 774–77; Roman, 196–202, 214–25; Romanesque, 343–55, 356; Romantic, 786–90, 810–13; Russian, 284–85; Spanish, 703–705; structural systems, 13, *14;* Sumerian, 47–48; trabeated, 236, *237;* twentieth-century, 927–36, 962–75; Venetian, 638–41. *See also* Cities and towns; Houses; Orders; Vaulting
Arcuated architecture, 236, *237*
Ardebil carpet, from tomb-mosque of Shah Tahmasp, *306,* 307
Area, 7
Arena Chapel, Padua, 537
Areogun: door from king's palace at Ikerre, 508, *508*
Argonaut Krater (Niobid Painter), 162–63, *162*
Aristophanes, 163
Aristotle, 49, 126, 127, 138–39, 161, 163, 169, 180, 373, 525
Arnolfo di Cambio: Florence Cathedral, 407–409

A 6
B 7
C 8
D 9
E 0
F 1
G 2
H 3
I 4
J 5